The Strategic Management of Intellectual Capital and Organizational Knowledge

The Strategic Management of Intellectual Capital and Organizational Knowledge

Edited by

Chun Wei Choo

Nick Bontis

UNIVERSITY PRESS

2002

OXFORD
UNIVERSITY PRESS

Oxford   New York
Auckland   Bangkok   Buenos Aires   Cape Town   Chennai
Dar es Salaam   Delhi   Hong Kong   Istanbul   Karachi   Kolkata
Kuala Lumpur   Madrid   Melbourne   Mexico City   Mumbai   Nairobi
São Paulo   Shanghai   Singapore   Taipei   Tokyo   Toronto

and an associated company in Berlin

Copyright © 2002 by Oxford University Press, Inc.

Published by Oxford University Press, Inc.
198 Madison Avenue, New York, New York 10016

www.oup.com

Oxford is a registered trademark of Oxford University Press

Library of Congress Cataloging-in-Publication Data
The strategic management of intellectual capital and organizational knowledge / edited
by Chun Wei Choo and Nick Bontis.
      p.   cm.
Includes bibliographical references and index.
ISBN 0-19-515486-X; 0-19-513866-X (pbk.)
    1. Intellectual capital.   2. Organizational learning.   3. Knowledge management.   I. Choo,
Chun Wei.   II. Bontis, Nick.
HD53.S773   2002
658.4'038—dc21   2001056034

9 8 7 6 5 4 3 2 1

Printed in the United States of America
on acid-free paper

I dedicate this book with deepest love and admiration to my beautiful wife, Stacy; my wise father, Charilaos; my inspirational mother, Despina; and my loyal sister, Panagiota. They fuel my spirit and guide my journey.

Nick Bontis

Dedicated to my father, Choo Hwee Ming, and the memory of my mother, Lily Low.

Chun Wei

Preface

Strategy management is concerned with understanding the causes and forces that explain performance differences between organizations. One approach analyzes industry structures as external determinants of competitive performance. An alternative view focuses on internal competencies and resources as the engine of superior achievement. In this view, organizational capabilities are bundles of physical assets, human know-how, and organizational routines that have evolved uniquely in each organization. This book adopts a knowledge-based perspective that sees the firm as a repository of knowledge resources and capabilities. The firm's knowledge base includes the expertise and experience of individuals, the routines and processes that define the distinctive way of doing things inside the organization, and the knowledge of customer needs and supplier strengths, among many others. To the extent that the knowledge and capabilities are unique and difficult to imitate, they confer sustainable competitive advantage on the firm. The extent to which the firm actually appropriates rents depends on how effective it is at combining knowledge and capabilities in configurations that deliver value to its market or community. Knowledge is cumulative, so the more the firm knows, the more it can apply what it knows to new areas of opportunity. Unlike traditional products, knowledge-based products and services can enjoy increasing returns, so the firm developing an early advantage has a better chance to grow market share through network externalities and customer familiarity effects.

The primary rationale for organizations is thus the creation and deployment of knowledge. Performance differences between organizations, then, are a result of their different stocks of knowledge and their differing capabilities in developing and deploying knowledge. Knowledge and competence have become the primary drivers of competitive advantage in advanced nations.

The field of intellectual capital poses special challenges. It has no legacy, few world-renowned researchers, and a modest literature. Defining its research agenda becomes a challenge. To complicate matters, the concept of intellectual capital arises in numerous disciplines, resulting in a mosaic of perspectives. For example, accountants are interested in how to measure it on the balance sheet; information technologists want to codify it in systems; sociologists want to balance power with it; psychologists want to develop minds because of it; human resource managers want to calculate a return on it; and training and development officers want to make sure that they can build it.

Purpose and Approach

The objective of the book is to bring together a balanced selection of core concepts as well as new perspectives that collectively articulate a knowledge-based view of strategy management. Three basic questions thread the discourse: How do organizations create knowledge and intellectual capital? How can organizations manage the accumulation and flow of knowledge and intellectual capital to sustain competitive advantage? What conceptual principles and action levers constitute a knowledge-based strategy of the firm?

Eleven countries are represented by the contributers to this collection: Britain, Canada, Finland, France, Ireland, Italy, Japan, Netherlands, Spain, Switzerland, and the United States. Each author is recognized for completing important work in this field, and several contributions are seminal in defining the scope and direction of knowledge and intellectual capital management.

As editors, we resisted the temptation to specify a formal framework and instead invited contributors to write what they believed would belong in a collection that seeks to define a knowledge-based view of strategy management. We welcomed divergent perspectives and did not attempt to guide the content of chapters into preselected schools or points of view. After all the chapters were received, we searched for unifying themes as well as interesting tensions, which we discuss in detail in the introduction (chap. 1).

Overview of the Topics

This book contains 41 chapters written by a total of ? authors. Of these chapters, 26–27 are original to this book. A significant number of chapters are collaborations between academics and practitioners. Of the seventeen reprint chapters, ten are accompanied by new commentaries from the authors. Several of the commentaries are substantial works in themselves and extend the original arguments significantly. While the majority of chapters are aimed at building theory, a good number focus on application and practice. The book is divided into seven parts, each of which is described briefly below.

Part I: Knowledge in Organizations

Knowledge in organizations is neither monolithic nor homogeneous, but is developed from different origins and engaged in different modes. Thus, there is knowledge consisting of what the organization believes about its identity and purpose, its capabilities, and its environment. Knowledge is embedded in the physical goods the organization produces and in the rules and routines that the organization develops. Individuals and groups possess knowledge derived from

experience, skillful practice, and personal and collective insight. Because tacit knowledge is uniquely embodied in practice and cannot be easily codified or imitated, it is generally perceived as a vital source of sustainable advantage. Explicit knowledge, on the other hand, is transferable, but this diffusibility can be yet another source of strategic advantage when organizations are seeking to standardize platforms, accelerate development of complementary products, or collaborate with other knowledge-rich organizations.

Part II: Knowledge-Based Perspectives of the Firm

A defining competitive feature of any organization will be its capacity to develop and apply new and existing knowledge to generate economic rent and social value. In strategy management, the dilemma is often stark: just as competitors cannot replicate the firm's knowledge, so the firm itself may not be able to exploit that same knowledge effectively. A knowledge-based theory of the firm differs from previous theories in that it must grasp the implications of managing invisible assets that behave both as resources and as processes (Itami 1987). A number of contributors to this volume have noted that standard economic theory does not cover the management of knowledge, intellectual capital, and organizational learning adequately or appropriately (see, e.g., chap. 10 by von Krogh and Grand, and chap. 11 by Huizing and Bouman). Spender and Grant (1996) observe that "the knowledge-based theory of the firm is a paradigmatic gateway, the point in the evolution of our field where we abandon the older concept of a theory as a blueprint for creating the firm, and move towards a more agricultural notion of management as the intervention in and husbandry of the natural knowledge-creating processes of both individuals and collectivities" (p. 9). A knowledge-based theory of the firm suggests that the boundaries and governance structure of the firm are determined not only by the considerations of lowering transaction costs, but also by the value to be derived from the deployment of its knowledge resources and capabilities.

Part III: Knowledge Strategy

An organization linking knowledge to strategy needs to balance a number of inherent tensions. The tacit knowledge of an organization's indi-

viduals and groups is unique to it. An organization must weigh the benefit of codifying this knowledge to facilitate sharing and operationalization against the risk of increasing the mobility of this knowledge and thus the likelihood of its being appropriated. Most organizations face the question of how to maximize the transfer and absorption of knowledge internally while controlling and directing the diffusion of that knowledge externally. Thus, Kogut and Zander (1992) wrote that "the central competitive dimension of what firms know how to do is to create and transfer knowledge efficiently within an organizational context" (p. 383). More recent research suggests a number of complementary approaches in formulating knowledge strategy. Bierly and Chakrabarti (1996) identify four generic knowledge strategy groups—explorers, exploiters, loners, and innovators—and observed that, at least in the U.S. pharmaceutical industry, firms in the innovator and explorer groups tended to be more profitable. Zack (1999; also chap. 15 this volume) suggests a gap analysis that compares an organization's strategic gap (between what a firm must do and what it can do) with its knowledge gap (between what a firm must know to execute its strategy and what it does know). Supporting the theory building is an expanding body of empirical research that scrutinizes the execution of knowledge strategies in industries such as biotechnology, financial services, pharmaceuticals, and semiconductors.

Part IV: Knowledge Strategy in Practice

The firm implementing a knowledge-based strategy faces daunting challenges. New knowledge is created by individuals, but this personal knowledge needs to be shared with others in the organization. Knowledge gained in one context has to be transferred and made usable in another process or problem. Knowledge-intensive organizations find it necessary to maintain a high degree of strategic flexibility: to be able to pursue multiple conflicting goals simultaneously and to be prepared to act on options that reveal themselves as the firm increases its learning and experience. An important focus of the knowledge strategy discussion is on new product development. In chapter 18, Helfat and Raubitschek show that knowledge, capabilities, and products coevolve, generating strategic opportunities for linking products within and across chains. Knott (chap. 19) attributes successful development of a model at Toyota to a knowledge strategy that

embraced both the creation of new knowledge and the exploitation of existing knowledge. Barabba, Pourdehnad, and Ackoff (chap. 20) introduce a systems approach to knowledge management and describe the design of a decision-support learning system at General Motors that tracks significant decisions, assumptions, and outcomes.

Part V: Knowledge Creation

One of the best known and most influential models in the knowledge strategy literature is the knowledge creation model developed by Nonaka and Takeuchi (1995). The model is concerned with how *organizations*, rather than *individuals*, create new knowledge. Organizations create knowledge by converting tacit knowledge into explicit knowledge. At the core of the framework is the interaction between tacit and explicit knowledge through a continuously expanding cycle of processes that involve socialization, externalization, combination, and internalization of the organization's knowledge. Subsequent extensions to the model include the concept of "Ba" or a shared context for knowledge creation; a taxonomy for classifying a firm's knowledge assets into experiential, conceptual, systemic, and routine knowledge categories; and the role of knowledge leadership in establishing conditions conducive to knowledge creation. The knowledge creation model provides the intellectual scaffolding for a growing number of empirical and theoretical studies in strategic knowledge management.

Part VI: Knowledge across Boundaries

An increasingly important strategy for adding depth to an organization's capabilities is to acquire knowledge from outside the organization's boundaries. Unfortunately, knowledge transferred is not the same as knowledge assimilated or applied. The outcome of the transfer is moderated by the embeddedness of the knowledge, and the capacity of the firm to absorb the knowledge. Thus, capability differences between organizations will influence the occurrence, direction, and result of the transfer of knowledge. The empirical study of U.S. nursing homes by Mitchell et al. (chap. 31) showed that transfer learning was both constrained and facilitated by the level and similarity of capabilities in component units and their chains. The capacity to absorb knowledge extends beyond preexisting

technical knowledge to organizational and social conditions. These would include organizational and alliance structures, the degree of trust between partner firms, and the extent to which norms and practices support knowledge sharing. Ciborra and Andreu (chap. 32) observe that web-based organizational arrangements such as open-source software development communities seem to challenge many conventional notions about coordination and governance, opportunism and free riding, and intellectual property rights protection.

Part VII: Managing Intellectual Capital

The idea of intellectual capital surfaced from the dialogue between researchers and practitioners seeking a more complete representation of the visible and invisible assets and processes that constitute a firm's capacity to create value (chap. 35). Conceptually, intellectual capital consists of human capital and structural capital. Human capital is a function of the competence, intellectual agility, and attitudes of the organization's members. Structural capital refers to the learning and knowledge that is enacted in processes (process capital); knowledge that is codified as documents, objects, and intellectual property (intellectual assets); and the reputation and relationships the organization has developed over time with customers and partners (relationship capital). Roos et al. (1998) observe the distinction between intellectual capital (IC) and organizational knowledge as follows: "While knowledge is a part of IC, IC is much more than just knowledge. Brands and trademarks as well as the management of relations with external parties (trade distributors, allies, customers, local communities, stakeholders in general and the like) are all dimensions of value creation" (p. 24). The strategic management of intellectual capital is concerned not only with the identification and measurements of stocks of organizational knowledge, but also with the control and alignment of knowledge flow across organizational levels in order to enhance performance.

The book concludes with an appendix excerpted from a research report published by the Conference Board in 2000 which analyzed data collected by a survey and interviews with a working group of senior executives from 12 global organizations. The report provides insights into the practice of knowledge management and organizational learning from the perspective of senior line and staff executives.

Audience

This book is designed to meet the needs of students, faculty, and researchers working in the areas of strategy management and knowledge management. It may be used as a core text or supplement, especially in departments of business policy and strategy within schools of business, and in departments of management information systems. The text would also be useful in schools and departments of information management or information science. The material in this book would be of significant interest to the growing numbers of managers, professionals, and practitioners who are leading, designing, or executing knowledge strategies in their organizations.

Acknowledgments

This book is the outcome of the generous knowledge sharing of the seventy-four authors who took part in this project. We are deeply indebted to each and every contributor who has created an original chapter for the volume. We salute the authors of the reprinted chapters for laying the foundation. We are grateful to Professor Ikujiro Nonaka for writing the foreword and to Professor Henry Mintzberg for suggesting the idea of adapting a chapter from *Strategy Safari*. We are grateful to the two reviewers who read the lengthy manuscript and provided helpful suggestions.

Katherine Young and John King, both graduate students of the Faculty of Information Studies at the University of Toronto, assisted with the preparation of the book. Over the years, interactions with students of the classes we teach at the University of Toronto and McMaster University have helped to sharpen some of the ideas presented here. The FIS Inforum library staff redefined customer service in responding to our requests. Finally, a special note of appreciation goes to the editors at Oxford University Press in New York. Kenneth MacLeod first approached one of us with the idea for this volume and advised the project through much of its duration. Martha Cooley, who joined the project later, effectively steered the project to completion. Paul Donnelly, the executive editor, guided the project during a transition period.

The intellectual breadth and diversity of this collection point to the energy and momentum driving this work. If we mark the beginning of

this research near the beginning of the 1990s, we are at a stage where reflection and synthesis of what we have learned so far will enrich the practice and inquiry of both strategy management and knowledge management. Our hope is that the book will contribute to our understanding of the link between strategy, knowledge, and intellectual capital, for there could be no more appropriate way to express our gratitude to the many colleagues and friends who took part in this enterprise.

Acknowledgments

chapter 3

Blackler, Frank. 1995. "Knowledge, Knowledge Work and Organizations: An Overview and Interpretation." *Organization Studies* 16(6):1021–1046. Copyright 1995 by Frank Blackler, Reprinted by permission of Frank Blackler.
The section entitled "Epilogue" is new material, copyright 2002 Oxford University Press.

chapter 7

Reprinted by permission, Kathleen Conner & CK Prahalad, "Resource-Based Theory of the Firm," *Organization Science*, vol. 7 no. 5, 1996. Copyright 1996, the Institute for Operations Research and the Management Sciences (INFORMS), 9001 Elkridge Landing Road, Suite 400, Linthieum, Maryland 21090-2909 USA.

chapter 14

Garud, R., and A. Kumaraswamy. 1995. "Technological and Organizational Designs to Achieve Economies of Substitution." *Strategic Management Journal* 16 (Special Issue):93–110. Copyright 1995 by John Wiley & Sons Limited. Reproduced by permission of John Wiley & Sons Limited. The section entitled "Commentary: Harnessing Intellectual Capital for Increasing Returns" is new material, copyright 2002 Oxford University Press.

chapter 15

Zack, Michael H. 1999. "Developing a Knowledge Strategy." *California Management Review* 41(3):125–145. Copyright 1999 by California Management Review. Reprinted by permission of California Management Review via the Copyright Clearance Center. The section entitled "Epilogue" is new material, copyright 2002 Oxford University Press.

chapter 18

Helfat, Constance, and Ruth Raubitschek. 2000. "Product Sequencing: Co-evolution of Knowledge, Capabilities and Products." *Strategic Management Journal* 21(10–11):961–979. Copyright 2000 by John Wiley & Sons Limited. Reproduced by permission of John Wiley & Sons Limited.
The section entitled "Epilogue: Product Sequencing, Knowledge, and E-Commerce" is new material, copyright 2002 Oxford University Press.

chapter 21

Starbuck, William H. 1993. "Keeping a Butterfly and an Elephant in a House of Cards: The Elements of Exceptional Success." *Journal of Management Studies* 30(6):885–921. Copyright 1993 by Blackwell Publishers Ltd. Reprinted by permission of Blackwell Publishers Ltd. The section entitled "Addendum: Wachtell, Lipton, Rosen and Katz" is new material, copyright 2001 Oxford University Press.

chapter 24

Nonaka, Ikujiro. 1994. "A Dynamic Theory of Organizational Knowledge Creation." *Organization Science* 5(1):14–37. Copyright 1994 by Institute for Operations Research & The Management Sciences. Reprinted by permission of Institute for Operations Research & The Management Sciences via the Copyright Clearance Center.

chapter 27

Leonard, Dorothy, Sensiper, Sylvia. 1998. "The Role Of Tacit Knowledge In Group Innovation." *California Management Review* 40(3):112–132. Copyright 1998 by California Management Review. Reprinted by permission of California Management Review via the Copyright Clearance Center.
The section entitled "Epilogue" is new material, copyright 2002 Oxford University Press.

chapter 30

Appleyard, M.M. 1996. "How Does Knowledge Flow? Interfirm Patterns in the Semiconductor Industry." *Strategic Management Journal* 17 (Winter):137–154. Copyright 1996 by John Wiley & Sons Limited. Reproduced by permission of John Wiley & Sons Limited.
The section entitled "Commentary" is new material, copyright 2002 Oxford University Press.

chapter 35

Bontis, Nick. 1999. "Managing Organizational Knowledge by Diagnosing Intellectual Capital: Framing and Advancing the State of the Field." *International Journal of Technology Management* 18(5–8):433–462. Reprinted by permission of Interscience Enterprises Ltd.

chapter 36

We fully acknowledge MCB University Press as copyright holder and first place of publication of: Bontis, Nick. 1998. "Intellectual Capital: An Exploratory Study That Develops Measures and Models." *Management Decision* 36(2):63–76.

chapter 38

Nahapiet, Janine, and Sumantra Ghoshal. 1998. "Social Capital, Intellectual Capital, and the Organizational Advantage." *Academy of Management Review* 23(2):242–266. Copyright 1998 by Academy of Management. Reprinted by permission of Academy of Management via the Copyright Clearance Center.

References

Bierly, P., and Chakrabarti, A. (1996) "Generic knowledge strategies in the U.S. pharmaceutical industry." *Strategic Management Journal* 17: 123–135.

de Geus, A.P. (1988) "Planning as learning." *Harvard Business Review* 66(2):70–74.

Itami, H. (1987) *Mobilizing Invisible Assets.* Cambridge, MA: Harvard University Press.

Kogut, B. and Zander, Y. (1992) "Knowledge of the firm, combinative capabilities, and the replication of technology." *Organization Science* 3(3):383–397.

Roos, J., Roos, G., and Dragonetti, N.C. (1998) *Intellectual Capital: Navigating in the New Business Landscape.* New York: New York University Press.

Spender, J.C. and Grant, R.M. (1996) "Knowledge and the firm: overview." *Strategic Management Journal* 17:5–10.

Zack, M.H. (1999) "Developing a knowledge strategy." *California Management Review* 41(3): 125–145.

Contents

*Original chapter.
**Reprinted chapter with new commentary by contributor(s).

*Original chapter.
**Reprinted chapter with new commentary by contributor(s).

*Original chapter.
**Reprinted chapter with new commentary by contributor(s).

Appendix

*Original chapter.
**Reprinted chapter with new commentary by contributor(s).

Contributors

RUSSELL L. ACKOFF, The Wharton School, University of Pennsylvania

PAUL S. ADLER, Marshall School of Business, University of Southern California

RAFAEL ANDREU, IESE, University of Navarra

MELISSA APPLEYARD, Darden School, University of Virginia

JANE BANASZAK-HOLL, School of Public Health, University of Michigan

VINCENT P. BARABBA, General Motors Corporation

JOEL A. C. BAUM, Rotman School of Management, University of Toronto

WHITNEY BERTA, Department of Health Administration, University of Toronto

PAUL BIERLY III, College of Business, James Madison University

FRANK BLACKLER, Lancaster University, Management School

MAX BOISOT, ESADE School of Business Administration, Barcelona

NICK BONTIS, DeGroote School of Business, McMaster University

WIM BOUMAN, Center of Excellence for Innovative Technologies in Organizations, Universiteit van Amsterdam

DILYS BOWMAN, School of Public Health, University of Michigan

JOYCE BROWN, Goizueta Business School, Emory University

DANIEL CHAUVEL, The Theseus Institute

CHONG JU CHOI, Judge Institute of Management Studies, University of Cambridge

CHUN WEI CHOO, Faculty of Information Studies, University of Toronto

CLAUDIO CIBORRA, London School of Economics

KATHLEEN R. CONNER, School of Business, University of Michigan

MARY CROSSAN, Ivey School of Business, University of Western Ontario

PAULA DALY, College of Business, James Madison University

DONNA MARIE DE CAROLIS, LeBow College of Business, Drexel University

CHARLES DESPRES, Graduate School of Business, Marseille-Provence

MICHAEL DEVAUGHN, School of Business, University of Wisconsin-Madison

AMY EDMONDSON, Harvard Business School, University of Wisconsin–Madison

RAGHU GARUD, Stern School of Business, New York University

SUMANTRA GHOSHAL, London Business School

SIMON GRAND, Institute for Management, University of St. Gallen, Switzerland

ROBERT M. GRANT, McDonough School of Business, Georgetown University, City University, London

BRIAN HACKETT, The Conference Board

CONSTANCE E. HELFAT, Amos Tuck School of Business Administration, Dartmouth College

ARD HUIZING, Faculty of Economic Sciences and Econometrics, Universiteit van Amsterdam

JOHN HULLAND, Ivey School of Business, University of Western Ontario

KAZUO ICHIJO, Graduate School of International Corporate Strategy, Hitotsubashi University

ALAINA KANFER, BORN Inc.

ANASTASIOS KARAMANOS, Judge Institute of Management Studies, University of Cambridge

ANNE MARIE KNOTT, The Wharton School, University of Pennsylvania

SEIJA KULKKI, Center for Knowledge and Innovation Research, Helsinki School of Economics and Business Administration

ARUN KUMARASWAMY, School of Business–Camden, Rutgers University

DOROTHY LEONARD, Harvard Business School

SHARON MATUSIK, Jesse Jones Graduate School of Management, Rice University

WILL MITCHELL, University of Michigan Business School

MIHNEA MOLDOVEANU, Rotman School of Management, University of Toronto

JANINE NAHAPIET, Templeton College, Oxford University

IKUJIRO NONAKA, School of Knowledge Science, Japan Advanced Institute for Science and Technology

STEVE PIKE, Intellectual Capital Services

JOSEPH PORAC, Goizueta Business School, Emory University

JOHN POURDEHNAD, Ackoff Center for Advanced Systems Approaches, University of Pennsylvania

C. K. PRAHALAD, School of Business, University of Michigan

RUTH S. RAUBITSCHEK, U.S. Department of Justice

GÖRAN ROOS, Intellectual Capital Services

ANNA RYLANDER, Intellectual Capital Services

RON SANCHEZ, IMD, Lausanne

SYLVIA SENSIPER, Harvard Business School

DEBORAH SOLE, Harvard Business School

J.-C. SPENDER, Fashion Institute of Technology

WILLIAM STARBUCK, Stern School of Business, New York University

GABRIEL SZULANSKI, The Wharton School, University of Pennsylvania

BEN TORREY, Accenture Inc.

KATSUHIRO UMEMOTO, Graduate School of Knowledge Science, Japan Advanced Institute of Science and Technology

GEORGE VON KROGH, Institute for Management, University of St. Gallen, Switzerland

JAMES B. WADE, School of Business, University of Wisconsin–Madison

SIDNEY G. WINTER, The Wharton School, University of Pennsylvania

YOUNGJIN YOO, Weatherhead School of Management, Case Western Reserve University

MICHAEL H. ZACK, College of Business Administration, Northeastern University

The Strategic Management of Intellectual Capital and Organizational Knowledge

1

Knowledge, Intellectual Capital, and Strategy

Themes and Tensions

Chun Wei Choo and Nick Bontis

The conversations in this volume about the role of knowledge in strategy management may be framed by seven basic questions:

1. What unique perspective does a knowledge-based view of the firm offer?
2. Should the organization focus on creating new knowledge or applying what it already knows?
3. How does an organization create new knowledge?
4. What knowledge should the firm share and transfer, and what knowledge should the firm protect?
5. Is a knowledge-based strategy the product of careful planning, or the outcome of learning and discovery?
6. What is the difference between managing knowledge and managing intellectual capital?
7. What are the main levers for designing a knowledge-based strategy?

Most of the chapters in this book directly or indirectly address these questions. We searched for

concepts that would increase our understanding, in two iterations. Below we first review the main ideas presented by contributors in each of the seven parts of the book, highlighting the ways in which they connect with or differ from each other. After these sectional reviews, we draw upon the principal themes presented by the contributors in an attempt to answer the questions raised above. We conclude this introductory chapter with a framework that brings together the major elements in our discussions about strategic knowledge management.

Review of the Sections

Knowledge in Organizations

We begin part I with two chapters that examine the fundamental ways that we look at organizations. Adler (chap. 2) revisits the market and the hierarchy as mechanisms for coordination and makes the observation that a third form of coordination based on trust and community will become more important in a knowledge-intensive economy. Moreover, this form of trust is new. Instead of being derived from tradition or loyalty, the new trust is built upon values of competence and integrity. This trust will be tempered by hierarchical rules to ensure stability, and by market competition to ensure flexibility. Blackler (chap. 3) sees the creation and use of knowledge as the collective outcome of social practice that he labels organizational knowing. As a phenomenon, knowing is situated, mediated, provisional, pragmatic, and contested. A promising framework to analyze knowledge work would be the version of activity theory developed by Yrjo Engestrom, which views human activity systems as multiple mediated interactions between individuals, communities or groups, tools, and concepts. Boisot (chap. 4) maps the creation and sharing of organization in his information space model. His focus is on the articulation and diffusion of knowledge. The articulation of organizational knowledge requires abstraction (creating cognitive categories to make sense of events) and codification (refining the categories to simplify distinguishing between them). The more abstract and codified the knowledge, the more diffusible it is. Diffusion results in use when the new knowledge is absorbed and embedded in practice. Choo (chap. 5) combines elements from Blackler's concept of organizational knowing and Boisot's information-based analysis. Strategy is seen as the outcome of organizational sensemaking, knowledge creation, and decision making. The greater the interplay between these three information processes, the more effective the organizational learning and adaptation. The final chapter by Despres and Chauvel (chap. 6) makes a broad survey of the literature and identifies seven concepts that structure the discussion on knowledge management: time, type or forms of knowledge, social space, context, transformation or dynamics, carriers or media, and knowledge culture.

Knowledge-Based Perspectives of the Firm

Conner and Prahalad (chap. 7) begin part II by contrasting a resource-based theory of the firm with the opportunism-based model of the firm in transaction cost economics. They note that the organizational mode (market or firm) through which individuals cooperate affects the knowledge they apply to business activity. Specifically, the organizational mode affects knowledge sub-

stitution (how present knowledge is employed) and knowledge flexibility (how future knowledge is acquired). In the choice of organizational mode, opportunism-independent considerations can outweigh opportunism-based ones. When the possibility for opportunism is low, transaction cost economics predicts the choice of a market mode. However, the resource-based theory predicts that a firm organization would nevertheless be selected in low-opportunism conditions when it results in more valuable knowledge being applied to the business activity.

Grant (chap. 8) points out that we do have a number of concepts that articulate a knowledge-based view of the firm: (1) Knowledge is the most important resource for generating market value and economic rent. (2) Explicit and tacit types of knowledge vary in their transferability. (3) Knowledge is subject to economies of scale and scope, and knowledge-intensive industries may experience increasing returns. (4) Knowledge is created by human beings, who need to specialize to be efficient in knowledge creation and storage. (5) Producing a good or service typically requires the application of many types of knowledge. Based on these observations, Grant asserts that firms exist to create conditions in which multiple individuals can integrate their specialist knowledge. He identifies four integration mechanisms (rules and directives, sequencing, routines, and group problem solving and decision making) that need to be supported by a base of "common knowledge" (common language, shared meanings, overlapping knowledge).

Spender (chap. 9) also examines the "integration" theme. He distinguishes two domains of knowledge management. One presumes that knowledge is objectifiable as an asset, while the other sees knowledge as the response to uncertainty arising from management's lack of knowledge on how to integrate what the firm knows explicitly. In the knowledge-based theory of the firm, knowledge thus has a front face that comprises knowledge about the elements of the firm's activities, and assumes that they are inherently designable; and a back face that analyzes the uncertainties of integrating the front-face elements. As does Grant, Spender considers "common knowledge" the key to this integration.

Von Krogh and Grand (chap. 10) specify that a knowledge-based theory of the firm would need concepts to explain knowledge origin, knowledge creation, how the firm establishes coherence, revolutionary versus evolutionary changes, and the link between managerial action and knowledge creation leading to success. On this last criterion, they suggest that knowledge management should focus on the management of conditions enabling knowledge creation. These enabling conditions include formulating a vision, enabling new experiences among members, structuring relationships among members, changing the relationships, changing the quality of the relationships, and creating knowledge-centered activism.

Huizing and Bouman (chap. 11) introduce the concept of information transaction space as the set of possible information exchanges available to an actor at a point in time: a "market for knowledge" where information seekers, providers and brokers organize arrangements for information exchange. The object of knowledge management is then the efficient allocation of the information transaction space. Four ideal-type governance modes are presented: (1) In the market mode, information demand and supply shape exchange relationships. (2) In the organized market, knowledge management helps solve the problem of finding reliable sources. (3) In the extended organized market, the focus is on finding sources *and* asking relevant questions unambiguously. (4) Finally, in the firm, the information space is organized to address all three problems of finding sources, asking relevant questions, and facilitating interpretation and use.

Knowledge Strategy

In part III, both Zack (chap. 15) and Bierly and Daly (chap. 16) provide definitions of knowledge strategy. Zack sees it as competitive strategy that is built around a firm's intellectual resources and capabilities. Bierly and Daly define it as the set of strategic choices addressing knowledge creation in an organization, which guide the development of intellectual capital and thus competitive advantage. These two chapters also present typologies of knowledge strategies that share the same pair of classificatory dimensions: the degree to which the firm creates or applies knowledge (exploration vs. exploitation), and the degree to which the firm learns or obtains knowledge internally or externally (internal vs. external). Zack suggests that aggressive knowledge strategies based on innovative knowledge that crosses boundaries would yield superior performance. Bierly and Daly describe "bimodal learners" that excel at both exploration and exploitation.

The three chapters by Winter and Szulanski (chap. 12), Sanchez (chap. 13), and Garud and Kumaraswamy (chap. 14) all elaborate on the exploitation theme of leveraging existing knowledge to derive competitive advantage. Winter and Szulanski show that the replication of organizational routines is an effective strategy for firms to exploit their knowledge assets. Moreover, firms pursuing replication are useful "laboratories" for studying differences in knowledge transfer and use. Garud and Kumaraswamy propose that in times of continuous and systemic change, firms need to take advantage of economies of substitution by reusing and retaining existing components when developing high-performing systems. To reduce the cost of component reuse, firms would need to simultaneously pursue elements normally viewed as antagonistic, for example, incremental and radical learning, markets, and hierarchies. Sanchez continues the discussion of knowledge reuse by focusing on the principle of modularity. Firms that systematically develop modular product and process architectures are specifying and articulating firm knowledge with the clarity needed to facilitate reuse, substitution, and reconfiguration of components. This in turn can promote strategic learning through leveraging current architectures as well as creating next-generation architectures.

Choi and Karamanos (chap. 17) observe that it is increasingly difficult to assess with high certainty the exchange value of knowledge-based goods. Instead of trying to value goods themselves, we rely on indices or indicators in the socioeconomic environment to identify certain actors and to certify their resources. Consequently, firms pursuing a knowledge strategy would need to understand what these indices are and how they may be managed.

Knowledge Strategy in Practice

The chapters in part IV describe and analyze knowledge management in practice in a range of settings: technology-intensive Japanese companies (Sony, Canon, NEC), Toyota Motor Company, General Motors, a highly regarded U.S. law firm, Accenture/ Andersen Consulting, a venture capital company, and a Canadian government agency. Helfat and Raubitschek (chap. 18) and Knott (chap. 19) examine knowledge creation and use in the context of cycles of product development over time and across different chains or families of products. Helfat and Raubitschek show that knowledge, capabilities, and products coevolve, so the firm's changing portfolios of products and knowledge open up strategic opportunities for linking products within and across chains. Knott examines the product development history of a successful Toyota car model and found evidence that the firm had executed a knowledge strategy based on combining exploitation and exploration. Rather than mutually exclusive, exploitation and exploration are complements that reinforce each other. Barabba et al. (chap. 20) apply a systems approach to knowledge management and present a design of a learning and adaptation support system that has been implemented at General Motors. The system tracks significant decisions, checks assumptions and outcomes, diagnoses deviations, and makes new learning available to others. The GM experience shows that the willingness to learn is high when users have confidence in the quality of diagnosis and error correction.

Moving from manufacturing to the services sector, Starbuck (chap. 21) takes an engaged and engaging look at the highly profitable and innovative U.S. law firm of Wachtell, Lipton, Rosen, and Katz. Starbuck attributes the success of the firm to its ability to assimilate what appear to be conflicting principles and to learn swiftly from experience, converting initial difficulties into opportunities. Yoo and Torrey (chap. 23) report interesting differences in how consultants of a global management consulting firm create, seek, and share knowledge in two countries. Differences in national cultures would account for the patterns that emerge. (Appleyard [chap. 30] in Part VI also reports differences in knowledge sharing between Japanese and U.S. employees in the semiconductor industry.) Multinational firms should recognize and manage the influence of national cultures, through, for example, training and ways of leveraging particular cultural traits. Moldoveanu (chap. 22) contrasts two epistemologies at work in a venture capital company and a government department as they decide whether to provide financial support for a high-technology start-up firm. Whereas the government department applied a rule-following "justificationist" approach, the venture capital company exercised a more open and questioning "falsificationist" approach. The latter's more adaptive belief revision strategy led to more robust causal models for guiding investment decisions.

Knowledge Creation

The common theme in part V is the knowledge creation model developed by Nonaka (chap. 24).

There are many aspects to the model (a full elaboration is in Nonaka and Takeuchi 1995), but among the most widely cited are the distinctions between tacit and explicit knowledge, and the cycle of four processes that create new knowledge by converting tacit knowledge into explicit knowledge (the socialization-externalization-combination-internalization, or SECI, model). Since 1995, more conceptual elements have been added to the basic model. Umemoto, a colleague of Nonaka, discusses in chapter 25 three major extensions in terms of concepts and applications: the concept of "Ba" or shared context for knowledge creation, sharing, and use; a typology of knowledge assets (experiential, conceptual, systemic, and routine knowledge assets); and knowledge leadership that provides "enabling conditions" conducive to knowledge creation. Ichijo (chap. 26) examines the tension between exploitation and exploration in the context of knowledge creation and suggests that both exploration (of firm-unique knowledge) and exploitation (of public knowledge) are necessary to increase intellectual capital and competitive advantage. Kulkki (chap. 28), who completed her doctoral work with Nonaka, expands the analysis of knowledge creation to global companies. She draws the distinction between local and global knowledge and investigates how some global firms are "architects of time" in the way that they "constitutively create their futures and their future markets with customers, partners, suppliers, and so on." This co-creation combines local and global innovation processes and is based on shared visions and experiences at the local and global levels. Leonard and Sensiper (chap. 27) suggest three ways that tacit knowledge is exercised in group innovation: problem solving, problem finding, and prediction and anticipation. In problem solving, experts overlay a problem with patterns derived from experience to quickly find a solution. In problem finding, tacit knowledge is used to frame a problem, often in a way that challenges assumptions or reveals hidden dimensions, so as to stimulate more radical innovation. In prediction and anticipation, tacit knowledge enables the prepared mind to follow hunches, listen to intuition, and take mental leaps to new ideas.

Knowledge across Boundaries

Transferring knowledge from beyond the firm's boundaries is an important strategy for organizations to add depth or breadth to their knowledge-based capabilities. In part VI, the review chapter by Fischer et al. (chap. 29) highlights findings in the research on knowledge transfer in alliances. Knowledge transferred is not necessarily assimilated or applied. The outcome of the knowledge transfer is conditioned by (1) the tacitness or causal ambiguity of the knowledge and (2) the capacity of the firm to absorb the knowledge, or absorptive capacity (Cohen and Levinthal 1990). Recent research has extended the concept of absorptive capacity beyond technical similarities to include such nontechnical similarities as organizational structures and compensation schemes. Fischer et al. suggest that conceptual frameworks from organizational learning and social network theory would be helpful when analyzing interfirm knowledge transfer. This same suggestion appears to have been taken up by other authors in this section without prior prompting. The effect of similarity between units in an organizational chain on the transfer of knowledge is examined empirically by Mitchell et al. (chap. 31). They found that transfer learning was both constrained and facilitated by the level and similarity of capabilities in component units and their chains. High-capability chains transferred knowledge to low-capability components, but low-capability chains required high-capability components to "regress" to capabilities the chain was more experienced with.

A second, related theme of this part of the book is the importance of social, cultural, or community norms that support knowledge sharing and contribution. The field study by Sole and Edmondson (chap. 33) suggests that in dispersed, cross-functional teams, members not only need to engage knowledge from diverse communities in order to surmount difficult problems, but also have to integrate this knowledge by developing congruent understandings of the structure and goals of the collective effort, and by developing norms and practices for communication and information sharing. Ciborra and Andreu (chap. 32) combine organizational learning with knowledge transfer as they develop the learning ladder model to analyze knowledge sharing within and between firms, and among firms collaborating in weblike networks. The way the Linux community has been able to operate successfully as a self-organizing weblike organization challenges conventional notions about coordination and governance, opportunism and free riding, and intellectual property rights protection.

A third theme in this part is the recognition that knowledge transfer is inherently two-way, so that some knowledge is given away even as new knowledge is acquired. Both Appleyard (chap. 30) and Matusik (chap. 34) propose a cost-benefit analysis approach to understand firms' decisions to share knowledge. Two categories of costs appear important: costs due to the loss of knowledge by the focal firm, and costs due to having to manage the knowledge transfer transaction. Appleyard's survey of U.S. and Japanese firms in the semiconductor industry also reveals interesting differences in their patterns of knowledge sharing. Employees in the United States relied more on private channels, while Japanese employees relied more on public channels. Thus, U.S. employees were approached more frequently for technical information, but Japanese employees were more likely to answer the (fewer) requests that they did receive. (See also Yoo and Torrey in [chap. 23] Part IV, who report differences in knowledge sharing by Korean and U.S. employees in a consulting firm.)

Managing Intellectual Capital

The chapters in part VII discuss intellectual capital and the stock of knowledge in the firm. Intellectual capital theorists Bontis (chaps. 35 and 36), Nahapiet and Ghoshal (chap. 38) and DeCarolis (chap. 39) propose a multifaceted description comprising human, structural, customer, relational, and social capital. Whereas the intellectual capital literature clearly identifies human capital and structural capital as distinct components, the final three seem to be intertwined and require further unraveling.

Bontis argues that customer capital is a subset of relational capital. In other words, the knowledge embedded in customers in the form of marketing and sales intelligence considers only one element of the integrated value chain. Presumably, organizations have knowledge embedded throughout their value chain, starting with their suppliers. Considering both directions of the value chain requires a broader conceptualization than originally proposed in the literature. Relational capital extends the definition of customer capital by including both sides of the value chain.

Nahapiet and Ghoshal expand the concept of social capital further by including all knowledge embedded in the social network of a firm beyond that of customers and suppliers. While the conceptualization of human and structural capital were initially focused inward, the advent of relational and social capital allows theorists to include an important environmental context as well. DeCarolis further develops the concept of social capital by providing an important link to entrepreneurial activities.

Pike et al. (chap. 37) bring two vital perspectives into the fold. Although essential for practitioners, accounting disclosure still remains an untapped research area for intellectual capital academics. Researchers recognize the importance of describing intellectual capital assets, but accounting policy makers are facing enormous roadblocks in implementing generally accepted principles that will be universally accepted. There is a tremendous opportunity for researchers to fill the void.

Crossan and Hulland (chap. 40) examine the links among learning, strategy, and knowledge management, and the role of leadership in organizational learning. They found a strong correlation between leadership and all elements of the organizational learning system. Moreover, there is also a strong correlation between the organizational learning system and organizational performance. They conclude that, over time, firms need to innovate through "feed-forward flow of learning" (exploration) while also ensuring financial returns through "feedback flow of learning" that institutionalizes new learning through the levels of the organization (exploitation). Crossan and Hulland show clearly how organizational learning can bring a dynamic, process perspective to the strategic management of stocks and flows of organizational knowledge.

Themes and Tensions

The collection of 41 chapters by seventy-four authors in this volume forms a rich pool of thinking and writing in which to look for patterns and motifs. Some of the themes are already apparent from the summaries above, but here our intent is to clarify and broaden these conceptual pathways, bringing in other related work that illuminates these themes.

What Unique Perspective Does a Knowledge-Based View of the Firm Offer?

Toward a Knowledge-Based Theory of the Firm

A theory of the firm seeks to answer at least three questions: Why do firms exist? What determines the scale and scope of firms? Why do firms differ? One widely applied approach to ad-dressing these questions is based on transaction cost economics. Williamson (1975, 1991) proposes that the unit of analysis in organizational study should be the transaction, or the exchange of a good or service. An organization is seen as a pattern of transactions between individuals or groups of individuals, and it therefore adopts the structure that offers the lowest transaction costs for the exchanges it wishes to enter into. Transactions of goods or services consist of contractual relationships. Williamson (1995) argues that the efficacy of the contracting mechanism is constrained by bounded rationality and subject to opportunism or "self-interest seeking with guile" (p. 26). Moreover, asset specificity arises when the firm is dependent on suppliers who have made specialized investment to engage in the transaction. Where bounded rationality, opportunism, and asset specificity occur together, transactions are better mediated by the private ordering of contracts. In the world of governance, the imperative is to organize transactions so as to economize on bounded rationality while safeguarding them against the hazards of opportunism. Williamson (1975) suggests that there are three generic governance structures: the market, the hierarchy, and a hybrid structure. Organizations move from the market to the hierarchy as transactions become more complex and uncertain. The hierarchy extends the bounds on rationality by allowing specialization in decision making and savings in communication; curbs opportunism by allowing incentive and control techniques; "absorbs" uncertainty and allows interdependent units to adapt to contingencies; resolves small-numbers indeterminacies by fiat; and reduces information gaps between exchange agents by allowing audits and other checks (Williamson 1975, p. 257).

The development of a knowledge-based theory of the firm is still in its infancy. One approach, first broached by Edith Penrose in 1959 (see Penrose 1995), is based on the idea that firms develop unique capabilities or "resources" as they develop products; build up research, production, and marketing capabilities; and learn from their customers. The resource-based view conceptualizes firms as bundles of resources that are heterogeneously distributed across firms. Moreover, these resources cannot be transferred between firms without cost, so a firm's resource differences will persist over time. Resources may include a firm's specific physical assets (e.g., equipment), human resources (e.g., expertise), and organizational processes (e.g., marketing).

When firms possess resources that are valuable (they bring about efficiency or effectiveness) and rare, they can produce competitive advantage. Additionally, when these resources are also inimitable (difficult to replicate) and nonsubstitutable (other resources cannot serve the same function), then the competitive advantage becomes sustainable (Barney 1991). Conner and Prahalad (chap. 7 this volume) show how the resource-based view predicts governance modes different from those predicted by transaction cost economics. When opportunism is low, transaction cost economics predicts the choice of a market mode. However, resource-based theory predicts that the firm structure would still be selected in low-opportunism conditions when it allows more valuable knowledge to be applied to the firm's activities. Ghoshal and Moran (1996) argue that firms are not mere substitutes for structuring efficient transactions when markets fail. The advantage of organizations over markets lies not in overcoming human shortcomings through hierarchy, but in leveraging the human ability to take initiative, cooperate, and learn, and the organizational ability to develop shared purpose. Thus, learning and trust would take the place of cost-economizing and opportunism.

In the ongoing debate between transaction cost economics (governance) and the resource-based (competence) perspective, Williamson (1999) observes that both views are needed:

> Given that both governance and competence are bounded rationality constructs and hold that organization matters, both share a lot of common ground. To be sure, there are differences. Governance is more microanalytic (the transaction is the basic unit of analysis) and adopts an economizing approach to assessing comparative economic organization, whereas competence is more composite (the routine is the unit of analysis?) and is more concerned with processes (especially learning) and the lessons for strategy. Healthy tensions are posed between them. Both are needed in our efforts to understand complex economic phenomena as we build towards a science of organization. (p. 1106)

Priem and Butler (2001a, b) evaluate the status of the resource-based view as a formal theory of the firm. They argue that its theoretical statements are true by definition and therefore tautological (e.g., "rare resources that enable a firm to implement specific value-creating strategies are a source of implementing strategies that are not being pursued by competitors"). The definition of "resources" is also problematic, since virtually anything associated with the firm can be a resource. Furthermore, the dependent variable ("value") lies outside the framework: value is determined by the product-market environment that is external to the firm. As a result, the theory is silent on "how" questions: "*How* can the resource be obtained? How and in which contexts does it contribute to competitive advantage? *How* does it interact/compare with other resources?" (Priem and Butler 2001a, p. 35).

In a rejoinder, Barney (2001) discusses a number of practical implications resulting from the resource-based logic. Firms experiencing strategic disadvantage can use the framework to identify those valuable and rare assets that they do not possess, and to indicate that these resources can be duplicated by imitation or substitution. Firms can also use the model to more completely evaluate their range of resources, and then to exploit these resources for sustained strategic advantage. Finally, firms can use resource-based reasoning to ensure that they nurture and maintain the resources that are the source of their current competitive advantage.

Spender (1994) asserts that the resource-based view may be too narrow. By concentrating on the acquisition and protection of critical resources, it underestimates the importance of how resources are brought together, coordinated, integrated, and put into use. Spender suggests that this coordinating capacity is the essence of the firm, and that the core of the rent-producing firm is its ability to learn by doing and to develop its coordinating capabilities. Grant (chap. 8 this vol.) notes that a knowledge-based perspective on economic organization implies that we are shifting our focus away from governance, toward the mechanisms and contexts through which coordination is achieved: "If the goal of organizational analysis is to predict the most efficient structures and systems for organizing production, a knowledge-based perspective suggests that the primary consideration is not so much the institution for governing transactions (markets vs. firms) as the mechanisms through which knowledge integration is achieved."

Teece et al. (1997) propose that the competitive advantage of the firm depends on its dynamic capabilities, conditioned by its specific asset positions (its portfolio of knowledge and complementary assets), and the evolution path that it has taken. Dynamic capabilities are defined as "the firm's ability to integrate, build, and reconfigure internal and external competences to address rapidly changing environments" (p. 516). Eisenhardt and Martin (2000) extend the concept of dynamic capabilities to include "the organizational and strategic routines by which firms achieve new resource configurations" (p. 1107). They point out that some dynamic capabilities integrate and reconfigure resources, while others allow the firm to acquire and release resources. The chapters in this volume provide many examples of firms deriving competitive advantage from this movement and integration of resources. Winter and Szulanski describe the strategic replication of routines in Banc One and Rank Xerox. Mitchell et al. analyze the transfer of learning in chains of U.S. nursing homes. Helfat and Raubitschek examine the coevolution of knowledge, capabilities, and products through product sequencing capabilities in Sony, Canon, and NEC. Knott describes a product development capability at Toyota that integrated exploitation and exploration. Garud and Kumaraswamy, and Sanchez show that modularity and modular product and process architectures can help articulate the firm's knowledge and facilitate knowledge reconfiguration and reuse.

Three concepts characterize the theory development so far: (1) Firms possess specific resources and capabilities that are heterogeneously distributed. (2) Competitive advantage depends on the firm's knowledge and ability to continuously configure and integrate resources into value-creating strategies. (3) The firm develops competitive advantage by expanding its unique knowledge and capabilities, and by knowing the specific product and market contexts in which this knowledge generates value. Thus, "resources, representing what can be done by the firm, and the competitive environment, representing what must be done to compete effectively in satisfying customer needs, are both essential in the strategy-making process" (Priem and Butler 2001b, p. 64).

Should the Organization Focus on Creating New Knowledge or Applying What It Already Knows?

Exploration and Exploitation

The tension between exploitation and exploration has been sharply observed in organization theory. An organization that engages exclusively in exploration will ordinarily suffer from the fact that it never gains the returns of its knowledge. An organization that engages exclusively in exploitation will ordinarily suffer from obsolescence. The basic problem confronting an organization is "to engage in sufficient exploitation to ensure its current viability and, at the same time, to devote enough energy to exploration to ensure its future viability" (Levinthal and March 1993, p. 105). The returns to exploitation are more certain, more immediate, and closer in space than are returns to exploration (March 1991). However, the effect of exploitation is to increase competency in existing domains while raising the opportunity cost of exploration, resulting in "the traps of distinctive competence" or "the success trap" (Levinthal and March 1993). The reverse is a firm caught in a spiral of exploration, constant change, and frequent failure ("the failure trap"). Frequent failure is unsurprising since good new ideas are hard to come by, and time and experience are needed to learn how to make a good idea work. An organization can control the balance between exploration and exploitation by adjusting aspirations, beliefs, feedback, incentives, and socialization or selection processes (Levinthal and March 1993). An organization can break out of the success trap by raising aspirations to levels that induce exploration or new knowledge creation, or by introducing feedback that exaggerates the high value of exploration. For example, if aspiration levels are tied to the best performers in an industry, then individuals may perceive themselves as performing substantially below the standard and are more likely to take risks and to explore. Symmetrically, an organization can break out of a failure cycle by lowering aspirations or by introducing a particularly good alternative. When individuals perceive themselves as operating above or close to aspiration levels, they become risk averse and refrain from exploitation. In other words, modest success is associated with risk aversion (March and Shapira 1987).

The tension between exploration and exploitation is one of the themes that appears most persistently among the chapters in this volume. For example, Conner and Prahalad contrast the effects of knowledge-substitution (exploiting current knowledge) and knowledge flexibility (exploring future knowledge). Bierly and Daly, and Zack, who independently developed typologies of knowledge strategies, both use the dimension of exploitation versus exploration for classifying knowledge strategies. As we discuss below, the chapters by Crossan and Hulland, Ichijo, and Knott also examine this tension.

The discussions in this volume point to three strategy options. The first would be to focus on exploitation. Exploitation is the use of the firm's existing stocks of knowledge and capabilities. A knowledge strategy focused on exploitation implies the codification of knowledge, rendering it explicit so as to promote reuse in multiple contexts, and to facilitate recombination with other sets of knowledge in the firm. This point of view may be discerned in the chapters by Sanchez, Garud and Kumaraswamy, and Winter and Szulanski. Sanchez recommends that firms develop modular product and process architectures so that knowledge components defined in the architecture can be reconfigured and reused. Garud and Kumaraswamy suggest that firms gain economies of substitution through partial retention and reuse of existing components when designing high-performance systems. Winter and Szulanski show the efficacy of replicating organizational routines in exploiting a firm's knowledge assets.

The second strategy option would be to focus on exploration. Exploration leads to the creation of new knowledge that is then applied in the development of new products and services. Exploration and new knowledge can also expand the capabilities and range of responses available to the firm. (Knowledge creation is examined as a major theme on its own in the next section.)

The third option is to embrace both exploitation and exploration. Several authors in this volume present the case for this option. Knott found empirical evidence that Toyota had executed a knowledge strategy combining exploitation and exploration as complements that reinforced each other. Exploitation led to learning curve cost reductions across product developments, while exploration led to product improvements and innovations. Crossan and Hulland also concluded from their field study that firms need two kinds of learning flows—feed-forward and feedback— that correspond to exploration and exploitation. Ichijo found that GE combined exploration of firm-unique knowledge with exploitation of public knowledge. Whereas Knott, and Crossan and Hulland describe the coexistence of exploitation and exploration across different *processes*, Ichijo describes the dual strategy working on different *categories* of knowledge. Finally, Bierly and Daly propose a category of "bimodal learners" for firms that are adept at both exploration and exploitation. Bimodal learners may be "ambidextrous" organizations (Tushman and Anderson 1996) with multiple cultures or subcultures that allow it to pursue both directions successfully, or "chameleon" organizations that can rapidly switch their focus between exploitation and exploration in response to environmental changes.

To summarize somewhat baldly, the benefit of exploitation is based on increased efficiency, that of exploration is based on increased innovation, and that of a bimodal combination is based on enhanced adaptability. The task for researchers and practitioners is to clarify the conditions under which exploitation, exploration, and/or bimodal learning would create sustainable advantage. Such conditions would probably relate to the type of industry, the nature of the knowledge, and the characteristics of the firm and its activity.

How Do Organizations Create New Knowledge?

The Knowledge to Create Knowledge

The model of knowledge creation developed by Nonaka (chap. 24 this vol.) and Nonaka and Takeuchi (1995) is one of the most cited theories in the knowledge management literature. At the core of the model is the distinction between tacit and explicit knowledge, and the analysis of the dynamics of knowledge creation through cycles of socialization, externalization, combination, and internalization (SECI cycles) that engage tacit and explicit knowledge across organizational levels.

All organizational knowledge is rooted in tacit knowledge. Yet, as long as tacit knowledge remains the private property of individuals or select groups, the organization cannot multiply its value in at least two important modes. First, the organization is limited in its ability to leverage that knowledge to gain economies of scale or strategic advantage:

> Unless able to train large numbers of individuals or to transform skills into organizing principles, the craft shop is forever simply a shop. The speed of replication of knowledge determines the rate of growth; control over its diffusion deters competitive erosion of the market position. For a firm to grow, it must develop organizing principles and a widely held and shared code by which to orchestrate large numbers of people and, potentially, varied functions. (Kogut and Zander 1992, p. 390)

Second, the organization is unable to sustain cycles of new knowledge generation that depend on the continuous conversion of tacit and explicit knowledge, and on the amplification of this knowledge across many levels of the organization (Nonaka and Takeuchi 1995). Knowledge conversion takes place when people share, externalize, combine, and internalize their knowledge. Knowledge expansion takes place when new ideas and concepts move to other parts of the organization to spark new cycles of knowledge creation.

The dichotomy between tacit and explicit knowledge has been emphasized so often that we need to remind ourselves that the two not only are complementary to each other, but also are in many ways interdependent. In an organization, the exercise of one form of knowledge almost always requires the presence and utilization of the other form. Thus, the exercise of tacit knowledge typically makes references to plans or blueprints, entails the handling of tools and equipment, and involves following written or oral instructions, all of which embody various kinds of explicit knowledge. Conversely, the application of explicit knowledge often requires individuals who can interpret, elaborate, demonstrate, or instantiate the formal knowledge with respect to a particular problem setting. Behind every formal knowledge system in an organization is an informal support structure that is just as important and necessary for the organization to function properly. Some of the most useful sources of knowledge in an organization are those that combine the tacit and the explicit, that articulate the judgmental or the conjectural, and that reveal the hidden or the unobvious.

Organizations face a number of issues with respect to the management of its tacit knowledge. Tacit knowledge grows in the soil of experience, so employees need to be given the time and opportunity to specialize and build up expertise in a certain area. As an alternative to cultivating its own tacit knowledge, an organization may consider contracting desired expertise on a "just-in-time" basis. This approach has limitations since tacit knowledge is not exercised in isolation, but needs to be contextualized and combined with the organization's explicit and cultural knowledge. Another basic concern is one of access: how does an organization find out and provide access to what its participants know, particularly when this personal knowledge defies codification and classification? As long as the personal knowledge remains tacit, it constitutes a unique competitive advantage for the organization, since the knowledge is hard for other organizations to copy. Unfortunately, this uniqueness is not permanent or

protected, since the tacit knowledge is lost should the individual decide to leave the organization (and perhaps join a competitor!). The organization managing its tacit knowledge has to deal with three major challenges: how to deepen its own stocks of tacit knowledge, how to access and activate this knowledge, and how to maximize the value derived from its use.

While the classification of organizational knowledge as tacit and explicit is widely discussed, the category of cultural knowledge is less often encountered. In epistemology, knowledge is sometimes defined as justified true belief (Audi 1998, Moser et al. 1998). An organization's cultural knowledge thus consists of the beliefs it holds to be true and justifiably so (based on experience, observation, reflection) about itself, its environment, and its way of doing business. Importantly, an organization's cultural knowledge is used to answer such questions as, What kind of business are we in? What is our business model? What knowledge would be valuable to the organization? What knowledge would be worth pursuing? Cultural knowledge consists of the assumptions and beliefs that are habitually used by organizational members to perceive and explain reality, as well as the criteria and conditions that are used to assign value and significance to new knowledge. Collins (1998) highlights two important roles of cultural knowledge: to understand and use facts, rules, and heuristics, and to make inductions in the same way as others in order to enable concerted action. Garud and Rappa (1994) suggest that the development of new knowledge based on technology is a sociocognitive process that rests on three definitions of technology: "technology as beliefs, artifacts, and evaluation routines" (p. 345). Technology development is guided by beliefs about what is possible, what is worth attempting, and what levels of effort are required. In their separate chapters in this volume, both Grant and Spender emphasize that knowledge integration in the firm is dependent on a base of "common knowledge" that consists of shared meanings, common language, and other forms of shared knowledge. Sole and Edmondson's chapter describes the need for dispersed teams to develop congruent understandings of the goals and structure of their collective effort in order to integrate knowledge.

Overall, an organization's beliefs about what technology or new knowledge is feasible and worth attempting, a part of its cultural knowledge, would influence the direction and intensity of the knowledge development effort, as well as the routines and norms by which new information and knowledge would be evaluated. In the context of knowledge creation, cultural knowledge plays the vital role of providing a pattern of shared assumptions so that the organization can assign significance to new information and knowledge. Cultural knowledge supplies values and norms that

> determine what kinds of knowledge are sought and nurtured, what kinds of knowledge-building activities are tolerated and encouraged. There are systems of caste and status, rituals of behavior, and passionate beliefs associated with various kinds of technological knowledge that are as rigid and complex as those associated with religion. Therefore, values serve as knowledge-screening and -control mechanisms. (Leonard 1995, p. 19)

There are familiar accounts of organizations in which cultural knowledge is misaligned with efforts to exploit tacit and explicit knowledge. For example, Xerox PARC in the 1970s had pioneered many innovations that Xerox itself did not exploit but other companies commercialized into products that defined the personal computer industry. PARC had invented or developed the bit-mapped display technology required for graphical user interfaces; software for on-screen windows and windows management; the mouse as a pointing device; the first personal computer, Alto; and an early word-processing software, Bravo, for the Alto (Hiltzik 1999). Xerox did not fully apprehend the application potential of these inventions because its perception of self and what kinds of knowledge it should pursue were bounded by its established position in the photocopier market, and its belief in a business model based on selling closed, integrated systems. Developing the new technologies would have been too radical and risky a departure from what Xerox believed was its core business. Many of the researchers working on these projects subsequently left PARC, taking their knowledge with them.

Nonaka and Takeuchi (1995) do include aspects of cultural knowledge in the way they divide tacit knowledge into technical and cognitive dimensions. The technical dimension encompasses practical know-how, while the cognitive dimension includes mental models, beliefs, and perspectives that are so ingrained that they are taken for granted and therefore cannot be easily

articulated. However, the suggestion here is that a separate category of cultural knowledge is helpful for the following reason. Tacit knowledge is personal knowledge that is lost to the organization when the individual leaves. Cultural knowledge, though to a large part not codified, remains with the organization as its membership changes. As beliefs and values that endure in the form of shared perceptions, incentive and reward systems, and evaluation methods and criteria, cultural knowledge has a powerful effect on the creation and adoption of new knowledge.

What Knowledge Should the Firm Share and Transfer, and What Knowledge Should the Firm Protect?

Moving Knowledge across Boundaries

Because of the substantial investment needed to create new knowledge and turn it into new products, coupled with the risk and uncertainty of the knowledge generation process, the distribution of valuable knowledge is unlikely to be uniform. As a result, the ownership of valuable knowledge can potentially earn both Ricardian and monopoly rents (Winter 1987). Ricardian rents are earned because the firm owning valuable knowledge possesses a factor of production that is more productive than its rivals. At the same time, monopoly rents are earned because the product developed with superior knowledge will be unique. The corollary of this reasoning is that the firm should protect its knowledge from appropriation or imitation (Liebeskind 1996). Spender and Grant (1996) note that "if knowledge is the primary resource upon which competitive advantage is founded, then its transferability determines the period over which its possessor can earn rents from it" (p. 7). Barney (1991) has identified inimitability as a criterion for assessing the ability of a resource to sustain strategic advantage.

Yet there are contexts where the deliberate sharing and transfer of knowledge constitute a strategic move. Firms in highly networked and densely connected industries where technologies and markets are still evolving may purposefully share knowledge in order to (1) encourage and enable the development of complementary products and services, (2) influence the development of common platforms, dominant designs, and de facto or formal standards, and (3) build up a critical mass of customers and users. Industries that experience network externalities where the value and usefulness of a good or service depend on the installed base of connected users may choose to share knowledge with customers, competitors, and collaborators. In addition to network externality effects, firms sharing knowledge may also stand to gain the advantage of increasing returns by establishing an early lead in a market or by developing a dominant position in an industry. The strategic challenge, then, becomes knowing what knowledge to transfer and what knowledge to retain as part of the firm's valuable, rare, inimitable, nonsubstitutable resources.

Boisot (chap. 4 this vol.) analyzes the paradoxical nature of the value of information goods using I-space (information space model). An information good maximizes its value when it is highly articulated (abstracted and codified), *and* when it is scarce. Paradoxically, the scarcity of highly articulated knowledge is difficult to maintain precisely because that knowledge has been codified and given structure and is therefore more diffusible. Boisot concludes:

> A critical skill for the knowledge-based firm will thus be to know what to share and what to hold on to. Recognizing when knowledge should be actively diffused to outsiders rather than hoarded, when it can be used to extend the firm's organizational reach beyond its boundaries, will become an important source of competitive advantage. Building up the capabilities of the networks a firm participates in through a judicious sharing of its knowledge strengthens its own competitive position within the network. Confining its internal focus to core strengths prevents it from overstretching what will always be limited cognitive resources. (chap. 4)

Sanchez (chap. 13 this vol.) suggests that the fear of losing explicit knowledge may be exaggerated. In a knowledge-intensive economy, organizations do not possess all the knowledge they need internally but increasingly rely on sharing or buying technologies or services from other organizations. The movement of knowledge within and between organizations is often in the form of transferring explicit knowledge. Because explicit knowledge is articulated knowledge, it is often assumed to be readily understood by others and can therefore diffuse more easily beyond an organization's boundary. Sanchez suggests that this assumption may not always be warranted. Even though the knowledge has been made explicit, the receiving organization may

experience problems of comprehension and valuation as it tries to understand and appraise the significance of the articulated knowledge. There may be several reasons: firms develop their own languages and vocabularies that others might not understand; different firms possess different levels of technical capability; different firms are at different stages of growth and development; the usefulness of the knowledge depends on its linkages with other knowledge, resources, and capabilities in the originating firm. Given these uncertainties, the assumption that explicit knowledge is fundamentally "less secure" than tacit knowledge may be simplistic. Each firm would need to identify the kinds of knowledge that constitute its distinctive competencies and maintain close control within the firm of the explicit or articulated knowledge that is most critical, while leveraging as broadly as possible with other firms knowledge that is strategically less critical.

Is a Knowledge-Based Strategy the Product of Careful Planning or the Outcome of Learning and Discovery?

Organizational Learning as Strategy Making

Three models of organizational learning as strategy making are presented in this volume. They share common assumptions and arrive at common implications: that the challenge of learning as strategy is managing the stocks and flows of knowledge across multiple levels of the organization in order to achieve both renewal and rent generation.

Crossan and Hulland (chap. 40 this vol.) show how organizational learning can bring a dynamic process perspective to the strategic management of stocks and flows of knowledge through the organization. The "4I framework" asserts that organizational learning takes place at the levels of the individual, group, and organization. These modes of learning are linked by social and psychological processes of intuiting, interpreting, integrating, and institutionalizing. The framework is operationalized as the "strategic learning assessment map" that describes and analyzes the stocks and flows of knowledge in a comprehensive organizational learning system. Their research suggests that the transference of learning across levels is one of the greatest challenges of managing organizational learning.

Another conceptualization of the levels of organizational learning is presented by Ciborra and Andreu (chap. 32 this vol.). They assert that learning occurs at the levels of (1) resources and work practices (routinization learning loop), (2) organizational routines (capability learning loop), and (3) firm goals and core capabilities (strategic loop). Each level of learning is dependent on resources and outcomes from the level beneath it, so the model resembles a "learning ladder." As do Crossan and Hulland, Ciborra and Andreu believe that it is the transformation of learning across these levels ("climbing up the rungs of the learning ladder") that poses the major strategic challenge.

In another dynamic, process view of strategic learning, Boisot (chap. 4 this vol.) describes a "social learning cycle" that is divided into the six phases: scanning (identifying threats and opportunities), problem solving (acquiring and codifying insights), abstraction (generalizing new insights), diffusion (sharing new insights with a population), absorption (applying insights through learning by doing), and impacting (embedding in concrete practices).

What Is the Difference Between Managing Knowledge and Managing Intellectual Capital?

The Intellectual Capital Turf War

The concepts of organizational learning, knowledge management, and intellectual capital overlap significantly, but it is possible to draw some helpful distinctions. Bontis et al. (2001) suggest that, at a general level of analysis, intellectual capital represents the "stock" of knowledge that exists in an organization at a particular point in time. Thus, it represents what the organization has learned in a cognitive sense. Managing this stock of knowledge in a firm as it flows and grows is the domain of knowledge management. The way that stocks of intellectual capital change and evolve over time is then dependent on knowledge management strategies. Finally, organizational learning expands the analysis to include behaviors at the individual, group, and organizational levels, as well as processes that create and utilize knowledge in order to understand more broadly how the "stocks" change and flow.

In his literature review, Bontis (this volume) describes both the benefits and challenges academic researchers face when studying the intellectual capital phenomenon. Its intuitive appeal allows ample opportunity for practitioners to work alongside academics in further understanding its complex inner workings. However, while both groups venture forward, functional biases seem to provide added resistance. While accountants concern themselves with disclosing intellectual capital, strategists maintain it is the Holy Grail for sustainable advantage. While finance researchers attempt to value it, technologists argue for its codification. While human resource researchers want to keep it, legal departments try to license it. Our fear in this turf war is that while intellectual capital increases in overall scope and popularity, the depth of our understanding from any single functional perspective will be limited. How can we pursue both depth and breadth?

Among the many directions the accelerating research trajectory of this field can follow, these are some of the tensions that we suggest require increased attention. From an accounting perspective, we have spent significant time talking about disclosing intellectual capital assets; should we not disclose intellectual capital *liabilities* as well? Caddy (2000) warns that for every positive there is a negative, and for every sunrise there is a sunset. Intellectual capital research would benefit from the same dual perspective. Microsoft Corporation and its loss in the famous antitrust case in 1999 would be a perfect example. What was once considered an arrogant and overreaching monopoly now suffers from an exodus of top executives. The considerable intellectual capital liability generated by the fallout in the public press puts significant downward pressure on Microsoft's market capitalization. The *Exxon Valdez* disaster in 1989 provides another setting for the study of intellectual capital liability. Even with over $3.5 billion spent on cleanup (Raeburn 1999), senior executives at Exxon Corporation are still limited in their strategic choices while environment groups watch them under a suffocating microscope.

Another suggestion we would like to make is that intellectual capital empirical research should be pursued with more fervor. We appreciate that studying an intangible, elusive, and ethereal phenomenon is never easy. However, the rewards of sound empirical research are countless. Most of the survey work done thus far (including Bontis (2000; chap. 36 this vol.) mainly reveals the intellectual capital topography of sampled firms (see also other survey researchers, e.g., Bornemann et al. 1999, Miller et al. 1999). More work is required that triangulates user perceptions with quantitative metrics over longitudinal time

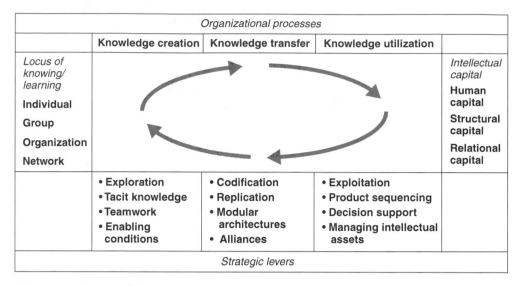

Figure 1.1 A framework for strategic knowledge management.

periods. Such a research program is not easy given that only a few firms in the world even have metrics that span more than a couple of years. However, the number of these firms is slowly increasing, and they are typically very enthusiastic about partnering with researchers who will enable them to be at the forefront of intellectual capital measurement.

A final suggestion on intellectual capital research comes from a user's perspective. Do we know that financial analysts want intellectual capital reports? Do we know that information technology administrators have bountiful knowledge repositories that are being used by all organizational members? Do we know that developing intellectual capital strategies is feasible in the long term from a cost-benefit perspective? Do we know that firms who report intellectual capital actually perform better? And finally, do we know that senior management teams that generate intellectual capital reports make better decisions? Unfortunately, the answer to all of these questions is no. The garden of opportunity awaits. We have an extremely fertile ground for future research.

What Are the Main Levers for Designing a Knowledge-Based Strategy?

A Framework for Strategic Knowledge Management

Figure 1.1 ties the main threads of our discussion in a single framework consisting of (1) organizational knowledge processes, (2) locus or levels of learning, (3) types of intellectual capital, and (4) strategic levers.

A firm generates value from what it knows through the organizational processes of knowledge creation, knowledge transfer, and knowledge utilization. In knowledge creation, the firm produces new knowledge through the dynamic conversion and externalization of its tacit, embedded knowledge. In knowledge transfer, knowledge is shared within a firm across different functional groups, product families, geographical locations, and time periods. Knowledge is also transferred between firms through interorganizational alliances and linkages. In knowledge utilization, the firm integrates and coordinates its different forms of knowledge in order to take action and to produce goods and services. Tacit knowledge plays a crucial role in knowledge creation; codified or explicit knowledge facilitates knowledge transfer; "common" knowledge or shared understanding about goals and purpose guides knowledge utilization.

Over time, the firm accumulates a stock of knowledge and capabilities that is unique to its learning and experience. This stock is the firm's intellectual capital, and it comprises human, structural, and relational capital that reside in its employees, organizational routines, intellectual property, and relationships with customers, suppliers, distributors, and partners. The stock of intellectual capital is continuously refreshed through new learning at various levels: the individual, the work group, the organization, and

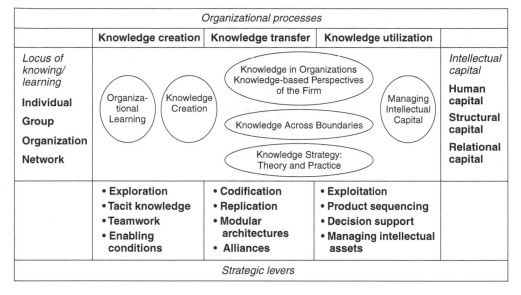

Figure 1.2 Conceptual structure of the book.

the network of organizations of which the firm is a part.

Within the framework composed by these elements, the chapters in this volume discuss a number of actions that a firm may pursue to leverage its knowledge. These "strategic levers" are shown in the lower part of figure 1.1. They include the following topics discussed by authors in this volume:

- Promoting "exploration" or knowledge creation through converting and sharing the organization's tacit knowledge (Nonaka)
- Forming cross-functional work teams that are able to access and integrate the diverse knowledge of members (Leonard and Sensiper, Sole and Edmondson)
- Establishing "enabling conditions" that are conducive to organizational knowledge creation (von Krogh and Grand, Umemoto)
- "Codifying" knowledge to facilitate diffusion (Boisot)
- Replicating organizational routines across different parts and locations of the firm as a way of exploiting knowledge assets (Winter and Szulanski)
- Developing "modular architectures" of product and process components and their interfaces in order to encourage recombination and reuse of knowledge (Sanchez, Garud and Kumaraswamy)
- Transferring knowledge and learning through alliances and organizational chains (Fischer et al., Mitchell et al.)

- Combining exploitation and exploration as complementary elements of the firm's knowledge strategy (Ichijo, Knott)
- "Sequencing" product development so as to take advantage of the path that organizational knowledge, capabilities, and product has coevolved over time (Helfat and Raubitschek)
- Using a cost-benefit calculus to decide on external knowledge transfer (Appelyard, Matusik)
- Designing decision support as a strategic learning and adaptation system (Barabaa et al.)
- Reconceptualizing the role of leadership in the context of learning and innovation (Crossan and Hulland)
- Purposefully measuring, evaluating, and managing the firm's intellectual assets (Bontis, Pike et al.)

The set of options shown is by no means exhaustive, but they suggest the kind of dynamic interplay between knowledge processes, types of intellectual capital, and the locus of learning and innovation that is necessary in crafting an effective knowledge-based strategy. The framework may also serve as a guide for positioning the seven parts of this book, as shown in figure 1.2.

Coda

Ultimately, there are no universal recipes on how a firm can best map out a knowledge-based strategy. Each organization would have to design its own responses and initiatives based on its aspirations, learning, and capabilities. These patterns of action would be shaped by conditions in the industry and the broader environment, as well as by the path that the organization has traveled. We recognize that organizations require many different kinds and levels of knowledge in order to be successful. Firms need knowledge to develop products; they need knowledge about customers and competitors in order to identify markets; they need knowledge about coordinating and integrating the flow and deployment of resources; and they need knowledge about how to continuously refresh and rejuvenate the intellectual capital and core capabilities they possess. We recognize that knowledge-based strategy is both an enactment and a response linking the firm's specific characteristics and the contingencies of the environment it thrives in. In an increasingly dynamic and complex world, firms would need the agility and dexterity to enfold what would traditionally be regarded as opposites: combining exploration with exploitation, sharing and protecting knowledge, managing the stocks and flows of intellectual capital. While there are no pat solutions, the contributors in this volume offer a rich suite of conceptual lenses and analytical tools that can help us better understand and manage knowledge and intellectual capital in the pursuit of superior organizational performance.

References

Audi, R. (1998) *Epistemology: A Contemporary Introduction to the Theory of Knowledge*. New York: Routledge.

Barney, J. (1991) "Firm resources and sustained competitive advantage." *Journal of Management* 17(1):99–120.

Barney, J. (2001) "Is the resource-based "view" a useful perspective for strategic management research?" Yes. *Academy of Management Review* 21(6):41–56.

Bontis, N., Chua, W., and Richardson, S. (2000) "Intellectual capital and the nature of business in Malaysia." *Journal of Intellectual Capital* 1(1): 85–100.

Bontis, N., Crossan, M., and Hulland, J. (2001) "Managing an organizational learning system by aligning stocks and flows." *Journal of Management Studies*, in press.

Bornemann, M., Knapp, A., Schneider, U., and Sixl, K. (1999) "Holistic measurement of intellectual capital." Paper presented at the International Symposium on Measuring and Reporting IC, Amsterdam, June.

Caddy, I. (2000) "Intellectual capital: recognizing both assets and liabilities." *Journal of Intellectual Capital* 1(2):129–146.

Cohen, W.M. and Levinthal, D.A. (1990) "Absorptive capacity: A new perspective on learning and innovation." *Administrative Science Quarterly* 35(1):128–152.

Collins, H. (1998) "Cultural competence and scientific knowledge," in R. Williams, W. Faulkner, and J. Fleck (eds.), *Exploring Expertise: Issues and Perspectives*, pp. 121–142. London: Macmillan.

Eisenhardt, K.M. and Martin, J.A. (2000) "Dynamic capabilities: what are they?" *Strategic Management Journal* 21(10–11):1105–1121.

Garud, R. and Rappa, M.A. (1994) "A sociocognitive model of technology evolution: the case of cochlear implants." *Organization Science* 5(3): 344–362.

Ghoshal, S. and Moran, P. (1996) "Bad for practice: a critique of the transaction cost theory." *Academy of Management Review* 21(1):13–47.

Hiltzik, M.A. (1999) *Dealers of Lightning: Xerox PARC and the Dawn of the Computer Age.* New York: HarperBusiness.

Kogut, B. and Zander, U. (1992) "Knowledge of the firm, combinative capabilities, and the replication of technology." *Organization Science* 3(3):383–397.

Leonard, D. (1995) *Wellsprings of Knowledge: Building and Sustaining the Sources of Innovation.* Boston: Harvard Business School Press.

Levinthal, D.A. and March, J.G. (1993) "The myopia of learning." *Strategic Management Journal* 14:95–112.

Liebeskind, J.P. (1996) "Knowledge, strategy, and the theory of the firm. *Strategic Management Journal* 17:93–107.

March, J.G. (1991) "Exploration and exploitation in organizational learning." *Organization Science* 2(1):71–87.

March, J.G. and Shapira, Z. (1987) "Managerial perspecives on risk and risk taking." *Management Science* 33(11):1404–1418.

Miller, M., Du Pont, B., Fera, V., Jeffrey, R., Mahon, B., Payer, B., and Starr, A. (1999) "Measuring and reporting intellectual capital from a diverse Canadian industry perspective." Paper presented at the International Symposium on Measuring and Reporting IC, Amsterdam, June.

Moser, P.K., Mulder, D.H., and Trout, J.D. (1998) *The Theory of Knowledge.* New York: Oxford University Press.

Nonaka, I. and Takeuchi, H. (1995) *The Knowledge-Creating Company: How Japanese Companies*

Create the Dynamics of Innovation. New York: Oxford University Press.

Penrose, E.T. (1995) *The Theory of the Growth of the Firm,* 3d ed. New York: Oxford University Press.

Priem, R. and Butler, J. (2001a) "Is the resource-based "view" a useful perspective for strategic management research?" *Academy of Management Review* 26(1):22–40.

Priem, R. and Butler, J. (2001b) "Tautology in the resource-based view and the implications of externally determined resource value: further comments." *Academy of Management Review* 26(1):57–66.

Raeburn, P. (1999) "It's time to put the *Valdez* behind US." *Business Week* 3622:90–93.

Spender, J.-C. (1994) "Organizational knowledge, collective practice and penrose rents." *International Business Review* 3(4):353–367.

Spender, J.-C. and Grant, R.M. (1996) "Knowledge and the firm: overview." *Strategic Management Journal* 17:5–10.

Teece, D.J., Pisano, G.P., and Schuen, A. (1997) "Dynamic capabilities and strategic management." *Strategic Management Journal* 18(7):509–533.

Tushman, M. and Anderson, P., eds. (1996) *Managing Strategic Innovation and Change: A Collection of Readings.* New York: Oxford University Press.

Williamson, O.E. (1975) *Markets and Hierarchies: Analysis and Antitrust Implications.* New York: Free Press.

Williamson, O.E. (1991) "Comparative economic organization: analysis of discrete structural alternatives." *Administrative Science Quarterly* 36:269–296.

Williamson, O.E. (1999) "Strategy research: governance and competence perspectives." *Strategic Management Journal* 20:1087–1108.

Winter, S.G. (1987) "Knowledge and competence as strategic assets," in D.J. Teece (ed.), *The Competitive Challenge: Strategies for Industrial Innovation and Renewal,* pp. 159–184. Cambridge: Ballinger.

I

Knowledge in Organizations

2

Market, Hierarchy, and Trust

The Knowledge Economy and the Future of Capitalism

Paul S. Adler

The Argument

This chapter is based on an article that was framed as part of an ongoing debate on the evolution of organizational forms. Recent conceptualizations of this evolution have focused on the relative importance of markets, hierarchies, and hybrid intermediate forms. I attempt to advance the discussion by distinguishing three ideal-typical forms of organization and their corresponding coordination mechanisms: market/price, hierarchy/authority, and community/trust. I argue that different institutions combine the three forms/mechanisms in different proportions. Economic and organizational theory have shown that, compared to trust, price and authority are relatively ineffective means of dealing with knowledge-based assets. Therefore, as knowledge becomes increasingly important in our economy, one should expect high-trust institutional forms to proliferate.

The chapter briefly reviews trends in employment relations, interdivisional relations, and interfirm relations and finds evidence suggesting that the effect of growing knowledge intensity may indeed be a trend toward greater reliance on

trust. There is also reason to believe that the form of trust most effective in this context is a distinctively modern kind—"reflective trust"—as opposed to traditionalistic, "blind" trust. Such a trend to reflective trust threatens the privileges of currently dominant social actors, and these actors' resistance, in combination with the complex interdependencies between price, authority, and trust mechanisms, imparts a halting character to the trend. But the momentum of this trend nevertheless appears to be self-reinforcing, which leads me to a neo-Schumpeterian conjecture: the trend to trust may ultimately challenge the foundations of our capitalist form of society while simultaneously creating the foundations of a new, postcapitalist form.

The implications for research on knowledge management are straightforward. We may be missing important trends if, in our simplifying zeal, we constrain our typology of organizational forms to a one-dimensional spectrum running between hierarchy and market. Nor should the three ideal-typical forms be treated as mutually exclusive alternatives. We need much more research on when, how, and with what effects they can combine.

The implications for practice lie in clarifying several dimensions of the trust phenomenon. Synthesizing prior research, I distinguish several sources of trust, mechanisms of trust, types of objects in which we trust, and the facets of those objects in which we invest our trust. I add a fifth dimension with the distinction between traditional and reflective trust. This last distinction has important implications for practitioners— particularly if my conjecture is correct, that modern trust facilitates knowledge management while traditional trust impedes it. But further research is needed to tease out these implications.

Background

Considerable attention has focused recently on data suggesting that the secular trend toward larger firms and establishments has stalled and may be reversing (Brynjolfsson et al. 1994). Some observers argue that the underlying new trend is toward the disintegration of large, hierarchical firms and their replacement by small, entrepreneurial firms coordinated by markets (Birch 1987). This argument, however, understates the persistence of large firms, ignores transformations underway within these firms, and masks the growth of network relations among firms. How, then, should one interpret the current wave of changes in organizational forms?

Zenger and Hesterly (1997) propose that the underlying trend is a progressive swelling of the zone between hierarchy and market. They point to a proliferation of hybrid organizational forms that introduce high-powered marketlike incentives into firms and hierarchical controls into markets (Holland and Lockett [1997] make a similar argument). This proposition is more valid empirically than is a one-sided characterization of current trends as a shift from hierarchy to market. The "swelling middle" thesis is also a step beyond Williamson's (1991) unjustified assumption that such hybrid forms are infeasible or inefficient. This chapter argues, however, that Zenger and Hesterly's thesis, too, is fundamentally flawed in that it ignores a third increasingly significant coordination mechanism: trust.

In highlighting the importance of trust, this chapter adds to a burgeoning literature (e.g., *Academy of Management Review* 1998; further references below); my goal is to pull together several strands of this literature to advance a line of reflection that positions trust as a central construct in a broader argument. In outline, the argument is, first, that alongside the *market* ideal-typical form of organization, which relies on the price mechanism, and the *hierarchy* form, which relies on authority, there is a third form, the *community* form, which relies on trust. Empirically observed arrangements typically embody a mix of the three ideal-typical organization forms and rely on a corresponding mix of price, hierarchy, and trust mechanisms. Second, based on a well-established body of economic and sociological theory, I argue that trust has uniquely effective properties for the coordination of knowledge-intensive activities within and between organizations. Third, given a broad consensus that modern economies are becoming increasingly knowledge intensive, the first two premises imply that trust is likely to become increasingly important in the mechanism mix. I present indices of such a knowledge-driven trend to trust within and between firms, specifically in the employment relationship, in interdivisional relations, and in interfirm relations. Fourth, I discuss the difficulties encountered by the trust mechanism in a capitalist society and the resulting mutation of trust itself. Finally, the concluding section discusses the broader effects of this intra- and interfirm trend to trust and argues that this trend progressively undermines the legitimacy of the capitalist form of society and simultaneously lays the foundations for a new form.

Both the theory and the data underlying these conclusions are subject to debate: I summarize the key points of contention, and it becomes obvious that we are far from theoretical or empirical consensus. In the form of an essay rather than a scientific paper, my argument is speculative and buttressed by only suggestive rather than compelling evidence. My goal, however, is to enrich organizational research by enhancing its engagement with debates in the broader field of social theory.

The Limits of Market and Hierarchy

Knowledge is a remarkable substance. Unlike other resources, most forms of knowledge grow rather than diminish with use. Knowledge therefore tends to play an increasingly central role in economic development over time. Increasing knowledge intensity takes two forms: the rising education level of the workforce (living or subjective knowledge) and the growing scientific and technical knowledge materialized in new equipment and new products (embodied or objectified knowledge).

Recapitulating a long tradition of scholarship in economics and organization theory, this section argues that neither market nor hierarchy, nor any combination of the two, is particularly well suited to the challenges of the knowledge economy. In order to draw out the implications of this argument, I will assume that real institutions, notably, empirically observed markets and firms, embody varying mixes of three ideal-typical organizational forms and their corresponding coordination mechanisms: (a) the hierarchy form relies on the authority mechanism, (b) the market form relies on price, and (c) the community form relies on trust. For brevity's sake, an organizational form and its corresponding mechanism will be referred to as an organizing "mode." Modes typically appear in varying proportions in different institutions. For example, interfirm relations in real markets embody and rely on varying degrees of trust and hierarchical authority, even if their primary mechanism is price. Similarly, real firms' internal operations typically rely to some extent on both trust and price signals, even if their primary coordination mechanism is authority.

Hierarchy uses authority (legitimate power) to create and coordinate a horizontal and vertical division of labor. Under hierarchy, knowledge is treated as a scarce resource and is therefore concentrated, along with the corresponding decision rights, in specialized functional units and at higher levels of the organization. A large body of organizational research has shown that an institution structured by this mechanism may be efficient in the performance of routine, partitioned tasks but encounters enormous difficulty in the performance of innovation tasks requiring the generation of new knowledge (e.g., Burns and Stalker 1961, Bennis and Slater 1964, Mintzberg 1979, Scott 1992, Daft 1998). When specialized units are told to cooperate in tasks that typically generate unanticipated problems requiring novel solutions, such as the development of a new product, the hierarchical form gives higher level managers few levers with which to ensure that the participating units will collaborate. By their nonroutine nature, such tasks cannot be preprogrammed, and the creative collaboration they require cannot be simply commanded. Similarly, the vertical differentiation of hierarchy is effective for routine tasks, facilitating downward communication of explicit knowledge and commands, but less effective when tasks are nonroutine, since lower levels lack both the knowledge needed to create new knowledge and the incentives to transmit new ideas upward. Firms thus invariably supplement their primary organizational mode, hierarchy/authority, with other modes that can mitigate the hierarchy/authority mode's weaknesses.

The market form, as distinct from the actual functioning of most real markets, relies on the price mechanism to coordinate competing suppliers and anonymous buyers. With standard goods and strong property rights, marginal pricing promises to optimize production and allocation jointly. The dynamics of competition, supply, and demand lead to a price at which social welfare is Pareto-optimal (i.e., no one's welfare can be increased without reducing someone else's). A substantial body of modern economic theory has shown, however, that the price mechanism fails to optimize the production and allocation of knowledge (Arrow 1962, Stiglitz 1994). Knowledge is a "public good"; that is, like radio transmission, its availability to one consumer is not diminished by its use by another. With knowledge, as with other public goods, reliance on the market/price mode forces a trade-off between production and allocation. On the one hand, production of new knowledge would be optimized by establishing strong intellectual property rights that create incentives to generate knowledge. On the other hand, not only are such rights difficult to enforce, but, more fundamentally, they block socially optimal allocation. Allocation of knowledge would be optimized by allowing free access because the marginal cost of supplying another consumer with the same knowledge is close to zero.

Over several decades, discussion of this trade-off between production and allocation was framed as a debate at a macroeconomic level over the relative merits of market, hierarchy in the form of central planning, and intermediate forms such as regulated markets and market socialism (Arrow and Hurwicz 1977, Stiglitz 1994). This "mechanism design" literature has more recently been applied to the analysis of individual firms (Miller 1992)—with the same results. On the one hand, hierarchy could simply mandate the free availability of knowledge and thus outperform market as far as allocation is concerned. On the other hand, hierarchy would have far greater difficulty than market in creating the incentives needed to optimize the production of new knowledge. Formal modeling has shown that neither market nor hierarchy nor any intermediate form can resolve the dilemma, leaving us stuck in a "second-best" equilibrium (Miller 1992).

Recent research on knowledge and coordination mechanisms has highlighted the importance of tacit knowledge. The recognition of the importance of tacit knowledge does little, however, to restore confidence in the ability of the market form to assure optimal outcomes. First, tacit knowledge brings with it all the challenges of hidden knowledge in principal/agent relations. Second, notwithstanding the current scholarly interest in tacit knowledge, codified forms of knowledge continues to be an important factor in economic growth. The reasons are straightforward: the transfer of knowledge is much more costly when the knowledge is of a tacit kind, and the generation of new knowledge is usually much faster when it builds on a base of explicit rather than tacit knowledge.

As knowledge becomes increasingly important in the economic development of firms and nations, the question of whether we can improve on the second-best allowed by market and hierarchy is posed with increasing urgency. Much recent economic scholarship has, however, argued for resignation: the second-best achievable in pure or mixed markets and hierarchies is redefined as the best feasible and "relatively efficient" (Alchian and Demsetz 1972, Williamson 1975). This resignation is not warranted. Hierarchy and market are not the only possible organizational forms. Community is an alternative (Ouchi 1980, Dore 1983, Bradach and Eccles 1989, Powell 1990).

The Power of Community and Trust

Community

Community is a term with many interpretations (Kirkpatrick 1986). However, the salience of some such notion is demonstrated by what we know of both intra- and interfirm relations.

Analysis of action within real firms reveals the ubiquity and importance of "informal" organization—this is one of the founding insights of organization theory (see Scott 1992, chap. 3). Views differ as to how best to conceptualize the informal organization and its differentiation from the formal structures of hierarchy. Without preempting this ongoing debate, we can posit that the informal organization constitutes its members as a community.

Analysis of real market relations between firms reveals a similar dependence on informal ties (Macaulay 1963). Pure spot market relations between anonymous buyers and sellers is in reality rather unusual. Firms transact primarily with long-standing partners, and in the continuity of their relations, shared norms and understandings emerge that have their own efficacy in shaping interactions.

Trust

Trust is the key coordinating mechanism in the community form. Following Gambetta (1988), one could define trust as the subjective probability with which actors assess that other actors or groups of actors will perform a particular action, both before they can monitor such action (or independently of his/her capacity ever to be able to monitor it) and in a context in which it affects their own actions. This broad definition captures many uses of the word "trust," including the possibility of feared as well as welcomed actions. Another, narrower, more benign definition is confidence in another's goodwill (Ring and Van de Ven 1992).

The difference between these definitions obliges us to make a short digression on the notion of trust. Both the generation of trust (i.e., its sources and mechanisms) and its targets (i.e., the objects and the features of those objects in which we invest our trust) are manifold (table 2.1). First, we can distinguish three *sources* of trust. Familiarity through repeated interaction can lead to trust (or distrust). Interests can lead to a calculative form of trust via a sober assessment of the costs and benefits to the other party of exploiting my vulnerability. Values and norms can engender trustworthy behavior that leads to confidence (Liebeskind and Oliver 1998). (I should note that there is some confusion in the literature about precisely what it is about values and norms that creates trust. We might reasonably distinguish a spectrum running from weaker forms of trust based on the predictability imparted to other actors' behaviors by their adherence to any stable norm, to stronger forms of trust based on the predicted benevolence of actors with whom we share norms that privilege trustworthiness. See Ring [1996].) Empirically, all three sources of trust are important in the real world of business (compare Williamson

TABLE 2.1 Dimensions and Components of Trust

Dimensions	Components
Sources	• Familiarity through repeated interaction • Calculation based on interests • Norms that create predictability and trustworthiness
Mechanisms	• Direct interpersonal contact • Reputation • Institutional context
Objects	• Individuals • Systems • Collectivities
Bases	• Consistency, contractual trust • Competence • Benevolence, loyalty, concern, goodwill, fiduciary trust • Honesty, integrity • Openness

1993), and in practice, although excessive focus on the calculative form can undermine the normative form, all three tend to be intertwined complements.

Second, we can distinguish three *mechanisms* by which trust is generated. As Coleman (1990) points out, trust can be engendered by direct interpersonal contact, by reputation through a network of other trusted parties, or by our understanding of the way institutions shape the other actor's values and behaviors. Like the three sources, the three mechanisms are primarily complements rather than substitutes—they tend to build on each other.

Third, we can distinguish three generic *objects* of trust: a person, an impersonal system, or a collectivity. Social psychologists have focused most of their efforts on individuals (Bigely and Pearce 1998), and indeed some social theorists would reserve the concept of "trust" for interpersonal relations and use the term "confidence" to refer to related assessments of abstract systems (Luhmann 1979, Seligman 1997). Notwithstanding the terminological issue, sociologists such as Barber (1983), Zucker (1986), Giddens (1990), and Shapiro (1987) highlight the importance to the functioning of contemporary society of confidence/trust in anonymous systems such as money and law. The concept of procedural justice (e.g., Brockner and Siegel 1996) is one form of system trust familiar to organizational re-

searchers. The importance to comparative economic performance of trust in a collectivity—that is, generalized trust in others who are part of that collectivity—is foregrounded by Fukuyama (1995).

Finally we can distinguish the features of those objects in which we feel trust, often referred to in the literature as the *bases* of trust. The list of bases invoked by various authors is long and partially overlapping, and none of the typologies has a strong theoretical foundation. They include the other party's consistency ("contractual trust"; Sako 1992), competence, benevolence (or loyalty, concern, or Sako's "goodwill trust"), honesty (or integrity), and openness. While much of the discussion of bases has taken interpersonal trust as its context, it is clear that system and collectivity trust also have diverse bases (see, e.g., Barber [1983] on fiduciary trust [i.e., benevolence] and competence trust in government). Like sources and mechanisms, both objects and bases are primarily complements: community, system, and interpersonal trust typically buttress each other, as do the various bases (e.g., Kurland 1996).

Community/Trust as a Third Mode

While trust is a complex, multifaceted phenomenon, the complementarities between the components of each of its four key dimensions enable trust to function as a highly effective coordinating mechanism. Groups whose cohesion is based primarily on mutual trust are capable of extraordinary feats. Trust is therefore usefully seen as a third coordination mechanism that can be combined in varying degrees with price and authority.

The thesis that trust constitutes a third coordination mechanism contrasts with three other views. Williamson (1991) suggests we see market and hierarchy as two discrete alternatives and declares trust to be irrelevant to business transactions. The "swelling middle" thesis invites us to see a continuum between these points but implicitly assumes a trade-off between mechanisms and still ignores trust. Ouchi's (1980) discussion includes trust but still implies a three-way trade-off.

It is more fruitful, I submit, to map institutions in three dimensions according to the salience of community/trust, market/price, and hiearchy/authority modes (figure 2.1). This three-dimensional representation has the ad-

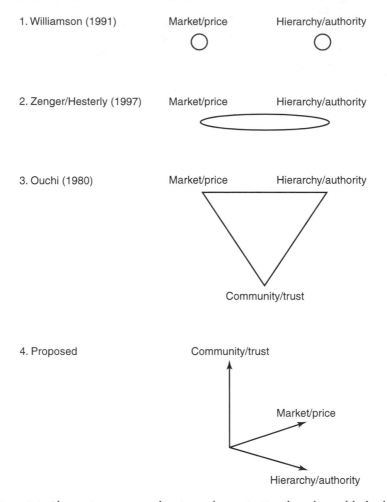

Figure 2.1 Alternative conceptualizations of organizational modes and hybrids.

vantage of allowing us to think of the ways the various modes combine in different settings. In the absence of trust, market coordination takes the form of spot markets. However, trust can be combined with the price mechanism in the form of "relational contracts" (Macneil 1980), as found in long-term partnership-type supplier relations (Bradach and Eccles 1989, Sako 1992, Uzzi 1997). Hierarchy often appears in a low-trust form, as reflected in the colloquial, pejorative use of the term "bureaucracy," and in cases such as those presented by Crozier (1964). However, hierarchy can be combined with trust, as in the "representative," "dynamic," and "enabling" types of bureaucracy described, respectively, by Gouldner (1954), Blau (1955), and Adler and Borys (1996).

Market and hierarchy are also often combined, as reflected in the mix of incentives and author-

ity typically found in employment relations, in relations between divisions and headquarters within large multidivisional firms, and in relations between firms and their suppliers. Sometimes this market/hierarchy mix takes a low-trust form, but sometimes trust is an important third ingredient. Within firms, high-trust hybrids can be found in "collaborative" multidivisional corporations characterized by high levels of interdivisional and interlevel trust (Eccles 1985). Between firms, high-trust hybrids can be found in keiretsu-type configurations characterized by high-trust, hierarchically structured, market relations (Gerlach 1992, Dyer 1996). Figure 2.2 summarizes these alternatives, building on the framework suggested by figure 2.1.

I should note that on this view, the growing importance of "network" forms of organization within and between organizations does not so

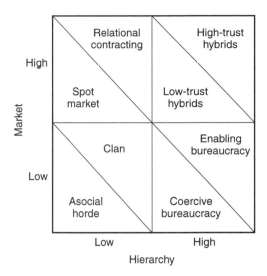

Figure 2.2 A typology of institutional forms. (Low-trust forms in lower left triangles; high-trust forms in upper right triangles.)

come an increasingly attractive mechanism to economic agents.

In the following sections, I will adduce some evidence—suggestive, but certainly not compelling—that firms are indeed being drawn to increasing reliance on trust. A constellation of somewhat contradictory trends is developing as firms attempt to deal more effectively with the knowledge management challenge. First, firms are sharpening marketlike processes. Second, they are developing more effective hierarchical processes. And third, in apparently growing numbers, they are adopting approaches to knowledge management that rely on community and trust between employees and managers, among divisions within the corporation, and between firms and their suppliers. The evidence I present for a trend to trust is not compelling, but given the stakes, it is sufficient to warrant a preliminary assessment and an exploration of its implications.

Employment Relations

Viewed over the longer period, the economy's growing knowledge intensity is pushing the employment relationship in several somewhat contradictory directions. A trend to trust may nevertheless be emerging.

First, one can identify a range of efforts to strengthen the authority mechanism in the employment relation. In response to competitive pressures, firms are fine-tuning their management structures and planning processes, demanding greater accountability of every level, and enforcing more discipline in the planning and execution of operations. The most common motivation for these efforts appears to be greater efficiency and control, but firms sometimes see this refinement of hierarchy as a path to more effective knowledge management, too. It is under this latter rationale that many firms are introducing more formalized procedures such as Total Quality Management and highly structured product and software development processes. Many firms are also developing more elaborate project planning and human resource planning techniques to ensure that the right mix of skills is available to support the development and launch of innovative products. They are developing more complex metrics, the "balanced scorecard," for example (Kaplan 1996), that go beyond market performance criteria for the assessment of these projects. Firms are attempting

much answer the question motivating this essay as it poses a further question: figure 2.1 suggests that we ask of these networks whether the content of their constituent ties is market exchange, hierarchical authority, or community trust. Korczynski (1996) and Carney (1998) contrast high-trust and low-trust network forms and show that the low-trust form can help lower costs but performs relatively poorly in generating or sharing new knowledge.

A Hypothesis: The Trend to Trust

Using these three-dimensional schemas, we can map the vector of change in the mix of organization modes associated with the increasing knowledge intensity of the economy. Compared to pure authority and price, trust makes possible an enlarged scope of knowledge generation and sharing. Trust can dramatically reduce both transaction costs—replacing contracts with handshakes—and agency risks—replacing the fear of shirking and misrepresentation with mutual confidence. Trust can thus greatly mitigate the coordination difficulties created by the public good character of knowledge. And insofar as knowledge takes a tacit form, trust is an essential precondition for effective knowledge transfer. Therefore, as knowledge management becomes an increasingly important performance determinant, I hypothesize that trust will be-to identify their "core competencies" and nurture development of these competencies over the longer term, even when purely market-based financial assessments do not support such risky investments.

Second, alongside these refinements of hierarchy, one sees efforts designed to strengthen the market form of the employment relation. Downsizing and contingent employment are sometimes seen as ways not only to reduce labor costs and increase "numerical" (head count) flexibility but also as paths to greater flexibility in the mix of knowledge and skills available to the firm (head content). Reliance on market-type mechanisms is also visible in the shift, albeit modest, toward contingent compensation at lower levels in the organizational hierarchy, creating higher powered incentives for performance in general and for risky innovation and knowledge creation in particular (Lawler et al. 1998). These efforts are most often motivated by efficiency and flexibility concerns, but here again, improvements in knowledge management capability are sometimes seen as another benefit. Firms such as Microsoft invoke both motives when they use market relations in the form of large pools of contingent, contract employees and high-powered stock incentives for regular employees.

Third, firms are trying to improve their knowledge management capabilities by strengthening employee trust. The rationale is explicit. Effective *development* of knowledge—whether new concepts in the research lab, new products in the development department, or process refinement suggestions on the shop floor—depends on employee commitment and on collaborative teamwork, for which mutual trust is a critical precondition (Bromiley and Cummings 1995). Effective *sharing* of knowledge depends equally critically on a sense of shared destiny, which in turn both depends on and engenders a sense of mutual trust (e.g., Nahapiet and Ghoshal 1998). Firms such as 3M and Hewlett Packard thus attempt to create high levels of community and trust by providing material and nonmaterial expressions of commitment to their employees (Collins and Porras 1994).

Trust is a crucial ingredient both in high-commitment vertical relations between employees and management and in collaborative horizontal relations between specialist groups. Building on many decades of research on the critical role of informal organization in innovation, community—particularly in the form of "communities of practice" (Wenger 1998)—is increasingly recognized as the organizational principle most effective in generating and sharing new knowledge.

In the language of transaction cost economics, we would say that when the firm needs high levels of firm-specific knowledge and when metering individual output is difficult—conditions that are arguably typical in knowledge-intensive firms—the most efficient form of the employment relation is that of a "relational team" (Williamson 1981). Notwithstanding Williamson's (1993) own reservations regarding the use of the notion of trust in sociological research, relational teams seem in practice to rely on high levels of trust. As illustration, consider a recent work on knowledge management by two particularly thoughtful observers of its practice, Thomas Davenport and Laurence Prusak (1998). They appear at first to advance a thesis contrary to mine, arguing for the need for improved "knowledge markets" within and between firms. But this turns out to be a metaphor for the need for trust, since the "currencies" of these markets are reciprocity, repute, and altruism and "mutual trust is at the heart of knowledge exchange" (p. 35).

Note the complex three-way tensions between market/price, hierarchy/authority, and community/trust. On the one hand, in some cases the three modes function as mutually exclusive substitutes. Efforts to sharpen market forms can undercut efforts to strengthen trust. Downsizing, for example, is rarely a propitious time for a shift toward teamwork. Efforts to improve hierarchical planning processes often require that market forms be moderated. And changes in the structure of hierarchy can be hampered by the long-term stability implied by strong trust. On the other hand, these three modes can be mutually supportive if they are designed and implemented appropriately. Employee participation, for example, is one way to link community and hierarchy so that the two are complements rather than substitutes (Adler et al. 1999). While figure 2.1 represents the three mechanisms as three orthogonal dimensions, it is not intended to preempt questions of substantive interdependencies. Unfortunately, these interdependencies have so far eluded compelling theorization (see Hirschman [1970] on the variable relationship between exit [read: market] and voice [read: community]). For now, all we can say is that hierarchy, market, and community are sometimes complements and sometimes substitutes.

Some Counterarguments

The hypothesis that as the knowledge intensity of the economy increases, firms will be drawn in increasing numbers to higher trust forms of the employment relation, runs counter to a long tradition in sociology. This tradition draws on several theoretical perspectives; here I review some that pertain directly to the employment relationship. In a subsequent section, I return to other perspectives of more general import.

A venerable line of sociological scholarship has argued that the capitalist employment relation is an essentially low-trust one. The hallmarks of the capitalist firm—scientific management and mass production—are engines of war against community: fragmenting workers' roles, separating conception and execution, and centralizing control. From this vantage point, writings in the human relations tradition and more recently on empowerment are seen as ideological inflation of a thin veneer of trust that managers try to overlay on the underlying reality of domination. Indeed, the concept of trust was rarely invoked in industrial sociology until Alan Fox's 1974 study—which argues that trust was systematically undermined in capitalist firms. His argument seemed so convincing that the topic essentially disappeared for another decade (Heisig and Littek 1995).

Some contributors to this sociological tradition work from the Marxist theoretical premise that the core of the employment relation is an inescapable struggle between workers and managers over work intensity (e.g., Braverman 1974, Burawoy 1979). Researchers working in this perspective highlight the deceptive nature of management efforts to inculcate a sense of trust in workers and the "false consciousness" of workers who take the bait.

Other contributors are grounded in Weber rather than Marx, and for these the hypothesis of a trend to trust in the employment relationship arouses skepticism rather than radical hostility. Weberians, like Marxists, remind us that a trend to trust would likely encounter enormous impediments in the rivalry of competing social groups. These scholars can point to a substantial body of research accumulated over many decades that documents the frequency and potency of both management and worker opposition to "progressive" management ideas. Enlightened self-interest does not diffuse easily in a society where so many personal, organizational, and con-textual factors encourage managers, and sometimes workers, to choose hierarchy and market over community/trust.

As a result of these impediments to trust, scholars in these traditions expect to find a trendless pattern of fluctuation in the employment relation's mechanism mix. Consistent with this interpretation, Ramsay (1977) argues that trust in the employment relation has fluctuated over the century as a function of the balance of power between labor and management. Barley and Kunda (1992) and Abrahamson (1997) document cyclical swings between the rhetorics of rational control and normative commitment in management discourse over the last century.

The Hypothesis Reaffirmed

These Marxist and Weberian objections are not convincing, however. The radical skepticism of trust in the traditional Marxist view is justified only if one accepts that the interests of workers and managers are never even partly congruent. This assumption appears empirically implausible. Moreover, it is based on an unfortunately narrow reading of Marx (Adler 1990). It ignores Marx's insights into the role of community within the firm, expressed in his analysis of "cooperation" and the "collective worker"—a collective that includes managers in their "productive," as distinct from "exploitative," roles (Carchedi 1977).

Once this facet of Marx's analysis is retrieved, it is no longer difficult to conceive of a progressive expansion of trust under capitalist relations of production. Trust, under this view, becomes a feature of work organization, and as such it is at the intersection of the forces of production (society's accumulated productive resources) and the relations of production (the structure of ownership and control of these resources)—embodying both structures simultaneously and subject to the dynamics of both (Adler 1997). Insofar as its trajectory is shaped by fundamentally antagonistic capitalist relations of production, the growth of trust is necessarily limited, but insofar as it is shaped by the forces of production, trust grows cumulatively with the progressive expansion of those forces. In sum, this alternative reading of Marx suggests the possibility of a trend to trust, albeit a trend that is limited in its form and extent by the persistence of capitalist relations.

The version of Weber invoked by those skeptical of a trend to trust is a somewhat truncated one, too. In its insistence on the enduring conflict between competing social groups, this reading downplays the importance Weber attached to rationalization in the development of modern society. As traditional bases of domination are displaced by rational-legal ones, the authority of managers within the firm is increasingly a function of the perceived legitimacy of their claim to expertise and to functional necessity. The brute assertion of positional prerogative loses legitimacy, and some kind of trust becomes increasingly critical to the exercise of authority. (Below, I take up the question of which kind of trust.)

Nor is an expansion of trust contradicted by evidence of fluctuations in the mix of mechanisms constituting employment relations. A closer look at the data cited by Barley et al. (1992) suggests that a secular trend underlies these cycles. In both the sequence of rational control phases (from scientific management, whose dominance Abrahamson dates from 1894 to 1921, to systems rationalism [1944–1971] and to reengineering [1990–]) and the sequence of normative commitment phases (from welfare and personnel management [1921–1944] to culture-quality [1971–1990]) we observe the growing importance of themes of employee consent and trust. In the normative approaches, for example, there is a clear shift from the earlier emphasis on paternalism, to relatively impersonal, bureaucratic norms of procedural justice, to the recent emphasis on empowerment and mutual commitment.

Perhaps more striking is the trend to trust found in the sequence of control rhetorics. Within two or three years of publishing a text popularizing a rather brutally coercive method of business process reengineering (Hammer and Champy 1993), both James Champy and Michael Hammer published new volumes (Champy 1995, Hammer 1996) stressing the importance of the human factor and the need for job redesigns that afford employees greater autonomy. The undeniably autocratic character of much early reengineering rhetoric and its rapid "softening" compares favorably with unilateral and enduring forms of domination expressed in post–World War II systems rationalism. It compares even more favorably with the even more unilateral and rigid rhetoric in turn-of-the-century scientific management: scientific management only softened its relations with organized labor after nearly two decades of confrontation (Nyland 1998).

Clearly there is a gap—often a huge one, as Marxist and Weberian commentators have pointed out—between these trends in rhetoric and the reality of the employment relation. However, this long-term evolution of rhetoric both reflects and reinforces a real trend to trust. It reflects the evolving expectations of an increasingly educated (read: knowledge-intensive) workforce and the evolving needs of an increasingly advanced (ditto) economy. And it reinforces that trend because the rhetoric of trust legitimizes the idea that management authority depends on employee consent.

Interdivisional Relations

Large multibusiness corporations are under increasing pressure to show real benefits for asserted synergies. A first result of this pressure is the trend to divest unrelated businesses in the interest of "focus." Therefore, the increasingly common configuration is that of related-diversified firms, that is, firms in which divisions are neither integrated vertically as suppliers and users nor totally independent of each other. However, in related-diversified firms, if divisions seek only to meet their own divisional objectives, they will behave in ways that are detrimental to the firm's global objectives. A second result of the performance pressure on large corporations is therefore a cluster of innovations that appear to be pushing beyond the limits of market and hierarchy.

The multidivisional corporation is in effect a miniature economy in which business units function as miniature firms. Such a corporation must struggle with precisely the dilemma of knowledge management articulated in the market/plan debate. Headquarters' hierarchical control over divisions might help assure the dissemination of existing knowledge across divisions, but such control undermines incentives for the divisions to create new knowledge. The more common approach gives divisions profit and loss responsibility and engenders the corresponding problems of the market form. When divisions function as autonomous profit centers and charge a market-based price for sales of intellectual assets to sister divisions, the effectiveness of the corporation as a whole suffers because the optimal allocation of knowledge assets is blocked (Kaplan 1984; for an example at TRW, see *Business Week* 1982). Since one division's use of these knowledge assets does not preclude their use by another, the corporation would benefit from a regime of free sharing among divisions.

Eccles (1985) finds that in the microeconomy of the firm there is no mix of transfer prices and hierarchical procedures that can simultaneously optimize incentives to invest in the development of new knowledge and to share the results of those development efforts. Not surprisingly, this finding supports at a microlevel the prediction of Arrow and Hurwicz's (1977) analysis of whole economies. The multidivisional form of the corporation was constructed to counterbalance the merits and limits of hierarchy, as embodied in the functional form, with those of market, as embodied in the holding-company form. In this, the multidivisional form resembles the intermediate cases of regulated market or market socialism mentioned above. But even this hybrid model becomes increasingly inefficient when the corporation must encourage simultaneously the creation of new knowledge within divisions and the sharing of existing knowledge across divisions (Miller 1992).

In response to these problems and to their growing urgency in an increasingly knowledge-intensive economy, multidivisional firms are actively experimenting with new ways to stimulate collaboration between profit centers within the firm. The notion of core competencies, as articulated by Prahalad and Hamel (1990), is premised on the insight that corporate competitiveness depends on bodies of expertise that are typically distributed across divisions rather than contained within them. Collaboration across divisions, therefore, is a critical rather than a secondary issue (see also Porter 1985, pt. 3 on "horizontal strategy"). Collins and Porras (1994) document a panoply of mechanisms designed to encourage a bond of common identity and a norm of sharing. Davenport and Prusak (1988) describe a range of methods used in large firms to enhance the trust and shared identity needed for the easy flow of ideas across divisional boundaries.

These shifts in interdivisional relations are reflected in changes in corporate control systems. Eccles's (1985) research shows that the most effective transfer pricing scheme in such cases is based neither on market prices nor on internal costs but on what he calls "rational trust." Under rational trust, division managers' confidence in top management's ability to evaluate and reward performance fairly is based on two measures: first, the judicious use of quantitative measures of subunit performance, and second, the enlightened use of subjective measures of the subunit managers' contributions to total company performance, even when these contributions hurt their subunits' own performance (p. 279).

Consistent with Eccles's argument, empirical research finds that in firms with relatively high levels of knowledge intensity, where collaboration between divisions is therefore at a premium, headquarters commonly use subjective judgments of how well division managers help their peers. These subjective judgments both assess and require trust, in contrast with the more traditional approaches that rely exclusively on quantitative, market performance–based formulas or hierarchical-bureaucratic criteria to determine division managers' bonuses (Gupta and Govindarajan 1986, Lorsch and Allen 1973, Salter 1973, Hill et al. 1992).

The shift to trust is not unproblematic, however. The ethos of common destiny that underpins trust blurs the allocation of accountability and decision rights at the heart of both hierarchy and market forms. Powerful actors resist this blurring. Within hierarchies, superiors resist giving up the ease of control afforded by the principle of accountability (see, e.g., Ashkenas et al. 1993, p. 125). Unilateral control is a far simpler organizational process to manage than is shared control. More fundamentally, as agents of owners, senior managers are themselves held accountable to brutally simple norms imposed by the product and financial markets. The implacable, anonymous irrationality of the market often makes a mockery of efforts to create and sustain trust. Senior executives, whose fortunes are tied to the firm's market performance, therefore cannot commit more than half-heartedly to trust (Hyman 1987).

Notwithstanding this resistance, increasing knowledge intensity appears to encourage a trend to trust in interdivisional relations. This trend might help explain the proliferation of titles such as chief technology officer and chief knowledge officer. These positions have broad responsibility for building cross-division knowledge and sharing, but typically they have no formal authority—they rely on trust in their attempts to build more trust (Adler and Ferdows 1992, Earl and Scott 1999). As firms learn how to infuse trust into the immensely complex task of coordinating action in multidivisional firms, and in particular as they learn how to combine trust with the necessary elements of hierarchy and market, Eccles's "rational trust" model appears to be gaining legitimacy.

Interfirm Relations

In parallel with these trends toward trust in employment and interdivisional relations, firms are increasingly infusing trust into their relations with other firms. Alliances and other forms of interfirm networks are proliferating, and the consensus in the field is that this proliferation is driven in large measure by the challenge of growing knowledge intensity. Here, too, firms are juggling market/price, hierarchy/authority, and community/trust modes, and scholars are debating their relative importance (e.g., *Organization Science* 1998). While some argue that trust is increasingly important in interfirm relations, others argue that firms are unlikely to suspend self-interest in alliances and that trust may often be a result rather than a cause (Koza and Lewin 1998). Whether trust plays an independent causal role is an open question; in this section, I present the case for the affirmative.

First, I should note the countertendencies. On the one hand, we see some firms imposing ever sharper market discipline on their suppliers by aggressively demanding lower prices and moving rapidly to cut off suppliers who cannot deliver (e.g., Ashkenas et al. 1993, p. 240). On the other hand, we see firms trying to force improvements in their supplier base by introducing more complex "hierarchical contracts" (Stinchcombe 1985) into their market relations. Such hierarchical elements control not only product specifications but also the supplier's internal processes. Korczynski (1996), for example, documents a trend toward a low-trust combination of market and hierarchical relations between management contractors and building contractors in the U.K. engineering construction industry in the 1980s and 1990s. Hancké (1997) makes a similar diagnosis of the evolution of subcontracting relations in the French automobile industry.

We also see, however, a growing number of firms building long-term, trust-based partnerships with their suppliers. A burgeoning body of research shows that when firms need innovation and knowledge inputs from suppliers rather than just standardized commodities, no combination of strong hierarchical control and market discipline can assure as high a level of performance as can trust-based community (Dyer 1996, Sako 1992, Helper 1991, Bensaou and Venkatraman 1995, Ring 1996, 1997). By contrast, Korczynski's (1996) study shows how low-trust relations

in the U.K. construction industry enabled schedule and cost improvements but were unable to stimulate the creation of new knowledge.

The hierarchy/authority mode of interfirm relations clearly risks impeding innovation by stifling the upward flow of new ideas from subordinate suppliers. Their narrow specialization leaves them without the technological knowhow needed for innovation, and their subordination leaves them few incentives to contribute innovative ideas to customers.

The market/price mode facilitates innovation by creating incentives to generate new ideas, but this mode, too, impedes innovation because suppliers and customers of innovations have difficulty agreeing on a price for these innovative ideas. The suppliers are not sure what price would cover their costs, for two reasons. First, the main source of a firm's innovative ideas is society's total stock of knowledge rather than assets held privately by the innovating firm. Given the public-good character of much of that knowledge stock, identifying or justifying a "raw materials" cost for new ideas generated from this knowledge stock is difficult. Second, an innovative idea is just as likely to arise during free time as on the job, so identifying a "transformation" cost is difficult. Whereas competition between suppliers of most other types of goods drives prices toward their marginal costs, no comparably grounded "supply schedule" guides the price of knowledge.

The customer side is no easier. The potential customer for an innovation typically cannot judge the worth of the idea without having its secret revealed, and intellectual property protection is cumbersome and expensive. Moreover, intellectual property rights, compared to property rights in other kinds of assets, lack a legitimating material substratum. We have already pointed out the difficulty of determining the price of knowledge based on its production cost; the alternative basis would be rent, but rent is a viable price form only when the asset in question is not reproducible and is rivalrous in use, whereas knowledge (at least in its codified forms) is reproducible at close to zero cost and nonrivalrous in use. Its price is therefore less grounded in any material considerations: it is purely a function of convention and relative power. Lacking a legitimating material basis, intellectual property is among the most contentious of forms of property. Perhaps that is why patent rights are so often bundled and bartered in dyadic trade rather than sold on open markets.

These implications of growing knowledge intensity for the market form were identified by Marx more than a century ago (1973, p. 700). The forces of production of modern industry are progressively socialized—increasingly, they take the form of society's total knowledge stock. As a result, labor inputs and production costs become increasingly irrelevant to the formation of prices, and the price mechanism becomes an increasingly unreliable basis for economic calculation. The difficulties encountered by efforts to create "metrics" for knowledge management are perhaps more fundamental than commonly recognized.

Hierarchy and market are relatively more effective for the governance of low-knowledge-intensity transactions where efficiency, rather than innovation, is critical. Where knowledge management is the critical task, the more effective approaches rely on long-term partnership-style relationships based on "goodwill" trust, as well as competence trust and contract trust (Sako 1992, Bensaou and Venkatraman 1995, Ring 1997). Thus, trust is at the heart of effective knowledge-intensive interfirm networks (Powell 1990).

As with the employment relation, the most effective approaches to knowledge management in interfirm relations deploy a complementary mix of price, authority, and trust mechanisms. Toyota, for example, rarely allows itself to become dependent on a single supplier and tries to maintain two sources for any noncommodity inputs. Toyota always makes these suppliers aware of the ultimate power of the market test. However, the relationships between Toyota and these suppliers are hardly composed of anonymous, arms'-length, spot-market transactions. First, these contracts embody a comprehensive set of documents specifying in detail the product requirements and management processes. Second, these hierarchical documents are embedded within a long-term, high-trust, mutual-commitment relationship.

While some observers might argue that Japanese firms such as Toyota put so much emphasis on trust because of the importance of this norm in the broader Japanese culture, the evidence appears strong that such a trust-heavy mix of mechanisms is productively superior in a broad range of cultures. Two indicators come from the U.S. auto industry. First, Dyer and Chu (1998) found that, as compared to their U.S.

counterparts, Japanese auto firms established recently in the United States were able to create higher trust relations rapidly with their U.S.-owned suppliers. Second, in response to this Japanese challenge, U.S. auto manufacturers have shifted toward higher trust relations with their suppliers. The percentage of U.S. auto parts producers who provide sensitive, detailed information about their production process to their customers grew from 38% to 80% during the 1980s (Helper and Sako 1995). However, in the case of supplier relations, unlike that of employment relations, research has not yet assessed whether such a shift is more than a swing of the pendulum back to what may have been relatively high-trust relations in interfirm relations in earlier periods of capitalism (see, e.g., Sabel and Zeitlin 1997).

Evidence for a trend to interfirm trust is stronger in the proliferation of multilateral network forms of organization for the most knowledge-intensive tasks and industries (Nelson 1988, Powell 1990, Liebeskind et al. 1996). The multiplication of such tasks and industries over time warrants the hypothesis that the proliferation of high-trust multilateral interfirm networks is not just a pendulum swing. Patent pooling and cooperative research and development consortia have multiplied in recent decades. Formal professional and technical societies and informal community ties among scientists constitute other, less direct forms of interfirm networking whose importance appears to be growing.

One should not ignore the countervailing forces. These high-trust network forms may be more productive, but since the market principle is also present, they suffer the risk of opportunistic defection. Self-interested behavior can sometimes encourage trustworthiness, particularly when the "shadow of the future" is long. But self-interest does not reliably ensure the diffusion and persistence of trust-based networks, and whole regions can find themselves stuck at low-trust and poor-performing equilibria. However, when these regions are subject to competition from regions that have attained a higher trust, higher performing equilibrium, one sometimes observes serious, sustained, self-conscious efforts to create trust (Sabel 1992). Some of these efforts succeed. One might hypothesize that if efforts to create trust as a response to competition do not succeed, economic activity will tend to shift to higher trust regions. In either case, the trend toward trust seems likely to emerge, if only at a more global level.

The Difficulties of Trust

The preceding overview of changes within and between firms suggests that all three coordination mechanisms—price, authority, and trust—have a role to play in the knowledge economy, but that trust is becoming increasingly important in this mix. Relative to their respective low-trust forms, the high-trust forms of intraorganizational, interdivisional, and interfirm relations encourage more effective knowledge generation and dissemination. The objective need for trust is, to be sure, counterbalanced by the resistance of those whose prerogatives would be threatened by it, but the defense of these prerogatives is increasingly inconsistent with the interests of economic performance. I leave empirical testing of this argument to another occasion and focus here on the theoretical obstacles. The section above on employment relations discussed several such obstacles. We must now broaden that discussion.

A first obstacle is posed by some economists and sociologists who argue that trust can never, even in principle, become a stable and dominant mechanism. Theoretical economists such as Arrow do not deny that trust would greatly improve the effectiveness of markets, and organizational economists such as Williamson add that trust would also no doubt improve the effectiveness of hierarchy. But economic theory argues that trust, like knowledge itself, is a public good, and that the spontaneous working of the price mechanism (assumed to be the dominant one) will generate too large a free-rider problem and consequently will fail to produce the optimal quantity of trust. In repeated games, tit-for-tat cooperation—a minimal form of community—may emerge, but the emergence of cooperation is neither necessary nor predictable. Economists therefore doubt that trust can ever become a stable, dominant mechanism.

The flaw in such reasoning is in the assumption that individuals' preferences are essentially egotistical and exogenous. If people have a propensity for altruism that coexists and competes with the propensity for egoism, and if the relative importance of these two propensities varies with the circumstances, then there is no reason to believe that trust cannot become an important, even dominant, mechanism of coordination in the right circumstances (Ring and Van de Ven 1992).

Some sociologists, too, have expressed skepticism of trust, based on the intuition that trust is far easier to destroy than to create and that its most powerful forms are those that accumulate over long periods (e.g., Putnam 1993, Hardin 1992). Evans (1996) contrasts this "endowment" view with a "constructibility" view of trust and social capital. While future empirical research might perhaps cast light on the relative merits of these views, common experience tells us that trust can be created, at least under some conditions. Sabel (1992) describes the processes by which previously distrustful actors can overcome the temptation to free ride and deliberately create the trust they recognize as being in their common interest (see also Ring 1997).

Assuming that trust can emerge, a second obstacle arises: trust has its own dark side. Trust can fail us because it makes betrayal more profitable (Granovetter 1985). More fundamentally, it can fail us because its success can prove dysfunctional. Trust-based institutions are often exclusivistic and elitist, particularly when the source of trust is shared norms or familiarity. These institutions are poorly equipped to deal with the knowledge management challenge. Social psychologists have shown that trust within teams can lead to complacency and poor performance in innovative tasks (Kim 1997). When trust based on familiarity or norms becomes the dominant mechanism, firms can come to look like premodern "clans" with the associated traditionalistic domination, and whether this domination takes an autocratic or a paternalistic form, such organizations are clearly handicapped in their knowledge management. When suppliers become trusted partners, the risk of discrimination against potential new suppliers grows correspondingly, reducing innovative potential (Uzzi 1997, Kern 1998). In the language of sociology, one would say that in settings governed by norm- or familiarity-based trust, ascribed status often replaces achieved status—which is surely not a promising step in a dynamic knowledge economy.

The most appropriate theoretical response to this challenge is to invoke the potential complementarities between price, authority, and trust. The downsides of trust and closed communities can be mitigated by the presence of market and hierarchy. Compared to traditional normative trust, the pure, low-trust market is a powerful lever for creating opportunities, especially opportunities for knowledge development. Uzzi's (1997) study of the New York women's apparel industry, for example, shows how firms combine arm's-length market relations with trust-based social relations in their supplier and customer networks. Uzzi argues that firms that balance trust and market can maintain the benefits of trust while avoiding the rigidity associated with exclusive reliance on trust relations. Communitarians sensitive to the risks of closed communities make a parallel argument for the importance of hierarchy: at the level of specific organizations, the pure, low-trust bureaucratic hierarchy is a powerful lever for assuring equity and stability, and at a more macrosocietal level, a healthy society needs a mutually supportive combination of community and hierarchy in the form of government and law (Walzer 1999).

A third and potentially greater obstacle is identified by several currents of social theory that argue that the overall dominance of the price mechanism in capitalist society tends over time to corrode the foundations of trust. Hirschman (1982) reviews these arguments in his discussion of a "self-destructive" view of market-based society. Scholars inspired by both Marxist and reactionary thought and by writers such as Weber, Simmel, and Durkheim have argued that the "cash nexus" characteristic of the market-based capitalist form of society progressively undermines the social conditions of capitalism's effectiveness. First, the market undermines the familiarity source of trust by corroding the traditional bonds of community and extended family, leading to the anonymity of urban life. And second, the market undermines the normative source of trust by corroding traditional shared beliefs, leading to "the dissolution of precapitalist bonds of loyalty and obedience" (Schumpeter 1942). Without the buttressing effect of familiarity and traditional shared norms, self-interested calculative trust alone provides only an unreliable foundation for capitalism: "[Self-]interest is what is least constant in the world" (Durkheim 1893; see also Ring 1996, on "fragile trust," and Barney and Hansen 1994, on "weak form" trust).

Hirschman points out, however, that this self-destructive view has competed with another, more benign view of the effect of the market of society. He labels this benign view the *doux commerce* (gentle commerce) thesis. Thomas Paine in *The Rights of Man* (1792): expressed it in the proposition: Commerce "is a pacific system, operating to cordialise mankind, by rendering Na-

tions, as well as individuals, useful to each other" (p. 215). Markets may undermine the strong ties of closed community, but they weave an ever broader web of weaker ties that draws us into "universal interdependence" (Marx and Engels 1959, p. 11). A host of observers (but few social theorists) argue that capitalism encourages the emergence of "modern" norms such as industriousness, frugality, punctuality, and probity (Rosenberg 1964, pp. 59–77). Some of these modern virtues are arguably propitious for the propagation of at least some forms of trust.

In the contest of these two views, the self-destruction thesis has fared better than the *doux commerce* view. Durkheim's celebration of organic versus mechanical solidarity, for example, echoes Paine's view of the importance of functional interdependence in modern society, but Durkheim was notably pessimistic concerning the possibility of the spontaneous emergence of the requisite normative foundations. Marx's celebration of capitalism's civilizing effects was eclipsed by his denunciation of its inhumanity. Indeed, Hirschman shows that the *doux commerce* thesis all but disappeared after the eighteenth century.

Toward Reflective Trust

My summary of the corrosive effects of the market distinguishes its effects on the three sources of trust: market society seems inimical to strong forms of familiarity trust; market society encourages calculative trust, but such trust alone is unreliable; and market society dissolves the traditional foundations of normative trust. Given the ineluctable quality of the first and second of these effects, the burden of a hypothesized trend to trust must fall on normative trust. Is there any reason to believe that normative trust can be sufficiently renewed to meet the challenge of the knowledge economy? Further research is needed to test the proposition, but the available evidence suggests that alongside the apparently irresistible decline of traditional trust, we might be observing the gradual emergence of a distinctively modern form of normative trust.

Leadership is one domain in which some of the tensions between the old and new forms of trust seem to manifest themselves. While some leaders at both the corporate and national levels still seek to legitimize their authority by reference to tradition, a growing number appear to have accepted that if leadership is going to support effective knowledge management, then leadership's legitimacy must be based on more rational norms. The trust that leaders build must be an inclusive, open, democratic kind, or knowledge creation and sharing will falter (Bennis and Slater 1964, Bennis and Nanus 1997). Charismatic bases of leadership, as Weber predicted, still wax and wane in popularity, continually finding new pertinence, but the balance between traditional and rational bases seems to be shifting progressively in favor of rationality. Within firms, leadership seems to have shifted toward a form of trust consonant with the ethos of "fact-based management," independent inquiry, and collaborative problem solving rather than traditionalist deference to established authority.

A modern form of normative trust can be distinguished from its premodern form. The modern form is less blind and tradition bound. It is more "studied" (Sabel 1992), "rational" (Eccles 1985), and "tentative" (Barnes 1981). Its rationality is not of the purely calculative kind assumed by economics—norms play a central role in modern trust, but these norms do not derive their legitimacy from affective sources such as tradition or charisma, or from their own calculative, purposive-rational utility. Rather, the legitimacy of modern trust is derived from grounding in open dialogue among peers. Habermas (1990) has attempted to characterize this form of legitimization in terms of the "ideal speech situation," and Apel (1987), in the "ideal community of communication."

The modern form of trust might be labeled "reflective." The values at work in modern trust are those of the scientific community: "universalism, communism, disinterestedness, organized skepticism" (Merton 1973, p. 270). Modern trust is inclusive and open. Referring to the discussion above of the bases of trust, one could hypothesize that whereas traditional trust elevates loyalty over the other bases (Schumpeter's "precapitalist bonds of loyalty and obedience"), modern trust ranks integrity and competence more highly (Butler and Cantrell 1984, Schindler and Thomas 1993, see Gates 1998 for a case study of the shift from loyalty to competence in the basis of trust among U.S. presidents' advisors).

From these considerations, I tentatively conclude that the efficacy of trust for knowledge management and the likelihood of its growth over time are maximized if (a) trust is balanced by hierarchical rules to ensure stability and equity, (b) trust is balanced by market competition to ensure flexibility and opportunity, and (c)

trust is modern and reflective rather than traditionalistic and blind. Space does not permit, but a parallel argument can be made concerning traditional and modern forms of community. Much of the debate around communitarianism has been diverted into an unproductive contrast between community and individual rights. As Lakoff (1996) argues, a more fruitful and urgent debate would be over alternative forms of community.

Trust and Universalism

Before exploring the broader implications of a trend toward reflective trust, one possible further objection should be addressed: as a norm, reflective trust appears to conflate the two poles of the fundamental Weberian distinction between particularism and universalism. Is reflective trust therefore a self-contradictory notion?

Heimer (1992) poses this problem nicely in her discussion of forms of organization based on interpersonal networks. Network forms of organization require a significant departure from the "universalist" orientation articulated by Weber and highlighted by Talcott Parsons as one of the distinguishing features of modernity. To build trust, actors must adopt a more "particularistic" orientation, acknowledging the obligation to reciprocity entailed by relations with specific others, rather than relying on universal norms to guide their conduct. To reinforce the point, Heimer quotes a quip about Parsons (an unfair one, I am told by others) to the effect that he was "so universalistic that he wouldn't help a friend" (p. 143). Is the idea of a modern form of trust that avoids the limitations of particularism essentially wrong-headed? If trust is necessarily particularistic, does it necessarily suffer the limitations of its traditional form? These limitations would hobble trust's ability to coordinate knowledge-intensive activity.

These questions call for a more nuanced analysis than space permits. For the present purposes, however, it is sufficient to point out that particularism and universalism need not be polarities on a one-dimensional spectrum. They might better be conceived as conceptually independent dimensions, even if broadly speaking they tend to occur in inverse correlation. Traditionalistic trust is indeed high on particularism and low on universalism, and both pure markets and pure bureaucracies are high on universalism and low on particularism, but we can easily imagine a normative orientation and an associated form of trust that are high on both dimensions. This is precisely the modern condition: the ethical dilemmas characteristic of the modern era are those engendered by simultaneous commitments to particular others and to universal principles.

It should be mentioned that under some construals, "modernity" would be characterized somewhat differently, as an epoch in which universalism prevailed and particularism was shunned—at least as the socially legitimate normative orientation, if not always in daily life. On this view, the current epoch should be seen as "postmodern" precisely because its ethos legitimates the simultaneous and paradoxical embrace of both universalism and particularism. Maxims such as "Think globally, act locally" come to mind.

Trust and Capitalism

So far, the argument has focused on the implications of an economywide trend—growing knowledge intensity—for intra- and interfirm relations. If, however, the trend to trust prevails, one must surely expect some reciprocal effect of firm-level changes at the aggregate, economywide level. Organizational research and social theory might both be enriched if these implications could be seen more clearly. The final set of speculations in this chapter leads to the hypothesis that if capitalism undermines traditional trust and fosters modern trust, a new form of society will likely emerge.

Schumpeter provides the starting point. Paraphrasing and extending Marx, Schumpeter (1946) wrote:

> Capitalism creates a critical frame of mind which, after having destroyed the moral authority of so many other institutions, in the end turns against its own; the bourgeois finds to his amazement that the rationalist attitude does not stop at the credentials of kings and popes but goes on to attack private property and the whole scheme of bourgeois values. (p. 143)

The capitalist process not only destroys its own institutional framework but it also creates the conditions for another. Destruction may not be the right word after all. Perhaps I should have spoken of transformation. The outcome of the process is not simply a void that could be filled by whatever might happen to turn up; things and souls are transformed in such a way as to become increasingly amenable to the socialist form of life. With every peg from under the capitalist structure vanishes an impossibility of the socialist plan. (p. 162)

In Schumpeter's view, large corporations developed means of institutionalizing innovation and regulating competition. The firm typical of competitive capitalism—owned and led by an entrepreneur—was thus progressively displaced by the large, bureaucratic firm with dispersed ownership and professional managers. Market was progressively displaced by hierarchy. Property was, in the process, progressively socialized—but not socialized enough to eliminate capitalism's tendency to periodic crises or its other negative externalities. The earlier form of capitalism derived legitimacy from its support for the entrepreneurial function: competitive capitalism's obvious flaws were the price to be paid for the productive energy of entrepreneurship. But capitalism's own development, and in particular the shift to large bureaucratically organized firms, makes capitalism's dysfunctions appear increasingly unnecessary and therefore intolerable: witness, for example, the U.S. government's bailout of Chrysler Corporation. The legitimacy of capitalism as a form of society based on private ownership of productive resources is progressively undermined. Moreover, by the same process, capitalist development "creates the conditions for another" institutional framework that replaces private ownership by public ownership—socialism.

The logic of the present essay argues for both the continuing pertinence of Schumpeter's thesis and the need to revise it. Schumpeter's underlying contrast was between market (externally coordinating entrepreneurial firms) and hierarchy (internally coordinating oligopolistic firms, and eventually coordinating activity across entire economies). This contrast and Schumpeter's analysis of it have continuing pertinence: both the persistent crisis tendencies of capitalism and the incapacity of markets to cope effectively enough with the growing knowledge intensity of modern society reinforce Schumpeter's concerns about the efficacy of market coordination. And the long-term trend toward larger firms and bigger government confirms his prognosis of the growing importance of hierarchy.

A critic might argue that this prediction is at variance with the real trends observed in the United States and elsewhere in the advanced industrial economies over the last couple of decades, where an intensification of global and domestic competition and a wave of deregulation have reasserted the dominance of the market. The Schumpeterian view invites us to enlarge our temporal horizon. If one considers the changes witnessed over the last 50–100 years, Schumpeter's prediction of the replacement of market by hierarchy becomes more plausible. The last couple of decades have made little progress in "turning back the clock." Even if the average size of establishments has stabilized, the weight of large firms relative to small in the economy has grown, as has the weight of (federal and state) government relative to private industry.

Schumpeter's thesis, however, also needs revision. Both the continued vitality of small entrepreneurial firms in the capitalist knowledge-creation process and the demise of state socialism give us reasons to doubt the efficacy of hierarchy alone as a form capable of effectively structuring firms and societies. Schumpeter's implicit market-hierarchy model must be extended to include trust—we must add a dialectic of trust to Schumpeter's market-hierarchy dialectic. On the one hand, over the longer run, the economy's increasing knowledge intensity undermines the efficacy and therefore legitimacy of (low-trust) market and hierarchy. Market's costly fluctuations and manifest failures and hierarchy's coercive domination and alienating specialization reveal the inadequacies of these two forms relative to the knowledge-management challenge. Low-trust market thus loses legitimacy as a model of governance of interfirm and interdivisional relations, and (low-trust) hierarchy loses legitimacy as a model of governance of employment relations. On the other hand, the gradual infusion of trust into hierarchies and markets popularizes and legitimates a range of more participative and democratic notions of how firms should be run (Levine 1995, Lawler et al. 1998) and of how society and the economy as a whole should be governed (Lodge 1975, Unger 1975, Etzioni 1988).

Do these trends, however, spell the demise of capitalism? Hirschman (1982) criticizes Schumpeter and other proponents of the self-destruction thesis for ignoring capitalism's ability to adapt to pressures such as these. Hirschman argues that through a series of innovations from factory legislation to social security to countercyclical macroeconomic management, demands to socialize the economy have been accommodated within a basically capitalist framework. At a microlevel of intra- and interfirm relations, one could follow Hirschman and point to the evidence that trust can indeed infuse hierarchy and market relations without provoking crisis—as argued above, the three forms are often complementary.

These complementarities should not, however, obscure the fact that in a capitalist society the varying combinations of market, hierarchy, and community operate under the overall predominance of the market. If, as I argue above, the three basic coordination modes are sometimes substitutes and only sometimes complements, then it follows that all three modes cannot peacefully coexist in any proportions: the greater the substitutability, the more likely one of them will dominate the other two and the more constraining will be that domination. There is little doubt which of the three dominates in advanced economies today. While the functioning of a market-based economy is greatly enhanced by modest doses of hierarchy and community, the dominance of the market form places limits on the growth of hierarchy and community. Whatever hierarchy and community are created within and between firms, market pressures that are beyond any actor's control—in the form of unpredictable market fluctuations and crises—can force management to renege on its commitments (laying off employees or breaking supply relationships) or can simply force the firm out of business. In an era of globalization, intensified competitive rivalry, and international financial crisis tendencies, the dominant role of the market has been brutally brought back into focus.

It is against this backdrop that Schumpeter's thesis acquires its force. The development of greater knowledge-management capability will necessitate the displacement of the market as the dominant form. However, whereas Schumpeter saw the progressive displacement of market by hierarchy, first in large corporations, then at the societal level in the form of socialism, this essay suggests a "friendly amendment" to Schumpeter's thesis: the institutional framework likely to emerge from capitalism's development is not any form of socialism but a form characterized by high levels of trust. If socialism can be construed as a form of society in which hierarchy dominates market at both the firm level and the economywide level, then the form of socialism that can successfully confront the challenges of modern, knowledge-intensive industry will have to be one in which hierarchy is combined with high levels of trust.

Opinions are divided as to whether the most viable form of postcapitalist society will prove to be one based on comprehensive centralized but democratic planning or on a form of market socialism in which markets supplement democratic planning (Nove 1982). What seems indubitable, however, is that the planning process must be one in which citizens feel a high degree of trust. Evidence for this assertion comes first from the demise of (decidedly low-trust) state socialism. While external pressures clearly played a role in this demise, low-trust central planning was also a key factor. Evidence also comes from research on the vitality of industrial districts in regions such as northern Italy. Whereas Putnam (1993) argues that long-standing community ties in those regions created a fabric of horizontal trust, which in turn led to high levels of civic engagement and economic prosperity, critics have shown the economic vitality of these regions stems not only from horizontal trust but also from the vertical trust earned and enjoyed by active local governments (e.g., Tarrow 1996). This is also the lesson of Evans's (1995) analysis of the importance for economic development of governments with high levels of "embedded autonomy."

The various configurations of capitalist and postcapitalist societal forms can be located in a typology that reflects at the macrosocietal level the typology presented earlier of institutional forms at the firm level (see figure 2.3). Indeed, substitution of the three terms of figure 2.2 (market, hierarchy, and community) with corresponding dimensions already well established in sociological analysis (market, state, and civil society) is conceptually straightforward. (Concerns voiced by critics of this market/state/civil society trichotomy focus on the way much prior research fell prey to "classificatory angst" [Edwards and Foley 1998, p. 128] and degenerated into arguments over whether a given institution falls into this or that type. The approach suggested by this chapter avoids that dead end by using these ideal types to understand the hybrids in which they are typically presented.)

For trust to become the dominant mechanism for coordination within organizations, broadly participative governance and multistakeholder control would need to replace autocratic governance and owner control—even if hierarchy, in a high-trust form, continued to characterize

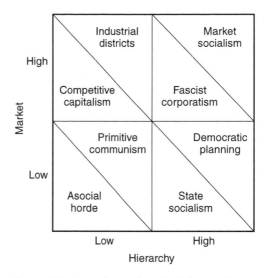

Figure 2.3 A typology of societal forms. (Low-trust forms in lower left triangles; high-trust forms in upper right triangles.)

large-scale enterprise. And for trust to become the dominant mechanism for coordinating between organizations, comprehensive but democratic planning would need to replace market competition as the dominant form of resource allocation—even if market retained an important subsidiary role. If capitalism can be defined as a form of society characterized by (hierarchically controlled) wage labor and (market coordinated) competing firms, then such a trust-based form of society would surely qualify as postcapitalist. A host of institutional components of capitalism, notably, property rights, corporate law, labor law, and even the form of government, would need to change accordingly. And "vertical trust"—trust in government—would have to be radically increased.

This extension of Schumpeter's thesis must immediately acknowledge that we know little about what any postcapitalist form of society might look like. The demise of state socialism has emphasized the importance of combining hierarchy with high levels of trust and the possible value of market as a subordinate mode. But whether and how such combinations can be attained and sustained is still an open question. Indeed, the central thesis of this essay is that the trends at work today in the fabric of intra- and interfirm relations might give us valuable clues to the answer.

References

Abrahamson, E. (1997) "The emergence and prevalence of employee management rhetorics: the effects of long waves, labor unions, and turnover, 1875–1992." *Academy of Management Journal* 40(3):491–533.

Academy of Management Review. (1998) "Special topic forum on trust in and between organizations." 23(3).

Adler, P.S. (1990) "Marx, machines and skill." *Technology and Culture* 31(4):780–812.

Adler, P.S. (1997) "Work organization: from Taylorism to teamwork." *Industrial Relations Research Association 50th Anniversary Magazine*, June, 61–65.

Adler, P.S. and Borys, B. (1996) "Two types of bureaucracy: coercive versus enabling." *Administrative Science Quarterly* 41(1):61–89.

Adler, P.S. and Ferdows, K. (1992) "The chief technology officer: a new role for new challenges," in L.R. Gomez-Mejia and M.W. Lawless (eds.), *Advances in Global High-Technology Management: Top Management and Executive Leadership in High Technology*, vol. 2, pp. 49–66. Greenwich, CT: JAI Press.

Adler, P.S., Goldoftas, B., and Levine, D.I. (1999) "Flexibility versus efficiency? A case study of model changeovers in the Toyota production system." *Organization Science* 10(1):43–68.

Alchian, A.A. and Demsetz, H. (1972) "Production, information costs, and economic organization." *American Economic Review* 62(5):777–795.

Apel, K.-O. (1987) "The problem of philosophical foundations in light of a transcendental pragmatics of language," in K. Barnes, J. Bohnmann, and T. McCarthy (eds.), *After Philosophy: End or Transformation?* pp. 250–290. Cambridge, MA: MIT Press.

Arrow, K. (1962) "Economic welfare and the allocation of resources for invention," in Universities-National Bureau Committee for Economic Research, *The Rate and Direction of Inventive Activity*, pp. 609–625. Princeton, NJ: Princeton University Press.

Arrow, K. and Hurwicz, L. eds. (1977) *Studies in Resource Allocation Processes.* Cambridge: Cambridge University Press.

Ashkenas, R., Ulrich, D., Jick, T., and Kerr, S. (1993) *The Boundaryless Organization.* San Francisco: Jossey-Bass.

Barber, B. (1983) *The Logic and Limits of Trust.* New Brunswick, NJ: Rutgers University Press.

Barker, J.R. (1993) "Tightening the iron cage: concertive control in self-managing teams." *Administrative Science Quarterly* 38:408–437.

Barley, S.R. and Kunda, G. (1992) "Design and devotion: surges of rational and normative ideologies of control in managerial discourse." *Administrative Science Quarterly* 37:363–399.

Barnes, L.B. (1981) "Managing the paradox of organizational trust." *Harvard Business Review* March–April, 107–116.

Barney, J.B. and Hansen, M.H. (1994) "Trustworthiness as a source of competitive advantage." *Strategic Management Journal* 15:175–216.

Bell, D. (1993) *Communitarianism and Its Critics.* Oxford: Clarendon Press.

Bennis, W.G. and Nanus, B. (1997) *Leaders: Strategies for Taking Charge*, 2d ed. New York: Harper-Business.

Bennis, W.G. and Slater, P.E. (1964) "Democracy is inevitable." *Harvard Business Review*, March–April.

Bensaou, M. and Venkatraman, N. (1995) "Configurations of interorganizational relationships: a comparison between U.S. and Japanese automakers." *Management Science* 41(9):1471–1492.

Bigely, G.A. and Pearce, J.L. (1998) "Straining for shared meaning in organization science: problems of trust and distrust." *Academy of Management Review* 23(3):405–421.

Birch, D.L. (1987) *Job Creation in America.* New York: Free Press.

Blau, P.M. (1955) *The Dynamics of Bureaucracy.* Chicago: University of Chicago Press.

Bradach, J. and Eccles, R. (1989) "Markets versus hierarchies: from ideal types to plural forms." *Annual Review of Sociology* 15:97–118.

Braverman, H. (1974) *Labor and Monopoly Capital.* New York: Monthly Review Books.

Brockner, J. and Siegel, P. (1996) "Understanding the interaction between procedural and distributive justice: the role of trust," in R.M. Kramer and T.R. Tyler (eds.), *Trust in Organizations*, pp. 390–413. Thousand Oaks, CA: Sage.

Bromiley, P. and L.L. Cummings (1995) "Transaction costs in organizations with trust," in R.J. Bies, R.J. Lewicki, and B.L. Sheppard (eds.), *Research on Negotiations in Organizations*, pp. 219–247. Greenwich, CT: JAI Press.

Brynjolfsson, E., Malone, T.W., Gurbaxani, V., and Kambil, A. (1994) "Does information technology lead to smaller firms?" *Management Science*, 40(12):1628–1644.

Burawoy, M. (1979) *Manufacturing Consent.* Chicago: University of Chicago Press.

Burns, T. and Stalker, G. (1961) *The Management of Innovation.* London: Tavistock.

Business Week. (1982) "TRW leads a revolution in managing technology." November 15, pp. 124–130.

Butler, J.K. and Cantrell, R.S. (1984) "A behavioral decision theory approach to modeling dyadic trust in superiors and subordinates." *Psychological Reports* 55:19–28.

Carchedi, G. (1977) *The Economic Identification of Social Classes*. London: Routledge and Kegan Paul.

Carney, M. (1998) "The competitiveness of networked production: the role of trust and asset specificity." *Journal of Management Studies* 35(4):457–479.

Champy, J. (1995) *Reengineering Management*. New York: HarperBusiness.

Coleman, R. (1990) *Foundations of Social Theory*. Cambridge, MA: Belknap Press.

Collins, J.C. and Porras, J.I. (1994) *Built to Last*. New York: HarperCollins.

Crozier, M. (1964) *The Bureaucratic Phenomenon*. Chicago: University of Chicago Press.

Daft, R.L. (1998) *Essentials of Organization Theory and Design*. Cincinnati: South-Western College Publishing.

Davenport, T.H. and Prusak, K. (1998) *Working Knowledge*. Boston: Harvard Business School Press.

Dore, R. (1983) "Goodwill and the spirit of market capitalism." *British Journal of Sociology* 34: 459–482.

Durkheim, E. (1893) *The Division of Labor in Society*, trans. W.D. Halls. Reprint, New York: Free Press, 1984.

Dyer, J.H. (1996) "Does governance matter? Keiretsu alliances and asset specificity as sources of Japanese competitive advantage." *Organization Science* 7(6):649–666.

Dyer, J.H. and W. Chu (1998) "The determinants of interfirm trust in supplier-automaker relationships in the U.S., Japan and Korea." Unpublished paper, Wharton School of Business.

Earl, M.J. and Scott, I.A. (1999) "What is a chief knowledge officer?" *Sloan Management Review*, Winter, 29–38.

Eccles, R. (1985) *The Transfer Pricing Problem*. Lexington, MA: Lexington.

Edwards, B. and Foley, M.W. (1998) "Civil society and social capital beyond Putnam," *American Behavioral Scientist*, 42(1):124–139.

Etzioni, A. (1988) *The Moral Dimension*. New York: Free Press.

Evans, P. (1995) *Embedded Autonomy: States and Industrial Transformation*. Princeton, NJ: Princeton University Press.

Evans, P. (1996) "Government action, social capital and development: reviewing the evidence on synergy." *World Development* 24(6):1119–1132.

Fox, A. (1974) *Beyond Contract: Work, Power and Trust Relations*. London: Faber and Faber.

Fukuyama, F. (1995) *Trust: The Social Virtues and the Creation of Prosperity*. New York: Free Press.

Gambetta, D., ed. (1988) *Trust: Making and Breaking Cooperative Relations*. Oxford: Basil Blackwell.

Gates, H.L. Jr. (1998) "The end of loyalty." *The New Yorker*, March 9, 34–44.

Gerlach, M.L. (1992) *Alliance Capitalism: The Social Organization of Japanese Capitalism*. Berkeley, CA: University of California Press.

Giddens, A. (1990) *The Consequences of Modernity*. Stanford, CA: Stanford University Press.

Gouldner, A.W. (1954) *Patterns of Industrial Bureaucracy*. New York: Free Press.

Granovetter, M. (1985) "Economic action and social structure: the problem of embeddedness." *American Journal of Sociology* 91:481–510.

Gupta, A.K. and Govindarajan, V. (1986) "Resource sharing among SBUs: strategic antecedents and administrative implications." *Academy of Management Review* 29(4):695–714.

Habermas, J. (1990) *Moral Consciousness and Communicative Action*. Cambridge, MA: MIT Press.

Habermas, J. (1993) *The Philosophical Discourse of Modernity*. Cambridge, MA: MIT Press.

Hammer, M. (1996) *Beyond Reengineering*. New York: HarperBusiness.

Hammer, M. and Champy, J. (1993) *Reengineering the corporation*. New York: HarperBusiness.

Hancké, B. (1997) "Trust or hierarchy? Changing relationships between large and small firms in France." *Small Business Economics* 11(3):237–252.

Hardin, R. (1992) "The street-level epistemology of trust." *Politics and Society* 21:505–529.

Harvey, D. (1990) *The Condition of Modernity*. Cambridge MA: Blackwell.

Heimer, C. (1992) "Doing your job and helping your friends: universalistic norms about obligations to help particular others in a network," in N. Noria and R.G. Eccles (eds.), *Networks and Organizations: Structure, Form, and Action*, pp. 143–164. Boston: Harvard Business School Press.

Heisig, U. and Littek, W. (1995) "Trust as a basis of work organization," in W. Littek and T. Charles (eds.), *The New Division of Labour: Emerging Forms of Work Organization in International Perspective*, pp. 17–56. Berlin: de Gruyter.

Helper, S. (1991) "Strategy and irreversibility in supplier relations: the case of the US automobile industry." *Business History Review* 65(4):781–824.

Helper, S. and Sako, M. (1995) "Supplier relations in the auto industry in Japan and the USA: are they converging?" *Sloan Management Review*, Spring, 7–84.

Hill, C., Hitt, M., and Hoskisson, R. (1992) "Cooperative vs. competitive structures in related and unrelated diversified firms." *Organization Science* 3(4):501–521.

Hirschman, A.O. (1970) *Exit, Voice, and Loyalty.* Cambridge, MA: Harvard University Press.

Hirschman, A.O. (1982) "Rival interpretations of market society: civilizing, destructive or feeble?" *Journal of Economic Literature* 20:1463–1484.

Holland, C.P. and Lockett, A.G. (1997) "Mixed mode network structures: the strategic use of electronic communication by organizations." *Organization Science*, 8(5):475–488.

Hyman, R. (1987) "Strategy or structure? Capital, labour and control." *Work, Employment and Society* 1(1):25–55.

Kaplan, R.S. (1984) "The evolution of management accounting." *Accounting Review* 59(3):390–419.

Kaplan, R.S. (1996) *The Balanced Scorecard: Translating Strategy into Action.* Boston: Harvard Business School Press.

Kern, H. (1998) "Lack of trust, surfeit of trust: some causes of the innovation crisis in German industry," in C. Lane and R. Bachmann (eds.), *Trust within and between Organizations*, pp. 203–213. New York: Oxford University Press.

Kim, P.H. (1997) "Working under the shadow of suspicion: the implications of trust and mistrust for information sharing in groups." Unpublished paper, University of Southern California.

Kirkpatrick, F.G. (1986) *Community: A Trinity of Models.* Washington, DC: Georgetown University Press.

Korczynski, M. (1996) "The low trust route to economic development: interfirm relations in the UK engineering construction industry in the 1980s and 1990s." *Journal of Management Studies*, 33(6):787–808.

Koza, M.P. and Lewin, A.Y. (1998) "The coevolution of strategic alliances." *Organization Science* 9(3):255–264.

Kurland, N.B. (1996) "Trust, accountability, and sales agents' dueling loyalties." *Business Ethics Quarterly* 6(3):289–310.

Lakoff, G. (1996) *Moral Politics: What Conservatives Know That Liberals Don't.* Chicago: University of Chicago Press.

Lawler, E.E. III, Mohrman, S.A., and Ledford, G.E. Jr. (1998) *Strategies for High Performance Organizations.* San Francisco: Jossey-Bass.

Levine, D. (1995) *Reinventing the Workplace: How Business and Employees Can Both Win.* Washington, DC: Brookings Institution.

Lewicki, R.J. and Bunker, B.B. (1996) "Developing and maintaining trust in work relationships," in R.M. Kramer and T.R. Tyler (eds.), *Trust in Organizations*, pp. 114–149. Thousand Oaks, CA: Sage.

Liebeskind, J.L. and Oliver, A.L. (1998) "From hand-shake to contract: trust, intellectual property, and the social structure of academic research," in C. Lane and R. Bachmann (eds.), *Trust within and between Organizations*, pp. 118–145. New York: Oxford University Press.

Liebeskind, J.L., Oliver, A.L., Zucker, L., and Brewer, M. (1996) "Social networks, learning and flexibility: sourcing scientific knowledge in the new biotechnology firms." *Organization Science* 7(4): 428–443.

Lodge, G.C. (1975) *The New American Ideology.* New York: Knopf.

Lorsch, J.W. and Allen, S.A., III. (1973) *Managing Diversity and Interdependence.* Boston: Division of Research, Graduate School of Business Administration, Harvard University.

Luhmann, N. (1979) *Trust and Power.* Chichester: Wiley.

Macaulay, S. (1963) "Non-contractual relations in business." *American Sociological Review* 28:55–70.

Macneil, I.R. (1980) *The New Social Contract.* New Haven, CT: Yale University Press.

Marx, K. (1973) *Grundrisse: Foundations of Political Economy.* Harmondsworth: Penguin.

Marx, K. and Engels, F. (1959) "Manifesto of the Communist Party," in L.S. Feuer (ed.), *Marx and Engels Basic Writings on Politics and Philosophy.* Garden City, NY: Doubleday.

Mashaw, J.L. (1983) *Bureaucratic Justice: Managing Social Security Disability Claims.* New Haven: Yale University Press.

Merton, R.K. (1983) *The Sociology of Science.* Chicago: University of Chicago Press.

Miller, G.J. (1992) *Managerial Dilemmas: The Political Economy of Hierarchy.* New York: Cambridge University Press.

Mintzberg, H. (1979) *The Structuring of Organizations.* Englewood Cliffs, NJ: Prentice-Hall.

Nahapiet, J. and Ghoshal, S. (1998) "Social capital, intellectual capital, and the organizational advantage." *Academy of Management Review* 23(2):242–266.

Nelson, R.R. (1988) "Institutions supporting technical change in the United States," in G. Dosi, C. Freeman, R. Nelson, G. Silverberg, and L. Soete (eds.), *Technical Change and Economic Theory*, pp. 312–329. London: Pinter.

Nove, A. (1982) *The Economics of Feasible Socialism.* London: Allen and Unwin.

Nyland, C. (1998) "Taylorism and the mutual-gains strategy." *Industrial Relations* 37(4):519–542.

Organization for Economic Cooperation and Development (OECD). (1996) *Employment and Growth in the Knowledge-Based Economy.* Paris:

Organization Science. (1998) Special issue on Managing Partnerships and Strategic Alliances. 9(3).

Ouchi, W. (1980) "Markets, bureaucracies and clans." *Administrative Science Quarterly* 25(1):125–141.

Paine, T. (1792) *The Rights of Man*. Reprint, New York: Dutton, 1951.

Porter, M.E. (1985) *Competitive Advantage*. New York: Free Press.

Powell, W. (1990) "Neither markets nor hierarchy: network forms of organization." *Research in Organizational Behavior* 12:295–336.

Prahalad, C.K. and Hamel, G. (1990) "The core competencies of the corporation." *Harvard Business Review* 86:79–91.

Putnam, R. (1993) *Making Democracy Work: Civic Traditions in Modern Italy*. Princeton NJ: Princeton University Press.

Ramsay, H. (1977) "Cycles of control: worker participation in sociological and historical perspective." *Sociology* 11(3):481–506.

Ring, P.S. (1996) "Fragile and resilient trust and their roles in economic exchange." *Business and Society* 35(2):148–175.

Ring, P.S. (1997) "Transacting in the state of union: a case study of exchange governed by convergent interests." *Journal of Management Studies* 34(1):1–25.

Ring, P.S. and Van de Ven, A.H. (1992) "Structuring cooperative relationships between organizations." *Strategic Management Journal* 13:483–498.

Rosenberg, N. (1964) "Neglected dimensions in the analysis of economic change." *Oxford Bulletin of Economics and Statistics*, 26(1):59–77.

Rothschild-Witt, J. (1979) "The collectivist organization: an alternative to rational-bureaucratic models." *American Sociological Review* 44:509–527.

Sabel, C.F. (1992) "Studied trust: building new forms of co-operation in a volatile economy," in F. Pyke and W. Sengenberger (eds.), *Industrial Districts and Local Economic Regeneration*, pp. 215–250. Geneva: International Institute for Labour Studies.

Sabel, C.F. and Zeitlin, J., eds. (1997) *World of Possibilities: Flexibility and Mass Production in Western Industrialization*. Cambridge: Cambridge University Press.

Sako M. (1992) *Prices, Quality and Trust: Interfirm Relations in Britain and Japan*. Cambridge: Cambridge University Press.

Salter, M.S. (1973) "Tailor incentive compensation to strategy." *Harvard Business Review* (March–April):94–102.

Satow, R.L. (1975) "Value-rational authority and professional organizations: Weber's missing type." *Administrative Science Quarterly* 20(December):526–531.

Schindler, P.L. and Thomas, C.C. (1993) "The structure of interpersonal trust in the workplace." *Psychological Reports* 73:563–573.

Schumpeter, J. *Capitalism, Socialism and Democracy*. Reprint, New York: Harper, 1976.

Scott, W.R. (1992) *Organizations: Rational, Natural, and Open Systems*. Englewood Cliffs, NJ: Prentice Hall.

Seligman, A.B. (1997) *The Problem of Trust*. Princeton, NJ: Princeton University Press.

Shapiro, S.P. (1987) "The social control of impersonal trust." *American Journal of Sociology* 93(3):623–658.

Sparrow, M.K. (1994) *Imposing Duties: Government's Changing Approach to Compliance*. Westport, CT: Praeger.

Spencer, M.E. (1970) "Weber on legitimate norms and authority." *British Journal of Sociology* 21(2):123–134.

Stiglitz, J.E. (1994) *Whither Socialism?* Cambridge, MA: MIT Press.

Stinchcombe, A.L. (1985) "Contracts as hierarchical documents," in A.L. Stinchcombe and C. Heimer, *Organization Theory and Project Management*. Bergen, Norway: Universitetsforslaget.

Tarrow, S. (1996) "Making social science work across space and time: a critical reflection on Robert Putnam's *Making Democracy Work*." *American Political Science Review* 90(2):389–401.

Unger, R.M. (1975) *Knowledge and Politics*. New York: Free Press.

Uzzi, B. (1997) "Social structure and competition in interfirm networks: the paradox of embeddedness." *Administrative Science Quarterly* 42(1):35–67.

Walton, R.E. (1985) "Toward a strategy for eliciting employee commitment based on policies of mutuality," in R.E. Walton and P.R. Lawrence (eds.), *HRM Trends and Challenges*, pp. 35–65 Boston: Harvard Business School.

Walzer, M. (1999) "Rescuing civil society." *Dissent* 46(1):62–67.

Weber, M. (1947) *The Theory of Social and Economic Organization*. New York: Free Press.

Wenger, E. (1998) *Communities of Practice*. New York: Oxford University Press.

Wicks, A.C., Berman, S.L., and Jones, T.M. (1999) "The structure of optimal trust: moral and strategic implications." *Academy of Management Review* 24(1):99–116.

Williamson, O.E. (1975) *Markets and Hierarchies*. New York: Free Press.

Williamson, O.E. (1981) "The economics of organization: the transaction cost approach." *American Journal of Sociology* 87:548–577.

Williamson, O.E. (1991) "Economic institutions: spontaneous and intentional governance." *Journal of Law, Economics and Organization 7: 159–187.

Williamson, O.E. (1993) "Calculativeness, trust, and economic organization." *Journal of Law and Economics* 36:453–502.

Zelizer, V.A. (1996) "Payments and social ties." *Sociological Forum* 11(3):481–496.

Zenger, T.R. and Hesterly, W.S. (1997) "The disaggregation of corporations: selective intervention, high-powered incentives, and molecular units." *Organization Science* 8(3):209–222.

Zucker, L.G. (1986) "Production of trust: institutional sources of economic structure, 1840–1920." *Research in Organizational Behavior* 8:53–111.

3

Knowledge, Knowledge Work, and Organizations

An Overview and Interpretation

Frank Blackler

Ever since Galbraith (1967) suggested that a powerful new class of technical-scientific experts was emerging, and Bell (1973) proposed that knowledge is a central feature of postindustrial societies, the significance of experts in contemporary society has attracted much comment (see Reed 1991 for a discussion of contemporary trends). Indeed, in recent years, the importance of expertise for competitive advantage has been emphasized again by economists and business strategists who have suggested that wealth creation is less dependent on the bureaucratic control of resources than it once was, and more dependent on the exercise of specialist knowledge and competencies, or the management of organizational competencies (e.g., Prahaled and Hamel 1990, Hague 1991, Reich 1991, Drucker 1993, Florida and Kenny 1993). This debate has found echoes in discussion about "knowledge-intensive firms," that is, organizations staffed by a high proportion of highly qualified staff who trade in knowledge itself (Starbuck 1992, 1993, Alvesson 1993a), in the suggestion that organizational competencies can be nurtured by the de-velopment of interorganizational links (Kanter 1989, Badaracco 1991, Wikstrom and Normann 1994) and in the proposal that, because of technological changes, team organization is becoming of crucial importance and employees generally should be managed as "knowledge workers" (Zuboff 1988).

Within the literature on the established professions the privilege suggested by the term *knowledge* and the opportunities it offers occupational groups to protect their positions and "black box" their skills (e.g., by claiming the authority of medicine, law, or other complex bodies of knowledge) have been well documented (e.g., Baer 1987, Abbott 1988). Writing in a special edition of the *Journal of Management Studies* on knowledge work, Alvesson (1993a) notes how specialists in the new generation of knowledge firms are, in exactly the same way, attracted to the mystique associated with the terms such as knowledge and knowledge worker; knowledge-intensive firms are, above all else, he suggests, systems of persuasion. Developing a similar point, Knights et al. (1993) suggest that the growing use of such terms may be regarded as a normalizing discourse that, as it legitimates a particular division of labor, distracts attention from the knowledge that is an essential characteristic of all forms of activity.

This chapter explores the relevance of the terms *knowledge, knowledge work,* and *knowledge-intensive firms* for organization studies, by developing an approach that seeks neither to perpetuate the mystique often associated with abstract, codified knowledge nor to present claims to knowledge merely as normalizing discourse. Conventional images of knowledge within the literature on organizational learning are first identified and are distinguished by the assumptions they make about the location of knowledge, that is, in bodies, routines, brains, dialogue, or symbols. Recent commentary on the emerging significance of knowledge work amounts to the suggestion that, in place of a strong reliance on knowledge located in bodies and routines (in the terminology of this chapter, in place of knowledge that is "embodied" and "embedded"), emphasis is increasingly falling on the knowledge that is located in brains, dialogue, and symbols (i.e., knowledge that is "embrained," "encultured," and "encoded"). Conventional assumptions about the nature of knowledge are not without their difficulties, however; a point that has emerged strongly from studies of the impact of new information and communication technologies. Inspired by such studies, and drawing from recent debates in philosophy, linguistics, social theory, and cognitive science, an alternative approach is outlined. Rather than regarding *knowledge* as something that people *have*, it is suggested that *knowing* is better regarded as something that they *do*. Such an approach draws attention to the need to research ways in which the systems that mediate knowledge and action are changing and might be managed. The conclusion of this chapter is that debate about the growing importance of esoteric experts and flexible organizations should be located within a broader debate about the nature of expertise and of the changing systems through which activities are enacted.

Images of Knowledge within Organization Studies

Within the organization studies literature, a variety of approaches to knowledge can be identified. One obvious place to begin exploring these is the literature on organizational learning. The metaphor of organizational learning is not new; it has attracted attention at least since Chandler (1962). Interest in the United States has been consistently high (see, e.g., Argyris and Schon 1978, Duncan and Weiss 1979, Nelson and Winter 1982, Daft and Weick 1984, Fiol and Lyles 1985, Nonaka and Johansson 1985, Levitt and March 1988, Zuboff 1988, Henderson and Clark 1990, Senge 1990, Brown 1991, Kochan and Useem 1992, Dixon 1994, and special editions of *Organization Science* 1991 and of *Organization Dynamics* 1993), although, especially in recent years, a strong interest has been developing in the United Kingdom and Europe also (Hedberg 1981, Garratt 1987, Pedler et al. 1991, Swieringa and Wierdsma 1992, Dodgson 1993; see also Douglas 1987).

At least five images of knowledge can be identified in this literature. Adapting and extending a categorization of knowledge types suggested by Collins (1993), these are knowledge that is *embrained, embodied, encultured, embedded,* and *encoded.*

Embrained knowledge is knowledge that is dependent on conceptual skills and cognitive abilities (what Ryles 1949 called "knowledge that" and James 1950 termed "knowledge about"). As discussed further below, within Western culture abstract knowledge has enjoyed a privileged status, and in the organizational learning literature a number of commentators have emphasized its importance. Fiol and Lyles (1985), for example, reflect the predominant view of the distinctive status of abstract knowledge when they contrast "routine" behavioral adjustments with what they term "higher level" abilities to develop complex rules and to understand complex causations. Perhaps the best known theorist of organization learning who has featured embrained knowledge is Argyris, whose theory of "double-loop" learning (e.g., Argyris and Schon 1978) encourages an explicit recognition and reworking of taken-for-granted objectives. A recent account in this tradition is Senge (1990), who synthesizes personal insights, models, systems thinking, and shared visions in a general account of organization learning.

Embodied knowledge is action oriented and is likely to be only partly explicit (what Ryles 1949 called "knowledge how" and James 1950, "knowledge of acquaintance"). A contemporary account of embodied knowledge is included in Zuboff (1988); such knowledge, she says, depends on people's physical presence, sentient and sensory information, physical cues, and face-to-face discussions; is acquired by doing; and is rooted in specific contexts. Other accounts include Scribner's (1986) description of "practical thinking," that is, problem-solving techniques that depend on an intimate knowledge of a situation rather than abstract rules; Hirschhorn's (1984) analysis of mechanization and his conclusion that operators' tacit understandings of machine systems are more important than their general knowledge; and Suchman's (1987) studies of how people spontaneously construct interpretations of technologies as they interact with them.

Encultured knowledge refers to the process of achieving shared understandings. Cultural meaning systems are intimately related to the processes of socialization and acculturation; such understandings are likely to depend heavily on language and hence to be socially constructed and open to negotiation. As Swidler (1986) indicated, in periods of social transformation explicitly formulated ideologies become the main vehicle for promoting new recipes for action. Following Pettigrew (1979) and Ouchi's (1980) discussions of organizational culture, there has, of course, been considerable interest in the relevance to organizations of such processes. Within the literature on organizational learning, Srivastva and Barrett (1988) demonstrated how the imagery in the language of a group can change over time: as people grasp for new insights, they experiment with new metaphors in their talk, which others may take up and develop; and Czarniawska-Joerges (1990) illustrated how consultants explicitly endeavor to manage this process. Other important contributions include Orr's (1990) account of stories shared by maintenance technicians about complex mechanical problems, and Nonaka's (1991, 1994) discussions of "knowledge-creating" organizations (these are discussed further below).

Embedded knowledge is knowledge that resides in systemic routines. The notion of "embeddedness" was introduced by Granovetter (1985), who proposed a theory of economic action that, he intended, would be neither heavily dependent on the notion of culture (i.e., "oversocialized") nor heavily dependent on theories of the market (i.e., "undersocialized"): his idea was that economic behavior is intimately related to social and institutional arrangements. Following Badaracco (1991), the notion of embedded knowledge explores the significance of relationships and material resources. Embedded knowl-

edge is analyzable in systems terms, in the relationships between, for example, technologies, roles, formal procedures, and emergent routines. This is how, for example, Nelson and Winter (1982) analyzed an organization's capabilities. They noted that an individual's skills are composed of subelements that become coordinated in a smooth execution of the overall performance, impressive in its speed and accuracy, with conscious deliberation being confined to matters of overall importance; thus, they maintained, may an organization's skills be analyzed. In addition to the physical and mental factors that comprise individual skills, however, organizational skills are made up of a complex mix of interpersonal, technological, and sociostructural factors. Similar approaches include Levitt and March's (1988) development of the notion of organizational routines (which, they suggest, make the lessons of history accessible to subsequent organizational members), while other writers refer to "organizational competencies" (Prahalad and Hamel 1990). A related orientation has been proposed by Henderson and Clark (1990), who distinguish between the knowledge of specialist elements in an organization ("component knowledge") and knowledge about how such elements interact ("architectural knowledge"); architectural knowledge is often submerged within an organization's taken-for-granted routines and interactions, yet is central to an understanding of its strengths and weaknesses.

Encoded knowledge is information conveyed by signs and symbols. To the traditional forms of encoded knowledge, such as books, manuals, and codes of practice, has been added information encoded and transmitted electronically. Zuboff's (1988) analysis of the "informating" power of information technologies explores the significance of this point for organizations: information encoded by decontextualized, abstract symbols is inevitably highly selective in the representations it can convey. Poster's (1990) thesis on how the new information technologies may be "culturally alien" and Cooper's (1992) analysis of the significance of technologies of representation for the theory of organization are among the writings that have complemented such lines of analysis.

Brown's (1991) account of efforts to develop Xerox as a learning organization provides an example of how the development of each of these different forms of knowledge may contribute to organizational learning. Brown pointed to the advantages for a company such as Xerox of undertaking new product development in close association with potential customers (i.e., in the terminology of this chapter, he identified the relevance of the embedded knowledge of Xerox's customers for an understanding of their reactions to new office machinery). He illustrated how design engineers at Xerox learned, from ethnographic studies of how people interact with machines (i.e., from studies of the ways in which encoded knowledge interacts with, and may disrupt, embodied knowledge) and he emphasized, too, how studies of communications between engineers in Xerox have revealed how essential dialogue is between them (i.e., encultured knowledge) to increase their effectiveness in solving problems. Finally, Brown emphasized the importance of encouraging senior managers to develop new appreciations of their company's established practices (i.e., he pointed to the importance of developing embrained and encultured knowledge at senior management levels).

Derived as it is from the literature on organizational learning, the five types of knowledge identified here do not focus on the commodification of knowledge into products, systems, or services. (Thus, economists' interests in the immediate competitive potential of industrial secrets, patents, etc. [see, e.g., Winter 1988] or with the cumulative advantages that such knowledge may provide [Arthur 1990] are not included within this typology). What the variety of images of knowledge identified here serves to emphasize is the complexity of issues that any discussion of knowledge within organizations must address. For example, it indicates that *all* individuals and *all* organizations, not just so-called "knowledge workers" or "knowledge organizations," are knowledgeable. As is discussed in the following sections, the typology can also be used to review claims that significant changes are presently taking place in the relationship between knowledge and economic success, and to introduce a critique of conventional approaches to analyzing such developments.

Organizations and Different Types of Knowledge

Drucker (1993) has offered a historical interpretation of the suggestion that, within the demands of contemporary capitalism, a shift is occurring in the relationship between knowledge and wealth creation. In the eighteenth century, he suggests, the basis for an economic system based on machines and factories was laid with the development of "technologies." These he describes as "knowledge applied to tools, processes and products" (in the terminology introduced above, this involved the development of new approaches to the study of embodied knowledge, i.e., craft skills, supported by the granting of patents to inventors and entrepreneurs). Later, in the early years of this century, F. W. Taylor's development of a technology of work analysis provided the basis for a further impetus to productivity. Drucker describes this as "knowledge applied to human work" (in the terminology used above this involved the systematic development of systems of embedded knowledge). Now, Drucker maintains, a society is emerging that is dependent upon the development and application of new knowledge: "Knowledge is being applied to knowledge itself." In the terminology of this paper, Drucker's thesis can be taken to imply that embrained and encultured knowledge are beginning to assume predominant importance.

Both the practical and the theoretical implications of Drucker's thesis are significant. Just as the nature of organization and management changed dramatically at the time of industrial revolution and later as a result of Taylorism, Drucker maintains that new approaches are now becoming necessary. Productivity is becoming dependent on the application and development of new knowledge, and on the contributions of specialist knowledge workers. Drucker's thesis is that knowledge workers are unlike previous generations of workers, not only in the high levels of education they have obtained, but principally because, in knowledge-based organizations, they own the organization's means of production (i.e., knowledge). Drucker suggests that, in these circumstances, familiar images of organizations as hierarchical, decentralized, or a matrix should be discarded. Alternative models can be developed from examples of organizations based on key specialist experts, such as hospitals, symphony orchestras, or the British Colonial administration in India.

In recent years, other American commentators have presented related ideas. Shortly before his appointment as U.S. Secretary of State for Labor, the political economist Reich (1991) suggested that the globalization of the world's economy is creating a split between the production of standardized products in low-wage economies, and high value-added problem solving, which may be undertaken wherever useful insights can be found. Accordingly, the maxim that a nation's chief economic assets are the skills and insights of its citizens assumes new significance. From his discussions with a range of senior executives in major American corporations, Reich believes that the strategies of big businesses no longer focus on products as such; rather, they are endeavoring explicitly to exploit the competitive advantage that specialized knowledge can provide. High value added depends on problem solving; in the international economy, value added accrues anywhere around the world where useful insights can be channeled to respond to the particular needs of individual customers. The tendency for manufacturing and service companies to concentrate on the provision of specialty services has become so advanced, Reich believes, that the traditional distinction in economics between goods and services has broken down. Moreover, he emphasizes the undesirable social consequences that are likely to result from the dependency of low-pay, low-status workers, in service industries or routine production, on highly paid, high-status "knowledge workers."

The skills of what Reich calls "symbolic analytic" workers are varied. They command high rewards, he believes, because they are difficult to duplicate. Such skills include problem solving (research, product design, fabrication), problem identification (marketing, advertising, customer consulting), and brokerage (financing, searching, contracting). When combined, Reich observes, these skills allow technical insights to be linked both to marketing know-how and to strategic and financial acumen. In the terminology suggested in this chapter, Reich is highlighting the contemporary significance of embrained knowledge. Such knowledge can be used to support new forms of organization based on networks, partnerships, or contractual arrangements.

Both Drucker and Reich attribute particular significance to knowledge workers. While Drucker's thesis is clearly influenced by Bell's theory of postindustrialization, Reich's analysis is strongly influenced by the current difficulties of the American economy, especially the reduced international dominance of American conglomerates, changes in American manufacturing industry, an influx of foreign capital, and acute social inequalities. Yet both claim their approaches reach beyond the American experience and locate their interpretations in a world perspective, suggesting that as national economies are integrated into the global economy, similar developments are occurring in other countries as well.

A less sophisticated account than either Drucker's or Reich's, but one that anticipated a number of their points, has been presented by a Swedish businessman and a British journalist in the mid 1980s. Sveiby and Lloyd (1987) developed an account for general managers not of knowledge workers but of knowledge *organizations*. Defining know-how as "value added information," they suggested that "know-how companies" provide a nonstandard, creative, problem-solving service. To be successful, know-how companies must, Sveiby and Lloyd suggested, be high on what they called professional skills, yet in itself this would be insufficient. The new breed of know-how organizations also need a high level of managerial skills (defined as "the ability to preserve added value"). Examples of professional know-how organizations that they provided included highly entrepreneurial (and very profitable) merchant banks, advertising agencies, software firms, and management, architectural, and engineering consultancies.

Sveiby and Lloyd's account is not without its problems, but their analysis of knowledge-intensive organizations (rather than capital, technology, or labor intensive) was unusual. Anticipating some of Drucker's observations, they noted how such firms present particular problems of organization and management (e.g., power in know-how companies stems primarily from ability and reputation; new forms of employment relationship may be demanded by know-how workers; high short-term profit is likely to be a mistaken goal for know-how companies—what matters is the company's ability to convince clients of the value of a long-term relationship). Rather than the specifics of their observations, it was the powerful image of the "professional know-how organization" that attracted the attention of academics. Starbuck in the United States and Alvesson in Sweden both preferred a different terminology, "knowledge-intensive firm," but their interests covered ground similar to Sveiby and Lloyd's. Thus, in presenting his comments on knowledge-intensive firms, Starbuck (1992) emphasized the economic significance of esoteric knowledge over common knowledge and pointed to the potential distinctions between specialist expertise and the skills of the established professions. He emphasized the importance of social skills and client relationships to the activities of knowledge workers and the success of their companies, and explored the difficulties that knowledge-intensive firms may have in developing their own learning (e.g., experts may not be receptive to new ideas). In a subsequent paper (Starbuck 1993) he further explores the distinctive identities of knowledge-intensive firms and the need to analyze them within their particular market situations.

Alvesson (1993b), on the other hand, has reported how the managers of knowledge-intensive firms may cope with their dependency on their specialist workers. In an analysis of a computer consultancy, he identifies the ideological controls that management used, striving to create a "strong" culture, by manufacturing a sense of community, using performance-related rewards, cultivating a positively buoyant outlook, and systematically intervening in an attempt to influence the ways in which employees thought of themselves and the company.

Recent commentaries on knowledge-intensive firms in the popular management literature have concentrated less on knowledge workers as the recipients of cultural manipulation and more on their active participation within their organization's dialogue. Daft and Weick's (1984) notion of organizations as systems of interpretation anticipated many of the issues that are now being raised: to survive, they argued, organizations must find ways to interpret events. Indeed, the processes of "sensemaking" that Daft and Weick highlighted are likely to be especially important for firms that concentrate on the solution of unfamiliar problems; thus, Peters' (1992) discussion of the consultancy firm McKinsey's points to the central role that communication plays in that organization where energetic efforts are made to share key reports, a data bank of project lessons is maintained to create "an internal marketplace of readily accessible ideas," and experienced consultants routinely make themselves available to other staff for comments or guidance. The conclusion that Webber (1993) takes from Peters' description is that, in a sense, conversations *are* McKinsey's.

Drawing from four of the knowledge types identified at the start of this chapter, an overview of the knowledge work literature reviewed in this section is offered in figure 3.1. Organizations that depend differentially on knowledge that is embodied, embedded, embrained, and encultured are distinguished in a two-by-two matrix. This is developed by distinguishing between organizations that, first, focus on problems of a routine kind versus those that are preoccupied with unfamiliar issues and, second, depend heavily upon the contributions of key individuals versus those that are more obviously dependent upon collective effort. Four kinds of organization are thus differentiated in the figure: (i) expert-dependent organizations, which depend heavily on embodied knowledge; (ii) knowledge-routinized organizations, which depend heavily on embedded knowledge; (iii) symbolic-analyst dependent, which depend heavily on embrained knowledge; and (iv) communication-intensive organizations, which depend heavily on encultured knowledge. This classification provides a way of summarizing key suggestions in the knowledge work literature. The arrows depicted in figure 3.1 highlight the trends many of the commentators reviewed in this section purport to have identified: that a shift is occurring away from dependence on the embodied and embedded knowledge toward embrained and encultured knowledge.

Encoded Knowledge, and Criticisms of Conventional Approaches to Knowledge

The accuracy of these very general claims can only, of course, be established by empirical investigation, and it may be that current developments are not all one way (e.g., there would appear to be a trend in the United Kingdom to organize certain professional bureaucracies in the public sector, not as symbolic-analyst-dependent or communication-intensive organizations, but as machine bureaucracies). However, there remains a more basic problem. In recent years, taken-for-granted assumptions about the nature of knowledge, which underpin the distinctions presented on figure 3.1, have been exposed as problematic. Studies of the ways in which new forms of encoded knowledge have affected organizations have played a major part in this reassessment.

It would be a mistake to regard the new generation of information and communication technologies as neutral tools that can merely be grafted onto existing work systems. Of particular interest to the present discussion is the way such technologies have been found to disrupt conventional practices, as Hirschhorn (1984) has noted of automated work systems, Zuboff (1988) of informated work systems, and Pava (1986) of how such technologies demand new approaches to sociotechnical systems design. The way the technologies intimately interlace with the minutiae of everyday practices is exposing processes that, previously, were taken for granted, ignored, or misunderstood.

Zuboff's studies, for example, document in detail how action-oriented skills (in the terms used here, embodied knowledge) are being displaced by computer technologies (encoded knowledge).

(ii) Knowledge-Routinized Organizations: *Emphasis on knowledge embedded in technologies, rules, and procedures* • Typically capital, technology, or labor intensive • Hierarchical division of labor and control • Low skill requirements *Example:* • "Machine bureaucracy" such as a traditional factory *Current issues:* • Organizational competencies and corporate strategies • The development of computer integrated work systems	**(iv) Communication-Intensive Organizations:** *Emphasis on encultured knowledge and collective understanding* • Communication and collaboration are the key processes • Empowerment through integration • Expertise is pervasive *Example:* • "Ad hocracy," "innovation mediated production" *Current issues:* • "Knowledge-creation," dialogue, sensemaking processes • The development of computer-supported cooperative work (CSCW) systems
(i) Expert-Dependent Organizations: *Emphasis on the embodied competencies of key members* • Performance of specialist experts is crucial • Status and power from professional reputation • Heavy emphasis on training and qualifications *Example:* • "Professional bureaucracy" such as a hospital *Current issues:* • Nature and development of individual competency • Computer displacement of action skills	**(iii) Symbolic-Analyst-Dependent Organizations:** *Emphasis on the embrained skills of key members* • Entrepreneurial problem solving • Status and power from creative achievements • Symbolic manipulation is a key skill *Example:* • "Knowledge-intensive-firm" (KIF) such as a software consultancy *Current issues:* • Developing symbolic analysts, the organization of KIFs • Information support and expert systems design

Emphasis on collective endeavor

Emphasis on contributions of key individuals

Focus on familiar problems   Focus on novel problems

Figure 3.1 Organizations and knowledge types. (Arrows summarize trends suggested in the knowledge work literature.)

The new technologies bypass the use of immediate, physical responses to situated cues; instead they require operators to interpret the selective, decontextualized and abstract symbols that machines present to them. Computers require sophisticated cognitive abilities; the skills of deduction and a knowledge of systems and procedures are essential for their satisfactory operation. Zuboff (1988) and Weick (1985) have suggested that it is foolish to believe that high-technology work systems can be managed as if conventional processes of sensemaking are outmoded. Talk *about* computer-mediated informa-

tion and the transformation of isolated problem-solving attempts into a shared activity are crucial to the effective operation of the "informated" organization. It is only through such processes that collective interpretation can be recreated. The point may be summarized in the suggestion that managers in informated organizations must contrive to develop the skills that are referred to here as encultured knowledge.

It is not only through their "informating" effects, however, that technologies based on microelectronics are transforming organizations. Such technologies are also associated with the changes precipitated by economic globalization. This is not to say that the transformations associated with contemporary capitalism are technologically determined. As Castells (1989) documents in his account of changes occurring in contemporary capitalism, governmental enactment of post-Keynesian policies in, for example, weakening trade unions, developing fiscally austere policies, retreating from policies of wealth redistribution, and reducing the size of the public sector are fundamental to an understanding of developments. By the operations they support, the new technologies are playing a vital role in facilitating the internationalization of capital, production, and labor processes. Castells summarizes how modern information technologies have transformed money markets and eroded the distinctions between mass markets and customized markets, and at the same time they make it possible for organizations to develop flexible methods of production, to disperse their operations, and to compete in alliances. The communication and control operations they support within organizations are also facilitating the demise of bureaucratic approaches of organization, promising vigorous internal networks, collaborative work relations, and significantly reduced hierarchical structures of control (developments explored in detail by Malone and Rochart 1991, Sproull and Kiesler 1991).

Thus, just as familiar working patterns are being transformed by the encodification of knowledge, at the same time, the new technologies are making it possible for organizations to operate relatively independently from geographical location, thereby blurring the boundaries between one organization and another and freeing internal communications within organizations. During the 1980s, much social science commentary on the relationship between information technologies and organizations emphasized how technologies are not deterministic in their effects (Buchanan and Boddy 1983). Instead, it was maintained, they open a range of options from centralization to decentralization, from automation to work enrichment. Current developments suggest, however, that rather than thinking of the new technologies as flexible tools for organizations to use as they believe is appropriate, it may be better to consider the technologies as the medium for organizing itself. Organizations that are heavily dependent on the new technologies are, simultaneously, being *imploded* into electronic codes and *exploded* into (global) information networks.

Some of the tensions involved in these processes are not new. The uneasy relationship that encoded knowledge may have to other forms of knowledge has been documented before. For example, Zuboff quotes the mediaeval historian Clanchy (1979), who recorded the slow and largely reluctant acceptance in eleventh- and twelfth-century England of written documentation: "both to ignorant illiterates and to sophisticated Platonists, a written record was a dubious gift, because it seemed to kill living eloquence and trust and substitute for them a mummified semblance in the form of a piece of parchment." Yet the extent of the disruption to knowledge bases associated with electronically encoded information *is* new. As summarized in figure 3.1, the new media of encoded knowledge not only affect embodied knowledge but may also affect the nature and significance of embrained knowledge (as information becomes ever more accessible and expert computer systems are developed), encultured knowledge (as new communication systems are introduced to support group working between individuals who are separated in time and space), and embedded knowledge (through, e.g., the development of integrated manufacturing systems).

The close relationship between encoded knowledge and the other images of knowledge highlighted in this discussion illustrate the point that it is a mistake to assume that embodied, embedded, embrained, encultured, and encoded knowledge can sensibly be conceived as separate one from the other. Knowledge is multifaceted and complex, being both situated and abstract, implicit and explicit, distributed and individual, physical and mental, developing and static, verbal and encoded. Analysis of the relationships between different manifestations of knowledge identified in this chapter is at least as important as any delineation of their differences.

From Theories of Knowledge to Theories of Knowing

Nonaka's (1991, 1994) description of the "knowledge-creating" organization provides a useful starting point for theorizing about the links between the different forms of knowledge identified in this chapter. Nonaka is concerned with the management of innovation. This he regards as an ongoing process in which organizations create problems, define them, then develop new knowledge for their solution. He develops the idea that knowledge is created out of a dialogue between peoples' tacit and explicit knowledge. Knowledge may move from tacit to tacit (e.g., in a craft apprenticeship), from explicit to explicit (e.g., when hitherto distinct but related bodies of information are brought together), from tacit to explicit (e.g., the study of craft skills), and from explicit to tacit (e.g., the internalization of new knowledge). Nonaka maintains that all four of these patterns exist in dynamic interaction in "knowledge-creating" companies. He does not wish to suggest, however, that the processes involved here are merely a recycling of knowledge. Knowledge creation, he believes, is closely associated with language and communications, requiring the creative use of metaphors, analogies, and models, and a resolution of the conflicts and disagreements that new approaches may provoke. In the terminology of this chapter, Nonaka is suggesting that encultured knowledge is intimately related to the development of embodied, embrained, and embedded knowledge. His approach traces the link between different forms of knowledge to the processes through which they are created.

In other respects, however, Nonaka's approach is rather traditional. He insists that knowledge is a specific entity, formed in the minds of individuals (albeit generated in interactions with others), and conceptually distinct from the material technologies around which organizations are structured (see Nonaka 1994). Similarly, while his concept of "knowledge-creation" pushes the distinction between knowledge and learning to its limits, he wishes to maintain a distinction between them.

To develop the analysis of the interrelations between different types of knowledge further, it is necessary to address the basic question, What *is* knowledge? (or perhaps as Pear 1972 asks, What is *not* knowledge?). In recent years there has been considerable debate about this issue. Postmodernists, for example, have challenged the idea of fundamental truth by suggesting that truth is a story (see, e.g., Lawson 1989); cognitive anthropologists, ethnomethodologists, and symbolic interactionists have queried the value of abstract plans and the notion of social structure and have demonstrated the significance of situated skills and pragmatic knowledge (e.g., Suchman 1987); and sociologists of science have challenged deep-rooted assumptions about the privileged status of explicit abstract knowledge by studying knowledge creation as a cultural process and by deemphasizing conventional dis-

tinctions between people and technology (e.g., Latour 1987, Law 1992).

The various implications of such approaches remain to be fully described. Yet it is becoming clear that traditional conceptions of knowledge as abstract, disembodied, individual, and formal are unrealistic. Polkinghorne (1992), for example, reviews the implications of postmodernism for the theory of practice. Practical knowledge, he suggests, is foundationless, partial, constructed, and pragmatic. A similar outlook is presented by Lave (1993), who reviews points of agreement between cognitive anthropologists, ethnomethodologists, and activity theorists. Such theorists agree, she says, that major difficulties occur when educationalists assume that knowledge can be divorced from context and transmitted either as abstract data or as universally applicable approaches to problem solving; learning is not a passive process, she argues, but an active one. Defining learning as a creative (and collective) interpretation of past experiences, she summarizes the emerging consensus between educational researchers as agreement that:

1. Knowledge always undergoes construction and transformation in use.
2. Learning is an integral aspect of activity in and with the world at all times. That learning occurs is not problematic.
3. What is learning is always complexly problematic.
4. Acquisition of knowledge is not a simple matter of taking in knowledge; rather, things assumed to be natural categories, such as "bodies of knowledge," "learners," and "cultural transmission," require reconceptualization as cultural, social products. (Lave 1993, p. 8)

Star (1992) has also presented a summary of patterns of agreement between contemporary social theorists, drawing on a literature similar to Lave's although placing a heavier emphasis on research studies in the actor-network tradition. The emerging consensus that conventional views of knowledge are unacceptable is so widespread, Star believes, that she refers to it as an "invisible college" and "an intellectual movement that as yet has no name." Reviewing detailed studies of technology and work, she echoes Lave's points in her observation that the boundaries of knowledge in complex organizations are fluid and overlapping. Star explains this by reviewing studies suggesting that cognitions are situated (as the circumstances of action shape even the most abstractly represented tasks), cognitions are collective (as practices are distributed socially and technologically), and that, rather than being a mere internal manipulation of ideas, cognitions are also forms of material practice (i.e., cognitions involve not only an internal manipulation of ideas but also physical, manual, and interactional actions).

Accounts such as these (see also Brown and Rogers 1991 for a similar approach developed for the theory of communication) provide a useful starting point for the development of a unifying theory of organizational knowledge. First, rather than talking of *knowledge*, with its connotations of abstraction, progress, permanency, and mentalism, it is more helpful to talk about the process of *knowing*. Second, to avoid segregating the forms of knowing identified in this chapter, old concepts (such as the split between the abstract and the specific, individuals and communities, and the social and the technical) need to be abandoned and new approaches to conceptualizing the multidimensional processes of knowing and doing need to be created. One approach to this task could be to develop from the insights that knowing is situated, distributed, and material.

Activity Theory, Knowing, and Doing

Out of the range of theoretical approaches that both Lave (1993) and Star (1992) include in their reviews, activity theory offers particular promise that might be of value in this project. Activity theory has its origins in the ideas of the Russian psychologist Vygotsky, who, working in the 1920s, endeavored to develop an understanding of mind and society that did not depend upon the dichotomies (e.g., mind vs. body, thought vs. action, individual vs. society, etc.) that have characterized mainstream Western thought (and that lend credence to the clear distinctions assumed between embodied, embedded, embrained, and encultured knowledge). Basic to the Vygotsky approach is the Marxist idea that it is not the consciousness of humans that determines their social being, but social experiences that shape their consciousness: psychological processes can only be understood by an appreciation of the culturally provided factors that mediate them. (Vygotsky thought, e.g., that it would be a mistake to think that children pass through a stage of egocentric speech before they use language socially; his view was the opposite, i.e., that children learn to internalize speech that is, from the

start, oriented to their external social environment; see Kozulin [1990].)

Contemporary versions of activity theory take a variety of forms. However, all are explicit in their attempts to develop a unified account of knowing and doing, and all emphasize the collective, situated, and tentative nature of knowing. Some (e.g., Brown et al. 1989, Lave and Wenger 1991) concentrate on the processes through which people develop shared conceptions of their activities. Others (e.g., Hutchins 1983, Engestrom 1987, 1993) model the relationships that exist between a community's conceptions of its activities and the material, mental, and social resources through which it enacts them. While the former approach develops a model of learning as socialization, the latter explores the circumstances in which communities may enact new conceptions of their activities.

Orr's (1990) analysis of Xerox maintenance technicians is in the Brown/Lave tradition of activity theory. He describes how the stories shared by maintenance personnel about complex technical problems are an essential part of their activities. In the first place, the stories they tell each other serve a key informational function, preserving and circulating essential news about particular problems. Second, the storytelling has an educational function: the technicians not only learn about particular faults on the machines but also help the participants develop their diagnostic and trouble-shooting skills. Finally, the stories provide an opportunity for the technicians to establish their identity within the community of technicians itself; as newcomers contribute to the storytelling process, they begin both to demonstrate their identity as professionals and to contribute to the collective wisdom of their group. In their discussion of the wider implications of this study, Brown and Duguid (1989) emphasize the general significance for organizations of such processes. Learning is a socially constructed understanding, they argue, that emerges from practical collaboration. Collective wisdom depends upon communal narratives. Note that this analysis suggests that it is not just esoteric consultancies like McKinsey (see Peters 1993, Webber 1993, discussed above) that benefit from lively internal communications; collective dialogue is also an essential aspect of life in other, less glamorous, organizations, developing skills and abilities which are distributed (often unnoticed) among the employees within them.

Engestrom's (1989, 1991) study of a medical practice in Finland illustrates a second version of activity theory. Partly through discourse analysis, partly from observation, and partly from accounts of the history of medicine, he was able to distinguish the variety of conceptions that doctors may have of their activity. Doctors may conceive of their work in biomedical, administrative-economic, psychiatric, sociomedical, or system-interactive terms. Doctors in the same medical practice may, perhaps unknowingly, be enacting different conceptions of health care, yet attempts to refocus priorities may not be easy to achieve. In Engestrom's study, attempts to reorientate priorities toward psychosomatic and sociomedical priorities were hampered by the resource system within which the doctors operated: (i) the division of labor between doctors and other health care professionals proved inflexible, (ii) the way patients are randomly allocated to doctors in the Finnish health care system created problems of continuity of care, and (iii) the biomedical concepts and techniques that the doctors had become accustomed to using encouraged them to continue treating health care problems as biomedical problems.

The analysis Engestrom offers of this and other work settings is explicitly intended to avoid separating the individual from the collective, or the social from the technical. Fundamental to his approach is the unit of analysis he adopts, namely, *the socially distributed activity system*. The general model he offers of such systems is shown in figure 3.2. Essential to such systems are the relations between agents, the community of which they are members, and the conception(s) people have of their activities (the inner triangle of relations in fig. 3.2). Such relations are mediated by a further series of factors, including the language and technologies used by participants within the system, the implicit and explicit social rules that link them to their broader communities, and the role system and division of labor adopted by the community.

A summary model of Engestrom's analysis of

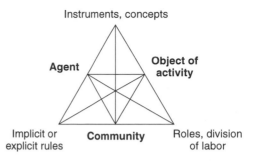

Figure 3.2 A general model of socially distributed activity systems. (Based on Engestrom 1987.)

the dynamics of the medical practice he studied is shown on figure 3.3. Note that the relations depicted in this figure are neither static nor are they necessarily harmonious. The three points of tension noted in Engestrom's fieldwork, detailed above, are featured on the model (see points i–iii). Indeed, Engestrom's approach suggests that, far from being unusual, tensions such as these are commonplace within distributed work systems. His analysis of the dynamics of activity systems is reminiscent of Perrow's (1984) suggestion that accidents are a normal feature of life in complex industrial work systems. Likewise, for the most part, everyday interruptions and breakdowns in the workings of activity systems are skillfully, regularly, and normally repaired (although system breakdown may sometimes occur). It is through their collective determination and skill, in both their actions and their language, that participants enact particular frames (i.e., impose conceptions of their activities on situations they believe appropriate) and maintain a (seemingly) smooth flow of events.

Note that the incoherencies, paradoxes, and conflicts that feature within activity systems provide a potential driving force for change. Engestrom's analysis suggests that organizations and institutions are a lot less stable and rational

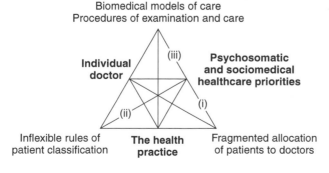

Figure 3.3 The tensions within a medical practice (adapted from Engestrom 1991; points i–iii mark points of tension within the activity system.)

than is usually recognized. The incoherencies and contradictions that feature within them are obscured, however, partly, no doubt, by conventional imagery of the organization as a rational machine, but also by the skills of participants who learn to work within the situation in which they find themselves. New ways of knowing and doing can emerge if communities begin to rethink what, in a different context, Unger (1987) has called the "false necessity" of everyday life, and to engage with the tensions in their activity systems. The complexities of socially distributed activity systems suggest that incoherencies and tensions are inevitable; the issue is not how can they be eradicated but how they should be treated.

Rethinking Knowledge and Organizations

As the review presented in the first part of this chapter indicated, current interest in knowledge and knowledge work marks a change of emphasis within contemporary capitalism away from knowledge that is embodied and embedded, to knowledge that is embrained, encultured, and encoded. The approach presented in the second part of this chapter offers a different orientation. To summarize:

(1) Lave suggests that knowledge should not be conceived as a timeless body of truth that experts have internalized and that organizations may harness. She suggests that the notion of "bodies of knowledge" (with its connotations of universal truth) is a problem in its own right. General abstractions are no more than resources to be used in specific circumstances where (in actions, improvisation, and dialogue) creativity is ubiquitous. By focusing on knowing rather than knowledge, the distinction that is conventionally assumed between knowledge and learning is avoided.

(2) Engestrom's interpretation of the dynamic relationships between individuals, their communities, and the objects of their activities provides a clear alternative to approaches that attempt to study such entities, or the factors that mediate the relationships between them, in isolation one from the other. His suggestion is that the appropriate unit of analysis is neither individuals nor organizations, but socially distributed activity systems. People act on the world, with others, utilizing (and contributing to the development of) the linguistic, material, and social resources currently available. Knowledge does

not appear as a separate category in Engestrom's model; rather, it permeates the relations he depicts. His approach models the dynamics of knowing: each moment is a compromise; the balance within an activity system changes constantly. Participants employ their situated knowledge in a situation that is itself constantly developing. In response to this changing situation, participants' knowledge and behavior will also inevitably develop.

(3) Activity theories in general argue that knowledge is constantly evolving. Analysis of the tensions that inevitably develop within socially distributed activity systems points to the opportunities for system development that (routinely) arise. Orr, and Brown and Duguid demonstrate how essential language is to this process. Talk enables collective interpretations, negotiates behavioral priorities, signals group membership, and helps to create a community. Language is an archetypal communal activity, integral to the enactment of practical actions.

Thus, helpful though it can be to characterize knowledge as embodied, embedded, embrained, encultured, and encoded, the concept of knowledge is problematic. Rather than studying knowledge as something individuals or organizations supposedly have, activity theory studies knowing as something that they do and analyzes the dynamics of the systems through which knowing is accomplished. Recast in this way, knowing in all its forms is analyzed as a phenomenon that is (a) manifest in systems of language, technology, collaboration, and control (i.e., it is mediated); (b) located in time and space and specific to particular contexts (i.e., it is situated); (c) constructed and constantly developing (i.e., it is provisional); and (d) purposive and object oriented (i.e., it is pragmatic).

Before considering how these conclusions can be used to inform debate about knowledge and knowledge work, however, it should be noted that, in at least one respect, an extension of activity theory is required. Activity theory is not alone in its attempts to draw attention to the need to rethink supposed distinctions between events and contexts, language and action, the social and the technical, and so on; as noted above, similar suggestions have also been made by anthropologists, social theorists, and linguists, and others. Of the comparisons that might be made between these various approaches, one point stands out: activity theory is weak in the analysis it offers of the relationship between knowledge and power. This is not to say that power as an issue does not occur at all in the writings of activity theorists. (E.g., in her criticism of the term "bodies of knowledge," highlighted above, Lave 1993 adopts Latour and Woolgar's [1979] terminology to suggest that claims to the possession of decontextualized knowledge are frequently no more than examples of erasure, collusion, or domination.) However, analysis of power in everyday life has featured far less in the writings of activity theorists than it has in the work of others who are theorizing practice from different traditions. This is well illustrated by the issues that preoccupied Ortner (1984) in her discussion of the relevance to anthropology of theories of practice (such as Bourdieu 1978, Giddens 1979) that were emerging in the early 1980s. Ortner supported the attempts being made in these writings to treat societies and cultures as integrated wholes and to avoid segregating social, economic, and political factors from values, ideals, and emotions, but she emphasized how it would be a mistake to treat all the elements of a social system as if they are of equal analytical significance. Social systems are fundamentally unequal. Gramsci's (1957) notion of hegemony and Foucault's (1980) notion of a "discourse of perversions" serve as reminders that any theory of knowing as a cultural activity must acknowledge the often self-reproducing dynamics of domination and subordination that are a feature of everyday life.

To the suggestion just made that knowing is *mediated, situated, provisional,* and *pragmatic* must therefore be added the point that it is also *contested.* As noted at the start of this chapter, this point has not passed unnoticed within the literature on knowledge work and knowledge-intensive firms (see Alvesson 1993a, Knights et al. 1993).

Applied to the study of knowledge work, the approach developed here suggests that, as an alternative to focusing on the kinds of knowledge that capitalism currently demands, attention should focus on the systems through which knowing and doing are achieved. Because of the changes that are occurring in capitalism touched on earlier (such as moves toward the globalization of markets and finance, new information and communication technologies, post-Keynesian governmental policies, new approaches to strategy, management and organization, etc.) activity systems are changing significantly. Rather than asking what sorts of knowledge are needed in contemporary capitalism and how may organizations harness them, the question thus becomes, How are systems of knowing and doing changing, and what responses would be appropriate?

This revised formulation promises to establish links between the knowledge work literature and broader studies of economic and organizational changes. The analysis of knowing as mediated, situated, provisional, pragmatic, and contested provides a basis for identifying research priorities:

Knowing as mediated. Research is needed into the dynamics of activity systems and how they are currently changing. As discussed above, changes associated with the new information and communication technologies are combining with other developments, such as new economic and organizational structures and new approaches to management to transform the contexts of action. Further work is needed into such changes. One key consequence of these developments is that activity systems that were previously segregated are becoming interlinked and, therefore, are growing larger and becoming more complex. Research is needed to document such developments. Detailed ethnographic studies are needed to illuminate the ways in which people improvise, communicate, and negotiate within expanded activity systems.

Knowing as situated. Work is needed to develop the relevance of the notion of situated knowledge to the knowledge work debate. As already noted, the concept of situated knowledge avoids the problems associated with abstract, decontextualized knowledge; it emphasizes the significance of peoples' interpretations of the contexts within which they act and the key role that "communities of practitioners" play in the acquisition and development of skill. The knowledge work debate draws attention to the differences in approach that may develop between employees whose work involves them in action skills or in the execution of procedural routines, and those who are involved in creative problem solving. Little is known about the ways in which peoples' understanding of their activities are changing as a consequence of the developing complexity of the contexts within which they are working.

Knowing as provisional. Research is needed into the idea that knowing is, essentially, provisional, and developing. Activity theory suggests that developments in systems of knowing and doing will occur constantly as tensions (inevitably) emerge within them. However, changes in activity systems may or may not be planned (e.g., the unanticipated impacts of advanced information and communication technologies) and may or may not be fully understood or articulated by participants (e.g., computer-mediated interactions may erode traditional practices in bureaucracies but people may continue to describe their organizations through a terminology that is familiar to them). Activity theory points to the opportunities that might be created to help participants become more proactive in the development of their activity systems. At a general level, research is needed into Engestrom's proposal that, by alerting people to the tensions in activity systems that would otherwise be ignored or tolerated, a process of dialogue, experimentation, and collective learning can be triggered that may transform participants' understandings of their activities and the systems through which they are enacted. Issues specific to the knowledge work debate include the study of the tensions within expert-dependent and knowledge-routinized organizations at the present time, and the ease with which they may transform themselves into symbolic-analyst-dependent and communication-intensive organizations.

Knowing as pragmatic. Central to activity theory is the idea that collective action is driven by the conceptions people have of the object of their activities. Further research is needed into the influence that "informated" and "communication-intensive" environments have on the approaches people take to their work. It seems likely that, as activity systems become interrelated and complex, traditional approaches to organizing are likely to be ineffective. Research is needed into the possibilities for developing communal narratives within expanded activity systems. Study is also needed of the anxiety that individuals and communities may experience in the face of significant, ongoing, and perhaps conflicting demands for changes in their work methods and priorities.

Knowing as contested. Finally, as noted above, the concepts of knowledge and power are interrelated. Conflicts are to be expected within and between the new generation of symbolic analysts and problem solvers, and established professionals and managers. Beyond this, the far-reaching social, technological, and economic changes that are at the heart of the knowledge work debate indicate that issues of domination and subordination are fundamental to the development of a general theory of knowing as praxis.

Inquiry along the lines sketched out here is unlikely to contradict the suggestion that symbolic-analytical work and communication-intensive organizations are of growing significance at the present time. Rather, it promises to explain why this is so and, by reframing the problem, to illuminate some of the difficulties associated with such developments. In summary, the approach introduced here extends the debate about the importance of creative experts and flexible organizations to the (more general) discussion of the nature of expertise and of the systems through which people enact their activities. The study of knowledge work and organizations is, in other words, best located within a broader analysis of knowing as a cultural phenomenon.

Note

This chapter was originally prepared for the E.U. Human Capital and Mobility Project "European Competitiveness in a Knowledge Society." I am most grateful to Colin Brown, David Courpasson, Bente Elkjaer, Manuel Graca, Henrik Holt Larson, Karen Legge, Yves-Frederic Livian, Mike Reed, and Alan Whitaker for their comments on an earlier version, and also to Arndt Sorge, Mats Alvesson, and anonymous reviewers.

References

Abbott, A. (1988) *The System of Professions: An Essay on the Division of Expert Labour.* Chicago: University of Chicago Press.

Alvesson, M. (1993a) "Organization as rhetoric: knowledge-intensive firms and the struggle with ambiguity." *Journal of Management Studies* 30:997–1016.

Alvesson, M. (1993b) "Cultural-ideological modes of management control: a theory and a case study of a professional service company," in S. Deetz (ed.), *Communication Yearbook*, vol. 16, pp. 3–42. London: Sage.

Argyris, C. and Schon, D. (1978) *Organizational Learning: A Theory of Action Approach.* Reading, MA: Addison-Wesley.

Arthur, W.B. (1990) "Positive feedbacks in the economy," *Scientific American*, February, 80–85.

Badaracco, J. (1991) *The Knowledge Link: How Firms Compete through Strategy Alliances.* Boston: Harvard University Press.

Baer, W. (1987) "Expertise and professional standards." *Work and Occupations* 13:532–552.

Bell, D. (1973) *The Coming of Post-industrial Society: A Venture in Social Forecasting.* New York: Basic Books.

Bourdieu, P. (1978) *Outline of a Theory of Practice.* Cambridge: Cambridge University Press.

Brown, J.S. (1991) "Research that invents the corporation," *Harvard Business Review*, January–February, 102–111.

Brown, J.S., Collins, A., and Duguid, P. (1989) "Situated cognition and the culture of learning." *Educational Researcher* 18:32–42.

Brown, J.S. and Duguid, P. (1989) "Innovation at the workplace, a perspective on organizational learning." Paper presented at the CMU Conference on Organizational Learning, May.

Brown, J. and Rogers, E. (1991) "Openness, uncertainty, and intimacy: an epistemological reformulation," in N. Coupland, H. Giles, and J. Wiemann (eds.), *Miscommunication and Problematic Talk*, pp. 146–165. London: Sage.

Buchanan, D. and Boddy, D. (1983) *Organizations in the Computer Age*. Aldershot: Gower.

Castells, M. (1989) *The Informational City: Information Technology, Economic Restructuring and the Urban-Regional Process*. Oxford: Blackwell.

Chandler, A. (1962) *Strategy and Structure*. Boston: MIT Press.

Clanchy, M. (1979) *From Memory to Written Record: England 1066–1307*. Cambridge, MA: Harvard University Press.

Collins, H. (1993) "The structure of knowledge." *Social Research* 60:95–116.

Cooper, R. (1992) "Formal organization as representation: remote control, displacement and abbreviation," in M. Reed, and M. Hughes (eds.), *Rethinking Organization: New Directions in Organization Theory and Analysis*, pp. 254–272. London: Sage.

Czarniawska-Joerges, B. (1990) "Merchants of meaning: management consultants in the Swedish public sector" in B. Turner (ed.), *Organizational symbolism*, pp. 139–150. Berlin: Gruyter.

Daft, R., and K. Weick (1984) "Toward a model of organizations as interpretation systems." *Academy of Management Review* 9:284–295.

Dixon, N. (1994) *The Organization Learning Cycle: How We Can Learn Collectively*. London: McGraw Hill.

Dodgson, M. (1993) "Organizational learning: a review of some literatures," *Organization Studies* 14(3):375–394.

Douglas, M. (1987) *How Institutions Think*. London: Routledge and Kegan Paul.

Drucker, P. (1993) *Post-capitalist Society*. Oxford: Butterworth-Heinemann.

Duncan, R., and Weiss, A. (1979) "Organizational learning: implications for organizational design," in B. Staw (ed.), *Research in Organizational Behaviour*, vol. 1, pp. 75–123. Greenwich, CT: JAI Press.

Engestrom, Y. (1987) *Learning by Expanding: An Activity Theoretical Approach to Developmental Research*. Helsinki: Orienta-Konsultit.

Engestrom, Y. (1989) "Developing expertise at the changing workplace; towards a redefinition of expertise," Technical Report 130. Centre for Information Processing, University of San Diego, La Jolla, California.

Engestrom, Y. (1991) "Developmental work research: reconstructing expertise through expansive learning," in M. Nurminen and G. Weir (eds.), *Human Jobs and Computer Interfaces*, pp. 265–290. Amsterdam: North-Holland.

Engestrom, Y. (1993) "Work as a testbed of activity theory," in S. Chaiklin and J. Lave (eds.), *Understanding Practice: Perspectives on Activity and Context*, pp. 65–103. Cambridge: Cambridge University Press.

Foucault, M. (1980) *The History of Sexuality*. New York: Vintage.

Fiol, C., and Lyles, M. (1985) "Organizational learning." *Academy of Management Review* 10:803–813.

Florida, R., and Kenney, M. (1993) "The new age of capitalism: innovation-mediated production." *Futures*, July–August, 637–651.

Galbraith, J. (1967) *The New Industrial State*. Boston: Houghton-Mifflin.

Garratt, B. (1987) *The Learning Organization, and the Need for Directors Who Think*. London: Fontana.

Giddens, A. (1979) *Central Problems in Social Theory: Action, Structure and Contradiction in Social Analysis*. Cambridge: Cambridge University Press.

Gramsci, A. (1957) *The Modern Prince and Other Writings*. New York: International Publishers.

Granovetter, M. (1985) "Economic action and social structure: the problem of embeddedness." *American Journal of Sociology* 91:481–510.

Hague, D. (1991) "Knowledge society, university challenge," *Marxism Today*, September, 12–17.

Hedberg, B. (1981) "How organizations learn and unlearn," in P. Nystrom and W. Starbuck (eds.), *Handbook of Organizational Design. Volume 1: Adapting Organizations to Their Environments*, pp. 3–27. Oxford: Oxford University Press.

Henderson, R., and Clark, K. (1990) "Architectural innovation: the reconstruction of existing product technologies and the failure of established firms," *Administrative Science Quarterly* 35:9–30.

Hirschhorn, L. (1984) *Beyond Mechanization: Work and Technology in a Post-industrial Age*. Cambridge, MA: MIT Press.

Hutchins, E. (1983) "Understanding Micronesian navigation," in D. Gentner and A. Stevens (eds.), *Mental Models*, pp. 191–225. Hillsdale, NJ: Erlbaum.

James, W. (1950) *The Principles of Psychology*. New York: Dover.

Kanter, R. (1989) *When Giants Learn to Dance.* New York: Simon and Schuster.

Knights, D., Murray, F., and Willmott, H. (1993) "Networking as knowledge work: a study of interorganizational development in the financial services sector." *Journal of Management Studies* 30:975–996.

Kochan, T. and Useem, M. eds. (1992) *Transforming organizations.* Oxford: Oxford University Press.

Kozulin, A. (1990) *Vygotsky's Psychology: A Biography of Ideas.* Hemel Hempstead: Harvester Wheatsheaf.

Latour, B. (1987) *Science in Action: How to Follow Scientists and Engineers through Society.* Milton Keynes: Open University Press.

Latour, B. and Woolgar, S. (1979) *Laboratory Life: The Social Construction of Scientific Facts.* London: Sage.

Lave, J. (1993) "The practice of learning," in S. Chaiklin and J. Lave (eds.), *Understanding Practice: Perspectives on Activity and Context,* pp. 3–32. Cambridge: Cambridge University Press.

Lave, J. and Wenger, E. (1991) *Situated Learning: Legitimate Peripheral Participation.* Cambridge: Cambridge University Press.

Law, J. (1992) "Notes on the theory of the actor-network ordering, strategy and homogeneity." *Systems Practice* 5:375–394.

Lawson, H. (1989) "Stories about stories," in H. Lawson and L. Appignanesi (eds.), *Dismantling Truth: Reality in the Postmodern World,* pp. ix–xxviii. London: Weidenfeld and Nicolson.

Levitt, B. and March, J. (1988) "Organizational learning." *American Review of Sociology* 14: 319–340.

Malone, T. and Rockart, J. (1991) "Computers, networks and the corporation." *Scientific American,* September, 92–99.

Nelson, R. and Winter, S. (1982) *An Evolutionary Theory of Organizational Change.* Cambridge, MA: Harvard University Press.

Nonaka, I. (1991) "The knowledge creating company," *Harvard Business Review,* November–December, 96–104.

Nonaka, I. (1994) "A dynamic theory of organizational knowledge creation." *Organization Science* 5:14–37.

Nonaka, I. and Johansson, J. (1985) "Japanese management: what about the 'hard' skills?" *Academy of Management Review* 2:181–191.

Orr, J. (1990) "Sharing knowledge, celebrating identity: community memory in a service culture," in D. Middleton and D. Edwards (eds.), *Collective Remembering,* pp. 169–189. London: Sage.

Ortner, S. (1984) "Theory in anthropology since the sixties." *Comparative Studies in Society and History* 26:126–166.

Ouchi, W. (1980) "Markets, bureaucracies and clans." *Administrative Science Quarterly* 25: 129–141.

Pava, C. (1986) "Redesigning sociotechnical systems design: concepts and methods for the 1990s." *Journal of Applied Behavioural Science* 22:201–221.

Pear, D. (1972) *What Is Knowledge?* Oxford: Basil Blackwell.

Pedler, M., Burgoyne, J., and Boydell, T. (1991) *The Learning Company: A Strategy for Sustainable Development.* London: McGraw-Hill.

Perrow, C. (1984) *Normal Accidents: Living with High-Risk Technologies.* New York: Basic Books.

Peters, T. (1992) *Liberation Management: Necessary Disorganization for the Nanosecond Nineties.* New York: Knopf.

Pettigrew, A. (1979) "On studying organizational cultures." *Administrative Science Quarterly* 24:570–581.

Polkinghorne, D. (1992) "Postmodern epistemology of practice," in S. Kvale (ed.), *Psychology and Postmodernism,* pp. 146–165. London: Sage.

Poster, M. (1990) *The Mode of Information: Poststructuralism and Social Context.* Cambridge: Polity Press.

Prahaled, C. and Hamel, G. (1990) "The core competence of the corporation." *Harvard Business Review,* May–June, 79–91.

Reed, M. (1991) "Experts, professions and organizations in late modernity: the dynamics of institutional, occupational and organizational change in advanced industrial societies." Unpublished paper, Department of Behaviour in Organizations, Lancaster University.

Reich, R. (1991) *The Work of Nations: Preparing Ourselves for 21st-Century Capitalism.* London: Simon and Schuster.

Ryles, G. (1949) *The Concept of Mind.* London: Hutchinson.

Scribner, S. (1986) "Thinking in action: some characteristics of practical thought, R. Sternberg and R. Wagner (eds.), *Practical Intelligence: Nature and Origins of Competence in the Everyday World,* pp. 13–30. Cambridge: Cambridge University Press.

Senge, P. (1990) *The Fifth Discipline: The Art and Practice of the Learning Organization.* London: Century Business.

Sproull, L. and Kiesler, S. (1991) *Connections: New Ways of Working in the Networked Organization.* Cambridge, MA: MIT Press.

Srivastva, S. and Barratt, F. (1988) "The transforming nature of metaphors in group development: a study in group theory." *Human Relations* 41:31–64.

Star, S. (1992) "The Trojan door: organizations,

work, and the 'open black box'." *Systems Practice* 5:395–410.

Starbuck, W. (1992) "Learning by knowledge intensive firms." *Journal of Management Studies* 29:713–740.

Starbuck, W. (1993) "Keeping a butterfly and an elephant in a house of cards: the elements of exceptional success." *Journal of Management Studies* 30:885–922.

Suchman, L. (1987) *Plans and Situated Actions.* Cambridge: Cambridge University Press.

Sveiby, K. and Lloyd, T. (1987) *Managing Knowhow: Add Value by Valuing Creativity.* London: Bloomsbury.

Swidler, A. (1986) "Culture in action: symbols and strategies." *American Sociological Review* 51: 273–286.

Swieringa, J. and Wierdsma, A. (1992) *Becoming a Learning Organization: Beyond the Learning Curve.* Reading, MA: Addison Wesley.

Unger, R. (1987) *False Necessity: Anti-necessitarian Social Theory in the Service of Radical Democracy.* Cambridge: Cambridge University Press.

Webber, A. (1993) "What's so new about the new economy?" *Harvard Business Review*, January–February, 24–42.

Weick, K. (1985) "Cosmos versus chaos: sense and nonsense in electronic contexts." *Organizational Dynamics*, Autumn, 50–64.

Wikstrom, S. and Normann, R. (1994) *Knowledge and Value: A New Perspective on Corporate Transformation.* London: Routledge.

Winter, S. (1988) "Knowledge and competence as strategic assets," in D. Teece (ed.), *The Competitive Challenge*, pp. 159–184. Cambridge, MA: Ballinger.

Zuboff, S. (1988) *In the Age of the Smart Machine: The Future of Work and Power.* New York: Basic Books.

EPILOGUE: KNOWLEDGE, KNOWLEDGE WORK AND, ORGANIZATIONS

The term *knowledge* conjures a promise of insight, skill, and power. Much of this appeal, however, derives from a desire for an ordered, predictable world. Scholars of management and organization would be advised to replace traditional images of knowledge with concepts grounded in pragmatism and the theory of activity.

This was the key message of this chapter. The first draft was written in 1993, before the current interest in "knowledge management," at a time when interest in knowledge work and knowledge-intensive firms was growing. I traced the growth of interest in these terms, then explored problems in the way they were used, recommended an alternative approach, and sketched out an associated research agenda.

Although the initial publication of this chapter attracted some interest, I am not sure that it has been well understood. For example, on two occasions in 2000 I heard conference presentations stating, "As Blackler demonstrated, knowledge can be embodied, embedded, embrained, encultured, or encoded." On the contrary, this chapter proposes an altogether different thesis: while such images of knowledge are common in the management literature, they are unsatisfactory. Commonsense approaches to the term *knowledge* need to be interrogated, I argued.

Rather than thinking of knowledge as a thing that people (or systems) possess, it is more helpful to analyze *knowing* as something that people *do*. Summarizing a range of work that supports this interpretation, and featuring activity theory, I suggested that knowing should be studied as a collective achievement that is mediated, situated, provisional, pragmatic, and contested.

The argument is counterintuitive. It blurs commonly assumed distinctions between knowledge and learning, cognition and behavior, the material and the mental, the social and the psychological. It suggests that knowing should be studied as practice, and practice should be studied as activity that is rooted in time and culture.

The particular approach that I recommended to address these difficult issues, Engestrom's (1987) version of activity theory, has not yet attracted the attention that I believe it deserves in management theory. Yet a cognate orientation has been quite widely discussed. This is Lave and Wenger's (1991) account of the centrality of "communities of practice" for situated learning (see, e.g., Brown and Duguid, 1991, 2000). Lave and Wenger's thesis resonates with the emphasis in activity theory on the fundamental importance of transformative, object-oriented activity. They stated that "in using the term community we do not imply some primordial culture-sharing entity. . . . Nor does the term community necessarily imply co-presence, a well-defined, identifiable group, or socially visible boundaries" (p. 97). Rather, they specified, the notion of community implies "participation in an activity system about which participants share understandings concerning what they are doing and what that means in their lives and for their communities. . . . The social structure of this practice, its power relations, and its conditions for legitimacy define possibilities for learning" (p. 98). Careful reading of such passages indicates that Lave and Wenger's thesis marked a departure from conventional assumptions about social processes. In particular, they do not prioritize norms and values, and they explicitly do not focus merely on teams. Instead, their approach focuses on *the social structure of object-oriented practices*. In activity theory terms, the suggestion is that an analysis of the emerging, "object of activity" that people are collectively working on is central to an understanding of practices (note the distinction between object and objective).

Note, however, that just as with the theory of knowledge advanced in "Knowledge, Knowledge Work, and Organizations," commentators do not always seem to have understood the significance of Lave's approach. Often they have assumed she is proposing a somewhat traditional notion of "community." Frequently, they seem confused about what she means by "practice." For example, Raelin (2000, pp. 74–82) is not unusual in the way he equates communities of practice with "learning teams," emphasizes normative integration in groups, and overlooks the ways in which power and learning are related.

To close my original piece, I suggested that, at the present time, activity systems are becoming larger, more complex, interpenetrated, abstract, and unstable. In these circumstances I suggested that it is important to study how systems of knowing and doing are changing and to consider how such developments might best be understood and influenced. After rereading the chapter my suggestion now is that one potentially very helpful approach to this task would be to explore what is distinctive about the relationship between so-called "knowledge workers" and the objects of their activity.

Knorr-Cetina's (1997, 2000) work is particularly promising in this respect. She suggests that a defining characteristic of contemporary knowledge work is the symmetrical relationship between the knowledge worker and the object of his or her activity. Knowledge workers obtain their sense of self, she suggests, through the respect they have for the perfection of the knowledge object. Taking scientific work as a model for the practices of financial traders, she illustrates how the object of such work is constantly developing, changing the characteristics it has, and acquiring new properties. Drawing from Lacan's (1975) theory of the mirror stage of development, she argues that this "unfolding sequence of absences" provides a milieu that is ideally suited for the sequence of wants that characterize peoples' developing sense of self. Her suggestion is that knowledge workers become bonded with their (emerging) knowledge object. This absorbing relationship mediates interactions with other people and overlays the breakdowns in more traditional processes of communal integration that are a feature of modern societies.

The thesis I proposed in "Knowledge, Knowledge Work, and Organizations" needs extension along these lines. Not only should the study of knowledge and organizations be undertaken within a broader analysis of knowing as a cultural phenomenon. It needs also to be located within the study of the changing nature of self and sociality.

References

Brown, J.S. and Duguid, P. (1991) "Organizational learning and communities of practice: toward a unified view of working, learning and innovation." *Organization Science* 2(1):40–57.

Brown, J.S. and Duguid, P. (2000) *The Social Life of Information.* Boston: Harvard Business School Press.

Engestrom, Y. (1987) *Learning by Expanding: An Activity Theoretical Approach to Developmental Research.* Helsinki: Orienta Konsultit.

Knorr Cetina, K. (1997) "Sociality with objects: social relations i+n postsocial knowledge." *Theory, Culture and Society* 14(4):1–30.

Knorr Cetina, K. (2000) "The market as an object of attachment: exploring postsocial relations in financial markets." *Canadian Journal of Sociology* 25(2):141–168.

Lacan, J. (1975) *The Language of Self.* New York: McGraw-Hill.

Lave, J. and Wenger, E. (1991) *Situated Learning: Legitimate Peripheral Participation.* Cambridge: Cambridge University Press.

Raelin, J. (2000) *Work-Based Learning: The New Frontier of Management Development.* Englewood Cliffs, NJ: Prentice-Hall.

4

The Creation and Sharing of Knowledge

Max Boisot

Historical Background

Most of the challenges posed by the effective management of knowledge resources are not particularly new. They have, in effect, been with us since the scientific revolution of the seventeenth century, if not before. The learned societies of the seventeenth century, the Académia dei Lincei in Rome (founded in 1603), the Royal Society in London (founded in 1660), and the Académie des Sciences in Paris (founded in 1666), were all concerned with the routinization of discovery and were all set up to promote the dissemination of useful knowledge (Shapin and Schaffer 1985). The European scientists of the day were grappling with the same sort of issues that confront knowledge management today: how to generate knowledge that is both valid and hopefully useful, how to share it, and how to keep in touch with each other as well as up to date (Sprat 1662).

In the eighteenth century, encyclopedias provided one way of storing and providing access to newly created knowledge. The nascent scientific community provided another. The key to the effective growth and management of scientific knowledge was thus as much social and institutional as it was technological. Technology, to be

sure, was a trigger: the scientific revolution would not have been possible without the development of printing, the substitution of vernacular languages for Latin, and the subsequent spread of literacy (Goody 1987). Yet the emergence of learned societies with their corresponding secretaries, their frequent meetings, and their periodical journals were as much the product of values and new habits of thought as they were of new means of communication (Schaffer and Shapin 1985, Foucault 1972).

If new knowledge could be first elicited and then made use of, then one obvious beneficiary would be the state. In mercantilist times, knowledge was perceived to contribute to the creation of national wealth and hence to the creation of a strong and competitive state. Unsurprisingly, therefore, the state attempted to foster the generation of new knowledge within its borders. Even in a later and somewhat more liberal age, the state retained—indeed, it deepened—its involvement in knowledge generation. The U.S. Congress, for example, was given the duty by the country's constitution "to promote the science of useful arts, by securing, for limited times, to authors and inventors, the exclusive right to their respective writings and discoveries." Was this granting of exclusive rights to the creators of new knowledge also intended to promote its sharing? In a roundabout way, yes, since it was only in return for a public disclosure of what would otherwise be privately held knowledge that a limited monopoly on its use was granted to its possessor.

Before the end of the nineteenth century, technological knowledge was neither generated nor disseminated in the same way as scientific knowledge. In the latter case, the scientific community would reward the creation of valid and useful knowledge by publicly acknowledging its source when use was being made of it. In this way, its creator was offered the esteem and recognition of his—or, more rarely, her—peers (Hagstrom 1965). In the former case, a broader community would reward the valid creation of technological knowledge by using it and, if it was suitably protected, paying for it. Thus, whereas the scientific community was engaged in what we might call "gift" exchanges, the technological community was engaged in trade.

It was not until the last three decades of the nineteenth century that a number of business enterprises—particularly those operating in the newly emerging chemical and electrical industries—began to concern themselves with the systematic creation and exploitation of knowledge for commercial purposes. It was at this time that the modern research laboratory first made its appearance (Chandler 1962, 1977). Research and development (R&D) activities systematically applied knowledge management principles inside one or two highly specialized departments within an organization. They greatly accelerated the pace of innovation and effectively helped to usher in the second industrial revolution (Landes 1969).

In sum, knowledge management has been around for some time—it is hardly a new kid on the block! Nevertheless, it is fair to say that it was only in the 1990s that managers in a large number of firms began to address issues that scientists have been grappling with for well over 300 years. What distinguishes corporate interest in knowledge management at the end of the twentieth century from what has gone before, perhaps, is that the kind of knowledge that is of interest today is as likely to arise *outside* the R&D laboratory as *inside* it. Indeed, it now emerges from the whole range of a firm's activities. Yet, instead of asking why firms have suddenly become interested in this area, one might reasonably ask, What kept them?

The Present

I offer three possible reasons for the interest in knowledge management at the end of the twentieth century:

1. Firms can only afford to concern themselves with what is observable and measurable, and in many cases—if not most—knowledge is neither. It often resides deep in people's heads, and it can be quite discontinuous in its effects. If firms have only recently become interested in managing their knowledge resources, it is because data capturing, processing, storage, and transmission costs have now dropped to the point where large quantities of data that were once beyond reach are now readily accessible. Whether knowledge—as opposed to data—has itself become any more accessible as a result of such falling costs is still a matter of controversy, the claims of some proponents of intellectual capital notwithstanding.

2. The rapid evolution of information and communications technologies has led to the "dematerialization" of economic activity—the substitution of data and information for physical resources—in many areas. Automobiles, for example, are getting lighter every year and are becoming "information rich" (Boisot 1998, Ayres 1994). And computers themselves are being miniaturized even as their data processing power continues to multiply. As we rejoice at the convenience and the energy savings made possible by this dematerialization, we suddenly find ourselves having to deal with ever larger quantities of data. In some cases, we become literally overwhelmed by the stuff, and overload threatens. The only way to deal with data overload is to extract useful information from it faster and more efficiently than before—that is, to increase the rate at which we metabolize data (Boisot 1995). Knowledge management might help us to achieve this increase.

3. Underpinning the recent interest in knowledge management is a belated recognition that while information may be substituted for energy in many fields, one cannot manage a knowledge resource as if it were a physical resource. Although some economists are now adopting a different approach, they have traditionally viewed knowledge with a certain schizophrenia, treating it at their convenience either as being completely appropriable—and hence behaving in economic terms like a tradeable physical good—or as being a public good whose supply is infinitely elas-

tic and whose consumption is not subject to crowding. Yet, as anyone involved in its creation will know, knowledge evolves over time and can move either in the direction of full appropriability or in the direction of free availability (Shapiro and Varian 1999). It is at its most interesting—and, unfortunately, at its most analytically intractable—when it is located somewhere between these two poles.

Outstanding Issues

Despite its growing appeal to practitioners, knowledge management faces three unresolved problems. The first is epistemological in nature: What exactly is it that is being managed? There are those who will count as knowledge only that which can be codified and durably stored. Here the focus is on knowledge as an objectively validated product to be inventoried (Dretske 1981). Then there are those who see knowledge as a largely tacit and more subjective phenomenon whose validation is problematic and that is not readily amenable to storing (Polanyi 1958). The first group would take Boyle's law as its exemplar of knowledge, whereas the second might well take Cézanne's painting of the *Mont Saint-Victoire*. Their different perspectives on what constitutes knowledge are not necessarily incompatible, but they have not as yet been reconciled in any way that commands wide assent.

The second problem concerns knowing as a social phenomenon: Is it, and can it ever be, a social phenomenon? The issue is not merely a philosophical quibble. It poses a problem of agency. If organizations do turn out to have something approximating "group minds" to direct their collective actions, then treating them as if they had individual personalities may end up being more than just a convenient legal fiction (Weick 1995). It also gives corporate culture a much larger role in the way that we conceptualize knowledge management than it has received hitherto. Cultures vary in their orientation to knowledge (Douglas 1973). Some are naturally inclined to hoard it; others, to share it. Much, of course, will depend on the nature of the knowledge that they deal with.

Power raises a third problem. From a purely societal perspective, knowledge is at its most useful when it is leveraged and shared. And public policy has often explicitly pursued leveraging and sharing as desirable policy goals. Yet it is also a commonplace that knowledge is power, and

never more so than when it is retained rather than shared (Foucault 1972, Crozier 1964). Of course, it is often the case that some knowledge first needs to be shared if whatever the knowledge that is then retained is to constitute a source of power. The most obvious illustration of this point is advertising. Here, some product information must be given away in order to stimulate a purchase. But when the good that is for sale is itself an information good, how much information should be shared and how much should be retained? In other words, at what point is one beginning to give away what one is actually trying to sell?

Lack of space prevents me from dealing with these problems in any detail in this chapter. In what follows, however, I present a three-dimensional conceptual framework, the information-space, or I-space, that helps to address them (Boisot 1995, 1998). I first briefly deal with the epistemological issues that confront knowledge management. We need to understand, for instance, what knowledge is and how it differs from data and information. In this section, I introduce the first two dimensions of the I-space, those of codification and abstraction. Then I examine some of the characteristics of knowledge flows that distinguish them from flows of physical resources. The focus in this section is on one of the issues that was being addressed at the very beginning of the scientific revolution: how new knowledge is generated. Next I address the issue of how such knowledge is shared, a second major concern of the period. In so doing, I introduce the third dimension of the I-space. The questions raised by knowledge sharing are still with us today—albeit, with the emergence of the Internet, they have taken on a radically new form. I assess the managerial implications of the analysis.

What Is Knowledge?

How does knowledge differ from data and information? The three terms are often used interchangeably in casual conversation, and this can lead to sloppy thinking on the subject of knowledge. One approach is to think of data as being located in the world and of knowledge as being located in agents, with information taking on a mediating role between them. Data can be viewed as a discernible difference between different energy states *only some of which* have information value for agents. Bateson (1972) defined this information as "the difference that makes a difference" to someone. Where data is thus informative, it will modify an agent's expectations and dispositions to act in particular ways—that is, what we call its knowledge base. Note that for our purpose an agent does not have to be a human being. It could be an animal, a machine, or an organization made up of other agents. All that we require for it to be "knowledgeable" is that its internal dispositions to act can be modified upon receipt of data that has some information value (Arrow 1984, Popper 1972, Latour 1986).

What follows from the distinctions we have drawn between data, information, and knowledge? First, if we accept them, then we must recognize that, in reality, it is never knowledge as such that flows between agents, but data. Some measure of resonance can be achieved between the knowledge states of two agents that are sharing the same data—we can call this "getting on the same wavelength." But because of differences in their prior experiences as well as differences in the way that they will process the data, two agents can never achieve identical dispositions to act and hence identical knowledge states. Thus, when I talk about "knowledge sharing" I will actually be referring to some degree of resonance being achieved between the knowledge states of two or more agents following some sharing of data among them.

Second, we must accept that if knowledge is dispositional and hence rooted in agency, then it is not a single "thing" with easily traced contours. As the cognitive neurosciences have now established, it is more like a set of complex activation patterns that can vary greatly from agent to agent, or from moment to moment within a single agent (Churchland 1989). Thus, how easily knowledge can be "shared," in the sense that the activation patterns of different agents can be made to resonate, will vary from case to case as a function of its complexity. If we both see the same cat, for example, there will be some overlap in the patterns of neurons that are activated in our respective brains. But significant differences will also occur, for example, if I had some bad prior experiences with cats that you did not.

Variations in activation patterns have many sources which we cannot discuss here. But one important source is the fact that some types of knowledge can be more easily articulated than other types: the data that transmits it can thus flow more readily. People are concerned with saving time and resources required to articulate and transmit knowledge. They are thus more likely to share knowledge that is clear and unambiguous than knowledge of a more tacit and elusive nature (Nonaka and Takeuchi 1995). It will be easier to transmit a list of stock market figures by fax, for example, than to faithfully describe a Jackson Pollock painting in detail over the telephone. We can better understand this by looking at the data processing requirements associated with the articulation and transmission of knowledge. The articulation of knowledge, in effect, calls for two kinds of cognitive efforts: abstraction and codification.

Abstraction either invokes or creates the minimum number of cognitive categories through which an agent makes sense of events. The fewer the categories an agent needs, the more abstract becomes its apprehension of events. Conversely, the larger the number of categories it requires, the more concrete its apprehension of events. Thus, for example, a problem in particle physics has a more abstract character than a business problem that has to address myriad concrete realities. It draws upon fewer categories even if the relationships between these can be quite complex. Selecting the relevant categories for abstraction, however, requires an understanding of the problem's underlying structure—that is, some prior knowledge of context.

Codification, by contrast, refines the categories that the agent invokes or creates so that it can use them efficiently and in discriminating ways. The fewer data an agent has to process to distinguish between categories, the more codified the categories that it has to draw upon. If, for example, the black and white surfaces on a wall are separated by a thin straight line, an agent will have no difficulty establishing whether a given point lies within the black or the white region. If, on the other hand, the black surface gradually fades into the white surface, then many points will lie in a gray zone that will be hard to readily assign to either the black or the white category. In this case, the agent will have to engage in further data processing in order to make an accurate assignment.

Abstraction and codification are mutually reinforcing. They make up two of the three dimensions of the conceptual framework of the I-space. The agent that is able to economize on its data processing resources through successive acts of codification and abstraction will be able to transact with other agents more economically and hence more extensively than will the agent that cannot. Phenomena that an agent can identify and describe parsimoniously can be readily referred to and discussed with others. Furthermore, knowledge that is well structured (codified and abstract) lends itself to appropriation and trading more readily than does knowledge that is not.

A problem arises, however, when much of the knowledge that is of potential value to other agents is of a more tacit nature and hence not readily amenable to trading. Much of an organization's technological know-how, for example, may be of this kind. It is the fruit of a slow accumulation of idiosyncratic experience, and it resides in the heads or the behaviors of employees, working singly or in groups. Such knowledge poses a problem of property rights. Because it is tacit, it cannot be clearly delimited or transferred to others in a controlled way. How can ownership claims to such knowledge be made good, then? Who, in effect, owns it?

In the days of the individual craftsman, such a question would have found a ready answer. Craftsmen invested in the acquisition of such knowledge and actually possessed it—that is, they carried it around in their heads. Therefore, since, as the saying goes, possession is nine-tenths of the law, it was clear that the craftsmen owned it. The craftsmen may, as Marx believed, have become alienated from the products of their labor, but they could not so easily be alienated from their knowledge unless they chose to be.

Yet, except for a few residual trades, the days of the individual craftsman are now pretty much over. Most new knowledge today is generated in groups and is therefore the possession of a group—in the R&D laboratory, in the engineering department, in the boardroom, and so on. The individual members of such groups may come and go, and when they go, they take part of the group's knowledge with them—one reason why some technologies are most effectively transferred through the movement of individuals. Are such individuals violating a group's property rights in knowledge when they take part of it with them? Here, the situation is complicated by the fact that the generation of much new knowledge is nonlinear in its effects—that is, small inputs of individual know-how can produce disproportionately large outputs of new knowledge—and often more so for new knowledge created by a group than for new knowledge created by an individual. The resulting whole is then worth more—and often much more—than the sum of the parts contributed by individuals.

Thus, knowledge creation, in contrast to the creation of most purely physical goods, is sometimes subject to increasing returns (Arthur 1994).

One view holds that, in the commercial case, these increasing returns belong to the firm employing such groups, which acts as a residual claimant. The firm, after all, brings individuals together, pays them, and generally creates the conditions under which group knowledge can emerge. Where such emergence is value adding, therefore, the firm has a claim on its fruits. The intellectual capital school goes further since it implicitly assumes that, in addition to having a residual claim to the emergent knowledge of groups and teams within the firm, the knowledge possessed by individual employees constitutes part of the firm's intellectual capital base and can therefore also be owned by the firm. It further assumes, however, that such knowledge can be subjected to firm-specific accounting measures, implying that it can be *possessed* by the firm as well as *owned* by it (Edvinsson 1997).

From an intellectual capital perspective, knowledge management is about the capture, storage, and retrieval of knowledge located either in the heads of employees, in the heads of outside collaborators, or in documents. Capture, storage, and retrieval are brought about through a firm's *structural capital*, defined by Edvinsson (1997) as "the embodiment, empowerment, and supportive infrastructure of human capital." Structural capital is also where the value added by the nonlinearities of the knowledge creation process is assumed to reside. Inputs to the knowledge creation process are provided by human capital, and the firm, acting as a residual claimant, captures the surplus. What we have here, in effect, is a new variant of the firm as *entrepreneur*. The firm is cast as the entrepreneurial purchaser and organizer of productive factors, and the value that it manages to extract over and above the cost of those factors constitutes a return on its organizing efforts. Yet it is not clear that the nonlinearities associated with creating new knowledge arise solely from bringing people together. If, for example, an intense group discussion at the workplace triggers a brilliant idea in the head of one participating individual, does the idea necessarily belong to the employer if it remains unstated? If so, given that possession is nine tenths of the law, how will the employer make good its ownership claim?

Yet even where structural capital can be considered a source of nonlinearities, does it necessarily follow that knowledge emerging within groups of organizational employees—such as communities of practice—belongs to the organization that employs them? Such a question has implications for the way that we look at competences and capabilities within firms. These are typically viewed as integrated streams of knowledge that are value adding yet hard to imitate or transfer (Prahalad and Hamel 1990). But is the integration of knowledge streams carried out by the firm as a whole? Or, rather, by groups within the firm? Or, indeed, by networks that cross organizational boundaries? Where the integration of streams of knowledge is tacit—a defining characteristic of a core competence, according to many scholars—then it cannot be traded by the firm (Foss and Knudsen 1996). But this is just another way of saying that it is likely to remain the possession of the group or groups that exercise the competence and that operate either within one firm or across firms. The organization might find it easier to exercise its ownership claim in the case of group knowledge than in the case of individual employees—the latter are more likely to come and go than are whole groups. Yet much of the group's tacit knowledge may still remain beyond the reach of ownership claims made by the firm. In short, it is by no means clear that the firm is either the sole or the natural residual claimant to such knowledge.

Knowledge management practices do take the firm to be the natural residual claimant to knowledge created within its boundaries. These practices aim to help a firm appropriate an individual or group's knowledge, tacit or otherwise, by having it systematically articulated and stored. In the case of tacit knowledge—and arguably, the most valuable components of an individual's knowledge is tacit in nature—they face two challenges.

The first challenge is that the process of articulating tacit knowledge can never be complete. As the philosopher Michael Polanyi put it, we always know more than we can say (Polanyi 1958). By their very nature, abstraction and codification are highly selective processes. Only a small part of a tacit knowledge base can ever be subject to articulation and structuring if genuine data processing economies are to be achieved. Thus, much tacit knowledge inevitably stays with its possessors whatever efforts at codifying and abstracting it has been subjected to—and much of this tacit knowledge will be valuable.

The second challenge is that the more tacit knowledge is articulated, the more readily diffusible it becomes. Although the articulation of knowledge makes it easier for a firm to exercise ownership claims over it, the process also allows knowledge to leak across organizational boundaries, often before such claims can be made good. This second challenge is discussed further below.

Learning and the Generation of New Knowledge

Knowledge, as I have argued, can be viewed as a stock of expectations or dispositions to act in particular ways conditional on the receipt of external information. From this perspective, learning amounts to a change of levels in such stocks. When learning adds to the range of contingencies over which one can entertain expectations (i.e., we learn to pay attention to events that we had hitherto ignored), the knowledge level goes up. Today, for example, we attend to and learn about many more environmental variables than we did, say, four decades ago. As a result, we now *know* more about the environment than we did then. When learning reduces the range (i.e., we decide that certain things can safely be ignored), the knowledge level goes down. Much folk learning about medicinal plants, for example, disappears when primitive societies are integrated into advanced civilizations. Learning can thus involve acquiring new knowledge or dropping old knowledge. When these two activities go on simultaneously, they serve to refine our stock of knowledge and adapt it to our changing needs.

Clearly, while learning is generally beneficial, we should not therefore assume that it only increases our knowledge stocks; it must also selectively decrease it as well. Unless we are able to metabolize our knowledge by eliminating those parts that are no longer useful, we risk information overload—that is, we would develop a disposition to respond to everything, and each piece of incoming data gets treated as potentially informative. In short, we would lose our capacity to be selective.

Social learning occurs when changes in the stocks of knowledge held by one or more agents in a given population trigger coordinate changes in the stocks of knowledge that are held by other agents in the population. The changes, of course, will not necessarily be all in the same direction for all agents, for it is how incoming information interacts with the existing stocks of knowledge held by different agents that determines the direction of the changes. Some agents, for example, will simply have their range of awareness expanded by the incoming information, while others will also experience a need to unlearn certain things if they are to make good use of it. The way that different agents internalize incoming information through adjustments to their existing stocks of knowledge, and the different meanings and interpretations that they attach to it, constitutes a source of further opportunities for generating new knowledge or discarding old knowledge—that is, for learning. The discussion below examines the process through which learning opportunities emerge and how they contribute to the generation of new knowledge. The following section looks at how newly created knowledge is shared and then internalized.

Learning Opportunities

Spotting an opportunity or a threat involves seeing potentially fruitful patterns in the data of experience. Although many people may possess the same data, they will not interpret it in the same way. And the less codified and abstract the data, the more scope there is for extracting idiosyncratic patterns out of it. In cases where the data enjoys many degrees of freedom, individual agents will be free to project whatever they want to see in it—just as they do in the inkblot test. Thus, in many cases, particularly those where the data is fuzzy and ambiguous, spotting a particular opportunity or threat will often turn out to be a singular event, something that goes on in the heads of, at most, a few agents.

Extracting novel patterns from data is a creative activity. It typically requires imagination and independent thought. Imagination allows one to see what is tentative and possible as well as what is probable and obvious. New insights often reside in the gap between these two poles (Klein 1998). Independent thought involves a willingness to resist the pressures of those who see only what is probable and obvious and feel threatened by alternative possibilities (Janis 1982). These pressures will vary from culture to culture—corporate or otherwise—but they will always intensify where novelty is perceived to be destructive of existing arrangements as well as creative.

Knowledge Generation

Once a possible new pattern has been identified, it needs to be stabilized and tested for robustness if it is to yield useful information. If it is

idiosyncratic, fuzzy, and ambiguous—and as discussed above, this will be more likely in the case of concrete and uncodified data than in the case of well codified and abstract data that readily lends itself to categorization—the pattern will have to be refined and worked up into something coherent.

We can treat this process of pattern elaboration as a problem-solving activity, one that involves teasing out whatever latent structures and forms that reside in the pattern and testing them against competing alternatives. In effect, over several iterations of generating alternative structures and forms, testing the evolving pattern against these, and selecting the best fit, the pattern is gradually being made more articulate and usable, that is to say, more codified and more abstract.

Emerging patterns correspond to provisional hypotheses that undergo testing and elaboration. As they compete with each other, many more hypotheses are discarded than are retained (Popper 1972). They are then lost to view. Clearly, then, the process of generating new knowledge involves forgetting as well as learning. Thus, although we frame the process as one of knowledge creation, it should be clear, following the above discussions, that knowledge destruction—the discarding of old knowledge—is a constituent part of the picture. Yet whatever is discarded, the process of forgetting it will always be partial. Many discarded hypotheses will maintain a tacit and twilight existence in the minds of those who entertained them, sometimes to be retrieved and reworked at a later stage. Do they therefore count as knowledge? This remains a controversial question. Having been discarded, such hypotheses do not form part of any formal and public body of knowledge, one that has been successfully refined and tested in accordance with some socially acceptable validation criteria. Yet to the extent that they are unconsciously retained and shape one or more persons' expectations and dispositions, they must count as knowledge of sorts—albeit a more personal and subjective kind of knowledge.

Social Knowing

Until the arrival of information and communication technologies (ICTs) that could handle the more personal and tacit kinds of knowledge discussed above, the prevailing assumption was that only well-codified and abstract knowledge that had been socially validated was a fit candidate for dissemination. After all, science gained credibility and respect as an institution only after it had successfully filtered out the dubious claims of charlatans and fraudsters—and it required three centuries to set up the appropriate safeguards (Butterfield 1931). From a scientific perspective, therefore, the only kind of knowledge worth having has tended to be the well-codified and abstract kind that has undergone rigorous public testing and is open to critical scrutiny and challenge.

The tradition of openness in science stands in sharp contrast to the tradition of secrecy in technology. In the latter case, the value of tacit and as-yet-undiffused knowledge, ignored as it is by official science, is much more readily recognized and prized (Rosenberg and Mowery 1989). After all, most valid and useful knowledge is wrought, directly or indirectly, from what is often initially dubious knowledge. Disdain and discard the dubious stuff and you lose the raw material out of which the valid stuff will eventually emerge. In the technological tradition, therefore, tacit and personal knowledge is treated as a rich uncle to be respected and courted rather than as a poor relation to be kept in the shadows. It is valued and not readily shared with outsiders.

Yet if it is to be put to some social use, all knowledge except personal knowledge needs to be shared to some minimal extent. For this reason, we take the diffusion of knowledge through a population of agents as the third dimension of the I-space. It is not enough to diffuse knowledge, however. Such knowledge also needs to be internalized by recipients if it is to become knowledge to them in the sense that it comes to form part of their dispositional repertoire. I discuss knowledge sharing and internalization next.

Knowledge Sharing

As discussed above, the tacit knowledge prized by the technological tradition is intrinsically hard to share. This is partly because uncodified and concrete knowledge is costly to communicate and does not easily diffuse. Yet even where ICTs have lowered the costs of sharing it—and in recent years they have done so dramatically—one still confronts the cognitive limitations of the human mind. Human attention is in limited supply (Simon 1982). Recall from the discussion above that it is never knowledge as such that flows between agents, but rather data from which

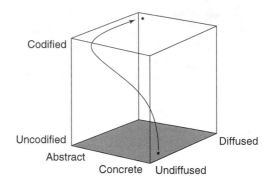

Figure 4.1 The codification-diffusion-abstraction curve in the I-space.

information has to be extracted and internalized. Only when information has been successfully internalized and forms part of an agent's repertoire of expectations and behaviors can it properly be called knowledge. All that knowledge sharing can really mean, therefore, is that some degree of resonance has been achieved between the repertoires of two or more agents. At best, ICTs can increase the quantity of *data* that flows between agents—sometimes massively so. But agents are still required to sift through the data in order to extract useful information from it. Beyond a certain volume of data, however, either the agent's extraction processes become increasingly random and arbitrary—it cannot see the wood for the trees—or the agent blows a fuse.

Knowledge needs some minimum degree of articulation (i.e., codification and abstraction) before it can be shared. How much articulation will depend on how extensively it needs to be shared. The tacit knowledge held by a Zen master, for example, need only be communicated to a few disciples in face-to-face situations. Even so, it can take years for a disciple to "get the message." The more codified and abstract type of knowledge held by a bond trader, by contrast—prices, quantities, and contract conditions—can be diffused worldwide by electronic means in a matter of seconds. The way that abstraction and codification affect the diffusibility of knowledge is depicted in figure 4.1.

Knowledge Internalization

But if articulating knowledge facilitates its diffusion and generally increases its availability, this by no means guarantees that it will be picked up, used, and subsequently internalized. If agents do not share the same codes, or if they operate with different conceptual schemes, then much readily available and diffused data will not register with anyone.

The absorption of external knowledge and information is a process whereby an agent's internal schemas assimilate external data and adapt to them (Piaget 1967). It is a process of interpretation and sensemaking in which new information is integrated with an existing knowledge base (Weick 1995). Three things are worth noting about this process. First, since, for reasons of differences in personal circumstances and biography, no two agents possess identical mental schemas, they will therefore assimilate and accommodate new knowledge in different ways. Thus, while the external data that different agents receive may be identical, what actually gets absorbed by each as knowledge will differ, even if only slightly, from case to case. Second, the absorption of new data goes hand-in-hand with a learning-by-doing or learning-by-using process that in the I-space—and following Williamson (1975)—we call "impacting." What is initially received from outside may well be well codified and abstract. But as it gets used and gradually internalized, layers of uncodified and concrete experience gradually build over it, layers that are then much harder to share with others. Freshman physics students, for example, will all be exposed to the same set of basic equations, but the way each of them will internalize them will depend on the unique and often idiosyncratic circumstances in which they may be required to put them into practice. Absorption and impacting are thus sources of variety. Finally, the successful integration of new data with the agent's existing knowledge base requires some positive fit between the two. If there is any incompatibility between them, then either the new knowledge will get distorted or rejected, or the existing knowledge base will need to be further modified—with some elements possibly being discarded—in order to achieve consistency between existing and new material.

Knowledge absorption and impacting, then, are personal and idiosyncratic processes. These processes effectively challenge any idea that knowledge is a "thing" that invariably maintains its identity as it is shared among agents. In the case of simple factual knowledge, maintaining a "thinglike" appearance may not be too difficult to achieve. For complex knowledge structures, however, it will be much more challenging.

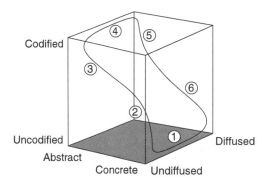

Figure 4.2 The six steps of a social learning cycle. See table 4.1 for details of the steps.

Differences in the way that new knowledge is absorbed and impacted by agents have sometimes been downplayed in knowledge management, particularly where it is driven by information technology. This is understandable since such differences are difficult to handle. Yet it is often in differences of interpretation and sensemaking, or in the difficulties of integrating new knowledge with an agent's existing and idiosyncratic knowledge base, that opportunities for identifying new patterns—and hence for generating new knowledge—in fact reside. Knowledge absorption and impacting, if properly understood and exploited, can thus help to initiate a social learning process that is cyclical in nature. A six-step social learning cycle is depicted in figure 4.2 and briefly summarized in table 4.1.

Managerial Implications

As suggested by the above discussion of opportunity spotting and knowledge generation, sharing, and absorption, information goods differ in important respects from physical goods and cannot be managed in the same way. Understanding how they differ is an important prerequisite to developing an effective knowledge management system. One important difference between them concerns the way that each is valued. This section examines some of the difficulties encountered in valuing information and knowledge goods: How do the production and distribution of knowledge differ from those of physical resources? Here I approach the production issue via the distribution one.

Physical resources are characterized by what physicists call "locality." Simply stated, if they

TABLE 4.1 The Six Phases of Social Learning Cycle

1. Scanning: identifying threats and opportunities in generally available but often fuzzy data—i.e., weak signals. Scanning patterns such data into unique or idiosyncratic insights that then become the possession of individuals or small groups. Scanning may be very rapid when the data is well codified and abstract, and very slow and random when the data is uncodified and context specific.
2. Problem Solving: the process of giving structure and coherence to such insights—i.e., codifying them. In this phase they are given a definite shape and much of the uncertainty initially associated with them is eliminated. Problem solving initiated in the uncodified region of I-space is often both risky and conflict laden.
3. Abstraction: generalizing the application of newly codified insights to a wider range of situations. This involves reducing them to their most essential features—i.e., conceptualizing them. Problem solving and abstraction often work in tandem.
4. Diffusion: sharing the newly created insights with a target population. The diffusion of well-codified and abstract data to a large population will be technically less problematic than that of data which is uncodified and context specific. Only a sharing of context among agents can speed up the diffusion of uncodified data; the probability of achieving a shared context is inversely proportional to population size.
5. Absorption: applying the new codified insights to different situations in a learning-by-doing or a learning-by-using fashion. Over time, such codified insights acquire a penumbra of uncodified knowledge that helps to guide their application in particular circumstances.
6. Impacting: the embedding of abstract knowledge in concrete practices. This embedding can take place in artifacts, technical or organizational rules, or behavioural practices. Absorption and impact often work in tandem.

are here, then they are not there. Furthermore, if they are here one minute, then they are also likely to be here the next. Knowledge shares this characteristic of locality only insofar as it is tied down to a physical substrate that itself has locality. Stone, for example, provides such a substrate, one reason why it has been a material of choice throughout the ages for the purposes of commemorating events and places. Yet even the knowledge carried by stone reaches us—via the retina—only by riding the electromagnetic waves. And when it does so, it leaves its substrate, thereby acquiring a certain measure of nonlocality. In ancient times, of course, knowledge could not ride electromagnetic waves very far, so it tended to stay mainly local. Today, such local knowledge can be captured through digital photography and transmitted worldwide in seconds. It can thus be here, there, and everywhere at the same time.

What are the consequences? When knowledge is tied down to a physical substrate, it partakes of the natural scarcity of that substrate, a scarcity imparted by locality in time and space. When knowledge can be prized loose from its substrate, however, it ceases to be scarce. Thus, to illustrate, an oil field is a knowledge-bearing structure that cannot be photocopied. Oil is therefore a naturally scarce commodity. Yet the chemical formula for benzene can indeed be photocopied and ubiquitously distributed. Having once been extracted from the oil, it no longer enjoys a scarcity status.

In dealing with the latter kind of knowledge, we face a *paradox of value* that is peculiar to knowledge goods and that affects their production.

The Paradox of Value

Extracting chemical information from oil is a costly and uncertain business. It requires extensive investments of time and effort, and results are not guaranteed. Yet whatever the costs incurred in first producing such information, the marginal costs of reproducing it are virtually nil—the cost of a photocopy. As just pointed out, the oil itself may be naturally scarce; the information extracted from it is not. Under such circumstances it may be hard to secure an adequate return on the extraction efforts.

Individuals create new knowledge for many reasons, not all of which are economic. Firms, by contrast, create new knowledge primarily in order to extract value from it, whether directly or indirectly. Economists see the value of a good as being a function of both its utility and its scarcity. The articulation of a knowledge good adds to its utility, so knowledge is at its most useful when it has been codified and made abstract. It can then be defined, made robust, standardized, and manipulated in value-adding ways. Such, for example, is the nature of chemical formulas. Yet it is precisely when a knowledge good has been so articulated that it is also most easily prized loose from its physical substrate. It

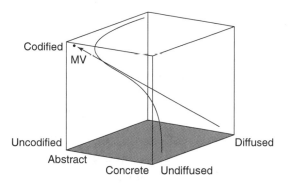

Figure 4.3 Maximum value (MV) in the I-space.

then can be replicated and travel rapidly and extensively in a compressed form, thus losing its scarcity. Knowledge goods, therefore, in contrast to physical goods, behave paradoxically with respect to value. The more we aim to increase their utility by making them more codified and abstract, the more difficult it is to maintain their scarcity. In the case of purely physical goods, utility and scarcity are typically independent of each other. In the case of information goods, they are inversely related. Since utility and scarcity jointly determine the economic value of a good, we must conclude that, in contrast to a physical object, knowledge is inherently unstable in value.

The paradoxical nature of information goods with respect to value is depicted in figure 4.3. The arrow points to the region of maximum value in I-space, where the utility of an information good is at its maximum because of its high degree of abstraction and codification, and where it achieves maximum degree of scarcity. It is also clear from the diffusion curve that it is also the region in which scarcity is most difficult to maintain given the inherent diffusibility of well-structured information.

Patents, copyrights, secrecy clauses, and the like, all indicate that at a practical and intuitive level we understand the paradox of value very well. These devices grant a temporary monopoly on the use of a newly created knowledge good in order to encourage investment in its codification and abstraction—that is, investment in its production. Thus, the scarcity of a knowledge good is achieved artificially, by institutional means. If the good had the locality of physical goods, then it would be naturally scarce. There would be no need to maintain its scarcity artificially in this way.

The inherent diffusibility of well-articulated

knowledge goods is what distinguishes them from physical goods, thus giving rise to the paradox of value. The paradox points to a challenge for the field of knowledge management. It suggests that we lack a workable theory of production and distribution for the information age. That is to say, we do not, as yet, have a political economy of information. We dichotomize knowledge, treating it one moment as if it is a physical good and hence appropriable, the next as a public good whose consumption does not reduce its supply.

Progress, to be sure, is being made. We do at least recognize that knowledge can evolve over time from one kind of thing to another. Yet we still tend to see the process as unidirectional: first we create new knowledge and try to keep it scarce; then as we articulate it, it loses its scarcity. This remains compatible with the idea that there is an equilibrium price for knowledge—its market price—that is reached when it is readily available to all who want it. Yet if, as I have argued above, knowledge is cyclical in the transformations that it undergoes, this equilibrium view is untenable. While in the knowledge generation phase it may become more codified and abstract, in the knowledge absorption phase it changes from codified and abstract to uncodified and concrete once more. It can then become idiosyncratic and local, thus reacquiring scarcity. As I have already shown, knowledge is not a thing in the way that physical objects are things, and it cannot be treated in the same way.

If the value of knowledge goods is inherently more unstable and transient than that of purely physical goods, then their production and exchange will require new theorizing. Without an adequate theory to guide us, we will find it difficult to devise efficient governance arrangements to facilitate and guide the process. In effect, managing a firm's knowledge resources presents new theoretical and practical challenges at three levels: governance, strategy and organization, and the operational level. Much of the literature on knowledge management has focused on the last of these. The first two are arguably more important. I conclude this section by briefly looking at challenges posed at each of the three levels.

Governance

The knowledge-based firm differs from the more traditional industrial firm in its governance requirements. In the latter, preserving shareholder value has meant fencing in the firm's asset base—for the most part physical in nature—and patrolling the firm's boundaries. The paradox of value makes this a dubious approach for the knowledge-based firm. Given the inherent diffusibility of useful knowledge, one may well end up fencing in an empty space, one from which the assets leaked out some time ago. Here, therefore, permanent firm boundaries matter much less. Rather, a dynamic stance is required, one that allows the firm to temporarily exploit a much more fluid and mobile class of assets: knowledge. These will, of course, pose new challenges of property rights. Is a knowledge worker who generates genuinely new knowledge, for example, to be treated as an employee of the firm or as an equity investor in the firm? If such an employee contributes to the firm's stock of intellectual capital, should he or she be considered on a par with external investors in the firm?

Strategy and Organization

If firm boundaries matter less, then the critical strategic and organizational skills shift from maximizing value creation behind well-protected and stable boundaries to rapidly extracting value from kaleidoscopic networks, both internal and external (Kogut 2000). It is not that the boundaries have disappeared; rather, they are now constantly being reconfigured by social learning processes that redistribute opportunity spotting, knowledge generation, knowledge sharing, and knowledge absorption within a community of players. Communities do not necessarily reduce to hierarchical forms of organization, and they often do not respect organizational boundaries. How do we manage and extract value from the fleeting networking and exchange processes through which new knowledge enters and leaves the knowledge-based firm?

Operational Level

How might a firm improve the numberless micro-interactions that take place between its own agents or between these and outsiders? And how might such improvements prepare the ground for opportunity spotting and knowledge generation, sharing, and absorption that make up a learning cycle? What transactional infrastructures and human resource systems need to be developed to discourage opportunistic behavior either by a firm's knowledge workers or, indeed, by the firm itself toward its knowledge workers?

Conclusion

Effective networking is built on reciprocity. A critical skill for the knowledge-based firm will thus be to know what to share and what to hold on to. Recognizing when knowledge should be actively diffused to outsiders rather than hoarded, when it can be used to extend the firm's organizational reach beyond its boundaries, will become an important source of competitive advantage. Building the capabilities of the networks a firm participates in, through a judicious sharing of its knowledge, strengthens its own competitive position within the network. Confining its internal focus to core strengths prevents it from overstretching what will always be limited cognitive resources.

In the information economy, a firm can sometimes come to know too much for its own good. It needs to avoid getting trapped by its own hard-won competencies while the world moves on (Leonard 1995), and it thus needs to unlearn as much and as fast as it learns. Knowledge has to be metabolized, and, as with any kind of metabolic processes, gluttony leads to indigestion—a challenge to the "more connecting and more collecting" perspective that is often promoted by knowledge management practitioners. Surprising as it may seem to some, managing the firm's knowledge resources does not necessarily mean maximizing them.

References

Arrow, K. (1984) "Information and economic behaviour," in *The Economics of Information: Col-*

lected Papers of Kenneth J. Arrow, pp. 136–152. Cambridge, MA: Belknap Press.

Arthur, B. (1994) *Increasing Returns and Path Dependence in the Economy*. Ann Arbor, MI: University of Michigan Press.

Ayres, R. (1994) *Information, Entropy and Progress: A New Evolutionary Paradigm*. Woodbury, NY: AIP Press.

Bateson, G. (1972) *Steps Towards an Ecology of Mind: Collected Essays in Anthropology, Psychiatry, Evolution and Epistemology*. St. Albans, Herts: Paladin.

Boisot, M. (1995) *Information Space: a Framework for Learning in Organizations, Institutions, and Cultures*. London: Routledge.

Boisot, M. (1998) *Knowledge Assets: Securing Competitive Advantage in the Information Economy*. Oxford: Oxford University Press.

Butterfield, H. (1931) *The Whig Interpretation of History*. Middlesex: Penguin.

Chandler, A. (1962) *Strategy and Structure: Chapters in the History of the American Industrial Enterprise*. Cambridge, MA: MIT Press.

Chandler, A.D. (1977) *The Visible Hand: The Managerial Revolution in American Business*. Cambridge, MA: Belknap Press.

Churchland, P.M. (1989) *A Neurocomputational Perspective: The Nature of Mind and the Structure of Science*. Cambridge, MA: MIT Press.

Crozier, M. (1964) *Le Phénonème Bureaucratique*. Paris: Seuil.

Douglas, M. (1973) *Natural Symbols: Explorations in Cosmology*. Middlesex: Penguin.

Dretske, F. (1981) *Knowledge and Flow of Information*. Cambridge, MA: MIT Press.

Edvinsson, L. (1997) *Intellectual Capital: the Proven Way to Establish Your Company's Real Values by Measuring Its Hidden Brainpower*. New York: HarperBusiness.

Foss, N. and Knudsen, C., eds. (1996) *Towards a Competence Theory of the Firm*. Studies in Business Organization and Networks, 2. New York: Routledge.

Foucault, M. (1972) *Histoire de la Folie à L'Age Classique*. Paris: Editions Gallimard.

Goody, J. (1987) *The Interface between the Written and the Oral*. Cambridge: Cambridge University Press.

Hagstrom, W. (1965) *The Scientific Community*. New York: Basic Books.

Janis, I.L. (1982) *Groupthink: Psychological Studies of Policy Decisions and Fiascos*. Boston: Houghton Mifflin.

Klein, G. (1998) *Sources of Power: How People Make Decisions*. Cambridge, MA: MIT Press.

Kogut, B. (2000) "The network as knowledge: generative rules and the emergence of structure." *Strategic Management Journal* 21(March):405–425.

Landes, D. (1969) *The Unbound Prometheus: Technological Change and Industrial Development in Western Europe from 1750 to the Present*. Cambridge: Cambridge University Press.

Latour, B. and Woolgar S. (1986) *Laboratory Life: The Construction of Scientific Facts*. Princeton, NJ: Princeton University Press.

Leonard, D. (1995) *The Wellsprings of Knowledge: Building and Sustaining the Sources of Innovation*. Boston: Harvard Business School Press.

Nonaka, I. and Takeuchi H. (1995) *The Knowledge Creating Company: How Japanese Companies Create the Dynamics of Innovation*. New York: Oxford University Press.

Piaget, J. (1967) *Biologie et Connaissance: Essai sur les Relations entre les Regulations Organiques et les Processus Cognitifs*. Paris: Gallimard.

Polanyi, M. (1958) *Personal Knowledge: Towards a Post-critical Philosophy*. London: Routledge and Kegan Paul.

Popper, K.R. (1972) *Objective Knowledge: An Evolutionary Approach*. Oxford: Clarendon Press.

Prahalad, C.K. and Hamel G. (1990) "The core competence of the corporation." *Harvard Business Review*, 68(3):79–91.

Rosenberg, N. and Mowery, D.C. (1989) *Technology and the Pursuit of Economic Growth*. Cambridge: Cambridge University Press.

Shapin, S. and Shaffer, S. (1985) *Leviathan and the Air Pump: Hobbes, Boyle, and the Experimental Life*. Princeton, NJ: Princeton University Press.

Shapiro, C. and Varian, H. (1999) *Information Rules: A Strategic Guide to the Network Economy*. Boston: Harvard Business School Press.

Simon, H.A. (1982) *Models of Bounded Rationality*. 2 vols. Cambridge, MA: MIT Press.

Sprat, T. (1662) *A History of the Royal Society*.

Weick, K. (1995) *Sensemaking in Organizations*. Thousand Oaks, CA: Sage.

Williamson, O. (1975) *Markets and Hierarchies: Analysis and Antitrust Implications*. New York: Free Press.

5

Sensemaking, Knowledge Creation, and Decision Making

Organizational Knowing as Emergent Strategy

Chun Wei Choo

This chapter introduces the perspective of strategy as the outcome of organizational sensemaking, knowledge creating, and decision making. The first three sections examine the processes by which an organization constructs meaning, creates knowledge, and makes decisions that drive patterns of action. The ensuing sections show how the three processes are interconnected to form cycles of learning and adaptation. Through these cycles, the organization traces out a growth trajectory that defines its strategic position.

An organization processes information to make sense of its environment, to create new knowledge, and to make decisions (Choo 1998). Sensemaking constructs the shared meanings that define the organization's purpose and frame the perception of problems or opportunities that the organization needs to work on. Problems and opportunities become occasions for creating knowledge and making decisions. An organization possesses three types of knowledge: tacit knowledge in the experience and expertise of individuals; explicit knowledge codified as artifacts, rules, and routines; and cultural knowledge held as assumptions, beliefs, and values. The creation of new knowledge involves the conversion, sharing, and combination of all three types of knowledge. The results of knowledge creation are innovations or extensions of organizational capabilities. Whereas new knowledge represents a potential for action, decision making transforms this potential into a commitment to act. Decision making is structured by rules and routines and guided by preferences that are based on interpretations of organizational purpose and priorities. Where new capabilities or innovations become available, they introduce new alternatives as well as new uncertainties. Decision making, then, selects courses of action that are expected to perform well given the understanding of goals and the conditions of uncertainty. Thus, the capacity to develop organizational knowledge is distributed over a network of information processes and participants. Rather than being centrally controlled and coordinated, the capacity to develop knowledge emerges from the complex, unpredictable patchwork of processes in which participants enact and negotiate their own meanings of what is going on, stumble upon and wrestle with new knowledge to make it work, and creatively improvise and bend rules and routines to solve tough problems.

Sensemaking

Weick (1979, 1995) presents a model of organizational sensemaking based on a conceptualization of organizations as "loosely coupled" systems in which individual participants have great latitude in interpreting and implementing directions. He stresses the autonomy of individuals and the looseness of the relations linking individuals in an organization. The purpose of organizational information processing is to reduce the *equivocality* of information about the environment. Weick summarizes his organizing model as follows:

> The central argument is that any organization *is* the way it runs through the processes of organizing. . . . This means that we must define organization in terms of organizing. Organizing consists of the resolving of equivocality in an enacted environment by means of interlocked behaviors embedded in conditionally related processes. To summarize these components in a less terse manner, organizing is directed toward information processing in general, and more specifically, toward removing equivocality from informational inputs. (Weick 1979, pp. 90–91)

Weick (1995) describes how people enact or actively construct the environment that they attend to by bracketing experience and by creating new features in the environment. Sensemaking is induced by changes in the environment that create discontinuity in the flow of experience engaging the people and activities of an organization (Weick 1979). These discontinuities constitute the raw data that have to be made sense of. The sensemaking recipe is to interpret the environment through connected sequences of enactment, selection, and retention (Weick 1979). In enactment, people actively construct the environments that they attend to by bracketing, rearranging, and labeling portions of the experience, thereby converting raw data from the environment into equivocal data to be interpreted. In selection, people choose meanings that can be imposed on the equivocal data by overlaying past interpretations as templates to the current experience. Selection produces an enacted environment that provides cause–effect explanations of what is going on. In retention, the organization stores the products of successful sensemaking (enacted or meaningful interpretations) so that they may be retrieved in the future.

Organizational sensemaking can be driven by beliefs or by actions (Weick 1995). In belief-driven processes, people start from an initial set of beliefs that are sufficiently clear and plausible and use them as nodes to connect more and more information into larger structures of meaning. People may use beliefs as expectations to guide the choice of plausible interpretations, or they may argue about beliefs and their relevance when these beliefs conflict with current information. In action-driven processes, people start from their actions and grow their structures of meaning around them, modifying the structures in order to give significance to those actions. People may create meaning to *justify* actions that they are already committed to, or they may create meaning to *explain* actions that have been taken to manipulate the environment. Figure 5.1 summarizes the sensemaking process.

An interesting corollary of Weick's model is that organizational action often occurs first and is then interpreted or given meaning. The con-

Model	Process	Dynamics
Sense making	Environmental change $\longrightarrow$ Enactment, selection, retention $\longrightarrow$ Enacted interpretations • Belief-driven processes • Action-driven processes	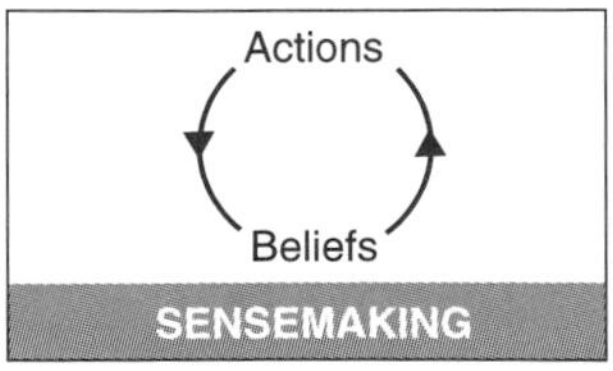 Actions Beliefs **SENSEMAKING**

Figure 5.1 Sensemaking.

nection between action and planning is thus topsy-turvy:

> Our view of planning is that it can best be understood as thinking in the future perfect tense. It isn't the plan that gives coherence to actions. . . . It is the reflective glance, *not* the plan per se, that permits the act to be accomplished in an orderly way. A plan works because it can be referred *back* to analogous actions in the past, not because it accurately anticipates future contingencies. . . . Actions never performed can hardly be made meaningful, since one has no idea what they are. They simply are performed and *then* made sensible; they *then* appear to be under the control of the plan. (Weick 1979, p. 102)

While Weick emphasizes retrospective sensemaking, Gioia and Mehra (1996) have suggested an important role for *prospective* sensemaking:

> If retrospective sense making is making sense of the past, prospective sense making is an attempt to make sense for the future. Retrospective sense making is targeted at events that have transpired; prospective sense making is aimed at creating meaningful opportunities for the future. In a loose sense, it is an attempt to structure the future by imagining some desirable (albeit ill-defined) state. It is a means of propelling ourselves forward—one that we conceptualize in the present but realize in the future. (p. 1229)

Sensemaking in strategy would then include both prospective "sense-giving" that articulates a collective vision for the organization and ret-rospective "sense-discovering" that notices and selects actions and outcomes that work well for the organization.

Knowledge Creating

An organization has three kinds of knowledge: tacit knowledge in the expertise and experience of individuals; explicit or rule-based knowledge in artifacts, rules, and routines; and cultural knowledge in the assumptions and beliefs used by members to assign value and significance to new information or knowledge. Knowledge creating is precipitated by the recognition of gaps in the organization's existing knowledge. Such knowledge gaps can stand in the way of solving a problem, developing a new product, or taking advantage of an opportunity. Organizations then create new knowledge by converting tacit to explicit knowledge, integrating and combining knowledge, and acquiring or transferring knowledge across boundaries (figure 5.2).

In *knowledge conversion* (Nonaka and Takeuchi 1995, Nonaka 1994, this volume), the organization continuously creates new knowledge by converting the personal, tacit knowledge of individuals who develop creative insight to the shared, explicit knowledge by which the organization develops new products and innovations. Tacit knowledge is shared and externalized through dialogue that uses metaphors and analogies. New concepts are created and the concepts are justified and evaluated according to its fit with organizational intention. Concepts are tested and elaborated by building archetypes or prototypes. Finally, concepts that have been created, justified, and modeled are moved to other levels of the organization to generate new cycles of knowledge creation.

Model	Process	Dynamics
Knowledge creating	Knowledge gap ⟶ Knowledge conversion, integration, transfer ⟶ New knowledge • Knowledge conversion • Knowledge integration • Knowledge transfer	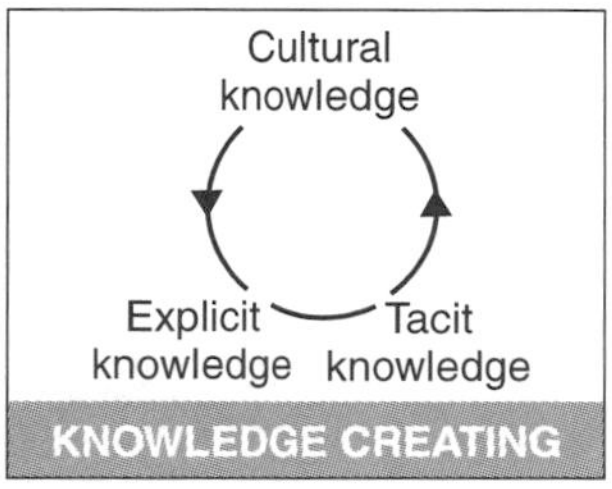 Cultural knowledge Explicit knowledge — Tacit knowledge **KNOWLEDGE CREATING**

Figure 5.2 Knowledge creating.

Grant (1996, chap. 8 this vol.) sees organizational capability as the outcome of *knowledge integration*—the result of the organization's ability to coordinate and integrate the knowledge of many individual specialists. In Grant's view, knowledge creation is an individual activity, and this means that the primary role of the organization is to apply knowledge rather than to create it. More specifically, the organization exists as an institution that "can create conditions under which multiple individuals can integrate their specialist knowledge" (p. 112). The fundamental task of the organization is to integrate the knowledge and coordinate the efforts of its many specialized individuals. The key to efficient knowledge integration is to establish mechanisms that combine efficiency in knowledge creation (which requires specialization) and efficiency in knowledge deployment (which requires integrating many types of knowledge).

Grant identifies four mechanisms for integrating specialized knowledge that economize on communication and coordination: rules and directives, sequencing, routines, and group problem solving and decision making. Rules and directives regulate the actions among individuals and can provide a means by which tacit knowledge is converted into readily comprehensible explicit knowledge. Sequencing organizes production activities in a time sequence so that each specialist's input occurs independently in a pre-assigned time slot. Routines can support relatively complex patterns of behaviors and interactions among individuals without the need to specify rules and directives. Group problem solving and decision making, in contrast with the other mechanisms, rely on high levels of communication and nonstandard coordination methods to deal with problems that are high in task complexity and task uncertainty. All four mechanisms depend upon the existence of common knowledge for their operation. Common knowledge may take the form of: a common language between organizational members, commonality in the individuals' specialized knowledge, shared meanings and understandings among individuals, and awareness and recognition of the individuals' knowledge domains (Grant 1996, this volume).

An organization may be perceived as a repository of capabilities, which are "determined by the social knowledge embedded in enduring individual relationships structured by organizing principles" (Kogut and Zander 1992, p. 396). These organizing principles establish a common language and set of mechanisms through which people in an organization cooperate, share, and transfer knowledge. They enable sets of functional expertise to be communicated and combined so that the organization as a whole can exist as integrated communities:

> Creating new knowledge does not occur in abstraction from current abilities. Rather, new learning, such as innovations, are products of a firm's *combinative capabilities* to generate new applications from existing knowledge. By combinative capabilities, we mean the intersection of the capability of the firm to exploit its knowledge and the unexplored potential of the technology. (p. 390)

While Kogut and Zander (1992), Grant (1996), and others regard organizations as institutions for combining and integrating knowledge, Tsoukas (1996) suggests that there may be limits to the extent that organizational knowledge may be integrated. Tsoukas views organizations as "distributed knowledge systems in a strong sense: they are de-centered systems. A firm's knowledge cannot be surveyed as a whole: it is not self-contained; it is inherently indeterminate and continually reconfiguring" (p. 13). The utilization of organizational knowledge cannot be known by a single agent—no single individual or agent can fully specify in advance what kind of knowledge is going to be relevant, when and where. There is no "master control room" where knowledge may be centrally managed:

> Organizations are seen as being in constant flux, out of which the potential for the emergence of novel practices is never exhausted—human action is inherently creative. Organizational members do follow rules but how they do so is an inescapably contingent-cum-local matter. In organizations, both rule-bound action and novelty are present, as are continuity and change, regularity and creativity. Management, therefore, can be seen as an open-ended process of coordinating purposeful individuals, whose actions stem from applying their unique interpretations to the local circumstances confronting them. . . . A necessary condition for this to happen is to appreciate the character of a firm as a discursive practice: a form of life, a community, in which individuals come to share an unarticulated

background of common understandings. Sustaining a discursive practice is just as important as finding ways of integrating distributed knowledge. (pp. 22–23)

Knowledge transfer across organizational boundaries can involve tacit, explicit, and cultural knowledge to varying degrees. In a small number of cases, the transfer is largely accomplished through a movement of explicit knowledge (e.g., an algorithm, a protein sequence). Transfers of such well-defined packages of codified knowledge typically require a substantial amount of collateral knowledge in the receiving organization to decode and apply the new information. In a larger number of cases, the transfer of explicit knowledge is accompanied and facilitated by human experts from the source organization. Experts interpret the meaning of the new information and deal with the detailed questions arising from trying to use the new information in its new setting. Thus, tacit knowledge is necessary to assimilate and apply new explicit knowledge effectively. There are important cases when the movement of explicit knowledge is not enough, even when accompanied by tacit knowledge—cultural knowledge is also necessary. This is especially so when organizations are trying to learn new practices or systems of work that are woven into organizational networks of roles, relationships, and shared meanings. Consider Toyota's production system, an example of a tight integration of tacit, explicit, and cultural knowledge:

> Toyota's knowledge of how to make cars lies embedded in highly specialized social and organizational relationships that have evolved through decades of common effort. It rests in routines, information flows, ways of making decisions, shared attitudes and expectations, and specialized knowledge that Toyota managers, workers, suppliers and purchasing agents, and others have about different aspects of their business, about each other, and about how they can all work together. (Badaracco 1991, p. 87)

When General Motors wanted to learn the Toyota production system, it established the NUMMI (New United Motor Manufacturing, Inc.) plant in 1984 as a joint venture with Toyota in order to facilitate the learning of "intimate, embedded knowledge." The NUMMI group took over a General Motors facility at Fremont, California.

Work at NUMMI was organized based on Toyota's lean production system that seeks to utilize labor, materials, and facilities as efficiently as possible. Although much has been published about Toyota's production system, without the NUMMI experience GM might have permanently missed the essence of Toyota's management process. Co-practice to learn the system was necessary because the capabilities were "tacit know-how in action, embedded organizationally, systemic in interaction and cultivated through learning by doing" (Doz and Hamel 1997, p. 570). Badaracco (1991) concluded that, through NUMMI, GM had the chance to learn first-hand Toyota's collaborative approach to worker and supplier relationships, just-in-time inventory management, and efficient plant operations. For Toyota, the project helped it learn about managing U.S. workers, suppliers, and logistics and about cooperating with the unions and the state and local governments.

> Scores of GM managers and thousands of workers have worked at NUMMI or at least visited the operation. It would have been much simpler for GM to buy from Toyota the manual *How to Create the Toyota Production System*, but the document does not exist and, in a fundamental sense, could not be written. Much of what Toyota "knows" resides in routines, company culture, and long-established working relationships in the Toyota Group. (Badaracco 1991, p. 100)

Many firms form alliances for the purpose of sharing and transferring knowledge. Only recently has research begun to examine the conditions and processes by which knowledge is exchanged in multifirm arrangements (Fischer et al., this volume). One finding is that the tacitness of the knowledge can influence knowledge sharing outcomes. A critical factor in a firm's ability to assimilate and utilize new knowledge is its "absorptive capacity" (Cohen and Levinthal 1990), which is a function of the level of prior related knowledge that the firm already possesses. The absorptive capacity argument has been broadened to include not only technical similarities (experience in related technical areas and complementary assets) but also nontechnical similarities (organizational structures, compensation practices). The exchange of knowledge between organizations involves both bringing in external knowledge and letting out (intendedly or inadvertently) internal knowledge. Thus, Appleyard (1996, chap.

30 this vol.) and Matusik (chap. 34 this vol.) examine the costs and benefits of interfirm knowledge sharing. Costs are incurred as a result of potential knowledge losses, protecting intellectual property, partner selection, decline in profitability, and transaction costs of the knowledge transfer. We may generalize that there are two categories of costs associated with interfirm knowledge transfer: those due to the loss of knowledge by the focal firm, and those due to managing the process of knowledge transfer.

Decision Making

Completely rational decision making involves identifying alternatives, projecting the probabilities and outcomes of alternatives, and evaluating the outcomes according to known preferences. These information gathering and information processing requirements are beyond the capabilities of any organization. In practice, organizational decision making departs from the rational ideal in important ways depending on the contingencies of the decision context. At least two features of the environment of decision making will be significant: (1) the structure and clarity of organizational goals that impinge on preferences and choices, and (2) the uncertainty or amount of information about the methods and processes by which the goals are to be attained. In a specific decision situation, goals may be fuzzy, and organizational groups may disagree about their relative importance. There is then *goal ambiguity or conflict* about which organizational goals to pursue. Moreover, uncertainty may arise because the specific problem is complex and there is not enough information about cause–effect relationships or appropriate approaches to be considered. Methods available to accomplish a task are not immediately evident, and the search space for solutions is ill-defined. There is therefore *technical or procedural uncertainty* about how goals are to be achieved.

Figure 5.3 positions four modes of decision making along the two dimensions of goal ambiguity/conflict and technical/procedural uncertainty that characterize a decision situation. In the *boundedly rational mode*, when goal and procedural clarity are both high, choice is guided by performance programs (March and Simon 1958). Thus, people in organizations adopt a number of reductionist strategies that allow them to simplify their representation of the problem situation by selectively including the

	Low goal ambiguity/conflict	High goal ambiguity/conflict
Low procedural uncertainty	Boundedly rational mode	Political mode
High procedural uncertainty	Process mode	Anarchic mode

Figure 5.3 Four modes of organizational decision making.

most salient features rather than attempting to model the objective reality in all its complexity (March and Simon 1993). During search, they "satisfice" rather than maximize; that is, they choose an alternative that exceeds some criteria rather than the best alternative. They also follow "action programs" or routines that simplify the decision-making process by reducing the need for search, problem solving, or choice.

In the *process mode* (Mintzberg et al. 1976), when strategic goals are clear but the methods to attain them are not, decision making becomes a process divided into three phases. The identification phase recognizes the need for decision and develops an understanding of the decision issues. The development phase activates search and design routines to develop one or more solutions to address a problem, crisis, or opportunity. The selection phase evaluates the alternatives and chooses a solution for commitment to action. The entire process is highly dynamic, with many factors changing the tempo and direction of the decision process: "They delay it, stop it, restart it. They cause it to speed up, to branch to a new phase, to cycle within one or between two phases, and to recycle back to an earlier point in the process. . . . [T]he process is dynamic, operating in an open system where it is subjected to interferences, feedback loops, dead ends, and other factors" (Mintzberg et al. 1976, p. 263).

In the *political mode* (Allison 1971, Allison and Zelikow 1999), goals are contested by interest groups but procedural certainty is high

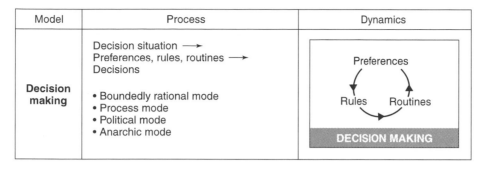

Model	Process	Dynamics
Decision making	Decision situation ⟶ Preferences, rules, routines ⟶ Decisions • Boundedly rational mode • Process mode • Political mode • Anarchic mode	Preferences Rules Routines **DECISION MAKING**

Figure 5.4 Decision making.

within the groups: each group believes that its preferred alternative is best for the organization. Decisions and actions are the results of the bargaining among players pursuing their own interests and manipulating their available instruments of influence. Political decision making may then be likened to game playing. Players take up positions, stands, and influence and make their moves according to rules and their bargaining strengths. In the political model, actions and decisions are produced as political resultants—political because decisions and actions emerge from the bargaining by individual members along regularized action channels; and resultants because decisions and actions are outcomes of the compromise, conflict, and confusion of the players with diverse interests and unequal influence (Allison 1971, Allison and Zelikow 1999).

In the *anarchic mode* (Cohen et al. 1972), when goal and procedural uncertainty are both high, decision situations consist of relatively independent streams of problems, solutions, participants, and choice opportunities arriving and leaving. A decision then happens when problems, solutions, participants, and choices coincide. When they do, solutions are attached to problems and problems to choices by participants who happen to have the time and energy to do it. Which solutions are attached to which problems is a matter of chance and timing, depending on which participants with which goals happen to be on the scene, when the solutions and problems are entered, and "the mix of choices available at any one time, the mix of problems that have access to the organization, the mix of solutions looking for problems, and outside demands on the decision makers" (Cohen et al. 1972, p. 16).

To be effective, organizations need to learn the full repertoire of decision-making modes (figure 5.4). Different choice situations call for different decision approaches. The (boundedly) rational mode would economize time and effort by invoking stored rules and routines for familiar, well structured situations. The dynamism and iterativeness of the process mode would help searches or designs for new solutions in unfamiliar but consequential situations. The political mode allows alternative points of view to be heard and may prevent complacency or parochialism. The anarchic mode is not dysfunctional, but rather is a way for organizations to discover goals and find solutions in unfamiliar, unclear situations.

The Organizational Knowing Cycle

Information flows continuously between sensemaking, knowledge creating, and decision making, so that the outcome of information use in one mode provides the elaborated context and the expanded resources for information use in the other modes, as shown in figure 5.5. Through sensemaking, organizational members enact and negotiate beliefs and interpretations to construct shared meanings and common goals. *Shared meanings and purpose* (fig. 5.5) are the outcome of sensemaking, and they set the framework for explaining observed reality and for determining saliency and appropriateness. Shared meanings and purpose help to articulate a shared organizational agenda, a set of issues that people in the organization agree on as being important to the well-being of the organization. While they may not agree about the content of a particular issue, and they may adopt diverse positions on how it should be resolved; nevertheless, there is collective recognition that these issues are salient to

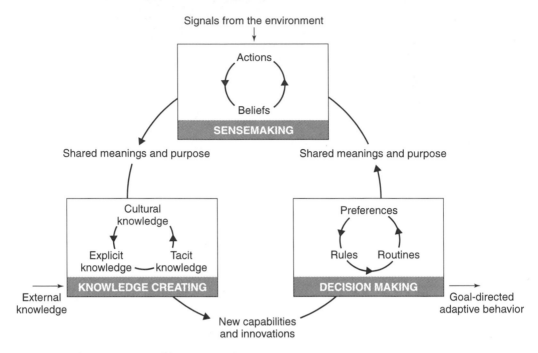

Figure 5.5 The organizational knowing cycle.

the organization. Shared meanings and purpose also help to define a collective organizational identity. Defining an organizational identity establishes norms and expectations about the propriety, accountability, and legitimacy of the organization's choices and behaviors. A framework of shared meanings and purpose is therefore used by organizational members to assess consequentiality and appropriateness and to reduce information ambiguity and uncertainty to a level that enables dialogue, choice, and action making. Where messages from the external environment are highly equivocal, shared meanings reduce ambiguity by helping members to select plausible interpretations. Where messages from the external environment are highly incomplete, shared meanings reduce uncertainty by supplying assumptions and expectations to fill in the voids. Shared meanings need to be continuously updated against new events and conditions. By allowing ambiguity and diversity in interpretations, an organization can constantly monitor its shared meanings against the environment to ensure that they are still valid.

Within the framework of its constructed meaning, agenda, and identity, the organization exploits current specializations or develops new capabilities in order to move toward its vision and goals. Movement may be blocked by gaps in

the knowledge needed to bridge meaning and action. When the organization experiences gaps in its existing knowledge or limitations in its current capabilities, it initiates knowledge seeking and creating, set within parameters derived from an interpretation of the organization's goals, agendas, and priorities. Organizational members individually and collectively fabricate new knowledge by converting, sharing, and synthesizing their tacit and explicit knowledge, as well as by cross-linking knowledge from external individuals, groups, and institutions. The outcome of knowledge creating are *new capabilities and innovations* (fig. 5.5) that enhance existing competencies or build new ones; generate new products, services, or processes; or expand the repertory of viable organizational responses. The value of new knowledge is assessed locally by its ability to solve the problem at hand, as well as generally by its ability to enhance the organization's capabilities in the long run. New knowledge enables new forms of action but also introduces new forms of uncertainty. The risks and benefits of untested innovations and unpracticed capabilities are compared and evaluated by invoking rules and preferences in the process of organizational decision making.

Shared meanings and purposes, as well as new knowledge and capabilities, converge on decision making as the activity leading to the selection and initiation of action. Shared meanings, agendas, and identities select the premises, rules, and routines that structure decision making. New knowledge and capabilities make possible new alternatives and outcomes, expanding the range of available organizational responses. By structuring choice behavior through roles and scripts, rules and routines, the organization simplifies decision making, codifies and transmits past learning, and proclaims competence and accountability. Rules and routines specify "rational" criteria for the evaluation of alternatives, "legitimate" methods for the allocation of resources, and "objective" conditions for distinguishing between normal states and novel situations that may necessitate the search for new rules.

Over time, the organization has learned and codified a large number of rules and routines, so choosing which rules to activate for a specific decision situation is itself problematic. Shared meanings and understandings about the nature and needs of a particular situation are used to guide rule activation. Shared interpretations help select which rules to apply by answering the questions, What kind of situation is this? What rules do we have for dealing with this type of situation? Shared interpretations may also select rules according to the criterion of appropriateness—What kind of organization are we? What would be appropriate behavior for an organization like ours in a situation like this one? (March et al. 2000). Sometimes shared interpretations indicate that the situation is novel, where none of the learned rules seems to apply. When rules break down, the organization attempts to make new meaning in time to initiate action, effectively prototyping new rules to prompt choice making. The end result of this interaction between shared meaning (in interpretations and understandings) and shared learning (in rules and routines) is the execution of a pattern of actions that allows the organization to move toward current goals while at the same time adapting to changed conditions in the environment. In this sense, the outcome of decision making is behavior that is both goal directed and adaptive.

While each organization adjusts its behavior to perceived changes in the environment, its responses are deflected and diffracted by the concurrent actions of other actors that participate in the same arena. Thus each organization is reacting to the actions of other organizations that are also reacting to it. The resultant meshwork of interactions configures new patterns and new conditions that pose fresh ambiguities and uncertainties. A continuous stream of new events and equivocal cues necessitates iterative cycles of information processing. Where meanings or purpose change as a result of reinterpreting the environment, or where rules or routines are altered as a result of acquiring knowledge and understanding, the organization is adapting to variation and feedback in its environment.

Organizational Knowing as Strategy Finding

Cycles of organizational knowing lead to the iterative development of organizational strategy. Strategies are patterns of actions that often appear to be rational or goal directed after the fact, with the benefit of hindsight. An organizational-knowing view of strategy suggests that an organizational "strategy" does not emerge fully formed. Rather, it is traced out through cumulative cycles of sensemaking, knowledge creation, and decision making. As described in the preceding section, the organization's initial beliefs prime it to notice and bracket certain events and signals. They also predispose the organization to be drawn to and consider certain actions. The pursuance of patterns of action involve creating knowledge to fill knowledge and capability gaps, as well as making operational and strategic decisions to commit resources and effort. The outcomes of organizational action generate new cycles of sensemaking, knowledge creating, and decision making.

The implication for an organization thriving in dynamic environments is that it would need to manage each of the three information processes effectively. In sensemaking, the organization would scan broadly (sensing), develop plausible interpretations quickly that enable action (sensemaking), and communicate purpose and vision to members (sense-giving). In knowledge making, tacit, explicit, and cultural knowledge are engaged simultaneously in the generation and utilization of knowledge. The more tightly integrated the three forms of knowledge, the more valuable, unique, and inimitable the organizational advantage. In decision making, rules and routines encode learning, economize effort, and add to the organization's tradable stocks of knowledge. At the same time, the organization must be able to recognize situations when existing rules are inadequate or irrelevant and be prepared to abandon them while inventing new rules.

The model also implies that the greater the interplay between the processes of sensemaking, knowledge creating, and decision making, the greater the organization's capacity to detect threats and opportunities, create valuable knowledge, and act on new knowledge. This interplay is necessarily fluid and open-ended, but it is not entirely random or without structure. The interplay is given coherence and direction through strong leadership (Crossan and Hulland, this volume), shared understandings about identity and purpose (Grant, this volume; Sole and Edmondson, this volume), and community norms and values (Adler 2001, Nahapiet and Ghoshal 1998, this volume). What drives the cycles of strategic learning is an inner logic and discipline that establishes a culture and a set of practices for revising and updating assumptions and beliefs, and for noticing, figuring, and trying things out.

References

Adler, P. (2001) "Market, hierarchy, and trust: the knowledge economy and the future of capitalism." *Organization Science* 12(2):215–234.

Allison, G.T. (1971) *Essence of Decision: Explaining the Cuban Missile Crisis.* Boston: Little Brown.

Allison, G.T. and Zelikow, P. (1999) *Essence of Decision: Explaining the Cuban Missile Crisis*, 2d ed. New York: Addison-Wesley.

Appleyard, M.M. (1996) "How does knowledge flow? Interfirm patterns in the semiconductor industry." *Strategic Management Journal* 17(Winter):137–154.

Badaracco, J.L. (1991) *The Knowledge Link: How Firms Compete through Strategic Alliances.* Boston: Harvard Business School Press.

Choo, C.W. (1998) *The Knowing Organization: How Organizations Use Information to Construct Meaning, Create Knowledge, and Make Decisions.* New York: Oxford University Press.

Cohen, W.M. and Levinthal, D.A. (1990) "Absorptive capacity: a new perspective on learning and innovation." *Administrative Science Quarterly* 35(March):128–152.

Cohen, M.D., March, J.G., and Olsen, J.P. (1972) "A garbage can model of organizational choice." *Administrative Science Quarterly* 17:1–25.

Doz, Y. and Hamel, G. (1997) "The use of alliances in implementing technology strategies," in M. Tushman and P. Anderson, eds. *Managing Strategic Innovation and Change*, pp. 556–580. New York: Oxford University Press.

Gioia, D.A. and Mehra, A. (1996) "Sensemaking in organizations: book review." *Academy of Management Review* 21(4):1226–1229.

Grant, R.M. (1996) "Prospering in dynamically competitive environments: organizational capability as knowledge integration." *Organization Science* 7:375–387.

Kogut, B. and Zander, U. (1992) "Knowledge of the firm, combinative capabilities, and the replication of technology." *Organization Science* 3(3):383–397.

March, J.G. and Simon, H.A. (1993) *Organizations*, 2d ed. Oxford: Blackwell.

March, J.G., Schulz, M., and Zhou, X. (2000) *The Dynamics of Rules.* Stanford, CA: Stanford University Press.

Mintzberg, H., Raisinghani, D., and Théorét, A. (1976) "The structure of 'unstructured' decision processes." *Administrative Science Quarterly* 21(2):246–275.

Nahapiet, J. and Ghoshal, S. (1998) "Social capital, intellectual capital, and the organizational advantage." *Academy of Management Review* 23(2):242–266.

Nonaka, I. (1994) "A dynamic theory of organizational knowledge creation." *Organization Science* 5(1):14–37.

Nonaka, I. and Takeuchi, H. (1995) *The Knowledge-Creating Company: How Japanese Companies Create the Dynamics of Innovation.* New York: Oxford University Press.

Simon, H.A. (1976) *Administrative Behavior: A Study of Decision-Making Processes in Administrative Organization*, 3d ed. New York: Free Press.

Tsoukas, H. (1996) "The firm as a distributed knowledge system: a constructionist approach." *Strategic Management Journal* 17:11–26.

Weick, K.E. (1979) *The Social Psychology of Organizing*, 2d ed. New York: Random House.

Weick, K.E. (1995) *Sensemaking in Organizations.* Thousand Oaks, CA: Sage.

6

Knowledge, Context, and the Management of Variation

Charles Despres and Daniele Chauvel

Knowledge management has apparently come of age. This concept now has a role in MBA and even PhD curricula, is a keyword in bibliographic databases, forms the conceptual nucleus of a developing literature, is sought after by leading firms, and is just as readily prescribed by all the major consultants. Professionals and academics apparently agree that knowledge management is a sensible approach to the new age of business, and an increasing number are working to develop its potential.

Just what they are working on enjoys less agreement. In a previous work (Despres and Chauvel 1999) we reported that the meanings associated with "knowledge management" are multiple rather than singular, and that the field has a set of intellectual roots that are neither incongruous nor consistent, but certainly different in their understanding of the matter. A scan for definitions of knowledge management in books, articles, and web sites reveals that most rely heavily on the distinction of data, information, and knowledge. One commonly encounters the metaphor of a hierarchy in this regard, with stimuli and data at the bottom, information in the middle, and meaningful knowledge at the upper levels. The objective is to act on high

value-adding knowledge rather than the comparatively less useful data and stimuli that surround our activities, and the prescribed ways of doing so differ from one knowledge architect to another.

Contexts

The hierarchy metaphor is a precarious cornerstone for thinking and action in the knowledge domain. Instead of ascending a hierarchy of knowledge in linear fashion, research and experience argue that we are propelled through time by a spiral of events that transmutes knowledge into noise as a function of the situation in play. We have all had the experience of having meaningful knowledge in one situation become a senseless sign in the next: financial analyses do not "make sense" in an emotional crisis, for example, x-rays are noise in a downsizing situation, and your car's oil level adds little value when coding a computer program. Academic schools of thought in the social sciences, ranging from idealism to conventionalism to poststructuralism, have made more profound observations of this sort for the last century. In large part it is our place in the trajectory of events—

our situation—that determines the meaning of phenomena around us; meaning does not exist in the phenomena themselves.

Said differently, knowledge is always knowledge in some context or situation. Knowledge cannot be extracted from its context, nor can it be defined apart from it, and some go so far as to claim that context is the knowledge determinant rather than the stimuli that circulate within it. It is instructive in this regard that the word *context* derives from the Latin *texere*, which means "woven together," and that today's social psychologists generally agree that humans weave together the phenomena around them, developing patterns that they then inscribe with meaning.

This is the first problem we will evoke in this chapter. The majority of the knowledge on knowledge management is naive regarding the complexities of the fundamental subject—which is knowledge itself. Most professionals make sweeping assumptions about what does and does not constitute "knowledge" in their workplace, and too many academics are content to brush aside the sticky issue of a root phenomenon (knowledge) whose essential nature is that of an intellectual chameleon.

Silver Bullets

The second problem derives from the first and involves that very human tendency to quickly, wholly, and often blindly embrace the latest, best way to do things better. The overwhelming tendency in knowledge management's professional literature is to prescribe a tool, method, or way of thinking for a large range (if not the entire range) of problems that a company encounters. The rallying cry appears to be, "One way, all problems, all companies."

There are at least two factors in play. One is a commercial dynamic that makes it natural for Oracle to endorse its database systems as the silver bullet where proponents of a social psychology would see communities of practice as the only way forward. While experienced managers will make allowances for "silver bullet" mentalities in their daily affairs, the balkanization of thinking among knowledge management providers is nonetheless alarming.

A second factor is that knowledge management as a field, hence those working within it as providers, does an inadequate job of accounting for the impact of context on the workings and dynamics of knowledge. The root phenomenon has been ignored, in effect, so managers charged with "doing" knowledge management are forced

to adapt off-the-shelf products or services to their situation. There are precious few providers that begin with a manager's situation and work toward a definition of the knowledge needed and how to manage it. The cart is before the horse, supply is not listening to demand, and the knowledge management profession—assuming it really exists—is working with deficient technology.

Adolescence

The neglect of knowledge contexts and the silver bullet syndrome result from the adolescence of knowledge management compounded by commercial interests that fuel enthusiasm on all sides of the question. Too often, the effect is to blot from awareness the accumulated wisdom in cognitive science, philosophy, information systems, natural language processing, semiotics, psychology, and related disciplines in a rush to apply techno-enabled solutions to what Tapscott (1997) has termed the "Age of Sand." Social and economic fundamentals may be changing fast, but business has yet to reach the shores of a chic, homogeneous e-World. Instead, the disciplines underpinning knowledge management insist on a fragmented mosaic of needs, interests, constraints, and contexts in which people and companies operate.

We therefore argue that it is time to move knowledge management to a more sophisticated level of thinking and application. We will attempt to partially unravel the issues involved by focusing on two areas. The first involves the structuring concepts that currently underlie Knowledge Management and its applications. The second involves the organizational forms that provide a framework for action.

In doing so, we will demonstrate that most of the models circulating in this field approach but do not embrace knowledge management as a situated construct that should account for organizational (contextual) variation. And since practice rests on the research and development underlying such models, the same is true for applications currently tendered by providers. At the same time, new thinking on organizational forms is such that a contingency framework may be useful.

Structuring Devices

The material in this section is adapted from work previously reported in Despres and Chauvel (2000) in which a set of models that currently inform knowledge management were deconstructed. A search of the literature spanning the period 1978 to October 1999 identified models and classification systems in the field of knowledge management on the assumption that such devices exert a structuring effect on the field to the extent they focus thinking on certain phenomena while ignoring others, establish the meaning of these phenomena and their interactions, and persuade members in a community as to their importance. This search yielded 72 books and articles that referred to or proposed a model of knowledge management (listed in appendix 1). The analysis eventually centered on the more robust models that are frequently cited in the literature, including works by Nonaka (1991, 1994, 1998), Hedlund (1994), Carayannis (1999), Wiig (1993), Edvinsson and Sullivan (1996), and Snowden (1999), as well as our own work (Despres and Chauvel 2000).

As an illustration, Nonaka's SECI model (1994) is founded on (a) two forms of knowledge (tacit and explicit), (b) an interaction dynamic (transfer), (c) three levels of social aggregation (individual, group, context), (d) four "knowledge-creating" processes (socialization, externalization, combination and internalization, SECI), and later (e) the concept of Ba, which is a space for knowledge conversion. Hedlund's N-form corporation (1994) is built around (a) two types of knowledge (tacit and articulated), (b) three forms of knowledge within each type (cognitive, skill, embodied), (c) four levels of carrier (individuals, small groups, organizations, the interorganizational domain), and (d) the dynamics of knowledge transfer and transformation.

We similarly deconstructed the remaining models and assembled the concepts thus extracted according to their commonalities. Our first observation was that each work was marked by two fundamental aspects, one structural and the other prescriptive. Authors tend to structure thought with a set of concepts that constrains and directs the perception/thinking process with regard to knowledge management. Once the field of action is delimited, each model leads to a set of explanations and prescriptions. The first aspect organizes things and the second provides a remedy. Nonaka's basic model, for example, directs us to "see" certain realities and, in particular, the interaction of tacit and explicit knowledge. Socialization, externalization, combination, and internalization (SECI) become the fundamental structuring devices around which Nonaka would have us weave much of our thinking.

Themes in the Community

More interesting is the commonality of basic concepts that inform these works. We divide these into two sets, which we term primary and secondary structuring devices (table 6.1). Primary structuring devices are held in common across all the models and classification systems reviewed for this chapter. They relate to fundamental issues and enjoy a high degree of commonality—frequent use and relatively stable definitional agreement. Secondary devices are those that authors employ frequently but dissimilarly. There is less definitional clarity in the way these devices are used, although the concepts being communicated are similar. Taken together, these seven devices appear to synthesize the thinking in the field of knowledge management. Only one author, Hedlund, includes all devices in his work, while others focus on some subset. Below we discuss the varieties of meaning associated with each device.

Time

An epistemological fundamental in Western science, it comes as no surprise that all of the authors reviewed here explicitly or implicitly employed time in some part of their work. It is explicitly present in Despres and Chauvel (2000),

TABLE 6.1 Themes in the Community.

Primary structuring devices	• Time • Types, forms, embodiments • Social space	Greater commonality ↑
Secondary structuring devices	• Context • Transformations and dynamics • Carriers and media • Knowledge culture	

Nonaka (1991, 1994, 1998), Carayannis and Van Buren (1999), for example, where a longitudinal view of the cognitive process is used to organize matters. It is less explicitly cited in Hedlund (1994), Snowden (1999), and Inkpen and Dinur (1998) but still clearly implicated. Given that it is difficult to conceive of the thinking process in a frozen, static state, it appears that the implication of time in knowledge management is a primary requirement. This argues against conceptions of knowledge as a store in organizations and, instead, points to the importance of knowledge processes.

Types, Forms, Embodiments

All authors drew on some classification of knowledge, with the tacit/explicit distinction popularized by Polyani (1967) so often employed that it may achieve the status of a banality in the near future. Other typologies of knowledge include the metaknowledge (knowledge of knowledge, awareness, consciousness) found in Earl (1998) and Carayannis (1999), the different embodiments of knowledge (products, routines, processes) found in Hedlund (1994) and Snowden (1999), and the more commercial approach of intellectual capital that views knowledge as stocks and assets (Van Buren 1999, Edvinsson and Sullivan 1996). As with the concept of time, the attempt to classify knowledge is no stranger to epistemological musings. Blackler and Whitaker (1993), for example, have outlined five different types: embrained (conceptual skills abilities), embodied (acquired by doing), encultured (acquired through socialization), embedded (organizational routines), and encoded knowledge (signs and symbols). And even cursory research in the history of science will reveal that the discussion goes far beyond: there is, in fact, little agreement on a universal classification of the types of knowledge but wide consensus that they are multiple and consequential.

Social Space

Once classified and fixed in time, all of the authors locate knowledge phenomena somewhere in social space, albeit with different levels of specificity. The most common approach is that involving the levels of social aggregation usually employed in organization studies: individuals, groups, and organizations. Carayannis (1999) and Hedlund (1994) go a step beyond to explicitly include the stakeholders outside a company's boundaries (industry/interorganizational context), the importance of which has clearly been demonstrated by institutional theory and elsewhere. In the discussions that ensue, most authors also recognize that the cornerstone of knowledge management is the individual, and that organization-level knowledge is a fiction. But having given individuals their due, most also recognize that knowledge is an inherently social construct, for how could anyone recognize a phenomenon inaccessibly locked in the confines of some brain as knowledge? This branches to a larger discussion on knowledge as action (Activity Theory), which we will leave aside to make the simpler observation that all authors define some unit of social and/or physical space.

Context

Context is also fundamental if one accepts the proposition that nothing has any meaning outside of a context. To introduce a broader view of the idea, consider Pierre Teilhard de Chadrin, who at the beginning of this century conceptualized a web of determinate human knowledge he termed the *nöosphere* and announced that it enveloped human consciousness on Earth (1947). He believed that this knowledge web gave substance to physical and social phenomena and that without it we were senseless as to the phenomena of gravity, rainfall, or the displacements of matter that constitute architecture. Business is to knowledge management what the *nöosphere* was to de Chadrin's concept of life on this planet. All authors recognize that a business context anchors their knowledge management devices, but they do so differently, varying from the firm's strategy to human interaction, group dynamics, and technological infrastructure. While some clearly set the boundaries of a context (e.g., Edvinsson's approach to the rents generated by thinking and knowledge in a firm), others are more elusive (e.g., Despres and Chauvel's use of values, culture, systems, and structures). That said, all make reference to the context of knowledge management in some way, but because of the lack of definitional agreement, we view this as a secondary structuring device.

Transformations and Dynamics

This is a normative and prescriptive device in that it carries the caveat that unless knowledge is transformed or dynamized in some way, it is essentially useless. The root idea is that knowledge becomes useful only when it goes into the forge of social interaction. Examples of transformations and dynamics include Nonaka's (1991, 1994, 1998) socialization, externalization, combination, internalization; Earl's (1998) inventorizing, auditing, experiencing, socializing; Hedlund's (1994) internalization, articulation, reflection, dialogue, expansion; Caryannis's (1999) interactivity and connectivity paths; and aspects of Van Buren's (1999) enablers. This is also consistent with authors such as Edvinsson who work on the transfer of human capability and knowledge to organizational structures, and those such as Hedlund who specifically target organizational routines.

Carriers and Media

Perhaps a subset of the preceding theme, we nonetheless distinguish carriers and media because of their presence in the literature. With this theme we mean to bring into evidence the systems and structures that specifically aim to facilitate the transfer and transformation of knowledge in an enterprise. While the theme of transformations and dynamics points squarely at knowledge processes, carriers and media are concerned with technologies of all kinds, both human and machine. They are, in a sense, the infrastructure of transformative/dynamic processes. Examples of this device include Nonaka's (1994) emphasis on physical proximity and interpersonal interaction for knowledge externalization and creation; the participation, in-company training, and cross-functionalism encouraged by Hedlund (1994); Snowden's (1999) emphasis on storytelling as a core knowledge mechanism; the auditing and socializing advised by Earl (1998); and the ensemble of Van Buren's (1999) enablers. Obviously included are the machine technologies familiar to anyone working in the field, including data warehouses, document management systems, groupware, Web-based communication, and so on. To the extent that transformations and dynamics are objectives in a knowledge management effort, carriers and media are the methods; the former are the "what" and the latter, the "how."

Knowledge Culture

Finally, a set of authors in our review make it clear that managing knowledge involves far more than the structures and systems that shuffle ideas back and forth. More important than knowledge itself, they say, is the context or ecology in which knowledge phenomena are nestled. This clearly branches to the organizational learning notion of double-loop learning, where "learning how to learn" becomes the critical competence. Having learned is one thing, but understanding the elements and dynamics of the learning process itself is quite another. This is analogous to the "knowledge culture" of Despres and Chauvel (2000). Authors such as Hedlund (1994) and Nonaka (1998) clearly emphasize the importance of knowledge management processes, which encourage awareness and knowledge creation, over systems and structures, which manage existing stores of knowledge. A knowledge culture requires such foundations but goes beyond. In the end, this device argues for reconceptualizing the firm as, for example, an N-form corporation or a knowledge-creating company.

Variation

These seven structuring devices achieve their meaning in organizations, where they are presumably deployed by managers who implement the prescriptions. Unfortunately, little due is paid the wicked problem of defining an "organization" despite the fact that underlying disciplines such as organization theory, sociology, and cognitive science agree that it is anything but a given. Knowledge management, a comparative newcomer, displays a troubling tendency to brush aside the definitional difficulties pertaining to "organization," has never (to our knowledge) dealt in depth with the interpretation/enactment conundrum (Weick 1969), and tends to steer clear of the complications posed by the view that organizational types are multiple and not singular. Office furniture can perhaps be as effectively installed in a government bureaucracy as an e-startup, but we doubt the same is true of technologies that undertake to manage the cognitive systems involved.

If it is useful to think in terms of different types of organizations, then it is reasonable to assume that knowledge management in one organization is not, and should not be, knowledge management in another. A simple illustration of the basic issues involved is displayed in figure 6.1. The horizontal axis represents the dichotomy that organizations are either all the same or different from one another, while the vertical axis represents whether the same or dif-

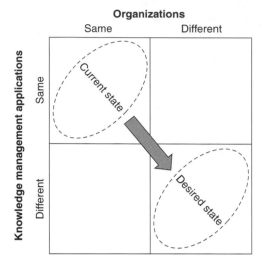

Figure 6.1 Basic issues.

ferent knowledge management applications are prescribed across these organizations.

Our assessment of the current situation is that a majority of authors define the same or similar programs of action for the entire range of organizations (the upper left quadrant: current state). Wenger's (1998) communities of practice and Snowden's (1999) storytelling are illustrative technologies that are often presented as generally appropriate and independent of the organizational characteristics that surround them. The question is whether this is reasonable given the variation in "organization" that has preoccupied several decades of research. The answer is that it is not, and that the variation in systems, structures, cultures, styles, and so on, in evidence is largely driven by environmental adaptation: "The assessment of an organization, and comparative studies across organizations, has shown that much of the variation in overall organization is explained by organizational context or domain" (Van de Ven and Ferry 1980, p. 88).

One conclusion is that a contingency framework (the lower right quadrant: desired state) is more appropriate since the effectiveness of different knowledge management programs is likely to vary across different organizational forms. We are thus led to suggest the benefits of a classical contingency framework to advance knowledge management toward the new age of business. This is not entirely original, for as we indicated above there are authors who propose that managing knowledge involves more than

the structures and systems that shuffle ideas back and forth. Hedlund (1994) and Nonaka (1998), for example, emphasize processes that are sensitive to context and not the systems and structures that manage existing stores of knowledge. Nonetheless, we are unaware of any research program or knowledge management product/provider that makes the contingency proposition—the "if–then" condition—the centerpiece of its approach. The basic formulation would be posed as follows: if we are dealing with an organization of type A, then we need to apply a knowledge management action program of type Y rather than type Z.

Organizational Types

The view exists that knowledge management is, in fact, a metaphor for the socioeconomic transformations (occasioned by the nexus of information technology, knowledge-intensive work, and globalization) that are leading to a new theory of the firm and, hence, to entirely new forms of organization (e.g., Spender 2000, Hedberg 2000, Grant 2000). This is an encouraging proposition for which we have sympathy, but it does not lift from practitioners the burden of implementing knowledge management action programs in existing organizations, today, and making them work. The current need is to advance theory and especially practice to more sophisticated levels, and in this regard, the respect for knowledge in context and recognition of variation across organizations are useful starting points.

To this end, and assuming one accepts the thinking represented in figure 6.1, two issues present themselves:

1. What typology of organizations facilitates the prescription and implementation of a knowledge management action program?
2. What is the effectiveness of a knowledge management action program across the types of organizations so defined?

Research pertaining to the first question has spawned a number of accepted perspectives, including the rationalist's contingency (Burns and Stalker 1961), resource dependence (Pfeffer and Salancik 1978), institutional (Zucker 1983), and population ecology (Hannan and Freeman 1977) approaches; the sociocultural work involving or-

TABLE 6.2 A Sample of Emerging Organizational Practices.

New Practices	Old Practices	Description
	PERTAINING TO STRUCTURE	
Flat organizations	Hierarchical layers	The existence, or not, of hierarchical levels that manage and control activities
Decentralization	Centralization	Investing subunits, or not, with decision-making authority and capability
Project-based structure	Functional or product structure	The organization of work according to organizational or results-oriented logics
	PERTAINING TO PROCESSES	
Vertical and horizontal	Constrained, formal interactions	The extent to which individuals are encouraged to cross boundaries
Information technology (IT) strategies and capabilities	Traditional strategies, limited technologies	The design of systems and structures that take IT as a starting point, or not
Organizational integration	Organizational segmentation	The existence, or not, of formally sanctioned partitions within the organization
	PERTAINING TO BOUNDARIES	
Downscoping and focus	Conglomerate strategies	Activities that focus on core competencies or on a portfolio
Outsourcing	In-house value chains	Conferring critical activities to others or performing all internally
Alliances	Autonomy	Engaging in partnerships or accomplishing all oneself

Source: Adapted from Whittington et. al. (1999, p. 589).

ganizational culture (Schein 1985); the symbolic interaction represented by enactment theory (Weick 1969); and others. The range of perspectives is impressive, and each yields a different typology of organizational forms that, when addressed to the first question above, can leave one in a state of postmodern paralysis.

For the purposes of this chapter, we will simply affirm the necessity of distinguishing organizational forms when developing a knowledge management program. A simple example may help to make the point in this regard. The idea of new, emerging organizational forms has received considerable attention over the last decade. One empirical study of such forms is found in the INNFORM project (Pettigrew et al., 2000), which recently surveyed organizational practices in Europe, Japan, and the United States. A review of the findings from this project (Whittington et al. 1999) suggests a simple dichotomy of organizational practices that illustrates the types of implementation issues a knowledge management practitioner faces across different organizations. Table 6.2 adapts a literature review presented by Whittington et al. (1999) and suggests certain characteristics of "old" and "new" organizations.

Whittington et al. write that the INNFORM project found "widespread but not revolutionary change in terms of organization structure, processes and boundaries" (p. 583). This being the case, and no matter what the fundamental drivers, environmental forces, or theoretical underpinnings may be, knowledge management practitioners are confronted with at least two sets of organizational characteristics that differ in fundamental ways. It is most certainly the case that a given knowledge management practice or technology is differentially appropriate to old and new organizational forms. Yet the practice literature is oddly silent on this matter, and the working assumption appears to be that all organizations are or should be flat, decentralized, project based, and so on.

Teece (2000) states that a modern firm, facing the challenges of a knowledge economy, "will need to evolve into a knowledge-generating, knowledge-integrating, and knowledge-protecting organization" (p. 42). But in his view the implementation of knowledge management will depend on the market in which the firms operate—their industrial context. He adds that "these challenges will obviously not simultaneously confront all the firms at the same time in the same manner" (p. 53) and predicts different fates depending on the ability of the firm to recognize the paradigm shift occurring in its macro-environment.

We agree with the fundamentals evoked by Teece and others, but caution that many proponents of knowledge management are working in an industrial context with a knowledge economy mindset. The purpose of this chapter has been to issue the warning that approaching organizations as a singular phenomenon is inappropriate and potentially damaging. Knowledge management will improve its effectiveness to the extent the action programs its models prescribe are refined to account for the variation in organizational forms.

References

Blackler, F., Reed, M., and Whitaker, A. (1993) "Editorial: knowledge workers and contemporary organizations." *Journal of Management Studies* 30(6):851–862.

Burns, T. and Stalker, G.M. (1961) *The Management of Innovation,* London: Tavistock.

Carayannis, Elias. (1999) "Fostering synergies between information technology and managerial and organizational cognition: the role of knowledge management." *Technovation* 19(4):219–231.

Despres, C. and Chauvel, D. (1999) "Knowledge management(s)." *Journal of Knowledge Management* 3(2):110–120.

Despres, C. and Chauvel, D. (2000) "A thematic analysis of the thinking in knowledge management," in C. Despres and D. Chauvel (eds.), *Knowledge Horizons: The Present and the Promise of Knowledge Management,* pp. 55–86. New York: Butterworth-Heinemann.

Earl, M. (1998) *What on Earth Is a CKO?* London: London Business School.

Edvinsson, L. and Sullivan, P. (1996) "Developing a model for managing intellectual capital." *European Management Journal* 14(4):356–364.

Grant, R. (2000) "Shifts in the world economy: the drivers of knowledge management," in C. Despres and D. Chauvel (eds.), *Knowledge Horizons: The Present and the Promise of Knowledge Management,* pp. 27–53. New York: Butterworth-Heinemann.

Hannan, M. and Freeman, J.N. (1977) "The population ecology of organizations." *American Journal of Sociology* 82:929–964.

Hedberg, B. (2000) "The new organizations: managing multiple arenas for knowledge creation," in C. Despres and D. Chauvel (eds.), *Knowledge Horizons: The Present and the Promise of Knowledge Management,* pp. 269–286. New York: Butterworth-Heinemann.

Hedlund, G. (1994) "A model of knowledge management and the N-form corporation." *Strategic Management Journal* 15:73–90.

Inkpen, A. and Dinur, A. (1998) "Knowledge management processes and international joint ventures." *Organization Science* 9(4):454–468.

Nonaka, I. (1991) "The knowledge creating company." *Harvard Business Review,* November–December, 96–104.

Nonaka, I. (1994) "Dynamic theory of organizational knowledge creation." *Organization Science* 5(1):14–36.

Nonaka, I. (1998) "The concept of "Ba": building a foundation for knowledge creation." *California Management Review* 40(3):40–54.

Pettigrew, A., Massini, S., Numagami, T. (2000) "Innovative forms of organising in Europe and Japan." *European Management Journal* 18(3):259–273.

Pfeffer, J. and Sálancik, G.R. (1978) *The External Control of Organizations: A Resource Dependence Perspective.* New York: Harper and Row.

Polanyi, M. (1967) *The Tacit Dimension.* New York: Anchor Day.

Schein, E.H. (1985) *Organizational Culture and Leadership.* San Francisco: Jossey-Bass.

Snowden, D. (1999) "The paradox of story." *Scenario and Strategy Planning* 1(5).

Spender, J.-C. (2000) "Managing knowledge systems," In C. Despres and D. Chauvel (eds.), *Knowledge Horizons: The Present and the Promise of Knowledge Management,* pp. 149–167. New York: Butterworth-Heinemann.

Tapscott, D. (1997) *The Digital Economy: Promise and Peril in the Age of Networked Intelligence.* New York: McGraw Hill.

Teece, D. (2000) "Strategies for managing knowledge assets: the role of firm structure and industrial context." *Long Range Planning* 33:35–54.

Teilhard de Chardin, Pierre (1947) *The Formation of the Noosphere.* http://www.technoetic.com/noosphere/.

Van Buren, M. (1999) "A yardstick for knowledge management." *Training and Development Journal* 53(5):71–78.

Van de Ven, A. and Ferry, D. (1980) *Measuring and Assessing Organizations.* New York: Wiley.

Weick, K.E. (1969) *The Social Psychology of Organizing.* Reading, MA: Addison-Wensley.

Wenger, E. (1998) *Communities of Practice: Learning, Meaning, and Identity.* New York: Cambridge University Press.

Whittington, R., Pettigrew, A., Peck, S., Fenton, E., and Conyon, M. (1999) "Change and complementarities in the new competitive landscape: a

European panel study, 1992–1996." *Organization Science* 10(5):583–600.

Wiig, K. (1993) *Knowledge Management Foundations*, vol. 1. Arlington, TX: Schema Press.

Zucker, L.G. (1983) "Organizations as institutions," in S.B. Bacharach (ed.), *Research in the Sociology of Organizations*, pp. 1–47. Greenwich, CT: JAI Press.

APPENDIX 1

Articles located via literature search spanning 1978 to October 1999 that referred to or proposed a model of knowledge management.

Albino, V., Garavelli, A., Claudio and Schiuma, G. (1999) "Knowledge transfer and inter-firm relationships in industrial districts: the role of the leader firm." *Technovation* 19(1):53–63.

Allerton, H. (1998) "News you can use." *Training and Development Journal* 52(2):9–10.

Anderson, N. (1998) "The people make the paradigm." *Journal of Organizational Behavior* 19(4):323–328.

Belasco, J. (1993) "The new organization." *Executive Excellence* 10(4):15–16.

Bienayme, A. (1988) "Technology and the nature of the firm." *International Journal of Technology Management* 3(5):563–578.

Blanning, R. (1984) "Expert systems for management: research and applications." *Journal of Information Science Principles & Practice* 9(4):153–162.

Buell, H. and Zuckerman, A. (1999) "Information, please." *Journal for Quality and Participation* 22(3):52–55.

Bukowitz, W. and Petrash G. (1997) "Visualizing, measuring and managing knowledge." *Research-Technology Management* 40(4):24–31.

Carayannis, E. (1999a) "Fostering synergies between information technology and managerial and organizational cognition: the role of knowledge management." *Technovation* 19(4):219–231.

Carayannis, E. (1999b) "Knowledge transfer technological hyperlearning in five industries." *Technovation* 19(3):141–161.

Chang, A.-M., Holsapple, C., and Whinston, A. (1993) "Model management issues and directions." *Decision Support Systems* 9(1):19–37.

Cisco, S. and Strong, K. (1999) "The value added information chain." *Information Management Journal* 33(1):4–15.

Cohen, L., Duberley, J., and McAuley, J. (1999) "The purpose and process of science: contrasting understandings in UK research establishments." *R&D Management* 29(3):233–245.

Cohen, S., and Backer, N.K. (1999) "Making and mining intellectual capital: method or madness?" *Training and Development Journal* 53(9):46–50.

Davenport, T., De Long, D., and Beers, M. (1998) "Successful knowledge management projects." *Sloan Management Review* 39(2):43–57.

Davies, J. and Waddington, A. (1999) "The management and measurement of intellectual capital." *Management Accounting-London* 77(8):34.

Demarest, M. (1997) "Understanding knowledge management." *Long Range Planning* 30(3):374–384.

Dolk, D. and Konsynski, B. (1984) "Knowledge representation for model management systems." *IEEE Transactions on Software Engineering* 10(6):619–628.

Dove, R. (1998) "A knowledge management framework." *Automotive Manufacturing and Production* 110(1):18–20.

Dove, R. (1999) "The avoidance of real knowledge management." *Automotive Manufacturing and Production* 111(5):16–17.

Dove, R. (1999) "Managing the knowledge portfolio." *Automotive Manufacturing and Production* 111(4):16–17.

Doz, Y. and Prahalad, C.K. (1987) "A process model of strategic redirection in large complex firms: the case of multinational corporations," In A. Pettigrew (ed.), *The Management of Strategic Change*, pp. 63–83. Oxford: Blackwell.

Earl, M. (1997) "Knowledge as strategy: reflections on Skandia International and Shorko Films," in L. Prusak (ed.), *Knowledge in Organizations*, pp. 1–17. New York: Butterworth-Heinemann.

Earl, M. (1998) *What on Earth Is a CKO?* London: London Business School.

Edvinsson, L. (1997) "Developing intellectual capital at Skandia." *Long Range Planning* 30(3):366–373.

Edvinsson, L. and Sullivan, P. (1996) "Developing a model for managing intellectual capital." *European Management Journal* 14(4):356–364.

Ford, N. (1989) "From information to knowledge management: the role of rule induction and neural net machine learning techniques in knowledge generation." *Journal of Information Science Principles and Practice* 15(4,5):299–304.

Frappaolo, C. (1998) "Defining knowledge management: four basic functions." *Computerworld* 32(8):80.

Grantham, C., Nichols, L., and Schonberner, M. (1997) "A framework for the management of intellectual capital in the health care industry." *Journal of Health Care Finance* 23(3):1–19.

Guenette, D. (1997) "Enterprising information." *EMedia Professional* 10(11):38–50.

Harvey, M. and Lusch, R. (1999) "Balancing the intellectual capital books: intangible liabilities." *European Management Journal* 17(1):85–92.

Hedlund, G. (1986) "The hypermodern—a heterarchy?" *Human Resource Management* 25(1).

Hedlund, G. (1994) "A model of knowledge management and the N-form corporation." *Strategic Management Journal* 15:73–90.

Hedlund, G. and Nonaka, I. (1993) "Models of knowledge management in the West and Japan," in P. Lorange et al. (eds.), *Implementing Strategic Process, Change, Learning, and Cooperation*, pp. 117–144. London: Blackwell.

Hildebrand, C. (1994) "The greater good." *CIO* 8(4): 32–40.

Inkpen, A. and Dinur, A. (1998) "Knowledge management processes and international joint ventures." *Organization Science* 9(4):454–468.

Johnson, W. (1999) "An integrative taxonomy of intellectual capital: measuring the stock and flow of intellectual capital components in the firm." *International Journal of Technology Management* 18(5–8):562–575.

Joyce, T. and Stivers, B. (1999) "Knowledge and innovation focus: a classification of US and Canadian firms." *International Journal of Technology Management* 18(5–8):500–509.

Kerssens-Van Drongelen, I., de Weerd-Nederhof, P., and Fisscher, O. (1996) "Describing the issues of knowledge management in R&D: towards a communication and analysis tool." *R&D Management* 26(3):213–230.

Lee, T. and Maurer, S. (1997) "The retention of knowledge workers with the unfolding model of voluntary turnover." *Human Resource Management Review* 7(3):247–275.

LeRoy, S. (1989) "Efficient capital markets and martingales." *Journal of Economic Literature* 27(4): 1583–1621.

Livanage, S., Greenfield, P., and Don, R. (1999) "Towards a fourth generation R&D management model—Research networks in knowledge management." *International Journal of Technology Management* 18(3,4):372–393.

Lynn, B. (1998) "Performance evaluation in the new economy: bringing the measurement and evalu-ation of intellectual capital into the management planning and control system." *International Journal of Technology Management* 16(1–3): 162–176.

Malone, M. (1997) "New metrics for a new age." *Forbes ASAP Supplement*, April 7, 40–41.

Mascitelli, R. (1999) "A framework for sustainable advantage in global high-tech markets." *International Journal of Technology Management* 17(3):240–258.

Maurer, H. (1998) "Modern WISs." *Communications of the ACM* 41(7):114–115.

Mirchandani, D. and Ramakrishnan, P. (1999) "Four models for a decision support system." *Information and Management* 35(1):31–42.

Nahapiet, J. and Ghoshal, S. (1998) "Social capital intellectual capital, and the organizational advantage." *Academy of Management Review* 23(2):242–266.

Nightingale, P. (1998) "A cognitive model of innovation." *Research Policy* 27:689–709.

Nonaka, I. (1989) "Organising innovation as a knowledge creation process: a suggestive paradigm." Working Paper N OBIR-41, University of California at Berkeley.

Nonaka, I. (1990) "Redundant, overlapping organizations: a Japanese approach to managing the innovation process." *California Management Review* 32(3):27–38.

Nonaka, I. (1991) "The knowledge creating company. *Harvard Business Review*, November–December, 96–104.

Nonaka, I. (1994) "Dynamic theory of organizational knowledge creation." *Organization Science* 5(1):14–36.

Nonaka, I. (1998) "The concept of "Ba": building a foundation for knowledge creation." *California Management Review* 40(3):40–54.

Odem, P. and O Dell, C. (1998) "Invented here: how Sequent Computer publishes knowledge." *Journal of Business Strategy* 19(1):25–28.

O'Hara, M., Watson, R., and Kavan, B. (1999) "Managing the three levels of change." *Information Systems Management* 16(3):63–70.

Oliver, A. and Liebeskind, J. (1997/1998) "Three levels of networking for sourcing intellectual capital in biotechnology: implications for studying interorganizational networks." *International Studies of Management and Organization* 27(4): 76–103.

Peters, T. (1996) "Know thy service." *Forbes ASAP Supplement*, October 7, 144.

Ram, S., Hayne, S., and Carlson, D. (1992) "Integrating information systems technologies to support consultation in an information center." *Information and Management* 23(6):331–343.

Silverman, B.G. (1985) "Toward an integrated cognitive model of the inventor/engineer." *R&D Management* 15(2):151–158.

Simatupang, T. and White, A. (1998) "A policy resolution model for knowledge acquisition in quality management." *Total Quality Management* 9(8):767–779.

Snowden, D. (1998a) "The ecology of a sustainable knowledge programme." *Knowledge Management* 1(6):15–20.

Snowden, D. (1998b) "Thresholds of acceptable uncertainty." *Knowledge Management* 1(5):1–9.

Snowden, D. (1999) "Creating a sustainable knowledge programme." Paper presented at Optimizing Knowledge Management conference, London, September 9–10.

Stauffer, D. (1999) "Why people hoard knowledge." *Across the Board* 36(8):16–21.

Swanson, R. and Holton, E. (1998) "Developing and maintaining core expertise in the midst of change." *National Productivity Review* 17(2):29–38.

Templeton, G. and Snyder, C. (1999) "A model of organizational learning based on control." *International Journal of Technology Management* 18(5–8):705–719.

Van Buren, M. (1998) "Virtual coffee klatch." *Technical Training* 9(5):42–46.

Van Buren, M. (1999) "A yardstick for knowledge management." *Training and Development Journal* 53(5):71–78.

Ward, A. and Leo, V. (1996) "Lessons learned on the knowledge highways and byways." *Strategy and Leadership* 24(2):16–20.

Wiig, K. (1993) *Knowledge Management Foundations*, vol. 1. Arlington, TX: Schema Press.

II

Knowledge-Based Perspectives
of the Firm

7

A Resource-Based Theory of the Firm

Knowledge versus Opportunism

Kathleen R. Conner and C.K. Prahalad

This chapter develops a resource-based theory of the firm. Its thesis is that the organizational mode through which individuals cooperate affects the knowledge they apply to business activity. For example, Y and Z might face a choice between working together as employees in a firm or completing the same task as independent contractors. There will be a difference in the knowledge that is brought to bear, and hence in their joint productivity, under the two options. This conclusion depends on the straightforward assumption that Y and Z each possess experience, insights, or skills that are to some extent different from those of the other. Tacit knowledge, which can be learned only through personal experience (Polanyi 1962, Nelson and Winter 1982, Nonaka 1994), is an example of know-how that is difficult to transfer ex ante. The difference in the knowledge that is brought to bear, once anticipated, affects the choice of organizational mode itself. Thus, as compared to opportunism-based, transaction-cost theory, we advance a separate (yet complementary) answer to the question, Why do firms exist?

As the literature makes increasingly clear, a knowledge-based view is the essence of the resource-based perspective. The central theme emerging in the strategic management resource-based literature is that privately held knowledge is a basic source of advantage in competition. The resource-based view generally addresses performance differences between firms using asymmetries in knowledge (and in associated competencies or capabilities; see, e.g., Amit and Schoemaker 1993, Barney 1991, Chen 1996, Henderson and Cockburn 1994, Peteraf 1993, Prahalad and Hamel 1990, Robbins and Wiersema 1995, Schoemaker and Amit 1994, Winter 1995). A resource-based theory of the firm thus entails a knowledge-based perspective.[1]

Using the standard established by Coase (1937), a theory of the firm generally addresses two issues: why firms exist, and what determines their scale and scope (Holmstrom and Tirole 1989). Of the two, the reason for the firm's existence is logically prior and is the primary subject of this chapter. In the literature, it is tantamount to asking why a firm exists instead of the alternative of market contracting between the same individuals.

Since received theory concentrates centrally (and virtually universally) on the effect of opportunistic behavior (see, e.g., Alchian and Demsetz 1972, Williamson 1975, 1985a, Klein et al. 1978, Grossman and Hart 1986, Kreps 1990, Milgrom and Roberts 1990), we stay away from opportunism in order to determine whether a resource-based theory of the firm has independent force. We do not claim, however, that resource-based theory constitutes the exclusive explanation of firms. Rather, the approach presented here accepts the validity—and, indeed, the remarkable intellectual achievement—of the opportunism-based view in explaining some of the motivation for firm organization.[2] Our aim is to identify additional, equally valid, empirically relevant causes. In particular, we argue that firms can exist because of knowledge-based transaction costs that are independent of the opportunistic considerations explored by Williamson. Recognition of knowledge-based transaction costs leads, we believe, to a fuller realization of Coase's (1937) original insights as to the reasons for firm organization.

We focus on basic choices: firm organization versus market contracting. We thus concentrate on polar organizational modes rather than complex or "hybrid" arrangements, such as joint ventures, alliances, or complicated corporate structures. Although the latter may be of great practical and scholarly interest, analysis of them is facilitated by studying the polar modes, since the more complicated structures can be seen as permutations of the polar ones. A joint venture, for example, may consist of blending aspects of firm organization and market contracting, while a geographically extended corporate structure, in contrast, may attempt to gain the basic advantages of firm organization repeatedly, through linking multiple layers or units. The polar cases are "basic particles" from which more elaborate arrangements are constructed. In addition, in this essay we are concerned with human, rather than physical, capital. We also are concerned with joint production between cooperating individuals, rather than simple exchange of discrete, separable products.[3] The analysis is presented, for simplicity, in terms of the choices of natural persons. However, it also applies to organizational entities, such as firms or organizational subunits, considering operating as one unit versus transacting autonomously.[4]

We begin by asking, "Why should strategic management and organizational scholars be interested in primary development of a theory of the firm?"[5] We contend that a theory of performance differences *between* firms requires, as an essential component, a theory of when advantage can be gained by organizing activity within a company instead of through arms-length markets. A logical nexus exists, therefore, between a theory of performance differences between firms and a theory of the firm itself, in that the former necessarily incorporates the latter.

Next we identify key concepts used in this study. These concern the nature of firm organization and individual behavior. We define the firm in a way consistent with Coase (1937), Simon (1951), Williamson (1975, 1985a), and Milgrom and Roberts (1988, 1990), among others. Firms are distinguished from markets based on an authority (employer-employee) relationship in the former, as compared to autonomous parties contracting in the latter. As to individual behavior, we assume bounded rationality (Simon 1957). This has an important corollary: cognitive limitations prohibit individuals from possessing identical stocks of knowledge. Individuals additionally are taken to behave truthfully. This ensures that we avoid opportunism-related reasons for the firm, allowing us to focus on other, knowledge-based considerations. In contrast to Williamson (1985a), we maintain that truthful behavior does not rule out market contracting frictions that can give rise to firm organization.

In the third section we present a resource-based theory of the existence of the firm. Organizational mode affects the knowledge applied to business activity in two ways: (1) how the parties' existing knowledge is blended and used and (2) how new learning or developments occurring during the course of the work are taken into account. We call these, respectively, the "knowledge-substitution" and "flexibility" effects of organizational mode. As to knowledge substitution, an employee sometimes acts according to the manager's direction rather than in conformity with what the employee otherwise would do. The manager's wisdom in such situations is substituted for the employee's.[6] If the employee cannot absorb the manager's wisdom before the employee profitably can apply it, the employee may opt to be directed by the manager and hence to be employed in a firm. In contrast, under market contracting, each person uses its own judgment to decide the specific responsibilities and duties that it will agree to carry out.[7] Indeed, the very notion of an autonomous market contractor means that the individual "retains the right or power of self-government" (*Merriam-Webster's* 1994) or, put differently, "works for itself." An individual will favor knowledge substitution—and hence, all else equal, a firm—when the manager's understanding (present or future) is believed to be of superior value compared to corresponding elements of the employee's.

The flexibility effect concerns the cost of altering an individual's responsibilities or duties on an ongoing basis, in order to respond to new learning or other developments arising during the course of the work. The cost of achieving flexibility under the two organizational modes differs, due to a fundamental distinction between firms and markets. As analyzed by Simon (1951), an employment contract need not be renegotiated when an employee undertakes a new or modified duty. In contrast, market contracts require renegotiation if responsibilities and duties are to be changed from the set originally agreed to. It is possible for either organizational mode to provide the cheaper flexibility, depending on the cost of operating the firm versus renegotiating the market contract. These costs need not depend on opportunistic potential.

Following this discussion of theory, we predict choice of organizational mode from the resource-based perspective. We identify whether firm organization or market contracting will result in the more valuable knowledge being applied to business activity, based on the combination of knowledge substitution and flexibility effects and independent of opportunism.

Next, we compare resource-based predictions of organizational mode with corresponding opportunism-related ones. The forecasts are identical in some instances and opposite in others. A principal point is that knowledge-based considerations can outweigh opportunism-related ones. For example, we predict firm organization in some situations in which opportunistic potential is too low for opportunism-based theory to do so. In others, we anticipate market contracting even though a firm would be chosen if opportunism-related factors were the only ones taken into account.

Resource-based limits to firm size and scope are then addressed in the following section. Since full treatment of this question is not possible in this chapter, our aim is to outline an approach

through which it might be addressed later. Concluding remarks follow.

Why Should We Be Interested in a Theory of the Firm?

In comparison to economists, less attention has been devoted by strategic management and organizational scholars to explicit development of a theory of the firm.[8] Some may have regarded theory of the firm as an essentially completed topic, given the works of Coase (1937), Williamson (1975, 1985a), and others. However, numerous fundamental issues remain unresolved and debated (see, e.g., Cheung 1983, Demsetz 1988, Dow 1987, Englander 1988, Kay 1992, Masten 1988, Milgrom and Roberts 1988, 1990, Nelson and Winter 1982, Postrel and Rumelt 1992, Williamson 1991a, 1991b, 1992, 1994).

Alternatively, primary development of a theory of the firm may not have been seen as directly germane to strategic management or organizational research. In particular, examining why a firm exists, as compared to a collection of market contracts, may not have been viewed as immediately related to the question of performance differences *between* firms.[9] Our aim in this section is to identify a theory of the firm as a necessary building block for addressing this broader issue.

Consider as an example two competing firms, *Red* and *Blue*. *Red* employs two persons, Y and Z, and *Blue*, two others, S and T. As illustrated in figure 7.1, although there are only two firms, each nonetheless competes against two other players. *Red* contends not only against the other firm, *Blue*, but also against the disaggregation of *Red*'s assets, Y and Z, into a market contracting arrangement. A parallel situation pertains to *Blue*. Direct competition between *Red* and *Blue*, portrayed within the dashed box in figure 7.1,

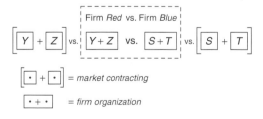

Figure 7.1 Competition between two firms (*Red* and *Blue*).

Component 1: $\boxed{Y} + \boxed{Z}$

Productivity under market contracting

Component 2: $\boxed{Y+Z} - \left[\boxed{Y} + \boxed{Z}\right]$

Extra margin of productivity created or lost by firm organization

Figure 7.2 Components of a single firm's (*Red*) productivity.

implicitly entails each already having had to "beat the market," in the sense that the employees of each firm deem firm organization to be superior to the alternative of market contracts. Indeed, disaggregation of the firms into autonomous relationships is the "stealth competitor" in any observable market contest.[10]

A single firm's productivity can be divided, for analytic purposes, into two components, as in figure 2. Using *Red* as the example, these are (1) the productivity that would be realized if the efforts of Y and Z were coordinated by means of a market contract, plus (2) the *extra margin* of productivity created (or lost) by applying firm organization to what Y and Z otherwise would achieve. Component 1 in figure 7.2 can be thought of as *Red's* "base" level of productivity, that is, the level that would be produced if the constituent assets, Y and Z, were completely self-directing. Component 2, on the other hand, is a change in the base level, which can be positive or negative. It is generated by altering the relationship between Y and Z, so that autonomous dealings are replaced by those occurring in a firm.[11]

Competition between *Red* and *Blue* can be analyzed as a contest over their relative standing as to the figure 7.2 components of individual firm productivity. As illustrated in figure 7.3, *Red* and *Blue* contend over the base level of productivity that each achieves, as well as over the *strength*

of benefits each provides because its employees are managed within a firm. Competition between firms can be divided into the two components shown in figure 7.3.[12]

The connection between a theory of the firm and a theory of performance differences between firms also is illustrated by figure 7.3. Specifically, one source of differential performance between firms is the degree to which each implements the productivity benefits arising from firm organization itself—component 2 in figure 7.3. Isolating the elements creating a difference in the productivity of a firm as compared to market contracting (i.e., a theory of the firm) is identical to identifying a subset of the factors determining why some firms outperform others. For example, if selecting firm organization over market contracting involves certain knowledge-related factors, then the comparative performance of firms will be affected by the relative strength of their implementation of these same factors. Our conclusion: a theory of performance differences between firms necessarily implies and incorporates a theory of the firm itself.[13]

We therefore have ample reason to be concerned with primary development of a theory of the firm. It is an essential building block for the more general theory to which resource-based analysis aspires. By developing a resource-based theory of the firm, we simultaneously take an important step toward the more complex task of creating a resource-based theory of performance differences between firms. In addition, we gain insight as to opportunism-independent, knowledge-based reasons for vertical integration itself.[14]

Definitions and Assumptions

A theory of the firm depends on the definitions and assumptions that form its basis. This section concerns two such aspects: firm organization and key parameters of individual behavior.

Firm *Red*		**Firm *Blue***
Component 1: $\boxed{Y} + \boxed{Z}$	vs.	$\boxed{S} + \boxed{T}$
Productivity under market contracting		*Productivity under market contracting*
Component 2: $\boxed{Y+Z} - \left[\boxed{Y} + \boxed{Z}\right]$	vs.	$\boxed{S+T} - \left[\boxed{S} + \boxed{T}\right]$
Extra margin of productivity gained or lost by firm organization		*Extra margin of productivity gained or lost by firm organization*

Figure 7.3 Components of competition between firms (*Red* and *Blue*).

Firm Organization

Establishing how the organizational modes differ is essential, since any extra rents to firm organization are returns to the difference between—characteristics that distinguish—firms and markets.[15] As reviewed in the appendix, defining firm organization has been problematic within the theory-of-the-firm literature (see, e.g., Masten 1988).

Our intent is to employ a firm–market distinction parallel to that generally used in opportunism-based, transaction-cost theory. Firm organization is distinguished from market contracting based on existence of authority in the former (i.e., employer over employee), as compared to the parties acting autonomously in the latter. Authority, or the possession of control rights, allows one person to direct—manage—the actions of another. Therefore, the firm represents a different capability to administer a given set of resources than does market contracting. As Dow (1987) suggests,

> efforts to explain internal organization inevitably center on the proposition that authority relations provide net benefits in organizing certain transactions, as compared with bargaining between autonomous agents. This proposition is defended by identifying certain desirable functions performed by authority relations which allegedly could not be performed as well or as cheaply through direct negotiation. (p. 19)

The specific conception of firm organization and market contracting used in this study is diagrammed in figure 7.4. It has been chosen for its simplicity and parsimony, in order to bare essential features of the resource-based argument. The "raw materials" (the individuals, Y and Z) are identical under the two organizational modes, as is traditional in theory-of-the-firm analyses.

Under market contracting, Y and Z each can be thought of as directors of their own, one-person firms (Demsetz 1988). They establish a contract, herein called a *market contract*, which sets out obligations of and compensation due to both. Once market contract terms are established, Y and Z are obliged to fulfill them.[16]

Under firm organization, on the other hand, Z is the manager, and Y, the employee. It may be typical to think of Z also as the legal owner of the firm, in the sense that Z is the sole share-

Y _____ Z	Y _____ Z
Market contract	*Employment contract*
(a) Market contracting	(b) Firm organization

Figure 7.4 The organizational modes.

holder if the firm is a corporation, or the owner if the firm is a sole proprietorship. Thus, it may be typical to think of Z as the "residual claimant" of the firm. For our purposes however, it is the *power to give direction*, with which Y is required to comply, rather than legal ownership per se, that is important. Thus, it is not necessary that Y be paid a wage by the firm, with Z, as residual claimant, being entitled to everything that remains after paying costs. As Demsetz (1988) puts it, "The direction of some by others catches the spirit of managed coordination" within a multiperson firm (p. 156).

Under firm organization, Y enters into an *employment contract* with Z, as compared to a market contract between them. In a seminal article, Simon (1951) addresses the nature of "[t]he authority relationship that exists between an employer and an employee, a relationship created by the employment contract" (p. 293).

> We will call our employer B (for "boss"), and our employee W (for "worker"). The collection of specific activities that W performs on the job (typing and filing certain letters, laying bricks or what not) we will call his *behavior*. We will consider the set of all possible behavior patterns of W and we will let x designate an element of this set. . . . We will say that B exercises *authority* over W if W permits B to select x. That is, W accepts authority when his behavior is determined by B's decision. In general, W will accept authority only if x_0, the x chosen by B, is restricted to some given subset (W's "area of acceptance") of all the possible values. (p. 294)

A central point is that, under an employment contract, the employer receives from the employee "the privilege of *postponing*, until some time after the contract is made, the selection of x," the employee's behavior (p. 295, emphasis added). Thus the authority an employer exercises as to an employee, that is, Z's right to "manage" Y, stems from Y giving Z the right to postpone final specification of the acts required of Y

until after an employment contract is established between them.[17]

In Simon's (1951) model, a market contract, in contrast, does not involve Y giving Z the right to specify Y's particular duties postcontractually or continuously.[18] Instead, in a market contract, Y and Z endeavor to lay out in the contract itself the particular acts required of each.

> Th[e] [employment] contract differs fundamentally from a . . . [market] contract. . . . In the . . . [market] contract each party promises a specific consideration in return for the consideration promised by the other. The buyer (like B) promises to pay a stated sum of money; but the seller (unlike W [in the context of an employment contract"]) promises in return a specified quality of a . . . specified commodity. (p. 294)

Of course, due to bounded rationality, the laying out of these requirements is never complete. But the essence of Simon's point is that some, and perhaps an extended, itemization of specific acts required of Y and Z is contained within a market contract, whereas in an employment contract, such itemization is replaced by Z being given the right to select the particulars of Y's duties postcontractually (within prescribed limits).

Williamson's (1975) view of firm organization does not appear to be contrary to that of Coase (1937) and Simon (1951):

> Among the most widespread characteristics of organizations is the prevalence of authoritative allocation. Virtually universally, in organizations of any size, decisions are made by some individuals and carried out by others. The fields in which an authority is valid may be limited; and the recipient of orders at one level may have his own field for authority. But within these limits, the giving and taking of orders, having someone tell someone else what to do, is an essential part of the mechanism by which organizations function. (Williamson 1975, p. 63)[19]

Williamson (1994) later makes the point even more strongly: "I argue that the main instrument to which firms have access that markets do not is fiat. . . . The exercise of fiat through hierarchy is . . . a very conscious, deliberate, and purposeful way of accomplishing coordination" (p. 324). A similar view characterizes the more recent, incomplete-contracting school.[20]

This chapter incorporates an authority-based—that is, managerially based—definition of the firm, consistent with Coase, Simon, and Williamson. Accordingly, the problem of choosing an organizational mode is equivalent to asking when Z's right to postpone selection of specific acts to be performed by Y (and Z) results in more profitable operation of the enterprise, than an ex ante specification of particular duties to be performed by Y and Z in a market contract, followed by potential renegotiation.

Behavioral Assumptions

We assume bounded rationality on the part of economic actors. This leads to an important corollary: cognitive limitations imply that no two individuals possess identical stocks of knowledge. However, unlike the opportunism-based approach, we focus on honest dealings between individuals.

As to bounded rationality, we suppose that individuals are "*intendedly* rational, but only *limitedly* so" (Simon 1957, p. xxiv). As a result, they possess finite cognitive abilities. Williamson (1975) characterizes these as follows:

> Bounded rationality involves neurophysiological limits on the one hand and language limits on the other. The physical limits take the form of rate and storage limits on the powers of individuals to receive, store, retrieve, and process information without error. . . . Language limits refer to the inability of individuals to articulate their knowledge or feelings by use of words, numbers, or graphics in ways which permit them to be understood by others. Despite their best efforts, parties may find that language fails them (possibly because they do not possess the requisite vocabulary or the necessary vocabulary has not been devised), and they resort to other means of communication instead. Demonstrations, learning-by-doing, and the like may be the only means of achieving understanding when such language difficulties develop. (pp. 21, 22)

Thus, tacit knowledge—knowledge that can be acquired only through personal experience (e.g., Polanyi 1962, Nelson and Winter 1982, Nonaka 1994)—is a result of bounded rationality.

A corollary of bounded rationality is that no two individuals possess identical stocks of knowledge, because cognitive limitations prohibit one person, such as Y, from absorbing the entire accumulated knowledge and skills of another, such as Z (and vice versa). Thus, each individual possesses experience, insights, or skills that are to some extent different from those of another.[21]

As a second principal assumption, we invoke what Williamson (1975) calls "stewardship" behavior.

> Opportunism is to be distinguished from . . . stewardship behavior. . . . [S]tewardship behavior involves a trust relation in which the word of a party can be taken as his bond. . . . Opportunistic behavior differs . . . because it involves making "false or empty, that is, self-disbelieved, threats and promises" in the expectation that individual advantage will thereby be realized. . . . (p. 26)

In this study, each player (Y and Z) is taken to tell the truth to the extent that it is known to that person (i.e., within the constraints of bounded rationality). Further, each knows that both will live up to whatever is agreed. However, Y and Z nonetheless acts in their own self-interest (again, within the constraints of bounded rationality). Thus, each tries to maximize its own return as well as possible within cognitive limitations, and without acting "in a self-disbelieved way" (Williamson 1975, p. 27).[22]

Williamson (1985a) claims that firms will not exist without opportunism, tantamount to arguing that a theory of the firm not based on opportunism is impossible.

> I . . . insist that bounded rationality notwithstanding, [market] contracting would be ubiquitous in the face of nonopportunism. . . . [E]x post contracting problems . . . [would] be annihilated by recourse to a "general clause" whereby parties to a contract promise to disclose all relevant information candidly and to behave in a cooperative fashion during contract execution and at contract renewal intervals. (p. 66)

Continuing, Williamson holds that

> [a]gents who value decision participation will . . . make this clear in the contracts they reach. All adaptations for which net gains can be projected will thereafter be realized without resistance within a community of nonopportunists. Should the nexus of con-

tracts need to be expanded or otherwise altered—for insurance purposes, for example—this will come about by displaying the relevant data in a fully objective way. Reversals of decision roles, due to aging, learning, or the like, will simply come about whenever net gains are in prospect, the disposition of these gains being distributed according to the gainsharing rule negotiated at the outset. (p. 66, footnote 1)

With market contracting frictions thus minimized, Williamson maintains that honest behavior will result in market contracting, since transaction costs would be negligible. We disagree with the proposition that honest behavior necessarily results in market contracting. As discussed below, contractual frictions of the sort that can produce firm organization can occur even when opportunism is held constant at zero.

The key is that some of each person's knowledge necessarily remains private, as established by the bounded-rationality corollary. Honest persons therefore may disagree about the best course of joint (or even individual) action or the division of gains. For example, a truthful individual may believe that it has identified a better way to proceed with a joint task and may argue for a concomitant change in approach that necessitates modifications by the entire group. The person's "discovery" may produce lengthy and costly negotiation, which includes efforts to convey to the others both the originator's analysis and the knowledge on which it is based. Because of irreducible differences in the knowledge possessed by the involved individuals, adoption of the innovation may not be automatic. Indeed, objections may never be surmounted, despite the originator's best (i.e., lengthy and costly) efforts.

Thus, we disagree with Williamson that "[a]ll adaptations for which net gains can be projected will . . . be realized without resistance within a community of nonopportunists." In our example, while the originator projects net gains from the innovation, those with whom the originator cooperates may believe, even after exhaustive discussion, that no gains, smaller gains, or even losses will result. Thus, an adaptation may not "be realized without resistance" under market contracting (or, indeed, may never be realized), even though net gains are projected (by at least the originator) and all are nonopportunists. The parties may have different expectations as to the nature of future gains (or losses), even after all, acting honestly, do their best to explain their reasoning to the others and to understand the alternative positions. Irreducible differences in the individuals' knowledge can lead them to make different judgments or expect different outcomes. Moreover, truthfulness in expressing an opinion or providing data need not erase all differences between the individuals' knowledge and judgments. Honest behavior, including the fullest possible disclosure of relevant data, does not guarantee that an "objective truth" will emerge that is easily recognized by all parties, as Williamson implies. The limits on information processing and knowledge articulation that Williamson describes (in an earlier-quoted passage) as characteristic of bounded rationality are the very factors that can prohibit honest individuals from reaching easy agreement. Similarly, it cannot be presumed that "[r]eversals of decision roles, due to aging, learning, or the like, will simply come about whenever net gains are in prospect," as Williamson maintains. Because individuals possess different knowledge, honest persons may disagree as to the best allocation of individual responsibilities, or whether a particular arrangement of decision roles has the potential to generate net gains.

We conclude that honesty does not rule out intense disagreement or haggling. Each party, acting truthfully, may have a different view of the factors (or their relative future importance) that should be taken into account in designing present and future courses of action based on predictions of uncertain, present or future, exogenous or endogenous, realities. For example, individuals' views of the best course of action may depend on their views of what a business rival will do, which presidential candidate or political party may win the next election, or what policies the new president or government will end up adopting (and how vigorously they will be implemented). The latter may include anticipating what particular political compromises will be struck (e.g., tax rates and mix, antitrust views, historical attitudes toward particular industries, dependence on the support of particular interest groups, etc.).[23] It is a commonplace that, even after (interminable) discussion, honest people still can disagree about what is going to happen. As a consequence, truthful individuals honestly may disagree about the best present and future course of action for their business activities. Or, the parties may possess different mindsets generally. Discord fundamentally derives from personal knowledge that cannot be communicated fully to others at the time of the disagreement.[24] Because each individual possesses different

knowledge, even truthful people may not reach agreement, nor can we be certain of the form (e.g., "rule governed") that concord will take if it can be reached.[25] Expressed in terms of the tenets of the incomplete contracting school, there may be no contract interval short enough that the parties are in complete agreement as to the preferred course of action. Because of irreducible differences in perspectives, experience, or skills, even the tiniest contract period may still involve substantive disagreement and hence negotiation and friction between truthful parties.[26]

Honest behavior, therefore, need not do away with firm organization. More specifically, honesty does not imply absence of transaction costs, that is, of the costs—frictions—of using market contracting (Coase 1937). Truthfulness does not guarantee automatic agreement, easy recognition of a present or future "common interest," or absence of haggling. Instead, these exist only if we eschew bounded rationality itself. Contrary to Williamson, frictions between economic actors can occur without opportunism, because of inevitable, irreducible differences in their knowledge. Expressed in another way, even in the absence of opportunism, knowledge-based transaction costs can exist. Further, knowledge variances between individuals generally will persist even as the contract interval shrinks, despite the individuals' best efforts to the contrary. These differences, as important to our view as opportunism is to Williamson's perspective, pave the way for a knowledge-based theory of the firm.

A Resource-Based Theory of the Existence of the Firm

We begin with an assumption that is standard in the theory-of-the-firm-literature: an individual's earnings depend on the profitability of the enterprise, be it autonomous contracting or employment within a firm.[27] Our problem becomes, therefore, to inquire when firm organization results in more profitable business activity than does market contracting. The analysis is related to, among others, Barney (1986, 1991), Cohen and Levinthal (1990), Conner (1991), Demsetz (1988), Hambrick (1989), Harrigan (1986), Kogut and Zander (1992), Langlois (1992), Prahalad and Hamel (1990), Rumelt (1984, 1995), Sanchez (1995), Silver (1984), Teece (1980, 1982), and Zajac and Olsen (1993).

Our thesis is that the organizational mode through which individuals cooperate affects the knowledge they apply to business activity. The difference in the knowledge that is brought to bear under the two organizational modes, once anticipated, affects the choice of mode itself. As we demonstrate below, no single organizational mode is always superior. Our objective is to establish a generalizable, empirically relevant relation between an organizational mode and the situations for which it is optimal, holding the probability of opportunistic behavior constant (at zero).

Organizational mode influences the knowledge applied to business activity in two ways: (1) how the parties' starting knowledge endowments are blended and used and (2) how learning or developments occurring during the course of the work are taken into account. Organizational mode thus affects both (1) the way in which *static* (i.e., presently possessed) knowledge is employed and (2) the *dynamics* of future knowledge acquisition and response to new developments. We refer to (1) and (2), respectively, as the "knowledge-substitution" and "flexibility" effects of organizational mode. In the theory developed below, an individual chooses between firm organization and market contracting according to which causes the individual to apply the more valuable understanding (net of applicable costs) to business activity, based on the combination of knowledge-substitution and flexibility effects and independent of opportunism.

The Knowledge-Substitution Effect

The knowledge-substitution effect concerns how presently held knowledge is applied to the activity. Under either organizational mode, Y obviously has access to its own knowledge.[28] One way for organizational mode to affect the understanding Y applies to the activity is to influence how Y uses Z's knowledge. Z can make its insights available to Y in many ways. A primary avenue is by giving directions (through Z's role as manager under firm organization) or making suggestions (as Y's contractual partner under market contracting).[29] The directions or suggestions are outcomes of Z applying its understanding to the particular problem or issue at hand.

Masten (1988) points out a fundamental, practical implication of the authority relationship in a firm, as compared to market contracting:

The overriding consideration expressed by the courts in . . . [disputes over the nature of a particular transaction] is the control exercised by an employer and, especially,

whether the latter is concerned with the manner in which the work is performed and not solely with its outcome. In evaluating [whether a] transaction [occurs within a firm or as part of a market contracting arrangement], "the first, and seminal, inquiry is whether the alleged employer . . . has the *right* to control . . . the details of the alleged employee's work" . . . whereas, "an 'independent' contractor is generally defined as one who in rendering services exercises an independent employment or occupation and represent his employer only as to the results of his work and not as to the means whereby it is to be done." . . . (p. 186, citations omitted)

Under market contracting, Y agrees to provide a service for a price. It is up to Y to decide *how* to produce the contracted-for service. In contrast, under firm organization, Z has the right to "control the details" of Y's performance, as Masten indicates. Z can direct Y as to the individual steps Y will take in creating a desired outcome. Indeed, exercising control as to individual work elements is an essential and legally recognized aspect of Z "managing" Y under firm organization, as compared to independent contracting, consistent with our earlier discussion on firm organization.

Remembering the focus on polar cases, if the market relationship is not to cross the boundary of becoming an authority-based (employment) one, then Y's own knowledge must be the final guide to its behavior. While Z, as market contracting partner, may make recommendations to Y during contract negotiations or afterward, Y will implement only those steps or actions that it comes to understand and agrees to perform, likely as part of a negotiated package. For as an autonomous contractor, Y retains "the right or power of self-government" (*Merriam-Webster's* 1994) or otherwise "works for itself." Z's knowledge thus will be used by Y if Y is able, either during contract negotiations or afterwards, to internalize enough of this knowledge so as to agree to act in a way different than Y would without it.

In contrast, under firm organization, Y can be called upon to act on the basis of Z's knowledge *prior* to Y internalizing it (or even if Y never does so). This occurs because the employment contract enables Z to give directions to Y. Hence Z can require Y to act (within the employment contract's boundaries) *according to Z's judgment*, rather than in conformity with Y's own. Knowledge-substitution takes place when Z tells Y to do something that Y, relying on its own knowledge and that which it has managed to absorb from Z, otherwise would not do.[30]

The knowledge-substitution effect thus involves the relationship between taking an action and internalizing the wisdom upon which it is based. An important question is why Y ever will favor a firm on knowledge substitution grounds, if firm organization causes Y to take actions that Y otherwise would not. The answer is that knowledge substitution is a fundamental response to cognitive limitations, having the effect of economizing on them. Knowledge substitution expands Y's productive capability without requiring fully concomitant knowledge absorption by Y. In effect, Z's knowledge becomes blended with Y's to a greater extent than would occur if Y had to internalize the relevant portions of Z's knowledge in their entirety. A primary effect of firm organization—of the authority relationship—is to cause an individual to use the knowledge of another *before* the former fully understands or agrees with it. Conversely, a main effect of market contracting—of an autonomous relationship—is to oblige knowledge to be internalized before the individual agrees to modify its actions on the basis of that knowledge.[31]

Thus, for knowledge substitution to be beneficial, there must be valuable aspects of Z's knowledge that Y cannot use autonomously until Y fully understands and absorbs them. An example is Z's tacit knowledge, which can be internalized by Y only through Y's personal experience, that is, only *after* Y has had practice developing or applying the knowledge. As an autonomous contractor, Y may doubt the value of a particular action suggested by Z, and hence not undertake it, because of Y's lack of experience with—and consequent lack of personal knowledge about—such a step. Under firm organization, on the other hand, Z simply can tell Y to take the action (thereby substituting Z's knowledge for corresponding elements of Y's).

Y's anticipation of knowledge-absorption difficulties can cause Y to favor a firm, because this mode is the organizational mechanism through which Y allows Z's judgment to dominate corresponding elements of Y's own. Conversely, market contracting is the organizational mechanism through which Y retains the right to exercise its own judgment, even at the cost of rejecting Z's. This point is related to Rumelt's (1995) conclusion that "[w]ithin the firm . . . it is possible to generate more and richer coordinative activity than can be accomplished in markets . . . it is the

gains to greater coordination that rationalize the firm" (p. 124). It also is consistent with Demsetz' (1988) insight that "[d]irection substitutes for education (that is, for the transfer of the knowledge itself)" (p. 172). It also underscores Cohen and Levinthal's (1990) conclusion that sufficient capacity for new-knowledge absorption is critical if a going concern (or individual) is to succeed (and stay independent).[32]

Seen in another way, firm organization and market contracting each create a particular relationship between people that stands in for the expanded individual abilities that otherwise would be needed to accomplish a similar outcome.[33] An essential function of market contracting, on the one hand, is to enable individuals to specialize in different aspects of business activity. Each person need not possess the full range of understanding or skills necessary to complete all aspects of the work by itself. The provisions of the market contract coordinate the individuals' efforts, so that a unified product (and hence specialization itself) can emerge.

On the other hand, firm organization also enables specialization, since it too provides a means for coordinating individual efforts. However, unlike market contracting, the firm entails a second means for minimizing the impact of limited cognitive abilities. Again looking at polar cases, because the employment contract creates the authority necessary for knowledge substitution, but a market contract does not, an employee need not internalize all the insights required to choose and carry out an action, while an independent contractor must. Thus, firm organization economizes on cognitive limitations through two methods: specialization and knowledge substitution. In contrast, market contracting economizes through specialization alone.[34]

The gains from implementing knowledge substitution will vary with the circumstances at hand. In highly creative or artistic endeavors, for example, knowledge substitution may be counterproductive or impossible. Some discernment (such as how to create a new product idea, strategy, or marketing campaign) may be *so* tacit that important aspects of it cannot be communicated. Even if they want to, "managers" may not be able to give sufficient directions to permit employees to come up with new breakthroughs.[35] Productivity instead may be enhanced by allowing each party to exercise its judgment independently. In contrast, if a manager's knowledge is not too tacit, then knowledge substitution can leverage it (Hamel and Prahalad 1993). More people can use the know-how because less individual internalization is required. In addition, a previously isolated individual's understanding purposefully can be leveraged by giving managerial responsibilities (and adopting a firm). Both firm organization and market contracting thus can be used proactively as elements of organizational design, in order to foster, respectively, knowledge leveraging or intellectual independence.

Accordingly, firm organization will not always be the organizational mode of choice on knowledge-substitution grounds. Y will consider which mode provides the greater *net* value. Either can be the better option as to knowledge substitution, depending on the relative knowledge-related advantages, balanced against the associated costs of operating each mode.

The cost of operating the firm includes negotiating the Y–Z employment contract, and the time and cost of Y receiving and digesting directions from Z. As discussed by Simon (1951), Y also bears the risk that Z's postcontractual directions will be, from Y's perspective, less as opposed to more desirable (notwithstanding that both are truthful and all Z's directions fall within the contractually established acceptable range). In addition, Y's evaluation of the quality of Z's knowledge will affect (interact with) some of the costs of obtaining it. For example, the greater the faith Y has in Z's judgment, the less may be the risk that Y believes it faces as to the palatability of Z's directions, the cheaper may be the costs of negotiating the boundary on Z's discretionary authority in the Y–Z employment contract, and the greater may be the likelihood that the boundary will not be excessively constrained.

Alternatively, the cost of carrying on market contracting includes the expense of negotiating the Y–Z market contract, and the cost of Y internalizing the knowledge of Z. Contract negotiation costs can be expected to be lower, the more quickly and cheaply the parties can transfer enough knowledge, settle differences, and arrive at agreement, and the lesser are legal costs. The degree of difference in perspectives between Y and Z will be important in this regard. If, for example, Y and Z come to diametrically opposite conclusions as to what needs to be done, market contract negotiation will be difficult and costly. This factor implies that firm organization is more likely to be preferred, all else equal, the *greater* the initial difference in the knowledge, culture, and so forth, of Y and Z (provided that

Y evaluates elements of Z's knowledge as superior to Y's).

Thus, depending on the value of Z's knowledge as compared to Y's, balanced against the cost of operating the firm as opposed to a market contract, either organizational mode can end up, as to knowledge substitution, being preferred. It is possible for either organizational mode to yield (1) the better blending and use of the parties' knowledge, and/or (2) the lower costs. Since Y will have some relationship with Z under either organizational mode (figure 7.4), Y may prefer either a stronger knowledge input by Z (under firm organization) or a weaker one (under market contracting), depending on the benefits and costs associated with each. We note that analysis of the knowledge-substitution effect has not depended on the potential for opportunistic behavior.

The Flexibility Effect

The flexibility effect accounts for the relative cost, under the two organizational modes, of altering the parties' duties and responsibilities on an ongoing basis, in order to incorporate learning or unexpected opportunities arising during the course of the work. The flexibility effect thus concerns the dynamics of future knowledge acquisition and application and response to new, internal or external developments. The modes carry different implications for the costs of adjusting duties and responsibilities to respond to events that were uncertain or simply unanticipated originally, as market contracting requires contract renegotiation in many situations in which firm organization does not. Y will take this difference into account in picking an organizational mode, since it affects the new knowledge that will end up being incorporated into the business activity and/or profitability.

Firm organization and market contracting each incorporate a mechanism for altering duties and responsibilities, in response to developments that were unforeseen or uncertain originally, or knowledge that was obtained after the initial contract was entered into. Under firm organization, the mechanism is an inherent part of the employment contract itself. Without engaging in contract renegotiation, Z, as manager, can reformulate previous directions or issue new ones. Under market contracting, in contrast, changes in duties and responsibilities require renegotiating the market contract itself, aside from those changes predetermined in the original market contract to become operative if certain, specified events occur. As to the latter, it will be difficult, if not impossible, for market contracts to provide for unanticipated acquisition of new knowledge, since it is axiomatic that the content of knowledge that may be obtained in the future is unknown at the present. Thus, market contracting flexibility as to unforeseen developments or new knowledge is achieved through engaging in a *series* of contracts.

Just as contractual mechanisms differ for achieving flexibility under the two organizational modes, so do the associated costs. The cost under firm organization is simply that of operating the firm over the relevant time frame. From Y's point of view, it includes, as before, the time Y spends receiving and digesting new directions, as well as the risk that (a truthful) Z will err by making changes unfavorable to the enterprise in general or to Y's productivity in particular.

Under market contracting, on the other hand, the cost of implementing flexibility is the expense of the market contract *renegotiations* required to attain it.[36] The renegotiation cost includes two aspects. The first and most obvious is the cost of conducting the renegotiation and redrafting the contract. As a factor contributing to these costs, it must be remembered that Y and Z have different knowledge sets (and potentially different associated linguistic conventions). This difference makes costly the transmission of ideas by Y to Z (and vice versa), which is itself an unavoidable part of the parties explaining to each other the reasons behind their respective new negotiating positions. Moreover, in a market contract, the onus is on the party seeking to convince the other to agree to disturb the status quo. The motivation is the former's perception that new, significant knowledge has been obtained, or that new circumstances or opportunities now beckon. Unless the stand-pat party can be convinced, the preexisting contract controls (if its term has not ended) or otherwise may exert a powerful force of inertia against change.

A second aspect concerns loss of coherent vision or cohesion as to the aim or conduct of the endeavor itself. This loss may be brought on through engaging in successive rounds of incremental compromises by Y and Z. Because each round of market contracting requires the parties to come to a priori agreement on the acts to be performed by each, the compromises made in one round can become the starting point for the next round. Over a succession of rounds, it is possible for the cohesion or coherence of the vi-

sions of, plans for, and activity of the endeavor as a whole to be diminished.[37]

Of course, the less important that flexibility is to the profitability of the endeavor, the less important is any cost difference between the organizational modes in obtaining it. The actual amount and value of flexibility that will be needed for efficient operations may become known only *after* entering into the contract— whether market or employment. We may think of Y as having an a priori probability distribution in its mind regarding this amount and value. Significant parts of the anticipated value that Y places on firm organization may turn on the amount (mean and variance) of flexibility that it anticipates to be necessary. The cost of flexibility in the market contract (e.g., the cost of renegotiation and redrafting) is an increasing function of the amount of flexibility that turns out to be necessary. Less needed flexibility translates into fewer negotiations and/or less important— and thus less contested—renegotiations.

Market contract renegotiation costs increase with the continuing degree of difference in perspectives between Y and Z. This difference, in turn, is likely to increase with the frequency, importance, and complexity of changes perceived to be necessary. If Y and Z continue to come to opposite (or very different) conclusions as to what needs to be done, renegotiation will be difficult and costly. The coherence/"short-sightedness" problem discussed above also may be intensified. In addition, in a turbulent, hypercompetitive (D'Aveni 1994) environment, the nature of tasks or required coordination may be concomitantly complex, and the sustainability of competitive advantage may be especially uncertain. As a result, the frequency, importance, and difficulty of market contract renegotiation may increase. Similarly, the greater the anticipated likelihood of frequent, important, and involved changes in the market environment, or in the knowledge that will be obtained in the future, the higher the likelihood of either a very short-term original market contract, or very costly negotiation of the original market contract. A very short-term original contract may exacerbate the coherence problem, and costly original negotiation may reflect attempts to anticipate and set the rules for dealing with a potentially chaotic future. This would reflect a parallel increase in the complexity of the work to be accomplished.

Thus, contrary to some views, firm organization is more likely to be preferred on knowledge-based flexibility grounds, the more dynamic and uncertain the competitive environment. Put another way, firm organization is likely to be preferred when the cognitive limitations imposed by bounded rationality, which are chief contributors to the unforseeability of events, and to the parties' differences in perspectives, may have a large impact on productivity and profitability. In such environments, commitment (Ghemawat 1991) on the part of Y, in the form of agreeing to abide by an employment contract and consequently Z's series of postcontractual directions, may add the advantage of stability of vision or strategic intent (Hamel and Prahalad 1989) to the endeavor. At the same time, the firm may preserve the lower cost flexibility as to Y's duties, by eliminating the need for successive contract renegotiations.

Accordingly, all else equal, if Y believes a priori that the mean and variance of the distribution on needed flexibility are small, Y is more likely to select market contracting. If the mean and/or variance is high, Y is more likely to select an employment contract with Z. We note, therefore, that either firm organization or market contracting can provide the lower cost flexibility as to amending duties and responsibilities, to reflect the dynamics of ongoing learning and new opportunities. As before, the effects discussed in this subsection do not depend on opportunistic potential.[38]

Resource-Based Predictions of Organizational Mode

Resource-based predictions of Y's choice of organizational mode are displayed in figure 7.5. In situation (i), substitution of Z's knowledge for some of Y's provides the higher value insights for the business activity. In addition, an employment contract produces the cheaper flexibility. Y therefore picks a firm, as this mode dominates on both counts. In situation (iii), these conditions are reversed, leading to Y's unambiguous choice of market contracting.

In situations (ii) and (iv), the direction of advantage is mixed, so Y picks either firm organization or market contracting, depending on the balance between opposing forces. In situation (ii), if the value of substituting Z's understanding for some corresponding elements of Y's is sufficiently large, and if market contract renegotiation provides the cheaper source of flexibility, but not by a lot, then the knowledge-substitution factor dominates and Y opts for a firm. Alterna-

		Knowledge-substitution provides positive net value:	
		Yes	No
Higher net value of flexibility provided by:	Employment contract	Firm (i)	Firm or (iv) market
	Market contract renegotiation	Firm or (ii) market	Market (iii)

Figure 7.5 Y's Resource-based choice of organizational mode.

tively, in situation (ii), if the value of knowledge substitution is small enough, and the flexibility-cost savings from market contracting are large enough (e.g., as might occur in a stable, mature industry), then Y picks market contracting. A parallel analysis applies to situation (iv), by reversing these conditions.

As illustrated by figure 7.5, the resource-based approach thus can be extended to a theory of the existence of the firm that incorporates predictive elements. Associated with the knowledge-substitution and flexibility effects are concepts such as strategy formulation, organizational culture, motivation, learning, organizational routines, barriers to transfer of knowledge, and strategic leadership, among others. For example, in assessing who has the superior judgment, Y is likely to consider how well Y and Z are each able to evaluate market opportunities and translate them into ideas for action leading to sustained competitive advantage. More broadly, Y's assessment of the value of firm organization will depend on the leadership and vision of Z—the value of Z's insights as compared to Y's. In addition, the organizational culture and shared values that can be built up under firm organization as opposed to market contracting, are likely to affect both the success of knowledge substitution and flexibility costs. Research on these and other concepts can be applied to the problem of predicting organizational mode, especially through their bearing on knowledge substitution and adaptive flexibility.[39]

Comparison of Resource- and Opportunism-Based Predictions

In figure 7.6, we compare resource-based predictions of organizational mode with corresponding opportunism-related ones. It is straightforward to see how the identical forecasts for situations (i) and (iii) in figure 7.6 arise. In situation (i), (a) the probability of opportunistic behavior is high, thus

Opportunism-based theory		Resource-based theory *Firm provides, on net. the more valuable, opportunism-independent knowledge*	
		Yes	*No*
Probability of opportunistic behavior is:	*High*	(i) RB - firm OB - firm	(iv) RB - firm or market OB - firm
	Low	(ii) RB - firm OB - market	(iii) RB - market OB - market

Figure 7.6 Comparison of resource- and opportunism-based predictions.

favoring a firm, and (b) a firm provides the more valuable, opportunism-independent knowledge.[40] Both approaches therefore anticipate firm organization. Situation (*iii*), in which neither does so, derives from reversing (a) and (b). We now turn to situations (*ii*) and (*iv*), which contain opposing forecasts.

Looking first at situation (*ii*), firm organization is not warranted from an opportunism-based view. Because the probability of opportunistic behavior is low, *Y* opts for market contracting. In contrast, the resource-based approach predicts the reverse: *Y* chooses a firm.

The key to the difference is that, in the choice of organizational mode, opportunism-independent knowledge considerations can outweigh opportunism-based ones. Even when opportunistic potential is too low to justify a firm, as occurs in situation (*ii*), firm organization nonetheless is selected from the resource-based perspective if it results in the more valuable knowledge applied to the activity. The resource-based approach thus implies that opportunistic potential is not all that *Y* considers in choosing an organizational mode.

Turning to situation (*iv*) of figure 7.6, (a) the probability of opportunistic behavior is high, and (b) market contracting provides the more valuable, opportunism-independent knowledge. While the opportunism-based approach anticipates a firm, resource-based theory forecasts *either* a firm or market contracting. The specific resource-based prediction depends on the balance of opposing forces.

As to this balance, it is not inconsistent with the resource-based approach that high probability of opportunistic behavior will lead to a firm, even if, absent the opportunism factor, the firm provides less valuable knowledge than market contracting. The benefit of minimizing opportunism, if sufficiently great, outweighs the loss imposed by this mode essentially "costing too much" for the opportunism-independent knowl-

edge that it provides. Alternatively, the gain from firm organization's reduction of opportunistic potential may be too weak to compensate for the loss this mode causes by providing the less valuable, opportunism-independent knowledge. In this case, the resource-based approach anticipates market contracting.

To establish that the resource- and opportunism-based theories have distinct predictive content, we must show that situations (*ii*) and (*iv*) are empirical possibilities. For example, will we ever observe a situation in which the probability of opportunistic behavior is low, but the firm nonetheless provides, on net, the more valuable opportunism-independent knowledge [situation (*ii*)]? We must examine whether factors that can produce a low probability of opportunistic behavior are compatible with those that can cause the firm to provide the more valuable opportunism-independent knowledge, and vice versa.

To show that these two sets of factors can be compatible, we supply a specific example. If *Y* and *Z* each stand to gain the same amount from cooperation and each must make the same-sized idiosyncratic investment in order to make the cooperation work, then opportunistic potential is balanced between the parties. If opportunistic potential is balanced, the probability of opportunistic behavior is low, since the parties are in a "stand-off" situation (Klein and Leffler 1981, Williamson 1983). Yet, equal specific investment by *Y* and *Z* and equal gain from cooperation do not imply that the factors giving rise to the knowledge-substitution and flexibility effects of firm organization must be absent. Equal specific investment and equal gain are compatible, for example, with a dynamic, highly uncertain competitive environment in which the flexibility and strategic coherence that a firm provides may be of great value. Similarly, equal specific investment and equal gain are compatible with the barriers to knowledge absorption that underlie the knowledge-substitution effect. Expressed in another way, equal specific investments and equal gains need not preclude obstacles to knowledge absorption or flexibility gains to firm organization. A parallel example can be developed to demonstrate the empirical possibility of situation (*iv*) in figure 7.6.[41]

Analysis of figure 7.6 also may help shed light on previously anomalous empirical findings. In an influential study of the costs of organization in naval shipbuilding, Masten et al. (1991) found that

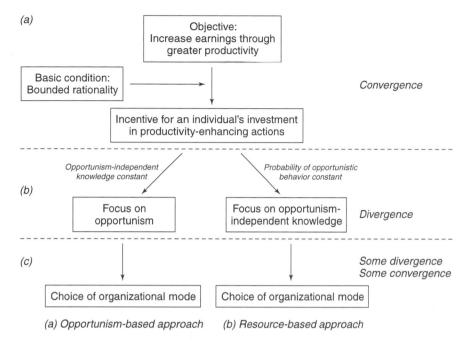

Figure 7.7 Comparison of resource- and opportunism-based approaches.

the second-stage estimates indicate that the correlation between human asset specificity and the likelihood of integration found in the first stage is a consequence of a decrease in internal organization costs rather than the increase in the costs of market exchange that the [opportunism-based, transaction-cost] theory predicts. (p. 19)

Masten et al. (1991) further comment that "[f]ully satisfactory explanations for these findings are elusive" (p. 21). Masten et al.'s results in this regard appear consistent with the analysis of situation (*ii*). From the resource-based perspective, a firm is chosen in situation (*ii*) because the human asset specificity—dependence of *Y* on direction by *Z*—thereby produced is more productive than the lesser level of dependence that would be generated by market contracting.

Speaking more broadly, the relationship of the resource- and opportunism-based theories is diagrammed in figure 7.7. As level (*a*) indicates, the basic purpose of firm organization under both approaches is to increase the productivity of cooperating individuals. The theories, therefore, are consistent as to this fundamental reason for a firm.[42]

As indicated in level (*b*) of figure 7.7, the divergence between the approaches is caused by different—opposite—ceteris paribus assumptions. We hold the probability of opportunistic behavior constant (at zero), in order to examine the opportunism-independent, knowledge-based influences of organizational mode more closely. Opportunism-based theory does the reverse. It implicitly holds opportunism-independent effects of organizational mode constant, in order to ascertain how organizational mode affects opportunistic potential.

Expressed in a different way, both theories are parsimonious in that each holds empirically relevant factors fixed in order to analyze others. Recognition of opportunism-based theory's implicit ceteris paribus assumption is the basis for Conner's (1991) earlier observation: "Transaction cost theory assumes that the *same* productive activity can be carried on either within a firm or by a collection of autonomous contractors: that is, except for problems of opportunism, the same inputs can be used equally productively in a firm or a market context" (p. 142).

It also may relate to Demsetz' (1988) statement that "[t]he emphasis that has been given to transaction cost . . . dims our view of the full picture by implicitly assuming that all firms can produce goods or services equally well" (p. 147).[43] Foss (1996) also maintains that:

> One problem in the contractual approach is that it is often implicitly assumed that what one firm can do on the level of production, another firm can do equally well, so that differences in economic organization are not allowed to turn on differences in production costs. . . . (p. 474)

The opposing predictions in situations (*ii*) and (*iv*) of figure 7.6, and the contrary ceteris paribus assumptions (fig. 7.7) that drive them, indicate the need for future theory development that incorporates both resource- and opportunism-based considerations into an explanation of the firm's existence. The now-conflicting predictions in figure 7.6 need to be replaced, through creation of new theory, with single, unified ones. The new forecasts would take into account, and the new approach would explain, how non-opportunism-based and opportunism-based factors interact and are balanced in the choice of organizational mode.

Limits to Size and Scope of the Firm

It is not possible within the present chapter to address in detail a theory-of-the-firm's second question—limits to firm size and scope. Instead, our objective here is to suggest a general approach through which this question subsequently might be treated from a resource-based perspective. Referring to limits on firm size as a "chronic puzzle," Williamson (1995a) holds that "[t]he upshot is that limitations on firm size of a comparative institutional kind have yet to be described" (p. 135).

The reason for this conclusion centers on the concept of "selective intervention." Its motivating question is, "Why can't a large firm do everything a collection of small firms can do and more?" (Williamson 1985a, p. 131). As Williamson (1992) puts it,

> Selective intervention is really the key. The idea is to replicate the market mode within the firm in all respects save those where the intervention is the source of expected net gains. If hierarchical control is reserved for the latter and if the firm replicates the market in all other respects, then the firm never

does worse than the market (by replication) and sometimes does better (through selective intervention). Accordingly, the firm will everywhere do as well and will sometimes do better than the market. (p. 339)

Williamson holds that the central issue in a theory of the limits of firm size is why selective intervention breaks down. The question is why a perfect blend of authority and market relationships cannot be achieved within the same firm, so that firm organization always outperforms the alternative of a collection of market contracts. Expressed differently, the issue is why a firm cannot accomplish a perfect mix of the right to direct employees' actions with the absence of rights to do so.[44]

A central challenge for resource-based theory is to evaluate whether selective intervention is an appropriate approach for assessing opportunism-independent, knowledge-based limits to the size and scope of the firm, or whether we should return to the marginal analysis originally suggested by Coase (1937).[45] For example, a question as to selective intervention might be, If there are places within a firm where firm management should *not* possess the right to direct employees, then what is the gain from having those places inside the firm? Resource-based theory as to existence of the firm predicts that if the manager adds, on net, insufficiently valuable knowledge to an employee's activity, then it will not be carried on inside the firm. For it to have independent force, the concept of selective intervention implies that factors additional to or simply different from those affecting whether an activity is included in the firm in the first place may determine the scope of an already established firm. The selective intervention concept thus may be reaching for a source of indivisibility between the activities or assets of an established firm, which simultaneously is not a factor (or is less of one) in deciding whether the activity or asset will be part of the firm in the first place. Such a factor could account for why parts of an already existing firm might be retained even though a theory of the existence of the firm would indicate that these parts would not be added de novo to the firm, or vice versa.

We believe that the selective intervention concept profitably can be interpreted as calling for a deeper understanding of the fundamental sources of incommensurability between the polar organizational modes. Indivisibilities pertaining to a firm's size but not to its existence, should they exist, are likely to be outgrowths of incommensurabilities between market contracting and firm organization themselves. Moreover, hybrid organizational modes, such as joint ventures or alliances, may be practical attempts to minimize inherent incommensurabilities between the polar modes and thus may constitute practical attempts to achieve "selective intervention."

Conclusion

Operationalizing the resource-based view through development of predictive theory is a significant challenge. We attempt to contribute by advancing a resource-based theory of the firm. Appreciating the substantial intellectual contribution of the opportunism-based, transaction-cost view, we seek to complement and build on it, through articulation of a knowledge-based perspective that is independent of opportunistic considerations. A resource-based theory of the firm is an important step, we believe, toward creation of more general, resource-based theory of performance differences between firms. It also provides knowledge-related reasons for vertical integration itself.

There have been at least three seminal contributions to the theory of the firm. Coase (1937) delineates the area as a research topic and establishes the comparative organizational reasoning crucial to a theory of the firm. Coase (1937) also introduces the fundamental concept of transaction costs, which he defines broadly. Simon (1957) advances the motivating behavioral assumption of bounded rationality. Simon (1951) also establishes the employment—authority—relationship as the incisive distinction between a firm and market contracting. Williamson (1975, 1985a) explores a powerful aspect of bounded rationality in the context of choosing an organizational mode: opportunistic potential. The predictive theory developed by Williamson operationalizes an important aspect of the transaction-cost approach.

While opportunistic potential may be an important ramification of self-interested, cognitively limited individuals choosing an organizational mode, it is not the only one. Holding that transaction costs arise only because of opportunism or the potential for it is, in our view, an incomplete interpretation of Coase's, Simon's, and Williamson's work. Transaction costs, or frictions within independent-contractor relationships, also may arise for knowledge-based reasons that are independent of opportunistic potential. Expressed in another way, bounded rationality has other important implications besides opportunism for how economic actors coordinate their productive activity. The implication upon which we focus is the difference in knowledge applied to business activity under the polar organizational modes of market contracting and firm organization.

The results obtained in this chapter complement those of Barney (1991) and others concerned with predictive power as to identifying "resources." A theory of the firm indicates a subset of the substantive areas of endeavor likely to be associated with a company's advantage vis-à-vis other firms. An implication of this study is that important resources, that is, factors contributing to above-normal earnings, may include those materially affecting (1) the quality of managerial as opposed to employee judgment (including, e.g., organizational culture and human resources policies) and (2) the cost of implementing flexibility as to what employees should do. Barney's (1991) tests of value, rarity, imperfect imitability, and nonsubstitutability can be applied to identify the specific assets within these areas that have the capability to generate competitive advantage.

An important future step is to explore the interaction between non-opportunism-based knowledge considerations and opportunism-related factors in the choice of organizational mode. The present knowledge-based approach also may be extended more specifically to organizational entities and to more complicated or hybrid modes, such as multilevel corporations, alliances, joint ventures, and legal partnerships. Examining situations involving physical as well as human capital also would be useful. In addition, opportunism-independent, knowledge-based limitations to the size and scope of an existing firm need to be explored.

Acknowledgment   We are grateful for the helpful comments and suggestions provided by Raphael Amit, Jay Barney, Jeffrey Conner, Aneel Karnani, Scott Masten, Will Mitchell, Elaine Mosakowski, Joanne Oxley, Richard Rumelt, José Santos, Ted Snyder, Neal Stoughton, Gordon Walker, and three anonymous referees. Kathleen Conner received financial support for this work from the University of Michigan Business School summer fellowship program.

APPENDIX

Defining Firm Organization

An essential element of the debate within the economics literature is whether an authority relationship can be said to separate firm organization from market contracting.[46] The use of authority to distinguish between firms and markets begins with Coase's (1937) original treatment. His approach depends on authority of employer over employee under firm organization, in contrast to market contracting. Coase (1937) defines a firm in terms of the managed direction of resources, instead of coordination being achieved through market processes:

> Outside the firm, price movements direct production, which is coordinated through a series of exchange transactions on the market. Within a firm, these market transactions are eliminated and in place of the complicated market structure with exchange transactions is substituted the entrepreneur coordinator, who directs production. . . . A firm . . . consists of the system of relationships which comes into existence when the direction of resources is dependent on an entrepreneur. (pp. 333, 339)

While Coase's (1937) and Simon's (1951) managerially based distinction between firms and markets may be intuitively appealing, Masten (1988) points out a weakness. He argues that neither Coase (1937) nor Simon (1951) establishes the firm as a *discrete* organizational mode as compared to market contracting. That is, Coase and Simon differentiate firms and markets as a matter of *degree* rather than *kind*. Indeed, as noted by Masten, Coase (1937) foreshadows this problem in his statement, "Of course, it is not possible to draw a hard and fast line which determines whether there is a firm or not. There may be more or less direction" (p. 337). And as to Simon (1951), Masten (1988) holds that

> [u]nder . . . [Simon's] definition . . . the employment relationship is analytically indistinguishable from any contract in which one party is empowered to alter some aspect of performance unilaterally. An example would be a fixed price, variable-quantity contract in which the buyer has the "authority" to determine the volume of trade under the agreement and can thus "direct" the produc-

tion level of the seller. Such arrangements are not at all uncommon in long-term contracts. But although they conform in a technical sense to Simon's definition of an employment transaction, the relationship between the buyer and seller in such contracts would not generally be considered that of employer and employee. At best, the distinction between employer and supplier is again a matter of degree. Only the details and not the type of contract entered separate an employment from a commercial transaction, and neither the label *firm* nor *employee* has any force beyond the provisions explicitly adopted in the contract itself. (p. 182)

The logical problem generated is substantial. If firms and markets differ only as to the degree of authority exercised, then it is difficult to identify in a general way the separation between market contracting and firm organization. For example, how *much* authority is needed for the relationship to constitute firm organization? Without a generalizable answer, a managerially based theory of the firm remains remote. In order to predict choice of organizational mode, it is necessary to be able to distinguish between modes.

An implicit answer to the question of how much authority is needed—as well as a significant challenge to the authority-based view as a whole—is presented by Alchian and Demsetz (1972). They argue that the authority exercised within a firm is no stronger or any different than that which occurs under market contracting. The Alchian-Demsetz approach therefore solves the problem of how much authority is enough to produce firm organization, by eliminating authority altogether as a variable of interest in a theory of the firm. According to Alchian and Demsetz (1972):

> It is common to see the firm characterized by the power to settle issues by fiat, by authority, or by disciplinary action superior to that available in the conventional market. This is delusion. The firm does not own all its inputs. It has no power of fiat, no authority, no disciplinary action any different in the slightest degree from ordinary market contracting between any two people. I can "punish" you only by withholding future

business or by seeking redress in the courts for any failure to honor our exchange agreement. That is exactly all that any employer can do. He can fire or sue, just as I can fire my grocer by stopping purchases from him or sue him for delivering faulty products. What then is the content of the presumed power to manage and assign workers to various tasks? Exactly the same as one little consumer's power to manage and assign his grocer to various tasks. . . . To speak of managing, directing, or assigning workers to various tasks is a deceptive way of noting that the employer continually is involved in renegotiation of contracts on terms that must be acceptable to both parties. (p. 777)

The Alchian-Demsetz view gives rise to defining the firm as a "nexus of contracts" (Jensen and Meckling 1976). The nexus-of-contracts approach underlies a significant portion of the agency-cost literature as well as of the "monitoring" school of transaction-cost economics (see, e.g., Williamson 1985a). Firms and markets are not seen to be separable entities on analytically substantive grounds. Firms are taken to be "legal fictions," that is, little more than nodes of intersection between (market) contracts.[47] An implication is that the theory of the firm (with the firm taken as a separable institution or substantive entity) would be replaced with a theory of contract. The latter would investigate why certain types of contracts emerge under certain circumstances. Presumably, the same type of contract could exist either under the legal fiction of "firm organization" or as a bona fide market relationship.[48]

In contrast, for firm organization to function as a "governance mode," firms and markets must be able to be defined as "discrete structural alternatives" (Williamson 1991b). Contrary to the nexus-of-contracts view, a substantive difference must exist between firms and markets for opportunism-based, transaction-cost theory (and ours) to apply. The difference between the polar organizational modes needs to be one of kind rather than simply degree. As Williamson (1981) puts it, "[t]he object [of transaction-cost analysis] is to match governance structures to the attributes of transactions in a discriminating way. Microanalytic attention to differences among governance structures and microanalytic definition of transactions are both needed in order for this to be accomplished" (p. 1544). As to the nexus-of-contracts view, Williamson (1994)

maintains that "[t]he argument that the firm 'has no power of fiat, no authority, no disciplinary action any different in the slightest degree from ordinary market contracting' (Armen Alchian and H. Demsetz 1972, p. 777) is exactly wrong: firms can and do exercise fiat that markets cannot" (p. 325).[49]

Masten (1988) and Williamson (1991a, 1991b, 1994) argue that the authority exercised under firm organization is of a different kind, as compared to the ability of parties to "direct" one another under market contracting. The authors analyze the law governing firm relations as opposed to market ones. Masten's (1988) purpose, for example, is to

> explor[e] the status of the employment relationship in the legal system and a comparison of corresponding doctrines in commercial contract law to see whether legal rules establish an institutional basis for the advantages and limitations most commonly associated with internal organization. . . . [T]he issue of whether the firm is a distinct institution is ultimately a question of fact: Are there mechanisms or sanctions available in employment transactions that are not similarly available to independent contractors? (pp. 182, 185)

Both Masten and Williamson find that the law indicates the traditional, authority-based notion of the firm. Masten (1988) observes, for example, that

> [e]ven a cursory examination of the case law governing the relationship between employers and employees . . . reveals a set of obligations and responsibilities that are indeed unique to employment transactions and which often coincide precisely with the traditional emphasis in economics on the information and authority advantages of internal organization. (p. 185)

Masten (1988) indicates that because of "differences in legal defaults, sanctions, and procedures governing commercial and employment transactions," there is "a basis for special managerial authority or access to information" traditionally attributed to firm organization (p. 195). Williamson (1994) maintains that "the (implicit) contract law of hierarchy is that of forbearance," under which "courts *will refuse* to hear disputes between one internal division and another" over technical issues that otherwise would be heard if the parties instead were market contractors (p. 325, emphasis in original).

While legal analysis is valuable in establishing differences of fact with respect to firm organization and market contracting, it leaves open the issue of the *cause* of the differences. In particular, *why* is authority—managerial direction—exercised by one party over another in some circumstances, but not in others? As Williamson (1994) comments, "I conjecture that forbearance law is the evolutionary product of business and the law groping for a contractual logic that 'worked,' which is to say that forbearance law was not consciously invented but mainly evolved" (p. 325). A theory of the firm emphasizing authority differences between the polar organizational modes can be seen as a way to explain why these differences have come to exist.

Notes

1. Examples of the knowledge-related emphasis in the resource-based and related literature include the following. Winter (1988) holds that "[f]undamentally, business firms are organizations that know how to do things. . . . Firms perform their function[s] as *repositories of knowledge*" (pp. 175, 177). Prahalad and Hamel (1990), in developing the concept of core competence, state that "[c]ore competencies are the collective learning in the organization, especially how to coordinate diverse production skills and integrate multiple streams of technologies" (p. 82). According to Teece et al. (1990), "it is not only the bundle of resources that matter, but the mechanisms by which firms learn and accumulate new skills and capabilities, and the forces that limit the rate and direction of this process" (p. 11). And Kogut and Zander (1992) comment that "the theoretical challenge is to understand the knowledge of a firm as leading to a set of capabilities that enhance the chances for growth and survival" (p. 384).

Lippman and Rumelt (1982) formally link the existence of privately held knowledge—in the form of causal ambiguity—to a firm's ability to earn above-normal returns through productive activity. As expressed separately by Barney (1986):

When firms seeking to acquire resources to implement a strategy . . . and firms who currently own or control these resources . . . have exactly the same, and perfectly accurate, expectations

about the future value of product market strategies before they are actually implemented, then the price of the resources needed to implement these strategies will approximately equal their value once they are actually implemented. . . . In such markets, all pure profits that could have been had when the strategy in question was implemented will be anticipated and competed away. (p. 1233)

Cyert et al. (1993) also conclude:

It is the existence of knowledge of internal production techniques or external opportunities in the hands of a small number of firms that creates the market imperfections necessary to generate rents for the firm. Put another way, it is proprietary knowledge that creates a comparative advantage for the firm. (p. 57)

2. Opportunism-based theory suggests that firms exist because of the potential for cheating that accompanies investments, when value "depends on the continuation of a particular relationship" (Milgrom and Roberts 1990, p. 62), creating asset specificity. Firm organization is seen as a method for reducing the net incentive to act opportunistically in situations in which asset specificity is present (see, e.g., Williamson 1975, 1985a).

3. Our interest coincides with Alchian and Demsetz' (1972) definition of teamwork: "Team production . . . is production in which several types of resources are used and the product is not a sum of separable outputs of each cooperating resource. An additional factor creates a team organization problem—not all resources used in team production belong to one person" (p. 779).

4. Hereafter, by "organizational mode," we mean whether actors join in a firm, or cooperate by means of a market contract (the polar cases).

5. We are grateful to an anonymous referee for suggesting that we address this issue.

6. We do not suppose that *all* of an employee's actions are so influenced, but rather that some of them necessarily are, if firm organization (management) is to have any effect.

7. Throughout the chapter, we use "it" as a personal pronoun, to avoid gender references and because the theory applies more broadly to entities, not just natural persons.

8. Exceptions include Bartlett and Ghoshal (1993), Borys and Jemison (1989), Conner (1991), Hennart (1991, 1994), Hill and Kim (1988), Kogut and Zander (1992), Ouchi (1980), Ring and Van de Ven (1992), Rumelt (1984, 1995), and Teece (1980, 1982). Some of these involve application of opportunism-based theory, while others focus on

opportunism-independent considerations, or both. The theory of the firm has been discussed as a strategic management or organization theory research issue by, among others, Argyres (1995), Collis and Montgomery (1995), Ghoshal and Moran (1996), Hesterley et al. (1990), Hoskisson et al. (1993), Mahoney (1992), Mahoney and Pandian (1992), Masten (1993), Montgomery (1995), Seth and Thomas (1994), Spender (1994), Van de Ven (1993), and Walker and Weber (1984, 1987).

9. This is a central issue in the strategic management literature (see, e.g., Barney 1986, 1991, Rumelt et al. 1994).

10. As Schumpeter (1950) put it in another context, this type of competition (from market contracting) "acts not only when in being but also when it is merely an ever-present threat. It disciplines before it attacks" (p. 85).

11. Components 1 and 2 in figure 7.2 include both asset stocks and flows, in Dierickx and Cool's (1989) sense.

12. From the early strengths-weaknesses-opportunities-threats (SWOT) analysis and accompanying concept of distinctive competence (e.g., Christensen et al. 1978), to the generic strategies and value chain approaches developed by Porter (1980, 1985), the emphasis in the strategic management field has been on a firm's competitive advantage as realized through superior productive activity, including, among other aspects, procurement of materials, manufacturing, distribution, marketing, and human resource policies. Given its intellectual roots within the strategic management field, it is not surprising that the resource-based perspective carries through the field's traditional emphasis on the firm "search[ing] for rent" (Bowman 1974, p. 47) through how it gains advantage from aspects of productive activity. This emphasis can be seen in Wernerfelt's (1984) initial treatment and virtually all of the resource-based and related literature.

13. Conner (1991) states in an earlier article that

> [b]ecause resource-based theory is centrally motivated by understanding performance differentials *between* firms . . . [the firm's] existence needs to be explained in terms of a firm's superiority to *two* alternative forms of organization: a collection of market contracts *and* other firms. By the latter, the intention is to raise the issue of why a particular firm exists, as opposed to its assets being distributed among other firms. (p. 139, italics in original)

Foss (1996) holds that such "separation of the existence issue into two parts is a non-issue." He maintains that a single, general explanation exists under opportunism-based, transaction-cost theory that "explains both the existence of the firm relative to the market and why a particular firm owns a particular combination of assets/resources" (p. 473). Our view is that existence of a firm, as opposed to other firms absorbing its assets, depends on the firm's performance in comparison to other firms, that is, on creating sustained competitive advantage. While a firm's survival in a firm-versus-firm context is affected by factors related to the theory of the firm (component 2 in figure 7.3), these are not the *only* influencing elements. Differences in the "base" assets controlled by competing firms also are significant (component in fig. 7.3). Thus, factors additional to those analyzed in a theory of the firm are required for a theory of performance differences between firms.

14. An additional reason for interest in a theory of the firm concerns its second aspect, namely, factors limiting the size and scope of firms. These factors relate to questions of diversification, vertical integration, and strategic alliances, among others, which are central in the strategic management literature.

15. As Alchian (1993) puts it, "Asking why 'firms' exist without clearly denoting what is meant by a 'firm' creates opportunities for dispute or nonrefutable generalities" (p. 367).

16. As described by Coase (1937), "Outside the firm . . . production . . . is co-ordinated through a series of exchange transactions on the market" (p. 333).

17. This view is consistent with that of Coase (1937), who earlier wrote that

> it is important to note the character of the contract into which a factor enters that is employed within a firm. The contract is one whereby the factor, for a certain remuneration (which may be fixed or fluctuating), agrees to obey the directions of an entrepreneur *within certain limits*. The essence of the contract is that it should only state the limits to the powers of the entrepreneur. Within these limits, he can therefore direct the other factors of production. . . . All that is stated in the contract is the limits to what the persons supplying the commodity or service is expected to do. The details of what the supplier is expected to do is not stated in the contract but is decided later by the purchaser. When the direction of resources (within the limits of the contract) becomes dependent on the buyer in this way, that relationship which I term a "firm" may be obtained. (p. 336–337, italics in original)

18. By "postcontractually," we mean after the formation of the contract, not after its term has ended.

19. Indeed, Williamson (1992) holds that "I expressly identify fiat as one of the distinguishing features of hierarchies, as compared with markets, in my very first article on transaction costs" (p. 339). This might seem contrary to his treatment of "peer groups," which Williamson (1975) takes to be "the simplest non-market alternative" (p. 41). Williamson holds that peer groups "do not entail subordination" (p. 42). However, Williamson (1985b) later indicates that "the hypothetical peer group is a romantic vision" and that "the pure peer group is unattainable" (p. 243, 244).

20. Receiving its start from Grossman and Hart (1986), the incomplete contracting perspective incorporates opportunistic behavior, but includes conceptual differences as compared to Williamson's framework and also involves mathematical formalization through game theory. A chief difference is that asset specificity is not seen necessary to generate firm organization. Instead, "the key to evaluating the efficacy of market transactions is the costs of negotiating suitably detailed short-term contracts" where "short-term refers to a period short enough so that all the information that is relevant for current decisions is already available" (Milgrom and Roberts 1990, p. 65). The basic concept is that if short-term intervals are allowed to be brief enough, then it is possible to define one in which, even given bounded rationality, the parties do not disagree regarding what should be done. The problem over a longer period thus is the cost of negotiating a sequence of such short-term contracts. It is held that a firm will be preferred when bargaining costs associated with negotiating this sequence (including opportunism-based ones) are sufficiently great. As to firm organization, Milgrom and Roberts (1990) comment that

> the crucial distinguishing characteristic of a firm is not the pattern of asset ownership but the substitution of centralized authority for the relatively unfettered negotiations that characterize market transactions. . . . [W]hat most distinguishes any centralized organization is the authority and autonomy of its top decision makers or management—that is, their broad rights to intervene in lower-level decisions and the relative immunity of their decisions from intervention by others. (pp. 72, 79)

In focusing on reputation effects, Kreps (1990) adopts a similar perspective:

> I develop . . . a dichotomy in transactions that correlates well with the distinction between firms and markets. . . . The dichotomy is between hierarchical transactions and, for lack of a better name, specified transactions. Roughly, in a specified transaction all terms are spelled out in advance. In a hierarchical transaction, certain terms are left unspecified; what is specified is that one of the two parties has, within broad limits, the contractual right to specify how the contract will be fulfilled. . . . Here I will concentrate on arrangements where one party has the authority to determine ex post fulfillment, comparing this with cases where there is no need for such authority. (This notion is far from original to me; see, for example, Simon 1951. (p. 99)

21. Differences in the knowledge possessed by different individuals is implicit in the concept of asset specificity, which figures prominently in opportunism-based, transaction-cost theory (Williamson 1985a). It also is involved in the condition of information impactedness (Williamson 1975). More broadly, these differences motivate individuals to specialize in various aspects of business activity, including management.

22. Williamson (1985a) states that

> [b]y opportunism I mean self-interest seeking with guile. This includes but is scarcely limited to more blatant forms, such as lying, stealing, and cheating. Opportunism more often involves subtle forms of deceit. . . . More generally, opportunism refers to the incomplete or distorted disclosure of information, especially to calculated efforts to mislead, distort, disguise, obfuscate, or otherwise confuse. (p. 47)

In our analysis, Y and Z engage in neither blatant nor subtle forms of opportunism. Thus, using Williamson's terminology, we assume "open or simple self-interest seeking" in which "individuals . . . [are] fully open and honest in their efforts to realize individual advantage. . . . " Williamson refers to this as a "semistrong form of self-interest seeking" (with opportunism being the strong form; p. 49). As a related point, implications of trustworthy behavior for strategy and competitive advantage are addressed by, among others, Barney (1990), Barney and Hansen (1994), Donaldson (1990a, 1990b), Ghoshal and Moran (1996), Hill (1990), Hosmer (1994, 1995), Mahoney et al. (1994), and Maitland et al. (1985).

23. The result for our analysis is the same, whether we formulate the issue as one of irreducible differences in knowledge because of

bounded rationality, or that, faced with the same information, individuals' hunches will differ about some future events as rivals' reactions or election outcomes, or about how those future events will impact the business.

24. An interesting question arises as to whether one party could simply pay the other to go along with the first when disagreements arise, therefore eliminating the negotiations and frictions that otherwise would be associated with market contracting. We can imagine, especially in the case of a one-time decision (e.g., where to place an oil well), that such a payment could be made, potentially resulting in market contracting being the preferred alternative. If, however, the work involves a series of future decisions, then one party would have to pay the other to agree to let the first have decision-making authority in the future. This amounts to an employment contract, and thus to firm organization as we have discussed it earlier.

25. Williamson (1985a) comments that

[p]lainly, if it were not for opportunism, all behavior could be rule governed. This need not, moreover, require comprehensive preplanning. Unanticipated events could be dealt with by general rules, whereby the parties agree to be bound by actions of a joint profit-maximizing kind. Thus problems during contract execution could be avoided by ex ante insistence upon a general clause of the following kind: I agree candidly to disclose all relevant information and thereafter to propose and cooperate in joint profit-maximizing courses of action during the contract execution interval, the benefits of which gains will be divided without dispute according to the sharing ratio herein provided. (p. 48)

26. Interestingly, Williamson (1991a) recognizes the problem as it pertains to the incomplete-contracting perspective. He states that "common knowledge is a very expansive assumption. . . . Is common knowledge reasonable even between the immediate parties?" (p. 174).

27. This statement is not the same as assuming that Y's or Z's compensation in a firm or market contract is an express function of the profit of the enterprise. Our point simply is that, the more profitable is the enterprise, the more Y or Z is likely to receive, whether as salary or profit sharing. And even a fixed-compensation individual cares that the enterprise takes in enough to be able to pay the fixed compensation.

28. Y's knowledge endowment is presumed to be the same, whether it picks firm organization or

market contracting. A parallel assumption pertains to Z.

29. We intend "direction" by Z to be interpreted broadly. For example, such directions can include giving detailed instructions on how to complete a task, assigning workgroup membership, deciding or agreeing to certain delegations of decision-making authority, setting the premises for decision by others, and taking actions that affect the norms or culture of the organization. In addition, by "contractual partner," we merely mean a party to a market contract.

30. There is no presumption that *all* of an employee's behavior under firm organization is so directed. As McNulty (1984) states, "[T]he employment contract is usually one in which the employee has a certain discretion and freedom to choose how he will use his time on the job" (p. 244).

31. In a related vein, Fredrickson (1986) suggests that "[o]rganizations that differ in their dominant structure are likely to make strategic decisions using a very different process" (p. 294).

32. Believing Z's knowledge to be valuable is required for Y to want to engage in joint production with Z, under either organizational mode. A useful area for future research concerns how Y evaluates the overall quality of Z's "package" of knowledge without knowing and understanding, in advance, all of the steps or elements that this knowledge incorporates. One possibility is that Y uses Z's reputation—past history—to help assess the likely quality of Z's knowledge (see, e.g., Weigelt and Camerer 1988).

33. Teece et al. (1994) make the related point that "[w]hile individual skills are of relevance, their value depends upon their employment in particular organizational settings" (p. 15).

34. We are indebted to Gordon Walker for pointing out that Cheung (1983) contains perhaps the first indication that a knowledge-substitution-like effect may exist, although Cheung expressly rejects it as a reason for the firm. Cheung asks, "Could it be that letting someone else make the decision [as to what to do] is often more productive? The answer is no. . . . Errors are bound to be less frequent when price information guides every activity performed" (p. 5). Cheung holds that a manager's judgment cannot be superior to an employee's, since the best guide to the employee's behavior would be for the employee to observe price signals itself and adjust its actions accordingly. Cheung's argument, however, presumes that the web of market contracts is so dense, complete and reproducible that (1) price signals exist for all relevant alternative courses of action, (2) price signals are easy to decipher and

separate into their components, and (3) an actor easily can find a contracting partner that will offer to replicate with the actor some other parties' observed market contract (and thus price). We believe that in many situations, the web is not very dense, complete or reproducible, so price signals will not be an adequate guide. Indeed, sustainable competitive advantage may depend on the absence of such price signals (see, e.g., Lippman and Rumelt 1982, Barney 1986). Because the manager and the employee have knowledge differences that are irreducible, the manager can be better (or worse) at interpreting the implications of market conditions that is the employee. Thus, letting someone else decide what to do indeed can be the more productive alternative.

35. The manager itself may be unable to ascertain how it creates the innovations. This is an example of the causal ambiguity explored by Lippman and Rumelt (1982).

36. The costs discussed in the previous subsection concern implementation of the original market contract.

37. Of course, there is a point at which, for both parties, the cost of backing down on desired points exceeds the value of the arrangement; if this point is reached, the relationship will be terminated once the contract expires.

38. The flexibility effect is related to one of Coase's (1937) originally identified transaction costs: "For this series [of market contracts] is substituted one" (p. 336). Coase's argument, like ours, does not depend on opportunism.

39. In taking issue with a knowledge-based approach, Foss (1996) holds that "[w]e cannot do without concepts such as opportunism if we wish to explain the existence of the firm" (p. 474). We believe that a contrary conclusion is indicated by the foregoing analysis, which relies on opportunism-independent, knowledge-based factors to explain why firms exist. Foss (1996) also maintains that a knowledge-based approach, such as in Conner (1991), "commit[s] the fallacy of technological determinism" (p. 473). To avoid the mistake of technological determinism, Williamson (1985a) provides the following test:

> A useful strategy for explicating the decision to integrate is to hold technology constant across alternative modes of organization and to neutralize obvious sources of differential economic benefit, such as transportation cost savings. . . . Technology is not determinative of economic organization if alternative means of contracting can be described that can feasibly employ, in steady state respects at least, the same technology. (pp. 88, 89)

As illustrated by figure 7.4 above, our model holds "technology" constant across organizational modes. Knowledge endowments are identical under both firm organization and market contracting, since the same actors participate in each. The only asymmetry in the model is that under firm organization, Z exercises authority as to Y, whereas under market contracting, Z does not. Since, using Williamson's test, the initial knowledge of the actors—and hence the technology open to them—is constant across modes, it is difficult to see how our approach is an example of "technological determinism" in his sense. Firm organization may lead to the better *use* of knowledge, or more valuable learning through greater flexibility and coherence of strategic vision over time. In other words, firms may have advantages over markets. But this is no more "technological determinism" than is opportunism-based theory's view that more valuable asset-specific investments will be made in firms because of this mode's reduction of opportunistic potential.

40. We use "more valuable, opportunism-independent knowledge" in this section in a broad sense, encompassing both the knowledge-substitution and flexibility effects discussed earlier.

41. A more formal treatment would examine the degree of positive or negative correlation, or lack thereof, between four sets of events: (a) high and (b) low probability of opportunistic behavior, and (c) affirmative and (d) negative answers to whether the firm provides, on net, the more valuable knowledge.

42. The linkage of opportunism-based theory to productivity is established through the concept of asset specificity. If firm organization lessens opportunistic potential, then cooperating individuals optimally invest in more productive molding to one another. This generates a gain in their joint productivity as compared to market contracting. (For discussion of the optimal degree of asset specificity under an opportunism-based approach, see, e.g., Riordian and Williamson [1985].)

43. Demsetz (1988) includes in "firms," both multiperson and single-person enterprises—the two organizational modes considered in this chapter.

44. Based on the concept of selective intervention, Williamson (1985a) eschews his earlier approach:

> I . . . [previously addressed] the firm size dilemma by invoking bounded rationality and noting that limited spans of control are thereby implied. If any one manager can deal directly with only a limited number of subordinates,

then increasing firm size necessarily entails adding hierarchical levels. Transmitting information across these levels experiences . . . losses . . . , which are cumulative and arguably exponential in form. As firm size increases and successive levels of organization are added, therefore, the effects of control loss eventually exceed the gains. A limit upon radical expansion is thus reached in this way. . . . Plausible as the argument seemed at the time, it does not permit selective intervention of the kind described above. Rather, [in my previous conception] the entire firm is managed from the top. (pp. 134–135)

Milgrom and Roberts (1990) also comment that

[m]any of the arguments purporting to explain the limits of organization fail when confronted with the policy of replacing previously autonomous units with semiautonomous ones in whose operations and decisions central managers intervene only when uncoordinated or competitively oriented decisions are inefficient. Any adequate explanation of why all economic activity is not brought under central management must confront this possibility. (p. 70)

45. Coase (1937) originally wrote:

First, as a firm gets larger, there may be decreasing returns to the entrepreneur function; that is, the costs of organizing additional transactions within the firm may rise. . . . Naturally, a point must be reached where the costs of organizing an extra transaction within the firm are equal to the costs involved in carrying out the transaction in the open market, or, to the costs of organizing by another entrepreneur. Second, it may be that as the transactions which are organized increase, the entrepreneur fails to place the factors of production in the uses where their value is greatest, that is, fails to make the best use of the factors of production. Again, a point must be reached where the loss through the waste of resources is equal to the marketing costs of the exchange transaction in the open market or to the loss if the transaction was organized by another entrepreneur. Finally, the supply price of one or more of the factors of production may rise, because the "other advantages" of a small firm are greater than those of a large firm. . . . Of course, the actual point where the expansion of the firm ceases might be determined by a combination of the factors mentioned above. The first two reasons given most probably correspond to the

economists' phase of "diminishing returns to management." (pp. 340–341)

46. As Masten (1988) comments,

Fifty years after the publication of Ronald Coase's seminal deliberations on the subject, economists have yet to reach a consensus on the nature of the firm. While many continue to regard the firm as a distinct institution, usually ascribing to it some superior control, information, or adaptive properties, others reject the notion that any unique governance advantages accrue to integration, noting that neither human nature nor technology or information are altered by the purely nominal act of "internalization." For the latter, the word *firm* is merely descriptive, a collective noun denoting a particular cluster of otherwise ordinary contractual relationships. (p. 181)

47. For example, according to Jensen and Meckling (1976),

[c]ontractual relations are the essence of the firm, not only with employees but with suppliers, customers, creditors, etc. . . . It is important to recognize that most organizations are simply *legal fictions which serve as a nexus for a set of contracting relationships among individuals.* . . . Viewed this way, it makes little or no sense to try to distinguish those things which are "inside" the firm (or any other organization) from those things that are "outside" of it. There is in a very real sense only a multitude of complex relationships (i.e., contracts) between the legal fiction (the firm) and the owners of labor, material and capital inputs and the consumers of output. (pp. 310–311, emphasis in original)

48. As Masten (1988) explains,

[s]uch criticisms have led many economists to deny the existence of administrative solutions to contractual failures, asserting that the same transactional frictions confront employers as independent contractors. The firm, at least in governance respects, thus becomes no more than a coalition or "nexus" of contractual relationships, and the choice faced by transactors is only among the details to include in the contract. (p. 183)

49. Dow (1987) also criticizes the nexus-of-contracts approach, as follows:

A venerable tradition in the economics of organization holds authority relations to be the distinguishing features of the firm (Coase 1937) and indeed of organization quite generally. . . . Authority relations form the bedrock of internal organization in a way which ownership or the degree of performance monitoring do not. For example, employment relationships are widely agreed to fall within the ambit of internal organization, although ownership of human and physical capital remains separated. Intensive monitoring often appears in conjunction with internal organization (Alchian and Demsetz 1972), but does not imply it, since such monitoring can equally well be used to enforce promises arrived at through bargaining in a market setting. Williamson is therefore correct to use "degree of autonomy" as the fundamental dimension along which governance structures are arrayed; another way of expressing this is to say that as one moves toward the "hierarchy" end of the contractual spectrum, authority relations grow in scope and complexity. (p. 16)

References

Alchian, A.A. (1993) "Thoughts on the theory of the firm." *Journal of Institutional and Theoretical Economics* 149:365–369.

Alchian, A.A. and Demsetz, H. (1972) "Production, information costs, and economic organization." *American Economic Review* 62:777–795.

Amit, R. and Schoemaker, P.J.H. (1993) "Strategic assets and organizational rent." *Strategic Management Journal* 14:33–46.

Argyres, N. (1996) "Evidence on the role of firm capabilities in vertical integration decisions." *Strategic Management Journal* 17:129–150.

Barney, J.B. (1986) "Strategic factor markets: expectations, luck and business strategy." *Management Science* 42:1231–1241.

Barney, J.B. (1990) "The debate between traditional management theory and organizational economics: substantive differences or intergroup conflict?" *Academy of Management Review* 15:382–393.

Barney, J.B. (1991) "Firm resources and sustained competitive advantage." *Journal of Management* 17:99–120.

Barney, J.B. and Hansen, M. (1994) "Trustworthiness and competitive advantage." *Strategic Management Journal* 15:175–190.

Bartlett, C.A. and Ghoshal, S. (1993) "Beyond the M-form: toward a managerial theory of the firm." *Strategic Management Journal* 14:23–46.

Borys, B. and Jemison, D.B. (1989) "Hybrid arrangements as strategic alliances: theoretical issues in organizational combinations." *Academy of Management Review* 14:234–249.

Bowman, E.H. (1974) "Epistemology, corporate strategy, and academe." *Sloan Management Review* 15:35–50.

Chen, M.-J. (1996) "Competitor analysis and interfirm rivalry: toward a theoretical integration." *Academy of Management Review* 21:100–134.

Cheung, S.N.S. (1986) "The contractual nature of the firm." *Journal of Law and Economics* 26:1–21.

Christensen, C.R., Andrews, K.R. and Bower, J.L. (1978) *Business Policy*. Homewood, IL: Irwin.

Coase, R.H. (1937) "The nature of the firm," *Economica* 4:386–405. Reprinted in G.J. Stigler and K.E. Boulding (eds.), *Readings in Price Theory*, pp. 331–351. Chicago: Irwin.

Cohen, W.M., and Levinthal, D.A. (1990) "Absorptive capacity: a new perspective on learning and innovation." *Administrative Science Quarterly* 35:128–152.

Collis, D.J. and Montgomery, C.A. (1995) "Competing on resources: strategy in the 1990s." *Harvard Business Review*, July–August, 118–128.

Conner, K.R. (1991) "A historical comparison of resource-based theory and five schools of thought within industrial organization economics: do we have a new theory of the firm?" *Journal of Management* 17:121–154.

Cyert, R.M., Kumar, P., and Williams, J.R. (1993) "Information, market imperfections and strategy," *Strategic Management Journal* 14:47–58.

D'Aveni, R.A. (1994) *Hypercompetition: Managing the Dynamics of Strategic Maneuvering*. New York: Free Press.

Demsetz, H. (1988) "The theory of the firm revisited." *Journal of Law, Economics, and Organization* 4:141–161.

Dierickx, I. and Cool, K. (1989) "Asset stock accumulation and sustainability of competitive advantage." *Management Science* 35:1504–1511.

Donaldson, L. (1990a) "The ethereal hand: organizational economics and management theory." *Academy of Management Review* 15:369–381.

Donaldson, L. (1990b) "A rational basis for criticisms of organizational economics: a reply to Barney." *Academy of Management Review* 15:394–401.

Dow, G.K. (1987) "The function of authority in transaction cost economics." *Journal of Economic Behavior and Organization* 8:13–38.

Englander, E.J. (1988) "Technology and Oliver Williamson's transaction cost economics." *Journal of Economic Behavior and Organization* 10:339–353.

Foss, N.J. (1996) "Knowledge-based approaches to the theory of the firm: some critical comments." *Organization Science*, 7(5):470–476.

Fredrickson, J.W. (1986) "The strategic decision process and organizational structure." *Academy of Management Review* 11:280–297.

Ghemawat, P. (1991) *Commitment: The Dynamic of Strategy*. New York: Free Press.

Ghoshal, S. and Moran, P. (1996) "Bad for practice: a critique of the transaction cost theory." *Academy of Management Review* 21:13–47.

Grossman, S.J. and Hart, O.D. (1986) "The costs and benefits of ownership: a theory of vertical and lateral integration." *Journal of Political Economy* 94:691–719.

Hambrick, D. (1989) "Putting top managers back into the strategy picture." *Strategic Management Journal* 10:5–15.

Hamel, G. and Prahalad, C.K. (1989) "Strategic intent." *Harvard Business Review*, 67(May–June): 63–76.

Hamel, G. and Prahalad, C.K. (1993) "Strategy as stretch and leverage." *Harvard Business Review* 71(March–April):75–84.

Harrigan, K.R. (1985) *Strategic Flexibility*. Lexington, MA: Lexington Books.

Henderson, R. and Cockburn, I. (1994) "Measuring competence? Exploring firm effects in pharmaceutical research." *Strategic Management Journal* 15:63–84.

Hennart, J.-F. (1991) "The transaction costs theory of joint ventures: an empirical study of Japanese subsidiaries in the United States." *Management Science* 37:483–497.

Hennart, J.-F. (1994) "The 'comparative institutional' theory of the firm: Some implications for corporate strategy." *Journal of Management Studies* 31:193–207.

Hesterley, W.S., Liebeskind, J., and Zenger, T.R. (1990) "Organizational economics: an impending revolution in organization theory?" *Academy of Management Review* 15:402–420.

Hill, C.W.L. (1990) "Cooperation, Opportunism, and the Invisible Hand: Implications for Transaction Cost Theory," *Academy of Management Review*, 15:500–513.

Hill, C.W.L. and Kim, W.C. (1988) "Searching for a dynamic theory of the multinational enterprise: a transaction cost model." *Strategic Management Journal* 9:93–104.

Holmstrom, B.R. and Tirole, J. (1989) "The theory of the firm," in R. Schmalensee and R.D. Willig (eds.), *Handbook of Industrial Organization*, vol. 1, pp. 61–133. Amsterdam: North Holland.

Hoskisson, R.E., Hill, C.W.L., and Kim, H. (1993) "The multidivisional structure: organizational

fossil or source of value." *Journal of Management* 19:269–298.

Hosmer, L.T. (1994) "Strategic planning as if ethics mattered." *Strategic Management Journal* 15: 17–34.

Hosmer, L.T. (1995) "Trust: the connecting link between organizational theory and philosophical ethics." *Academy of Management Review* 20: 379–403.

Jensen, M.C. and Meckling, W.H. (1976) "Theory of the firm: managerial behavior, agency costs and ownership structure." *Journal of Financial Economics* 3:305–360.

Kay, N.M. (1992) "Markets, false hierarchies and the evolution of the modern corporation." *Journal of Economic Behavior and Organization* 17:315–333.

Klein, B., Crawford, R.A., and Alchian, A.A. (1978) "Vertical integration, appropriable rents, and the competitive contracting process." *Journal of Law and Economics* 21:297–326.

Klein, B. and Leffler, K. (1981) "The role of market forces in assuring contractual performance." *Journal of Political Economy* 89:615–641.

Kogut, B. and Zander, U. (1992) "Knowledge of the firm, combinative capabilities, and the replication of technology." *Organization Science* 3:383–397.

Kreps, D.M. (1990) "Corporate culture and economic theory," in J.E. Alt and K.A. Shepsle (eds.), *Perspectives on Positive Political Economy*, pp. 90–143. Cambridge: Cambridge University Press.

Langlois, R.N. (1992) "Transaction-cost economics in real time," *Industrial and Corporate Change* 1:99–127.

Lippman, S.A. and Rumelt, R.P. (1982) "Uncertain imitability: an analysis of interfirm differences in efficiency under competition." *Bell Journal of Economics* 13:418–438.

Mahoney, J.T. (1992) "Organizational economics within the conversation of strategic management." *Advances in Strategic Management* 8: 103–155.

Mahoney, J.T., Huff, A.S., and Huff, J.O. (1994) "Toward a new social contract theory in organization science." *Journal of Management Inquiry* 3:153–168.

Mahoney, J.T. and Pandian, J.R. (1992) "The resource-based view within the conversation of strategic management." *Strategic Management Journal* 13:363–380.

Maitland, I., Bryson, J., and Van de Ven, A. (1985) "Sociologists, economists, and opportunism." *Academy of Management Review* 10:59–65.

Masten, S.E. (1988) "A legal basis for the firm." *Journal of Law, Economics, and Organization* 4:181–197.

Masten, S.E. (1993) "Transaction costs, mistakes,

and performance: assessing the importance of governance." *Managerial and Decision Economics* 14:119–129.

Masten, S.E., Meehan, J.W., Jr., and Snyder, E.A. (1991) "The costs of organization." *Journal of Law, Economics, and Organization* 7:1–25.

McNulty, P.J. (1984) "On the nature and theory of economic organization: the role of the firm reconsidered." *History of Political Economy* 16: 233–253.

Merriam-Webster's Collegiate Dictionary, 10th ed. Springfield, MA: Merriam-Webster.

Milgrom, P. and Roberts, J. (1988) "Economic theories of the firm: past, present, and future." *Canadian Journal of Economics* 21:444–458.

Milgrom, P. and Roberts, J. (1990) "Bargaining costs, influence costs, and the organization of economic activity," in J.E. Alt and K.A. Shepsle (eds.), *Perspectives on Positive Political Economy*, pp. 57–89. Cambridge: Cambridge University Press.

Montgomery, C.A. (1995) "Of diamonds and rust: a new look at resources," in C.A. Montgomery (ed.), *Resource-Based and Evolutionary Theories of the Firm*, pp. 251–268. Boston: Kluwer.

Nelson, R.R. and Winter, S.G. (1982) *An Evolutionary Theory of Economic Change*. Cambridge, MA: Belknap Press.

Nonaka, I. (1994) "A dynamic theory of organizational knowledge creation." *Organization Science* 5:14–37.

Ouchi, W.G. (1980) "Markets, bureaucracies, and clans." *Administrative Science Quarterly* 25: 129–141.

Peteraf, M.A. (1993) "The cornerstones of competitive advantage: a resource-based view." *Strategic Management Journal* 14:179–191.

Polanyi, M. (1962) *Personal Knowledge*. Chicago: University of Chicago Press.

Porter, M.E. (1980) *Competitive Strategy*. New York: Free Press.

Porter, M.E. (1985) *Competitive Advantage*. New York: Free Press.

Postrel, S. and Rumelt, R.P. (1992) "Incentives, routines, and self-command." *Industrial and Corporate Change* 1:397–425.

Prahalad, C.K. and Hamel, G. (1990) "The core competence of the corporation." *Harvard Business Review* 68(May–June):79–91.

Ring, P.S. and Van de Ven, A.H. (1992) "Structuring cooperative relationships between organizations." *Strategic Management Journal* 13:483–498.

Riordan, M.H., and Williamson, O.E. (1985) "Asset specificity and economic organization." *International Journal of Industrial Organization* 3:365–378.

Robins, J. and Wiersema, M.F. (1995) "A resource-based approach to the multibusiness firm: empirical analysis of portfolio interrelationships and corporate financial performance." *Strategic Management Journal* 16:277–300.

Rumelt, R.P. (1984) "Toward a strategic theory of the firm," in R. Lamb (ed.), *Competitive Strategic Management*, pp. 556–570. Englewood Cliffs, NJ: Prentice-Hall.

Rumelt, R.P. (1995) "Inertia and transformation," in C.A. Montgomery (ed.), *Resource-Based and Evolutionary Theories of the Firm*, pp. 101–132. Boston: Kluwer.

Rumelt, R.P., Schendel, D., and Teece, D.J. (1994) *Fundamental Issues in Strategy*. Cambridge, MA: Harvard Business School Press.

Sanchez, R. (1995) "Strategic flexibility in product competition." *Strategic Management Journal*, 16:135–160.

Schoemaker, P.H.J. and Amit, R.H. (1994) "Investment in strategic assets: industry and firm-level perspectives," in P. Shrivastava, A.S. Huff, and J.E. Dutton (eds.), *Advances in Strategic Management: Resource-Based View of the Firm*. Greenwich, CT: JAI Press.

Schumpeter, J.A. (1950) *Capitalism, Socialism, and Democracy*. New York: Harper and Row.

Seth, A. and Thomas, H. (1994) "Theories of the firm: implications for strategy research." *Journal of Management Studies* 31:165–191.

Silver, M. (1984) *Enterprise and the Scope of the Firm*. Oxford: Martin Robertson.

Simon, H.A. (1951) "A formal theory of the employment relationship." *Econometrica* 19:293–305.

Simon, H.A. (1957) *Administrative Behavior*. New York: Macmillan.

Spender, J.-C. (1994) "Organizational knowledge, collective practice and Penrose rents." *International Business Review* 3:353–368.

Teece, D.J. (1980) "Economies of scope and the scope of the enterprise." *Journal of Economic Behavior and Organization* 1:223–247.

Teece, D.J. (1982) "Towards an economic theory of multiproduct firm." *Journal of Economic Behavior and Organization* 3:39–63.

Teece, D.J., Pisano, G., and Shuen, A. (1990) "Firm capabilities, resources, and the concept of strategy." Mimeo, University of California, Berkeley. Haas School of Business.

Teece, D.J., Rumelt, R., Dosi, G., and Winter, S. (1994) "Understanding corporate coherence: theory and evidence." *Journal of Economic Behavior and Organization* 23:1–30.

Van de Ven, A.H. (1993) "The institutional theory of John R. Commons: a review and commentary." *Academy of Management Review* 18:139–152.

Walker, G. and Weber, D. (1984) "A transaction cost approach to make-or-buy decisions." *Academy of Management Journal* 29:373 391.

Walker, G. and Weber, D. (1987) "Supplier competition, uncertainty, and make-or-buy decisions." *Academy of Management Journal* 30:589–596.

Weigelt, K. and Camerer, C. (1988) "Reputation and corporate strategy: a review of recent theory and applications." *Strategic Management Journal* 9: 443–454.

Wernerfelt, B. (1984) "A resource-based view of the firm." *Strategic Management Journal* 5:171–180.

Williamson, O.E. (1975) *Markets and Hierarchies: Analysis and Antitrust Implications*. New York: Free Press.

Williamson, O.E. (1981) "The modern corporation: origins, evolution, attributes." *Journal of Economic Literature* 19:1537–1568.

Williamson, O.E. (1983) "Credible commitments: using hostages to support exchange." *American Economic Review* 73:519–540.

Williamson, O.E. (1985a) *The Economic Institutions of Capitalism*. New York: Free Press.

Williamson, O.E. (1985b) "Employee ownership and internal governance: a perspective." *Journal of Economic Behavior and Organization* 6:243–245.

Williamson, O.E. (1991a) "Economic institutions: spontaneous and intentional governance." *Journal of Law, Economics, and Organization* 7: 159–187.

Williamson, O.E. (1991b) "Comparative economic organization: the analysis of discrete structural alternatives." *Administrative Science Quarterly* 36:269–296.

Williamson, O.E. (1992) "Markets, hierarchies, and the modern corporation: an unfolding perspective." *Journal of Economic Behavior and Organization* 17:335–352.

Williamson, O.E. (1994) "Visible and invisible governance." *American Economic Association Papers and Proceedings*, 323–326.

Winter, S.G. (1988) "On Coase, competence, and the corporation." *Journal of Law, Economics, and Organization* 4:163–180.

Winter, S.G. (1995) "Four Rs of profitability: rents, resources, routines and replication," in C.A. Montgomery (ed.), *Resource-Based and Evolutionary Theories of the Firm*, pp. 147–178. Boston: Kluwer.

Zajac, E.J. and Olsen, C.P. (1993) "From transaction cost to transactional value analysis: implications for the study of interorganizational strategies." *Journal of Management Studies* 30:131–145.

8

The Knowledge-Based View of the Firm

Robert M. Grant

During the early part of the 1990s, a number of ideas and streams of research converged to produce what has come to be described as "the knowledge-based view of the firm." These streams include the resource/capability analysis of the firm (Barney 1986, 1991, Prahalad and Hamel 1990, Grant 1991), epistemology (including contributions from Polanyi 1962, 1966, Hayek 1945, Krogh et al. 1994), and organizational learning (Levitt and March 1988, Huber 1991). The outcome was not so much a new theory of the firm as a number of explorations into aspects of the firm and the organization of production that were unified by their focus on the role of knowledge as a factor of production. Among the key contributions to this literature have been Demsetz's (1991) knowledge-based analysis of firm boundaries, Brown and Duguid's (1991) examination of knowledge-based organization, Kogut and Zander's (1992) view of the firm as a knowledge-processing institution, and Nonaka's (1994) analysis of knowledge creation within the firm. In an earlier essay I attempted to reconcile and integrate some of these contributions (Grant 1996a).

Since then, we have experienced a flood of publication in knowledge management, organizational learning, and the knowledge-based approaches to the firm. A major part of this literature has comprised practical guides to knowledge management, advising managers as to how companies can create, store, transfer, and deploy knowledge in order to increase business effectiveness. At the same time, there is a growing academic literature that has analyzed the role of knowledge in different aspects of the firm—new product development, interfirm collaboration, best practice transfer, and organizational design, to name but a few—as well as exploring more fundamental questions about the role of knowledge in determining the existence and boundaries of the firm. In this chapter, I focus on the more academically orientated stream of literature in an attempt to draw together some of the emerging themes. My goal is to consider whether there is any such thing as a "knowledge-based view of the firm" and, if so, what it is and what use we can derive from it. I begin by considering the context. Is interest in knowledge-based approaches to the firm the result of the evolution of ideas, or is it the result of a fundamental transformation in the nature of the economy where the old theories no longer apply?

Background: Is There a "New Knowledge Economy"?

Interest in a knowledge-based approach to the theory of the firm has been closely linked to the recognition of the fundamental economic changes resulting from the acceleration in the accumulation and availability of knowledge during the past two decades. The emerging knowledge-based, postindustrial economy widely referred to as the "new economy" exhibits several characteristics. In terms of factors of production, the role of knowledge in today's economy corresponds to that of land in the preindustrial, agrarian economy and that of capital in the industrial economy of the nineteenth and early twentieth centuries (Quinn 1992, Drucker 1993, Burton-Jones 2000). Second, it is focused on intangibles rather than tangibles (Stewart 1997, Edvinsson and Malone 1997). In terms of output this means a predominance of services over goods. In terms of inputs it means that the primary assets of firms are intangibles such as technology and brands rather than physical and financial assets. This is reflected in firms' valuation ratios: on May 31, 2000, the ratio of market value to book value of the world's five most valuable companies (GE, Intel, Cisco, Microsoft, and Exxon Mobil) was 14.8 (*Business Week* 2000, p. 67). Third, it is networked: unprecedented interconnectivity has resulted from new communication media. Fourth, it is increasingly digital. Digitization of information has had a huge impact on the capacity for transferring, storing, and processing information. Fifth, it is virtual. The virtual organization is just one example of the transition from real to virtual work made possible by digitization and networking (Hagel and Armstrong 1997). The growing role of virtual (i.e., electronic) money, virtual transactions, virtual communities, and virtual vacations is dissolving the boundaries between the real and imaginary worlds to the point where futurists Jim Taylor and Watts Wacker (1998) claim that we are entering an age where anything we can dream we can do. Finally, the new economy is subject to rapid change. The rapid pace of innovation and the speed of diffusion has accelerated the pace of technological change and compressed the life cycles of products and technologies, helping to create what Davis and Meyer (1998) call the "blur" economy.

The outcomes of these trends are a number of structural changes within the business sectors of the advanced industrialized nations. Particularly gratifying to both central bankers and ordinary citizens has been the upturn in labor productivity since 1996. The startling rise in U.S. productivity represents a reversal in the declining trend of labor productivity since the mid-1960s. Although, as Paul Romer (1998) reminds us, looking much longer term, the rate of labor productivity is not just a recent phenomenon; it is a general feature of the "soft revolution" of the last century. At the sectoral level, the acceleration of technological change is redrawing the boundaries of industries. The convergence of computing and communication, the impact of new materials, and the circumvention of traditional channels of distribution ("disintermediation") are all aspects of the convergence of some industries and the redefinition of others. Finally, the new knowledge economy has seen an unprecedented increase in globalization. The Internet and other media for global communication and information transfer reinforce Peter Drucker's dictum that "knowledge knows no boundaries."

How far these changes go toward amounting to the emergence of a new model of business activity is debatable. The evidence of human development over the past five millennia suggests that knowledge has been the basis of cultural and economic advances since mankind first graduated from a primitive hunter-gatherer society. Similarly, it is difficult to argue that today's software engineer, Web designer, or management consultant is any more a knowledge worker than was Stradevario, Rembrandt, or Brunel. Different workers use different types of knowledge, and it is difficult to compare the knowledge intensity of different occupations.

My own conclusion is that, despite the increasing importance of knowledge within the economy and the far-reaching changes caused by the digital revolution, the recent surge of interest in knowledge and its management is not primarily the result of external changes in the business environment. More important, in my opinion, has been the burst of intellectual activity that has accompanied the recognition of knowledge as a productive resource, the rediscovery of the discussion of knowledge by writers such as Hayek (1945), Polanyi (1962), Arrow (1962), and March and Simon (1958), and the wave of new thinking concerning the characteristics of knowledge and its role within the firm. Thus, most of the developments in the concepts and techniques of knowledge management and the knowledge-based view of the firm that appeared during the 1990s were not specific to the present digitally based, postindustrial economy. Indeed, some of the powerful tools of knowledge management that have recently emerged are concerned not with the flows of information and codified knowledge that have characterized the information revolution of recent decades, but with the oldest form of knowledge known to society: tacit knowledge. My argument is that recent developments in knowledge management and knowledge-based approaches to the firm do not represent new principles for a new era. Rather, they represent the recognition of aspects of the firm and its management that are valid in any era. Hence, the main contribution of this surge of interest in the economics and management of knowledge has been in shedding light on the fundamental issues of the business enterprise that have long been central to strategy, organization, and human resource management. What knowledge management and the knowledge-based view of the firm offer us is insight into aspects of the firm and its management that we have failed to understand properly because of our failure to consider the nature and characteristics of knowledge.

Previously (Grant 2000) I offered two examples of how recognition of the characteristics and role of knowledge can offer insight into management and provide a bridge between different theories of management. Two of the most important contributions to management practice during the last century were scientific management and total quality management (TQM). Although these two approaches shared a common basis of applying a rigorous, scientific methodology to the analysis of management problems, their implications for decision making and the role of managers were very different. These differences between the two can be traced to their different assumptions concerning the characteristics of knowledge within the firm.

In Frederick Taylor's (1916) "scientific management," the basic division of labor is between workers, who undertake operational tasks, and managers, who—because of their superior intelligence and knowledge of management principles—make decisions. Through analyzing and redesigning employees' tasks and working methods in line with scientific principles, Taylor demonstrated that his methods could achieve remarkable increases in productivity. However, a critical assumption of the approach is that managers can access the knowledge held by workers. This implicit assumption that managers have ready access to the knowledge of their subordinates is a central weakness, not just of scientific management but also of hierarchical models of decision making more generally. If managers have limited access to the knowledge held by subordinates, decision making becomes severely impaired and the logic of hierarchical, authority-based structures begins to unravel.

The interesting feature of TQM is that, though also based on scientific principles, its management implications are quite different from those of scientific management. Though founded on statistical analysis and cause and effect relationships, it makes very different assumptions about the distribution and characteristics of knowledge: TQM recognizes that knowledge is not easily transferable. Given that good decisions require the application of the knowledge relevant to those decisions, TQM favors the transfer of decision making concerning each employee's production tasks to the employees who are undertaking the tasks. Hence, the emphasis in TQM is not to pass operational decision making up to specialized decision makers called managers, but to develop the decision-making capacities of those undertaking the operations work. This outcome also rests upon a second implicit assumption about knowledge that is inherent in TQM: that human beings are intelligent and capable of learning. Hence, the continuous training of workers in statistical process control and problem solving is a central feature of TQM.

My point is this: the rekindling of interest in the role of knowledge within the firm has certainly been stimulated by the accelerating rate of technical change—particularly in information and communications technologies. However, this is not the primary force driving interest in knowledge management and the knowledge-based view of the firm. What my discussion of scientific management and TQM reveals is that, once we take account even of quite elementary aspects of the nature of knowledge (such as the ease with which it can be communicated from one person to another), then we gain substantial insight into the theories and principles of organization and management. Thus, the real contribution of knowledge-based approaches to management and the firm is not so much in offering a new theory that can revolutionize our thinking about the existence and management of companies; it is more in providing a perspective that can augment and extend, possibly even transform, existing theory and management techniques.

Fundamentals of the Knowledge-Based View of the Firm

The emerging knowledge-based view of the firm is not a theory of the firm in any formal sense. It is more a set of ideas about the existence and nature of the firm that emphasize the role of knowledge. At its foundation are a number of assumptions and observations concerning the nature of knowledge and its part in production:

1. Knowledge is the overwhelmingly important productive resource in terms of market value and the primary source of Ricardian rents (Machlup 1980, Grant, 1996a).
2. Different types of knowledge vary in their transferability. Explicit knowledge can be articulated and easily communicated between individuals and organizations. Tacit knowledge (skills, know-how, and contextual knowledge) is manifest only in its application—transferring it from one individual to another is costly and slow (Nonaka 1994, Kogut and Zander 1992).
3. Knowledge is subject to economies of scale and scope. A characteristic of all knowledge is that its initial creation is more costly than its subsequent replication. As I have already argued, economies of scale in knowledge together with the complementarity of different types of knowledge imply increasing returns in knowledge-intensive industries—a fundamental feature of the "new economy" (Arthur 1994). To the extent that knowledge is not specific to the production of a specific good, economies of scale translate into economies of scope. The extent of economies of scale and scope vary considerably among different types of knowledge. They are especially great for explicit knowledge, information in particular, which is "costly to produce, but cheap to reproduce" (Shapiro and Varian 1999, p. 3). Tacit knowledge tends to be costly to replicate, but these costs are lower than those incurred in its original creation (Winter 1995).
4. Knowledge is created by human beings, and to be efficient in knowledge creation and storage, individuals need to specialize (Simon 1991, p. 127).
5. Producing a good or service typically requires the application of many types of knowledge (Kogut and Zander 1992).

An important implication of these assumptions is the dichotomy between two types of knowledge-based activity in the economy. There are those activities that are concerned with increasing the stock of knowledge—what March (1991) refers to as "exploration" and Spender (1992) calls "knowledge generation"—and those activities concerned with deploying knowledge in order to produce goods and services—what March (1991) refers to as "exploitation" and Spender (1992) calls "knowledge application." Reconciling the dichotomy between knowledge creating and knowledge applying activities represents a key challenge for economic organization: knowledge creation requires specialization (items 3 and 4 above), while knowledge application requires diversity of knowledge (item 5). Given the limited transferability of knowledge (item 2), this presents considerable difficulty for the institutions of production. The solution lies in some process of knowledge integration that permits individuals to apply their specialized knowledge to the production of goods and services while preserving the efficiencies of specialization in knowledge acquisition (Demsetz 1991).

Knowledge and Economic Organization: Coordination in the Firm

The problem of economic organization may be viewed in terms of this challenge of reconciling efficiency in knowledge creation with efficiency in knowledge deployment. In order to create and store knowledge, individuals must specialize. This is a feature not just of today's sophisticated, knowledge-based society, but also of Adam Smith's pin workshop (Smith 1776). For more complex products, for example, a jet engine or a feature-length movie, production is likely to require the combined efforts of many thousands of different specialists. Specialization increases the efficiency of knowledge creation and storage, but it also creates the need for integration once knowledge is applied to production. Integrating a wide range of different knowledge bases represents an immense organizational task.

These problems of organizing fall into two categories: the problems of *cooperation* and the problems of *coordination*. The cooperation problem results from the fact that different organizational members have different goals. The coordination problem is the technical problem of how to integrate the separate efforts of multiple individuals. Most organizational analysis has focused upon the problem of cooperation. This is true of both the analysis of alternative institutions and the analysis of organizational structure. The analysis of the relative efficiency of alternative institutions has been dominated by transaction cost economics, in particular, the costs arising from the opportunistic behavior by the parties to a contract. The analysis of organizational structure, too, has been dominated by issues of control, goal alignment, and incentives. This is true of traditional organizational theory, which has been primarily concerned with issues of hierarchical control. It is also evident in organizational economics, which has focused upon misalignment of goals, especially between principals and agents.

The potential for a knowledge-based perspective to further our analysis of organization is primarily in relation to the problem of coordination. Even if we abstract from problems of goal conflict among individuals and groups, the problem of organizing is far from trivial. The members of a parent-teacher association may be united in their desire to put on an event to raise funds for the school, but in the absence of coordination, the fund raiser will not happen. Focusing on knowledge as the critical resource in the production of all goods and services helps us clarify the central issues of coordination. The challenge of coordination is to devise mechanisms through which the knowledge resources of many different individuals can be deployed in the production of a particular product. For such deployment mechanisms to be efficient, they must preserve the efficiencies of specialization in knowledge creation. Hence, any system of production that requires each individual to learn what every other individual knows is inherently inefficient. As Demsetz (1991) notes, "Although knowledge can be learned more effectively in specialized fashion, its use to achieve high living standards requires that a specialist somehow uses the knowledge of other specialists. This cannot be done only by learning what others know, for that would undermine gains from specialized learning" (p. 172).

However, until recently, the primary driving force behind the development of a knowledge-based approach to the existence of firms has been based less upon the need to understand internal coordination within the firm as upon the quest for a theory of the firm that is independent of the tenets of transaction cost economics (TCE). The desire for an alternative to TCE is a consequence of distaste for the behavioral assumptions that underpin the theory—notably, the presupposition that people behave opportunistically (Ghoshal and Moran 1996, Williamson 1996)—as well as dissatisfaction with the theoretical basis of TCE (Zajac and Olsen 1994, Demsetz 1995) and empirical evidence that contradicts some of the predictions of TCE (Holmstrom and Roberts 1998).

Demsetz's (1991) contribution to developing a knowledge-based view of the firm was in developing a theory of firms' vertical boundaries based on the observation that markets are efficient only where knowledge can be embodied in products, such that the use of the product by the purchaser is not dependent upon accessing the knowledge necessary for producing the product. Kogut and Zander (1992) took this idea further, arguing that coordination is fundamentally different within the firm than between individuals transacting across markets. They argued that the nature of economic activity that occurs within the firm is fundamentally different from that which occurs in the market. Kogut and Zander (1992) stated that "organizations are social communities in which individual and social expertise is transferred into economically useful products and services by the application of a set of higher order organizing principles. Firms exist because they provide a social community of voluntaristic action structured by organizing principles that are not reducible to individuals" (p. 384). In later work, Kogut and Zander (1996) are more explicit about the identity and operation of these "higher organizing principles," emphasizing the role of social identity as a basis for coordination. Ghoshal and Moran (1996) also identify the firms' capacity to undertake different types of activity than those undertaken by markets, pointing to firms' ability to achieve dynamic efficiency and innovation through "purposeful adaptation."

Despite a lively debate over the relative merits of TCE and knowledge-based approaches to the existence of the firm (e.g., Foss 1996, Conner and Prahalad 1996), no obvious reconciliation of the different approaches has been reached. While the promoters of knowledge-based approaches point to the versatility of the firm in coordinating production activities, the advocates of TCE point to the critical role of transaction costs: in the absence of these costs, firms can replicate any kind of coordination that is possible within the firm. Foss argues that the knowledge-based theorists "commit the fallacy of technological determinism when they argue that the need for shared codes, languages, etc. . . . necessitates firm organization in a way that can be seen in isolation from considerations of opportunism/moral hazard" (Foss 1996, p. 473). Although the gains from "higher order organizing principles" may be necessary to explain the existence of the firm, they are not sufficient. According to Foss, "Agents (human resources) could simply meet under the same factory roof, own their own capital equipment or rent it to each other, and develop value-enhancing higher-order organizing principles among themselves (as a team)" (p. 474). Illustrating this point, Milgrom and Roberts (1992, p. 198) quote the case of the nineteenth-century English traveler in China who, shocked at the ferocity with which the overseer whipped the oarsmen of a passenger ferry, was informed that the oarsmen hired the overseer in order to prevent slacking by individual oarsmen.

My own reading of the literature pushes me toward the view that the knowledge-based and TCE theories of the firm are complementary rather than competitive. Knowledge-based approaches depend heavily on the failure of markets for information and other types of knowledge (Arrow 1962). At the same time, TCE tells us a lot about market transactions but has little to say about the administrative processes within the firm. According to TCE, firms exist primarily to avoid the costs associated with market transactions. But this offers little insight into what firms actually do, or the nature of the economic activities that give rise to transactions in the first place. The key contribution of the knowledge-based approach is in offering understanding of the process in which knowledge inputs are converted into goods and services and the role of the firm in this process.

Mechanisms for Knowledge Integration

One of the reasons that some economists and management theorists have been dissatisfied with knowledge-based approaches to the firm is that a number of writers on knowledge and the firm (e.g., Kogut and Zander 1992, Nonaka 1994, Spender 1995) base much of their analysis on the concept of "organizational knowledge." Once we view organizations as knowing entities, then it is difficult to discern the mechanisms through which individuals link together their separate skills and knowledge bases to create this collective knowledge. An alternative approach that is consistent with Simon's dictum that "all knowledge resides in human heads" is to dispense with the notion of organizational knowledge and to regard all collective knowledge as the result of aggregating and integrating individuals' knowledge.

Earlier (Grant 1996a) I suggested some of the mechanisms through which firms (and other or-

ganizations) might achieve the integration of individuals' knowledge into the production of goods and services. As I have already argued, the key to efficiency in knowledge integration is to create mechanisms that reconcile the efficiency in knowledge creation (which requires specialization) with efficiency in knowledge deployment (which requires integrating many types of knowledge). Drawing upon the existing literature, I proposed four mechanisms for knowledge integration:

1. *Rules and directives.* "Impersonal" approaches to coordination involve "plans, schedules, forecasts, rules, policies and procedures, and standardized information and communication systems" (Van de Ven et al. 1976, p. 323). Rules may be viewed as standards that regulate the interactions among individuals. Thus, in society at large, rules in the form of etiquette, politeness, and social norms are essential to facilitating human interaction. The efficiency of these mechanisms in achieving coordination extends beyond their ability to minimize communication (Galbraith 1973). As recognized by Demsetz (1991), *direction* is a "low-cost method of communicating between specialists and the large number of persons who either are nonspecialists or who are specialists in other fields" (p. 172). Such rules and directives provide a means by which tacit knowledge can be converted into readily comprehensible explicit knowledge. Thus, it is highly inefficient for a quality engineer to teach every production worker all that he knows about quality control. A more efficient means of integrating his knowledge into the production process is for him to establish a set of procedures and rules for quality control.

2. *Sequencing.* Probably the simplest means by which individuals can integrate their specialist knowledge while minimizing communication and continuous coordination is to organize production activities in a time-patterned sequence such that each specialist's input occurs independently through being assigned a separate time slot. Thompson (1967) viewed sequential interdependence as technologically determined. Certainly, the characteristics of the product, its physical inputs, and its production technology strongly influence the potential for sequencing: a product composed of multiple components facilitates sequencing much more than a commodity produced by continuous processes. However, in most production activities there is discretion over the extent of sequencing. For example, new product design can be fully sequen-

tial, overlapping sequences, or concurrent (Nonaka 1990, Clark and Fujimoto 1991).

3. *Routines*. An organizational routine is a "relatively complex pattern of behavior . . . triggered by a relatively small number of initiating signals or choices and functioning as recognizable unit in a relatively automatic fashion" (Winter 1987, p. 165). While a routine may be a simple sequence, their interesting feature is their ability to support complex patterns of interactions between individuals in the absence of rules, directives, or even significant verbal communication. There are two main dimensions to this complexity. First, routines are capable of supporting a high level of simultaneity of individuals' performance of their particular tasks, for example, navigation of a ship (Hutchins 1991), surgical operating teams and pit crews in auto racing (Grant 1996b), and the operations of fast food restaurants (Leidner 1993). Second, routines can permit highly varied sequences of interaction. While Nelson and Winter (1982) and Gersick and Hackman (1990) have emphasized the automatic nature of routines, Pentland and Rueter (1994) have shown that a routine can be a varied repertoire of responses in which individuals' moves are patterned as "grammars of action."

4. *Group problem solving and decision making*. While all the above mechanisms seek efficiency of integration through avoiding the costs of communication and learning, some tasks may require more personal and communication-intensive forms of integration. Galbraith (1973) points to the need for "impersonal" coordination through rules and plans to be supplemented by "personal" and "group" coordination modes, the last taking the form of meetings. Reliance upon high-interaction, nonstandardized coordination mechanisms increases with task complexity (Perrow 1967) and task uncertainty (Galbraith 1973, Van de Ven et al. 1976). Hutchins (1991) documents the switch from routine-mode to group-problem-solving mode in a crisis. The main contribution of the knowledge-based view to this discussion is recognition of the limits and high costs of consensus decision making given the difficulties associated with the communication of tacit knowledge.

The Role of Common Knowledge

While these mechanisms for knowledge integration are necessitated by the differentiation of individual's stocks of knowledge, all depend upon the existence of some measure of *common knowledge* for their operation. At its most simple, common knowledge comprises those elements of knowledge common to all organizational members—the intersection of their individual knowledge sets. The importance of common knowledge is that it permits individuals to share and integrate aspects of knowledge that are *not* common among them. There are different types of common knowledge, each of which is likely to fulfill a different role in permitting knowledge integration.

Language. The existence of a common language is fundamental to integration mechanisms that rely on verbal communication among individuals, namely, integration through rules and directives, and integration through group problem solving and decision making. The lack of a common language among production workers in the United States and other polyglot communities represents a considerable barrier to the introduction of integration-intensive manufacturing techniques such as TQM.

Other forms of symbolic communication. The ability of organizational members to speak the same tongue is but one aspect of commonality of language. If language is defined to embody all forms of symbolic communication, then literacy, numeracy, and familiarity with the same computer software are all aspects of common language that enhance the efficiency and intensity of communication. The experiences of companies such as Motorola, Texas Instruments, and Toyota confirm that the higher the level of common knowledge in the form of literacy, numeracy, and basic statistics (e.g., the ability to interpret Pareto charts), the more effective are rules, procedures, and directives in implementing sophisticated levels of TQM.

Commonality of specialized knowledge. While language is the core aspect of common knowledge that provides a platform for communication-based modes of knowledge, the level of sophistication that communication-based modes of knowledge integration achieve depends on the extent of commonality in their specialized knowledge. There is something of a paradox in this. The benefit of knowledge integration is in meshing the specialized knowledge of different individuals—if two people have identical knowledge, there is no gain from integration—yet if the individuals have entirely separate knowledge bases, then integration cannot occur beyond the most primitive level.

Shared meaning. The problem of communication-based modes of knowledge integration is that they require the conversion of tacit knowledge into explicit form. Such conversion typically captures only a portion of the tacit knowledge. However, tacit knowledge can be communicated through the establishment of shared understanding between individuals. Polanyi (1966) notes that "a teaching which appears meaningless to start with has in fact a meaning which can be discovered by hitting on *the same kind of indwelling* as the teacher is practicing" (p. 61, emphasis added). The organizational learning literature points to the role of common cognitive schemata and frameworks (Weick 1979, Spender 1987), metaphor and analogy (Nonaka and Takeuchi 1995), and stories (Brown and Duguid 1991) as vehicles for molding, integrating, and reconciling different individual experiences and understandings. The underlying theory of the mutual cognitions necessary for coordination in social actions has been developed within social psychology (Leudar 1992).

Recognition of individual knowledge domains. Common cognition is only one element in the development of shared understanding among individuals that is critical to integrating their tacit knowledge. Another is the requirement that each individual be aware of the repertoire of know-how and stock of explicit knowledge possessed by the other individuals. In any situation of reciprocal or group interdependence, a soccer team or a debating team, the integration requires *coordination by mutual adjustment* (Thompson 1967, p. 56). Achieving this without explicit communication requires that each team member recognize the tasks and actions that the other can perform exceptionally well. Such mutual recognition permits successful coordination even in novel situations where routines have not been established.

The Efficiency of Firms, Alliances, and Markets in Deploying Knowledge

The case for the existence of the firm as a unit of economic organization rests on the superiority of the firm over markets in supporting these knowledge integration mechanisms. To achieve coordination through these different mechanisms of integration requires authority (to permit direction), centralized decision making, colocation, and common knowledge (to permit communication). All these conditions are provided more readily within firm than in any other type of organization.

By contrast, market contracts suffer from the familiar sources of transaction cost that afflict exchange transactions in knowledge. Information and other forms of explicit knowledge suffer problems of nonexclusivity of use and the difficulty of concluding contracts without first revealing the knowledge involved (Arrow 1962). Tacit knowledge is also problematic because, in order to mesh their areas of know-how, transacting parties are likely to require a "common language or . . . overlaps in cognitive frameworks. . . . This requires time and effort: investments which are to some extent . . . transaction specific . . . [hence] yield issues of dependence and lock-in" (Nooteboom 1996, p. 331). Within the firm, these problems are ameliorated by a social context characterized by a common identity of organizational members (Kogut and Zander 1996) and the ability of the firm to appropriate knowledge rents through secrecy (Liebeskind 1996). In addition, markets are less able than firms to support either direction or routine. While routines develop within markets, market-based routines are often less adaptable and less effective in integrating the individuals' specialist knowledge than are those within a single firm.

Alliances can avoid many of the costs associated with knowledge transactions across markets. Alliances limit opportunism by converting single-period into multiperiod games and fostering investments in trust (Ring and Van de Ven 1992, Teece 1992, Gulati 1995, Simonin 1997). Yet inevitably, alliances are inferior to firms in terms of their ability to integrate knowledge through "higher order organizing principles." They typically lack the authority-based relationships needed for rules and directives, and although many alliances are very long-lasting, most lack the close, continuous association conducive to developing routines.

Are there any circumstances where alliances can be superior to firms in knowledge integration? The key problem for knowledge integration within the firm is that, whether integration is by direction or routine, the efficiency of integration tends to decline as the firm's knowledge domain expands. As with any complex system, large-scale knowledge integration requires hierarchy (Simon 1962), with loose coupling of components and subsystems (Weick 1976, Sanchez and Mahoney 1996). The efficiency of directives and rules as integrating devices depends on the extent to which they can be standardized (March and Simon 1958, Thompson 1967). Similarly with organizational routines: to the extent that they are embedded within organizational values and norms, the common culture of an organization limits the variety of routines that can be efficiently performed. Thus, as the range and diversity of knowledge increases, so integration mechanisms need to be increasingly differentiated, resulting in rising marginal costs of knowledge integration within the firm.

In these circumstances, efficiency of integration may be maximized through separate firms integrating knowledge at the component or subsystem level, with overall integration through an alliance among the firms. Thus, the rapid growth in strategic alliances within biotechnology reflects the advantages of alliances between dedicated biotechnology companies and large, integrated pharmaceutical companies, as compared to mergers and acquisitions. Any benefits of full merger in terms of closer integration are likely to be offset by the difficulty of reconciling the different routines and operating rules required in the pharmaceutical business from those required for leading-edge biotechnology research (Barley et al. 1996, Powell 1998). Similarly in semiconductors: although firms are more effective than alliances in sharing and developing knowledge (Almeida et al. 1998), as the range of knowledge required for the design and manufacture of semiconductors continues to expand, so alliances have proliferated, both between semiconductor design companies and between designers and fabricators (Macher 2000). Within alliance networks, however, one firm tends to act as overall system integrator (Lorenzoni and Baden-Fuller 1994). Such a role requires some duplication of knowledge between firms since, in order to efficiently integrate across multiple areas of knowledge, the integrating firm must continue to maintain some knowledge base in each knowledge area. As Prencipe (1997) has shown, the role of aircraft engine manufacturers as "systems integrators" for many hundreds of suppliers of components and subsystems requires that they maintain a residual level of research and development (R&D) in the component technologies that they are responsible for integrating.

In addition, alliances also allow fuller utilization of firms' knowledge resources. Grant and Baden-Fuller (1995) point to the problems firms face in achieving an efficient match between their knowledge domain and their product domain. This issue becomes critical because, if limits to firm growth within individual markets constrain a firm's ability to fully exploit scale economies in specific types of knowledge, then economies of scope emerge as crucially important to achieving efficient utilization of knowledge. However, different types of knowledge have different product domains, which raises the problem of *fit* between the firm's knowledge domain and its product domain. If much of the firm's knowledge is not product specific and is subject to economies of scope, excess capacity in knowledge encourages the firm to expand its product scope (Penrose 1957). Efficient utilization of knowledge is achieved where the knowledge domain of the firm matches exactly the knowledge requirements of the product domain of the firm, with no overlap and, thus, no underutilization of knowledge. The problem, however, is that different types of knowledge are applicable to different sets of products. Through importing certain knowledge requirements from other firms, and exporting to other firms knowledge available in excess within the firm, the efficiency of knowledge utilization is increased. Because of the familiar sources of transaction costs in market contracts for knowledge, such arrangements are best achieved through strategic alliances. Thus, alliances tend to be more frequent in sectors where knowledge requirements are broad, where knowledge tends not to be product specific, and where economies of scope in knowledge are substantial, such as aerospace, automobiles, and consumer electronics, than in sectors where knowledge is more product specific, such as iron and steel, metal fasteners, and textiles. The tendency for alliances to increase over time reflects the broadening knowledge requirements of most goods and services and the breadth of application of newer technologies such as microelectronics, materials sciences, imaging, microengineering, and digital communication.

One implication of a knowledge-based perspective on economic organization is that, by concentrating upon the need for knowledge integration in production, it shifts the focus of attention away from institutions per se and more toward the mechanisms through which coordination is achieved and the appropriate contexts for these mechanisms. Given the difficulties economists have experienced even in agreeing upon a definition of the firm, this may well be a useful step. It is notable that Demsetz (1995) has chosen to avoid the term "firm" altogether: he refers to "firmlike institutions." If economists cannot agree on what the firm is, there is little hope of consensus between economists, sociologists, and lawyers. However, if the goal of organizational analysis is to predict the most efficient structures and systems for organizing production, a knowledge-based perspective suggests that the primary consideration is not so much the institution for governing transactions (markets vs. firms) as the mechanisms through which knowledge integration is achieved. Thus, if the main mechanisms for integrating the knowledge required for production are rules and organizational routines, we can identify the conditions needed to support these mechanisms. We can then go on to make general hypotheses about the efficiency of particular institutions in supporting these mechanisms (e.g., firms tend to outperform both markets and alliances because they permit relationships of authority among individuals and groups and because they provide stability of relationships conducive to developing organizational routines. However, such analysis can also permit finer grained analysis of why, in certain circumstances, collaborative relationships between separate firms can achieve superior knowledge integration than that achieved in single corporations. Thus, the MIT automobile study observed:

> The make-or-buy decision that occasioned so much debate in mass production firms struck Ohno and others at Toyota as largely irrelevant as they began to consider obtaining components for cars and trucks. The real question was how the assembler and the supplier could work together smoothly to reduce costs and improve quality, whatever formal, legal relationship they might have. (Womack et al. 1990)

Focusing on coordination mechanisms, rather than economic institutions, may permit a broader view for the institutions through which productive activity takes place. Thus, Brown and Duguid (1991) identify "communities of practice" within which knowledge is shared and problems solved. These loose-knit informal institutions created through common interests and shared experiences are likely to overlap formal organizational boundaries, yet they may be much more effective in integrating and transferring knowledge than the more formalized processes of the firm.

Implications for Firm Structure and Design

Some of the most potentially interesting applications of knowledge-based approaches to the theory of the firm lie in the area of organizational design. As has been recognized by many commentators, our understanding of the determinants of organizational structure and principles of organization design are underdeveloped, and a widening gap appears to be opening between the evolution of organizational structures in the real world and our ability to explain, let alone predict, these developments.

Let us consider two areas in which the knowledge-based view of the firm has influenced our thinking about organizational structure: The design of hierarchical structures and the distribution of decision making in the organization.

Designing Hierarchical Structures: Authority and Modularity

Hierarchy is a solution to the problems of both cooperation and coordination. However, the analysis of hierarchy in organizational theory has not drawn a clear distinction between the two. The focus has been to emphasize issues of cooperation. Thus, conventional models of hierarchy envisage a pyramid of individuals (or "offices") arranged in vertical authority-based relationships to one another. Progress in the analysis of organizational structure requires a separation of the issues of coordination and goals alignment. While principal-agent theory addresses the issues of aligning different goals, information science and general systems theory have explored the pure coordination aspects of organizing. Hierarchy is as fundamental to system-based approaches to the analysis of organizations as it is to the theory of bureaucracy. However, its rationale is quite different. Hierarchy is a feature of all complex systems to the extent that all complex systems (whether biological, mechanical, or social) can be decomposed into subsystems. The primary rationale for hierarchy in complex systems is that it promotes adaptation (Simon 1962).

This approach is useful in deriving principles for grouping activities and people within complex organizations and designing the relationships between the different groups. If hierarchy within a classical organization theory is defined in terms of delegation of authority, hierarchy within a systems perspective is defined by *mod-*

ularity. Activities and processes where coordination needs are most intense are organized into modules. This idea of hierarchies organized around intensity of interaction is fundamental to Simon's concept of the "nearly decomposable" systems (Simon 1981) and Williamson's "vertical decomposition principle" (Williamson 1975). The analysis of coordination and the articulation of the principles of organizing on the basis of intensity of coordination needs were articulated by Thompson (1967). Thompson classified interactions from the loosest ("pooled" interdependence), through intermediate ("sequential" interdependence), to the most intense ("reciprocal" interdependence) and argued for the design of hierarchies based, first, on identifying those tasks and activities characterized by reciprocal interdependence, then forming hierarchies around the successive levels of interdependence. The analysis of interdependence has been extended by the MIT Center for Coordination Science, which proposes a framework for disaggregating organizational processes and classifying their dependencies in terms of resource usage (Malone et al. 1999).

The performance advantages of the hierarchical structure in terms of pure coordination arise from its potential for adaptability. The critical issue here is the "loose coupling" of modules such that individual modules can innovate and adapt while not having to coordinate continually with all other modules. The concept of loose coupling between organizational units is closely associated with Weick (1976), who argued that, where departments are able to vary independently, this promotes sensitivity to detecting environmental variation, opportunistic adaptation to local circumstances, simultaneous adaptation to conflicting demands, and the maintenance of overall organizational stability while individual departments adapt to outside change.

The best-developed applications of the principles of hierarchical design based on modularity and loose coupling relate to new product development. The problems presented by the need for fast, low-cost development of highly complex products such as automobiles, aircraft, and sophisticated computer software have spawned a number of empirical and theoretical studies of the organization of product development. The basic idea is that product design is based on modules organized as subsystems and components, with standardized interfaces between them, and that the design process is organized in modular form to parallel the modular design of the prod-

uct (Sanchez and Mahoney 1996, Bayliss and Clark 1997). Cusumano's (1997) account of how Microsoft's leadership in operating system and applications software has been supported by a modular approach to software design offers insight into the advantages of modular, hierarchical structures in reconciling complexity, flexibility, and speed. The essential requirement for such modularization is the establishment of interfaces that permit the modules to work together. Key features of Microsoft's "synch and stabilize" approach are imposition of rules that permit flexibility and innovation within teams, but ensure coordination of the project as a whole. Critical aspects of interface management include common development languages, clearly defined goals for each module in terms of features and functions, and daily and weekly builds that occur at fixed times. The advantages of a modular, loosely coupled structure over a tightly integrated structure were apparent in the tortuous evolution of Netscape's Navigator browser. The tightly coupled structure of Netscape's initial version of Navigator and the frequency of "spaghetti code" handicapped Netscape's ability to upgrade and extend the product. The resulting rewriting of Navigator around a modular architecture delayed upgrading the product, allowing Microsoft to gain leadership in the browsers' market (Cusumano and Yoffie 1998).

Modular structures are an efficient response to the problem of knowledge integration. If the greater part of the knowledge used by firms is tacit, then it can be transferred only at high cost. Modularity is a means of achieving integration across a broad range of different knowledge bases while minimizing the costs of knowledge transfer. The essence of the efficiency benefit of modular structures is that each unit is capable of integrating knowledge among the individuals within the unit, while avoiding the need to continuously transfer knowledge between units. The critical issues for organizational design are then the allocation of the activities of the organization into separate modules and definition of interfaces between the modules. The establishment of interfaces is critical. It is the interfaces that provide the basis for knowledge integration between modules.

In the case of products, interface design relates to the physical specification of how one component fits with another. Thus, standardizing the way in which a light bulb fits into a light socket permits light bulb makers and lamp manufacturers to work independently on design and innovation in each product area. Indeed, the success of such an interface in economizing on knowledge transfer between the two is indicated by the fact that light bulb manufacturers and lamp manufacturers are typically separate firms.

Most applications of the principles of modularity to organizational design have concentrated on the organization of new product development. Here the basic principle is that product development is organized around the same modular structure of the product that is being developed: "Microsoft divides projects in a way that mirrors the structure of its products. This helps teams create products with logical efficient designs and results in project organizations with logical, efficient groupings of people" (Cusumano 1997, pp. 16–17). The challenge for the theory of organizational structure is to extend the principles of modularity to the design of organizations in general. The principles upon which modules are to be defined have been articulated fairly clearly. The essential principle is intensity of interdependence. From a knowledge-based perspective, the most intense interdependencies are likely to involve the integration of tacit knowledge in team-based activities that require organizational routines and/or joint problem solving.

Less progress has been made on the design of common interfaces between modules that allows the different modules to work together. Sanchez and Mahoney (1996) argue that "[e]mbedding coordination in fully specified and standardized component interfaces can reduce the need for much overt exercise of managerial authority across the interfaces of organizational units developing components, thereby reducing the intensity and complexity of a firm's managerial task" (p. 73). But what are these "standardized interfaces" between organizational units? For the most part, these interfaces are the standardized control systems through which overall coordination is achieved. In traditional conglomerates, such as ITT or Hanson, the main interface linking the modules was the financial management system. Because each business was deemed to be technologically and strategically independent, the operation of each division as an independent entity with very little interdivisional knowledge integration was highly feasible. Where higher levels of knowledge integration are required among modules, the interfaces need to be more complex and less standardized. Typically, the more closely related the businesses of a corporation, the greater the requirements for knowledge integration and the more complex the integration mechanisms. Thus, the typical multibusiness corporation established formal integration through a financial control system, a strategic planning system, and a human resource planning and appraisal system. In addition, there are ad hoc and informal mechanisms, including company meetings and conferences, systems for best practice transfer, and various "extracurricular" activities.

The Distribution of Decision Making within the Firm

What determines the optimal distribution of decision making within an organization, in particular, the balance between centralization and decentralization? If, as I have already established, the quality of decision making depends critically upon the co-location of decision-making rights with the knowledge relevant to that decision, then we can specify two approaches: decision making can be devolved to where the knowledge resides, or knowledge can be transferred to the desired seat of decision-making authority.

The critical issue here is the mobility of knowledge. This depends upon whether the relevant knowledge can be codified. Where knowledge is fully codifiable (e.g., information on the inventories of different food products held by Safeway Stores), not only can the knowledge be transferred at low cost, but it can also be aggregated at a single location. Given economies of scale in decision making, it is desirable to centralize such decisions. Hence, in most companies, treasury functions, including cash management and foreign exchange hedging, are centralized in a single corporate treasury. Similarly with the purchasing of standardized items by different departments within an organization: these activities, too, are easy to centralize. Conversely, highly tacit knowledge cannot be codified and is extremely difficult to transfer and to aggregate. Hence, where the relevant knowledge is tacit, then decision-making power must be distributed to where the tacit knowledge is located. For example, a financial planner's knowledge of the characteristics, circumstances, and preferences of different customers is the combination of factual knowledge and tacit understanding. It is very difficult to codify and centralize this information. Hence, firms of financial planners tend to devolve most decision making about selling tactics to their individual financial planners.

Recent moves toward "empowerment" have been justified primarily in terms of motivation and philosophies of individualism and self-determination. Our knowledge-based approach provides an efficiency-based argument for empowerment decisions: when knowledge is tacit or, for whatever reason, is not readily codifiable. In such circumstances, decision-making quality (and speed) is enhanced where decision-making authority is delegated to those with the relevant knowledge. However, the trend of the 1990s has not been in one direction. While the dominant trend was toward decentralization, developments in information technology and artificial intelligence have increased the potential for knowledge to be codified. Such developments have encouraged increased centralization of decision making in some areas. For example, centralization trends are apparent within fast food chains, where the information technology has encouraged a shift of decision making over menus, pricing, and production scheduling from individual restaurant managers and franchisees to the corporate and regional headquarters.

However, as Jensen and Meckling (1998) point out, the optimal allocation of decision-making rights is not exclusively about the co-location of knowledge and decisions. There exists a trade-off between benefits of co-locating decision making with knowledge and the costs of agency. As decision making is devolved to those with the know-how relevant to those decisions, so the costs of agency arising from the inconsistent objectives of different organizational members tend to increase. Hence, Jensen and Meckling identify an optimal degree of decentralization where, at the margin, the cost reductions from distributing decision rights to individual employees is equal to the rising agency costs associated with moving decision rights further from the CEO's office.

Conclusion

The above discussion summarizes a few of the areas in which the knowledge-based view of the firm has illuminated the nature of the firm and the theory and practice of organizing. It is notable that, despite the profound philosophical issues concerning the nature of knowledge, some of the most important insights have derived from considering very basic characteristics of knowledge. For example, the distinction between explicit and tacit knowledge has yielded far-reaching implications for the strategy and organizational design.

At the same time, progress in developing a knowledge-focused theory of the firm has been constrained by a failure to clearly define concepts and looseness in specifying the relationship between concepts. In addition, there is a risk that a number of directions taken in the knowledge-based approach to management and organization may turn out to be blind alleys. For instance, the present enthusiasm for organizational learning risks losing sight of the efficiencies in specialization in the creation, acquisition, and storage of knowledge. As Leadbeater (2000) has recognized, the obverse of the knowledge-based society is the pervasiveness of ignorance. As the total stock of knowledge within society increases, so the proportion that lies within the knowledge domain of each individual must diminish. A key issue for companies, as it is for society, is the management of ignorance. How does an entrepreneur setting up an Internet-based florist business deal with the fact that he knows little about the technologies he is using: IP, WAP, agent-based software, or encryption technology? The need to manage ignorance has important implications for the "learning organization." Companies must recognize not only that learning is costly, but also that it is impossible to encompass within the firm all the knowledge that it uses. The interest of companies is not to maximize learning among organizational members, but to clarify what areas of knowledge need to be acquired by each individual and to devise mechanisms that permit effective integration of different individuals' knowledge bases while minimizing cross-learning.

There are also areas where the impact of knowledge-based thinking has yet to make its mark. Knowledge-based approaches offer some hope for filling the widening gap between the evolution of organizational forms in the business sector and the capacity for organizational theory to explain them (Daft and Lewin 1993). For example, consideration of the characteristics and role of knowledge may assist the analysis and design of team-based organizations as manufacturing and service companies increasingly emulate the team-based structure of project-based organizations such as consulting, engineering, and construction firms. Potential contributions of knowledge-based thinking to the design of teams and team-based organizations include, first, principles of modularity discussed above, and second, the role of knowledge integration among team members. If no one outside the team has access to the knowledge within the team or, by extension, to the design of the integration mechanisms within the team, then the implication is that effective knowledge integration within teams is likely to require a significant level of self-management.

Complex management issues also relate to the management of knowledge integration among teams. Even though we may view a modular hierarchy as a hierarchy of knowledge integration, it is also true that teams closer to the apex of knowledge integration cannot easily access the knowledge being integrated by teams closer to the base. Thus, new product development is an activity that must integrate knowledge from nearly all the functions of the firm: R&D, engineering, design, marketing, manufacturing, purchasing, finance, and so on. Yet, simply by having a product development organization formed by the heads of all the individual functions does not necessarily permit effective access to (or integration of) the knowledge available in each function. During the late 1980s and early 1990s, U.S. automobile companies moved away from product development by committees of functional-level heads in favor of semi-autonomous, multifunctional product development teams comprising lower level personnel within each function, each product development team typically led by a "heavyweight" product manager (Clark and Fujimoto 1991).

Key issues also relate to the boundaries of firms. Even though firms may be superior institutions for supporting mechanisms for knowledge integration, increasingly firms are recognizing that the domain of knowledge they can effectively encompass is limited, and they must rely on strategic alliances for acquiring the full range of knowledge resources that are needed within their businesses. However, knowledge-based considerations are also pointing to the effective design of such alliance arrangements. In particular, the need for firms to act as "systems integrators" for knowledge (and components goods and services) supplied by strategic partners means that firms must maintain a minimal level of knowledge in order to perform integration roles.

Within alliance networks, however, one firm tends to act as overall system integrator (Lorenzoni and Baden-Fuller 1994), such a role requires some duplication of knowledge between firms since, in order to efficiently integrate across multiple areas of knowledge, the integrating firm must continue to maintain some knowledge base in each knowledge area. As Prencipe (1997) has shown, the role of aircraft engine manufacturers as "systems integrators" for many hundreds of suppliers of components and subsystems requires that they maintain a residual level of R&D in the component technologies that they are responsible for integrating.

References

Almeida, P., Grant, R.M., and Song, J. (1998) "The role of international corporations in cross-border knowledge transfer in the semiconductor industry," in M.A. Hill, J.E. Ricart, I. Costa & R.D. Nixon (eds.), *Managing Strategically in an Interconnected World*, pp. 119–148. New York: Wiley.

Arrow, K. (1962) "Economic welfare and the allocation of resources for invention," in National Bureau of Economic Research, *The Rate and Direction of Inventive Activity*, pp. 609–625. Princeton, NJ: Princeton University Press.

Arthur, B.W. (1994) *Increasing Returns and Path Dependency in the Economy*. Ann Arbor: University of Michigan Press.

Baldwin, C.Y. and Clark, K.B. (1997) "Managing in an age of modularity." *Harvard Business Review*, September–October, 84–93.

Barley, S.R., Freeman, J., and Hybels, R.C. (1996) "Strategic alliances in commercial biotechnology," in N. Nohria and R.G. Eccles (eds.), *Strategy and Networks*. Boston: Harvard Business School Press. pp. 311–347.

Barney, J.B. (1986) "Strategic factor markets: expectations, luck and business strategy." *Management Science* 32:1232–1241.

Barney, J.B. (1991) "*Firm resources and sustained competitive advantage*." Journal of Management 17:99–120.

Brown, J.S. and Duguid, P. (1991) "Organizational learning and communities-of-practice: toward a unified view of working, learning and innovation." *Organization Science* 2:40–57.

Burton-Jones, A. (2000) *Knowledge Capitalism*. Oxford: Oxford University Press.

Business Week. (2000) "The *Business Week* global 1000." European ed., July 10, 44–85.

Clark, K.B. and Fujimoto, T. (1991) *Product Development Performance*. Boston: Harvard Business School Press.

Conner, K.R. and Prahalad, C.K. (1996) "A resource-based theory of the firm: knowledge versus opportunism." *Organization Science* 7:477–501.

Cusumano, M.A. (1997) "How Microsoft makes large teams work like small teams." *Sloan Management Review*, Fall, 9–20.

Cusumano, M.A. and Yoffie, D.B. (1998) *Competing on Internet Time: Lessons from Netscape and Its Battle with Microsoft*. New York: Free Press.

Daft, R.L. and Lewin, A.Y. (1993) "Where are the theories for the 'new organizational forms'? An editorial essay." *Organization Science* 4:i–vi.

Davis, S. and Meyer, C. (1998) *Blur*. New York: Addison-Wesley.

Demsetz, H. (1991) "The theory of the firm revisited." In *The Nature of the Firm*, pp. 159–178. New York: Oxford University Press.

Demsetz, H. (1995) *The Economics of the Business Firm: Seven Critical Commentaries*. Cambridge: Cambridge University Press.

Drucker, P.F. (1993) *Post-capitalist society*. New York: HarperBusiness.

Edvinsson, L. and Malone, T. (1997) *Intellectual Capital*. New York: HarperBusiness.

Foss, N.J. (1996) "Knowledge-based approaches to the theory of the firm: some critical comments." *Organization Science* 7(5):473.

Galbraith, J. (1973) *Designing Complex Organizations*. Reading, MA: Addison-Wesley.

Gersick, C.J.G. and Hackman, J.R. (1990) "Habitual routines in task-performing groups." *Organizational Behavior and Human Decision Processes* 47:65–97.

Ghoshal, S. and Moran, P. (1996) "Bad for practice: a critique of transaction cost theory." *Academy of Management Review* 21:13–47.

Grant, R.M. (1991) "The resource-based theory of competitive advantage: implications for strategy formulation." *California Management Review* 33(Spring):114–135.

Grant, R.M. (1996a) "Toward a knowledge-based theory of the firm." *Strategic Management Journal* 17:109–122.

Grant, R.M. (1996b) "Prospering in dynamically competitive environments: organizational capability as knowledge integration." *Organization Science* 7:375–387.

Grant, R.M. (2000) "Shifts in the world economy: the drivers of knowledge management," in D. Chauvel and C. Despres, (eds.), *Knowledge Horizons: The Present and the Promise of Knowledge*, pp. 27–53: Butterworth-Heinemann.

Grant, R.M. and Baden-Fuller, C. (1995) "A knowledge-based theory of inter-firm collaboration." *Academy of Management Best Paper Proceedings*, pp. 57–59. Academy of Management.

Gulati, R. (1995) "Does familiarity breed trust? The implications of repeated ties for contractual choice in alliances." *Academy of Management Journal* 38:85–112.

Hagel, J. and Armstrong, A.G. (1997) *Net Gain: Expanding Markets through Virtual Communities*. Boston: Harvard Business School Press.

Hayek, F.A. (1945) "The use of knowledge in society." *American Economic Review* 35:519–532.

Holmstrom, B. and Roberts, J. (1998) "The boundaries of the firm revisited." *Journal of Economic Perspectives* 12(4):81–94.

Huber, G.P. (1991) "Organizational learning: the contributing processes and literatures." *Organization Science* 2:88–115.

Hutchins, E. (1991) "Organizing work by adjustment." *Organization Science* 2:14–39.

Jensen, M.C. and Meckling, W.H. (1998) "Specific and general knowledge and organizational structure," in M.C. Jensen (ed.), *Foundations of Organizational Strategy*, pp. 103–125. Cambridge: Harvard University Press.

Kogut, B. and Zander, U. (1992) "Knowledge of the firm, combinative capabilities, and the replication of technology." *Organization Science* 3:383–397.

Kogut, B. and Zander, U. (1996) "What firms do: coordination, identity, and learning." *Organization Science* 7:502–518.

Leadbeater, C. (2000) *The Weightless Society*. London: Texene.

Leidner, R. (1993) *Fast Food, Fast Talk: Work and Routinization of Everyday Life*. Berkeley: University of California Press.

Leudar, I. (1992) "Sociogenesis, coordination and mutualism." *Journal for the Theory of Social Behavior*, 21:197–220.

Levitt, B. and March, J.G. (1988) "Organizational learning." *Annual Review of Sociology* 14:319–340.

Liebeskind, J. (1996) "Knowledge, strategy, and the theory of the firm." *Strategic Management Journal* 17(Winter):93–108.

Lorenzoni, G. and Baden-Fuller, C. (1994) "Creating a strategic centre to manage a web of partners." *California Management Review* 37(3): 146–163.

Macher, J.T. (2000) "Vertical disintegration and process innovation in semiconductor manufacturing: foundries versus integrated producers." Discussion paper, Haas School of Business, University of California, Berkeley.

Machlup, F.M. (1980) *Knowledge: Its Creation Distribution and Economic Significance*. Princeton, NJ: Princeton University Press.

Malone, T.W., Crowston, K., et al. (1999) "Tools for inventing organizations: toward a handbook of organizational processes." *Management Science* 45(3):559–574.

March, J.G. (1991) "Exploration and exploitation in organizational learning." *Organization Science* 2(1):71–87.

March, J. and Simon, H. (1958) *Organizations*. New York: Wiley.

Milgrom, P. and Roberts, J. (1992) *Economics, organization and management*. Englewood Cliffs, NJ: Prentice-Hall.

Nelson, R. and Winter, S. (1982) *An Evolutionary Theory of Economic Change*. Cambridge, MA: Belknap Press.

Nonaka, I. (1990) "Redundant, overlapping organization: a Japanese approach to managing the innovation process." *California Management Review*, Spring, 27–38.

Nonaka, I. (1994) "A dynamic theory of organizational knowledge creation." *Organization Science* 5:14–37.

Nonaka, I. and Takeuchi, H. (1995) *The Knowledge Creating Company*. New York: Oxford University Press.

Nooteboom, B. (1996) "Transaction costs and technological learning," in J. Groenewegen (ed.), *Transaction Cost Economics and Beyond*, pp. 327–350. Boston: Kluwer.

Penrose, E. (1957) *Theory of the growth of the firm.* Oxford: Blackwell.

Pentland, B.T. and Rueter, H. (1994) "Organizational routines as grammars of action." *Administrative Science Quarterly* 39:484–510.

Perrow, C. (1967) "A framework for the comparative analysis of organizations." *American Sociological Review* 32:194–208.

Polanyi, M. (1962) *Personal Knowledge: Towards a Post-critical Philosophy*. Chicago: University of Chicago Press.

Polanyi, M. (1966) *The Tacit Dimension*. New York: Anchor Day.

Prahalad, C.K. and Hamel, G. (1990) "The core competences of the corporation." *Harvard Business Review*, May–June, 79–91.

Prencipe, A. (1997) "Technical competencies and products' evolutionary dynamics: a case study from the aero engine industry." *Research Policy* 25:1261–1276.

Quinn, J.B. (1992) *Intelligent Enterprise*. New York: Free Press.

Ring, P.S. and Van de Ven, A.H. (1992). "Structuring cooperative relationships between organizations." *Strategic Management Journal* 13:483–498.

Romer, P. (1998) "The soft revolution." *Journal of Applied Corporate Finance*, Summer.

Sanchez, R. and Mahoney, J.T. (1996) "Modularity, flexibility, and knowledge management in product and organisation design." *Strategic Management Journal* 17(Winter):63–76.

Shapiro, C. and Varian, H. (1999) "Information rules." *California Management Review* 4–1(Spring): 8–32.

Simon, H.A. (1962) "The architecture of complexity." *Proceedings of the American Philosophical Society* 106:467–482.

Simon, H.A. (1981) *The Sciences of the Artificial*, 2d ed. Cambridge, MA: MIT Press.

Simon, H.A. (1991) "Bounded rationality and organisational learning." *Organization Science* 2: 125–134.

Simonin, B.L. (1997) "The importance of collaborative know-how: an empirical test of the learning organisation." *Academy of Management Journal* 40:1150–1174.

Smith, A. (1776) *An Inquiry into the Nature and Consequences of the Wealth of Nations.* Reprint, New York: Modern Library Edition, 1937.

Spender, J.-C. (1987) *Industry Recipes*. Oxford: Blackwell.

Spender, J.-C. (1992) "Limits to learning from the West: how Western management advice may prove limited in Eastern Europe." *International Executive* 34(5):389–410.

Spender, J.-C. (1995) "Organizational knowledge, collective practices and Penrose rents." *International Business Review* 3:353–367.

Stewart, T. (1997) *Intellectual Capital: The New Wealth of Organizations*. New York: Doubleday.

Taylor, F.W. (1916) "The principles of scientific management." *Bulletin of the Taylor Society*. Reprinted in J.M. Shafritz and J.S. Ott (eds.), *Classics of Organization Theory*, pp. 66–81. Chicago: Dorsey, 1987.

Taylor, J. and Watts, W. (1998) *The 500 Year Delta: What Happens after What Comes Next.* New York: HarperBusiness.

Teece, D.J. (1992) "Competition, co-operation, and innovation." *Journal of Economic Behaviour and Organization* 18:1–25.

Thompson, J.D. (1967) *Organizations in Action.* New York: McGraw-Hill.

Van de Ven, A.H., Delbecq, A.L., and Koenig, R. (1976) "Determinants of coordination modes within organizations." *American Sociological Review* 41:322–338.

von Krogh, G., Roos, J., and Slocum, K. (1994) "An essay on corporate epistemology." *Strategic Management Journal* 15(Summer):53–71.

Weick, K.E. (1976) "Educational organizations as loosely-coupled systems." *Administrative Science Quarterly*, March 21, 1–19.

Weick, K.E. (1979) "Cognitive processes in organizations." *Research in Organizational Behavior* 1:41–74.

Williamson, O.E. (1975) *Markets and Hierarchies.* Englewood Cliffs, NJ: Prentice-Hall.

Williamson, O.E. (1996) "Economic organization: the case for candor." *Academy of Management Review* 21:48–57.

Winter, S.G. (1987) "Knowledge and competence as strategic assets," in D.J. Teece (ed.), *The Competitive Challenge*, pp. 159–184. Cambridge, MA: Ballinger.

Winter, S.G. (1995) "Four Rs of profitability: rents, resources, routines, and replication," in C. Montgomery (ed.), *Resource-Based and Evolutionary Theories of the Firm: Towards a Synthesis*, pp. 147–177. Hinham, MA: Kluwer.

Womack, J., Jones, D., and Roos, D. (1990) *The Machine That Changed the World*. New York: Rawson Associates.

Zajac, E.J. and Olsen, C.P. (1993) "From transaction cost to transaction value analysis." *Journal of Management Studies* 30:131–145.

9

Knowledge Management, Uncertainty, and an Emergent Theory of the Firm

J.-C. Spender

Where Is the Knowledge Discourse Leading?

The recent attention to organizational knowledge has done much to reinvigorate theorizing about organizations and the way they operate. This is partly because organizational knowledge (K) is a broader concept than organizational rules and performance—the underpinning concepts of bureaucratic theory—and more precise than organizational climate—for those who remember that literature. But it is also because the K-discourse has provoked new cross-disciplinary thinking, most notably between developmental psychologists interested in human learning, economists interested in the nature of the firm and its evolution, institutional theorists interested in the nature and evolution of social cooperation, and organizational theorists grappling with the bounded rationality challenge thrown down by Simon (1957).

A knowledge-based approach allows us to relax our assumption that firms compete with identical products and moves us through the notion of industry or strategic groupings (Porter 1980, Spender 1989) toward the notion of firms as uniquely evolved (Penrose 1959) and thus en-gaged in monopolistic competition (Chamberlin 1947, Triffin 1947). As soon as we take knowledge and information seriously, we recognize that information is neither free nor plentiful. Rather, it is costly to acquire and difficult to manage. These costs and difficulties lead to strategically significant information asymmetries, and thus give new meaning to strategic management. The K-approach has also provided a point of access for those exploring the impact of modern information technologies on organizations, markets, and societies. And, not to be wholly overlooked, the K-approach has pushed academe to rethink its own activity—the business of knowledge generation and diffusion.

These "knowledge effects" are so pervasive that we readily speak of the coming of the information age, a time of such unparalleled dynamism in global social, technological, and economic affairs that each of us must now pay explicit attention to the management of our own knowledge. We see that career-long learning is both normal and essential as we zigzag through our professional lives. These are some positive things about the K literature. Negatives are that knowledge is a puzzling concept, tough to measure, so we cannot take a scientific approach or perform robust empirical research. For instance, while patents are easy to count, they are clearly a poor measure of an organization's total knowledge.

The idea of researching knowledge may itself be odd, for it presents us with interesting conundrums, such as:

> What is the status of a statement about knowledge? Is it simply another item of knowledge, or some form of meta-knowledge that presupposes the possibility of objective statements about knowledge?

or

> Is knowledge that which is held in the mind to guide human action—either decision making or movement—or can it also be "embodied" and stored in codes and objects that exist independent of human action? Conversely, is everything that guides human action knowledge, or do we presume an alternative irrational domain of nonknowledge?

There are many similar questions, and they are the meat and potatoes of the epistemologist's work. Their reach goes beyond the debate in the philosophy department, for such answers as can be found tell us something profound about the limits to our theorizing about organizational knowledge and its strategic, economic, and administrative implications.

Distinguishing Organizational Theorizing from Epistemology

The first point is that our theorizing about organizational knowledge needs to be bounded by some epistemological assumptions that position it as a subset of the broader field of philosophical inquiry. We need to keep a careful eye on the utility of our theorizing, whether our conclusions can ever be reattached to our discipline's established empirical work in economics, strategy, competition, institutional theorizing, management, and so forth. Perhaps our conclusions can leverage our field's achievements rather than sweep them aside in the pursuit of a new field of organizational inquiry with its own research language and methods (e.g., Wiig 2000). We might also pay renewed attention to the needs of all types of practitioners as they grapple with the challenges of the new economy and the new world order.

Every advancing academic field experiences periodic calls for standardization of terms and methods, typically advanced by those with vested interests in preventing disciplinary fragmentation and disputes, and resisted by those protesting censorship and the policing of academic thought and imagination. The evident fragmentation of the writing on organizational knowledge is sure to generate such calls soon. And, as so often in the past, the calls will turn out to be a storm in an academic teacup, capable of promoting or derailing individual academic careers, but making few long-term marks on the evolution of the field. That said, however, it is clear that knowledge management presents us with special challenges that go beyond methodological debate and strike deep at the definitional bases on which we work.

The point here is that rather than police the field with standardized terms and methods, we can ask K-researchers to do more to surface and state the typically nontestable epistemological assumptions that bound their inquiry so that their readers may see them more clearly. These authors seldom appeal to a correspondence theory of truth in the way natural scientists make assumptions about the reality embraced by their theories. The assumptions and definitions offered by K-researchers would actually be answers to the questions philosophers would ask as they attempt to identify the epistemological subset being explored—knowing that such answers could never be definitive.

In general, I believe it would benefit researchers, students, and practitioners alike to get greater insight into the different territories being explored rather than—as we have at present—an expanding field that seems to be unfragmented yet is evidently muddied by a considerable definitional confusion and conceptual variation (e.g., Allee 1997, Arbnor and Bjerke 1997, Brown and Duguid 2000, Davenport and Prusak 1998, von Krogh et al. 1998, von Krogh et al. 2000, Myers 1996, Ruggles 1997, Scarbrough 1996). Many readers would find it clarifying to have these authors explain how they would define data, information, and knowledge—should they intend to use these terms in a theoretically substantial manner. My call, therefore, is for a more explicit bounding of our theorizing, rather than an attempt to prevent exploration beyond the boundaries laid down by others' definitions.

In this spirit I attempt to describe here some boundaries around my own area of interest, in order to distinguish clearly between problems that arise because my choices differ from those of other authors and those that arise because of the way I work within those assumptions. I would also hope to provoke some discussion of these definitional boundaries so that we may all better understand how the various streams of work now appearing as "knowledge management" might, or might not, relate to each other.

Our Field's Primary Distinction: The Problematicity of Knowledge

I would argue that our field is separated into two radically distinct domains—one in which knowledge is conceived to be ultimately objectifiable, understandable in a scientific sense, and inherently unproblematic, and a second, less explored domain wherein the term knowledge is considered to extend beyond that which can ever be objectified or otherwise made explicit. In this second domain we go beyond reasoning into intuition, emotion, judgment, and skilled action.

In the first, objectifiable domain, the topic of interest is not knowledge itself, but rather the question of how the management of organizational knowledge differs from the management of the organization's more conventional assets and resources. It often becomes a discussion of how knowledge interacts with nonknowledge aspects, such as individual personalities, market institutions, and organizational structure. We explore the first domain in the next few paragraphs. In the second domain researchers focus more on managing the problems created by or inherent in knowledge. The best-known writings here stem from the work of Polanyi (1962) and his proposition that there are two types of knowledge, explicit and tacit. This distinction, quite different from the first domain's assumptions about knowledge, leads to completely new questions, such as how the two types of knowledge interrelate and whether tacit knowledge can be managed at all in the conventional sense of the term management. In the second domain it is often easier to frame the epistemological problem that derives from the assumed nature of knowledge than it is to identify the managerial problem. Indeed, it is often so difficult to frame the managerial problem that some dismiss the second domain as irrelevant to organizational theorizing.

The border territory between the two domains is occupied by those such as Nonaka and Takeuchi (1995) who, adopting Polanyi's assumptions about knowledge, argue that a knowledge approach does not really change management's

problems. They assume knowledge assets are of two types, explicit and tacit. They remain focused on maximizing the return on the organization's assets and relationships even though their K-based approach opens up new questions about managing the interaction of the explicit and tacit K-assets. To make this work, they assume that all relevant tacit knowledge can eventually be made explicit. There is an important precursor to their position in the work of Frederick Winslow Taylor, arguably among the first to be interested in a knowledge-based theory of the firm (Spender and Kijne 1996). Scientific management codified the best of the practical knowledge developed on the shop floor and articulated it optimally into mandated practices and equipment—what we might now call "best practices."

While a scientific approach dominates in the first K-research domain, it offers little in the second—as Taylor noted. Thus, we can observe various attempts to bring a knowledge approach to economics by supposing that organizational knowledge is simply another organizational asset, to be evaluated and managed in much the same way as all the other assets. This is nontrivial and interesting when the difference between K-assets and other assets leads to new conclusions (e.g., Teece 2000). The added value here is the observation that knowledge assets are less tangible and harder to identify and manage. There are important implications for those managing investment in "soft" assets such as brand names, strategic alliances, and personnel skills. Such thinking leads, for instance, to human capital accounting and the kind of organizational practices made famous by Skandia (e.g., Hedberg 2000).

The vast bulk of today's managerial interest in knowledge management, as reflected in the special units set up recently by the major accounting, computing, and consulting firms, lies within this first domain. Knowledge, information, and data are not thought of as being fundamentally different. It follows from these assumptions that it makes good economic sense to gather all the firm's knowledge (information or data) into one searchable database and provide immediate access to those around the firm who need it. They can then, for instance, find out if previous investments provide answers to their present problems. Absent this, the poor communications that characterize most organizations not only give rise to efficiency-draining disputes, but also require further investment to create new knowledge assets that are ultimately underused in their turn.

Here the value added by a K-approach is not simply cosmetic, with terms that non-computer-oriented managers can use without being concerned that they will be embarrassed by database and network specialists. Nor is it simply a matter of raising the organization's communications efficiency. We see that the knowledge management insights turn on the special and extensible nature of knowledge assets. Unlike most of the corporate assets, knowledge is not consumed when it is applied to solving the organization's problems. On the contrary, a knowledge asset's value is generally maintained and often enlarged by its application—while conventional assets must be depreciated and replaced. Hence, K-assets must be managed differently. A key part of Penrose's (1959) theory of the growth of the firm is the presumed extensibility of the firm's knowledge, the possibility of extracting further economic value without further investment.

But the difference between the firm's tangible assets—those itemized on the balance sheet—and its knowledge assets may lie only in the latter's fluidity, the ease with which they, and the revenues they can attract, flow to others. The managerial implications of fluidity are radically different from those of the assumption of extensibility. In particular, the management theory that emerges from this assumption focuses less on what goes on within the firm than in the institutional apparatus that lies outside the firm, in its legal and institutional context. An interesting mark of most Western industrial civilizations is that knowledge and ideas can be transformed into tangible assets. Thus, patents are evidence both of research investment and an institutional fabric in which the rights to highly mobile knowledge assets can be protected.

The converse of fluidity is that knowledge is "sticky" and that the organization's internal institutions prevent also the efficient transfer of knowledge from one part of the firm whose function it is to generate knowledge, such as its research labs, to other parts that are to transform knowledge into revenue, such as its production engineers and marketing managers. The managerial implications of this framing are quite different from those suggested by the other K-assumptions.

Different again is the assumption that managing the processes that generate knowledge assets is fundamentally different from managing the creation of either revenue or more tangible assets. First, the extensibility of knowledge assets makes identifying the return on investment

difficult, more a matter of judgment than of science. Second, the process of creating knowledge seems different from that of applying professional knowledge in the creation of the organization's conventional assets—such as machines, plants, buildings, and finished goods—or in the management of the organization itself. And these differences go beyond the distinction between creativity versus rational decision making to embrace intangible issues that cannot be captured in explicit planning and project management.

In short, even within the domain bounded by the notion that knowledge can be objectified and treated as an organizational asset, there are many subdomains differentiated by additional underpinning assumptions. Better maps of this domain would be extremely useful to show us how the various versions of the knowledge approach can add significant and practical value to organizational theorizing and research.

Into the Second Domain

In the second domain knowledge itself is perceived as problematic. This is the territory that Simon pointed toward with his work on bounded rationality. Though he only took us to the boundary wall separating the domains and pointed over it rather than actually reconnoitering into the region beyond. I believe the deeper import and promise of the knowledge-based approach is that it tempts us to push into this strange territory. Perhaps here we can begin to deal with uncertainty, ambiguity, and aspects of organizational leadership, intuition, praxis, and shrewdness that have baffled us so far. Though it is clear that not everyone in the field of knowledge management wishes to head this way, if one wished to, how could that be done? I believe there are two approaches. Though they seem to differ in their objectives, I suspect that they simply differ in methodologies, each part of the other much as the wave and particle theories of light turn out to be complementary.

The first approach is to argue that we humans know things in different ways. Polanyi introduced us to a distinction between explicit and tacit knowing. The first is associated with conscious reasoning; the second, with skill and nonconscious judgments. The first is demonstrated by explanation; the second, in activity. The first is the stuff of well-structured language; the second, of the activity in which the knowledge appears embedded. Each is an epistemological world unto itself, and there is a fundamental discontinuity between the two.

The idea that humans are capable of knowing in significantly different ways is well established and precedes the ancient philosophers. Detienne and Vernant (1974) noted that some Greek philosophers distinguished *metis* (cunning) from *techne* (the how-to pragmatic knowledge implied in the term technology), *phronesis* (sociopolitical skills) and *episteme* (theoretical knowledge). Ihde (1993) likewise noted another Greek tradition that differentiated *noesis* (pure abstraction) from *diainoia* (mathematical truths), *pistis* (perceptions), and *eikasia* (images of objects). Some contemporary neuroscientists suggest, in a manner anticipated by the phrenologists, that different kinds of knowledge are stored in different parts of the brain (Penrose 1989). Reber (1993) describes a particular spin on this, that the brain as a multipart evolved organ, with the older parts (cerebellum) knowing in ways different from the more recently evolved parts (cerebrum), thus differentiating intuitive or "animal" knowledge from reasoned conscious knowledge.

Another kind of K-distinction lies external to the knower, rather than internal. Durkheim and Halbwachs appealed to an equally ancient tradition that differentiates what is collectively known, as evidenced in collective behavior that is not readily explained by any of the individuals making up the collective, from that which is individually known and can be explained by such individuals (Sandelands and Stablein 1987, Connerton 1989, Spender 1998).

As soon as we assume that there can be different types of knowing, there are legions of distinctions on which to draw. But so what? At one level this is an interesting idea, especially since it seems to reach beyond the positivistic tradition into which most of us were trained—one that focuses on "truth" as a single objective/scientific type of knowledge. Given this assumption, we might argue that the different types of knowledge suggest different types of learning and memory, and maybe communication, too. We must speak explicit knowledge and show tacit knowledge, and so on. At another level we might argue that there are several different theories of the firm, and different theories of managing, one for each kind of knowledge. An accounting or bureaucratic model works with explicit knowledge; a social or evolutionary model works with the implicit. The first is a theory of explicit rational decision making. The second might be a theory

of the firm as a collective, or as a set of tacit knowledge–manifesting practices or "routines" (Nelson and Winter 1982).

We might find one of these theories more interesting than another, but would there be any way of establishing which is "best"? A Baconian "critical experiment" would miss the point, since that would merely privilege explicit knowledge and so lead us to ignore the nonscientific types of theorizing and knowing. Another approach would be to argue that the best theory would be that which best captures the phenomena of interest, be they growth rate, market share, competitive activity, robust adaptiveness, or whatever. That takes us back to the puzzle about how we decide how firms differ (Chamberlin 1947, Triffin 1947, Nelson 1991). We are also caught in a Kuhnian paradox, for we must presume something to observe a phenomenon, and that necessarily orients us toward one or other of these alternative theories. Hence, our sense of the "best" actually follows from our assumptions rather than from the evidence. Having a set of paradigmatically discontinuous alternative theories derived from alternative types of knowledge is interesting, but in itself does not lead to much clarification. It merely reflects the unresolved complexity of our prior assumptions about the phenomena of interest.

But we can take a major step forward and see that the assumption that we know things differently is simply a special way of defining knowledge as problematic. Popper's (1969) way of making scientific knowledge problematic depended on the difference between theory and empirical evidence, showing that they can never be wholly reconciled for they are, in fact, somewhat different ways of knowing. Popper's work led us to a more sophisticated notion of positivist science. Previously the relationship between prediction and outcome was considered unproblematic, with confirmation as evidence that the theory was correct and "true." Popper's answer is that such resolution is not possible. Instead, he proposed a different and more vulnerable criterion for "truth," falsification: a single instance in which the outcome runs counter to the prediction shows the falsity of the theory. Thus, provided theoretical knowledge seems to work and remains open to empirical criticisms, it is considered reliable—albeit temporarily.

Popper's work showed us a complementary part of the previous assumption that we humans seem to know in different ways. For even when this is true we also seem to achieve a coherent sense of self and situation; that is, we manage to integrate these discontinuous types of knowledge into a coherent world view. From this vantage point we can argue that Simon (1957) was searching for ways to integrate organizational decision making across the boundaries to complete rationality, or that Thompson (1967) was integrating core rationality with some extrarational boundary-spanning principles. It is within this notion of integration that Nonaka and Takeuchi's (1995) work proposed a theory of the firm as an apparatus that integrates the organization's tacit and explicit knowledge.

The point here is that by using the assumption of knowing in different ways to suggest that knowledge is inherently problematic, we can point to an entirely new kind of knowing, that necessary to integrate the types of organizational knowledge we presume distinct. With this different type of knowing—about integration—comes a new theory of the firm.

A New K-Based Theory of the Firm

It is at this point that the knowledge-based approach intersects with traditional theories of the firm, especially those from economics and organization theory. There are theories that derive from Adam Smith and his assumption of the firm as an apparatus that integrates and transforms the factors of production: land, labor, and capital. Likewise, microeconomic theories focus on the integration of production and consumption. Bureaucratic theories are about the integration and transformation of different kinds of asset and knowledge—such as design, production, and marketing. As Grant (1996) has argued persuasively, there is a long and rich literature defining the firm as an integration mechanism.

So we need to find out if using the term knowledge, so general, powerful, and yet so vague, adds anything substantive to this literature, whether it enables us to see or say something new. But now we are focused on integration knowledge as the crucial type shaping the new theory of the firm. Hence I would extend the earlier point about the two domains and argue that the real value of a K-based approach is that it drives a wedge between theories that regard the firm's integration as logical and inherently unproblematic, and those that argue to the contrary, suggesting that some new knowledge is needed. Microeconomic theory presupposes information completely adequate to the task of

bringing the firm and the market together rationally and optimally. Likewise, most of organization theory frames the managerial problem as one of bringing together completely known elements in much the same way as one would design an aircraft—hence the bureaucratic "machine" metaphor. The parts are each known completely and designed to come together to create a preconceived functionality—the organization's predefined purpose. The aircraft needs to be test-flown to bridge the gap between the manipulation of symbolic knowledge and its physical construction. But we have some fundamental ideas about why it is going to fly, and these are designed in at the beginning. Can this same rational approach be adequate to designing the viable firm? For Simon, this is the challenge presented by bounded rationality, and to make progress we have to pay special attention to the notion of uncertainty. While Knight's (1921) distinction between risk and uncertainty set the theoretical stage for Simon and others, it is largely ignored today. Uncertainty is the absence of the data or information necessary to make an informed judgment. It should not be confused with risk, which is knowing instances as members of a population (Spender 1989, p. 42). Action under conditions of risk is amenable to analysis. Action under conditions of uncertainty is only explainable by adding a judgment that cannot be logically related to the data available.

In Spender (1989) I followed Knight (1921) and Simon's (1952) little referenced paper on the challenge of bringing together microeconomic theory (F-theory) and organization theory (O-theory). I argued that the discontinuities between the assumptions underpinning these two disciplines could be used to define the principal uncertainty that needed to be resolved by the theory of the firm and, parenthetically, the process of strategy making. To have a strategy is to have a coherent body of organizational knowledge, free of the uncertainties that would arrest reasoned action about the organization of the firm—and its interactions with the environment. I argued that even though managers do not think like microeconomists or organization theorists, the uncertainties arising from the discontinuities between the ideas they actually adopt are of the same type as that addressed in Simon's article. Thus, epistemological or K-based uncertainty could be defined as the fundamental problem with which entrepreneurial managers need to deal as they strategize for their firms. The idea was that they have to deal with uncertainties arising from many sources—the market, the behavior of employees and subcontractors, and the unpredictable consequences of previous decisions and activity. But they also have to deal with a more fundamental uncertainty, that arising because what they know is known in many different ways. Thus, I redefined strategy making as the active process of resolving the epistemological uncertainties inherent in what management knows about the firm's situation.

While we can redefine strategy making as the creation of a coherent body of organizational knowledge, the uncertainties are never fully resolved. The organization's body of knowledge is inherently Popperian, tentative, flawed, and always open to rebuttal by exposure to experience. The appropriate criterion for acceptance is whether the knowledge is adequate to enable management to choose from among the range of strategic decisions or actions available. That is, does it "satisfice" for action?

The Industry Recipe

Having framed management's strategic problem this way, I went on to argue that the firm-level uncertainties were often partially resolved collectively—by judgments that managers added to their knowledge of their firm's situation but drew from an "industry recipe" (Spender 1989, p. 60). This recipe was known throughout the industry. The idea was that managers often perceived themselves to be members of a trade or strategic group, and this group developed and shared views of the world that helped resolve each manager's firm-level uncertainties. I followed Marshall and E. A. Robinson, who tended to define "industry" in terms of the managers' self-perceptions rather than in terms of the tangible resource thinking that produced the SIC coding. Though the latter is focused on the firm's tangible inputs and outputs, it seems poorly related to the body of knowledge actually being applied in the conversion process and so generates much confusion about the comparability of firms. I also followed North's (1990) sense of social institutions as collective responses to the uncertainties of social life (Spender 1996). Of course the notion of an industry recipe stands opposed to the idea that these strategy-making managers are "entrepreneurs," inventing new solutions to the uncertainties they face.

I went on to show that an industry recipe was widely shared within an industry—while accepting the circularity that the firms industry observers denote as being industry members were those that shared recipes. To break this circularity, I showed that, despite a common logical structure, the recipe's components were highly specific to each industry and not shared across other industries. I also showed that workable recipes comprised only a few components—around 12–15—so a recipe is not hugely complex. Each component defined a strategic question to be answered before a coherent sense of the firm could develop.

The resulting industry recipe is not known explicitly by the managers in the industry. It is somewhat available to those such as cultural anthropologists—and consultants who do much the same thing—who make explicit many of the recipe's tacit components. But their most difficult challenge is to achieve that sense of coherence, the point where one understands the other's world enough to feel one could act mindfully within it (Goodenough 1966). In this theory managers are part of the world they seek to understand and influence. They are not separated from it, or above it, as most organization theory assumes by positioning strategic managers as designers and decision makers. So the recipe emerges from the industry's activities, unbidden and undesigned, into the judgments of the managers, whose decisions and actions shape the industry. Marshall (1964) likewise observed that the mysteries of the trade were learned unconsciously, as if they were "in the air" (p. 152).

What is implicit and not spelled out in this approach is the additional knowledge that produces that coherence. The puzzle is to see what must be learned before the different things that managers know become integrated in their sense of the firm as a coherent and more or less manageable entity.

Is Integration Evidence of New Knowledge? And If So, of What Type?

At this point I have proposed that there are two fundamentally different types of knowledge: (1) evident elements, such as core competencies, to be absorbed into the body of knowledge that comprises the firm and (2) that which integrates these elements into a coherent workable whole—albeit not integrated into what logicians might call a sound "well-formed" theory of the firm. Rather, we have a Popperian theory, tentative, replete with contradictions and uncertainties, falsifiable, but adequate to the task of choosing from among the immediately available actions. It is also dynamic, open to learning from error, and evolutionary (Spender, 1996).

Uncertainties are resolved by knowledge, so it may be more useful to define knowledge types in terms of the uncertainties resolved rather than in terms of the arbitrary epistemological or neurological frameworks mentioned above. For instance, some uncertainties prevent reasoned logical conclusions. There might be lack of (a) a theoretical framework or model or (b) the situation-specific data that one needs to apply the model. This is to distinguish general laws from factual assertions (e.g., Hempel 1966, p. 51), the two types of scientific knowledge that complement the two kinds of uncertainty permissible within the positivist framework. It is the rigorous integration of these two types of knowledge that sets the conventional framework for scientific discovery.

Polanyi introduced the notion that there were things that one knew—and could do—that could not be fitted into this kind of explanation-based model, hence his phrase "we know more than we can say." Knowledge, such as balancing a pushbike or swimming, can be manifest in skilled action even though it cannot be explained or modeled. The uncertainty lies in one's ability to act under particular circumstances rather than in one's inability to explain that action. Tacit knowledge—as Polanyi defined it—resolves uncertainty in the domain of action, integrating knowledge and context. His point was that having explanation-type knowledge is insufficient to determine skilled action, and exemplary scientific research is always the outcome of highly skilled action. Czikszentmihalyi's (1988) notion of "flow," action completely disconnected from conscious thought, emphasizes the nature of the tacit knowledge necessary to achieve peak performance under high stress.

But we can go further and look at champion players, for instance, those in tennis or golf, who clearly combine superb physical skills with high-quality reasoning about the strategic opportunities open within the framework of a formal game. We get a sense of a rather different kind of uncertainty and corresponding knowledge associated with integration. The knowledge necessary to keep one's game "together" under pressure is neither exclusively tacit nor exclusively explicit. Nor is it expressly psychological. It seems all-pervading and holistic. It grasps all of the above and is intimately tied up with the player's dynamic, and thus inevitably fragile, sense of self. This self-knowledge is an underpinning knowledge in which the person's explicit and tacit knowledge are both embedded, in which they are brought together in action. It is a deeply buried and embracing type of knowledge—akin to Popper's body of collective social experience.

We can experience ourselves how panic interrupts our sense of self and arrests both thought and movement. The point here is that integration—and its absence—is pretty easy to observe in people and organizations alike. Organizations and people become befogged and disoriented (Baumard 1996, 1999). The presence of underpinning knowledge of integration is tied up with the presence or absence of an integrated sense of self in the particular dynamic context. Real contexts are replete with uncertainties and threats to the self. Although organizations and people are quite different, and I use a psychological model to illustrate the point about self-knowledge, I certainly presuppose something analogous to consciousness and self-image for the firm. The point of strategy making is to produce an integrated body of knowledge and, as in a mission statement, the firm's discrete sense of itself. I would point to Fayol's (1949) notion of *esprit de corps*, or the integrated outcome of effective leadership. I shall go on to argue that this integration knowledge is also the epistemological context that gives all the organization's knowledge elements their meaning. I see this notion as the key to Penrose's (1959) theory of the firm as a knowledge context in which its managers are embedded, that enables transformation of all incoming knowledge. Resources become revalued in terms of the actions they enable. We can also see it as knowledge or confidence shared by those comprising the firm. I also draw on Peirce's notion of "indexicality," the unstated and unstatable experiential knowledge that gives meaning to conversational terms such as "here" and "now."

Microeconomics takes the firm's integration for granted and focuses on the need to integrate firm and market. Organization theory presumes the firm to be problematic and focuses on the integration of the firm's various components. Thus, both give us ways of examining uncertainties that challenge the firm's self-identity. But, as Simon (1952) noted, neither gives us a framework for examining the background into which each theory must be embedded. Absent this, we have no theory of the firm that can embrace the full range of uncertainties that management must clearly resolve. Integration adds materially and fundamentally to the types of knowledge we have identified. Once integrated, there is more knowledge present than was entailed by the simple sum of the assumptions prior to their synthesis and transformation. Grant (1996) focused directly on how knowledge sharing and integration takes place within organizations. I argued that transferring knowledge is not an efficient approach to integrating knowledge (p. 114), and noted the distinctions between Thompson's (1967) pooled, sequential, and reciprocal types of interdependence. He also noted Ouchi's (1980) proposal for three social integrating mechanisms, market, bureaucracy, and clan, itself merely a re-presentation of Etzioni's (1971) three bases of social power. He then focused on Van de Ven's richer notion of group coordination and cited Hutchins's study of collective cognition on board aircraft carriers. He arrived at the notion of an underpinning "common knowledge" (Grant 1996, p. 115) as the prerequisite to group coordination.

The question now is whether or not this common or background knowledge is one of the previously identified types of organizational knowledge. Grant (1996) did not address this point directly, though his comment that at its most simple common knowledge is the intersection of the individuals' knowledge-sets, as in a Venn diagram (p. 115), suggests that he did not see it as fundamentally different, or at a different epistemological level. As a result, Grant was unclear whether coordinated activity required the generation of new knowledge to augment that possessed by the group's members prior to their collaboration. He did pursue the notion that common knowledge could be of several types: language, other forms of symbolic communication, commonality of specialized knowledge, shared meaning, and recognition of individual knowledge domains (p. 116). All of these ideas are helpful, but I want to focus less on the similarities among common knowledge and the other types of organizational knowledge than on their differences. Examining the differences surfaces our assumptions, and it is from these that we spin our theories about what managers need to accomplish.

In short, my argument is that integration requires additional knowledge. This must be present before the individuals can coalesce into a team, before there is a firm. Integration knowledge is a different and more profound kind of background knowledge. This assumption set us

up with some new strategic problems to address with our new theory: how to (a) create the background knowledge—or indicate how it emerges—and (b) integrate it with the more readily identified "foreground" types of knowledge. Again, I would appeal to the reader's personal experience and argue that team building (Belbin 1981, Larson and LaFasto 1989) is a distinct knowledge-creating activity. The team members' sense of it may be that they are discovering the others' capabilities and learning how to adjust their own activities accordingly, as Grant (1996) implied. But there may be more to it than that—in that there may be crucial tacit and collective aspects of which the members are relatively unaware, at least until the common knowledge is in place. This becomes most evident when the team surprises itself with its performance.

The Nature and Growth of Common Knowledge

We can think about common knowledge in a number of ways, for instance, as the source of meaning in language, or the source of self-identity, or what one has to know before one can acquire a message, the kernel of absorptive capacity (Cohen and Levinthal 1990). I like the term "common knowledge" because it connotes common sense, what one needs to makes one's way in the world irrespective of one's "book learning" or physical skills. It is contextualized because it is related to a specific aspect of the world. It is also the basis on which one can develop a pragmatic sense of self by comparing oneself with contextually relevant others. This is especially the case for organizations, for they are often unrealistic about themselves and their competitive position. As advertising people sometimes remark, there is nothing more dangerous than believing one's own hype. I do not use the term "common knowledge" in the same way as Dixon (2000) used it. Although she was not entirely consistent about the nature of organizational knowledge, she was primarily concerned with knowledge sharing in the sense dismissed by Grant (1996). Seeing no discontinuities between common knowledge and elements of organizational knowledge, she argued elements of knowledge become common when shared.

The point here is that common knowledge is both visceral and the platform for everything else. It lies deep and brings together, in contextualized thought and action, all the other types of knowledge that are judged relevant—for it is the source of such judgments. Since it is also tied up with self-knowledge, it implies a degree of consciousness, objectivity, and self-awareness and the ability to observe the self and compare it to others, in so doing becoming aware of both similarities and differences. To lose the sense of self is to become unable to place oneself in the experienced world. To have a sense of self is to be able to make sense of the world—to keep one's game together despite the many threats the world presents. This sense is dynamic, both fragile in its falsifiability and vulnerability, and robust, being able to absorb the uncertainties that experience brings. The most profound outcome of effective strategy making is this coherent sense of organizational self. Certainly one might harness the outcome to the task of creating competitive advantage with the resources that are at hand or are available. But the process is not the reverse, that one first has capabilities or advantages that then suggest a strategy. Here I agree with Grant (1996, p. 116), who argued that organizational capabilities are the outcome of knowledge integration. Though he referred to specific team-based productive activities, I suspect we disagree about the nature of the outcome.

Knowledge management writers sometimes assume that only individuals know, and an organization cannot. After Durkheim and his followers, I would disagree, but not in the trivial sense of assuming an organizational mind that stands independent of its members. Instead, I would argue that the individual's sense of self is partially, though not wholly, a reflection of the social and organizational context in which the individual lives, learns, and works. To have a sense of self that is relevant and effective in the organizational context requires one to know that context in very specific ways—not simply to know it objectively, so generating explicit knowledge, but know it experientially and understand the collective practices that are appropriate to that context (Connerton 1989). In addition, one has to know it morally and emotionally since it is not neutral in either respect. As every experienced manager can tell us, organizational decisions and actions have meaning and are irrevocably value laden, irrespective of and discontinuous from the logic or reasoning that preceded them.

Most of us have experienced the process of learning the common knowledge of an organization when we joined a community and became socialized into its practices and meanings. Sometimes this process can be painful. We may see we have made a mistake but do not understand its exact nature. We may discover "things are not done that way around here," and it is difficult to be precise about what we do not yet know. In retrospect, after some weeks or months, we begin to see much to which we were previously blind. It is not so much the explicit facts about who does what, or how this or that works, or the tacit skills required to deal with this or that person or topic. Rather, it is the process of acquiring deep or "thick" knowledge, an emerging realization of the organization's integrated identity or "chemistry."

We have no trouble conceiving common knowledge as dynamic, endlessly responsive to the learning that comes from new experiences and to the creative contributions of individuals throughout the organization. After all, common knowledge's fundamental nature is to integrate the other types of knowledge, and they, too, are ever changing. The theoretical challenge is to understand how organizations ever acquire their common knowledge in the first place. This is a "big bang" type of origin problem—with a difference since we know that organizations, unlike societies, begin as instruments of purposive human action (Toennies 1971).

Front-Face and Back-Face

My assumption is that background common knowledge emerges as a result of interactions around those comprising the organization's first members. On the one hand, it is likely to reflect the founder's own common knowledge and sense of self. Organizational research has shown us that the founder's way of seeing and doing things is likely to shape an organization for a long time, often long after the founder has departed. On the other hand, recalling the sociological interest in the unintended consequences of human action, common knowledge also begins as a reaction to the uncertainties involved in bringing the firm's components together. As soon as the process of firm building begins, its knowledge base immediately comprises two types of knowledge that we might call "front-face" and "back-face." Front-face knowledge comprises the knowledge of the firm's elemental parts, activities, and understandings: material inputs, performance objectives, transformation processes and resources, market segments, distribution channels, and so forth. This is the stuff that can be identified, either explicitly or as skilled performance. But it is not integrated. Profound uncertainties exist about how the elements are to be brought together to generate robust, viable, purposive, and responsive organizational activity. Back-face knowledge comprises the common knowledge that integrates them.

Under many circumstances, rules and directives will prove insufficient to the task of generating purposive activity. We can consider this proposition from a number of different vantage points. Rules are always general and bounded by ceteris paribus assumptions, while action is always specific. Real situations often seem to fall outside the circumstances presumed by the rules. Rules are matters of the mind and apply to the realm of decision, while action exists in the world. But at bottom is the fact that the actors must already know something—some of which must be beyond specification—before they can absorb the rules. This knowledge is visceral and must be adequate to the task of integrating the knowledge provided by the rules and the knowledge of the action situation.

Vygotsky (1962, 1978), whose work is sometimes dubbed "activity theory," argued that an individual's consciousness and sense of self emerges from and is thus shaped by active involvement with the environment. Likewise, Abram (1996) argued that the beginnings of consciousness are reflections of the sensed world. The point here is not to retrace the whole discussion of consciousness since Descartes, but rather to argue that the initial human circumstance is uncertainty—about everything, including oneself, the other, and the world. The firm also begins by confronting uncertainty about how to act, survive, and grow. As its members strive to integrate the resources they bring to the firm, they must select those that are appropriate. But they cannot do this through logic alone since that would demand unbounded rationality.

A rather different way of illustrating this point is provided by Kusterer's (1978) research into how shop-floor operatives actually get their work done. He revealed that many tricks of the trade, fudges, fixes, and adjustments must be applied before even the most elementary instructions can be executed. These elements must also be added to and integrated with the rules, objectives, and other explicit elements of organizational knowledge. The back-face common knowl-edge is especially rich in indicating which fixes are necessary to deal with specific situations. Operators learn the quirks of their machines just as managers learn the quirks of the different work teams, the salesmen of their customers, and so forth.

Thinking about where front-face and back-face knowledge comes from, I presume knowledge is generated by both individuals and social collectives in response to their exposures to uncertainty. Thus, back-face common knowledge is generated only after the problem of integration is present—and this must always take place in a context that contains its own uncertainties. Hence, back-face knowledge is always contextualized. The team's sense of self cannot be present before the members begin to work together, and that reflects the circumstance in which it happens. The front-face knowledge comprises the resources brought to the firm, and these typically exist before the firm develops its sense of self (or back-face common knowledge). The land, capital, and labor resources exist before the enterprise is formed. Even if the founders have a sense or vision of what they would like to create, contact with the world in which the firm must operate brings an entirely unexpected universe of challenges. Of course, once the firm begins, it is capable of generating new front-face knowledge resources—which then pose new internally generated integration challenges. Since the back-face knowledge follows exposure to the realities of integrating the firm's elements, core competencies, shop-floor fixes, or whatever, it is largely emergent. Even though managers might intentionally or unintentionally copy others, the core of the industry recipe idea, their integration problems are still unique. The industry recipe can never be the whole answer. Being emergent, the resulting back-face knowledge also tends to be self-regulating and self-sustaining.

It is clearly neither possible nor valuable to strive to completely integrate any organization. This would involve resolving all the uncertainties that could result from interaction with the world or those generated as unintended consequences of previous actions. Complete "local" rationality is not an appropriate objective. In the spirit of Popper, a more appropriate heuristic might be to caution the actors to deal only with those uncertainties that arrest their reasoned purposive activity as they attempt to pursue their planned objectives. This involves creativity, either their own or by others whom they can copy. Knowing who to copy, and when, is part of self-identity. Knowing how and what to copy is a matter of absorptive capacity. The industry recipe merely suggests one pattern of copying that resolves many of the firm's uncertainties.

Where Does This Leave Us?

I believe the knowledge management field holds considerable promise in its ability to embrace phenomena and problems that have been persistently ignored or underconsidered in economic and organization theory. The key, as I have noted before (Spender 1989, p. 212), lies in the treatment—or avoidance—of uncertainty.

In this essay my principal purpose is to help sharpen the knowledge management field's methods by exploring the assumptions that underpin it. In particular, I distinguish two principal domains of knowledge management work. One presumes knowledge is an organizational asset and focuses on the management implications of differences between the organization's knowledge and other assets. The second focuses on knowledge as the response to uncertainty, most particularly the uncertainties arising from management's lack of knowledge about how to integrate what they know explicitly—such as the firm's core competencies—into a coherent body of knowledge. This integration produces the firm's identity and its sense of itself and its place in the world. This is the principal outcome of the strategy-making process.

Of course, others have remarked on integration as something theoretically significant, while offering very different treatments (Kogut and Zander 1992, Amit and Schoemaker 1993). Following Grant (1996), though disagreeing on several assumptions, I argue that the key to integrating the different kinds of knowledge that comprise the firm is its "common knowledge." This is knowledge of a different type than has been previously considered in the knowledge management literature. Yet, paradoxically, all of us know this type of knowledge well and have experienced it as we joined organizations and learned to find our way around, make our contributions, and get our jobs done.

My assumption is that common knowledge grows—emerges—out of the interactions among the firm's parts and context. There is considerable opportunity to facilitate the process by borrowing from relevant others, so leveraging the firm's sense of identity into membership in a community of practice that some, following Marshall and Robinson, would call "their industry." In previous work along these lines I showed that researching the industry recipe—aspects of the industry's firms' common knowledge—is fairly straightforward cultural anthropology. I would argue that strategy consultants do something like this as a matter of course.

The emerging knowledge-based theory of the firm is dialectical in the sense that it has a front face that is inherently designable, the elements that need to be integrated, and a back face that is inherently emergent, resolving the uncertainties experienced when trying to integrate the front-face elements in a particular context. Thus, common knowledge is contextualized and bounded by the context in which it emerges. Bounded rationality is that which is articulated but is also "local" in that it is supported by a specific and limited common knowledge.

I believe we can do much to resolve the problems of integrating the knowledge management field's literature by adopting a two-knowledge domain model of the firm. Knowledge management work in the first domain illustrates the principles of front-face design. Notions of organicism and self-regulation, a recurrent theme in organization theory, arise from the back face and can best be reached through an analysis of the uncertainties of integrating the front-face elements. The broad sweep of organization theorizing over the last century has shown us the limitations of thinking only about front-face issues and presuming certain knowledge. Questions about uncertainty, leadership, strategy, creativity, entrepreneurship, growth, and appropriate firm size and operational complexity persist and have been little illuminated (Barnard 1938, Graham 1995).

While the approach sketched here may seem complex, I would argue it is merely unfamiliar as discourse. I believe we have adequate knowledge of these matters from our own experience of living in a contextualized and uncertain world, and that these ideas may be readily mapped into our theorizing about firms. Actually, our literature offers many indications of what it means to have a theory of the firm that can embrace both the familiar forms of organizational knowledge and the uncertainties that we so frequently ignore. The work of Barnard (1938), Penrose (1959), Simon (1957), and some of the previous generation of industrial economists can be augmented by a new generation of developmental psychologists and learning theorists to give us new insight into some of our field's most problematic questions: What is strategy? What is organizational learning? How are managers to influence either?

References

Abram, D. (1996) *The Spell of the Sensuous: Perception and Language in a More-Than-Human World*. New York: Vintage Press.

Allee, V. (1997) *The Knowledge Evolution: Expanding Organizational Intelligence*. London: Butterworth-Heinemann.

Amit, R. and Schoemaker, P. (1993) "Strategic assets and organizational rent." *Strategic Management Journal* 14(1):33–46.

Arbnor, I. and Bjerke, B. (1997) *Methodology for Creating Business Knowledge*, 2d ed. London: Sage.

Barnard, C. (1938) *The Functions of the Executive*. Cambridge, MA: Harvard University Press.

Baumard, P. (1996) "Organizations in the fog: an investigation into the dynamics of knowledge," in B. Moingeon and A. Edmondson (eds.), *Organizational Learning and Competitive Advantage*, pp. 74–91. Thousand Oaks, CA: Sage.

Baumard, P. (1999) *Tacit Knowledge in Organizations*. London: Sage.

Belbin, R. (1981) *Management Teams: Why They Succeed or Fail*. London: Heinemann.

Brown, J. and Duguid, P. (2000) *The Social Life of Information*. Boston: Harvard Business School Press.

Chamberlin, E. (1947) *The Theory of Monopolistic Competition: A Re-orientation of the Theory of Value*. Cambridge, MA: Harvard University Press.

Cohen, W. and Levinthal, D. (1990) "Absorptive capacity: A new perspective on learning and innovation." *Administrative Science Quarterly* 35:128–152.

Connerton, P. (1989) *How Societies Remember*. New York: Cambridge University Press.

Czikszentmihalyi, M. (1988) "The flow experience and its significance for human psychology," in M. Czikszentmihalyi and I.S. Czikszentmihalyi (eds.), *Optimal Experience: Psychological Studies of Flow in Consciousness*, pp. 15–35. New York: Cambridge University Press.

Davenport, T. and Prusak, L. (1998) *Working Knowledge: How Organizations Manage What They Know*. Boston: Harvard Business School Press.

Detienne, M. and Vernant, J. (1974) *Les Ruses de l'Intelligence: Le Metis des Grecs*. Paris: Flammarion.

Dixon, N. (2000) *Common Knowledge: How Companies Thrive by Sharing What They Know*. Boston: Harvard Business School Press.

Etzioni, A. (1971) *A Comparative Analysis of Complex Organizations*. New York: Free Press.

Fayol, H. (1949) *General and Industrial Management*. London: Pitman.

Goodenough, W. (1996) "Cultural anthropology and linguistics," in B. Hymes (ed.), *Language in Culture and Society*, pp. 36–48. New York: Harper and Row.

Graham, P., ed. (1995) *Mary Parker Follett: Prophet of Management*. Boston: Harvard Business School Press.

Grant, R. (1996) "Toward a knowledge-based theory of the firm." *Strategic Management Journal* 17(Winter):109–122.

Hedberg, B. (2000) "The new organizations: managing multiple arenas for knowledge creation," in C. Despres and D. Chauvel (eds.), *Knowledge Horizons: The Past and the Promise of Knowledge Management*, pp. 269–286. Boston: Butterworth-Heinemann.

Hempel, C. (1966) *Philosophy of Natural Science*. Englewood Cliffs, NJ: Prentice-Hall.

Ihde, D (1993) *Philosophy of Technology: An Introduction*. New York: Paragon House.

Knight, F. (1921) *Risk, Uncertainty and Profit*. New York: Harper and Row.

Kogut, B. and Zander, U. (1992) "Knowledge of the firm, combinative capabilities, and the replication of technology." *Organization Science* 3:383–397.

Kusterer, K. (1978) *Know-how on the Job: The Important Working Knowledge of the "Unskilled" Workers*. Boulder, CO: Westview Press.

Larson, C. & LaFasto, F. (1989) *Teamwork: What Can Go Right and What Can Go Wrong*. Thousand Oaks, CA: Sage.

Marshall, A. (1964) *Elements of Economics of Industry*. London: Macmillan.

Myers, P., ed. (1996) *Knowledge Management and Organizational Design*. London: Butterworth-Heinemann.

Nelson, R. (1991) "Why do firms differ, and how does it matter?" *Strategic Management Journal* 12(Winter):61–74.

Nelson, R. and Winter, S. (1982) *An Evolutionary Theory of Economic Change*. Cambridge, MA: Belknap Press.

Nonaka, I. and Takeuchi, H. (1995) *The Knowledge-Creating Organization: How Japanese Companies Create the Dynamics of Innovation*. New York: Oxford University Press.

North, D. (1990) *Institutions, Institutional Change, and Economic Performance*. New York: Cambridge University Press.

Ouchi, W.G. (1980) "Markets, bureaucracies, and clans." *Administrative Science Quarterly* 25: 129–141.

Penrose, E. (1959) *The Theory of the Growth of the Firm*. New York, Wiley.

Polanyi, M. (1962) *Personal Knowledge: Toward a Post-critical Philosophy*. Chicago: University of Chicago Press.

Popper, K. (1969) *Conjectures and Refutations: The Growth of Scientific Knowledge*, 3d ed. London: Routledge and Kegan Paul.

Porter, M. (1980) *Competitive Strategy: Techniques for Analyzing Industries and Competitors*. New York: Free Press.

Reber, A. (1993) *Implicit Learning and Tacit Knowledge: An Essay on the Cognitive Unconscious*. New York: Oxford University Press.

Ruggles, R., ed. (1997) *Knowledge Management Tools*. London: Butterworth-Heinemann.

Sandelands, L. and Stablein, R. (1987) "The concept of organizational mind." *Research in the Sociology of Organizations* 5:135–161.

Scarbrough, H., ed. (1996) *The Management of Expertise*. Basingstoke, Hampshire: Macmillan.

Simon, H. (1952) "A comparison of organization theories." *Review of Economic Studies* 20(1): 40–48.

Simon, H. (1957) *Administrative Behavior*, 2d ed. New York: Macmillan.

Spender, J.-C. (1989) *Industry Recipes: The Nature and Sources of Managerial Judgement*. Oxford: Blackwell.

Spender, J.-C. (1996) "Making knowledge the basis of a dynamic theory of the firm." *Strategic Management Journal* 17(Winter):45–62.

Spender, J.-C. (1998) "The geographies of strategic competence: Borrowing from social and educational psychology to sketch an activity and knowledge-based theory of the firm," In Alfred D. Chandler, Peter Hagstrom, and Örjan Sölvell (eds.), *The Dynamic Firm: The Role of Technology, Strategy, Organization, and Regions*, pp. 417–439. New York: Oxford University Press.

Spender, J.-C. and Kijne, H. (1996) *Scientific Management: F. W. Taylor's Gift to the World?* Norwell, MA: Norwell.

Teece, D. (2000) "Managing knowledge assets in diverse industrial contexts," In C. Despres and D. Chauvel (eds.), *Knowledge Horizons: The Past and the Promise of Knowledge Management*, pp. 131–147. Boston: Butterworth-Heinemann.

Thompson, J. (1967) *Organizations in Action: Social Sciences Bases of Administrative Theory*. New York: McGraw-Hill.

Toennies, F. (1971) *On Sociology Pure, Applied, and Empirical*. Chicago: University of Chicago Press.

Triffin, R. (1947) *Monopolistic Competition and General Equilibrium Theory*. Cambridge, MA: Harvard University Press.

von Krogh, G., Roos, J., and Kleine, D., eds. (1998) *Knowing in Firms: Understanding, Managing, and Measuring Knowledge*. London: Sage.

von Krogh, G., Ichijo, K., and Nonaka, I. (2000) *Enabling Knowledge Creation: How to Unlock the Mystery of Tacit Knowledge and Release the Power of Innovation*. New York: Oxford University Press.

Vygotsky, L. (1962) *Thought and Language*. Cambridge, MA: MIT Press.

Vygotsky, L. (1978) *Mind in Society: The Development of Higher Psychological Processes*. Cambridge, MA: Harvard University Press.

Wiig, K. (2000) "Knowledge management: an emerging discipline rooted in a long history," in C. Despres and D. Chauvel (eds.), *Knowledge Horizons: The Past and the Promise of Knowledge Management*, pp. 3–26. Boston: Butterworth-Heinemann.

10

From Economic Theory toward a Knowledge-Based Theory of the Firm

Conceptual Building Blocks

Georg von Krogh and Simon Grand

Open Issues and Overall Argumentation

There is consensus among entrepreneurs, managers, academics, and consultants that we are about to embark on a new economic order: a knowledge-based economy, playing by a new set of rules (Day and Schoemaker 2000, Hamel 2000). In recent years we have seen an increasing interest in firm knowledge and innovation as the source of competitive advantage, which can be traced back to the emergence of the resource-based perspective of the firm (Wernerfeld 1984, Dierickx and Cool 1988, Barney 1991, Mahoney and Pandian 1992, Peteraf 1993, Teece et al. 1997), the growing literature on innovation (Dosi 1982, Foster 1986, Tushman and Anderson 1986, Henderson and Clark 1990, Utterback 1994, Bower and Christensen 1995, Christensen 1997), organizational learning (Hedlund 1994, Argyris and Schon 1996, Wenger 1998), and most explicitly in the recent development of a knowledge-based perspective of strategy (Nonaka 1994, von Krogh et al. 1994, Spender 1996, Grant 1996).

Strategic management thereby refers to industrial organization and microeconomic theories of the firm (Porter 1991, Rumelt et al. 1994) as the conceptual foundation to explain competitive success. Economic theory discusses various sources of abnormal returns and rents (Montgomery 1995, Winter 1995), including monopoly rents generated from the product markets, Ricardian rents resulting from the factor markets, and Schumpeterian rents gained through innovation (Schmalensee 1989, Tirole 1989). Interestingly, economic theory does not refer explicitly to knowledge and learning as key sources of competitive success, though it implicitly alludes to knowledge issues in its narratives (McCloskey 1986). As a consequence, understanding and conceptualizing how companies appropriate returns from innovation and knowledge creation in order to create competitive advantage becomes one of the key issues for the advancement of strategic management.

The present chapter argues that conceptual limitations imply that standard economic theory cannot fully contribute to this advancement, since its underlying theoretical architecture does not cover knowledge and innovation issues appropriately (see Nelson and Winter 1982, Dosi 1982). The theoretical attempts to conceptualize innovation, technological development, standard setting, and industry emergence discuss some limitations. The more recent attempts to build a resource-based theory of the firm add further arguments. But, while they share important points of criticism, they only partially provide theoretical alternatives, referring to evolutionary theories (Nelson 1991, 1995, Montgomery 1995). The present chapter will discuss both the conceptual advancements and the limitations of evolutionary theorizing.

Evolutionary theory, as the theoretical core of most innovation research and part of the resource-based theory of the firm, heavily refers to organizational knowledge as being at the core of competitive success and advantage, often without making the argument explicit. The recent developments of a knowledge-based perspective, on the contrary, provide a detailed analysis of the mechanisms underlying organizational knowledge creation and transfer, though without demonstrating its impact on competitive success. Elaborating on the gap between insisting on the importance of organizational knowledge as a source of competitive success and analyzing the mechanisms of knowledge creation and transfer is at the core of strategy research.

There have been many attempts to further elaborate and specify this agenda (Connor 1991, Spender 1996, Grant 1996, Williamson 1999, Foss 1999). These contributions either defend economic theory as the theoretical core of strategic management (Grant 1996, Williamson 1999), or they argue in the perspective of an evolutionary theory (Szulanski 1996), or they lose sight of competitive success as the core issue of strategic management (Spender 1996, Tsoukas 1993, von Krogh et al. 1994), or they end up with an eclectic comparison of various isolated perspectives without discussing their mutual interdependencies and contradictions (Conner 1991, Foss 1999). The present chapter demonstrates why these approaches are limited and attempts to contribute theoretical building blocks toward a knowledge-based theory of the firm.

First, we analyze the theoretical architecture of economic theory as a paradigm of strategic management and discuss its conceptual limitations to appropriately cover innovation and knowledge creation and transfer. Second, we discuss the contributions of the resource-based view, on the one hand, and of innovation research

based on evolutionary theory, on the other, as two recent attempts to resolve some of the major strategic issues not covered by economic theory. Third, we introduce some building blocks for a knowledge-based view that explicitly include return appropriation and competitive success as the core issue for any contribution in strategic management. Finally, we conclude with implications for both strategy research and managerial action.

When following this argument, the chapter systematically compares and relates important contributions to strategic management, as well as to a knowledge-based theory of the firm. While various established contributions try to relate arguments from economic theory to recent insights on organizational knowledge (Grant 1996, Williamson 1999), other contributions follow a resource-based perspective (Montgomery 1995, Teece et al. 1997) or an evolutionary perspective (Cohen and Levinthal 1990) as more promising alternatives. Or, they combine all three theoretical lenses within one single argumentation (Foss 1999). The present chapter argues that all four approaches suffer from analytical limitations and conceptual contradictions, which must be explicitly resolved by any robust contribution to a knowledge-based theory of the firm.

This overall argument can be visualized as shown in figure 10.1, which shows the different research strategies dominating strategy research. They will be subsequently analyzed and diagnosed in this chapter.

Strategic Management and Economic Theory

Return Appropriation in Strategic Management

Strategy research has taken shape around a common framework (Andrews 1971, Mintzberg et al. 1998), focusing on the match between what a firm can do, its organizational strengths and weaknesses, within the environment of what it might do, its environmental opportunities and threats (Foss et al. 1995). In order to elaborate and refine this basic concept, the microeconomic theory of the firm as well as industrial organization has had a profound influence on the strategy field (Rumelt et al. 1994).

Strategic management identified as its primary mission the analysis of diversity of performance among firms as well as the impact on

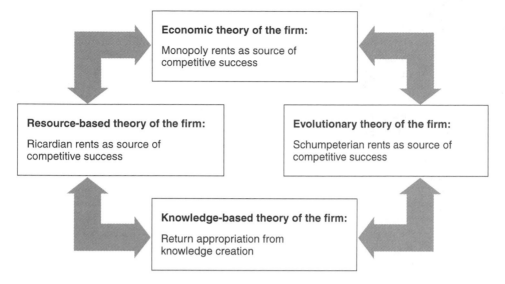

Figure 10.1 Overview research strategies.

competitive success (Porter 1991). In order to understand and explain differences in firm success, the analysis profits from various traditions in economic theory (Winter 1995).

Traditional industrial organization, based on the structure-conduct-performance paradigm, identifies attractive product market environments as the primary source of abnormal profits. Successful strategic management thus results from identifying attractive industry constellations and optimally positioning the firm. The attractiveness of an industry depends on the actual rivalry within the industry, as well as future changes in the competitive situation, due to market entries of new competitors, changes in the behavior of competitors, or changes in the broader technological, economic and sociocultural environment (Porter 1980, 1985, 1991, Foss et al. 1995). Empirical research only partially supports this explanation; the industry structure accounts for only a modest fraction of the variation in performance differences among firms (for this controversy, see Schmalensee 1989, Rumelt 1991).

As a consequence, strategic management is forced to elaborate on an alternative model of competitive success, drawing performance differences back to Ricardian rents. Ricardian rents result from differences among firms in their access to input factors, as well as in their efficient transformation into valuable products and services through procedures internal to the firm (Montgomery 1995, Winter 1995). While the competitive position on the factor markets is

modeled in industrial organization terms, the internal processual efficiency is modeled in terms of transaction costs, incomplete contracts, and incentive structures (Williamson 1991, 1999). It is at this point in the argument that the significance of organizational knowledge as an important driver behind differences in internal processes between firms is raised, however, without any explicit discussion (Williamson 1991; see critique in Ghoshal and Moran 1996).

Given the importance of technological innovation for industry transformations and changing competitive landscapes in most industries, strategic management increasingly refers to Schumpeterian rents as another source of competitive success (D'Aveni 1994, Nelson 1991, 1995, Winter 1995). Schumpeterian rents result from differences in the ability of companies to create first-mover advantages by proactive innovation (Lieberman and Montgomery 1988). In this perspective, firm differences result from dynamic evolutionary processes (Dosi 1982), where companies enact their environments through innovations (Weick 1995) and judge environmental responses by selecting the most robust initiatives (March 1991, Nelson 1995). At this point however, knowledge is implicitly seen as an input to the innovation process, without any further elaboration.

All three perspectives contribute to strategy research to the extent that they recognize, understand and explain conduct and performance differences across firms (Winter 1995). While industrial organization focuses on the competitive forces in the relevant industrial environment on both the product and factor markets, transaction cost theory focuses on contractual arrangements and coordination mechanisms leading to specific firm conduct (Williamson 1991, 1999). Based on the economic assumptions about internal and market efficiency, firm strategies, and behaviors become more homogeneous over time, due to strategic interaction and imitative learning, which lead to decreasing returns. As a consequence, established industry structures are challenged by proactive strategic moves and innovative initiatives, in order to create new industry constellations and to realize first-mover advantages therein (Lieberman and Montgomery 1988).

Economic Theory and the Production of Knowledge

While these arguments implicitly assume the importance of organizational knowledge creation and innovation, they provide no illumination to questions dealing with how the organizational knowledge and existing range of technological alternatives came into existence and to the nature of the specific forces generating them (Rosenberg 1976, Dosi 1982, Rumelt 1984, Teece et al. 1994). This bias can be explained by the underlying architecture of neoclassical economic theory, assuming methodological individualism and rational optimizing agents (firms or individual actors) with given preference and production functions, focusing on the forces driving toward equilibrium states, and excluding chronic information problems, radical uncertainty, and divergent ambiguous perceptions (Hodgson 1994). Innovation and knowledge creation are thus seen as the result of the rational choice among previously given technical and structural alternatives.

While the above argumentation explains competitive strategies from the outside, the internal processes and organizational knowledge that lead to innovative initiatives and unique abilities are more difficult to explain within economic theory itself. It is not surprising, then, that economic theory only recently has begun to garner interest in information and knowledge and their relations to a theory of the firm (Arrow 1962, 1975). Unlike other assets, knowledge and information still have a quality of being highly arbitrary concepts, which are difficult to observe and to theorize about. At the same time, however, it remains an empirical fact that knowledge and in-

formation are important for innovation and economic growth (Morrison and Siegel 1997), and much of the knowledge creation in the economy is done within the firm (Nelson and Winter 1982).

As a consequence, knowledge gains in importance as a research topic in economic theory:

> Information and knowledge are at the heart of organizational design, because they result in contractual and incentive problems that challenge both markets and firms. Indeed, information and knowledge have long been understood to be different from goods and assets commonly traded in markets. In light of this, it is surprising that the leading economic theories of the firm have paid almost no attention to the role of organizational knowledge. (Holmström and Roberts 1998, p. 90)

While economic theory typically suggests that knowledge creation is exogenous to the firm, more recent economic theories of the firm suggest that firms play an extraordinary role in creating and transferring knowledge within an economy and that firm performance in terms of innovation is endogenous (Holmström and Roberts 1998).

One key issue remains open, however: If knowledge is created within the firm, contributing to competitive success, what, then, are the processes by which this occurs? This cannot be ignored, as it will help to uncover the mechanisms underlying important firm activities that affect economic growth. A glimpse "inside the black box" helps economic theory to provide a more comprehensive view of the way firms tie in with innovation and the overall knowledge production of society.

In order to approach these questions, economic theory refers to one of its central concepts: the production function that describes the technical relations between outputs and inputs in a production process. Organizational knowledge is thus conceptualized as the outcome of a knowledge production function (Griliches 1979, Kamien and Schwartz 1982, Jaffe 1986). Knowledge production is formalized as a knowledge output (e.g., number of patents; see Crepon and Duguet 1997) being a function of certain input factors (industry research and development [R&D] expenditures, university R&D expenditures), which is further specified by including interactive effects between a university and industry R&D (e.g., due to co-location of R&D facilities; Jaffe 1989). The knowledge production function itself is seen as resulting from exogenous processes of technological evolution.

This approach has also been criticized for the difficulty to specify input, activities, and output of knowledge production appropriately (Acs and Audretsch 1990, Stiglitz 1996), as well as for the invisible nature of knowledge flows (spillover, input, output) in general (Krugmann 1991). More important, the knowledge production function model assumes the firm to be exogenous, engaging in the pursuit of new knowledge in order to generate innovation, which is endogenous. Whereas this might be arguable for large firms with established routines for allocating R&D investments, small firms do not have the same access to internal resources. However, considerable innovations and patents in high-tech industries are created by small firms (Scherer 1992, Audretsch and Stephan 1999).

Thus, what happens in the black box of the knowledge production function is vague and ambiguous at best. The exact links between knowledge sources and the resulting innovative output remain invisible and unknown. In many instances, external knowledge is absorbed and used by existing firms. In other cases, however, the development of new knowledge provides an incentive for the establishment of new firms. In addition, a major part of the knowledge input is shared by communities of specialists beyond the boundaries of any specific firm. If we want to make a prediction on knowledge production and knowledge spillovers involving firms, in order to understand how firms accrue private returns from new knowledge, there is a need to open the black box of the knowledge production function.

Toward an Evolutionary Perspective on Strategic Management

Organizational Knowledge and the Resource-Based View

The clear conceptual advantages of the industrial organization model to deduce an analytical framework for an industry and competitive analysis (Porter 1991) are offset by its focus on conceptualizing the impact of innovation and organizational knowledge creation on return appropriation and strategic advantages. Beyond a predominance of environmental factors over mechanisms internal to the firm, there are various limitations to economic theory that matter in our context.

Contrary to predictions of economic theory, there is a growing body of empirical evidence that firms differ largely and sustainably in their resource endowments (Rumelt 1984, Cool and Schendel 1988, Hansen and Wernerfeldt 1989, Grant 1991, Barney 1991, Mahoney and Pandian 1992). Since the basic tenet of microeconomic theory is that competitive advantages are not sustainable in the long run, or in the short run in case of free entry (Schoemaker 1993), it basically contradicts the intention of strategic management to understand the sources of lasting competitive advantages. As a consequence, innovation research analyzing the sources of Schumpeterian rents, and the resource-based view of strategy elaborating the concept of Ricardian rents in combination with a closer look at the role of firm-specific resources further advance strategic management.

The initial building blocks for a resource-based view of strategy intended simply to broaden the economic perspective: "For the firm, resources and products are two sides of the same coin. By specifying the size of the firm's activity in different product markets, it is possible to infer the minimum necessary resource commitments; by specifying a resource profile for a firm, it is possible to find the optimal product-market activities" (Wernerfeldt 1984, p. 171). Thereby, resources are defined as those tangible and intangible assets that are tied semipermanently to the firm at a given point in time (Wernerfeld 1984, based on Penrose 1959). Contrary to economic theory, resources are assumed to develop as a result of limited rational and discretionary decisions through time that cumulate in a given set of organizational capabilities (Amit and Schoemaker 1993).

Based on these initial conceptual building blocks, strategy research started to investigate the necessary characteristics of resources, which could generate market imperfections and abnormal returns (Barney 1986, 1991, Dierickx and Cool 1989, Peteraf 1993, Amit and Schoemaker 1993): resources that create value while being scarce have the potential to create rents and thus competitive advantage (rent creation; this part of the argument is still in line with economic theory), but only resources that are difficult to imitate and only imperfectly substitutable create sustainable advantages (inimitability). This second point contradicts the standard microeconomic argument that firm differences will erode over time due to imitative learning. The mechanisms that preserve the heterogeneity of firms' resource endowments become the cornerstone of a resource-based view of strategy (Lippmann and Rumelt 1982).

The isolating mechanisms that create ex post limits to competition (Peteraf 1993) are manifold (Rumelt 1984, Mahoney and Pandian 1992): path dependency or historicity makes competence building time dependent and context specific (Dierickx and Cool 1989); competence interconnectedness implies that certain assets create their value only as complementary assets (Kogut and Zander 1992, Teece 1990); causal ambiguity means that there is uncertainty about the ways in which competences create valuable outcomes (Reed and DeFilippi 1990). These arguments share the insight that it is necessary to leave economic theorizing in order to explicitly model firm-specific knowledge-related production.

Despite its considerable progress, the resource-based view still suffers from several weaknesses (see Williamson 1999). Theoretical progress has been made in identifying resources and characterizing what makes them valuable (Dierickx and Cool 1989); however, it is often difficult to identify which of the concrete resources account for success, leading to tautological argumentation. At the very least, the identification process often has a distinct ex post quality; once a firm is recognized as successful, the resources behind the success are labeled as valuable. If observed in another setting, it is not clear that the resources would be valued in the same way (Montgomery 1995).

The difficulty in assessing the value of resources is related to the fact that it is impossible to measure them in isolation and out of the particular context in which the firm finds itself. Resources are valuable only if they allow firms to perform activities that create advantages in particular markets (Porter 1991). Another contextual factor to consider is the presence of complementary assets. The value of an individual resource is likely to be at least partially contingent upon the presence of other resources; that is, it may be a system of resources that matters, not the individual resources taken separately. Further, the value of resources will change over time (Foss et al. 1995).

While the resource-based view uses equilibrium arguments from industrial organization to analyze rent creation, when identifying sources of abnormal returns and competitive success from an economic perspective, it relies on process arguments to understand inimitability, based on such concepts as emergence, path dependence, and learning. At this point, there is a need for new theoretical building blocks that explicitly model the dynamic character of rent appropriation from resources and competences.

Toward an Evolutionary Theory of Strategy

Economic theory assumes that the knowledge about the input and output in the production function, as well as the actual transformation, is explicit and possible to formalize (Arrow and Hahn 1971). Furthermore, economic theory assumes that this knowledge is articulated and accessible to other firms in a way that they can adopt the most efficient production function through imitative learning. The remaining differences between firms result from the indefinite costs of sharing the information or of measuring the value of that information for another firm (Hallwood 1997). As a consequence, substantial differences in firm structures, procedures, and behaviors will basically disappear over time due to imitation and adaptive learning, except for certain procedures that are protected by specific property rights regulations and measurement costs.

The distinguishing characteristic of the evolutionary approach in strategy research is precisely that it goes to the question of where firm differences come from and how they are created, maintained, and defended over time (Nelson 1991, p. 1005). These path-dependent, firm-specific procedures, routines, resources, and competencies ultimately differentiate a firm from other firms, leading to unique profit-seeking strategies. Thereby, firm-specific resources and competencies cannot be acquired simply through imitative learning, but are the result of firm-specific processes of competence building, routinization, and knowledge creation.

Contrary to conventional economic theory, an evolutionary perspective will conceptualize firms as being motivated by profit and engaged in search for new ways to improve their profits, but their actions are not assumed to be profit maximizing over well-defined and exogenous choice sets (Nelson and Winter 1982). There is a general tendency for the most profitable firm to drive the less profitable ones out of business, however, without assuming hypothetical states of industry equilibrium as a reference point. In parallel, firm behavior does not result from any maximizing strategic decision-making process: "[F]irms are modeled as simply having, at any given time, certain capabilities and decision rules which are modified as a result of both deliberate problem-solving efforts and random events" (Nelson and Winter 1982, p. 4).

If one is to adopt an evolutionary perspective, the issue remains as to what forces drive the evolutionary process, the basic elements being variation, selection, and retention (Campbell 1965). In the perspective of strategic management, the search for profitable opportunities is a primary force of variation generation (Schumpeter 1934, Baumol 1993). Thereby, entrepreneurial activity can occur within the context of established firms as well as being associated with the founding of new enterprises (Burgelman and Sayles 1986, Block and MacMillan 1993). Within the firm, appropriate incentives and internal selection mechanisms are key in creating as well as sorting out innovative options (Burgelman 1983a, 1983b). Another way to generate variation is organizational search (March and Simon 1958). A critical feature of organizational search is that it tends to be local. By implication, if capabilities are enhanced via a search process, then the capabilities that emerge will be path dependent. While the resource-based perspective takes the firm, as a bundle of resources, as its unit of analysis, the evolutionary perspective focuses on technological evolution and the resulting competition among firms as bundle of routines (Foss et al. 1995).

From an evolutionary perspective, firm behavior is nevertheless important, since it is on this level where retention processes should be found. Concepts such as adaptation, learning, search and path dependence mostly relate to the level of the firm. In this view, firms are conceptualized as possessing path-dependent knowledge bases, forming bundles of hierarchically arranged routines. Routines thereby include a wide range of firm-specific procedures, including technical routines, production processes, investment policies, research and development activities, and business strategies. Together, they aggregate to persistent patterns of behavior (Nelson and Winter 1982). The notion of routines provides a rationale for the relative rigidity that is necessary for the successful application of selection arguments. However, to the grief of many strategists who go down this route, evolutionary theory is less interested per se in the strategies that individual firms articulate on

the basis of these knowledge bases (Foss et al. 1995).

As a consequence, evolutionary theory provides deep insights into the broader functions of organizational competencies and knowledge (Nelson 1991, 1995). Whereas economic theory reduces organizational knowledge to formalized knowledge production, evolutionary theory sees knowledge as encompassing and embedded in the firm (Winter 1995, Levinthal 1996). People solve tasks in ways that deviate from formal procedures, and they learn through experimenting with new tasks. Firms are heterogeneous in their factor inputs by selecting, modifying, and adapting the input to fit with the established routines, or sometimes adapting certain routines to changing inputs. Routines that prove successful for the firm are replicated over time, while unsuccessful routines are replaced by new ones (Nelson and Winter 1982, Szulanski and Winter unpublished manuscript).

Innovation and organizational knowledge creation can be interpreted as shifting the border between technically possible and technically impossible production activities. Traditional economic theorizing assumes that knowledge production can be interpreted as extending what is physically possible. This implies that knowledge extends beyond current activities, the boundary of the actual production set being the boundary of the actual organizational knowledge. While economic theory has to conceptualize these mechanisms as exogenous, evolutionary theory indicates that knowledge is subject to some form of transformation as a result of searching and learning (Nelson and Winter 1982).

If accompanied by basic uncertainty and ambiguity, industry transformation and technological evolution confront firms with difficult investment choices and limited rationality for managerial decision making. In particular, transformation and technological evolution make limited rationality about the resources to be invested a particularly prominent feature. Technological shifts are also important because they are likely to have a cascading effect on the value of the existent resource base. Because technologies exist in a broader system of complementary assets (Teece 1986, Christensen 1997), shifts in technology are likely to induce changes in the value of supporting or complementary assets. While the resource-based view focuses on firm-specific competences, an evolutionary perspective opens for considering industrywide value constellations (Christensen

1997) as well as relational advantages (Dyer and Singh 1998).

Implications for Return Appropriation and Knowledge Creation

Equilibrium models are the cornerstone of economic thinking, both in neoclassical industrial organization and in the resource-based view of strategy. Equilibrium models imply that all known possibilities for decision alternatives, as well as for economic exchange, have been exploited; it is an end-state of a process of opportunity discovery, modeled as if the discovery process itself did not matter much. This basic conceptualization hinders the resource-based perspective from appropriately covering the dynamic character of competence building and competence destruction over time (Leonard-Barton 1992; see the more recent attempts by Teece et al. 1997). On the contrary, Schumpeterian competition, as a cornerstone of evolutionary theory, describes the processes through which innovations are made and imitated, as being inherently nonequilibrium. As a consequence, evolutionary theory implies an entirely new way of defining firm success, resulting in a new understanding of the issue of return appropriation.

According to Schumpeterian theorizing, evolutionary theory identifies innovation with the carrying out of recombining existing routines and competencies (Schumpeter 1934, p. 65f). Innovation in the economic system consists to a substantial extent of a recombination of conceptual and physical building blocks that were previously in existence (Nelson and Winter 1982). New routines and competencies are created through a combination of existing knowledge and existing routines in new ways. This search for new combinations is not purely arbitrary, but follows heuristics as principles and devices contributing to the reduction in the average search efforts to find an appropriate solution (Newell et al. 1962). In this sense innovation and knowledge creation can be interpreted as resulting from a recombination of already existing organizational routines (Nelson and Winter 1982).

This straightforward conceptualization of innovative activities in the perspective of evolutionary theory dominates much of current innovation research (Dosi 1982, 1988, Teece 1984, 1990, Dosi and Marengo 1993, Hodgson 1993, 1994, Teece et al. 1994, Nelson 1995, Dosi et al. 1998). Evolutionary theory is considered to be

the appropriate meta-theory to explain both technological innovation and industry development. While the initial work on innovation processes referred to a broad and unspecified evolutionary perspective (Abernathy and Utterback 1978, Abernathy and Clark 1985, Tushman and Andersen 1986, Utterback 1994), more recent contributions extensively draw from evolutionary theorizing (Kauffman 1989, 1993, 1995, Anderson 1999). Hence, it does not come as a surprise that industry and technologic evolution is increasingly being conceptualized as local adaptive search on a fitness landscape. Thus, observed differences in strategic behavior, organizational forms, and firm-specific resources and competencies "may in large part reflect variation in founding conditions in conjunction with local search on a rugged landscape" (Levinthal 1995, p. 26f).

Evolutionary theory therefore does an adequate job of conceptualizing incremental adaptation processes. For example, the punctuated equilibrium paradigm shapes most argumentations in innovation research (Eldredge and Gould 1972, Gersick 1991, Romanelli and Tushman 1994): "relatively long periods of stability (equilibrium), punctuated by compact periods of qualitative, metamorphic change (revolution)" (Gersick 1991, p. 11). However, it remains unclear how phases of revolutionary change and disruption can be conceptualized. Recent theorizing suggests that given the inertia and path dependence of established firms, small entrepreneurial companies (Christensen 1997), as well as proactive changes within established firms (Hamel 2000), become key. However, proactive innovation, competence building, and knowledge creation fall outside much of the current evolutionary theorizing. As a consequence, it seems a theory of knowledge creation is required that explicitly explains how new ideas and local initiatives turn into radical changes in firm competencies and behavior.

Whereas the resource-based view sees strategy as having a strongly intentional element (Barney 1986, 1991, Porter 1991, Hamel and Prahalad 1993, 1994), evolutionary theories are traditionally much more pessimistic about the possibilities for significant, managerially led, proactive change (see also Witt 1994). The question of intentionality becomes particularly salient when considering how a firm sets out to build a given set of capabilities. Because resources that support a competitive advantage are by definition inimitable, and high measurement costs (Hallwood 1997) are a sufficient condition for inimitability, it follows that managerially led initiatives are also difficult to understand and model. In short, strategists following this path can give little advice to managers on how they should invest in order to build a competitive advantage. As a consequence, a theory of knowledge creation, in order to be practically useful as well as to become a real theoretical contribution, has to reintegrate managerial discretion into its theory of strategic behavior and return appropriation.

On the level of the economic knowledge production function, evolutionary theory (Nelson and Winter 1982) sees the importance of knowledge for the production set and capability building in general, however, addressing the notion of input in relation to knowledge output in a cursory manner. For example, what are the relations between receiving new procedures through knowledge spillover and routinizing them in new patterns of behavior? If firms have access to similar knowledge through knowledge spillover, do they differ in the application of this knowledge? There are possible indications that they should. Loasby (1998) suggests, for example, that

> capabilities are endogenous, and should be analyzed in the context of change. They result from specialization, and need to be coordinated, but in ways which do not inhibit their continuing development; the capability of managing coordination while fostering learning . . . is worth particular attention. But since capability is know-how, manifested in action, and accumulated rather than the product of logical analysis, it does not fit comfortably into conventional economic theory. (p. 157)

Another problem in recent evolutionary thinking on firm behavior is that of coherence (Teece et al. 1994). This question focuses on what it is that fundamentally distinguishes the viable firm as a historical entity, rather than just an arbitrary collection of businesses, competencies, and activities. While economic theory is strong at explaining firm coherence, as the result of strategic decisions in the perspective of transaction costs and property rights, it remains unclear how evolutionary theory might structure this open issue. As a consequence, a theory relating knowledge creation and return appropriation must cover the creation and development of firm coherence.

In summary, it can be said that evolutionary theory conceptualizes knowledge creation as being internal to the firm. Its innovative activities are centered around combining knowledge and routines in new ways to achieve competitive success and appropriate returns from this new knowledge. Private returns from these new combinations might be appropriated by tacit routines and intellectual property rights. However, a reading of evolutionary theory also leaves some questions open. For example, is the combination of existing routines the only source of new knowledge, or are there any other sources or ways by which the firm can achieve this (Witt 1994)? Are intellectual property rights and routinization the only ways to protect knowledge, or are there other mechanisms directly related to the process of knowledge creation (as discussed in the resource-based view)? Both issues are key if we intend to carefully examine potential strategies for return appropriation from innovation and knowledge creation.

Building Blocks for a Knowledge-Based Theory of the Firm

Conditions for a Knowledge-Based Theory of the Firm

In order for a knowledge-based theory of the firm to achieve its appropriate status as a theoretical as well as managerial contribution, it must satisfy at least five conditions. First, it needs a concept of knowledge origin. Evolutionary as well as conventional economic theory lacks a concept of knowledge that can explain the origin of new knowledge, a process central to the creation of rent and competitive advantage. However, whereas the current status of a "knowledge-based theory" includes many attempts to conceptualize knowledge and relate this to overall organizational activity (Tsoukas 1993), it has failed to explain the relation between firm rent appropriation and its knowledge-creation activities. Therefore, as a second condition, it needs a concept of knowledge creation as an ongoing firm activity that itself could become a source of rent, due to its valuable but unique character (i.e., the process is a source of advantage, not the knowledge itself). Third, a view of the firm as a collage of resources, processes, and competences is overly simplistic and might divert attention away from the underlying dynamics of establishing coherence in patterns of firm activity and development. Therefore, the theory needs to identify necessary and sufficient conditions for a "corporate coherence." Fourth, a knowledge-based theory of the firm must explain, and if possible predict, revolutionary versus evolutionary changes at the level of firms and industries. In particular, it must link the level of change affecting the firm to the creation of coherence in the firm. Therefore, a knowledge-based theory of the firm needs a comprehensive concept of change. A cornerstone in the strategic management discipline is that managerial activity and decision making matter for success (Grinyer 1998a, 1998b). Therefore, in order to claim value in this discipline, as a fifth condition, a knowledge-based theory of the firm must establish a link between managerially led initiatives and competitive advantage, and therefore a concept of intentionality is called for.

Condition 1: A Concept of Knowledge Origin

A prominent philosophical notation of knowledge is "justified true belief" (Nonaka 1994). Knowing means holding certain beliefs about the world, this knowledge being justified in experience and current observations as well as conceptual reasoning and thinking. However, "[b]eliefs alone are not sufficient to cause action: they would fail to motivate the action" (Saidel 1998, p. 24). As a consequence, economic theory uses a more actionable distinction on knowledge between "knowledge-that" and "knowledge-how" (based on Ryle 1949). While knowledge-that captures knowledge that is publicly available, knowledge-how represents the capabilities of firms at making sense of this publicly available knowledge, as well as solving tasks (Loasby 1998). If knowledge can be seen as the capacity for action (both knowledge-what and knowledge-how), we have to consider that various forms of organizational knowledge compete to be translated into action (Lammers 1974). Knowledge-how implies action whereas knowledge-what is not necessarily tied directly to action. But knowledge-what (to do) can also be designed in such a way from the outset as to enable action rather than to simply enhance understanding of a phenomenon.

As a consequence, we must further differentiate: "Knowledge is both a medium of social action and the result of human conduct" (Stehr 1992, p. 4). Knowledge informs social action and, by this, enhances the capacity for the creation of new knowledge. In order to capture this duality, and the competition entailed in knowledge production, knowledge-how implies both action knowledge as knowledge that has been translated into action, and practical knowledge as knowledge that from the beginning is designed to serve as a capacity for action. When action knowledge is encoded and translated into rules, procedures, and action plans, it becomes practical knowledge. In the production function of orthodox economic theory, knowledge is limited to practical knowledge about potential technologies, their intended consequences, and guidelines for their applications. In this respect, technology is practical knowledge in terms of means–end relationships.

Given this concept of knowledge, where does knowledge originate? Orthodox economic theory and evolutionary theory assume knowledge originates first and foremost through combinations of existing knowledge: "As a rule, the new combinations must draw the necessary means of production from some old combinations. . . . [D]evelopment consists primarily in employing existing resources in a different way, in doing new things with them" (Schumpeter 1934). Combination corresponds ideally to declarative and practical knowledge, because they are of an explicit kind and thus allow easy combination (Weitzman 1998). This model reduces the knowledge origin to existing knowledge and to the creation or processing capacity.

One key extension in the perspective of a knowledge-based theory of the firm is to consider the difference, yet interconnectedness, of explicit knowledge (declarative and practical) and tacit knowledge (action) (Polanyi 1958). Tacit knowledge is difficult if not impossible to codify, only transmittable through direct observation of activities and imitation of task solutions. Cognition thus works not only by combining new ideas but also by drawing on a variety of human experiences. This experience in turn may remain beyond investigation and scrutiny by the holder of that experience (Varela et al. 1991), hence beyond straightforward combination. A pure combinatorial approach to knowledge creation remains silent on where such knowledge first originated, whereas recent efforts suggest that such experience might be the very essence of knowledge, both tacit and explicit (Varela 1996). Human experience as the origin of knowledge should in turn be studied at the levels of both individuals and groups (Cook and Brown 1999), and perhaps even at the level of firms, at least as contexts that provide individuals and groups with particular and universal, regular and ephemeral, and individual and collective experiences. The attention to experience is vaguely reminiscent of the earlier elaborations of experience effect, scale economies, and cost advantage and in industrial organization and strategic management. But what is new here is that experience, in its broadest sense, might be the foundation for a knowledge-based theory of the firm rather than the by-product of operating a manufacturing technology (see Nelson and Winter 1982, p. 260).

This attention to human experience as the foundation for human knowledge has led to a stronger focus (or reinvention) of phenomenology in the cognitive sciences (Globus 1995). What the consequences of this may be for economics is quite premature to suggest, but since phenomenology is concerned with the object of perception and what the senses notice, one could envisage a stronger attention to the differences rather than uniformity of the *perception* or *experience* of the firm. Strategic management has already started to pay greater attention to the phenomenological method and its consequences (Mir and Watson 2000), making way for a new approach to the study of the origins of knowledge, perhaps resolving some of the existing tautologies in the resource-based theory of the firm, where a distinction between knowledge and competitive advantage cannot be made.

Condition 2: A Concept of the Knowledge Creation Process

A second cornerstone in a knowledge-based theory of the firm is the concept of a knowledge-creation process as an activity description of what the firm does or does not do. Though the root of knowledge is experience, there is still some uncertainty related to the process whereby the firm creates knowledge. How do firms process information and create new knowledge about input conditions (declarative knowledge), technologies (practical knowledge), and output conditions (declarative knowledge) to generate economic activity (action knowledge) under conditions of limited processing capabilities?

Knowledge has a highly distributed and fragmented character (Spender 1996, Tsoukas 1993), and whereas knowledge creation through combination seems deterministic at first glance, closer examination reveals that it is highly stochastic. Knowledge creation contains several random elements due to numerous organizational,

individual (Nonaka and Takeuchi 1995, von Krogh et al. 1994, von Krogh et al. 2000, Levinthal and March 1993), and governance-related obstacles (Williamson 1999). For a knowledge-based theory of the firm, what matters are the necessary conditions for knowledge creation to occur. In general terms, we argue that connectivity can be seen as basically shaping knowledge creation as well as the robustness of new knowledge being processed by the firm (von Krogh et al. 1994). Connectivity is an expression of the proximity of the source and the user of knowledge in the knowledge-creation process. Weak connectivity implies that there is very limited physical contact between the source and the user of knowledge. Experiences may be regular, but they remain individual and particular. Strong connectivity implies a lack of identifiable demarcation between the source of knowledge and the user of knowledge (Wenger 1998). Experiences may be regular, and collective and universal as well.

In this perspective, the enabling conditions for knowledge creation are as follows: While the creation of declarative and practical knowledge, based on other declarative and practical knowledge, and the creation of declarative knowledge based on action knowledge assume weak connectivity between the source and the user of the knowledge, the creation of action knowledge, rooted in declarative and practical knowledge, and the creation of practical knowledge based on action knowledge require semistrong connectivity. The creation of action knowledge based on action knowledge requires strong connectivity. This knowledge is only accessible through the membership in a group or in the firm (Wagner 1987; see Winter 1991, p. 185).

Given this extended model of knowledge creation and the conditions of connectivity, the firm can be understood as a network of agents (nodes), built of sources and users of knowledge, relationships between these, and knowledge-creation activities (Granovetter 1985). The firm combines existing knowledge into new knowledge as in evolutionary theory, but it also internalizes this knowledge into action knowledge, externalizes action knowledge into explicit knowledge, socializes action knowledge and so forth (Nonaka, Takeuchi 1995). In any network analysis, the type of connections have to be described in terms of "relational contents" (Knoke and Kuklinski 1991). The agents in the network comprise the source and user of knowledge, whereas the connection itself comprises the activity of knowledge creation. The implication of this is that every relationship in the firm should be viewed as carrying the potential for knowledge creation. Thus, the firm emerges as a portfolio of relationships with the potential to create new knowledge. These relationships might be characterized among several dimensions, such as levels (group to group), frequency, strength (Granovetter 1985), authority and hierarchy (Weber 1958), trust (Nonaka and Takeuchi 1995), or care (von Krogh 1998).

The interesting consequence of this view is that in order to fully understand knowledge-creation processes in firms, we need to unmask the processes of establishing knowledge-creating relationships as well. Hence, a firm's advantage might be found in its ability to quickly establish strong relationships among previously unrelated agents, for the purpose of innovating or for the purpose of searching in a solution space.

What is clear, however, is that the processes of establishing relationships are subject to competition for attention, as well as to competition for justification. Competition for attention originates from a psychological view of human cognition, recognizing that agents' observational range and search for knowledge is affected by human experience (Kaplan and Kaplan 1991, Varela 1996). Competition for justification originates from a social view of knowledge, emphasizing that the value of knowledge is subject to shared beliefs in the firm (Stehr 1992, Nonaka and Takeuchi 1995, von Krogh and Grand 2000).

In line with Weizmann (1998), competition for attention assumes that the firm has more knowledge than it has the capacity to process; it stores more than it can possibly use. The growth of knowledge with the potential to be converted into action is exponential, whereas the capacity to process this knowledge and to generate economic activity is linear. Because an agent must be involved when knowledge is communicated and utilized (Dopfer 1994), knowledge will compete for attention in the firm, in the form of a competitive bidding process. New practical and declarative knowledge is generated through combination or externalization, and the sources "keep on firing" knowledge at the users. The user of knowledge senses knowledge relevant to his needs or task at hand, selects knowledge among competitive knowledge available by strengthening the connection to the source, and activates the use of the knowledge (Drougol et al. 1992). At the same time, agents can be seekers of knowledge and expertise in the firm, searching

for the knowledge "best suited" to fulfill the local needs. The firm thereby carries a certain history of connections that prevails and wins out over other potential connections. In other words, the firm tends to favor connections that have already been established (Nelson 1991, 1995, Levinthal and March 1993).

The principle of competition for attention explains how the firm creates knowledge but neglects the fact that some activities have an inhibitory character that tends to favor some connections over others. Competition for justification addresses this. A closer inspection of knowledge creation reveals that not all knowledge in an organization can be combined, externalized, internalized, or socialized. Agents might resist working with other agents (Elster 1998), as agents favor established knowledge over new knowledge (frequently referred to as the endowment effect; Rabin 1998). Knowledge users might not trust the knowledge source (Loasby 1991, Szulanski 1996) when knowledge is presented in such a form that the benefit to the user is not obvious or when costs involved in comprehending the knowledge outweigh the benefits to the user. For knowledge to prevail, it has to be justifiable in the firm (von Krogh et al. 2000). Only knowledge that can be justified by the source and/or seeker is further processed in the firm. If justification cannot be achieved, knowledge gradually loses its ability to influence new knowledge or even at some point shape human experiences.

This view of knowledge creation should fit comfortably with economic analysis, due to its focus on exchange relationships in the typical firm. However, knowledge-creating relationships are more than pure exchange relationships, generating new experiences and action knowledge. Moreover, knowledge is subject to competition for attention, which should be a straightforward complement to Weizmann's (1998) analysis of knowledge creation as combination. But there are also subtle processes at work that scrutinize knowledge for its value as experienced by agents in the firm (Nonaka and Takeuchi 1995). These processes are of importance to rent-seeking behavior of firms: while new knowledge might be created within the firm that has value in the marketplace, whether or not the firm can appropriate returns from this knowledge depends on whether or not this knowledge can be justified within the firm. If the legitimization structures of competing firms allow knowledge to spill over to this firm's web of relationships, a shift of return appropriation from the originator to the applier of that knowledge might occur. A firm without evolving relationships and appropriate legitimization structures *cannot* appropriate returns from knowledge.

Condition 3: A Concept of Corporate Coherence

Evolutionary theories search for ways to conceptualize "corporate coherence," and resource-based theories look for higher order, organizing principles that give some stability and connection to the constant flow of knowledge, changes in resource base, and evolution of capability. As mentioned, orthodox economic theory can explain coherence by strategic choices and related property rights arrangements, but evolutionary theory must conceptualize coherence as a historically grown phenomenon. Corporate coherence can be understood as the glue or logic underlying strategic decisions (Prahalad and Bettis 1986, Spender 1989; Bettis and Prahalad 1995). Implicit in this understanding is that the firm adapts to a changing environment. Evolutionary theory sees such adaptation as an evolutionary process fraught with uncertainty and ambiguity. Hence, corporate coherence can perhaps best be understood as the firm's ability to weather various types of crisis or its capacity to adapt as a unit.

From this perspective, where knowledge is rooted in experience, corporate coherence emerges as the ability of the firm to provide regular, individual and collective, particular and universal experiences. Moreover, corporate coherence emerges as the ability of the firm to retain knowledge-creating relationships over time. Given the network characteristics of knowledge creation, corporate coherence might be best understood as an evolutionary process. Corporate coherence can thus be understood as resilience in solving problems found in its ongoing relationships, as evidenced by the firm's solution to two types of crises, the attention crisis and the justification crisis. In line with evolutionary theory and resource-based theory, new knowledge is constantly needed for the firm's adaptation to a changing environment, that is, its ability to sustain rent-generation activity. Yet, for some reason this knowledge is not created and hence does not represent itself as a new potential to the firm (action). Relationships can break down because sources and seekers of knowledge are not aware of each other's presence and activities. Moreover, the relationships might

be too manifold; each node in the network might be exposed to too many sources of knowledge. Corporate coherence should enable seekers and sources to realign their relationships, strengthen selected ongoing relationships, build new relationships, and improve the knowledge creation in these select relationships.

Empirical work on knowledge creation in organizations (Latour 1987, 1998) further shows that knowledge is not value-free but rather is inherently contested. Although it might be individually rational for a seeker of knowledge to make use of available knowledge in the organization, negative emotional states are evoked by the new knowledge, resulting in lack of trust in the source. In short, knowledge does not "travel" for subtle reasons of justification. Here, corporate coherence should enable the justification of new knowledge created, if this knowledge is relevant for changes. Such justification operates largely at the value system of the firm, enabling the firm to distinguish new relevant from new irrelevant knowledge.

Not unexpectedly, the challenge for a knowledge-based theory of the firm is phenomenological: to describe and classify the events and consequences of crisis. A firm's reaction to a crisis in knowledge creation, essentially the failure to create new knowledge needed for change, could be comparative. Given an observable change in the industry, such as demand conditions, concentration, entry barriers, or differentiation, economists and strategists alike can assess the impact on the knowledge-creation activity in the firm before, during, and after the transition. Whereas condition 2 deals with the appropriation of rent from knowledge creation itself, condition 3 deals explicitly with the firm's ability to sustain rent generation in the face of an attention and/or a justification crisis.

Condition 4: A Concept of Change

Based on condition 3, it is inevitable that firms will be subject to path dependencies in knowledge creation. The original idea of knowledge creation resulting from excessive combination is at its limits (Weitzman 1998). Knowledge is created in network connections that are weakened and strengthened over time; ideas are not only generated in a combinatoric process, but also based on competitive bidding for attention and justification. While new practical and declarative knowledge might not be limiting in the firm, the creation of action knowledge through socialization and internalization is. Attention and justification are in limited supply, and agents must choose what knowledge to amalgamate and ameliorate further within a framework of corporate coherence. Under these conditions, seekers and sources of knowledge have a tendency to lock into relationships that work for the creation of new knowledge.

In this regard, human learning and organizational knowledge creation bear strong similarities to the economy as a complex evolving system, where there is a potential for lock-in effects and path dependencies (Arthur 1997). Agents in a network of knowledge creation can be seen as overexploiting knowledge that pays off, receiving both attention (Kaplan and Kaplan 1991) and justification (von Krogh and Grand 2000). Knowledge creation relationships that prove successful tend to prevail over time, reinforcing the connectivity between the source and the seeker. Under corporate coherence, relationships develop into "networks of commitment" between the source and the user (see also Winograd and Flores 1987). Justification, tightly connected to the perceived benefit of the knowledge for the user, is unlikely to change if the payoffs of using new knowledge that comes to attention of the user are random: "[K]nowledge gained in earlier problems may be carried into later, similar ones in the form of expectations or prior beliefs" (Arthur 1997, p. 153).

Path dependency and lock-in create a double-edged sword. On the one hand, path dependencies create suboptimal solutions when firms need to adapt to changing environmental conditions, but on the other hand, it is the only way firms can deal coherently with the rising complexities of connections, knowledge, and agents. Hence, some environmental changes might indeed go beyond the firm's ability to resolve justification and attention crisis, to the very concept of attention and justification.

As for condition 3, competition for attention in knowledge creation can be treated as a given, dependent on individual cognitive resources and exposure to information and decisions (March and Shapira 1987). On the other hand, recent arguments would suggest that attention structures "are the social, economic, and cultural structures that govern the allocation of time, effort, and attentional focus of organizational decision makers" (Ocasio 1997, p. 195). Various levels of values and norms, to some extent shaped by the cultural context in which the knowledge creation activity occurs, affect joint attention of agents within that context (Tomasello 1998). Hence, it

seems that if the rules underpinning the competition for attention are to change in order to allow radically new knowledge to be created by forging new relationships and focus on new knowledge, a deeper cultural change is needed in the firm. Since relationships are not static structures, but reproducible entities over time, this suggests that a theory of the firm needs to have a concept of change of the very capacity to reproduce those relationships. Relationships need to take on new qualities that lead to new behavior, which in turn leads to new knowledge created.

One of these fundamental changes could be the transformation from transactive relationships between knowledge seekers and sources into caring relationships (von Krogh et al. 2000) or changes in the context whereby these relationships are realized (Nonaka and Konno 1998). In this sense, Heidegger's idea of care for the world as a driver of attention (you are alert to those things you care for) could finally be realized as a conceptual progress in theory. Caring relationships can be instrumental for the forging of new collective and universal experiences that go beyond the individual and particular experiences. In consequence, if changes in the industry require a new fundamental response from the firm by way of creating new types of tacit knowledge, the quality and nature of relationships need to change.

Likewise, fundamental change involves changes in justification mechanisms and rules in order for new knowledge to emerge, dependent on values, norms, and managerial discourses (von Krogh and Grand 2000). A plethora of mechanisms that constitute justification mechanisms need to be changed, including what passes for a legitimate knowledge and what passes for acceptable and legitimate procedures, routines, and managerial explanations related to the firm's reason for being in business, its technologies, and way of conducting the business. Changes in rules underlying the competition for justification are encompassing, covering values, norms, language, and behavior.

Unless a theory of the firm is equipped with a concept of change covering both the mechanisms for reproducing relationships and the cultural context, it will fail to explain how firms sustain rent generation and rent appropriation in the face of dramatic changes in the industry. So far, perspectives on knowledge and the firm, including the resource-based theory of the firm as well as most evolutionary contributions, have not discussed such changes explicitly, and this could have prevented the emergence of a robust theoretical framework. Teece et al.'s (1997) work holds high prominence in this regard. It is the only contribution we are aware of that discusses the changing resources, positions, and revenue streams of firms and attempts to link such changes to the broader industry perspective. However, they have not yet dealt explicitly with the knowledge-creation process, and hence, their theory has yet to be further developed in explaining why firms succeed or fail in delivering new knowledge, products, and services.

Condition 5: A Concept of Management

So far, the discussions of the various conditions have not dealt explicitly with management, but rather with the building blocks necessary to understand the nature of knowledge and its creation and change. However, in order for a knowledge-based theory of the firm to be of use in strategic management, it needs an explicit concept of management. At this point it would be tempting to discuss management under the label of "knowledge management," but as it should be apparent from condition 1 and 2, such a term would indeed be a misnomer since this would imply the management of individual and collective experiences, which inherently are unmanageable given a private sphere of perception of the phenomena. Management, therefore, refers more to the management of those conditions enabling the creation of knowledge (von Krogh et al. 2000). Based on the foregoing discussion, management covers (1) formulating a vision for the knowledge creation of the firm, coherent with industry level changes; (2) enabling new experiences among organizational members; (3) structuring relationships among organizational members; (4) changing relationships; (5) changing the quality of relationships; and (6) creating knowledge-centered activism.

First, the most important role of managers in the business enterprise is to secure the rent-seeking behavior of their firms. But as we discussed above, rent appropriation and generation need to be as tightly coupled to the nature of knowledge and knowledge creation as possible. Based on case study material, Nonaka and Takeuchi (1995) suggest that a knowledge vision expresses what knowledge needs to be created given changes at the level of the industry. A knowledge vision suggests fields of expertise to be developed, new technologies to be developed, and their relation to the existing activities of the firm. The knowledge vision represents top management's outlook on the industry and the requirements to the firm, but a "good knowledge vision" might need bottom-up initiatives as well. The knowledge vision in turn can be implemented through training programs, new hiring and staffing, research and development projects, and product and market development projects.

Second, since the origin of new knowledge is human experience, management needs to provide organizational members with new experiences counter to specialization (Grant 1996). Incentive schemes can motivate organizational members to embark on new tasks and challenges. Job-rotation programs can secure a wider exposure to various parts of the organization. Cross-functional, divisional, and company project work can stimulate people's insights and new knowledge. The knowledge vision can function as a roadmap for such programs, linking the overall direction of the firm with new experiences of employees.

Third, since knowledge is created in relationships, managers need to structure relationships. Such structuring activity encompasses formal hierarchical relationships, networked relationships through information and communication technologies, and community-based relationships. Whereas the first two relationships require a strong top-down approach by management, the last one requires sufficient time and resources to let community interactions emerge around interests, common tasks, or knowledge (Wenger 1998). It is important to note that conditions 2 and 3 would suggest that some relationships must extend beyond the firm's boundaries. This, in turn, implies that firm boundaries cannot be defined by its possession of stocks of knowledge, but rather by its knowledge-creation processes. External partners provide knowledge to the firm, which in turn creates new knowledge based on this relationship, while experts might leave the firm. Both relate the definition of firm boundaries to the dynamic nature of knowledge, leading to a concept of the firm as the boundary of its knowledge-creation activities.

Fourth, as argued above, in order for the firm to create radically new knowledge needed to continue its rent generation, it also needs new relationships. Managers can change hierarchical relationships and information and communication technology, and thereby change relationships between knowledge seekers and sources. They can also withdraw or allocate more time and resources to the emerging communities in the organization. Ideally, managers would attempt to align changes in relationships, the need for changes, and the new knowledge created. Managers can attempt to change attention structures by signaling to the organization what they perceive as important (Ocasio 1997), or incentivizing a new focus among organizational members.

Fifth, managers can also attempt to change the quality of relationships to foster new knowledge-creation processes. This is often referred to as organizational development and might involve smaller reorganization of work, reflection and change on the way people work together, incentivizing caring behavior, mentoring programs, or training programs in social competence. Organizational development is likely to be sought when radically new knowledge must be created and when existing knowledge creation and relationships cannot secure this supply of new knowledge.

Sixth, a certain level of activism is needed in the organization in order to foster new knowledge creation (von Krogh et al. 2000). Activists are internal entrepreneurs that not only motivate new projects but also create links between projects and between projects and the overall knowledge vision of the firm. Activists are both insiders and outsiders in the knowledge-creation process. As insiders, they actively engage in relationships, participate in projects, and create new knowledge. As outsiders, they serve an instrumental role in connecting seekers and sources of knowledge and developing these relationships. In this sense, they lubricate the competitive process of justification and attention, guiding the search for patterns and connections between seemingly unconnected knowledge-creation processes.

Conclusion: Appropriating Returns from Knowledge Creation

Economic theory and evolutionary theory are two of the most predominant theoretical frameworks underlying research in both strategic management and innovation research. While they provide important insights into the nature of competitive dynamics, strategic returns, and technological evolution, they suffer from a series of limitations with respect to both scientific research and managerial practice. In parallel, recent insights into the nature and dynamics of organizational knowledge creation provide important new opportunities to transcend some of these key limitations, however, implying fundamentally different theoretical premises. An appropriate theoretical framework for a knowledge-based theory of the firm is thus still lacking.

For a knowledge-based theory of the firm to achieve its appropriate status as a robust, coherent theoretical as well as managerial perspective, such theory has to elaborate conceptual building blocks along five major dimensions:

1. First, a concept of knowledge origin is required. Evolutionary as well as conventional economic theory lacks a concept of knowledge that explains the origin of new knowledge. A key extension in the perspective of a knowledge-based theory of the firm is to consider the difference, yet interconnectedness, of explicit knowledge (declarative and practical knowledge) and tacit knowledge (action knowledge) as well as their dynamic interplay. The firm is understood as creating knowledge by combining existing knowledge into new knowledge (as in evolutionary theory), but it also internalizes this knowledge into action knowledge, externalizes action knowledge into explicit knowledge, socializes action knowledge, and so forth. The implied explicit focus on human experience as the foundation for human knowledge requires one to integrate (or reinvent) a phenomenological perspective, as it appears in the new cognitive sciences.

2. As a second condition, such a theory needs a concept of knowledge creation as an ongoing firm activity. Knowledge has a highly distributed and fragmented character. Connectivity is thus key in shaping knowledge creation as well as the robustness of new knowledge being processed by the firm. The firm must be understood as a network of agents (nodes), sources, and users of knowledge, relationships among these, and knowledge-creation activities. A firm's advantage can be found in its ability to establish strong relationships among previously unrelated agents, in order to create new knowledge. The process of establishing relationships is thereby subject to competition for attention as well as to competition for justification. Competition for attention originates from a psychological view of human cognition recognizing that an agent's observational range and search for knowledge is affected by human experience. Competition for justification originates from a social view of knowledge emphasizing that the value of knowledge is subject to shared beliefs in the firm.

3. Third, a view of the firm as a collage of resources, processes, and competencies is overly simplistic and might divert attention away from the underlying dynamics of establishing coherence in patterns of firm activity and development. In a perspective where knowledge is rooted in experience, corporate coherence emerges as

the ability of the firm to provide regular, individual and collective, particular and universal experiences. Moreover, corporate coherence emerges as the ability of the firm to retain knowledge-creating relationships over time. Corporate coherence can thus be understood as resilience in solving problems found in its ongoing relationships, as evidenced by the firm's solution to two types of crises; the attention crisis and the justification crisis. Thereby, the challenge for a knowledge-based theory of the firm is, not surprisingly, phenomenological, as well: to interpret and classify the events and consequences of crises.

4. Fourth, a knowledge-based theory of the firm must explain, and if possible predict, revolutionary versus evolutionary changes at the level of firms and industries. Since relationships are not static structures, but reproducible entities over time, this suggests that a theory of the firm needs to have a concept of change of the very capacity to reproduce those relationships. Relationships need to take on new qualities that lead to new behavior, which in turn leads to new knowledge created. In this network perspective, path dependency and lock-in are key; path dependencies thereby create suboptimal solutions when firms need to adapt to changing environmental conditions, while allowing firms to deal coherently with the rising complexities of connections, knowledge, and agents. Some environmental changes might indeed go beyond the firm's ability to resolve justification and attention crises, leading to changes in the concept of attention and justification. Unless a theory of the firm equipped with a concept of change covering the mechanisms for reproducing both the relationships and the cultural context, it will fail to explain how firms sustain rent generation and rent appropriation in the face of dramatic changes in the industry.

5. A cornerstone in the strategic management discipline is that managerial activity and decision making matter for success. Therefore, in order to claim value in this discipline, as a fifth condition, a knowledge-based theory of the firm must establish a link between managerially led initiatives. At this point it would be tempting to discuss management under the label of "knowledge management," but as should be apparent from conditions 1 and 2, such a term would indeed be a misnomer since this implies the management of individual and collective experiences, which inherently are unmanageable given a private sphere of perception of the phenomena. Management, therefore, refers more to the management of those conditions enabling the creation of knowledge. Based on the foregoing discussion, management covers formulating a vision for the knowledge creation of the firm coherent with industry-level changes, enabling new experiences among organizational members, structuring relationships among organizational members, changing relationships, changing the quality of relationship, and creating knowledge-centered activism.

Given this knowledge-based theory of the firm, how do firms appropriate returns from knowledge creation? Essentially firms cannot appropriate the returns from the knowledge itself if the knowledge originates in experience and remains as action knowledge of the individual organizational member. If this knowledge is used for the creation of practical and declarative knowledge, only in rare instances of intellectual property rights protection can the firm appropriate returns from knowledge directly. The firm can appropriate returns from the knowledge-creation process, however, if new knowledge leads to innovation. Whereas many firms might share access to the same practical knowledge, only some firms are able to move from this to create valuable action knowledge, turning potential opportunities into actual strategic initiatives, leading to strategic returns.

This innovation process encompasses knowledge-creation activities, and therefore relationships start to matter for return appropriation. The firm is now seen as a structure of relationships for creating knowledge, where human experience is the starting point of this process. We might even speak of "relational rents" (see especially Dyer and Singh 1998), but this time, these sources of relational rents are found within the organization. Industry level transitions influence the firms' abilities to cope with various types of breakdown and crisis in knowledge-creation relationships. In consequence, corporate coherence and change processes matter for the firm's ability to sustain rent generation over time. Moreover, management takes an active role in fostering knowledge creation, and by itself, excellent management on the listed activities could be a source of rent.

References

Abernathy, W.J. and Clark, K.B. (1985) "Innovation: mapping the winds of creative destruction." *Research Policy* 14:3–22.

Abernathy, W.J. and Utterback, J.M. (1978) "Patterns of industrial innovation." *Technology Review* 80:40–47.

Acs, Z.J. and Audretsch, D.B. (1990) *Innovation and Small Firms*. Cambridge, MA: MIT Press.

Amit, R. and Schoemaker, P.J.H. (1993) "Strategic assets and organizational rent." *Strategic Management Journal* 14:33–46.

Anderson, P. (1999) "Complexity theory and organization science." *Organization Science* 10(3): 216–232.

Andrews, K.R. (1971) *The Concept of Corporate Strategy*. Reprint, Homewood, IL: Dow-Jones Irwin, 1981.

Argyris, C. and Schon, D. (1996) *Organizational Learning II*. Reading, MA: Addison-Wesley.

Arrow, K.J. (1962) "Economic welfare and the allocation of resources for invention," reprinted in D.M. Lamberton (ed.), *The Economics of Communication and Information*. Cheltenham: Edward Elgar, 1996.

Arrow, K.J. (1975) "Vertical integration and communication." *Bell Economic Journal* 6:173–182.

Arrow, K.J. and Hahn, F.H. (1971) *General Competitive Analysis*. San Francisco: Holden-Day.

Arthur, W.B. (1997) "Path-dependence, self-reinforcement, and human learning," in W.B. Arthur (ed.), *Increasing Returns and Path Dependence in the Economy*, Ann Arbor: University of Michigan Press, pp. 133–158.

Audretsch, D.B. and Stephan, P.E. (1999) "Knowledge spillover in biotechnology: sources and incentives." *Journal of Evolutionary Economics* 9:97–107.

Barney, J.B. (1986) "Strategic factor markets: expectations, luck, and business strategy." *Management Science* 32:1231–1241.

Barney, J.B. (1991) "Firm resources and sustained competitive advantage." *Journal of Management* 17:99–120.

Baumol, W.J. (1993) *Entrepreneurship, Management, and the Structure of Payoffs*. Cambridge, MA: MIT Press.

Bettis, R.A. and Prahalad, C.K. (1995) "The dominant logic: retrospective and extension." *Strategic Management Journal* 16:3–14.

Block, Z. and MacMillan, I. (1993) *Corporate Venturing*. Cambridge, MA: Harvard Business School Press.

Bower, J.L. and Christensen, C.M. (1995) "Disruptive technologies: catching the wave." *Harvard Business Review*, January/February, 43–53.

Burgelman, R.A. (1983a) "A model of the interaction of strategic behavior, corporate context, and the concept of strategy." *Academy of Management Review* 8:61–70.

Burgelman, R.A. (1983b) "A process model of internal corporate venturing in the diversified major firm." *Administrative Science Quarterly* 28: 223–244.

Burgelman, R.A. and Sayles, L. (1986) *Inside Corporate Innovation*. New York: Free Press.

Campbell, D.T. (1965) "Variation and selective retention in socio-cultural evolution," in H.R. Barringer, G.I. Blanksten, and R.W. Mack (eds.), *Social Change in Developing Areas*, Schenkman. Cambridge, MA: pp. 19–49.

Christensen, C. (1997) *The Innovator's Dilemma. When New Technologies Cause Great Firms to Fail*. Cambridge, MA: Harvard Business School Press.

Cohen, W.M. and Levinthal, D.A. (1990) "Absorptive capacity: a new perspective on learning and innovation." *Administrative Science Quarterly* 35:128–152.

Connor, K. (1991) "A historical comparison of resource-based theory and five schools of thought within industrial organization economics: do we have a new theory of the firm?" *Journal of Management* 17:121–154.

Cook, S.D.N. and Brown, J.S. (1999) "Bridging epistemologies: the generative dance between organizational knowledge and organizational knowing." *Organization Science* 10:381–400.

Cool, K.O. and Schendel, D. (1988) "Performance differences among strategic group members." *Strategic Management Journal* 9:207–223.

Crepon, B. and Duguet, E. (1997) "Estimating the innovation function from patent numbers: GMM on count panel data." *Journal of Applied Econometrics* 12:243–263.

D'Aveni, R. (1994) *Hypercompetition: Managing the Dynamics of Strategic Maneuvering*. New York: Free Press.

Day, G.S. and Schoemaker, P.J.H. (2000) *Wharton on Managing Emerging Technologies*. New York: Wiley.

Dierickx, I. and Cool, K. (1989) "Assets, stock accumulation and sustainability of competitive advantage." *Management Science* 35:1504–1511.

Dopfer, K. (1994) "How economic institutions emerge: institutional entrepreneurs and behavioral seeds," in Y. Shionoya and M. Perlman (eds.), *Innovation in Technology, Industries, and Institutions: Studies in Schumpeterian Perspectives*, pp. 299–329. Ann Arbor: University of Michigan Press.

Dosi, G. (1982) "Technological paradigms and technological trajectories." *Research Policy* 11:147–162.

Dosi, G. (1988) "Sources, procedures, and microeconomic effects of innovation." *Journal of Economic Literature* 26:1120–1171.

Dosi, G. and Marengo, L. (1993) "Some elements of an evolutionary theory of organizational competences," in R.W. England (ed.), *Evolutionary Concepts in Economics*, pp. 157–178. Ann Arbor, MI: University of Michigan Press.

Dosi, G., Teece, D.J., and Chytry, J. (1998) *Technology, Organization, and Competitiveness: Perspectives on Industrial and Corporate Change.* New York: Oxford University Press.

Drougol, A., Ferber, J., Corbarra, B., and Fresneau, D. (1992) "A behavioral simulation model for the study of emergent social structures," in F. Varela and P. Bourgine (eds.), *Toward a Practice of Autonomous Systems*, pp. 161–170. Cambridge, MA: MIT Press.

Dyer, J.H. and Singh, H. (1998) "The relational view: cooperative strategy and sources of interorganizational competitive advantage." *Academy of Management Review* 23(4):660–679.

Eldredge, N. and Gould, S.J. (1972) "Punctuated equilibria: an alternative to phyletic gradualism," in T.J.M. Schopf (ed.), *Models in Paleobiology*, pp. 82–115. San Francisco: Freeman Cooper.

Elster, J. (1998) "Emotions and economic theory." *Journal of Economic Literature* 36(March):47–74.

Foss, N.J. (1999) "Research in the strategic theory of the firm: 'isolationism' and 'integrationism.'" *Journal of Management Studies* 36(6):725–755.

Foss, N.J., Knudsen, C., and Montgomery, C.A. (1995) "An exploration of common ground: integrating evolutionary and strategic theories of the firm," in C.A. Montgomery (ed.), *Resource-Based and Evolutionary Theories of the Firm*, pp. 1–18. Boston: Kluwer.

Foster, R. (1986) *Innovation: The Attacker's Advantage.* New York: Summit Books.

Gersick, C.J. G. (1991) "Revolutionary change theories: a multilevel exploration of the punctuated equilibrium paradigm." *Academy of Management Review* 16:10–36.

Ghoshal, S. and Moran, P. (1996) "Bad for practice: a critique of the transaction cost theory." *Academy of Management Review* 21:13–47.

Globus, G. (1995) *The Post-Modern Brain.* New York: Benjamin.

Granovetter, M. (1985) "Economic action and social structure: the problem of embeddedness." *American Journal of Sociology* 91:481–510.

Grant, R.M. (1991) "The resource-based theory of competitive advantage: implications for strategy formulation." *California Management Review* 33:114–135.

Grant, R.M. (1996) "Toward a knowledge-based theory of the firm." *Strategic Management Journal* 17(2):109–123.

Griliches, Z. (1979) "Issues in assessing the contribution of R&D to productivity growth." *Bell Journal of Economics* 10:92–116.

Hallwood, C.P. (1997) "An efficient capital asset pricing theory of the firm." *Journal of Institutional and Theoretical Economics* 153(3):532–544.

Hamel, G. (2000) *Leading the Revolution.* Cambridge, MA: Harvard Business School Press.

Hamel, G. and Prahalad, C.K. (1993) "Strategy as stretch and leverage." *Harvard Business Review* March/April:75–85.

Hamel, G. and Prahalad, C.K. (1994) *Competing for the Future.* Boston: Harvard Business School Press.

Hansen, G. and B. Wernerfeldt (1989) "Determinants of firm performance: the relative importance of economic and organizational factors." *Strategic Management Journal* 10:399–411.

Hedlund, G. (1994) "A model of knowledge management and the N-form corporation." *Strategic Management Journal* 15(Summer):73–90.

Henderson, R.M. and Clark, K.B. (1990) "Architectural innovation: the reconfiguration of existing product technologies and the failure of established firms." *Administrative Science Quarterly* 35:9–30.

Hodgson, G. (1993) *Economics and Evolution. Bridging Life Back into Economics.* Cambridge, MA: Polity Press.

Hodgson, G. (1994) "Critique of neoclassical microeconomic theory," in G. Hodgson, W.J. Samuels, and M.R. Tool (eds.), *The Elgar Companion to Institutional and Evolutionary Economics*, pp. 128–134. Vermont: Edward Elgar.

Holmström, B. and Roberts, J. (1998) "The boundaries of the firm revisited." *Journal of Economic Perspectives* 12(4):73–94.

Jaffe, A. (1986) "Technological opportunity and spillovers of R&D: evidence from firms' patents, profit and market value." *American Economic Review* 76:984–1001.

Jaffe, A. (1989) "Real effects of academic research." *American Economic Review* 79:957–970.

Kamien, M.I. and Schwartz, N.L. (1982) *Market Structure and Innovation.* Cambridge: Cambridge University Press.

Kaplan, M.L. and Kaplan, N.R. (1991) "The self-organization of human psychological functioning." *Behavioral Science* 36:161–178.

Kauffman, S.A. (1989) "Adaptation on rugged fitness landscapes," in D.L. Stein (ed.), *Lectures in the Science of Complexity. The Proceedings of the 1988 Complexity Systems Summer School.* Santa Fee, NM: Reading.

Kauffman, S.A. (1993) *The Origins of Order. Self-organization and Selection in Evolution.* New York: Oxford University Press.

Kauffman, S.A. (1995) "Escaping the red queen effect." *McKinsey Quarterly* 1(95):119–129.

Knoke, D. and Kuklinski, J.H. (1991) "Network analysis: basic concepts," in G. Thompson, J. Frances, R. Levacic, and J. Mitchell (eds.), *Markets, Hierarchies, and Networks*, pp. 173–182. London: Sage.

Kogut, B. and Zander, U. (1992) "Knowledge of the firm, combinative capabilities, and the replication of technology." *Organization Science* 3:383–397.

Krugmann, P.A. (1991) *Geography and Trade*. Cambridge, MA: MIT Press.

Lammers, C.J. (1974) "Mono- and polyparadigmatic developments in natural and social sciences," in R. Whitey (ed.), *Social Process of Scientific Development*, pp. 123–147. London: Routledge and Keegan Paul.

Latour, B. (1987) *Science in Action*. Cambridge, MA: Harvard University Press.

Latour, B. (1998) *Pandora's Hope*. Cambridge, MA: Harvard University Press.

Leonard-Barton, D. (1992) "Core capabilities and core rigidities: a paradox in managing new product development." *Strategic Management Journal* 13:111–125.

Levinthal, D.A. (1995) "Strategic management and the exploration of diversity," in C.A. Montgomery (ed.), *Resource-Based and Evolutionary Theories of the Firm*, pp. 19–43. Boston: Norwell.

Levinthal, D.A. (1996) "Learning and schumpeterian dynamics," in G. Dosi and F. Malerba (eds.), *Organization and Strategy in the Evolution of the Enterprise*, pp. 27–41. Basingstoke, Hampshire: Houndmills.

Levinthal, D.A. and March, J.G. (1993) "The myopia of learning." *Strategic Management Journal* 17(2):95–112.

Lieberman, M.B. and Montgomery, D. (1988) "First-mover advantages." *Strategic Management Journal* 8:441–452.

Lippmann, S.A. and Rumelt, R.P. (1982) "Uncertain imitability: an analysis of interfirm differences in efficiency under competition." *The Bell Journal of Economics* 13:418–438.

Loasby, B.J. (1991) *Equilibrium and Evolution*. Manchester: Manchester University Press.

Loasby, B.J. (1998) "The organization of capabilities." *Journal of Economic Behaviour and Organization* 35:139–160.

Mahoney, J. and Pandian, R. (1992) "The resource-based view within the conversation of strategic management." *Strategic Management Journal* 13(5):363–380.

March, J.G. (1991) "Exploration and exploitation in organizational learning." *Organization Science* 2:71–87.

March, J.G. and Shapira, Z. (1987) "Managerial perspectives on risk and risk taking." *Management Science* 33:1404–1418.

March, J.G. and Simon, H.A. (1958) *Organizations*. New York: Oxford University Press.

McCloskey, D.N. (1986) *The Rhetoric of Economics*. Madison: University of Wisconsin Press.

Mintzberg, H., Ahlstrand, B., and Lampel, J. (1998) *Strategy Safari. A Guided Tour through the Wilds of Strategic Management*. New York: Free Press.

Mir, R. and Watson, A. (2000) "Strategic management and the philosophy of science: the case for a constructivist methodology." *Strategic Management Journal* 21:941–953.

Montgomery, C.A., ed. (1995) *Resource-Based and Evolutionary Theories of the Firm*. Boston: Kluwer.

Morrison, C.J. and Siegel, D. (1997) "External capital factors and increasing returns in U.S. manufacturing." *The Review of Economics and Statistics* 79:647–654.

Nelson, R.R. (1991) "Why do firms differ, and how does it matter?" *Strategic Management Journal* 12:61–74.

Nelson, R.R. (1995) "Recent evolutionary theorizing about economic change." *Journal of Economic Literature* 33:48–90.

Nelson, R.R. and Winter, S. (1982) *An Evolutionary Theory of Economic Change*. Cambridge, MA: Harvard University Press.

Newell, Shaw, Simon 1962

Nonaka, I. (1994) "A dynamic theory of organizational knowledge creation." *Organization Science* 5(1):14–37.

Nonaka, I. and Konno, N. (1998) "The concept of 'Ba': building a foundation for knowledge creation." *California Management Review* 40:40–54.

Nonaka, I. and Takeuchi, H. (1995) *The Knowledge-Creating Company*. New York: Oxford University Press.

Ocasio, W. (1997) "Towards an attention-based view of the firm." *Strategic Management Journal* 18(Summer):187–206.

Penrose, E.T. (1959) *The Theory of Growth of the Firm*. London: Blackwell.

Peteraf, M. (1993) "The cornerstones of competitive advantage: a resource-based view." *Strategic Management Journal* 14:179–191.

Polanyi, M. (1958) *Personal Knowledge*. Chicago: University of Chicago Press.

Porter, M.E. (1980) *Competitive Strategy. Techniques for Analyzing Industries and Competitors*. New York: Free Press.

Porter, M.E. (1985) *Competitive Advantage: Creating and Sustaining Superior Performance*. New York: Free Press.

Porter, M.E. (1991) "Towards a dynamic theory of strategy." *Strategic Management Journal* 12:95–118.

Prahalad, C.K. and Bettis, R.A. (1986) "The dominant logic: a new linkage between diversity and performance." *Strategic Management Journal* 7(6):485–501.

Rabin, M. (1998) "Psychology and economics." *Journal of Economic Literature* 36(March):11–46.

Reed, R. and DeFilippi, R. (1990) "Causal ambiguity, barriers to imitation, and sustainable competitive advantage." *Academy of Management Review* 15:88–102.

Romanelli, E. and Tushman, M.L. (1994) "Organizational transformation as punctuated equilibrium: an empirical text." *Academy of Management Journal* 37:1141–1166.

Rosenberg, N. (1976) *Perspectives on Technology*. Cambridge, MA: Cambridge University Press.

Rumelt, R.P. (1984) "Towards a strategic theory of the firm," in B. Lamb (ed.), *Competitive Strategic Management*, pp. 91–108. Englewood Cliffs, NJ: Prentice-Hall.

Rumelt, R.P. (1991) "How much does industry matter?" *Strategic Management Journal* 12:167–185.

Rumelt, R.P., Schendel, D.E., and Teece, D.J. (1994) *Fundamental Issues in Strategy. A Research Agenda*. Cambridge, MA: Harvard Business School Press.

Ryle, G. (1949) *The Concept of Mind*. Chicago: University of Chicago Press.

Saidel, E. (1998) "Beliefs, desires, and the ability to learn." *American Philosophical Quarterly* 35(1):21–37.

Scherer, F.M. (1992) "Schumpeter and plausible capitalism." *Journal of Economic Literature* 30(3):1416–1433.

Schmalensee, R. (1989) "How much does industry matter?" *The American Economic Review* 75:341–351.

Schoemaker, P.J.H. (1993) "Strategic decisions in organizations. Rational and behavioral views." *Journal of Management Studies* 30(1):107–129.

Schumpeter, J.A. (1934) *The Theory of Economic Development*. Cambridge, MA: Harvard University Press.

Spender, J.-C. (1989) *Industry Recipes. The Nature and Sources of Managerial Judgment*. Oxford: Blackwell.

Spender, J.-C. (1996) "Making knowledge the basis of a dynamic theory of the firm." *Strategic Management Journal* 17:45–62.

Stehr, N. (1992) *Practical Knowledge: Applying the Social Sciences*. London: Sage.

Stiglitz, J.E. (1996) "Information and economic analysis: a perspective." *Economic Journal* 95:21–41.

Szulanski, G. (1996) "Exploring internal stickiness: impediments to the transfer of best practice within the firm." *Strategic Management Journal* 17(S2):27–44.

Teece, D.J. (1984) "Economic analysis and strategic management." *California Management Review* 26:87–110.

Teece, D.J. (1986) "Profiting from technological innovation. Implications for integration, collaboration, licensing and public policy." *Research Policy* 15:285–305.

Teece, D.J. (1990) "Contributions and impediments of economic analysis to the study of strategic management," in J.W. Frederickson (ed.), *Perspectives on Strategic Management*.

Teece, D.J., Rumelt, R.R., Dosi, G., and Winter, S. (1994) "Understanding corporate coherence. Theory and evidence." *Journal of Economic Behavior and Organization* 23:1–30.

Teece, D.J., Pisano, G., and Shuen, A. (1997) "Dynamic capabilities and strategic management." *Strategic Management Journal* 18:509–533.

Tirole, J. (1989) "The theory of industrial organization." Cambridge, MA: MIT Press.

Tomasello, M. (1998) "Reference: Intending that others jointly attend." *Pragmatics and Cognition* 6:219–234.

Tsoukas, H. (1989) "The missing link: a transformational view of metaphors in organization science." *Academy of Management Review* 16(3):566–585.

Tsoukas, H. (1993) "Analogical reasoning and knowledge creation in organization theory." *Organization Studies* 14:323–346.

Tushman, M.L. and Anderson, P.C. (1986) "Technological discontinuities and organizational environments." *Administrative Science Quarterly* 31:439–465.

Utterback, J.M. (1994) *Mastering the Dynamics of Innovation*. Cambridge, MA: Harvard Business School Press.

Varela, F. (1996) "Neurophenomenology: a methodological remedy for hard problems." *Journal of Consciousness Studies* 3(4):330–349.

Varela, F., Thompson, E., and Rosch, E. (1991) *The Embodied Mind: Cognitive Science and Human Experience*. Cambridge, MA: MIT Press.

von Krogh, G. (1998) "Care in knowledge creation: Special issue of knowledge and the firm." *California Management Review* 40(3):133–145.

von Krogh, G. and Grand, S. (2000) "Justification in knowledge creation. Dominant logic in management discourses," in G. von Krogh, I. Nonaka, and T. Nishiguchi (eds.), *Knowledge Creation. A New Source of Value*. London: Macmillan.

von Krogh, G., Roos, J., and Slocum, K. (1994) "An essay on corporate epistemology." *Strategic Management Journal* 15(Summer):33–71.

von Krogh, G., Ichijo, K., and Nonaka, I. (2000) *Enabling Knowledge Creation: Unlocking the Mystery of Tacit Knowledge and Unleashing the Power of Innovation*. New York: Oxford University Press.

Wagner, R.K. (1987) "Tacit knowledge in everyday intelligent behavior." *Journal of Personality and Social Psychology* 52(6):1236–1247.

Weber, M. (1958). *From Max Weber: Essays in Sociology*. Gerth, H.H. and Mills, C.W. (eds.). New York: Oxford University Press.

Weick, K.E. (1995) *Sensemaking in Organizations*. Reading, MA: Sage.

Weitzman, M.L. (1998) "Recombinant growth." *Quarterly Journal of Economics* 113(2):331–360.

Wenger, E. (1998) *Communities of Practice*. Cambridge: Cambridge University Press.

Wernerfeldt, B. (1984) "A resource-based view of the firm." *Strategic Management Journal* 5:171–180.

Williamson, O.E. (1991) "Strategizing, economizing, and economic organization." *Strategic Management Journal* 12:75–94.

Williamson, O.E. (1999) "Strategy research: governance and competence perspectives." *Strategic Management Journal* 29(12):1087–1108.

Winograd, T. and Flores, F. (1987) *Understanding Computers and Cognition: A New Foundation for Design*. Reading, MA: Addison-Wesley.

Winter, S. (1991) "On coase, competence, and the corporation," in O.E. Williamson and S. Winter (eds.), *The Nature of the Firm: Origins, Evolution, and Development*, pp. 179–195. Oxford: Oxford University Press.

Winter, S. (1995) "Four Rs of Profitability: Rents, Resources, Routines and Replication," in C.A. Montgomery (ed.), *Resource-Based and Evolutionary Theories of the Firm*, pp. 147–178. London: Dordrecht.

Winter, S. and Szulanski, G. (2002) "Replication as strategy." *Organization Science*, in press.

Witt, U. (1994) "Imagination and leadership: the neglected dimension of the (evolutionary) theory of the firm." Working paper, Max-Planck-Institute for Research into Economic Systems, Jena.

11

Knowledge and Learning, Markets and Organizations

Managing the Information Transaction Space

Ard Huizing and Wim Bouman

The field of knowledge management lacks a comprehensive analysis from the economic perspective. While numerous benefits are claimed in literature, for instance, increased productivity and the creation of innovative products and services, it is broadly acknowledged that the business or strategic value of knowledge management is hard to demonstrate (Davenport et al. 1998, Zack 1999).

The aim of this chapter is to help develop an economic foundation for knowledge management. We view knowledge management as an organizational discipline bridging information demand and supply in support of learning processes within organizations. The fundamental task of organizing is generally to achieve purposeful, coordinated action from organizations that consist of many specialized individuals and other resources that can be deployed in different ways and for different purposes (Douma and Schreuder 1991, Grant 1996). To better exploit the potential productivity of these resources and to learn from the experiences, a vast network of information exchange is necessary. We call this complex and chaotic network of human interaction "the information transaction space" and see it as the object of knowledge management. It represents the set of all possible information exchanges—economists say "transactions"—available to any actor at any time.[1]

The productive possibilities of resources can be enhanced through exchange. In economics, exchange performs two roles. It can improve efficiency as it enables the continual reallocation of resources to more productive uses, and it can rearrange the bundle of resources economic actors have at their disposal, which can stimulate the perception of new, productivity-enhancing combinations among these resources (Penrose 1959, Moran and Ghoshal 1999). Regarding knowledge, exchange allows actors to better exploit existing knowledge by reallocating it to better known uses, and it can improve their ability to access, deploy, and develop this knowledge, that is, to learn and innovate. The first role of exchange is related to "allocative efficiency"; the second, to "adaptive" or "dynamic" efficiency (Williamson 1999).

Transaction-cost economics (Coase 1937, Williamson 1975, 1985) and agency theory (Jensen and Meckling 1973, Fama and Jensen 1983) address coordination as the fundamental organization problem from a cost perspective and emphasize allocative efficiency. In both economic theories of organization, competitive advantage results from capturing economic rents[2] stemming from organization-level efficiency advantages. In knowledge-based views of the firm as outgrowths of resource-based thinking, coordination is seen as a dynamic management task, which requires learning by doing (Grant 1999a). In this view, managers' coordinating and learning capabilities are the primary sources of a competitive advantage and of adaptive efficiency.

We develop a dynamic framework for managing the information transaction space that incorporates the considerations of all these economic theories, integrating the coordination, cost, and learning perspectives. It intends to help managers orient their knowledge policies, decisions, and practices as well as to advance knowledge-based views of the firm. The framework goes beyond the usual market-hierarchy dichotomy inherent in economic theories by developing four governance structures for knowledge management: the market, the organized market, the extended organized market, and the firm. These alternatives are based on the three generic information problems inhibiting any process of information exchange: (1) the relevant questions have to be posed unambiguously, (2) reliable information sources have to be found, and (3) the information acquired has to be interpreted and translated to a unique social practice. These information problems limit organizations' rent-generating potential as they restrict the free flow of knowledge and cause exchange inefficiencies. The goal of knowledge management is to help solve these problems. Its rationale is to increase the allocatively and adaptively efficient use of the information transaction space.

The essence of strategy is to maximize economic rent over time through creating and sustaining sources of competitive advantage (Boisot 1999). For that, organizations have to be allocatively and, in particular, adaptively efficient. We argue that such economic development is dependent on management's "interpretative flexibility" (Spender 1996) while managing the information transaction space. Managers have to continually assess and reassess the knowledge domains into which the information transaction

space can be divided, decide which of the four governance structures is the most efficient for each domain, and use investment opportunities to adjust cost structures leading to productive organizational change, while acknowledging the organization's contingency factors and path dependencies. Organization members learn, and managers have to learn how they learn best. In that sense, the dynamic ability to make the best use of the information transaction space is a defining competitive dimension of any organization.

Criticism of Knowledge Management

The way knowledge management is represented in theory and applied in practice is subject to growing criticism. Four arguments summarize this criticism. First, knowledge is frequently seen as a relatively static phenomenon, not capturing the ongoing cycle of action taking and knowledge acquisition found in learning theories (Crossan et al. 1999). In today's dynamic world, however, learning processes constitute organizational learning, rather than the time-limited knowledge that is accumulated as a result of these processes (Dixon 1997). Best practice descriptions, for instance, can lead to learning traps when conditions change (Lant and Mezias 1990). Knowledge from others may therefore inform people's thinking, but it cannot replace it.

Second, the prevailing notion of knowledge often rests on a naively objectivist model of learning (Leidner and Jarvenpaa 1995, Tenkasi and Boland 1996, Cook and Seely Brown 1999). Knowledge is dealt with as an "it" or a disembodied object that is made up of discrete and transferable granules of understanding that can be added to an existing heap of knowledge (Spender 1996, Davenport et al. 1998). Equating learning with making information available, and information and communication technology as primarily used to automate the information delivery function, is typical for this kind of reasoning.

Third, many knowledge initiatives are biased toward the supply of information (Manville and Foot 1996, Alavi and Leidner 1999). The main problem addressed is how to structure reality into generalized representations and to "push" that information to the users who will uncritically absorb it. This approach underestimates the active role users play in seeking and creating knowledge. It also negates the fact that, increasingly, information demand, and not supply, is the scarce factor in knowledge economies (Pine and Gilmore 1999). User attention is the currency of the information age (Davenport and Prusak, 1998). Hence, there is a need to rebalance the demand and supply sides in knowledge management, based on a reexamination of the notions learning, knowledge, and information.

Fourth and last, knowledge initiatives often take place within organizational boundaries or within a limited network of organizations that may run counter to the borderless learning behavior of information seekers. Presented with questions, problems, ambiguities, or uncertainties, information seekers do not passively wait for ideas or experiences to be broadcast by the supply side. Instead, they actively search for or "pull" information and create meaning from it for themselves. They learn their way into the future. For that, they participate in all kinds of social networks constituting distinct communities socialized in unique practices (Spender 1996, Choo 1998, Wenger 1998), both formal and informal, within and outside their organizations. While there can be legitimate reasons to partially seal up an organization—for instance, to protect precious knowledge (Liebeskind 1999)—the pitfall of an inward-looking perspective on knowledge management is that organizations become blind to valuable and perhaps more efficient external knowledge sources.

View on Knowledge Management

Faced with such criticism, what can knowledge management possibly mean for organizations? We view knowledge management as an organizational discipline bridging information demand and supply in support of learning processes within organizations. Learning occurs if information is used to construct new understandings to guide actions (Berger and Lockman 1966, Dixon 1997) or if it changes the range of potential behavior (Huber 1991, Anderson 1995). Knowledge is defined as the relatively permanent record of the experience underlying learning (Anderson 1995). This definition of knowledge is intentionally broad. It encompasses declarative (facts), procedural (know-how), and conditional knowledge (knowing under what circumstances the knowledge applies), in both its implicit and explicit dimensions. Our view implies that information can contribute to people's knowledge through learning. It acknowledges

that information has little meaning in and of itself and has to be interpreted in processes of construction and reconstruction to make sense out of it, and convert it into knowledge (Berger and Lockman 1966, Weick 1995). In that sense, knowledge cannot be managed. One person's knowledge is just too subjective, fluid, and context specific to be more than another's information.[3] What can be managed are the processes of information exchange between information demand and supply, which are crucial to learning. We therefore see these processes of information exchange as the basic units of analysis in knowledge management.

The Dual Role of Exchange

In resource- and knowledge-based views of the firm, it has become conventional to distinguish knowledge from other resources (Spender 1996). On their own, few resources—defined as all tangible and intangible means potentially contributing to the satisfaction of human needs such as skills, computer systems, and brands—are productive. Productive activity requires that heterogeneous resources are combined and coordinated to transform them into higher value products and services. Most resources, however, can be used in different ways and for different purposes. Consequently, the value-adding processes of an organization and its products and services depend on how resources and resource combinations are viewed, which is a function of the knowledge applied to them (Tsoukas 1996). The more an organization learns about the different ways of coordinating and leveraging resources, the greater the potential productivity of any given set of resources and the attendant prospects of successful action will be (Penrose 1959).

Learning about deploying resources includes understanding how exchange can enhance their productive possibilities. Resources are scarce and should therefore be used and developed efficiently. In this regard, exchange performs two roles. The first role is that exchange is seen as a principal mechanism to improve efficiency as it enables the continual reallocation of resources to more productive uses. Another role of exchange is that it rearranges the set of resources that people and organizations have at their disposal, which can stimulate the perception of new, productivity-enhancing combinations among these resources (Penrose 1959, Moran and Ghoshal 1999). In a Schumpeterian sense, new combinations can intendedly or unintendedly lead to the creation of more productive resources or more efficient ways of creating resources. Regarding knowledge, exchange not only allows actors to better exploit existing knowledge by reallocating it to better known uses, it can also improve their ability to access, deploy, and develop this knowledge, that is, to learn and innovate. In particular, this latter role of exchange—sometimes referred to as "adaptive" or "dynamic" efficiency (Moran and Ghoshal 1999, Williamson 1999) as opposed to the "allocative efficiency" related to the first role of exchange—is essential to value creation or rent generation.

Object of Knowledge Management: The Information Transaction Space

Ideally, all possible information exchanges that could be expected to increase the organization members' knowledge on how resources can be deployed in an allocatively and adaptively efficient manner should take place. The more information within an actor's reach, the more productive possibilities there will be. All knowledge resides in humanity, but no one knows everything and everyone knows something (Lévy 1997). To fully exploit the productive possibilities of resources and resource combinations, a vast network of information exchange is needed, as unfettered as possible. We call this network of human interaction the "information transaction space," representing the set of all possible information exchanges available to any actor at any moment in time. It can be seen as a "market for knowledge" where navigating information seekers in search of explicit and tacit information, insights, and understanding of others reach mutual agreements with information providers and information brokers.[4] This information transaction space is the *object* of knowledge management.

To determine what is productive and to affect the possibilities likely to be seen as such, organizations can delineate the information transaction space by defining a number of knowledge slices. These slices are the knowledge domains offering the most opportunities to enhance the organization's strategic capabilities and the productive possibilities of its resources. They are the constraints shaping the human interactions that bind the organization's resources together. The consultancy firm Ernst & Young, for instance, has 22 knowledge networks focused on industries, consulting approaches, and key technology areas (Davenport et al. 1998). Another example

is a traditional dairy food producer that had to develop knowledge of fast-moving consumer goods when making the transition to a food company focusing on brands instead of products. To help realize the new business models, it explicitly defined knowledge slices: marketing, logistics, distribution, and research and development business functions.

Rationale and Goal of Knowledge Management

Whether or not knowledge slices are defined, in practice only a fraction of all possible information transactions will ever be made. Unrestricted information exchange maximizing the productive possibilities of resources and resource combinations is a fiction. As a result, there is always and everywhere a gap between what is possible and would be productive and what is realizable at any given time. The economic *rationale* for knowledge management is to narrow this gap. Its *goal* should be to help smooth the three fundamental and generic information problems contributing to the existence of the gap and causing inefficiencies in any process of information exchange: (1) the relevant questions have to be posed in terms that can not be misunderstood, (2) knowledgeable and trustworthy information sources have to be found (internal or external people, Web sites, or databases), and (3) the information gathered has to be interpreted to create meaning from it and applied to the context-specific practice of the information user. Whether individually or collectively, people learn through social interaction. For knowledge management to be instrumental in these learning processes, all knowledge initiatives should be related to at least one of the three information exchange issues.

Knowledge and Strategy

Much of the current interest in knowledge management can be explained from the economic perspective. The phrase "if we only knew what we know" implies that actors can benefit from knowledge of others but that they have difficulty in locating, accessing, interpreting, and applying it. These frictions hamper the free flow of information and cause exchange inefficiencies. As a result, they limit the potential of actors for future development and economic rent generation. The essence of strategy is to maximize economic rent over time through creating and sustaining sources of competitive advantage (Boisot 1999). Due to competition, organizations have to continually renew their sources of competitive advantage. For that, they need to be allocatively and, in particular, adaptively efficient. Viewed as such, adaptation is the central problem of economic organization.[5]

The prospect of efficiency gains, new resource combinations, and ultimately, competitive advantage strengthens the view that the primary role of knowledge management is to draw information demand and supply together. It also lends this view strategic importance: insofar as economic growth is increasingly fueled by ideas and knowledge and less by traditional resources (Drucker 1983, Tenkasi and Boland 1996, Quinn et al. 1999), the dynamic ability to make the best use of the information transaction space is a defining competitive dimension of any organization. At the end of the chapter, we return to this argument and relate it to resource- and knowledge-based views of the firm. Before we do that, however, we first explore the opportunities for knowledge management provided by transaction-cost economics and agency theory.

Organizing Exchange

Transaction-cost economics (Coase 1937, Williamson 1975, 1985) and agency theory (Alchian and Demsetz 1972, Jensen and Meckling 1973, Fama and Jensen 1983) are economic theories of organization. Together, they permit a comparative assessment of market, organizational, and hybrid forms of organizing knowledge management, explain inefficiencies in information exchange, and show the relevant cost components to balance in knowledge decisions.

Every exchange or transaction has to be coordinated. That raises the question of whether there are different ways to coordinate exchanges, and if so, what form of organization or governance structure is the most expeditious and least costly. A governance structure is a set of rules and institutions for administering exchange relationships. It is a means by which to infuse order into a relationship where potential conflict threatens to undo or upset opportunities to realize mutual gains (Williamson 1999). Transaction-cost economics claims that there are two governance modes: transactions may take place across markets or within organizations. Markets use the price system as the coordina-

tion mechanism, and organizations have an array of nonprice devices available, such as authority, the standardization of skills, and mutual adjustment.[6] This view opposes conventional neoclassical economics, which states that perfect markets are maximally efficient (Hayek 1945, Douma and Schreuder 1991). Perfect competition means, among other things, that all the information needed to make decisions is collected and communicated to all economic actors by the price system and that any piece of new information is instantaneously reflected in a price change. Hence, it is assumed that everybody is always perfectly informed. Organizations are represented as reactors responding to price changes (Rowlinson 1997), as "black boxes" transforming the factors of production into output with the sole objective of maximizing profits or the organization's market value (Jensen and Meckling 1973). The costs of generating and marketing the output—the production or operations costs—is thus the only relevant cost component in the neoclassical theory.

Transaction-cost economics acknowledges that markets do not function perfectly. It accounts for the fact that in the real world, information is unevenly distributed among actors. These information asymmetries indicate that nobody is perfectly informed. Two key features of human actors explain market imperfections: people are boundedly rational and sometimes also display opportunistic behavior (Williamson 1975, 1985). *Bounded rationality* means that a human being's capacity to formulate and solve complex problems is limited. As a result, people tend to aspire to what is acceptable rather than what is optimal. *Opportunism* implies that, just to take advantage of particular situations, information can be manipulated, concealed, or distorted. Both these human characteristics cause markets to operate inefficiently, for they prevent information from flowing freely. Consequently, transaction costs occur, which are the costs associated with the inefficiencies in exchange processes.[7] To put it differently, transaction costs are the costs involved in using imperfect markets to coordinate the exchange (Coase 1937, Williamson 1975, 1985). Examples are the costs of acquiring information from alternative knowledge brokers and negotiating a deal with them. Economic analyses should therefore include not only operations costs, as is assumed in neoclassical economics, but also transaction costs.[8]

Agency theory focuses on organizational problems arising from information asymmetries between actors and on how these problems can be overcome (Jensen and Meckling 1973, Fama and Jensen 1983). Agency relationships exist in any situation where one actor—the principal—depends on the action of another actor—the agent. Agents (e.g., employees) are supposed to perform services on behalf of the principal (e.g., managers). However, the behavioral assumptions underlying agency theory predict that they will not always fulfill the agreements made with principals. They will rather try to maximize their own individual utility, paying little attention to the welfare of the principal or to nonpecuniary virtues such as honor and integrity. As in transaction-cost economics, information asymmetries can lead to opportunism.[9] The neoclassical view of the organization as a unified "black box" with a single brain is therefore rejected. It does not allow for an analysis of situations in which the behavior of organization members is inconsistent with profit maximization. Instead, an organization is seen as a nexus of contracts between self-interested individuals. The costs incurred as a result of the goal divergence between these individuals or, better, the internal coordination costs to bridge these conflicts of interests are called agency costs.[10] An example is the costs to adjust the general evaluation and compensation structure in an organization to discourage the hoarding of information.

Hence, information asymmetries causing exchange inefficiencies play a pivotal role in economic theories of organization. Organizations and any organizational arrangement, including knowledge initiatives, surface as solutions to these information problems that cannot be resolved by the price system. They are seen as substitutes for the market mechanism in coordinating exchange. In practice, however, organizational and market governance structures are usually mixed (Malone et al. 1987, Douma and Schreuder 1991), leading to a market–firm continuum of different combinations of price and nonprice coordination mechanisms. The actual mix as found in any situation depends on the information requirements of that situation (Douma and Schreuder 1991, Gurbaxani and Whang 1991, Ciborra 1993).

Below we identify four ideal types of governance structures based on the three generic information problems mentioned above, which also have their roots in information asymmetry. Given their bounded rationality and the hazards of opportunism, whenever information seekers enter the information transaction space, they are faced with the problems of asking the relevant questions, finding reliable information sources, and interpreting and applying the information acquired to specific contexts. These information problems inhibit the reallocation of information to more productive uses and the ability to envisage new combinations with this information. Organizations can help their members by organizing knowledge initiatives that will address one or more of the three information problems. Which information problems are tackled determines which of the four governance structures applies. These governance structures are the market, the organized market, the extended organized market, and the firm. We explore these alternative ways of coordinating information exchange and their different allocative and adaptive efficiency properties. Before turning to this subject, however, we first specify the cost components that have to be dealt with in knowledge management.

Relevant Cost Components

It follows from the preceding section that organizations and organizational endeavors are alternative governance structures for the market, created to reduce the sum of transaction costs, agency costs, and operations costs. In terms of allocative efficiency, the economic rationale for knowledge management is to minimize these costs. Note that these costs are mainly information costs, for the essence of coordination involves communicating and processing information (Malone et al. 1987).

Transaction Costs

In a knowledge setting, transaction costs are the coordination costs associated with using the market mechanism to organize information exchange. Consider a company hiring a consultancy firm to help implement a groupware system. This company incurs *search costs* when collecting and interpreting information on the market, possible candidates, prices, and other terms of doing business. Further inquiries into track records, suggested consultancy approaches, and so on, lead to communication processes with a selected number of candidates. This results in a variety of transaction-specific information-processing costs: *communications costs* to better understand the situation, which include costs of miscommunications and opportunity costs due

TABLE 11.1 Three Cost Components

Cost Components	Types of Costs
Transaction costs	Search costs
	Communications costs
	• Costs of communications and miscommunications
	• Opportunity costs due to delays in communications and poor or misinterpreted information
	Documentation costs
	Contracting costs
	• Costs of negotiation and writing contracts
	• Costs of enforcing contracts
	Redundancy costs
	• Costs of reinventing the wheel
	• Opportunity costs due to inventing square wheels
	• Costs of recurring mistakes
Agency costs	Monitoring costs
	Bonding costs
	Residual loss
Operations costs	Costs of information representation: acquiring, refining, storing, and disseminating information
	Protection costs

to delays in communications and poor or misinterpreted information, and *documentation costs* to record the information gathered. These costs are partly out-of-pocket expenses and partly opportunity costs, which are costs that are foregone by not putting the organization's resources to their best uses. Reaching an agreement with a consultancy firm further entails *contracting costs*—the costs to negotiate, write, and enforce a contract.

Moreover, there are *redundancy costs*, which we define as the costs of needlessly repeating the same transactional activities as a result of not sharing information. Due to specialization, differentiation, and departmentalization, organization members frequently are unaware of the existence or whereabouts of information possessed or stored by others (Huber 1991). This lack of information can result in costs to reinvent the wheel that could have been avoided if the information had been shared in one way or another. Parts of this are opportunity costs due to inventing square wheels, which result from someone acting upon poor or misinterpreted information while a colleague in the organization had superior yet undisclosed knowledge. Finally, not sharing information promotes the recurrence of mistakes, leading to yet another kind of cost.

Table 11.1 includes the five types of transaction costs relevant to knowledge management. All these costs are closely related to bounded rationality and opportunism. While search is fundamental to intelligent behavior (Newell 1990), bounded rationality limits the time and effort people spend on searching. This increases the chance for decisions to be made on the basis of inferior or incomplete information. Another example is contracting costs, the main purpose of which is to prevent the other party from acting opportunistically. Yet, transaction costs do not add value to the business. They are inefficiencies in information exchange. Organizations can economize on bounded rationality and mitigate the hazards that come with opportunism by taking transactions out of the market and organizing them internally (Williamson 1999). To proceed with the example of hiring a consultancy firm, organizations can choose from a whole array of organizational arrangements. They could, for instance, store knowledge in standard operating procedures or routines, collect experiences with consultancy firms into an easily accessible organizational memory, and appoint internal consultants who partly take over the external experts' job. Each of these organizational measures has the intention of significantly reducing transaction costs.

Agency Costs

The second relevant cost component is agency costs. Knowledge management is replete with agency problems. One source of these problems is shareholder–management conflicts. Knowledge management often leads to the creation of a specialized business function that can consist of multiple levels of new roles such as the chief knowledge officer, knowledge reporters, and network facilitators (Davenport and Prusak 1998). New business functions may evoke a whole range of new coordination issues. For instance, knowledge managers, like any manager, can suffer from the "empire-builder" syndrome (Gurbaxani and Whang 1991) and overconsume organization resources at the expense of the shareholders. To them, a large budget, a large staff, the finest computer equipment, and a large office, for example, can be signs of power and career success.

Other sources of agency problems are manager–employee conflicts and conflicts between peers. Information exchange is often seen as an unnatural act (Davenport et al. 1998, Quinn et al. 1999). Organization members may be reluctant to share their tacit and explicit information because they see it as crucial to maintaining their value as employees. Without any concrete compensation in return, they may be unwilling to spend precious time in helping colleagues. They may hoard information to advance their careers. A struggle to get organization members to contribute to repositories or use discussion databases, and rivalry between all tasks and activities demanding attention would fit in this picture. As many organizations have experienced, rewarding and recognizing knowledge-sharing behavior to combat opportunism is a major concern of knowledge management (Hackett 2000). Moreover, conflicting interests between the knowledge management function and other business functions may give rise to agency problems.

Agency structures have two major devices for overcoming agency problems: monitoring and bonding (Fama and Jensen 1983, Douma and Schreuder 1991). The costs associated with both ways of ensuring that agents act in the interests of principals are agency costs. By definition, they add bureaucratic costs (Williamson 1999). *Monitoring costs* are costs of observing the behavior of agents, and *bonding costs* are costs agents incur in reporting and documenting their activities, consuming resources that could have been spent on other, value-adding activities. Examples are investigations into information use patterns, and the introduction of performance-based compensation schemes and other motivational instruments. In addition, a *residual loss* remains,

which means that opportunistic behavior cannot be completely banished by monitoring and bonding activities, thus leading to partial welfare losses for principals.

Operations Costs

The third and last relevant cost component—operations costs—can be divided into costs of information representation and protection costs. Knowledge must be represented in some fashion to be used, told, or thought (Newell 1990). Best practices, for instance, are representations abstracted from reality. They contain knowledge, yet they are not the knowledge itself. The *costs of information representation* are the costs of making representations involving single identifiable processes comprising linked sets of activities to acquire, refine, store, and distribute information (Gurbaxani and Whang 1991, Meyer and Zack 1996, Choo 1998). These typical information management costs include costs to develop and use information systems, products, and services that add value to the represented information and assist users in asking better questions, finding better information sources, making better sense of situations, and taking more effective action.

Finally, there are *protection costs* when organizations choose to protect parts of their knowledge from appropriation or imitation by their competitors (Liebeskind 1999). Inserting confidentiality clauses into employee contracts, implementing computer protection systems, and establishing employee conduct rules are examples of adding to these costs.

Four Governance Structures for Knowledge Management

We distinguish four ideal type governance modes for knowledge management on the basis of the three generic information problems in information exchange: the market, the organized market, the extended organized market, and the firm. As mentioned above, a governance structure is a set of rules and institutions for administering exchange relationships. In the market, these rules and institutions refer to market coordination, which implies that the exchange relationships are mainly shaped by information demand and supply forces. The organizing principle is "self-organization," as organizations consciously or unconsciously refrain from deliberate knowledge initiatives or outsource them. The rules and institutions in the other three governance modes increasingly relate to organizational coordination. In the organized market, the organizing principle is "paving the road to experts," meaning that knowledge management is solely deployed to help solve the information problem of finding reliable information sources. The two remaining information problems are left to market governance. When organizational coordination is also focused on helping information seekers ask the relevant questions unambiguously and on "guiding information asking" by clarifying and specifying information needs, we speak of the extended organized market. Finally, in the firm, the organization of the information transaction space is directed toward all three information problems. In this case, the organizing principle also includes "facilitating information interpretation" in order to promote information use and feedback.

The following sections elaborate on the four governance structures for knowledge management, which are summarized in table 11.2.[11] On the basis of economic theories, coordination as the fundamental task of organization is approached from a cost and a learning perspective. We then continue to explore the different allocative and adaptive efficiency properties of the four governance modes. Finally, the strategic relevance of managing the information transaction space is addressed.

The Market

The information transaction space can be viewed as a "market for knowledge" where information seekers, providers, and brokers reach mutual agreements. These agreements can involve the exchange of money, but often information is transacted freely. Free exchange, however, does not mean that the market mechanism is not at work (Douma and Schreuder 1991, Davenport and Prusak 1998). Maximizing one's utility can also include the exchange of intangible scarce factors such as favors, reputation, and affection. Bounded rationality and opportunism indicate that people act on the basis of perceived self-interest and expect to financially or nonfinancially benefit from the information transactions they engage in. These two human characteristics also explain inefficiencies in information exchange and the resulting relatively high transaction costs. They are therefore crucial in understanding how knowledge markets operate.

Even if social relationships are based on trust, it is important to realize that people rarely give away valuable information without expecting something in return.

Given that organizations exist, market governance means that organizations follow a laissez-faire approach to knowledge management, which implies that they do not take specific knowledge actions to back their members. Organizations that have not yet considered knowledge initiatives, or expect no benefits from them, fall into this category. This mode can also attract organizations that are convinced it is the best strategy to nurture individual and collective learning processes. Refraining from deliberate knowledge initiatives does not imply that organization members will not learn. In fact, they learn all the time as they constantly pull information from different sources, make sense of it by themselves, and use it for purposeful actions. To satisfy their information needs, they actively contribute to formal networks and informal communities of practice, both within and across organizational boundaries. Moreover, they use existing information systems and channels, improvise, install new systems, and share the outcome of their information organization with others.

Communities of practice, in particular, have recently gained attention in management literature as the new "organizational frontier" (Wenger 1998, Wenger and Snyder 2000). Such communities are self-organizing and informal groups of people sharing experiences and knowledge in free-flowing creative ways to better deal with never-ending new developments, exploring potential solutions to structured and unstructured problems, and developing and implementing new ideas. They are organic, spontaneous, and informal market places where people coordinate their information exchanges to learn from each other and build new socially constructed knowledge around knowledge slices attracting all the group members. Allegedly, the best way to learn is to engage in social practices with people sharing similar interests and goals (Wenger 1998, Storck and Hill 2000).

Hence, even if organizations adopt a laissez-faire market approach to knowledge management, bottom-up and self-organizing initiatives emerge that can intentionally or unintentionally result in allocative and adaptive efficiency gains. Organizations adhering to this view see their employees as professionals performing best without too much supervision, interference, and top-down structures. They act on the belief that

TABLE 11.2 Framework for Managing the Information Transaction Space

	The Market	The Organized Market	The Extended Organized Market	The Firm
Organizing principle	Self-organizing	(1) Paving the road to experts	(1), plus (2) guiding information asking	(1) and (2), plus (3) facilitating information interpretation and use
Coordination mechanisms				
Finding reliable information sources	Market mechanisms	Nonmarket mechanisms, outsourced market mechanisms	Nonmarket mechanisms, outsourced market mechanisms	Nonmarket mechanisms, outsourced market mechanisms
Asking the relevant questions unambiguously	Market mechanisms	Market mechanisms	Nonmarket mechanisms, outsourced market mechanisms	Nonmarket mechanisms, outsourced market mechanisms
Understanding and applying information	Market mechanisms	Market mechanisms	Market mechanisms	Nonmarket mechanisms
Examples of practices	Communities of practice, knowledge brokers	Strategic communities, expert directories, portals, agents, libraries	"Frequently asked questions," meaning-based search engines, interactive guiding systems	Feedback systems such as learning histories and storytelling
Transaction costs	+ + + +	+ + +	+ +	+
Agency costs	+	+ +	+ + +	+ + + +
Operations costs	+	+ +	+ + +	+ + + +
Relationship between learning and the rent-generating potential of the organization	Performance is best served with employees shaping their own learning processes	(1) Performance can be improved by paving the road to reliable experts	(1), plus (2) performance can be enhanced by guiding employees in their search processes	(1) and (2), plus (3) performance can be increased by helping employees interpret and use information
Contingency factors	Degree of bureaucratization Degree of "politicalness" Degree of individualism Degree of knowledge fluidity Degree of dispersion of information sources			

The designations + + + +, and so on, refer only to relative comparisons between columns, not to absolute values.

the professionals themselves know best how to shape their own learning processes, put the greatest trust in their abilities to deal effectively with the intricacies and subtleties of bounded rationality and opportunism, and take the relatively high transaction costs for granted.

The high transaction costs of the free market approach offer rich business opportunities for external knowledge brokers. These infomediaries have the same reason for being as do internal knowledge initiatives: they interfere in free market interaction and create physical and virtual marketplaces to reduce transaction costs. These developments are spurred on by information and communication technology, which facilitate the creation of new markets where none existed before or improve existing ones (Ciborra 1993). As a result, external and internal knowledge structures increasingly compete with each other for the attention of information users, information providers, and their organizations. In some cases, organizations can put resources to more productive use if they access them through outsourcing (Williamson 1999). We will elaborate on this subject in the following sections.

The Organized Market

The relatively high transaction costs of market coordination can inspire organizations to consider internal knowledge initiatives. Information seekers often have difficulties in finding the right information sources, in reaching these sources, and in assessing their quality and reliability. In their turn, information providers are frequently not aware of whom their information could benefit, and so do not share or store it. In this governance mode, knowledge management is confined to this generic information problem, which specifically causes search and redundancy costs to be high.[12] Choosing this mode implies that knowledge management is viewed as a means of keeping track not so much of the information itself, but of who possesses it and how to access them (Alavi and Leidner 1999). Such a view fits organizations that see their members as professionals responsible for what they need to learn and how, but whose productivity can be substantially improved by helping them find their way (Moreland et al. 1996).

Paving the road to experts involves accessibility, availability, quality, and reliability issues. To address these issues, many exchange-enhancing arrangements can be applied. For instance, managers can create dedicated information trans-action spaces for communities of practice or "strategic communities" that will enhance the organization's strategic capabilities, and stimulate every employee to join them. Strategic communities are communities of practice that have a defined relationship to formal organizational objectives (Storck and Hill 2000). The social and affective bonds in both types of communities constitute information channels that reduce not only the amount of time and investment required to gather information (Nahapiet and Ghoshal 1998), but also uncertainties about the quality and reliability of the information and its sources.[13] Identifying and cultivating communities and defining their knowledge domains are organizational capabilities maximizing such "economies of communication."

Other arrangements intend to create information-transfer infrastructures leveraging human interactions. They often combine organizational, behavioral, and technological measures. Elements of such infrastructures are "registration systems"—such as competence databases (or expert directories), document scanning and management systems, libraries, and calendaring and scheduling systems—and "communication systems"—such as corporate portals offering personalized single points of access to multiple information sources, desktop videoconferencing systems, and intra- and extranets. As mentioned above, people have to be motivated to contribute to such systems and to be available for information-seeking colleagues. This governance structure therefore results in higher operations and agency costs, which should be counterbalanced with the decreasing transaction costs.

If applied, all these arrangements to some extent organize the knowledge market. They partly replace market governance with organizational coordination. In communities, "mutual adjustment" in collegial networks is the primary coordination mechanism, agency problems suggest the use of "authority," and "standardization" is the effect of information-transfer infrastructures and the related motivational instruments. In the latter case, organization members are suggested to use preselected and tested information sources, and tailored search tools and patterns are suggested to help solve the generic problem of finding reliable information sources. The other two information problems remain the responsibility of the actors involved. That is, the problems of asking the relevant questions unambiguously and that of interpreting and applying the information to context-specific practices are left to market coordination. This option is thus a hybrid governance structure, a mix of market and organizational coordination devices.

The transparency of knowledge markets can also be increased by external infomediaries. In their role as expert, information source, or producer (Choi et al. 1997), they categorize, filter, and prune the information supply. Technological developments such as meaning-based search engines and intelligent agents and filters share this intention, and application service providers offer opportunities to outsource software and databases. Initiatives to draw information seekers and providers together abound on and off the Internet. On the Internet, there are knowledge fairs based on the idea to "sell what you know, buy what you don't," community builders where questions asked are routed to the right expert's door, auctions to exchange any imaginable knowledge product, and interactive plazas fostering dialogues between knowledge experts. Many of these initiatives can be seen as new market mechanisms intended to put fair market values on knowledge. By facilitating the sharing of dispersed information, the Internet enables the emergence of such "communities of knowing" (Boland and Tenkasi 1995). Similar infomediaries emerge off the Internet. The services they provide range from simple information transactions to complex and specialized knowledge brokering.

The Extended Organized Market

Another hybrid governance structure emerges when organizations not only correct market imperfections related to finding reliable information sources, but also to asking the right knowledge questions unambiguously. In particular, when people face ambiguous problems or opportunities, find themselves in highly uncertain situations, or merely have some indeterminate feelings that something should be done, articulating information needs can be a difficult search process in itself. As a result of posing vague or wrong questions, people can learn something incorrectly or can correctly learn something incorrect, even if the answers received are representative (Huber 1991). Organizations realizing that such difficulties in information exchange may occur can choose this option to further increase the productivity of employees and the organization's performance.

Organizational arrangements directed toward this second generic information problem focus

on guiding organization members in their search processes. We call such arrangements "interactive systems" to indicate that genuine guiding requires real-time interaction in successive questions and answers. Practices vary from search engines capable of first verifying what the information seeker means before presenting the search results and expert-system software programs for more structured searches, to enhanced library functions and experts employed for every designated knowledge slice to help with unstructured searches. In its simplest form, organizations can create databases with "frequently asked questions" and past search results. Depending on the percentage of repetitive questions, such organizational coordination can lead to substantial *informational economies of scale*: the average costs per information transaction will be lower for high-frequency transactions. In other words, the value of information increases as more people use it. In all these cases, mutual adjustment and standardization are used as the coordination mechanisms to reduce transaction costs. This reduction will be at least partly offset by the costs incurred for the necessary investments in and maintenance of the interactive systems, and for the monitoring and bonding activities.

Guiding services to help information seekers pinpoint their information needs before they are referred to the right information source are also provided by external knowledge brokers. An example is Teltech—Research and Knowledge Management Services. This broker provides a technical referral service connecting over 3,000 technical experts and thousands of online databases with clients who occasionally have questions or problems in technical knowledge slices. When a client calls Teltech, he or she gets assistance from a knowledge analyst. They collaboratively browse appropriate databases, elicit the client's true information needs, and discuss the search results. Especially when questions are not articulated well, client and knowledge analyst together engage in such dialogues, which may extend over a couple of days. Among others, by effectively guiding the client to information, Teltech adds value to information.[14] Whether the client understands the information gathered and is capable of using it in his or her context remains the client's responsibility. It is also the realm of the last governance structure for knowledge management distinguished by us, the firm.

External infomediaries such as Teltech can be so efficient that outsourcing becomes an alternative road to travel in attempts to economize on transaction costs. It complicates the trade-offs to be considered in knowledge decisions. The costs of internalizing information transactions have to be compared not only with the costs of transacting on the market, but also with the costs of outsourcing.

The Firm

The last governance structure is directed toward all three generic information problems. Compared to the extended organized market, it also includes the problem that information has to be understood to be able to formulate statements and actions that are meaningful and purposeful for the practices in which organization members collectively work. The intention is to ease information interpretation in order to support information use and feedback. It is for organizations viewing learning as essential to rent generation and future development, but that also believe it does not come about spontaneously or that it can be more efficiently coordinated internally. Here we encounter the issue of organizational learning: individual people learn, but we cannot be sure that organizations learn as well. Individuals learn as they develop their unique knowledge bases by constantly constructing new understandings to guide actions. Whether organizations learn depends on their abilities to synergistically use and integrate these distinct knowledge bases. That requires a process of mutual perspective taking to exchange individual knowledge among organization members (Tenkasi and Boland 1996), mutual engagement and a shared repertoire (Wenger 1998), the construction of collective meaning (Dixon 1997), or uniform understandings across organization members of possibly different interpretations (Huber 1991). For any coordinated action to take place, it is essential to (partly) know what others know. The issues involved in these delicate processes constituting learning and adaptive efficiency are, among others, the stickiness of information (Szulanski 1996) and proprietary and political concerns related to agency problems.

Most knowledge projects aim at organizational learning. As stated in the beginning of this chapter, however, these projects can often be characterized as supplier-focused, centralized approaches pushing commodified information to users, which hardly facilitate learning at the organizational level. In terms of the coordination mechanisms applied, most initiatives strive for efficiency gains through the "standardization of knowledge." Inviting one expert to write a "best practice" for all colleagues to copy is an example of such standardization. If information *could* be used in this way, it *would* greatly reduce transactions costs and lead to substantial informational economies of scale. However, as a study of the best practice databases we conducted in three large organizations has shown, "standard solutions" contain too little information to come close to what is needed for mutual perspective taking. Typically, they lack information on historical contexts, situational factors, assumptions used, personal reflections, and on their validity and generalizability. The study has also demonstrated that sometimes sensitive yet crucial information is excluded from best practice descriptions, and that intermediary "knowledge officers" are often focused more on the maintainance side of the information systems than on raising the value of the information stored. We argue that knowledge projects relying on standardization result in a less than expected decrease of transaction costs and higher agency costs due to "not-invented-here syndromes" and increased reluctance to use standard solutions.

Managers can cultivate learning, but they cannot force it. Instead of having knowledge officers trying to control for quality, organizations can give the learners themselves control of their learning processes (Leidner and Jarvenpaa 1995) and support them in pulling the information they need. Rather than relying solely on centralized information delivery, they can create situations that help group members learn from each other (Storck and Hill 2000) and develop practices that make use of information in new and more productive ways (Cook and Seely Brown 1999). In particular, people learn by giving and receiving feedback information showing how actions can reinforce or counteract each other (Senge 1990). Mutual perspective taking often boils down to knowing how others deploy resources and relate organizational actions to outcomes. To ensure the collection and analysis of such feedback and to increase its accuracy, organizations can use feedback systems such as learning histories (Kleiner and Roth 1997), storytelling (Boyce 1996, Barry 1997), scenario planning (Van der Heijden 1996), and open discussion spaces (Tenkasi and Boland 1996). All these recent developments in organization theory indicate that organizational learning only occurs in relatively small groups or communities sustaining close relations of mutual engagement based on trust and freely exchanging explicit and tacit information to achieve benefits for all. We therefore prefer to speak of collective instead of organizational learning. Organizations consist of many groups or collectivities, each situated in unique practices and demanding tailored learning processes.

In the governance structure of the firm, the function of the external knowledge market is largely taken over by the organization itself, for the allocation of resources and the abilities to access, deploy, and develop them are primarily seen as internal affairs. There are, however, infomediaries that facilitate rather than standardize individual and collective learning processes. These expert networks are always specialized on particular industries, knowledge domains, or professionalisms, place high demands on those who may call themselves experts, and offer space for rich conversations between information demand and supply. In contrast to the knowledge exchanges, knowledge communities, and knowledge auctions mentioned above, they constantly intervene in these conversations to stimulate learning processes and share responsibility for the quality of the information exchanged. An example is the Cambridge Information Network, an online community of 4,000 senior ICT executives from around the world. Outsiders such as consultants, scientists, journalists, lower management, and employees are excluded. Due to this closeness, members can openly collaborate, share experiences or questions, and glean advice from colleagues. The organization's staff is highly active in maintaining and extending the community. They start, moderate, and close discussions. They conduct surveys and provide members with in-depth research, white papers, and columns. In other words, expert networks promote members to give and receive feedback information to support their learning processes.

As to the cost effects of this governance structure, collective learning requires regular interaction and mutual interest in groups of limited size. This implies that information exchange is mainly coordinated by mutual adjustment within and between all groups to be distinguished within the organization (Grant 1996). Compared to standardization, mutual adjustment leads to higher governance costs as it greatly reduces the potential informational economies of scale. Mutual adjustment enhancing adaptive efficiency, therefore, may result in less allocative efficiency. That, however, is the consequence of combining push and pull strategies for knowledge management, of believing

that collective learning requires intense and reciprocal social and affective bonds that facilitate mutual understanding taking a long time of sustained effort to build, which cannot be bought and can be destroyed "in a second."

Managing the Information Transaction Space

The Coordination and Cost Perspectives

The four ideal types of governance structures for knowledge management are different solutions to the information problems inherent in information exchange processes. They have different allocative and adaptive efficiency properties. Which of the four options is to be preferred under what conditions?

From a cost perspective, the answer would be that this is determined by the relative cost of transacting using these alternatives. Based on transaction-cost economics and agency theory, we have argued that there are three cost components relevant to knowledge management: transaction, agency, and operations costs. Both theories emphasize building a competitive advantage through capturing economic rents stemming from fundamental organization-level efficiency advantages. To comparatively assess the four governance structures, the costs of market imperfections (i.e., transaction costs) should be compared with the costs of internalizing knowledge transactions (i.e., agency and operations costs). Moreover, if other organizations are capable of organizing the same information transactions, the costs of outsourcing alternatives should also be considered. Such comparative assessments between governance structures should be conducted for every knowledge slice distinguished by the organization to enhance its strategic capabilities and the productive possibilities of its resources. This implies that the coordination mechanisms used can be attuned to the specific conditions met in each knowledge domain.

As figure 11.1 shows, the transaction costs decrease while the agency and operations costs increase as organizations rely more heavily on internal coordination. The optimal point for any organization is located where the sum of these costs is minimized.[15] In this way, the boundaries between the alternative governance structures are set by the economics of exchanging information. The exact location of this point cannot be given in general, for it depends on the spe-

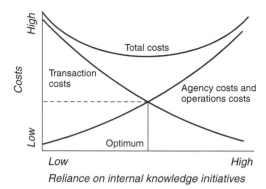

Figure 11.1 Minimization of total costs.

cific cost structure of the organization, which in itself is contingent upon factors such as the degree of bureaucratization, of "politicalness," of individualism, of dispersion of information sources, and of knowledge fluidity.[16] If, for instance, the organization's culture is characterized as relatively bureaucratic, political, or individualistic, agency theory predicts that the agency costs will be comparatively high in that organization. This could lead to a shift toward more market coordination to avoid the high agency costs, or toward specific actions and investments to fight these costs. If the relevant information sources are geographically dispersed or if knowledge is highly fluid, the transaction costs will be relatively high, which might stimulate organizations to coordinate the information transactions internally. Hence, in practice the shapes of the cost curves can deviate from those depicted in figure 11.1 and should therefore be investigated if knowledge decisions are to be made from a cost perspective.

So far we have used a *static* analysis to assess comparative economic organization. By incorporating three intertemporal considerations into our framework for managing the information transaction space (see table 11.2), it becomes *dynamic*.[17] First, investments can change the underlying cost structures of the organization and its knowledge slices. To some extent, managers can choose the cost components they want to minimize. For instance, cost-effective information and communication technology can reduce transaction costs and can lead an organization to increase its use of markets. However, it can also be deployed to decrease agency and operations costs, suggesting more organizational governance. Examples are intranets supporting infor-

mation sharing, and tools to monitor the agents' performance, respectively. In all, therefore, the net effect of investments on the boundaries between the four options is not so obvious and depends upon other factors.

Second, managers have to continually assess and reassess the strategic knowledge domains they want to excel in. For instance, in 1995 the Internet was not important to most organizations. By the year 2000 it was. Consequently, knowledge slices continually compete with each other for the attention of managers and employees.

Third, managers have to dynamically decide which governance structure is the most appropriate for each distinguished knowledge slice. Learning from failed knowledge projects, changing opinions and beliefs as to what is and what is not feasible with knowledge management, the emerging of innovative technologies, and new services offered by external knowledge brokers can all change the relative desirability of governance structures. What was efficient yesterday may not suffice today. Hence, in each knowledge slice, the four options for knowledge management are continually involved in a dynamic process of competition. These dynamic considerations affect not only the organization's allocative efficiency, but also its adaptive efficiency.

The Coordination and Learning Perspectives

Resource-based and knowledge-based theories of the firm follow a different logic. In the resource based view, superior performance is based on developing competitively unique (and therefore scarce) resources and capabilities, deploying them in a well-conceived strategy, and protecting them from imitation (Grant 1999a, Teece et al. 1999). Resources are generally seen as the source of capabilities and capabilities as the source of competitive advantage and the organization's rent-generating potential. Originally, the issues of value or rent appropriation (i.e., sustaining the existing competitive edge) and its distribution (i.e., shareholder value) were emphasized (Moran and Ghoshal 1999). More recently, the focus has been broadened to include the issue of rent creation, that is, the continual renewal of competitive advantage through learning and innovation and the development of new resource bundles and capabilities (Spender 1996, Teece et al. 1999, Grant 1999a). The essence of strategy, then, is to dynamically balance rent creation and rent appropriation. Strategy formulation should not be concerned as much with the maximization of current rents as with the maximization of rents *over time* (Boisot 1999).

In knowledge-based theories as outgrowths of the resource-based view, performance differences among organizations are a result of their different knowledge bases and differing capabilities in developing and deploying knowledge (Bierly and Chakrabarti 1999). Thus, differential allocative and adaptive efficiency between organizations is the key. The attention is particularly focused on the largely implicit knowledge and skills required to coordinate heterogeneous resources in distinct, organization-specific resource bundles in such a way that current capabilities are leveraged and new ones created (Tsoukas 1996, Spender 1999). As in transaction-cost economics and agency theory, achieving purposeful, coordinated action from organizations consisting of many specialized individuals and other resources is the fundamental problem of organizations and their management. Perfecting such coordination requires learning through repetition (Grant 1999a). Hence, managers' coordinating and learning capabilities are seen as the principal sources of a competitive advantage and of adaptive efficiency.

The coordination and learning perspectives are reflected in our framework (see table 11.2). The four options for knowledge management show that organizations can achieve equally efficient, yet differentiated approaches to coordination and learning. We expect most organizations to require a mixture or "institutional pluralism" (Moran and Ghoshal 1999), not just a single form. All four governance structures are needed for allocatively and, in particular, adaptively efficient economic development. That is, for each distinguished knowledge slice, managers have to determine what relationship between the rent-generating potential of the knowledge domain and learning will be most fruitful, and apply the corresponding (mix of) coordination mechanisms. If, for instance, intellectual property rights are an issue, strategic considerations can lead to the internalization of the associated knowledge activities and the erection of knowledge barriers as isolating mechanisms, thus improving the possibilities to protect valuable knowledge from appropriation or imitation by competitors (Liebeskind 1999). For other knowledge slices, however, access to broader knowledge bases may be needed to keep abreast of cutting-edge developments and increase the organization's flexibility to create

new competitive opportunities (Bierly and Chakrabarti 1999). In one situation, collective learning demands specific organizational and motivational actions, while in other situations self-organizing communities of practice offer a better way to adopt this role.[18] In the market option, transaction costs can be pervasive, distorting perceptions of the nature of available resources and their accessibility, quality, and usability. On the other hand, in the firm option, any disregard of market incentives can be inefficient, leading to, for example, relatively high agency costs to increase the efficiency of information exchange. Therefore, from the perspective of the total organization, both "spontaneous adaptation" through markets and "cooperative adaptation" through internal coordination are needed. In this regard, it is essential to realize that learning cannot be mandated, implying that whatever option for knowledge management is applied, command-and-control structures are highly inefficient means to foster learning processes (Grant 1999b, Spender 1996). To create a climate of openness and trust, more can be expected from actions enhancing unencumbered communication and free information exchange between information demand and supply (Smith et al. 1996), which we have mentioned before as the goal of knowledge management.

Differentiating knowledge approaches according to the knowledge slice under consideration, however, is just one facet of managing the information transaction space. Organization members learn and managers have to learn how members learn best. Management's dynamic capabilities to manage the information transaction space relate to their "interpretative flexibility" (Spender 1996) to define and redefine strategic knowledge slices, explore and exploit institutional pluralism, and use investment opportunities to adjust cost structures leading to productive organizational changes, while acknowledging the organization's contingency factors and path dependencies. The ability to manage the information transaction space is to configure and reconfigure the total mix of governance structures to better fit the organization's competitive context. This open-ended process of coordinating and learning from the experiences gained may be more important in creating and sustaining a competitive advantage and economic rent than the specific knowledge acquired. In that sense, management's dynamic ability to make the best use of the information transaction space is a defining competitive dimension of any organization.

Notes

1. Although they focus on exchange in general and not on information transaction as we do, we are indebted to the work of Moran and Ghoshal (1999) for this line of argument.

2. The term "rent" is used in the academic literature due to the ambiguity associated with accounting definitions of profit. Rent is the abnormal return to resources, which is the surplus of revenue over the "real" or "opportunity cost" of the resources used in generating that revenue (Grant 1999a).

3. Although we adhere to this distinction between information and knowledge as much as possible, the term "knowledge" is so ingrained in the business parlance that we use both concepts interchangeably in this chapter.

4. A resource is exchanged whenever the right to use it is transferred.

5. Transaction-cost economics has been criticized for being a static theory that needs to be made dynamic (Douma and Schreuder 1991, Liebeskind 1996, Moran and Ghoshal 1999). We agree with Williamson (1999), who argues that there are no fundamental impediments to the inclusion of dynamic, intertemporal considerations into the transaction cost economics project. While he acknowledges that intertemporal issues have not been worked out in a satisfactory way yet, they are considered to be central to this project.

6. Originally, coordination mechanisms in transaction-cost economics were confined to the "hierarchy," that is, to vertical coordination based on authority (Williamson 1975). We follow Douma and Schreuder (1991), who argue that Williamson and other proponents of transaction-cost economics took too narrow a view on nonmarket coordination and adopt the six organizational mechanisms proposed by Mintzberg (1989). Authority or direct supervision is but one of the organizational coordination devices. Therefore, we prefer speaking about "organizations" or "firms" instead of "hierarchies." See also Grant (1996).

7. Nobel Prize winners D. North and J. Wallis have estimated the magnitude of transaction costs to be 45% of total costs (Carroll 1998).

8. Transaction-cost economics has been criticized for focusing on transaction costs and ignoring production costs. Later, however, this bias has been corrected (Riordan and Williamson 1985).

9. Transaction-cost economics and agency theory have been criticized for excluding trust as a basis for lasting social relations (Douma and Schreuder 1991, Davenport and Prusak 1998, Liebeskind 1999). Without trust it would be difficult to understand how people can cooperate within and across organizational boundaries. However, to concede opportunism is not to celebrate it (Williamson 1999). In other words, transaction cost economics and agency theory are positive theories describing "what is." Publications on trust, on the other hand, are always normative, advancing "what should be." If trust is seen as the absence of opportunism, both views are not mutually exclusive.

10. Researchers of transaction-cost economics and agency theory do not fully agree on the definitions of "operations costs," "transaction costs," and "agency costs" (Gurbaxani and Whang 1991). Even economists complain that if you cannot understand it, it must be transaction costs (Rowlinson 1997). Our use of the three terms is based on the opposite directions these cost components take if information transactions are taken out of the external market and are organized internally; see the following sections.

11. We agree with the idea that trust can positively affect the allocative and adaptive efficiency of knowledge markets, which should therefore be cultivated. However, we do not agree with researchers who criticize transaction-cost economics and agency theory for not paying attention to the issue of trust. Fighting opportunism is to build trust. See also note 9.

12. Search entails both "scanning" and "focused search." Scanning is the sensing of the organization's external environment, while focused search occurs in a narrow segment of the organization's internal or external environment, often in reaction to actual or suspected problems or opportunities (Huber 1991).

13. Uncertainty about the quality of information stems from information asymmetry between actors. It can result in the withdrawal of high-quality information from the market, leaving it with low-quality information. This so-called "lemons problem" arises in markets when it is difficult to assess the quality of products, services, or information prior to their use or purchase (Choi et al. 1997).

14. For more information on Teltech, see *www.teltech.com* or *www.bus.utexas.edu/kman/telcase.htm*.

15. Economists say that the optimal point is located where the marginal cost of organizing an additional transaction internally equals the marginal cost of executing the same transaction on the market, and equals the marginal cost of organizing the same transaction in another organization.

16. Except for the degree of knowledge fluidity, these contingency factors closely relate to the notion of path dependency. This notion expresses

that the organization's previous investments and its repertoire of routines constrain its future behavior (Teece et al. 1999).

17. See note 5.

18. Resource- and knowledge-based theorists commonly state that knowledge and capabilities are generally inappropriable by means of market transactions (Grant 1996, Teece et al. 1999), that market contracts are unlikely to achieve the stability of long-term relationships needed for learning and are likely to cause all the problems of opportunism that transaction-cost economics and agency theory predict (Grant 1996, Hodgson 1998), and that organizations exist because they can more efficiently coordinate collective learning processes than market organization is able to do (Foss 1996, Grant 1996). We agree with these arguments if only "markets" and "firms" are allowed as alternative governance structures, if the price is the only market coordination mechanism, and "authority" the only organizational coordination mechanism. However, when these assumptions are relaxed, a richer framework emerges in which more autonomously governed structures (like a market) can be compared with more purposely governed ones (like a "hierarchy"). Moreover, as illustrated before, problems of opportunism also occur within organizations. It is not opportunism in the outside world versus altruism inside organizations.

References

Alavi, M. and Leidner, D.E. (1999) "Knowledge management systems: issues, challenges, and benefits." *Communications of the Association for Information Systems* 1:1–37.

Alchian, A.A. and Demsetz, H. (1972) "Production, information costs and economic organization." *American Economic Review* 62(5):777–795.

Anderson, J.R. (1995) *Learning and Memory: An Integrated Approach*. Chichester: Wiley.

Barry, D. (1997) "Telling changes: from narrative family therapy to organizational change and development." *Journal of Organizational Change Management* 10(1):30–46.

Berger, P.L. and Lockman, T. (1966) *The Social Construction of Reality: A Treatise in the Sociology of Knowledge*. New York: Anchor Books.

Bierly, P. and Chakrabarti, A. (1999) "Generic knowledge strategies in the U.S. pharmaceutical industry," in M.H. Zack (ed.), *Knowledge and Strategy*, pp. 231–250. Boston: Butterworth-Heinemann.

Boisot, M.H. (1999) "Is your firm a creative destroyer? Competitive learning and knowledge flows in the technological strategies of firms," in M.H. Zack (ed.), *Knowledge and Strategy*, pp. 251–274. Boston: Butterworth-Heinemann.

Boland, R.J. and Tenkasi, R.V. (1995) "Perspective making and perspective taking in communities of knowing," *Organization Science* 6(4):350–372.

Boyce, M.E. (1996) "Organizational story and storytelling: a critical review." *Journal of Organizational Change Management* 9(5):5–26.

Carroll, P. (1998) "Law and disorder: three interviews with influential thinkers who predict a new wave of change in the rules of commerce." *Context Magazine*, http://www.contextmag.com/archives/199809/LawAndDisorder.asp

Choi, S.-Y., Stahl, D.O., and Whinston, A.B. (1997) *The Economics of Electronic Commerce*. Indianapolis: Macmillan.

Choo, C.W. (1998) *The Knowing Organization*. New York: Oxford University Press.

Ciborra, C.U. (1993) *Teams, Markets and Systems—Business Innovation and Information Technology*. Cambridge: Cambridge University Press.

Coase, R.H. (1937) "The nature of the firm." *Economica* 4:386–405.

Cook, S.D.N. and Seely Brown, J. (1999) "Bridging epistemologies: the generative dance between organizational knowledge and organizational knowing." *Organization Science* 10(4):381–400.

Crossan, M.M., Lane, H.W., and White, R.W. (1999) "An organizational learning framework: from intuition to institution." *Academy of Management Review* 24(3):522–537.

Davenport, T.H. and Prusak, L. (1998) *Working Knowledge*. Boston: Harvard Business School Press.

Davenport, T.H., De Long, D.W., and Beers, M.C. (1998) "Successful knowledge management projects." *Sloan Management Review* Winter, 43–57.

Dixon, N.M. (1997) "The hallways of learning." *Organizational Dynamics* 25(4):23–34.

Douma, S. and Schreuder, H. (1991) *Economic Approaches to Organizations*. London: Prentice-Hall.

Drucker, P.F. (1983) *Post-capitalist Society*. Oxford: Butterworth-Heinemann.

Fama, E.F. and Jensen, M. (1983) "Agency problems and residual claims." *Journal of Law and Economics* 26(2):327–349.

Foss, N.J. (1996) "Firms, incomplete contracts, and organizational learning." *Human Systems Management* 15(1):17–26.

Grant, R.M. (1996) "Toward a knowledge-based theory of the firm." *Strategic Management Journal* 17:109–122.

Grant, R.M. (1999a) "The resource-based theory of competitive advantage: implications for strategy formulation," in M.H. Zack (ed.), *Knowledge and Strategy*, pp. 3–24. Boston: Butterworth-Heinemann.

Grant, R.M. (1999b) "Prospering in dynamically competitive environments: organizational capability as knowledge integration," in: M.H. Zack (ed.), *Knowledge and Strategy*, pp. 133–153. Boston: Butterworth-Heinemann.

Gurbaxani, V. and Whang, S. (1991) "The impact of information systems on organizations and markets." *Communications of the ACM* 34(1):59–73.

Hackett, B. (2000) *Beyond Knowledge Management: New Ways to Work and Learn*. New York: Conference Board.

Hayek, F.A. (1945) "The use of knowledge in society." *American Economic Review* 35(4):519–530.

Hodgson, G. (1998) "Competence and contract in the theory of the firm." *Journal of Economic Behavior and Organization* 35(April):179–201.

Huber, G.P. (1991) "Organizational learning: the contributing processes and the literatures." *Organization Science* 2(1):88–114.

Jensen, M.C. and Meckling, W.H. (1973) "Theory of the firm: managerial behavior, agency costs and ownership structure." *Journal of Financial Economics* 3:305–360.

Kleiner, A. and Roth, G. (1997) "How to make experience your company's best teacher." *Harvard Business Review*, September-October, 172–177.

Lant, T.K. and Mezias, S.J. (1990) "Managing discontinuous change: a simulation study of organizational learning and entrepreneurship." *Strategic Management* 11(Summer):147–179.

Leidner, D.E. and Jarvenpaa, S.L. (1995) "The use of information technology to enhance management school education: a theoretical view." *MIS Quarterly*, September, 265–291.

Lévy, P. (1997) *Collective Intelligence: Mankind's Emerging World in Cyberspace*. New York: Plenum Press.

Liebeskind, J.P. (1999) "Knowledge, strategy, and the theory of the firm," in M.H. Zack (ed.), *Knowledge and Strategy*, pp. 197–219. Boston: Butterworth-Heinemann.

Malone, T.W., Yates, J., and Benjamin, R.I. (1987) "Electronic markets and electronic hierarchies." *Communications of the ACM* 30(6):484–497.

Manville, B. and Foote, N. (1996) "Harvest your workers' knowledge." *Datamation*, July, 78–81.

Meyer, M.H. and Zack, M.H. (1996) "The design and development of information products." *Sloan Management Review*, Spring, 43–59.

Mintzberg, H. (1989) *Mintzberg on Management*. New York: Free Press.

Moran, P. and Ghoshal, S. (1999) "Markets, firms, and the process of economic development." *Academy of Management Review* 24(3):390–412.

Moreland, L.M., Argote, L., and Krishnan, R. (1996) "Socially shared cognition at work: transactive memory and group performance," in J.L. Nye and A.M. Brower (eds.), *What's Social about Social Cognition? Research on Socially Shared Cognition in Small Groups*, pp. 57–84. Thousand Oaks, CA: Sage.

Nahapiet, J. and Ghoshal, S. (1998) "Social capital, intellectual capital, and the organizational advantage." *Academy of Management Review* 23(2):242–266.

Newell, A. (1990) *Unified Theories of Cognition*. Cambridge, MA: Harvard University Press.

Penrose, E. (1959) *The Theory of the Growth of the Firm*. New York: Wiley.

Pine, B.J. and Gilmore, J.H. (1999) *The Experience Economy*. Boston: Harvard Business School Press.

Quinn, J.B., Anderson, P., and Finkelstein, S. (1999) "Leveraging intellect," in M.H. Zack (ed.), *Knowledge and Strategy*, pp. 275–300. Boston: Butterworth-Heinemann.

Riordan, M. and Williamson, O.E. (1985) "Asset specificity and economic organization." *International Journal of Industrial Organization* 3:365–378.

Rowlinson, M. (1997) *Organisations and Institutions*. Houndmills: Macmillan.

Senge, P.M. (1990) *The Fifth Discipline—The Art and Practice of The Learning Organization*. New York: Doubleday.

Smith, K.A., Vasudevan, S.P., and Tanniru, M.R. (1996) "Organizational learning and resource-based theory: an integrative model." *Journal of Organizational Change Management* 9(6):41–53.

Spender, J.-C. (1996) "Organizational knowledge, learning and memory: three concepts in search of a theory." *Journal of Organizational Change* 9(1):63–78.

Spender, J.-C. (1999) "Organizational knowledge, collective practice and Penrose rents," in M.H. Zack (ed.), *Knowledge and Strategy*, pp. 117–132. Boston: Butterworth-Heinemann.

Storck, J. and Hill, P.A. (2000) "Knowledge diffusion through 'strategic communities.'" *Sloan Management Review*, Winter, 63–74.

Szulanski, G. (1996) "Exploring internal stickiness: impediments to the transfer of best practice within the firm." *Strategic Management Journal* 17:27–44.

Teece, D.J., Pisano, G., and Shuen, A. (1999) "Dynamic capabilities and strategic management," in M.H. Zack (ed.), *Knowledge and Strategy*, pp. 77–116. Boston: Butterworth-Heinemann.

Tenkasi, R.V. and Boland, R.J. (1996) "Exploring knowledge diversity in knowledge intensive firms: a new role for information systems." *Jour-*

nal of *Organizational Change Management* 9(1):79–91.

Tsoukas, H. (1996) "The firm as a distributed knowledge system: a constructionist approach." *Strategic Management Journal* 17:11–26.

van der Heijden, K. (1996) *Scenarios—the Art of Strategic Conversation*. Chichester: Wiley.

Weick, K.E. (1995) *Sensemaking in Organizations*. Thousand Oaks, CA: Sage.

Wenger, E.C. (1998) *Communities of Practice— Learning, Meaning, and Identity*. Cambridge: Cambridge University Press.

Wenger, E.C. and Snyder, W.M. (2000) "Communities of practice: the organizational frontier."

Harvard Business Review, January-February, 139–145.

Williamson, O.E. (1975) *Markets and Hierarchies: Analysis and Antitrust Implications*. New York: Free Press.

Williamson, O.E. (1985) *The Economic Institutions of Capitalism: Firms, Markets, Relational Contracting*. London: Free Press/Collier Macmillan.

Williamson, O.E. (1999) "Strategy research: governance and competence perspectives." *Strategic Management Journal* 20:1087–1108.

Zack, M.H. (1999) "Introduction," in M.H. Zack (ed.), *Knowledge and Strategy*, pp. vii–xii. Boston: Butterworth-Heinemann.

III

Knowledge Strategies

12

Replication of Organizational Routines

Conceptualizing the Exploitation of Knowledge Assets

Sidney G. Winter and Gabriel Szulanski

The fundamental problem of improving knowledge utilization in organizational settings continues to attract considerable attention. This interest manifests itself under such rubrics as organizational learning (Argote 1999, Garvin and Oliver 2000), knowledge sharing (Hansen 1999, Dixon 2000), internal transfer of knowledge and best practices (O'Dell et al. 1998), and closing the knowing–doing gap (Pfeffer and Sutton 2000).

It would appear that interest in leveraging knowledge assets outstrips the ability to achieve results in that domain. For example, a recent survey of 431 U.S. and European organizations conducted by Ernst & Young shows that only 14% of the respondents judged satisfactory the performance of their organization in transferring existing knowledge internally (Ruggles 1998). There seems to be ample room for improvement.

Organizations can learn from experience how to exploit knowledge assets. Such learning is generally more effective when selected key aspects of the exploitation effort are varied while the rest is kept constant or comparable. This way, causal explanations of success or failure in exploiting organizational knowledge can be rigorously assessed. For such quasi-experimental conditions to occur in a real-life setting, there must be numerous attempts to exploit knowledge, for example, to transfer best practices, attempts that are comparable in all but those aspects that are being manipulated, which means that such efforts must be simultaneous or adjacent in time if they are to remain comparable. Such conditions are rare, especially when each attempt is in and of itself a large-scale effort.

This is why few settings rival replicating organizations—organizations that intentionally replicate internal processes and business systems—in their promise to illuminate fundamental problems of knowledge management. Such organizations routinely conduct efforts to replicate knowledge, often hundreds of times each year. Examples of such organizations are McDonald's, Starbucks, and Mail Boxes Etc, three chain organizations that have each opened several hundred new stores worldwide over the past year. In all cases, they replicate outlets uniformly, to the extent possible, each outlet the implementation of a sophisticated business concept.

Such replicators can be regarded as natural laboratories for studying the leveraging of knowledge assets.

Yet systematic study of the exploitation of knowledge assets in such settings requires conceptual infrastructure that is not yet fully in place. Economics and other disciplines that employ the theoretical tools of decision theory to analyze organizational action presume that those actions that would be needed to exploit knowledge are familiar and, for the most part, readily available (Dosi et al. 2000, p. 10). Such treatment of knowledge utilization typically relies on the signaling metaphor (Shannon and Weaver 1949), which portrays the transfer of knowledge as an instantaneous and costless act—rather than as a costly and protracted process (Rogers 1994, Putnam et al. 1996). While useful to highlight the basic elements of the transfer, such a view blurs the process by which exploitation occurs or does not occur. As a consequence, the process of utilization is not well understood and is typically, often mistakenly, assumed to be trivial (Teece 1976, Szulanski 1994, Bradach 1998). Theory development efforts in this domain have been relatively rare and modest in scope.

The replication of organizational routines offers a conceptual lens that could remedy this theoretical deficiency. The replication perspective applies to a broad class of exploitation situations where an organization attempts to reproduce at multiple internal sites the outcome of an existing activity (Nelson and Winter 1982). In this chapter, we begin the effort toward a more complete specification of replication as an analytical approach. First, we distinguish replication from conceptual neighbors such as the transfer of technology and the diffusion of innovations between and within organizations. We then outline theoretical dimensions of replication. Next, we illustrate those dimensions of replication of routines with two examples drawn from in-depth fieldwork. We conclude the chapter by raising broader theoretical considerations that we believe must also be part of a discussion of knowledge utilization in productive settings.

Defining Replication of Routines

Leveraging idiosyncratic profit opportunities latent in existing knowledge endowments often takes the form of replicating the firm's productive routines in the quest for greater profit. In a straightforward descriptive sense, replication involves the creation of "replicas"—that is, of a series of local routines that are quite similar to the original routine in significant respects. At the microlevel, a routine in operation at a particular site can be conceived as a web of coordinating relationships connecting specific resources; without those resources it could not exist. Considered as an abstract activity pattern, however, "that same routine" may be in operation also at a different site, where a different but similar set of resources is coordinated by a very similar web of relationships. It is in that sense that routines can be replicated (Winter 1995, pp. 149–150).

Replication of routines is one important process by which organizations reuse knowledge that is already in use. Seen that way, replication has several conceptual neighbors, including the diffusion of innovations and horizontal transfers of technology between and within organizations, that also involve the transfer of knowledge embodied in organizational routines, practices, and cultures. Despite many similarities, there are important, sometimes subtle, differences among these.

Differentiating Replication from Conceptual Neighbors

The connotations of "replication" include the theoretically significant idea that there is an original that is being copied. We use the term "template" or "template site" to refer to this working example.[1] Perhaps the most salient difference between replication and conceptually similar processes hinges on the fact that, unlike conceptual alternatives, replication allows explicitly for the possibility that the target routine, the routine that is being replicated, is only partially understood at the source. In other words, the target routine is causally ambiguous (Lippman and Rumelt 1982).

This assumption has two important implications. The first is that replication is likely to be a costly and difficult process. A causally ambiguous target routine would normally have some features that are irrelevant or even detrimental to its effectiveness and others that, though desirable, are impossible to replicate— such as unique human capital. Furthermore, some of its features may be tacit (Polanyi 1966, Kogut and Zander 1992, Nonaka 1994). Such tacit knowledge must be recreated by the recipient, rather than obtained through a single act of transmission and absorption (Rosenberg 1982, Attewell 1992, Zander and Kogut 1995). Replication thus could be a protracted iterative process rather than a single directional transfer, because several iterations may be necessary to produce an acceptable replica.

Second, and implied by the first, the replication of routines is an organizational capability that is learned by doing. Specifically, through repetition, the organization learns to increase the scope and speed of replication. For example, Bradach (1998) notes how the central organizations of five restaurant chains progressively improved their ability to grow by replication by developing expertise in site selection, building outlets faster, and operating them more efficiently. Likewise, Love (1995, p. 277) reports that McDonald's doubled its central real estate and construction staff to implement its ambitious acceleration of growth in the late 1960s. Firm-level factors that may play an important role in creating and sustaining superior performance at the subunit level may include skill in site selection, human resource practices, and logistics or economies of scale in purchasing.

The contribution of the center can be conceptualized as the differential ability of the organization to access the template or target routine, when compared to that afforded to an imitating outsider. As Nelson and Winter (1982) explain, when problems arise in the replica, the replicating organization can attempt to resolve them by closer scrutiny of the original (p. 123): subtle features of the template site, the fine detail of its productive routines, and the accompanying input flows. Such scrutiny may even extend to recollections of the process by which the template was constructed.

Attention to the role of the focal firm distinguishes replication from the diffusion of innovations in a population of organizations—on which there is a large literature (Rogers 1995)—and from an even closer neighbor, but one on which the literature is much smaller, intraorganizational diffusion (Cool et al. 1997). For the most part, the diffusion literature treats the recipient (adopting) organizations as the key locus of decision making and gives little or no attention to the source or promoting organization—this notwithstanding the fact that informing the decisions of the latter organizations has been from the start an important practical rationale of the research interest in the area.

Studies of the transfer of practices and technologies do reveal the same sort of activism in the source firm that we find in replication strategy, and in this respect the subjects are close relatives. Such studies tend to be of "one-off" examples. Partly as a result, they tend to neglect the evolving role of the "center" when there is one. This difference looms larger in intrafirm contexts.

Dimensions of Replication

In what follows, we expand Nelson and Winter's (1982) definition of replication as the costly, time-consuming process of copying an existing pattern of productive activity, by outlining theoretical dimensions of replication.

Intended versus Unintended Replication

We seek to understand the managerial challenges of leveraging knowledge. Our focus, then, is on replication as an intentional activity. In saying this, however, we recognize that the early manifestations of knowledge reuse in a given firm may not necessarily indicate an explicit effort to replicate, but that it might lead to such an orientation. At the opposite end of the spectrum, we find firms where replication of routines to leverage knowledge is a standard feature of the organizational reality that is taken for granted. The managerial challenges are most prominent in the broad zone between the "emergent" and "taken-for-granted" extremes.

What could be called unintended replication is a staple of the literature on firm behavior, under such rubrics as organizational inertia and the persistence of routines and cultures. These issues do impinge on our topic, in the role of obstacles to profitable replication. Also, when replication seeks to transform an existing business, established cultures and routines may offer resistance.

Spatial versus Temporal Replication

We are primarily interested in the spatial replication of routines, that is, replication in another geographical location with a different set of specific resources. The specific resources involved in the performance of the activity at a new locale are entirely, or almost entirely, different from those at the source or template site—but the activity itself is, from a functional point of view and in many of its details, highly similar to what goes on at the template site. Spatial replication stands in obvious contrast to temporal replication—the reproduction of activity through time at a given site.[2]

In many respects, however, the two forms of replication are close cousins. Spatial and temporal replication both rely on the existing example provided by the ongoing activity to be replicated. If, in a temporal replication, the process does not work today but it did work yesterday, diagnostic effort is naturally guided by the question, What changed? If, in a spatial replication, the process does not work at the new site but it still works at the old site, the natural question is, What is different? The former effort must rely partly on memory, while the latter can be supported by direct comparison. Neither sort of effort is guaranteed success, but in both cases the space of possibilities searched is vastly smaller than is required to diagnose the cause of a failure when the available reference is only a plan or concept of what success might look like.[3]

Broad and Narrow Scope

Replication involves knowledge transfers of varying scope. In general, the notion of a routine involves no commitment regarding size—large routines are typically structured sets of medium-sized routines—nor does it make any assumptions about significance. The relative size of a routine could be loosely defined by its share of the productive activity of the organization. A large routine confers upon an organization's management a set of decision options for producing significant outputs of a particular type. Such a large routine is referred to by Winter (2000, p. 983) as a "high-level" routine or as a "capability." In contrast, a small routine could be entirely invisible and unknown to decision makers and may be triggered automatically by external events to the organization.

The transfer of a large routine is deemed to be of *broad* scope. The transfer of large routine will create or greatly modify the organizational context of the target organization, possibly defining or redefining its identity. In contrast, a transfer of a small routine—even though it could be a large effort in absolute terms—is considered of *narrow* scope because the organizational context of the target organization will remain relatively stable. In a transfer of narrow scope, the locus of adaptation activities will be primarily internal and will consist mostly of modifications to the transferred routine, with possibly some minor accommodating changes made to the inner organizational environment (Downs and Mohr 1976, Leonard-Barton 1988). In a broad-scope transfer, adaptation efforts seek to align the target organization to the characteristics of its external environment.

Replication may involve the creation of a new establishment, with a work force consisting for the most part of employees new to the organization, or it may involve the conversion of an existing establishment with a substantial carry-over of the previous work force. In the latter case, the establishment as a whole may be relatively new to the organization, or it may have a longer history in it.

Obviously, in a narrow-scope replication that involves sets of practices or key systems, rather than an entire business model, there must be an existing establishment in which the change takes place. A characteristic set of issues arises involving possible interference between new and old ways of doing particular things, dysfunctional interactions between the new ways and complementary parts of the existing organization, or cultural incompatibilities.

These same issues tend to loom larger as the scope of the change increases and are most prominent when a new and comprehensive business model is imposed on an existing organization. More typically, when an entire business model is replicated, a new establishment is created at the same time. This avoids the pitfalls associated with the legacy of the past, but the creation of an adequately coordinated productive organization where there was none before involves substantial learning costs.

True versus False Replication

Replication is concerned with leveraging existing organizational processes. Any changes that may occur in the characteristics and the quality of products and services, in the customer satisfaction, or in the firm's reputation are seen as indirect consequences of replicating routines and therefore as possible indicators of outcome.

Thus, it is important to distinguish replication of routines from *faux replication*, that is, from the replication of superficial features of the template without costly involvement with internal organizational processes. This approach seeks to derive marketing advantages from the general expectation that similar-looking things will prove to be similar. Faux replication is more likely to be a tempting strategic option in contexts where even a short-lived favorable reputation is well rewarded.

Narrow-scope replications are often directed at improving internal efficiency. At this end of the spectrum, the customer may not carry away any distinct impression as a direct result of the replicated practices. Sometimes, however, even a small routine may have a noticeable impact on reputation. One example is McDonald's french fries. The fries are the product of a standard process that is carefully replicated and monitored (Hayes et al. 1996); they also constitute an important feature of McDonald's reputation—for most people, an affirmative reason for seeking out a McDonald's stand.

Below, we illustrate the theoretical dimensions of replication with two examples drawn from in-depth fieldwork.

Replicating Routines at Rank Xerox

Rank Xerox is a European multinational with operations in all Western European countries and also in Africa and in Asia.[4] In 1992, it had 26,000 employees and a turnover of four billion ECUs. The early 1990s had been a time of substantial change at both European Rank Xerox and its parent company, Xerox Corporation, headquartered in Stamford, Connecticut. To match the financial performance of the U.S. operations, Managing Director Bernard Fournier launched the Rank Xerox 2000 initiative in September 1992. An im-

portant part of the initiative consisted of a reorganization designed to shorten the "line of sight" between headquarters and customers to match the customer responsiveness levels achieved by the business division structure of Xerox US. A main thrust of the RX-2000 initiative was to identify and transfer "best practices" across countries. Fournier formed a series of expert teams to meet these objectives. In the most ambitious initiative, Team C had the goal of increasing incremental revenues by identifying, documenting, and transferring best practices associated with discrete sales and marketing processes.

Wave 1 of the Team C initiative began in 1994. Its goal was to identify, document, and transfer best practices to bring specific products to market to increase revenues. Team C searched for discrete best practices that were contained entirely in a specific location. These best practices would be then transferred to other locations, with the originating unit offering the working example of that practice, for others units to consult and emulate. Team C selected nine validated best practices for revenue growth. The units where best practice was found and validated were designated as benchmarks. The team then prepared and distributed a set of easy-to-understand books detailing those practices. Table 12.1 below details the nine best practices.

TABLE 12.1 Best Practices as Identified by Team C for RX-2000

1. MajestiK	An initiative to increase market share in the European color copier market
2. Customer Retention	A plan to encourage current customers to repurchase equipment from Rank Xerox by providing special incentives to salespeople for customer retention as well as technological database aids for tracking customer equipment stocks, usage requirements, and contract expiration dates
3. DocuTech	An initiative to sell offset printers to commercial and educational users by focusing on overall document solutions rather than on traditional product or price selling
4. New Business Major Accounts	A plan to establish salespeople whose sole responsibility is generating new business
5. DocuPrint	A plan to accelerate sales of the newly launched line of high-speed network printers, particularly to the banking and insurance industries, by emphasizing the product's image printing capabilities and systems integration features
6. CSO Competitive MIF Identification	An initiative for rapid updating of the Rank Xerox companywide sales database to track competitive information and provide salespeople with reliable leads
7. Analyst Time Billing	A plan to sell the value-adding, problem-solving consulting services of Rank Xerox technical analysts
8. XBS	A plan to educate salespeople on how to sell facilities management services effectively through the creation of simple packages and pricing options (i.e., Rank Xerox providing to the customer a packaged service consisting of both equipment and manpower)
9. Secondhand CEP	An initiative to regain control of the secondhand market for centralized mainframe printers (typically found in data centers) by repurchasing secondhand machines, refurbishing them, and reselling them to targeted accounts for which price sensitivity is very high

Team C's wave 1 initiative was started and closely tracked by the senior management team. The steps taken by Team C to collect best practices, document them, and diffuse them exemplify possible roles of the "center," in a situation that involves deliberate, conscious choice, that is, intended replication.

Replication, however, is not a fully institutionalized part of the organizational fabric at Rank Xerox. The original implementation goals of wave 1 were tentative and relatively modest: 50% of the opportunities to transfer best practice would be pursued in 75% of the regional units. The corporate office asked each regional unit to choose at least four from the set of nine practices. These voluntary features undoubtedly mitigated the problem of fit between the transferred routines and their new organizational environments. Even though the wave 1 project met overall expectations, the different initiatives experienced varying degrees of success. Some surpassed expectations, others merely met expectations, and some failed to meet expectations. Team C's wave 1 initiative increased revenues by $106 million in the first year and by $150 million in 1995, at an estimated cost of roughly $1 million per year.

Wave 1 also exemplifies spatial replication. The effort aimed to reproduce those practices in different national subsidiaries. Team C's wave 1 initiative concentrated primarily on leveraging small routines, consisting exclusively of narrow-scope replications. Yet the internal processes represented by these routines did have some impact on the customer's perception of Rank Xerox.

Replicating Routines at Banc One

From 1982 until 1993, Banc One, a regional retail bank, grew its asset base from $5 billion to over $46 billion mainly by acquiring and affiliating 36 banks (Banc One Corporation 1991, p. 10).[5] In that period, Banc One grew its assets 15 times, from $5 billion to over $75 billion. By 1997, Banc One Corporation was one of the United States' largest bank holding companies, with assets of over $101.8 billion and 1,502 offices in Arizona, Colorado, Illinois, Indiana, Kentucky, Louisiana, Ohio, Oklahoma, Texas, Utah, West Virginia, and Wisconsin. Increasingly larger new affiliates were converted to a standardized product line supported by common data processing (DP) systems through the "affiliation" process.

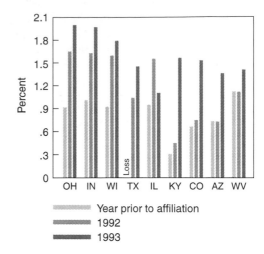

Figure 12.1 Performance in state holding companies' return on average assets.

An important part of that process was the "conversion" of the bank to common DP systems and operating procedures. Banc One relies on standardization of deposit and loan products and implementation of "common systems" of data processing. Their conversion process is admired by the industry, in both its quickness and its completeness. In general, a bank can close its doors Friday evening, switch over to Banc One systems and operating procedures, and reopen on Monday morning with a completely different appearance and operating practices.

Figure 12.1 illustrates the state holding companies' return on average assets the year prior to their affiliation to Banc One and after their conversion was completed. Banc One virtually doubled the return on average assets of the banks it acquired in this period. At its 1997 size of $100 billion in assets, roughly $1 billion per year of returns on average assets could be attributed to successful replication of Banc One practices.

The benefits that Banc One derives from replication are not, however, limited to a once-and-for-all improvement in new affiliates. Rather, the common systems implemented in all Banc One banks provide the foundation for continuing comparison, knowledge sharing, and performance incentives. Thus, the whole corporate performance standard is lifted because of the replication-induced comparability of the outlets.

The informal process used to convert early affiliates became progressively formalized. Because even brief malfunctions of converted affiliates were prohibitive, achieving flawless implementa-

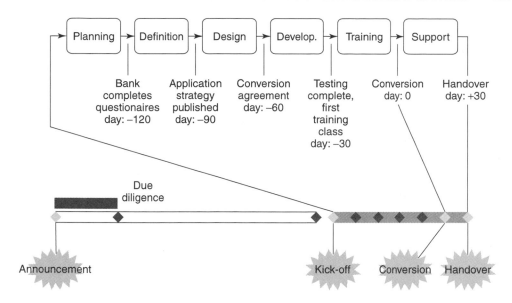

Figure 12.2 Summary of the six steps in Banc One's conversion process.

tion of conversions was of utmost importance to Banc One. Indeed, as converted banks grew larger, corporate efforts to make conversions work smoothly took precedence over efforts to develop new products (see Uyterhoeven 1994, p. 17).

Banc One's conversion process has six phases spanning approximately 200 days: (1) planning the project scope and resources; (2) definition, where the converting bank's and Banc One's current and desired environments are defined; (3) design, where the converting bank's postconversion environment is designed; (4) development, where the computer programs and the bank's new work environment are developed; (5) training, where the bank is prepared for the postconversion environment; and (6) support, when the bank begins to operate in its new environment. Each phase begins and ends with an event; however, different application areas may be in different phases at the same time. Figure 12.2 summarizes the process. At Banc One, responsibility for replication resides in a corporate unit created for the purpose, the Banc One Systems Corporation (BOSC). Interaction between BOSC and the new affiliate is intense at the beginning and end of the process, when information on the existing state of the affiliate is gathered and the conversion team assembled, and later in the training and support phases surrounding the conversion date. Design and development, by contrast, are largely processes internal to BOSC.

Significant and measurable events during the process are called deliverables. The timing of their delivery is relative to the conversion weekend or, more precisely, to "day 0"—the first day of the affiliate's operation with Banc One systems. Specific deliverables mark the termination of one phase and the beginning of another. Once the conversion date is chosen, the calendar for that specific conversion project is automatically set. For this reason, conversions are taken-forgranted aspects of Banc One's organizational reality and considered largely automatic from the top management perspective.

Indeed, the hallmark of a good conversion is that, for everybody but those directly involved in the conversion, the transition from the affiliate's existing systems to Banc One systems is a nonevent. Banc One's corporate management essentially assumes that a conversion will be completed successfully, and thus their awareness of the conversion process rarely encompasses more than issues related to setting the conversion date. They will devote time and effort to the conversion process only when delays in the completion of a key deliverable seriously disrupt the conversion process or when cost overruns are so significant as to impair Banc One's ability to conduct other planned conversions on the same budgetary year. This has happened; not all conversions are noneventful.

This noneventful nature of a good conversion is to a large extent also true for the existing customers of the affiliate, even though they are directly affected by the conversion because the product offerings change and because the reports issued by the affiliate may change. In a successful conversion, the affiliate's customers are given advance notice of these changes. This transforms them into little more than small and predictable inconveniences. Thus, in a successful conversion the bank should not lose customers because of the conversion.[6]

At Banc One, replication efforts concentrate on processes, and efforts to replicate process knowledge are explicit and central. In some cases but not all, these processes had a direct impact on the customer's experience. Banc One converts affiliates to its "common systems," the set of systems that are standard to the corporation at any given time. Although the exact composition of common systems varies as new applications are developed and old ones discarded, three groups of applications are usually covered: strategic banking systems (SBS), branch automation systems (BA), and credit (overdraft line of credit) and deposit (checking, savings, certificate of deposit) applications. Banc One offers over 75 different credit and deposit products, each supported by its own dedicated application. The BA systems have two separate subsystems: teller automation and platform automation. Within a single workstation, teller automation provides the tellers with all the information and transaction capabilities they need to identify customers and to review account relationships, transactions, activity, and balances. Platform automation supports sales and service of banking products by allowing service representatives to open accounts on line and by generating automatically the necessary forms. Information common to numerous accounts is entered only once and transferred by the system to the respective application systems. The SBS, developed primarily to expedite the introduction of new products and to give banks a total and accurate picture of the customers' relationships, acts as an integrating application by providing the capability to process customer information and deposit and credit accounts all in one system.

To operate with Banc One systems, the branches and the back office of a bank need suitable operating procedures. To address this need, BOSC offers affiliates a set of generic operating procedures, in the form of guidelines or flowcharts, that the new affiliate can customize for its own use by filling in the blanks and expanding some details. For example, step-by-step procedures instruct tellers how to handle commercial loans, utilities, installment loans, money orders, or food stamps. Similarly, they provide instructions that platform operators could follow to open a new savings account or sell loans, stocks, or treasury notes. These codified procedures support and complement the detailed training provided to the affiliate's personnel.

A Banc One affiliate that undergoes conversion essentially unlearns its own identity to become a member of the Banc One family. Converting data processing systems means that a new affiliate abandons one tool to do business and unlearns the accompanying operating procedures in order to learn new ones that suit the new set of tools. By adopting Banc One's systems and operating procedures, a new affiliate adopts the same set of tools that all other members of the Banc One family are using to conduct their business, and thus its tools can be supported by BOSC and its results directly compared with those of other units. Subsequently, responsibility for keeping the systems operational and current falls to BOSC.

Converting a new affiliate means installing new applications[7] in the affiliate's computer system and converting its existing data files on customers to a format that is compatible with the new applications. The new affiliate's personnel are trained and then supported until they can comfortably operate the new systems on their own. After a conversion, a new affiliate will have changed its standard operating procedures and supporting assets and systems in irreversible ways—and this provides strong protection against "backsliding" to old routines. The precise nature of the conversion is tailored to the affiliate's new operating environment, not its existing identity, and its old practices are effectively discarded. Thus, the organizational change at the local level is much more fundamental than in a typical example from the diffusion of innovations literature.

During a replication, Banc One selects a "sister" bank to provide a realistic scenario for the postconversion operating environment of a new affiliate. The new affiliate can visit the sister bank to see how it operates and how it is structured. This helps the new affiliate to make conversion-related decisions with more confidence. This also reduces the likelihood that the converted bank will repeat avoidable errors. Sister banks can help train a big new affiliate and may even temporarily lend specialists to new affiliates to help them solve transition problems. To select a sister bank, Banc One looks for a bank that has converted recently to a similar set of products and systems, and that operates in a similar market context.

Banc One has also started to develop a different sort of template in the form of a "model" bank, which consists of a functioning laboratory model of a retail bank's front office and back office, where the latest corporate standards, operating procedures, and work flows are implemented. Every new system that is made part of Banc One's common systems is also made part of the model bank. The role of the model bank is to complement the sister bank approach to support conversions before, during, and after they occur. It provides a forum where pilot trials and experiments can be conducted without disrupting the functioning of an actual bank.

In short, Banc One provides an example of intentional replication, where replication activities have been routinized. Replications at Banc One are of broad scope. High-level routines that substantially affect the capabilities and identity of the acquired bank are the object of replication.

Theoretical Considerations in the Replication of Routines

So far we have refined the notion of replication of routines by specifying some of its theoretical dimensions and outlining differences with neighboring concepts. We have then illustrated our theoretical discussion with two in-depth examples. We now raise broader theoretical considerations that we believe must also be part of a discussion of replication of routines as a mechanism of knowledge utilization in productive settings.

Relevance of the Information Economics Paradigm

Our theoretical approach to replication is grounded in the economics of information. Fundamental to the modern literature on this subject is the recognition that information has properties that distinguish it from typical economic commodities and consequently requires a distinctive theoretical analysis (Arrow 1962, Stewart 1997, Shapiro and Varian 1999). Although a particular item of information may be very costly to discover or create, the costs of additional use of it once it is in hand are typically low. An idealization that is often close to the truth—and more often as information technology advances—is that information is costly to produce but (relatively) costless to reproduce, store, and transfer through space. Given this idealization, it is clear that the second receipt of given information by a specific recipient is essentially of no consequence, since the recipient can costlessly derive as much use as desired from the first re-

ceipt—an economic attribute that contrasts sharply with the situation that obtains for the second carload of wheat or the second acre of land.

A familiar point in the strategy literature is the difficulty of appropriating rents from a fully codified innovation, unless the innovation is well protected by intellectual property rights or can be exploited secretly. The force of this point arises precisely from the fact that the secret only has to get out once to undermine the innovator's claim on the rent stream. Even within the context of effective intellectual property rights protection, the economics of costly original creation and cheap reproduction is a dominant strategic theme in such areas as pharmaceuticals, movies and videos, software, and publishing. The relationship between the costs of original creation and the magnitude of demand for the product (as modified by efforts to increase it) is the key to profitability.

However, replication exemplifies a class of nonstandard examples of these information economics ideas. In standard examples, there is typically little occasion to distinguish among three separable aspects of the notion that information is cheap to reproduce: (1) the "nonrivalrous" character of information, that is, the fact that reproduction does not diminish the information content of the source; (2) the absence of ambiguity about the information content of the "original" that is reproduced; and (3) relatively low costs of the reproduction process. In the printing of an issue of a newspaper, for example, the discovery, development, and organization of the information that constitutes the content of the newspaper is a cost that has to be incurred only once for the issue, independent of the copies subsequently printed. Once rendered in a form capable of generating a single copy of the newspaper, that content unambiguously expresses an "original" in symbolic form, and it is a fact of technology and economics that the per copy costs of reproduction are extremely low relative to the cost of creation of the original. By contrast, replication—and many other situations—illustrates that aspect 1 need not be accompanied by aspects 2 and 3.

The teaching of a tacit skill through apprenticeship or coaching provides a basic illustration of these "nonstandard" situations. Certainly the teacher's command of the skill is typically not diminished by the effort to convey it to the student; it may well be enhanced. Thus, aspect 1 prevails. On the other hand, the fact that the content is a tacit skill means precisely that the content of the original cannot be adequately and usefully rendered in symbolic form, and with that comes an inevitable ambiguity about what the content amounts to and whether the student's command matches the teacher's. For example, the degree of transferability of the skill to novel contexts is likely affected by the way it is taught, but not in straightforward and easily characterized ways. Finally, imparting skills in this way requires at least the substantial time investments of teacher and student and perhaps also the services of some valuable apparatus on which to practice—a tennis court, an aircraft, a surgery patient. Thus, while the information content of the teacher's skill is per se nonrivalrous in use, that fact implies neither that it can be delineated precisely nor that it can be reproduced cheaply.

Replication presents these same issues and attributes, but on a large scale. While standard information economics logic may apply, for example, to the printing of menus and manuals, or to outlet décor, there are typically also requirements for training in tacit skills, including particularly the outlet manager's tacit appreciation of the coherence of the total process—the sense of how the whole thing fits together. The problem of the ambiguity of the original presents itself with particular force, because replication efforts quite typically begin with an observed business success at one or a few local outlets. The aspiring replicator entertains the cheerful hypothesis that the success is attributable to nonrivalrous business information that can be successfully replicated at other locations and confer benefit in excess of costs—but what it is that is to be replicated, and how, is unknown at the start. This logic, clearly illustrated in the examples of Banc One and Rank Xerox, is of central relevance to a broad range of business situations.

The application of the information economics paradigm to replication thus presents a variety of issues; some of them illustrate the kinship to the standard examples and hence seem familiar in that perspective, while others are clearly deviant. Beginning with the first category, we note that the various outlets of a business systems replicator resemble each other closely in appearance. They look like "copies." Economic sense suggests that the likely explanation for the existence of all these copies is that there are gains to be had by making them; from this it is easy to infer the substantial economic value of the original creation that lies behind them. This interpretation is underscored by managerial words and actions that affirm the value of making high-

fidelity copies, such as those observed in our two examples.

Appearance, however, is not the relevant test. In the language above, resemblance in appearance might only be indicative of "faux leveraging." Consider the classic case of McDonald's. Creating a large chain of outlets with strong superficial resemblance to McDonald's stands in matters of décor, menus, and so forth would be expensive, but it is not difficult from a knowledge viewpoint. Such resemblance at a superficial level is easily produced. Producing strong resemblance among a number of different outlets in terms of internal processes and customer experience is another matter, especially when it comes to details like the flavor of the french fries. Each outlet is a functioning organization in its own right, though perhaps a small one, and the task of creating such an organization is far more complex than the printing of another copy of a newspaper, producing another 100 doses of some drug, or putting up golden arches. It requires not only that the requisite plant and equipment be put in place, but also that a work force be recruited and that the relevant skills and routines be imparted to that work force, one way or another. Each local outlet has a manager with a distinct personality, and that fact alone is enough to suggest that the organizational cultures of different outlets cannot be precisely the same. Differences in culture, stemming from this source and others, can in turn affect the details of organizational routines, perhaps to the point where there are readily observable differences in the outcomes realized by customers.

Viewing the start-up of an outlet in the perspective of organizational learning and organizational knowledge suggests additional considerations illustrating the nonstandard character of the information economics analysis of replication. The term "information" is often used in a way that implicitly assumes the existence of a symbolic medium by which information is conveyed, and of an infrastructure for encoding, decoding, and (most important) interpreting it. Further, there is assumed to be no binding constraint on the capacity of this infrastructure. In fact, communication in organizations typically involves specialized language (or "codes") understood only by the participants in the organization at a given time (Arrow 1974, Nelson and Winter 1982).

Thus, leveraging knowledge by replication of routines necessarily involves an investment in communication infrastructure, at least in the form of training in the organization's specialized language. Adequate command of the language requires, however, substantial knowledge of organizational context: the link of information to action typically depends on the knowledge-based interpretive powers of individual human beings. Hence, the organizational use of symbolic information depends on the stocks of knowledge held by the participants; much of this is tacit and/or context dependent, and it reflects the accumulation of local experience. Under these circumstances, the creation of the requisite knowledge stocks at a new outlet can be accomplished only through a variety of costly processes that are substantially less straightforward than a standard notion of transmission of information would suggest. It often includes processes that both require support from a template site and involve a significant component of new organizational learning at the new outlet.

To adapt the information economics paradigm to the analysis of replication, we need conceptual apparatus that captures the standard and nonstandard features and the linkage between them. Without denying the complex, costly, and problematic character of a "copying" process that involves causal ambiguity, knowledge transfer, and learning, we can still affirm the basic validity of the idea that a successful business model or set of routines is at least potentially a valuable template: it may contain what we will call an "Arrow core"—an abstract, quasi-informational source of economic merit that can be replicated by embodiment in new resources at new locations and yield a surplus over the combined costs of the new resources and the replication process. Such a surplus represents successful leveraging of the idiosyncratic knowledge asset the firm possesses in the template.

The Arrow core is (by definition) informationlike in the important sense that it is nonrivalrous in use: it is not used up in the process of replication. Hence, the extent of the leveraging is not limited from the "supply side" by the scarcity of the Arrow core—a situation quite analogous to what happens in the standard examples of information economics logic, such as book publishing.

On the other hand, the template as an ongoing business entity *is* rivalrous in use; efficient allocation of its activity between direct production and contribution to replication is a consideration affecting the appropriate rate and method of replication. Similarly, the resources of the new outlet are rivalrous in use; for example, it would not suffice for only one teller in a new Banc One affiliate to be familiar with the new

systems. The structure of the situation parallels that of a teacher imparting knowledge to a group of students. It is fundamental that the knowledge in the teacher's head be nonrivalrous in use; the knowledge is still there after it has been imparted to the students (unlike the teacher's copy of the textbook). However, the teacher's time *is* rivalrous in use, and so is that of the students and the classroom and other support services. So the fact that there is nonrivalrous knowledge in the teacher does not make teaching students free. There is economic magic in the nonrivalrous character of information and knowledge, but it is not magic of unlimited power.

Obviously, the firm's ability to achieve these good outcomes would be enhanced by good information on the relevant considerations. Equally obviously, this sort of information is likely to be very scarce in the early stages of a replication strategy. This fact enhances the relative importance of the initial conceptualization of the replicable advantages; this "mental model" will be much more controlling of initial efforts to leverage a particular resource, for example, than actual but yet unknown circumstances. In this sense, it can learn replication by doing it.

As the replicator accumulates experience in transferring knowledge, it learns about the transfer process itself. It may make substantial investments in resources specialized to the replication activity, and establish organizational units that are dedicated to this activity, gradually accumulating the sorts of resources featured in the analysis of Dierickx and Cool (1989).

The higher order capabilities created in this way are likely to present a stronger barrier to imitation than the visible activities of local outlets, since access to the firm-level template can be more effectively restricted. It is one thing to contemplate imitating a Starbucks coffee bar, quite another to consider imitating a set of organizational capabilities that makes it possible to locate, design, build, furnish, and train personnel for new coffee bars at the Starbucks rate of about one store a day.

Sustainability

Attempts to leverage knowledge assets are obviously of greater strategic interest when the advantage so derived is sustainable, that is, cannot be easily eroded by imitation. Our analysis of the leveraging of knowledge assets through the conceptual lenses of the replication of routines suggests some of the keys for sustainability. First, the replicator has superior access to the template, a working example of the successful business model or set of routines. The significance of this point is enhanced to the extent that key features of the routines are not readily observed in a local outlet and to the extent that the routines involve tacit components that can only be acquired through "hands-on" training by a qualified trainer, and with equipment that is itself idiosyncratic and not accessible to an imitator.

Second, the replicator learns from experience and often makes specialized investments to facilitate replication. The challenge facing the imitator is not to copy a local outlet at whatever cost, but to acquire a replication capability that can compete in terms of cost, effectiveness, and speed with that of the challenged firm. These higher order capabilities are likely to be both less observable and, as the fruit of experience, intrinsically less imitable on the basis of mere observation than are the local outlet routines.

Third, apart from capabilities directly related to knowledge transfer, the replicator may have other firm-level advantages in replication capabilities, such as site selection and acquisition. When suitable sites for the type of business are scarce and differentiated, the combination of site selection capabilities and first-mover advantages provides a paradigmatic example for the point that a firm can profit from its superior information about its own intentions. The replicator that first introduces a particular business model can acquire good sites at prices reflecting their value in inferior uses; subsequent challengers are left to pick over inferior sites in what has become a better informed market—and then to compete with the established incumbent. A frontal challenge may actually be deterred in some locales—not every McDonald's has a Burger King nearby.

Fourth, the replicator may also develop further layers of protection by cultivating operating superiority in such areas as logistics, supplier relations, quality control, economies of scale in purchasing, and perhaps upstream integration in key inputs. While each of these advantages might be overcome, their individual and collective effect is to extend the period of time required for a challenger to break even.

While our analysis of sustainability refers implicitly to advantages derived from broad-scope replication, the analysis of sustainability of advantages derived through narrow-scope replication follows a similar logic. Each individual attempt at narrow-scope replication is likely to be less significant but also less observable. While each one of a series of individual attempts may be easier to imitate in isolation, a mosaic of narrow-scope replication efforts would be more difficult to decipher and thus imitate. The logic of specialized investments and the role of the center could apply to this situation as well.

Laboratories of Knowledge Utilization

Our analysis of replication identifies variables that could be manipulated to further our understanding of knowledge utilization. Specifically, our analysis points out two aspects of a routine: (1) the tangible aspect embodied in the working example or template and (2) the intangible aspect that we called the Arrow core. It also points to the importance of considering the size of such routines and the scope of their replication, whether the replication occurs in space versus over time, and the degree to which replication is a genuine effort to recreate the working of productive routines versus a more superficial concern with mere appearances of similarity.

We have suggested that replication provides a relatively transparent window on knowledge issues in general. Thus, in settings where replication is attempted with sufficient frequency, such variables can be manipulated systematically to isolate how they affect the gains from replication. For example, one deeply entrenched belief in international business posits that there are no global best practices. Rather, practices must be tailored in advance to the characteristics of different national contexts to be effective. This is a specific manifestation of the fundamentally important problem of transfer of learning: what is learned in one context may be useful in others— but which learning specifically, and which other contexts? Some organizations such as chain organizations pursue broad-scope replication as their strategy. Others pursue replication of internal processes of smaller scale. In dealing with those challenges, such firms are ideal settings for systematic study of thorny issues of knowledge management.

The attractiveness of replication settings as a laboratory arises, above all, from its pervasive "one-to-many" structure. At least over a short time frame, a given replicator is reasonably viewed as engaged in an effort to accomplish "the same thing" in different places. The same "treatment" is being applied in a variety of environments; measurable differences in environmental conditions therefore provide powerful probes to determine how (or whether) success is affected by those differences. Note that the concept of attempting "the same thing" can be applied flexibly in this sort of analysis; for example, when the replication process involves an element of routinized responsiveness to local conditions, there is still an underlying identity of treatment at the level of the application of the same routinized process. Changes in the policies of a given replicator over time, or contrasts in the contemporaneous policies of similarly positioned replicators, provide additional sources of analytically interesting variance. For example, by examining contrasts and similarities in the ways that Mail Boxes Etc. (MBE) master licensees approach the problem of building MBE networks in different countries, and relating these to their success, we hope to build a case that there are indeed global "best practices."

A secondary but nevertheless significant virtue of replication settings is that they abound in practices that, while quite sharply defined, are not particularly esoteric. The observer is therefore in a position not only to understand in general terms the content of the knowledge that is being transferred, but also to probe its details to the extent necessary. This means that the list of possible explanations for transfer difficulties need not include highly technical issues that may be beyond the observer's ability to assess.

Ernest Rutherford, 1908 Nobel Prize winner in chemistry, once said, "If you need statistics for your experiment you ought to have designed a better experiment." Alas, the field of knowledge management is not yet at a stage in which it could profitably apply statistics, much less the advanced stage at which it could dispense with them. It lacks the theoretical infrastructure to design experiments and the settings in which to conduct them. We believe that the replication of routines could provide a paradigm for the systematic study of the leveraging of knowledge assets. And companies that regularly attempt to copy their business process internally could be appropriate settings to conduct the needed experiments. We hope this chapter will inspire new experiments. We hope replication of routines will help realize the promise of gaining systematic knowledge about knowledge management.

Notes

We acknowledge useful comments from Arie Lewin, Bruce Kogut, Mark Bonchek, Hank Chesbrough, Ned Bowman, Chun Wei Choo, Hans Pennings, Connie Helfat, Mark Bonchek, Alice Rivlin, Mary Tripsas, Michael Porter, Jan Rivkin, two anonymous referees, and participants of the Conference on Risks, Managers and Options, held at Wharton to honor Ned Bowman. We acknowledge also Deepti Chauhan's research assistance. Research support was provided by the Reginald H. Jones Center Management, Policy, Strategy and Organization and the Emerging Technologies Program of the Huntsman Center for Global Competition and Innovation.

1. The role of template may be played by a "flagship" example that is not the original in a historical sense but now stands out as an appropriate model of the type.

2. See Garud and Nayar (1994) for a discussion of temporal replication in relation to the firm's ability to maintain its technological competence in a changing world.

3. The HBS Case *Corning Glass Works: The Z-Glass Project* presents an interesting example of a struggle to diagnose the cause of failure in a process that was previously working well. It is clear that an actual working example would be a better basis for diagnosis—and codification, the objective in the case—than a previously working example.

4. This section is based on Szulanski's fieldwork for his dissertation, *Appropriating Rents from Existing Knowledge—Intra-firm Transfer of Best Practice* (1995). For discussion of research methods and further detail on the Banc One example, see Szulanski, G. (2000). Appriopriability and the challenge of scope: Banc One routinizes replication. *The Nature and Dynamics of Organizational Capabilities*. G. Dosi, R. Nelson and S. G. Winter. Oxford, UK, Oxford University Press.: 69–98.

5. This section is based on Szulanski's fieldwork for his dissertation (Szulanski 1995), which also contains a discussion of research methods and further detail on the Banc One example.

6. A striking contrast with Banc One's smoothly routinized conversion process is provided by the Wells Fargo acquisition of First Interstate in April 1996. Wells targeted a seven-month process for converting First Interstate to Wells's computer system. As it turned out, the computer system did not have the capacity to handle the combined load, and the bank's entire computer system went down for two days in September. Repercussions included losses of market share in loans and deposits; in early 1997 Wells was losing accounts at a rate of 1.5% a month (Hansell 1997).

7. The term "application" means a software program closely associated with a particular financial product and necessary to deliver that product. Applications may be developed by Banc One or supplied by an outside vendor.

References

Argote, L. (1999) *Organizational Learning: Creating, Retaining, and Transferring Knowledge.* Boston: Kluwer.

Arrow, K.J. (1962) "Economic welfare and the allocation of resources for invention," in R. Nelson (ed.), *The rate and direction of inventive activity*, pp. 609–625. Princton, NJ: Princeton University Press.

Arrow, K.J. (1974) *The limits of organization.* New York, NY, Norton.

Attewell, P. (1992) "Technology Diffusion and Organizational Learning: The Case of Business Computing." *Organization Science* 3(1):1–19.

Banc One Corporation (1991) Annual report. Columbus, OH: Banc One.

Bradach, J.L. (1998) *Franchise Organizations.* Boston: Harvard Business School Press.

Clark, K.B. (1997) Corning Glass Works: The Z-Glass Project. Harvard Business School Case 681091.

Cool, K.O., Dierickx, I., et al. (1997) "Diffusion of innovations with organizations: electronic switching in the Bell System, 1971–1982." *Organization Science* 8:543–559.

Dierickx, I., and Cool, K. (1989) "Asset stock accumulation and sustainability of competitive advantage." *Management Science* 35(December):1054–1511.

Dixon, N.M. (2000) *Common Knowledge: How Companies Thrive by Sharing What They Know.* Boston: Harvard Business School Press.

Dosi, G., Nelson, R.R., et al., eds. (2000) *The Nature and Dynamics of Organizational Capabilities.* Oxford: Oxford University Press.

Downs, G.W., and Mohr, L.B. (1976) "Conceptual issues in the study of innovation." *Administrative Science Quarterly* 21:700–714.

Garud, R., and Nayar, P.R. (1994) "Transformative capacity: continual structuring by intertemporal technology transfer." *Strategic Management Journal* 15(5):365–385.

Garvin, D.A. and Oliver, R.W. (2000) *Learning in Action.* Hinsdale, IL: Audio-Tech Business Book Summaries.

Hansell, S. (1997) "Banking with a heavy hand; Wells Fargo risks becoming a victim of its own power." *New York Times*, July 26, sec. 1, p. 33.

Hansen, M. (1999) "The search-transfer problem: the role of weak ties in sharing knowledge across organization subunits." *Administrative Science Quarterly* 44:82–111.

Hayes, R.H., Pisano, G.P., et al. (1996) *Strategic Operations: Competing through Capabilities.* New York: Free Press.

Kogut, B. and Zander, U. (1992) "Knowledge of the firm, combinative capabilities and the replication of technology." *Organization Science* 3(3):383–397.

Leonard-Barton, D. (1988) "Implementation as mutual adaptation of technology and organization." *Research Policy* 17 (5 October):251–267.

Lippman, S. and Rumelt, R. (1982) "Uncertain imitability: an analysis of interfirm differences in efficiency under competition." *Bell Journal of Economics* 13:418–438.

Love, J.F. (1995) *McDonald's: Behind the Arches.* New York: Bantam.

Nelson, R. and Winter, S. (1982) *An Evolutionary Theory of Economic Change.* Cambridge: Belknap Press.

Nonaka, I. (1994) "A dynamic theory of organizational knowledge creation." *Organization Science* 5(1):14–37.

O'Dell, C.S., Grayson, C.J., et al. (1998) *If Only We Knew What We Know: The Transfer of Internal Knowledge and Best Practice.* New York: Free Press.

Pfeffer, J. and Sutton, R.I. (2000) *The Knowing–Doing Gap: How Smart Companies Turn Knowledge into Action.* Boston: Harvard Business School Press.

Polanyi, M. (1966) *Personal Knowledge: Towards a Post-critical Philosophy.* Chicago: University of Chicago Press.

Putnam, L., Phillips, N., et al. (1996) "Metaphors of communication and organization," in S. Clegg, C. Hardy, and W. Nord, (eds.), *Handbook of Organizational Studies*, pp. 375–408. London: Sage.

Rogers, E. (1995) *The Diffusion of Innovations*, 4th ed. New York: Free Press.

Rogers, E.M. (1994) *A History of Communication Study: A Biographical Approach.* New York: Free Press.

Rosenberg, N. (1982) *Inside the Black Box: Technology and Economics.* Cambridge: Cambridge University Press.

Ruggles, R. (1998) "The state of the notion: knowledge management in practice." *California Management Review* 40(3):80–89.

Shannon, C.E. and Weaver, W. (1949) *The Mathematical Theory of Communication.* Chicago: University of Illinois Press.

Shapiro, C. and Varian, H.R. (1999) *Information Rules: A Strategic Guide to the Network Economy.* Boston: Harvard Business School Press.

Stewart, T.A. (1997) *Intellectual Capital: The New Wealth of Organizations.* New York: Currency.

Szulanski, G. (1994) *Intra-firm Transfer of Best Practices Project: Executive Summary.* Houston, TX: INSEAD and International Benchmarking Clearinghouse.

Szulanski, G. (1995) *Appropriating Rents from Existing Knowledge: Intrafirm Transfer of Best*

Practice Management. Fontainebleu, INSEAD: 154. UMI Code 9600790.

Szulanski, G. (2000) "Appriopriability and the challenge of scope: Banc One routinizes replication," in G. Dosi, R. Nelson, and S.G. Winter (eds.), *The Nature and Dynamics of Organizational Capabilities*, pp. 69–98. Oxford: Oxford University Press.

Teece, D.J. (1976) *The Multinational Corporation and the Resource Cost of International Technology Transfer.* Cambridge, MA: Ballinger.

Uyterhoeven, H., and Hart, M. (1996) Banc One–1993. Harvard Business School Case 394043.

Winter, S.G. (1995) "Four Rs of profitability: rents, resources, routines and replication, in C.A. Montgomery (ed.), *Resource-based and Evolutionary Theories of the Firm: Towards a Synthesis*, pp. 147–178. Norwell, MA: Kluwer.

Winter, S.G. (2000) "The satisficing principle in capability learning." *Strategic Management Journal* 21:981–996.

Zander, U. and Kogut, B. (1995) "Knowledge and the speed of the transfer and imitation of organizational capabilities: an empirical test." *Organization Science* 6(1):76–92.

13

Modular Product and Process Architectures

Frameworks for Strategic Organizational Learning

Ron Sanchez

In recent years management theory and practice have begun to take note of the increasingly important role of product architectures in product market competition (Morris and Ferguson 1993, Sanchez 1995, Sanderson and Uzumeri 1997). As growing numbers of firms adopt architectural approaches to managing their products and processes, however, some managers and researchers have begun to understand that architectural approaches to creating new products and processes can offer a substantial benefit beyond new product strategies and improved market success. Architectures can also help organizations to identify and manage key knowledge assets and to discover their most strategically beneficial opportunities for acquiring new knowledge and capabilities. Among the architectures that a firm might adopt, *modular product and process architectures* offer an especially powerful framework both for managing current knowledge assets effectively and for guiding strategic organizational learning (Sanchez and Mahoney 1996). This chapter investigates the nature of modular product and process architectures and

their roles in supporting effective knowledge management and strategic organizational learning. Our discussion is organized in the following way.

A presumption often evident in much writing on knowledge management is that firms may lose competitive advantage by converting their tacit knowledge into articulated, explicit knowledge. I therefore first consider some fundamental arguments why organizations should try to make key forms of knowledge explicit and organizational rather than leaving such knowledge in tacit, personal form. This discussion provides the essential strategic justifications for using architectures to identify and articulate an organization's strategically important knowledge used in creating new products and processes.

I next define product and process architectures and identify the key forms of technical and market knowledge used in creating product and process architectures. I then consider the special characteristics of *modular* architectures and how processes for creating and using modular architectures help an organization to develop its technical and market knowledge and make those key forms of knowledge explicit within the organization.

I then explain how using modular architectures to make knowledge explicit can also help an organization to discover the knowledge deficits and "capability bottlenecks" that limit its ability to create and realize new products. Extending this architectural perspective on organizational learning, I identify four forms of strategic learning that an organization can undertake to overcome its current capability bottlenecks.

This chapter concludes by explaining the essential features of a new approach to managing product creation processes that uses modular architectures systematically to identify, leverage, and continuously improve an organization's technical and market knowledge. (Examples of modular architectures at work may be found in Sanchez [2001] and Sanchez [1999].)

Organizational Knowledge: Better Left Tacit, or Better Made Explicit?

It is often asserted by strategic management scholars writing on knowledge management that an organization's strategically important knowledge is best left in tacit, personal form. The basic argument in support of this approach to managing knowledge goes like this: if strategically important knowledge held by individuals in an organization is articulated and made explicit, that knowledge can readily diffuse outside the organization, be absorbed by competitors, and lose its ability to be a source of competitive advantage once all competitors possess and use the knowledge.

While seemingly plausible, observation of knowledge management practices in many firms suggests that this argument greatly overestimates the potential for knowledge that is articulated and made explicit in one organization to be absorbed and used by competing organizations. In addition, this argument ignores the significant risks and competitive disadvantages of leaving knowledge that is important to an organization in tacit, personal form (Sanchez 1997). As a preface to the discussion of the role of architectures in helping organizations to make important forms of knowledge explicit, I summarize below the arguments that support knowledge management strategies premised on making strategically important knowledge explicit within an organization.

First consider the inherent limitations and risks to an organization of leaving important knowledge in tacit form. When key knowledge—such as technical and market knowledge about an organization's products—is left in tacit form in the minds of individuals, the ability of the organization to use that knowledge advantageously is limited by the amount of time each individual can spend in personally applying his or her knowledge in the value-creation processes of the organization. Moreover, applying the personal knowledge of individuals in new projects or trying to transfer one employee's tacit knowledge to other employees generally requires moving key "knowledge workers" from one location to another—something that is generally costly and time consuming and may meet with resistance from those employees. More critically, an organization will lose knowledge that is left in tacit form when a person having such knowledge leaves the organization. In essence, leaving strategically important knowledge in tacit form exposes an organization to the risk that critical knowledge will simply "walk out the door" as employees retire, fall ill, change jobs, or—in the worst case scenarios—take positions in competing firms. Even if a person with important tacit knowledge remains in an organization, he or she may use the threat of withholding that knowledge to acquire organizational power and advance his or her personal interests at the expense of the organization as a whole (Salancik and Pfeffer 1977).

By contrast, articulating the tacit knowledge of individuals into explicit organizational knowledge makes it possible to disseminate knowledge rapidly and widely within the organization. As an intellectual asset, explicit knowledge is free of the limitations of time and space that constrain the use of physical assets (including human assets with tacit knowledge). Once articulated, explicit knowledge may be shared with many employees quickly and globally through information technology and communication systems. Compared to relying on moving individual "tacit knowledge carriers" around an organization, electronically disseminating explicit knowledge throughout an organization enables strategically important knowledge to be applied extensively throughout an organization and with maximum speed. Making key forms of knowledge explicit also helps all members of an organization to discuss, debate, test, and improve the organization's knowledge—something that cannot be done when knowledge remains in tacit form in the mind of an individual. Finally, articulating the tacit knowledge of individuals into the explicit knowledge of an organization can greatly mitigate the potential for individuals to use their personal tacit knowledge to acquire and use power for personal advantage within an organization.

In principle, explicit knowledge that diffuses beyond the boundaries of an organization and is absorbed and used by competitors could lose its value as a source of competitive advantage. In practice, however, there are a number of reasons why knowledge that has been made explicit within an organization would be unlikely to lose its strategic value in this way. First, because organizations often create their own contextual "corporate languages" for discussing key issues and strategically important factors (von Krogh et al. 1994), knowledge may be articulated in terms that are readily understood within an organization but not understood by people outside the organization. For example, I once worked for a trade association that had a set of 13 rules governing the interactions of employees with people outside the association. Twelve of the rules provided guidelines for dealing with specific kinds of situations, but the rule 13 literally said, "If none of the 12 prior rules seems to apply, do something intelligent." Over time, stories of how employees had successfully followed "rule 13" in various situations created a legacy of examples that gave specificity to the notion of "doing something intelligent" in similar situations. In this way, the phrase "rule 13" stood for a set of actions that were explicitly understood internally by members of the organization, but the phrase conveyed no meaning to people outside the organization.

Even when knowledge is articulated in the terms of a standard language that is not unique to a given organization, the full meaning of explicit statements of some form of knowledge may not be grasped by people with experience, education, and capabilities different from those of the people who articulated the knowledge. Chemical formulas, engineering drawings, design methodologies, and other articulated forms of knowledge used within a firm may not be understood by outsiders—even competitors—with different skill sets, knowledge bases, and work processes. Moreover, even when the meaning of an explicit statement of knowledge is understood by someone, it is not at all certain that this person will recognize the potential strategic value of that knowledge when applied in the most effective way in its best uses. Further, simply understanding something intellectually is not sufficient to enable effective application of the knowledge in practice (Heene 1993). Applying some explicit knowledge effectively may require a complex set of supporting skills and assets that even the direct competitors of an organization may lack. In effect, because the value of any form of knowledge derives from its use in a system of complementary skills and assets, a bit of explicit knowledge that may be of great strategic value in one organizational context may be of limited usefulness and value in another organizational context (Sanchez and Heene 1997). Finally, if appropriate steps are taken to control important forms of explicit knowledge within an organization—such as Intel's policy of providing employees access to explicit knowledge only on a "need-to-know" basis—the risk that explicit knowledge will diffuse to competitors in the first place can be greatly moderated.

Boisot (1995) has coined the term "paradox of value" to refer to the simultaneous benefits and risks that an organization may face when it makes its knowledge explicit. The analysis here suggests, however, that the risks of making knowledge explicit within an organization may be less threatening and more manageable than commonly imagined. The analysis further suggests that with proper management of an organization's explicit knowledge, the "paradox of value" may be transformed into something more like the biblical "miracle of the loaves," in which one person's knowledge, once made explicit, may be shared among and help to sustain thousands of people within an organization.

With these perspectives on the strategic limitations and risks of *not* making organizational knowledge explicit, as well as the strategic benefits that may be obtained when knowledge is made explicit within an organization, the next section considers ways in which well-defined product and process architectures can help organizations to identify and articulate key organizational knowledge used in creating new products and processes.

Product and Process Architectures in Knowledge Articulation

The term "architecture" refers to two fundamental properties of a product or process design. (1) The way in which a product design is decomposed into *functional components* and the way in which a process design is decomposed into

1. A decomposition of the overall functionalities of a product into specific functions and **functional components:**

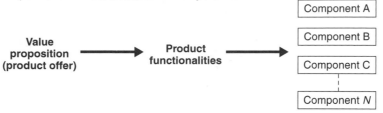

2. The full specification of the **component interfaces**—the inputs and outputs of each component—that define how components *interact* in the product as a system:

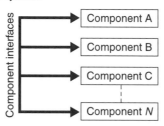

Figure 13.1 Two elements of a product architecture.

functional activities. For simplicity in this discussion, I will use the term "components" to refer to the functional elements of both product and process designs. (2) The ways in which the functional components interact in a product or process design. In the designs of products and processes, the interactions of functional components and activities are represented in the form of *interface specifications* that define how components or activities "interface" or interact with each other when they function together as a system[1] (Sanchez 1995, 1999, 2002). Figures 13.1 and 13.2 illustrate the decomposition of product and process designs into functional components and the use of interface specifications to define how components interact in those designs.

Carefully defining the architectures of its products and processes helps an organization to articulate strategically important knowledge in at least two ways. First, organizations create designs of products and processes in an effort to create "value propositions"—that is, product offers that create value for customers. By carefully analyzing how each kind of functional component in its product and process designs creates value for customers, an organization can develop deeper insights into ways that its technological capabilities can be applied to create specific customer benefits. Thus, analyzing how the overall benefits a firm seeks to bring to customers can

best be decomposed into specific product and process components can lead to much clearer, more precise, and more explicit understanding of how the firm's technology can be applied to create value for targeted customers.

Of course, a collection of components must function together effectively and reliably as a system to create benefits and value in the marketplace. Creating effective, reliable products and processes therefore requires knowledge about the *system behaviors* of the components an organization uses in its products and processes. The system behaviors of components are defined and controlled through the interface specifications an organization establishes for its products and processes. In organizations that are focused on creating products rather than on understanding and managing the component structure of their product designs, interface specifications are usually regarded as a technical detail to be worked out during product development. In some organizations, the interface specifications for their various product designs may not even be clearly documented at the end of a development process. An organization that adopts an architectural approach to managing product creation, however, will soon understand that the interface specifications it develops for the components it uses constitute a "balance sheet" of the organization's explicit knowledge about the system behaviors

1. A decomposition of the overall functionalities of a process into specific functions and **functional activities:**

2. The full specification of the **process activity interfaces**—the inputs and outputs of each activity—that define how various process activities *interact* in the process as a system:

Figure 13.2 Two elements of a process architecture.

of those components when used in the organization's products and processes. Interface specifications therefore become a primary vehicle for articulating and making explicit the organization's collective technical knowledge about the system behaviors of the components it uses in its products and processes.

Modular Product and Process Architectures in Learning and Knowledge Articulation

Modular architectures are a special kind of architecture in which the interfaces between components have been specified to allow the *substitution of a range of component variations* into an architecture and thereby enable the ready configuration of a range of product variations based on different combinations of components (Langlois and Robertson 1992, Garud and Kumaraswamy 1993, Sanchez 1995). The possibility of "mixing and matching" a range of "plug-and-play" compatible components within a single modular architecture suggests new kinds of product strategies and new possibilities for product creation processes (Sanderson and Uzumeri 1997). Rather than focusing product strategy and development processes on creating individual new products, organizations may create modular architectures that can serve as "platforms" for leveraging a broad range of product variations based on combinations of different component variations.

The leveraging of product variations based on mix-and-match combinations of plug-and-play

modular components makes possible new marketing strategies that support new forms of market learning (Sanchez 1999). Modular architectures may enable a firm to learn about consumer preferences in "real time" by testing consumer reactions to a range of modular product variations. Modular architectures may enable the leveraging of larger numbers of product variations to support more extensive market exploration and segmentation.

Modular architectures may also be designed to allow the substitution of higher performing components to support the rapid technological upgrading of products as higher performing components are developed in the future. In addition, modular architectures may be used to lower overall costs of maintaining high levels of product variety and change through careful use of common components in many product models and by reusing component designs in successive generations of products (Sanchez 1995, 1999, Sanchez and Sudharshan 1993).

Creating modular architectures to support these new kinds of product strategies can greatly stimulate and deepen an organization's technical learning about both component designs and interface specifications. When a firm follows a traditional product-focused development process, its primary concern during product development is to devise specific component designs that will enable each component to perform its function in the desired new product. In traditional product development, an organization's learning about components therefore tends to become narrowly focused on finding "local," context-dependent component design solutions that will work in a specific product design. Such learning tends to produce "sticky" contextual knowledge about components that often cannot readily be transferred to other product development projects (von Hippel 1994).

By contrast, when an organization pursues a modular development process in which the output is conceived as an architecture that will serve as a platform for leveraging product variations based on mix-and-match combinations of component variations, the organization will have an incentive to explore the full set of component designs that may be used in the modular architecture. Creating modular architectures rather than single new product designs therefore tends to result in broader organizational learning about feasible component designs. This expanded component-level learning helps to develop broader and more explicit organizational knowledge about the feasible range of variations in functions, features, performance levels, and costs that various kinds of components can bring to the organization's products.

Modular architectures also stimulate more extensive and explicit organizational learning about the behaviors and interactions of components in products and process designs. When a firm follows a conventional product development process, interface specifications tend to be viewed in a narrowly pragmatic way. The primary (and sometimes only) concern in product-focused development processes is to specify a set of component interfaces that will enable a given set of component designs to work together reliably in a specific new product design. In this mode, learning about the systemic behaviors of the different types of components an organization uses in its products tends to become "spotty" and contextually dependent on the specific component designs used in the product designs a firm has developed.

However, when a firm creates modular architectures intended to support the plug-and-play mixing and matching of a broad range of component variations, there are incentives—and indeed imperatives—to develop more fundamental knowledge about how different kinds of component variations will behave when combined with other kinds of component variations. Learning about component interfaces therefore becomes elevated from solving a problem of controlling the interactions of specific components used in a single product design to developing broader, more explicit knowledge about the behaviors and systemic interactions of many kinds of components and component variations that is needed to define robust interface specifications for a modular architecture.

Because creating modular architectures requires more fundamental, more explicit knowledge of feasible component designs and the systemic behaviors of components than is required when an organization simply develops single new product designs, creating modular architectures helps an organization to discover the current limits of its fundamental knowledge about components and their interactions. These technical knowledge deficiencies implicitly act as "capability bottlenecks" that limit an organization's ability to create and realize new products and to launch more aggressive, exploratory, and flexible product strategies. By using modular development processes to define more explicitly what an organization currently knows about the components it may use in its product architectures, the organization can begin to "see" more clearly strategically useful forms of technical knowledge that it currently lacks.

Creating modular architectures can therefore bring an organization two important knowledge management benefits. Modular architecture development processes help an organization to define more explicitly "what we know" as an organization about creating new component designs and controlling their interactions within modular architectures. With a clearer understanding of what it is currently capable of in this regard, an organization can leverage its current knowledge more quickly, widely, and effectively in creating flexible, robust product and process architectures. At the same time, by using modular architecture development processes to make explicit the limits of "what we know about component behaviors" an organization can more readily identify specific opportunities for developing new technical knowledge in component design and interface specification that can overcome the organization's current capability bottlenecks and bring definable strategic benefits to the organization.

Four Forms of Strategic, Systematic Learning in Creating Modular Architectures

An architectural perspective on the knowledge used in creating new products and processes suggests that there are four forms of strategic learning that an organization can undertake in overcoming its current capability bottlenecks. As outlined in figure 13.3, organizational learning in an architectural framework may consist of

	Incremental	Radical
Component-Level Learning	Development of component variations based on familiar technologies	Development of new kinds of components based on new technologies
Architectural-Level Learning	Improvement of interface specifications for controlling current components	Development of new interface specifications for controlling new kinds of components

Figure 13.3 Four forms of learning in an architectural framework.

component-level learning and architectural-level learning. Component-level learning may take the form of either "incremental" learning about current kinds of components or more "radical" learning about new kinds of components. In general, incremental component-level learning occurs when an organization develops variations on existing component designs based on familiar technologies, while radical component-level learning occurs when developing new designs for new kinds of components that use new technologies to bring new kinds of functionalities to a product.

Similarly, incremental architectural-level learning involves the development of better interface specifications that improve and extend the ability of an organization to control the system behaviors of the kinds of components it currently uses in its products. Radical architectural-level learning occurs when an organization develops interface specifications that enable a new kind of component (usually based on new technology and/or providing new functionality) to be used reliably within a product architecture.

These four forms of technical learning may be managed strategically in a new kind of development process that systematically uses modular architectures as a framework for managing organizational learning, as summarized in figure 13.4. In this modular approach to strategically managing technical learning, the organizational processes for undertaking each form of component and architectural learning are carefully separated and coordinated (Sanchez and Mahoney 1996, Sanchez and Collins 2001). As illustrated in the lower "learning loop" of figure 13.4, incremental learning about components takes place during the leveraging of a current modular product architecture. As a firm uses the flexibility of its current modular architecture to explore cus-

tomer reactions to different combinations of component-based functions, features, and performance levels offered at different price points, a firm may improve its knowledge of the component-based benefits consumers most desire from the firm's product and of the price elasticity of consumer demand for those benefits. This market knowledge may then drive incremental component-level learning through developing more component variations to serve the strongest, most profitable consumer preferences for component-based benefits.

In the top learning loop of figure 13.4, the long-term strategic planning processes of an organization integrate technology road mapping and market trend forecasting to define future generations of modular architectures that would try to take greatest advantage of future technological possibilities to serve future market opportunities. Defining future generations of modular architectures enables a firm to identify new kinds of components that could be based on new technologies expected to be available in the future and that would provide new kinds of functions and benefits to customers. The organization's long-term strategic learning can then be focused on radical learning about how to design the expected new kinds of components and how to specify interfaces that will control the system behavior of the new kinds of components when used with other components.

Unlike traditional research and development that produces only "proof of concept" and then relies on product development processes to create reliable designs for new components, these two forms of radical learning lead to a new form of organizational knowledge that may best be called *proof of component*—that is, the ability to specify and control the system behavior of a new kind of component. New kinds of components—once their basic designs are established and system behaviors understood—may then be placed in an organization's "design library" of proven, explicitly understood component designs that can be used in developing the next generations of product architectures.[2]

The middle section in figure 13.4 represents the incremental architectural learning involved in improving a firm's interface specifications for components to be used in an organization's next-generation product architecture and the incremental component learning involved in creating new component variations (but not new kinds of components) to be used in a next-generation product architecture. This incremental learning benefits from feedback about the reliability and

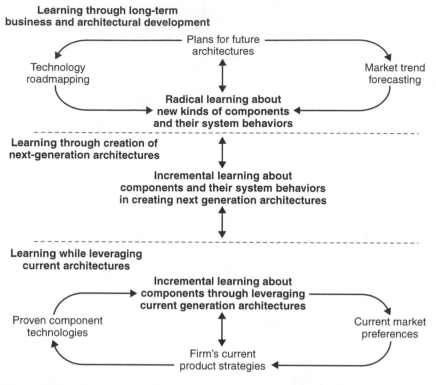

Figure 13.4 Architectures as frameworks for systematic, strategic learning.

performance of its current architecture gained through experiences in leveraging product variations from its current product architecture. Incremental learning in next-generation architecture development also benefits from "feedforward" from its radical learning processes that have developed new component designs with proven system behaviors.

This new modular approach to managing product creation rests on the principle of making explicit the knowledge within an organization about the kinds of components that can produce benefits for customers, the kinds of component designs that can perform reliably in given kinds of product and process architectures, and the interface specifications needed to assure reliable performance and interactions of each component in a system of components.

Conclusion

This discussion has suggested several ways in which adopting a modular architectural approach to product development can stimulate organiza-

tional learning about markets and technologies. The need to understand and control components' system behaviors within a modular architecture also helps to make the collective technical knowledge of an organization more explicit and, by being explicit, more manageable strategically. Once made explicit, the current technical knowledge of an organization can be leveraged more effectively, quickly, and widely through the configuration of an expanded range of product variations based on mixed-and-matched, plug-and-play modular component variations. Once the current technical knowledge of an organization is made explicit, the limits of that knowledge and its associated capability bottlenecks can be recognized more clearly. Organizational learning may then be strategically focused on developing new knowledge that will remove those capability bottlenecks. In some firms, these strategic learning processes are now being organized in a new model of product creation that uses the creation of modular architectures as a framework for driving both incremental and radical learning about components and their interactions (Sanchez and Collins 2001).

Notes

1. Interface specifications define and manage the following seven kinds of interactions between product components: (1) how components physically *attach* to each other; (2) what *space* within the overall arrangement of components in a product a given component will occupy; (3) what is *transferred* into and out of a component as the component performs its primary function in the product as a system (e.g., transformation of electrical power, of chemical energy into mechanical energy, of a bit stream from one format to another, etc.); (4) how one component *signals* to a second component what state it is in, and how the second component signals to the first component whether to stay in that state or change to another state—this interface generally includes the critical *timing* coordination among components in a product with internal dynamics; (5) how each component interacts with the *user* of the product; (6) how each component must interact with the intended *ambient environment*—that is, the intended environmental context of use of the product (intended range of temperature, humidity, shock, vibration, and so forth; and (7) how each component will interact with the *internal environment* of the product in unintended ways—that is, how the functioning of each component may generate heat, emit electromagnetic fields, or produce effects that can affect the functioning of other components in undesirable ways. For a more detailed discussion of component interfaces, see Sanchez (2002).

2. Radical component and architectural learning is a form of technology development that some firms are now defining as an intermediate process between traditional research and development and traditional product development. Achieving "proof of component" before using components in product development essentially removes most technological uncertainty from product development per se (or more precisely, from next-generation architecture development), and as a result can greatly accelerate product development and make its outcomes much more predictable (Sanchez and Collins 2001, Sanchez 2002).

References

Boisot, M.H. (1995) *Information Space*. London: Routledge.

Garud, R. and Kumaraswamy, A. (1993) "Changing competitive dynamics in network industries: an exploration of Sun Microsystems' open systems strategy." *Strategic Management Journal* 14(5): 351–369.

Heene, A. (1993) "Classifications of competence and their impact on defining, measuring, and developing 'core competence'." Paper presented at the second International Workshop on Competence-Based Competition, EIASM, Brussels, November.

von Hippel, E. (1994) "Sticky information and the locus of problem solving." *Management Science* 40(4):429–439.

von Krogh, G., Roos, J., and Slocum, K. (1994) "An essay on corporate epistemology." *Strategic Management Journal* 15:53–71.

Langlois, R.N. and Robertson, P.L. (1992) "Networks and innovation in a modular system: lessons from the microcomputer and stereo component industries." *Research Policy* 21(4):297–313.

Morris, C.R. and Ferguson, C.H. (1993) "How architecture wins technology wars." *Harvard Business Review* 71(2):86–96.

Salancik, G.R. and Pfeffer, J. (1977) "Who gets power—and how they hold on to it: a strategic-contingency model of power." *Organizational Dynamics* (Winter):3–21.

Sanchez, R. (1995) "Strategic flexibility in product competition." *Strategic Management Journal* 16(Summer):135–159.

Sanchez, R. (1997) "Managing articulated knowledge in competence-based competition," in R. Sanchez and A. Heene (eds.), *Strategic Learning and Knowledge Management*, pp. 163–187. Chichester: Wiley.

Sanchez, R. (1999) "Modular architectures in the marketing process." *Journal of Marketing* 63:92–111.

Sanchez, R. (2001) *Modularity, Strategic Flexibility, and Knowledge Management*. Oxford: Oxford University Press.

Sanchez, R. and Collins, R.P. (2001) "Competing—and leaving—in modular markets." *Long-Range Planning*. in press.

Sanchez, R. and Heene, A., eds. (1997) *Strategic Learning and Knowledge Management*. Chichester: Wiley.

Sanchez, R. and Mahoney, J.T. (1996) "Modularity, flexibility, and knowledge management in product and organization design." *Strategic Management Journal* 17(Winter):63–76.

Sanchez, R. and Sudharshan, D. (1993) "Real-time market research: Learning-by-doing in the development of new products." *Marketing Intelligence and Planning* 11(7):29–38.

Sanderson, S.W. and Uzumeri, M. (1997) *Managing Product Families*. Chicago: Irwin.

14

Technological and Organizational Designs for Realizing Economies of Substitution

Raghu Garud and Arun Kumaraswamy

The Schumpeterian era during which "gales of creative destruction" brought about revolutionary changes over long periods of time (Schumpeter 1942) is past. In recent times, we have entered a neo-Schumpeterian era where technological change appears to be ceaseless. To survive in this new era, firms have to innovate continually (Klein 1977). Continual innovation, however, imposes limits on a firm's ability to realize scale economies. Moreover, rapid change dampens the diffusion of new technologies as customers postpone purchases due to fear of obsolescence (Rosenberg 1982). Slower diffusion of technological changes creates problems for firms attempting to recoup investments made in technologies that change continually.

There is another facet to this new era that renders contemporary environments different from those prevalent during Schumpeter's time. Specifically, many of these technologies are "systemic" in nature (Winter 1987); that is, they are embodied in multicomponent products that connect to each other. The development and production of such technological systems require significant investments in several complementary technologies (Hakansson 1989, Powell and Brantley 1992, Quinn 1992, Teece 1987). It is difficult for any one firm to invest in all complementary technologies because, after a point, bottlenecks arise in the form of overextended scientists, engineers, and manufacturing personnel (Penrose 1959, Teece 1980). Such congestion imposes limits on the firm's ability to realize scope economies.

How may firms deal with these challenges? We propose that firms take advantage of a different source of economies—economies of substitution—instead of relying exclusively on economies of scale and scope. We use the term "substitution" to suggest that technological progress may be achieved by substituting certain components of a technological system while reusing others. The potential for such economies increases if technological systems are modularly upgradable. By designing modularly upgradable systems, firms can reduce product development time, leverage their past investments, and provide customers with continuity.

Additionally, we suggest that firms reorganize their internal and external relationships to

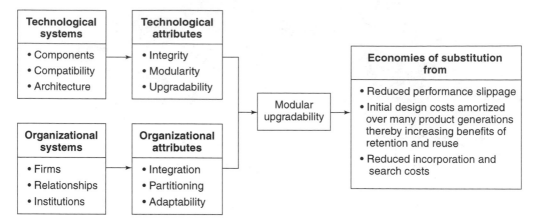

Figure 14.1 Organization of the chapter, based on our core thesis.

reduce the costs of component reuse, while enhancing associated benefits. The network mode of governance, with its emphasis on knowledge sharing, adaptability, and continual innovation, appears to be best suited for this task (Powell 1990). Indeed, networks form the basis for a variety of arrangements ranging from giant Japanese "keiretsus" to small Italian firms linked by cooperative associations (see Best 1990, Kenney and Florida 1993, Nelson and Wright 1992, Piore and Sabel 1984, Porter 1990, Quinn 1992). Increasingly, these network forms are challenging traditional "Fordist" organizations based on Taylor's scientific management principles.

Figure 14.1 summarizes our core thesis and depicts the organization of this chapter. First, we discuss how technological systems are built of components that interact with one another under an overall system architecture. We identify three system-level attributes: integrity, modularity, and upgradability. All three attributes must be considered while designing technological systems for economies of substitution. We substantiate why technological systems must be modularly upgradable to yield economies of substitution. Then, we explore organizational issues that arise in realizing these economies of substitution. We emphasize the similarity between the design of technological systems and organizational systems for realizing substitution economies. Just as technological systems are composed of components interacting with one another within an overall architecture, these organizational systems are composed of individual firms interacting with each other within an overall institutional framework. We explore how modularly upgradable organizational systems

may be created, and how modular upgradability gives rise to both cooperative and competitive dynamics. Finally, we discuss the implications of our thesis for firms operating in the neo-Schumpeterian era.

Technological Systems for Economies of Substitution

A technological system comprises a set of components that, together, provide utility to customers. System performance is dependent not only on the performance of individual components, but also on the extent to which they are compatible with one another (Garud 1987, Henderson and Clark 1990, Tushman and Rosenkopf 1992). Compatibility is a relative attribute that defines rules of fit and interaction between components across boundaries called interfaces. The overall set of rules that describes acceptable fit and interactions constitutes the system's architecture.

The degree of compatibility among components defines three important attributes of technological systems: integrity, modularity, and upgradability. *Integrity* represents "the consistency between a product's function and its structure: the parts fit smoothly, components match and work together, the layout maximizes available space" (Clark and Fujimoto 1990: 108). Although individual system components may have been designed to yield high performance, a lack of compatibility among them results in suboptimal system performance. In other words, incompatibility between components compromises the integrity of a technological system.

Firms may ensure system integrity by custom-designing components and assembling them through an iterative process of rework to obtain requisite fit and interaction, as in craft production (Cox 1986, Womack et al. 1990). Firms may also ensure system integrity by designing and producing components to standard dimensional and interface specifications. Conformance to standard specifications enables the production of identical (and therefore interchangeable) components in large numbers, as in mass production (Marshall 1961).

Production of components conforming to standard interface specifications also leads to modularity. *Modularity* allows components to be produced separately and used interchangeably in different configurations without compromising system integrity (Demsetz 1993, Flamm 1988, Garud and Kotha 1994).[1] The degree of modularity of a technological system varies, depending on whether interfaces are standardized within only a single firm or throughout an industry. In the former case, components may be used interchangeably only within a firm's own product lines. In the latter case, components manufactured by different firms may be mixed and matched. This ability to mix and match allows firms to offer a variety of system configurations and to economize on product development investments (Baldwin and Clark 1994, Pine 1993, Sanchez 1995). At the same time, it offers customers the flexibility to buy components from different firms and create technological systems that are most appropriate for their requirements (Matutes and Regibeau 1988).

In rapidly changing environments, a third system-level attribute—*upgradability*, or the ease with which system performance can be enhanced over time—also becomes important. If a system is not upgradable, performance improvements may involve its complete redesign. Such a process entails the destruction of existing knowledge and competence. Given the rapidity of technological change, the repetitive destruction and creation of knowledge and competencies for each new generation may increase firms' research and development (R&D) investments to levels that cannot be recouped within ensuing short product life cycles. At the same time, customers will be wary of adopting new technologies that become obsolete rapidly, thereby decreasing the rate at which these technologies diffuse (Rosenberg 1982).

To be upgradable, a technological system must possess degrees of freedom that enable improvements in existing capabilities and the addition of new capabilities.[2] To understand how degrees of freedom may be created, we have to appreciate the hierarchical organization of components within a technological system (Clark 1985, Hughes 1987, Simon 1962). Component choices at any given level of the hierarchy outline operational boundaries for lower order components. For instance, the performance capability of a computer is dependent on the speed of its microprocessor. Over time, technological advances in microprocessor design have led to significant increases in the speed of the entire computer. These innovations in microprocessor design represent a movement "up the system hierarchy" and, typically, represent revolutionary changes where system foundations are built afresh (Clark 1985). Movement up the system hierarchy makes it more difficult to maintain compatibility between product generations because core components are replaced.

Firms, however, may design higher order components with performance capabilities that are not fully exploited at early design stages. These unutilized degrees of freedom in higher order components can be exploited progressively through innovations in lower order components. Clark (1985) labels such innovations as a movement "down the system hierarchy." Specifically, movement down the hierarchy represents incremental change where core components are preserved even as innovations occur in lower order components. In this case, it is easier to maintain compatibility between product generations because innovations occur only in lower order components.

In sum, firms may impart upgradability to technological systems by designing unutilized degrees of freedom into higher order components. These unutilized degrees of freedom enable designers to enhance system performance by substituting only those lower order components whose potentials have been exhausted. However, the benefits of upgradability and associated retention of components must be weighed against the costs of component reuse. We now explore these benefits and costs in greater detail, and suggest how to design technological systems that yield economies of substitution.

Economies of Substitution

Economies of substitution exist when the cost of designing a higher performance system through the partial retention of existing components is lower than the cost of designing the system afresh (Garud and Kumaraswamy 1993). Component retention yields several benefits. The most obvious benefit is the reutilization of the existing base of knowledge associated with the retained components. Other benefits include savings in testing and production costs. Savings in testing costs arise when test programs developed for retained components are reused. This benefit is especially valuable in cases where test program development takes as much time as the actual design of the system itself. For instance, Texas Instruments (TI) cites such savings in testing costs as one of the main benefits that it expects to receive from its new PRISM methodology, which allows circuit modules to be combined in different configurations to create new chips (*Texas Instruments* 1992). Additionally, the reuse of circuit modules enables TI to standardize chip fabrication processes, thereby yielding significant savings in production costs. In general, savings in production costs accrue from the reutilization of capital equipment and production routines associated with reused components.

Yet, these benefits have to be balanced against performance slippage and several costs incurred in reusing components. *Performance slippage* may occur when designers try to incorporate newly developed components into a technological system. This is because newly developed components may not fit or interact well with existing components, thereby compromising system integrity.

Designers can minimize performance slippage by using gateway technologies, such as adapters and converters, that enable the coexistence of incompatible components within a technological system (David and Bunn 1990). Gateway technologies, however, imply higher costs because they involve the development and usage of additional components. Moreover, gateway technologies seldom restore system integrity completely. Therefore, they may not provide the best way for firms to realize economies of substitution.[3]

A better way for firms to realize economies of substitution is by designing modularity into technological systems. Modularity minimizes performance slippage arising from incompatibility between the newly designed and reused components. Additionally, modularity makes it easier for designers to integrate newly developed components into the existing system; that is, modularity reduces *incorporation costs* for both designers and customers. Incorporation costs in

a modular system are limited to eliminating incompatibilities that are not anticipated while designing standard interfaces.

Therefore, modularity and upgradability are both important system attributes for realizing economies of substitution. Modularity increases the ease with which system designers can substitute certain system components while retaining all others. Upgradability provides designers with the opportunity to work on an already-established technological platform, thereby preserving their core knowledge base (Wheelwright and Clark 1992). In this manner, modular upgradability simplifies the task of coping with very short life cycles.

Besides enabling the preservation of knowledge over successive generations, modular upgradability creates new knowledge that enhances, rather than destroys, existing knowledge. This competency-enhancing knowledge (Tushman and Anderson 1986) derives from experience as designers gain a deeper appreciation of (1) which aspects of the platform will lead to future improvements, (2) which aspects of the platform will lead to dead ends, and (3) how new lower order components fit in with the base platform.

Modular upgradability leads to economies of substitution in another way. Modular upgradability allows firms to listen to customer feedback and modify their systems accordingly by substituting some components while retaining the others. Rosenberg (1982) points out that such learning by using is essential for the evolution of complex multicomponent systems whose optimization only occurs through large-scale customer trials. Insofar as the system design incorporates modular upgradability, designers will find it easy and economical to carry out modifications. Wheelwright and Clark (1992) call this process "rapid prototyping."

Increasingly, firms competing in neo-Schumpeterian environments are designing modularly upgradable systems to enable component reuse. In computer hardware, for instance, Sun Microsystems had created the modularly upgradable Sparcstation10 family of computer workstations (see Garud and Kumaraswamy [1993] for more details). In computer software development, object-oriented programming (OOP), a technique that allows reuse of program modules and easy upgradability, has gained in popularity and usage by firms. By using OOP techniques, Brooklyn Union Gas Company created 20% more functionality (over the previous non-object-oriented system) with 40% fewer lines of code; Shearson Lehman, Inc., reduced development costs by 30% through reuse of objects (*Business Week* 1991); and the U.S. Marine Corps reduced prototype time from the normal six to eight weeks to just two weeks. In general, OOP users report two- to fivefold increases in programmer productivity (*Financial Executive* 1991).[4]

Firms in the automobile industry, too, have designed models that allow for the sharing and reuse of key components. For instance, Honda developed a single basic 1994 Accord model and customized it later for different markets. Honda held its total development costs down by reusing components from other models. All versions of the 1994 Accord had at least 50% common components (*Business Week* 1992). Additionally, Honda reduced retooling and procurement costs by (1) reusing components, (2) designing new components so that these could be manufactured using existing equipment in its Japanese and U.S. plants, and (3) delegating design of certain components entirely to its suppliers (*Wall Street Journal* 1993).

However, modularly upgradable technological designs alone are inadequate for firms to realize economies of substitution. This is because several costs are implicit in the design of modularly upgradable systems: initial design costs, testing costs, and search costs. *Initial design costs* refer to the additional costs that designers incur in creating components for reuse over and above those incurred in designing components for one-time use. These additional costs are incurred up-front to impart additional degrees of freedom to a system, such as standardized interfaces or the design of higher order components with unutilized capabilities. For instance, analysts of OOP estimate that initial design costs of reusable objects may be as high as 3–10 times the costs incurred in building an object for one-time use (Balda and Gustafson 1990, Kain 1994).

Baldwin and Clark (1994) highlight that *testing costs* constitute a high proportion of product innovation costs. They suggest that the ability to perform tests at the component level (rather than at the system level) is essential for reducing testing costs. Although testing at the component level and the reuse of testing programs reduce costs, overall testing costs increase cumulatively with the number of modular components to be tested. Additionally, as Baldwin and Clark point out, designers of different components must strike prior agreements on the interface specifications and the encompassing system architecture to develop testing programs. This increases initial design costs.

Finally, designers incur *search costs* to locate reusable components. Typically, search costs increase with the proliferation of modular, reusable components. For instance, in OOP, Banker et al. (1993) found that reuse percentage decreased with an increase in the number of reuse candidates. They cite the case of Carter Hawley Hale Information Services, where reuse dropped by more than 15% when the number of reusable objects in the firm's repository grew by four times. In these cases, even libraries that allowed searches by key words did not promote reuse.

To realize economies of substitution, then, initial design costs and testing costs need to be amortized over a number of reuses, and search costs need to be minimized. These demands raise issues concerning the design of appropriate organizational systems. For instance, consider a firm that does not consciously encourage component reuse. In such a firm, the extra costs associated with the creation of modularly upgradable components may not be amortized fully. Consequently, the firm will not realize economies of substitution. Or consider a firm that does not institute effective mechanisms to search for reusable components. In such a firm, high search costs may prevent reuse altogether, or even if reuse occurs, costs may outweigh benefits. Again, the firm will not realize economies of substitution.

Organizational Systems for Economies of Substitution

Technological systems consist of components that together provide utility to users. Similarly, firms that manufacture the components of a technological system together comprise an organizational system for that technology. Relationships between these firms are analogous to interactions between components of the technological system. The mosaic of rules, procedures, and norms that comprise the institutional environment of this organizational system parallels the architecture of a technological system.

A key challenge in realizing economies of substitution is the design of organizational systems that enhance component retention or reuse while reducing associated costs. We suggest that this challenge be met by designing organizational systems to be "modularly upgradable." A modularly upgradable organizational system allows constituent members to work independently and in unison, even as they evolve over time.[5]

Intrafirm Issues

Realization of economies of substitution requires knowledge sharing and the reuse of components. Traditional hierarchical and Strategic Business Unit (SBU) structures, however, inhibit realization of these economies. Specifically, these traditional structures result in "knowledge hoarding" by independently functioning units. To encourage "knowledge sharing," Prahalad and Hamel (1990) propose that firms organize themselves around core competencies. Garud and Nayyar (1994) recommend that firms enhance knowledge sharing and reuse by cataloguing, updating, and distributing lists of available "shelved projects" (see also Kogut and Zander 1992). Kotha (1995) reports how the National Bicycle Company rotates personnel between its plants, thereby creating a mechanism for the sharing of tacit knowledge (see also Nonaka 1994). Indeed, Hill et al. (1992) report that related-diversified firms that install mechanisms to promote cooperation and knowledge sharing between constituent units tend to perform well.

Cusumano (1991) illustrates how a knowledge-sharing organization might look in his description of Toshiba's software production facilities. Toshiba has instituted elaborate procedures to evaluate, catalogue, store, and disseminate reusable software throughout the company, thereby reducing search costs. Toshiba has also created special "committees," "departments," and "centers" to ensure that designers create reusable software and reduce incorporation costs by conforming to companywide standards. Additionally, committees help overcome the short-term concerns that may arise with knowledge sharing and reuse.

There are yet other challenges involved in designing reusable components, and in reusing components designed by others. As Mary Wells, erstwhile training program manager at Tektronix Inc., asserted: "There will always be tension between those pushing for a library and reuse, and those trying to get a job done. People focusing on reuse want to make (objects) as general as possible while the application developers want things as specific as possible" (*Datamation* 1989, p. 90). In a similar vein, Graham (1994) states: "We are used to rewarding analysts and programmers according to the amount of code they produce rather than the amount of other people's code they reuse. . . . Furthermore, project managers are paid to make projects come in on time and not to write code for the benefit of subsequent projects" (also see Banker et al. 1993, Cusumano 1991). Therefore, firms need to realign their incentives to encourage reuse.

Cusumano (1991) describes Toshiba's integrated set of incentives and controls associated with knowledge sharing and reuse. At the beginning of each project, managers at Toshiba agree to productivity targets that can be met only if a certain percentage of software specifications, designs, or code is reused. Design overview meetings held at the end of each phase in the development cycle monitor progress against reuse targets. Moreover, when building new software, management requires project members to register a certain number of components in databases for reuse in later projects. Personnel receive awards for registering particularly valuable or frequently reused modules, and their formal evaluations from superiors report on whether they have met their reuse targets. An overall committee, meanwhile, monitors reuse levels at Toshiba as well as deviations from targets at both the project and individual levels, and provides regular reports to managers.

Although reuse and knowledge sharing lead to economies of substitution, they have the potential to trap firms within the confines of old knowledge. To overcome this eventuality, Garud and Nayyar (1994) suggest that firms must continually create new knowledge through a combination of the old (see also Jelinek and Schoonhoven 1990). Moreover, Hamel and Prahalad (1994) note that firms must upgrade their core competencies over time, partially by continually retraining employees. Lei et al. (1995) provide a more complete thesis on how firms can update core competencies through a meta-learning process that consists of information transfer, continuous improvement based on experimentation, and the development of firm-specific skills based on dynamic routines.

These arguments, and the Toshiba example in particular, establish a firm's capabilities to reorganize its structure, routines, and incentives to encourage reuse and realize economies of substitution. However, there are limits to the number of activities any one firm can perform within the purview of its administrative structure. To appreciate these limits, we have to compare the costs of internalizing activities within the firm with the costs of sharing some of these activities with other firms.

Internalizing activities within a firm involves two costs: managerial and production costs. *Managerial costs* increase with the number of components produced in-house (lateral integration) and with the number of stages required to produce a given component (vertical integration). First, as the extent of vertical and lateral integration increases, managerial costs of coordinating different activities increase disproportionately (Demsetz 1993, Piore 1992). These coordination costs will increase further if congestion occurs in the deployment of scarce resources among competing activities (Teece 1980). Second, cognitive complexity faced by managers also increases. This is particularly true in neo-Schumpeterian environments where each change brings with it disproportionate cognitive demands. As cognitive complexity increases, at some point, it becomes more costly for a firm to undertake any more activities in-house than it is to delegate them to other firms.

Additionally, in-house *production costs* will increase if the demand experienced by a firm is low or uncertain. In such circumstances, the firm cannot justify production facilities that operate at a minimum efficient scale for each component.[6] However, a specialized firm that consolidates demand for a particular component can justify building a minimum efficient scale plant, thereby realizing scale economies.[7]

Thus, in neo-Schumpeterian environments, increases in managerial and production costs are key forces for the disaggregation of activities. To understand fully why disaggregation is occurring, however, we must trade off the benefits of depending upon external component manufacturers with increases in transactions costs (Langlois and Robertson 1992). Transactions costs arise from asset specificity under uncertainty, and from the potential for opportunistic behavior under conditions of information asymmetry and bounded rationality (Williamson 1985). However, the advent of information technologies (such as electronic data interchange) allows firms to coordinate activities more closely (Manzi 1994), thereby reducing information asymmetry and opportunism. Furthermore, a steady movement in many systemic industries toward industrywide standards has reduced asset specificity and small numbers bargaining. Consequently, transactions costs are progressively decreasing (Malone et al. 1987, Quinn 1992). With decreases in transactions costs and increases in managerial and production costs, firms are focusing on a set of conceptually related activities and outsourcing the rest (Demsetz 1993, Langlois 1992, Piore 1992, Piore and Sabel 1984, Richardson 1972).[8]

Interfirm Issues

As firms manufacture only some components and outsource others, they implicitly "partition" the technological system.[9] Partitioning a technological system can create an organizational system whose organizational modules (firms) can engage and disengage in response to market and technological changes (also see Miles and Snow 1986, Sanchez and Mahoney 1994). However, to accomplish such "flexible specialization" (Piore and Sable 1984), it is important that these organizational modules coordinate among themselves to design and produce compatible components. Otherwise, performance slippage and the costs associated with integrating the various components into a technological system will become prohibitively high.

A key question is whether such integration should be left to markets, or whether some other governance mode is required. If we were dealing with a static technological system, perhaps markets could serve as a forum for integration. However, when technological systems are changing rapidly, the cost of creating and maintaining interface standards within a market mode of governance will be prohibitively high. Standardization requires much closer coordination among firms than markets can offer.

Coordination between vertically interdependent firms requires an approach to contracting that emphasizes long-term relationships based on trust and reputation (Macneil 1980, Powell 1990).[10] Analogous to the notion of unutilized degrees of freedom in technological systems, relationships between firms are defined broadly, allowing enough latitude for evolution over time. Once relationships are established, continual interactions (including the exchange of strategic information, personnel, and knowledge) among collaborating firms create an environment that engenders trust and mutual accommodation. That is, the relationships between firms become "upgradable." Indeed, as Morgan (1986) points out, the broadest agreement would be one in which only those eventualities that definitely must be avoided (noxiants) are specified.

The classical approach to contingent claims contracting reduces such upgradability. This is because contingent claims contracts create a rigid framework for relationships by attempting to prespecify performance under all likely contingencies (Macneil 1980). However, when technology is evolving rapidly and it is difficult to foresee the future, the very notion of a contingent claims contract becomes questionable.[11]

Furthermore, a zero-sum mentality that prescribes that firms should view buyer–supplier relationships as a source of competition also inhibits upgradability (Garud 1994). For instance, Porter (1980) has suggested that firms should develop "bargaining advantage" over suppliers to "squeeze out the best deal." Such a zero-sum mentality engenders distrust (Kelley and Stahelski 1970, Weick 1979) and leads to conflict in a self-fulfilling way. Eventually, such a mentality destroys the coordination required to realize economies of substitution.

There are indications that some firms in the United States are increasing their emphasis on upgradable relational contracts. For instance, vertically related firms are focusing on the practical aspects of building relationships and trust among themselves. In particular, some firms are reducing the number of suppliers and focusing their energies on building long-term relationships with this core group.[12] Such long-term relationships seek to ensure that "[e]ach player's destiny will be joined with that of the other. And mutual dependence will characterize the relationships" (Davidow and Malone 1993, p. 142).

The advent of new information-mediated technologies (Zuboff 1984) makes coordination between firms all the more possible (Fombrun and Astley 1982). If we view firms as modules of knowledge, mechanisms such as electronic data interchange (Malone et al. 1987) enable connections between these modules and promote interfirm coordination. These information technologies reduce transaction costs, thereby improving the management of disaggregated systems (Quinn 1992).

A neo-Schumpeterian industrial landscape requires cooperation between horizontally interdependent firms as well. As technologies change, firms may find that they do not have all the required competencies to create a viable technological system. These competencies may be resident in their rivals. Given the difficult task of creating new competencies rapidly as and when they are required, firms may be compelled to forge hybrid arrangements with rivals.[13] Taligent is one such hybrid arrangement. IBM and Apple, two direct competitors, created the Taligent collaborative venture and gave it wide latitude to create a common object-oriented operating system.

Another form of cooperation between horizontally interdependent firms is knowledge sharing without the formation of a formal alliance such as a joint venture (Langlois and Robertson 1992). Knowledge sharing between rivals is desirable to the extent that it increases the density of firms manufacturing technological systems that conform to a common standard. As the density of firms manufacturing systems to a common standard increases, so do the benefits to customers, who get a wider choice of complementary products from which to create their preferred system configurations (see Wade 1994). The larger customer base, in turn, provides incentives to manufacturers of complementary components to invest in innovation.

In their study of the music and computer industries, for instance, Langlois and Robertson (1992) note that a firm can earn higher profits by sharing knowledge with rivals than by attempting to appropriate all the benefits itself. They add that "when a component maker is unable to offer customers enough variety to justify the purchase of associated components in a modular system, the most successful firms will be those that abandon a proprietary strategy in favor of membership in a network of competitors employing a common standard of compatibility" (p. 301).

Eventually, distinctions between horizontal and vertical interdependence become blurred. As vertically interdependent firms learn from one another, they may become horizontally interdependent over time (Hamel et al. 1989). For instance, Donnelley Corporation, a supplier of glass for making mirrors, became a rival to its own buyers when it built a plant to supply Honda with exterior mirrors (*Fortune* 1994a). As winners and losers arise in a technological race, firms that were horizontally interdependent may become vertically interdependent over time. For instance, Next Corporation, an erstwhile rival to workstation manufacturers such as Hewlett Packard and Sun Microsystems, exited the workstation hardware markets and currently supplies its object-oriented tools and operating system software to these companies. Moreover, two firms that are vertically interdependent in one organizational system may become horizontally interdependent in another organizational system. In the telecommunications industry, for instance, AT&T supplies wireless communications equipment to the Baby Bells. However, with its acquisition of McCaw, AT&T also competes with the Baby Bells in the cellular services market.

In summary, the partitioning of the technological system among specialized manufacturers confers modularity on the organizational system. The coordination of specialized firms manufacturing components of the partitioned technological system occurs under a governance mode that is neither a hierarchy nor a market (Best 1990, Powell 1990, Richardson 1972). This governance mode is characterized by a "lattice-type" network of relationships (Powell and Brantley 1992) wherein the distinction between horizontal and vertical relationships becomes blurred. This network structure must be generally, rather than specifically, defined to allow enough latitude for interfirm relationships within the organizational systems to evolve with time. The result is a modularly upgradable organizational system.

Piore and Sabel (1984) note that the partitioning of tasks in the production process need not map neatly on to customers' preferred system configurations. In this regard, intermediary firms, commonly known as value-added resellers or system integrators, play an important role. Such firms perform two functions. First, they provide customized solutions to meet specific customer needs. In doing so, they reduce the cognitive complexity customers confront in mixing and matching the components manufactured by different firms. Second, when performance slippage occurs due to incompatibilities created by technological change, these firms ensure that the integrity of the technological system is maintained. To this extent, the role of system integrators in an organizational system is analogous to the role of gateway technologies in a technological system.[14]

Whereas system integrators reduce cognitive complexity, their presence increases transaction costs. These costs can be minimized to the extent that members of an organizational system subscribe to a common set of standards. According to Astley and Brahm (1989), for "the functional integration of modules as part of a coherent system, an overarching 'framework' of planning and coordination would be necessary" (p. 258; see also Toffler 1985). Indeed, we are now witnessing a growing movement toward "open standards" in the institutional environment of standards. Open standards act as mechanisms for coordinating the emerging network mode by reducing transaction costs. We now direct our attention to the institutional aspects of open standards creation.

Institutional Issues

Langlois and Robertson (1992) distinguish between two types of networks: "centralized" and "decentralized." They suggest that a centralized network is one in which network members are tied to a "lead" firm, as in the Japanese automobile industry. A decentralized network is one in which no one firm exercises exclusive control over common standards; moreover, any firm that tries to dictate standards in a decentralized network risks being isolated if network members and customers do not follow its lead.

Increasingly, we are witnessing the growth of such decentralized networks in rapidly changing systemic environments, because of network externalities (Rotemberg and Saloner 1991). Network externalities arise when the benefits a user derives from a product increase from current levels as others use compatible products (e.g., Farrell and Saloner 1986, Katz and Shapiro 1985).[15] In the presence of network externalities, the larger the network, the greater is its attraction. In such a situation, firms are finding it in their best interests to adhere to industrywide standards and promote compatibility, thereby increasing network benefits.[16] Even the largest of firms have been forced to participate in the joint setting of industrywide standards. For instance, in the computer industry, dominant computer manufacturers (e.g., IBM in the United States and NEC in Japan) were reluctant to adopt open standards, fearing loss of market control. However, over time, customers have compelled even these firms to offer systems based on open standards.[17]

Although the impetus for open standards stems from market demands for compatibility, the actual process of standard setting is political—one that unfolds in the institutional environment of standards-setting bodies. The political process manifests itself in the form of broad agreements on system architecture, rather than in the form of precise definitions of standards. Indeed, only such broad agreements provide organizational and technological systems with the degrees of freedom required for future evolution. Recognizing the importance of this upgradability, Graham (1994) suggests that open standards must be specified at a high level of abstraction to allow greater degrees of freedom. At the same time, if standards are specified too loosely, they may result in the creation of incompatible components.

Working with open standards leads to decentralized innovation wherein individual firms can autonomously create differentiated components. At an extreme, a proliferation of components occurs, thereby increasing the costs involved in identifying and selecting appropriate components (both for system manufacturers and users). Under these circumstances, specialized information brokers arise to reduce these search costs. For instance, in the case of OOP, the Object Management Group has created an information brokerage that provides information as well as a market for component software. Participating firms list their products with the brokerage, along with descriptive information and product specifications (Object Management Group 1994, p. 1).

Thus, open standards reduce asset specificity and information asymmetry between interdependent firms manufacturing complementary components of a larger system. Moreover, with open standards, the negative consequences of opportunistic behavior are mitigated because no one firm can change industrywide standards on its own. No firm is held hostage by others because open standards create second sources for the supply of components. Therefore, as more firms embrace open standards, transaction costs decline. In turn, a reduction in transaction costs makes it possible for firms to form dynamic networks (Miles and Snow 1986). In these dynamic networks, coordination occurs through institutional mechanisms that comprise both the standards-setting bodies and the open standards they foster. While modularity in the organizational system makes it highly adaptive to external contingencies, the overarching institutional umbrella of standards maintains overall consistency of action.

In sum, just as relational contracting imparts hierarchylike characteristics to the network organizational system, the institutional environment of open standards imparts marketlike characteristics to it. Reliance on open standards allows firms to "trade" knowledge encapsulated in reusable components. Just as markets comprise regulatory bodies and institutional arrangements to guarantee efficiency, the organizational system comprises autonomous bodies to maintain and guarantee conformance to open standards. In markets, changes in customer demand result in resource reallocation between competing activities. In organizational systems, too, customers play an important role in providing incentives for

firms to conform to a common set of standards. Specifically, customers are the arbiters of whether or not a technological system has greater network benefits, and firms that offer "incompatible" systems pay a price. At the same time, institutionalized standards endow memory on the organizational system—a feature missing in traditional atomistic markets. Thus, open standards create a unique institutional environment that coordinates activities of the organizational system.

Cooperative and Competitive Dynamics in a Modularly Upgradable World

We have introduced three levels of analysis—intrafirm, interfirm, and institutional—to explain how organizational systems may be designed to realize economies of substitution. A fundamental attribute of these emerging organizational systems is the presence of both cooperation and competition at each of the three levels. Within the firm, for instance, competition for a limited pool of resources between individuals creates incentives for increasing current performance even at the expense of future performance. Contributions to current performance provide instant recognition and rewards, whereas contributions to future performance (through the design of reusable components) may yield little recognition or reward. Moreover, creators of reusable components may have to face an additional burden when problems arise with their reusable components. Consequently, there will be a tendency to avoid or postpone the creation of reusable components. In addition, there may be a reluctance to reuse components designed by others (even if created). Clearly, cooperation is required to create and reuse such components. Firms need to balance the tension between cooperation and competition by instituting appropriate systems, structures, and incentives to encourage the creation of reusable components.

This tension between cooperation and competition manifests at the interfirm level as well. Firms confronting a rapidly changing technological system will have to rely on others for complementary components even as they focus on the creation of core components. Indeed, firms will have to share knowledge with one another to ensure that the components they manufacture are compatible. Knowledge sharing, in turn, increases competitive pressures on firms.[18] In such a situation, firms have to innovate continually, destroying some core competencies and enhancing others to suit current requirements (see Lei et al. [1995] for a detailed discussion of how core competencies can be changed over time).

As Powell and Brantley (1992) and Mowery and Rosenberg (1989) suggest, these efforts to extend and adapt core competencies essentially serve as a "ticket of admission" into the wider organizational network to which they belong. Indeed, from this perspective, the main question is not whether to "make or buy." Rather, it is, What competencies are complementary to our own? so that access to these may be secured through appropriate realignment of relationships within organizational networks (Quinn 1992; see also Black and Boal 1994). Depending on how firms answer this question, they may terminate some relationships and forge new ones to create a dynamic learning environment that enables them to adapt to the demands of an evolving technological system.

The tension between cooperation and competition pervades the institutional level as well. Because of network benefits, firms will try to create or join as large a network as possible. As we showed above, this implies the creation of, or conformance to, open standards. To this extent, cooperation is required. However, confronting the prospect of subscribing to common standards, firms would want to be proactive in shaping these standards to suit their competencies better. Specifically, each firm would want its own component specifications built directly into emerging standards. To this extent, firms compete to define standards that favor their own conceptualization of the technological system.

Thus, firms operating in a neo-Schumpeterian world of rapidly changing system technologies have to focus their attention on some core components while depending upon others for complementary ones. To ensure compatibility between these components, firms have to share their knowledge with others and subscribe to open standards. Such cooperation leads to competition as firms differentiate their activities through innovation and attempt to shape their institutional environment of standards. In this way, the tension between cooperation and competition manifests between levels of the organizational systems.

Conclusion

Kenney and Florida (1993) state that the "challenge facing American industry is similar to that faced by Britain at the turn of the century—the need to restructure according to the organizational principles of a new production paradigm in the face of social inertia resulting from the legacy of a past industrial order." These authors caution that American industry may lose its global leadership role if contemporary industrial challenges are not articulated in appropriate technological and organizational terms.

This chapter is an attempt to pose these challenges in appropriate technological and organizational terms. Specifically, firms are operating in a neo-Schumpeterian environment where systemic technologies are changing rapidly. In such an environment, firms have to design technological systems to yield economies of substitution and, at the same time, design organizational systems to exploit these economies.

Implicit in the design of technological and organizational systems for economies of substitution is an ability to manage what were once considered to be mutually exclusive concepts—incremental versus radical technological change, markets versus hierarchies, cooperation versus competition, and craft versus mass production. Already, we can see a trend toward the coexistence of these mutually exclusive concepts as evidenced by the prevalence of terms such as "modular upgradability" (*New York Times* 1991), "networks" (Powell 1990), "co-opetition" (Mr. Sam Albert in *Fortune* 1994b), and "mass customization" (Pine 1993). Clearly, we need new theoretical frames to understand the basis for these concepts.

Our chapter provides a basis for understanding how these new terms are the order of the new industrial landscape. For instance, consider the dichotomy between radical and incremental technological change. As our chapter suggests, technological change need not be radical breakthroughs that destroy previous knowledge.[19] Innovating from scratch each time is difficult, if not impossible, given the systemic nature of technologies and the rapidity of change. At the same time, reliance on incremental change may stifle technological progress and lead to stagnation. Instead, firms may create higher performing systems by reusing some components and substituting others, thereby building on existing knowledge and reaping economies of substitution. Thus, the technological change process need not be either incremental or radical, but can incorporate aspects of both.

Similarly, consider the traditional dichotomy between markets and hierarchies. As our chapter suggests, the network mode of governance integrates both the decentralization of market governance and the coordination of hierarchical governance. Moreover, we argue that the network mode requires reconceptualization of current practices at the intrafirm, interfirm, and institutional levels. For instance, at the intrafirm level, we need to design systems, incentives, and structures that promote knowledge sharing rather than knowledge hoarding. At the interfirm level, we need to conceptualize alliances and relationships in fluid terms calling into attention relational aspects of contracting. At the institutional level, we need to explore the sociopolitical processes involved in the creation and evolution of self-regulatory mechanisms such as open standards. Emphasizing the unique status of networks, Powell (1990) declared that they are "neither fish nor fowl, nor some mongrel hybrid, but a distinctly different form" (p. 299). Indeed, Powell argues that network governance is the most appropriate mode for organizing complex and idiosyncratic exchanges (such as knowledge) under dynamic conditions.

Next, consider the dichotomy between cooperation and competition. As our chapter suggests, firms need to cooperate and compete with one another simultaneously. Firms need to cooperate with suppliers and even rivals to secure complementary resources, skills, or components. At the same time, they may have to compete with their collaborators in the product markets. For instance, standards creation requires cooperation among firms; at the same time, these firms compete with one another to ensure that their own technical specifications are included in the evolving standards.

Together, the technological and organizational designs that we have described in this chapter address another dichotomy—the trade-off between craft and mass production. Specifically, modular upgradability makes it possible for customers to mix and match components to create customized solutions to their technological needs. At the same time, modular upgradability allows firms to realize scale and scope economies. For instance, firms realize scale economies when they partition the system and specialize in mass producing specific components (an aspect that Baldwin and Clark [1994] term modularity in production). Firms realize scope economies by reusing components across different product lines (Goldhar and Jelinek 1983). Thus, modular upgradability leads to mass customization (Pine 1993).

Although our chapter provides a framework with which to view these emerging phenomena, it is but a first step. As is the case with most new frameworks, ours raises as many questions for future research as it attempts to answer. For instance, what are the limits to economies of substitution? Clearly, after a point, modularity results in too many options, thereby increasing cognitive complexity and search costs for designers, manufacturers, and customers. Upgradability too has its limits; the degrees of freedom built into a system will be exhausted eventually. How can firms anticipate these limits and plan ahead to sustain continual innovation?

Consider another issue. How can firms create organizational systems that balance conflicting demands created by the coexistence of cooperation and competition? We offered one description of a network form that is illustrative of industries characterized by network externalities and built around technological systems. Others have reported network forms in industries ranging from biotechnology to textiles (Best 1990, Kenney and Florida 1993, Nelson and Wright 1992, Piore and Sabel 1984, Porter 1990, Powell 1990, Quinn 1992). What are the idiosyncratic features of these network forms? These are but illustrative questions that we as researchers and practitioners need to address. Indeed, our ability to raise the appropriate questions and address them is critical for the continued success of American firms in the emerging industrial order.

Notes

We thank several colleagues for their comments at various stages of this chapter's development. These include participants at the Strategic Management Society Conference held at Chicago, 1993; anonymous reviewers for the *Strategic Management Journal*; editors of the special issue, Richard Bettis and Michael Hitt; participants of a conference on "Technological Transformation and the New Competitive Landscape" held at the University of North Carolina, Chapel Hill, 1994; and Warren Boeker, Deborah Dougherty, Roger Dunbar, Rebecca Henderson, Sanjay Jain, and Praveen Nayyar. We also thank Ian Graham for graciously sharing with us chapters of his book on object-oriented programming and Chris Stone of the Object Management Group.

1. Baldwin and Clark (1994) make a useful distinction among modularity in design, modularity in production, and modularity in use. In this chapter, we make a general argument that encompasses all three types of modularity. Specifically, *modularity in design* creates a potential for the reuse of components and knowledge, *modularity*

in production arises from the partitioning of production tasks, and *modularity in use* provides customers the benefits of speed and scope flexibility.

2. The design of cochlear implants provides an illustration of all three system-level attributes. Cochlear implants are biomedical devices that provide the profoundly deaf with a sensation of sound. For illustrative purposes, consider two parts of the implant: the electrode that is implanted within the cochlea, and the processor that is worn outside the body. Here, system integrity represents how well the processor works with the electrodes to create a sensation of sound. Modularity refers to the decoupling of the electrode from the processor. Recipients may disconnect the processor when desired, even though they are compelled to wear the electrode in the cochlea. Moreover, modularity provides the recipient with the flexibility to use different types of processors. The type of electrode implanted (single-channel or multichannel), however, limits the benefits that a recipient may derive from processor improvements. It is here that the notion of upgradability is best illustrated. A multichannel electrode possesses greater technological degrees of freedom. Therefore, it allows recipients to benefit from the development of new processing schemes that utilize more than one channel in the implanted electrode. In contrast, a single-channel electrode has fewer degrees of freedom, thereby limiting its upgradability (see Garud and Rappa [1994] for more details). Moreover, in attempting to migrate from a single-channel device to a multichannel device, designers have not been able to retain either the electrode or the processing scheme associated with the single-channel device. This is because it is difficult to create a multichannel device by replacing only one or the other subsystem of the single-channel device. Both subsystems need to be replaced, thereby entailing a complete redesign of the device.

3. However, for systems that were originally designed for obsolescence, gateway technologies remain the only way to retain or reuse existing components. See Toffler (1971) for reasons why systems were designed for obsolescence in earlier periods.

4. Several researchers have studied and catalogued the actual costs and benefits of employing OOP techniques. Based on these studies, several simulation models that perform cost-benefit analysis for OOP and predict productivity increases and returns on investment have been generated (e.g., Banker et al. 1993, Gaffney and Durek 1989, Graham 1994, 1995, Henderson-Sellers 1993, Pfleeger 1991). As data on the costs and benefits

of employing OOP have accumulated, these simulations are yielding more accurate estimations of productivity and return on investment.

5. Following Weick (1976) and Granovetter (1985), we must design various elements of an organizational system such that they are coupled neither too tightly nor too loosely. Very tight coupling between elements will constrain the evolution of the system. Very loose coupling, on the other hand, will undermine the coordination required for system elements to function in an integrated manner.

6. A firm could establish minimum efficient scale plants and sell excess production to other system manufacturers. But, as the number of system components manufactured in-house increases, the firm will encounter greater cognitive complexity and higher coordination costs in dealing with multiple activities in several different markets.

7. Even with the usage of flexible manufacturing technologies, eventually cognitive complexity will set in as the variety of product configurations increases.

8. For several illustrations, see a recent *Fortune* (1994b) article that discusses the benefits of outsourcing and provides examples of firms that benefited from outsourcing.

9. Von Hippel (1994) offers the notion of sticky data to explain why such a task partitioning is important. Data are sticky when there are costs associated with replicating and diffusing location-specific information. Consequently, if different components of a technological system require conceptually different kinds of knowledge, it makes sense to partition the system into modules that different members can manufacture in a distributed manner.

10. Relational contracting is an important characteristic of the Japanese keiretsu system (Abegglen and Stalk 1985, Aoki 1990, Piore and Sable 1984, Womack et al., 1990). Keiretsus are characterized by a governance mode that possesses features of both markets and vertically integrated hierarchies while being neither. Reflecting on the benefits of such a "quasi-integrated" system, Aoki (1990) states: "A key to an understanding of Japan's industrial performance can be found in the ability of firms in certain industries to coordinate their operating activities flexibly and quickly in response to changing market conditions and to changes in other factors in the industrial environment, as well as to emergent technical and technological exigencies" (p. 3).

11. This line of reasoning has led many researchers to suggest that these types of transactions be internalized within firms. However, as we

noted above, there are limits to the different kinds and number of activities that can be internalized.

12. A recent *Fortune* (1994a) article describes these emerging practices in the United States. For instance, AMP, a manufacturer of electronic connectors, supplied Silicon Graphics, a workstations manufacturer, with an order over the weekend to replace defective connectors (supplied by a competitor) on the basis of just a phone call. Similarly, Donnelley Corporation built a new plant to manufacture exterior mirrors for Honda based on a verbal agreement to initiate a new partnership. From Honda's point of view, too, this agreement involved a lot of trust, because Donnelley had neither prior experience in making exterior mirrors nor the requisite production facilities.

13. In dynamic environments, in-house development of components as and when they are required is prohibitively expensive because of time compression diseconomies (Dierickx and Cool 1989). Time compression diseconomies arise when an attempt is made to reduce the time taken to accomplish a set of activities by allocating additional resources. The diseconomies result because the resources additionally required are disproportionately more than the benefits that accrue from time compression.

14. For instance, in OOP, several firms, including Visual Edge Software Ltd., Iona Technologies Inc., and Digital Equipment Corporation, have created products to bridge various systems based on incompatible object models from Object Management Group (OMG) and Microsoft Corporation (*Computerworld*, 1994c, p. 8.). Recently, however, Microsoft and OMG have agreed to make their object models compatible with each other (*Computerworld*, 1994a, p. 1).

15. The importance of compatibility in OOP is captured by Graham (1994), who states: "Object technology can succeed against the inertia of existing practice only if users can achieve the confidence in moving to it that they require from a move to open systems. If object-oriented applications are all mutually incompatible, if object-oriented databases cannot interwork with each other and with relational databases and if there are no standard notations and terms for object-oriented analysis there is little hope of this (success)" (p. 5).

16. See Arthur (1988), David (1993), and Garud and Kumaraswamy (1993) for a deeper appreciation of why the presence of network externalities is leading to the creation of open standards in contemporary environments.

17. For instance, the Network Applications Consortium, a group of 25 large users with an-nual revenues of almost $200 billion, hopes to use its buying capacity to exert pressure on hardware and software vendors to conform to standards, so that applications, operating systems, and network services from various vendors can work smoothly together (*Computerworld* 1994b).

18. For instance, Motorola, Apple, and IBM have had to share technical knowledge with one another in order to create the Power PC microprocessor; this effort eventually will increase competitive pressures on each firm to innovate (*Fortune* December 1994).

19. We are not alone in suggesting this. Usher (1954) offers the thesis of cumulative synthesis where invention occurs through accumulation of incremental progress in seemingly unconnected areas until such time the stage is set for an act of insight (the actual invention) to take place. Similarly, Dougherty (1992) suggests that product innovations do not occur in a vacuum, but typically build upon available knowledge.

References

Abegglen, J. and Stalk, G. Jr. (1985) *Kaisha: The Japanese Corporation*. New York: Basic Books.

Aoki, M. (1990) "Toward an economic model of the Japanese firm." *Journal of Economic Literature* 28:1–27.

Arthur, W.B. (1988) "Self-reinforcing mechanisms in economics," in P. Anderson, K. Arrow, and D. Pines (eds.), *The Economy as an Evolving Complex System*, pp. 9–31. Reading, MA: Addison-Wesley.

Astley, W.G. and Brahm, R. (1989) "Organizational designs for post-industrial strategies: the role of interorganizational collaboration," in C. Snow (ed.), *Strategy, Organization Design, and Human Resources Management*, pp. 233–270. Greenwich, CT: JAI Press.

Balda, D. and Gustafson, D. (1990) "Cost estimation models for the reuse and prototype software development life-cycles." *ACM SIGSOFT Software Engineering Notes* 15(3):42–50.

Baldwin, C. and Clark, K. (July 1994) "Modularity-in-design: an analysis based on the theory of real options." Working paper, Harvard Business School, Boston.

Banker, R., Kaufman, R., and Zweig, D. (1993) "Repository evaluation of software re-use" *IEEE Transactions on Software Engineering* 19(4): 379–389.

Best, M. (1990) *The New Competition: Institutions of Industrial Restructuring*. Cambridge, MA: Harvard University Press.

Black, J.A. and Boal, K.B. (1994) "Strategic resources: traits, configurations and paths to sustainable competitive advantage." *Strategic Management Journal* 15(Summer):131–148.

Business Week (1991) "Software made simple." September 30, pp. 92–97.

Business Week (1992). "How Honda hammered out its new Accord." December 21, p. 86.

Clark, K. (1985) "The interaction of design hierarchies and market concepts in technological evolution." *Research Policy* 14:235–251.

Clark, K. and Fujimoto, T. (1990) "The power of product integrity." *Harvard Business Review* 68(6):107–118.

Computerworld (1994a) "Object standard accelerates: Microsoft blesses emerging standard." September 5, p. 1.

Computerworld (1994b) "Group brings order to interoperability." September 12, p. 4.

Computerworld (1994c) "Object standard conflict rises . . . as compatibility issue gets an 'Edge.'" October 3, p. 8.

Cox, B. (1986) *Object Oriented Programming: An Evolutionary Approach*. Reading, MA: Addison-Wesley.

Cusumano, M. (1991) *Japan's Software Factories: A Challenge to US Management*. New York: Oxford University Press.

Datamation (1989) "Cultural barriers slow reusability." November 15, pp. 87–92.

David, P. (1993) "Path-dependence and predictability in dynamic systems with local network externalities: a paradigm for historical economics," in F. Dominique and C. Freeman (eds.), *Technology and the Wealth of Nations: The Dynamics of Constructed Advantage*, pp. 209–231. New York: Pinter.

David, P. and Bunn, J.A. (1990) "Gateway technologies and network industries," in A. Heertje and M. Perlman (eds.), *Evolving Technology and Market Structure*, pp. 121–156. Ann Arbor, MI: University of Michigan Press.

Davidow, W. and Malone, M. (1993) *The Virtual Corporation*. New York: HarperCollins.

Demsetz, H. (1993) "The theory of the firm revisited," in O.E. Williamson and S.G. Winter (eds.), *The Nature of the Firm: Origins, Evolution, and Development*, pp. 159–178. New York: Oxford University Press.

Dierickx, I. and Cool, K. (1989) "Asset stock accumulation and sustainability of competitive advantage," *Management Science* 35:1504–1511.

Dougherty, D. (1992) "A practice-centered model of organizational renewal through product innovation." *Strategic Management Journal* 13(Summer):77–92.

Farrell, J. and Saloner, G. (1986) "Installed base and compatibility: Innovation, product preannouncements and predation." *American Economic Review* 76:940–955.

Financial Executive (1991) "Major technology trends for the 1990s." July/August, pp. 11–15.

Flamm, K. (1988) *Creating the Computer: Government, Industry and High Technology*. Washington, DC: Brookings Institution.

Fombrun, C. and Astley, W. (1982) "The telecommunications community: an institutional overview." *Journal of Communications* 32:56–68.

Fortune (1994a) "The new golden rule of business." February 21, pp. 60–64.

Fortune (1994b) "Outsourcing." December 14, special advertising section.

Gabel, H.L. (1987) "Open standards in the European computer industry: the case of X/OPEN," in H.L. Gabel (ed.), *Product Standardization and Competitive Strategy*, pp. 91–123. New York: Elsevier.

Gaffney, J. Jr., and Durek, T. (1989) "Software reuse—key to enhanced productivity: some quantitative models." *Information and Software Technology*, 31(5):258–267.

Garud, R. (1994) "Cooperative and competitive behaviors during the process of creative destruction." *Research Policy* 23(4):385–394.

Garud, R. and Kotha, S. (1994) "Using the brain as a metaphor to model flexible production systems." *Academy of Management Review* 19:671–698.

Garud, R. and Kumaraswamy, A. (1993) "Changing competitive dynamics in network industries: an exploration of Sun Microsystems' open systems strategy." *Strategic Management Journal* 14(5):351–369.

Garud, R. and Nayyar, P. (1994) "Transformative capacity: Continual structuring by inter-temporal technology transfer." *Strategic Management Journal* 15(5):365–385.

Garud, R. and Rappa, M. (1994) "A socio-cognitive model of technology evolution: the case of cochlear implants." *Organization Science* 5(3):344–362.

Goldhar, J. and Jelinek, M. (1983) "Plan for economies of scope." *Harvard Business Review* 61(6):141–148.

Graham, I. (1994) *Object Oriented Methods*, 2d ed. Workingham, UK: Addison-Wesley.

Graham, I. (1995) *Migrating to Object Technology*. Workingham, UK: Addison-Wesley.

Granovetter, M. (1985) "Economic action and social structures: the problems of embeddedness." *American Journal of Sociology* 91:481–510.

Hakansson, H. (1989) *Corporate Technological Behavior: Cooperation and Networks*. New York: Routledge.

Hamel, G. and Prahalad, C.K. (1994) *Competing for*

the Future. Boston: Harvard Business School Press.

Hamel, G., Doz, Y., and Prahald, C.K. (1989) "Collaborate with your competitors—and win." *Harvard Business Review* 67(1):133–139.

Henderson, R. and Clark, K. (1990) "Architectural innovation: the reconfiguration of existing product technologies and the failure of established firms." *Administrative Science Quarterly* 35:9–30.

Henderson-Sellers, B. (1993) "The economics of reusing library classes." *Journal of Object-Oriented Programming* 6(4):43–50.

Hill, C., Hitt, M., and Hoskisson, R. (1992) "Cooperative versus competitive structures in related and unrelated diversified firms." *Organization Science* 3:501–521.

von Hippel, E. (1994) " 'Sticky information' and the locus of problem solving: implications for innovation." *Management Science* 40:429–439.

Hughes, T. (1987) "The evolution of large technological systems," in W.E. Bijker, T.P. Hughes, and T.J. Pinch (eds.), *The Social Construction of Technological Systems*, pp. 51–82. Cambridge, MA: MIT Press.

Jelinek, M. and Schoonhoven, C.B. (1990) *The Innovation Marathon: Lessons from High Technology Firms*. Cambridge, MA: Basil Blackwell.

Kain, J.B. (1994) "Measuring the ROI of reuse." *Object Magazine*, June, pp. 49–54.

Katz, M. and Shapiro, C. (1985) "Network externalities, competition, and compatibility." *American Economic Review* 75:424–440.

Kelley, H. and Stahelski, A. (1970) "Inference of intentions from moves in prisoners-dilemma games." *Journal of Experimental Social Psychology* 6:401–419.

Kenney, M. and Florida, R. (1993) *Beyond Mass Production: The Japanese System and Its Transfer to the U.S.* New York: Oxford University Press.

Klein, B. (1977) *Dynamic Economics*. Cambridge, MA: Harvard University Press.

Kogut, B. and Zander, U. (1992) "Knowledge of the firm, combinative capabilities, and the replication of technology." *Organization Science* 3:383–397.

Kotha, S. (1995) "Mass customization: implementing the emerging paradigm for competitive advantage." *Strategic Management Journal* 16 (Summer):21–42.

Langlois, R. (1992) "External economies and economic progress: the case of the microcomputer industry." *Business History Review* 66:1–50.

Langlois, R. and Robertson, P. (1992) "Networks and innovation in a modular system: lessons from the microcomputer and stereo component industries." *Research Policy* 21:297–313.

Lei, D., Hitt, M., and Bettis, R. (1995) "Dynamic core competence through meta-learning and strategic context." *Journal of Management* 22(4): 549–569.

Macneil, I. (1980) *The New Social Contract: An Inquiry into Modern Contractual Relations*. New Haven, CT: Yale University Press.

Malone, T., Yates, J., and Benjamin, R. (1987) "Electronic markets and electronic hierarchies." *Communications of the ACM* 30(6):484–497.

Manzi, J. (1994) "Computer keiretsu: Japanese idea, U.S. style." *New York Times*, February 6, money section, p. 15.

Marshall, A. (1961) *Principles of Economics*. London: Macmillan.

Matutes, C. and Regibeau, P. (1988) " 'Mix and match': product compatibility without network externalities." *Rand Journal of Economics* 19: 221–234.

Miles, R. and Snow C. (1986) "Organizations: new concepts for new forms." *California Management Review* 27(3):62–73.

Morgan, G. (1986) *Images of Organization*. Beverly Hills, CA: Sage.

Mowery, D. and Rosenberg, N. (1989) *Technology and the Pursuit of Economic Growth*. New York: Cambridge University Press.

Nelson, R. and Wright, G. (1992) "The rise and fall of American technological leadership: the postwar era in historical perspective." *Journal of Economic Literature* 30:1931–1964.

New York Times. (1991) "Tandon's modular upgradability." June 25, p. C9.

Nonaka, I. (1994) "A dynamic theory of organizational knowledge creation." *Organization Science* 5:14–37.

Object Management Group. (1994) "Objects get online with the Information Brokerage." Press information bulletin, July 25.

Penrose, E. (1959) *The Theory of the Growth of the Firm*. Oxford: Basil Blackwell.

Pfleeger, S. (1991) "Model of software effort and productivity." *Information and Software Technology* 33(3):224–231.

Pine, B.J., II. (1993) *Mass Customization*. Boston, MA: Harvard Business School Press.

Piore, M. (1992) "Fragments of a cognitive theory of technological change and organizational structure," in N. Nohria and R.G. Eccles (eds.), *Networks and Organizations: Structure, Form and Action*, pp. 430–444. Boston: Harvard Business School Press.

Piore, M. and Sabel, C. (1984) *The Second Industrial Divide*. New York: Basic Books.

Porter, M. (1980) *Competitive Strategy*. New York: Free Press.

Porter, M. (1990) *The Competitive Advantage of Nations*. New York: Free Press.

Powell, W. (1990) "Neither market not hierarchy: Network forms of organization." *Research in Organizational Behavior* 12:295–336.

Powell, W. and Brantley, P. (1992) "Competitive cooperation in biotechnology: learning through networks," in N. Nohria and R.G. Eccles (eds.), *Networks and Organizations: Structure, Form and Action*, pp. 366–394. Boston: Harvard Business School Press.

Prahalad, C.K. and Hamel, G. (1990) "The core competence of the corporation." *Harvard Business Review* 68(3):79–91.

Quinn, J. (1992) "The intelligent enterprise: a new paradigm." *Academy of Management Executive* 6(4):48–63.

Richardson, G. (1972) "The organization of industry." *Economic Journal* 82:883–896.

Rosenberg, N. (1982) *Inside the Black Box: Technology and Economics*. Cambridge: Cambridge University Press.

Rotemberg, J. and Saloner, G. (1991) "Interfirm competition and collaboration," in M. Morton (ed.), *The Corporation of the 1990s: Information Technology and Organizational Transformation*, pp. 95–121. New York: Oxford University Press.

Sanchez, R. (1995) "Strategic flexibility in product competition: an options perspective on resource-based competition." *Strategic Management Journal* 16(Summer):135–159.

Sanchez, R. and Mahoney, J. (1994) "The modularity principle in product and organization design: achieving flexibility in the fusion of intended and emergent strategies in hypercompetitive product markets." Office of Research working paper #94-0139. University of Illinois at Urbana-Champaign.

Schumpeter, J. (1942) *Capitalism, Socialism and Democracy*. New York: Harper.

Simon, H. (1962) "The architecture of complexity." *Proceedings of the American Philosophical Society* 106:467–482.

Teece, D. (1980) "Economies of the scope and the scope of the enterprise." *Journal of Economic Behavior and Organization* 1:223–247.

Teece, D.J. (1987) "Profiting from technological innovation: Implications for integration, collaboration, licensing and public policy," in D.J. Teece (ed.), *The Competitive Challenge: Strategies for Industrial Innovation and Renewal*, pp. 185–219. Cambridge, MA: Ballinger.

Toffler, A. (1971) *Future Shock*. New York: Bantam.

Toffler, A. (1985) *The Adaptive Corporation*. New York: McGraw-Hill.

Texas Instruments (September 1992). News release #SC-92075, SC-92076. September.

Tushman, M. and Anderson, P. (1986) "Technological discontinuities and organizational environments." *Administrative Science Quarterly* 31: 439–465.

Tushman M. and Rosenkopf L. (1992) "Organizational determinants of technological change: toward a sociology of technological evolution," in B. Staw and L. Cummings (eds.), *Research in Organizational Behavior*, vol. 14, pp. 311–347. Greenwich, CT: JAI Press.

Usher, A. (1954) *A History of Mechanical Inventions*. Cambridge, MA: Harvard University Press.

Wade, J. (1994) "Dynamics of organizational communities and technological bandwagons: an empirical investigation of community evolution in the microprocessor market." Working paper, University of Illinois at Urbana–Champaign.

Wall Street Journal (1993) "Redesign of Honda's management faces first test with unveiling of new Accord." September 1, p. B1.

Weick, K. (1976) "Educational organizations as loosely coupled systems." *Administrative Science Quarterly* 21:1–19.

Weick, K. (1979) *The Social Psychology of Organizing*. New York: Random House.

Wheelwright, S. and Clark, K. (1992) *Revolutionizing Product Development: Quantum Leaps in Speed, Efficiency, and Quality*. New York: Free Press.

Williamson, O. (1985) *The Economic Institutions of Capitalism*. New York: Free Press.

Winter, S. (1987) "Knowledge and competence as strategic assets," in D.J. Teece (ed.), *The Competitive Challenge: Strategies for Industrial Innovation and Renewal*, pp. 159–184. Cambridge: Ballinger.

Womack, J., Jones, D., and Roos, D. (1990) *The Machine That Changed the World*. New York: Rawson Associates.

Zuboff, S. (1984) *In the Age of the Smart Machine: The Future of Work and Power*. New York: Basic Books.

COMMENTARY

Harnessing Intellectual Capital for Increasing Returns

Among practitioners and academicians alike, there is an increasing appreciation of knowledge as a strategic asset (Winter 1987). Indeed, Alcoa's erstwhile CEO, Paul O'Neil, suggested that we are witnessing nothing short of another industrial revolution (one that James Belasco calls "intellectual capitalism") where artisans are "using their heads and not their hands" (*Fortune* 1991). In a similar vein, an article in *Business Week* (1992) suggested that "competitive advantage no longer belongs to the biggest or those blessed with abundant natural resources or the most capital. In the global economy, knowledge is king."

Reflecting on the economics of knowledge, Arthur (1991) pointed out that intellectual capital has properties that are different from other traditional resources such as land, labor, and financial capital. Rather than diminishing returns that set in with the use of such traditional resources, intellectual capital can yield increasing returns. That is, the returns accruing from intellectual resources can increase with use not at a diminishing rate but at an increasing rate. However, such increasing returns are possible only if we manage knowledge in a manner that generates such economics.

Our essay on economies of substitution, reproduced in this chapter, offers several suggestions on how technological and organizational systems may be designed to generate increasing returns. Technological systems, which embody the knowledge produced through organizational processes, represent the demand side of the increasing returns generation process. Organizational systems, within which knowledge required for producing technological solutions is created and embedded, represent the supply side of this process. Together they constitute a knowledge ecosystem wherein artifacts and actors coevolve (Moore 1996, Garud et al. 1999).

Economies of Substitution

In developing the notion of economies of substitution, we had suggested that economies of scale and scope—though important—are not sufficient to generate increasing returns. It is important to harness additional economies that derive from an ability to add, subtract, or modify components within a larger architecture, thereby generating new functionality. We labeled these "economies of substitution." Specifically, economies of substitution arise when the cost of designing a higher performance system through the partial retention of existing components is lower than the cost of designing the entire system afresh.

Modularity is one important system attribute that helps generate these economies. Modularity refers to an ability to disaggregate and aggregate system components to rapidly create different functionality (cf. Simon 1962, Langlois and Robertson 1992, Garud and Kumaraswamy 1993, Sanchez and Mahoney 1996, Baldwin and Clark 1997, Schilling 2000). Such ability is especially important in network industries—industries built around systemic products comprising a set of components that together provide utility to users. Although systemic products and network industries have existed in earlier times, network benefits have become accentuated with the advent of "unbounded" technologies such as the World Wide Web. Indeed, as our knowledge ecosystem has become unbounded, it has also become increasingly complex. One way to deal with this complexity is to modularize.

Modularity offers several benefits. For instance, modularity can generate options value inherent in technological and organizational architectures by facilitating retention and reuse of system components (Garud and Nayyar 1994, Garud and Kumaraswamy 1996, Baldwin and Clark 1997). Modularity also provides firms with an opportunity to harness external economies—economies deriving from the efforts of other firms comprising the knowledge ecosystem (Langlois and Robertson 1992). Especially in the case of complex and systemic products, such an ability to harness external economies is critical as no one firm will possess all the competencies required to produce the goods and services valued by customers (Hughes 1983). Indeed, modularity enhances the speed and scope of innovation by providing an opportunity to mix and match components of the knowledge ecosystem to rapidly create new technologies, products, and services (Garud and Kotha 1994).

For modularity to deliver these and other benefits, however, one has to pay attention to the overall "architecture" that underlies technological and organizational systems (Morris and Ferguson 1993). Manifest in the form of compatibility standards, the architecture refers to a set of rules and processes that defines acceptable fit and interactions among a system's various components. To the extent that different actors and actants of a system subscribe to the same set of standards, the overall system is able to operate with some *integrity*, a second important system attribute.

Yet integrity comes at a price. As Schumpeter (1942) pointed out, any system designed to be efficient *at* a point in time is likely to be inefficient *over* time. Specifically, a system optimized for efficient performance now may not be able to evolve to new functionality in the future. Therefore, besides modularity and integrity, a third system attribute—*upgradability*—is also necessary. Upgradability exists to the extent that the system architecture possesses sufficient degrees of freedom to evolve over time (Garud and Kumaraswamy 1993).

Underlying this discussion of system attributes is a host of issues that cut across technological and organizational domains. For instance, it is clear that a common standard can enhance the integrity of the system. Indeed, there are considerable network benefits for firms that subscribe to the same technological standard (Katz and Shapiro 1985, David and Greenstein 1990, Garud et al. 2002). Yet, these very standards may constrain the evolution of the system. A key question, then, is, How should standards be designed to enhance the benefits of coordination even while minimizing the constraints imposed by standardization?

In this regard, it is useful to recognize that technological and organizational systems are embedded in the standards that govern their overall functioning (Garud and Kumaraswamy 1994, Garud and Jain 1996). The specific degree of embeddedness can have a critical impact on the dynamics of change within network industries. Systems that are overembedded may become prisoners of the standards that enable their use, as is the case with the QWERTY keyboard (David 1985). Systems that are underembedded may be unable to generate the momentum or critical mass required for widespread adoption and use of the system, as was the case with IBM's OS/2 operating system or Apple's Macintosh computers. Systems that are "just" embedded in the standards that govern and enable their functioning may be able to preserve dynamic capa-

bilities required to continually evolve to new functionality, as may be the case with Sun Microsystem's Java technology.

Just-embeddedness implies that standards and technological capabilities coevolve. Such coevolution also requires loose coupling between innovations or enhancements in technological capabilities and the standards that prescribe compatibility rules. Indeed, given strategic considerations in the sponsorship of proprietary technologies as standards, a standard is as much a set of rules that firms agree upon as a set of rules that they plan to depart from (Garud et al. 2002).

Knowledge Ecosystem Dynamics

So far, we have suggested that knowledge embedded in organizational systems and embodied in associated technological systems constitutes a knowledge ecosystem. One way for the knowledge ecosystem to generate increasing returns is by harnessing economies of substitution. To harness these economies, it is not sufficient to focus only on modularity as a system attribute. In addition, we need to take into consideration two other system attributes—integrity and upgradability. The interplay between these system attributes draws attention to the overall architecture of the knowledge ecosystem. In sum, we need to understand not only the partitioning of the knowledge ecosystem into components, but also the relational aspects among these components and the sociopolitical processes through which standards that govern the functioning of the knowledge ecosystem emerge.

This view recognizes that the knowledge ecosystem can operate in a manner that is distributed and in parallel—a key facet of the new economy (Garud and Kotha 1994). In the old economy, competence was localized and sequentially activated as in a typical mass production assembly line. The new information economy, however, offers the potential to generate increasing returns through the activities of distributed knowledge modules that can operate in parallel within an overall architecture that is itself evolving continually.

To facilitate the parallel processing of distributed knowledge modules, it is possible to design the system such that it consists of a nested interrelated set of modules, each module encapsulating a knowledge of how, why, and what is required for its functioning (Garud 1997, Langlois 1999). Moreover, such knowledge need not be static. Each component of knowledge stock can be continually replenished by underlying learning processes.

By encapsulating knowledge of how, why, and what along with associated learning processes into self-sufficient but interrelated modules, we confer on each module an ability to generalize from its experiences even as it "refreshes" itself over time. Such an ability to generalize is possible because knowledge creation and accumulation is a natural by-product of any activity and knowledge of how, why, and what are co-located. Consequently, each module is scalable—that is, it can continue to upgrade its functionality without much loss of integrity (Garud and Kumaraswamy 2001).

Scalability across modules requires continual adjustment among modules. Continual adjustments ensure that the whole system is able to evolve through local interactions over time. These local interactions also allow for the diffusion of knowledge of how, why, and what across modules. Feedback to a module, then, comes not only from internal operations but also from its interactions with other knowledge modules that simultaneously enable and constrain the scope of its actions.

These relational dynamics occur within a larger architecture that shapes and is shaped by the activities of each knowledge module. Because the architecture directs the activities of modules and interactions among them, changes in standards create a new reality for modules constituting the knowledge ecosystem. Confronting this new reality, each module may modify its competencies and, in the process, change the type and nature of its relationships with other interdependent modules. In turn, these changes may result in the creation of new knowledge that existing standards cannot handle. Consequently, standards have to be "extensible" so that they can integrate the new knowledge and yield useful applications (Jain 2001).

We characterize this overall process of change as being metamorphic in nature (Garud and Kumaraswamy 1994, Garud et al. 1998). Individually and collectively, modules of the ecosystem continue to change based on feedback from using, testing, and doing (Garud and Karnoe 2001, 2002). As this process unfolds, it is difficult to distinguish between any two adjacent stages of the overall process. Over time, however, differences can be dramatic. That is, the change process is neither incremental nor radical. Instead, it combines elements of both. It is like rebuilding a ship plank by plank even as it sails.

Conclusion

Knowledge modules that operate in a distributed yet parallel manner within an overall architecture constitute a knowledge ecosystem that is continually in the making (Garud et al. 1995). This represents a key facet of the new economy—one in which competitive advantages are transient, firm boundaries are porous, and firms continually attempt to shape standards. To survive in this dynamic environment, it is essential to harness economies of substitution through the partial retention and reuse of components of the knowledge ecosystem even as it evolves over time.

References

Arthur, B. (1991) "Now capital means brains not bucks." *Fortune*, January 14, pp. 31–32.

Baldwin, C.Y. and Clark, K.B. (1997) "Managing in an age of modularity." *Harvard Business Review*, September–October, pp. 84–93.

Business Week. (1992) "Industry policy: call it what you will, the nation needs a plan to nurture growth." April 6, pp. 70–104.

David, P. (1985) "Clio and the economics of QWERTY." *Economic History* 75:227–332.

David, P. and Greenstein, S. (1990) "The economics of compatibility standards: an introduction to recent research." *Economics of Innovation and New Technology* 1:3–41.

Fortune. (1991) "The most fascinating ideas for 1991: managing." 123(1):30–33.

Garud, R. (1997) "On the distinction between know-how, know-why and know-what in technological systems," in J. Walsh and A. Huff (eds.), *Advances in Strategic Management*, pp. 81–101. Stamford, CT: JAI Press.

Garud, R. and Jain, S. (1996) "Technology embeddedness." *Advances in Strategic Management* 13:389–408.

Garud, R. and Karnoe, P. (2002) "Bricolage vs. breakthrough: Distributed and embedded agency in technology entrepreneurship." *Research Policy*, in press.

Garud, R. and Karnoe, P. (2001) "Path creation as a process of mindful deviation," in R. Garud and P. Karnoe (eds.), *Path Dependence and Creation*. Mahwah, NJ: Earlbaum.

Garud, R. and Kotha, S. (1994) "Using the brain as a metaphor to model flexible productive units." *The Academy of Management Review* 19:671–698.

Garud, R. and Kumaraswamy, A. (1993) "Changing competitive dynamics in network industries: an exploration of Sun Microsystems' open systems strategy." *Strategic Management Journal* 14:351–369.

Garud, R. and Kumaraswamy, A. (1994) "Coupling the technical and institutional faces of Janus in network industries," in R. Scott and S. Christensen (eds.), *Advances in the Institutional Analysis of Organizations: International and Longitudinal Studies*, pp. 226–242. Thousand Oaks, CA: Sage.

Garud, R. and Kumaraswamy, A. (1996) "Technological designs for retention and reuse." *International Journal of Technology Management* 11:883–891.

Garud, R. and Kumaraswamy, A. (2001) "Infosys: the architecture of a scalable organization." *Working Paper*, New York University.

Garud, R. and Nayyar, P. (1994) "Transformative capacity: continual structuring by intertemporal technology transfer." *Strategic Management Journal* 15:365–385.

Garud, R., Kumaraswamy, A., and Prabhu, A. (1995) "Networking for success in cyberspace," in *IEEE Proceedings of the International Conference on Multimedia Computing and Systems*, pp. 335–340.

Garud, R., Jain, S., and Phelps, C. (1998) "Metamorphic change: exploration and exploitation in the web browser market." Paper presented at the Academy of Management Annual Meetings, San Diego.

Garud, R., Jain, S., and Kumaraswamy, A. (1999) "An integrative perspective for managing knowledge," in R. Garud and J. Porac (eds.), *Cognition, Knowledge and Organization*, pp. 195–214, Stamford, CT: JAI Press.

Garud, R., Jain, S., and Kumaraswamy, A. (2002)

"Orchestrating international processes for technology sponsorship: The case of Sun Microsystems and Java." *Academy of Management Journal*, in press.

Hughes, T.P. (1983) *Networks of Power*. Baltimore: Johns Hopkins University Press.

Jain, S. (2001) "Rolling the bandwagon: the emergence of compatibility standards in the local area networking industry, 1980–1995." Unpublished doctoral dissertation, New York University.

Langlois, R. (1999) "Modularity in technology, organization, and society." Paper presented at IN-FORMS, November 8, Philadelphia.

Langlois, R.N. and Robertson, P.L. (1992) "Networks and innovation in a modular system: lessons from the microcomputer and stereo component industries." *Research Policy* 21:297–313.

Moore, J.F. (1996) *The Death of Competition: Leadership and Strategy in the Age of Business Ecosystems*. New York: HarperBusiness.

Morris, C. and Ferguson, C.H. (1993) "How architecture wins technology wars." *Harvard Business Review*, March–April, pp. 86–96.

Sanchez, R. and Mahoney, J.T. (1996) "Modularity, flexibility and knowledge management in product and organizational design." *Strategic Management Journal* 17:63–76.

Schilling, M.A. (2000) "Towards a general modular systems theory and its application to interfirm product modularity." *Academy of Management Review* 25:312–334.

Schumpeter, J. (1942) *Capitalism, Socialism and Democracy*. New York: Harper.

Simon, H.A. (1962) "The architecture of complexity." *Proceedings of the American Philosophical Society* 106:467–482. Reprinted in H.A. Simon, *The Sciences of the Artificial*, 2d ed. Cambridge: MIT Press, 1981.

Winter, S. (1987) "Knowledge and competence as strategic assets," in D.J. Teece (ed.), *The Competitive Challenge: Strategies for Industrial Innovation and Renewal*, pp. 159–184. Cambridge, MA: Ballinger.

15

Developing a Knowledge Strategy

Michael H. Zack

Business organizations are coming to view knowledge as their most valuable and strategic resource. They are realizing that to remain competitive they must explicitly manage their intellectual resources and capabilities. To this end, many organizations have initiated a range of knowledge management projects and programs.[1] The primary focus of these efforts has been on developing new applications of information technology to support the digital capture, storage, retrieval, and distribution of an organization's explicitly documented knowledge (e.g., Davenport et al. 1996, Goodman and Darr, 1996). A smaller number of organizations, on the other hand, believe that the most valuable knowledge is the tacit knowledge existing within peoples' heads, augmented or shared via interpersonal interaction and social relationships. To build their intellectual capital, those organizations are utilizing the "social capital" that develops from people interacting repeatedly over time (Nahapiet and Ghoshal 1998). Many are experimenting with new organizational cultures, forms, and reward systems to enhance those social relationships (Quinn et al. 1996).

Technical and organizational initiatives, when aligned and integrated, can provide a comprehensive infrastructure to support knowledge management processes. However, while the appropriate infrastructure can enhance an organization's ability to create and exploit knowledge, it does not ensure that the organization is making the best investment of its resources or that it is managing the right knowledge in the right way. How should an organization determine which efforts are appropriate, or which knowledge should be managed and developed?

My research with more than 25 firms has found that the most important context for guiding knowledge management is the firm's strategy. An organization's strategic context helps to identify knowledge management initiatives that support its purpose or mission, strengthen its competitive position, and create shareholder value. Intuitively, it makes sense that the firm that knows more about its customers, products, technologies, markets, and their linkages should perform better. However, the link between knowledge management and business strategy, while often talked about, has been widely ignored in practice.[2]

Many executives are struggling to articulate the relationship between their organization's competitive strategy and its intellectual resources and capabilities. They do not have well-developed strategic models that help them to link knowledge-oriented processes, technologies, and organizational forms to business strategy, and

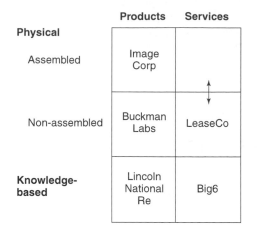

	Products	Services
Physical Assembled	Image Corp	
Non-assembled	Buckman Labs	LeaseCo
Knowledge-based	Lincoln National Re	Big6

Figure 15.1

they are unsure of how to translate the goal of making their organizations more intelligent into a strategic course of action. They need a pragmatic, yet theoretically sound model of what I call *knowledge strategy.*

This article provides a framework for describing and evaluating an organization's knowledge strategy. The framework is illustrated using examples from five companies representing the spectrum of physical and knowledge-based products and services (see figure 15.1). "Image Corp."[3] is a leading photographic imaging firm manufacturing physical assembled products such as film and photoprocessing equipment. Buckman Labs is a leading manufacturer of specialty chemicals, a physical nonassembled product. Lincoln Re, one of the world's largest life/health reinsurers, provides knowledge-based products and services. "LeaseCo," an industrial garment and small equipment-leasing firm, provides a service based on physical products, some requiring assembly. "Big6" is a leading public accounting and professional services firm, providing knowledge-based services. Together, these companies demonstrate the importance of knowledge strategy regardless of industrial sector.

Business Strategy

The strengths-weaknesses-opportunities-threats (SWOT) framework is perhaps the best-known approach to defining strategy, having influenced both practice and research for over 30 years (Andrews 1971). Performing a SWOT analysis involves describing and analyzing a firm's internal capabilities—its strengths and weaknesses—relative to the opportunities and threats of its competitive environment. Organizations are advised to take strategic actions to preserve or sustain strengths, offset weaknesses, avert or mitigate threats, and capitalize on opportunities. Strategy can be seen as the balancing act between the external environment (opportunities and threats) and the internal capabilities of the firm (strengths and weaknesses).

Application of the SWOT framework has been dominated over the last 20 years by Porter's (1980) "five-forces" model. This model focuses on the external side of strategy, helping firms analyze the forces in an industry that give rise to opportunities and threats. Industries that are structured so as to enable firms to dictate terms to suppliers and customers as well as to provide barriers to new entrants and substitute products are seen as favorable. Strategy becomes a matter of choosing an appropriate industry and positioning the firm within that industry according to a generic strategy of either low cost or product differentiation.

While enjoying much popularity (in no small part because it was perhaps the first attempt to apply solid economic thinking to strategic management in a practical and understandable way), Porter's model has come under criticism (Teece 1984, Barney 1991). The main argument is that the model addresses the profitability of industries rather than individual firms and therefore does not help particular firms to identify and leverage unique and sustainable advantages. Its underlying economic theory assumes that the characteristics of particular firms per se do not matter with regard to profit performance (Connor 1991). Rather, it is the overall pattern of relationships among firms in the industry that makes the difference. If the industry as a whole is structured properly (i.e., with sufficient barriers and other impediments to competition), then all firms should realize excess returns.

It turns out, however, that unique characteristics of particular firms within an industry *can* make a difference in terms of profit performance (Nelson 1991, McGahan and Porter 1997, Rumelt 1991). To put balance back into the original notion of business strategy, recent work in the area of strategic management and economic theory has begun to focus on the internal side of the equation—the firm's resources and capabilities.[4] This new perspective is referred to as the *resource-based view* of the firm (Barney 1996, Collis and Montgomery 1995, Grant 1991,

Prahalad and Hamel 1990). Strategic management models traditionally have defined the firm's strategy in terms of its product/market positioning—the products it makes and the markets it serves. The resource-based approach suggests, however, that firms should position themselves strategically based on their unique, valuable, and inimitable *resources and capabilities* rather than on the products and services derived from those capabilities. Resources and capabilities can be thought of as a platform from which the firm derives various products for various markets (Kogut and Kulatilaka 1994). Leveraging resources and capabilities across many markets and products, rather than targeting specific products for specific markets, becomes the strategic driver. While products and markets may come and go, resources and capabilities are more enduring. Therefore, a resource-based strategy provides a more long-term view than does the traditional approach, and one more robust in uncertain and dynamic competitive environments. Competitive advantage based on resources and capabilities therefore is potentially more sustainable than that based solely on product and market positioning.

Knowledge as a Strategic Resource

While having unique access to valuable resources is one way to create competitive advantage, in some cases either this may not be possible, or competitors may imitate or develop substitutes for those resources. Companies having superior knowledge, however, are able to coordinate and combine their traditional resources and capabilities in new and distinctive ways, providing more value for their customers than can their competitors (Penrose 1980, Romer 1995, Teece et al. 1997). That is, by having superior *intellectual* resources, an organization can understand how to exploit and develop its traditional resources better than competitors, even if some or all of those traditional resources are not unique. Therefore, *knowledge* can be considered the most important strategic resource, and the ability to acquire, integrate, store, share, and apply it is the most important capability for building and sustaining competitive advantage (Grant 1996, Kogut and Zander 1992, Penrose 1980, Spender 1994, Teece et al. 1997, Winter 1987). The broadest value proposition, then, for engaging in knowledge management is that it can enhance the organization's fundamental ability to compete.

What is it about knowledge that makes the advantage sustainable? Knowledge—especially context-specific, tacit knowledge embedded in complex organizational routines and developed from experience—tends to be unique and difficult to imitate. Unlike many traditional resources, it is not easily purchased in the marketplace in a ready-to-use form. To acquire similar knowledge, competitors have to engage in similar experiences. However, acquiring knowledge through experience takes time, and competitors are limited in how much they can accelerate their learning merely through greater investment.

LeaseCo, for example, recognized this opportunity by occasionally bidding aggressively on complex, novel, or unpredictable lease opportunities (e.g., leasing personal computers in 1980) to gain unique and leverageable knowledge from those experiences, while attempting to prevent its competitors from gaining that same knowledge. LeaseCo realized a double benefit over its competitors, first by investing in its strategic knowledge platform and second by learning enough about the particular client to competitively and profitably price leases for future opportunities with the same client. Often, enough mutual learning occurred between LeaseCo and its client that the client contracted with LeaseCo for future leases without going out for competitive bids. In essence, LeaseCo created a sustainable (or renewable) knowledge-based barrier to competition. Lincoln Re, as part of its "experimental underwriting" process, similarly invested in its learning by insuring strategically selected novel and difficult classes of risk at favorable rates.

Knowledge-based competitive advantage is also sustainable because the more a firm already knows, the more it can learn (Cohen and Leventhal 1990). Learning opportunities for an organization that already has a knowledge advantage may be more valuable than for competitors having similar learning opportunities but starting off knowing less (Goldstein and Zack 1989). For example, Big6 invested heavily in capturing and sharing knowledge about key engagements across the firm so that it could sustain its areas of advantage by always building on its latest knowledge, rather than "reinventing the wheel" while giving its competitors a chance to catch up.

Sustainability may also come from an organization already knowing something that uniquely complements newly acquired knowledge, which provides an opportunity for knowledge synergy not available to its competitors. New knowledge is integrated with existing knowledge to develop unique insights and create even more valuable knowledge. Organizations should therefore seek areas of learning and experimentation that can potentially add value to their existing knowledge via synergistic combination. For example, Lincoln Re's unique (and patented) capability for capturing and distributing medical risk knowledge via expert systems—above and beyond the knowledge stored in these systems—enabled it to outperform competitors. Combining newly acquired risk management knowledge with its "meta-knowledge" (of how to document, codify, and structure that knowledge) provided Lincoln Re a greater benefit that either alone. As an additional benefit, by designing its expert system to function as a generic knowledge platform, Lincoln Re was able to apply it to additional knowledge domains at essentially no additional cost (except for that to codify the content knowledge of those new areas), thus providing an economic advantage for entering new markets.

Sustainability of a knowledge advantage, then, comes from knowing more about some things than do competitors, combined with the time constraints faced by competitors in acquiring similar knowledge, regardless of how much they invest to catch up. These examples represent what economists call *increasing returns* (Romer 1995, Teece 1998). Unlike traditional physical goods that are consumed as they are used (providing decreasing returns over time), knowledge provides *increasing* returns as it is used. The more it is used, the more valuable it becomes, creating a self-reinforcing cycle. If an organization can identify areas where its knowledge leads the competition, and if that unique knowledge can be applied profitably in the marketplace, it can represent a powerful and sustainable competitive advantage.

Organizations should strive to use their learning experiences to build on or complement knowledge positions that provide a current or future competitive advantage. Systematically mapping, categorizing, and benchmarking organizational knowledge not only can help make knowledge more accessible throughout an organization, but by using a knowledge map to prioritize and focus its learning experiences, an organization can create greater leverage for its learning efforts. It can combine its learning experiences into a "critical learning mass" around particular strategic areas of knowledge.

For example, LeaseCo proactively searched for opportunities to build continually on what it knew about leasing formal dress apparel to appearance-conscious organizations. It became one of the most knowledgeable firms in the industry regarding this premium market. Buckman Labs took a similar approach by focusing its learning to maintain and grow its superior knowledge of the pulp and paper industry. Big6 implemented a computer system that tracked its employees' experience, and formal training and matched their capabilities to the knowledge and skills required of its current and future engagements. Big6 focused its training, assignments, and recruiting on continually building the knowledge base to support its most strategically important competitive positions.

While a knowledge advantage may be sustainable, building a defensible competitive knowledge position internally is a long-term effort, requiring foresight and planning as well as luck. For example, as part of its prospective risk management process, Lincoln Re has an "early-warning" process in place to monitor research in the medical field for anything that eventually may improve its mortality and risk management knowledge. Using its unique expertise for translating commonly available research data into an estimate of actual experience, Lincoln Re is able to effectively learn about and profitably insure emergent risk management opportunities sooner than its competitors.

Long lead time explains the attraction of strategic alliances and other forms of external ventures as potentially quicker means for gaining access to knowledge. It also explains why the strategic threat from technological discontinuity tends to come from firms outside of or peripheral to an industry (Utterback 1994). New entrants often enjoy a knowledge base different than that of incumbents, one that can be applied to the products and services of the industry under attack. This has been especially evident in industries where analog products are giving way to digital equivalents. For example, Image Corp. is experiencing a significant shift from physical film substrates to digital imaging. Its knowledge base is built on the science and technology of a physical consumable packaged good. Digital imaging, on the other hand, requires knowledge of computer systems and peripherals, imaging software, electronic distribution channels, and an economic model entirely different than for consumable physical products. The strategic challenge for the firm is to develop sufficient knowledge to support a shift to those new technologies and markets before nontraditional competitors make significant inroads in those markets. At the same time, it must not abandon its years of experience and knowledge about physical imaging that is supporting its core business.

This long learning lead time or "knowledge friction" highlights the importance of benchmarking and evaluating the strengths, weaknesses, opportunities, and threats of an organization's current knowledge platform and position, as this knowledge provides the primary opportunity (and constraint) from which to compete and grow over the near to intermediate term. This must in turn be balanced against the organization's long-term plans for developing its knowledge platform.

The Knowledge–Strategy Link

The traditional SWOT framework, updated to reflect today's knowledge-intensive environment, provides a basis for describing a knowledge strategy. In essence, firms need to perform a *knowledge-based* SWOT analysis, mapping their knowledge resources and capabilities against their strategic opportunities and threats to better understand their points of advantage and weakness. They can use this map to strategically guide their knowledge management efforts, bolstering their knowledge advantages and reducing their knowledge weaknesses. Knowledge strategy, then, can be thought of as balancing knowledge-based resources and capabilities to the knowledge required for providing products or services in ways superior to those of competitors. Identifying which knowledge-based resources and capabilities are valuable, unique, and inimitable and identifying how those resources and capabilities support the firm's product and market positions are essential elements of a knowledge strategy.

To explicate the link between strategy and knowledge, an organization must articulate its strategic intent (Hamel and Prahalad 1989), identify the knowledge required to execute its intended strategy, and compare that to its actual knowledge, thus revealing its strategic knowledge gaps.

Linking Knowledge to Strategy

Every firm competes in a particular way—operating within some industry and adopting a competitive position within that industry. Competitive strategy may result from an explicit grand decision—the traditional perspective on strategy—or from an accumulation of smaller incremental decisions (Quinn 1980). It may even be revealed in hindsight, by looking back on actual behaviors and events over time (Mintzberg 1994, Weick 1987). Regardless of the strategy formation process, organizations have a de facto strategy that must first be articulated.

Every strategic position is linked to some set of intellectual resources and capabilities. That is, given what the firm believes it must do to compete, there are some things it must know and know how to do. The strategic choices that companies make—regarding technologies, products, services, markets, processes—have a profound influence on the knowledge, skills, and core competencies required to compete and excel in an industry.

On the other hand, what a firm *does* know and knows how to do limits the ways it can actually compete. The firm, given what it knows, must identify the best product and market opportunities for exploiting that knowledge. For example, Buckman Labs competed on value-added services, requiring it to develop and maintain superior knowledge of how to use its chemicals in various microbial treatment applications to solve its customers' problems. In some markets, Buckman Labs had well-developed knowledge and expertise. In others, it was more limited. Most important, it recognized the difference and managed and developed its strategic knowledge accordingly.

Lincoln Re competed directly via the high quality of its knowledge about particular classes of medical risk as well as its knowledge about how to combine ancillary services into an integrated packaged solution for its clients' risk management problems. Lincoln Re, however, knew less about property and casualty risk than did some of its competitors, and its competitive strategy reflected this. LeaseCo, which specialized in novel and customized leases, had to know more about the economics of pricing a complex lease than its competitors. LeaseCo did not know as much as its competitors about low-cost, high-volume production or high-volume inventory management. Image Corp. had extensive knowledge and expertise regarding its traditional imaging technologies and products and how they could best be marketed to consumer and industrial customers. Their knowledge regarding digital imaging was much less developed, potentially limiting their ability to compete in that emerging market. Given the strategic importance of the digital imaging market, they were aggressively moving to close this gap.

So-called category killers such as Circuit City and Toys 'R' Us focus their retailing knowledge on one product category at the expense of others. In comparison, many broad-line retailers, led by Wal-Mart, have taken a different competitive knowledge position. They have come to realize that while they know some things about retailing tens of thousands of products to the consumer market, their suppliers are able to develop a more focused understanding about the particular products each supplies. Rather than try to be the consumer expert on every product, these retailers have recognized the limits to what they know and can know. They are asking their suppliers to take responsibility for understanding consumption habits, practices, needs, and buying patterns and to share that knowledge with the retailer. The retailer is, in fact, operating as a knowledge integrator, integrating the knowledge of many suppliers to better serve consumers.

In each case, an organization's competitive position created a knowledge requirement, while its existing knowledge created an opportunity and a constraint on selecting viable competitive positions. Success required dynamically aligning those knowledge-based requirements and capabilities.

A Strategic Framework for Mapping Knowledge

Assessing an organization's knowledge position requires cataloging its existing intellectual resources by creating what is commonly called a knowledge map. Knowledge can be characterized in many ways. Popular taxonomies distinguish between tacit and explicit knowledge, general and situated context-specific knowledge, and individual and collective knowledge (Demsetz 1988, Polanyi 1966, Spender 1996). Knowledge can also be categorized by type, including declarative (knowledge about), procedural (know-how), causal (know why), conditional (know when), and relational (know with). While these distinctions are useful for mapping and managing knowledge at the process level once a knowledge strategy has been formulated, our purpose requires a knowledge taxonomy oriented toward strategy that reflects the competitive uniqueness of each organization.

Categorizing or describing what a business firm knows and must know about its industry or competitive position is not easy. Although firms

within particular industries, firms maintaining similar competitive positions, or those employing similar technologies and other resources often share some common knowledge, there are no simple answers regarding what a firm must know to be competitive—if there were, then there would be no sustainable advantage.

Each company I have worked with has developed an approach to describing and classifying its strategic or competitive knowledge that is in some ways unique. In fact, each firm's general awareness of and orientation to the link between knowledge and strategy tends to be somewhat unique and may, itself, represent an advantage. Regardless of how knowledge is categorized based on content, every firm's strategic knowledge can be categorized by its ability to support a competitive position. Specifically, knowledge can be classified according to whether it is core, advanced, or innovative.

Core knowledge is that minimum scope and level of knowledge required just to "play the game." Having that level of knowledge and capability will not assure the long-term competitive viability of a firm, but does present a basic industry knowledge barrier to entry. Core knowledge tends to be commonly held by members of an industry and therefore provides little advantage other than over nonmembers.

Advanced knowledge enables a firm to be competitively viable. The firm may have generally the same level, scope, or quality of knowledge as its competitors, although the specific knowledge content will often vary among competitors, enabling knowledge differentiation. Firms may choose to compete on knowledge head-on in the same strategic position, hoping to know more than a competitor. They instead may choose to compete for that position by differentiating their knowledge. LeaseCo, for example, competed with others for the custom lease market but used its knowledge of lease pricing and equipment sourcing rather than garment finishing or equipment integration to compete for that position. Buckman Labs competed in certain markets based on its superior knowledge of how to apply its chemicals to solve the process treatment problems of its customers. Big6 knew how to deliver accounting, tax, and consulting solutions of a quality sufficient to enable it to attract and retain high-quality clients.

Innovative knowledge is knowledge that enables a firm to lead its industry and competitors and to significantly differentiate itself from its competitors. Innovative knowledge often enables a firm to change the rules of the game itself (Markides 1998). LeaseCo, based on its extensive knowledge of cost accounting and lease economics, challenged the traditional way leases were priced in its industry. Not only did this confuse the competition to LeaseCo's advantage, but it also allowed LeaseCo to identify many profitable opportunities passed over by competitors while avoiding potentially unprofitable ventures. Lincoln Re developed highly innovative knowledge not only about assessing risk, but also about how to codify, structure, distribute, leverage, and market that knowledge using expert systems. Big6 developed expertise in particular industries and services that clearly led its competitors. Buckman Labs developed innovative knowledge for delivering more comprehensive solutions to its customers to help increase their overall processing plant efficiency and quality.

Knowledge is not static, and what is innovative knowledge today will ultimately become the core knowledge of tomorrow. Thus, defending and growing a competitive position requires continual learning and knowledge acquisition. The ability of an organization to learn, accumulate knowledge from its experiences, and reapply that knowledge is itself a skill or competence that—beyond the core competencies directly related to delivering its product or service—may provide strategic advantage.

Although knowledge is dynamic, this strategic knowledge framework (figure 15.2) does offer the ability to take a snapshot of where the firm is today vis-à-vis its desired strategic knowledge profile (to assess its internal knowledge gaps) and vis-à-vis its competitors (to assess its external knowledge gaps). Additionally, it can be used to plot the historical path and future trajectory of the firm's knowledge. The framework may be applied by area of competency or, taking a more traditional strategic perspective, by single business unit, division, product line, function, or market position. Regardless of the particular way each firm categorizes its knowledge, each category can be further broken down into elements that are core, competitive, or innovative to produce a strategic knowledge map.

Gap Analysis

Having mapped the firm's competitive knowledge position, an organization can perform a gap analysis. The gap between what a firm must do to compete and what it actually *is* doing represents a *strategic* gap. Addressing this gap is the

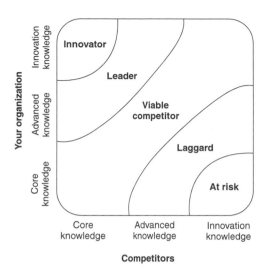

Figure 15.2

stuff of traditional strategic management. As suggested by the SWOT framework, strengths and weaknesses represent what the firm can do; opportunities and threats dictate what it must do. Strategy, then, represents how the firm balances its competitive "cans" and "musts" to develop and protect its strategic niche.

At the same time, underlying a firm's strategic gap is a potential *knowledge* gap. That is, given a gap between what a firm must do to compete and what it can do, there may also be a gap between what the firm must know to execute its strategy and what it does know. Based on a strategic knowledge and capabilities map, an organization can identify the extent to which its various categories of existing knowledge are in alignment with its strategic requirements. The result is a set of potential knowledge gaps. In some cases, an organization might even know *more* than needed to support its competitive position. Nevertheless, a knowledge strategy must address any possible misalignments. The greater the number, variety, or size of the current and future knowledge gaps, and the more volatile the knowledge base because of a dynamic or uncertain competitive environment, the more aggressive the knowledge strategy required. A firm not capable of executing its intended or required strategy must either align its strategy with its capabilities or acquire the capabilities to execute its strategy.

Having performed a strategic evaluation of its knowledge-based resources and capabilities, an

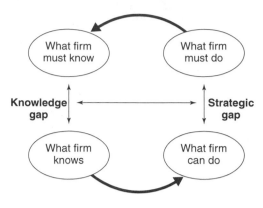

Figure 15.3

organization can determine which knowledge should be developed or acquired. To give knowledge management a strategic focus, the firm's knowledge management initiatives should be directed toward closing this strategic knowledge gap. The important issue is that the knowledge gap is directly derived from and aligned with the strategic gap (see figure 15.3). This simultaneous alignment of strategy and knowledge is a crucial element of a firm's knowledge strategy. In many firms, knowledge management efforts are divorced from strategic planning and execution. However, having an appropriate knowledge strategy in place is essential for assuring that knowledge management efforts are being driven by and are supporting the firm's competitive strategy. For example, to ensure alignment, Lincoln Re placed responsibility for knowledge management and corporate strategy within the same senior executive position.

A Knowledge Strategy Framework

A knowledge strategy, paralleling the traditional SWOT analysis, describes the overall approach an organization intends to take to align its knowledge resources and capabilities to the intellectual requirements of its strategy. It can be described along two dimensions reflecting its degree of aggressiveness. The first dimension addresses the degree to which an organization needs to increase its knowledge in a particular area versus the opportunity it may have to leverage existing but underutilized knowledge resources—that is, the extent to which the firm is primarily a creator versus user of knowledge. The second dimension addresses whether the primary sources of knowl-

edge are internal or external. Together these characteristics help a firm to describe and evaluate its current and desired knowledge strategy (Bierly and Chakrabarti 1996, March 1991).

Exploration versus Exploitation

To the extent that an organization finds itself to be at a lower level of knowledge than required to execute its strategy or to defend its position, it requires a high level of knowledge processing to close its *internal* knowledge gap. To the extent that many competitors in an organization's industry are operating at higher levels of knowledge across many more knowledge positions, a high level of knowledge processing is required to close the *external* competitive knowledge gap. To the extent that knowledge in the industry is changing rapidly, the organization may need to be creating new knowledge just to keep pace. In these situations, the organization's requirement is to be an *explorer*—a creator or acquirer of the knowledge required to become and to remain competitive in its strategic position.

On the other hand, when knowledge resources and capabilities significantly exceed the requirements of a competitive position, the organization has the opportunity to further exploit that knowledge platform, possibly within or across other competitive niches. In this situation, the organization's requirement is to be a knowledge *exploiter*. For example, Dow Chemicals screened its portfolio of 29,000 patents to see which should be exploited (and by whom), which could be licensed, and which should be abandoned. This generated $125 million in licensing income and $40 million in savings over 10 years (Cohen 1998). Big6 aggressively sought to sell additional engagements leveraging its experiences, and Lincoln Re aggressively sought reinsurance deals that exploited its existing knowledge regarding insurance risk, service integration, and deal making.

Exploitation and exploration are not mutually exclusive. An organization may need to develop one area of knowledge while simultaneously exploiting another. Ultimately, the ideal for most companies is to maintain a balance between exploration and exploitation within all areas of strategic knowledge. Exploration provides the knowledge capital to propel the company into new niches while maintaining the viability of existing ones. Exploitation of that knowledge provides the financial capital to fuel successive rounds of innovation and exploration. Exploration without exploitation cannot be economically sustained over the long run unless it is subsidized or directly generates a revenue stream (e.g., a research institute). Exploitation without exploration will ultimately result in trying to pump from a dry well. Eventually knowledge becomes stale or obsolete. Those companies that closely integrate knowledge exploration and exploitation I refer to as *innovators*.

Firms that are extremely efficient in exploiting others' knowledge may enjoy some long-term success as an exploiter. However, given the difficulty in transferring knowledge, these cases are rare. Success in those cases usually requires competing against firms whose ability to exploit is not well developed and who make their tacit knowledge accessible to outsiders. For example, recall Apple's exploitation of Xerox's development of the personal computer graphical user interface. The value from knowledge exploitation may be greater when done by the firm creating it or via some form of joint venture between explorer and exploiter firms.

Exploration and exploitation typically occur in different parts of an organization and are often separated temporally and culturally as well as organizationally. Balancing exploitation and exploration requires a well-developed internal knowledge transfer capability between functions such as research and development (R&D), sales, marketing, manufacturing, and customer service. This requires a culture, reward systems, and communication networks that support the flow of knowledge and a well-functioning organizational memory (as embedded both in humans and in technology) to transcend the time delays between developing and applying knowledge as well as between applying and developing the next round of knowledge. This knowledge transfer and integration capability is itself strategic.

The creation of unique, strategic knowledge takes time, forcing the firm to balance short- and long-term strategic resource decisions. The firm therefore must determine whether its efforts are best focused on longer term knowledge exploration, shorter term exploitation, or both. It must then balance its knowledge-processing resources and efforts accordingly. For example, Image Corp. focused its recruiting and training on the knowledge required to support its future digital products and services. It also implemented computer-based conferencing technologies and created opportunities for face-to-face interaction to support knowledge transfer between its few highly knowledgeable technical, sales, and mar-

keting people in the growing digital products division and their counterparts in traditional products divisions. It did not, however, abandon its existing analog imaging niche but implemented a computer-based knowledge-sharing capability among its sales and marketing personnel to exploit as much of their existing knowledge about selling and marketing traditional products as possible.

It is not enough for an organization merely to engage in both exploration and exploitation. More important, those activities must be linked and coordinated so that they can reinforce one another. For example, Big6 turned its learning experiences first into semistructured documents that could be accessed and reused by others immediately and eventually into formal, structured methods for efficiently delivering the service. They established organizational units having explicit responsibility for this function. In this way, they actively managed the exploitation of their exploratory knowledge. New insights gained in the field from reapplying and adapting this knowledge to different contexts were subsequently captured and integrated into existing methods, closing the exploitation/exploration loop. Lincoln Re explored new areas of risk via its prospective R&D process, using the knowledge gained to create new risk management products and services. Those products generated a loss-experience history that could be monitored and analyzed to create additional learning, closing the loop. Image Corp. and Buckman Labs linked their R&D personnel and technical specialists to their field-based marketing, sales, and technical support staffs to ensure that new products were developed with the customers' needs in mind and that customer needs were quickly and accurately communicated to the product development group. New knowledge and insights were therefore more effectively exploited in the marketplace in the form of better products, while interaction with the customers generated knowledge to guide future developments. LeaseCo aggressively attempted to explore knowledge via taking on novel leases and to exploit that learning across its other clients and markets.

Internal versus External Knowledge

A second way to orient a knowledge strategy is to describe the firm's primary sources of knowledge (Bierly and Chakrabarti 1996). Knowledge resources may lie within or outside the firm. Internal knowledge may be resident within peoples' heads; embedded in behaviors, procedures, software, and equipment; recorded in various documents; or stored in databases and online repositories. Common sources of external knowledge include publications, universities, government agencies, professional associations, personal relations, consultants, vendors, knowledge brokers, and interorganizational alliances.

Knowledge generated within the firm is especially valuable because it tends to be unique, specific, and tacitly held. It is therefore more difficult for competitors to imitate, making it strategically valuable. Knowledge from outside the firm—while more abstract, more costly to obtain, and more widely available to competitors— can provide for fresh thinking and a context for benchmarking internal knowledge. Commonly available external knowledge combined with unique internal knowledge can still result in new and unique insights. Buckman Labs, for example, maintains close links to universities, taking the generic body of microbiological knowledge and reapplying it within the specific context of its own products and customer applications. Lincoln Re has similarly obtained and reapplied knowledge through its university ties. Joint ventures provide an important means to obtain external knowledge that is tacit, has not been widely distributed, and therefore retains its competitive value (Badaracco 1991). The biotechnology industry, for example, thrives on the collaboration that occurs among firms (Powell 1998).

Many externally oriented organizations create opportunities for ongoing dialog with their customers to exchange knowledge. These mechanisms range in formality and include user groups, joint ventures, beta-testing, web sites, electronic mail, toll-free numbers, customer care centers, customers advisory boards, conferences, and social gatherings. For example, Lincoln Re maintains strong relationships with its clients through a company-sponsored user group. An advisory council and periodic conferences also provide many opportunities for Lincoln Re to gain access to valuable external customer knowledge and to share its internal knowledge regarding its products and markets. Often, firms use computer-based conferencing systems to supplement face-to-face interaction. They also are creating electronically based repositories to be used for collecting external knowledge, both informal and formal. These materials include papers and presentation slides from conferences, comments, and observations acquired in the field,

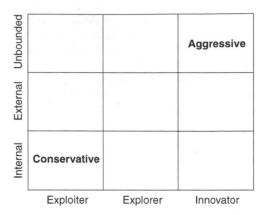

Figure 15.4

knowledge picked up at trade shows, and lessons learned from interactions with customers. Buckman Labs is quite well known for its worldwide online conferencing capability and its efforts to build customer-focused knowledge repositories.

Aggressive versus Conservative

Combining the knowledge exploitation versus exploration orientation of the firm with its internally acquired versus externally acquired orientation toward knowledge sources provides a more complete picture of a firm's knowledge strategy (figure 15.4). Firms oriented toward exploiting internal knowledge exhibit the most conservative knowledge strategy, while unbounded innovators (those that closely integrate knowledge exploration and exploitation without regard to organizational boundaries) represent the most aggressive strategy. In knowledge-intensive industries, firms that pursue an aggressive knowledge strategy tend to outperform those competitors that pursue less aggressive knowledge strategies over time (Bierly and Chakrabarti 1996).

In cases where a firm's knowledge significantly lags its competitors or the firm is defending a knowledge position, an aggressive knowledge strategy will be required to remain viable (Kim 1998). Buckman Labs, for example, prioritized its knowledge management efforts by focusing on several markets where its treatment applications knowledge lagged its current or potential competitors, although to maintain existing advantages it continually created and renewed its knowledge of all markets. It took a more aggressive knowledge strategy in those markets than in markets where its knowledge led the industry. LeaseCo claimed the premium, upscale-garment, service-intensive market as a competitive niche and aggressively sought to learn as much as possible about serving that market. Image Corp. found itself needing to aggressively acquire knowledge about digital imaging to ward off both traditional and new competitors. Lincoln Re staked out superior knowledge of risk underwriting and pricing as well as how to integrate multiple services into innovative and comprehensive risk management solutions, and it put in place an aggressive knowledge strategy to maintain this competitive differentiation.

Industry Learning Cycles

Knowledge strategy cannot be formulated in isolation of what competitors are doing. Comparing aggressive and conservative strategies, then, also requires looking at the overall flow of industry knowledge. At the industry level, there is the potential for knowledge to diffuse out from the firm and into the industry at large, where it can be absorbed by competitors. At the same time, a similar process may be occurring with other firms in the industry, creating the opportunity for the firm to absorb knowledge from the industry.

Firms taking a conservative strategy view knowledge primarily as a proprietary asset to be protected. They attempt to create barriers to its diffusion or transfer outside of the firm. Aggressive firms, however, take a Schumpeterian view of knowledge as an ongoing process of creative destruction. Rather than wait for a competitor to destroy the value of their knowledge, these firms aggressively seek to make their own knowledge obsolete, always staying one step ahead of the competition. Aggressive firms are less concerned with erecting barriers to the diffusion or transfer of knowledge; rather, they protect their knowledge resources by recruiting and developing intelligent, loyal, and committed employees and supporting them with a culture of learning, commitment, and collaboration. The firm's advantage comes from being able to absorb external knowledge and integrate it with their internal knowledge to develop new insights faster than the competition. For example, Lincoln Re's competitors were often able to acquire and imitate the underwriting guidelines Lincoln Re provided its clients. However, they were not able to replicate Lincoln Re's skilled medical and actuarial researchers, its deep understanding of

how the medical research related to managing and pricing risk, and its unique process for experimenting with that publicly available research to improve and expand its existing knowledge.

The strategic knowledge environment of an industry can be viewed as the sum of the interactions among the knowledge strategies of the individual firms in the industry. In industries with many firms pursuing conservative knowledge strategies, knowledge leaks into the industry slowly and the opportunities to learn from the industry at large may be limited. In industries with many aggressive firms, knowledge flows between individual firms and the industry at large relatively quickly. Only those firms with the best learning capability and the greatest capacity for absorbing external knowledge will survive. Lincoln Re, Buckman, Big6, and Image Corp. were all operating in industries where knowledge was changing rapidly enough that an aggressive strategy was needed just to keep up with the pace of change. Buckman Labs was faced with adding service expertise to its product and manufacturing knowledge. Lincoln Re and Big6 were selling their knowledge directly, transferring it out of the organization at a price. This opened the way for diffusion among competitors and further drove the need to aggressively and continually learn and develop new knowledge.

Positioning

Knowledge can profoundly change the way an organization positions itself in its industry and, in doing so, can radically change the organization itself. Buckman Labs exemplified this in its shift from selling chemical products to providing broad microbicidal treatment solutions. Lincoln Re similarly repositioned itself from selling reinsurance to selling its knowledge in the form of comprehensive risk management solutions. The case of Bay State Shippers provides an even more profound example. Originally a freight forwarder (a "travel agent for freight"), Bay State took responsibility for physically routing a shipment from its point of origin to its intended destination, potentially via several modes of transportation (e.g., truck, rail, ship). Using satellite systems, barcodes, and other information technologies, Bay State created the ability to track a package throughout its multimodal trip, functioning as "information central." While these tracking data were useful to customers, Bay State found a way to add significantly more value while at the same time repositioning itself from a freight handler to a knowledge broker. Bay State was sitting on a huge amount of transaction data describing point-to-point travel times for various routings and modalities. By analyzing this information and combining it with its employees' experience, it learned how to predict shipment transit times for particular routes and modalities, and it was able to learn about travel patterns in great detail. For example, it might find that particular goods shipped by train through a certain part of Iowa always ran into delays at a particular freight yard on Fridays. Bay State combined this knowledge with its ability to track shipments in real time and to create an early warning system for customers. Customers could list their shipments on a computer screen. Shipments highlighted in green were expected to deliver on time. Yellow indicated the freight was running behind forecasted time. If red, the shipment was expected to arrive late. Customers could now plan and react more intelligently. Beyond this freight control capability, Bay State was able to use its routing knowledge to recommend the most efficient and effective routing for the customer's needs, helping them to avoid de-

lays in the first place. Bay State used its superior knowledge to carve out a significant competitive advantage. In fact, Bay State (like American Airlines and its Sabre reservation system, and Lincoln Re and its Life Underwriting System) eventually saw enough value in the knowledge-based routing system to create a company to sell the system.[5]

Conclusion

Knowledge is the fundamental basis of competition. Competing successfully on knowledge requires either aligning strategy to what the organization knows or developing the knowledge and capabilities needed to support a desired strategy. Organizations must strategically assess their knowledge resources and capabilities, and they need to broadly conceptualize their knowledge strategy to address any gaps. A summary of the process is outlined in table 15.1. An organization's knowledge strategy must then be translated into an organizational and technical architecture to support knowledge creation,

TABLE 15.1 Assessing and conceptualizing knowledge resources, capabilities, and strategies

Step	Key Question	Action
1	How do you want to play the game?	Articulate desired or intended strategy
2	What do you need to know?	Articulate strategy → knowledge link
3	What *do* you know?	Create internal knowledge map
4	What is your internal knowledge gap?	Compare what you need to know to what you do know
5	What do your competitors know?	Create external (competitor/industry) knowledge map
6	What is your external knowledge gap?	Compare what you know to what your competitors know
7	What is your learning cycle?	Assess your dynamic learning capabilities and intentions
8	What are your competitors' and industry's learning cycles and capabilities?	Assess your industry's and competitors' dynamic learning capabilities and intentions
9	What is your learning gap?	Compare your dynamic learning capabilities to those of your competitors and your industry
10	What is your internal strategic gap?	Assess how your internal knowledge gap affects your current strategy
11	What is your external strategic gap?	Assess how your external knowledge gap affects your current strategy
12	What is your industry cycle strategic gap?	Assess how your dynamic learning gap affects your future strategy
13	What is your new current and future strategy?	Determine if and how your knowledge and learning gaps require a revision in strategy
14	What is your knowledge strategy?	Determine how aggressive you will be to close your knowledge gaps: —regarding exploration vs. exploitation —regarding internal vs. external sources

management, and utilization processes for closing those gaps.[6]

If knowledge management is to take hold rather than become merely a passing fad, it will have to be solidly linked to the creation of economic value and competitive advantage. This can be accomplished by grounding knowledge management within the context of business strategy. Given the state of the art in knowledge management, firms just starting to build a knowledge management infrastructure are not far behind their more established rivals. By developing the proper strategic grounding, they will be able to focus and prioritize their investments in knowledge management and come out ahead of competitors who have not grounded their efforts in strategy.

Notes

I thank Nicholas Athanassiou, Dr. Arthur DeTore (Director of Strategy and Knowledge Management, Lincoln Re), and William Habeck (CEO, TIE Logistics) for their helpful comments.

1. For a good overview of knowledge management, see Davenport and Prusak (1998).

2. For example, strategy was not identified as a motivating factor or key evaluation criterion regarding knowledge management efforts in a field study of 31 projects in 24 companies (Davenport 1998), a survey of 431 U.S. and European companies (Ruggles 1998), or a survey of 100 U.S. and European companies (Leidner 1998).

3. Image Corp., LeaseCo, and Big6 are pseudonyms.

4. While many authors distinguish (often not consistently) between capabilities and competencies, the term "capabilities" as used here is meant to include both.

5. In 1992, Bay State Shippers spun off their software product, COMMAND, into Tie Logistics, Inc. In 1993, Tie Logistics won the Computerworld Smithsonian Transportation Award for innovative use of information technology in transportation, and COMMAND was made part of the permanent Information Age exhibit at the Smithsonian National Museum of American History. C.H. Robinson Worldwide, Inc., acquired Bay State in 1994.

6. For a good discussion, see Davenport and Prusak (1998) and Zack (1999).

References

Andrews, K.R. (1971) *The Concept of Corporate Strategy.* Homewood, IL: Dow-Jones Irwin.

Badaracco, J., Jr. (1991) *The Knowledge Link: How Firms Compete through Strategic Alliances.* Boston: Harvard Business School Press.

Barney, J.B. (1991) "Firm resources and sustained competitive advantage." *Journal of Management* 17:99–120.

Barney, J.B. (1996) "The resource-based theory of the firm." *Organization Science* 7(5):469–476.

Bierly, P. and Chakrabarti, A. (1996) "Generic knowledge strategies in the U.S. pharmaceutical industry." *Strategic Management Journal* 17 (Winter):123–135.

Cohen, D. (1998) "Toward a knowledge context: report on the first annual U.C. Berkeley Forum on Knowledge and the Firm." *California Management Review* 40(3):22–39.

Cohen, W. and Leventhal, D. (1990) "Absorptive capacity: a new perspective on learning and innovation." *Administrative Science Quarterly* 35: 128–152.

Collis, D.J. and Montgomery, C.A. (1995) "Competing on resources: strategy in the 1990s." *Harvard Business Review* 73(4):118–128.

Connor, K.R. (1991) "A historical comparison of resource-based theory and five schools of thought within industrial organization economics: do we have a new theory of the firm?" *Journal of Management* 17:121–154.

Davenport, T. and Prusak, L. (1998) *Working Knowledge.* Cambridge, MA: Harvard Business School Press.

Davenport, T., De Long, D.W., and Beers, M.C. (1998) "Successful knowledge management projects." *Sloan Management Review* 39(2):43–58.

Davenport, T., Jarvenpaa, S., and Beers, M. (1996) "Improving knowledge work processes." *Sloan Management Review* 37(4):53–66.

Demsetz, H. (1998) "The theory of the firm revisited." *Journal of Law, Economics and Organization* 4(1):141–161.

Goldstein, D.K. and Zack, M.H. (1989) "The impact of marketing information supply on product managers: an organizational information processing perspective." *Office, Technology and People* 4(4):313–336.

Goodman, P. and Darr, E. (1996) "Exchanging best practices through computer-aided systems." *The Academy of Management Executive* 10(2):7–19.

Grant, R.M. (1991) "The resource-based theory of competitive advantage: implications for strategy formulation." *California Management Review* 33(3):114–135.

Grant, R.M. (1996) "Prospering in dynamically competitive environments: organizational capability as knowledge integration." *Organization Science* 7(4):375–387.

Hamel, G. and Prahalad, C.K. (1989) "Strategic intent." *Harvard Business Review* 67(3):63–76.

Kim, L. (1998) "Crisis construction and organizational learning: capability building in catching up at Hyundai Motor." *Organization Science* 9(4): 506–521.

Kogut, B. and Kulatilaka, N. (1994) "Options thinking and platform investments: investing in opportunity." *California Management Review* 36(2): 52–71.

Kogut, B. and Zander, U. (1992) "Knowledge of the firm, combinative capabilities, and the replication of technology." *Organization Science* 3(3):383–397.

Leidner, D.E. (1998) "Organization and information cultures in knowledge management initiatives." Panel presentation at the sixth European Conference on Information Systems, Aixen Provence, June.

Markides, C. (1998) "Strategic innovation in established companies." *Sloan Management Review* 39(3):31–42.

McGahan, A.M. and Porter, M.E. (1997) "How much does industry matter, really?" *Strategic Management Journal* 18:15–30.

Mintzberg, H. (1994) "The fall and rise of strategic planning." *Harvard Business Review* 72(1):107–114.

Nahapiet, J. and Ghoshal, S. (1998) "Social capital, intellectual capital, and the organizational advantage." *Academy of Management Review* 23(2):242–267.

Nelson, R. (1991) "Why do firms differ and does it matter?" *Strategic Management Journal* 12 (Winter):61–74.

Penrose, E.T. (1980) *The Theory of the Growth of the Firm.* White Plains, NY: Sharpe.

Polanyi, M. (1966) *The Tacit Dimension.* Garden City, NY: Doubleday.

Porter, M.E. (1980) *Competitive Strategy: Techniques for Analyzing Industries and Competitors.* New York: Free Press.

Powell, W.W. (1998) "Learning from collaboration: knowledge and networks in the biotechnology and pharmaceutical industries." *California Management Review* 40(3):228–240.

Prahalad, C.K. and Hamel, G. (1990) "The core competence of the corporation." *Harvard Business Review* 68(3):79–91.

Quinn, J.G. (1980) *Strategies for Change: Logical Incrementalism.* Homewood, IL: Irwin.

Quinn, J.G., Anderson, P., and Finkelstein, S. (1996) "Leveraging intellect." *Academy of Management Executive* 10(3):7–27.

Romer, P.M. (1995) "Beyond the knowledge worker." Paper presented at World Link, Davos '95, January/February.

Ruggles, R. (1998) "The state of the notion: knowledge management in practice." *California Management Review* 40(3):80–89.

Rumelt, R.P. (1991) "How much does industry matter?" *Strategic Management Journal* 12(3):167–185.

Spender, J.-C. (1994) "Organizational knowledge, collective practice and Penrose rents." *International Business Review* 3(4):353–367.

Spender, J.-C. (1996) "Organizational knowledge, learning and memory: three concepts in search of a theory." *Journal of Organizational Change Management* 9(1):63–78.

Teece, D.J. (1984) "Economic analysis and strategic management." *California Management Review* 26(3):87–110.

Teece, D.J. (1998) "Capturing value from knowledge assets: the new economy, markets for know-how, and intangible assets." *California Management Review* 40(3):55–79.

Teece, D.J., Pisano, G., and Shuen, A. (1997) "Dynamic capabilities and strategic management." *Strategic Management Journal* 18(7):509–533.

Utterback, J.M. (1994) *Mastering the Dynamics of Innovation: How Companies Can Seize Opportunities in the Face of Technological Change.* Boston: Harvard Business School Press.

Weick, K.E. (1987) "Substitutes for strategy," in D.J. Teece (ed.), *The Competitive Challenge: Strategies for Industrial Innovation and Renewal*, pp. 221–233. Cambridge, MA: Ballinger.

Winter, S.G. (1987) "Knowledge and competence as strategic assets," in D.J. Teece (ed.), *The Competitive Challenge: Strategies for Industrial Innovation and Renewal*, pp. 159–184. Cambridge, MA: Ballinger.

Zack, M.H. (2002) "An architecture for managing explicated knowledge." *Sloan Management Review*, in press.

EPILOGUE: DEVELOPING A KNOWLEDGE STRATEGY

This epilogue presents additional observations and findings I have made as I continue to research the knowledge–strategy link first described in the preceding article in 1999. First I discuss the extent to which this link appears to be missing in many of today's corporations. I then clarify the term knowledge strategy and attempt to distinguish it from other similar terms in use today. Next I raise the need for taking an external view toward benchmarking a firm's knowledge against its competitors to identify knowledge opportunities and threats, rather than focusing only on internal strengths and weaknesses, and expand the above discussion on strategic learning. Last, I close with some implications of the knowledge strategy approach for market segmentation, organizational structure, new product development, and strategic alliances.

The Basic Premise Revisited

In introducing the knowledge strategy framework, I made two assertions in the introduction above:

1. The link between knowledge management and business strategy, while often talked about, has rarely been put into practice.
2. Executives are in need of a framework to help them understand the knowledge–strategy link.

The evidence from further research in this area continues to overwhelmingly support those assertions. While many of the organizations recognize the importance of developing a strategic rationale for investing in knowledge creation and exploitation, they continue to be, for the most part, driven by focused, short-term, first-order outcomes rather than by broader, longer term strategic goals.

Those organizations that do attempt to make the knowledge–strategy link typically begin by developing a knowledge management initiative and then trying to work "backward" to determine its impact on the organization's strategy. They assume that knowledge management is "strategic" because it potentially improves knowledge creation and sharing. They frame knowledge strategy generically, in terms of knowledge exploration/creation versus exploitation/codification (March 1991, Hansen et al. 1999) and the configuration of organizational and technological resources to support these orientations. These categories, however, are process oriented and do not speak to the issue of *what* knowledge needs to be exploited or created. This results in organizations attempting to share what they know without first understanding what they need to share. They are attacking their knowledge *process* gaps without considering their strategic knowledge *content* gaps. This is not to say that knowledge processing and organizational learning are not strategic capabilities with their own intrinsic value. However, the mere act of processing knowledge itself does not guarantee strategic advantage.

As an example, consider Image Corp. described above. They were doing an excellent job managing the exploration and exploitation of knowledge related to physical/analog cameras and film. They had an appropriate culture, a useful technology, and well-designed knowledge management roles and processes. They judged their knowledge management initiatives a success— and from a process perspective they were. Their competitive strategy, however, called for a rapid move to digital imaging. Unfortunately, the organization did not know much about how to develop, manufacture, distribute, fund, price, or service information systems hardware and software—the foundation of digital photography. And they were not systematically managing the acquisition, creation, or sharing of this missing knowledge. While they were enjoying a near-term success, they were facing a potential future catastrophe. In the same vein, I studied a Fortune 50 firm whose strategy was to move from an engineering to a marketing focus without having the necessary marketing knowledge and skills. They did not systematically diagnose or manage this knowledge gap, and their knowledge management initiatives were focused elsewhere.

Similarly, I observed many firms whose strategy dictated a move to an e-business model without the requisite knowledge and skills or a knowledge management initiative to address those knowledge gaps. Others were migrating from selling products to selling knowledge-based services and solutions, without first understanding what they knew (or did not know) about being a service provider, or identifying the unique value (if any) to be found in their existing knowledge. As explained by executives of one organization:

> While you try to wrap as much knowledge around product as possible, it's different when you're solving customer problems throughout the whole application process as opposed to focusing on just [the product].

> You might have understood everything about this [product], but let's get away from the [product] and figure out how you apply it so that the customer gains an advantage through the application. What is it about that product that the customer sees value in, or how can you enhance that product so that the customer gains benefit?

Again, their knowledge management programs, while effective from a process and infrastructure perspective, were not addressing key strategic content gaps. In contrast, the knowledge strategy framework suggests that firms start with strategy and its link to knowledge before initiating formal knowledge management programs—let the firm's strategy guide the management of its intellectual resources and capabilities.

I have found generally that the degree to which firms are attempting to link their intellectual resources and capabilities to strategy is associated with the extent to which their core product or service is knowledge based. For example, consulting firms—in the business of selling knowledge—will tend to consider managing knowledge as a strategic issue more than will firms producing physical products or services. However, surprisingly, I even have observed several consulting firms and others selling knowledge-based products that have not directly linked the management of their intellectual capital with their strategic processes.

One indicator of the degree to which knowledge is viewed strategically is the organizational linkage between those responsible for strategy and those responsible for knowledge management. I have found that the most strategically aware organizations have tightly integrated the responsibility for strategic management and knowledge management. For example, at Lincoln Re described above, the same executive is responsible for both corporate strategy and knowledge management. At Xerox, the corporate knowledge management function reports to the office of strategy. Others have created separate organizational units linked via the strategic planning process. Most, however, maintain separate groups that may have little to no ongoing communication or coordination between them.

A secondary indicator of the degree to which an organization views knowledge strategically is the extent of public relations directed toward building an image of the company as a knowledge-based organization. One organization I observed employed a public relations staff to manage external communication to ensure a consistent message supporting the image of the company as knowledge based. They reinforced this in their annual report, press releases, speaking opportunities at conferences, trade journal articles, and other communication outlets.

Clarifying the Term "Knowledge Strategy"

The term knowledge strategy is coming into greater use but is being used in various ways in the literature and the practitioner community. To bring some precision to the term, I make two distinctions. The first is between knowledge strategy and knowledge management strategy. They are not the same. *Knowledge strategy*, as used in my article above, implies a notion of knowledge-based strategy, that is, competitive strategy built around a firm's intellectual resources and capabilities. Once a firm identifies opportunities, threats, strengths, and weaknesses related to its intellectual resources and capabilities, then actions it may take to manage knowledge gaps or surpluses (e.g., recruiting for particular skills, building online document repositories, establishing communities of practice, acquiring firms, licensing technologies, etc.) are guided by a *knowledge management strategy*. Knowledge strategy is oriented toward understanding what knowledge is strategic and why. Knowledge management strategy guides and defines the processes and infrastructure (organizational and technological) for managing knowledge. Knowledge management strategy typically includes broad generic components (e.g., emphasizing tacit vs. explicit knowledge, knowledge exploration vs. exploitation, or organizational vs. technical mechanisms for knowledge exchange) as well as those that are firm specific (e.g., support for globally distributed field technicians). Regardless, it should focus action on strategic knowledge gaps or surpluses.

The second distinction is between knowledge strategy and strategic knowledge management. To effectively formulate strategy, firms need to know things about themselves (their strengths and weaknesses regarding their resources and capabilities) and their competitive environment (opportunities and threats). The processes and infrastructures firms employ to acquire, create, and share knowledge for formulating strategy I call *strategic knowledge management*. It is a type of knowledge management. It is *not* knowledge strategy. It involves all the things we have come to associate with knowledge management, such as communities of practice, information technologies, and knowledge management roles. But the knowledge management activities are directed toward providing knowledge for formulating strategy and making strategic decisions. For example, one company I observed created a formal strategic planning community that included people representing various functional and geographical units of the organization, supported by an online discussion area and document repository. Another created an online mechanism to gather competitive environmental knowledge from field technicians and sales people and make it available to those formulating strategy. In both cases, they were engaged in strategic knowledge management, the results of which could then be used to formulate a knowledge strategy.

A third distinction can be made between strategic knowledge management and operational (or tactical) knowledge management. In addition to the knowledge needed to formulate strategy, firms need to know and know how to do particular things well in order to execute their strategy. This may include servicing customers better than their competitors can or building higher quality products. The knowledge required to support more efficient and effective operations is the focus of traditional knowledge management. I call this type of knowledge management *operational knowledge management.* Operational knowledge management supports the day-to-day activities and processes needed to execute a firm's strategy. For example, one organization I observed created formalized communities of practice around various aspects of automobile assembly. Another built an online capability for salespeople to share tips and techniques across sales regions. A consulting firm made its engagement documents accessible to other consultants. Another provided an online mechanism for locating expertise across the organization when trying to solve a client's problem. These are the familiar knowledge management examples and initiatives that we read about. They should be aligned with the firm's business strategy to provide long-term value. Firms, therefore, must practice effective *strategic* knowledge management to enable informed strategic decision making. They must practice effective *operational* knowledge management to ensure that they bring all required knowledge to bear on executing their strategy. However, to start, they must formulate a knowledge strategy to understand what knowledge they should be managing.

The Internal versus the External View

Most firms have directed their knowledge management activities toward understanding and sharing what they currently know. The premise is that they have available somewhere all the knowledge they need. Their approach is to identify what they know and provide a mechanism for locating and sharing that knowledge. This usually starts with some type of knowledge mapping process. Knowledge mapping for that purpose is an operationally focused adjunct of knowledge management. The strategic use of a knowledge map, however, is not merely to catalog existing knowledge, but to map existing knowledge against what is required to formulate and execute the organization's strategy. Further, the map can be used to evaluate how an organization's knowledge compares with its competitors. If we think of strategy as defending *knowledge* positions rather than product/market positions, then competitive knowledge benchmarking is crucial for evaluating the firm's competitive position. Where a firm holds a strong strategic knowledge position, it may be prudent to invest to maintain that position. Where it holds a weak knowledge position, it may be prudent to invest to gain strength. These knowledge management decisions must be made within the context of knowledge-based competitive opportunities and threats.

Most organizations I have observed do not attempt to systematically understand what their competitors know. Some organizations have a unit engaged in business intelligence or similar scanning function. However, business intelligence typically is not part of the knowledge management function; therefore the benchmarking of an organization's knowledge against competitors is rarely done. Further, most business intelligence functions attempt to identify what competitors are doing, not what they know. However, it is possible to infer competitor knowledge based on their actions, products, and services. One company I observed learned about competitors' stages of knowledge by debriefing people they hired who had worked for the competition or had interviewed with them. According to one senior executive, "I know [competitor X] is not interested in a lot of the tools that we're using in sales and marketing because the person that's designed most of those is somebody that we hired from them. He had these great ideas, and they said, 'We're not going that way.' So I know I'm way out in front of them on that."

Knowing versus Learning

The article above identified one source of the strategic value of knowledge as lying in its sustainable uniqueness based on increasing returns. Applying the notions of time compression, asset mass efficiencies, and asset complementarity (Dierickx and Cool 1989) to intellectual resources, I discuss how knowledge advantage is sustainable if the knowledge-superior firm continues to learn from experience at least as well as its competitors. The article, while addressing issues of exploration and learning, goes on to focus more on knowledge superiority than on learning superiority. However, the dynamics of firm learning capabilities and industry learning cycles need more attention (especially in these turbulent times of e-business). Further thought and field observations have led me to propose that learning superiority will dominate knowledge superiority. A firm that does not have superior knowledge but is a better learner than the knowledge-superior firm eventually should attain knowledge superiority. A firm that has strategically superior knowledge and is a superior learner should be able to maintain its dominant competitive position.

Therefore, firms need to focus as much on their strategic learning gaps as on their knowledge gaps. And so the gap analysis should focus not only on what the firm needs to know versus what it does know, but also on how much, how rapidly, and how effectively it needs to learn to execute its strategy and defend its knowledge position.

Learning must be externally benchmarked not only against particular competitors, but also against the firm's industry in general. In the article I raised the notion of a learning cycle for a firm and an industry. Firms develop and transfer knowledge among themselves within their industry, similar to Nonaka's (1994) framework whereby tacit knowledge developed within one organizational unit is made explicit, transferred to another unit, applied within the new unit, and thereby made tacit again. An organization develops tacit knowledge as a by-product of its activities. This knowledge may be made explicit to facilitate its transfer among other units of the organization. In doing so, it may leak out of the organization into the industry at large. At the same time, the organization may be absorbing knowledge leaking out of other firms within its industry and internalizing that knowledge through its reapplication within the firm. Each firm in an industry has some capability for engaging in this learning cycle. It may be more or less capable of identifying its own tacit knowledge, explicating and sharing it within the firm,

limiting its transfer out of the firm, absorbing external knowledge from the industry, and reapplying that external knowledge in some unique and strategic way.

The strategic knowledge environment of an industry can be viewed as the sum of the interactions among the knowledge strategies of the individual firms in the industry. Firms taking a conservative approach to knowledge strategy tend to be more internally focused and attempt to create barriers to knowledge transferring outside their organization. The objective is to financially exploit the knowledge for as long as possible. If the industry is characterized by conservative knowledge-strategy firms, then little knowledge moves through the industry and little is available to be absorbed from the outside. We can characterize the industry, then, as one having slow learning cycles. A conservative strategy may make sense for firms in industries where knowledge diffuses slowly, has a relatively long "shelf life," and therefore provides the opportunity to exploit that knowledge via explication and reuse without great exposure to imitation by competitors.

Barriers to knowledge diffusion may take several forms (Teece 1998). Strong patents may provide sufficient protection in some industries, for example, pharmaceuticals. Barriers may also occur in industries that are based on technologies whose transfer is "sticky." Stickiness may occur when the technology does not adhere to an industry standard or where no standard exists, making adoption risky, for example, in electronics (e.g., the introduction of 56K modems or VHS vs. Betamax video formats). It may also arise where the technology lacks well-defined interfaces to other firms' existing technologies, is embedded in a complex web of complementary technologies, or requires tight coupling to the other firms' existing technologies, making adoption difficult and complex (e.g., enterprisewide information system software packages). Adoption may be costly or diffusion irrelevant where knowledge is highly specific to the source firm's context for application and use. And some knowledge may be just too confusing for the rest of the industry to understand and adopt (Lippman and Rumelt 1982, Reed and DeFillippi 1990). For example, LeaseCo, described above, was unable to explain its pricing scheme to a competitor it was attempting to acquire. The approach was so different from that of the industry that the competitor could not make sense of the economic framework and assumptions on which it was based.[1]

Firms adopting an aggressive knowledge strategy accept the premise that continual learning is the key to maintaining a knowledge advantage. They are less concerned with what they know at any point in time, assuming they or their competitors will render that knowledge obsolete in the near future. For example, CapitalOne has made this premise an explicit part of its strategy. Rather than concentrate on creating barriers to knowledge diffusing into the industry, they focus more on maintaining its capacity to learn and to absorb knowledge from the industry. Organizationally, they recognize the value of the tacit knowledge of its employees and focus on retaining them via an attractive culture and work environment. While the leaner, more abstract explicit knowledge may diffuse out of the firm, the richer tacit knowledge providing the firm its sustainable knowledge advantage still remains within the firm. That tacit knowledge is what enables the firm to learn faster and to develop more creative and valuable insights than its competitors.

Having strong barriers to knowledge diffusion or operating in a slow-cycle industry does not preclude firms taking a more aggressive knowledge strategy. However, it suggests that in that context a moderately aggressive knowledge strategy may provide sufficient advantage. For example, knowledge diffusion in LeaseCo's industry occurred slowly. LeaseCo therefore had an incentive to invest in and to explicate its strategic knowledge because it could exploit this knowledge over a long enough period to recoup its investment while having low exposure to knowledge diffusion. LeaseCo in fact captured much of its knowledge in electronic documents and a computer-based decision support system, enabling the knowledge to be easily, efficiently, and consistently distributed to and used by a wide range of employees. It had perhaps a more aggressive knowledge strategy than needed and took more knowledge-building risks than required to compete in their industry, a reflection of LeaseCo's culture and the CEO's personal desire to "keep things interesting." The result, however, was a clear and persistent dominance in its markets accompanied by high profit margins relative to the industry.

In industries characterized by aggressive knowledge strategy firms, knowledge moves through the industry rapidly. We can characterize the industry, then, as one having rapid learning cycles. In general, more knowledge in total should be available for absorption from outside the firm than the amount diffusing out of any individual firm. However, only those firms with the best learning capability and the greatest capacity for absorbing external knowledge will benefit the most. Firms implementing an aggressive knowledge strategy from a strong existing knowledge position supplemented by an effective learning capability should gain more knowledge than they lose and be able to maintain their strong knowledge position.

Ultra-aggressive firms proactively transfer their knowledge out of the firm to accelerate the learning cycle. One approach is to transfer out only part of the knowledge, creating a knowledge dependency on the remainder of the knowledge that is more highly protected. This is similar to the strategy taken by software companies that protect their main program source code but distribute sufficient knowledge of the program's workings to enable others to develop compatible programs with seamless interfaces. Other firms offer their knowledge in hopes of creating or influencing de facto industry standards. An example of perhaps the most aggressive strategy is that of the open-source movement used, for example, to develop the Linux computer operating system, which makes public the core source code to take advantage of those innovations others may develop.[2]

A firm's strategy, by placing it within an industry, also places it within some industry learning cycle and therefore determines the learning capabilities it must maintain. Likewise, a shift in business strategy can move firms to industries with learning cycles different than they are used to. Even having adequate knowledge to enter a new competitive position may not be sufficient if the learning capability of the firm is inadequate. For example, Image Corp., facing a major technological discontinuity, was shifting from the more conservative learning cycle of the physical consumer goods industry to the highly aggressive industry learning cycle of computer software and systems.

In industries characterized by aggressive innovation cycles, firms may have to adopt an aggressive knowledge strategy or fall by the wayside. Firms without a learning capability, the ability to understand, acquire, and absorb industry knowledge, or the knowledge management infrastructure to support unbounded innovation may need to search for a more compatible strategic position.

Knowledge-Based Customer Segmentation

The focus on strategic learning has resulted in several organizations I have observed changing the notion of customer segmentation from a product/market orientation to one focused on knowledge and learning. That is, they categorize customers not by what the firm can sell them, but by the value of the learning opportunity those potential customers may provide. Customers might then be pursued not for the current revenue they could generate, but for the opportunity to learn how to provide new products and services leading to additional revenue in the future. A "good" customer would be one that requires a significant amount of customer-specific knowledge to service, yet provides a long-term return sufficient to recoup the investment in learning required. If the relationship is one of a contractual nature (e.g., leasing, insurance, real estate, auditing, and various services, etc.), then the objective is to acquire the contract (even at a potential initial loss) and learn enough about serving the customer to preclude less knowledgeable competitors from obtaining the business when up for rebid. If the relationship is noncontractual, then the goal is to become sufficiently more knowledgeable about the customer than are competitors and to combine that knowledge with the product or service, giving the customer an incentive not to do business with competitors. Because of the increasing returns to knowledge, if the firm is at least as good at learning as its competitors (and is willing and able to turn its learning into action [Pfeffer and Sutton 2000]), it should continue to retain the customer's loyalty as long as serving the customer requires unique, inimitable, and nonsubstitutable knowledge. Firms not taking a customer-specific learning-based approach will find customers having less unique knowledge requirements to be more suitable.

Some customers, particularly those under contractual relationships, may provide enough revenue potential that they directly pay back the investment in learning. For example, Buckman Labs, described above, obtained a sole-source contract to manage the chemical consumption of the Fort Howard paper company. This is one of the first contracts in the industry where the supplier takes the risk for managing the customer's cost of operations. Typically, chemical companies maximize revenue by selling as much product as possible. Key strategic knowledge has traditionally been product oriented, including the ability to manufacture, sell, and distribute a low-cost, high-quality product. While the industry has been migrating to value-added services, the Buckman/Fort Howard deal has taken this to its extreme. Because Buckman is paid a flat rate based on production volume, Buckman now has an incentive to *minimize* the amount of chemical sold. Profitability now depends on applying its knowledge of the customer's total manufacturing system and how to run it efficiently, not merely knowledge of its own products. In fact, Buckman, to maximize mill performance (and its own profitability), may have to provide competitors' products in certain cases where it does not carry a needed chemical.

In addition to customer-specific learning, most learning-intensive customers provide the ability to reapply that unique knowledge elsewhere with other potential customers. For example, Lincoln Re contracts to reinsure difficult or novel risks so that it can learn how to develop new products and markets for these new classes of risk management. Its unique knowledge and learning opportunities give it an advantage over competitors in those new markets.

Knowledge-Based Organization Design

Organizations are typically designed to maximize communication, coordination, and interaction among those performing similar or interdependent tasks. Knowledge-focused organizations, however, seek opportunities to maximize communication, coordination, and interaction among units to create knowledge synergies. For example, an information technology industry research firm I studied (Zack 1996) originally created separate organization units around its various product and service domains (e.g., data warehousing, client-server computing, and groupware). However, it realized that the knowledge being created within various units could be combined to generate new insights and, ultimately, new research products for its clients. For example, knowledge management technology represents the intersection of many existing areas, such as business intelligence, intranets, online learning, data mining, and groupware. By bringing traditional units together into "virtual" lines of business, the firm was able to create entirely new sets of knowledge that could be spun off into new products.

Similarly, units may be combined because they provide better learning opportunities together than when separated by products or markets. For example, public accounting firms have traditionally organized by function: tax, audit, and consulting. However, some are finding that by bringing these functions together by customer or industry, they can create greater insights into customers' problems and requirements than each can individually.[3]

Knowledge Surpluses

The knowledge strategy framework also accommodates a positive knowledge gap—a situation where a firm knows "more" than it needs given its current strategy. This suggests the firm has knowledge it is not exploiting fully. The typical case is where firms hold patents they are neither using nor licensing. Patent management has become more active recently (Rivette and Klein 1999). However, again I did not observe many cases where firms systematically considered whether or not they could further exploit their tacit or nonpatented knowledge in new products or markets. They may do this, but it is not explicitly or directly linked to the strategic planning process.

Knowledge Alliances

I observed several firms engaged in a significant level of alliance activity. However, the alliances, while often made to acquire knowledge, skills, and technologies, were not mapped to the firm's strategic knowledge gaps. Again, those responsible for formulating alliances were not connected to those responsible for managing the firm's intellectual resources and capabilities.

Conclusion

If one accepts the premise that knowledge is the (or at least one of the) most strategic resources of a firm, then a firm' s business strategy should reflect the role of knowledge in helping the firm to compete. Once the link between strategy and knowledge is defined, then other aspects of strategic management such as resource allocation, organization design, product development, and market segmentation can be configured to bolster knowledge strengths, reduce knowledge weaknesses, capitalize on knowledge-based competitive opportunities, and mitigate knowledge-based competitive threats.

Where strategic knowledge is strong, knowledge management can focus on enabling knowledge sharing and distribution, and ensuring that learning is focused on maintaining a strong competitive knowledge position. Where opportunities abound, knowledge management can focus on exploiting the firm's "knowledge platform" by deriving new products or services from or by locating new markets for its knowledge. Where weaknesses exist, knowledge management must focus on acquiring knowledge, for example, through training, recruiting, or alliances. Where threats loom, knowledge management must focus on providing sufficient learning opportunities and capabilities to strengthen the firm's knowledge position. In all cases, a firm's strategic agenda and competitive context should drive the priorities for knowledge management.

Notes

1. It may have been that the pricing scheme was so illogical and ill-conceived that no firm would be expected to understand it. However, in this case, LeaseCo's unique approach proved to provide a significant competitive advantage, enabling it to profitably service several markets without encountering significant competition.

2. For the rationale behind the open source movement, see Raymond (1998).

3. On the other hand, they are constrained, of course, by the SEC's concern with objectivity, especially as it relates to firms auditing the work of their tax and consulting divisions.

References

Dierickx, I. and Cool, K. (1989) "Asset stock accumulation and sustainability of competitive advantage," *Management Science* 35(12):1504.

Hansen, M.T., Nohria, N., and Tierney, T. (1999) "What's your strategy for managing knowledge?" *Harvard Business Review* 77(2):106.

Lippman, S.A., and Rumelt, R.P. (1982) "Uncertain imitability: an analysis of interfirm differences in efficiency under competition." *Bell Journal of Economics* 13:418–438.

March, J.G. (1991) "Exploration and exploitation in organizational learning." *Organization Science* 2(1):71–87.

Nonaka, I. (1994) "A dynamic theory of organizational knowledge creation." *Organization Science* 5(1):14–37.

Pfeffer, J. and Sutton, R. (2000) *The Knowing-Doing Gap: How Smart Companies Turn Knowledge into Action*. Boston: Harvard Business School Press.

Raymond, E.S. "The cathedral and the bazaar." 1998/05/13 17:29:31. Available at http://sagan.earthspace.net/~esr/writings/cathedral-bazaar/cathedral-bazaar.html.

Reed, R. and DeFillippi, R.J. (1990) "Causal ambiguity, barriers to imitation, and sustainable competitive advantage." *Academy of Management Review* 15(1):88–102.

Rivett, K. and Kline, D. (1999) *Rembrandts in the Attic: Unlocking the Hidden Value of Patents*. Boston: Harvard Business School Press.

Teece, D.J. (1998) "Capturing value from knowledge assets: the new economy, markets for know-how, and intangible assets." *California Management Review* 40(3):55–79.

Zack, M.H. (1996) "Electronic publishing: a product architecture perspective." *Information and Management* 31(2):75–86.

16

Aligning Human Resource Management Practices and Knowledge Strategies

A Theoretical Framework

Paul E. Bierly III and Paula Daly

According to a knowledge-based view of organizations, the principal function of a firm is the creation, integration, and application of knowledge (Grant 1996, Spender 1994, Nonaka 1994, Conner and Prahalad 1996). The essence of strategy, the development of sustainable competitive advantages, can then be viewed as the identification, development, and application of key resources, and in most cases the resource that ultimately leads to a sustainable competitive advantage is the firm's unique knowledge base (Grant 1996, Barney 1991, Peteraf 1993). This *knowledge base* comprises the firm's intellectual capital, which can be viewed as the tangible and intangible knowledge, experience, and skills of employees in an organization. The set of strategic choices addressing knowledge creation in an organization comprise the firm's *knowledge strategy*, which provides the firm with guidelines for developing intellectual capital and therefore creating competitive advantage (Bierly and Chakrabarti 1996a, Zack 1999). For any firm, the best of all possible worlds would be *not* having to make strategic choices due to resource con-

straints. This is seldom the case, and therefore most firms must carefully evaluate their strategic choices in order to allocate resources in a way that maximizes their knowledge base. As with other strategy typologies (e.g., Porter 1980), for each type of knowledge strategy there should be internal consistency between strategic actions and other organizational practices and systems. Most important, for a knowledge strategy to be successful, it must be properly aligned with the human resource management (HRM) practices of the firm.

Many researchers in the area of strategic HRM have discussed the importance of having HRM practices support a firm's strategy. For example, Schuler and Jackson (1987) contend that HRM practices can create or enhance competitive advantage by fostering and reinforcing role behaviors that help to lower costs and/or strengthen product differentiation. They successfully illustrate how different practices could support each of Porter's (1980) generic strategies of low cost and differentiation. Snell (1992) also views HRM as a source of competitive advantage and argues

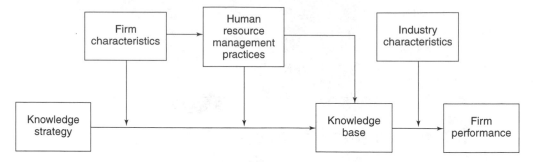

Figure 16.1 Moderating effects of human resource management practices on the relationship between knowledge strategies and performance.

that managers should link existing human resource practices to the strategic posture of firms. Lado and Wilson (1994) use a resource-based view of the firm to examine how HRM systems can facilitate the development and utilization of organizational competencies or inhibit exploitation of, even possibly destroy, these competencies. However, an extensive literature review has shown that no other researchers have examined the potential benefits of the alignment of HRM and organizational knowledge strategies.

Theoretical Model

The basic premise of our model is that a firm can enhance its knowledge base, and thereby positively affect firm performance, when HRM practices are congruent with the firm's knowledge strategy. The knowledge base of the firm will positively affect overall organizational effectiveness through the creation of sustainable competitive advantages. Internal and external factors can also moderate this process. Firm characteristics, such as firm size, structure, and culture, will influence the choice of HRM practices and will determine how a specific knowledge strategy changes the firm's knowledge base. Certain industry characteristics, such as the market structure and the strength of its existing regime of appropriability, will determine how the evolution of a firm's knowledge base will lead to superior performance. Our overall model is depicted in figure 16.1.

Knowledge Strategy

In its basic form, a knowledge strategy can be viewed as a firm's set of strategic choices regarding two knowledge domains: (1) the creation or acquisition of new knowledge and (2) the ability to leverage existing knowledge to create new organizational products and processes. We propose a typology of knowledge strategies based upon these two core dimensions, as displayed in figure 16.2.

The most crucial element of a firm's knowledge strategy is whether the firm focuses more of its resources on generating new, radical knowledge or on incrementally enhancing the existing knowledge base. According to Argyris and Schon (1978), organizations tend to focus on one of two distinctly different types of learning processes, single-loop or double-loop. Those organizations that strive to incrementally increase the current knowledge base typically do so within an existing frame of reference, thus engaging in single-loop learning. In contrast, organizations that seek out new, radical knowledge must challenge existing assumptions, values, and mental models in order to move forward, a process Argyris and Schon call double-loop learning.

March (1991) also addressed the trade-offs associated with either (but not both) a radical or

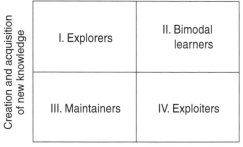

Figure 16.2 A typology of firm knowledge strategies.

incremental knowledge strategy. The continuous and incremental exploitation of current knowledge maximizes profits in the short run, whereas the exploration of radical new knowledge is more likely to maximize long-term success. Pursuing a strategy of exploration entails higher costs and increased risk for a firm, but is more likely to lead to a sustainable competitive advantage. However, concentrating resources too heavily on exploration may prevent firms from reaping the benefits that come from developing these knowledge breakthroughs. Focusing on exploration tends to slow down the developing and refining of skills and processes associated with the firm's current competencies. A strong commitment to an exploitation strategy entails trade-offs as well. According to March (1991), organizations that focus on incremental knowledge gain may find themselves experts in areas that have become obsolete, getting better and better at things that customers no longer value.

Few firms are successful at developing both radical and incremental knowledge, primarily due to limited resources within the firm (Levinthal and March 1993). Explicitly focusing on either exploration or exploitation as a means of enhancing the knowledge base generally implies not focusing on the other approach. As researchers (e.g., Volberda 1996, Hedlund 1994) have pointed out, focusing on new, radical knowledge and focusing on incrementally enhancing a current knowledge base often require very different types of organizational cultures, skills, and structures.

Explorers

Explorers, in quadrant 1 of figure 16.2, are firms that excel at developing new, radical knowledge but are not strong at exploiting existing knowledge. They continually try to "hit the home run." Explorers will be most successful in industries that have strong regimes of appropriability. That is, they will be successful when they can prevent others from imitating them and utilize first-mover advantages through long lead times, an effective patent system, the establishment of a reputation as an industry leader, and the capture of critical supply and distribution channels (Lieberman and Montgomery 1988). To be successful, explorers need to recruit, select, and develop individuals who are highly creative and routinely think "outside the box." They typically have effective product champions who can push new ideas past organizational resistance, and an organizational culture that promotes risk

taking and accepts failure. According to March (1991), an internal environment that fosters exploration incorporates relatively slow socialization of new organizational members and has moderate employee turnover. This environment promotes fresh new ideas that challenge conventional wisdom, without detrimental side effects such as job insecurity.

Exploiters

Exploiters, in quadrant 4 of figure 16.2, are firms that successfully exploit existing knowledge areas but are not effective in generating radically new knowledge. These firms are excellent at refining and leveraging existing knowledge, and focus on becoming very efficient at current practices. Exploiters typically stress flexibility throughout their organizational structure, systems, and human resource practices in order to increase their adaptability. Total quality management and continuous improvement techniques are often useful tools for exploiters. In relatively mature industries where efficiency and cost reduction are crucial and new advances are less common, the exploitation strategy is generally successful. It enables the firm to develop a competitive advantage by refining existing knowledge areas, thus reducing concerns regarding competitors' advances in the firm's area of expertise. The exploiter strategy is not a good fit in very dynamic industries where competitors frequently introduce radically new innovations.

Bimodal Learners

Bimodal learners, in quadrant 2 of figure 16.2, are firms that excel at developing new, radical knowledge but are also strong at exploiting existing knowledge. These are the rare paradoxical companies that can be either (a) an "ambidextrous organization" (Tushman and O'Reilly 1996) that successfully goes both directions simultaneously, with multiple cultures within the organization, or (b) a "chameleon organization" that rapidly changes focus back and forth from exploration to exploitation, as the environment changes. Instead of fitting the typical molds of explorers or exploiters, bimodal learners possess the seemingly contradictory skills and competencies of both. They can be creative and pragmatic, loose and tight, chaotic and efficient. They allow substantial freedom yet maintain control. These companies have complex organizational cultures and structures that not only accept conflict but thrive on it. Flexible organizational forms (Volberda 1996), modular organizational structures (Sanchez and Mahoney 1996), and N-form organizations (Hedlund 1994) have been proposed to manage such a paradox within an organization, mostly by designing the organization to facilitate knowledge transfer and integration. Large companies usually have an advantage over small companies in being bimodal learners because large companies have access to the resources required to have a more complex structure and are better able to manage multiple subcultures.

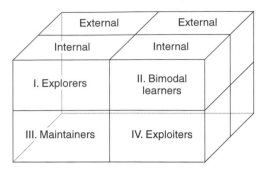

Figure 16.3 An extended typology of firm knowledge strategies.

Maintainers

Maintainers, in quadrant 3 of figure 16.2, are firms that do not excel at developing new, radical knowledge and are not strong at exploiting existing knowledge. In other words, they are poor learners and are content to stay where they are and defend their current position. They do not follow an aggressive approach to expanding the firm's knowledge base. Companies in this category focus on maintaining their current knowledge level to best serve existing customers. The focus is on "tried-and-true" products, practices, and processes. An effort is made not to "tinker with" the products and processes that have brought the company success. Typically, these companies have a strong history and emphasize tradition and stability when training employees. The obvious problem with this strategy is that there is no creation of a new competitive advantage. The only situation where this strategy can be implemented over a long period of time is in a very stable industry where a company already has some type of competitive advantage well established, such as strong brand name or superior location. Most maintainers will eventually face a period of decline and will be faced with the difficult challenge of radically changing their knowledge strategy and corporate culture.

Internally versus Externally Sourced Learning

Within each knowledge strategy type, firms may be further classified according to their primary source of knowledge, internal or external. Internal learning is the creation, integration, and dispersal of knowledge within the boundaries of the firm. External learning refers to a two-step process in which organizational members are exposed to knowledge from an outside source, and that information is then transferred to other members inside the organization. To excel at both internal and external learning would be the ideal for most firms, yet few achieve this goal. Limited resources, lack of managerial attention, and the specific nature of a firm's culture generally predispose the firm to either internal or external learning. For example, firms that excel at benchmarking (gathering external information about industry leaders) may become experts at product and/or process improvement within a specific frame of reference, but may lack the creativity and outside-the-box thinking required to internally generate new ideas. Conversely, firms that develop a strong sense of pride in being leaders in innovation in a particular field may be skeptical of, and resistant to, external sources of information. Thus, the two-factor typology developed above can be expanded to include this third dimension (source of learning), as illustrated in figure 16.3: explorers, exploiters, bimodal learners, and maintainers are further differentiated by having a primarily external or primarily internal learning focus.

Which type of learning is most crucial to the development of core competencies, competitive advantages, and superior profits? That depends upon the unique nature and goals of the organization. For a core competency to be unique and inimitable, it must be internally developed, not obtained from an outside source that is also available to competitors. Additionally, there are certain types of knowledge that are inherently internal. Systemic knowledge, which is defined as knowledge that is complexly integrated with multiple knowledge areas in the organization, is tacit in nature. It must be developed internal to the firm, allowing firm members to better understand and control the development process

(Chesbrough and Teece 1996). The tacit nature of systemic knowledge essentially precludes its being obtained from an outside source. Successful internal learning requires organizational systems and culture that promote and reward the expression of creative new ideas, and a skilled labor pool that has the ability to initiate new ideas.

A strong focus on external learning also provides several potential advantages to a firm. External knowledge sources allow the firm to develop a broader knowledge base and to monitor and evaluate technological advances. A broader knowledge base enables greater strategic flexibility and adaptability in rapidly changing environments (Bierly and Chakrabarti 1996b, Grant 1996). An additional benefit is reduced costs, since there is less "reinventing the wheel." The skills required to excel at external learning are (a) expertise in external monitoring (e.g., benchmarking); (b) an ability to understand, value, and apply external knowledge (which Cohen and Levinthal [1990] refer to as absorptive capacity); and (c) skill at integrating the external knowledge with existing, internal knowledge. However, overreliance on external learning has a serious drawback. Failure to develop internal sources of knowledge may degrade a firm's internal learning skills to the extent that it is difficult to maintain core competencies and sustainable competitive advantages. For example, Hitt et al. (1991) found that reductions in both research and development (R&D) inputs and outputs are often associated with increased reliance on acquisitions as a source of new products. This study exemplifies (in a limited fashion) the trade-offs between internal and external learning, and the difficulty firms encounter when trying to excel at both.

The above trade-offs concerning the development of knowledge within firms leads one to believe that there are several generic positions available to firms. Our first proposition simply contends that these generic knowledge strategies exist. Other researchers (March 1991, Bierly and Chakrabarti 1996a, Zack 1999) have made similar claims; however, there has been almost no empirical research conducted in this area. Using a cluster analysis, Bierly and Chakrabarti (1996a) did find the existence of knowledge strategies similar to those proposed here, but their study was limited to large pharmaceutical companies. Specifically, we propose:

Proposition 1: Organizations can be categorized as one of the following based on their strategic choices regarding acquisition and creation of new knowledge and leverage of existing knowledge: explorers, exploiters, maintainers, bimodal learners.

Proposition 1a: Within each knowledge strategy type, organizations can be further categorized based on a tendency to focus predominantly on either internal or external learning.

Aligning HRM Practices with Knowledge Strategies

We propose that the degree to which a firm's knowledge strategy develops or degrades its knowledge base is partially determined by the HRM engaged by the firm. If human resources support the firm's strategic knowledge focus, then the knowledge base is strengthened, potentially creating a competitive advantage for the firm. When HRM practices are not congruent with the firm's knowledge focus, the knowledge base remains static or is eroded, and thus negatively affects firm performance. In the strategic human resource management (SHRM) literature, the contingency perspective conceptualizes the organization's strategic posture as the moderator of the relationship between HRM practices and firm performance (Youndt et al. 1996). In this study we have framed the relationships among these variables differently, contending that the impact of knowledge strategies on the knowledge base of the firm (and subsequently on overall performance) is conditioned by HRM practices. We also propose that firm characteristics, such as size, culture, and structure, influence the appropriateness of certain HRM practices and that HRM practices may, additionally, directly influence the development of the knowledge base independent of which knowledge strategy the firm follows (see figure 16.1).

Strategic HRM Practices

By definition, SHRM practices are theoretically or empirically linked to overall organizational performance. Delery and Doty (1996) have used the theoretical works of Osterman (1994), Sonnenfeld and Peiperl (1988), Kerr and Slocum (1987), and Miles and Snow (1984), to identify seven practices that are consistently defined as strategic HRM practices. These are (1) internal career opportunities (hiring within or outside of the firm), (2) formal training systems (amount of formal training), (3) appraisal measures (based on behavior or results), (4) profit sharing (pay tied to organizational performance), (5) employment security, (6) voice mechanisms (grievance systems and participation in decision making), and (7) job definition (narrow or broad). Many of these seven elements are included on the lists of best HRM practices compiled by Delaney et al. (1989), Arthur (1992), Pfeffer (1994), Huselid (1995), and MacDuffie (1995).

The focus of most research in SHRM has been on large firms, but a growing body of literature that targets small firms has provided additional insights. For example, recent research in the fields of entrepreneurship and small business management, areas often characterized by innovation, has focused on the relationship between human resource practices and firm performance. Smaller firms often have resource constraints that limit strategic and operational choices. Yet, in order to compete in a global quality-based market, small businesses need to have highly motivated and highly skilled workers (Holt 1993). Deshpande and Golhar's (1994) work supports this view, concluding that workforce characteristics such as concern for the firm's success and worker self-discipline are perceived to be key elements in small firm success. Marlow and Patton (1993) argue that effective management of employees is crucial to the survival of small firms because of several unique small business characteristics, including a smaller likelihood of hiring HRM professionals and of being unionized, a tremendous variety in the amount and availability of training, and failure to consciously try to gain competitive advantage through the use of HRM practices. The link between firm performance and HRM management was also highlighted in McEvoy's (1984) research, where lack of progressive HRM practices was found to be the leading cause of failure of small firms.

The need for integrated sets of HRM practices, described in the literature as HRM "bundles," has been discussed in several recent studies (e.g., Huselid 1995, MacDuffie 1995, Wright and Snell 1991). Drawing on resource-based theory, Barney and Wright (1998) described how purposefully bundling HRM practices according to unique firm characteristics and needs is more likely to lead to a sustainable competitive advantage than a more traditional HRM approach. They argue that a system of integrated HRM practices that support the firm's strategy can provide a sustainable competitive advantage because unique bundles of HRM practices are valuable,

rare, and difficult to imitate. Baron and Kreps (1999) contend that consistency among HRM practices is desirable because it supports the organizational learning process. Consistent HRM practices can be used to reinforce core values and beliefs in the organization. Conversely, inconsistent HRM practices can send mixed messages and cause confusion and conflict in the organization. Even though it appears obvious that firms should have a coordinated set of HRM practices, in reality few companies actually do this (Barney and Wright 1998). A study of small- and medium-sized manufacturing firms by Duberley and Walley (1995) shows a wide variety of HRM practices used across firms, with very few companies using a strategic approach to the management of human resources.

We contend that, although some *individual* HRM practices are generally viewed as positive regardless of situation, there is no one best *bundle* of HRM practices for all firms. Each generic knowledge strategy we have identified is associated with a particular set of critical capabilities (e.g., creativity, flexibility, continuous improvement). These critical capabilities are, in turn, best supported by a particular, complementary set (bundle) of HRM practices. We propose that the purposeful application of a knowledge strategy (development and use of intellectual capital) in conjunction with the use of HRM practices that are congruent with the chosen strategy, is a way for firms to create and sustain competitive advantage.

Knowledge Base

The knowledge base of the organization includes the tangible and intangible knowledge, experience, and skills of employees in the organization, along with the knowledge embedded in equipment, culture, structure, and routines of the organization. Several different facets of the knowledge construct must be taken into consideration when exploring the concept of an organizational knowledge base. First, it is important to differentiate between individual, group, and organizational knowledge. All knowledge is initiated (created or acquired) at the individual level (Simon 1991). Individual learning must take place prior to organizational learning. According to Brown and Duguid (1991), individual knowledge is transmitted to other "close" individuals in an organization who share similar interpretation frameworks, a social network referred to as a *community of practice*. March (1991) contends that this social context of knowledge transfer between individuals is an extremely important part of the organizational learning process. "Expert" individuals in the organization have two key skills: first, the ability to create or interpret new ideas from outside sources, and second, the social skills to transmit the knowledge to others. Once transmitted, the collective knowledge of the group often becomes more than just the sum of all individual knowledge. Synergies are created as the knowledge is integrated and reinterpreted by organizational members (Spender 1994). Group norms may also develop that are used to store certain types of knowledge and pass them on to others in the organization.

The integration of group knowledge, which takes place primarily at the middle management level, results in what is known as organizational knowledge (Nonaka 1994). Theoretically, organizational knowledge is a body of knowledge that has been disseminated throughout the entire organization. However, in reality true organizational knowledge rarely exists due to individual differences in ability to interpret and understand the new knowledge. Horizontal transfer of knowledge among work groups may be limited due to specialized areas of expertise or lack of incentive. It is essential, however, that vertical upward knowledge transfer takes place so that resources can be appropriately allocated by strategic decision makers in the firm. Some knowledge that reaches the top of the organization becomes institutionalized and forms the basis for new organizational rules, procedures, and routines, which are the means by which the knowledge is stored within the organization. These new organizational beliefs are transferred to incoming members through the socialization process (March 1991). This cyclical process of mutual individual and collective learning constantly changes the knowledge base within the organization.

A second element critical to understanding the organization's knowledge base is the distinction between tacit and explicit knowledge. *Explicit knowledge* is information that is articulable or codifiable; thus, it can be transferred from one individual to another using some type of formal communication system. In contrast, *tacit knowledge* is commonly understood to be knowledge that cannot be formally communicated (Polanyi 1966). Personal experience and an individual's unique "mental model" provide the framework for generating and interpreting tacit knowledge. This distinction between explicit and tacit

knowledge is particularly important when evaluating competitive differences between firms. Tacit knowledge (as compared to explicit knowledge) is much more difficult for competitors to imitate; thus, it is more valuable and more likely to lead to a sustainable competitive advantage (Winter 1987, Kogut and Zander 1992, Zander and Kogut 1995). When there is causal ambiguity, that is, when the knowledge is complex and combined with other types of knowledge in an unclear and systemic fashion, inimitability is further enhanced (Kogut and Zander 1992, Lippman and Rumelt 1982). Although tacitness is a broad and difficult construct to measure, a few attempts have been made. For example, Kogut and Zander (1993) and Zander and Kogut (1995) measured the overall concept of tacitness by developing three more specific constructs: codifiability, teachability, and observability.

The third aspect of the knowledge base that must be examined is size. The size of the knowledge base can be evaluated by assessing two dimensions—depth and breadth (Leonard-Barton 1995). Most firms perform better when they focus on specific domains of knowledge (core competencies) so that they can become leaders in those industries or areas (Hamel and Prahalad 1994). This strategy entails developing unique core products and depth of knowledge in a few critical areas of expertise. However, for some firms the opposite approach may actually be more successful. Firms that have a broad knowledge base are able to combine related technologies in a more complex manner than are firms with a deep but narrow knowledge base. This can create causal ambiguity and, therefore, sustainable competitive advantages (Reed and DeFillipi 1990). Core capabilities developed within a very narrow knowledge base may evolve into core rigidities if the firm lacks the ability to monitor and adapt to advances in different but related knowledge areas (Leonard-Barton 1992). Increased strategic flexibility and the ability to react more quickly to changes in the external environment are two of the benefits generally associated with a broader knowledge base (Grant 1996, Volberda 1996).

Linking Knowledge Strategy Dimensions with HRM Practices

Each generic knowledge strategy is associated with a particular set of critical capabilities (e.g., creativity, flexibility, continuous improvement), which in turn are best supported by a particular set (bundle) of HRM practices. The critical capabilities and key HRM practices for each generic strategy type are discussed below and are summarized in table 16.1. These HRM practices are discussed in the context of five general human resource management areas: (1) staffing—including recruitment, selection, and placement; (2) training and development—which also includes socialization; (3) performance management—covering appraisal and feedback; (4) compensation—including incentives and rewards; and (5) job design. These five areas encompass the seven strategic HRM practices discussed above.

Explorers

Explorers' competitive advantage is based on their ability to generate and apply new, radical knowledge. This requires "outside-the-box" thinking and a culture that fosters creativity, encourages risk taking, and accepts failure. Nonaka and Takeuchi (1995) have identified five enabling conditions that are particularly important for knowledge development to take place: organizational intention, autonomy, fluctuation and creative chaos, information redundancy, and requisite variety. Similar elements can be found in Leonard-Barton's (1995) discussion of the management strategies necessary to support knowledge building: clear understanding of strategic intent and core capabilities, a climate supportive of experimentation, development of signature skills and cognitive diversity, and importing external knowledge. This research helps to explain why the HRM practices discussed below are likely to enhance the knowledge base of firms pursuing an explorer strategy.

We contend that the explorer strategy is best supported by the following HRM practices. With regard to *staffing*, explorers should target recruitment sources that provide access to candidates with new knowledge and cutting-edge technology (e.g., universities with specialized programs, or geographic hotbeds of high-tech talent such as Silicon Valley). Effort should be made during the recruitment and selection process to identify individuals who are comfortable with nonconformity, experimentation, and failure in pursuit of success (McCune 1997). This can be accomplished by using assessment tools such as personality tests and problem-solving exercises. Additionally, explorers should maintain a moderate level of external hiring. Bantel and Jackson (1989) contend that recruiting from

outside the organization brings in employees with fresh, new ideas, something that is especially important for firms that require innovation and creativity. March (1991) found that moderate external hiring, which results in moderate turnover, is optimal because outsiders bring diversity and different perspectives that benefit the organization, yet not too much individual knowledge leaves the organization.

In the area of *training and development*, existing research shows a link between firm strategy and appropriate types and amounts of employee training (Raghuram and Arvey 1994). More specifically, firms focusing on innovation and product development (i.e., explorers) need to focus training efforts on enhancing specific areas of technical expertise, helping to develop a culture that values creative thinking and analysis, and providing management training in facilitation and feedback. To be successful at developing new, radical knowledge, organizations must develop a deep understanding of a specific knowledge area (Leonard-Barton 1995). Therefore, formal training should focus on enhancing "signature skills" (areas of specialization), and informal skill development should be encouraged through individual experimentation and "learning by doing." During the socialization process it is crucial that explorers clearly convey the vision, or strategic intent, of the firm to new employees. Because many explorer employees have a high degree of autonomy, idiosyncratic jobs, and high intrinsic motivation, they must clearly understand what types of new knowledge (innovations) will be most valuable to achieving organizational goals. Finally, it is important that explorer employees be allowed to pursue increased responsibility through managerial or administrative positions while retaining their ability to work in specialized technical or research areas.

As for *performance management*, appraisal in the explorer firm should be very results oriented, focusing on *what* was achieved rather than *how* it was achieved. This conveys the message that there are many different ways to achieve effective performance and that experimentation and failure are not only accepted but expected. Thus, the firm encourages innovation and risk taking, and helps to reduce employees' fear of failure. Using outcome-based appraisal criteria is most successful in a culture of high autonomy and trust where employees assume accountability for the way in which successful results are achieved (e.g., use of resources). Additionally, research by

TABLE 16.1 Aligning Generic Knowledge Strategies with HRM Practices

Generic Knowledge Strategy	Critical Capabilities	Key HRM Practices
Explorer	Creativity, innovation, risk taking, experimentation, deep knowledge areas	*Staffing:* recruiting for new knowledge and technology, moderate external hiring, maximizing person-culture fit *Training/Development:* enhancing specialized skill areas, encouraging individual experimentation, high socialization regarding strategic intent, and dual (technical/managerial) career tracks *Performance Management:* results-oriented appraisal, individualized goals and feedback *Compensation:* linking individual innovation to team performance and firm profitability, customized compensation packages, "lifestyle benefits," employee ownership (e.g., stock options) *Job Design:* loose job definitions, high challenge and autonomy, cross-functional teams, alternative work schedules
Exploiter	Flexibility, continual improvement, employee participation, tacit knowledge transfer and integration	*Staffing:* internal hiring *Training/Development:* on-site and on-the-job training, formal ongoing training in new technology, cross-training, team building, leadership training, interpersonal skills and diversity training *Performance Management:* combination of behavior-based and short-term outcome-based appraisal, frequent performance feedback, participative goal setting, balancing team and individual goals *Compensation:* pay for performance, individual and team production incentives, rewards for employee participation *Job Design:* self-managed work teams
Bimodal learner	Managing complexity, creativity, flexibility and adaptability, organizational commitment	Combination of key explorer and exploiter HRM practices, plus a comprehensive and flexible HRM system to accommodate the diversity of HRM practices, and training in interpersonal and organizational skills, communication, negotiation, and conflict resolution to deal with the complexity and conflict inherent in the bimodal strategy
Maintainer	Stability, socialization of new members, respect successful past/tradition	*Staffing:* internal hiring, clear career paths *Training/Development:* high socialization in company history, traditions, and behavioral norms, formal orientation to standard policies and procedures, formal job- or task-specific training, employee development grooms select number of lower level employees for management positions *Performance Management:* primarily behavior-based appraisal, individualized goals and feedback *Compensation:* traditional monetary compensation structure, rewards for seniority *Job Design:* tight job definitions, traditional hierarchical relationships

Gupta and Singhal (1993) demonstrates that companies that highly value innovation and creativity must develop appraisal systems that clearly link individual innovation to team performance and firm profitability. Explorer employees need to participate in setting individualized goals that connect their signature skills to desired organizational outcomes. Similarly, explorer employees should receive feedback that provides information on how their unique knowledge, skills, and abilities are affecting goal attainment. This helps keep employees motivated and aligned with the firm's strategic intent.

In terms of *compensation*, an increasing number of explorer firms operate on a basis of resource attraction rather than resource allocation. Resource attraction means firms are acting as venture capitalists would, competing to attract the best new ideas via talented human resources (Hamel 1999). Under this system, talent migrates to firms that offer the most appealing jobs and the greatest potential earnings. According to Ermel (1997), customizing compensation packages to meet individual needs may be the best way to attract and retain skilled employees, particularly in high technology areas (where the explorer strategy is commonly used). Emrel states that a firm's ability to offer challenging work, recognition for contributions, and "lifestyle benefits" (e.g., on-site child care) gives it an advantage in attracting and retaining skilled employees such as engineers, scientists, and information systems professionals. Employee ownership (e.g., stock option programs) is another HRM tool that can be used to successfully support the explorer strategy. Although employee ownership can be implemented under any of the four generic strategies, we believe it has the largest potential impact for an explorer firm. Top talent may bypass offers of high annual salaries for the possibility of future wealth through stock ownership. In addition employee ownership may enhance organizational commitment and provide incentive for long-term performance.

Lastly, in the area of *job design*, we believe the explorer strategy is best supported by loose job definitions, high challenge and autonomy, the use of cross-functional teams, and alternative work schedules. Loosely structured jobs allow employees the freedom to experiment, use their signature skills in unique and innovative ways, and engage in intrapreneurial activity. Creative employees are crucial to a successful explorer strategy, and according to Amabile (1997), creativity thrives under intrinsic motivation. In a discussion of the componential theory of organizational creativity and innovation, Amabile proposes that creativity is most likely to occur when employees' skills overlap with their greatest intrinsic interests, and that the level of creativity is positively correlated with level of expertise, creative-thinking skill, and intrinsic task motivation. Thus, a job in an individual's area of expertise that is personally challenging and loosely structured should engender higher levels of creativity as well as increased job satisfaction. Bringing people together from different areas of specialization to work in cross-functional teams creates what Leonard-Barton (1995) calls "creative abrasion." By helping employees develop integrative skills, managers can harness the creative energy produced by this process to generate new ideas and solutions.

> *Proposition 2:* Companies that align HRM practices with a specific knowledge strategy will be more successful in developing a knowledge base that provides sustainable competitive advantage than companies that do not align HRM practices and knowledge strategy.

> *Proposition 2a:* Companies that implement an explorer knowledge strategy in conjunction with HRM practices that promote creativity and risk-taking (e.g., moderate external hiring, results-oriented appraisal, loose job definitions) will be more successful in developing a knowledge base that provides sustainable competitive advantage, than explorer companies that do not use this set of HRM practices.

Exploiters

Exploiters' competitive advantage is that they can leverage existing knowledge better than other firms. Leveraging existing knowledge means continual modification and improvement of a firm's products and processes in pursuit of competitive advantage. Often this is accomplished using a total quality management approach that incorporates employee empowerment. Because decentralization of decision making is inherent to empowerment, this approach increases employee participation at all levels of the organization. This increased participation affects each of the HRM areas and encourages practices such as employee input into hiring decisions, employee determination of training content and methods, peer (or 360-degree) evaluation, participative goal setting, incentives and rewards for employee suggestions and improvements, and self-managed work teams (Glew et al. 1995, Cotton 1993, Lawler et al. 1992). Regarding *staffing*, exploiters should rely heavily on internal hiring. By filling vacancies above entry-level positions through promotion and transfer, firms can capitalize on employee familiarity with the knowledge base, use existing networks and relationships to promote knowledge sharing, protect proprietary information, and strengthen the existing culture. Internal hiring will result in a higher than average individual level of experience and tacit knowledge, but may do so at the expense of initiating radically new ideas.

In the area of *training and development*, successful exploiters will emphasize formal frequent or ongoing training in new technologies in order to keep the knowledge base abreast of changes in the market. Given the exploiter's preference for internal knowledge sourcing, much of the training should be offered on-site and many positions will require on-the-job training, thus encouraging the transfer of tacit knowledge among employees. Cross-training, team building, and interpersonal skills and diversity training emphasize the need for exploiter employees to communicate openly, understand each other's areas of expertise, and share knowledge in order to consistently and incrementally enhance the existing knowledge base. In a discussion of knowledge sharing, Greengard (1998) identifies three common problems firms may encounter. First, employees may believe that sharing their best ideas may impair their ability to move up in the firm. Second, employees are reluctant to use other people's ideas for fear it makes them look less knowledgeable and overdependent on others. Last, many employees like to perceive themselves as experts and are reluctant to collaborate. These concerns can be addressed through performance management and compensation practices as well as through the training and development practices mentioned above.

Performance management in the exploiter firm should be a combination of behavior-based and short-term outcome-based appraisal. Because the exploiter is concerned with incremental improvement, efficient use of resources, and cost containment, *how* results are achieved may be as important as the outcome itself. It is only by understanding, standardizing, and then teaching new processes or product innovations that firms can rapidly modify existing knowledge to

meet new customer expectations. Whereas explorers' appraisals are more long-term results oriented, exploiters' appraisals will focus on shorter term goals, thus encouraging more rapid action (e.g., bringing a new variation of a product to market). This fosters comparatively small, well-understood, and lower risk improvements that can be implemented relatively quickly and inexpensively.

Additionally, since many exploiters use a team-based structure, the appraisal process must balance individual and team goals in order to maximize performance from each. Allowing employees to participate in individual and team goal setting improves acceptance and commitment to these goals. Similarly, in the area of *compensation*, exploiters should incorporate both individual and team production incentives. Rewards should be tied to performance and how individual or team suggestions/innovations affect firm profitability. Knowing that employee participation encourages knowledge sharing and development of tacit knowledge, exploiters should also reward high levels of employee participation. Experienced employees will be the primary source of improvements based on tacit knowledge, and thus it is critical that they actively participate in the innovation process. The most crucial elements of *job design* in the exploiter strategy are the use of cross-training and teams. These practices help ensure that employees will know how their suggestions/innovations affect other members of the firm, encourage knowledge sharing across firm boundaries, and expedite implementation of new ideas.

Proposition 2b: Companies that implement an exploiter knowledge strategy in conjunction with HRM practices that promote flexibility, continual improvement, and the integration of tacit knowledge (e.g., internal hiring, teams, formal training, short-term results-oriented appraisals, rewards for employee participation) will be more successful in developing a knowledge base that provides sustainable competitive advantage, as compared to exploiter companies that do not use this set of HRM practices.

Maintainers

The maintainer's strategy is based on preserving the status quo. Their critical capabilities are stability, consistency, standardization, maintaining proven products and processes, and preserving company tradition and reputation. Preventing erosion of the knowledge base takes precedence over expanding or improving it. For *staffing*, maintainers rely heavily on internal hiring in order to maximize consistency and minimize disruption of operations when vacancies are filled. Preference in hiring goes to those individuals who have a proven track record in the organization and have worked their way up the advancement ladder in a systematic fashion. Recruitment sources are limited, and candidates are often found through internal job posting or referral by current employees. Career paths in the firm are very clear and advancement happens in a slow and deliberate fashion.

The socialization aspect of the *training and development* area is very important to maintainers. A high level of socialization is necessary for new employees to ensure familiarity with company history and traditions, image and reputation, standard operating procedures, and strong behavioral norms. This ensures that most employees understand, are familiar with, and actively support "the way we do things here." Rapid and thorough socialization of new employees limits challenges of existing practices and encourages these employees to value the rich tradition of the organization. Training will be formal and narrowly focused, used primarily to train employees in job- or task-specific skills. Employee development is primarily found in the grooming of a select number of lower level employees for management positions.

Performance management in the maintainer firm uses behavior-based appraisal. This helps to ensure that employees use standard operating procedures to meet existing production standards. The emphasis is on consistency and conformity. Goals are specific to an individual's position, and feedback is primarily used to remedy inconsistency or lack of conformity. *Compensation* is primarily monetary, based on traditional salary and hourly wage components, and is largely determined by position and seniority. Bonus pay may be a part of the compensation package but is not linked to an individual's impact on departmental goal attainment or firm profitability (e.g., annual Christmas bonus). Regarding *job design*, maintainer employees have tight job definitions, where tasks, duties, and responsibilities are clearly prescribed and narrowly defined within specialized skill areas.

Proposition 2c: Companies that implement a maintainer knowledge strategy in conjunc-

tion with HRM practices that promote stability and rapid socialization of new members (e.g., internal hiring, formal training, behavioral appraisals, narrow job definitions, clear career paths) will be more successful in maintaining a knowledge base that provides sustainable competitive advantage, as compared to maintainer companies that do not use this set of HRM practices.

Bimodal Learners

Bimodal learners must develop HRM practices that are supportive of both the development of new, radical knowledge and the exploitation of existing knowledge. Thus, they must incorporate the most critical HRM practices of both explorers and exploiters. Some practices, such as high employee participation or loose job definitions, will support both of these learning styles, for the reasons outlined above. However, in some areas there may be conflict in the sense that contradictory HRM practices are required. For example, the development of new, radical knowledge will thrive with less formal training (more experimentation) and a more long-term-results focus concerning appraisals, compensation, and goals, but the exploitation of existing knowledge will thrive with more formal training and a more short-term focus. These areas of contradiction for bimodal learners are the areas where managers need to give most attention and provide the strongest leadership. For these areas of conflict, the organization must either find some midrange compromise position or incorporate a combination of apparently contradictory practices. Different HRM practices may need to be applied to different departments and individuals in the organization, which will create greater complexity and greater potential for confusion. Thus, the overall HRM system must be very flexible and adaptable. Additionally, teams and open communications are needed to deal with the complexity and conflict of these types of companies.

Examples of firms that are successful at both the development of new, radical knowledge and the exploitation of existing knowledge are Johnson and Johnson, ABB (Asea Brown Boveri), and Hewlett-Packard (Tushman and O'Reilly 1996). All three of these companies are simultaneously tight and loose concerning their organizational structure, culture, and processes. They all rely on decentralized, autonomous operating units that allow for the use of different practices and strategies, and the development of different subcul-

TABLE 16.2 Aligning Knowledge Sourcing Strategies with HRM Practices

Knowledge Sourcing Strategy	Critical Capabilities	Key HRM Practices
Internal sourcing	Internal expertise, innovative culture, tacit knowledge transfer and integration	*Staffing:* internal hiring. *Training/Development:* high degree of socialization, formal standardized on-site training, on-the-job training, mentoring *Performance Management:* used for developmental as well as evaluative purposes. *Compensation:* rewards for new ideas and sharing knowledge *Job Design:* teams
External sourcing	Absorptive capacity, external monitoring/benchmarking, integrating external explicit knowledge with internal knowledge base	*Staffing:* moderate external hiring. *Training/Development:* broad-focused training from experts outside the organization, encourage participation in research and professional activities (e.g., conferences, workshops, trade shows, etc.), reimbursement for continuing education, and networking with customers, suppliers, and competitors. *Performance Management:* professional/skill development as performance evaluation criteria. *Compensation:* market competitive to attract top external people *Job Design:* loose job definition

tures. But they also are centralized in certain ways to take advantage of their size advantages, strong brand names, and strong corporate cultures that foster and provide direction for successful innovation.

Proposition 2d: Companies that implement a bimodal learner knowledge strategy in conjunction with HRM practices that promote managing complexity, creativity, and flexibility (e.g., flexible HRM system, teams, rewards and practices that promote open communications) will be more successful in developing a knowledge base that provides sustainable competitive advantage, as compared to bimodal learner companies that do not use this set of HRM practices.

Knowledge Sourcing Strategies

Additionally, the firm's focus on either internal or external learning will further determine which HRM practices will best enhance the firm's knowledge base (see table 16.2). More specifically, if the focus is internally sourced learning, where success is highly dependent on creativity and internal expertise in certain areas, congruent practices would include extensive formal training to develop expertise, and incentive compensation designed to encourage new ideas. These HRM practices that promote an innovative culture (e.g., compensating employees for suggestions that are implemented), which values risk taking, openness in communications, and teamwork, will be critical to successful internal learning (Starbuck 1992). Additionally, a major advantage of internal sourcing is the creation of tacit knowledge, which is difficult for competitors to imitate and a source of sustainable competitive advantage. These HRM practices should be developed that facilitate the transfer and integration of tacit knowledge, which can be supported by the use of cross-functional teams where members from different areas can best share their unique experiences and tacit knowledge. More internal hiring and lower turnover will also help increase the experience level of employees in the company and better enable them to manage tacit knowledge. Essentially, the firm must ask, What does it take to excel at internal learning? and then adopt HRM practices that foster that particular knowledge dimension.

Proposition 3a: Companies that implement an internal knowledge sourcing strategy in conjunction with HRM practices that promote internal expertise, innovative culture, and tacit knowledge integration (e.g., internal hiring, extensive formal training, rewards for new ideas and sharing knowledge, teams) will be more successful in developing a knowledge base that provides sustainable competitive advantage, as compared to maintainer companies that do not use this set of HRM practices.

Strength in externally sourced learning requires absorptive capacity and access to external sources of knowledge. Certain HRM practices can support external learning by exposing employees to many alternative ideas: (a) training that focuses on new ideas initiated by outside sources (rather than expanding on an existing strength), (b) employee access to "cutting-edge" ideas discussed at conferences, trade shows, and university research groups and in trade journals, and (c) external hiring in order to bring new ideas and fresh perspectives into the organization. Most of the knowledge brought into the organization from external sources will be more explicit in nature. By definition, tacit knowledge is difficult to codify and pass on to others outside the work environment. Thus, firms that predominantly follow an external sourcing strategy should focus on ways of transferring more explicit knowledge throughout the company. Computer systems provide an excellent medium for the transfer and storage of such explicit knowledge. Many companies have designated a top manager responsible for this function, often called chief information officer or chief knowledge officer. Additionally, firms that excel at external sourcing should have HRM practices that assist in reducing the natural internal political resistance to externally generated ideas, a phenomenon known as the not-invented-here syndrome (Katz and Allen 1982). To overcome this resistance to individuals bringing knowledge into the organization, frequently called boundary-spanning individuals, firms should have a strong network of internal and external connections and should encourage development of both technical and social skills (Tushman and Scanlan 1981). Training programs, rewards, and appraisal systems should promote these individual strengths.

Proposition 3b: Companies that implement an external knowledge sourcing strategy in conjunction with HRM practices that promote absorptive capacity, external monitoring, and integrating external knowledge with internal knowledge base (e.g., external hiring, training from outsiders, attending conferences and trade shows) will be more successful in developing a knowledge base that provides sustainable competitive advantage,

as compared to maintainer companies that do not use this set of HRM practices.

The Role of Other Firm Characteristics

The focus of our model is the alignment of knowledge strategies and HRM practices, but there are also other firm characteristics that moderate the relationship between the firm's knowledge strategy and the development of its knowledge base (see figure 16.1). Specifically, consideration of organizational size, structure, and culture is important to understanding the primary relationships depicted in the model. The size of the organization is an important factor in two ways. First, large firms usually have the advantage of access to more resources. This is particularly important for firms that follow a bimodal learner strategy since they must simultaneously support a broad array of learning projects. Second, smaller firms tend to have the advantage of being more flexible and able to respond more quickly to a changing environment (Chen and Hambrick 1995). Smaller firms may also be less conservative and more willing to "bet the farm" on something radically new, which is necessary to be a successful explorer.

Organizational structure can either facilitate or hinder the learning process. Generally speaking, a centralized, hierarchical organizational structure usually inhibits the learning process because it makes knowledge diffusion and integration across the organization difficult (Fiol and Lyles 1985); this inhibits both internal and external learning. Whereas it is generally accepted that a more decentralized organizational structure is best for developing creative new ideas, it can be argued that a more centralized structure is better for the rapid implementation of ideas (Tushman and O'Reilly 1996). More complex structures will be required for more complex knowledge strategies, such as the bimodal learners, where the company is attempting to pursue many different goals simultaneously.

A different type of culture is required for each of the different knowledge strategies, supporting the critical capabilities we outlined above. However, a firm's culture is strongly influenced by the values of the founder and is very difficult to change (Schein 1983). To a degree, HRM practices, through effective performance appraisals and appropriate reward systems, can be used to adjust a culture to better support a particular strategy. However, an organizational crisis and/or new and powerful leadership is usually the catalyst for major alterations in a firm's culture (Lorsch 1985, Wilkins and Ouchi 1988). Thus, a firm may find it difficult to establish congruency between an evolving knowledge strategy and an entrenched culture.

Proposition 4: The influence of a firm's knowledge strategy on its knowledge base will be moderated by the firm's size, organizational culture, and structure.

Intellectual Capital, Industry Characteristics, and Firm Performance

A general assumption in the knowledge management literature is that a superior knowledge base will lead to superior firm performance (i.e., Senge 1990, Garvin 1993). However, this is a generalization that should be questioned. The most knowledgeable firms are not always the most profitable. Knowledge only leads to superior firm performance if the industry characteristics enable the knowledgeable company to appropriate the profits from their new ideas (see figure 16.1). When environmental factors enable innovators to appropriate a large portion of profits from a new idea, the industry is referred to as a strong regime of appropriability (Teece 1986). When competitors/imitators, suppliers, or customers benefit more from an innovation and the company that comes up with the new idea is not able to realize a significant profit, the industry is referred to as a weak regime of appropriability (Teece 1986). Generally speaking, appropriability is determined by the degree others can understand and imitate the innovating firm's new knowledge. Appropriability is determined by the following factors.

1. Effectiveness of legal instruments protecting intellectual property: patents, copyrights, trademarks, and trade secrets are effective in some industries (e.g., the use of patents in the pharmaceutical industry) but are ineffective in many other industries, depending on the types of products and processes in the industry and their established norms (Levin et al. 1987).
2. Industry lead times: long lead times give the innovating firm a window of opportunity that allows them to generate high initial profits and build on their initial advantage before competitors enter the industry. Lead times are longer in industries where

competitors are less flexible, due to previous commitments (Ghemawat 1991). For example, if large capital investments are needed in manufacturing, firms committed to other processes probably are not able to quickly replace their established plant with a new facility.
3. The nature of the knowledge associated with products and processes of the industry: the more tacit, systemic, and complex knowledge is, the more difficult it is for others to understand and imitate.

An interesting paradox exists concerning firms' knowledge, industry characteristics, and performance. Fast-cycle industries (e.g., hypercompetitive industries) are usually industries with weak regimes of appropriability, where intellectual capital does not necessarily lead to sustainable high performance because others quickly imitate and disrupt advantages (D'Aveni 1994). Fast-cycle industries, as compared to slow-cycle industries, more often have short lead times, legal instruments that are not effective, and products and processes based on tacit and complex knowledge. However, competition in fast-cycle is usually based on firms' ability to generate new knowledge, whereas competition in slow-cycle industries is often based on less knowledge-intensive factors, such as economies of scale, brand image, and access to distribution channels. Fast-cycle industries typically have more firms that excel at organizational learning, but developing a strong knowledge base does not guarantee success because of the competitors. In slow-cycle industries, a firm with a superior knowledge base is more likely to have a competitive advantage that is sustainable over a longer period of time. Thus, the relationship between a firm's knowledge base and performance depends on competitors. In a sense, performance is not based on a specific measure of a firm's knowledge base, but instead it is based on a firm's knowledge base relative to its competitors' knowledge bases.

Measures of performance across industries differ to the extent that some industries are more attractive and profitable than others. According to Porter (1980), industries are more attractive if they have high entry barriers, low bargaining power of buyers, low bargaining power of suppliers, few substitutions, and low rivalry. Thus, if the industry is more attractive, a firm's knowledge base will more likely result in a higher level of performance than will that of a similar firm in a less attractive industry. Of course, this is only a generalization, since there are also many companies that have been extremely successful in unattractive industries, such as Wal-Mart and Southwest Airlines.

Proposition 5: The influence of a firm's knowledge base on its performance will be moderated by industry characteristics.

Conclusion

Research Implications

Studying knowledge in organizations is obviously a very difficult task. We strongly believe many critical issues related to knowledge management can be studied using carefully designed surveys and archival data (e.g., patent and citation data), particularly when they are supplemented with qualitative research methods (e.g., interviews) to improve the richness of the data. Several recent empirical studies have successfully produced important findings about the nature of organizational knowledge and should be used as guides to further research (Nonaka et al. 1994, Kogut and Zander 1993, Zander and Kogut 1995, Bierly and Chakrabarti 1996a, 1996b, Szulanski 1996, Henderson and Cockburn 1994, Pisano 1994, Appleyard 1996, Almeida 1996).

This chapter proposes relationships among organizational knowledge strategies, human resource practices, organizational knowledge bases, industry characteristics, and organizational performance. The most critical link, we argue, is the alignment of knowledge strategies and HRM practices. We suggest that this fit between knowledge strategies and HRM practices be examined in two ways, first from a gestalt perspective (Miller 1981) and second as a moderated relationship. The gestalt perspective is a multivariate approach that is free of criteria (e.g., organizational effectiveness) and minimally precise, thus allowing the researcher to identify recurring clusters of attributes (Venkatraman 1989). This initial phase of research will help to determine whether specific knowledge strategies are inherently coupled with specific HRM practices. The second examination of fit is based on an interaction perspective, that the presence or absence of specific HRM practices determines the extent to which a specific knowledge strategy enhances the firm's knowledge base, and therefore organizational effectiveness. According to this conceptualization, the impact of knowledge strategy (the predictor variable) upon intellectual capital (the criterion variable) is dependent upon HRM practices (the moderating variable). The current knowledge base of the organization has a direct effect on firm performance. Measures of firm characteristics and industry characteristics (e.g., firm size, industry dynamism, and industry competitiveness) should be used as control variables.

Managerial Implications

The theoretical framework developed in this chapter has practical implications for managers. The propositions are relatively straightforward but deal with issues frequently neglected and misunderstood by most managers. Our advice to managers is to take a knowledge-based perspective of strategic issues and to strive for internal consistency throughout the organization. Specifically, we offer the following recommendations:

1. Firms should have a clear knowledge strategy. The design of their future knowledge strategy should be based on their past knowledge strategy, their current knowledge base, their unique resources, and an identification of key industry characteristics.
2. Firms should bundle their HRM practices, such that they consistently support the same goals of the organization.
3. Firms should align their HRM practices with their future knowledge strategy. The HRM practices must support the knowledge strategy.
4. There should be internal consistency throughout the organization. The firm's HRM practices and knowledge strategy should also fit well with (a) the firm's size, structure, and culture and (b) the external environment.

References

Almeida, P. (1996) "Knowledge sourcing by foreign multinationals: patent citation analysis in the U.S. semiconductor industry." *Strategic Management Journal* 17(Winter):155–165.

Amabile, T.M. (1997) "Motivating creativity in organizations: on doing what you love and loving what you do." *California Management Review* 40:39–58.

Appleyard, M.M. (1996) "How does knowledge flow? Interfirm patterns in the semiconductor industry." *Strategic Management Journal* 17 (Winter):137–154.

Argyris, C. and Schon, D. (1978) *Organizational Learning: A Theory of Action Perspective*. Reading, MA: Addison-Wesley Publishing.

Arthur, J.B. (1992) "The link between business strategy and industrial relations systems in American steel minimills." *Industrial and Labor Relations Review* 45:488–506.

Bantel, K. and Jackson, S. (1989) "Top management and innovations in banking: Does the composition of the top team make a difference?" *Strategic Management Journal* 10:107–124.

Barney, J. (1991) "Firm resources and sustained competitive advantage." *Journal of Management* 17(1):99–119.

Barney, J. and Wright, P.M. (1998) "On becoming a strategic partner: the role of human resources in gaining competitive advantage." *Human Resource Management* 37(1):31–46.

Baron, J.N. and Kreps, D.M. (1999) "Consistent human resource practices." *California Management Review* 41(3):29–53.

Bierly, P. and Chakrabarti, A. (1996a) "Generic knowledge strategies in the U.S. pharmaceutical industry." *Strategic Management Journal* 17: 123–135.

Bierly, P. and Chakrabarti, A. (1996b) "Technological learning, strategic flexibility, and new product development in the pharmaceutical industry." *IEEE Transactions on Engineering Management* 43:368–380.

Brown, J.S. and Duguid, P. (1991) "Organizational learning and communities-of-practice: toward a unified view of working, learning, and innovation." *Organization Science* 2:40–57.

Chen, M.J. and Hambrick, D.C. (1995) "Speed, stealth and selective attack: how small firms differ from large firms in competitive behavior." *Academy of Management Journal* 38:453–482.

Chesbrough, H.W. and Teece, D.J. (1996) "When is virtual virtuous? Organizing for innovation." *Harvard Business Review*, January–February, pp. 65–73.

Cohen, W.M. and Levinthal, D.A. (1990) "Absorptive capacity: a new perspective on learning and innovation." *Administrative Science Quarterly* 35:128–152.

Conner, K.R. and Prahalad, C.K. (1996) "A resource-based theory of the firm: knowledge versus opportunism." *Organization Science* 7(5):477–501.

Cotton, J.L. (1993) *Employee Involvement: Methods for Improving Performance and Work Attitudes*. Newbury Park, CA: Sage.

D'Aveni, R.A. (1994) *Hypercompetition*. New York: Free Press.

Delaney, J.T., Lewin, D., and Ichniowski, C. (1989) *Human Resource Policies and Practices in American Firms*. Washington, DC: U.S. Government Printing Office.

Delery, J.E. and Doty, D.H. (1996) "Modes of theorizing in strategic human resource management: tests of universalistic, contingency, and configurational performance predictions." *Academy of Management Journal* 39(4):803–835.

Deshpande, S.P. and Golhar, D.Y. (1994) "HRM practices in large and small manufacturing firms: a comparative study." *Journal of Small Business Management*, April, pp. 49–56.

Duberley, J.P. and Walley, P. (1995) "Assessing the adoption of HRM by small and medium-sized manufacturing organizations." *International Journal of Human Resource Management* 6(4):891–909.

Ermel, L. (1997) "Responding to a tight labor market: using incentives to attract and retain talented workers." *Compensation and Benefits Review* 27:25–29.

Fiol, C.M. and Lyles, M.A. (1985) "Organizational learning." *Academy of Management Review* 10: 803–813.

Garvin, D.A. (1993) "Building a learning organization." *Harvard Business Review*, July–August, pp. 78–91.

Ghemawat, P. (1991) *Commitment: The Dynamic of Strategy*. New York: Free Press.

Glew, D.J., Griffin, R.W., and Van Fleet, D.D. (1995) "Participation in organizations: a preview of the issues and proposed framework for future analysis." *Journal of Management* 21:15–37.

Grant, R.M. (1996) "Prospering in dynamically-competitive environments: organizational capability as knowledge integration." *Organization Science* 7(4):375–387.

Greengard, S. (1998) "Will your culture support KM?" *Workforce* 77(10):93–94.

Gupta, A.K. and Singhal, A. (1993) "Managing human resources for innovation and creativity." *Research Technology Management* 36:41–48.

Hamel, G. (1999) "Bringing Silicon Valley inside." *Harvard Business Review* 77(5):70–84.

Hamel, G. and Prahalad, C.K. (1994) *Competing for the Future*. Boston: Harvard Business School Press.

Hedlund, G. (1994) "A model of knowledge management and N-form corporation." *Strategic Management Journal* 15(Summer):73–90.

Henderson, R. and Cockburn, I. (1994) "Measuring competence? Exploring firm effects in pharmaceutical research." *Strategic Management Journal* 15(Winter):63–84.

Hitt, M.A., Hoskisson, R.E., Ireland, R.D., and Harrison, J.S. (1991) "Effects of acquisitions on R&D inputs and outputs." *Academy of Management Journal* 34:693–706.

Holt, D.H. (1993) *Management Principles and Practices*, 3d ed. Englewood Cliffs, NJ: Prentice Hall.

Huselid, M.A. (1995) "The impact of human resource management practices on turnover, productivity, and corporate financial performance." *The Academy of Management Journal* 38(3): 635–672.

Katz, R. and Allen, T.J. (1982) "Investigating the not invented here (NIH) syndrome: a look at the performance, tenure, and communication patterns of 50 R&D project groups." *R&D Management* 12:7–19.

Kerr, J.L. and Slocum, J.W. (1987) "Linking reward systems and corporate cultures." *Academy of Management Executive* 1(2):99–108.

Kogut, B. and Zander, U. (1992) "Knowledge of the firm, combinative capabilities, and the replication of technology." *Organization Science* 3:383–397.

Kogut, B. and Zander, U. (1993) "Knowledge of the firm and the evolutionary theory of the multinational corporation." *Journal of International Business Studies* 24(4):625–645.

Lado, A.A. and Wilson, M.C. (1994) "Human resource systems and sustained competitive advantage: a competency-based perspective." *Academy of Management Review* 19(4):699–727.

Lawler, E.E., Mohrman, S.A., and Ledford, L.E., Jr. (1992) *Employee Involvement and Total Quality Management: Practices and Results in Fortune 1000 Companies.* San Francisco: Jossey-Bass.

Leonard-Barton, D. (1992) "Core capabilities and core rigidities: a paradox in managing new product development." *Strategic Management Journal* 13:111–125.

Leonard-Barton, D. (1995) *Wellsprings of Knowledge.* Boston: Harvard Business School Press.

Levin, R.C., Levorick, A.K., Nelson, R.R., and Winter, S.G. (1987) "Appropriating the returns from industrial research and development." *Brookings Papers on Economic Activity*, p. 794.

Levinthal, D. and March, J.G. (1993) "The myopia of learning." *Strategic Management Journal* 14 (Winter):95–112.

Lieberman, M. and Montgomery, D. (1988) "First-mover advantages." *Strategic Management Journal* 9:41–58.

Lippman, S.A. and Rumelt, R.P. (1982) "Uncertain imitability: an analysis of interfirm differences in efficiency under competition." *Bell Journal of Economics* 13:418–438.

Lorsch, J.W. (1985) "Strategic myopia: culture as an invisible barrier to change," in R.H. Kilman, M.J. Saxton, R. Serpa, and Associates (eds.), *Gaining Control of the Corporate Culture*, pp. 84–102. San Francisco: Jossey-Bass.

MacDuffie, J.P. (1995) "Human resource bundles and manufacturing performance: organizational logic and flexible production systems in the world auto industry." *Industrial and Labor Relations Review* 48(2):197–221.

March, J.G. (1991) "Exploration and exploitation in organizational learning." *Organization Science* 2:71–87.

Marlow, S. and Patton, D. (1993) "Managing the employment relationship in the small firm: possibilities for human resource management." *International Small Business Journal* 11(4):57–64.

McCune, J.C. (1997) "Making lemonade: companies must try and (sometimes) fail in order to succeed." *Management Review* 86:49–53.

McEvoy, G.M. (1984) "Small business personnel practices." *Journal of Small Business Management*, October, pp. 1–8.

Miles, R.E. and Snow, C.C. (1984) "Designing strategic human resource systems." *Organizational Dynamics* 13(1):36–52.

Miller, D. (1981) "Toward a new contingency perspective: the search for organizational gestalts." *Journal of Management Studies* 18:1–26.

Nonaka, I. (1994) "A dynamic theory of organizational knowledge creation." *Organization Science* 5(1):14–37.

Nonaka, I. and Takeuchi, H. (1995) *The Knowledge-Creating Company: How Japanese Companies Create the Dynamics of Innovation.* New York: Oxford University Press.

Nonaka, I., Byosiere, P., Borucki, C.C., and Konno, N. (1994) "Organizational knowledge creation theory: a first comprehensive test." *International Business Review* 3:337–351.

Osterman, P. (1994) "How common is workplace transformation and who adopts it?" *Industrial and Labor Relations Review* 47(2):173–188.

Peteraf, M.A. (1993) "The cornerstones of competitive advantage: a resource-based view." *Strategic Management Journal* 14(3):179–191.

Pfeffer, J. (1994) *Competitive Advantage through People: Unleashing the Power of the Work Force.* Boston: Harvard Business School Press.

Pisano, G.P. (1994) "Knowledge, integration, and the locus of learning: an empirical analysis of process development." *Strategic Management Journal* 15(Winter):85–100.

Polanyi, M. (1966) *The Tacit Dimension.* London: Routledge and Kegan Paul.

Porter, M. (1980) *Competitive Strategy.* New York: Free Press.

Raghuram, S. and Arvey, R.D. (1994) "Business strategy links with staffing and training practices." *Human Resource Planning* 17:55–73.

Reed, R. and DeFillipi, R.J. (1990) "Casual ambiguity, barriers to imitation, and sustainable competitive advantage." *Academy of Management Review* 15:88–102.

Sanchez, R. and Mahoney, J.T. (1996) "Modularity, flexibility, and knowledge management in product and organization design." *Strategic Management Journal* 17(Winter):63–76.

Schein, E.H. (1983) "The role of the founder in creating organizational culture." *Organization Dynamics* 12:13–28.

Schuler, R.S. and Jackson, S.E. (1987) "Linking competitive strategies with human resource management practices." *Academy of Management Executive* 1(3):207–219.

Senge, P.M. (1990) *The Fifth Discipline*. New York: Doubleday.

Simon, H.A. (1991) "Bounded rationality and organizational learning." *Organization Science* 2: 125–134.

Snell, S.A. (1992) "Control theory in strategic human resource management: the mediating effect of administrative information." *Academy of Management Journal* 35:292–327.

Sonnenfeld, J.A. and Peiperl, M.A. (1988) "Staffing policy as a strategic response: a typology of career systems." *Academy of Management Review* 13(4):588–600.

Spender, J.C. (1994) "Organizational knowledge, collective practice and Penrose rents." *International Business Review* 3(4):353–367.

Starbuck, W.H. (1992) "Learning by knowledge-intensive firms." *Journal of Management Studies* 29:713–740.

Szulanski, G. (1996) "Exploring internal stickiness: impediments to the transfer of best practice within the firm." *Strategic Management Journal* 17(Winter):27–43.

Teece, D.J. (1986) "Profiting from technological innovation: implications for integration, collaboration, licensing and public policy." *Research Policy* 15:285–305.

Tushman, M.L. and O'Reilly, C.A. (1996) "The ambidextrous organization: managing evolutionary and revolutionary change." *California Management Review* 38(4):1–23.

Tushman, M.L. and Scanlan, T. (1981) "Boundary spanning individuals: their role in information transfer and their antecedents." *Academy of Management Journal*: 24:289–305.

Venkatraman, N. (1989) "The concept of fit in strategy research: toward verbal and statistical correspondence." *Academy of Management Review* 14(3):423–444.

Volberda, H.W. (1996) "Toward the flexible form: how to remain vital in hypercompetitive environments." *Organization Science* 7:359–374.

Wilkins, A.L. and Ouchi, W.G. (1988) "Toward culturally sensitive theories of cultural change." *Academy of Management Review* 13:534–545.

Winter, S. (1987) "Skill and knowledge as strategic assets, in D. Teece (ed.), *The Competitive Challenge*, pp. 159–184. Cambridge, MA: Ballinger.

Wright, P.M. and Snell, S.A. (1991) "Toward an integrative view of strategic human resource management." *Human Resource Management Review* 1:203–225.

Youndt, M.A., Snell, S.A., Dean, J.W., Jr., and Lepak, D.P. (1996) "Human resource management, manufacturing strategy, and firm performance." *Academy of Management Journal* 39(4):803–836.

Zack, M.H. (1999) "Developing a knowledge strategy." *California Management Review* 41(3): 125–145.

Zander, U. and Kogut, B. (1995) "Knowledge and the speed of the transfer and imitation of organizational capabilities: an empirical test." *Organization Science* 6:76–92.

17

Knowledge and the Internet

Lessons from Cultural Industries

Chong Ju Choi and Anastasios Karamanos

The traditional resource-based theory of the firm posits that firms outperform competition when they enjoy rents arising from the possession of unique albeit mobile valuable assets (Amit and Schoemaker 1993). Because assets are treated by the traditional resource-based theory as perfectly mobile, firms are thought to have unlimited exchange opportunities as long as they can locate these assets. Firms enter interfirm exchanges in order to acquire mobile assets that deliver value. Thus, exchanges are defined as relationships between parties that involve the clear and obvious transfer of goods or services from the party that values them less to the party that values them more (Podolny and Phillips 1996). In line with Barney (1996) and Grant (1996), we define the value of interfirm exchanges as the usefulness of the asset exchanged to the recipient, who can either be the end user or use it as an input to subsequent value-adding processes. Accordingly, exchanges are the unit of analysis regardless of the position of the exchange partners along the value chain. In this chapter we seek the underlying fundamental premises that guide exchanges regardless of their position along the value chain. If an exchange takes place early in the value chain, we can call it a resource exchange, whereas if it happens at the last stage of the value chain it is a product exchange. We therefore use the words resources and products interchangeably as the subjects of exchanges.

The knowledge-based theory of the firm goes further to suggest that firms outperform competition when they enjoy rents arising from the imperfect mobility of assets that are able to generate greater rents within the focal firm than within any other firm. Such rents are largely derived from invisible and organization-specific assets that are not easily imitable by other firms (Reed and DeFillippi 1990). Creating, transferring, applying, and managing such invisible assets, which behave both as resources and as processes, is crucial to sustaining competitive advantage (Barney 1996; Itami and Roehl 1987) and to achieving superior firm performance (Prahalad and Hamel 1990). However, the knowledge-based view of the firm maintains that not all exchange opportunities are valuable because the value of a firm's knowledge base is not necessarily obvious (Coff 1999). Knowledge-intensive exchanges pose fundamental value assessment problems (Chi 1994) that lead to significant transaction costs of searching for reliable and valuable partners (Kranton 1996) and to potential exchanges falling through (Arrow 1974). In other words, the value of exchanges becomes less manifest as the knowledge content and the inherent intangibility associated with it increases (Spender 1996, Zander and Kogut 1995). This assertion moves the focus of analysis away from the perfect competition paradigm to a more behaviorally based theory of economic exchange that takes into account the effects of social externalities, such as interfirm relations and social structure. Economic exchanges thus need to be analyzed in the context of their socioeconomic ecological system. Complexity theory, which stems from the study of dynamic systems in natural sciences, has been adopted as an appropriate tool for the study of the organization of socioeconomic systems (Anderson et al. 1988).

In the light of these observations, this chapter's main objective is to use complexity theory as the background for building a paradigm for determining value in knowledge-intensive exchanges, which also incorporates externalities arising from a firm's socioeconomic environment. Although researchers have explored extensively the issues of knowledge intangibility, value tacitness, and the risks associated with knowledge exchanges, there has been less emphasis on how to ascertain value in knowledge exchanges. Our paradigm will be primarily grounded on evidence from the cultural industries, and we purport to draw parallels with business on the Internet (henceforth called e-business). Cultural industries such as filmmaking, music, broadcasting, and performing arts are characterized by high knowledge content, demand uncertainty, and ambiguity in terms of drivers of success. Nevertheless, valuations take place, and some cultural products enjoy great success while others flop. Our main thesis is that social conventions that determine self-enforcing patterns of behavior (Schelling 1960, Ellickson 1991, Young 1996) shape valuations in knowledge-intensive exchanges. In other words, the intangibility of value of knowledge-intensive exchanges shifts the focus of valuation away from the exchanges themselves toward how the socioeconomic system selects certain actors in the business and identifies their assets. We will analyze the drivers of identification that lead to self-reinforcing demand for selected actors' assets and exceptional success in the context of the cultural industries and e-business.

Cultural Industries and E-business: Parallel Directions

A concise comparison between cultural industries and e-business will demonstrate their common features that allow for parallels to be drawn. Their fundamental similarity is that in e-business and the cultural industries there is "content" to be sold to an "audience." More specifically, in e-business, firms create modular products constituted by information-based resources, and products reach the customers through many independent distribution points (Werbach 2000). This is also the case with cultural industries—for instance, in the movie industry studios supply films to different distributors and cinema businesses. In fact, cultural industries are increasingly intertwined with the new technologies of the information highway to fashion a new, combined mega-information/entertainment industry (Herther 1993). E-business and cultural industries are thus no longer parallel; with the advent of the Internet they are gradually becoming convergent entities. Below we will group the supply and demand side parallels between the cultural industries and e-business.

Supply Side

Product Modularity

Cultural products are modular in that they are made up of different constituent resources. What is more, modularity breeds product uniqueness in the sense that "every film is different, combining the different artistic and creative talents of numerous individuals from the initial ideas, through script development, design, acting, photography, background music and editing, to marketing the final product, including advertising and promotion" (MMC 1994, para. 4.12). Unlike the case of tangible products, the quality of cultural products is ambiguous because the value of their constituent resources, the exact relationships between these resources, and the link between constituent resources and the attributes of successful cultural products are far from explicit and quantifiable (Choi and Hilton 1995). In other words, a cultural product like a theater play or a music show is complex in that it is more than the mere sum of its modules and constituent resources.

E-products are also modular and information intensive, and the exact relationships between their constituent resources are hard to fathom.

This is evident, for instance, in the case of the Internet company called E*Trade (Werbach 2000): E*Trade is a financial information provider that relies on its core expertise for acquiring and building relationships with its on-line customers. E*Trade products are made up of syndicated information from an array of suppliers. However, what distinguishes E*Trade from competitors is not the information they provide as such but the way it is tailored to the customer, packaged, and priced: "Just like a television station, it is in the business of aggregating and distributing syndicated content as well as providing other in-house services such as trade execution" (Werback 2000, p. 86).

Resource Abundance

Cultural industries are characterized by the abundance of constituent resources, such as scripts, actors, musicians, singers, and so forth. For instance, in the mid-1970s in the United States there were about 3000 full-time self-employed writers and about 1 million people striving to make a living through writing (Tebbel 1976). Yet production companies must cope with this oversupply and the associated uncertainty, select what they think will be a successful project (made up of winning combination of modules), and pour significant capital resources to their production and promotion. Similarly, there is a plethora of easily accessible e-business resources that provide endless product opportunities for companies in the form of syndication—network building aimed at acquiring or building product modules. The Internet company Cisco Systems is an exemplar of syndication, where alliance partners are treated as part of the company because they are an integral part of the company's ability to deliver the product to the customer. Syndication "enables businesses to choose where they wish to concentrate their efforts and to piggyback a myriad of other businesses that can handle the remaining elements of a complete end-to-end service. Unlike outsourcing, it does not restrict flexibility. Syndication relationships can change rapidly—by the second, in fact—and companies can quickly shift between different roles" (Werback 2000, p. 90).

Demand Side

For the consumer, uncertainty stems from time constraints combined with the oversupply of cultural and e-business products: the time people spend "using" cultural products is limited and in that limited time they want to maximize the expected product utility, that is, minimize alternative opportunities forgone in terms of the psychological and emotional effects these products induce. Utility is defined primarily as "a measure of the desirability of a commodity from the psychological viewpoint of the consumer" and secondarily as "a measure of usefulness or need" (Barrett 1974, p. 79). This is also true for e-business when, for instance, one considers the true utility to the customer of a commercial web site when currently there are about 1.6 million on the Internet, the majority of which offer similar services (Hoffman and Novak 2000). In this situation, measurement costs for the consumer are very high, and it is likely that on the usefulness scale most commercial web sites rate similarly. Consequently, psychological factors must be considered as significant drivers of product differentiation, selection, and patronage.

Expected utility of cultural and Internet products is affected by both monetary and nonmonetary factors. For example, the film industry typically expects that only about one in five new movies will make a healthy profit from their theatrical release, a further one fifth will break even, and the remaining will lose money (though some films will recoup their losses from ancillary markets), because in the end the public decides which films succeed and which fail (MMC 1994, para. 4.12). Public taste is notoriously unpredictable because perceived cultural product value is largely socially and culturally defined (Maruca 2000) and susceptible to self-reinforcing social phenomena, such as fashions and fads (Vogel 1998). We can identify two reasons why cultural industries and e-business are sensitive to such phenomena: difficult product valuations and a shortened time period to measure product utility.

Product valuations can be difficult not only before but also after consumption. This is because cultural products and e-products consist primarily of information-based resources, and information cannot be consumed in the traditional sense of the word (Werback 2000). For example, a play by Shakespeare is timeless because it can never be consumed as can a physical product. In other words, cultural products are credence products—their quality is rarely known precisely even after consumption (Darby and Karni 1973). This is not to suggest that consumers cannot make personal judgments about a product's utility after experiencing it, but that their judgment is probably never a final one, as further experience and time can alter it. If later the consumer experienced a product they enjoyed more and made a more favorable judgment about it, the utility of the first product would drop in the eye of that consumer.

Second, in today's era of extreme short product cycles and rapid diffusion of innovation it is possible that the time incurred measuring the value of a resource can reduce its utility. For instance, the use of computers and digital technology is affecting the entire film production industry, and the quality of computer-generated animation is increasing and the price dropping every year. For example, the computer-animated movie *A Bug's Life,* made in 1998, far exceeded *Toy Story* (made in 1995) in "facial expressiveness" (*The Economist* 1998, 15). Accordingly, an exchange of the latest technology, film, or visual arts can become less valuable if the exchange partner can only make use of it after investing time appraising it. This is so because during the appraisal process the resource utility attenuates as new and improved resources appear, capable of inducing stronger psychological and emotional effects.

Complexity Theory and Market Externalities

Markets are conceived of as sites where individuals and institutions come together to communicate, share ideas, and conduct exchanges. Markets do not exist in isolation but they are intertwined with the regional economy, which is in turn intertwined with society and the global economy. Market participants are not perfectly rational actors—as assumed in neoclassical economics—and they live and act in the wider context of society (Arthur 1994). We adopted North's (1990) definition of institutions as "the rules of the game in a society or, more formally, the humanly devised constraints that shape human interaction" (p. 3), which implies that society plays an institutional role in the markets. In light of these observations, the economy can be treated as a complicated system of socioeconomic relations with constituent subsystems— such as regional economies, societies, and local markets—down to individuals. Socioeconomic interactions are human—competitive and hardly predictable (Thietart and Forgues 1995)—and the constituent subsystems interact through myriads of enormously intricate socioeconomic ties and feedback links. The economy can then be modeled as a "complex" system or "a set of

interdependent parts that together make up a whole in that each contributes something and receives something from the whole, which in turn is interdependent with some larger environment" (Thompson 1967, p. 6). Complex systems' interactions at microlevel drive self-reinforcing dynamics that yield nonanticipated, emergent, self-organizing macrolevel system behavior, which is distinct from the mere sum of individual actions of the system's constituent components (Baumol and Benhabib 1989, Stacey 1996). Such system behavior is the subject of complexity theory.

The economy as a complex system is also an evolutionary system. The constituent actors of socioeconomic systems are boundedly rational (Arthur 1994)—their behavior coevolves as actors observe other actors' behavior and the arrangement of their ties to the rest of the system changes. The uncertain nature of human behavior, combined with resource imbalances due to technological capability differentials, subjects socioeconomic systems to evolutionary dynamics. More specifically, socioeconomic system behavior is driven by random variation, exploitation, and exploration mechanisms (Young 1996). System outcomes are driven by random effects and by a feedback process where information regarding past system dynamics is fed back into the system to alter its structure and influence subsequent dynamics (Savit 1991). The evolution of socioeconomic systems is then said to be "path dependent."

The evolution of complex systems' outcomes displays two fundamental processes that create order out of apparently random system behavior, which also underpin two fundamental metaphors for the study of the organization of socioeconomic systems (Polley 1997):

- *Bifurcation.* A system can have more than one stable equilibrium outcome without anyone being dominant. Small variations at the microlevel can become critical and may be the source of instability and subsequent selection of a new macrolevel system-equilibrium outcome.
- *Deterministic chaos.* The long-term evolution of macrolevel equilibrium outcomes takes place within basins of attraction called "strange attractors." Whatever the transient evolutionary path of the chaotic system outside a strange attractor, most of the iterations over the long term fall inside the strange attractor, such that if transient evo-

lutionary paths are omitted, we are left with the strange attractor. The order, however, in which each point in the evolutionary path inside the strange attractor is visited will be unpredictable because small differences between starting points make major differences in the outcome path, and the probability of the system revisiting a previous equilibrium will be extremely low.

Bifurcation and deterministic chaos phenomena have the following metaphorical demonstrations in the case of socioeconomic systems:

Bifurcation Metaphor

First, the dynamics of socioeconomic systems are sensitive at an infinite level to initial conditions, and thus, system equilibrium outcomes can be quite diverse even for similar systems starting from similar initial conditions. Second, in socioeconomic systems, random shocks at a constituent level can cause systems to flip from one equilibrium outcome to another, for example, from one mindset to another, or from one technical standard to another, or from one product dominating the market to another. A socioeconomic system's sensitivity to random shocks and bifurcations is dependent on the weight of its history on its subsequent evolution. If history is increasingly and indefinitely weighing upon current evolution, then system sensitivity to bifurcation is small, perturbations are not strong enough to shake the system away from its current equilibrium, and lock-in effects appear over the long-term evolution (Arthur 1994). When system history has a finite weight on present evolution, then the system can periodically flip to alternative equilibrium outcomes under the influence of random shocks created by external forces (Polley 1997).

On the supply side of cultural industries and e-business, lock-in effects can be demonstrated by the example of Microsoft's attempt to set the technological standard for software for set-top boxes (computer boxes needed to convert digital television signals to pictures, which also allows interactivity and fast Internet access). Microsoft's aim was to develop a lock-in effect similar to the situation with Windows software for personal computers, where they would be the sole suppliers and they could exert monopoly power to cable operators. However, the attempt was undermined by U.S. cable operators, which did not accept Microsoft's software and instead

agreed on common technical standards and a multiplicity of suppliers for set-top boxes (*The Economist* 1998, p. 22). In e-business, market domination through lock-in effects have been the target of many successful high-tech companies. For example, Microsoft gives away the Internet Explorer Web browser, Qualcomm the Eudora e-mail program, and Sun Microsystems the Java computer language in an attempt to lock in as many users as possible, build loyalty, and capture revenues from a premium product or ancillary services. Lock-in effects are also used to repel competition, as in the case of Sun Microsystems giving away the Java language to deter Microsoft from entering the workstation market.

A geographical example of a supply-side lock-in effect in cultural industries comes from Storper (1989), who observed a process of transition from mass production to flexible specialization in the U.S. film industry, which involved the weakening of internal scale economies in favor of external economies. Moreover, external economies and geographical concentration have been shown to be linked in positive feedback relationships: Storper and Christopherson (1987) explained the geographical concentration of the U.S. film production around Los Angeles using a rationale for "increasing returns due to locational advantages." Pratten and Deakin (1999) note that "[e]xamples of locational advantages . . . include 'agglomeration' or 'clustering' between buyer and supplier firms and the emergence of localised pools of skilled labour, which in each case give rise to positive externalities in the form of scale economies and specialisation in the division of labour" (p. 17).

Deterministic Chaos Metaphor

We showed that socioeconomic system evolution is largely driven by exploitation and exploration forces in constant tension. The poised balance between the two makes socioeconomic system outcomes nonrandom, but not entirely predictable either. In other words, system behavior displays deterministic chaos—outcomes are unpredictable but demonstrate order in that they fall within an area of likely behavior (i.e., within a strange attractor). Deterministic chaos has been observed by institutional theorists who have noted the tendency of organizations in the same sector to take up similar forms (DiMaggio and Powell 1983) or the emergence of collective rationality among firms within industries—"industry mindsets" or "industry cultures"—as the backdrop underlying firm strategy and behavior (Huff 1982, Spender 1989). A further demonstration of deterministic chaos includes emergent firm communities, within interfirm networks, where macrocultures develop. Macrocultures are "the relatively idiosyncratic, organization-related beliefs that are shared . . . across organizations" (Abrahamson and Fombrun 1994, p. 730). The development of macrocultures at the firm community level is a demonstration of the "local conformity effect" (Young 1996)—whereby system actors follow local rules. In the long run, we expect the emergence of different firm communities displaying different macrocultures because socioeconomic system evolution is path dependent. This is called the "global diversity effect" (Young 1996)—whereby there is a variety of local rules at global scale.

In the same vein, just as macrocultures develop in islands of firms within interfirm networks, conventions develop in socioeconomic systems. These are social interpretations, norms, rules, and legitimization processes that constrain action and create typical behavior patterns (Jones et al. 1997). Conventions regulate social life and direct socioeconomic systems (as well as emerging from the system itself) toward new equilibrium outcomes. In fact, "it would scarcely be an exaggeration to say that almost all economic and social institutions are governed to some extent by convention" (Young 1996, p. 105). In this context, conventions work not as teleological mechanisms but as coevolving ones, which create order out of the uncertainty and randomness of socioeconomic system behavior.

In socioeconomic systems the bifurcation and deterministic chaos metaphors are not mutually exclusive, but rather work in a complementary manner that drives the evolution of system behavior. In natural science terminology, this would be the type of system behavior where "coherent structures . . . propagated, grew, split apart, and recombined in a wonderfully complex way" (Waldrop 1992, p. 226). The emergence of coherent structures reflects the deterministic chaos metaphor, and their evolution emerges through a series of bifurcations. In other words, socioeconomic systems evolve through a series of equilibria, and within subsystems order emerges in the form of the local conformity effect. Thus, the complete metaphor for the evolution of socioeconomic system behavior could be stated as follows:

> Small variations at the constituent level tend to bring about changes in the system's fundamental tenets, which in turn create emergent conventions and lead to the establishment of new emergent and unpredictable system equilibrium outcomes, ad infinitum.

Conventions and Identification

How do conventions arise? A typical setting would be two cars approaching from opposite directions in a two-way road when there is no law to determine which side each should take. In game theory terminology, this is a situation with more than one Nash equilibrium, and there is nothing intrinsic to the game itself that would allow rational actors to deduce what side they should take (Sugden 1989). This is where conventions come into play, and a convention is defined as an established pattern of behavior "that is . . . expected and self-enforcing," or, using systems terminology, a convention is "an equilibrium that everyone expects in interactions that have more than one equilibrium" (Young 1996, p. 105). Conventions have the power to direct the system toward a given equilibrium because any one of its components conforms to it and expects the others to conform to it, and conforming is in all components' best interest when they all plan to conform (Lewis 1969). Also, conventions have efficiency properties because they reduce transaction costs. For instance,

> consider the cost of having to switch freight from one type of railroad car to another whenever a journey involves both a wide-gauge and a narrow-gauge railroad line. This was a common circumstance in the nineteenth century and not unknown in the late twentieth: until recently, Australia had different mil gauges in the states of New South Wales and Victoria, forcing a mechanical switch for all trains bound between Sydney and Melbourne. (Young 1996, p. 106).

Following Arrow (1971, p. 22) and Young (1996), we distinguish between "formal" and "informal" conventions.

Formal Conventions

Formal conventions are defined as being designed and dictated from the top. Expanding on Young's (1996) argument we believe there are two ways in which formal conventions become internalized by the population: *sheer enforcement* and *positive predisposition*. People follow formal conventions because of the enormous power that the notion of authority has over the human mind (Shiller 2000). Sheer authoritative power can cause us to internalize convention, as demonstrated by the case of the French Academy of Arts during the Renaissance: As soon as painters were elevated to the ranks of the Academy and their work accepted at the so-called "salons," the artists were immediately acknowledged as excellent, and only then they could have a career and reap rewards in terms of resources (Crow 1983, White and White 1993). In this case, there is no need for the people involved to have certain shared values or experiences, but only to accept the central authority that is imposing the convention and the social practices that follow from the central authority's decision. Accordingly, formal conventions established through sheer enforcement are not emergent socioeconomic system outcomes. They are system outcomes that are intentionally selected and identified by a powerful authority on behalf of the actors of the socioeconomic system.

Positive predisposition seems to be able to promote the internalization of formal conventions. Government policy and education can be conducive toward the establishment of positive predisposition, as exemplified by the case of government support for the arts: "national-government support [for the performing arts] has a much longer and deeper tradition in Europe than in the United States" and "such support has educational benefit" (Vogel 1998, p. 288). In other words, the government initiative to culturally educate people—thus conditioning them to be at least positive toward the arts—has created a formal convention that drives demand for the arts. The power of positive predisposition for the establishment of formal convention is also demonstrated in the case of the French government decree to drive on the right side. This formal convention was unopposed and unanimously accepted by the French people not only because of fear of the new authority but also because people shared the common value of "democracy": "The previous custom had been for carriages to keep left and for pedestrians to keep right, facing the oncoming traffic. Changing the custom was symbolic of the new order: going on the left had become politically incorrect because it was identified with the privileged classes; going on the right was the habit of the common man and therefore more 'democratic'" (Young 1996, p. 106). This example demonstrates that the two mechanisms for internalizing formal conventions—sheer enforcement and positive predisposition—are not mutually

exclusive and can work together in a self-reinforcing manner.

Moreover, as Shiller (2000) pointed out, people follow authority not only because they possess an instinct of obedience, but also because they seem to be conditioned to deferring to experts—they accept the judgment of someone whom they are convinced knows more than they do. We posit, then, that positive predisposition can be induced via expert opinion. However, the less people believe someone is an expert, the less they tend to value and follow the expert's authority. Therefore, expert authority depends also on "people's past learning about the reliability of authorities" (Shiller 2000, p. 151). So, as long as the authority that decrees a formal convention can persuade people of its expertise, the convention survives and works. In this case, the internalization of a formal convention is conditional on the parties involved sharing certain values, in this case values regarding the reliability of experts. The case of the French Academy of Arts during the Renaissance is not a case of positive predisposition via expert opinion, because the French Academy, although an expert, did not need to assert its expertise, as it had draconian control over the arts. Thus, when sheer enforcement is hard to impose, positive predisposition can work toward the internalization of formal conventions. In this case, positive predisposition can be induced via expert opinion. Formal conventions established through positive predisposition are partly emergent system outcomes. They are system outcomes that are selected by a powerful authority, but their internalization by the socioeconomic system actors is dependent on conventions being positively identified by expert opinion.

Informal Conventions

Informal conventions are defined as emerging from the base rather than being decreed from the top. The establishment of informal conventions is rooted in the fundamental human ability to relentlessly communicate facts from one person to another—word-of-mouth communication. People are very good at word-of-mouth communication of facts about everyday life (rather than abstract notions), and word-of-mouth communication has the most powerful impact on our behavior (Shiller 2000). Informal conventions are "information cascade" phenomena (Bikhchandani et al. 1992), which arise when there is uncertainty in the environment and difficulty in assessing quality. It has been observed that decision makers follow the decisions made by previous decision makers in making their own decisions, even when their own information suggests doing something quite different. Thus, the act of using information contained in the decisions made by others makes each person's decision less responsive to his or her own information and hence less informative to others. Hence there is a "failure of information about true fundamental value to be disseminated and evaluated" (Shiller 2000, p. 152). Information cascade accelerates network externalities, such as herding toward certain choices, lock-ins, and increasing returns for those "selected" choices (Arthur 1994, Choi and Lee 1996, Schelling 1978). In sum, informal conventions established through information cascade phenomena direct identification and select certain socioeconomic system outcomes in an emergent manner.

As discussed above, identification of certain socioeconomic system outcomes can be deterministic (formal conventions through sheer enforcement), semi-emergent (formal conventions through positive predisposition), and purely emergent (informal conventions). However, in this day and age, informal conventions are increasingly dominating formal ones because of the increasingly pluralistic nature of society. For instance, in the nineteenth century the Impressionists managed to substitute the institutional role (central authority creating conventions by decree) that the Academy used to enjoy in the French arts, for a more pluralist institutional environment made up of a network of art critics, museums, and dealers (Wijnberg and Gemser 1999). This example demonstrates that with time societies move to more pluralistic states. Hence, although conventions can be formal and informal, in today's socioeconomic environment conventions can rarely be imposed from the top and almost always arise from the base.

This is why complexity theory is employed and the process of identification of socioeconomic system outcomes is modeled as an emergent process primarily driven by informal conventions. The theory posits that a complex system cannot be intentionally forced toward a predetermined outcome. Therefore, we cannot expect formal conventions per se to push socioeconomic systems toward desired equilibria. However, formal conventions through positive predisposition play an ancillary role of reinforcing the establishment of informal conventions. Then, formal and informal conventions can work in tandem to identify and establish socioeconomic

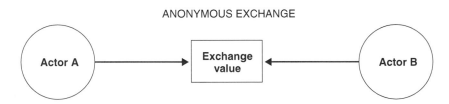

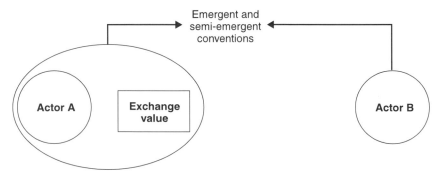

Figure 17.1 Conventions and exchange value.

system outcomes. The identification of exchange value associated with certain socioeconomic actors is treated as a socioeconomic system outcome driven by conventions, as shown in figure 17.1. In other words, we posit that when conventions are absent, exchanges follow the anonymous market mechanism, whereas with conventions present, exchange value becomes directly associated with actor identification.

Exchange Value Identification

The identification process then follows the model of information cascade dynamics, such as word-of-mouth communication of ideas. The mechanism of word-of-mouth communication of ideas has been modeled along the lines of the spread of diseases (Bartholomew 1967). When a new idea is introduced, it will start being adopted as soon as the "infection" rate is greater than the "removal" rate (i.e., of those encountering the idea, more adopt than reject it), and the difference between the infection and removal rates is the rate of adoption. In terms of the success of an idea—the proportion of adopters in the total population—it will peak at the point where infection rate equals removal rate, and it will start declining at the point where the infection rate falls below the removal rate. By the time all the population becomes aware of the idea, the number of adopters will stabilize to some value below the peak value. It is obvious, then, that the success of the idea will be greater under two scenarios: (1) the adoption rate is slow, so the peak occurs at a point where a very high proportion of the population has encountered the idea (this is the case when people have difficulty catching on to an idea but the people who adopt it become very loyal supporters); (2) the rate of adoption before the peak is very much higher than the rate of negative adoption (loss of support) after the peak. We believe that the first scenario is probably more appropriate to model the spread of hardcore ideology (e.g., political ideas) whereas the second scenario is more suitable to modeling how everyday facts of life are communicated, including information that identifies exchange value.

We will concentrate on how informal conventions drive positive or negative identification of socioeconomic actors, for informal conventions are dominant in the modern pluralistic society. The rate of adoption of a particular identification spreading, such as an informal convention, increases when people's behavior is herded around certain collective contextual cues called *focal points* (Schelling 1960, 1978; otherwise conceptualized as a shared notion of *prominence* or *salience*). "A focal point for agreement often owes its focal character to the fact that small concessions would be impossible, that small encroachments would lead to more and larger ones. . . . [It] is supported mainly by the rhetorical question, 'If not here, where?' . . . We are dealing with the players' shared appreciations, preoccupations, obsessions, and sensitivities to suggestion" (Schelling 1960, pp. 111–114). But why are informal conventions through focal points able to coordinate behavior and reduce measurement costs? The answer was given by psychologists Deutsch and Gerard (1955), who showed that when a random sample of people are placed into a large group, their judgment on a question of simple fact they don't know the answer to tends to agree with the prevailing judgment of the group. This is because people believe that the judgment of a large group cannot be wrong and they unconsciously convince themselves to agree to it. In sum, herding around focal points increases the adoption rate of identification as an informal convention.

Focal Points as Drivers of Exchange Value Identification

Focal points are context specific and depend on the culture in which the social actors are embedded (Schelling 1960). In this section, we examine what forms focal points can take in the context of value identification. Could focal points be what Spence (1974) defined as signals? The latter are observable quality indicators with the following two characteristics: (1) they can be at least partially manipulated by the firm, and (2) they incur nonzero marginal cost that is inversely proportional to the firm's level of quality. Podolny's (1993) definition of status as a signal of the underlying "quality of . . . [a] producer's products in relation to the perceived quality of that producer's competitors' products" (p. 830) satisfies the two criteria for signals but demonstrates that signals are unreliable because they are based on perceptions that can be manipulated by impression management tactics (Elsbach and Sutton 1992). Implicitly Podolny (1993) appreciated the limitations of signals when he stressed that the loose linkage between status and quality is mediated by the focal actor's socioeconomic relations. Similarly, Carter and Manaster (1990), Cadmic (1992), and

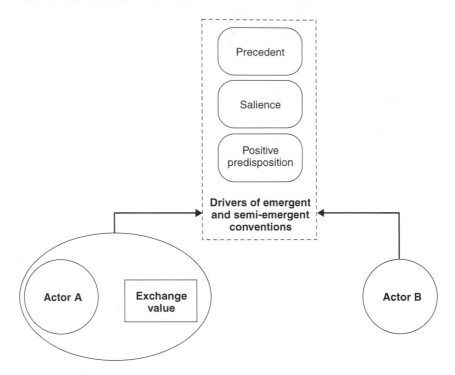

Figure 17.2 Indices of exchange value identification establish emergent and semi-emergent conventions.

Haunschild (1994) have shown that a firm's position in the socioeconomic structure can not only affect rewards but also reduce its ability to interact with firms of different social status. Therefore, the link between status—or, for that matter, any signal—and value must be socially reinforced to be reliable. Socially reinforced signals are indices—"statements or actions that carry some inherent evidence the image projected is correct because they are believed to be inextricably linked to the actors' capabilities or intentions" (Jervis 1985, p. 26). Accordingly, indices are socially reinforced signals that perform the role of focal points, which generate conventions and drive exchange value identification. From our previous analysis of conventions we can identify three forms of indices, as shown in figure 17.2: precedent, salience, and positive predisposition.

Precedent

The first index of exchange value identification that works as a focal point to induce informal conventions is common precedent among social actors (Young 1996, Sugden 1989). Precedent works as a focal point because, as shown by Barzel (1982), exchange parties choosing products over time can be satisfied with the average quality level that identifies their partner. In other words, it is in the interest of both exchange parties not to measure the exact value of what is being exchanged at every single transaction but to follow the precedent that has established an informal convention guaranteeing an average quality. Precedent in the market can work as an index for subsequent exchange identification. This is the case when certain choices are repeated over others and gain in practice, in turn making them more prominent (a focal point) and thus easier to follow (Arthur 1994, Young 1996). For example, studios know that a sequel of a hit movie is more likely to have a successful opening weekend (Frank and Cook 1995).

Brands are also an important tool used to facilitate emergent conventions that identify exchange value through the establishment of precedent. Brands have the potential of providing customers with a variety of pleasant or unpleasant experiences (Schmitt 1999a) and, hence, become focal points as they elicit word-of-mouth communication around these experiences. Brands are flexible strategic tools because they allow for precedent to be transferred to multiple artistic means of communication (e.g., from printed cartoon to film). Therefore, entertainment companies do not simply sell movies, games, or television programs separately, but bind them under brands. As discussed in *The Economist* (1999), brands are "often launched with an 'event' movie, as with Disney's *Lion King* or Sony's *Godzilla*, but brands can start life in all sorts of ways. Viacom's *Rugrats*, which has just been turned into a movie, came from a children's cable channel, Nickelodeon; Time Warner's *Batman* is an old and revered comic-book character that . . . translate[s] nicely into a live-action movie" (p. 8). In fact, *Rugrats* has also been turned into a book and a Web site, as well as being sold via all kinds of merchandise (*The Economist*, 1999, p. 83). Precedent through brand building is invaluable in e-business when one considers the expansion of customer reach that the Internet offers compared to traditional business. For instance, Amazon.com stores some 4.5 million titles and reaches some 25 million computer screens, compared with the largest physical branch of Barnes & Noble book stores, which stores only 200,000 titles. Careerpath.com—an on-line agency that links employers with job seekers—has a classified ads market 50 times larger than any printed newspaper (Evans and Wurster 1999).

Precedent in the market can also occur through an actor's network of clients. As an example of identification of an actor via his clients, Rupert Murdoch's "publishing company, HarperCollins, rejected a manuscript for a book by Chris Patten of his years as governor of Hong Kong, which it had earlier agreed to publish. The book was critical of the Chinese government, whose favour Mr Murdoch needs to help his Star TV satellite broadcaster" (*The Economist* 1998, p. 7). It is evident that HarperCollins was aware that it would have been hampering other Murdoch business interests in China had it gone ahead with the Patten deal. In this case, identification with the specific client was considered negative, and it would have led to negative feedback effects for Murdoch's business interests. In another case, when Silicon Graphics got the contract from animation designers Industrial Light & Magic to provide workstations for animation design for the movie *Jurassic Park*, it used it to spur future sales, first, by making the movie a showcase of its workstations and, second, by complementing the workstations with the specialized software developed for *Jurassic Park*,

thus making its product more valuable (Shapiro and Varian 1999). In other words, serving important clients can be influential when these clients have the power within an industry to shape product development, because smaller customers will tend to adopt product development specified by your big client.

Salience

A focal point is by definition a salient point. Salience can be induced, as demonstrated by HBO's Jeff Bewkes: "We don't care how many people watch our shows. We just want people to decide at the end of the month that it's worth renewing their subscription." This implies that the customer base is divided into segments and that if every segment "was wild about one thing . . . screened, and hated the rest, they have done the job. If all their programmes are mildly, but not very interesting to everybody, they haven't." This strategy is based on positive feedback effects within the multiple market segments, because "it is news, far more than soaps, that people gossip about in the office" (*The Economist* 1998, p. 13). So, for people who were excited about a particular program, it was a memorable experience. Subsequently, they will maintain their subscription and hype the program to their peers, reinforcing word-of-mouth mechanisms and positive feedback demand effects for their choice of program.

The central role excitement plays in creating memorable experiences was noted by Hutton (1995), who quotes Daniel Kahnemann's "peak and end rule"—"that our memory of an event is conditioned by the peak of emotion we experienced during its course and how we felt when it ended; how long it lasted and thus what the true full experience was has little impact on our recollection" (p. 230). Therefore, we can posit that among the thousands of web sites purporting to perform similar tasks, those that excite people and offer memorable experiences can be more popular. The Internet, in conjunction with new technologies, allows customers not simply to browse passively through what a web site has to offer but to participate and connect with the content. Internet technologies "such as interactive games, . . . chat rooms, . . . motion-based simulators, and virtual reality" whereby "customers can view, hear, and touch—as well as drive, walk of fly—through myriad product possibilities" can encourage memorable experiences of various degrees of customer participation in, absorption of, or immersion into the web site content (Pine and Gilmore 1998, pp. 99–102).

We believe that salience mechanisms are also at work through an actor's networks of competitors, clients, and collaborators. The idea behind this assertion is that there exist groups of competitors, clients, and collaborators with specific characteristics who identify with and are identified by established group norms. Thus, a focal actor linked with a particular group of competitors or collaborators is selected and identified as adhering to some shared values and norms. For example, a play showing on Broadway belongs to the group of plays that are competitors on Broadway—a very specific group of plays with strong characteristics that identify the focal play. Another example is the Goodwill Games—started by Ted Turner and considered a member of his business empire: "HBO [a sports pay channel] organised the boxing, its speciality, which was covered mainly on the Turner networks and promoted in *Sports Illustrated*" (*The Economist* 1998, p. 11). On the Internet, firms join membership shopping clubs (such as cuc.com), which are virtual clubs regulated by the participating firms, where customers can search according to price, attributes, or brand name and can choose among a list of products that meet their entered criteria.

Collaboration seems to be another means of strengthening a firm's salience in the marketplace. Increasingly, even traditional competitors such as print and television rivals are coming together to collaborate. For instance, the *Washington Post* and NBC News jointly developed a web page that "prominently displays the *Post*'s lead story, as well as the latest news from NBC's flagship shows such as *Today* and *Nightly News with Tom Brokaw*" (*The Guardian* 1999b, p. 6). In the Internet era, forming alliances with respected rival organizations is becoming widespread because it answers the question of how to gather quality news around the clock. Alliances work to this effect, provided the partners remain independent; hence, "*Washington Post* and NBC are keen to stress that editorial independence will be fiercely maintained under the[ir] new alliance" (p. 7). Another example is the 1995 merger of Disney with ABC broadcasting network and ESPN cable sports network, which was an attempt by these three companies to carry each other's brands and promote each other's products through as many distribution channels as possible (*The Economist* 1999, p. 83).

Film and television stars and collaborators who are perceived as leaders function as another driver of salience. For example, Simonet (1977) showed that film commercial success is dependent on star directors and actors, and Kindem (1982) demonstrated that they also account for 23% of the variance in box office revenues. This was noted by film director John Boorman: "Because films go out to hundreds of cinemas across America at the same time, they need very expensive advertising. . . . This means the audience needs a recognition factor of a simple story and stars they can identify with" (*The Guardian* 1999a, p. 2). In the software industry, Sun Microsystems used salient players who endorsed its products to induce other companies to buy them. Their strategy proved successful, and they even managed to get Bill Gates to announce Microsoft's support for Java (Shapiro and Varian 1999). Similarly, Internet-based companies can collaborate with influential players who endorse their products and become salient focal points for potential customers, as Amazon.com and America Online (AOL) did in 1997 (Sandberg 1997).

Positive Predisposition

Positive predisposition is the third index of exchange value identification, and it is induced via expert opinion that drives semi-emergent formal conventions. Positive predisposition can be established through relations with or support of legitimate institutions—regulatory agencies, magazines, journals, or influential critics. Support for this claim can be found in a recent study of the German music industry (Choi et al. 1999). The study sought to analyze why over 50% of sales are generated by the 16–29 age group and why the over-30 group has a nonbuyer motivation. One explanation offered was that people over 30 are less sociable and spend more time and money on family and home. Thus, they do not reach critical mass that younger people reach through reading magazines and discussing among themselves the latest music trends. If some expert music opinion was introduced in the over-30 group and it was received by a large proportion of them, then critical mass could possibly be achieved.

Examples of identification by expert opinion are drawn from the world of visual arts (Wijnberg and Gemser 1999): museums of living artists—such as modern art museums—play the role of certification of living artists. "Precisely because of the presumption of the modern art museum that the way in which it categorizes and displays art works adds significantly to the understanding of the art consumer, the museum has become so important an agent in certifying the quality of these art works" (p. 16). Expert identification also occurs through art dealers and galleries. For example, the first Impressionist painters were promoted by so-called "ideological" dealers like Durand-Ruel, Petit, and Theo van Gogh—who were not simply motivated by money but promoted a certain genre or artistic style (Jensen 1994)—the Impressionist movement. Finally, expert selection identification is also crucial. For example, dealers who bought Impressionists needed the contribution of art experts to help them place the painters in their historical context and provide legitimacy, as well as convince the consumers of the value of Impressionist works (Jensen 1994, Wijnberg and Gemser 1999). In fact, nowadays the experts have become so powerful that it seems as if they are more important than the artist or as if they are the real artists and the artists are just the persons who provide the raw input (Sandler 1996). Moreover, different expert identification mechanisms can work in parallel, as demonstrated in the case of the Impressionists, where museums, art dealers, and critics started working together in a mutually reinforcing manner that eventually established the Impressionists as a worthwhile art movement (Wijnberg and Gemser 1999).

In the Internet era, exchange value identification by expert opinion is taking a new turn in the form of virtual experts. Experts as physical parties are being slowly superseded by Internet chat rooms and virtual communities—web sites such as epinions.com, feedbackdirect.com, and eComplaints.com, where customers voice their views, suggestions, and experiences on products: "eComplaints is your chance to fight back. It's your chance to be heard by the company at fault and more importantly, by your fellow consumer. . . . Neatly sorted into categories we all recognise from the big search engines, these websites allow customers very easily to convey their concerns to a broad audience" (Schmitt 1999b, p. 7). Similarly, "Microsoft CarPoint provides car buyers with the data and software to compare alternative models along 80 objective specifications. Physical dealers never offer that kind of information. Nor (quite rationally) do the car makers on their proprietary web sites. Microsoft can do

this because Internet technology enables such rich information to be assembled from wide-reaching sources at negligible cost" (Evans and Wurster 1999, p. 89). This is a case of a formal convention creation by positive predisposition through expert opinion where the actual virtual expert opinion is emergent. It is therefore a semi-emergent form of conventions establishment.

Selected versus Nonselected Actors

Our exchange value identification scheme is a competitive dynamics paradigm based on value identification through socioeconomic relations. We posited that exchange value identification is driven by emergent conventions established through information cascade dynamics, and we identified the drivers of these dynamics as the three indices: precedent, salience, and positive predisposition. With the introduction of indices as drivers of exchange value identification, perfect competition becomes distorted because information cascade dynamics induce positive feedback effects that lead to the selection and favorable identification of a few actors among the competing set. Then the opportunities of an actor to establish its product (or resource) as a leader are shaped by the availability of information about the actor and the product and that information is channeled through the indices of identification. Because the indices induce positive information cascade effects, the availability of information related to selected actors and their products or resources is much higher than for nonselected actors. In other words, selected actors acquire "social capital" through the indices, which is a resource similar to financial or human capital that exists within the social relations in which an actor is embedded (Loury 1987). Therefore, selected actors enjoy the additional resource of social capital that nonselected actors do not have, which brings them more opportunities as more information about them cascades through the market. As shown in figure 17.3, increased opportunities translate into the selected actors moving in a virtuous spiral of success and supernormal returns that nonselected actors do not enjoy. Also, the success spiral of selected actors further distorts the nature of competition, which becomes disproportionate (Choi and Baden-Fuller 1995)—where the interaction of markets, relations, and identification in the social structure selects winners and makes

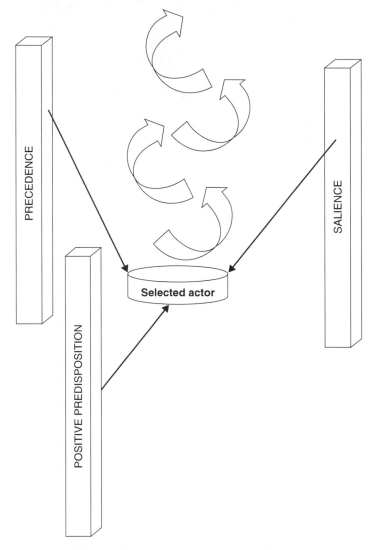

Figure 17.3 The spiral of success of actors selected by conventions.

it particularly difficult for the unselected actors to succeed.

The spiral can be further reinforced in two ways: (1) the more selected actors become embedded into progressively denser networks of socioeconomic relations, "directing information flows in the building and maintaining of social capital" (Walker et al. 1997, p. 111), the more opportunities will abound, and (2) new opportunities will lead to new exchanges, some of which can be gateway events (Gell-Mann 1994) where "small changes . . . escalate into major qualitative changes in outcomes" (Stacey 1995, p. 483). In summary, selected actors enter a spiral of in-

creasing social capital and success that leads to disproportional availability of opportunities and disproportional success.

Conclusions and Strategy Implications in the Internet Era

With the advent of the Internet, the field of strategy has become increasingly interdisciplinary, as has already happened with organization theory. Research into e-business requires overlap between strategy, knowledge management, and market valuation theories. All three are inextricably linked, because market valuations are heavily driven by a firm's knowledge management strategy, which nowadays does not simply involve a firm's internal resources but also seeks to identify and develop the knowledge assets and relationships of the firm's knowledge environment. Accordingly, strategy as a means to success and favorable valuations cannot be isolated from a firm's knowledge management.

In this chapter, we link strategy, knowledge management, and Internet research, relying on a parallel analysis of cultural industries. Our main thesis is that uncertainty of exchange value shifts the focus of valuation away from the resources themselves toward how the socioeconomic environment identifies certain actors in the business and certifies their resources. We posit that in cultural industries and e-business, conventions—patterns of behavior that are customary and socially self-enforcing—drive self-reinforcing success because they provide identification in the market for certain actors. We distinguish between emergent and semi-emergent conventions and we specify their function in legitimizing value and moderating measurement costs. Conventions are primarily established through focal points, which are socially reinforced signals and carry some inherent evidence that the projected image is true. These are called indices, and we identified three families of indices: precedent, salience, and positive predisposition.

We believe that in the Internet era, strategy development has to incorporate knowledge management in the form of putting in place the three families of indices. One aspect of strategy should dwell on establishing the index of salience, which is associated with making the enjoyment of a product an experience for the consumer, with the firm's network of collaborators and competitors, and its association with exceptional contributors and stars. Firms should not be afraid to establish cooperative ventures with other companies to bring benefits to the customer and carry each others' names, particularly when one of the parties involved has an established star quality. Such agreements are expensive, as the case of America Online shows, which by August 1997 had sold space on its web site to more than 70 retailers or content providers for $125,000 per year plus commission of 5–60% (Shapiro and Varian 1999). However, the explosive expansion of the Internet makes this a small price to pay for making your firm more salient, reducing the consumers' search costs and making it easier for them to find out about your products.

Strategy must also manage the index of precedent, which is principally associated with the firm's brands and network of clients. Establishing and maintaining brands is pivotal in the Internet era because they create precedents that facilitate favorable customer expectations. Brands must be carried through as many conduits as possible, in which case salience and precedent indices become mutually reinforcing mechanisms because brands become stronger the higher the percentage of customer population they reach through salience mechanisms. Finally, we identified positive predisposition as an index of identification driven by expert opinion. Product preannouncements and prereleases to expert users as well as subsequent third-party information (e.g., consumer reports) can create focal points that elicit positive expectations. As physical experts tend to be replaced by virtual experts, so firms need to have active involvement in the Internet and freely expose their offerings to discussion groups and virtual communities, as well as being fast in incorporating feedback.

In e-business, precedent, salience, and positive predisposition can work in a complementary fashion to each other. For instance, firms in search of salience collaborate with on-line consumer clubs and web sites specializing in particular products, such as Virtual Vineyards at virtualvin.com and Software Net at software.net, to promote their product. Besides, these web sites offer expert reviews, such as an expert called CorkDork at Virtual Vineyards, who "shares his tasting notes with consumers who can then compare these recommendations to their own expressed taste preferences" (Klein 1998), which drive the positive predisposition index. Moreover, these web sites offer consumers reviews and experiences through bulletin boards, which drive the precedence and positive predisposition indices. In turn, positive predisposition can kickstart further salience and precedent positive feedback mechanisms by accelerating the establishment of customer base and strengthening brand position. In the case of CarPoint, Microsoft offers this on-line car expertise service because it allows Microsoft to carry its brand, build salience, and create precedent with the customers to navigate them to its core-business-related web sites.

Another mutually reinforcing connection between indices is that of precedent (created by brands) and salience (arising from memorable experiences). As Evans and Wurster (1999) put it,

> Brand-as-experience . . . is not . . . defined by . . . statements about it or by . . . product specifications. Barbie is a fantasy world for young girls and a collectible for adults. Mattel devotes enormous resources to creating and preserving the consistency with which that fantasy world is presented. Barbie-as-experience will be magnified by richer channels of communication. When Mattel can reach young girls in a broadband, interactive, customized environment [enabled by Internet technology] . . . it can enrich the Barbie fantasy world with dress up, storytelling, and conversations. This enhances the brand, but it also enhances the product and the experience of owning it. Indeed the brand, the product, and the experience are really one and the same. (p. 93)

This chapter also raised the importance of heterogeneity between selected and nonselected actors. Drivers of exchange value identification distort perfect competition, and identified actors are selected and enjoy disproportionate success. We believe that the selected versus nonselected competitive dynamics paradigm in cultural industries and e-business is relevant to other knowledge-intensive industries. Accordingly, future research should thus focus on what the identification drivers are in these industries, how they are formed, and how they evolve over time. This would be a significant step toward understanding the competitive dynamics and institutional influences in knowledge-intensive industries.

Acknowledgment   We thank George Syrpis for his helpful comments on earlier drafts of this chapter.

References

Abrahamson, E. and Fombrun, C. (1994) "Macrocultures: determinants and consequences." *Academy of Management Review* 19:328–355.

Amit, R. and Schoemaker, P. (1993) "Strategic assets and organisational rents." *Strategic Management Journal* 14:33–46.

Anderson, P.W., Arrow, K.J., and Pines, D. (1988) *The Economy as an Evolving Complex System.* Reading, MA: Addison-Wesley.

Arrow, K.J. (1971) "Political and economic evaluation of social effects and externalities," in M. Intriligator (ed.), *Frontiers of Quantitative Economics*, pp. 3–25. Amsterdam: North-Holland.

Arrow, K.J. (1974) *The Limits of Organization.* New York: Norton.

Arthur, B. (1994) *Increasing Returns and Path Dependency in the Economy.* Ann Arbor: University of Michigan Press.

Barney, J.B. (1996) *Gaining and Sustaining Competitive Advantage.* Reading, MA: Addison-Wesley.

Barrett, N.S. (1974) *The Theory of Microeconomics Policy.* Lexington, MA: Heath.

Bartholomew, D.J. (1967) *Stochastic Models for Social Processes.* New York: Wiley.

Barzel, Y. (1982) "Measurement cost and the organisation of markets." *Journal of Law and Economics* 25:27–48.

Baumol, W.J. and Benhabib, J. (1989) "Chaos: significance, mechanism, and economic applications." *Journal of Economic Perspectives* 3(1): 77–105.

Bikhchandani, S.D., Hirshleifer, D., and Welch, I. (1992) "A theory of fashion, social custom and cultural change." *Journal of Political Economy* 81:637–654.

Cadmic, C. (1992) "Reputation and predecessor selection: Parsons and the institutionalists." *American Sociological Review* 57:421–445.

Carter, R. and Manaster, S. (1990) "Initial public offerings and underwriter reputation." *Journal of Finance* 45:1045–1068.

Chi, T. (1994) "Trading in strategic resources: necessary conditions, transaction cost problems, and choice of exchange structure." *Strategic Management Journal* 15(4):271–290.

Choi, C.J. and Baden-Fuller, C. (1995) *Disproportionate Competition.* Mimeo, City University Business School, London.

Choi, C.J. and Lee, S.H. (1996) "A knowledge based view of co-operative interorganizational relationships," in P. Beamish and P. Killing (eds.), *Co-operative Strategies: European Perspectives.*

Choi, C.J., Kretschmer, M., and Klimis, G.M. (1999) "Increasing returns and social contagion in cultural industries." *British Journal of Management.*

Coff, R.W. (1999) "How buyers cope with uncertainty when acquiring firms in knowledge-intensive industries: caveat emptor." *Organization Science* 10(2):144–161.

Crow, T. (1983) *Painters and Public Life in Eighteenth-Century Paris.* New Haven: Yale University Press.

Darby, M. and Karni, E. (1973) "Free competition and the optimal amount of fraud." *Journal of Law and Economics* 16:67–88.

Deutsch, M. and Gerard, H.B. (1955) "A study of normative and informational social influences upon individual judgment." *Journal of Abnormal and Social Psychology* 51:629–636.

DiMaggio, P.J. and Powell, W. (1983) "The iron cage revisited: institutional isomorphism and collective rationality in organizational fields." *American Sociological Review* 48:147–161.

The Economist. (1998) "Technology and Entertainment Survey." November 21.

The Economist. (1999) "Two sharks in a fishbowl." September 11, pp. 83–84.

Ellickson, R. (1991) *Order without Law*. Cambridge, MA: Harvard University Press.

Elsbach, K.D. and Sutton, R.I. (1992) "Acquiring organizational legitimacy through illegitimate actions: a marriage of institutional and impression management theories." *Academy of Management Journal* 35:699–738.

Evans, P. and Wurster, T.S. (1999) "Getting real about virtual commerce." *Harvard Business Review*, November–December, pp. 84–94.

Frank, R.H. and Cook, P.J. (1995) *The Winner-Take-All Society*. New York: Free Press.

Gell-Mann, M. (1994) *The Quark and the Jaguar: Adventures in the Simple and the Complex*. London: Little, Brown.

Grant, R.M. (1996) "Prospering in dynamically-competitive environments: organizational capability as knowledge integration." *Organization Science* 7(4):375–387.

The Guardian 2. (1999a) "They're not just rich and famous. They're in charge." November 19, pp. 2–3.

The Guardian 2. (1999b) "Sleeping with the enemy." November 22, pp. 6–7.

Haunschild, P. (1994) "How much is that company worth? Interorganizational relationships, uncertainty and acquisition premiums." *Administrative Science Quarterly* 39:391–411.

Herther, N.K. (1993) "The next information revolution. *CD-ROM Professional*, July.

Hoffman, D.L. and Novak, T.P. (2000) "How to acquire customers on the Web." *Harvard Business Review* 78(3):179–183.

Huff, A.S. (1982) "Industry influence on strategy reformation." *Strategic Management Journal* 3:119–131.

Hutton, W. (1995) *The State We're In*. London: Vintage.

Itami, H. and Roehl, T.W. (1987) *Mobilizing Invisible Assets*. Cambridge, MA: Harvard University Press.

Jensen, R. (1994) *Marketing Modernism in Fin-de-Siécle Europe*. Princeton, NJ: Princeton University Press.

Jervis, R. (1985) *The Logic of Images in International Relations*. Princeton, NJ: Princeton University Press.

Jones, C., Hesterly, W., and Borgatti, S. (1997) "A general theory of network governance: exchange conditions and social mechanisms." *Academy of Management Review* 22:911–945.

Kalish, E. (1991) In E. Penzer, How to guard against box-office flops. *Incentive*, March.

Kindem, G. (1982) "Hollywood's movie star system: a historical overview," in G. Kindem (ed.), *The American Movie Industry: The Business of Motion Pictures*, pp. 79–94. Carbondale: Southern Illinois University Press.

Klein, L.R. (1998) "Evaluating the potential of interactive media through a new lens: search versus experience goods." *Journal of Business Research* 41:195–203.

Kranton, R. (1996) "The formation of cooperative relationships." *Journal of Law, Economics, and Organization* 12:214–233.

Lewis, D. (1969) *Convention: A Philosophical Study*. Cambridge, MA: Harvard University Press.

Loury, G. (1987) "Why should we care about group inequality?" *Social Philosophy and Policy* 5: 249–271.

Maruca, R.F. (2000) "Mapping the world of customer satisfaction." *Harvard Business Review* 78(3):30–31.

Monopolies and Mergers Commission (MMC). (1995) *Report on the Supply of Films for Exhibition in Cinemas in the UK*. London: Her Majesty's Stationery Office.

North, D.C. (1990) *Institutions, Institutional Change and Economic Performance*. New York: Cambridge University Press.

Pine, J.B., II and Gilmore, J.H. (1998) "Welcome to the experience economy." *Harvard Business Review*, July–August, pp. 97–105.

Podolny, J. (1993) "A status-based model of market competition." *American Journal of Sociology* 98:829–872.

Podolny, J. and Phillips, D.J. (1996) "The dynamics of organizational status." *Industrial and Corporate Change* 5(2):453–472.

Polley, D. (1997) "Turbulence in organizations: new metaphors for organizational research." *Organization Science* 8(5):445–457.

Prahalad, C.K. and Hamel, G. (1990) "The core competence of the corporation." *Harvard Business Review*, May–June, pp. 79–91.

Pratten, S. and Deakin, S. (1999) *Competitiveness Policy and Economic Organisation: The Case of the British Film Industry*. Working Paper 127.

Cambridge: ESRC Centre for Business Research, University of Cambridge.

Reed, R. and DeFillipi, R. (1990) "Casual ambiguity barriers to imitation and sustainable competitive advantage." *Academy of Management Review* 15:88–102.

Sandberg, J. (1997) "Retailers pay big for prime Internet real estate." *Wall Street Journal* (23 July): C1.

Sandler, I. (1996) *Art of the Postmodern Era*. New York: HarperCollins.

Savit, R. (1991) "Chaos on the trading floor," in N. Hall (ed.), *The New Scientist Guide to Chaos*, pp. 115–136. London: Penguin Books.

Schelling, T.C. (1960) *The Strategy of Conflict*. Cambridge, MA: Harvard University Press.

Schelling, T.C. (1978) *Micromotives and Macrobehavior*. New York: Norton.

Schmitt, B. (1999a) *Experiential Marketing: How to Get Customers to Sense, Feel, Think, Act and Relate to Your Company and Brands*. New York: Free Press.

Schmitt, B. (1999b) "Branding puts a high value on reputation management." *Financial Times* 13 (June):6–7.

Shapiro, C. and Varian, H.R. (1999) *Information Rules: A Strategic Guide to the Network Economy*. Boston: Harvard Business School Press

Shiller, R.J. (2000) *Irrational Exuberance*. Princeton, NJ: Princeton University Press.

Simonet, T. (1977) "Regression analysis of prior experience of key production personnel as predictors of revenues from high grossing motion pictures in American release." Doctoral diss., Temple University.

Spence, M. (1974) *Market Signaling*. Cambridge, MA: Harvard University Press.

Spender, J.-C. (1989) *Industry Recipes*. Oxford: Blackwell.

Spender, J.-C. (1996) "Making knowledge the basis of a dynamic theory of the firm." *Strategic Management Journal* 17(Winter):45–62.

Stacey, R.D. (1995) "The science of complexity: an alternative perspective for strategic change processes." *Strategic Management Journal* 16:477–495.

Stacey, R.D. (1996) "Emerging strategies for a chaotic environment." *Long Range Planning* 29(2):182–189.

Storper, M. (1989) "The transition to flexible specialisation in the US film industry: external economies, the division of labour, and the crossing of industrial divides." *Cambridge Journal of Economics* 13:273–305.

Storper, M. and Christopherson, S. (1987) "Flexible specialization and regional industrial agglomerations: the US film industry." *Annals of the Association of American Geographers* 77:1 04–117.

Sugden, R. (1989) "Spontaneous Order." *Journal of Economic Perspectives* 3:85–97.

Tebbel, J. (1976) "The book business in the USA," in D. Daiches and A. Thorlby (eds.), *The Modern World: Reactions*, Vol. 3, pp. 251–280. London: Aldus.

Thietart, R.A. and Forgues, B. (1995) "Chaos theory and organization." *Organization Science* 6(1):19–31.

Thompson, J.D. (1967) *Organizations in Action*. New York: McGraw-Hill.

Vogel, H.L. (1998) *Entertainment Industry Economics: A Guide for Financial Analysis*, 4th ed. Cambridge: Cambridge University Press.

Waldrop, M. (1992) *Complexity: The Emerging Science at the Edge of Order and Chaos*. New York: Simon and Schuster.

Walker, G., Kogut, B., and Shan, W. (1997) "Social capital, structural holes and the formation of an industry network." *Organization Science* 8(2): 109–125.

Werback, K. (2000) "Syndication: the emerging model for business in the Internet era." *Harvard Business Review* 78(3):84–93.

White, C. and White, H.C. (1993) *Canvases and Careers: Institutional Change in the French Painting World*, 2d ed. New York: Wiley.

Wijnberg, N.M. and Gemser, G. (1999) *Groups, Experts and Innovation: The Selection System of Modern Visual Art*. Working Paper 99B39. Gröningen: Research Institute of Systems, Organisation and Management. University of Gröningen.

Young, P. (1996) "The economics of convention." *Journal of Economic Perspectives* 10:105–122.

Zander, U. and Kogut, B. (1995) "Knowledge and the speed of the transfer and limitation of organizational capabilities." *Organization Science* 6(1):76–92.

IV

Knowledge Strategy in Practice

18

Product Sequencing

Coevolution of Knowledge, Capabilities, and Products

Constance E. Helfat and Ruth S. Raubitschek

Why are firms different? This is one of the fundamental questions in strategic management, because the sources of firm heterogeneity underlie competitive advantage (Rumelt et al. 1994). The resource-based view (Barney 1991, Peteraf 1993, Wernerfelt 1984) and knowledge management approaches (Grant 1996) suggest that capabilities and knowledge form the basis for differential firm performance. But how do successful firms get to the point where they have superior resources and knowledge, and how do firms maintain this superiority through time? Dynamic capabilities that enable firms to introduce new products and processes and adapt to changing market conditions play an important role (Teece et al. 1997, Helfat 1997). But exactly how do firms build and deploy capabilities? We provide a conceptual model that explains how organizations can successfully build and utilize knowledge and capabilities, over long time spans, in single and multiple product markets, for continuing competitive advantage. The model further highlights the importance of products, supported by vertical chains of complementary assets and activities, to the development and exploitation of capabilities and knowledge. That is, we bring the role of products back into the analysis of resources, capabilities, and knowledge. We also provide an explicitly dynamic framework that tracks stages of organizational evolution through time, across markets, and in the context of products and vertical chains. This in turn yields a model of the *coevolution* of knowledge, capabilities, and products.

At the heart of the model are sequences of products within and across vertical chains, supported by an underlying system of knowledge and systems of learning. At any given point in time, an organization's portfolio of products serves as a platform for future product sequences. These product platforms evolve over time in concert with knowledge and capabilities, and provide opportunities for competitive advantage through the strategic linkage of products up, down, and across vertical chains.[1]

The chapter proceeds as follows. We first set up some basic building blocks for the model. Next we explain the components of the model: the *system of knowledge* that underpins vertical chains of activities and supports *product se-*

quencing within and across vertical chains over time, based on *systems of learning*. Then we present three company case histories that illustrate the model. We conclude with an explanation of the contributions of the model to several related literatures, including the resource-based view, dynamic capabilities, and knowledge management.

Basic Setting and Building Blocks

The model applies to technology-intensive companies, and to firms that require complex coordination of knowledge and activities more generally. Such firms include those in high-technology industries, as well as businesses that are not considered to be high technology but require complex or technologically sophisticated knowledge in order to design and operate plant, equipment, and services. For example, an oil refinery consists of many complex, interrelated pieces of equipment requiring substantial technological know-how to design, build, and deploy. Our analysis also applies to companies that rely heavily on information technology, even if the companies themselves are not in high-technology industries (e.g., retailers such as Wal-Mart). Additionally, the analysis encompasses service businesses that make less use of information technology but nevertheless require complex coordination of activities (e.g., financial services prior to the widespread use of computers). Thus, the model applies to a wide range of companies.

Within this setting, we focus on *organizational* knowledge and its relation to *organizational* capabilities, activities, and products. Tacit knowledge, for example, has the characteristic that it is not easily communicated in words, numbers, or pictures, but instead requires people, and often teams of people—that is, organizations—to effect knowledge transfer and utilization (Winter 1987, Leonard and Sensiper 1998). The creation of tacit organizational knowledge also generally requires repeated interactions among people over time. Because we are interested in organizational knowledge and capabilities, we do not analyze the sort of knowledge that can be easily transferred independent of people. Thus, we do not seek to explain phenomena such as the decoupling of semiconductor chip design and manufacturing fabs, enabled by the codifiability of chip designs.[2] We do, however, analyze more complex coordination of codified knowledge that requires organizational mechanisms.[3]

The product sequencing model utilizes two well-established concepts. The first is that of complementary assets and resources surrounding a core technology (Teece 1986). The second, closely related concept is that of a value chain (Porter 1985). Teece (1986) points out that capturing value from what he terms "core technological know-how" frequently requires complementary assets that reside in different stages of a vertical chain, such as finance, manufacturing, and marketing. A separate literature on vertical chains is associated with Porter (1985) in particular, who focuses on the "value chain" within firms.[4] The stages of the value chain are "activities" such as manufacturing and marketing, and we adopt that terminology here.

The basic unit of analysis in our model is a vertical chain in combination with the product it supports.[5] To simplify the exposition, we use the term "product" to denote either a product or a service. We do not analyze the internal workings of individual stages in a vertical chain (e.g., research, manufacturing) or factors related to design of the product, nor do we deal with issues of organizational design. Additionally, we abstract from boundary of the firm issues. Our analysis requires only a long-term relationship among stages of vertical (or horizontal) chains, in order to build and utilize knowledge, regardless of whether this takes place in a single firm or in multiple firms (see, e.g., Dyer and Singh 1998). Figure 18.1 provides an overview of the model.

To begin the analysis, we describe the *system of knowledge* that underlies a set of activities and products in a vertical chain. Then we analyze *product sequencing* within and across vertical chains, as well as the required *systems of learning*.

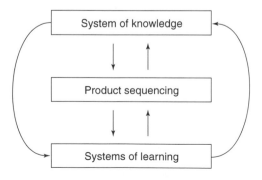

Figure 18.1 Product sequencing model.

System of Knowledge

The system of knowledge[6] in our model is composed of *core knowledge* and *integrative knowledge*. A more detailed explanation of each follows.

Core Knowledge

In technology-intensive industries, a fundamental resource of the firm is its technology base.[7] We define *core knowledge* as knowledge—often scientific or technological—that is at the heart of, and forms the foundation for, a product or service. Core knowledge also is specific to a particular vintage of technology or state of knowledge development. For example, knowledge of integrated circuit technology formed the basis for semiconductor chips beginning in the 1960s. This vintage of electronics technology was preceded by transistors and vacuum tubes before that.

Henderson and Clark (1990) note that an individual product consists of multiple components, each of which has a separate "component knowledge" consisting of the basic knowledge underlying the component. In order to talk about basic knowledge for a product rather than a component, we focus on the critical aspects of the knowledge underlying a particular product. Such aspects of core knowledge for a product frequently relate to technology, and may include component knowledge underlying critical components of the product, as well as architectural knowledge that links components.

Core knowledge in vertical chains has the following characteristic:

> *Proposition 1:* Core knowledge can form the foundation for multiple products and stages not only in different vertical chains, but also within vertical chains.

The logic behind this proposition is similar to the rationale for related diversification, involving expansion into different product markets (and vertical chains) based on shared knowledge, resources, and capabilities (see, e.g., Montgomery 1994). As an example of this phenomenon within a vertical chain,[8] rather than across vertical chains as in related diversification, consider the relationship between refined oil products and basic petrochemicals (Helfat 1988). A basic petrochemical plant converts a refined oil or natural gas product into ethylene, propylene, and by-products. The core knowledge underlying both refined oil products and basic petrochemicals has to do with the process technologies used to refine crude oil and to process refined oil products into petrochemicals, respectively. In particular, production of basic petrochemicals utilizes a refining process that relies on technological knowledge similar to that used to refine crude oil. Additionally, both oil refineries and petrochemical plants consist of complex, interrelated pieces of equipment (no two oil refineries are exactly alike) that require considerable tacit knowledge in order to operate the equipment together smoothly. As this example demonstrates, oil refining and basic petrochemicals production takes place within a vertical chain, yielding separate products that rely on similar core technological knowledge and core capabilities.

Integrative Knowledge

In addition to core knowledge, we define *integrative knowledge* as knowledge that integrates, or knowledge of how to integrate, different activities, capabilities, and products in one or more vertical chains. Integrative knowledge enables organizations to coordinate activities within a vertical chain or across vertical chains, to obtain market feedback from customers about products, and to obtain feedback either from within vertical chains or from external markets regarding technology.[9]

The nature of coordination within and across vertical chains depends in part on the sorts of knowledge that must be coordinated, such as tacit versus codified knowledge. For example, Monteverde (1995) refers to "unstructured technical dialog" involving the "unstructured uncodifiable, generally verbal, and often face-to-face communication demanded by integrated project management" of product design and manufacturing (p. 1629; see also Wheelwright and Clark 1992). In this situation, coordination of tacit knowledge that resides in multiple stages of a vertical chain requires somewhat tightly coupled organizational mechanisms.[10]

In contrast, the product and organizational design literature on modularity (Baldwin and Clark 2000, Sanchez and Mahoney 1996) suggests that coordination often can take place via standardized rules when the knowledge in different activities that must be coordinated is codified and well understood. Coordination of codified knowledge, however, does not necessarily preclude the need for integrative knowledge. As an example, consider "just-in-time" manufacturing and distribution of goods to final sales outlets that requires close coordination among suppliers, manufacturers, and distributors (Flaherty 1996). Although the information that flows between the various stages of the supply chain is largely codified (e.g., number of widgets needed), the complexity of coordinating these information flows may require integrative organizational mechanisms and knowledge. More generally:

> *Proposition 2:* Integrative knowledge is required not only for coordination of tacit knowledge, but also for complex coordination of codified knowledge, within and across vertical chains.

As an example, consider the ways in which Wal-Mart uses information technology to help integrate multiple stages of a vertical chain (Bradley and Ghemawat 1995). The company obtains daily information from its stores about shelf-stocking needs (derived from cash register scanner information), which it then relays to its suppliers, who deliver the requested goods to Wal-Mart warehouses within 24 hours. Then a portion of the supplier delivered goods is immediately cross-docked directly onto company trucks for store delivery, without any holding of inventory in Wal-Mart warehouses. All of this greatly reduces inventory costs at Wal-Mart stores and warehouses, and improves customer satisfaction (and presumably leads to repeat customers) because store shelves are more fully stocked.

Wal-Mart's system, which requires underlying knowledge of how to integrate activities and sales in a vertical chain, has several aspects that merit attention. First, the system involves complex coordination of codified information. Second, the system has feedback from customers built into it, in the form of daily information about what consumers are buying at each store. Third, information about the "product" itself (i.e., retail sales) affects other activities in the chain. Fourth, Wal-Mart gains valuable information that it can use to forecast future coordination needs and consumer buying for its complete network of suppliers, distribution centers, and stores. Finally, Wal-Mart provides an example of how integrative knowledge can be embodied in organizational mechanisms and routines—in this case, facilitated by the use of information technology—that link activities and products.

Many other companies have made similar use of information technology to coordinate multiple stages of a vertical chain, including Federal Express (Rivkin 1998), for example. We note that Wal-Mart and Federal Express are service companies. Their core products are retail sales and express delivery service, respectively, and therefore the core knowledge underlying these products has to do with the attributes of the products themselves (e.g., knowledge of customer needs). But in addition, integrative knowledge and integrative capabilities allow the companies to more cost effectively deliver their products and to gain more information about their customers' needs, which the companies can then use to improve their core knowledge.

Product Sequencing

Both core and integrative knowledge can lead to economies of scope. Core knowledge reduces joint costs of production via sharing of intangible assets such as technological know-how (Bailey and Friedlander 1982, Teece 1980), not only across product markets (in different vertical chains), as in related diversification, but also across product markets within a single vertical chain. Integrative knowledge also reduces joint costs of production between stages of a single vertical chain and across vertical chains via improved coordination and consequent cost reductions, as illustrated by Wal-Mart's lower inventory costs.[11] But perhaps more important, in the spirit of Penrose (1959), firms can utilize core and integrative knowledge to introduce sequences of new products that in turn may provide new bases for economies of scope and platforms for future expansion.

> *Proposition 3:* A system of core and integrative knowledge provides the basis for a matrix of product-market expansion paths, traced out by a series of new product introductions that we term product sequencing.

We classify product sequencing strategies into the following types: (1) new generations of an existing product, (2) replacement products, designed to partially or fully supplant customer usage of a company's prior product, (3) horizontal expansion (e.g., related diversification), (4) vertical expansion, and (5) complex sequences that combine two or more of the prior sequencing strategies.

The simplest product sequencing strategy involves new generations of a product, in the same product market, generally using the same vertical chain. This strategy builds most directly on prior core knowledge and likely requires the least alteration of the associated activities and integrative knowledge in the vertical chain. Manufacturing techniques frequently are similar, the distribution channels often remain the same, and marketing usually occurs to similar groups of customers. Additionally, integrative knowledge that links activities in the vertical chain facilitates the launching of new product generations in an organization's current market.

Like new generations of a product, some replacement products may be introduced in an organization's current market. Other sorts of replacement products, however, may be introduced in a separate market, essentially involving horizontal expansion. For example, the market for television differs from the market for radios, which televisions partially replaced. As this example also makes clear, a replacement product need not fully displace the prior product. Although replacement products may utilize previous core knowledge, they also may require new core knowledge and may require changes in manufacturing techniques. Distribution, marketing and sales, and customer service also may require changes to accommodate new customers and ways to reach them. Integrative knowledge, in turn, may need to adapt as well.

Opportunities for product sequencing in markets new to the organization encompass not only some forms of replacement product sequencing, but also horizontal expansion, as in related diversification, as well as product expansion up or down a vertical chain.[12] Consistent with proposition 1, vertical product sequencing generally extends core knowledge underlying a product in one stage of a vertical chain to the introduction of a product in another stage of the same vertical chain. Horizontal product sequencing also extends core knowledge to another market, but across vertical chains. Like replacement product sequencing, both vertical and horizontal product sequencing may entail changes to integrative knowledge as well.

At some point of course, organizations may reach limits of integrative knowledge to coordinate across vertically and horizontally related markets, potentially with multiple generations of products in each. Moreover, expansion into new product markets, including perhaps different customers, may require additions to core and integrative knowledge.[13] Additions to knowledge in this system, and product sequencing based on the system of knowledge, require learning, as we next explain.

Systems of Learning

Proposition 4: Accumulation of core and integrative knowledge can be conceptualized as consisting of two systems of learning that run in parallel, each linked to one another and to the current system of knowledge and portfolio of products. The first system involves incremental learning, and the second system involves what we term step function learning.

We next explain the two systems of learning in more detail.[14]

Incremental Learning

Incremental learning improves upon but does not fundamentally depart from current knowledge. Incremental learning in core knowledge may underpin new product generations, as in, for example, Sony's continual introduction of new Walkman and Discman models. These new models involved incremental improvements in the underlying technological knowledge of personal tape recorder and CD player technology and hardware design.[15] Incremental extensions of core knowledge also can involve new product development in another stage of a vertical chain, or in closely related horizontal markets.

Incremental learning also applies to integrative knowledge. As an example, consider Wal-Mart's addition of cross-docking (the unloading of supplier deliveries directly onto Wal-Mart store delivery trucks) to its distribution system. The integrative mechanisms linking supplier and company trucks changed, since Wal-Mart required greater coordination between supplier deliveries and store deliveries.

Rosenberg (1982, chap. 6) focuses on two forms of incremental learning: learning by doing and learning by using. The learning curve, where production costs decline as cumulative volume increases, typifies learning by doing in manufacturing. Additionally, learning by doing about productive processes can lead to alterations in the design of the product (Monteverde 1995). In this instance, integrative knowledge that links manufacturing and product design activities facilitates incremental learning in core knowledge of the product.

With regard to learning by using, customer experience with a product can provide information about the relationship between specific product characteristics and product performance. Firms then can incorporate this information into design modifications (Rosenberg 1982), including in new models or generations of a product (Von Hippel 1976, 1986). Here again, incremental learning in core knowledge benefits from integrative knowledge, in this case involving feedback from customers that is linked to product design.

Incremental learning by doing and using is cumulative (Cohen and Levinthal 1990) and also relies on local search for new knowledge in the neighborhood of existing knowledge. In general, cumulative learning combined with local search creates path dependence in the direction of organizational learning (Nelson and Winter 1982, Helfat 1994). Incremental learning therefore is path dependent, as are the product sequences that result. For example, as new generations of a product evolve, learning becomes more engineering and user oriented and specific to the particular product (Rosenberg 1982, p. 122). Improvements typically require familiarity with the product (Gomory 1987, Gomory and Schmitt 1988). Thus, incremental learning, the knowledge underlying the product, and the product itself are inextricably linked to one another, and to the history of product sequencing over time.

Step Function Learning

In contrast to incremental learning, what we term "step function learning" involves fundamental changes to core or integrative knowledge. Step function learning presents difficult challenges for organizations, and the literature is replete with examples of firms that failed because they could not adapt to new technologies in particular. But some firms have successfully managed to accomplish step function learning, with regard to both core knowledge and integrative knowledge, using processes that we next describe.

Step function learning at a minimum requires ongoing feedback about products, markets, and technologies that points to the need for new and different knowledge. For example, Kao, a leading Japanese household and chemical products maker, has developed what it calls the ECHO system for processing and analysis of customer questions and complaints about Kao products

(Nonaka and Takeuchi 1995). Phone operators in Kao's customer service organization enter customer questions and complaints into a computer system that in turn generates reports used in various activities throughout the vertical chain. Kao also uses this feedback system directly in product refinement, involving incremental learning in core knowledge. But in addition, Kao obtains information regarding shifts in customer desires (Quinn et al. 1997), which provides a basis for step function learning in core knowledge and for new product development.[16]

As with core knowledge, step function learning in integrative knowledge requires ongoing feedback mechanisms that point to the need for new knowledge. Benchmarking of competitors, for example, can provide feedback such that wide gaps in performance may signal the need for a major rethinking of integrative mechanisms.

In addition to recognizing the need for fundamentally new knowledge, organizations must acquire and learn to utilize the knowledge. This may require teams and organizational units dedicated specifically to the learning effort. For example, with regard to core knowledge, when Sony decided to develop what became the Trinitron color TV, the firm set up a team of researchers focused on this effort.[17] As an example involving integrative knowledge, the opportunity for GM to learn from Toyota about just-in-time supply chains came about through a new organizational unit in the form of the NUMMI joint venture between the two companies (Badaracco 1988).[18]

Product Sequencing and Linked Systems of Learning

The product sequencing strategies outlined above rely on incremental and step function systems of learning, upon which the system of core and integrative knowledge is built. Not only are the systems of incremental and step function learning linked to the current system of knowledge, but also the two systems of learning are linked to one another in the following ways. First, incremental learning is likely to build upon step function learning. For example, incremental learning in core knowledge that leads to new generations of a product builds upon step function learning in core knowledge embodied in the initial product. Additionally, step function learning may build upon prior incremental learning. For example, although Sony required new core knowledge to develop the Trinitron color TV tube, which differed fundamentally from black-

and-white TV tubes, Sony also adapted the new tube to the company's prior TV design, which embodied incremental learning related to black-and-white TVs.

By employing the two parallel linked systems of incremental and step function learning, organizations learn to effectively manage the product sequencing process within markets, as well as up, down, and across vertical chains and product markets, based on a system of core and integrative knowledge. The systems of learning create an understanding of the potential as well as the limitations of core and integrative knowledge, of the nature of the family of products that can be developed using the underlying system of knowledge, and of the markets for these current and potential products. Products are linked to one another at a point in time in different markets and through time, and coevolve with the underlying knowledge and capabilities.

Product Sequencing and Competitive Advantage

The system of knowledge and portfolio of products, in combination with the two systems of learning provide "real options" (Kogut and Kulatilaka 1997, Brown and Eisenhardt 1997) for future product sequences. As Bowman and Hurry (1993) state, "options come into existence when existing resources and capabilities allow preferential access to future opportunities" (p. 762). In creating access to new opportunities, however, the history of product sequencing also constrains options for future product sequences.[19] More specifically, creation of new products and new knowledge depends on existing products, along with the underlying path-dependent knowledge and capabilities. This dependence on history matters not only for incremental (and, hence, path-dependent) learning and the products it supports, but also for step function learning. For example, integrative mechanisms in the current system of knowledge often alert the organization to the need for step function learning: existing integrative knowledge therefore shapes the direction of step function learning. Moreover, step function learning in turn may build on some aspects of existing core knowledge.

Over time, a system of core and integrative knowledge may generate more real options than an organization has the organizational, productive, and financial resources to pursue.[20] Managers must make choices of paths to pursue and place bets (Raubitschek 1988a), and the choices made will alter the options for future product sequencing, due to built-in path dependence. There is no certain "right" path to future success, since feedback that occurs in the process of developing, making, and selling each new product is not known ahead of time.

The product sequencing model implies differential firm success and competitive advantage. Different organizations rarely enter a market at the same time with the exact same initial sets of knowledge, products, and systems of learning, nor do these organizations necessarily make the same choices of product sequences over time. Therefore, due to path dependence, organizations will evolve different systems of knowledge, systems of learning, and portfolios of products. Furthermore, successful bets on products provide a richer set of real options and product platforms upon which to base future product sequences than do unsuccessful bets. Success may breed success and failure may make future success more difficult. And superior systems of learning that form the basis for continued product sequences can turn short-term competitive success into longer term advantage.

Examples of Product Sequencing Strategies

To illustrate the product-sequencing model, we next provide abbreviated histories of new product introductions over time in three technology-intensive Japanese firms: Sony, Canon, and NEC. These histories rely on publicly available sources of information, and as a result, the histories contain more information about core than integrative knowledge. Where possible, we identify the types of knowledge (core or integrative) and learning (incremental or step function) in the product sequences. Following the three histories, we discuss their implications as a group for the product sequencing model.

Sony

When incorporated as Tokyo Telecommunications Engineering Corporation (also called Totsuko) in 1946, Sony repaired radios and made radio upgrade kits that converted AM radios into short-wave receivers, among other products.[21] By 1950, Sony produced magnetic audio tapes as well as tape recorders (step function learning related to audio magnetic recording for the company). Like radios, tape recorders were electromagnetic audio devices with mechanical parts.

In 1953, Sony licensed the basic technology underlying transistors from Bell Laboratories, and building on this technology developed a high-frequency transistor for radios (step function learning in electronics for the company). Sony went on to introduce the first Japanese transistor radio in 1955 (horizontal product sequencing from audio tapes and recorders into radios), as well as a "pocket-size" transistorized radio in 1957. Then in 1958, after having further developed transistors so that radios could receive FM signals, Sony introduced the first portable AM/FM transistor radio (replacement product sequencing in radios). For both its radios and the transistor inputs (vertical product sequencing), Sony utilized and extended its core knowledge of electronics. Additionally, with its transistor radios, Sony developed core knowledge involving miniaturization of electronic products.

Continuing its transistor research, in 1958 Sony developed a portable transistorized video tape recorder (VTR) (horizontal and vertical product sequencing) followed by new, lower priced VTR models throughout the next decade (new-generation product sequencing). With the VTR, Sony added to its core knowledge of electronics and also fundamentally extended its knowledge of audio magnetic recording to video magnetic recording (step function learning).

Then, extending its research in transistors even further,[22] Sony developed a semiconductor type of television receiver. Sony combined this development with its core knowledge of miniaturization and by 1960 introduced the first all-transistor, black-and-white, portable, small-screen television set (horizontal product sequencing into TVs and vertical product sequencing of semiconductor inputs for TVs, based on core knowledge of electronics). Then in 1969 Sony introduced its extremely successful Trinitron color TV (replacement product sequencing in televisions), which produced a superior picture due to its unique technology. In order to develop a color TV, Sony had initially licensed a new TV tube technology based on the work of Nobel Prize–winning physicist O.E. Lawrence, but its efforts to commercialize the technology were unsuccessful. These efforts, however, aided Sony in its subsequent development of the Trinitron technology (step function learning), which the company also combined with its knowledge of TV design from black-and-white TVs (incremental learning). While Sony's first Trinitron

TV was again a small set, utilizing its core knowledge of miniaturization, this product was extremely successful, and Sony subsequently introduced a series of new models with larger screens (new-generation product sequencing).

In 1971, building on its experience with televisions, video recording, tapes, radios, and semiconductors, Sony developed a video recorder that used bulky video cassettes (replacement product sequencing for reel-to-reel VTRs). This "U-Matic" machine became the standard format in the institutional market[23] and formed the basis for Sony's subsequent Betamax video cassette recorder (VCR) and for competing VHS machines, both sold to the home market. Sony introduced its Betamax-type VCR in 1975, and in 1976 JVC introduced the VHS-type VCR, which was not compatible with Betamax and had a longer recording time. This began the Betamax–VHS video war, which lasted until the early to mid 1980s, when VHS emerged as the industry standard (Cusumano et al. 1992).

Sony's failure with Betamax provides a cautionary tale that core technological knowledge alone cannot support effective product sequencing. Early on, JVC worked to line up other consumer electronics firms that would sell VHS-format VCRs. JVC's partners, especially its parent Masushita, provided technical feedback and assistance to JVC during development of the VHS machine, which led to improvements in product features such as longer recording and playback time (suggestive of integrative knowledge). Masushita also pursued large market share for the VHS format in order to obtain economies of scale, and therefore produced VCRs for other consumer products companies to market using their own brand names—which Sony refused to do. Additionally, Masushita held a dominant share of the retail appliance store market in Japan, giving the company guaranteed distribution outlets for its VCRs.

Masushita's large share of retail outlets in Japan also provided the company with good information about consumer reaction to its VCRs. In addition, JVC and Masushita, through their partners, gained early knowledge of the evolving importance to consumers of compatible prerecorded video software. JVC and Masushita had several partners in Europe, where video rentals become popular more quickly than in the United States. And one of Masushita's earliest partners in the United States was RCA, which saw consumer video software as important due to its videodisk business. As demand increased for prerecorded video tapes, consumers purchasing VCRs had to choose between two different video tape formats, and constraints on shelf space made stores reluctant to carry both formats. Masushita sped acceptance of the VHS format as a standard not only by manufacturing VCRs for other consumer electronics companies, but also by developing high-speed VHS video tape duplication equipment that it supplied at low cost to producers of prerecorded video tapes, which in turn increased availability of VHS tapes in stores.

In summary, throughout its history, Sony established strong links among its products based on core technological knowledge. With the VCR, however, Sony lagged JVC and Masushita in understanding customer needs and building market share in a market with network externalities, where small players often lose. Here we see the importance of feedback from consumers, feedback from partner companies, and integrative knowledge that facilitates this.

Canon

Founded in 1933 as the Precision Optical Research Laboratories,[24] Canon relied on core technologies of precision optics (involving the grinding of lenses to exact specifications) and mechanics to produce mechanical cameras.[25] During the next half century, Canon introduced new camera models and further accumulated skills in precision optics and mechanics (incremental learning and new-generation product sequencing).

One of Canon's relatively early ventures beyond mechanical cameras involved photocopiers, which essentially are cameras that take a picture in a different way. To introduce its first copier in 1965 (horizontal product sequencing), Canon used technology licensed from RCA. Then in 1968 Canon announced that, based on its own research on plain-paper copiers, it had developed a new process technology that provided the first alternative to Xerox's patented technology (step function learning). This new process reflected Canon's development of core knowledge in chemicals, which the company combined with its core knowledge of precision optics and mechanics to introduce a copier with dry toner in 1970 (replacement product sequencing). Canon then introduced a second-generation copier with liquid toner in 1972 (new-generation product sequencing) and a color copier in 1973. Because Canon lacked strong industrial marketing, the

company licensed the technology to Japanese and foreign competitors. While providing royalty income, licensing inadvertently strengthened the competition, which gained manufacturing experience and brand recognition.

During the same time period, Canon entered the calculator business. In 1964, Canon introduced the world's first 10-key pad electronic desk calculator, which utilized the company's core knowledge of mechanics and which contributed to the development of core knowledge of electronic circuitry. Then in the early 1970s, Canon introduced hand-held electronic calculators, but was bested by Sharp's superior "thin" calculator, which it could not quickly duplicate. Nevertheless, with its hand-held calculator initiative, Canon developed knowledge of miniaturized electronic circuitry that contributed to the company's platform for further product sequencing, as we next explain.

In 1976, Canon revolutionized the 35 mm camera market by introducing the AE-1 camera—the world's first electronically controlled, fully automatic, single-lens reflex (SLR) camera with a built-in microprocessor unit (replacement product sequencing in cameras). In developing the AE-1, Canon combined its core knowledge of precision optics and mechanics (from cameras) with that of miniaturized electronic circuitry (from hand-held calculators) in a completely new way, to essentially put an electronic brain into what previously were mechanical cameras (step function learning).[26]

Improving on its marketing performance with copiers, Canon spent over a million dollars for a spectacular promotion on American television to introduce the AE-1 camera—the first time that 35 mm cameras were advertised on TV. Canon also priced the camera at more than $100 below other cameras. Relying on experience gained in producing electronic calculators, the AE-1 used 20% fewer parts than did conventional SLR cameras, resulting in significant cost reductions. In addition, Canon drew on knowledge it had gained in manufacturing mechanical cameras to construct new automatic equipment that helped to lower production costs. This learning in manufacturing from electronic calculators and mechanical cameras, and learning from copiers about the need for effective marketing, suggest that Canon may have had integrative mechanisms to facilitate knowledge transfer. The AE-1 became the world's best-selling 35 mm SLR camera, which Canon followed with new models that continued to attract consumer interest for many years (incremental learning and new-generation product sequencing).

Following the AE-1, Canon again hit the jackpot, this time with a personal copier introduced in 1979 and sold to the office market (replacement product sequencing in copiers). Canon had developed a new photocopying process, which the company did not license, and which it incorporated into the typewriter-size copier (step function learning). Then, in 1982, Canon introduced another personal copier (replacement product sequencing) that combined its new copying process with a disposable cartridge that incorporated the toner, developing assembly, and photoconductive drum, thus utilizing the company's core knowledge of chemicals. The cartridge eliminated the need for Canon to build a service network, a major barrier to entry in this market, by putting all parts that are likely to break down into a disposable cartridge.

To market the copier, Canon expanded its distribution channels and launched a major marketing campaign resembling its previous successful campaign for the AE-1 (suggestive of integrative knowledge in marketing across products). The company set a low price for the copier as well, relying in part on cost reductions obtained from redesign of the copier production line. These cost reductions in turn benefited from integrative mechanisms that facilitated knowledge transfer, in that Canon's copier product development group worked closely with the production engineering unit to utilize its camera-manufacturing know-how. Over time, Canon introduced new generations of personal copiers with features never before offered in the low-end price segment (new-generation product sequencing).

As yet another example of Canon's complex product sequencing strategy, in the early 1980s the company introduced a personal printer for desktop computers (horizontal product sequencing) that had higher speed and better quality text and graphics than existing daisywheel and dot matrix printers. Canon's personal printer relied on a copierlike printer engine and, like the copier, used a disposable cartridge. Canon offered the printer engine to other (original equipment) manufacturers of printers at a price such that, when configured with the necessary control electronics, the printers were priced competitively with the inferior daisywheel and dot matrix machines. Canon achieved this price breakthrough by using its experience in high-volume manufacturing of small copiers, and by employing

common components in its copiers and printers, again suggestive of integrative knowledge across products in manufacturing. The Canon printer engine became an industry standard, used by many original equipment manufacturers, including Apple and Hewlett-Packard.

In summary, Canon evolved from a simple new-generation product sequencing strategy in mechanical cameras to a complex product sequencing strategy in many markets. To introduce new products, Canon built on and extended its core knowledge of precision optics and mechanics, and developed completely different areas of core knowledge in electronics and chemicals (step function learning). Additionally, the evidence suggests that integrative knowledge across products in marketing and manufacturing may have played an important role in Canon's product sequencing strategy.

NEC Corporation

NEC was formed in 1899 as a joint venture between Japanese investors and Western Electric, the manufacturing arm of AT&T, to produce telecommunications equipment in Japan.[27] In its long and complicated history, NEC also enjoyed strong ties to ITT and Sumitomo.

Using Western Electric technology, NEC initially built telephone communication equipment and later using this expertise entered radio communication systems (horizontal product sequencing). Both sets of products relied on electromagnetic waves, although at different frequencies with different carrying mediums, and utilized electronics technology. Subsequently, NEC integrated backward into vacuum tubes (step function learning in electronics), an important input to its telephone and radio broadcasting equipment (vertical product sequencing based on core knowledge of electronics). NEC also established its own radio research unit and later began research on microwave communication systems. Over time, the company grew to the point where toward the end of World War II, it was a major producer of radio equipment, vacuum tubes, telephone equipment, and telephone carrier transmission equipment (complex vertical and horizontal product sequencing). At the conclusion of the war, however, NEC's operations came to a standstill due to bombing of its facilities and severe shortages of personnel and materials.

Following the war, Japan enacted two reforms aimed at restructuring and remaking its communication infrastructure, which allowed NEC to quickly rebuild. One reform permitted commercial broadcasting, and the resulting boom in broadcasting created a huge demand for broadcasting equipment. The other reform created Nippon Telegraph and Telephone Public Corporation (NTT) as the monopoly provider of domestic telecommunications in Japan, although NTT was not allowed to manufacture its own equipment.

NEC reentered the communications business, providing broadcasting equipment and telephone communication systems, and became NTT's lead supplier. By 1950, NEC had begun research on transistors (the semiconductors of the time) out of concern that the transistor would replace the vacuum tube. After the war, NEC also resumed work on microwave communication technology involving extremely high-frequency transmissions used in both telephone and broadcasting systems. And in 1954, the necessity for complex calculations in telecommunications spurred NEC to enter computer research.

All of these efforts converged as follows. In 1958, NEC began mass production of transistors, primarily for industrial applications with some internal consumption (step function learning in electronics and replacement product sequencing whereby transistors replaced vacuum tubes). This advance in transistor development benefited in part from NEC's research and development and production of silicon diodes for its microwave communication systems. And NEC's advances in transistors further enabled the company by 1959 to develop the first Japanese transistorized computer targeted for the general public (step function learning, resulting in complex vertical and horizontal product sequencing involving core knowledge of electronics).

During this period, again building on core knowledge of electronics, NEC in 1955 invented a method for improving the FM receiver threshold. This led to over-the-horizon microwave communications systems used to connect telephone networks, which NEC produced in 1959, and ultimately to NEC's highly successful entry into satellite communication systems (horizontal product sequencing), which essentially involve microwave relay links in space.

In 1960, NEC also began development of integrated circuits, the vintage of semiconductors that followed transistors. By 1962, NEC had developed its own integrated circuits (step function learning in electronics for the company and replacement product sequencing in semiconductors), and over a period of two decades the company introduced a series of semiconductor devices (new-generation product sequencing). By the mid 1980s, NEC was the world's biggest producer of semiconductors.

NEC continued its development of computers as well. In 1965, NEC unveiled the Series 2200 family of computer systems sharing a common hardware and software architecture, which made it easy for users to connect the machines to one another and to trade up to more expensive machines. With these products, each linked to one another at a point in time and over time, NEC became a major computer manufacturer in its domestic market. Then, in 1972, NEC became the first Japanese company to develop a microcomputer (horizontal product sequencing), utilizing its semiconductors as inputs (vertical product sequencing based on core knowledge of electronics), which it followed with even more powerful versions (new-generation product sequencing).

In the early 1970s, NEC also increased its output of consumer electronics products, building on an electrical household appliance business originally established in the 1950s. Once again, NEC employed vertical product sequencing in electronics, incorporating microelectronic control functions into new consumer products, such as a color TV set with an electronic tuning system introduced in 1973.

In 1977, Koji Kobayashi, then chairman of the board of NEC, expressed the concept behind the strategy that NEC pursued through the 1980s. He called it C&C—integration of computers and communications. Kobayashi early on recognized trends whereby advances in semiconductors supported the development of computers and communications networks throughout the world. NEC, with its strong presence and core knowledge of electronics in all three markets, could utilize the company's knowledge and product base to capitalize on integration of these markets and technologies. By the mid 1980s, NEC was the only company in the world to achieve the "Triple Crown" in electronics: NEC alone ranked among the top companies in the world in the three most important markets of the electronics industry, semiconductors, computers, and telecommunications.

Discussion

The histories of Sony, Canon, and NEC highlight several aspects of the product sequencing model. First, per proposition 1, NEC's and Sony's core knowledge provided the foundation for upstream as well as downstream products in vertical chains. For example, core knowledge of electronics underlay NEC's businesses in vacuum tubes (upstream) and telephone and radio communication systems (downstream). NEC also utilized core knowledge of a later vintage of electronics to produce semiconductors (upstream) as well as computers, consumer electronics, and telecommunication and broadcast systems (downstream). Similarly, Sony's core knowledge of electronics underlay semiconductors (upstream) and radios, VTRs, VCRs, and TVs (all downstream).

The company histories also demonstrate the importance of integrative knowledge, per proposition 2. For example, Canon's copier product development group worked closely with the camera production engineering group to redesign the copier production line. Canon also benefited from learning across products in manufacturing and marketing for its electronic cameras and printers, suggestive of integrative knowledge. Sony's failure and Masushita's success in VCRs points to the importance of integrative knowledge as well.

Per proposition 3, each of the companies' product sequences traces out a matrix of product-market expansion paths across or within vertical chains, building on previous core and integrative knowledge. For example, knowledge of audio and video technology, combined with core knowledge of electronics and miniaturization, are key links in Sony's horizontal product sequencing in radios, VTRs, TVs, and VCRs, supplemented by vertical integration into semiconductors. Canon built on its initial core knowledge of precision optics and mechanics in mechanical cameras, and combined this knowledge with core knowledge of electronics and chemicals to develop calculators, electronic cameras, copiers, and printers. And NEC's expansion based on core knowledge of electronics made it a leading player in the markets for semiconductors, computers, and communications.

Step function learning, per proposition 4, also plays an important role in the product sequences. We see the importance that being in a market and making a product had in pointing to opportunities for related products and to the need to deal with emerging technologies. For example, by virtue of being in the markets both for vacuum tubes and for downstream communication systems that used vacuum tubes, NEC understood the threat posed by transistors. As a result, NEC undertook semiconductor research and made the leap from vacuum tubes to transistors.

Also with regard to step function learning, the desire to make a new type of product sometimes led the companies to combine previous areas of core knowledge and extend them in fundamentally new ways. For example, Canon's development of the electronically controlled AE-1 camera combined and extended the company's prior knowledge of precision optics and mechanics and electronic circuitry in a fundamentally new way. We also see how companies learned from their mistakes, as in Canon's ill-fated hand-held calculator initiative. From this endeavor, Canon gained a great deal of knowledge regarding miniaturized electronic circuitry, which it then employed in its highly successful AE-1 electronic camera.

Finally with regard to step function learning, we see how firms adapted to radical changes in technology and markets, and also shaped the evolution of products and markets. For example, NEC successfully managed the transition from vacuum tubes to transistors, a "radical" shift in technology and the underlying core knowledge. And Canon's development of the AE-1 camera, along with its aggressive marketing, shifted the consumer camera market away from mechanical cameras to electronically controlled cameras.

A critical element in the product sequencing of these companies, but not brought out in the histories, has to do with the role of top management. In Sony, founders Morita and Ibuka often initiated and played a large role in decisions regarding product sequencing and acquisition of any new knowledge required. In NEC, Kobayashi was critical to the company's product sequencing strategy involving integration of computers and communications. Notably, these leaders played important integrative roles within their organizations, as well as scanning the environment for new technologies and generating new ideas.

Overall, the product sequencing histories illustrate the continued coevolution of knowledge and products through time, involving both incremental and step function learning. We also see how these systems of learning essentially constitute dynamic capabilities that enabled the firms to continually introduce new products and adapt to changing technological and market conditions.

Conclusion

The product sequencing model provides a dynamic framework that enables us to track, step by step, how knowledge, capabilities, activities, and products coevolve over time and across markets. Admittedly, this is a large undertaking, and the model is a first step in unpacking the evolution of capabilities and products.

The model has several features that differ somewhat from existing models. As noted above, the concept of knowledge shared across products is a well-known explanation for related diversification, but is not usually applied to vertical expansion. The oil–petrochemical example used above, as well as the histories of the electronics companies, suggests not only that core knowledge forms the foundation for multiple products and stages in a vertical chain, but also that it applies to industries that contribute large shares to the world economy and that can be highly profitable. With regard to integrative knowledge, although the concept has been applied to linkages of activities within a vertical chain (e.g., Armour and Teece 1980, Clark and Fujimoto 1991, Iansiti and Clark 1994), it has not been applied frequently to expansion into new product markets either vertically or through diversification across vertical chains. More generally, the literatures on diversification and product development have not focused on the dynamic aspects of how expansion into new product markets unfolds over time,[28] or on the importance of product platforms.

The product sequencing model has implications for several closely related literatures, including the resource-based view, knowledge management, dynamic capabilities, organizational learning, firm and industry evolution, and business history. First, the model highlights the importance of products to the resources and capabilities of firms. The analysis also helps to make the idea of resource and activity bundles (Rumelt 1984, Conner 1991) more concrete,[29] particularly with regard to knowledge and learning. The model further draws attention to the role of knowledge as a resource that supports capabilities, activities, and products, and that in turn arises from experience gained in making and selling products. Additionally, the model relates specific types of knowledge in specific ways to vertical chains of activities, and further suggests that it is useful to characterize the evolution of firms and industries in terms of vertical chains and products.[30] Thus, we may be able to gain greater understanding of changes in scale and scope (Chandler 1990) over the course of business history by asking questions about exactly what types of knowledge and systems of learning formed the basis for expansion, and how

these were linked to specific products. We also can examine deficiencies in knowledge and learning over the course of history.

With regard to change over time, the product sequencing model extends the analysis of dynamic capabilities as well. As noted above, the parallel systems of learning in the model are prime examples of dynamic capabilities (Teece et al. 1997), since these systems are fundamental to the ability of organizations to innovate and to adapt to changes in technology and markets, including the ability to learn from mistakes. We also bring in the role of products that coevolve with and contribute to specific systems of knowledge and learning.

With regard to organizational learning and innovation more generally, step function improvement in integrative knowledge is akin to architectural innovation (Henderson and Clark 1990), but at the firm rather than the product level. The model also contributes to the limited literature that points to the possibility that firms can achieve both evolutionary and revolutionary change (Tushman and O'Reilly 1996). Our analysis highlights the dual systems of incremental and step function learning that facilitate evolutionary and revolutionary change, respectively.

The product sequencing model does not necessarily yield generic predictions about the appropriate direction of expansion for broad categories of firms.[31] As an example, consider the costs of learning required for product sequencing. These costs depend in part on how "close" the new knowledge that must be acquired is to current knowledge, as well as on the extent of technological opportunity (or opportunity for knowledge advancement more generally) in a particular market. Although in general we would expect lower costs for incremental than step function learning, it is not clear a priori whether horizontal or vertical expansion, for example, will have lower costs of incremental learning, since both forms of expansion may build on current core and integrative knowledge. Nor is it clear a priori whether step function learning is less costly for vertical or horizontal expansion. Instead, costs of learning depend on the situation of the individual firm, and more specifically on how "close" the knowledge base required for a product expansion is to the current knowledge base of the firm, regardless of the direction of expansion.

In focusing on the knowledge bases and product sequencing of individual firms, the model alerts managers to factors to consider when making decisions regarding innovation, new product introduction, and market entry. Managers must consider the firm's core technological knowledge, as well as information regarding the likely future trajectories of technologies and markets (gained from integrative knowledge), the firm's learning capabilities (systems of learning), and any new knowledge and capabilities the firm may need to acquire. Given this information, managers in essence place bets on product sequences, and scenario analysis can help managers plan in such situations (Raubitschek 1988b).

In addition, using the model retrospectively, we can trace the progression of organizational knowledge and products through time using both qualitative historical analysis and statistical techniques if we can obtain appropriate data. The model predicts that, for each individual firm, successful product sequencing builds on and also augments the knowledge and capability base of the firm. More generally, we can start to unpack the evolution of firms (and other long-term organizational arrangements) and, by implication, the evolution of industries into the evolution of the underlying systems of knowledge and learning, capabilities, and products.

Notes

This chapter has benefited from discussions with Paul Almeida, Betsy Bailey, Therese Flaherty, Rob Grant, Quintus Jett, Bruce Kogut, Dan Levinthal, Marvin Lieberman, David Mowery, Yiorgos Mylonadis, C.K. Prahalad, James Brian Quinn, Dick Rosenbloom, Lori Rosenkopf, Nicolaj Siggelkow, Harbir Singh, and Sid Winter. We also benefited from presenting earlier versions at the 1999 annual meetings of the Academy of Management and INFORMS, the Tuck/CCC conference on the Evolution of Firm Capabilities, and the Helsinki School of Economics and Business Administration. The views expressed herein are not purported to represent those of the U.S. Department of Justice.

1. Kim and Kogut (1996) use the term "platform technologies" to denote technologies that form the basis for diversification over time. The product platforms in our model serve a related purpose.

2. Grant (1996, p. 330) notes that more advanced chips require closer coordination of design and fabrication, which has reversed some of the separation of the design and fab stages.

3. Moreover, simply because knowledge is codified does not mean that it is necessarily well understood by all recipients of such knowledge. For

example, most nonphysicists would have difficulty understanding a highly technical physics journal article. We thank Bruce Kogut for pointing this out. See also Zander and Kogut (1995) on the transfer of knowledge.

4. In operations management, a vertical chain is referred to as a "supply chain" that may involve more than one firm (Flaherty 1996).

5. Our analysis is in the spirit of Porter's (1996) recent focus on the entire activity system, with multiple linkages among different stages of the vertical chain. Fine (1998) also refers to "capability chains."

6. Leonard and Sensiper (1998) refer to "system knowledge" as "collective tacit knowledge . . . developed communally, over time, in interactions among individuals in the group" (p. 121). Our use of the term "system of knowledge" also incorporates an important role for tacit knowledge among individuals, in our case involving stages of vertical chains that support specific products.

7. For this reason, Teece (1986) makes "core technological know-how" the centerpiece of his wheel of complementary assets, although he does not explicitly define the term.

8. Argyres (1996) refers to the idea of shared knowledge that is common to adjacent stages of a vertical chain but does not elaborate on the concept.

9. Integrative knowledge, as defined here, is in part a firm-level analogue to architectural knowledge (Henderson and Clark 1990) that links components of a product.

10. We note that "learning by monitoring" (Helper et al. 1999) can mitigate pitfalls of tightly coupled systems. Learning by monitoring includes simultaneous engineering across groups (e.g., sharing of designs in real time), as well as error detection and correction systems (e.g., stopping the assembly line when a worker spots a defect). These continuous adjustments prevent problems in one part of the chain from continually causing problems throughout the chain. Additionally, greater experimentation can take place, because the system provides a means of resolving potential consequences of experimentation in one stage of a chain for other stages in the chain.

11. For products in two contiguous stages of a vertical chain, economies of scope occur when $C(y_i,y_j) < C(y_i,0) + C(0,y_j,p_i) - p_i y_i(y_j,p^*)$, where y_i = upstream output, y_j = downstream output, p_i = market price for the intermediate product, $y_i(y_j,p^*)$ = derived demand for the intermediate product, and p^* = vector of all input prices at the downstream stage (including p_i). This formula comes from Kaserman and Mayo (1991), who focused on avoidance of transactions costs and of monopoly pricing markup as an explanation of

vertical integration, rather than on core and integrative knowledge.

12. Winter (1993) briefly discusses the possibility that knowledge may form the basis for the growth of firms via vertical integration.

13. We note also that integrative knowledge itself can provide the basis for horizontal product-market expansion. Federal Express, for example, is developing a new business as a logistics supplier, based on integrative knowledge developed in its express mail business (Smart 1999).

14. The concepts of incremental and step function learning are similar to March's (1991) exploitation and exploration in organizational learning, respectively.

15. This statement is based on information in Patton (1999).

16. Kao's use of its customer service organization provides an example of Christensen's (1997) point that information from companies' less attractive customers (such as those that complain) may point to the need for what we term step function learning.

17. We are grateful to James Brian Quinn for suggesting the Trinitron TV example. The references for the Sony example here and elsewhere in the chapter are given at the end.

18. General Motors, however, had difficulty taking full advantage of the opportunity NUMMI presented. For example, GM had difficulty transferring knowledge gained at the NUMMI plant throughout the rest of the company (Badaracco 1988).

19. Ghemawat et al. (1999) make the more general point that investments in resource commitments and capabilities are often irreversible.

20. An essential element of options is that less promising options can be allowed to expire.

21. The sources for this history of Sony are Bartlett (1992), *Broadcasting* (1983), Browning (1986), Burgess (1999), *Business Week* (1987), Cieply (1983), Cusumano et al. (1992), *Economist* (1982, 1983a, 1983b), Gerson (1978), Ibuka (1975), Lyons (1976), Morita et al. (1986), Nathan (1999), Pollack (1999), Rosenbloom and Cusumano (1987), Rubinflen et al. (1988), and Smith (1987).

22. Semiconductors, made of substances that are between conductors and insulators, are the class of devices that replaced vacuum tubes. Transistors were the first generation of semiconductor microelectronics technology.

23. In 1970, Sony, Masushita, and JVC entered into a cross-licensing agreement for video recording patents that allowed the U-Matic to be adopted by all three companies as the standard for institutional use.

24. The sources for this history of Canon are Beauchamp (1988), Blum (1978), Cavuoto (1984), Canon, Inc. (2000), *Economic World* (1976), *Electronic Business* (1984), Heller (1983), Helm (1985), Hof and Gross (1989), Ishikura and Porter (1983a, 1983b), Johansson (1986), Kraar (1981), Meyer (1985), Moore (1982), Port (1987), Sutherland (1988), Trachtenberg (1987), and Yamanouchi (1989).

25. This abbreviated history includes many but not all of Canon's product areas. The history does not, e.g., cover Canon's optical products (semiconductor production equipment, broadcasting equipment, and medical equipment), which also utilize Canon's core knowledge.

26. This provides an excellent example of the power of combinative capabilities (Kogut and Zander 1992).

27. The sources for this history of NEC are Browning (1985), *Business Week* (1982), *Economist* (1984, 1986), Hayashi (1987), *IEEE Spectrum* (1986), Joseph (1986), Kobayashi (1986), Mead (1985), NEC (1984), Smith (1984), and Sullivan (1988).

28. Teece et al. (1994) and Kim and Kogut (1996) are notable exceptions.

29. As an alternative approach with a somewhat different focus, Milgrom and Roberts (1990) provide a model of strong complementarities between groups of activities. See also Cockburn et al. (1999).

30. Thus, the model adds a dynamic element to the literature on activity systems and value chains, which heretofore have often been analyzed in static terms (with notable exceptions: Ghemawat et al. 1999, McKelvey 1999, Siggelkow 1999).

31. In this, we depart from Teece et al. (1994). We also differ somewhat from them in our explanation of vertical linkages.

References

Argyres, N. (1996) "Evidence on the role of firm capabilities in vertical integration decisions." *Strategic Management Journal* 17(2):129–150.

Armour, H. and Teece, D.J. (1980) "Vertical integration and technological innovation." *Review of Economics and Statistics* 62:470–474.

Badaracco, J.L., Jr. (1988) *General Motors' Asian Alliances*. Case no. 9-388-094. Boston: Harvard Business School.

Bailey, E.E. and Friedlander, A. (1982) "Market structure and multiproduct industries." *Journal of Economic Literature* 20:1024–1048.

Baldwin, C.Y. and Clark, K.B. (2000) *Design Rules:*

The Power of Modularity. Cambridge, MA: MIT Press.

Barney, J.B. (1991) "Firm resources and sustained competitive advantage." *Journal of Management* 17:99–120.

Bartlett, C.A. (1992) *Phillips and Masushita: A Portrait of Two Evolving Companies*. Case No. 9-392-156. Boston: Harvard Business School.

Beauchamp, M. (1988) "From Fuji to Everest." *Forbes*, May, pp. 35–36.

Blum, E. (1978) "Japan's camera makers wage fierce battle in U.S. SLR boom." *Economic World*, September, pp. 4–11.

Bowman, E.H. and Hurry, D. (1993) "Strategy through the option lens: an integrated view of resource investments and the incremental-choice process. *Academy of Management Review* 19: 760–782.

Bradley, S.P. and Ghemawat, P. (1995) *Wal-Mart Stores, Inc.* Case No. 9-794-024. Boston: Harvard Business School.

Broadcasting. (1983) "Sony nearly 40 years of making it better and/or smaller." 104(20):51–56.

Brown, S.L. and Eisenhardt, K.M. (1997) "The art of continuous change: linking complexity theory and time-paced evolution in relentlessly shifting organizations." *Administrative Science Quarterly* 42:1–34.

Browning, E.S. (1985) "NEC's telephone products, computers hit trouble: but it keeps on trying." *Wall Street Journal*, March 25, p. A1.

Browning, E.S. (1986) "Sony's perseverance helped it win market for mini-CD layers." *Wall Street Journal*, February, A1. p. 27.

Burgess, J. (1999) "Sony's co-founder Akio Morita dies." *Washington Post*, October 4, pp. A1, A14.

Business Week. (1982) "NEC's solo strategy to win the world. 2746(July 5):79–80.

Business Week. (1987) "Sony's challenge." 3001 (June 1):64–69.

Canon, Inc. (2000) "The Canon story/Canon fact book." Available at: http://www.canon.co.jp/story-e/fact/fact01.html.

Cavuoto, J. (1984) "Laser printers: a status report." *Lasers and Applications*, October, pp. 69–72.

Chandler, A.D. (1990) *Scale and Scope: The Dynamics of Capitalism*. Cambridge, MA: Harvard University Press.

Christensen, C.M. (1997) *The Innovator's Dilemma: When New Technologies Cause Great Firms to Fail*. Boston: Harvard Business School Press.

Cieply, M. (1983) "Sony's profitless prosperity." *Forbes*, October 24, pp. 128–134.

Clark, K.B. and Fujimoto, T. (1991) *Product Development Performance: Strategy, Organization, and Management in the World Auto Industry*. Boston: Harvard Business School Press.

Cockburn, I., Henderson, R., and Stern, S. (1999) "Exploring the diffusion of science driven drug discovery in pharmaceutical research." Working paper, MIT.

Cohen, W.M. and Levinthal, D.A. (1990) "Absorptive capacity: a new perspective on learning and innovation." *Administrative Science Quarterly* 35:128–152.

Conner, K.R. (1991) "A historical comparison of resource-based theory and five schools of thought within industrial organization economics: do we have a new theory of the firm?" *Journal of Management* 17:121–154.

Cusumano, M., Mylonadis, Y., and Rosenbloom, R. (1992) "Strategic maneuvering and mass market dynamics: the triumph of VHS over Beta." *Business History Review* 66:51–94.

Dyer, J. and Singh, H. (1998) "The relational view: cooperative strategy and sources of interorganizational competitive advantage." *Academy of Management Review* 23:660–679.

Economic World. (1976) "Canon AE-1 breaks price barrier for electronic SLRs." September, pp. 56–57.

Economist. (1982) "The giants in Japanese electronics." 282(February 20):80–81.

Economist. (1983a) "Sony and JVC: video wars." 288(July 9):66–69.

Economist. (1983b) "Sony: Beta minus." 289(December 24):75–76.

Economist. (1984) "NEC: a lightning semiconductor." 292(7372):84–85.

Economist. (1986) "Kobayashi's triple play." April 12, pp. 73–75.

Electronic Business. (1984) "Laser printers: HP rushes in where IBM fears to tread." 10(19):36.

Fine, C.H. (1998) *Clockspeed: Winning Industry Control in the Age of Temporary Advantage*. Reading, MA: Perseus.

Flaherty, M.T. (1996) *Global Operations Management*. New York: McGraw-Hill.

Gerson, R. (1978) "1978 marks year of recovery for Sony." *Economic World*, May, pp. 26–29.

Ghemawat, P., Collis, D.J., Pisano, G.P., and Rivkin, J.W. (1999) *Strategy and the Business Landscape: Text and Cases*. Reading, MA: Addison-Wesley.

Gomory, R.E. (1987) "Dominant science does not mean dominant product." *Research and Development* 29:72–74.

Gomory, R.E. and Schmitt, R.W. (1988) "Science and product." *Science* 240:1131–1204.

Grant, R.M. (1996) "Toward a knowledge-based theory of the firm." *Strategic Management Journal* 17(Winter):109–122.

Hayashi, A. (1987) "NEC takes the Triple Crown in electronics." *Electronic Business*, September 15, pp. 40–48.

Helfat, C.E. (1988) *Investment Choices in Industry*. Cambridge, MA: MIT Press.

Helfat, C.E. (1994) "Evolutionary trajectories in petroleum firm R&D." *Management Science* 40: 1720–1747.

Helfat, C.E. (1997) "Know-how and asset complementarity and dynamic capability accumulation: the case of R&D." *Strategic Management Journal* 18(5):339–360.

Heller, R. (1983) "What makes Canon boom." *Management Today*, September, pp. 62–71.

Helm, L. (1985) "Canon: a dream of rivaling Big Blue." *Business Week*, May 13, pp. 98–99.

Helper, S., MacDuffie, J.P., and Sabel, C. (1999) "The boundaries of the firm as a design problem." Working paper, Wharton School, University of Pennsylvania.

Henderson, R. and Clark, K. (1990) "Architectural innovation: the reconfiguration of existing product technologies and the failure of established firms." *Administrative Science Quarterly* 35:9–30.

Hof, R. and Gross, N. (1989) "Silicon Valley is watching its worst nightmare unfold." *Business Week* 63:67.

Iansiti, M. and Clark, K. (1994) "Integration and dynamic capability: evidence from product development in automobiles and mainframe computers." *Industrial and Corporate Change* 3:557–606.

Ibuka, M. (1975) "How Sony developed electronics for the world market." *IEEE Transactions of Engineering Management* 22(February):15–19.

IEEE Spectrum. (1986) "Assessing Japan's role in telecommunications." 23(6):47–52.

Ishikura, Y. and Porter, M.E. (1983a) *Canon, Inc.* Case No. 9-384-151. Boston: Harvard Business School.

Ishikura, Y. and Porter, M.E. (1983b) *Note on the World Copier Industry in 1983.* Case No. 9-384-152. Boston: Harvard Business School.

Johansson, J.K. (1986) "Japanese marketing failures." *International Marketing Review* 3(3):33–46.

Joseph, J. (1986) "Japan begins forging dominion in optical communications." *Data Communications* 15(4):66–68.

Kaserman, D.L. and Mayo, J.W. (1991) "The measurement of vertical economies and the efficient structure of the electric utility industry." *Journal of Industrial Economics* 39:483–502.

Kim, D. and Kogut, B. (1996) "Technological platforms and diversification." *Organization Science* 7:283–301.

Kobayashi, K. (1986) *Computers and Computers: A Vision of C&C.* Cambridge, MA: MIT Press.

Kogut, B. and Kulatilaka, N. (1997) "Capabilities as real options." Paper prepared for the conference on Risk, Managers, and Options, Wharton School, University of Pennsylvania.

Kogut, B. and Zander, U. (1992) "Knowledge of the firm, combinative capabilities, and the replication of technology." *Organization Science* 3:383–397.

Kraar, L. (1981) "Japan's Canon focuses on America." *Fortune*, January 12, pp. 82–88.

Leonard, D. and Sensiper, S. (1998) "The role of tacit knowledge in group innovation." *California Management Review* 40:112–132.

Lyons, N. (1976) *The Sony Vision.* New York: Crown.

March, J.G. (1991) "Exploration and exploitation in organizational learning." *Organization Science* 2:71–87.

McKelvey, B. (1999) "Avoiding complexity catastrophe in coevolutionary pockets: strategies for rugged landscapes." *Organization Science* 10: 294–321.

Mead, T. (1985) "Patience pays off for NEC America." *Electronic Business*, February 1, pp. 56–62.

Meyer, M. (1985) "Can anyone duplicate Canon's personal copiers' success?" *Marketing and Media Decisions*, Spring, pp. 97–101.

Milgrom, P. and Roberts, J. (1990) "The economics of modern manufacturing: technology, strategy, and organization." *American Economic Review* 80:511–528.

Monteverde, K. (1995) "Technical dialog as an incentive for vertical integration in the semiconductor industry." *Management Science* 41:1624–1638.

Montgomery, C.A. (1994) "Corporate diversification." *Journal of Economic Perspectives* 8:163–178.

Moore, T. (1982) "Canon takes aim at the snapshooter." *Fortune* 106(2):38–39.

Morita, A., with Reingold, E.M. and Shimomura, M. (1986) *Made in Japan: Akio Morita and Sony.* New York: Signet.

Nathan, J. (1999) *Sony: The Private Life.* New York: Houghton-Mifflin.

NEC. (1984) *NEC Corporation: The First 80 Years.* Tokyo: NEC Corporation.

Nelson, R.R. and Winter, S.G. (1982) *An Evolutionary Theory of Economic Change.* Cambridge, MA: Harvard University Press.

Nonaka, I. and Takeuchi, H. (1995) *The Knowledge-Creating Company.* New York: Oxford University Press.

Patton, P. (1999) "Humming off key for two decades." *New York Times*, July 29, p. E1.

Penrose, E.T. (1959) *The Theory of the Growth of the Firm.* Wiley: New York.

Peteraf, M.A. (1993) "The cornerstones of competitive advantage: a resource-based view." *Strategic Management Journal* 14(3):179–191.

Pollack, A. (1999) "Akio Morita, co-founder of Sony and Japanese business leader, dies at 78." *New York Times*, October 4, pp. A28–A29.

Port, O. (1987) "Canon finally challenges Minolta's mighty Maxxum. *Business Week*, 2987(2 March): 89–90.

Porter, M.E. (1985) *Competitive Advantage: Creat-*

ing and Sustaining Superior Performance. New York: Free Press.

Porter, M.E. (1996) "What is strategy?" *Harvard Business Review* 74(6):61–78.

Quinn, J.B., Baruch, J.J., and Zien, K.A. (1997) *Innovation Explosion: Using Intellect and Software to Revolutionize Growth Strategies*. New York: Free Press.

Raubitschek, R.S. (1988a) "Hitting the jackpot: product proliferation by multiproduct firms under uncertainty." *International Journal of Industrial Organization* 6:469–488.

Raubitschek, R.S. (1988b) "Multiple scenario analysis and business planning." *Advances in Strategic Management* 5:181–205.

Rivkin, J. (1998) *Airborne Express (A)*. Case no. 9-798-070. Boston: Harvard Business School.

Rosenberg, N. (1982) *Inside the Black Box: Technology and Economics*. Cambridge: Cambridge University Press.

Rosenbloom, R.S. and Cusumano, M.A. (1987) "Technological pioneering and competitive advantage: the birth of the VCR industry." *California Management Review* 22:51–76.

Rubinflen, E., Ono, Y., and Landro, L. (1988) "A changing Sony aims to own the 'software' that its products need." *Wall Street Journal*, December 3, p. A1.

Rumelt, R.P. (1984) "Towards a strategic theory of the firm," in B. Lamb (ed.), *Competitive Strategic Management*. pp. 556–570. Englewood Cliffs, NJ: Prentice-Hall.

Rumelt, R.P., Schendel, D.E., and Teece, D.J. (1994) Fundamental issues in strategy," in R.P. Rumelt, D.E. Schendel, and D.J. Teece (eds), *Fundamental Issues in Strategy: A Research Agenda*, pp. 9–53. Boston: Harvard Business School Press.

Sanchez, R. and Mahoney, J.T. (1996) "Modularity, flexibility, and knowledge management in product and organization design." *Strategic Management Journal* 17(Winter):63–76.

Siggelkow, N. (1999) "Change in the presence of fit: the rise, the fall, and the renaissance of Liz Claiborne." Working paper, Wharton School, University of Pennsylvania.

Smart, T. (1999) "Delivering packages, partnerships." *Washington Post*, May 2, pp. H1, H8.

Smith, L. (1984) "Japan's two-fister telephone maker." *Fortune* 109(13):30–36.

Smith, L. (1987) "Sony battles back." *Fortune* 111(8):26–38.

Sullivan, K. (1988) "Key word at NEC: applicability." *Business Month* 131(3):48–49.

Sutherland, D. (1988) "Still video: anything there for marketers?" *Business Marketing* 73(10):64–70.

Teece, D.J. (1980) "Economies of scope and the scope of the enterprise." *Journal of Economic Behavior and Organization* 1:223–247.

Teece, D.J. (1986) "Profiting from technological innovation: implications from integration, collaboration, licensing and public policy." *Research Policy* 15:285–305.

Teece, D.J., Pisano, G., and Shuen, A. (1997) "Dynamic capabilities and strategic management." *Strategic Management Journal* 18(7):509–534.

Teece, D.J., Rumelt, R., Dosi, G., and Winter, S. (1994) Understanding corporate coherence: theory and evidence. *Journal of Economic Behavior and Organization* 23:1–30.

Trachtenberg, J.A. (1987) "I am betting my destiny." *Forbes* 139(5):66.

Tushman, M.L. and O'Reilly, C.A. (1996) "The ambidextrous organization: managing evolutionary and revolutionary change." *California Management Review* 38:8–30.

Von Hippel, E. (1976) "The dominant role of users in the scientific instrument innovation process." *Research Policy* 5:212–239.

Von Hippel, E. (1986) "Lead users: a source of novel product concepts." *Management Science* 32:791–805.

Wernerfelt, B. (1984) "A resource-based view of the firm. *Strategic Management Journal* 5(2):171–180.

Wheelwright, S. and Clark, K.B. (1992) *Revolutionizing Product Development*. New York: Free Press.

Winter, S.G. (1987) "Knowledge and competence as strategic assets," in D.J. Teece (ed.), *The Competitive Challenge: Strategies for Industrial Innovation and Renewal*, pp. 159–184. Cambridge, MA: Ballinger.

Winter, S.G. (1993) "On Coase, competence, and the corporation," in O.E. Williamson and S.G. Winter (eds), *The Nature of the Firm: Origins, Evolution, and Development*, pp. 179–195. New York: Oxford University Press.

Yamanouchi, T. (1989) "Breakthrough: the development of the Canon personal copier." *Long Range Planning* 22(5):11–21.

Zander, U. and Kogut, B. (1995) "Knowledge and the speed of the transfer and imitation of organizational capabilities: an empirical test." *Organization Science* 6:1–17.

EPILOGUE: PRODUCT SEQUENCING, KNOWLEDGE, AND E-COMMERCE

The product sequencing model in our original article links the evolution of knowledge to new product introductions over time in technology intensive or operationally complex organizations. As such, we can use the model to help us understand some of the potential benefits as well as possible limitations of perhaps the most exciting new businesses today—those involved in the emerging digital economy (U.S. Department of Commerce 2000).

The digital economy spans a wide range of businesses and services. Here we focus on electronic commerce on the Internet, defined as purchases and sales of goods and services transacted over the Internet. Two primary forms of electronic commerce involve business-to-consumer and business-to-business transactions. In what follows, we use the product sequencing model to analyze well-publicized examples of each of these forms of business. The Internet businesses on which we focus—retail sales and mass customization (business-to-consumer) and electronic buyer–supplier online marketplaces (business-to-business)—are still in the early stages of their development. Like all other aspects of electronic commerce and the digital economy more generally, it is difficult to predict the ultimate form that these businesses will take. We can, however, use the product sequencing model to track the evolution of these businesses, to understand the nature of the knowledge required for the current visions of these businesses, and to analyze how firms may be able to use this knowledge to create new products and services over time.

Business-to-Consumer Electronic Commerce

Internet Retailers

Well-known examples of business-to-consumer retailers include those such as Amazon or Barnes & Noble (Ghemawat and Baird 1998) that sell retail products directly to consumers over the Internet. These retailers include start-up companies that began life as Internet companies, as well as established "bricks-and-mortar" and catalogue mail order retailers that added Internet retail stores to their existing businesses. As discussed in our original article, like all retailers, the core knowledge of these companies relates specifically to retail sales, such as knowledge related to the mix of products desired by consumers. Integrative knowledge for these Internet businesses links the retailer to its suppliers and customers, conceptually similar to the integrative knowledge employed by Wal-Mart (Bradley and Ghemawat 1995) in the example in our article.

Like Wal-Mart, Internet retailers may find integrative knowledge helpful to incremental learning related to core knowledge about retail sales, because integrative knowledge enables retailers to obtain feedback about customer buying patterns. Compared to bricks-and-mortar retailers, Internet retailers can more easily obtain information about the buying habits of individual customers, which the companies can then use to do more targeted selling and thus improve the "product" of retail sales. In order to capitalize on the potential of the Internet in this manner, existing bricks-and-mortar and catalogue mail order companies need to alter their integrative knowledge, via either incremental or step function learning. Start-up Internet retailers face at least an equally challenging task. Since the companies are starting from scratch, they require step function learning in both core knowledge and integrative knowledge.

Mass Customization

Another example of business-to-consumer electronic commerce involves mass customization, such as that pioneered by Dell Computer (Rangan and Bell 1998). In mass customization, customers configure their own products from a set menu of modular choices offered by the seller. Dell, which made its name as a mail order personal computer company engaged in mass customization, provides an example of moving mail order business to the Internet.[1]

A company like Dell is both a retailer and a producer. Like other Internet retailers, mass customizers can use integrative knowledge to obtain feedback from customers via purchasing patterns. For example, the companies can see trends in customer demand for product features and can further use this information to experiment by offering new product features to customers. Here again, integrative knowledge is helpful for learning related to core knowledge about the nature of the product, and for product sequencing based on this learning. In addition, established companies such as Dell need to alter their integrative knowledge, via incremental or step function learning, in order to move their current operations to the Internet. Start-up mass customizers must build both core and integrative knowledge simultaneously.

Business-to-Business Electronic Commerce

One of the most talked about forms of business-to-business electronic commerce on the Internet involves the formation of online marketplaces by consortia of buyers, often large established companies in a particular industry such as automobiles, chemicals, or retailing (U.S. Department of Commerce 2000). These buyers intend to use the Internet to purchase inputs from suppliers, who will bid to supply the inputs.[2] We can think of these planned online marketplaces as performing a similar function to electronic data interchange (EDI) systems that individual companies maintain to link themselves to their suppliers, such as the internal system employed by Wal-Mart.[3] Like EDI systems, online exchanges are best suited to commodities or to inputs that have codified designs, because the required attributes of the inputs can be completely and accurately specified using electronic communication.

In order to develop and utilize these online exchanges effectively, the buyers in these networks need to develop new integrative knowledge, both within the company itself and within any new entity that manages the exchange. This may involve step function learning in integrative knowledge in order to take advantage of the large cost reductions that are foreseen using the Internet relative to EDI networks (U.S. Department of Commerce 2000). Utilization of these online marketplaces to purchase standardized inputs, however, does not by itself create the potential for product sequencing by the purchasers over time. In order to provide a basis for development of new products by the buyers in these networks, the exchanges must incorporate feedback from suppliers or customers in a way that affects the core knowledge underlying the end products (e.g., chemicals, automobiles).

As an illustration of the potential for feedback from suppliers in these networks, suppose the auto companies make computer-aided designs for parts available on these exchanges. If an entire network of actual and potential suppliers had easy access on the Internet to the whole set of designs that comprise a product, such as a car, for example, these suppliers might be able to provide valuable advice to the producer. Such advice might involve improvements in how various parts could be made to fit together better, and how the designs for individual parts could be improved as well. This is just one example of the potential of these exchanges to alter the core knowledge underlying products. As another example, suppose the exchanges could include links to consumers, such as Wal-Mart does using its EDI system. Again, companies could use feedback from their customers as the basis for learning in core knowledge and for development of new products.

Conclusion

The foregoing examples of electronic commerce on the Internet indicate ways in which companies in both the business-to-business and business-to-consumer segments of the market can take advantage of opportunities for development of new knowledge and for product sequencing over time. We examined only a few prominent examples. There are many other forms of business emerging on the Internet, and we really have little idea of how these and other yet unknown businesses will evolve over time. But we can use the product sequencing model to illuminate where some of the challenges lie, especially with regard to development of new knowledge, and where the potential lies for product sequencing. More generally, we did not require an entirely new model to analyze the changes taking hold in e-commerce. And like the e-commerce examples briefly analyzed here, the product sequencing model applies equally well to other businesses involved in the digital economy, including the many technology-intensive businesses that provide the products and services that comprise the infrastructure underlying the Internet.

Notes

The views expressed herein are not purported to represent those of the U.S. Department of Justice. This chapter benefited from discussions with Jan Hammond and Roy Shapiro. We are entirely responsible for its contents.

1. In addition to sales to individuals, Dell sells directly to businesses. Although the latter portion of Dell's sales over the Internet is sometimes termed business-to-business e-commerce, it has some similar implications for knowledge and product sequencing as do Dell's mass customization sales to individuals over the Internet.

2. Concerns have been raised about the potential for firms to use business-to-business electronic marketplaces to reduce competition (U. S. Department of Commerce 2000, Federal Trade Commission 2000).

3. In fact, most of the current business-to-business electronic commerce takes place over private EDI networks (U.S. Department of Commerce 2000).

References

Bradley, S.P. and Ghemawat, P. (1995) *Wal-Mart Stores, Inc.* Case No. 9-794-024. Boston: Harvard Business School.

Federal Trade Commission. (2000) "FTC to hold public workshop to examine competition issues in business-to-business electronic marketplaces." Available at: http://www.ftc.gov/opa/2000/05/b2bworkshop.htm, May 4.

Ghemawat, P. and Baird, B. (1998) *Leadership Online: Barnes & Noble vs. Amazon.com (A)*. Case No. 9-798-063. Boston: Harvard Business School.

Rangan, V.K. and Bell, M. (1998) *Dell Online*. Case No. 9-598-116. Boston: Harvard Business School.

U.S. Department of Commerce (2000) *The Digitial Economy 2000*. Available at: http://www.doc.gov.

19

Exploration and Exploitation as Complements

Anne Marie Knott

One of the more persistent themes in the management literature is the tension between success in a competitive environment versus survival in a changing environment. Success in the competitive environment involves exploitation of a firm's existing capabilities; survival in a dynamic environment involves exploration for new capabilities (March 1991, Levinthal and March 1993). In the early work, exploration and exploitation were often characterized as perfect substitutes. Strategic choice was thus presented as positioning along a continuum from exploration (high variance in activities/knowledge) to exploitation (low variance in activities/knowledge). The challenge for firms then, was "picking" the point on the exploration/exploitation continuum corresponding to the underlying rate of change in the environment.

A more recent perspective suggests that exploration and exploitation are imperfect substitutes, such that there are greater returns to specialization. Once a firm engages in substantial exploitation, it is more cost-effective to increase exploitation than it is to engage in exploration, and vice versa. From this perspective, the optimal strategies for firms are the extremes of static op-

timization (exploitation) and dynamic optimization (exploration)—balancing is impractical.

This chapter explores a third perspective—that exploration and exploitation are actually complements. If so, then engaging in exploitation makes firms more effective at exploration, and vice versa. What motivates this perspective is the observation that product development appears to combine exploration and exploitation in a single activity. If exploration and exploitation are imperfect substitutes, as the recent literature suggests, then such combination should be inefficient. I believe that empirical examination of product development may provide insights into the exploration and exploitation of knowledge and may help us characterize the nature of their interdependence.

I define exploration in a product development context to be the addition of new characteristics or higher performance with each new product introduction, and I define exploitation to be regular reduction in product cost with each new product introduction (learning curve behavior).[1] I assert that if product development introduces new features that improve product quality, then product development represents *exploration* for new capabilities within the firm. Similarly, I assert that if sequential product developments exhibit learning curve behavior, then product development represents an *exploitation* of some form of knowledge within the firm. Further, if product development exhibits *both* exploration and exploitation behavior, this is evidence that the two strategies are likely complements since it is non-optimal to combine them if they are substitutes.

The chapter begins by reviewing the literature on the exploration/exploitation tension. Next I characterize product development along these two dimensions. I then empirically examine sequential product developments in a single firm over a 28-year period: I look quantitatively at changes in unit cost across product developments to determine if there is evidence of exploitation in product development. And I look qualitatively at the nature of changes to the product over the period to determine if there is evidence of exploration in product development.

I find evidence of both exploration and exploitation in product development. This evidence, combined with the fact that the firm I describe is the most profitable in its industry, suggests that exploration and exploitation are likely complements, rather than substitutes. I strengthen that argument by identifying organizational features that engender the complementarity.

The Exploration/Exploitation Tension

The tension between improving current operations (exploitation) and expanding into new operations (exploration) is a common theme in the management literature. In the classical organization theory literature, the tension was resolved by assigning the disparate activities to different individuals in the organization. Simon (1945) distinguished between an administrator and a legislator. The administrator was charged with monitoring the internal environment—maintaining links among subunits. Decision making at that level was within given reference frames. In contrast, the legislator was charged with linking the organization with the external environment, developing policy where reference frames for decision making had to be constructed. Similarly, Selznick (1957) distinguished between administrative management that emphasized methods versus goals, and institutional leadership concerned with the evolution of the organization's goals and capabilities. Selznick was concerned that with improper balance means might displace ends. In theories of growth of the firm, Penrose (1959) distinguished between an administrator and an entrepreneur. The role of the administrator was to implement entrepreneurial ideas as well as to supervise existing operations. That of the entrepreneur was to choose the expansion path for the firm by introducing new ideas with respect to products, markets, and technology and by making fundamental changes in the organization. Chandler (1962) defined executives who allocated resources as entrepreneurs, and those who coordinated and planned operations with the means allocated as managers. This classical perspective was generally agnostic about whether the two activities were complements or substitutes. The literature's primary contribution was identifying that both activities were important to firms.

Beginning with contingency theory, the solution to the exploration/exploitation tension rose above individual roles to organizational structure. Burns and Stalker (1961) asserted that there were two extreme forms that organizations should adopt in response to the rate of industrial change. For static environments, firms should adopt mechanistic structures like those in theories of bureaucracy (Weber 1920, Fayol 1923, Gulick 1936); for dynamic environments, firms need organic forms where tasks are continually redefined, with network structures rather than hierarchies, and communication in the form of advice rather than instruction. Later, population ecologists raised solutions to a population level. Hannan and Freeman (1989) adopted solutions from biology (MacArthur and Levins 1964): Opportunist strategies, or r-strategies, were suited to open environments in which there were no resource or competition constraints. The strategies led to many reproductive events with few resources invested in each attempt—thereby maximizing population growth rate in open environments. In contrast, k-strategies were suited to competitive environments. Here the strategies produce a small number of reproductive events with much time and energy invested in each event. K-strategies maximize a population's ability to expand in the face of competitive pressure by giving individual offspring good life chances. The advantage of the r-strategies is rapid exploitation of new opportunity; their disadvantage is low capacity to withstand dense competition. In contrast, k-strategies can withstand competition but are slow to respond in changing environments. While the ecological solution nominally refers to populations of firms, it holds implications for multidivisional firms as well. Both the contingency theory and population ecology literature tend to suggest that exploration and exploitation are *perfect substitutes*, lying on opposite ends of a continuum. The managerial challenge is one of determining the underlying rate of change in the environment and then choosing the corresponding organizational form.

More recently, the tension has been couched from a decision theoretic perspective in the organizational learning literature. March (1991) and Levinthal and March (1993) distinguish between exploration and exploitation. Exploration is the search for new knowledge, whereas exploitation is the use and development of things already known. The risk in excessive exploitation is obsolescence in a changing environment. The risk in excessive exploration is failure to harvest the value of any single discovery. Relatedly, Ghemawat and Ricart i Costa (1993) distinguish between static efficiency and dynamic efficiency: static efficiency is optimization within a given production function, whereas dynamic efficiency is changing production functions in profitable ways. The tension between them is modeled as constrained information processing: to search for improvements within a framework of fixed beliefs, or to reconsider the beliefs themselves. This decision theoretic literature tends to suggest that exploration and exploitation are *imperfect substitutes* such that each incremental increase in one activity comes at increasing cost to the other activity.

I propose a third perspective: that exploration and exploitation are *complements* rather than substitutes. What prompts this perspective is the observation that product development appears to combine the two activities in a single function. Such combination, while consistent with the contingency theory perspective of a linear continuum (perfect substitutes) between exploration and exploitation, would not be expected in the decision theoretic perspective. Since the decision theoretic perspective holds that the returns to specialization are greater than those to combination, combination of exploration and exploitation should be nonoptimal. This chapter empirically examines the "anomaly" of product development in order to determine if the underlying relationship between exploration and exploitation is that of perfect substitutes (contingency theory), imperfect substitutes (decision

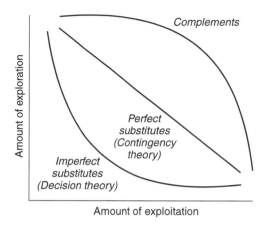

Figure 19.1 Posited relationships between exploration and exploitation.

theory), or complements (my hypothesis). Figure 19.1 captures the distinction between these three perspectives graphically.

Product Development

Product development appears to combine exploration and exploitation in a single activity. Certainly firms engage in product development to introduce new versions of products (which on the face appears to be evidence of exploration). What is less clear, but potentially feasible, is that firms may actually become better at product development over time, much like they become better at manufacturing over time. If so, then product development also constitutes exploitation.

While I am hopeful that product development is exploitive, there are many reasons to suspect that learning phenomena such as those exhibited by manufacturing are not possible in product development environments. Knowledge acquisition, interpretation, recording, and retrieval (Levitt and March 1988, Huber 1991) are all likely to be more difficult for product development than they are for manufacturing. *Acquisition* is difficult because the period between stimulus and response can be quite long. Designers may have to wait an entire development period (which in the case of the automobile industry is 4–10 years; Clark and Fujimoto 1991) to incorporate the knowledge gained from prior design decisions. *Interpretation* of experience is more difficult because the causal structures of product development are complex. Product development teams are often very large, involving many people from diverse disciplines working with new technologies. *Recording* of experience (Levitt and March 1988) may be less likely because participants are pulled away from projects at different points in time (Hayes et al. 1988) possibly before they even see the outcome of their contributions. Further, managers are often unwilling to spend money to document experience, preferring instead to press forward with the next project (Wheelwright and Clark 1992). *Retrieving* experience from prior product developments can be difficult. Product developments are generally infrequent, and thus nonencoded information is likely to be clouded by intervening events. Further, the people involved in development projects are likely to be physically dispersed once a project is concluded, either to their functional area or to a new project (Hayes et al. 1988). Under such circumstances reconstruction of information may be inhibited by the inability to bring together all those who contributed to a given design. Finally, product development suffers from paucity of experience. Whereas the intervals between manufacture of one unit and the next are measured in minutes, those between product developments are often longer than a year. Such infrequency yields inadequate observation opportunities relative to the complexity and instability of history (Levitt and March 1988).

In addition to the structural characteristics that inhibit learning from product development, there are perceptual problems as well. Since product development is generally considered to be an innovative process, managers resist efforts to control it or learn from it. According to one manager interviewed, "No two projects are the same—there are too many variables, too much random noise to make sense of anything" (Hayes et al. 1988, p. 336). In some sense, however, the very conditions that inhibit product development learning are also the conditions making it valuable in a dynamic environment. The complexity and variety of experience are likely to lead to learning that is explorative rather than exploitive (March 1991, Levinthal and March 1993). Such exploration is likely to produce greater likelihood of survival in a changing environment.

While the picture just painted seems bleak, there are reasons to expect that learning from one product development to the next is possible. First, learning likely takes place at the individual level. Engineers assigned to product development often are "development engineers" who work on a series of product developments. Thus, they ought to learn better how to execute their own function. Second, there is structure to

product development: development progresses through predictable stages of developing top-level specifications, allocating those performance goals and constraints (weight, volume, power consumption, etc.) across the various subsystems, designing the subsystems, prototyping, and system integration and testing. This structure presents an opportunity for some level of routinization. Finally, the product is generally well documented in drawings, test results, change requests, and so forth. Thus, at least the raw data to support learning exists. The challenge may be in synthesizing the data into useful summaries.[2]

In short, there are several factors that impede product development learning and several other factors that facilitate it. The question of whether product development learning (exploitation) occurs is an empirical one. I explore that question here in conjunction with the question of exploration.

My primary goal for the empirical test is to demonstrate the coexistence of exploration and exploitation in product development. By so doing, I hope to challenge the notion that the two activities (exploration and exploitation) are substitutes and to contribute to the view that they are actually complements. A secondary goal is to understand the processes that generate exploration and exploitation. In so doing, I hope to form prescriptions about how to best combine the two activities. To accomplish both goals, I conducted a quantitative test of learning curve behavior (exploitation) in a single firm over time and examined qualitative evidence of improvement in product quality (exploration).

Method

Toyota Motor Company was chosen as the subject of the study because I felt product development learning would be easiest to detect there. This stems from characteristics of the auto industry in general, and Toyota in particular. The auto industry is characterized by several generations of product development for which the scope of innovation between generations is fairly uniform. Of the firms in that industry, Toyota has exhibited the most remarkable productivity growth and is therefore most likely to exhibit any form of learning.[3] Finally, Toyota vehicle production data at the model level were publicly available.

Data for Toyota were gathered from multiple sources. Firm-level data on sales and production levels as well as factor utilization are from the studies of the automobile industry by Lieberman (1987), Lieberman and Weiers (1993), and Lieberman et al. (1990). Model production levels are from the Motor Vehicles Manufacturers Association's (MVMA) motor vehicle data books (several years). Data on prices and year of product introduction are from *Automotive News* market data yearbooks (several years). Data on product development innovations are from *Wards, Motor Trend, Car and Driver,* and *Consumer Reports* (several years).

Test of Exploitation

Empirical Model

To test exploitation in product development, I first developed a structural model of product development learning. I then adapted the model to the specific data available at Toyota. I used the adapted model to test for the significance of product development learning effects.

The foundation for the product development learning model is the basic form of the learning curve from manufacturing (see Yelle 1979 for a historical review):

$$y = Ax^b \tag{19.1}$$

Where

y is the unit cost for producing the xth unit of a product

A is the unit cost for producing the first unit of that product

x is the cumulative number of units produced

b is the learning exponent, generally $\varepsilon(-1,0)$

Thus, y is the estimated cost to produce the xth unit of a product, given the cost of the first unit, A, and the learning exponent, b. The underlying assumption in the model is that each unit produced is a "learning episode." Each time workers install their respective widgets, they have an opportunity to both observe the outcome of their installation and improve the installation process. Under this assumption, the cumulative experience that drives learning is the number of units produced.

To model product development learning, I made the assumption that the relevant "learning episode" is a major product development.

Thus, each time engineers complete a product development, they have an opportunity to observe its outcome relative to their goals and consider how they would modify future products or future product development processes. Under this assumption, the cumulative experience that drives learning is the number of product developments rather than the number of units produced. Equation 19.1 is modified accordingly:

$$A_i = A_1 i^d \tag{19.2}$$

Where:

i is the model number (number of prior product developments)

A_i is the cost of the first unit of model i

A_1 is the cost of the first unit of the first product

d is the product development learning exponent

If there is such a thing as product development learning, I expect it to occur in organizations where there is also manufacturing learning, since for reasons mentioned above, product development learning is more difficult than manufacturing learning. The combined learning is exhibited graphically in figure 19.2 for a notional firm with 70% manufacturing learning and 70% product development learning. Figure 19.2 shows the manufacturing cost for several sequential products. The figure assumes that the life of each product is four years, 100,000 units of the product are produced in each of those four years, and the first unit costs $1,000,000 to produce.

Given these assumptions, we see that the 100,000th unit of model 1 costs $2700 to produce. In contrast, the final 400,000th unit of

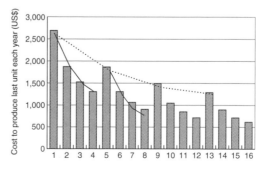

Figure 19.2 Combined effects of product development and manufacturing learning.

model 5 costs $700 to produce. This dramatic reduction in cost occurs because of manufacturing learning that reduced the average cost of a model 75% over its life (solid lines connecting manufacturing years within each model) and product development learning that reduced the cost for each new model by 30% (dotted line connecting new models). What is interesting is that even though we have dramatic learning in both manufacturing and product development, there are periods of "apparent unlearning" when new models are introduced. In other words, the average cost for the 100,000th unit of model 2 production is 50% higher than the cost for the last unit of model 1. This apparent unlearning occurs as workers give up their competency with the previous model and become familiar with the new model (Hall 1957, Yelle 1979).

To ensure that this empirical test truly captures product development learning rather than misinterprets manufacturing learning as such, I need to control for manufacturing learning. To do so, I combine equations 19.1 and 19.2:

$$y_{ik} = A_1(i^d)(x_{ik}^b) \qquad (19.3)$$

Where:

x_{ik} is the cumulative production of model i up to unit k

y_{ik} is the cost to produce the kth unit of model i

While this is a simple equation, in practice firms do not know the cost to produce any single unit. They merely know the *average unit cost* over a production period. I take that into account here by integrating equation 19.3 over the production interval:

$$Y_{it} = \int A_1 (i^d) (x_{ik}^b) \qquad (19.4)$$

$$Y_{it} = A_1 (i^d) / (b + 1) (x_{it}^{b+1} - x_{i(t-1)}^{b+1}) \qquad (19.5)$$

For simplicity, I combine the constants[4]:

$$Y_{it} = C(i^d) (x_{it}^{b+1} - x_{i(t-1)}^{b+1}) \qquad (19.6)$$

Where:

Y_{it} is the total cost to produce all units of i in period t

C is $A_1 / (b + 1)$

Finally, because production cost data are available only at the aggregate level (over all models), I sum equation 19.6 over all products:

$$Y_t = C \Sigma_i (i^d) (x_{it}^{b+1} - x_{i(t-1)}^{b+1}) \qquad (19.7)$$

Equation 19.7 is the baseline model for decomposing manufacturing learning and product development learning. Note that, for the purposes at hand, manufacturing learning is merely a control variable, to ensure that I am not incorrectly attributing manufacturing learning to product development. My main goal is to test the hypothesis that product development is exploitive (exhibits learning curve behavior):

H[1]: $d < 0$

Data

The quantitative data set comprises 28 years (1961–1988)[5] of production volumes for each model and annual aggregated production cost at Toyota. (Production cost for each model is not available directly; thus, I will be solving for it indirectly using aggregated cost and variance in model volume.) Figure 19.3 gives the volume for each model in each year from 1960 to 1988. Incidentally, figure 19.3 indicates that rapid output growth at Toyota has been achieved through the addition of models rather than through increased volume of any given model. This suggests that there must not be significant scale economies at the model level once minimum efficient scale (MES) is achieved.

Because we are working with time series data, I present time lines of salient variables rather than the standard data summary. These are shown in figure 19.4, which indicates that average model volume increased rapidly until 1965, then fell dramatically. This trend suggests a shift

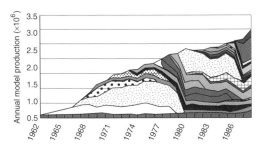

Figure 19.3 History of Toyota model volume.

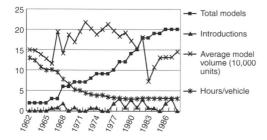

Figure 19.4 Temporal study of Toyota data.

in strategy for Toyota, possibly from one of exploiting manufacturing (scale) advantage to one of developing market advantage through more variety/shorter product life. Figure 19.4 also indicates that Toyota enjoys decreasing unit cost even as average volume is dropping. Thus, cost savings seem to be coming from something other than scale economies.

Product Quality Weights

Equation 19.7 compares total production cost against total vehicles produced. Implicit in the equation is an assumption that all products have comparable manufacturing cost. However, automobile manufacturers in general, and Toyota in particular, produce a broad range of product qualities. One means to account for product quality is to use a price index for each product. However, Toyota data indicate that price was increased annually, even in the absence of changes to the product. Moreover, these price increases were not strictly consumer price index (CPI) adjustments, since the annual percentage price increase for each product was a function of product quality—higher quality models increased price at a faster rate than did lower quality models. Accordingly, we chose vehicle weight as a more fundamental measure of product quality. Industry studies have tended to show that vehicle weight is the best aggregate predictor of manufacturing cost.

Product Sequence Numbers

Product introductions need to be indexed to establish the variable i for cumulative product developments. This indexing is complicated by the fact that products carrying the same nameplate undergo a number of redesigns over their life. Some of these are major; others are mainly cos-

metic. To restrict study to major product development efforts, new introductions for existing nameplates were defined as changes in wheelbase size (equivalently platform changes).[6] When more than one model shared the same wheelbase, the set of models was treated as a single model. Once introduction order was determined, products were assigned a model number i, ranging from 1 to 33, representing their order of introduction.

Incremental Innovation

My qualitative analysis will show that there is incremental innovation between major product developments. This incremental innovation justifies the annual increases in real prices (above CPI) for each model. I attempt to control for incremental innovation by adding a factor g for quality growth.

I modify equation 19.7 to include vehicle weights, model-specific quality constants, and incremental innovation:

$$Y_t = C \, \Sigma_i \, (i^d) \, w_i \, (x_{it}^{b+1} - x_{i(t-1)}^{b+1})g^t \quad (19.8)$$

Where:

w_i is the weight (1000 pounds) of model i

g is the coefficient for annual quality improvement

t is time (years)

Analysis

Equation 19.8 is inherently nonlinear, leading to nonlinear regression using maximum likelihood (see Greene 1993, chap. 11; Judge 1988, chap. 12; White 1990, chap. 19). The regression consists of one equation with 60 variables but only three coefficients. Given 28 observations, there are only 25 degrees of freedom. Thus, it will be difficult to obtain significant results. Because the data are time series and because the estimation method assumes normally distributed errors, I specified an AR1 (first-order autoregressive) transform of the variables (see Greene 1993, chap. 15; Judge 1988, chap. 9; White 1990, chap. 11). I also ran the model alternatively with second-order transformation and without transformation and found the first-order transform to provide the best fit. The correlation coefficient, ρ, used in the transform is included for each regression in table 19.1.

TABLE 19.1 Regression Output

	Types of learning				
	Model 0: OLS	Model 1: All Mfg	Model 2: Model Mfg	Model 3: Dvlp	Model 4: Dvlp + Mfg
C	−6.085	−515.240	0.002	0.066	0.010
	(−12.220)	(−0.133)	(0.350)	(0.645)	(0.710)
$b + 1$	0.400	0.614	1.257	1.132	
	(3.563)	(1.369)	(7.751)		(8.600)
d				−4.633	−4.711
				(0.824)	(−0.967)
Time			1.059	1.106	1.091
			(36.958)	(14.548)	(14.884)
ρ		1.053	0.981	1.085	1.086
		(25.816)	(14.805)	(63.156)	(65.815)
MLE of σ^2		3.37E + 11	9.55E + 10	2.40E + 10	2.39E + 10
Adjusted r^2	0.830				

Dependent variable = total manufacturing cost; n = 28 years. OLS = ordinary least squares. MLE = maximum likelihood estimator.

Numbers in parentheses are t-statistics. Scale (physical capital) was tested as a control variable in all models—it was never significant, nor did it add to model explanatory power. I tested alternative orders of autocorrelation and found first order to provide the best fit (the only model for which linear approximation was plausible). This had no effect on results. Time is not added to models 0 and 1 because cumulative output (over all models) and time are perfectly correlated.

Results for Quantitative Test of Exploitation

The results for quantitative test of exploitation (eq. 19.8) are presented in table 19.1 (model 4). The results indicate substantial but only mildly significant (83% level) product development learning. The −4.7 coefficient for d corresponds to a product development learning curve of 4% ($=2^{-4.7}$). Thus, for each doubling of product introductions, the cost of the first unit of the new product decreases by 96%. This result is robust to the deletion of manufacturing learning (model 3) and time (not shown).[7] Thus, there appears to be some support for hypothesis 1, that product development exhibits learning curve behavior and thus exploits knowledge within the firm.

Before becoming too enthusiastic about the results, it is worth restating the fact that this is not an ideal data set. I am using aggregate cost data over all 33 models for only 28 years in an effort to characterize product development learning. In addition, I have to control for manufacturing learning. Thus, I have only 25 degrees of freedom. The ideal database would have annual cost data for each model. Unfortunately, this was unavailable (and efforts to obtain private data from Toyota suggested the data may not exist). I compensated for the data set limitations by conducting supplementary tests of the data, which I discuss now.

Nonlinear regression (NLR) is an iterative method that searches for the best fit, rather than the simple linear algebra of ordinary least squares (OLS) regression. Accordingly, I wanted an OLS baseline that provided a test of reasonableness of the NLR results. This OLS baseline is a simple regression of manufacturing learning using equation 19.1. This regression, like most others examining manufacturing learning, uses average unit cost over an annual interval as the dependent variable. Thus, it is not strictly correct. However, results for that regression (model 0) provide a baseline estimate of learning at Toyota over all models and years. That estimate suggests that Toyota enjoys a 66% learning curve ($2^{(0.4 - 1)}$). Note that this coefficient, like those of most prior tests of learning, attributes both manufacturing and product development learning effects (to the extent that both exist) to manufacturing.

The OLS regression is thus a proxy for NLR without product development learning and with cumulative (rather than model specific) manufacturing output. This is a further simplification of equation 19.5:

$$Y_{it} = A_1 / (b + 1) (X_t^{b+1} - X_{(t-1)}^{b+1}) \quad (19.9)$$

Results from test of equation 19.9 are given in Table 19.1 (model 1). While the coefficients $b + 1$ are not the same across the two regressions, they do appear to be comparable (0.4 in OLS, 0.61 for NLR). The nonlinear regression provides a more conservative estimate of learning (76%) than does OLS. Thus, I have some confidence in the mechanics of the nonlinear approach (in addition to knowledge that it, rather than OLS of eq. 19.1, is structurally correct given the data).

Armed with that knowledge, I then proceeded to test equation 19.8 (model 4). The results for product development learning were reported above. I now want to mention the results for manufacturing learning. The results indicate that when we consider manufacturing learning within a model, for example, from the first Celica off the line to the last Celica off the line, there is no manufacturing learning. In fact, there appears to be unlearning—the coefficient of 1.13 corresponds to an increase in unit cost of 9.6% for each doubling of output. This result is robust to the deletion of development learning (model 2) and time (not shown).

This is a troublesome result. I thought perhaps that the result was due to the inherent multicollinearity in the data—the fact that the same output and cost data were being used to decompose manufacturing and product development learning. Thus, I wondered if the manufacturing coefficient was arbitrarily created in the regression's effort to decompose the two forms of learning. Accordingly, I tested models with manufacturing learning alone (model 2), and development alone (model 3). Comparison of these models with the main model (model 4) suggests this is not the case. The coefficients for d and $b + 1$ are similar across the models—indicating that the results are fairly reliable.

Finally, I thought that the implicit increased manufacturing cost might be due to real increases in input prices. Thus, I added price deflators to equation 19.8. This had no real effect on the results other than to reduce the model fit. Similarly, I added scale (dollar value of capital equipment) to the model. The scale coefficient was never significant, and its inclusion did not improve the model fit.

I want to mention the coefficient for quality improvement (time). It is characterized in equation 19.8 as an annual growth factor, and the results in models 2–4 are consistent with that. The estimated annual growth is 6–11% (1.059–

1.106)—within the range of Toyota's price growth (figure 19.5). Thus, time appears to be a reliable control for incremental improvement.

Thus, the main result—product development learning and manufacturing unlearning—appears to be reliable. We discuss plausible interpretations of this result in the discussion section. At this point, however, there does seem to be evidence supporting hypothesis 1, that product development is exploitive. Given evidence of exploitation in product development, I now test for exploration using qualitative data of product innovations.

Test of Exploration—Qualitative Review of Toyota Innovations

Approach

The qualitative study has two components. First, a top-level summary of product innovation across all Toyota product lines examines the evolution of product specifications to paint a picture of Toyota's overall innovation strategy. This top-level summary is followed by an in-depth narrative of innovations in a single product line. What I want to demonstrate with both components of the qualitative review is evidence that product development is explorative—that each product development introduces new product characteristics that improve quality (through enhanced performance, comfort, or styling). This provides the exploration counterpart to the exploitation pattern associated with cost improvement.

The Celica was chosen as the featured product line in the narrative for three reasons. First, the product line had a long life. It was introduced in the United States in 1971 and remained in production through 1988. Second, it catered to the middle market and thus was subject to nominal innovation pressure, that is, more than economy models such as the Tercel but less than "enthusiast" models—thus, it is representative of the "average" product development process. Finally, because the Celica was Toyota's best-selling model, it received substantial press attention (from which to gather the qualitative data).

To support the conclusion that the Celica is representative of Toyota's product development, we compiled specification data for each Toyota model in each year of the observation period (subject to data availability). These data are sum-

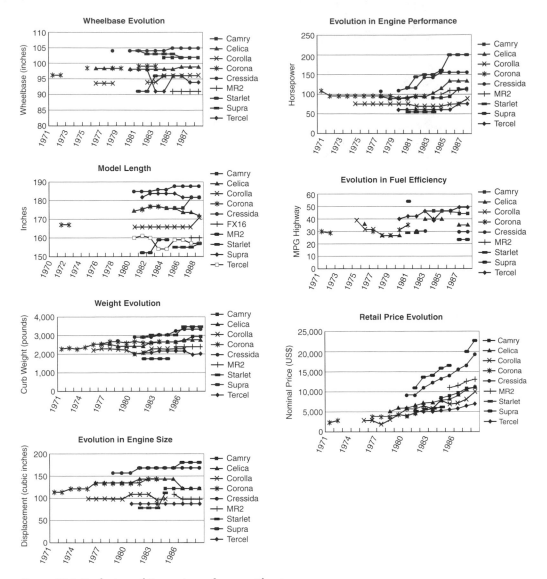

Figure 19.5 Evolution of Toyota's product specifications.

marized in figure 19.5, which characterizes the evolution of a particular automobile specification across all the Toyota models for all available years 1971–1988. I include three specifications pertaining to performance (engine size, power, and fuel efficiency) and three pertaining to body size (curb weight, wheelbase, and body length). These charts provide a sense of the overall frequency and magnitude of innovation across all the models.

While not a specification, the evolution of models' prices is also included. Price evolution is interesting because it captures Toyota's product

proliferation and model positioning. This can provide some insight for interpreting the evolution of other attributes.

Observations on Toyota Product Evolution

Toyota entered the U.S. market in 1971 with the Corolla, the Corona, and the Celica. While all three models were classified as "small cars" at the time, they had distinct positioning. The Corolla was the economy subcompact (least expensive of the three), the Corona was a family sedan, and the Celica (the most expensive of the three models) was a sporty coupe. Over time, Toyota expanded its product offerings to include two more less expensive models (the Tercel and the Starlet), and four more expensive cars: Supra (sports car), Cressida (high-end sedan), MR2 (affordable sports car), and the Camry (mid-market sedan).

Model Size Specifications

The wheelbase is the most durable of the auto specifications, since components are all fitted to the chassis. In terms of Henderson and Clark (1990) typology, wheelbase defines the physical architecture of an automobile. A change in the wheelbase represents an architectural change.[8] Except in the case of the Tercel, the wheelbase is fairly stable. What appears to happen with the Tercel is that it adopts the wheelbase of different models over time, rather than creating a unique wheelbase. Changes in length and weight (representing changes in styling rather than complete redesign) occur with somewhat greater frequency. Notice that there is a tendency toward increasing the weight of the higher end models while preserving the weight of the less expensive models. Since weight is one of the primary drivers of cost (and perceived quality), this appears to be an effort to increase the price of the higher end models over time.

Performance Specifications

The engine is the major performance component of the automobile. Changing the engine allows (and often requires) a change to the other mechanical components. Thus, engine size, like wheelbase, is a fairly durable commitment. While engine size tends to be quite stable for the models, engine performance improves for all models except the Corolla and the Corona. It appears that beginning in 1981, Toyota makes performance improvements for all models almost on an annual basis. Until I review the qualitative data, I cannot determine whether these changes are improvements at the engine manufacturer or changes by Toyota in complementary components. I expected that fuel efficiency would provide another indication of performance improvement. While the data are spotty, it appears that with the exception of the Tercel, Toyota moves away from fuel efficiency as a design goal in favor of heavier, higher performance

automobiles. This is most notable for the Corolla. This finding likely reflects Toyota's response to changes in customer preferences.

Summary

In summary, evolution of the specifications tends to suggest a pattern of continuous innovation of each model superimposed on infrequent major product developments. The in-depth review below of Celica's history will confirm whether this is the case and should provide insight into the mechanics of the actual innovation process. More important for my purposes, the charts in figure 19.5 indicate that Celica is a reasonable model to examine because it is in the middle of the product range and seems to track the general pattern of innovation (magnitude and frequency) of the set of product lines.

Narrative of Innovations to the Celica

1971

The Toyota Celica series was launched in the United States at the May 1971 Los Angeles Auto Expo. The car was a front-engine, rear-wheel-drive coupe powered by a four-cylinder, 1858 cc single-overhead-cam (SOHC) engine (taken from the Corona), with a four-speed manual transmission. "The little 2 + 2 filled the needs of buyers who wanted a sports sedan at a modest price, good fuel economy and passenger comfort" (*Motor Trend*, 1976). The original Celica, at least in Toyota's view, created the modern sporty subcompact field" (*Motor Trend* 1981).

1971–1975

For the first several years following introduction, innovation took the form of expanding the body styles, trimlines, and options available for the Celica, rather than improving the base model. The general pattern seemed to be one of offering innovations first as options, then as new "body styles" (essentially packages of options with some styling differences). For example in 1973, Toyota offered options for a larger (2000 cc) engine and an automatic transmission. Then, in 1974, Toyota introduced the Celica GT. The GT had a larger engine (2000 cc vs. 1858 cc for the ST), five-speed transmission, and a superior suspension (stiffer springs, bigger tires, and wider rims).

An exception to "innovation through product line extension" was the Electro Sensor Panel (ESP). The ESP, a panel of indicators ("dummy lights") mounted in the cabin above the windshield, was adopted by all the Celicas (from the Corona) in 1974.

1976

The first major product development for the Celica after initial launch was for the 1976 model. That development effort led to several engineering and styling changes across all the Celica body styles, but also produced a new body style—the Liftback, which won Motor Trend's Import Car of the Year award.

Global changes for all Celicas included a new, vertically cropped front end profile, a larger frame (3 inch longer and 1.5 inch wider wheelbase), fatter steel-belted radial tires on larger wheels (185/70 HR 14 steel-belted radials in place of the '75 GT's smaller 13-inchers), and new suspension (MacPherson strut coil spring front suspension and a solid rear axle also on coils and held in alignment by four trailing link arms). Changes to the frame, tires, and suspension were motivated by goals of improving the Celica's handling while preserving comfort. Additional performance changes included a new larger engine (type 20R, 2189 cc SOHC, four-cylinder engine with a cast iron block and an aluminum cylinder head).

The Celica's interior was revamped with new upholstery trim and greater functionality. The interior redesign included an all-new instrument panel with easier-to-read gauges, easier-to-use heater controls, repositioned air vents that improved circulation, and more accessible controls for lights, turn signals, wiper, and washer (levers mounted on the steering column rather than push-pull dashboard switches).

The new Liftback was mechanically the same as the Celica GT. The main functional difference of the liftback relative to the GT was, as the name implies, the "third door." To take full advantage of the hatch, the car had an adjustable rear seatback that extended the cargo area to 56 inches of carpeted flat floor, a tonneau cover for the rear load space to keep valuables out of sight, and an adjustable hold-down strap to keep things from sliding around. Other incidental features, exclusive to the Liftback, included a roof-mounted map light and rear seat litter boxes set in each side panel, just below the flush-mounted stereo speakers.

1978

While there were no real changes to the Celica in 1977, it underwent major restyling for 1978 and again won Motor Trend's Import Car of the Year award. The primary goals of the restyling appear to have been aesthetics, though secondary emphasis was placed on aerodynamics and comfort. Aerodynamics were geared not only toward decreasing fuel consumption, but also, perhaps more important, at reducing the wind noise that plagued earlier designs.

The redesign led to a sleeker, longer Celica. While the two body styles (coupe and Liftback) retained distinct roof profiles, both redesigns yielded low beltlines and large glass areas for a European-type look and increased visibility. Black bumpers, blacked-out accents around the windows, and black rubber molding replaced the chrome trim of prior models. Cast aluminum wheels replaced wheelcovers. A brushed-aluminum targa band was added. Further contributions to aerodynamics came from distinctive speed-styled mirrors, and from embedding the antenna in the windshield glass. A sliding steel sun roof was introduced as an option.

Performance improvements over the older Celica included increased rear wheel travel, further improved weight distribution, a 2.2-inch increase in rear track (for handling), and a slight weight reduction (for performance and fuel economy). A five-speed transmission became standard in all Celicas, while automatic transmission was available as an option. Power-assisted steering was also introduced as an option. Other options such as air and automatic transmission were carried over from the prior year.

Interior improvements included comfort and convenience enhancement. Comfort was improved through increased front shoulder room. The driver's seat on the two GT models added driver's seat controls for the back cushion (with three different degrees of lumbar support) as well as the bottom cushion. Rear seat shoulder room was increased 4.6 inches due to curved side glass and a wider rear track, and rear seat knee and headroom were also increased. Adjustable ventilation grilles for the rear seats were added to the B-pillars.

Convenience enhancements included oil pressure and ammeter gauges that replaced idiot lights, intermittent speeds added to the windshield wipers, and a quartz clock. The air vent to the right of the dash was fitted with a grille that defrosted the side window as well as directing air into the cockpit. Remote cable releases for the hatchback and locked gas cap were positioned on the floor to the left of the driver's seat.

Functional improvements unique to the Lift-back included a split-bench design for the rear seats such that they folded separately, a rear window wiper/washer, and an automatic lamp for the cargo area triggered by raising the hatchback.

1979

Existing Celica models (ST base coupe, GT coupe, GT Liftback) underwent only minor change for 1979, including longer front seat travel, a visor vanity mirror on GT models, and more complete color keying of interior console equipment.

The real innovation for the Celica was introduction of the Supra model. The larger and more luxurious Supra was 8 inches longer and used the 2600 cc fuel-injected 110-horsepower, six-cylinder engine from the Cressida sedan. While the Celica ST and GT models had a five-speed manual transmission as standard equipment and a three-speed automatic as an option, the Supra used the four-speed overdrive automatic (also from the Cressida).

The Supra was fully loaded with standard equipment, including power steering, power windows, wider tires, four-wheel disc brakes, air conditioning, and cruise control. The cruise control was set into the center console. Driver conveniences included six-position adjustment of the steering column height, a center armrest between the front seats whose top flipped up to reveal a small storage compartment and a mobile map light with a magnetic back, and a small coin box and the controls for the power windows mounted in the driver-side arm rest.[9]

1981

There were no significant changes to the Celica for 1980. The major change for the 1981 Celica was the new 22R 2.4-liter four-cylinder SOHC engine (from the Toyota pickup). Also new as options were cruise control, electronic radio/cassette, a two-tone paint package, and the Supra's four-speed overdrive automatic transmission.

Again, the major innovation was the addition of a new body style: a limited edition 10-year anniversary version of the Celica, the GTA, with the four-speed overdrive automatic transmission. On the exterior, the GTA had a two-tone paint package with color-keyed polyurethane bumpers and mudguards, pin striping, an exclusive honeycomb grille, and cast aluminum wheels (borrowed from the Cressida). On the inside, the GTA was essentially a Supra, with beige cloth seats and door trim, a leather-wrapped steering wheel (three spokes), console with map light, padded armrests, seatback pockets, cruise control, power windows, lighted visor vanity mirror, and fully carpeted trunk and package tray. The biggest single component of the package was the digital sound system (taken from the Cressida). Air conditioning, power steering, and a sunroof were available as separate options.

1982

The Celica was completely restyled for the 1982 model year toward a goal of "sportiness and high performance coupled with comfort and low fuel consumption" (Akihiro Wada, chief designer of the Celica, as quoted in *Motor Trend* 1981, p. 36).

The major emphasis of the Celica redesign appeared to be aerodynamic styling. The new nose peeled back from the bumper at 45 degrees. New halogen lights lay flush with the body angle when not in use and rocked up to vertical at the click of the light switch. The new body was 90 pounds lighter than its predecessor and achieved the lowest drag coefficient of any Japanese production car (0.34 for the Liftback, 0.38 for the coupe), very close to those for the Porsche 924.

The engine and transmission were carried over from the 1981 model (other than for slightly rearranged ratios). Also continued from 1981 hardware were the solid rear axle with four-link location and coil springs and MacPherson strut front suspension, though caster was increased for stronger self-centering action and better stability. New mechanical features were rack-and-pinion steering to improve road feel, and vented disk brakes from the new Supra.

Everything in the interior was taken from the Supra except for the Supra's eight-way adjustable seats. The Supra seats were available as an option, as were the Supra wheels and flares.

1986

There were minor changes to the Celica between 1983 and 1985. For example, the Celica front end was restyled in 1984 to include concealed headlamps and an enlarged front air dam. In 1986, however, "Toyota unveiled a completely redesigned sporty car for the '86 model year: an aerodynamically styled front-drive Celica coupe and hatchback [coup]" (*Wards* 1986, p. 151).

The body styling was a radical departure from earlier Celicas: the sides had a slightly sensuous, curvy little Coke-bottle flare that wrapped around the rear where the windows and fenders wound into the car's tail. The B- and C-pillars were hidden, such that the roofline seemed suspended over the rear windows with no real support. The aerodynamic result was a drag coefficient of 0.33.

The prior body styles (Liftback and notchback) were carried forward, as were the two trim lines (ST and GT). Toyota also introduced a third trim line for both body styles, the GT-S (including rear spoiler, 14 × 6.0 alloy wheels, and Bridgestone 205/60 HR 14 tires). There were two engines, both 2 liters; the single-cam 28E in the ST and GT versions, and the twin-cam 16-valve 38-GE for the GT-S. There were three transmission options: a five-speed manual and two four-speed automatics (the GT-S transmission was electronic and had a numerically higher final drive).

No new functionality was added to the interior. The main impact of the redesign was layout. Gauge faces were redesigned and housed in a pod; a center console housed all the heating/ventilation/sound system controls. A tilt wheel became standard equipment on the ST and GT, and the GT-S came with eight-way power-adjusted seats and a sound system with an electronic one-touch equalizer that automatically adjusted for music type, such as jazz, classical, or rock 'n' roll. (The sound system was optional on the GT.)

The fully independent chassis had struts front and rear, the front struts located by rigid lower arms affixed to a special crossmember to inhibit structural flex. Additionally, there was adjustment for precise setting of camber, and the tops of the strut towers were linked to the firewall by a triangulating brace. In the rear, the struts were positioned by a single trailing link and a pair of lateral links per side. All the links were visibly larger than those of other cars. Rear toe could be set exactly through cam-type adjusters. All models had gas-filled shock absorbers and antiroll bars with spherical joint link attachments, both front and rear.

The driveshaft diameter was enlarged to increase rigidity, increase structural stiffness, and improved rigidity of the steering column support. This resulted in less wheel hop. To minimize torque steer, driveshaft angularity was reduced to 4 degrees (from a front-drive norm of 6 degrees). All models had ventilated brake rotors in front; ST and GT versions had drums in the rear, while the GT-S featured rear discs with small drums inside for the parking brake.

The ST and GT models were powered by the 2S-E SOHC engine from the Camry (2 liter, 97 horsepower with full electronic engine management, including control of the fuel injection and spark advance). The GT-S engine was the 3S-GE, based loosely on the 2S-C, but with twin cams and 16 valves, also governed by full electronic management, like the Toyota Variable Induction System (also in the MR-2) that closes off half the intake ports below 4350 rpm and opens up above that. The engine generated 135 horsepower (67.5 horsepower per liter—putting it above several turbo-charged cars).

Beyond 1986

There were no significant changes to the Celica between the 1986 restyling and the 1988 model year (the last year of data for the quantitative test).

Summary of Qualitative Review of Exploration

Taken together, the specification evolution charts and the qualitative review of Celica's evolution tend to suggest a pattern of minor annual innovations punctuated by less frequent but more substantial redesigns. The goal in all innovations appears to be improvements in quality rather than reduction in cost. In fact, with the exception of the economy models, Toyota appears to pursue a deliberate strategy of *increasing cost/price* for its automobiles—moving up the food chain.

The quality improvements take on several forms: driving performance (engine, transmission, steering, and braking), styling (cleaner, more aerodynamic bodies), comfort (noise reduction, cabin space, seat, temperature control), and convenience (human factors for the controls). While there is some attention to all of these design goals in the major product developments, it appears that particular goals take precedence in each redesign. For example, the primary goal in 1976 was handling, in 1978 it was aesthetics, and in 1982 it was aerodynamics. Thus, I can say with some confidence that Toyota is pursuing "exploration"—creation of new features.

With regard to the actual innovation process, some patterns are worth noting:

1. It appears that many of the Celica's innovations are imported from other products in the Toyota lines: the pickup truck for the 1981 engine, the Cressida for the 1981 four-speed automatic overdrive transmission. Thus, innovations appear to be introduced first in the lines where their advantages command the most value. Once these innovations become more producible at lower cost, they can be incorporated in models where they have lower incremental value (a form of perfect price discrimination).

2. Relatedly, it appears that these innovations each follow a life cycle of high marginal value to table stakes. Innovations appear first as options on high-end nameplates. Next they appear as standard equipment on high-end body styles of less expensive nameplates, and are offered as options on base body styles of those nameplates. Finally, they become standard equipment on the base models. We saw this with the four-speed overdrive automatic transmission. The transmission was originally developed for the Cressida, then was adopted by the Supra in 1980 and was standard on the GTA in 1982, when it also became an option on the ST and GT. This cascading effect is best captured in the Celica's innovation timeline in figure 19.6.

3. It appears that Toyota maintains a high degree of modularity across its product lines. This makes it possible to drop the Cressida engine in the Celica chassis without having to do a complete product development. Thus, Toyota can enjoy incremental innovation in each product line, without resorting to full-scale development.

4. Ultimately, to take maximum advantage of component innovations, it appears Toyota needs to do a full-scale product development. As an example, Toyota dropped a new 2.8 liter engine in the 1981 Supra. This boosted horsepower by 5% and acceleration by 2%. But it took the 1982 product development to fully exploit the new engine. Through several simultaneous and interdependent design changes (new DOHC cylinder head and cover, electronic fuel injection, transistorized ignition, and transmission tailored to the new engine's torque curve), the Supra was able to boost horsepower an additional 25% and acceleration an additional 22%.

Thus, I conclude that Toyota was in fact engaged in exploration. Toyota continually introduced new innovations to the Celica to increase its quality over time. The most direct evidence that these innovations increased quality is that performance improved over time. Less direct but perhaps more compelling evidence that these innovations increased quality was the fact that Toyota was increasing the price of the Celica at an average rate of 10% per year, from 1978 to 1988. Since these price increases were well above the average CPI increases over the same period (6.1%), they should cause sales to fall, if quality is held constant. However, the Celica actually *increased* annual sales over much of the period. This was true even in the face of increasing competition in the product category.

Discussion

My primary goal for this chapter was to test whether exploration and exploitation were substitutes or complements. To do so, I first asserted that coexistence of exploration and exploitation would be evidence of complementarity because combining the two activities is nonoptimal if they are substitutes. Thus, to demonstrate complementarity, I merely needed to demonstrate coexistence. I then tested whether exploration and exploitation coexist in a setting where it appears possible—product development. I assert that regular reduction in product cost with each product development (learning curve) is evidence of exploitation; I further assert that regular improvements in product quality with each new product development is evidence of exploration. I then tested for learning curves and product improvement across sequential product developments at Toyota. I did indeed find evidence of both exploration and exploitation and thus demonstrated their coexistence.

Through quantitative examination of cost and output data, I was able to show that there was substantial (3.8%) learning curve, though only mildly significant learning across product developments. Thus, I had evidence of exploitation. Through qualitative examination of the history of changes to the Celica, I found that Toyota follows a pattern of small annual improvements punctuated by less frequent major product developments. These improvements were of sufficient value that Toyota was able to increase the price of the Celica at a rate 67% higher than CPI increases. Thus, I had evidence of exploration.

Together the results indicate that exploration and exploitation can coexist even within the

Model Year

Innovation	'71	'72	'73	'74	'75	'76	'77	'78	'79	'80	'81	'82	'83	'84	'85	'86
2000 cc engine			opt	GT												
Auto transmission			opt													
5-speed transmission				GT				std								
Superior suspension				GT												
Electric sensor panel				std												
20R engine						std										
Column control						std										
Sun roof								opt								
Aluminum wheels								std								
Aerodynamic shape								std								
Increased cabin room								std								
Gauges (vs. lights)								std								
Intermittent wipers								std								
Split bench								lift								
Rear wiper/washer								lift								
Remote releases								std								
Longer seat travel									std							
Visor mirror									std							
2600 cc engine									Sup							
4-speed overdrive transmission									Sup		Opt/GTA					
Power steering									Sup		Opt/ GTA					
Power windows									Sup		Opt/ GTA					
4-wheel disc brakes									Sup							
Cruise control									Sup		Opt/ GTA					
Column adjust									Sup							
22R engine (2.4 liter)											std					
2.8 liter engine											Sup					
Electronic radio/cassette player											opt					
Performance handling											Sup/opt					

Figure 19.6 Summary of innovations to the Celica.

Model Year

Innovation	'71	'72	'73	'74	'75	'76	'77	'78	'79	'80	'81	'82	'83	'84	'85	'86
Spoilers											Sup/opt					
Low drag body											Sup/opt					
8-way adjustable seats											Sup					
Halogen headlights												std				
Rack and pinion steering												std				
Vented disc brakes												std				
2.8 liter DOHC engine												Sup				
5-speed overdrive												Sup				
Variable boost steering												Sup				
Power assisted brakes												Sup				
Independent rear suspension												Sup				
10 extra horsepower														Sup		

Opt = option on ST (base model)   Sup = Supra
std = standard on all models
lift = liftback

Figure 19.6 (*Continued*)

same function-product development and thus that the two activities are complements. This suggests that more attention should be paid to mechanisms for optimally combining exploration and exploitation rather than choosing between them. To aid that endeavor, I attempt to integrate observations from the qualitative examination of Toyota's product evolution, and the quantitative examination of the cost evolution.

The first observation pertains to temporal patterns in exploration versus exploitation. While Toyota engages in annual incremental innovation, the big boosts in vehicle performance and cost reduction coincide with major product developments. My results indicate that each major development reduces product cost by 96%. Our qualitative results indicate that the major developments integrate independent component innovations into a coherent whole. The new product that emerges from a major development achieves higher performance than the sum of the separate innovations (Mintzberg 1983).

While I am reluctant to rely on the finding of increasing manufacturing cost over the product life, the finding is consistent with Toyota's strategy of expanding product lines rather than exploiting scale and learning within a product line. If there were substantial scale economies or manufacturing learning within a product line, Toyota would likely have fewer lines with longer life.[10]

Similarly the finding of increasing manufacturing cost is consistent with the observation in the qualitative data that it took major product developments to realize the bulk of the performance gains from incremental innovation to the Celica. Incremental innovation to a product already in production may be costly in that the changes do not form a coherent whole. Rather, changes are costly appendages to both the product and its corresponding production system. Neither is optimized. The real promise from these changes is realized when all the components that contribute to performance can be jointly optimized in the next major product development. This characterization of incremental versus major change would explain both the high learning from one product development to the next *and* the negative manufacturing learning across the product life. This characterization is also consistent with the Tyre and Orlikowski (1996) finding that learning takes place in bursts rather than continuously (as the learning curve literature has tended to indicate). The practical implication seems to be that while exploration can be continuous, exploitation of that exploration should be episodic.

The second observation pertains to the source of innovations. Few improvements to the Celica were initiated on that platform. In several instances what was exploration for the Celica was exploitation of innovation elsewhere at Toyota. It would be wrong to conclude through backward induction that there is no exploration. The steady stream of innovation on the Celica is only possible because there is exploration somewhere at Toyota, else at some point the innovation would be exhausted. The more appropriate conclusion is that exploration and exploitation are nested, just as product and process innovation are nested. What is a product innovation to a photolithography equipment manufacturer is a process innovation to a semiconductor manufacturer. What is exploration for the Celica is exploitation for the Cressida. The theoretical implication is that what is defined as exploration versus exploitation is necessarily specific to context.

The practical implication is that the ability to exploit an innovation elsewhere in the organization requires both a large organization and commonality across the organization. In 1988 Toyota had 19 nameplates in production. Commonality across the nameplates was accomplished through product modularity (Baldwin and Clark 2000). This allowed an engine from the Cressida to be dropped in the Supra between product developments. Modularity not only increases opportunities for exploitation by providing more homes for any innovation, but in so doing it also increases the gains to exploration. To the extent a firm has more opportunities to exploit an innovation, it is more likely to engage in exploration (Schumpeter 1942). Thus, exploration and exploitation are positively rather than negatively related—they are complements rather than substitutes.

A final observation from the Toyota data is that there appears to be a natural flow of innovation from the more expensive nameplates to the less expensive nameplates. This is a mechanism that accomplishes near-perfect price discrimination, in that consumers purchase the product near the price they are willing to pay (no consumer surplus). More interesting, perhaps, is the fact that this mechanism also provides Toyota the dynamic means (profits) and incentives (broader opportunities for exploitation of each innovation) to continually invest in cost reduction for each innovation (Adner and Levinthal 1998). Sales of the innovation in a nameplate at any given level provide the funds necessary to pursue the cost reduction necessary for adoption by the next lower level of name-plate. The practical implication is that not only should firms have a wide product range with modularity within and across products, but also these products should be vertically differentiated. To fuel dynamic exploitation for each innovation, firms need to have products that attract the entire Rogers (1962) spectrum of innovators, early adopters, early majority, late majority, and laggards. These groups, and their corresponding willingness to pay for an innovation, define the innovation's negative sloping demand curve. The strategies of near-perfect price discrimination and dynamic exploitation of the innovation require access to all these customer classes.

The observations I make are inferential. I have evidence of exploration and exploitation, and some sense of the structure producing them, but I do not know exactly *how* knowledge flows within the firm to take maximum advantage of the exploration and exploitation opportunities. This would likely require an ethnographic study of development inside Toyota. The mechanisms that improve performance within a given product development (Hoopes and Postrel 1999) may be the same as those that produce learning across product developments.

I recommend caution in generalizing the results of the study. First, the study derived learning curves inferentially from aggregate production cost data. A more exhaustive study should compare model cost and model production volume. Second, this study is for one firm in a single, mature industry. I am fairly confident that opportunities and incentives to engage in exploration and exploitation will vary across firms as well as across industries. Further insight into exploration/exploitation will come from studies comparing firms as well as industries.

Notes

1. An alternative definition of exploitation would be regular reduction in the cost of the development process itself. I prefer embedded cost reduction both because it is more valuable—typically the cost of development is small relative to the cost of production over the product life—and because embedded exploitation is a parallel construct to the embedded exploration that we discuss here.

2. A very interesting experiment by Ingram and Bhardwaj (1998) shows that when data are raw, managers tend to ignore it, but when the same data are summarized in charts, managers use the information to update their strategies.

3. Remember that I am merely trying to demonstrate that exploration and exploitation can co-exist, *not* the extent to which all firms take advantage of that potential. In essence, I am trying to characterize the efficient frontier, not the mean tendency of firms.

4. Later when I have an empirically derived values for C and b, I can solve for the A_1.

5. This essentially captures Toyota's relevant experience since inception. In 1961 Toyota had cumulative production of 100,000 units over two models. Prior to 1961, Toyota was operating well below the minimum efficient scale in the auto industry (100,000 units annually).

6. I compared this definition with Clark and Fujimoto's (1991) definition of new car development as 50% new parts. Looking both at publicly available data and the data available in Clark and Fujimoto, the only number we could even roughly compare to assess definition of major development was average model life. Clark and Fujimoto indicate that the average model age for Japanese manufacturers using their definition of model was 4.6 years. My model definition yields an average life of 11 years. Thus, my new model definition is more conservative than is theirs.

7. In fact, the coefficient increases in magnitude and significance if time is deleted.

8. Because the set of components that actually comprise an automobile is stable, Henderson and Clark (1990) might argue that this is not an architectural change. The reason I feel the term is appropriate here is that a frame change is of such a significant scope that designers are able to re-think much of the configuration.

9. While the Supra remained part of the Celica line until 1986, it ultimately gained its own nameplate. Because the two models diverged so dramatically, I restrict further attention to the Celica ST and GT.

10. Remember, too, that Toyota's unit cost was decreasing even as they were reducing scale and shortening each product line.

References

Adner, R. and Levinthal, D. (2001) "Demand heterogeneity and technology evolution: Implications for product and process innovation." *Management Science* 47(5):611–628.

Alchian, A. (1950) "Uncertainty, evolution and economic theory." *Journal of Political Economy* 211.

Baldwin, C. and Clark, K. (2000) *Design Rules*, Vol. 1. Cambridge: MIT Press.

Burgelman, R. (1983) "Corporate entrepreneurship and strategic management: insights from a process study." *Management Science* 29:1649–1664.

Burns, T. and Stalker, G. (1961) *The Management of Innovation*. New York: Oxford University Press.

Chandler, A. (1962) *Strategy and Structure: Chapters in the History of the American Industrial Enterprise*. Cambridge, MA: MIT Press.

Clark, K. and Fujimoto, T. (1991) *Product Development Performance in the World Auto Industry*. Boston: Harvard Business School Press.

Fayol, H. (1923) *The Administrative Theory in the State*. Address before the Second International Congress of Administrative Science.

Ghemawat, P. and Ricart i Costa, J. (1993) "The organizational tension between static and dynamic efficiency." *Strategic Management Journal* 14(2): 59–74.

Greene, W. (1993) *Econometric Analysis*. New York: Macmillan.

Gulick, L. (1936) *Notes on the Theory of Organization*, Memorandum for President's Committee on Administrative Management.

Hall, L. (1957) "Experience with experience curves for aircraft design changes." *NAA Bulletin* 39(4):59–66.

Hannan, M. and Freeman, J. (1989) *Organizational Ecology*. Cambridge, MA: Harvard University Press.

Hayes, R., Wheelwright, S., and Clark, K. (1988) *Dynamic Manufacturing*. New York: Free Press.

Henderson, R. and Clark, K. (1990) "Architectural innovation: the reconfiguration of existing product technologies and the failure of established firms." *Administrative Science Quarterly* 35:9–30.

Hoopes, D. and Postrel, S. (1999) "Shared knowledge, 'glitches', and product development performance." *Strategic Management Journal* 20(9): 837–865.

Huber, G. (1991) "Organization learning: the contributing processes and literatures." *Organization Science*.

Ingram, P. and Bhardwaj, G. (1998) "Strategic persistence in the face of contrary industry experience: two experiments on the failure to learn from others." Paper presented at the annual meeting of the Academy of Management, Boston.

Judge, G., Hill, R., Griffiths, W., Lutkepohl, H., and Lee, T. (1988) *Introduction to the Theory and Practice of Econometrics*. New York: Wiley.

Levinthal, D. and March, J. (1993) "Myopia of learning." *Strategic Management Journal* 14(2): 95–112.

Levitt, B. and March, J. (1988) "Organizational learning." *Annual Review of Sociology* 14:319–340.

Lieberman, M. (1987) "Learning curve, diffusion, and competitive strategy." *Strategic Management Journal* 8:441–452.

Lieberman, M. and Weiers, B. (1993) "How are the gains from productivity growth distributed: a comparative study of US and Japanese Auto Manufacturers. Mimeo, UCLA.

Lieberman, M., Lau, L., and Williams, M. (1990) "Firm level productivity and management influence: a comparison of US and Japanese automobile producers." *Management Science* 36(10): 1193–1215.

MacArthur, R. and Levins, R. (1964) "Competition, habitat selection and character displacement in a patchy environment." *Proceedings of the National Academy of Sciences (USA)* 51:1207–1210.

March, J. (1991) "Exploration and exploitation in organizational learning." *Organization Science* 2:71–87.

Mintzberg, H. (1983) *Structure in Fives: Designing Effective Organizations*. Englewood Cliffs, NJ: Prentice-Hall.

Motor Trend (various issues).

Penrose, E. (1959) *The Theory of the Growth of the Firm*. New York: Wiley.

Rogers, E. (1962) *Diffusion of Innovations*. New York: Free Press.

Schumpeter, J. (1942) *Capitalism, Socialism and Democracy*. New York: Harper.

Selznick, P. (1957) *Leadership in Administration*. New York: Harper and Row.

Simon, H. (1945) *Administrative Behavior*. New York: Macmillan.

Tyre, M. and Orlikowski, W. (1996) "The episodic process of learning by using." *International Journal of Technology Management* 11(7,8):790–798.

Ward's Automotive Yearbook (various years).

Weber, M. (1968) "Economy and society," in G. Roth and C. Wittich (eds.), *Economy and Society*. New York: Buckminster Press.

Wheelwright, S. and Clark, K. (1992) *Revolutionizing Product Development*. New York: Free Press.

White, K., Wong, S., Whistler, D., and Haun, S. (1990) SHAZAM *Econometrics Computer Program*. New York: McGraw Hll.

Yelle, L. (1979) "Learning curve, historical review." *Decision Science* 10(2):302.

20

Above and Beyond
Knowledge Management

Vincent P. Barabba, John Pourdehnad, and Russell L. Ackoff

It is important to understand the differences between a systemic approach to learning and adaptation and the conventional way of managing the use of knowledge. The conventional way has been responsible for the increasingly negative attitude toward the subject. For example, according to *The Economist* (2000), "[a] widely spurned tool is knowledge management, something that consultancies such as Bain go in for a lot, but their clients, especially those outside North America, find a failure" (pp. 60–61).

A systems approach starts out with the belief that in any enterprise seeking success, the performance of the whole is taken to be not the sum of the performances of its parts, but the product of their interactions. Knowledge management and data-and-information warehousing—based on "inventorying" what is known—are ideas whose value is passing because they focus on a part of a system taken separately, not interactively. From a systems thinking perspective, the collection, dissemination, and use of not only data, information, and knowledge but also understanding and wisdom require a decision support system that promotes organizational learning and adaptation. And such a system, of course, requires a clear understanding of the differences

among these different types of mental content: "It's a huge mistake to be blinded to the real and powerful distinctions in the meanings of data, information, and knowledge. . . . The differences between data, information, and knowledge are as crisp as those between calculus differentials or quantum levels" (Perelman 1997, p. 5). And those between knowledge, understanding, and wisdom are equally crisp.

An appropriate learning and adaptation support system can distribute a free flow of inputs into a series of productive dialogues. These can take place continuously across the functions within the firm, as well as among the enterprise and its extended alliances, including the ultimate consumers of its products and services.

A distinction between two metaphors helps illustrate the importance of the differences between the conventional and systemic approaches to "knowledge management." The mechanistic mindset of the industrial age encouraged us to think about managing businesses as if they were made of replaceable parts—like pieces of a jigsaw puzzle. The metaphor fits reasonably well for that era. When one starts a puzzle, one knows how many pieces one is supposed to have, and the chances are that they are all there. Each of the parts will interact with only a small portion of the other parts, and sometimes a part seems to have no connection with any other part. If one has trouble trying to put the pieces together, there is a picture on the box that reveals the one ultimate solution.

But today's business challenges are more complex than that. We operate in a world characterized by increasing complexity and an accelerating rate of change, that is, by turbulence. It is an environment consisting of constantly changing processes, relationships, and components; it is more like the DNA molecule than a jigsaw puzzle. Depending on how the elements come together, we can end up with an entirely different outcome than we expect. We cannot always know up front what we are creating; unexpected consequences can almost always be expected.

Most of the purveyors of knowledge management are anchored in the industrial-age way of thinking; they assume a predictable world rather than one in which uncertainty, if not chaos, is commonplace. They also raise the question of how to place value on intellectual assets. There is no question that these assets have value, but the attempt to assign values to each of them separately is bound to fail because they interact and form a system; and a system is a whole that cannot be divided into independent parts (and a corporation is a system).

The learning and adaptation support system described below has been applied at General Motors Corporation, among others. The experience of implementing it has been of great value because it requires the corporation to create an environment that stresses the interdependence of the users and providers of data, information, knowledge, understanding, and wisdom. It destroys silos within the organization and makes it more ready, willing, and able to change.

The Management of Change

Managers are in much the same position as the old farmer who, when confronted by a young county agent telling him how to modernize his farm, said, "Go away, young man, and stop bothering me. I'm already not doing as well as I know how." If organizations are reluctant to do as well as they know how, it seems clear that they are even more reluctant to do better than they know how. Organizational resistance to change has been explained in many ways, but these explanations tend to be superficial and do not yield

operationally meaningful ways of reducing or eliminating such resistance. Here we try to present one such way of addressing this deep issue.

There are only two sources of learning: experience and others. The others from whom we learn have learned either from experience or from still others who have learned from experience. All learning ultimately derives from experience, but not from all experience. One learns nothing from doing something right because one already knows how to do it. But it can confirm what one believes is right. *One can only learn from mistakes.*

For example, John Chambers, Cisco's president and chief executive, tells of an important lesson he learned while working at Wang about the need for open and clear communication within an enterprise. At that time he had the opportunity to encourage Wang to move to personal computers when the firm had the option to make the move. Chambers felt that he was in a better position than anyone else to challenge the revered Dr. Wang on this particular issue. In fact, he did raise the issue with him—causing Dr. Wang to get mad at Chambers for the first time. Because of respect and admiration for Dr. Wang—and also influenced from other members of Wang's leadership team—Chambers chose to back off and not to push harder. Chambers believes that because he had not changed Dr. Wang's mind on resisting the move to a personal computer platform, Chambers had to go through the personal pain of eventually laying off 5,000 people in his organization. The lesson he learned from that decision has stayed with him—and it is reflected in the manner in which he leads Cisco by constantly encouraging, indeed demanding, open and frank communication throughout the enterprise.

Mistakes are of two types: doing something that should not have been done (errors of commission), and not doing something that should have been done (errors of omission). An examination of corporations that have been in serious trouble (whether or not they have recovered) reveals that the source of their trouble is much more likely to be what they did not do rather than what they did do. For example, IBM got into trouble in the 1980s because it did not develop and produce small computers. Apple got into trouble because it did not permit cloning of its computers; Sears, because it did not react to the emergence of Wal-Mart.

Despite the greater importance of errors of omission, corporate accounting systems reveal only errors of commission. Therefore, managers need not worry about errors of omission since they do not show up on the books. If, in addition, the organization looks askance at mistakes, as is so often the case, the best strategy for a security-seeking manager is to avoid only errors of commission. Therefore, avoidance of punishable mistakes is best assured by doing as little as possible—hence the reluctance to change.

If an organization is to encourage change, it must record and evaluate decisions not to do things as well as decisions to do them; it must raise to consciousness and reveal errors of omission. This is the most effective way of overcoming an organization's reluctance to change. It requires development of a system that encourages and facilitates learning from mistakes of both types.

From Data to Wisdom

Learning by primarily relying on others runs the significant risk that what is obtained from others is ignorance disguised as knowledge. There is no amount of ignorance that, when shared, produces knowledge.

A major obstruction to organizational learning is the exclusive focus on information—as in management information systems—or even the more recent extension of these systems to cover knowledge. Information and knowledge do not exhaust the content of the human mind and are not even the most important. The mind can capture not only *data, information,* and *knowledge,* but also *understanding* and *wisdom.*

Information is more valuable than data, knowledge more valuable than information, understanding more valuable than knowledge, and wisdom more valuable than understanding. Nevertheless, the attention and effort that most organizations spend on acquiring these are inversely related to their importance. This is due in part to the fact that organizations are not aware of the differences among them, let alone the differences in their value. Unfortunately, the difficulty in obtaining information, knowledge, understanding, or wisdom is proportional to their value. There is no easy way out.

Data consist of symbols that represent the properties of objects and events. In general, data, much like iron ore, are useless until processed into information (like iron). Information is contained in *descriptions,* answers to questions that begin with such words as *who, where, when,*

what, and *how many.* Knowledge is contained in *instructions,* answer to *how* questions. (Knowledge also has a second meaning, *awareness,* as in "I know you are here," which is not what we mean here.) Understanding is contained in *explanations,* answers to *why* questions.

Data, information, knowledge, and understanding are concerned with efficiency—the likelihood of attaining one's objectives or the amount of resources consumed in obtaining them—but not effectiveness. The difference is that effectiveness additionally takes into account the value of the outcome of one's behavior. This is what wisdom does. Peter Drucker made the point when he said that there was a big difference between doing things right (efficiency) and doing the right things (effectiveness).

The *righter* one does the wrong thing, the *wronger* one becomes. If one makes a mistake while doing the wrong thing and corrects it, he or she becomes *wronger.* However, correcting a mistake while doing the right thing makes things *righter.* Therefore, it is better to do the right thing wrong than the wrong thing right.

Information reveals the properties or behavior of a system; knowledge reveals how it works; understanding reveals why it works the way it does; and wisdom reveals how it ought to work. Learning should focus on understanding and wisdom as well as information and knowledge. But understanding and wisdom are rarely generated by our current pattern of thought, *analysis.*

Changing Our Pattern of Thought

Organizations are systems, and understanding of systems cannot be obtained by analyzing them. A different way of thinking is required. Einstein saw this clearly when he wrote, "Without changing our pattern of thought, we will not be able to solve the problems we created with our current pattern of thought." To understand this we need a precise definition of *analysis* and *system.*

Analysis is a three-step process:

1. Take the entity or event to be understood apart, disassemble it.
2. Explain the behavior or properties of each part taken separately.
3. Aggregate the understanding of the parts into an understanding of the whole.

For example, business schools tacitly assume that the way to understand a business is first to understand each of its parts: production, marketing, finance, personnel, and so forth. The atomic theory in physics, the periodic table in chemistry, the cell in biology, the phoneme in linguistics, are all the products of taking things apart until alleged indivisible parts are reached. However, *no amount of analysis of a system can explain its properties or behavior*. For example, no amount of disassembly of an American automobile will explain why, until recently, it was designed for six passengers. The explanation lies outside the system, not inside: to serve the average American family, which contained 5.6 people at the time. Today, it contains only between three and four. Explanations of a system's behavior or properties always lie outside the system, in its function(s), in its external, containing system(s). To understand this we must know something about a system.

Every system has a function or functions in one or more containing systems. The automobile, a mechanical system, is defined by its ability carry things external to it from one place to another. It is part of a transportation system. A corporation has two principal functions in society: to produce and distribute wealth.

A system is a whole that consists of two or more essential parts. Essential parts are ones without which a system cannot perform its defining function. For example, a motor and battery are essential for an automobile. The ash tray and cigarette lighter are not.

The essential parts of a system must satisfy three conditions.

1. Every essential part of a system can affect the properties or behavior of that system.
2. No essential part has an independent effect on the whole; its effect depends on at least one other essential part. The essential parts form a completely connected set.
3. Every possible subgrouping of essential parts has the same properties as an essential part: they can affect the properties or behavior of the whole, but they cannot do so independently.

Therefore, a system is a whole that cannot be divided into independent parts. The defining properties and behavior of a system derive from the interactions of its essential parts, not their actions considered separately. When a system is disassembled, it loses all of its defining properties and behavior, and so do its parts. For example, a disassembled automobile cannot move peo-

ple from one place to another. Its motor, without which it cannot move people, when separated from the automobile cannot move anything, including itself.

Now we can see why analysis cannot explain the properties or behavior of a system: analysis begins by taking a system apart. When this is done to a system, it loses all its essential properties, hence cannot be explained. A different pattern of thought is required, *synthetic thinking*. This, too, involves three steps, but ones that are opposite to those in analysis:

1. Identify one or more containing systems of which the system to be explained is a part (e.g., an automobile is part of a transportation system).
2. Identify the function(s) of the containing system(s) (e.g., the transportation system has the function of moving things from one place to another).
3. Disaggregate the function(s) of the containing system(s) and identify the role or function within it of the system to be explained (e.g., the automobile has the function of transporting people from one place to another under their control).

Analysis of a system yields knowledge, reveals *how it works*, its structure. When a system stops working properly, analysis can be used to identify the defective part(s). Synthetic thinking can reveal a system's function, its role in one or more containing systems: *why it works the way it does*. Evaluation of that function, which is wisdom, reveals whether or not the system is doing the right thing, that is, *how it ought to work*. For example, the automobile ought to be less energy consuming, less polluting, and safer. It could be all of these if *designed* wisely. Design is to synthetic thinking what research is to analysis.

Required Support for Organizational Learning

A system that encourages and facilitates organizational learning must enable it to acquire and transmit understanding and wisdom as well as data, information, and knowledge. To do so, it must perform the following steps:

1. Identify every decision of significance (including decisions not to do something) and produce a record of it that contains its ex-

pected effect, by when that effect is expected, the assumptions on which this expectation is based, the inputs to the decision (information, knowledge, etc.), the way the decision was made, and by whom.

2. The decision should then be monitored to reveal whether an assumption on which it is based turns out to be incorrect, or the expectation is not being realized.

3. Such deviations from expectations and assumptions are errors that should then be diagnosed—their causes determined—and corrected. The correction of such an error constitutes learning. However, the correction itself involves a decision that should be treated as the decision from which the error derives. Then, if these "second-order" decisions are corrected, the system *learns how to learn*. This enables it to increase the speed and effectiveness of learning.

4. What is learned from any decision should be available to anyone in the organization who needs it. It should be made available to those who have a relevant interest whether or not they need it at the time. Organizational learning, in contrast to individual learning, takes place when whatever an individual in the organization learns is available to others in the organization when they need or want it, even after the person who learned it is no longer available.

5. The organization and its environment should be under continuous surveillance to determine when either one changes in ways that require responses from the organization.

6. Finally, it should be a system that those who use it can learn to use more effectively over time.

The Design of a Learning and Adaptation (L&A) Support System

The following design is meant to be treated as a theme around which each organization should write its own variation, one suited to the uniqueness of its structure, business, and environment. No two applications of this design have ever been exactly the same. For example, its application in the North American Organization of General Motors is very different from its application in one of the divisions of DuPont. It should be noted that the apparent complexity of the design derives from the not-so-apparent complexity of the processes of learning and adaptation. All the

functions contained in the model are often carried out in the mind of one person who learns from experience, usually unconsciously.

The numbers and letters in parentheses refer to figure 20.1. The boxes shown in this figure represent functions, not individuals or groups. As we will show, they may be performed by individuals, groups, or even a computer and related technologies.

Since the support of learning should be continuous, a description of it can begin at any point, but it is easiest to follow if we begin with the generation of inputs (1) (data, information, knowledge, and understanding and wisdom) about the behavior of the part of the organization managed (which may be the whole organization) and its environment. These inputs are received by the input supply subsystem.

Ackoff (1967) argued that management suffers more from an overabundance of irrelevant information than from a shortage of relevant information. Therefore, he suggested that a management support system should *filter* incoming messages for relevance and *condense* them so as to minimize the times required to acquire their content. These two functions have received relatively little attention in the learning literature. This is a serious deficiency.

Because data must be processed to convert them into information, knowledge, understanding, or wisdom, data processing is a necessary part of the input supply subsystem. Inputs (2) are transmitted to the decision makers in response to their requests (3).

When the decision makers receive the inputs, they do not always find them useful. They may find them unreadable or incomprehensible, doubt their validity, or question their completeness. Therefore, the receipt of inputs (2) often leads them to additional requests (3). Such requests require two additional capabilities of the input supply subsystem. This subsystem must be able to generate new data—that is, inquire (4) into the part of the organization managed and its environment so that the additional inputs (2) required can be obtained. It must also have the ability to reuse data, information, knowledge, or understanding previously received or generated. This means that it must be able to store data in retrievable form. A data-storage facility is a "file" whether it resides in a drawer or computer. It is a part of the input supply subsystem.

Once the new or old data have been processed to provide the information believed to be responsive to the request received from the deci-

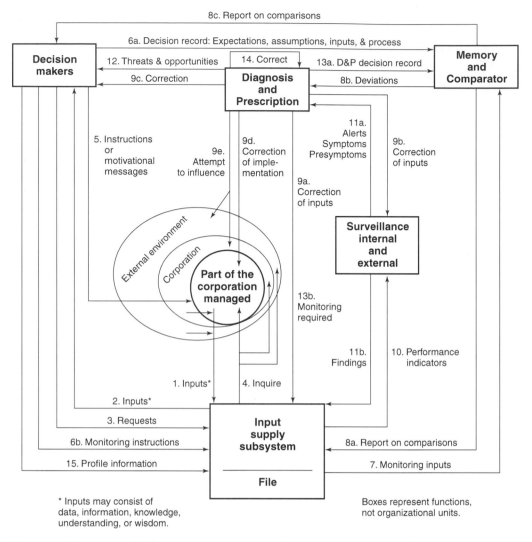

Figure 20.1 Learning and Adaptation (L&A) Support System. Boxes represent functions, not organizational units. *Inputs may consist of data, information, knowledge, understanding, or wisdom.

sion makers, it is transmitted back to them. This request-fulfillment cycle may continue until the decision makers either have all the inputs they want or have run out of time and must make a decision with whatever they have. In some cases they may believe that the time and cost of further inquiry is not likely to be justified by the improvement or increase of inputs that they believe is possible.

The expected value of information-to-wisdom (henceforth referred to as information+) should be estimated before any inputs are requested and used. A judgment should be made as to whether the maximum amount the decision maker(s) is willing to pay for the input is justified by the value expected from using it. Unfortunately,

those making requests for information+ frequently act as though their fulfillment is costless.

The output of a decision to do something is a message that is either an instruction or a motivational message (5) and is addressed to those in the part of the corporation managed whose responsibility it is to carry out the instructions or whose motivation is the target. An instruction is a message to others or oneself that is intended to increase or maintain the *efficiency* of the organization. A motivational message is one intended to affect the values of an organization or some of its (internal or external) stakeholders, hence the organization's *effectiveness*. A decision, of course, may be to do nothing as well as to do something. When a decision to do nothing

DECISION RECORD

Date: _____

Identification Number: _____

Report Prepared by: _____

Report Checked by: _____

INFORMATION USED: _____

_____

_____

WHO PARTICIPATED IN MAKING THE DECISION: _____

_____

_____

KEY WORDS: _____

_____

_____

THE DECISION MAKING PROCESS: _____

_____

_____

_____

DESCRIPTION OF ISSUES: _____

_____

_____

IS ISSUE PRIMARILY AN:

_____ Opportunity OR _____ A Threat (check one)

WHO IS RESPONSIBLE FOR IMPLEMENTATION (if anyone)?

_____

_____

_____

OUTCOME (check one):

_____ No decision   _____ Decision to Do Nothing

_____ Decision to Do Something (Describe)

_____

_____

IMPLEMENTATION PLAN: _____

_____

_____

ARGUMENTS PRO: _____

_____

_____

OBSERVATIONS AND COMMENTS: _____

_____

ARGUMENTS CON: _____

_____

_____

_____

_____

EXPECTED CONSEQUENCES OR EFFECTS AND WHEN THEY ARE EXPECTED: _____

_____

_____

ASSUMPTIONS ON WHICH EXPECTATIONS ARE BASED:

_____

_____

Figure 20.2 An example of a decision record.

is made, no instructions may be required, but a decision record (6a) is.

Every decision has only one of two possible purposes: to make something happen that otherwise would not, or to keep something from happening that otherwise would. In addition, there is always a time by which the effect of the decision is expected. Therefore, to control a decision, its expected effects and expected times of their realizations should be made explicit and recorded. All this is equally true of decisions involving the implementation of a decision. If, for example, a decision has been made to build a new factory, there are expectations about when it

should be completed, what it should cost, and so on. Implementation decisions should be separately recorded and tracked. In addition to recording the expected effects and when they are expected, for each decision a record should be kept of the information and assumptions on which the expectations are based and the process by which the decision was reached, by whom, and when.

All this should be recorded in the decision record (6a) that should be placed and stored in an inactive memory and comparator (an example of a decision record is shown in figure 20.2), which we will discuss further below. Because human memories are inclined to modify their content over time, especially forecasts and expectations, it is important that the memory employed be completely inactive. Inactive storage of inputs may be the only thing a computer can do that a human cannot.

A version of the decision record (6a), monitoring instructions (6b), should be sent to the input supply subsystem, which has responsibility for checking the validity of the expectations, assumptions, and information+ used in making the decision and its implementation. When obtained, information about the validity of the expected effects, the relevant assumptions, and the information+ used should be sent to the memory and comparator as monitoring inputs (7). Then, using the information on the decision record (6a) stored in the memory, and the monitoring inputs (7) a comparison should be made of the actual and expected effects, and the assumptions and relevant occurrences.

When the comparator finds no significant difference between expectations/assumptions and the performance actually observed and reported in the monitoring inputs (7), nothing need be done other than enter a report on comparisons (8a) in the memory for future reference and to the decision makers (8c). This record preserves what is known or believed. Therefore, it should be stored in an easily retrievable form; for example, by the use of key words. However, if significant differences are found, they are reported as deviations (8b) to the diagnosis and prescription function.

Such deviations indicate that something has gone wrong. A diagnosis is required to determine what has, and what should be done about it. The purpose of the diagnosis is to find what is responsible for the deviations and to prescribe corrective action. In other words, the diagnostic function consists of *explaining* the mistake and, therefore, producing *understanding* of it.

There are only a few possible sources of error, each of which requires a different type of corrective action.

1. The inputs (2) used in making the original decision were in error, and therefore the input supply subsystem requires correction of inputs (9a) so that it will not, or is less likely to, repeat that type of error. The information used in decision making can also come from the surveillance function, which is described below. Therefore, it too may require correction of inputs (9b).

2. The decision-making process may have been faulty. In such a case, a correction (9c) of this process should be made. It can be wrong in several different ways: it made incorrect assumptions; it drew incorrect conclusions from the information+ available to it—hence formulated unrealizable expectations; it did not have sufficient information+ available to make a correct decision; or it incorrectly formulated the objective(s) to be pursued or problem(s) to be solved—that is, it either did the wrong thing or committed a so-called *type 3 error* (Mitroff and Featheringham 1974). This input supply subsystem should create and maintain a file of correct and incorrect assumptions, expectations, and decision-making processes against which decision records (6a) can be checked before instructions (5) are issued. This would enable this function to provide quality assurance of decisions.

3. The decision may have been correct but it was not implemented properly. In such a case a correction of implementation (9d) is required for the behavior of those in the part of the corporation managed that was responsible for the implementation.

4. The environment may have changed in a way that was not anticipated. Though the environment is not subject to control, it may be subject to influence (9e). What may additionally be needed is a better way of either anticipating environmental changes or decreasing sensitivity to them. This may require corrections of any of the types (9a–9d).

Through these types of corrective actions, the diagnosis and prescription function assures both learning and adaptation.

Now consider how threats and opportunities that are not related to previous decisions are identified and formulated. A *symptom* indicates the presence of a threat or an opportunity. It is one of a range of values of a variable that usually occurs when something is exceptionally right or wrong, but seldom when things are normal. For example, a fever is an abnormally high body temperature that is seldom associated with good health but frequently with illness. Abnormally low temperature is also a symptom of something wrong.

Variables used as symptoms are properties of the behavior of the organization managed or its environment. Such variables can also be used dynamically as *presymptoms* or *omens*: indicators of future opportunities or problems. A presymptom is *nonrandom normal behavior*, for example, a trend, a (statistical) run, or a cycle. Therefore, a trend of rising body temperature measurements, each of which is separately within the normal range, is a predictor of a coming fever. There are many statistical tests for nonrandomness, hence presymptoms, but the naked eye and common sense can identify many of them.

A complete L&A support system regularly obtains information on a number of internal and external performance indicators (10), some of whose values are found to reveal symptoms and presymptoms to the surveillance function. When symptoms and presymptoms are found, they are sent (11a) to the diagnosis and prescription function and are recorded (11b) in the file of the input supply subsystem. Once a diagnosis is obtained, the threats and opportunities (12) revealed are reported to the decision makers.

Whenever the diagnosis and prescription function prescribes a change, a D&P decision record (13a) of it should be prepared. This record is sent to the memory and comparator, where its content can be compared with the facts supplied by the input supply subsystem in response to the monitoring required (13b) issued by the diagnosis and prescription function. Deviations (9a) are then reported to the diagnosis and prescription function, where corrective action should be taken. Such corrective action may involve correction (14) of the diagnosis and prescription function or any of the types of change previously referred to. Such changes are what makes *learning how to learn and adapt* possible.

An individual information+ support system can be superimposed on the system described here. All it requires is a way of identifying an individual's interests (15)—for example, by key words—and identification of all entries into the file by the same key words. Individuals can then be notified of entries that are relevant to them. Such an individual-service system can be adaptive, subject to change as the individual's interests change. A detailed description of one such system can be found in Ackoff et al. (1976, chap. 3).

If a diagonal is drawn in figure 20.1 from the upper lefthand corner to the lower righthand corner, the system is divided into the part that already exists to some extent in most companies below the diagonal, and the part above the diagonal is missing in most companies. The usefulness of the part that exists (usually called a management information system, MIS) is very limited until it is embedded in the more comprehensive system that incorporates the functions shown above the diagonal. An MIS alone has relatively little effect on individual and organizational learning because it does not deal with one's own mistakes and their correction. Infrequently, and at best, an MIS informs one only about mistakes made by others. Vicarious experience is not a good substitute for one's own.

An Application

In 1997, while flying home from a business trip, a GM executive was reading a corporate report and noticed a very poor performance compared to expectations (sales volumes, penetrations, unit profitability, unit cost) for two of the company's products. He wrote the following memo: "How come these products are performing so poorly vs. our expectations when the products were conceived? What went wrong?" This question coincided with the company's decision to develop a system to facilitate organizational learning and adaptation based on the conceptual framework described above.

The L&A model was utilized to reconstruct the decisions that led to creating the underperforming products. Retrospective decision records were prepared identifying the decision makers, the strategic context for the decisions, arguments pro and con, expected outcomes, assumptions on which the expected outcomes were based, who were responsible for the implementation, key information used, and the decision-making process employed. This process was similar to retrieval of data from the black boxes in the commercial aviation system described below.

First, in the case described above, expected outcome variables such as design cost, capital investment, volume, market share, profit, quality, warranty, and so on, were identified and tracked. Second, assumption variables on which the expectations were based were identified through the study of the program development charters and business plans as well as from interviewing the decision makers. The assumptions covered such things as market segment growth, product life cycle, program potential, pricing, and customer preferences. By retrospectively collecting data relevant to these assumptions and plotting their "behavior over time," it became apparent that the product programs were off course right from the time of launch.

Next, the challenge for the investigative team was to understand why this was the case and why the attempts to correct these errors did not bear results for the product management teams. The first significant finding was that the assumptions were never made explicit, hence not monitored by the product managers in the early stages of development. If these assumptions had been identified and tracked, changes that were taking place in the market segment affecting segment growth negatively would have been detected and would have provided an early warning of poor product performance. If these errors had been recognized at the early stages of product development, particularly before the launch, it would have led the management team to reframe its expectations and perhaps change its decisions, hence the outcomes.

It was important to demonstrate how the different variables were interacting to create a system of problems for the product programs. By creating an "influence diagram," it became apparent that isolating problem areas and applying local remedies (e.g., increasing the advertising budget) did not help with the overall performances of the programs. Because of these findings, the investigative team recommended the total redesign of these product programs and change in the company's prevailing product development paradigm, one that also reduced development cycle times.

Today, parts of GM use a system that is based on the L&A model to improve strategic decisions by accelerating the organization's ability to learn and adapt. An organizational unit has been created to help with training and incorporation of learning functions into the so-called "common processes" (e.g., the product development process). A standard format for capturing decisions in "real time" and committing a record of them to the organization's "memory" has been developed. Assistance with tracking and comparison of the relevant expected outcomes and associated assumption variables is provided in order to determine if there are any significant deviations. After diagnosis of the cause(s) of errors, assistance in prescribing corrective actions is provided.

A cross-functional team has been developed that is responsible for supporting units in their efforts to construct and use an L&A support system. The team has addressed a variety of decisions, including assessment of the impact of incentives on the sale of vehicles, innovations in vehicle scheduling, and establishing the appropriateness of vehicles in the marketplace. And GM has learned that there is a considerable willingness to learn and adapt when the quality of the diagnosis and correction of error is high. Leaders have demonstrated a great desire to learn when they are confident in the validity of these processes.

One of the more unusual applications of the system has been to assess consulting contracts. On special projects GM frequently uses consulting firms. Too often the consultants learn more about GM than do GM personnel. This challenges the organization's ability to learn from and with consultants. Moreover, does the decision to obtain external help improve company performance? Does the company receive the benefits it expects when it contracts for such assistance? Such questions are now dealt with in the L&A support system.

But GM has avoided the common error of making the accumulation of information, knowledge, understanding, and wisdom the objective of its system; its objective is their *use* and evaluation. Their capture is not enough; their effective use is.

A Parallel Case

Historical data on airline safety show that in the early days of commercial aviation, airline fatality rates were approximately 1,500 times higher than those of railroads and 900 times higher than those of bus lines. Today it is commonly known that air travel is safer, in terms of passenger miles, than travel by automobile, bus, or railroad. In 1930, there were 28 passenger fatalities for each 100 million passenger-miles. Today, the number is less than one (*Comptons* 2000). *This improvement in air safety exemplifies a successful learning and adaptation (L&A) system.*

Since human errors are considered to contribute to more than 70% of aviation accidents, the major focus of learning in the aviation system is on improving decision making by pilots and other key stakeholders. In recent years, study of pilot judgment and aeronautical decision making (ADM) has been a mission of the Federal Aviation Agency (FAA) and the National Aeronautics and Space Administration.

Although great effort is directed at raising the competency level of all those who work within the system, mistakes do occur. In order for the aviation industry to learn and improve, it must and does have a way of identifying errors. A "black box" is on every commercial aircraft. It consists of flight data and cockpit voice recorders. Faith (1997) wrote that black boxes are the best single source of information for investigators. As a memory, they provide data on the long series of events that occur during a flight. Crucially, black boxes are completely objective. Because they record events as they occur, they are exempt from interference and influence. Analysis of the data in black boxes enables investigators to compare expected happenings with what actually happened and to determine where differences between them have occurred.

Determining what caused deviations from expectations is the responsibility of the National Transportation Safety Board (NTSB). Its main function is diagnosis and prescription—to investigate accidents, identify their causes, and recommend improvements. In order to achieve a high standard of excellence, the NTSB is a professional body with its own investigators and methodology. Faith (1997) makes this point: "[A]ir-accident investigators, or 'tin-kickers,' are a very special breed. In one sense they're detectives operating in a very specialized field, but, at a senior level, they have to be capable of co-coordinating, and thus of comprehending, a far wider range of professional skills than their equivalents in the criminal field" (p. 24).

Despite its responsibilities, the NTSB has no regulatory or enforcement powers. Once the cause of an accident has been determined, its recommendations for action are sent to the FAA, which sets and enforces air safety standards. In addition, the FAA plays a major role in assuring system efficiency, regulatory reform, and sharing and analysis of safety information, surveillance, inspection, and accident prevention.

In order to provide high-quality input to relevant decision makers, the FAA has created the Aviation Safety Reporting System (ASRS). It collects voluntarily submitted aviation safety incident reports in order to reduce the likelihood of aviation accidents. In this way ASRS captures information about such things as emergency landings, mechanical/maintenance problems, security, injuries and illnesses, operational problems, passenger disturbances, and health-related fatalities. This information is used to identify and remedy deficiencies and discrepancies in the national aviation system. Lessons from mistakes

are documented and organized for easy access and made available to those who need and are authorized to receive it. In this setting, there is constant support for policy formulation and system improvement. Also, in many instances, expertise is leveraged across the system.

In Conclusion

What can be learned extends well beyond information and knowledge to understanding and wisdom, which are more valuable than information and knowledge. The system described here can capture such extended learning. Since all learning eventually derives from experience, we have designed and implemented a system that maximizes what can be learned from experience under both constant and changing conditions. The experience dealt with in this system is that which follows making decisions either to do something or not do something. Since the learning this system facilitates derives from the identification of mistakes and their correction, the mistakes made in correcting these mistakes are also subject to identification and correction. The correction of these mistakes makes *learning how to learn* possible. This can significantly accelerate learning and make continuous self-improvement of the system possible.

References

Ackoff, R.L. (1967) "Management misinformation systems." *Management Science* 14:B147–B156.

Ackoff, R.L., Cowan, T.A., Sachs, W., Meditz, M., Davis, P., Emery, J., and Elton, M.C. (1976) *Designing a National Scientific and Technological Communication System*. Philadelphia: University of Pennsylvania Press.

Compton's Encyclopedia. (2000) "Air safety." Available at: http://Comptomssv3.web.aol.com.

Faith, N. (1997) "Black box: why air safety is no accident." *Motorbooks International*, pp. 24–25. Oceola, WI: Motorbooks International.

Mitroff, I.I. and Featheringham, T.R. (1974) "On systematic problem solving and the error of the third kind." *Behavioral Science* pp. 383–393.

21

Keeping a Butterfly and an Elephant in a House of Cards

The Elements of Exceptional Success

William H. Starbuck

Where Tandoori Can Lead

My wife and I were eating dinner with Donna and Joe.

Joe asked what I had been doing lately.

I explained that I had been studying knowledge-intensive firms—ones that earn revenues from specialized expertise. I cited the Rand Corporation and Arthur D. Little as examples, and briefly described their work.

Joe, a partner in a prominent Park Avenue law firm, asked if I had studied any law firms.

With insufficient tact and excessive confidence, I told him I had not. I understood law firms to make most of their revenues by routinely generating standardized documents such as contracts, stock offerings, or wills. Because legal word-processing systems are widely available, because all lawyers have adequate basic knowledge, and because law firms employ lawyers with diverse skills, clients can readily substitute one law firm for another. My interest lay, I said, in firms that are renowned for their unusual expertise.

Joe replied quietly that he thought I was misjudging law firms in general, and more important, that some law firms do have reputations for unusual expertise.

I asked him to suggest such a firm for me to study.

He proceeded to tell me about Wachtell, Lipton, Rosen & Katz (Wachtell), another Park Avenue firm not far from his own. The very high quality of Wachtell's work and its distinctive culture had impressed him.

I did not really understand what Joe was telling me. I got the idea, which he later corrected, that he was saying Wachtell specializes in merger-and-acquisition cases and that clients seek out the firm because of this expertise. Doubting that any law firm stands out from the others, I listened to Joe's description with skepticism. As a result, it was roughly a year before I got around to writing to Martin Lipton and Herbert Wachtell, asking if I might interview them.

Had I known how exceptional their firm is, I would have waited not one day.

When I finally did interview people in Wachtell, I came away fascinated and impressed. When I later compared Wachtell statistically with other law firms, I was utterly astonished.

This chapter reports my observations.

A Few of My Many Biases

While living in Berlin in the early 1970s, Wolfgang Müller and I became statistical consultants to a research project that was searching for side-effects of contraceptive pills. Because it sought to find rare or unusual side-effects, the project observed 30,000 women for five years.

Statistical analyses showed the main determinants of side-effects to be doctors. Because some doctors noticed coronary disease, women who went to these doctors were more likely to have been diagnosed as having coronary disease and less likely to have been diagnosed as having other ailments. Other doctors noticed pulmonary disease, and women who went to these doctors were more likely to have been diagnosed as having pulmonary disease and less likely to have been diagnosed as having other ailments. And so on.

The same notion applies, of course, to social science. I tend to notice certain phenomena and to neglect others. Thus, readers need to beware of my biases.

Using Nonrigorous Methods and Focusing on Narrow Categories

During the 1960s and 1970s, many researchers attempted to find generalizations about all organizations. Widespread beliefs of that period, to which I subscribed, said that social science ought to use "rigorous" methods to produce generalizations of very broad applicability. Unfortunately, practical experience demonstrated that these beliefs were ill-founded.

For example, the original Aston study examined eight autonomous organizations and 38 subunits of organizations and analyzed the data as if subunits were organizations. "We included manufacturing firms that made strip steel, toys, double decker buses, chocolate bars, injection systems, and beer, and service organizations such as chain stores, municipal departments, transport companies, insurance companies and a savings bank" (Pugh, 1981, p. 141). Some of these organizations focused on local areas and others sold nationally. Further, the researchers carefully chose measures that would be equally meaning-

ful in all organizations. "It is the strength and the weakness of this project that no items were used unless they were applicable to *all* work organizations, whatever they did; several possible items of information had to be sacrificed to this end. Since the research strategy was to undertake a wide survey to set the guidelines, the result was superficiality and generality in the data" (Pugh et al. 1968, p. 69).

Of course, the drive to generalize has induced researchers to ignore or de-emphasize the properties that make organizations distinctive. Imagine comparing a hospital with a steel plant but ignoring the fact that one treats injuries and cares for sick people while the other operates blast furnaces and rolls hot steel.

Such studies showed that "rigorous" methods contain many inherent traps. In application, methods that were labeled rigorous turned out to be formalistic, and the researchers who used rigorous methods lost sight of the commonsense content in their data. Their findings depended very strongly on assumptions embedded in their measures, assumptions of which they were unaware. The very process of following methodological prescriptions induced researchers to substitute ritual for understanding. As a result, rigorous studies had commonsense interpretations that were very different from the meanings implied by the names of variables (Starbuck 1981).

Although some might blame this outcome on the researchers, the people who did this research were bright, well educated, sincere, and among the intellectual leaders of their time. Their findings appeared in the most prestigious journals and were widely cited in other research and in textbooks. Thus, these studies showed deficiencies of rigorous methods rather than peculiarities of specific studies: So-called rigorous methods are very prone to yield deceptive data that lack validity.

Thus, I generally eschew "rigorous" methods in order to weaken the influence of my prior beliefs, to strengthen the validity of my data, and to heighten my understanding of what I observe. Most of my observations about Wachtell come from conversations with lawyers who work there. My informants are bright and articulate people who earn very high incomes because clients want the benefit of their perception and understanding: They well understand organizations and interpersonal relations. These people became my collaborators, as they not only answered my questions but also told me what is-

TABLE 21.1 Codes Identifying the Sources of Quotations

A	An associate in Wachtell
C	A lawyer who has been a client of Wachtell
L	A document that Martin Lipton wrote in 1987 and then revised for the firm's 25th anniversary in 1990
O	A lawyer from a competing firm who has opposed or collaborated with Wachtell
P	A partner in Wachtell, including both junior and senior ones
S	A member of Wachtell's nonlawyer support staff

sues I ought to explore and with whom I should talk. Of course, my informants had agendas of their own, but their attempts to influence me afford useful data in themselves. Not only is it fun to spot inconsistencies and efforts to shape my perceptions, but the interviews I found least useful are those in which I said too much, especially at the outset. That is, I learned more by listening than by talking. One result is that I have grown even more skeptical of interviews that follow preplanned agendas.

This chapter assumes that readers also enjoy dealing with inconsistent and unprocessed information. I often let people speak for themselves. Their choices of words add to the basic information about organizational properties, but they do not portray Wachtell as a coherent, unambiguous system, and there are contradictions in what they say. I will leave these for readers to spot because I think the contradictions are rather clear and because identifying contradictions helps one to think through the issues.

Before each quotation is a letter that denotes its source, as shown in table 21.1. The interviewed clients are all General Counsels of major corporations. The opposing lawyers include several of New York's most successful ones. The statements by associate lawyers came from questionnaires they submitted to the *American Lawyer* in 1990 or 1992 rather than from interviews.

The generalization-seeking studies have built up evidence that the properties shared by all organizations are superficial, obvious, or unimportant (Starbuck 1981). Again and again, these studies have rediscovered weak relationships that organizational researchers had observed "nonrigorously" many years earlier—possibly many centuries earlier. For instance, the strongest consistent "finding" of the Aston studies was that larger organizations tend to be more bureaucratic. Two of the strongest consistent "findings" from statistical studies of organizational populations have been that larger organizations have lower risks of failure than do smaller ones, and that well-established organizations have lower risks of failure than do infant ones.

Even apart from the measurement methods used in studies, the properties shared by all organizations ought to be uninteresting and unimportant. One reason is that people create new organizations to pursue goals that existing organizations are not achieving. If left free, people will create organizations that complement the existing ones, and the new organizations will emphasize properties that the founders believe are both important for success and neglected by previous organizations. The overall population of organizations will grow more diverse, and diversity will increase primarily in the dimensions that are important to organizational survival or goal attainment. Many industries encompass firms that complement each other, and of course, industries complement each other (Carroll 1985, Starbuck and Dutton 1973). Thus, to see how certain properties foster success, one needs to look at the differences among organizations, and one of my goals in studying knowledge-intensive firms (KIFs) is to focus on a special category that differs from the general mass of organizations.

This chapter focuses much more narrowly yet. Far from claiming that Wachtell is a representative law firm, this article argues that Wachtell's extraordinary success derives from its individuality. Not only does Wachtell differ in important ways from all organizations, it differs in important ways from the mass of law firms and it even differs in important ways from other highly successful law firms. Wachtell is quite distinctive, and other law firms have not imitated its distinctive properties.

Nor does this chapter claim to make findings that generalize to other times. A firm may have to forgo some short-run profits in order to build relationships that foster longevity, so an extremely profitable firm takes some risk of transience. Also, Wachtell illustrates both the effects of passing fads and fashions and the diverse forces that undermine exceptional success—or other peculiarities. These forces promote regression to the mean and make exceptional success transitory.

Avoiding Averages

A second reason why shared properties tend to be uninteresting and unimportant is that organizations cannot gain exceptional success by imitating other organizations and exploiting shared properties (Starbuck 1992). Although not all organizations seek exceptional success, its determinants and consequences interest me.

Focusing on exceptional success had not been my explicit initial goal. I had set out to study firms having distinctive expertise. Expertise is hard to separate from its effects because clients judge advice to be good if it produces good results. Thus, after studying a few firms, I realized I had been looking at especially successful ones. This realization forced me to re-examine my goals.

North American and English social science has been paying far too much attention to averages. The study of averages has become so prevalent that social scientists do not even have to explain why they think averages are the appropriate variables to study. Other social scientists often accuse the deviates who fail to study averages of doing valueless work, as if averages were the only information of value.

A statistical principle, established over 50 years ago (Robinson 1950, Thorndike 1939), states that a correlation across a population may not recur in subsets of that population. Indeed, a true statement about averages across a population may be false for every subset of that population, including every individual in the population. For instance, in the study that introduced the concept of a strategic group, Schendel and colleagues observed a positive correlation between profits and firm size across the population of brewing companies (Schendel and Hatten 1977, Schendel and Patton 1978). But when they divided the brewing companies into size categories, they found negative correlations between profits and firm size within every size category.

Although statements about averages bother very few, they ought to bother many. For instance, scholars often state "hypotheses" of the form "Managers do such and such" and then support these hypotheses with statistically significant correlations computed across many managers. In such cases, one can nearly always point to at least one manager in the analyzed data who did not do such and such. Typically, many of the analyzed managers did not do such and such; and it is possible that none of the analyzed managers did such and such. Is not something wrong when analysis supports a hypothesis that is violated by most or even all specific instances? Why do scholars not specify the fraction of managers who do such and such? What are scholars doing when they state "Managers do such and such," even though some managers do not? I suggest that they are engaging in a stylized sense-making ritual rather than science.

Social scientists not only focus on averages, but they also often calculate averages that lack meaning because they arise from arbitrary categories with undefined boundaries. For instance, averages across a sample of KIFs would be meaningless because no clear definition of KIFs has wide acceptance. Scholars advocate multitude definitions of knowledge and hold disparate notions about the proper definitions for KIFs (Starbuck 1992). Although one can point to specific organizations that almost everyone will agree are KIFs, the boundaries of the KIF category are obscure.

Fixation on averages makes social science blind to individuality, peculiarity, excellence, complexity, interaction, and subcultures. Similarity should not be the dominant property of people, groups, organizations, or societies because there are many criteria for what is good, many solutions for most problems, and many opportunities to exploit. All people, groups, organizations, and societies are peculiar and unique and seeing how people, groups, organizations, and societies differ is as least as important as seeing how they look similar. In study after study, it turns out that few instances closely resemble the averages (Starbuck and Bass 1967).

Averages usually tell nothing about outlying cases such as exceptionally successful firms. In most industries, the modal firms make low profits and have short lives (Starbuck and Nystrom 1981). An exceptionally successful firm has to be unique in a way that exploits the peculiarities of its environments: It gains high profits and long survival through distinctive competencies that take advantage of its environments' unusual needs and capabilities.

Not only do its environments reflect and exploit the unique properties of an exceptionally successful firm, but also the existence of a highly successful firm induces its environments to act as if the firm does exist. Thus, an observer nearly always sees marginal adjustments and rarely glimpses the complex dynamics that occur sometimes. An observer who averages across time will overlook the intricate and unusual, yet these may be the most important.

Produced by decomposition and simplification, simple relations among averages often misrepresent ecological interactions (Martin 1992). Should one describe Beethoven's Ninth Symphony only in terms of pure sine waves, as Fourier proved one can? No musicologist would do so. Should one describe Van Gogh's *Starry Night* only in terms of cyan, magenta, and yellow, as one can in principle? No art critic or historian would attempt it.

Studies of Averages

Gilson and Mnookin (1985) reported, mainly via footnotes, that lawyers in larger law firms receive higher compensation than those in smaller firms, that more Stanford graduates had been taking jobs in large law firms, and that the largest law firms are growing larger. They then argued that law firms have been growing larger in order to diversify and that diversification helps to explain law firms' commitment to "lockstep compensation." Lockstep compensation makes seniority the sole determinant of lawyers' wages and of partners' profits. Gilson and Mnookin (1985, pp. 328–9) explained: "The lawyer cannot diversify his human capital investment. He cannot be both a securities law specialist and a bankruptcy law specialist." Because domains of specialization become more or less lucrative as demands for their services fluctuate, lawyers find it useful to create "full-service" firms and to agree "that the returns to [human capital investments in different specialties] will be shared on a predetermined basis rather than in accordance with actual outcomes."

Later, Gilson and Mnookin (1989, p. 585) reported:

First, firm leverage [the ratio of nonpartner associate lawyers to partners] is directly related to firm profit: the higher the firm's leverage, the higher the firm's per partner profit. When one outlier is eliminated, our regression analysis of data from the *American Lawyer*'s compilation of the one hundred most successful corporate law firms for 1987 discloses that differences in leverage explain 34.3% of the differences among

firms in per partner profitability. Second, the degree of firm leverage appears to be determined, in part, geographically: the same data indicate that among these one hundred firms, those based in New York City had an average associate/partner ratio of 2.55, while those based outside New York had an average ratio of only 1.66; the leverage of New York firms was greater by some 54%. . . .

The outlier is Wachtel [*sic*], Lipton, Rosen, & Katz, a firm specializing in hostile [*sic*] takeover work. In 1987, Wachtel was reported to have an average profit per partner of $1,405,000—the top in the nation— although its ratio of associates per partner was only 1.05. This firm bills for takeover work on a transaction, rather than a per-hour, basis, which significantly reduces the importance of leverage. If Wachtel, Lipton is included in the regression, differences in leverage explain 20.9% of the differences among firms in per-partner profits.

Note that Gilson and Mnookin based their generalizations on averages and that their wording illustrates the widespread usages cited in the preceding section.

Samuelson and Jaffe (1990, p. 190) remarked:

The major source of profitability for firms has traditionally been an army of associates who receive a salary equal to only a fraction of the revenues they generate, with the lion's share divided among the partners. Associates have been willing to cooperate with this system because they have had a good chance of being promoted to partnership. Thus, they anticipated that, in the relatively short period of six to twelve years, they would be sharing in the economic surplus generated by associates. Since partners have grown to expect an income based on a ratio of at least one (and ideally more) associates to each partner, firms suffer under an enormous growth imperative. Each time an associate is promoted to partnership, two or three new associates must be hired.

Price Waterhouse has been sending long questionnaires to the managing partners of "well-managed" law firms since 1961. Roughly 600 firms participate in the Statistical Survey and 300 in the Compensation Survey. Samuelson and Jaffe persuaded Price Waterhouse to allow them to analyze the responses submitted by 219 firms

TABLE 21.2 Determinants of Profit
per Partner

Variable	Incremental Correlation
Number of associates	0.25
Number of partners (negative effect)	0.13
Hours billed per associate	0.10
Nonlegal staff	0.06
Computer workstations	0.02
Hours billed per partner	0.01
Being in New York City	0.01
Lockstep compensation	0.01

Samuelson and Jaffe 1990

that responded to both questionnaires in both 1985 and 1986. These firms employed from eight to 645 lawyers, the average being 115.

Samuelson and Jaffe used step-wise regression to estimate the effects of various variables on profits per partner. Table 21.2 lists the statistically significant variables.

Samuelson and Jaffe struggled with these findings because they had expected profitability to correlate with total lawyers and with leverage. They concluded (a) that total lawyers adds no "explanatory value" beyond the number of associates and (b) that leverage adds no "explana-

tory value" beyond the combination of associates and partners. One should, however, view their analysis and interpretations cautiously because of correlations among the alternative independent variables. A linear combination of associates and partners might afford a fair approximation of leverage, and associates plus partners equals total lawyers.

These studies say that law firms achieve higher profits by exploiting associates—either by exploiting more associates or by exploiting associates more.

High-Revenue, High-Profit Law Firms

Now consider some statistics about 20 of America's largest 100 law firms. Figures 21.1 to 21.6 graph four-year averages, based on estimates made by the *American Lawyer*. Some of these estimates are more accurate than others because the *American Lawyer* is able to get more information or more reliable information about some firms than others. The firms shown are the ones that ranked at the top on either revenue per lawyer or profit per partner during 1989 or 1990.

Figure 21.1 shows that Wachtell not only had the highest revenue per lawyer, its revenue per lawyer was fully 55% above that of any other firm.

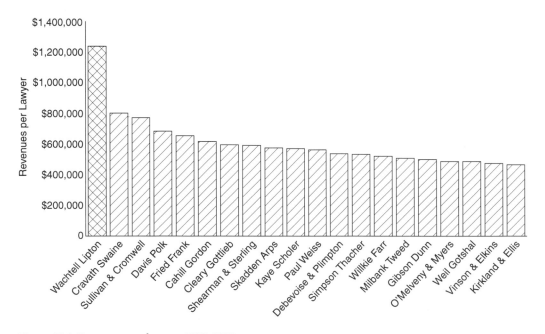

Figure 21.1 Revenues per lawyer, 1989–1990

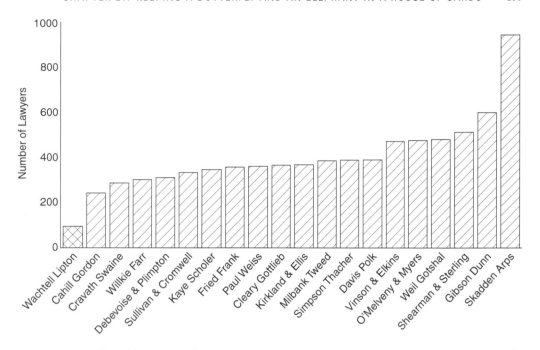

Figure 21.2 Number of lawyers per firm, 1989–1990

Figure 21.2 indicates that Wachtell is the smallest firm in this group. Indeed, Wachtell is the smallest firm among the largest 100.

Of course, with fewer lawyers than the others, Wachtell would likely have fewer partners, and it does. However, figure 21.3 implies that Wachtell has disproportionately more partners for its size. For instance, Wachtell had 39% as many lawyers as Cahill Gordon and 33% as many as Cravath Swaine, but it had 94% as many partners as Cahill Gordon and 79% as many partners as Cravath Swaine.

Figure 21.4 traces the implications of figures 21.2 and 21.3, that Wachtell has disproportionately few associates per partner—very low "leverage." Indeed, Wachtell had only 0.8 associates per partner. In this group of firms, only Vinson & Elkins had fewer than two associates per partner. Excepting Wachtell, the group averaged 2.8 associates per partner. The two firms that most nearly resembled Wachtell in the previous figures—Cahill Gordon and Cravath Swaine—had 3.3 associates per partner.

Of course, the preceding statistical analyses imply that Wachtell must have very low profit per partner. According to Gilson and Mnookin, leverage determines profit per partner, and Wachtell had the lowest leverage among the largest 100 firms. According to Samuelson and

Jaffe, highly profitable firms have many associates and few partners, and Wachtell has the fewest associates and disproportionately many partners. Yet figure 21.5 says Wachtell had the second highest profit per partner, falling between Cravath Swaine and Cahill Gordon. It is no wonder that Gilson and Mnookin excluded Wachtell from their calculations.

Despite the firm's high ranking on this measure, Wachtell's senior partners would say profit per partner is not a good measure of their firm's performance because profit per partner places too much emphasis on partners and too little on associates. (The *American Lawyer* says its estimates of profit per partner are less reliable than other statistics, partly because some firms have various partnership classes.)

Figure 21.6 shows another astonishing differential between Wachtell and the other firms: Its profit amounts to 68.5% of its revenue. No other firm has profits that exceed 52.8% of revenue.

Wachtell stands out as a work environment as well. Each summer, large law firms employ "summer associates" or "interns"—students who have finished at least one year of law school. Summer employment allows the interns to see potential employers and allows the firms to appraise prospective employees. In 1989 and 1991, the *American Lawyer* surveyed these interns,

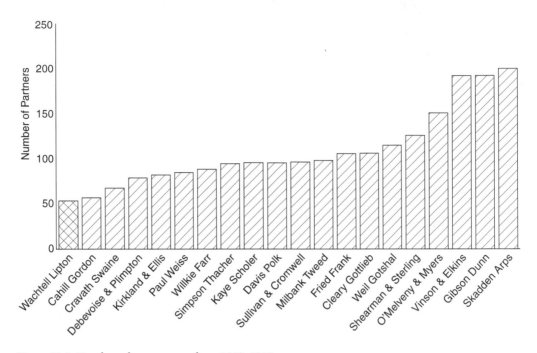

Figure 21.3 Number of partners per firm, 1989–1990

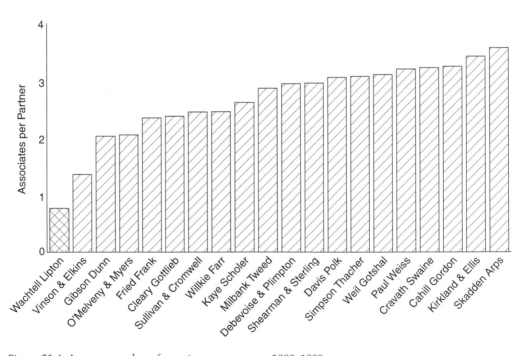

Figure 21.4 Average number of associates per partner, 1989–1990

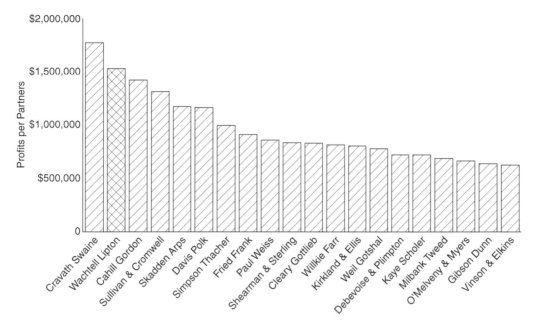

Figure 21.5 Profit per partner, 1988–91 (1992 dollars)

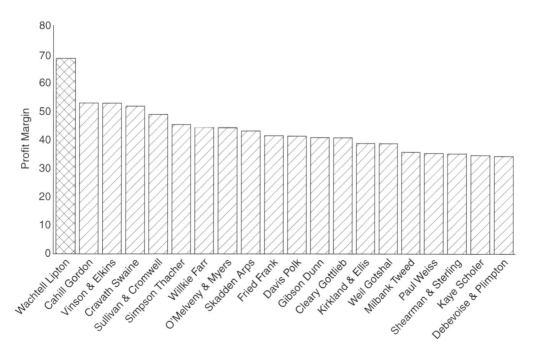

Figure 21.6 Profit margin

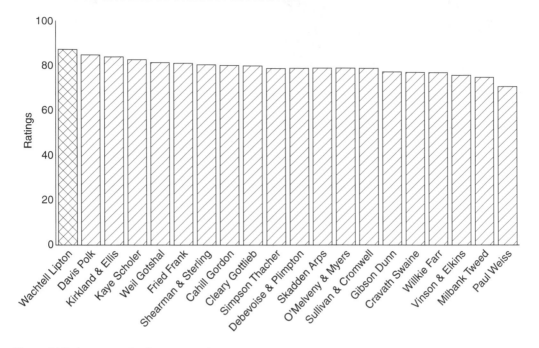

Figure 21.7 Average rating by summer interns

asking their reactions to the experience and to the firms. Figure 21.7 shows that the interns gave Wachtell higher average ratings than any other firm in this high-revenue, high-profit group.

Similarly, in 1988, 1990, and 1992, the *American Lawyer* surveyed third-to-fifth-year associates, asking their reactions to their work experiences and to their employing firms. Figure 21.8 reveals that Wachtell's associates have given it the highest average ratings in this high-revenue, high profit group. In 1992, Wachtell's associates rated it highly for client contact, level of responsibility, collegiality among associates, treatment of associates by partners, training of associates, associates' knowledge of their partnership chances, and compensation.

Overall, figures 21.1, 21.2, 21.4, 21.6, and 21.8 suggest that Wachtell is an entirely different business than the other top law firms. Although Cahill Gordon, Cravath Swaine, or Vinson & Elkins may contain subunits that generate very high revenues per lawyer, the earnings of these subunits are being averaged with much lower earnings from other subunits. Further, it is extremely unlikely that high-profit subunits in other firms have as few associates per partner as Wachtell, or associates who indicate as much pleasure with their working conditions as those at Wachtell.

How Wachtell Works

The Beginning

Ironically, one of the most profitable law firms in the world was founded by men seeking "interesting work rather than lucrative" (P).

In 1965, four friends and alumni of New York University's Law School decided to form their own law firm. Their organizing plan and early decisions portray them as idealists in headlong pursuit of financial failure. P: "We wanted an old-fashioned partnership rather than a business. . . . We didn't want a hierarchy, didn't want a managed business. Our goal was a congenial home for people who can't function in a hierarchy. One early decision was better legal products at the cost of administrative waste." This "congenial home" would have strong egalitarian norms: every lawyer would write his own first drafts of briefs, and every lawyer would do his own library research.

These values partly derived from personal experience. P: "We tried to avoid the bad things. We didn't like imperious senior partners using people instead of developing a firm. We wanted to have a different relationship with our [junior] colleagues than we'd had with the people we had worked for." They had also seen friends and for-

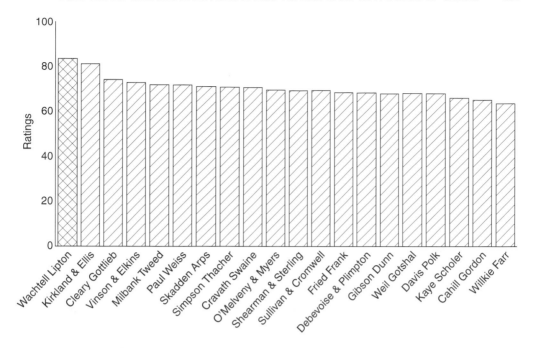

Figure 21.8 Associate lawyers' ratings, 1988, 1990, and 1992

mer classmates working long hours for low wages while highly paid partners spent their evenings at home. P: "In a lot of ways we didn't know what we were doing. We didn't think these things through in a logical way. We just said we don't want the unpleasantness we had and we've observed in other places."

They vowed to refuse routine assignments even if this meant earning less money. Wachtell would not offer a full range of legal services. It would try to excel in corporate law, creditors' rights, and litigation. (Katz also did real estate.) To ensure that legal expertise would count for more than social skills, every lawyer with the same seniority would receive the same pay. There would be no special incentives to encourage the courting of clients.

O: "They thought they could form a terrific law firm and make a lot of money. Marty Lipton is a great securities lawyer and Herb Wachtell is a brilliant litigator, so they were taking no chances. It was the next generation that took the chances—Nussbaum, Fogelson, Katcher. . . ."

A Transactional Practice

During Wachtell's first year and a half of operation, in 1965 and 1966, one corporate client accounted for two-thirds of its revenue. Then dur-

ing the firm's second year, contending groups within this key client asked Wachtell to favor them in ways that made the partners very uncomfortable. The partners resigned the relationship . . . and thus lost two-thirds of their income. P: "We had to call a future employee and say 'We may not be in business next year.' "

The partners' immediate reaction was to "go out and scramble" for work. However, after they had dealt with the immediate crisis, the partners adopted policies that would keep a single client from becoming so important again: P: Initially, they agreed that Wachtell would "emphasize transactional representation rather than across-the-board general representation." They would base relations with clients on short-term agreements about specific matters. L: "The Firm encourages its clients to maintain relationships with other law firms." Around 1976, after some experience, the partners adopted a more sweeping limitation: L: "Firm does not have retainer relationships with the retainer fee applicable to any services the client desires."

Had Wachtell become an ordinary law firm, its transactional emphasis might have been very costly. However, the firm turned out to be anything but ordinary. It has become one of the rare ones to which corporations turn when they are most desperate, when their normal legal resources seem inadequate—at least, when they do not want to find out whether their normal legal resources would be adequate, or when they do not want to risk Wachtell's aiding their opponents.

Wachtell's transactional relations with clients have become an asset. Transactional practice means that it has few conflicts of interest arising from ties to long-standing clients, so it is likely to be available to new clients. Partners in Wachtell say transactional practice also implies that other law firms can enlist Wachtell as co-counsel without fearing that it might try to steal their clients, and that clients need not fear that Wachtell will "play politics" and disturb existing client-lawyer relations.

C: "They are basically a litigation law firm and a firm that specializes in deal making and transactions. . . . Where would we use them? Examples would be if we were going to make a major acquisition, or when we adopted a shareholder-rights plan (sometimes called a poison pill), or when we have shareholder suits against us."

O: "As an opponent and one who has been in the same area [of the legal practice], I'd rather have them against me—no, not really against me, with me as co-counsel—than any other firm because they're very bright and creative."

O: "I'd be afraid they'd steal the client."

Case Selection and Innovation

Wachtell has adhered to its founders' ideal of refusing to perform routine legal chores. It does not regularly produce "green goods" such as stock registration statements and loan agreements, and it focuses on "a limited number of interesting and difficult specialities" (L). P: "We are selective about cases. The partners would be bored with routine, repetitive work such as prospectuses, underwriting, due-diligence." P: "Wachtell is always 'special counsel.' It deals with unusual problems and boardroom situations, such as suits against directors. The client's CEO is involved. Such cases have high visibility." P: "We try to make the cases not-labor-intensive. We can't handle cases that require a lot of labor."

Wachtell can be choosy because even in a slump, clients offer it twice as many cases as it can handle. In a boom, it turns down seven cases for each it takes. P: "The firm could be 500 lawyers today if it took all of the work available." P: "We could be an 800-lawyer firm today. We chose not to do that, to keep ourselves small." P: "We are insulated against downturns by our small size. We've always had more work offered to us than we wanted."

P: "We never went 100% M&A [mergers and acquisitions]. We didn't want to do only that. The work is too intense, and the work might go away, so we always maintained a lot of other work." P: "The takeover and buyout businesses have declined, but bankruptcies and litigation have ballooned." O: "I have to believe that in the 90s, the corporate lawyers there [at Wachtell] are doing green-goods work."

P: "Transactional business requires a special kind of excellence—flexibility, creativity, and innovation." L: "The Firm encourages innovations and has been successful in developing many, such as cross-border equity mergers, mortgage-pass-through securities, the poison pill, the state business combination takeover laws, and innovative forms for merger and acquisition transactions." P: "Herb [Wachtell] has ideas that people think are crazy but they win cases." P: "Marty [Lipton] not only has good ideas every day, but also every five years, he produces a radical innovation. He wrote the law review article about the business-judgment rule that became the basis for our M&A practice." P: "No one anywhere rivals him [Lipton], but a number of the younger partners have come up with innovations."

One of Wachtell's most important innovations was the idea that, instead of being paid by the hour, lawyers' compensation should reflect their clients' benefits. P: Wachtell sometimes "bases its fee in part on the amount involved in the transaction and Firm's contribution to the accomplishment of the client's objective." Thus, in 1988, Wachtell received $20,000,000 for two weeks of work defending Kraft against a takeover attempt (Cohen 1991, p. D6), P: "and obtaining billions more for the shareholders than originally offered." O: "How they got compensated in the 80s is history. It's no longer true today. It was . . . almost an anomaly."

O: "Lawyers should not be partners with their clients. That type of compensation can raise questions about the lawyers' objectivity." O: "The two or three cases in which the courts criticized the defense all involved Lipton. In effect, the courts said 'You overstepped the bounds.' Is it a case in which your fee arrangement makes you more aggressive?"

Mergers and Acquisitions

P: "We would have been intellectually successful, but perhaps not as financially successful, without M&A." P: "M&A has evolved rapidly.

Many firms have come in and dropped out. Wachtell has stayed with it every step of the way." L: "The Firm's success in takeover field is *not* attributable to other firms not being willing to handle takeovers—those other firms were practicing in the takeover area before the Firm—they were not successful and lost the practice because they were not structured to operate on a task force basis and were unwilling to test corporate innovations—like the poison pill—in litigation." P: "Takeovers are good examples of crisis-team situations. These provide good training grounds because you see a whole case from beginning to end in two months. You see two or three complete cases the first year." O: "It's perfectly clear to me that Marty and Joe [Flom of Skadden Arps] saw this whole area of hostile transactions developing long before other people recognized it. They saw it coming and got into it and just out-marketed the hell out of other law firms. Also, what they did do was bring together the various disciplines. . . . This task-force idea was very effective in selling to clients." P: "Wachtell focuses on takeover defense, Skadden on offense." C: "One thing I did notice. During the 80s, the firm prided itself in only representing the targets of takeovers. And then a couple of years ago, they began to represent the other side."

Staying on top requires staying out in front. The specific actions of law firms are easy to imitate. For example, in 1982, Martin Lipton invented the "poison pill" defense against hostile corporate takeovers. According to Powell (1986, pp. 21–2):

> Prior to the Chancery Court's decision upholding the poison pill [in 1985] ten companies had accepted the advice of Lipton and adopted his innovation, and in the eleven months between that ruling and the affirmation of the Delaware Supreme Court only an additional seventeen companies followed suit (*Corporate Control Alert* April 1986). This was a period of very cautious adoption by a few Wachtell Lipton clients who viewed themselves as highly vulnerable to a hostile takeover attempt. Law firms other than Wachtell Lipton did not recommend the pill to their clients because its future was still uncertain; it was a radical innovation, not just some minor tinkering with corporate charters. The slow diffusion of the poison pill was not due to inadequate information about the new device, however. News of Lipton's innovation spread rapidly through

the legal and business presses and Lipton himself promoted the poison pill in client memoranda, interviews and addresses to lawyers. . . .

> Once, however, the Delaware Supreme Court had put its seal of approval on the poison pill, its diffusion occurred very rapidly. Indeed, within nine months of the court's decision a total of 263 companies had poison pills in place, including many of America's largest corporations.

O: "Gotta hand it to Marty though. That poison pill was a great thing. [Long pause.] *His* pill though didn't work! The court ruled against him in the Crown Zellerbach case. *We* added a feature to the pill that *made* it work."

One informant opined that the poison pill changed the nature of acquisitions, by devaluing the nonmonetary components of deals and escalating the monetary values. O: "Marty's creation, the poison pill, the courts held that it was legal because he clothed it in a garb in which the courts looked only at the formality of it and not at the substance of it. . . . The way the poison pill turned out was that only cash counted. Any other kind of offer could be turned down. Negotiation disappeared. Junk bonds made it possible to raise the [large amounts of] money."

Selective Hiring

To attain and retain its status, Wachtell has had to recruit exceptional lawyers, P: "Wachtell's strategy is rooted in personnel: Don't compromise standards. Each generation should be as good as the founders." P: "There is an external perception of a quality difference at Wachtell. Maintaining that perception depends on recruiting. There is only a small pool of qualified applicants." O: "We recently did a [very big] deal with Wachtell. They had a young tax lawyer who ran rings around my whole crew. Just beat them into the ground. He wasn't even a partner. They've got some wonderful people there."

During Wachtell's early years, its hiring benefited from its founders' disadvantages: it looked attractive to Jews, and it had an inside track at the New York University (NYU) law school. Although discrimination had been declining since the 1940s, the large American corporations and the banks and law firms that served them had long traditions of anti-Semitism. NYU had a tradition of serving the children of recent immigrants to America; and during the decades when elite law schools were applying quotas to Jewish applicants, NYU's doors had been open equally to all. During the 1960s and 1970s, NYU's law school had very high standards and was graduating some excellent lawyers; but because the school was much less well known than the elite ones, its graduates had restricted job opportunities. The founders of Wachtell taught at NYU's law school and participated in alumni activities, and the deans of NYU's law school advised outstanding graduates to consider Wachtell. P: "For years, two-thirds to three-fourths of the [Wachtell] lawyers were NYU graduates." C: "They were able to people this firm with some lawyers who might not have been acceptable at other firms—some Jews, some Irish, some Greek, some Italians, Polish—who might have been welcome as associates at other firms but would never had made partner."

These demographic advantages gained strength from Wachtell's small size and its policies of egalitarian pay, egalitarian work, and every-associate-can-become-a-partner. P: "I wanted a small collegially structured firm that works on the most sophisticated matters." P: "I joined Wachtell because I wanted a small firm with intelligent people, highly regarded people." P: "I was attracted by Wachtell's small size. I was also attracted by the promise that associates can make partner if they're good enough. Other firms don't do this; they reject some deserving people." P: "The odds of becoming partner are far higher here. This helps to attract top-notch people. We never hire people just to ease the burden of work. We've wanted the firm to grow slowly; wanted to retain collegiality." L: "Partnership decision is made early, with associates becoming partners at the end of six years. The basic premise is that every associate will become a partner."

Of course, the conditions that existed when Wachtell began have all but disappeared. Discrimination against Jews has become largely insignificant in the New York law firms; NYU's law school has become highly respected; and Wachtell itself has become an icon. P: "Wachtell is the hardest firm in the U.S. to get a job in." P: "We have insanely tight criteria on whom we let in." P: "Most firms have many associates and few partners. The partners make money on the associates' excess value. These firms need 50–100 new associates each year. They can't hire 50–75 superstars in one year, so they hire a lot of not-so-terrific lawyers and weed out. We only take in superstars at Wachtell. No fixed number. We take as many or as few as look promising."

Nearly all of Wachtell's hiring is out of summer jobs. Each year, around 1200 law students apply to Wachtell for jobs as interns, and the firm chooses 20 to 25. At summer's end, it offers long-term employment to 12 to 15 of the interns who are beginning their last year of law school. Six or seven accept the offers.

Associate lawyers receive appraisals after three, four, and five years. The senior partners make these appraisals quite frank so that the final partnership decision surprises no one. The partnership decision occurs earlier than at other leading firms.

Of those who start at Wachtell, over 40% become partners. Figure 21.9 shows the percentages. Wachtell's percentage is three times the average and 60% higher than the next highest one. The data for the other firms come from the *New York Law Journal* (May 29, 1990; June 11–12, 1992). The data describe 27 of the 30 largest New York firms and lawyers who graduated from law school from 1979 through 1983.

P: "In Wachtell's history, only one person has been brought in as a partner." P: "When I joined the firm as an associate in February it was with the expectation that by year end I would be made a partner, if everything worked out. That is a euphemism for 'if everyone likes you and respects you'" (Lederman 1992, p. 59).

High Quality

C: "I've had nothing but the best experiences with them and I've always had the impression that there's something they do that is unique." P: "The advantages of working at Wachtell are always dealing with very smart people, also highly motivated people who look further for evidence. Imaginative ideas. Good theories. It's a spectacular environment. Our clients are always amazed and happy with the people who work on their cases. Also, clients get partners, not associates, working on their matters." P: "People are wildly self-motivated. Their drive to do a spectacular job is so great that they'll drive themselves nuts. The success of the firm came from lousy marriages." P: "Wachtell is also somewhat arrogant. We believe we are as good as any firm in the U.S." P: "It is a true academic environment in the best sense of that term. There are never any political issues. The only thing to think about is what is the best way to do it. Never, never compromise anything." O: "I think that what has distinguished the Wachtell firm is that they have consistently gone out and hired first-class minds." O: "If they say 'We are the best there is' and they try to behave that way, that is what makes it real."

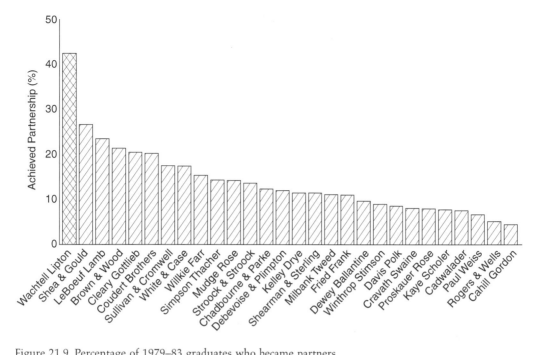

Figure 21.9 Percentage of 1979–83 graduates who became partners

L: "The Firm has not deviated from the basic premise on which it was founded twenty-five years ago—if you do a superior job there will be more demand for your services than you can meet." P: "People come to us because they perceive us as very good lawyers." P: "Wachtell's attraction to clients is basic things. People really care. They'll work 20 hours more to improve a document 2%." P: "Wachtell has quality consistency far higher than any other law firm." O: "They can be a little slovenly." P: "I always knew that I could work as many hours as I wanted to do the best job I could and nobody would ever second guess me." P: "I'm successful because I'm scared. All you have to do is screw up once or twice."

O: "When I was sued, they were my first choice to represent me."

O: "I've been involved in many situations where we've bested them. Like the . . . case. It was just marvelous." So how does one go about beating Wachtell? "There's no consistent theme to it. They don't have any glaring weakness. Marty, of course, became more doctrinaire as he matured in the practice."

C: "Are they better than other lawyers? I find it easier to talk about individuals. We use other firms as well. I'm enormously impressed by the associates at Cravath; I think they're the best associates I've ever met. At Wachtell, there's an enormous consistency at an exceptionally high level—mainly among the partners." O: "There are differences in degree in what they do, and there are differences in how hard their partners work. There is not a significant difference in the kind of work or quality of work. They have been able to do it on a more profitable basis and to have less chicken shit in what they do."

Commitment, Stress, and Self-confidence

Why do only half of those to whom Wachtell offers jobs accept? Who would not welcome an opportunity to work in such an organization? After all, it is a very prestigious firm that offers high pay and high probabilities of partnership, that provides an egalitarian, collegial work environment, and that practices on the leading edge of the law.

Obviously, some lawyers see a downside to working at Wachtell, but without interviews with those who turned down offers, one can only speculate about their reasons. One factor may be the lawyer's commitment to career achievement and hard work. A second factor may be the lawyer's attitude toward stress. A third factor may be the lawyer's self-confidence.

Wachtell resembles an emergency medical team. Their clients are desperate and demanding.

Although willing to pay very high prices, the clients want immediate results, and they expect Wachtell to deliver products that their normal law firms cannot—legal innovations, remarkable arguments, extreme quality.

L: "The Firm's operations are geared to the needs of its practice—24-hour-7-day full service; always prepared to do a deal, fight an injunction or give an opinion on an overnight basis." P: "Wachtell treats everything as a crisis. Clients get upset if lawyers slow things down." P: "My wife says this firm is built on failed marriages." P: "Our creed is being there when the client wants you, getting it done expeditiously, turning out the best possible piece of work, and being scared. You're worrying so that [the client] doesn't have to worry." C: "You give them something, they're interested in it. I call up at 3:30 in the afternoon, they'll be in my office at 5:30, maybe 8:30 the next morning. If I ask for Marty, he'll call me back in half an hour. He might be in Europe or on the West Coast, but he calls me back. Since most of our work is litigation, we don't use him that much, but still, I like that relationship."

P: "Wachtell people take a lot of pride in what they do." P: "Wachtell people work harder than others. They agonize over important calls and major matters." S: "We just *know* that it's last minute." O: "I suspect that they work harder than other lawyers." O: "Another thing I've always been impressed by over there is their dedication to hard work."

To call these extremely self-confident people would be gross understatement. To attract Wachtell's attention initially, they had to have outstanding records in law school. They know they are brighter than almost everyone. They know they can accomplish more than almost everyone. Those who joined Wachtell before it became well known were putting their own judgments ahead of general opinion. P: "Most law students saw Wachtell as a gamble [when I graduated]. Wachtell wasn't well known among most students at [my law school]." Even those who join Wachtell today are choosing an unconventional path.

Then Wachtell offers them positions as junior associates who have unusual responsibility. To take these positions, they have to regard themselves as ready to practice law on an equal basis with the best. They will be working among people who are at least as able as themselves.

Recall that the founders wanted a firm in which associates do not do grunt work for partners and partners work as hard as associates. As the firm developed, the founders augmented their initial ideas with three more notions: (a) that new graduates from law school would have major responsibilities, (b) that no lawyer would be hired or retained unless they expected him to become a partner, and (c) that major cases would be shared by teams of lawyers representing different specialties.

P: "You're about as good a lawyer as you are ever going to be after your first year in law school." L: "Associates get full responsibility as soon as they are ready." A: "I feel I have been granted a surprising degree of responsibility." A: "By third year, an associate often will be the primary contact on a number of matters and negotiating major portions of transactions. I find I am given more responsibility than associates I come across at other firms—no matter what class year they are in." A: "It is hard for me to imagine any firm where I would get more responsibility and consistently excellent work." A: " 'Partner' functions and roles are often not clearly distinguishable from 'associate' functions and roles." O: "They can delegate responsibility to people who aren't ready for it."

P: "There is prompt feedback when you screw up." P: "Employees have to expect to be treated as autonomous professionals or they wouldn't join Wachtell." P: "You never feel afraid of telling Wachtell or Lipton 'I just don't understand this. Explain it to me.' " C: "The [Wachtell] partners have a presence. They have a certain style. It's a commanding style. They're not background people. They tend to be forceful advocates of what they think is the right legal judgment."

P: "The main disadvantage of working at Wachtell is not enough associates to handle matters. The partners feel overworked and complain. The partners would like more help." P: "Everyone drafts briefs; everyone does research; everyone deals with clients. In other firms, the senior partner goes home at 5 P.M. and leaves the work for inexperienced associates. At Wachtell, no one does that." P: "No one works harder than Marty Lipton."

Egalitarian Compensation

Wachtell's compensation system reinforces its egalitarian norms.

One of the firm's most unusual policies is that it takes no markup on associates' time; clients pay proportionately less for the work done by associates. P: "Wachtell has no leverage. Instead, we get top-dollar for what we do."

Thus, the firm has no incentive to employ associates instead of partners. Indeed, the financial incentives promote the opposite. P: "Partners do a lot of low-level work" but charge clients proportionately more for it. P: Wachtell is a "bottom-loaded partnership because there are so many younger ones." P: This strategy is "protected by the excess demand for our services."

C: "We use them because they are very good. They work very hard. We can call them on a Friday afternoon and they'll work through the weekend. They're expensive, but they're not *that* expensive because they don't use so many people. They never overstaff there. Where another firm might use six or eight people, Wachtell might use two or three. The aggregate bill may be not that much higher. Why do you pay a little more? Well, the quality of the work, the timeliness."

Partners too have egalitarian compensation in comparison with many firms. P: According to Wachtell's lockstep formula: "The three founders get 125% of the average. Other seniors get 100%. Younger partners progress toward 100%. A new partner would get around 33%." P: These percentages are "determined entirely by seniority. No one is compensated for client clout." L: "Hours worked, client contact, firm administration all do not affect partnership shares."

P: This compensation system "can only work where everyone is sharing the workload. No one is seriously considering changing the system. It requires trust among partners, sharing, beneficence by the seniors." P: "No one came to this firm for dollars; no one stays for dollars." P: "We can move associates around because no partner is responsible for a specific client. Also, there is no reticence to bring someone else into a client relationship. Lockstep is very important."

P: "Lockstep fosters cooperation. But the question is: can we afford it in terms of decreased entrepreneurship? Lipton gave up income to buy loyalty, but he also gained more control, more decision power." Partners conjectured that Lipton would be making 3–6 times as much if he were in another firm. O: "Lawyers tend to be risk-averse—even a great lawyer like Marty Lipton. If he went to another firm, would he have a senior litigator as good as Bernie Nussbaum?"

Collegiality and Culture

KIFs face serious obstacles to creating and maintaining distinctive cultures (Starbuck 1992). Although skilled experts share values, standards, habits, mental frameworks, and language, the culture they share is supra-organizational (Smigel 1964). As a result, few KIFs closely resemble what Maister (1985) called the "one-firm firm."

According to Maister, a one-firm firm devotes much effort to selecting and training personnel; grows slowly while choosing clients and tasks carefully; takes service to clients very seriously; stresses cooperative teamwork, group identity, and institutional commitment; de-emphasizes autonomous profit centers, entrepreneurship, and internal competition; encourages free communication among personnel; and gives information freely to its personnel, including financial information. Maister also warned that one-firm firms tend to grow complacent and habit-bound and to lack entrepreneurship and diversity.

All of the KIFs I have studied select expert personnel carefully, use teams extensively, take their missions seriously, manage growth cautiously, and encourage open communication; and all of them depart from the one-firm model in decentralizing activities and not involving everyone in decision-making. However, only Wachtell approximates the one-firm model in discouraging internal competition, emphasizing group work, disclosing information, and eliciting institutional loyalty. Wachtell's personnel disagree about whether it lacks entrepreneurship.

P: "Wachtell is a special place. It has a culture. It is structured differently. No one is hired who is expected to leave. People treat each other well. There is no pyramid of partners and associates. There is no competition among the associates." P: "Excellence as a lawyer is cherished. A lot of people teach [in law schools]. Education is valued. Comradeship is also valued. The one-to-one ratio lets partners spend time on associates, help them develop. There is much loyalty to the firm. The associates rated Wachtell first in New York City." A: "I am . . . impressed with how informal and nonhierarchical relationships between partners and associates are." P: "One of my surprises on becoming a partner was the very collegial atmosphere among the partners." P: "I came to Wachtell because it looked different—smaller, less widely known at [my law school]. The Wachtell people seemed very smart, bound together some way but not socially—young aggressive people. I didn't understand the structural difference between Wachtell and other firms." P: "Wachtell doesn't abuse human capital." S: "We all feel part of a very big family. . . . Every person feels that the firm cares about them. If you need money, if you need medical advice, even if you're abroad, there's always someone here. . . . People have been here 15 to 20 years. They don't leave. They feel it's just family. . . . People come here to be spoiled. . . . If someone decides they want a different soda, or a different flavor cookie, it's here. It's a firm that does everything for everybody. It's because we care."

P: "People like each other, and in large part, it's because the things that cause dislikes are eliminated." P: "Doors are open. Everyone has a first name, and people use them." A former partner, Lederman (1992, p. 57), recalled: "All office doors were always open, fostering a communal workplace. Everyone treated the office like home, and no one felt any need to knock on doors or to hesitate to cross a threshold. Lawyers would walk into your office, demand attention (almost always bringing cookies or coffee or soda from the small kitchen), and begin talking about what was bothering them, while offering you food, even though you were with someone else or on the phone. . . . Without any privacy, everybody knew what everyone else was doing, which meant that knowledge was shared, making the informality more effective than seminars or luncheons arranged for the dissemination of information. George Katz, one of the founding partners, embodied this family style. He visited all the offices almost every day, bringing encouragement or news or gossip, a practice which he continued until his premature death in 1989. Always optimistic, George would report on current matters and ask for advice from everyone on thorny legal questions, giving even the new junior associates the sense that their participation was valuable."

O: "They're pretty nice even though they're tough. There are some law firms that pride themselves on being mean. Wachtell doesn't play those games. They're not a bunch of mean pricks." O: "It's an interesting place and the people are fun. They're interesting people to be with." C: "It's a very informal firm. You walk into Cravath, it's a little bit stuffy. At Wachtell, they're in their shirt sleeves. Nothing oppressive, nothing standoffish. Some people might want more of a white-shoe atmosphere. We don't. These people are extremely smart and extremely capable. That's what *we* want." C: "You get a different feeling at Wachtell. Maybe collegial isn't the best word but it's the only one I can think of."

O: "Wachtell has limited itself to two or three disciplines, so when they talk about communi-

cation across disciplines they don't know what real communication problems are."

L: "The Firm is not a business; it is an old fashioned professional partnership; there is no partnership agreement—only a handshake among friends." Lederman (as quoted by Cohen 1991, p.D6): "The ethic there [at Wachtell] is, if you're in, it's your life. If you're partly in, you're out." S: "People here often don't understand how different other firms are. A lot of strange things happen in other firms."

Task Forces

L: "The Firm approaches all matters on a task force basis. An ad hoc group of tax, antitrust, litigation, creditor rights, real estate, corporate or other lawyers, as needed, is formed for each matter. . . . The task forces overlap with a particular lawyer leading one or more and assisting on one or more. There is considerable overlapping of the composition of the task forces so that each matter has the benefit of the best thinking the Firm can bring to bear on that matter." P: "Our success in takeover cases arose from marrying different kinds of expertise. In the beginning, Wachtell was a small firm working for big corporations, so we had to work together. Everyone shared every project. We had a collegial atmosphere. We learned how to create task forces. Other firms had departments, and it took them ten years to learn to make task forces." O: "They were a ragtag bunch of people who pulled together, bonded by the fact that they weren't tied to anything else."

P: "Task forces are the essence of expertise. Critical. Life and death. Other firms don't copy task forces well. People at Wachtell work together well. People know each other very well. There are few partners and they have had long relationships. Lipton is exceedingly generous."

Management and Control

Wachtell has also applied its founders' ideas about organizing. P: "This place would go bananas if we tried to put in systems and turn it into an efficient organization." P: "Our overhead costs are twice that of most firms." Figure 21.10 graphs ratios of support staff to lawyers and indicates that Wachtell had a higher staffing ratio than any of the largest New York firms during 1990 and 1991; Wachtell's ratio was 61% above the average. The data for the other firms come from the *New York Law Journal* (December 2, 1991).

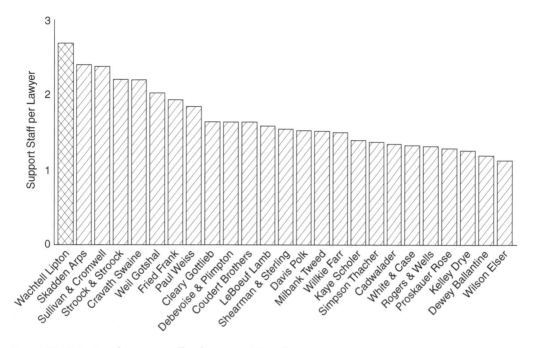

Figure 21.10 Ratios of support staff to lawyers, 1990 and 1991

Nelson (1988, pp. 205–28) remarked on lawyers' ambivalence about power and organizational control. On the other hand, they spoke of collegiality and every partner having a say in firm governance; on the other hand, a very few lawyers dominated each firm, "not unlike the father does in many families" (p. 212).

P: "Management devolves on those who will do it." P: "Occasionally, we lean on people." In late 1991, four people made case assignments at Wachtell: Herbert Wachtell and Bernard Nussbaum [former Legal Counsel to President Clinton] did so for litigation, Leonard Rosen for bankruptcy and creditors' rights, and James Fogelson for major assignments and antitrust.

P: "Three committees manage the firm. The Administration and Coordinating Committees overlap. The Recruiting Committee is the most important one." Who is on the Recruiting Committee? P: "Whoever wants to be on the Committee shows up." P: "The Administration Committee handles paper clips. At one partners' meeting, no one knew who was on it." P: "Wachtell is a frustrating institution sometimes. It doesn't plan very well." P: "We need more structuring within the firm."

Martin Lipton says, "I have never gone to a committee meeting." P: "Marty doesn't participate in management but no one can do anything

without consulting him so decisions get changed. There is some grumbling about this."

P: "Suppose there is an issue as to whether we should take up a new matter from a nontraditional client. This produces a group discussion in the creditors' rights department. In corporate or litigation, the decision is centralized."

P: "Up to now, policy decisions have been made by consensus. But 60 partners makes getting everyone to agree very, very tough. Ten percent dissent can be overcome, but a 60–40 split leads to slow decisions. Ultimately some kind of smaller decision-making system will have to get put into place. Now, a lot of major decisions get made by the three main partners over lunch. If this system hadn't been benevolent, it would have been deposed." P: "Most decisions are made ad hoc, not at partnership meetings." O: "The desire to stay small is an important feature of the way they do business. It allows them to maintain control in a way that you can't do in a larger organization."

P: "Twice someone at Wachtell has been involved in insider trading. In both cases, a small group made the decision and someone was dismissed. There was no partnership meeting." (Lederman 1992, pp. 226–61, describes both cases.) O: "In [a small collegial firm], how did they end up with two partners within a few years who became involved in insider trading? No other firm that I know of has had two partners who did that. How did this happen?"

Rainmaking

Service KIFs generally give client relations higher priority than technical expertise (Starbuck 1992). The experts with greater social skills become client-relations specialists, and these receive higher compensation and wield greater power than other experts. Their power arises from the possibility that client-relations specialists might depart and take long-term clients with them.

Informally, American lawyers put the label "rainmakers" on the lawyers whom clients seek out. This term symbolizes the mystery, magic, and power of client relations.

Most law firms reward rainmaking, of course, and Wachtell does not. P: "Getting new business is irrelevant to people's performance [ratings]. The criterion is always excellent legal work." P: "The only thing that matters in terms of becoming a partner is whether you're any good." C: "Of course, by doing such good work, you don't have to market yourself. Your work speaks for itself."

Some Wachtell personnel see the firm's disregard of rainmaking as a corollary to its transactional practice. P: "Wachtell isn't dependent on long-term relationships with clients. Wachtell has a transactional practice." P: "No clients account for more than 3, 4, 5, 10% of revenues, so we don't have to worry about pissing any clients off." P: "We have a huge client base. Many, many more client contacts than most firms, and they are contacts at high levels. Not the assistant counsel. Usually the chief counsel, the CFO, or the CEO." P: "Our clients are mainly lawyers who represent corporations" and who know how to evaluate legal services. P: "The firm tries to make all clients the firm's clients rather than individuals' clients." P: "Marty spreads it around. Over the years, he's succeeded in introducing the world to the rest of the firm. I think there is very little question that the firm will survive the retirements of Wachtell, Lipton, and Rosen."

O: "The thing that distinguishes a Cravath, Wachtell, or Davis Polk is that the clients come to them because they have big problems. They're not looking for a lawyer they can schmooze with. With the high-pressure investment banker, with the Type-A personality we usually see, there's not much room for social skills."

Other Wachtell personnel worry that the firm may be undercutting its future. P: "We need more people generating new business." P: "We haven't spread rainmaking as much as we should have. We've been too busy, so junior people haven't been encouraged to rainmake. It's happening now [during the recession] more than it was however."

Still other Wachtell personnel are trying to make rain. P: "Rainmaking in our kind of practice is [a matter of] doing a good job and getting to know other people. There is not a need for rainmaking [in another sense]. We get business because we do a good job. We also have to stay in touch with clients." The latter speaker then explained how he keeps in touch with clients. He has Wachtell's library watch for ticker-tape items and articles in the business press that relate to firms he regards as his clients. When the library turns up an item on which he has insight, he telephones a senior manager or the corporate counsel, explains that he has noticed the item, and suggests that the client consider doing such and such. Thus, he lets clients know that he is watching out for their interests and that he has expertise relevant to their current problems; by giving advice away he implies that he could bring even greater expertise to bear.

Marty

P: "Marty was leading. He recognized that M&A was a good way to go. We just followed him." P: "Marty Lipton is a business genius. He has strategic planning insight." P: "Marty is charismatic, confident, usually right, and he dominates. Herb is similar, yet they get along."

O: "Marty was one of the best securities lawyers in the country; there were maybe half a dozen others. Unlike the others, Marty was not at a firm that would necessarily frown on aggressive hostile actions. Unlike the others, Marty was willing to deploy task forces. Finally, of the great security lawyers, Marty had the best business sense." O: "Marty is the most honorable guy. He doesn't communicate any sleaze to anybody." O: "Marty has a big ego and sometimes he comes across too strong." O: "I have very high regard for Marty Lipton. He is a fine lawyer. He is innovative. He is superb with clients. He is the force at that firm. They have other fine lawyers, but without Marty Lipton. . . ."

O: "Lipton's genius was he chose to be on one side [defense against takeover]. He realized that they were prepared to pay because . . . they were never around afterward. You couldn't win so it was a matter of how much money you could raise for the losers. Everybody hired Marty to keep them independent, but this just wasn't possible. I believe the financial results justified the earnings, and I believe [Wachtell's] actual earnings were much higher than" the estimates made by the *American Lawyer*.

P: "Wachtell has one phenomenal rainmaker. We've practiced in the puddle created by his rain. But he's not politically well connected or socially well connected. He's an extremely good lawyer who makes contacts because people want him to work on their cases." P: "Lipton would be sorely missed. His business life is interwoven with his social life. He's a genius and we all benefit from it." P: "Lipton is one of the most brilliant lawyers in the United States, maybe the most brilliant. He's also entrepreneurial, and he networks." P: "No one this side of the Mississippi could replace Marty Lipton. However, many lawyers in Wachtell have close relations with various clients." P: Marty is unbelievably smart. Comes up with these ideas." P: "Marty is unique." P: "Even if Lipton's not here, he's here. 'What would Marty say?'"

What Lies Ahead?

Will Growth Drive Wachtell Back to the Mean?

P: "We need more associates, especially in litigation. Young people are willing to do the routine work. They have more energy, more enthusiasm. Without young people you feel isolated, put upon. The young work cheaper, so there is less client complaint."

Galanter and Palay (1991) argued that the up-or-out rule—which dictates that associates must either become partners or depart—locks law firms into exponential growth. Maintaining constant sizes requires firms to appoint new partners no faster than current partners retire or die. Maintaining leverage requires having more associates and fewer partners. But associates remain so for only a few years whereas partners remain so for many years, so to keep the same sizes, law firms must promote very few associates to partnership. When firms grow, the ratios become more severe because there are fewer partners near retirement and because firms tend to grow by adding associates rather than partners.

Galanter and Palay said that around 1960 the prominent New York City law firms were more or less in equilibrium: They had 1.36 associates per partner, and they were promoting between one-seventh and one-fifteenth of these associates to partnerships. They also allowed a few associates to hold that status indefinitely. Firms outside New York had just 1.03 associates per partner, but they were promoting about half of their associates to partnership. According to Galanter and Palay (1991, p. 36), "For big firms, circa 1960 was a time of prosperity, stable relations with clients, steady but manageable growth, and a comfortable assumption that this kind of law practice was a permanent fixture of American life and would go on forever."

Of course, what Galanter and Palay saw as comfortable stability, Katz, Lipton, Rosen, and Wachtell saw as exploitation and bureaucratization. The story of Wachtell suggests that the structure of 1960 was promoting the creation of new specialist law firms that did what they did better than their old, large competitors. In 1976, Brill (1976, p. 55) speculated, "Flom's and Lipton's success seems to be part of a trend in New York that has seen younger firms spring up in the last two decades to challenge the supremacy of the old Wall Street firms. The younger firms, many of which were started by Jewish lawyers who were not as welcome then at the old-line firms, enjoy reputations among job-seeking students at major law schools as 'sweatshops' or as 'places where the action is,' depending on the student's outlook." Because similar developments were occurring in investment banking and financial brokerage, the new law firms could find clients who did not have established ties.

From 1960 to 1985, according to Galanter and Palay, law firms adhered to the up-or-out rule while their operations changed dramatically. Government regulations and an increasingly litigious society led corporations to search for more specialized and higher legal skills. Many corporations terminated their long-standing relationships with full-service law firms, created in-house legal departments to handle routine matters, and divided their outside legal work among specialists in governmental regulation, labor relations, mergers, pensions, taxes, and so on. The large law firms responded by bringing in former government officials as partners, by raiding each other to obtain the specialists in greatest demand, by merging with firms having complimentary specialties, and by expanding geographically. Most large law firms have opened offices in Europe and in several U.S. cities.

Nelson argued that Galanter and Palay overstated the importance of the up-or-out rule in these developments and understated the importance of lawyers' ideologies and their desire for profits. He (1992, pp. 745–6) opined that "corporate law firms began to mimic the aggressive entrepreneurialism of the corporate and financial actors they represented. In a corporate environment that did not value institutional loyalty, traditionally oriented law firms risked looking flabby or out-of-touch." Furthermore, "corporate law firms simultaneously define professional achievement in terms of status and economic returns" (1992, p. 747). "Law partnerships maintain the promotion-to-partnership tournament, not because it is the only way to arrange these exchanges, but because it is an effective surplus-producing mechanism" (1992, pp. 746–7). (Sander and Williams [1992] also disagreed with Galanter and Palay's interpretation.)

Of course, Wachtell promotes associates to partnerships, even though the firm does not extract surpluses from its associates.

Whatever the reasons, the large law firms grew 8% annually from 1975 to 1985. Since much of this growth came through recruitment at the bottom, leverage went up. Leverage probably also rose because competition among law firms for new graduates drove up starting salaries. In New York, leverage had risen to 1.82 associates per partner by 1985; and figure 21.4 says it had gone much higher in the top firms by 1990.

Although Wachtell has resisted an increase in leverage, it has not escaped growth. Some of its partners wonder if Wachtell has already grown too big. P: "One hundred lawyers pose managerial problems—personnel, recruiting, space, mail, word processing." P: "Participatory democracy doesn't work as well with 100 lawyers as with 50." P: "Maintaining the culture was easier with 30 partners than with 60 partners." O: "I don't happen to believe that when you've got a hundred lawyers, there's that great communication!"

Others wonder how much longer the firm can continue to expand without radically altering its culture and standards. P: "Will growth dilute the partnership interest? Will Wachtell be a victim of its success?" P: "Can Wachtell find enough new hires who are good enough to sustain the one-to-one ratio?" O: "The biggest problem you run into with a large law firm is: the bigger you get, the more conflicts [of interest] you get into. . . . It's a huge limiting factor."

Wachtell has also resisted expansion to other sites. Responding to pressure from clients, Wachtell did experiment with an office in London, but then closed it. P: "Our staff are 'homegrown.' We need to monitor quality. It's difficult to do that with just one office; multiple offices make it an impossibility. We don't want to work with people we haven't worked with before. We've been able to serve all the business by getting on airplanes. Ours is a transaction business." P: "We believe that to survive, you don't need 2,000 lawyers all over the world. Of course, the world may pass us by; we may be an anachronism. We're not trying to do everything."

Does Wachtell Need Long-Term Strategies?

People in Wachtell debate the need for long-term strategic planning. P: "Wachtell needs an overall strategy as the firm gets bigger. There may be trouble in, say, 1995 when the firm has grown to 140–150 lawyers and the founders are gone." P: "We have no long-term strategy. Held a weekend meeting of partners. It was a bust." P: "We held a Retreat two years ago to talk about how to identify what is most fundamental. Everyone is struggling cooperatively with the issues. Three guys discuss the issues at lunch and agree, but they don't push their solution on others." P: "Do we need to plan? Yes. Lipton encourages us to plan. But he's the planner, together with Fogelson and Wachtell."

Others see little need for long-term strategies. P: "Our long-term strategy is 'more of the same.'" P: "Fine tuning will suffice. We have enough work for 150 partners." We think restructuring is going to be the next five years. Litigation and creditors' rights boom in a bad economy. Corporate goes the other way." P: "People here believe that if you're good at what you do and you do the best job you can, there will always be people who come to you. The work will always be there. There's not a whole lot of concern about the future."

What Will Happen When the Founders Depart?

Succession is an ancient problem. For instance, Marshall (1920, p. 316) remarked that "after a while, the guidance of the business falls into the hands of people with less energy and less creative genius, if not with less active interest in its prosperity."

Wachtell's founders see this issue and aspire to create an exceptional institution that will long survive them. The L quotations above have a formal tone that reflects Lipton's vision of Wachtell as an institution. The example of Cravath Swaine proves that extreme excellence and unusual ways of organizing can memorialize those who created them (Nelson 1988, pp. 71–3; Swaine 1946–48). Still, no one is confident that Wachtell's excellence will survive its founders' departure.

O: "These were four extraordinary lawyers. Emotionally, if I were part of that firm, I'd feel enormous gratitude to them." O: "Len Rosen— I'm told he's the best bankruptcy practitioner in the country." P: "It is a law-firm tradition: The original partners get diluted. The next generation is not as good as the founders. Wachtell hopes to break out of this." P: "There's a generation gap between the 30-year-olds and the 60-year-olds." P: "The organization has to get over the parental problem. Wachtell, Lipton, and Rosen stand in the parental role. The younger partners resist responsibility" for management. P: "We have to pass relationships down to the younger generations." C: "I have a relationship with the two top people. I can call Marty. I can call Herb."

James Fogelson, whom some regarded as Wachtell's likely leader for the 1990s, died in September 1991 at the age of 48. P: "Fogelson was a great administrator. He kept track of everything."

The Elements of Exceptional Success

What explains Wachtell's exceptional success? This question has many answers, all of which may be correct, and there is no way to find out whether some of these answers are truly essential. Here is a concise analysis by one of Wachtell's competitors who knows the firm well.

What factors have led Wachtell to be so profitable? The first is that Wachtell was and is a major factor in takeover work. Virtually all of the most successful firms have been major presences in takeover work.

A second factor is that Wachtell has limited lines of business. That is to me a function of its age. . . . Old law firms are like snowballs rolling down the hill. Not only

can't you get rid of the bad business, it keeps growing. The theory that diversification is risk-averse is wrong. It's wrong because an unprofitable line is never going to become profitable again.

The third factor—Wachtell has the best work ethic of any firm in the country. A higher percentage of Wachtell's personnel have a diligent work ethic than any other law firm in the country. This too is a function of the age of the firm. Wachtell has relatively few people who are over 48–50, and the people at Wachtell who are over that age are a very diligent group. They deserve credit, a lot of credit, for maintaining that work ethic. I'd guess that 90% of Wachtell's lawyers share their work ethic. At a firm like this one, there might be [one-seventh of the] lawyers who have that work ethic.

It takes all three factors. If they just had the other factors but not the takeover work, they'd have been very successful but not as successful as they have been. If they just had takeover but not the other factors, they'd have been very successful but not as successful as they have been.

Wachtell is an intricate house of cards. The preceding analysis seems too simple. It also overstates the importance of M&A work. As the analyst observed, "Virtually all of the most successful firms have been major presences in takeover work." Indeed, Wachtell was far from the dominant presence in M&A cases. Powell (1986, p. 40) noted, "Skadden Arps . . . was involved in 60% of all major mergers and acquisitions during 1985 and Wachtell Lipton in 45% (*Corporate Control Alert* February 1986)."

Every concise analysis seems too simple. Wachtell contains many elements that fit together and reinforce each other. Each element is individually a flimsy component with which to build an institution, and some elements are individually farfetched. Yet, they fit together so well that removing one element might undermine the whole structure.

I found it impossible to array the quotations in a cleanly linear fashion: For example, Wachtell's success with M&A cases arose partly from its ability to innovate, partly from its use of teamwork, partly from its willingness to practice law 168 hours a week, partly from its self-confidence, and partly from the personalities and abilities of its founders. These elements in turn interrelate with its high recruiting standards, culture, compensation systems, transactional practice, history, and social environment.

The cards forming a house stay up because they oppose each other. Likewise, Wachtell is internally inconsistent, in conflict with itself. For instance, in a profession that emphasizes individualism, it hires supremely self-confident lawyers and asks them to subordinate their individuality to teamwork. Although it specializes in difficult areas of practice and emphasizes the high quality of its work, it gives early responsibilities to associate lawyers, makes partnership decisions early, and promotes a high percentage of associates to partner. Although its policies call for transactional practice and some lawyers emphasize their independence of clients, rainmaking is on many minds. Whereas the mythology says "management devolves on those who will do it," it is senior partners who make case assignments, who "lean on people," and who make "a lot of major decisions . . . over lunch." The firm's founders say they have given low priority to income, and they seem to be forgoing personal income to build a firm. Thus, the founders are hoping to attract lawyers like themselves, yet no potential or current employee can ignore the very high incomes that Wachtell offers. Lawyers who were social underdogs have become the professional elite.

A house of cards can grow stronger as the builder adds cards, but growth also makes the structure less stable. Policies of early promotion and high rates of promotion, and possibly clients' resistance to high fees, compel Wachtell to grow; yet growth is posing serious challenges of socialization, recruiting, and demand for services. The current 100-plus-lawyer firm is probably much less integrated and less stable than the 24-lawyer firm of 1974.

Wachtell is an elephant. Like the blind men who tried to describe the elephant, various participants in and observers of Wachtell see different organizations. Wachtell's complexity is one cause of ambiguity, and its internal inconsistencies are another.

To explain Wachtell's success, one must point to many factors—converting disadvantages into advantages, successful recruiting, case selection, lawyers' efforts to live up to their own aspirations, a culture that promotes supreme effort, emphasis on high quality, disdain for administrative costs, the M&A fad, collegiality, teamwork, an extreme ethic of client service, founders who are willing to trade financial rewards for organizational ones, the differing personalities and values of the four founders, success that feeds on success, and luck.

It is no wonder that the partners disagree about what Wachtell should do next. The firm is not a coherent unity, and it justifies different interpretations of "reality." Is control more democratic in creditors' rights than in corporate law or litigation? Is there enough entrepreneurship? Does Wachtell offer a warm, collegial work environment or does it consume its personnel? Is Wachtell egalitarian or paternalistic, or is paternalism a prerequisite for egalitarianism? Does the firm's success arise from its method of organizing or from the exceptional abilities of a very few? Does Wachtell need a strategy or does it already have one? "Task forces are the essence of expertise," and "if you do a superior job there will be more demand for your services than you can meet."

Law firms, and other KIFs, tend to attribute their successes and failures to individuals. For example, Gilson and Mnookin (1989, p. 572) wrote:

> At the time of the initial hiring decision, the law firm is unable to tell which among its pool of new associates will come to possess the knowledge and personal attributes that the firm requires in a partner. The firm is uncertain not only about an associate's legal skills, but also about more subjective personal characteristics—for example, co-operativeness, maturity, the ability to gain respect of existing clients and to recruit new ones—that traditionally have been important to the partnership decision.

Such interpretations assume that "personal characteristics" are indeed personal. The Wachtell case suggests that personal characteristics reflect organizational culture and policies. Wachtell has no better information about prospective employees than any other law firm, yet more of Wachtell's associates achieve partnerships and do so earlier, and Wachtell's partners have external reputations for unusually high quality and especially hard work.

Wachtell is a butterfly. Butterflies are elegant creatures, airy and colorful. They seem barely to touch down on flowers, branches, or leaves. Although butterflies are easily injured and short-lived, nothing lives forever. Some butterflies might choose to live longer at the cost of less beauty; others might risk their lives to attain more beauty. Wachtell too is an elegant, colorful creation that flits from one success to another, and almost no one will be surprised if Wachtell metamorphoses into something more ordinary.

Wachtell flits because it opportunistically goes where the flowers look brightest. Some observers allege smugly that Wachtell's success is a result of a fad—the M&A one. To me, this appears to be a correct statement, but not in the sense that its speakers intend.

Fads always happen. Social changes are inevitable and frequent. The important point is not that Wachtell benefited from a fad, but that Wachtell turned a fad into an opportunity. Indeed, several of Wachtell's opponents suggested that the firm both helped to stimulate the M&A fad and took actions that shaped its character. When the M&A fad faded and recession developed, Wachtell shifted to creditors' rights and bankruptcies. And when the recession ends, Wachtell will turn to something else. It doesn't require a specific social current because its personnel are very proactive and very, very able; they might be able to turn almost any social current into an opportunity. In 1993, Wachtell is emphasizing, more than before, its capabilities in taxation, antitrust, and real estate; and it is promoting its expertise in bank mergers and in recapitalizations of and regulatory compliance by financial institutions.

Some people protest that one should not hold Wachtell up as an example for imitation. They say the firm makes an appalling prototype because it turns an occupation into an all-consuming passion. One response to this protest is that people have the right to dedicate their lives to their occupations if they so choose and it is not only those who work at Wachtell who do this. A second response is that Wachtell cannot serve as a prototype for many firms because it is so difficult to imitate.

Wachtell is more unique. All organizations are unique, but Wachtell is more so. Although it shares many properties with other law firms, it pushes a few properties to extremes that no other law firm attains; it combines properties in a way that no other firm duplicates; and it may possess a few unique resources.

Wachtell is very much a product of a time and a place. Its founders' values fit into the 1960s, and its founding reflects the New York City legal system of the 1960s and New York City's ethnic diversity. Wachtell is also very much a product of specific people—Lipton and Wachtell with charisma and off-beat ideas, Katz and Rosen with commitments to democracy and teamwork. What if Wachtell's first major client had not posed difficulties that stimulated the founders to opt for a transactional practice? Indeed, what if Martin Lipton is truly the best corporate lawyer in America and what if the firm is basically an amplifier for his talents? How would an imitator obtain a Martin Lipton?

One strong evidence that Wachtell is difficult to imitate is the lack of a twin. Although other law firms crave Wachtell's high status and stratospheric fees, either they cannot reproduce the conditions necessary to elicit these or they have refused to make the required trade-offs. Observers often contrast Wachtell with Skadden, Arps, Slate, Meagher & Flom. Skadden Arps opposed Wachtell in many M&A battles, and Joseph Flom's reputation for creativity and good sense equals Martin Lipton's. Skadden Arps very likely received fees for M&A work resembling those paid to Wachtell. But Skadden Arps used this injection of wealth to try to become "a complete financial services company." It has allied with affiliate law firms in a dozen countries, and in 1990, it employed 1,113 lawyers.

Deviance plays a powerful role in Wachtell's success. The law industry needs and can support very few firms of last resort, very few emergency medical teams. One can imagine a second Wachtell or even a third, but not five or ten. If there were five law firms with similar abilities, they would not have several times as much work as they could do, they would not be able to choose their cases, and they would not be able to charge significantly higher fees than other firms.

Nevertheless, someone could probably create a second or third law firm like Wachtell. O: "I don't think it's a formula anybody could follow but it could happen again." O: "Why hasn't it been repeated? There's no question in my mind that it can be repeated. It hasn't been because lawyers are so risk-averse and we pay them so much."

Someone could also create KIFs like Wachtell in other industries. Maister (1985) pointed to one-firm firms in accounting, consulting, investment banking, law, and the military, and one can visualize them in education, marketing research, product development, scientific research, and software. But complexity and peculiarity do make Wachtell difficult to imitate. This firm's story seems to show that it is not sufficient to assemble two or three crucial elements or to assemble many conventional elements. Those who aspire to exceptional success must integrate many elements, some of which are abnormal, and must put them together in unique combinations that may not work or that may meet environmental hostility. Indeed, the fusion of complexity and peculiarity are probably what makes exceptional success rare. Furthermore, both complexity and peculiarity offer bases for the destruction of exceptional success. Complexity means that there is a high probability of losing a few crucial elements out of many, or of opposing elements getting out of balance. Peculiarity means that there is a high probability of the peculiar elements being lost.

Wachtell's story says a great deal about what it takes to attain exceptional success, but it also says exceptional success is very difficult to attain and something most people would be unwilling or unable to attain. Like the Grand Canyon or the British Royal Family, Wachtell challenges the premise that something is only worth observing in order to imitate it.

Note

I owe thanks to many who contributed data, time, ideas, insights, and contacts. This chapter reflects help from Murray Bring, Andrew Brownstein, Joan Dunbar, William Evan, Arthur Fleischer, Joseph Flom, Blaine Fogg, James Fogelson, Stephen Fraidin, Eliot Freidson, Melvin Heineman, Dennis Hersch, Ruth Ivey, Morris Kramer, Robert Landes, Joanne Laurence, Karen Legge, Martin Lipton, Joanne Martin, Joanna Martinuzzi, Alan Meyer, Theodore Mirvis, Connie Monte, Robert Nelson, Harold Novikoff, Lawrence Pedowitz, Fioravante Perrotta, Joseph Post, James Ringer, Lawrence Rosenberg, Stephen Volk, Herbert Wachtell, Alan Whitaker, and some who asked for anonymity.

References

Brill, S. (1976) "Two tough lawyers in the tender-offer game." *New York*, June 21, 52–61.

Carroll, G.R. (1985) "Concentration and specialization: Dynamics of niche width in populations of organizations." *American Journal of Sociology* 90:1262–83.

Cohen, R. (1991) "Denting a legal Galahad's armor." *New York Times*, October 16, D1, D6.

Galanter, M. and Palay, T.M. (1991) *Tournament of Lawyers: The Transformation of the Big Law Firm*. Chicago: University of Chicago Press.

Gilson, R.J. and Mnookin, R.H. (1985) "Sharing among the human capitalists: An economic inquiry into the corporate law firm and how partners split profits." *Stanford Law Review* 37: 313–92.

Gilson, R.J. and Mnookin, R.H. (1989) "Coming of age in a corporate law firm: The economics of associate career patterns." *Stanford Law Review* 41:567–95.

Lederman, L. (1992) *Tombstones: A Lawyer's Tales from the Takeover Decades*. New York: Farrar, Strauss.

Lipton, M. (1990) "The firm at twenty-five." Unpublished document.

Maister, D.H. (1985) "The one-firm firm: What makes it successful." *Sloan Management Review* 27:3–13.

Marshall, A. (1920) *Principles of Economics* (8th Ed.). New York: Macmillan.

Martin, J. (1992) *Cultures in Organizations: Three Perspectives*. New York: Oxford University Press.

Nelson, R.L. (1988) *Partners with Power: The Social Transformation of the Large Law Firm*. Berkeley: University of California Press.

Nelson, R.L. (1992) "Of tournaments and transformations: Explaining the growth of large law firms." *Wisconsin Law Review*: 733–50.

Powell, M.J. (1986) "Professional innovation: Corporate lawyers and private lawmaking." Manuscript, Department of Sociology, University of North Carolina, Chapel Hill.

Pugh, D.S. (1981) "The Aston program of research: retrospect and prospect." In Van de Ven, A. and Joyce, W. (eds.), *Perspectives on Organization Design and Behavior*, pp. 135–166. New York: Wiley.

Pugh, D.S., Hickson, D.J., Hinings, C.R., and Turner, C. (1968) "Dimensions of organization structure." *Administrative Science Quarterly* 13:65–105.

Robinson, W.S. (1950). "Ecological correlations and the behavior of individuals." *American Sociological Review* 15:352–7.

Samuelson, S.S. and Jaffe, L.J. (1990) "A statistical analysis of law firm profitability." *Boston University Law Review* 70:185–211.

Sander, R.H. and Williams, E.D. (1992) "A little theorizing about the big law firm: Galanter, Palay, and the economics of growth." *Law & Social Inquiry* 17:391–414.

Schendel, D. and Hatten, K. (1977) "Heterogeneity within an industry: Firm conduct in the U.S. brewing industry." *Journal of Industrial Economics* 25:97–113.

Schendel, D. and Patton, R. (1978) "A simultaneous equation model of corporate strategy." *Management Science* 24:1611–21.

Smigel, E.O. (1964) *The Wall Street Lawyer: Professional Organization Man?* New York: Free Press.

Starbuck, W.H. (1981) "A trip to view the elephants and rattlesnakes in the Garden of Aston." In Van de Ven, A. and Joyce, W. (Eds.), *Perspectives on*

Organization Design and Behavior, pp. 167–198. New York: Wiley.

Starbuck, W.H. (1992) "Learning by knowledge-intensive firms." *Journal of Management Studies* 29:6, 713–40.

Starbuck, W.H. and Bass, F.M. (1967) "An experimental study of risk-taking and the value of information in a new product context." *Journal of Business* 40:155–65.

Starbuck, W.H. and Dutton, J.M. (1973) "Designing adaptive organizations." *Journal of Business Policy* 3:21–8.

Starbuck, W.H. and Nystrom, P.C. (1981) "Designing and understanding organizations." In Nystrom, P.C. and Starbuck, W.H. (eds.), *Handbook of Organizational Design*. Vol. 1, pp. ix–xxi. Oxford: Oxford University Press.

Swaine, R.T. (1946–48) *The Cravath Firm and Its Predecessors, 1819–1947*. New York: Privately printed, two volumes.

Thorndike, E.L. (1939) "On the fallacy of imputing the correlations found for groups to the individuals or smaller groups composing them." *American Journal of Psychology* 52:122–4.

ADDENDUM: WACHTELL, LIPTON, ROSEN AND KATZ
William H. Starbuck

What Happened?

People often ask me what happened to Wachtell after I completed the study in 1993. When I interviewed them in 1992–93, several of Wachtell's opponents had predicted that the wave of mergers and acquisitions had ended, and hence that Wachtell would no longer be able to achieve such extreme financial success. Many people, both inside and outside the firm, wondered how dependent Wachtell was on the talents and values of its founding partners.

The years 1994 and 1995 did indeed bring fewer mergers nationally and less merger work for Wachtell. But in that period, there were many corporate bankruptcies and many bank reorganizations, and Wachtell suddenly emerged as a leading U.S. firm in these two areas of practice. Leonard Rosen, one of the founding partners,

had long been recognized for his expertise in bankruptcy and creditors' rights, and the firm included a small group specializing in this area of practice. When bankruptcies grew prevalent in the early 1990s, this group gained prominence and took on more business. Also, one of Wachtell's partners was widely recognized for his exceptional expertise in bank reorganization. When the 1990s brought many bank reorganizations, his specialty gained prominence and the firm took on more such business.

The decline in merger activity was short-lived, and after just a few years, Wachtell again had more M&A work. Table 21A.1 shows the recent M&A activity by top U.S. law firms.

In 1999, Wachtell continued to stand out in general performance measures. Figures 21A.1, 21A.2, and 21A.3 show revenues per lawyer, profits per partner, and profit margins for the top

TABLE 21A.1. M&A Activity by U.S. Law Firms

Ranked by M&A Deal Value in 1998	Ranked by Proceeds from M&A in 1999	Ranked by Number of M&A Deals from 1990 to 1999
Wachtell, Lipton	Skadden, Arps	Skadden, Arps
Skadden, Arps	Cravath, Swaine	Sullivan, Cromwell
Sullivan, Cromwell	**Wachtell, Lipton**	Dorsey & Whitney
Shearman, Sterling	Davis Polk	Simpson Thacher
Cleary, Gottlieb	Shearman, Sterling	Shearman, Sterling
Davis Polk	Simpson Thacher	Gibson, Dunn
Simpson Thacher	Cleary, Gottlieb	Latham & Watkins
Jones, Day	King & Spalding	Davis Polk
Dewey Ballantine	Weil, Gotshal	**Wachtell, Lipton**
Baker & Botts	Sullivan, Cromwell	Wilson Sonsini

American Lawyer, April 1999 and April 2000; *Mergers and Acquisitions Journal*, Feb. 1, 2000)

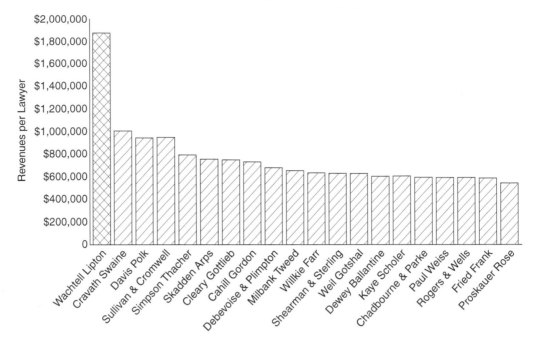

Figure 21A.1

20 U.S. law firms. Indeed, one could argue that Wachtell occupied a more outstanding position in 1999 than it had in 1989–90. According to Alison Frankel (2000):

> In the last 10 years we've seen an increasing percentage of the highest-end (and best-paying) litigation and deal work consolidating at

fewer and fewer elite firms—all New York-based. In fact, throughout the 1990s, just 10 firms—again, all headquartered in New York—dominated our revenue-per-lawyer and profits-per-partner rankings. They are the Winners of the Nineties, listed here in order of their dominance: Wachtell, Lipton, Rosen & Katz; Cravath, Swaine & Moore;

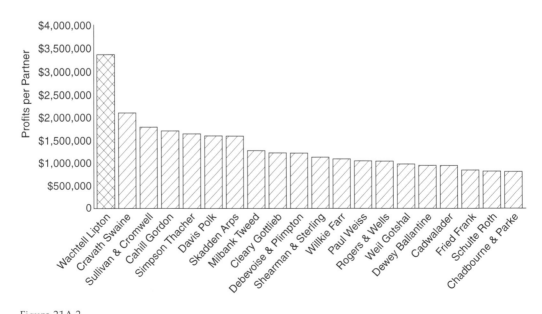

Figure 21A.2

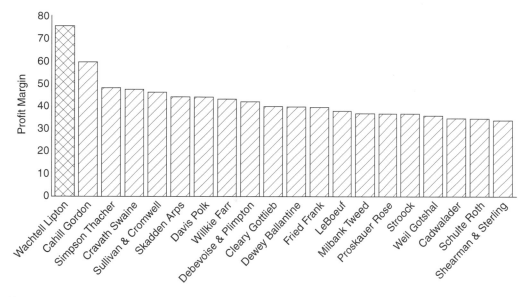

Figure 21A.3

Sullivan & Cromwell; Davis Polk & Wardwell; Cahill, Gordon & Reindel; Simpson Thacher & Bartlett; Cleary, Gottlieb, Steen & Hamilton; Skadden, Arps, Slate, Meagher & Flom; Debevoise & Plimpton; and Shearman & Sterling.

Figures 21A.4, 21A.5, and 21A.6 show the numbers of lawyers working in these firms, the numbers of partners, and the numbers of lawyers per partner (leverage). Wachtell has expanded about 40%, but the number of partners has increased only 10%, so there are now more associates per

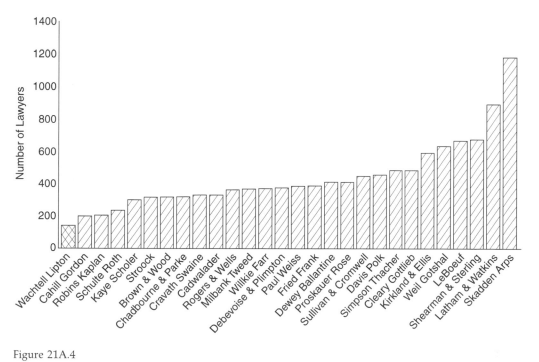

Figure 21A.4

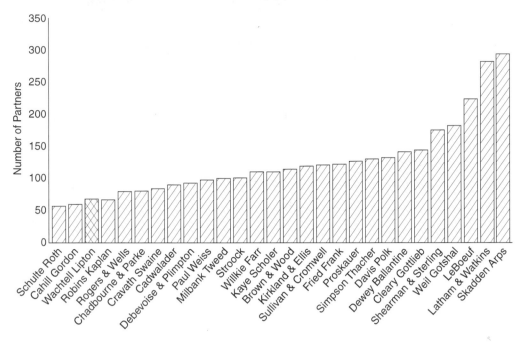

Figure 21A.5

partner. Still, Wachtell has the lowest ratio of associates per partner among the top firms.

Figures 21A.1 to 21A.6 are based on data published in the *American Lawyer* in July 2000.

As the three surviving founders have continued to practice law, there is no evidence about the effects of succession. But a new challenge or opportunity has surfaced—"The New Economy." As one result, in the summer of 2000, Wachtell was again considering whether to open a branch office outside New York City, this time in Silicon Valley.

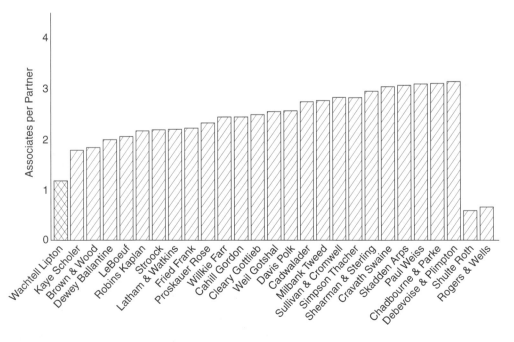

Figure 21A.6

Learning How to Compete from Experience

The original article did not give enough emphasis to one component of Wachtell's success: the firm's repeated ability to extract effective strategic policies from its experience. The founding partners' experiences as associate lawyers led them to formulate Wachtell's radical personnel policies. An early difficulty with a very important client, together with the need to surmount entry barriers, inspired an emphasis on transactional practice. Experience working together while the firm was still very small triggered an emphasis on teamwork. Interaction with investment bankers suggested the possibility of fees based on outcomes rather than hours worked. Observing that a large corporation had been unable to obtain legal service over a weekend led Wachtell to adopt a policy of 24-hour-7-day service. Success in circumventing established precedents taught lessons about surprise and innovation. After initial success with the poison pill, Wachtell created poison pills for many clients.

Although many, many law firms must have had experiences similar to Wachtell's, the other firms did not convert those experiences into ideas about how they might be able to innovate. Furthermore, after Wachtell innovated, the other firms were slow to imitate Wachtell's innovations and they usually made weak commitments to the innovations. One reason for this might be the loose, individualistic structures of most law firms. Managing partners often lack authority and they may not receive much respect; central coordination is usually weak and individual partners usually have much autonomy. By contrast, especially during the early years, the founding partners of Wachtell operated as a unified coalition that was small enough to formulate innovative policies and strong enough to control the other partners. Evidently, this coalition was also good at extracting valuable lessons from the firm's experience.

References

Frankel, A. (2000) "Edifice Lex." *American Lawyer*, July 5, 2000.

22

Epistemology in Action

A Framework for Understanding Organizational Due Diligence Processes

Mihnea Moldoveanu

When people like us invest in a company, nothing about it is real. A thicket of claims, predictions, and projections always surrounds a new investment and makes the kernel of truth almost impossible to discern. . . . The company amounts to little more than a figment of someone's imagination. When we summon up the conviction to invest, we do so based on our belief of what someday might come true. If a pattern of future success were glaringly obvious, it would be too late to make a glaring venture capital investment.

Michael Moritz, Partner,
Sequoia Capital

22.1 Applied Epistemology as a Form of Knowledge Strategy

Organization A is considering whether or not to make a significant investment in a start-up company working in a new and quickly growing industry. The business plan put forth by the start-up's founders presents a series of forecasts and predictions of firm and market-level revenues and net income, which are in turn derived from a series of assumptions about the firm's technology, the behavior of the market's consumer base, and the costs of materials for the firm's products. Together, these various propositions form the "business case" of the start-up—or the causal model—complete with assumptions and initial and boundary conditions—that explains how the start-up firm will register supernormal profits at some time in the future if it is funded in the present.

Organization A uses the facts, figures, and forecasts in the start-up's business plan as hypotheses to be tested and performs its own market studies aimed at refuting the propositions that the firm's business case is built on. It confronts the start-up's founders with the evidence statements that apparently refute the claims of the business plan and incorporates the founders' responses in the "new" business plan that is again taken for a "test ride" in the market. Organization A simultaneously checks for the internal consistency of the assumptions on which the start-up's claims are based (confronts the founders with inconsistencies and incorporates their answers in the new business plan, if required) and, time allowing, attempts to obtain refuting evidence for the assumptions in question from subsequent market studies. Organization A proceeds in similar fashion with several other start-up firms up to a deadline, at which the funds in its charge must be invested, at which time it selects the most vigorously tested and least frequently refuted of the various business cases that it has come across.

By contrast, organization B (performing due diligence on the same start-up firm for the purpose of awarding a convertible loan, for instance) must satisfy a set of internal guidelines (regarding likely sales levels within the next five years, likely number of employees at a particular geographic location, mix of technological skills of the employees, suitability of the firm's strategy for a particular market segment, and so forth). These guidelines have, embedded in them, assumptions about the consequences of investments in various types of start-up firms, usually accumulated on the basis of "painful precedents": a "past debtor," for instance, failed reportedly because they entered the market "too late," leading to the drafting of a guideline specifying a minimum period of time to market entry that must be apparent in the candidate firm's business plan. The assumptions embedded in the guidelines of organization B are inductively derived from such past experiences. If a firm that fulfilled every guideline at the time of its loan inception fails miserably, a new guideline is drafted to cover similar cases. On the other hand, no firm that does not pass all or most of the guideline requirements is considered as a likely candidate, and therefore organization B cuts off its access to the projected funding.

The grant application of the start-up firm is judged by managers in organization B according to whether or not it passes the various tests that have been set up in the form of formal guidelines. If a particular feature of the start-up's business plan is logically consistent with the relevant guideline, then the business plan is said to pass the "local test." Organization B chooses to award grants to the firms that pass most of the guideline-oriented tests. In its calculus of reasons and judgments, each successful "match" between the business case of the start-up firm and a particular guideline set internally represents a "reason for" granting funds to the start-up, and each failure to pass a particular guideline test represents a reason against granting funds to the start-up. Thus, the due diligence strategy of organization B is aimed at identifying the firms that have the highest "net score" in the guideline clearance process: the highest difference, in other words, between crucial tests passed and crucial tests failed.

There are clear differences in the two processes. These differences can be captured in many different ways, but one particularly salient distinction is between the *falsificationist* approach used by organization A (searching for evidence-based reasons against particular business cases and choosing—albeit provisionally—the most severely tested and least refuted among the various business cases put forth) and the *justificationist* approach used by organization B (looking for reasons *for* the validity of its internal guidelines through its process of selecting among competing projects, and using a justificationist calculus of reasons in order to decide among competing projects). We can use this distinction to compare due diligence processes in organizations with the process of scientific discovery (or creation) of explicit knowledge ostensibly referring to external phenomena and to map different due diligence processes to different patterns of the evolution of scientific theories. Stages of scientific creation (or discovery) correspond—in the framework I am advancing—to stages in the process of formulating models and theories, subjecting them to tests and selecting among them on the basis of these test results that characterize processes of due diligence.

I will reconstruct—in what follows—arguments for various forms of epistemic rationality that establish the relative advantages of falsificationist strategies over justificationist strategies and will illustrate falsificationist and justificationist due diligence strategies "in action" in case studies of processes of due diligence carried out by a venture capital firm and a government agency on the same high-technology start-up firm. These case studies—together with the underlying argument for the superior "performance" of falsificationist strategies—supply an alternative explanatory hypothesis for the abnormally high rate of return of venture capital funds relative to other organizations investing in similar industries. If certain processes of due diligence lead to better outcomes, we have reason to ask, "How can these processes be created or brought about in an organization?" The final section of the chapter makes a start toward answering these questions. It connects individual epistemology to individual cognitive psychology and argues that it is generally *unlikely* that falsificationist organizations are made up of falsificationist individuals (as most individuals are justificationist or dogmatists in their approaches to belief validation and selection). Thus, I argue that further work should be devoted to understanding the differences between organizational and individual deliberation and inquiry processes, and in particular to understanding how justificationist individual minds can be brought together to form falsificationist groups or organizations.

22.1.1 Due Diligence Processes and the Construction of Scientific Knowledge: Similarities and Differences

The argument about to unfold relies on a model of *processes of due diligence as processes of scientific knowledge creation*. Managers put forth hypotheses about the opportunity presented for investment that are tested against observation statements related to the opportunity. The hypotheses are derived from underlying *models and theories*. These form, together, the manager's assumption base. The statements making up the assumption base may or may not be empirically testable. If they are empirically testable, they may or may not have been tested, and they may or may not be tested as part of the due diligence process. The aim of the due diligence process—like the aim of the scientific endeavor—is to come up with maximally accurate, objective, justified, or truthlike statements about the underlying opportunity. Not all of these goals are treated equally, however. For example, whereas the aim to provide a justified account of why one is investing in an opportunity will stress the gathering of reasons *for* and *against* investing, followed by a weighing of the available reasons against each other for the purpose of increasing the justificatory value of the account, stressing truthlikeness as a criterion for model or theory choice will emphasize gathering reasons *against* the account in question, reasons *against* those reasons, and so forth. These differences, we shall see, give rise to differences between *justificationist* and *falsificationist* processes of due diligence.

Treating the managers conducting a due diligence process as a group of scientists and likening their cognitive activities to the cognitive activities of scientists conducting a scientific investigation opens up due diligence processes to study, using the tools of classical epistemology and the sociology of science. The underlying assumptions and beliefs of managers about the opportunity presented are akin to the scientific theory that is being tested. The questions that the managers conducting due diligence processes ask of the people presenting the opportunity and the data gathering process are akin to the process of testing empirically testable hypotheses derived from an underlying scientific theory. The process of selecting among various opportunities on the basis of data gathering and selection is akin to the scientist's choice among various competing theories that vie to explain the same evidentiary base.

Internal and external validity, reliability, parsimony, and procedural rationality in the selection of theories are as important to a community of scientists investigating a phenomenon or solving a problem as they are to managers conducting an empirical inquiry into the structure and nature of an opportunity. These standards—often argued by methodologists (Cook and Campbell 1979) and philosophers (Kuhn 1970) as the hallmark of normative theorizing—can be used to characterize the nature of an organizational due diligence process. Organizational activities can be judged relative to the ways in which they address these normative criteria for adequate scientific processes of inquiry.

Internal Validity

Internal validity refers to the internal coherence or consistency of the assumptions or axioms of a theory. Internally inconsistent axioms do not preclude one from holding any belief whatsoever: if one believes that "p is true" and one believes at the same time that "p is not true" (or any statement implying that "p is not true"), then one is logically committed to believing any other statement (Popper 1940). Thus, internally inconsistent theories cannot function as useful discriminators between alternative states of the world, because they do not disallow any state of the world from being observed. The product of organizational due diligence processes can—like scientific theories—be judged according to the internal consistency of the causal models and theories that they produce, and organizational due diligence processes can be judged according to whether or not they seek out and correct inconsistencies in their assumptions sets.

External Validity

External validity refers to the degree to which a theory or a model is corroborated by intersubjectively agreed-upon observation statements. It is a measure of the degree to which changes in the underlying theory track changes in the underlying data set. Empirically untestable theories, for example, may be said to lack external validity because changes in the evidentiary base will not cause a change in the underlying theory. Like scientific theories, the set of beliefs that result from due diligence processes can be judged in terms of their responsiveness to observation statements—the degree to which they track some external data set.

Reliability

Reliability refers both to the replicability of empirical tests of a theory across time and replicability of the empirical tests across different observers. It is a measure that contributes to the perception of the objectivity of a theory. If an observation statement cannot be replicated, then it may not be reliable. If a theory does not lead to similar reported results when used by two different investigators, then it is not reliable. If its results cannot be replicated in time, then it is not reliable. Just as intertemporal and intersubjective reliability can be used to gauge the relative merits of scientific theories, they can also be used to gauge the relative merits of the causal models (models that map present conditions to future payoffs achievable through purposive actions causally related to the conditions and the payoffs) that result from due diligence processes. More or less reliable means for testing models' beliefs may be used in the due diligence process. These will lead to more or less reliable causal models and more or less reliable action strategies.

Parsimony

Parsimony has historically been judged to be one of the qualities of a "good theory," since the time of the Scottish philosopher Occam, but more recently causal accounts—based on evolutionary arguments—have been put forth that explain why a more parsimonious theory is likely to have greater validity than another, less parsimonious theory (Quine and Ullian 1970): if by "validity" we mean "greater predictive power," then, by Quine and Ullian's explanation, "innate subjective standards of simplicity that make people prefer some hypotheses to others will have survival value insofar as they favor successful prediction. Those who predict best are likeliest to survive and reproduce their kind, in a state of nature anyway, and so their innate standards of

simplicity are handed down." A more parsimonious theory explains the observation statements in its domain with fewer axioms and ad hoc assumptions than a less parsimonious theory does. Just as parsimony can be held as a standard of scientific rationality, it can also be held as a standard of rationality for the products of due diligence processes. A model of the opportunity (linking current conditions to future payoffs causally linked to imminent actions and impending changes in the environment) based on many different ad hoc assumptions may be less valid than a model of the opportunity based on fewer ad hoc assumptions and initial conditions.

Procedural Rationality

Procedural rationality refers to the degree to which the processes of scientific enterprise (or organizational due diligence) conform to some external principles that govern the processes by which people should select among alternative theories and beliefs. All the standards of substantive rationality outlined above (external and internal validity, parsimony, reliability) can be transformed into standards of procedural rationality (governing the processes that safeguard compliance with the standards of substantive rationality). In addition, procedural rationality also includes the processes by which alternative beliefs are tested against observation statements and alternative theories are selected as most worthy of belief. These processes will be treated in detail in section 22.2, where they will be used to articulate a model of organizational epistemology.

The Role of Theory and Paradigms in the Investigation Process

Recent psychological and sociological studies of communities of scientists (Greenwald et al. 1986) have revealed that a priori commitment to some theory or paradigm can "blind" scientists to some counterarguments, even though these counterarguments are empirically corroborated or testable. In an individual setting, "theories of the self"— or theories of individual identity—can blind individuals to relevant observation statements that may change their identities, if they are duly considered (Greenwald 1980). A theory—though externally valid—may not be responsive to challenges from alternative theories and thus may fail to incorporate all of the relevant evidential base in its workings. Such failures are not typically considered to be failures of validity, reliability, or parsimony, but nevertheless they affect the all-things-considered predictive value of a theory. Open-mindedness is the closest positive norm that captures the value of a reflective approach to the practice of inquiry. Just as we would expect scientists to be "open-minded" to alternative empirically testable theories, we would also expect organizational actors to be open-minded in their consideration of relevant alternative theories and hypotheses. Open-mindedness as a norm will be related to the processes of belief selection and validation, as discussed in section 22.3.

22.1.2 Applied Epistemology and Organizational Learning: The Broader Picture and Outline of the Chapter

Organizational learning is not only about organizations producing adaptive behavior in response to market signals (Weick 1991). Rather, organizational learning is also about the production of organizational knowledge through the interpretation of market signals (Daft and Weick 1984) and the transformation of implicit knowledge (inner and outer-directed) into explicit knowledge (Nonaka 1994). As such, organizational learning resembles the learning that takes place in communities of scientists concerned with a particular subject matter ("organizations," say), advancing models and theories and confronting those models with observation statements, ideally with a view to *refuting* the models (Popper 1959), but quite often prey to the temptation of protecting these models from refutation or criticism (Greenwald et al. 1986). That is, organizations can be looked at as *communities of knowledge*. The models, theories, and frameworks that they use to interpret market signals can be looked upon as scientific models and theories. Market data can be seen as "scientific data." Due diligence and inquiry processes can be modeled as processes of experimentation and data gathering, specification or construction (depending on which side of the realist/constructivist debate one falls on). Thus, organizational learning can be studied through the lens provided by sociological and philosophical studies of the process of the creation or discovery of scientific knowledge (Barnes et al. 1996).

This is the task that this chapter undertakes. It uses insights from classical epistemology (Popper 1959, Lakatos 1974) to provide a framework for understanding organizational learning processes—which include the processes by which organizations specify and gather data and make

sense of that data in order to synthesize a pattern of decisions. This chapter considers the following questions:

1. How are beliefs, models, and theories within the organization selected for testing and then tested? How are the test results incorporated into the organizational models and frameworks?
2. How are the organizational models and frameworks modified to accommodate various empirical results? How does organizational epistemology reflect itself in organizational behavior? What are the observable implications of different organizational epistemologies?

Questions grouped under (1) are addressed in section 22.2, which provides a general framework for the study of belief selection, corroboration, and revision processes within organizations. Section 22.3 addresses the questions in (2) through a longitudinal case study of due diligence processes performed by venture capital firms, commercial banks, and government institutions on the same high-technology start-up firm.

22.2 Organizational Epistemology: Mapping the Processes by which Beliefs Are Selected in Organizations

The literature on organizational learning is usually silent about the *processes* by which organizational beliefs, models, and theories are acquired or selected from among all the possible candidates. These topics are much more likely to be deferred to the study of managerial cognition (Kahneman and Lovallo 1994, Eisenhardt and Zbaracki 1992), where managerial cognition is studied by the same analytical tools used to study cognitive frames and biases in the laboratory. Such studies assume there is a "correct" approach to forming judgments about uncertain events—based on the probability calculus and the Bayesian logic of confirmation and belief kinematics—and proceeds to measure deviations from the correct logic of belief, as exhibited by subjects' behavior on forced choice experiments. These studies do not explicitly consider whether or not a market signal will be registered and accounted for by the organization, and how different market signals are incorporated in the organization's models and frameworks used to

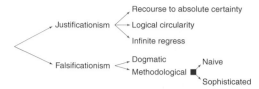

Figure 22.1 Epistemological styles: a meta-cognitive map.

make sense of its environment. Studies of cognition simply tell us whether or not subjects' reasoning conforms to the logic of belief deemed normative by the researcher.

The epistemological literature reveals that belief selection processes come in many different kinds, as shown in figure 22.1 (Lakatos 1974, Albert 1985, Moldoveanu 2000a). One can hold a belief *for* a particular reason, in the sense that the belief is a logical consequence of the reason in question. Knowledge, on this view, is considered to be *proven* knowledge (Lakatos 1974). One also seeks reasons *for* holding a belief rather than *against* holding it, and therefore it is unlikely that refuting evidence will be sought out and incorporated into one's belief system. This represents a *justificationist* approach to holding a belief. A justificationist organization might either ignore evidence that refutes its basic premises about how the market is likely to evolve or might develop fortified theories that account for the negative evidence, but will rarely, if ever, abandon a model or theory in favor of another.

22.2.1 Kinds of Justificationism

There are several different kinds of justificationism (Albert 1985), according to the strategies that one uses in order to justify a particular belief, model, or theory (see figure 22.2). *Regressive justificationism* is a justification strategy that seeks out reasons for a belief, reasons for those reasons, and so forth. Each reason becomes, in turn, a belief demanding another reason to justify it. As Albert (1985) points out, this strategy leads to an infinite regress. Justificationist organizations that are regressive in their strategies might be expected to be inert to changes in the evidence base because their theories are *entrenched* very deeply in the minds of the individual organization members. Each regressive justification chain forms a large cognitive *sunk cost* by the organization as a whole, which may preclude the organization (through well-known overcommitment biases [Staw 1976]) from seriously considering relevant alternatives and refuting evidence. Key decision makers in the Baby Bells, for example, at the time of the "wireless revolution" might believe that the wireless phenomenon is short-lived, might justify those beliefs by reference to past market "follies," which in turn are deemed relevant to the current events because of a belief in the recurrence of past patterns, which in turn is believed to be relevant here because of a belief in the logic of induction, which . . . (Noda 1995, Noda and Bower 1996). In such a firm, disconfirming evidence will not be easily incorporated into the model of the market, as such evidence

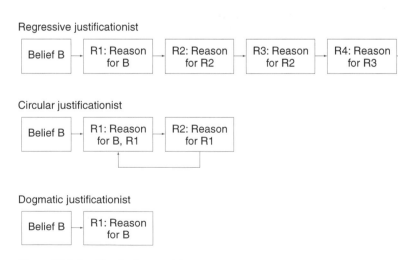

Figure 22.2 Justificationist cognitive maps.

will not only challenge a first-order belief or model about the market, but also an entire set of beliefs that may be central as coordination mechanisms for the organization as a whole.

One can also justify a belief circularly, by appealing to a second belief, which in turn is justified by the first belief. One may believe, for instance, that individual people maximize their utility functions having observed that they make a series of choices that have been in the first instance interpreted as utility-maximizing acts. A circularly regressive organization will display belief systems that are inert not because they are cognitively deep, but rather because they are unresponsive to counterarguments (including refuting evidence). If one believes A because B and B because A and is a justificationist (seeks reasons for rather than against a theory or model), then one is not likely to notice or incorporate arguments or evidence statements that refute A or B.

A dogmatic justificationist will hold a belief for a reason (or a chain of reasons) that one will hold with absolute certainty, that is, without the need for further justification. "I just know it is so," the dogmatic justificationist says of his beliefs. One might believe, without recourse to appeal, for instance, that markets are in a state of equilibrium and use that assumption in order to *interpret* evidence from actual markets, thus precluding the possibility of disconfirming the underlying, dogmatically held assumption.

The different kinds of justificationism may—in one form or another—provide the cognitive foundation for the organizational defenses that Chris Argyris has written about (Argyris 1990). Justificationists do not either seek or generally find refutations of their positions. All three forms of justificationism, in fact, can be understood as willful attempts by individual minds or collections of individual minds to make their assumptions as difficult to refute as possible: Regressive justificationism pushes the assumptions base further and further away into logical space, thus insulating it from immediate empirical refutation. Circular justificationism makes the assumption base self-contained in that it does not depend on any external propositions for its credence. Dogmatic justificationism makes the assumption base unassailable in that it will not consider any kind of challenge to this assumption base from the "external world." Thus, to the extent that organizational learning has to do with the creation of knowledge by the interac-

tion between minds and the world, justificationist strategies provide a logical map for understanding the processes by which learning fails.

22.2.2 Kinds of Falsificationism

Unlike justificationists, falsificationists hold their beliefs provisionally, in the absence of reasons against holding them, while looking for reasons and arguments against those beliefs. The attention of the falsificationist organization is directed at finding evidence *against* a particular model, belief, or theory. The selection criteria of the falsificationist focus on the degree to which a theory, model, or belief has survived repeated attempts at refutation rather than the degree to which it has been adequately supported with different reasons for accepting it.

As with justificationism, there are several different kinds of falsificationism, masterfully mapped out by Imre Lakatos (1974). One can also hold a belief in the absence of a contradictory belief that has an empirical basis, while holding the latter belief as true beyond doubt. This would make one a dogmatic falsificationist. The dogmatic falsificationist organization is one with a very short "attention span." Early "bad experiences" can lead to the abandonment of an entire theory, model, or framework. A single evidence point against the "working model" can acquire the status of dogma within the company.

By contrast to the dogmatic falsificationist, the *methodological* falsificationist believes that all statements, including evidence statements, are criticizable or falsifiable. Evidence statements also have "provisional" status, just as theories do. Here, another distinction is helpful, one between naïve and sophisticated methodological falsificationism. The naïve methodological falsificationist believes that all theories, models, or beliefs are likely to be false and looks for evidence against them (see figure 22.3 for a cognitive map of the thought processes of a naïve methodological justificationist). He has, however, no criterion of choice among alternative theories and so can make no commitment to a particular model in order to guide purposeful action (Lakatos 1974).

The naïve methodological falsificationist organization may be the typical organization of "nay-sayers" described by Pfeffer and Sutton (1999), wherein new ideas and models are "shot down" by overzealous managers. Naïve methodological falsificationist organizations are likely to

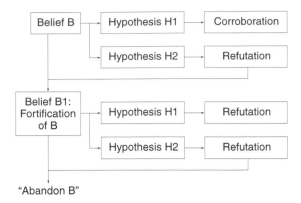

Figure 22.3 Naïve falsificationist cognitive map.

remain in a noncommittal status quo. New ideas and models are eliminated from consideration, but there is no organizational commitment to a particular model or theory (about itself or about the market) that guides the organization to a concerted action plan. A naïve falsificationist approach to understanding an industry's future evolution might be one of performing a series of market tests aimed at refuting various beliefs about the evolution of the market, in a process where the aim of producing a viable strategy becomes secondary to the aim of "shooting down" alternative models and beliefs.

One can hold a belief that has been tested and even possibly contradicted by some empirical statements in the absence of some alternative belief that has been more thoroughly tested and received a greater level of corroboration from empirical investigations, which would make one a sophisticated methodological falsificationist.

The sophisticated methodological falsificationist organization cultivates beliefs and models provisionally, looks for reasons against them (and designs market tests of those beliefs), and commits to the beliefs or models that have been least severely damaged by critical testing (see figure 22.4 for a cognitive map).

22.3 Epistemology in Action: A Study of Due Diligence Processes

To illustrate the application of the collective epistemology framework outlined above, a comparative study of due diligence processes in two organizations was performed. The two organizations were a U.S.-based venture capital firm and a Canadian federal agency that provided financial assistance in the form of limited-recourse

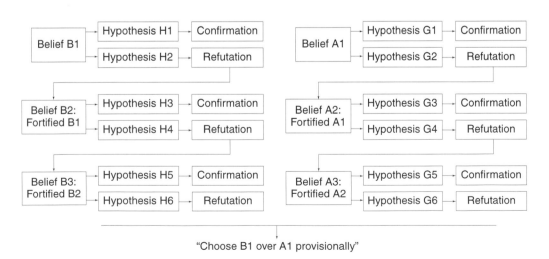

Figure 22.4 Sophisticated falsificationist cognitive map.

loans and grants to promising high-technology manufacturers located in Canada. I studied both organizations' due diligence processes around *the same* high technology start-up firm—High-line Inc., or HI, henceforth—seeking both venture capital financing and financial assistance from the federal government. Both due diligence processes yielded "go-ahead" decisions on the project the two organizations researched—albeit for different reasons and on different grounds. Because the study involved participation in all of the significant discovery-oriented meetings between HI and the two organizations, it gives a complete picture of all of the inquiry "moves" made by the venture capital firm's managers and the government agency, involving direct contact with the HI managers, and allows us to reconstruct the learning strategy of these organizations, as experienced by HI.

22.3.1 Research Design

The research project took place over a period of four months and involved the researcher in all of the meetings between the management of HI and the two organizations from whom financing was sought, as well as in-depth interviews with all of the HI managers taking part in the due diligence and negotiations process, as well as with all of the nine board members of HI. Five such meetings occurred between HI's management and the venture capital firm's principals and directors tasked with the due diligence process. Four such meetings occurred between HI's management and employees of the federal government agency that did research on the HI business plan and capability to repay the loan from sales based on the business plan projections. Many sources of heterogeneity were accounted for by studying the same company and the same project within that company, for which financing was sought.

Both due diligence processes resulted in positive outcomes for HI, embodied in a term sheet from the venture capital firm and a letter of intent from the federal granting agency. Thus, the study resulted in a "natural experiment," where heterogeneities were controlled in three ways: by studying the same firm, by studying the same project for which financial participation from the organizations doing due diligence was sought, and by studying two processes that yielded the same outcome, albeit through very different processes. The purpose of the study was to produce a cognitive map of the due diligence processes so as to reconstruct the epistemologies of the organizations doing the due diligence work.

22.3.2 Situational Analysis

HI was a private Canadian high-technology start-up company designing chips and systems for the emerging fixed broadband wireless communications infrastructure. The company employed 35 engineers in Canada and Europe, had produced a prototype system allegedly offering order-of-magnitude performance improvements over alternative technologies in a set of newly allocated frequency bands, and was preparing to manufacture and market system in Canada, the United States, and worldwide. To finance its market entry plans, HI sought $15 million (Cdn) in first-round financing from several U.S.-based venture firms and government agencies offering 50% matching funding for venture financing for high-technology start-up firms. If successful on both of the money-raising projects, HI would have raised $15 million from venture capital firms and another $7.5 million from the federal agency. The venture capital funds were to be invested in return for one-third of the equity of HI. The federal money, on the other hand, was to be disbursed to HI in the form of a loan, repayable from profits that HI registered over the next seven years that were directly traceable to the work performed in the two years after the disbursement of the loan proceeds, or converted into HI equity at an equivalent rate to the venture firm's valuation, in the event of a takeover of HI by a foreign firm. The federal granting agency was looking for a 10–15% compound annual rate of return on the total value of the loan. The venture capital firm was looking for a tenfold increase in the value of its investment over the three to five years following the investment decision. Historically, the federal loan program had recovered only about 10% of the funds loaned to start-up companies. By contrast, the venture capital fund had historically returned four to five times the investment of its limited partners, over a period of three to five years.

22.3.3 The Business Plan and the Market Data: Elements of the Cognitive Map

The same business model, marketing plan, financial projections, and technology strategy map were submitted by HI's managers to both the government agency and the venture capital firm.

The plan called for the development of a fixed wireless broadband system that could be used in access-point and bridge configurations to offer Internet service providers and local telecommunications carriers with a "last-mile" infrastructure that would outperform existing "last mile" technologies, such as cable modems and digital subscriber line modems. The plan called for a design that was based on custom gate arrays to hit the market during the following eight months, targeting commercial users, and a design that was based on application-specific integrated circuits (ASIC's) to be brought to market in another four to eight months after the initial market entry, targeting small-office/home-office (SOHO) environments with an integrated access point modem that would cost less than existing last-mile system solutions. The financial forecasts were based on a compilation of market data from major research firms (Frost and Sullivan, Inc., IDC, Inc.) and were used to support the HI revenue forecast of $10 million in the first sixteen months of operation and $500 million per year in the fifth year of operation.

The venture firm's managers and the federal agency's managers had their own sets of beliefs, models, theories, and observation statements that constituted their background knowledge, including proprietary data about the industry that HI was targeting, knowledge of alternative business scenarios that may have been equally well supported by the *same* data used by HI, and knowledge about the *sources* of the data that HI was basing its forecasts on, that may not have been accessible to HI. In addition, both the government agency and the VC firm relied on idiosyncratic but abundant information about "comparable" deals that each had done in the past, as well as the particular outcomes of those deals. The federal agency's managers, moreover, had codified their idiosyncratic knowledge about the outcomes of past dealings with high-technology start-ups in the form of a set of guidelines and rules of thumb that they deferred to in evaluating the substantive claims made by HI managers, either orally or in the written HI business plan.

22.3.4 Mapping the Due Diligence Process

Both due diligence processes could be divided up in roughly five phases, following the initial approach of the venture capital firm and the federal agency by the HI management team and board members. The reconnaissance phase entailed preliminary information gathering on the HI opportunity through presentations of the HI business plan and financial projections, verification of references of the HI managers and HI itself on the basis of the list provided by HI managers, and comparison of the HI prognostications about the market with market reports from financial analysts. A period of *tatonnement*—of mutual feeling-out with no specific strategy for asking questions or uncovering information—followed, in which seemingly "random" questions about valuation and the planned use of proceeds were sent out to the HI managers. Their answers were in some cases challenged on the basis of available data on comparable firms, and in some cases tested against the internal data base of the organization performing due diligence.

The period of *tatonnement* was focused on gathering information from HI that was not written in any of the business plans and slide presentations that HI's managers had put together in the case of the venture capital firm, and on helping HI prepare a proposal that conformed to internal guidelines in the case of the federal agency.

A full-fledged inquiry process followed, in which the answers provided by HI managers to earlier queries were recorded and checked for internal consistency in the case of the venture capital firm and checked for external validity against a wealth of private and public data sources. The "fit" between the HI plans and the "data" against which the validity of these plans was gauged was evaluated and, in the case where the fit was poor, HI's managers were asked to provide explanations of the discrepancies. These explanations were then again tested against the private information base of the organization performing the due diligence process.

A period of deliberation followed. This period of "deliberation" was used by the federal granting agency to clear the internal hurdles to securing the financing. It was used by the venture capital firm to inform the rest of the limited partnership's members about the proposed investment, as well as to check references on HI and HI's management that were *not* provided by the latter. A commitment phase followed, in which the terms of the deal were laid out to the HI managers, and the terms that would make up the term sheet in the case of the venture capital firm and the letter of intent in the case of the federal granting agency were agreed upon.

Reconnaissance

The reconnaissance stage started in both cases with a two-hour presentation by the HI CEO to members of the two organizations performing the due diligence search. In the case of the federal agency, several senior managers that were judged to be able to understand and judge the validity of the technological approach being put forth were assembled to listen to the presentation. Their interactions with the HI management team present at the gathering were largely confirmatory of the technological strategy that HI had adopted. They deferred to the HI chief technical officer on questions of technological feasibility and limited their questions to queries about the precise market positioning of the HI product.

Once these questions were answered, most of the discussion turned in ways in which HI could work together with various government-sponsored laboratories in order to accelerate its time-to-market, and on the evaluation of various HI proposals in which time-to-market could be shortened by working together with the federal laboratories. Once again, there was little overt criticism of the HI proposal. Most of the questions from the federal agency representatives were aimed at clarifying the kinds of work that HI would need to perform within the two years following the investment.

The presentation to the venture fund's managers proceeded with an outline by HI top managers of the market opportunity and the likely size of the market once HI could deliver its technology into a marketable product. The venture fund's managers showed themselves very interested in the technology and excited about the potential opportunity. It seemed as if they were searching for reasons to invest in the deal and encouraging HI's managers to provide those reasons. Encouraged by the positive response, HI's managers articulated many of the potential pitfalls that could befall the deal going forward, such as competitive threats and technological risks. Several kinds of questions were raised: questions that directly challenged HI management's assumptions (such as the viability of building up a remote engineering design team in Europe: the answers of HI's managers were duly recorded and not further challenged but flagged as potential areas of future discussions); questions that sought to elicit falsifiable answers from HI's managers on the size of the market and the percentage of the market that HI could seize

over various periods of time (the answers were not challenged, but recorded, for the purpose of due diligence); and clarificatory questions that aimed to turn the HI business plan into a set of propositions that could be confronted with market data (such as the timing of various standards ratification processes and the precise definition of the market segment that HI was trying to address).

Tatonnement

The period of *tatonnement* was used by the two organizations in very different ways. The government agency directed HI's management to write a marketing plan that conformed to a set of internal guidelines that had evolved over time and as a result of a sequence of positive and negative antecedent cases. The HI business model was tweaked to conform with the expectations of the federal agency's managers about market entry, sales levels over the next five years, and expected ability to repay the proceeds of the loan made by the federal agency to HI. There was little interaction between HI's managers and the federal agency during this period of time. The efforts of the HI managers were guided by a consultant working closely with both HI and the federal agency's managers, who served as a conduit for the expectations of the latter about the business models and projections that HI was undertaking to live up to.

The main activity during the period of *tatonnement* for the HI managers was one of making point modifications to its business model in order to get it to conform with the terms and conditions under which the federal agency was prepared to make its investment. No assumptions about the market were "made up" in order to justify the compliance of HI's sales projections with the expectations of the federal agency's managers. However, expectations about market entry points, market shares, and timing were modified in order that figures would "work out" to the repayment terms required by the guidelines in question. Working from the assumption that all statements about the future are equally suspect, HI's managers started from the current market conditions that they believed were supported by market reports and modified HI's plans in order that, together with the realistic characterization of current market conditions, the overall result would correspond to the expectations that had been channeled to them through their consultant.

During the *tatonnement* period, the venture capital firm's managers repeatedly approached HI's managers with questions about factual issues of potential relevance to the business case that HI had put forth, which were, however, not in the original HI business model. Questions asked included: questions about new and potential competitors and their market strategies, questions about new technologies for broadband wireless access modems that could be competitive with HI's own approach; and questions about the management team that HI had put in place and about HI's strategy for rounding out its organizational structure. Questions during the *tatonnement* period referred almost exclusively to information that was missing from the original HI plan. The answers given by HI's managers were recorded and it was *these* answers that were compared with the overall business plan of the company. For example, answers by HI about the viability and cost of alternative technologies for broadband wireless access were checked for consistency with HI's competitive advantage markers and with their overall technological strategy.

Inquiry/Advocacy

In the case of the venture capital firm, the period of *tatonnement* escalated smoothly into a full-fledged investigation of HI once it was established that the HI business plan, team, and technology constituted a potentially interesting investment opportunity. The venture fund's managers moved from a "discovery" process into a "validation" process, in which they sought references for most of the key HI managers and technical project leaders both from references supplied by HI managers themselves and from references not supplied by HI managers but traced by using the resumes of the HI managers. The venture firm's managers set up meetings between HI's managers and top technical and business managers in firms with similar technological capabilities but noncompeting business models, for the explicit purpose of gauging the capabilities of the HI team. The venture fund's managers then interviewed the HI managers about the relative strengths and weaknesses of the firms used as "expert witnesses," interviewed the "expert witness firms" about the relative strengths and weaknesses of the HI managers, and then presented to the HI managers the "data" that was gathered from the "expert witness" firms, and recorded the responses of the HI managers to their comments and queries. Inconsistencies between the HI managers' responses and the stated assumptions of the HI business plan were flagged for further discussion and conversations. The venture fund also set up meetings between HI's managers and potential HI customers, and once again used the "bootstrapping" approach to get bilateral validation between the HI managers' impressions and the impressions of the potential customers.

The venture fund's managers visited HI's headquarters, took part in a demonstration of the HI wireless access technology, and interviewed three of the key technical and operations managers in HI. These interviews were ostensibly aimed at validating the design and roll-out schedules that the HI management team had presented to the venture firm and had predicated most of their sales projections on. To this end, each one of the HI employees interviewed by the venture fund's managers was individually asked about his own view about the firm's product launch schedule. The discrepancies—small in this case, amounting to no more that a 10% deviation from the HI projections—were not explicitly flagged to the HI CEO and top management team but were made obvious enough. Although the venture fund repeatedly promised to get outside experts to evaluate the substantive technological claims of HI, no expert was eventually brought in to evaluate the technology.

The inquiry period in the venture firm's due diligence cycle corresponded to an advocacy or "presentation phase" in the relationship between HI and the federal agency. During the presentation phase, managers in the federal agency packaged the HI plan so that it could be "sold" to other, higher-level managers within the hierarchy. Although the packaging process could not be directly monitored, it was nevertheless reconstructed from the questions that HI managers had to field from the agency's managers. These questions were prompts for clarification about the way in which the funds would be disbursed, questions about the staffing requirements of HI during the period of time for which financial assistance was sought, and questions about the fit between HI's market entry plans and the required repayment terms for the loan that was being contemplated. Individual managers within the federal agency were "coached" by HI's managers on answering questions that might come up during the deliberation phase from higher level managers within the federal agency. The purpose of the coaching process was to gather enough information about HI so as to competently portray HI as being sufficiently different from "notable" failures that constituted a sort of "common law" at the federal agency, on which most of its internal policies and guidelines were based.

Deliberation

The deliberation phase was once again very different in the two cases. The venture fund's managers, having completed their own inquiry processes, now presented the opportunity to invest in HI under a "hot deals action memo" to the rest of the general partners in the fund during a series of meetings. The outcome of these meetings was a set of follow-up interviews and meetings between HI's managers and partners and associates in the venture fund, who had not previously been part of the due diligence process. Their questions and queries concentrated on clarifying the business model of HI and boiling the HI prognostications down to a set of immediately testable propositions. They related to such topics as, "How quickly can the engineering effort be ramped up within the next few months, given a sufficient level of funding?" "What would be the expected revenues of HI within the following 24 months, and how would the revenues be generated?" "Who would be the first three or four customers of HI, and why would they want to buy the HI product?" Answers from HI's managers were recorded and tested in interviews between the venture fund's managers and decision makers working for potential clients of HI, who were also corporate limited partners of the venture fund or in some other way associated with the venture fund's managers.

The deliberation phase in the federal agency entailed the development of an accurate model of the HI opportunity that was logically connected to (a) the HI projections, technological capabilities summary, and business model, and (b) the internal guidelines that had been developed for the purpose of approving or rejecting such applications. Again, this process could not be directly monitored but was reconstructed from observations of the interactions that HI's managers had with managers in the federal granting agency. As the HI managers had been fully briefed on the internal guidelines of the agency (through the consultant that had been hired, with mutual consent, by HI and paid on a contingency basis by HI for the purpose of securing the loan), the HI man-

agers had prepared a set of "normative" answers to the questions asked by the managers in the federal agency, which appeared to satisfy the inquirers' questions.

Commitment

Although both of the due diligence processes turned up positive results (in the form of term sheets and letters of offer from the venture fund and the federal agency, respectively), the form of the commitment was very different. The venture fund's term sheet tied the valuation of the company to the achievement of specific technological and market-based milestones that were revealed to be crucial to the short-run success of the company from the venture fund's analysis of the business model and the technological capabilities summary of HI. Such issues as the rounding out of the management team and the deployment of a test system to beta customers were specifically tied to the venture fund's investment in HI at a specific valuation level. Moreover, the timing of the venture fund's investment was also tied to specific performance milestones from HI, including such issues as the development of a field-ready prototype for the system. All the milestones were based on directly observable results, which could be ascertained by the VC fund's managers without requiring outside expert assistance. Thus, no payments were specifically tied to the achievement of internal technological milestones (such as the integration of some subcomponent of the HI wireless system), as the venture fund's managers did not have the expertise to evaluate whether or not the internal milestones had been met.

By contrast, the letter of offer from the federal agency did not tie payments or terms of repayment of the proceeds of the loan to any kind of observable milestones at HI. The agency did require that HI's financial statements be audited on a yearly basis (they had already been audited on a quarterly basis to satisfy the existing shareholders' agreements) and that such audit reports be filed with the federal agency's managers in due course. Repayment terms were specified as a percentage of the net income realized from sales of products, whose development was directly attributable to work performed after the approval of the loan to HI; however, given that HI had already developed a significant portion of the technology that would ultimately be used in their products in the field, there was considerable ex ante ambiguity about the conditions under which the product would be said to utilize technology that had been developed as a result of the financial assistance offered by the federal agency. This ambiguity was not explicitly addressed in the term sheet, and therefore no empirically testable set of propositions about what precisely would constitute the part of the product directly attributable to the agency's financial participation was articulated.

22.4 Analysis of the Due Diligence Process

Both due diligence processes can be represented as processes of scientific discovery (figures 22.5 and 22.6). A theory about the underlying opportunity is formulated and hypotheses that follow from the theory are tested against observation statements. The various processes by which theories are tested are refined, outlined in section 22.2 above, and can be used as a framework for understanding how each of the organizations studied here approached the due diligence process: how they formulated their theories or models, how they derived their hypotheses, and how they used the resulting observation statements in order to revise their initial assumptions.

The main differences in the two approaches can be captured by looking at the processes by which evidence was sought out during the due diligence process and the ways in which such evidence was incorporated into the knowledge base that eventually led to a decision (figures 22.7 and 22.8). While the federal agency's managers made an early cognitive commitment to the deal on the basis of initial "fit" between the characteristics of the project and the guidelines for investment that had emerged over a period of time within the agency, the venture fund started out by creating a model of the HI opportunity during the initial reconnaissance period, and then testing the model by looking for reasons to refute it (and with it, to reject the opportunity pre-

Figure 22.6 Cognitive strategy in government grant due diligence process.

sented by HI) during subsequent periods. Let us look more carefully at the two due diligence processes, with an eye to characterizing them as scientific discovery processes and examining their performance in promoting external and internal coherence.

22.4.1 Epistemology in Action: External Coherence

The main concern of the federal agency's managers seemed to be the justification of the guidelines that had been internally set forth for regulating investment decisions. The guidelines themselves were a mixture of "if-then" statements that emerged either from very successful or very unsuccessful past experiences, and included revenue expectations and expectations about the use of engineering resources for the company to whom the funds would be disbursed. These guidelines were treated as irrefutable axioms during the due diligence process, as they would be by a dogmatic justificationist. Indeed, if a set of guidelines is taken as true and infallible, then there is no opportunity to ascertain whether or not these guidelines may be incorrect, because the only test that would reveal their inadequacy is precisely the one that is forbidden by strict adherence to them, which is the fund-

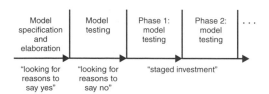

Figure 22.5 Cognitive strategy in the venture capital due diligence process.

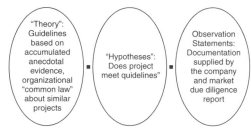

Figure 22.7 Cognitive map of the due diligence process, government agency.

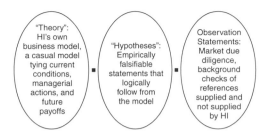

Figure 22.8 Cognitive map of the due diligence process, venture capital firm.

ing of a firm that does *not* meet them but is nevertheless successful. In our case, if there was a discrepancy between the company's business model and sales projections on the one hand, and the internally developed guidelines on the other, then the decision to reject a particular claim (or to ask for a modification of the model in order to suit the guidelines) was automatic. Moreover, the "data" that was assembled during the due diligence process by the federal agency's managers was largely data provided by HI's managers, which had in turn been selected, based on the HI's consultant's advice, to correspond with the guideline-mandated expectations of the agency. Such data was considered to settle arguments about whether or not the HI project fulfilled the guideline in question.

By contrast, the venture firm's due diligence process stressed the fallibility of *any* statement, including the evidence statements generated by the venture firm's own due diligence process. They did not, as a dogmatic falsificationist might have, consider market evidence that refuted the HI managers' assumptions as immediately conclusive about the HI business case. Rather, HI's managers were confronted with discrepancies between the venture firm's findings and the managers' own models and projections and asked to explain these discrepancies. Just like a methodological falsificationist would, the venture firm's managers then turned around and treated these explanations of the discrepancies as potentially falsifiable hypotheses in themselves, seeking evidence statements against them. The HI managers were invited to respond to discrepancies between their own model and projections on the one hand, and the data turned up by the due diligence process on the other hand. Typical of this process was the venture fund's approach to checking references. A negative reference was

not simply held, by itself, to be conclusive about the validity of the business plan. Rather, HI's managers were confronted with the results of the reference-checking process and invited to respond. Their responses were then taken into consideration, and the credibility of the person providing the reference was adjusted to factor in the nature of the personal relationship between him or her and the HI manager for whom the reference was provided.

Finally, just like a sophisticated methodological falsificationist would, the venture firm's managers reached a *decision* on moving forward with the investment, in spite of having found many different areas in which the statements initially made by the HI managers had been refuted. Falsificationism, in its sophisticated methodological form, does not mean "nihilism," or the *identical* rejection of all theories and models. Purposive action is still possible, even though it is action that is undertaken in the shadow of doubt, not in the light of certainty.

22.4.2 Epistemology in Action: Internal Coherence

Not less important than the process by which the two organizations sought evidence for or against the claims in the HI business plan was the process by which they each formulated and revised their internal models of the opportunity. The internal coherence of a model is important to the process of scientific inquiry because, should the assumptions of the model or the theory being tested be internally inconsistent, the theory or model can explain *any* evidence statement. This is a direct consequence of the analytical truth that, from two mutually inconsistent propositions, any other proposition can follow (Popper 1940). A model or theory that can explain anything, in turn, is just as unhelpful to the practitioner as a model or theory that can explain nothing at all. Thus, it is important to gauge the degree of *diligence* of the two organizations under study in formulating and updating the model of the HI opportunity that they tested against the data gathered during the due diligence process.

A model or theory of the opportunity, as explained above, is a causal map that links current conditions and managerial actions to a set of future payoffs. The assumptions on which such a model or theory rests have to do with the mechanisms by which the company was to have established a significant enough market share and technological lead in the wireless broadband access modems in order to return supernormal profits in the case of the venture firm or to provide assurance of ability to repay the loan made by the federal agency. For example, one can assume that a patentable technology in a standards-compatible product would assure HI of both access to the market in a world where the major carrier-class telecommunications equipment manufacturers looked for a "second source" for their products, which is based in turn on the well-corroborated assumptions that the availability of a standard correlates with the availability of second sources, and that a patented technology provides a sufficient short-term barrier to entry to guarantee supernormal profits, at least until the original invention is "patented around" or superseded by the inventions of competing firms. Articulating these assumptions coherently and making sure that they are internally coherent is the part of the due diligence process that we are now concentrating on.

The venture group took the HI business plan itself as the working model or theory to be tested. They analyzed the prima facie internal consistency of the assumptions embedded in the business models by first attempting to uncover those assumptions and then asking HI's managers to help them resolve any apparent inconsistency in the model. This first-order internal validity check was followed by higher-order internal validity checks. HI's managers were confronted with disconfirming evidence that emerged from the venture group's due diligence process and asked to respond. If their response implied an alteration of the underlying business model, then the internal validity of the resulting, "fortified" model was once again verified.

This bootstrapping approach to the iterative modifications to the underlying model was nicely illustrated by the exchange between HI's managers and the venture group around the problem of the market focus of HI. The original market focus of the company was the provision of chips and systems to the wireless broadband communications market. Chips were to be marketed to systems manufacturers, and systems were to be marketed to network manufacturers and systems integrators. The main objection raised by the venture fund managers was that, even though it made good technological sense to build chips that would be used in the wireless access points, which would confer significant idiosyncratic competitive advantage and self-determination on HI, it made no sense to sell both

chips and systems, as the likely customers for the chips would also be HI's competitors on the systems side. The "dual role" of competitor and supplier was, in their experience, a difficult one to play for a small company, which was likely to quickly run into conflicts with large clients that wanted to build systems. Once the HI managers agreed with the basic premise behind the venture fund managers' objection, they altered the original business plan of HI in order to focus the company on a pure systems play. In turn, changes in the technological infrastructure and the hiring plans of the company were made in order to reflect the firm's new focus. These changes were submitted to the same "consistency check" as the original business model of the company, and further changes were made based on queries from the venture fund managers about the internal consistency of the resulting, systems-oriented business model.

By contrast, the federal agency treated the HI business plan as *data* that either confirmed or disconfirmed the set of guidelines and heuristics that had accumulated within the bureaucracy as a result of past experience with similar loans. It was these guidelines and heuristics that functioned as the model or theory in the federal agency's approach to the due diligence process. The guidelines, however, were not necessarily submitted to any critical inquiry, either externally, from the data (if the firm's plans ran afoul of the guidelines, then they would either have to be modified [via information passed to the firm by the go-between that had been hired by the firm] or the firm's proposal would be rejected)— or internally, via consistency checks. It was not checked, for example, that the expectations about product introductions and return on investment would match the technological profile of HI (as the guidelines had been derived from a database of firms in very different technological fields), and that the technological development work that would be funded by the agency would be consistent with the financial goals that would function as "litmus tests" for the success or failure of the program. As a result, tensions in the business plan of HI (such as "chips versus systems") went unnoticed in the federal agency's due diligence process and were not brought up in discussions with HI managers. Moreover, when HI's business plan changed as a result of discussions with members of the venture group, the federal agency's managers did not reexamine HI's standing application for internal consistency, but simply insisted that the new figures be made to conform to the guidelines that had internally been set forth.

22.5 Organizational Epistemology and Due Diligence Processes: A Summary and Further Research Questions

The processes described in this chapter can be paraphrased as follows. Due diligence is akin to scientific discovery. A model of the opportunity is articulated and then tested against observation statements that are collected during the due diligence process. The results of these tests are then incorporated back into the model, the model is revised accordingly, and the process begins anew. At some point, a decision has to be made concerning the validity of the model. One has to decide whether or not, given the model and the balance of the evidence, the model is to be accepted or rejected. Classical epistemology contributes several frameworks for understanding the processes of discovery, which in turn can be used to understand and cognitively map due diligence processes. Justificationist procedures focus on seeking evidence for the model in question. Various forms of justificationism focus on shielding the assumptions of the model from refutation by observation statements. Dogmatic justificationism, the most common and straightforward form of justificationism, simply holds the assumptions of the model as a set of axioms that must be true independently of the observation set. By contrast, falsificationist approaches to due diligence processes focus on seeking evidence against a particular model and therefore on (a) making the hypotheses that logically follow from the model testable against observation statements, and (b) conducting tests that aim to falsify rather than verify the core assumptions of the model. In methodological forms of falsificationism, the observation statements are themselves fallible. They can be criticized using other theories (as in the case of optical and cognitive illusions) or by observation statements that challenge the credibility of the initial observation statements (as in the process of checking references on the credibility of a particular reference and incorporating these reports in the initial model).

The government agency displayed a prototypically justificationist approach to the due diligence process. Its model or theory was the set of internally derived guidelines about what constitutes a viable opportunity. Only viable opportunities are to be approved. Once the opportunity

"passed" an initial set of hurdles, the process of due diligence turned into one of finding reasons for investing in the firm from among the data supplied by the company. The credibility of the data seemed to be taken for granted, possibly because of the desire to fund the company once the initial guidelines were met. One possible explanation for this is the typical circular justificationist argument that a noncredible company would not have passed the initial hurdles raised by the approvals process, therefore, if the company passed these hurdles, then it must be the case that it conforms to the prototype of a successful company. One attribute of a successful company is the credibility of its data, as action predicated on poor data is bound to produce failure. One can deduce that the firm's data must be credible, given that its proposal conforms to the "successful" company prototype. Information about what the agency's managers expected would be that the attributes of a successful company had been passed to the firm by the consultant hired to make the process go more smoothly on both sides. Therefore, the company had all the information required to make its project conform to the mental image of a project approved by the federal agency's managers. Thus, there was, indeed, no opportunity to disconfirm these models.

By contrast, the venture firm's approach to due diligence more closely resembled that of a sophisticated methodological falsificationist. The model was derived from the business plan presented by the company. The assumptions of the model were checked for internal consistency. This is crucial to the process of subsequent validation, as any statement whatsoever can follow from a set of mutually contradictory statements, and therefore any observation statement can be said to confirm or disconfirm an internally inconsistent set of propositions. The inquiry process that followed stressed the search for reasons against accepting the firm's business model. Testable implications of the model were checked against market data and the private information of members of the venture fund. Moreover, any claim in an official document is a claim to *truthfulness*, not just truthlikeness. In putting forth a set of propositions that mapped current market conditions to their own actions and a set of future payoffs for the firm's backers, HI's managers made a claim to veracity, not just a claim to accuracy. Accordingly, their own credibility was considered part of the propositional set that was to be tested. Extensive reference checks, using both names supplied by the managers and names not supplied by the managers (including credit reporting agencies), were performed by the venture fund's managers. Apparent discrepancies between the data collected and the business models and the implicit claims to veracity of the managers were not simply held to be conclusive about the opportunity. In true methodological falsificationist fashion, the observation statements were considered to be fallible, and the venture fund's managers turned to the best possible critics of these observation statements: the fund's managers themselves, who were confronted with many of the negative tests of their model and core assumptions. Their comments and rebuttals were incorporated in a "revised" model of the opportunity that was again submitted to critical testing.

Obviously, if the process is typical of due diligence processes in venture funds, then several opportunities are tested in parallel, and a decision is made to go forward with the projects that have stood up most favorably to the due diligence process. It is important to note, however, that due to the "negative" nature of the due diligence process, "most favorably" does not mean "most positively," but rather "least negatively."

The "negative heuristic" (Lakatos 1974) that the falsificationist approach to checking models and theories entails commits the inquirer to picking "the best of the least" rather than "the best of the best," as in the case of the justificationist, who picks the model or theory *for* which he or she has the most reasons. However, the substantial differential in returns between venture capital funds on the one hand and large organizations that are more likely to use a justificationist model of inquiry on the other hand may be partly explained by the difference in the validity of the models produced by the very different approaches to due diligence that these various organizations have.

References

Albert, H. (1985) *Treatise on Critical Reason* Princeton: Princeton University Press.

Argyris, C. (1990) *Overcoming Organizational Defenses: Facilitating Organizational Learning.* Needham: Allyn and Bacon.

Barnes, B., Henry, J., and Bloor, D. (1996) *Scientific Knowledge: A Sociological Analysis.* Chicago: University of Chicago Press.

Daft, R. and Weick, K.E. (1984) "Toward a model of organizations as interpretation systems." *Academy of Management Review* 9:284–295.

Eisenhardt, K. and Zbaracki, M.J. (1992) "Strategic decision making." *Strategic Management Journal* 13:17–37.

Kahneman, D. and Lovallo, D. (1994) "Timid Choices and Bold Forecasts: A Cognitive Perspective on Risk Taking," in R.P. Rumelt, D.E. Schendel, and D. Teece (eds.), *Fundamental Issues in Strategy.* Boston: Harvard Business School Press.

Kuhn, T. (1970) *The Structure of Scientific Revolutions.* Chicago: University of Chicago Press.

Lakatos, I. (1974) "Falsification and the Methodology of Scientific Research Programmes," in I. Lakatos, and A. Musgrave (eds.), *Criticism and the Growth of Knowledge.* New York: Cambridge University Press.

Levitt, B. and March, J. (1988) "Organizational Learning." *Annual Review of Sociology* 14:319–340.

March, J. (1991) "Exploration and Exploitation in Organizational Learning." *Organization Science* 2:71–87.

Noda, T. (1995) "The Dynamics of New Business Development in Large Complex Firms." D.B.A. diss., Harvard Business School.

Noda, T. and Bower, J.L. (1996) "Strategy Making as Iterated Processes of Resource Allocation." *Strategic Management Journal* 21:417–433.

Nonaka, I. (1994) "A Dynamic Theory of Organizational Knowledge Creation." *Organization Science* 5:22–46.

Pfeffer, J. and Sutton, R. (1999) *The Knowing/Doing Gap.* Boston: HBS Press.

Popper, K.R. [1940] (1972) *Objective Knowledge.* London: Routledge.

Popper, K.R. [1959] (1992) *The Logic of Scientific Discovery.* London: Routledge.

Quine, W.v.O. and Ullian, D. (1970) *The Web of Belief.* Cambridge: Harvard University Press.

Seeley-Brown, J. and Duguid, P. (1991) "Organizational learning and communities of practice: Toward a unified view of working, learning and innovation." *Organization Science* 2:40–57.

Staw, B.M. (1976) "Knee-Deep in the Big Muddy: A Study of Organizational Commitment to a Chosen Course of Action." *Organizational Behavior and Human Performance* 16:27–44.

Weick, K.E. (1991) "The Non-traditional Quality of Organizational Learning." *Organization Science* 2:35–45.

23

National Culture and Knowledge Management in a Global Learning Organization

A Case Study

Youngjin Yoo and Ben Torrey

The vast size of modern global enterprises; the speed with which the markets move; the increased knowledge of clients, customers, and competitors; and increased demands for personalization and specialization in products and services all come together to demand that organizations be as smart and knowledgeable as they can be. The only way that this is possible is for the members of the organization to share their knowledge rapidly and widely within the organization and for each person to make use of the best and most current knowledge. In order to support such knowledge sharing systematically, many companies have adopted knowledge management practices and implemented worldwide knowledge management systems utilizing global communications networks and groupware technology.

If, however, the tools and processes designed to manage the knowledge and facilitate the sharing do not take into account the differing national cultures represented by the different parts of the organization, there will be severe impediments preventing the vital circulation of the modern enterprise's life's blood—knowledge. In much the same way, enterprises built and operated within cultures that do not recognize the need for such knowledge sharing or that do not understand or accept modern knowledge management practices are at a distinct disadvantage in the global arena unless they address these issues.

While much has been written about the role of organizational culture in knowledge management and knowledge sharing, the role of national culture in these practices needs to be explored. Occasional mentions of experiences where differences in national culture affected knowledge management efforts appear in the literature, but there is little theoretical and systematic empirical work (Torrey and Datta 1999).

To fill this void, we hope, in this chapter, to show how vital it is to address the issue of national culture as it relates to knowledge sharing.

To this end, we review the literature with an aim to better understand the potential role of national cultures in various aspects of knowledge management. In particular, we are interested in differences between Eastern and Western cultures. We then present a case study conducted at Accenture, known as Andersen Consulting at the time of the study, to illustrate how different national cultures influence individual consultants in their daily knowledge management and knowledge sharing behaviors. We end the chapter with a discussion of the implications of our findings for future research and for knowledge management practices by suggesting possible ways to address some of the issues raised by our conclusions.

National Culture and Knowledge Management

Much has been made of the importance of organizational culture for the success or failure of knowledge management and knowledge sharing in the modern enterprise. Studies have shown that culture can make or break efforts to manage knowledge effectively within an organization (Orlikowski 1992, Bair et al. 1997, Skyrme and Amidon 1997, Davenport and Prusak 1998, Wenger 1998, Leonard-Barton 1995). Yet, in all that has been written, the influence of national culture on knowledge sharing in multinational corporations is relatively unexplored. The existing works on the role of national cultures in relation to knowledge management (Nonaka and Takeuchi 1995, Hedlund 1994, Lam 1997) often rely on comparisons between Japanese companies and Western companies, making it difficult to distinguish the role of national and organizational culture. Furthermore, by emphasizing the differences between Japanese and Western "organizations," these prior works have not fully explored the differences in behavioral and cognitive differences among "individuals" in different cultures.

Yet, as we think about knowledge, knowledge management, and knowledge sharing, we are struck with how laden with values these concepts and practices are. Knowledge is closely related to truth and power. Sharing knowledge relates to trust, integrity, and status. Managing knowledge involves people at some of their deepest levels of emotion and belief. We are dealing with something much more than the practices of organizations—we are dealing with very personal matters.

Existing literature suggests that national culture influences the world of business, global enterprises, national economies, diplomacy, and so forth (Hofstede 1984, Hofstede 1991, Hampden-Turner and Trompenaars 1997). Hofstede (1991) has shown that organizational culture is really a matter of practices, whereas the core of national culture is values. He identifies five such values: power distance, individualism, masculinity, uncertainty avoidance, and long-term orientation. He shows that these values, which "are programmed early in our lives," are strong determinants of our assumptions and behaviors. Members of a given society or nation will have generally similar values; this forms the basis of a culture (Hofstede 1984). While organizations may have a common set of symbols, heroes, and rituals (with values, the four components of national culture) that may give it a sense of culture, without the values, these are only shared practices. In truth, the *values* of the organization's founders become the *practices* of the employees (Hofstede 1991).

Through more than 15 years of research with attendees at more than 1,000 cross-cultural training programs in more than 20 countries and with some 30 multinational firms, yielding a database of 30,000 completed questionnaires, Hampden-Turner and Trompenaars (1993, 1997, Trompenaars and Hampden-Turner 1998) have explored their question, "if any of the American management techniques and philosophy we were brainwashed with in many years of the best business education money could buy would apply in the Netherlands or the UK, where we came from, or indeed in the rest of the world" (Trompenaars and Hampden-Turner 1998, p. 1). Viewing culture as the way in which a group of people solves problems and reconciles dilemmas (Trompenaars and Hampden-Turner 1998, p. 6, Schein 1985), they point out how the many different groups that make up global society have developed many different ways to solve the same or similar problems. They categorize these as dilemmas that arise from human relationships, the passage of time, and relations with the environment. In much the same way that Hofstede ranks cultures on a scale of values between opposite extremes, so do they contrast a number of things. Adopting Parsons's five relational orientations as their starting point (Parsons 1951), they look at universalism and particularism, individualism and communitarianism, neutral and emotional, specific and diffuse, and achievement and ascription. They also examine attitudes to time and to nature. They point out how these perspectives, these problem-solving orientations pervade every aspect of one's life—private and public, personal and corporate (Trompenaars and Hampden-Turner 1998).

Given that the influence of national culture is so pervasive, one can expect that the way in which individuals manage knowledge in their work would also be influenced by national culture. Below, we examine how national cultures might influence individuals' knowledge management practices, including knowledge creation, knowledge seeking, and knowledge preservation and sharing.

Creating Knowledge

Before knowledge can be either owned or shared, it must be created. How knowledge is created is one of the fundamental aspects of knowledge management that would seem to be affected profoundly by culture. Different perspectives on what knowledge is cannot help but impinge on this process. Nonaka and Takeuchi (1995) explore this issue at length, showing how the process works in Japanese companies, contrasting it to Western habits of thought. They compare the greater emphasis in Japan on collective effort, the use of metaphors to trigger thinking, and the reliance on sharing tacit knowledge in informal contexts and through observation with the Western reliance on individual effort, explicit knowledge transfer (manuals, documentation, etc.), and the careful, conscious articulation of exact ideas for knowledge creation. Hampden-Turner and Trompenaars (1997), in their *Mastering the Infinite Game*, make a similar point as they contrast East Asian and Western thought. They note that "[w]hile Sino-Japanese culture saw latent, uncodified knowledge as the well-springs of knowledge itself, Western cultures felt this barely qualified as knowledge at all, unless it was in the process of being codified in which case it would literally 'count'" (p. 197). We see here the concept that knowledge almost "grows" from preexisting knowledge, whereas the Western perspective sees it as the result of accountable, planned activity.

Ideas about collaboration and competition can also have a profound effect on knowledge creation and on how individuals work harmoniously in groups or competitively as individuals. Hampden-Turner and Trompenaars (1997) discuss the East Asian ideas about complementarity—the harmonizing of yin and yang, of opposites. They contrast the Western attitudes that result in "finite games" with the "infinite games" of the East. "East Asian cultures are ancient frameworks for comprehending the complementarity of values, which most Western cultures lack. What we see depends on how we look and what our values are . . . complementarity is at the roots of scientific inquiry" (p. 17). Rather than seeing things as an "either/or" situation, they are seen as "both/and." This sense of combining, rather than excluding, would seem to influence significantly the way ideas are combined to create new knowledge—possibly to synthesize disparate ideas and experiences in ways that might not occur to Western practitioners. Reflecting the East Asian emphasis on complementarity and dialectic synthesis, Nonaka and Takeuchi (1995) explore the importance of combination in the process of knowledge creation in the Japanese context.

Seeking Knowledge

Attitudes toward authority—whether it be organizational or informational—would have a profound effect on where one looks for knowledge or expects to find that which is valuable, as well as how freely one shares one's thoughts and ideas, whether or not one is willing to risk contradicting accepted authority, or even if there is a risk in so doing. Different cultures exhibit very different behavior toward authority. As noted earlier, Hofstede (1991) has identified power distance as one of five fundamental values that differentiate cultures. According to him, power distance refers to the degree of inequality among people that the population of a country accepts as "normal." As such, individuals in cultures with a low power distance would be likely to take any official pronouncement as something to be immediately and openly challenged, while those in contrasting cultures would not even think of voicing a contradictory idea. Similarly, in cultures with high power distance, juniors take their cues from seniors concerning information, processes, and so forth rather than trust equals to set direction and those under them to provide valuable input.

This difference raises several questions related to individuals' knowledge-seeking behaviors. Can an organization depend on meaningful collaboration and knowledge sharing if its members are afraid to challenge the ideas of "authorities"—real or perceived? On the other hand, can the vehicles that allow for modifying the established understanding in cultures that resist challenge to authority be effective in contrasting cultures? Also, is it possible to capitalize on regard for authority in redirecting individuals to other sources of knowledge—seniors directing juniors to consult certain peers or to use certain sources or even to contribute their own tacit knowledge?

Another factor that might affect the seeking and use of knowledge is Hofstede's "uncertainty avoidance." Uncertainty avoidance refers to the degree to which people in the culture prefer structured over unstructured situations. One might think that in those cultures that tend to have a low uncertainty avoidance, there would be a greater ease in taking various types of explicit knowledge from various sources of less-assured quality and integrating them to create something new. This would contrast with a high uncertainty avoidance, which would lead a knowledge seeker to look for precise matches to his or her need and to look for the authoritative version.

On Hofstede's scale, the English-speaking countries all rank low on both power distance and uncertainty avoidance, while the Hispanic countries are uniformly quite high on the uncertainty avoidance index and tend to be high on power distance. Thus, one can expect that while English speakers would find it much easier to draw from different sources and to integrate the results, Spanish speakers might be more likely to require authoritative, finished, explicit knowledge. Yet still another perspective would be the East Asian. An interesting factor is that these countries all score high on power distance but are split when it comes to uncertainty avoidance; some are quite high (Korea, Japan), some are quite low (Hong Kong, Malaysia, China), and a few are somewhat above the mean (Taiwan, Thailand). The question can be raised as to how complementarity might or might not counter uncertainty avoidance and whether it might affect the process of synthesizing less specific and more diverse knowledge content.

Preserving and Sharing Knowledge

Sharing knowledge is one of our most fundamental imperatives. Without it, we would be unlikely to survive childhood. Beginning with the first things a mother teaches her infant, to the parental nurturing and the "mental programming" that imparts to us our culture, the experiences shared with playmates through the years of formal education and into adulthood, we are the beneficiaries of shared knowledge and the richness of all the relationships involved. Almost from the beginning, we, in turn, become sharers of knowledge, passing along to others the excitement of our discoveries, the experiences that we have, the ideas that become our passion (Vigotsky 1978).

Such knowledge, gained within the give and take of shared experience, becomes the memories upon which we build our lives. The literature has shown the shared nature of memory and the importance of the group for building these foundations (Hutchins 1995, Resnick et al. 1991, Levine et al. 1993, Giddens 1984). Halbwachs (1952, p. 38) states succinctly that "[i]t is in society that people normally acquire their memories. It is also in society that they recall, recognize, and localize their memories. . . . It is in this sense that there exists a collective memory and social frameworks for memory; it is to the degree that our individual thought places itself in these frameworks and participates in this memory that it is capable of that act of recollection." He further notes that the individual and the group together create and remember memories by noting that "[o]ne may say that the individual remembers by placing himself in the perspective of the group, but one may also affirm that the memory of the group realizes and manifests itself in individual memories" (p. 40).

If knowledge sharing is so universal an aspect of the human experience and crucial to relationships, then why is there an issue when it comes to sharing in the organizational context? Precisely because it is such a relational activity. To share knowledge is to expose oneself to others, to give power to others, to demonstrate one's ability (or lack thereof) (Wenger 1998). These are not done lightly. Since it is also a communal act—especially in the context of knowledge management and the modern enterprise—our attitudes toward the community become extremely important. These attitudes are based on the values that form the core of our culture.

This raises questions about how certain values may be called on to encourage the sharing of knowledge—to overcome the barriers. For example, do different cultures have different attitudes to such things as experiences, lessons learned, or technical material—specifications, product or process descriptions? How do culturally specific attitudes toward the preservation of the past affect knowledge sharing? Similarly, different perspectives on the relationship between the individual and the group would most likely have an effect on what is remembered and passed on, as well as the "how" of this. For example, the strong sense of community found in the East might be brought into play to overcome barriers that come from attitudes toward authority (Torrey and Datta 1999).

Related to cultural values are ideas about organizations themselves. In some cultures, there is a strong sense that organizations are and should be hierarchical and patriarchal, while in others, egalitarianism and flatter structures are the accepted norms (Hofstede 1991, Trompenaars and Hampden-Turner 1998). These assumptions would affect how people share knowledge within the organization, both vertically and horizontally. Rigid hierarchical structures may prevent knowledge being shared up the hierarchy as suggestions or feedback, and also laterally, if it is assumed that all knowledge comes down the hierarchy from above. Egalitarian structures, on the other hand, may indicate strong individualism that may inhibit the acceptance of knowledge shared by others. Structures that keep individuals in closed circles may experience a "silo" effect that prevents knowledge from being shared from one group to another within the organization. A number of examples of this effect have been described by Pfeffer and Sutton (2000).

Time is another factor. It has been pointed out that East Asian cultures tend to reflect a very different perspective on time than do Western cultures. There is less concern for immediate return and a greater ease with allowing events to take their time and run their course. Persistence and the long-term view are of more value than attempts to "seize the moment" or catch every wind of change (Hofstede 1991, Hampden-Turner and Trompenaars 1993, Hampden-Turner and Trompenaars 1997). In contrast to this view, the field of knowledge management seeks to address the need for the rapid dissemination of knowledge in the present commercial environment, where speed is of the essence—at least as it is seen in the West. The ways in which such differences in time focus would affect knowledge sharing processes in global organizations would be a key question to explore.

Finally, storytelling is one of the most ancient means of sharing knowledge, but, as Orr (1990) has demonstrated, it is extremely important in the modern day as well. Orr describes the process of transferring tacit knowledge among photocopier repair technicians. He posits "community memory" as the repository of largely tacit knowledge related to the successful servicing of clients' machines. Storytelling is crucial in this context. As the knowledge management community confronts the need for increasing tacit-to-tacit knowledge transfer in the modern environment, where the speed of change and the press of work inhibit the process of making tacit knowledge explicit by creating documentation, articles, etc., practitioners are looking to storytelling as a serious knowledge sharing mechanism and the recording of stories as an easier way to explicate tacit knowledge. Since storytelling is such an ancient practice and one with many cultural aspects, the question certainly arises as to how culture would affect this in the modern business context.

Case Study

To begin to understand the influences of national culture on individuals' daily knowledge management and knowledge sharing practices, we conducted a field study at Accenture ("the firm," hereafter). The firm has offices in 80 different countries and has about 65,000 consultants. To support effective knowledge management and knowledge sharing at a global level, the firm has developed and implemented a global knowledge management system called the Knowledge Xchange System ("Knowledge Xchange," "KX system," or "KX," hereafter). Furthermore, the leadership of the firm consistently emphasizes the importance to the firm's success of effective knowledge management and knowledge sharing among individual consultants.

Accenture was chosen for the study for three primary reasons: (1) the firm is recognized as an early and effective adopter of knowledge management practices and systems; (2) it has a strong global presence and has implemented knowledge globally; and (3) it has a strong organizational culture (often referred to as the "Andersen way") that includes an in-residence program for all new recruits from around the world at its training campus in St. Charles, Illinois, as well as various standard methodologies used by consultants in different areas. As pointed out earlier, previous studies in this area have looked primarily at Japanese firms, confusing the effects of national and organizational culture. By focusing on one global company with a strong organizational culture, we are able to examine the role of the different national cultures on individuals' knowledge management and knowledge sharing practices.

The firm's primary knowledge management system is the Knowledge Xchange. Conceived in 1991, the system was fully implemented by 1993 and rolled out across the global enterprise. The Horizon 2000 report, released in March 1992, contained the following statement: "We will establish 'Knowledge Management' as a new function within Accenture. Key responsibilities will be to ensure the leading edge currency of our knowledge capital, and to keep the Knowledge Exchange demand driven rather than supply driven." The Knowledge Xchange is currently a system of 4500 Lotus Notes databases, containing both internal and external information in document repositories, special applications known as practice aids, discussion databases, and directories. This system and all knowledge management practices within the firm are supported by over 500 full-time knowledge management professionals. Internal knowledge capital in the repositories consists of such things as client deliverables, white papers, evaluations, presentations, proposals, methodologies, best practices, and tools. External information includes subscription databases provided by arrangement with content vendors, Internet newsgroups and Internet based services, news feeds, and the like. The Knowledge Xchange is available for all employees to access from laptop or desktop PCs over Accenture's global area network, by dialing in to the network remotely, through the networks at client sites where connectivity arrangements have been made, or over the local area networks in each Accenture office. The KX system is constantly undergoing development and revision in order that content remain current, to adapt to changing needs, and to reflect changes in the firm's organization and priorities. New technologies are applied as needed.

We conducted our study in two countries: Korea and the United States. According to previous cross-cultural studies, these two countries differ substantially in all dimensions of Hofstede's theory. As shown in table 23.1 below, on a scale from 0 to 100, Hofstede indicates that, compared with Americans, Koreans are more likely to respect authority (high "power distance"), think in terms of community rather than the individual (low "individualism"), be more concerned about care for others and quality of life (low "masculinity"), look for longer-term results (high "long-term orientation"), and feel more threatened by uncertainty and ambiguity (high "uncertainty avoidance"). Furthermore, although Korean culture is similar to that of other Asian countries in that it is heavily influenced by Confucian philosophy, it differs from that of China and Japan. For example, in Korea, the focus is on *inwha* (harmony based on respect for hierarchical relationships and obedience to authority), while in China, the focus is on *guanxi* (personal relationships) and in Japan on *wa* (group harmony and social cohesion) (Alston 1989).

Given the differences in the various cultural dimensions, we expect that individual consultants' knowledge management behaviors in these two countries—within and outside the firm's knowledge management system—would reflect the cultural differences between them. The purpose of our study was to examine empirically whether and how these cultural differences manifest themselves in individual consultants' daily knowledge management and knowledge sharing practices.

The data were collected primarily by in-depth individual interviews with 53 consultants—22 in Korea and 31 in the United States. All interviewed consultants had been with the firm between two and five years. The average ages of Korean and American consultants were 29.6 and 28.3, respectively. All interviews in Korea were conducted in Korean and in the United States in English. All interviews were tape recorded and transcribed for data analyses.

Each interview lasted about an hour and was conducted in the native language of the interviewee. We conducted semistructured interviews, using a critical incident method. Specifically, we asked each consultant his or her most recent and significant experiences in knowledge creation, seeking, and preservation and sharing. Thus, each interviewed consultant told us three

TABLE 23.1 Values for Hofstede's five dimensions for South Korea and the United States

	Power Distance	Individualism	Masculinity	Long-term Orientation	Uncertainty Avoidance
South Korea	60	18	39	75	85
United States	40	91	62	29	46

recent critical incidents, one for each phase of knowledge management. We probed the nature of the incidents by asking follow-up questions. We also asked consultants about their general perceptions of the KX system including usefulness, impediments to effective use, and the perceived usage of the systems.

The data were analyzed by the first author, who is fluent in both languages. Following the recommendations by Eisenhardt (1989) and Yin (1994), each interview transcript was treated as a single case. Each interview transcript was subjected to a within-case analysis that involved repeatedly reading the transcript and taking thorough notes. For each case, we summarized into a few short phrases the key aspects of the interviewee's experience in knowledge creation, knowledge seeking, and knowledge preservation and sharing. After the individual interviews had been analyzed, we began cross-case comparisons that involved listing similarities and differences between the U.S. and Korean consultants in the sample.

Results

The interviews identified major differences between the U.S. and Korean consultants along the dimensions identified above. In this section, we summarize these differences.

Creating Knowledge

We asked consultants to describe their most recent significant experiences with knowledge creation. With the exception of a few U.S. consultants, who described their involvement in leading-edge technology development projects, most consultants in both countries described their knowledge creation as a rather minor activity; however, we observed several stark differences in the knowledge creation process in terms of forms, outcomes, and collaboration. These differences seem to arise from differences in long-term orientation and individualism between the two cultures.

First, in both countries, two common forms of knowledge creation were observed: invention and integration. Although consultants in both countries mentioned both forms of knowledge creation, there was a strong emphasis on integration among Korean consultants.

In more than 70% of the cases, U.S. consultants believed that new knowledge was invented

as a result of their activities. This form of knowledge creation is similar to the notion of "problem-solving" as a source of innovation, as observed by Leonard-Barton (1995). For example, one U.S. consultant said, "I guess there wasn't any previously documented or laid out procedures that we could follow and . . . model after. There were a few, but we basically had to go in and . . . document the 'as is' of how the company was functioning and then go ahead and brainstorm and look at different pieces of information from other . . . places and companies and try to come up with our own model."

Another U.S. consultant said, "We had never used the tool and we had never completely integrated with that GUI, the test management tool. And, I had looked around and asked about other projects, and specifically people had done it, but no one had done it with the SAP per se."

On the other hand, integration and modification were the frequently described forms of knowledge creation by Korean consultants. Furthermore, many Korean consultants had difficulty finding an example of creating new knowledge. This is similar to combination and internalization as conceptualized by Nonaka and Takeuchi (1995). For example, one Korean consultant stated[1]

> I typically work on data warehousing projects and, although you can get deliverables of similar projects stored in [Accenture's] knowledge base, many of them need to be customized for the situations in Korea and the client. Therefore, nothing fits perfectly, so I can say almost everything I did was re-created by myself. . . . [Accenture] provides issues that we need to be aware of (learned from other projects), templates, standardized processes, and the methodology. Using those, we went to the client site and received the new requirements, and modified our methodology to fit with the requirements.

Another Korean consultant who received a Ph.D. in the United States said

> I used to work for [a local Korean consulting company] for about three years. At that time, we did not have any particular methodology, so we continued to study and develop new methodologies for our projects. That experience can be very helpful for basic consulting approaches in general. I have shared much of my experiences with my

team members. . . . Although Andersen has many methodologies, I often graft my experiences into those general methodologies.

We also found differences in the perceived outcome of knowledge creation processes. When asked to describe the outcomes of the knowledge creation process, about half of Korean consultants described the outcomes of their knowledge creation as templates or models that can be readily used by other individuals in the firm, while only one-third of U.S. consultants expressed general knowledge as the outcomes of their knowledge creation processes. On the contrary, about 75% of U.S. consultants viewed client-specific deliverables as the outcomes of their knowledge creation processes. This difference is related to the long-term versus short-term orientation of the two cultures. According to Hofstede (1991), Korean culture shows much stronger long-term orientation than U.S. culture. Korean consultants' tendency to focus on standards and templates seems to reflect this long-term orientation, while U.S. consultants' focus on deliverables seems to reflect the short-term orientation of their culture.

Another difference observed was that while more than half of Korean consultants viewed their knowledge creation as a group effort, over 80% of U.S. consultants said it was an individual effort, even though both groups generally work in teams, seldom as individuals. This clearly reflects the collective and individualistic natures of Korean and U.S. cultures, respectively (Hofstede 1993, Kim and Nam 1998).

Seeking Knowledge

Despite the strong organizational culture of knowledge sharing and the universal training on and access to the KX system, evidence from the study clearly shows different patterns of knowledge search by individual consultants in Korea and the United States. We observed differences in consultants' knowledge seeking behavior both using and not using the KX system. These differences appear to stem from the different cultural orientations toward power and authority in the two cultures. As evidenced by Hofstede (1991) and others (e.g., Alston 1989), Korean culture is highly hierarchical, valuing seniority and position.

When using the KX system, Korean consultants focused on "best practices" or the latest version of templates or the methodology, while U.S.

consultants seldom mentioned the term "best practices" in the context of knowledge seeking. It seems Korean consultants' and their clients' primary motivation for using the knowledge repository is to establish the "authority" of their solutions by importing the best practices implemented in other leading global companies. The following comments are revealing.

The most difficult part of the search was to identify what was the latest version.

Although we can come up with the solution through brainstorming, we always look for the best practice—this way we can confirm. These best practices are confirmed guidelines stored in the KX system. We tend to modify these best practices.

The biggest benefit of the KX system to me is to be able to say that I know that there is the best practice for such a case. If I cannot show the best practice and have to make it up by myself, I cannot even speak in front of the client.

On the other hand, some U.S. consultants were skeptical about the notion of best practices, as reflected in the following comments.

Because by nature of our business, our solutions are always tailored for specific clients' needs, though it's going to be very rare that you're going to actually find something that was used on another project that is, you know, exactly meeting your client's needs.

Everything is unique, even though you can use general basic guidelines and general, you know, general approaches, you can't, I don't think you should ever, I don't think you could ever really overlay.

Similarly, while both Korean and U.S. consultants have had no experience of finding in the KX system a solution that fit the problem perfectly, their thinking about this was quite different. More than 80% of Korean consultants believed that someone in the global Accenture organization possessed the knowledge that they sought, and the reason that they could not find the knowledge was because of the limitations of the KX system. For example, one Korean consultant said "in reality, there are people who're holding answers for my problem. We have collected that information in one place. It is a database about engagements. I can look at the list of people in the database to contact them. Frankly, although that is the right process and I try it out, I don't expect to hear from others, because I am in the Seoul office."

Another Korean consultant echoed a similar opinion. "I believe that the KX system has what I need, although each client is different. . . . If you really need to get the real solution, you need to contact the people, which is frustrating."

On the other hand, a much smaller number of U.S. consultants expect to find a perfect solution for their problems, because they feel that every situation is unique and requires different approaches. For example, one U.S. consultant said

I would fall over if I found a 100 percent ready solution. Because every client is so different and the variables that just go into the project, I mean, there's so many things that can change or be a little bit off here or a little off there and even if your situation's the same, you could have two clients with the same situation and their management will ask for something different. So I would never expect to find a 100 percent solution. Usually what I'm looking for is a good starting point. I'm looking for a good basis to go forward from.

In addition to respect for authority, these differences seem to reflect the differences in uncertainty avoidance between the two cultures. The American culture is tolerant toward uncertainty and ambiguity for the sake of exploration, while Korean society traditionally values stability and certainty.

Korean and U.S. consultants showed differences in their search patterns, as well. One such difference was related to the credibility of the knowledge source. When a consultant conducts a key word search on a particular topic in the KX system, the system returns a list of documents along with author names and synopses of the documents. From the list, the consultant can decide which documents to "order" for downloading from the system. None of the U.S. consultants said they paid attention to the author's name in this process. Instead, they focused exclusively on the synopsis to determine the usefulness of the document for their problem. In contrast, several Korean consultants said that they developed a "preferred author list" and ordered documents developed by those authors

first. One Korean consultant who was involved in several training projects said "first, the topic and then it is the author name. I look at the author name because I can trust certain names. . . . There is a person who did many training-related projects. . . . I encountered his name in many searches and found that he did lots of training projects. So, it is better just to order his latest training project."

Another Korean consultant expressed a similar experience. "After all, I tend to order documents from the same author again and again. . . . I didn't intend to order documents from the same person, but now I look at his/her documents a lot."

Korean and U.S. consultants also showed several differences in their knowledge search patterns outside the KX system. While about half of U.S. consultants preferred to get help from their peers, virtually all Korean consultants expressed their reliance on their superiors, as evidenced by the following comment of one Korean consultant. "I don't know how he did it, but my project manager contacted someone for the topic, probably someone within Andersen in the U.S., and forwarded the reply to me. He told me that I would need that information."

Interestingly, this reliance on superiors influenced Korean consultants' usage of the KX system as well. That is, in many cases, Korean consultants verified with their superiors the way they conducted searches on the KX. Two Korean consultants made the following comments.

My project managers gave me the initial set of key words for my search. It was very helpful.

When I cannot find what I need from the KX system, I go to my project manager and tell him that I have difficulty in finding what I need. Then, usually he tells me do this, do that, and they are very helpful. . . . If I can only think of keyword A, my project manager who has more experience can tell me to do a search on A1, A2, A3, etc.

Similarly, there was a clear hierarchical differentiation of roles in the Seoul office that was manifested in several different ways. First, Korean consultants felt that posting their project results on the KX was their superiors' responsibility. Second, Korean consultants felt that contacting foreign "experts" was also their superiors' responsibility. In certain situations, consultants communicate with foreign experts using their superior's e-mail account to "legitimize" themselves by leveling themselves up, as is shown in the following comment. "I didn't know whether it was appropriate to contact these people. Some of them were partners. So I asked my project managers whether I should contact these people. He told me that I should send e-mail using his name and e-mail address."

In the context of knowledge seeking outside the KX, Korean and U.S. consultants showed another stark difference in terms of with whom they communicated beyond their immediate team members. More than half of U.S. consultants included software and hardware vendors, expert user groups on the Internet, and other publicly available reports such as those published by the Gartner Group. On the other hand, several Korean consultants often referred to their own friends from college and high school as an important source of knowledge when they needed to search beyond the boundary of the firm. In some cases, this social network seemed to work effectively, even between friends employed by competing companies, as demonstrated by the following Korean consultant.

Next, my college friends are at different consulting companies and they gave me a few leads for this problem. . . . My background is computer science and my friends are working at other foreign consulting companies or companies like IBM or Oracle. I needed information about those companies and fortunately, I had at least one friend at each of those companies. So I called them up.

This seems to imply that the use of weak ties in knowledge search and transfer (Hansen 1999, Constant et al. 1996) may not be as effective in Korea or other similar Eastern cultures as it is in Western culture.

Preserving and Sharing Knowledge

We also examined the differences between the two cultures in the context of knowledge preservation. Individual consultants in both countries employ various mechanisms to preserve individual knowledge such as journaling, preserving interim documents and final deliverables, and keeping personal collections of documents from the KX. A significant number of consultants in both countries do not try to preserve know-how and skills acquired through their own personal experiences in explicit documents. Many of them said they simply take "mental notes." Consultants in both countries felt that the documents they produce capture only about 20% to 30% of what they learned from their experiences.

A clear difference between the two cultures seemed to exist in the way they share knowledge within the organization. Compared with U.S. consultants, Korean consultants share their knowledge through informal social settings (e.g., project team dinners) or weekend workshops voluntarily organized by the consultants. This difference seems to reflect flexible boundaries between social and work realms in Korean culture. It is also a way to preserve the knowledge within the community, making it become a part of each person, rather than preserving it as an abstract object in an impersonal system.

When we finished one project, it was a project that we did first in Seoul, we learned a lot. Before we moved on to the next phase, we prepared a lessons learned session for people in our office. We have this kind of workshop about once a month. Only those who are interested in the topic participate. . . . Teams voluntarily prepare such workshops.

About once every other month, all the team members get together to go out for dinner and drink. It is a very important and useful forum for knowledge sharing. . . . We also have regular formal meetings. Both formal and informal meetings are important. They serve different purposes. . . . The formal meetings are where we make decisions. The informal meetings are where we share ideas and opinions much more freely.

Few Korean consultants contribute to the KX system to preserve their knowledge. Those who do are project leaders. On the other hand, U.S. consultants view the KX system as their primary vehicle for knowledge preservation. Although occasionally, U.S. consultants used workshops or seminars to preserve and share their knowledge within the organization, these were rare cases serving specific purposes. All U.S. consultants contributed to the KX system at least once, and most of them did it voluntarily. Also, there were a few U.S. consultants who participated in virtual communities of practices through conference calls.

This difference seems to come from the differences in epistemology in the two countries. As pointed out earlier, while knowledge is often considered as an extension of self, dwelling within the knower in Eastern culture (e.g., Nonaka and Takeuchi 1995), in Western culture, knowledge is often treated as an object, separate from the knower. Also, as noted by Hutchins (1995), often knowledge is considered to be embedded in technological artifacts. These perspectives are reflected in the following comments by U.S. consultants.

> I was in the process of packaging [my knowledge about the project] all up to hand to someone else to do anyway.

> So what we did as a project team is upon completion or near completion of our project, we thoroughly documented the processes that we had defined, the tools that we used to manage the project and to facilitate the transition itself, and captured a lot of those and then saved those out on our Knowledge Xchange for others to use.

This shows that if one looks at the contribution to computerized knowledge repository as the only measure of organizational knowledge preservation and knowledge sharing, the results can produce a very misleading picture. That is, in cultures like Korea, much of organizational knowledge sharing occurs through informal and social settings, not by creating knowledge objects and storing them in systems.

Other Differences

While U.S. consultants did not perceive major differences between U.S. offices and other Accenture offices in foreign countries, Korean consultants often distance themselves from Accenture. Despite the strong global corporate culture and global training systems, Korean consultants frequently referred to the global Accenture organization as "them" and the global KX system as "their" system, while referring to the Seoul office as "us" and its local knowledge repository as "our" system. This seems to reflect the fact that Korea is an ancient country with a single people who speak a single language that often makes its culture very ethnocentric. It may also be related to Korea's strong communitarian orientation, as shown by Hofstede and others. (Korea has a value of 18 on the individualism index compared with 91 for the United States.)

We also asked the consultants how frequently they use the KX system, using two five-point Likert scale questions, in which 1 = "very infrequent" and 5 = "very frequent." We ran a simple t-test to examine the differences in individual consultants' usage of the KX system. The results showed that Korean consultants utilize the KX system more frequently than U.S. consultants ($t = 2.741$, $p < 0.01$). Given the lack of contribution to the KX system by Korean consultants, this result suggests that Korean consultants utilize the KX system to search for best practices and the latest applications of new management skills and methodologies. At the same time, they seem to utilize their social network to share their own experiences and knowledge with other Korean consultants. This disparity in the use of knowledge management systems in the search and preservation of knowledge locally in a global company, which seems, at least in part, to stem from cultural differences between the two countries, can be a significant impediment to effective knowledge management at the global level. We will discuss the managerial and strategic implications of these findings in the next section.

Implications and Conclusions

Strategic Imperative

As organizations compete more and more within a global marketplace and grow to become multinational, it is imperative that they consider, exploit, and compensate for increasing cultural diversity, as evidenced in our study. To the business manager raised and trained in the West, who assumes that the business practices and management techniques developed in Western Europe and North America represent the epitome of progress in these areas, the fact that much of the world operates from very different values and assumptions and within very different contexts frequently comes as a great surprise. Such a manager often assumes that the "foreign" workers just don't understand or simply will not cooperate. Unfortunately, it is the Western manager who usually does not understand and who misses many opportunities for creating cross-cultural synergies that would prove immensely valuable in the marketplace. This is especially true for the realm of knowledge management since it is deeply tied to values.

In this section, we will attempt to explore the implications of our findings for multinational organizations and to suggest some possible ways to address the issues involved, pointing out how these may well provide the organization with significant competitive advantage.

Creating Knowledge

We have seen how the American and Korean consultants differed in their approaches to knowledge creation. The Americans tended to invent more and to take existing knowledge as a starting point or one of many factors to consider. In Korea, on the other hand, consultants were more likely to integrate and modify existing knowledge, which they looked upon as providing the best practice or the industry standard. Both approaches have value—and both can be found in either group, although one will be more the norm in one culture than in the other. We also saw differences in the perceived outcomes of the knowledge creation process. Koreans, taking a longer-term view, looked on their efforts as creating models and templates for future use by others, while Americans focused on immediate deliverables.

Would it not be possible to harness these different perspectives and working styles within multicultural teams working together to both invent and modify, to address the immediate need while creating knowledge objects that may be useful for the longer term through taking a model-creating point of view?

With a sound knowledge of the different cultural tendencies (it is important to remember that we are dealing with tendencies and norms—any given individual may differ considerably from the norm), it should also be possible to develop and carry out specialized training designed to address the cultural differences in meeting the organization's strategic goals. Koreans could be given training that emphasizes the inventive techniques commonly used by the Americans and be encouraged to explore individually, while Americans could be trained to take a longer-term view and focus on working collaboratively. In both cases, it might prove quite valuable to use culturally aware instructors from the "other" culture. Not only would this provide an excellent opportunity to tap the riches of different cultures, but it would also do much to integrate the different cultures within the global enterprise, producing a powerful, highly competitive workforce. Taking a lesson from the East, an organization may orient itself toward a "both/and" approach rather than the West's "either/or."

Seeking Knowledge

The contrast in practices that we have seen between Korean and American consultants in relation to seeking out needed knowledge poses some interesting challenges. While Accenture has a strong focus on developing best practices and defining specific methodologies (items sought more by Koreans than Americans), much of the firm's Knowledge Xchange knowledge management system is more easily used for gathering contact information and for finding examples of prior work. In the context of a highly competitive marketplace, where speed is considered to be essential, it is more rare than not that the types of knowledge objects sought out by Korean consultants are posted to the repository. The heavy emphasis on contacts—even to the creation of directories of subject matter experts—as opposed to highly synthesized, universally applicable knowledge seems to have left the Koreans at a disadvantage. Given the realities of the market for consulting services, it is less likely that types of knowledge objects desired by Korean consultants will be created and posted. This would indicate that special emphasis in training to compensate for some of these tendencies might prove valuable for this and other global firms.

On the other hand, it is important for organizations to keep in mind that national markets have the same cultural values as the consultants native to those cultures. Korean clients may want the same assurance that the materials being used are considered to be "best practices" and industry standards. One way to meet this need might be through a process designed to obtain a "seal of approval" from a recognized expert quickly and painlessly. This approval could be applied to material gleaned and synthesized by the Korean consultant, thereby *making* it a "best practice." If done well, this could also add a valuable level of quality assurance to the development process.

The Koreans' respect for superiors might be exploited by having seniors require juniors to do more in the way of seeking out knowledge on their own and creating new materials rather than relying on supervisors in these areas.

As noted above, the Korean consultants demonstrated a tendency to rely on existing inner-facing social networks in seeking out needed knowledge, rather than exercising the boundary-spanning activities of the Americans, who would frequently look to vendors and other external sources. It has been recognized that this type of behavior can build upon itself, leading to "core rigidity" problems that inhibit innovation (Leonard-Barton 1995, Hansen 1999, Granovetter 1973). This could be addressed through training.

Training in using knowledge resources could be designed with a sensitivity to different attitudes toward power distance, uncertainty avoidance, and affinity to reflect the realities in different cultures.

Preserving and Sharing Knowledge

A very interesting development in the world of knowledge management is the growing recognition of the importance of sharing tacit knowledge directly from person to person, rather than by the process of first making it explicit, then combining and socializing it (Nonaka and Takeuchi 1995, Wenger 1998). It would seem that the Korean practice has an advantage here, in that this appears to be the primary means of knowledge preservation and sharing exercised there. Even so, the explicit packaging of knowledge is still important, and that need will not go away.

This area, again, may be a place where a global organization could exploit the different practices and tendencies of its various national units by recognizing the different values in each and exploring ways to make good use of them. Practitioners skilled in and accustomed to each process could be called on to train and encourage those who are not so comfortable with them. It would be very important to make sure that everyone involved understands that culturally important factors are involved and proceeds with sensitivity toward an understanding of these matters.

Again, the difference in attitudes toward supervisors comes into play. The organization may determine that it is in its best interest to encourage lateral and upward feedback among members of cultures that would have considerable difficulty with this. It may also want to encourage juniors to be more active in capturing and posting their knowledge to the knowledge management system. Experience indicates that it may be possible to harness these very attitudes by having the supervisors promote the value of these practices to the group and make them a required part of the job (Torrey and Datta 1999).

Finally, in considering training itself, it is most important to explore the cultural implications of the growing shift that is taking place from classroom teaching to computer-based self-study and Internet-based distance learning. This classic method of knowledge sharing is undergoing major changes in the new electronic economy. Traditionally, the classroom has been a place where both tacit and explicit knowledge were transferred. While electronic tools do enable the transfer of tacit knowledge over distance from teacher to student or from student to student, it is generally not as easy as with face-to-face instruction. Distance learning would seem to put more emphasis on the individual rather than the group—another factor with clear cultural implications.

Directions for Future Research

We have begun a process of research and reflection that we believe will start to open up new possibilities for knowledge sharing throughout the world. Given the lack of prior empirical research in this particular area, the nature of our research was exploratory and our results, therefore, should be interpreted as suggestive rather than definitive, although they are consonant with expectations derived from general cross-cultural research literature. We hope that a response to our efforts here will be an increase in research and the application of future findings. Here, we conclude our chapter with a few suggestions for future research. First, findings from our study need to be further validated and expanded by including more cultures and countries. Often, we hear a simple contrast between Western versus Eastern. One should recognize, however, that there are substantial differences among different cultures in the West and in the East. Second, we observed similarities as well as differences between the two cultures. While it is interesting and important to note the differences between cultures, identifying similarities—particularly the ones that lead to more effective knowledge management—can be fruitful. One can examine the behavioral and cognitive characteristics that are found globally among high performers in different cultures. Third, we noted that epistemology is culture specific, which seems to affect all aspects of knowledge management. Particularly, knowledge sharing and the use of technological artifacts to preserve knowledge seem to be deeply related to an individual's epistemology. Further theoretical and empirical examination of this issue would bear results with significant practical implications.

We believe that effective knowledge management is critical for the survival and progress of modern organizations. We believe organizations functioning in a global society must be concerned with the effects of national culture on that knowledge management. And we believe that there lies within the world's many cultures great potential for enhancing knowledge sharing within the global enterprise.

Note

1. All excerpts of interviews with Korean consultants were translated by the first author.

References

Alston, J.P. (1989) "*Wa, guanxi* and *inhwa*: Managerial principles in Japan, China, and Korea." *Business Horizons* 32(2):26–31.

Bair, J., Fenn, J., Hunter, R. and Bosik, D. (1997) "Foundations for enterprise knowledge management." Gartner Group.

Constant, D., Sproull, L. and Kiesler, S. (1996) "The kindness of strangers: The usefulness of electronic weak ties for technical advice." *Organization Science* 7(2):119–135.

Davenport, T.H. and Prusak, L. (1998) *Working Knowledge: How Organizations Manage What They Know*. Boston: Harvard Business School Press.

Eisenhardt, K.M. (1989) "Building theories from case study research." *Academy of Management Review* 14(4):532–550.

Giddens, A. (1984) *The Constitution of Society*. Berkeley: University of California Press.

Granovetter, M.S. (1973) "The strength of weak ties." *American Journal of Sociology* 6:1360–1380.

Halbwachs, M. (1952) *On Collective Memory*. Chicago: University of Chicago Press.

Hampden-Turner, C. and Trompenaars, A. (1993) *The Seven Cultures of Capitalism: Value Systems for Creating Wealth in the United States, Japan, Germany, France, Britain, Sweden, and The Netherlands*. New York: Doubleday.

Hampden-Turner, C. and Trompenaars, A. (1997) *Mastering the Infinite Game: How East Asian Values Are Transforming Business Practices*. Oxford: Capstone.

Hansen, M.T. (1999) "The search-transfer problem: The role of weak ties in sharing knowledge across organization subunits," *Administrative Science Quarterly* 44:82–111.

Hedlund, G. (1994) "A model of knowledge management and the N-form corporation," *Strategic Management Journal* 15:73–90.

Hofstede, G. (1984) *Culture's Consequences* (abridged ed.). Newberry Park, CA: Sage.

Hofstede, G. (1991) *Cultures and Organizations: Software of the Mind*. New York: McGraw-Hill.

Hofstede, G. (1993) "Cultural constraints in management theories." *Academy of Management Executive* 7:81–94.

Hutchins, E. (1995) *Cognition in the Wild*. Boston: MIT Press.

Kim, J.Y. and Nam, S.H. (1998) "The concept and dynamics of face: Implications for organizational behavior in Asia." *Organization Science* 9(4) 522–534.

Lam, A. (1997) "Embedded firms, embedded knowledge: Problems of collaboration and knowledge transfer in global cooperative ventures," *Organization Studies* 18(6):973–996.

Leonard-Barton, D. (1995) *Wellsprings of Knowledge: Building and Sustaining the Sources of Innovation*. Boston: Harvard Business School Press.

Levine, J.M., Resnick, L.B. and Higgins, E.T. (1993) "Social foundation of cognition." *Annual Review of Psychology* 44:585–612.

Nonaka, I. and Takeuchi, H. (1995) *The Knowledge-Creating Company: How Japanese Companies Create the Dynamics of Innovation*. New York: Oxford University Press.

Orlikowski, W. (1992) "Learning from notes: Organizational issues in groupware implementation," in *ACM 1992 Conference on Computer-Supported Cooperative Work*.

Orr, J. (1990) "Sharing knowledge, celebrating identity: War stories and community memory in a service culture," in D.S. Middleton and D. Edwards (eds.), *Collective Remembering: Memory in Society*. Beverly Hills, CA: Sage.

Parsons, T. (1951) *The Social System*. New York: Free Press.

Pfeffer, J. and Sutton, R.I. (2000) *The Knowing-Doing Gap: How Smart Companies Turn Knowledge into Action*. Boston: Harvard Business School Press.

Resnick, L.B., Levine, J.M. and Teasley, S.D. (1991) *Perspectives on Socially Shared Cognition*. Washington, D.C.: American Psychological Association.

Schein, E.H. (1985) *Organizational Culture and Leadership*. San Francisco: Jossey-Bass.

Skyrme, D. and Amidon, D. (1997) "The knowledge agenda." *Journal of Knowledge Management* 1(1):27–37.

Torrey, B. and Datta, V. (1999) "Knowledge across the globe," *Journal of Knowledge Management* 2(8):26–31.

Trompenaars, A. and Hampden-Turner, C. (1998) *Riding the Waves of Culture: Understanding Diversity in Global Business*. New York: McGraw-Hill.

Vigotsky, L.S. (1978) *Mind in Society*. Cambridge, MA: Harvard University Press.

Wenger, E. (1998) *Communities of Practice: Learning, Meaning, and Identity*. Cambridge: Cambridge University Press.

Yin, R.K. (1994) *Case Study Research: Design and Methods*. Thousand Oaks, CA: Sage.

V

Knowledge Creation

24

A Dynamic Theory of Organizational Knowledge Creation

Ikujiro Nonaka

It is widely observed that the society we live in has been gradually turning into a "knowledge society" (Drucker 1968, Bell 1973, Toffler 1990). The ever increasing importance of knowledge in contemporary society calls for a shift in our thinking concerning innovation in large business organizations—be it technical innovation, product innovation, or strategic or organizational innovation.[1] It raises questions about how organizations process knowledge and, more important, how they create new knowledge. Such a shift in general orientation will involve, among other things, a reconceptualization of the organizational knowledge creation processes.

The theory of organization has long been dominated by a paradigm that conceptualizes the organization as a system that "processes" information or "solves" problems. Central to this paradigm is the assumption that a fundamental task for the organization is how efficiently it can deal with information and decisions in an uncertain environment. This paradigm suggests that the solution lies in the "input-process-output" sequence of hierarchical information processing. Yet a critical problem with this paradigm follows from its passive and static view of the organization. Information processing is viewed as a problem-solving activity which centers on what is given to the organization—without due consideration of what is created by it.

Any organization that dynamically deals with a changing environment ought not only to process information efficiently but also create information and knowledge. Analyzing the organization in terms of its design and capability to process information imposed by the environment no doubt constitutes an important approach to interpreting certain aspects of organizational activities. However, it can be argued that the organization's interaction with its environment, together with the means by which it creates and distributes information and knowledge, are more important when it comes to building an active and dynamic understanding of the organization. For example, innovation, which is a key form of organizational knowledge creation, cannot be explained sufficiently in terms of information processing or problem solving. Innovation can be better understood as a process in which the organization creates and defines problems and then actively develops new knowledge to solve them. Also, innovation produced by one part of the organization in turn creates a stream of related information and knowledge, which might then trigger changes in the organization's wider knowledge systems. Such a sequence of innovation suggests that the organization should be studied from the viewpoint of how it creates information and knowledge, rather than with regard to how it processes these entities.

The goal of this chapter is to develop the essential elements of a theory of organizational knowledge creation. In the sections which follow, the basic concepts and models of the organizational knowledge creation are presented. Based on this foundation, the dynamics of the organizational knowledge creation process are examined and practical models are advanced for managing the process more effectively.

Basic Concepts and Models of Organizational Knowledge Creation

The following subsections explore some basic constructs of the theory of organizational knowledge creation. They begin by discussing the nature of information and knowledge and then draw a distinction between "tacit" and "explicit" knowledge. This distinction represents what could be described as the epistemological dimension to organizational knowledge creation. It embraces a continual dialogue between explicit and tacit knowledge which drives the creation of new ideas and concepts.

Although ideas are formed in the minds of individuals, interaction between individuals typically plays a critical role in developing these ideas. That is to say, "communities of interaction" contribute to the amplification and development of new knowledge. While these communities might span departmental or indeed organizational boundaries, the point to note is that they define a further dimension to organizational knowledge creation, which is associated with the extent of social interaction between individuals that share and develop knowledge. This is referred to as the "ontological" dimension of knowledge creation.

Following a consideration of the two dimensions of knowledge creation, some attention is given to the role of individuals and, more specifically, to their "commitment" to the knowledge creating process. This covers aspects of their "intention," the role of autonomy, and the effects of fluctuations or discontinuities in the organization and its environment.

Next, a "spiral" model of knowledge creation is proposed which shows the relationship between the epistemological and ontological dimensions of knowledge creation. This spiral illustrates the creation of a new concept in terms of a continual dialogue between tacit and explicit knowledge. As the concept resonates around an expanding community of individuals, it is developed and clarified. Gradually, concepts which are thought to be of value obtain a wider currency and become crystallized. This description of the spiral model is followed by some observations about how to support the practical management of organizational knowledge creation.

Knowledge and Information

Knowledge is a multifaceted concept with multilayered meanings. The history of philosophy since the classical Greek period can be regarded as a never-ending search for the meaning of knowledge.[2] This essay follows traditional epistemology and adopts a definition of knowledge as "justified true belief." It should be noted, however, that while the arguments of traditional epistemology focus on "truthfulness" as the essential attribute of knowledge, for present purposes, it is important to consider knowledge as a personal "belief," and emphasize the importance of the "justification" of knowledge. This difference introduces another critical distinction between the view of knowledge of traditional epistemology and that of the theory of knowledge creation. While the former naturally emphasizes the absolute, static, and nonhuman nature of knowledge, typically expressed in propositional forms in formal logic, the latter sees knowledge as a dynamic human process of justifying personal beliefs as part of an aspiration for the "truth."

Although the terms "information" and "knowledge" are often used interchangeably, there is a clear distinction between information and knowledge. According to Machlup (1983), information is a flow of messages or meanings which might add to, restructure, or change knowledge. Dretske (1981) offers some useful definitions. In his words:

> Information is that commodity capable of yielding knowledge, and what information a signal carries is what we can learn from it (Dretske 1981, p. 44). Knowledge is identified with information-produced (or sustained) belief, but the information a person receives is relative to what he or she already knows about the possibilities at the source. (p. 86)

In short, information is a flow of messages, while knowledge is created and organized by the very flow of information, anchored on the commitment and beliefs of its holder. This understanding emphasizes an essential aspect of knowledge that relates to human action.

The importance of knowledge related to action has been recognized in the area of artificial intelligence. For example, Gruber (1989) addresses the subject of an expert's "strategic knowledge" as that which directly guides his action and attempts to develop the tools to acquire it. Since the 1980s, the development of cognitive science has been based on a serious reflection on behavioralist psychology's neglect of such traditional questions as, "Why do human beings act in a certain way?", which was a central issue for so-called folk psychology (Stich 1986). Searle's discussion on the "speech act" also points out a close relationship between language and human action in terms of the "intention" and "commitment" of speakers (Searle 1969). In sum, as a fundamental basis for the theory of organizational creation of knowledge, it can be argued that attention should be focused on the active, subjective nature of knowledge represented by such terms as "belief" and "commitment" that are deeply rooted in the value systems of individuals.

The analysis of knowledge and information does not stop at this point. Information is a necessary medium or material for initiating and formalizing knowledge and can be viewed from "syntactic" and "semantic" perspectives. The syntactic aspect of information is illustrated by Shannon's analysis of the volume of information which is measured without regard to its meaning or value. A telephone bill, for example, is not calculated on the basis of the content of a conversation but according to the duration of time and the distance involved. Shannon said that the semantic aspects of communication, which center on the meaning of information, are irrelevant to the engineering problem (Shannon and Weaver 1949). A genuine theory of information would be a theory about the content of our messages, not a theory about the form in which this content is embodied (Dretske 1981).

In terms of creating knowledge, the semantic aspect of information is more relevant as it focuses on conveyed meaning. The syntactic aspect does not capture the importance of information in the knowledge creation process. Therefore, any preoccupation with the formal definition will tend to lead to a disproportionate emphasis on the role of information processing, which is insensitive to the creation of organizational knowledge out of the chaotic, equivocal state of information. Information, seen from the semantic standpoint, literally means that it contains new meaning. As Bateson (1979, p. 5) put it, "information consists of differences that make a difference." This insight provides a new point of view for interpreting events that make previously invisible connections or ideas obvious or shed light on unexpected connections (Miyazaki and Ueno 1985). For the purposes of building a theory of knowledge creation, it is important to concentrate on the semantic aspects of information.

Two Dimensions of Knowledge Creation

Although a great deal has been written about the importance of knowledge in management, relatively little attention has been paid to how knowledge is created and how the knowledge creation process can be managed. One dimension of this knowledge creation process can be drawn from a distinction between two types of knowledge—*tacit knowledge* and *explicit knowledge*. As Michael Polanyi (1966, p. 4) put it, "We can know more than we can tell."[3] Knowledge that can be expressed in words and numbers only represents the tip of the iceberg of the entire body of possible knowledge. Polanyi classified human knowledge into two categories. "Explicit" or codified knowledge refers to knowledge that is transmittable in formal systematic language. On the other hand, "tacit" knowledge has a personal quality, which makes it hard to formalize and communicate. Tacit knowledge is deeply rooted in action, commitment, and involvement in a specific context. In Polanyi's words, it "indwells" in a comprehensive cognizance of the human mind and body.

Whereas Polanyi articulates the contents of tacit knowledge in a philosophical context, it is also possible to expand his idea in a more practical direction. Tacit knowledge involves both cognitive and technical elements. The cognitive elements center on what Johnson-Laird (1983) called "mental models," in which human beings form working models of the world by creating and manipulating analogies in their minds. These working models include schemata, paradigms, beliefs, and viewpoints that provide "perspectives" that help individuals to perceive and define their world. By contrast, the technical element of tacit knowledge covers concrete know-how, crafts, and skills that apply to specific contexts. It is important to note here that the cognitive element of tacit knowledge refers to an individual's images of reality and visions for the future, that is to say, what is and what ought to be. As will be discussed later, the articulation of tacit perspectives—in a kind of "mobilization" process—is a key factor in the creation of new knowledge.

Tacit knowledge is a continuous activity of knowing and embodies what Bateson (1973) has referred to as an "analogue" quality. In this context, communication between individuals may be seen as an analogue process that aims to share tacit knowledge to build mutual understanding. This understanding involves a kind of "parallel processing" of the complexities of current issues, as the different dimensions of a problem are processed simultaneously. By contrast, explicit knowledge is discrete or "digital." It is captured in records of the past such as libraries, archives, and databases and is assessed on a sequential basis.

The Ontological Dimension: The Level of Social Interaction

At a fundamental level, knowledge is created by individuals. An organization cannot create knowledge without individuals. The organization supports creative individuals or provides a context for such individuals to create knowledge. Organizational knowledge creation, therefore, should be understood in terms of a process that "organizationally" amplifies the knowledge created by individuals and crystallizes it as a part of the knowledge network of organization.

In this line, it is possible to distinguish several levels of social interaction at which the knowledge created by an individual is transformed and legitimized. In the first instance, an informal community of social interaction provides an immediate forum for nurturing the emergent property of knowledge at each level and developing new ideas. Since this informal community might span organizational boundaries—for example, to include suppliers or customers—it is important that the organization is able to integrate appropriate aspects of emerging knowledge into its strategic development. Thus, the potential contribution of informal groups to organizational knowledge creation should be related to more formal notions of a hierarchical structure. If this is done effectively, new knowledge associated with more advantageous organizational processes or technologies will be able to gain a broader currency within the organization.

In addition to the creation of knowledge within an organization, it is also possible that there will be formal provisions to build knowledge at an interorganizational level. This might occur if informal communities of interaction, that span the link between customers, suppliers, distributors, and even competitors, are put on a more formal basis, for example, through the formation of alliances or outsourcing.

Commitment on the Part of the Knowledge Subject: Intention, Autonomy, and Fluctuation

The prime movers in the process of organizational knowledge creation are the individual members of an organization. Individuals are continuously committed to re-creating the world in accordance with their own perspectives. As Polanyi noted, "commitment" underlies human knowledge creating activities. Thus, commitment is one of the most important components for promoting the formation of new knowledge within an organization. There are three basic factors that induce individual commitment in an organizational setting: "intention," and "autonomy," and a certain level of environmental "fluctuation."

Intention

Intention is concerned with how individuals form their approach to the world and try to make sense of their environment. It is not simply a state of mind, but rather what might be called an action-oriented concept. Edmund Husserl (1968) called this attitude on the part of the subject "intentionality." He denied the existence of "consciousness" per se, which was generally assumed by psychologists in the nineteenth century, and argued that consciousness arises when a subject pays attention to an object. In other words, any consciousness is a "consciousness of something." It arises, endures, and disappears with a subject's commitment to an object.

Eigen (1971) argued, in his evolutionary theory, that evolution involves the process of acquiring environmental information for better adaptation. Eigen insisted that the degree of meaningfulness of information, or a value parameter, needs to be introduced to explain this system. Human beings, as organic systems, derive meaning from the environment which is based on their ultimate pursuit of survival (Shimizu 1978). Man cannot grasp the meaning of information about his environment without some frame of value judgment.

The meaning of information differs according to what a particular system aims to do (manifest purpose or problem consciousness) and the broader environment in which that system exists (context). It is more concerned with the system's future aspirations than its current state. Weick (1979) explains this "self-fulfilling prophecy" of a system as the "enactment" of the environment, which may be a projection of its strong will for self-actualization. While mechanistic information-processing models treat the mind as a fixed capacity device for converting meaningless information into conscious perception, in reality, cognition is the activity of knowing and understanding as it occurs in the context of purposeful activity (Neisser 1976). Intention becomes apparent against this background. Without intention, it would be impossible to judge the value of the information or knowledge perceived or created. "The intentionality of the mind not only creates the possibility of meaning, but also limits its form" (Searle 1983, p. 166).

Autonomy

The principle of autonomy can be applied at the individual, group, and organizational levels— either separately or all together. However, the individual is a convenient starting point for analysis. Individuals within the organization may have different intentions. Every individual has his or her own personality. By allowing people to act autonomously, the organization may increase the possibility of introducing unexpected opportunities of the type that are sometimes associated with the so-called garbage can metaphor (Cohen et al. 1972). From the standpoint of creating knowledge, such an organization is more likely to maintain greater flexibility in acquiring, relating, and interpreting information. In a system where the autonomy of individuals is assured, or where only "minimum critical specification" (Morgan 1986) is intended, it is possible to establish a basis for self-organization.

Individual autonomy widens the possibility that individuals will motivate themselves to form new knowledge. Self-motivation based on deep emotions, for example, in the poet's creation of new expressions, serves as a driving force for the creation of metaphors. A sense of purpose and autonomy becomes important as an organizational context. Purpose serves as the basis of conceptualization. Autonomy gives individuals freedom to absorb knowledge.

Fluctuation

Even though intention is internal to the individual, knowledge creation at the individual level involves continuous interaction with the external world. In this connection, chaos or discontinuity can generate new patterns of interaction between individuals and their environment. Individuals re-create their own systems of knowledge to take account of ambiguity, redundancy, noise, or randomness generated from the organization and its environment. These fluctuations differ from complete disorder and are characterized by "order without recursiveness"—which represents an order where the pattern is hard to predict in the beginning (Gleick 1987).

Winograd and Flores (1986) emphasize the role of periodic "breakdowns" in human perception. Breakdown refers to the interruption of an individual's habitual, comfortable "state-of-being." When breakdowns occur, individuals question the value of habits and routine tools, which might lead to a realignment of commitments. Environmental fluctuation often triggers this breakdown. When people face such a breakdown or contradiction, they have an opportunity to reconsider their fundamental thinking and perspectives. In other words, they begin to question the validity of basic attitudes toward the world. This process necessarily involves deep personal commitment by the individual and is similar in context to Piaget's (1974) observations about the importance of the role of contradiction in the interaction between the subject and its environment in such a way that the subject forms perceptions through behavior.

Knowledge Conversion and the Spiral of Knowledge

It is now possible to bring together the epistemological and ontological dimensions of knowledge creation to form a "spiral" model for the processes involved. This involves identifying four different patterns of interaction between tacit and explicit knowledge. These patterns represent ways in which existing knowledge can be "converted" into new knowledge. Social interaction between individuals then provides an ontological dimension to the expansion of knowledge.

The idea of "knowledge conversion" may be traced from Anderson's ACT model (Anderson 1983) developed in cognitive psychology. In the ACT model, knowledge is divided into "declarative knowledge" (actual knowledge) that is expressed in the form of propositions and "procedural knowledge" (methodological knowledge) which is used in such activities as remembering how to ride a bicycle or play the piano. In the context of the present discussion, the former might approximate to explicit knowledge and the latter to tacit knowledge. Anderson's model hypothesizes that declarative knowledge has to be transformed into procedural knowledge in order for cognitive skills to develop. This hypothesis is consistent with Ryle's classification (1949) of knowledge into categories of knowing that something "exists" and knowing "how" it operates. Anderson's categorization can be regarded as a more sophisticated version of Ryle's classification. One limitation of the ACT model is the hypothesis that transformation of knowledge is unidirectional and only involves transformations from declarative to procedural knowledge, while it can be argued that transformation is bidirectional. This may be because the ACT model is more concerned with maturation than with the creation of knowledge.

Four Modes of Knowledge Conversion

The assumption that knowledge is created through conversion between tacit and explicit knowledge allows us to postulate four different "modes" of knowledge conversion: (1) from tacit knowledge to tacit knowledge, (2) from explicit knowledge to explicit knowledge, (3) from tacit knowledge to explicit knowledge, and (4) from explicit knowledge to tacit knowledge.

First, there is a mode of knowledge conversion that enables us to convert tacit knowledge through interaction between individuals. One important point to note here is that an individual can acquire tacit knowledge without language. Apprentices work with their mentors and learn craftsmanship not through language but by observation, imitation, and practice. In a business setting, on-the-job training (OJT) uses the same principle. The key to acquiring tacit knowledge is experience. Without some form of shared experience, it is extremely difficult for people to share each others' thinking processes. The mere transfer of information will often make little sense if it is abstracted from embedded emotions and nuanced contexts that are associated with shared experiences. This process of creating tacit knowledge through shared experience will be called "socialization."

The second mode of knowledge conversion involves the use of social processes to combine different bodies of explicit knowledge held by in-

dividuals. Individuals exchange and combine knowledge through such exchange mechanisms as meetings and telephone conversations. The reconfiguring of existing information through the sorting, adding, recategorizing, and recontextualizing of explicit knowledge can lead to new knowledge. Modern computer systems provide a graphic example. This process of creating explicit knowledge from explicit knowledge is referred to as "combination."

The third and fourth modes of knowledge conversion relate to patterns of conversion involving both tacit and explicit knowledge. These conversion modes capture the idea that tacit and explicit knowledge are complementary and can expand over time through a process of mutual interaction. This interaction involves two different operations. One is the conversion of tacit knowledge into explicit knowledge, which will be called "externalization." The other is the conversion of explicit knowledge into tacit knowledge, which bears some similarity to the traditional notion of "learning" and will be referred to here as "internalization." As will be discussed later, "metaphor" plays an important role in the externalization process, and "action" is deeply related to the internalization process. Figure 24.1 illustrates the four modes of knowledge conversion.

Three of the four types of knowledge conversion—socialization, combination, and internalization, have partial analogs with aspects of organizational theory. For example, socialization is connected with theories of organizational culture, while combination is rooted in information processing and internalization has associations with organizational learning. By contrast, the concept of externalization is not well developed. The limited analysis that does exist is from the point of view of information creation (see Nonaka 1987).

	Tacit knowledge *To*	Explicit knowledge
Tacit knowledge	Socialization	Externalization
From Explicit knowledge	Internalization	Combination

Figure 24.1 Modes of knowledge conversion.

Theories of organizational learning do not address the critical notion of externalization and have paid little attention to the importance of socialization, even though there has been an accumulation of research on "modeling" behavior in learning psychology. Another difficulty relates to the concepts of "double-loop learning" (Argyris and Schön 1978) or "unlearning" (Hedberg 1981), which arises from a strong orientation toward organization development (OD). Since the first integrated theory of organizational learning presented by Argyris and Schön, it has been widely assumed, implicitly or explicitly, that double-loop learning, that is, the questioning and reconstruction of existing perspectives, interpretation frameworks, or decision premises, can be very difficult for organizations to implement by themselves. In order to overcome this difficulty, they argue that some kind of artificial intervention such as the use of organizational development programs is required. The limitation of this argument is that it assumes implicitly that someone inside or outside an organization knows "objectively" the right time and method for putting double-loop learning into practice. A mechanistic view of the organization lies behind this assumption. Seen from the vantage point of organizational knowledge creation, on the contrary, double-loop learning is not a special, difficult task but a daily activity for the organization. Organizations continuously create new knowledge by reconstructing existing perspectives, frameworks, or premises on a day-to-day basis. In other words, double-loop learning ability is "built into" the knowledge creating model, thereby circumventing the need to make unrealistic assumptions about the existence of a "right" answer.

Modal Shift and Spiral of Knowledge

While each of the four modes of knowledge conversion can create new knowledge independently, the central theme of the model of organizational knowledge creation proposed here hinges on a dynamic interaction between the different modes of knowledge conversion. That is to say, knowledge creation centers on the building of both tacit and explicit knowledge and, more important, on the interchange between these two aspects of knowledge through internalization and externalization.

A failure to build a dialogue between tacit and explicit knowledge can cause problems. For example, both pure combination and socialization have demerits. A lack of commitment and neglect of the personal meaning of knowledge might mean that pure combination becomes a superficial interpretation of existing knowledge, which has little to do with here-and-now reality. It may also fail to crystallize or embody knowledge in a form that is concrete enough to facilitate further knowledge creation in a wider social context. The "sharability" of knowledge created by pure socialization may be limited and, as a result, difficult to apply in fields beyond the specific context in which it was created.

Organizational knowledge creation, as distinct from individual knowledge creation, takes place when all four modes of knowledge creation are "organizationally" managed to form a continual cycle. This cycle is shaped by a series of shifts between different modes of knowledge conversion. There are various "triggers" that induce these shifts between different modes of knowledge conversion. First, the socialization mode usually starts with the building of a "team" or "field" of interaction. This field facilitates the sharing of members' experiences and perspectives. Second, the externalization mode is triggered by successive rounds of meaningful "dialogue." In this dialogue, the sophisticated use of "metaphors" can be used to enable team members to articulate their own perspectives and thereby reveal hidden tacit knowledge that is otherwise hard to communicate. Concepts formed by teams can be combined with existing data and external knowledge in a search of more concrete and sharable specifications. This combination mode is facilitated by such triggers as "coordination" between team members and other sections of the organization and the "documentation" of existing knowledge. Through an iterative process of trial and error, concepts are articulated and developed until they emerge in a concrete form. This "experimentation" can trigger internalization through a process of "learning by doing." Participants in a "field" of action share explicit knowledge that is gradually translated, through interaction and a process of trial-and-error, into different aspects of tacit knowledge.

While tacit knowledge held by individuals may lie at the heart of the knowledge creating process, realizing the practical benefits of that knowledge centers on its externalization and amplification through dynamic interactions between all four modes of knowledge conversion. Tacit knowledge is thus mobilized through a dynamic "entangling" of the different modes of knowledge conversion in a process which will be

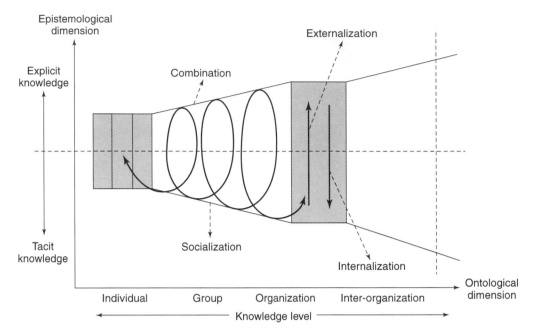

Figure 24.2 Spiral of organizational knowledge creation.

referred to as a "spiral" model of knowledge creation, illustrated in figure 24.2. The interactions between tacit knowledge and explicit knowledge will tend to become larger in scale and faster in speed as more actors in and around the organization become involved. Thus, organizational knowledge creation can be viewed as an upward spiral process, starting at the individual level moving up to the collective (group) level, and then to the organizational level, sometimes reaching out to the interorganizational level.

From Metaphor to Model: Methodology of Knowledge Creation

Before concluding this presentation of the basic constructs of the theory, it is helpful to consider some general principles for facilitating the management of knowledge conversion. One effective method of converting tacit knowledge into explicit knowledge is the use of metaphor. As Nisbet (1969, p. 5) noted, "(m)uch of what Michael Polanyi has called 'tacit knowledge' is expressible—in so far as it is expressible at all—in metaphor." "The essence of metaphor is understanding and experiencing one kind of thing in terms of another (Lakoff and Johnson 1980, p. 5)." Even though the metaphor is not in itself a thinking process, it enables us to experience a

new behavior by making inferences from the model of another behavior. The use of metaphor is broader than the traditional, lexical definition of the term (meta = change; phor = move). According to Lakoff and Johnson: "metaphor is pervasive in everyday life, not just in language but in thought and action. Our ordinary conceptual system, in terms of which we both think and act, is fundamentally metaphorical in nature" (Lakoff and Johnson 1980, p. 3).

As a method of perception, metaphor depends on imagination and intuitive learning through symbols, rather than on the analysis or synthesis of common attributes shared by associated things. Rosch (1973) suggested that man describes the world, not in the formal attributes of concepts, but in terms of prototypes. For example, the robin could be seen as a better prototype than the turkey for a small bird. Prototypes provide a mechanism for recognizing the maximum level of information with a minimum of energy.

Metaphor is not merely the first step in transforming tacit knowledge into explicit knowledge; it constitutes an important method of creating a network of concepts which can help to generate knowledge about the future by using existing knowledge. Metaphor may be defined as being "two contradicting concepts incorporated in one word." It is a creative, cognitive process which relates concepts that are far apart in an individual's memory. While perception through prototype is in many cases limited to concrete, mundane concepts, metaphor plays an important role in associating abstract, imaginary concepts. When two concepts are presented in a metaphor, it is possible not only to think of their similarity, but also to make comparisons that discern the degree of imbalance, contradiction, or inconsistency involved in their association. The latter process becomes the basis for creating new meaning.[4] According to Bateson (1973) metaphors cut across different contexts and thus allow imaginative perceptions to combine with literal levels of cognitive activities. This experience, he further argues, will promote the type of "presupposition-negation" learning that is closely related with the formation of new paradigms.

Contradictions incorporated in metaphor may be harmonized through the use of analogies. Analogy reduces ambiguity by highlighting the commonness of two different things. Metaphor and analogy are often confused. The association of meanings by metaphor is mostly driven by intuition and involves images. On the other hand, the association of meanings through analogy is more structural/functional and is carried out through rational thinking. As such, metaphors provide much room for free association (discontinuity). Analogy allows the functional operation of new concepts or systems to be explored by reference to things that are already understood. In this sense, an analogy—that enables us to know the future through the present—assumes an intermediate role in bridging the gap between image and logic.

It follows from the preceding discussion that tacit knowledge may be transformed into explicit knowledge by (1) recognizing contradictions through metaphor, and (2) resolving them through analogy. Explicit knowledge represents a model within which contradictions are resolved and concepts become transferable through consistent and systematic logic. In the business organization, a typical model is the prototype that represents the product concept. The prototype's specification is then explicit knowledge. It has been pointed out that metaphor, analogy, and model are all part of the process of scientific discovery.[5] Whether the metaphor-analogy-model sequence is indispensable in all such processes will depend upon the nature of the question under study; yet in creating new concepts, the model is usually generated from a metaphor.

The Process of Organizational Knowledge Creation

The theoretical constructs and models described in the previous section may now be related to organizational knowledge creation in a corporate organizational setting. This will be approached by assessing the processes that enable individual knowledge to be enlarged, amplified, and justified within an organization.

The Enlargement of an Individual's Knowledge

The prime mover in the process of organizational knowledge creation is the individual. Individuals accumulate tacit knowledge through direct "hands-on" experience. The quality of that tacit knowledge is influenced by two important factors. One factor is the "variety" of an individual's experience. If this experience is limited to routine operations, the amount of tacit knowledge obtained from monotonous and repetitive tasks will tend to decrease over time. Routine tasks mitigate against creative thinking and the formation of new knowledge. However, increasing the variety of experience is not sufficient by itself to raise the quality of tacit knowledge. If the individual finds various experiences to be completely unrelated, there will be little chance that they can be integrated to create a new perspective. What matters is "high quality" experience which might, on occasion, involve the complete redefinition of the nature of a "job."

A second factor that determines the quality of tacit knowledge is "knowledge of experience." The essence of "knowledge of experience" is an embodiment of knowledge through a deep personal commitment into bodily experience. Varela et al. (1991) have pointed out that the embodied nature of human knowledge has long been neglected in Western epistemological traditions that have followed from Descartes. They define embodiment as "a reflection in which body and mind have been brought together" (1991, p. 27). Yuasa (1987) describes this "oneness of body-mind" as the free state of minimal distance between movement of the mind and of the body, as for example in the dynamic performance of a master actor on a stage (1987, p. 28). As Merleau-Ponty (1964) pointed out, bodily experience plays a critical role in the process of crystallization. Commitment to bodily experience means an intentional self-involvement in the object and situation which transcends the subject-object distinction, thereby providing access to "pure experience" (Nishida 1960). This notion is prevalent in Oriental culture. As Yuasa mentions:

> One revealing characteristic of the philosophical uniqueness of Eastern thought is presupposed in the philosophical foundation of the Eastern theories. To put it simply, true knowledge cannot be obtained simply by means of theoretical thinking, but only through "bodily recognition or realization" (*tainin* or *taitoku*), that is, through the utilization of one's total mind and body. Simply stated, this is to "learn with the body" not the brain. Cultivation is a practice that attempts, so to speak, to achieve true knowledge by means of one's total mind and body. (1987, pp. 25–26)

A good case in point is "on-the-spot-ism" in Japanese management. In developing the products and identifying the markets, Japanese firms encourage the use of judgment and knowledge formed through interaction with customers—and by personal bodily experience rather than by "objective," scientific conceptualization. Social interaction between individuals, groups, and organizations are fundamental to organizational knowledge creation in Japan. Nevertheless, since this approach uses hands-on experience and action, it sometimes falls in the category of "experiencism" which neglects the importance of reflection and logical thinking. It tends to overemphasize action and efficiency at the expense of a search for higher level concepts which have universal application.

While the concepts of "high-quality experience" and "knowledge of experience" may be used to raise the quality of tacit knowledge, they have to be counterbalanced by a further approach to knowledge creation that raises the quality of explicit knowledge. Such an approach may be called a "knowledge of rationality," which describes a rational ability to reflect on experience. Knowledge of rationality is an explicit-knowledge-oriented approach that is dominant in Western culture. It centers on the "combination" mode of knowledge conversion and is effective in creating digital, discrete, declarative knowledge. Knowledge of rationality tends to ignore the importance of commitment, and instead centers on a reinterpretation of existing explicit knowledge.

In order to raise the total quality of an individual's knowledge, the enhancement of tacit knowledge has to be subjected to a continual interplay with the evolution of relevant aspects of explicit knowledge. In this connection, Schön (1983) pointed out the importance of "reflection in action," that is, reflecting while experiencing. Individual knowledge is enlarged through this interaction between experience and rationality and crystallized into a unique perspective original to an individual. These original perspectives are based on individual belief and value systems and will be a source of varied interpretations of shared experience with others in the next stage of conceptualization.

Sharing Tacit Knowledge and Conceptualization

As we saw in the previous section, the process of organizational knowledge creation is initiated by the enlargement of an individual's knowledge within an organization. The interaction between knowledge of experience and rationality enables individuals to build their own perspectives on the world. Yet these perspectives remain personal unless they are articulated and amplified through social interaction. One way to implement the management of organizational knowledge creation is to create a "field" or "self-organizing team" in which individual members collaborate to create a new concept.

In this connection, it is helpful to draw on the concept of an organization's "mental outlook" as articulated in Sandelands and Stablein's (1987) pioneering work on "organizational mind." While making caveats about the dangers of reification and anthropomorphism, these authors use the analogy of "mind" to identify the process by which organizations form ideas. Mind is distinct from the brain in the same way that computer software is distinct from hardware. Against this background, intelligence may be seen as the ability to maintain a working similarity between mind and nature.

The development of ideas associated with organizational mind requires some form of physical substrate (i.e., hardware) which Sandelands and Stablein (1987) argue might be derived from "patterns of behavior traced by people and machines" (p. 139). Organizational behaviors can convey ideas and, like the firing of neurons in the brain, may trigger other behaviors and so form a trace of activation.

In the brain, whether or not one neuron influences another depends on a complex set of factors having primarily to do with physical proximity, availability of pathways, intensity of the electrochemical signal, and whether or not the target neuron is inhibited by other neurons. Similarly, whether one behavior influences another in social organizations depends on a complex of factors primarily concerned with physical access, lines of communication, power, and competition from other behaviors. At an abstract formal level, at least, the politics of the social organization and the physiology of the brain share much in common. (Sandelands and Stablein 1987, p. 140)

It is human activity that creates organizational mind as individuals interact and trigger behavior patterns in others. Managing a self-organizing team involves building an appropriate degree of flexibility into the system which can accommodate a diversity of imaginative thinking in the pursuit of new problems and solutions.

Constructing a Field: Building a Self-organizing Team

To bring personal knowledge into a social context within which it can be amplified, it is necessary to have a "field" that provides a place in which individual perspectives are articulated, and conflicts are resolved in the formation of higher-level concepts. Berger and Luchman (1966) say that reality in everyday life is socially constructed. Individual behavior ought to be relativized through an interactive process to construct "social reality."

In the business organization, the field for interaction is often provided in the form of an autonomous, self-organizing "team" made of several members coming from a variety of functional departments. It is a critical matter for an organization to decide when and how to establish such a "field" of interaction in which individuals can meet and interact. It defines "true" members of knowledge creation and thus clarifies the domain in which perspectives are interacted.

The team needs to be established with regard to the principles of self-organization. In Lewin's (1951) development of the field theory in social psychology, a group is defined as "a dynamic

whole based on interdependence rather than on similarity." Some indication of the number of members and the composition of their background can be achieved using the principle of "requisite variety" (Ashby 1956). According to our observation of successful project teams in Japanese firms, the appropriate team size may be in the range between 10 and 30 individuals, with an upper limit arising because direct interaction between all the group members tends to decrease as group size increases. Within the team, there are usually four to five "core" members who have career histories that include multiple job functions. These core members form focal points in the team and could be seen as the organizational equivalent of the central element in a series of nested Russian dolls.[6] That is to say there is a radical pattern of interaction with other members, with closer links being associated with key individuals. Core members play a critical role in assuring appropriate "redundancy" of information within the cross-functional team. Other attributes of members such as formal position, age, gender, etc. might be determined with regard to Morgan's (1986) four principles of "learning to learn, requisite variety, minimum critical specification, and redundancy of functions."

The span of team activities need not be confined to the narrow boundary of the organization. Rather, it is a process that frequently makes extensive use of knowledge in environment, especially that of customers and suppliers. As Norman (1988) argues, the mental outlook of an organization is shaped by a complex pattern of factors within and outside the organization.[7] In some Japanese firms, for example, suppliers of parts and components are sometimes involved in the early stages of the product development. The relationship between manufacturers and suppliers is less hierarchical and arm's length than in Western countries. Some other Japanese companies involve customers in the field of new product planning. In both cases, sharing tacit knowledge with suppliers or customers through coexperience and creative dialogue play a critical role in creating relevant knowledge.

The significance of links between individuals that span boundaries, both within and outside the organization, has been highlighted by Brown and Duguid's (1991) revealing insight into the operation of "evolving communities of practice." These communities reflect the way in which people actually work as opposed to the formal job descriptions or task-related procedures that are specified by the organization. Attempts to solve practical problems often generate links between individuals who can provide useful information. The exchange and development of information within these evolving communities facilitate knowledge creation by linking the routine dimensions of day-to-day work to active learning and innovation. Collaboration to exchange ideas through shared narratives and "war stories" can provide an important platform on which to construct shared understanding out of conflicting and confused data.

By contrast with conceptions of groups as bounded entities within an organization, evolving communities of practice are "more fluid and interpenetrative than bounded, often crossing the restrictive boundaries of the organization to incorporate people from outside" (Brown and Duguid 1991, p. 49). Moreover, these communities can provide important contributions to visions for future development. Thus, these communities represent a key dimension to socialization and its input to the overall knowledge creation process.

The self-organizing team triggers organizational knowledge creation through two processes. First, it facilitates the building of mutual trust among members and accelerates creation of an implicit perspective shared by members as tacit knowledge. The key factor for this process is sharing experience among members. Second, the shared implicit perspective is conceptualized through continuous dialogue among members. This creative dialogue is realized only when redundancy of information exists within the team. The two processes appear simultaneously or alternatively in the actual process of knowledge creation within a team.

Before discussing these two processes further, it is necessary to mention another dimension of the knowledge creating process that can be associated with the self-organizing team. Scheflen (1982) proposed an idea of "interaction rhythms," in which social interactions were viewed as being both simultaneous and sequential. The management of interaction rhythms among team members, that is, that of divergence and convergence of various interaction rhythms, plays a critical role in accelerating the knowledge creation process. Within the team, rhythms of different speed are first generated and amplified up to a certain point of time and level, and then are given momentum for convergence toward a concept. Therefore, the crucial role of the team leader concerns how to balance the rhythm of divergence and convergence in the process of dialogues and shared experience.

In sum, the cross-functional team in which experience sharing and continuous dialogue are facilitated by the management of interaction rhythms serves as the basic building block for structuring the organization knowledge creation process. The team is different from a mere group in that it induces self-organizing process of the entire organization through which the knowledge at the group level is elevated to the organizational level.

Sharing Experience

In order for the self-organizing team to start the process of concept creation, it first needs to build mutual trust among members. As we shall see later, concept creation involves a difficult process of externalization, that is, converting tacit knowledge (which by nature is hard to articulate) into an explicit concept. This challenging task involves repeated, time-consuming dialogue among members. Mutual trust is an indispensable base for facilitating this type of constructive "collaboration" (Schrage 1990). A key way to build mutual trust is to share one's original experience—the fundamental source of tacit knowledge. Direct understanding of other individuals relies on shared experience that enables team members to "indwell" into others and to grasp their world from "inside."

Shared experience also facilitates the creation of "common perspectives" which can be shared by team members as a part of their respective bodies of tacit knowledge. The dominant mode of knowledge conversion involved here is socialization. Various forms of tacit knowledge that are brought into the field by individual members are converted through coexperience among them to form a common base for understanding.

As was mentioned earlier, tacit knowledge is a distinctly personal concept. Varela et al. (1991) point out the limitation of the cognitivist view of human experience in comparison with the non-Western philosophical view, and suggest that cognitive experience is "embodied action" rather than a mere representation of a world that exists independent of our cognitive system. The mutual conversion of such embodied, tacit knowledge is accelerated by synchronizing both body and mind in the face of the same experience. Coexperience with others enables us to transcend the ordinary "I-Thou" distinction and opens up the world of common understanding, which Scheflen (1982) called "Field Epistemology." Condon (1976) shared this view that communication is a simultaneous and contextual phenomenon in which people feel a change occurring, share the same sense of change, and are moved to take action. In other words, communication is like a wave that passes through people's bodies and culminates when everyone synchronizes himself with the wave. Thus, the sharing of mental and physical rhythm among participants of a field may serve as the driving force of socialization.

Conceptualization

Once mutual trust and a common implicit perspective have been formed through shared experience, the team needs to articulate the perspective through continuous dialogues. The dominant mode of knowledge conversion here is externalization. Theories of organizational learning have not given much attention to this process. Tacit "field-specific" perspectives are converted into explicit concepts that can be shared beyond the boundary of the team. Dialogue directly facilitates this process by activating externalization at individual levels.

Dialogue, in the form of face-to-face communication between persons, is a process in which one builds concepts in cooperation with others. It also provides the opportunity for one's hypothesis or assumption to be tested. As Markova and Foppa (1990) argue, social intercourse is one of the most powerful media for verifying one's own ideas. As such, dialogue has a congenetic quality, and thus the participants in the dialogue can engage in the mutual codevelopment of ideas. As Graumann (1990) points out, dialogue involves "perspective-setting, perspective-taking, and multiperspectivity of cognition." According to the theory of language action suggested by Austin (1962) and Searle (1969), illocutionary speech does not only involve a description of things and facts but also the taking of action itself. The expression "language is behavior," therefore, implies that language is a socially creative activity and accordingly reveals the importance of the connection between language and reality created through dialogue.

For these purposes, dialectic is a good way of raising the quality of dialogue. Dialectic allows scope for the articulation and development of personal theories and beliefs. Through the use of contradiction and paradox, dialectic can serve to stimulate creative thinking in the organization. If the creative function of dialectic is to be exploited to the full, it is helpful to pay regard to certain preconditions or "field rules." First, the dialogue should not be single-faceted and deterministic but temporary and multifaceted so that there is always room for revision or negation. Second, the participants in the dialogue should be able to express their own ideas freely and candidly. Third, negation for the sake of negation should be discouraged. Constructive criticism substantiated by reasoned arguments should be used to build a consensus. Fourth, there should be temporal continuity. Dialectic thinking is a repetitive, spiral process in which affirmation and negation are synthesized to form knowledge. Strict and noncontinuous separation of affirmation and negation will only result in logical contradictions and thus hamper the creation of knowledge. Team leaders, therefore, should not discourage the dramatic and volatile dimensions of dialogue. If these conditions are met, dialogue will add much to the potential of the group in knowledge creation.

The process of creating a new perspective through interpersonal interaction is assisted by the existence of a degree of redundant information. Making and solving new problems are made possible when its members share information by obtaining extra, redundant information which enables them to enter another person's area and give advice. Instances of "learning by intrusion" (Nonaka 1990) are particularly widespread in Japanese firms.[8] In the meantime, redundancy of information also functions to determine the degree to which created perspectives are diffused. It may sound paradoxical; yet the degree of information redundancy will limit the degree of diffusion. In this sense, information redundancy can serve to regulate the creation of perspectives.

It is now possible to turn to the question of how to conceptualize new perspectives created from shared tacit knowledge. According to Bateson (1979), concepts are created through deduction, induction, and abduction. Abduction has a particular importance in the conceptualization process. While deduction and induction are vertically oriented reasoning processes, abduction is a lateral extension of the reasoning process which centers on the use of metaphors. Deduction and induction are generally used when a thought or image involves the revision of a preexisting concept or the assigning of a new meaning to a concept. When there is no adequate expression of an image, it is necessary to use abductive methods to create completely new concepts. While analytical methods can be used to generate new concepts via inductive or deductive reasoning, they may not be sufficient to create more meaningful—or radical—concepts. At the early stages of information creation, it is very useful to pursue creative dialogues and to share images through the metaphorical process by merging perspectives, that is, tacit knowledge.

Crystallization

The knowledge created in an interactive field by members of a self-organizing team has to be crystallized into some concrete "form" such as a product or a system. The central mode of knowledge conversion at this stage is internalization. Crystallization may then be seen as the process through which various departments within the organization test the reality and applicability of the concept created by the self-organizing team. These internalization processes are facilitated by encouraging experimentation. It should be noted that because the instrumental skill, a part of tacit knowledge, is exploited in this process, a new process of knowledge creation is triggered by crystallization. While this usually leads to refinement of the concept, sometimes the concept itself is abandoned and fundamentally re-created.

The process of crystallization is a social process which occurs at a collective level. It is realized through what Haken (1978) called "dynamic cooperative relations" or "synergetics" among various functions and organizational departments. This relationship tends to be achieved most effectively when redundancy of information creates scope for critical knowledge conversion processes to take place. In an organization where there is redundancy of information, the initiative for action can be taken by the experts who have more information and knowledge. This characteristic is what McCulloch (1965) called "the principle of redundancy of potential command." In this principle, all parts of a system carry the same degree of importance, and each part's impact upon the system is determined by the importance of information it contains in each specified context. In sum, each part has the potential of becoming the leader of the entire system when there exists redundancy of information.

The speed at which Japanese firms develop new products seems to be assisted by information redundancy. In the product development process of Japanese firms, different phases of the process are loosely linked, overlapping in part, and the creation and realization of information is carried out flexibly. The loosely linked phases, while simultaneously maintaining mutual independence, have redundant information that activates their interactive inquiry, thereby facilitating cyclical generation and solution of problems (Imai et al. 1985). This "rugby-style" product development is equipped with the flexible capability of knowledge conversion. Clark and Fujimoto (1991) showed that Japanese firms take relatively less time for product development than American and European firms.

The specific characteristics of the product development in Japanese firms is its lateral breadth covering the whole organization. In other words, it is overlapping and synthetic rather than analytic or linear. In this system, development staff can traverse overlapping phases and, to a certain extent, share each other's functions. This is far different from the usual product development process of U.S. firms, which have definite partitions between phases over which a baton is relayed. In the Japanese "rugby-style" product development (Takeuchi and Nonaka 1986), staff involved in one phase may also be involved in the next phase. Thus, some development staff can be involved in all phases of development. Sometimes this process also involves those outside the organization such as suppliers and customers in order to mobilize an explicit environmental knowledge.

One problem with this developmental style is the potential risk of confusion if, for example, the design changes or other alterations take place. Participants might have to exert more effort to organize the process due to the lack of strict specifications at each phase and definite boundaries between them. However, these risks are counterbalanced by a tendency to create and realize concepts quickly and flexibly in an integral fashion. In this context, redundant information can play a major role in facilitating the process.

The Justification and Quality of Knowledge

While organizational knowledge creation is a continuous process with no ultimate end, an organization needs to converge this process at some point in order to accelerate the sharing of created knowledge beyond the boundary of the organization for further knowledge creation. As knowledge is conventionally defined as "justified true belief," this convergence needs to be based on the "justification" or truthfulness of concepts. Justification is the process of final convergence and screening, which determines the extent to which the knowledge created within the organization is truly worthwhile for the organization and society. In this sense, justification determines the "quality" of the created knowledge and involves criteria or "standards" for judging truthfulness.

What matters here are the evaluation "standards" for judging truthfulness. In the business organizations, the standards generally include cost, profit margin, and the degree to which a product can contribute to the firm's development. There are also value premises that transcend factual or pragmatic considerations. These might be opinions about such things as the extent to which the knowledge created is consistent with the organization's vision and perceptions relating to adventure, romanticism, and aesthetics. The inducements to initiate a convergence of knowledge may be multiple and qualitative rather than simple and quantitative standards such as efficiency, cost, and return on investment (ROI).

In knowledge-creating organizations, it is the role of top or middle management to determine the evaluation standard. Determining the turning point from dissipation to convergence in the creation process is a highly strategic task which is influenced by the *aspiration* of the leaders of the organization. Justification standards have to be evaluated in terms of their consistency with higher-order value systems. The ability of leaders to maintain continuous self-reflection in a wider perspective is indispensable when it comes to increasing the quality of knowledge created.

Networking Knowledge

The realization of new concepts, described above, represents a visible emergence of the organization's knowledge network. During this stage of organizational knowledge creation, the concept that has been created, crystallized, and justified in the organization is integrated into the organizational knowledge-base which comprises a whole network of organizational knowledge. The organizational knowledge base is then reorganized through a mutually inducing process of interaction between the established organizational vision and the newly created concept.

Speaking in sociological terms, this mutually-inducing relationship corresponds to the relationship between a grand concept and a middle-range concept. A middle-range concept is induced from an equivocal knowledge base as a grand concept and then is condensed into concrete form. The grand concept is not fully understood at the organizational level unless these middle-range concepts are verified on site. This verification also induces the creation or reconstruction of a grand concept, causing the interactive proliferation of grand concepts presented by top management, and middle-range concepts created by middle management. This interaction, mediated by the concrete form as condensed information, is another dynamic self-organizing activity of knowledge network that continuously creates new information and meaning.

It should be noted that the process of organizational knowledge creation is a never-ending, circular process that is not confined to the organization but includes many interfaces with the environment. At the same time, the environment is a continual source of stimulation to knowledge creation within the organization. For example, Hayek (1945) pointed out that the essential function of market competition is to discover and mobilize knowledge "on-the-spot," that is, the implicit, context-specific knowledge held by market participants.

In the case of business organizations, one aspect of the relationship between knowledge creation and the environment is illustrated by reactions to the product by customers, competitors, and suppliers. For example, many dimensions of customer needs take the form of tacit knowledge that an individual customer or other market participants cannot articulate by themselves. A product works as a trigger to articulate the tacit knowledge. Customers and other market participants give meaning to the product by their bodily actions of purchasing, adapting, using, or not purchasing. This mobilization of tacit knowledge of customers and market will be reflected to the organization, and a new process of organizational knowledge creation is again initiated.

The total process of organizational knowledge creation is summarized in figure 24.3. Even though the figure is illustrated as a sequential model, the actual process progresses forming multilayered loops. Respective stages can take place simultaneously or sometimes jump forward or backward.

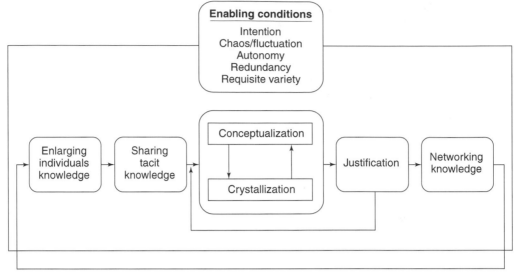

Process of generating information/knowledge in the market

Figure 24.3 Organizational knowledge creation process.

Managing the Process of Organizational Knowledge Creation: Creative Chaos, Redundancy, and Requisite Variety

This section draws on preceding arguments in order to develop a practical perspective on the management of organizational knowledge creation. Its main purpose is to complement the aspects of "individual commitment" to the knowledge creating process (i.e., intention, autonomy, and fluctuation) with, what could be seen as, "organization-wide" enabling conditions that promote a more favorable climate for effective knowledge creation[9] (see figure 24.3). An analysis of these enabling conditions—creative chaos, redundancy of information, and requisite variety—is developed below, prior to making specific proposals for two management models: "middle-up-down management" and a "hypertext" organization. The former model relates to management style, while the latter centers on organizational design.

As was mentioned earlier, environmental fluctuation is one of the three factors that induce individual commitment. At an organizational level, environmental fluctuation can generate "creative chaos" which triggers the process of organizational knowledge creation. When the organization faces nonrecursiveness that cannot be dealt with by existing knowledge, it might try to create a new order of knowledge by making use of the fluctuation itself. According to the principle of "order out of noise" proposed by von Foerster (1984), the self-organizing system can increase its ability to survive by purposefully introducing its own noise. In the context of evolutionary theory, Jantsch (1980) argues: "In contrast to a widely held belief, planning in an evolutionary spirit therefore does not result in the reduction of uncertainty and complexity, but in their increase. Uncertainty increases because the spectrum of options is deliberately widened; imagination comes into play" (1980, p. 267).

This represents a circular process in which chaos is perceived in its interaction with cosmos and then becomes a cosmos, which in turn produces another chaos.

Creative chaos is generated naturally when the organization faces a real "crisis" such as rapid decline of performance due to changes in technologies or market needs, or the realization of a significant competitive advantage on the part of a rival firm. It can also be generated intentionally when leaders of an organization try to evoke a "sense of crisis" among organizational members by proposing challenging goals. This creative chaos increases tension within the organization and focuses attention on forming and solving new problems. In the information processing paradigm, a problem is simply given and a solution is reached through a process of combining relevant information based on a preset algorithm. But this process ignores the importance of problem setting—defining the problem to be solved. In reality, problems do not present themselves as given but instead have to be constructed from the knowledge available at a certain point in time and context.

It should be noted, however, that this process takes place only when organizational members reflect on their actions. Without reflection, the introduction of fluctuation tends to produce "destructive" chaos. As Schön (1983) observed, "When someone reflects while in action, he becomes a researcher. He is not dependent on the categories of established theory and technique, but constructs a new theory of the unique case" (1983, p. 68). The knowledge-creating organization is required to institutionalize this reflection-in-action in its process as well as in its structure to make the chaos truly "creative."

A second principle for managing organizational knowledge creation is redundancy. In business organizations, this means the conscious overlapping of company information, business activities, and management responsibilities. To Western managers, the term "redundancy," with its connotations of unnecessary duplication and waste, may sound unappealing. Nevertheless, redundancy (Landau 1969 and Nonaka 1990) plays a key role, especially in the process of knowledge creation at the level of the organization. Redundant information can be instrumental in speeding up concept creation. A concept that was created by an individual or a group often needs to be shared by other individuals who may need the concept immediately. The redundancy of information refers to the existence of information more than the specific information required immediately by each individual. The sharing of extra information between individuals promotes the sharing of individual tacit knowledge. Since members share overlapping information, they can sense what others are trying to articulate. Especially in the concept development stage, it is critical to articulate images rooted in tacit knowledge. In this situation, individuals can enter each others' area of operation and can provide advice. This allows people to provide new information from new and different perspectives. In short, redundancy of information brings about "learning by intrusion" into an individual's sphere of perception.

Redundant information can be an instrumental factor in reducing the impact of managerial hierarchy. That is to say, redundant information

provides a vehicle for problem generation and knowledge creation which follows procedures that are different from those specified by the "official" organizational structure. This concept of "nonhierarchy" has been described by Hedlund (1986) as "heterarchy." The important point to note is that redundancy of information makes the interchange between hierarchy and nonhierarchy more effective in problem solving and knowledge creation. It enables all members of the organization to participate in the process on the basis of consensus and equal preparation. In this sense, redundancy of information is an indispensable element in inducing the "synergetics" and to realize the "principle of redundancy of potential command."

Deep, mutual trust between the members of the organization—the creators of knowledge—can be promoted through information redundancy and, in this way, the organization can control its knowledge creation. If an organization contains enough redundancy of information to deal with as many contingencies as possible, it can generate various combinations of information flexibly. This redundancy also facilitates interaction among organizational members and consequently makes it easier to transfer tacit knowledge among them. Redundancy can eliminate cheating among organizational members and facilitates establishment of mutual trust. Williamson (1975) argues convincingly that opportunism tends to appear less frequently in internally organized activities than in market transactions. Close interaction and trust based upon sharing of redundant information minimizes the possibility of cheating. Since "trust is a critical lubricant in social systems" (Arrow 1974), it would be impossible to form "synergetics" needed for knowledge creation without trust.

Sharing of extra information also helps individuals to recognize their location in the organization, which in turn increases the sense of control and direction of individual thought and behavior. This state is different from the one in which all members are scattered with no relationship to each other. Redundancy of information connects individuals and the organization through information, which converges rather than diffuses.

There are several ways to build redundancy into the organization. One is to adopt an overlapping approach and internal competition in product development. As was stressed in the section on crystallization, Japanese companies manage product development as an overlapping, "rugby-style" process where different functional divisions work together in a shared division of labor. Some of them also divide the product-development team into competing groups that develop different approaches to the same project and then argue over the advantages and disadvantages of their proposals. Internal rivalry encourages the team to look at a project from a variety of perspectives. Under the guidance of a team leader, the team eventually develops a common understanding of the "best" approach. In one sense, such internal competition is wasteful. But when responsibilities are shared, information proliferates, and the organization's ability to create and implement concepts is accelerated.

Another way to build redundancy into an organization is through strategic rotation, especially between different areas of technology and between functions such as R&D and marketing. Rotation helps members of an organization understand the business from a multiplicity of perspectives. This makes organizational knowledge more fluid and easier to put into practice. Wide access to company information also helps build redundancy. When information differentials exist, members of an organization can no longer interact on equal terms, which hinders the search for different interpretations of new knowledge.

Since redundancy of information increases the amount of information to be processed, it is important to strike a balance between the creation and processing of information. One way of dealing with this issue is to determine the appropriate location of information and knowledge storage within an organization. Ashby (1956) has suggested the concept of "requisite variety" which refers to the constructing of information process channels that match the information load imposed by the environment. According to the principle of requisite variety, an organization can maximize efficiency by creating within itself the same degree of diversity as the diversity it must process. Following Ashby, requisite variety may be seen as the third principle of organizing knowledge creating activities.

Efficient knowledge creation requires quick inquiry and preprocessing of existing knowledge and information. Therefore, it is a practical requirement here that everyone is given access to necessary information with the minimum number of steps (Numagami et al. 1989). For this purpose, (1) organizational members should know who owns what information, and (2) they should be related to the least number of colleagues so

that they are not loaded with information in the excess of each one's cognitive capacity.

Middle-Up-Down Management: Leadership for Parallel Process

In an earlier work, a new model of management called "middle-up-down management" was proposed and contrasted with typical "top-down" management or "bottom-up" management (Nonaka 1988b). This middle-up-down management model is suitable for promoting the efficient creation of knowledge in business organizations. The model is based on the principle of creative chaos, redundancy, and requisite variety mentioned above; much emphasis is placed on the role of top and middle management for knowledge creation, which has been almost neglected in traditional accounts of managerial structure.

The essence of a traditional bureaucratic machine is top-down information processing using division of labor and hierarchy. Top managers create basic managerial concepts (the premises of decision making) and break them down hierarchically—in terms of objectives and means—so that they can be implemented by subordinates. Top managers' concepts become operational conditions for middle managers who then decide how to realize the concepts. Again, middle managers' decisions constitute operational conditions for lower managers who implement their decisions. In consequence, the organization as a whole executes a huge amount of work that can never be done by individuals.

If we visualize the dyadic relations between top versus middle managers, the middle versus lower members, an organization assumes a tree-shaped or pyramidal structure. In this "top-down" model, it is desirable to organize the whole structure in the way it will conform to the above relations. To clearly break down the end-means relations, it is necessary to get rid of any ambiguity or equivocality in the concepts held by top managers. In sum, the concepts anchor on the premise that they only have one meaning. By corollary, the concepts are also strictly functional and pragmatic. An implicit assumption behind this traditional model of organization is that information and knowledge are processed most efficiently in a tree structure. The division of labor taking place within such a bureaucratic organization is associated with a hierarchical pattern of information processing. Moving from the bottom to the top of the organization, information is processed selectively so that people at the peak would get simple, processed information only. Moving in the reverse direction, on the other hand, information is processed and transformed from the general to the particular. It is this deductive transformation that enables human beings with limited information processing capacity to deal with a mass of information.

It should be noted that information processing by middle and lower members in this model is of minor relevance to knowledge creation. Only top managers are able and allowed to create information. Moreover, information created by these top managers exists for the sole purpose of implementation; therefore, it is a tool rather than a product. On the contrary, in the bottom-up model, those who create information are not top managers, but middle and lower managers. In a typical bottom-up managed company, intracompany entrepreneurs or "intrapreneurs" (Pinchot 1985) are fostered and developed by the system. In reality there are not many large firms that have bottom-up management style. In this model, top managers remain sponsors for individual employees who function as intracompany entrepreneurs—including knowledge creation. However, this model is also anchored on the critical role of the individual as an independent, separate actor as in the top-down model.

Unlike the above two models, the middle-up-down model takes all members as important actors who work together horizontally and vertically. A major characteristic of the model regarding knowledge creation is the wide scope of cooperative relationships between top, middle, and lower managers. No one major department or group of experts has the exclusive responsibility for creating new knowledge.

But this is not to say that there is no differentiation among roles and responsibilities in this style of management. In the middle-up-down model, top management provides "visions for direction" and also the deadline by which the visions should be realized. Middle management translates these visions into middle-range visions, which are to be realized in the fields—the groups. Middle managers create their visions out of those from top and lower managers and materialize them vis-à-vis the two levels. In other words, while top management articulates the dreams of the firm, lower managers look at the reality. The gap between these two forms of perspectives is narrowed by and through middle management. In this sense, it is a leadership style that facilitates the parallel knowledge creation process taking place simultaneously at top, middle, and lower management, respectively.

Table 24.1 summarizes the comparison of the three models, top-down, bottom-up, and middle-up-down management, in terms of knowledge creator, resource allocation, structural characteristics, process characteristics, knowledge accu-

TABLE 24.1 A Comparison of Three Management Models

	Top-Down	Middle-Up-Down	Bottom-Up
Agent of knowledge creation	top management	self-organizing team (with middle managers as team leaders)	entrepreneurial individual (intrapreneur)
Resource allocation	hierarchically	from diverse viewpoints	self-organizing principle
Pursued synergy	"synergy of money"	"synergy of knowledge"	"synergy of people"
Organization	• big and powerful hq. • staff use manuals	• team-oriented • affiliated firms by intrapreneurs	• small hq. • self-organizing suborganizations
Management processes	• leaders as commanders • emphasis on information processing • chaos not allowed	• leaders as catalysts create organizational knowledge • create/amplify chaos/noise	• leaders as sponsors create personal information • chaos/noise premised
Accumulated knowledge	explicit computerized/ documented	explicit and tacit shared in diverse forms	tacit incarnated in individuals
Weakness	high dependency on top management	• human exhaustion • lack of overall control of the organization	• time consuming • difficult to coordinate individuals

Source: Nonaka (1988b).

mulation, and inherent limitation. The roles and tasks of lower, top, and middle managers in the middle-up-down management will now be discussed in detail.

Frontline employees and lower managers are immersed in the day-to-day details of particular technologies, products, and markets. No one is more expert in the realities of a company's business than they are. But, while these employees and lower managers are deluged with highly specific information, they often find it extremely difficult to turn that information into useful knowledge. For one thing, signals from the marketplace can be vague and ambiguous. For another, employees and lower managers can become so caught up in their own narrow perspective, that they lose sight of the broader context. Moreover, even when they try to develop meaningful ideas and insights, it can still be difficult to communicate the importance of that information to others. People do not just passively receive new knowledge; they actively interpret it to fit their own situation and perspectives. Thus, what makes sense in one context can change or even lose its meaning when communicated to people in a different context. The main job of top and middle managers in the model of middle-up-down management is to orient this chaotic situation toward purposeful knowledge creation. These managers do this by providing their subordinates with a conceptual framework that helps them make sense of their own experience.

In both top-down management and bottom-up management, a high degree of emphasis is given to charismatic leadership. By contrast, middle-up-down management views managers as catalysts. In this role as a "catalyst," top management sets the direction, provides the field of interaction, selects the participants in the field, establishes the guidelines and deadlines for projects, and supports the innovation process.

Top management gives voice to a company's future by articulating metaphors, symbols, and concepts that orient the knowledge-creating activities of employees. In other words, they give form to "organizational intention" that is beyond the personal intention of top management as an individual. This is achieved by asking the questions on behalf of the entire organization: What are we trying to learn? What do we need to know? Where should we be going? Who are we? If the job of frontline employees and lower managers is to know "what is," then the job of top management is to know "what ought to be." In other words, the responsibility of top man-

agement in middle-up-down management is to articulate the company's "conceptual umbrella": the grand concepts expressed in highly universal and abstract terms identify the common features linking seemingly disparate activities or businesses into a coherent whole. Quinn (1992) called this conceptual umbrella a "future vision" that gives intellectual members of organizations some challenges for intellectual growth and develops their capacity for continuous change.

Another way in which top management provides employees with a sense of direction is by setting the standards for justifying the value of knowledge that is constantly being developed by the organization's members. As earlier comments on the "justification" of knowledge indicated, deciding which efforts to support and develop is a highly strategic task. In order to facilitate organizational knowledge creation, qualitative factors such as truthfulness, beauty, or goodness are equally important to such qualitative, economic factors as efficiency, cost, or ROI.

In addition to the umbrella concepts and qualitative criteria for justification, top management articulates concepts in the form of committed, equivocal visions, which are open-ended and susceptible to a variety of, and even conflicting, interpretations. If a vision is too sharply focused, it becomes more akin to an order or instruction, which will not foster the high degree of personal commitment. A more equivocal vision gives employees and self-organizing teams the freedom and autonomy to set their own goals. The final role of top management in middle-up-down management is to clear away any obstacles and prepare the ground for self-organizing teams headed by middle management. Knowledge creation, in this type of management, takes place intensively at the group level, at which middle managers embody top managers' visions. Middle managers are selected by top management, and therefore staffing is an important strategic consideration. Top managers should be able to provide middle managers with a sense of challenge or crisis and trust them.

As we have seen before, teams play a central role in the process of organizational knowledge creation. The main role of middle managers in middle-up-down management is to serve as a team leader who is at the intersection of the vertical and horizontal flows of information in the company. The most important knowledge creating individuals in this model are neither charismatic top managers nor the entrepreneur-like lower managers, but every employee who works in association with middle managers. It is the middle manager who takes a strategic position at which he or she combines strategic, macro, universal information and hands-on, micro, specific information. They work as a bridge between the visionary ideals of the top and the often chaotic reality on the frontline of business. By creating middle-level business and product concepts, middle managers mediate between "what is" and "what ought to be." They even remake reality according to the company's vision.

In addition, middle management forms the strategic knot that binds the top-down and bottom-up models. As the self-organizing team, headed by middle management moves up and down the organization, much redundancy and fluctuation can be created. As such, the organization with middle-up-down management naturally has a strong driver of self-reorganization. The middle management sometimes plays the role of "change-agent" for the self-evolution of the organization.

In sum, middle managers synthesize the tacit knowledge of both frontline employees and top management, make it explicit, and incorporate it into new technologies and products. They are the true "knowledge engineers" of the knowledge creating organizations.

Hypertext Organization: A Design Prototype of a Knowledge-Creating Organization

Finally, an image can be presented of organizational design that provides a structural base for the process of organizational knowledge creation. Middle-up-down management becomes most efficient if supported by this infrastructure. The central requirement for the design of the knowledge-creating organization is to provide the organization with a strategic ability to acquire, create, exploit, and accumulate new knowledge continuously and repeatedly in a circular process. Earlier work has described an image of organizational design equipped with such a dynamic cycle of knowledge under the concept of a "hypertext organization" (Nonaka et al. 1992). This term is borrowed from a concept of computer software where "hypertext" allows users to search large quantities of text, data, and graphics by means of a friendly interface. It links related concepts and areas of knowledge to allow a problem to be viewed from many angles. In many ways, this is analogous to the ability of individuals to relate stories in different ways according to the nature of the audience. The same knowledge might be used but in different for-

mats, making it easier to draw relationships between different sets of information.

The core feature of the hypertext organization is the ability to switch between the various "contexts" of knowledge creation to accommodate changing requirements from situations both inside and outside the organization. Within the process of organizational knowledge creation, it is possible to distinguish several "contexts" of knowledge creation such as the acquisition, generation, exploitation, and accumulation of knowledge. Each context has a distinctive way of organizing its knowledge creation activities. Nonhierarchical, or "heterarchical" self-organizing activities of teams are indispensable to generate new knowledge as well as to acquire "deep" knowledge through intensive, focused search. On the other hand, a hierarchical division of labor is more efficient and effective for implementation, exploitation, and accumulation of new knowledge as well as acquisition of various information through extensive unfocused search.

Hypertext organization design first distinguishes the normal routine operation conducted by a hierarchical formal organization from the knowledge creating activities carried out by self-organizing teams. But it does not mean that the two activities need to operate separately and independently. Rather, it stresses the need for the careful design of the two activities which takes account of their distinctive contributions to knowledge creation. The important point to note is that the design of the hierarchy and self-organizing teams should enable the organization to shift efficiently and effectively between these two forms of knowledge creation. In terms of the theory of organizational knowledge creation, while hierarchical formal organization mainly carries out the task of combination and internalization, self-organizing teams perform the task of socialization and externalization. This also improves the ability of an organization to survive. By establishing the most appropriate organizational setting for the two activities, an organization can maximize the efficiency of its routine operation, which is determined by bureaucratic principles of division of labor and specialization, and also the effectiveness of its knowledge creation activities. In this type of organization, the knowledge creating activities of self-organizing teams work as a measure which serves to prevent the so-called reverse function of bureaucracy (Merton 1957).

Thus, the hypertext organization combines the efficiency and stability of a hierarchical bureaucratic organization with the dynamism of the flat,

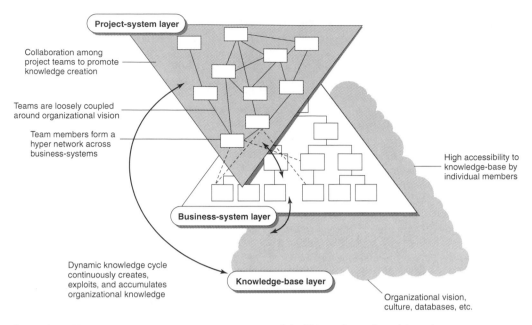

Project-system layer

Collaboration among
project teams to promote
knowledge creation

Teams are loosely coupled
around organizational vision

Team members form a
hyper network across
business-systems

High accessibility to
knowledge-base by
individual members

Business-system layer

Dynamic knowledge cycle
continuously creates,
exploits, and accumulates
organizational knowledge

Knowledge-base layer

Organizational vision,
culture, databases, etc.

Figure 24.4 Hypertext organization—an interactive model of hierarchy and nonhierarchy.

cross-functional task-force organization. Nevertheless, it should be noted that a critical factor for the design of the hypertext organization lies in the coordination of time, space, and resources to realize the "requisite variety." Jacques (1979) pointed out that positions in the hierarchical organization have responsibility of different time-span. This implies that the hierarchical organization is a coordination device for these works of diverse time-span and generates a "natural frequency" by "orchestrating" various rhythms. As the previous section indicated, each self-organizing team also creates its own "natural frequency" by synchronizing various rhythms brought into the field by members from diverse positions in hierarchical organization. The hypertext organization is an organizational structure that enables orchestration of different rhythms or "natural frequency" generated by various project teams and the hierarchical organization. It coordinates the allocation of time, space, and resource within the organization so as to compose an "organizational" rhythm that makes organizational knowledge creation more effective and efficient. In this sense, the hypertext organization is a structural device to build "requisite variety," which cannot be secured solely by middle-up-down management.

The image of the hypertext organization is illustrated in figure 24.4. It can be visualized as a multilayered organization comprised of three layers; knowledge-base, business-system, and project team. At the bottom is the "knowledge-base" layer which embraces tacit knowledge, associated with organizational culture and procedures, as well as explicit knowledge in the form of documents, filing systems, computerized databases, etc. The function of this archival layer may be seen in terms of a "corporate university." The second layer is the "business-system" layer where normal routine operation is carried out by a formal, hierarchical, bureaucratic organization. The top layer relates to the area where multiple self-organizing project teams create knowledge. These teams are loosely linked to each other and share in the "joint creation of knowledge" using "corporate vision." Thus, the hypertext organization takes different "forms," depending on the perspective from which it is observed.

The process of organizational knowledge creation is conceptualized as a dynamic cycle of knowledge and information traversing the three layers. Members of project teams on the top layer are selected from diverse functions and departments across the business-system layer. Based on the corporate vision presented by top management, they engage in knowledge creating activities interacting with other project teams. Once the task of a team is completed, members move "down" to the knowledge-base layer at the bottom and make an "inventory" of the knowledge acquired and created in the project. After categorizing, documenting, and indexing the new knowledge, they come back to the upper business-system layer and engage in routine operation until they are called again for another project. A key design requirement in the hypertext organization is to form such a circular movement of organization members, who are the fundamental source and subject of organizational knowledge creation. From the vantage point of strategic management, the true "core competence" (Prahalad and Hamel 1990) of the organization, which produces sustainable competitive advantage, lies in its management capability to create relevant organizational knowledge (Nonaka 1989, 1991). This is a continuous process and the ability to switch swiftly and flexibly between the three layers in the hypertext organization is critical to its success.

Conclusion

The theory of organizational knowledge creation proposed here has been constructed mainly on the basis of hands-on research and practical experience of Japanese firms. Nevertheless, it should be stressed that the principles described have a more general application to any organization, either economic or social, private or public, manufacturing or service, in the coming age despite their field of activities as well as geographical and cultural location. The theory explains how knowledge held by individuals, organizations, and societies can be simultaneously enlarged and enriched through the spiral, interactive amplification of tacit and explicit knowledge held by individuals, organizations, and societies. The key for this synergetic expansion of knowledge is joint creation of knowledge by individuals and organizations. In this sense, the theory of organizational knowledge creation is at the same time a basic theory for building a truly "humanistic" knowledge society beyond the limitations of mere "economic rationality."

Organizations play a critical role in mobilizing tacit knowledge held by individuals and provide the forum for a "spiral of knowledge" creation through socialization, combination, externalization, and internalization. All of these conversion modes interact in a dynamic and continuous "entanglement" to drive the knowledge creation process. These modes operate in the context of an organization and, while acknowledging the role of individuals as essential actors in creating new knowledge, the central theme of this chapter has been to address the processes involved at an organizational level.

By concentrating on the concept of organizational knowledge creation, it has been possible to develop a perspective which goes beyond straightforward notions of "organizational learning." In the language of the present discussion, learning can be related to "internalization" which is but one of the four modes of conversion required to create new organizational knowledge. Taken by itself, learning has rather limited, static connotations, whereas organizational knowledge creation is a more wide-ranging and dynamic concept.

Finally, hypertext and middle-up-down management have been offered as practical proposals for implementing more effective knowledge creation. As knowledge emerges as an ever more important feature of advanced industrial development, it is necessary to pay increased attention to the processes by which it is created and the assessment of its quality and value both to the organization and society.

Notes

I thank Arie Y. Lewin, John Seeley Brown, Takaya Kawamura, doctoral student at Hitotsubashi University, and Tim Ray for their insightful comments and assistance.

1. See Lewin and Stephens (1992) for arguments on challenges to and opportunities for organizational design in the post-industrial society.

2. Discussion on epistemology here is based on such classical accounts as Plato's *Theaetetus* and *Phaedo*, Descartes's *Discourse on Method*, Locke's *An Essay Concerning Human Understanding*, Hume's *An Enquiry Concerning Human Understanding*, and Kant's *Critique of Pure Reason*. For interpretation of these works, see Hospers (1967), Dancy (1985), Hallis (1985), Moser and Nat (1987), and Winograd and Flores (1986).

3. See also Polanyi (1958) and Gelwick (1977).

4. Metaphor should not be understood as mere rhetoric or an issue of expression; it is deeply connected with knowledge creation. For this point, see Black (1962) and McCormac (1985).

5. For comprehensive discussion on metaphor, analogy, and model, see Leatherdale (1974) and Tsoukas (1991).

6. The self-organizing team may be depicted by Maturana and Varela's (1980) concept of an "autopoietic system." Living organic systems are

composed of various organs, which are again composed of numerous cells. Each unit, like an autonomous cell, is self-regulating. Moreover, each unit determines its boundary through self-reproduction and is separate from the environment. This self-referential or self-reflecting nature is a quintessential feature of autopoietic systems.

7. Gibson (1979) suggested an interesting hypothesis that knowledge lies in the environment itself, contrary to the traditional epistemological view that it exists inside the human brain. According to him, man perceives information ("affordance") which natural objects afford to human cognitive activity, i.e., according to the degree of affordance of the environment. Information on chair, knife, and cliff are revealed when the actions of sitting, cutting, and falling are made, in other words, in the course of interactions between the subject and the object of perception.

8. Jaikumar and Born (1986) pointed to this as the characteristic of Japanese firms' production methods. According to them, the production method for most American firms is clearly defined as the function of the basic manufacturing technology, assigned works, organizational goals, and environment. In this mode of production, then, workers are well aware of their work and thus simply follow the routine procedure. On the other hand, Japanese workers do not get prior knowledge and thus become part of the given work, rather than being separate from the work itself. Therefore, anomaly, or nonroutine nature, of the work itself becomes an important opportunity for learning.

9. The development of these concepts are based on a series of theoretical and empirical research studies (Kagono et al. 1985, Takeuchi et al. 1986, and Nonaka 1988a).

References

Anderson, J.R. (1983) *The Architecture of Cognition.* Cambridge, MA: Harvard University Press.
Argyris, C. and Schön, D.A. (1978) *Organizational Learning.* Reading, MA: Addison-Wesley.
Arrow, K.J. (1974) *The Limits of Organization.* New York: John Brockman Associates.
Ashby, W.R. (1956) *An Introduction to Cybernetics.* London: Champan & Hall.
Austin, J.L. (1962) *How to Do Things with Words.* Oxford: Oxford University Press.
Bateson, G. (1973) *Steps to an Ecology of Mind.* London: Paladin.
Bateson, G. (1979) *Mind and Nature: A Necessary Unity.* New York: Bantam Books.

Bell, D. (1973) *The Coming of Post-industrial Society: A Venture in Social Forecasting.* New York: Basic Books.
Berger, P.L. and Luchman, T. (1966) *Social Construction of Reality.* New York: Doubleday.
Black, M. (1962) *Models and Metaphors.* Ithaca, NY: Cornell University Press.
Brown, J.S. and Duguid, P. (1991) "Organizational Learning and Communities of Practice: Towards a Unified View of Working, Learning and Organization." *Organization Science* 2(1):40–57.
Clark, K.B. and Fujimoto, T. (1991) *Product Development Performance.* Boston, MA: Harvard Business School Press.
Cohen, M.D., March, J.G., and Olsen, J.P. (1972) "A Garbage Can Model of Organizational Choice." *Administrative Science Quarterly* 17:1–25.
Condon, W.S. (1976) "An Analysis of Behavioral Organization." *Sign Language Studies*, 13.
Dancy, J. (1985) *Introduction to Contemporary Epistemology.* New York: Basil Blackwell.
Dretske, F. (1981) *Knowledge and the Flow of Information.* Cambridge, MA: MIT Press.
Drucker, P. (1968) *The Age of Discontinuity: Guidelines to Our Changing Society.* New York: Harper & Row.
Eigen, M. (1971) "Self-Organization of Matter and the Evolution of Biological Macro-Molecules." *Naturwissenshaften* 58.
Gelwick, R. (1977) *The Way of Discovery: An Introduction to the Thought of Michael Polanyi.* Oxford: Oxford University Press.
Gibson, J.J. (1979) *The Ecological Approach to Visual Perception.* Boston, MA: Houghton-Mifflin.
Gleick, J. (1987) *Chaos.* New York, Viking.
Graumann, C.F. (1990) "Perspectival Structure and Dynamics in Dialogues," in I. Markova and K. Foppa (eds.), *The Dynamics of Dialogue.* New York: Harvester Wheatsheaf.
Gruber, T.R. (1989) *The Acquisition of Strategic Knowledge.* San Diego, CA: Academic Press.
Hallis, M. (1985) *Invitation to Philosophy.* Oxford: Basil Blackwell.
Haken, H. (1978) *Synergetics: Nonequilibrium Phase Transitions and Self-Organization in Physics, Chemistry and Biology.* 2nd ed. Berlin: Springer.
Hayek, F.A. (1945) "The Use of Knowledge in Society." *American Economic Review* 35(4):519–530.
Hedberg, B.L.T. (1981) "How Organizations Learn and Unlearn," in P.C. Nystrom, and W.H. Starbuck (eds.), *Handbook of Organizational Design.* Oxford: Oxford University Press.
Hedlund, G. (1986) "The Hypermodern MNC—A Heterarchy?" *Human Resource Management* 25(1).

Hospers, J. (1967) *An Introduction to Philosophical Analysis*. 2nd ed. London: Routledge & Kegan Paul.

Husserl, E. (1968) *The Ideas of Phenomenology*. Hague: Nijhoff.

Imai, K., Nonaka, I., and Takeuchi, H. (1985) "Managing the New Product Development Process: How Japanese Companies Learn and Unlearn," in K.B. Clark, R.H. Hayes and C. Lorenz (eds.), *The Uneasy Alliance: Managing the Productivity-Technology Dilemma*. Boston, MA: Harvard Business School Press.

Jacques, E. (1979) "Taking Time Seriously in Evaluating Jobs." *Harvard Business Review* (September–October):124–132.

Jaikumar, R. and Born, R.E. (1986) "The Development of Intelligent System for Industrial Use: A Conceptual Framework." *Research on Technological Innovation, Management and Policy* 3, JAI Press.

Jantsch, E. (1980) *The Self-Organizing Universe*. Oxford: Pergamon Press.

Johnson-Laird (1983) *Mental Models*. Cambridge: Cambridge University Press.

Kagono, T., Nonaka, I., Sakakibara, K., and Okumura, A. (1985) *Strategic vs. Evolutionary Management*. Amsterdam: North-Holland.

Lakoff, G. and Johnson, M. (1980) *Metaphors We Live By*. Chicago: University of Chicago Press.

Landau, M. (1969) "Redundancy, Rationality, and the Problem of Duplication and Overlap." *Public Administration Review* 14(4).

Leatherdale, W.H. (1974) *The Role of Analogy, Model and Metaphor in Science*. Amsterdam: North-Holland.

Lewin, A.Y. and Stephens, C.V. (1992) "Designing Post-industrial Organization: Theory and Practice," in G.P. Huber and W.H. Glick (eds.), *Organization Change and Redesign: Ideas and Insights for Improving Managerial Performance*. New York: Oxford University Press.

Lewin, K. (1951) *Field Theory in Social Science*. New York: Harper.

Machlup, F. (1983) "Semantic Quirks in Studies of Information," in F. Machlup and U. Mansfield (eds.), *The Study of Information*. New York: John Wiley.

Markova, I. and Foppa, K. (eds.) (1990) *The Dynamics of Dialogue*. New York: Harvester Wheatsheaf.

Maturana, H.R. and Varela, F.J. (1980) *Autopoiesis and Cognition: The Realization of the Living*. Dordrecht, Holland: Reidel.

McCormac, E.R. (1985) *A Cognitive Theory of Metaphor*. Cambridge, MA: MIT Press.

McCulloch, W. (1965) *Embodiments of Mind*. Cambridge, MA: MIT Press.

Merleau-Ponty, M. (1964) *The Structure of Behavior*. Boston, MA: Beacon Press.

Merton, R.K. (1957) *Social Theory and Social Structure*. New York: Free Press.

Miyazaki, K. and Ueno, N. (1985) *Shiten* (The View Point). Tokyo: Tokyo Daigaku Shuppankai (in Japanese).

Morgan, G. (1986) *Images of Organization*. Beverly Hills, CA: Sage Publications.

Moser, P.K. and Nat, A.V. (1987) *Human Knowledge*. Oxford: Oxford University Press.

Neisser, U. (1976) *Cognition and Reality*. New York: W. H. Freeman.

Nisbet, R.A. (1969) *Social Change and History: Aspects of the Western Theory of Development*. London: Oxford University Press.

Nishida, K. (1960) *A Study of Good* (Zen no kenkyu). Tokyo: Printing Bureau, Japanese Government.

Nonaka, I. (1987) "Managing the Firm as Information Creation Process." Working Paper, January (published in J. Meindl (ed.) (1991) *Advances in Information Processing in Organizations* 4, JAI Press.

Nonaka, I. (1988a) "Creating Organizational Order Out of Chaos: Self-Renewal in Japanese Firms." *California Management Review* 15(3):57–73.

Nonaka, I. (1988b) "Toward Middle-Up-Down Management: Accelerating Information Creation." *Sloan Management Review* 29(3):9–18.

Nonaka, I. (1989) "Organizing Innovation as a Knowledge-Creation Process: A Suggestive Paradigm for Self-Renewing Organization." Working Paper, University of California at Berkeley, no. OBIR-41.

Nonaka, I. (1990) "Redundant, Overlapping Organizations: A Japanese Approach to Managing the Innovation Process." *California Management Review* 32(3):27–38.

Nonaka, I. (1991) "The Knowledge-Creating Company." *Harvard Business Review* (November–December):96–104.

Nonaka, I., Konno, N., Tokuoka, K., and Kawamura, T. (1992) "Hypertext Organization for Accelerating Organizational Knowledge Creation." *Diamond Harvard Business* (August–September) (in Japanese).

Norman, D.A. (1977) *The Psychology of Everyday Things*. New York: Basic Books.

Numagami, T., Ohta, T., and Nonaka, I. (1989) "Self-Renewal of Corporate Organizations: Equilibrium, Self-Sustaining, and Self-Renewing Models." Working Paper, University of California at Berkeley, no. OBIR-43.

Piaget, J. (1974) *Recherches sur la Contradiction*. Paris: Presses Universitaires de France.

Pinchot, G. III (1985) *Intrapreneuring*. New York: Harper & Row.

Polanyi, M. (1958) *Personal Knowledge*. Chicago: University of Chicago Press.

Polanyi, M. (1966) *The Tacit Dimension*. London: Routledge & Kegan Paul.

Prahalad, C.K. and Hamel, G. (1990) "The Core Competition of the Corporation." *Harvard Business Review* (May–June):79–91.

Quinn, J.B. (1992) *Intelligent Enterprise*. New York: Free Press.

Rosch, E.H. (1973) "Natural Categories." *Cognitive Psychology* 4:328–350.

Ryle, G. (1949) *The Concept of Mind*. London: Huchinson.

Sandelands, L.E. and Stablein, R.E. (1987) "The Concept of Organization Mind." *Research in the Sociology of Organizations* 5.

Scheflen, A.E. (1982) "Comments on the Significance of Interaction Rhythms," in M. Davis (ed.), *Interaction Rhythms*. New York: Free Press.

Schön, D.A. (1983) *The Reflective Practitioner*. New York: Basic Books.

Schrage, M. (1990) *Shared Minds: The New Technologies of Collaboration*. New York: John Brockman.

Searle, J.R. (1969) *Speach Acts: An Essay in the Philosophy of Language*. Cambridge: Cambridge University Press.

Searle, J.R. (1983) *Intentionality: An Essay in the Philosophy of Mind*. Cambridge: Cambridge University Press.

Shannon, C.E. and Weaver, W. (1949) *The Mathematical Theory of Communication*. Urbana, IL: University of Illinois Press.

Shimizu, H. (1978) *Seimei o toraenaosu* (Capturing the Nature of Life). Tokyo: Chuo koronsha (in Japanese).

Stich, S. (1986) *From Folk Psychology to Cognitive Science: The Case Against Belief*. Cambridge, MA: MIT Press.

Takeuchi, H. and Nonaka, I. (1986) "The New New Product Development Game." *Harvard Business Review* (Jan.–Feb.): 137–146.

Takeuchi, H., Sakakibara, K., Kagono, T., Okumura, A., and Nonaka, I. (1986) *Kigyo no jiko kakushin* (Corporate Self-renewal). Tokyo: Chuo koronsha (in Japanese).

Toffler, A. (1990) *Powershift: Knowledge, Wealth and Violence at the Edge of 21st Century*. New York: Bantam Books.

Tsoukas, H. (1991) "The Missing Link: A Transformation View of Metaphor in Organizational Science." *Academy of Management Review* 16(3): 566–585.

Varela, F.J., Thompson, E., and Rosch, E. (1991) *Embodied Mind: Cognitive Science and Human Experience*. Cambridge, MA: MIT Press.

von Foerster, H. (1984) "Principles of Self-organization in a Socio-Managerial Context," in H. Ulrich and G.J.B. Probst (eds.), *Self-organization and Management of Social Systems*. Berlin: Springer-Verlag.

Weick, K.E. (1976) *The Social Psychology of Organizing*. 2nd ed. Reading, MA: Addison-Wesley.

Williamson, O.E. (1975) *Market and Hierarchies: Antitrust Implications*. New York: Free Press.

Winograd, T. and Flores (1986) *Understanding Computer and Cognition*. Reading, MA: Addison-Wesley.

Yuasa, Y. (1987) *The Body: Toward an Eastern Mind-Body Theory*, T.P. Kasulis (ed.), trans. S. Nagatomi and T.P. Kasulis. New York: State University of New York Press.

25

Managing Existing Knowledge Is Not Enough

Knowledge Management Theory and Practice in Japan

Katsuhiro Umemoto

The 1990s has witnessed a remarkable surge of interest in knowledge as the ultimate source of competitive advantage not only for business companies but also for nations or regions (Toffler 1990; Drucker 1993). And knowledge management (KM) has become a most lucrative industry in itself, as evidenced by scores of KM books being sold worldwide, KM programs being promoted by consulting firms, and KM software being marketed by IT vendors.[1]

Professor Ikujiro Nonaka, dubbed "Mr. Knowledge" by *The Economist* magazine (May 31, 1997 issue), is one of the most influential thinkers in the KM movement, since he published the now-classic *Harvard Business Review* article titled "The Knowledge-Creating Company" (Nonaka 1991),[2] which was later enlarged and enriched into another article (Nonaka 1994, see also chapter 24, this volume) and a book with the same title (Nonaka and Takeuchi 1995).

Knowledge management in Japan has naturally been influenced by Professor Nonaka. Though KM goes usually by its Japanese pronunciation, it can be translated into two Japanese terms, namely (*chishiki kanri*) and (*chishiki keiei*). While the former means only management of *existing* knowledge, the latter term, promulgated by Nonaka and Konno (1999), goes beyond it to further imply "management by creating *new* knowledge *continuously*." According to this view, current IT-based KM practices, through its impressive diffusion, still remains at the former level.

Being dissatisfied with it, Professor Nonaka and his colleagues have continued their efforts to further develop his theory of organizational knowledge creation as the basis of (*chishiki keiei*) (Nonaka et al. 1996, von Krogh et al. 1997, Nonaka and Konno 1998, Nonaka and Konno 1999, Nomura and Kametsu 1999, Nonaka et al. 2000, von Krogh et al. 2000, Nonaka, Reinmoeller, and Senoo 2000, Nonaka, Toyama, and Konno 2000, Nonaka, Reinmoeller, and Toyama, forthcoming). This chapter aims to provide the reader with the recent theoretical developments and current Japanese KM practices in Japan.

Recent Developments in KM Theory and Practice in Japan

As of 2000, Nonaka's theory of organizational knowledge creation consists of four major elements: (1) the SECI model, the process of creating new knowledge through interaction and conversion between tacit and explicit knowledge (see previous chapter); (2) *ba* or a shared context for knowledge creation; (3) knowledge assets as inputs and outputs of the knowledge-creating process; and (4) knowledge leadership that provides enabling conditions conducive to the process. These four elements interact with each other in "management by creating *new* knowledge *continuously*."

Because no single company can represent all aspects of Nonaka's theory, we present minicases of Japanese companies that are practicing each of the four elements: that is, the SECI model, *ba*, knowledge assets, and knowledge leadership, respectively. Needless to say, however, practice cannot be the same as theory. In reality, therefore, the Japanese companies presented below have adapted, with varying degrees, the four elements.

SECI as the Self-Transcending Process

Since the SECI model is discussed in the previous chapter, this section presents only notable points and developments to deepen your understanding of the model. First, the knowledge-creating process takes the form of a *spiral*, not a circle. In the "knowledge spiral," the interaction between tacit and explicit knowledge is amplified through the four modes of knowledge conversion. The spiral becomes larger in scale as it enriches knowledge contents and moves up the ontological levels from individual to group to organizational (and often to interorganizational), and then back to the individual level. It is a dynamic, never-ending process, starting at the individual level and expanding as it moves through communities of interaction that transcend individual, sectional, departmental, divisional, and organizational boundaries (see figure 25.1).

Second, organizational knowledge creation is the self-transcending process in which an individual finds his or her new identity, first within a group, and next in an organization, thereby discovering him- or herself enriched with new experience and knowledge. In socialization, individuals acquire skills by sharing direct (i.e., real)

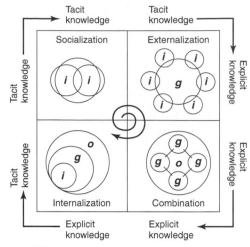

i : individual
g : group
o : organization

Figure 25.1 Knowledge creation as the self-transcending process. *Source:* Nonaka and Konno (1998), p. 43.

experiences with others in the same time and space, like in apprenticeship or OJT, and empathize another person's way of looking at the same situation by "putting oneself into another person's shoes." In externalization, those who empathize along with their separate tacit knowledge in mental models get integrated into a group's mental model, which is then articulated into explicit concepts through dialogues. In combination, new explicit concepts created by the group are combined with existing explicit knowledge (embodied into component technologies) to form a systemic knowledge (in the form of a new product and/or service) at the organizational level. And in internalization, again, individuals (e.g., factory workers, service engineers, customers) accumulate tacit knowledge of know-how by producing, doing, or using the product and/or service.

Practicing an Elaborated SECI model at Fuji Xerox

Fuji Xerox has defined its mission as "Build an Environment for the Creation and Effective Utilization of Knowledge."[3,4] The leading copier-maker has developed an intranet-based knowledge-sharing system called "Z-EIS or *Zen-in* Engineering Information System" (*Zen-in* means everyone) and built a "*Zen-in* Design

Room" or a meeting room, where designers and engineers come together from every stage of the development process to have discussion over three-dimensional, visualized models.

The development of the knowledge-sharing and -creating systems started in the early 1990s, when the company's R&D managers decided to solve the problem of prolonged lead time due to design changes in the last stage of development. Engineers responsible for the last stage, who are also closer to users, had to wait for a prototype. To solve the problem, therefore, designers and engineers of the whole development process had *interacted* with one another to have discussions in search of solutions. They noticed the importance of know-how or tacit, on-the-site knowledge of designers and engineers, which often becomes explicit only in front of prototypes. Thus, they started visiting each site of the development stage, trying to *capture* the tacit, on-the-site knowledge (Socialization).

In the meantime, they came up with the concept of *"Zen-in* Design" or "Design by Everyone," which means that "every engineer must participate in the whole design process by making comments or suggestions for better designs while taking responsibility in each area." Yet, a problem of how to *organize* the captured knowledge remained. To that purpose, an on-line engineering information-sharing system was developed and named Z-EIS, into which designers and engineers started articulating and inputting (i.e., *formalizing*) their on-the-site know-how (Externalization).

Because not every piece of formalized knowledge is useful enough to be shared among all designers and engineers, middle managers of each development stage have to *identify* only usable items to be officially registered on Z-EIS. In addition to the on-the-site know-how, three-dimensional graphic models, parts specifications, market data, patents information, and product management data are input into Z-EIS. Thus, 4,500 pieces of articulated on-the-site knowledge are *shared* among 500 designers and 4,100 engineers, and about 50,000 inquiries come to Z-EIS every month, as of 1999 (Combination).

For the registered items of know-how to become really significant, they must be actually utilized and lead to action. To effectively and efficiently utilize the articulated know-how, therefore, the most useful knowledge is *selected* and compiled into the "Quality Assurance List," that is, new explicit knowledge to be utilized for design reviews. Thus, the explicit knowledge of de-

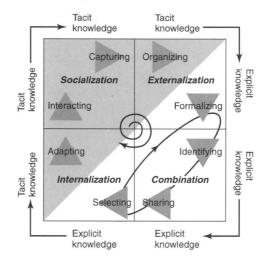

Figure 25.2 Elaborated SECI model at Fuji Xerox. Adapted from Nomura and Kametsu (1999), p. 64.

sign and development know-how are utilized and *adapted* on the site, thereby becoming tacit again (Internalization).

As noted above, the SECI process is not a cycle but a *spiral*. Therefore, the knowledge-creating process goes on, *expanding* and entering into socialization again. Designers and engineers with enriched and embodied tacit knowledge come together and *interact* with one another at the *Zen-in* Design Room. Nomura and Kametsu (1999) pointed out that the currently prevalent KM practice of utilizing merely existing knowledge forms the *cycle* of actions from formalizing to selecting, thereby contributing to some increase in efficiency but little in the way of creativity in organizations (see figure 25.2).

Ba: Shared Context for Knowledge Creation

Nonaka and Konno (1998) introduced the concept of *ba* to the KM field.[5] They defined it as "a shared context in which knowledge is created, shared, and utilized." *Ba* can be physical (e.g., office), virtual (e.g., teleconference), mental (e.g., shared experiences, ideas, or ideals), or any combination of them.

For knowledge to be created, it needs a context. Contrary to the Cartesian view of knowledge that asserts the absolute and context-free nature of knowledge, the knowledge-creating process is necessarily context-specific. Social, cultural, and historical contexts provide the basis for us to interpret information and create meaning. *Ba* is a context where information is interpreted and integrated into knowledge. Also, *ba* provides a platform for individuals to participate in each mode of knowledge conversion and to move along the knowledge spiral.

A key concept in understanding *ba* is interaction. Knowledge is created through interactions among individuals or between individuals and their environments rather than by an individual operating alone. Interactions may be real or virtual (i.e., IT-based) or a mix of them. Especially in socialization and externalization, it is essential for participants to interact face-to-face in the same time and space (i.e., in a real *ba*), because these modes deal with tacit knowledge that is difficult to be transmitted via electronic media (Nonaka et al. 1997). *Ba* is the context shared by those who interact with each other to create knowledge, and both *ba* and its participants co-evolve toward self-transcendence.

There are four types of *ba*: originating *ba*, dialoguing *ba*, systemizing *ba*, and exercising *ba*, each of which corresponds roughly to socialization, externalization, combination, and internalization, respectively.

Originating *ba* is defined by real, face-to-face interactions. It is a place where individuals share actions, cognitions, and emotions. It offers mainly a context for socialization, since real, face-to-face interaction is the only way to capture the full range of physical senses and psycho-emotional reactions such as ease or discomfort, which are important elements in sharing tacit knowledge. Originating *ba* is an existential place in the sense that it is the world where an individual transcends the boundary between self and others by empathizing with others. From originating *ba* emerge care, love, trust, and commitment that form the foundation for knowledge conversion among individuals.[6]

Dialoguing *ba* is defined by collective, face-to-face interactions. It is the place where individuals' mental models are shared, translated into common language, and articulated into concepts through dialogues among participants. Therefore, dialoguing *ba* offers mainly a context for externalization. Also, the articulated knowledge goes back into each individual and interacts with the remaining tacit knowledge, thereby promoting further articulation through reflection. Dialoguing *ba* can be built more intentionally than originating *ba*. When possible, selecting individuals who have the right mix of specific knowledges and capabilities is the key to promoting knowledge creation in dialoguing *ba*.

Systemizing *ba* is defined by collective, indirect (i.e., increasingly virtual or IT-based) interactions. It offers mainly a context for combination of existing explicit knowledge that can be easily transmitted to a large number of people in written form. Information technology (e.g., TV conference, intranet, groupware, and the Internet) provides a virtual collaborative environment for the building of systemizing *ba*. Today, many organizations use such media as electronic mailing lists and news groups through which participants can exchange necessary information or answer each other's questions to collect and disseminate knowledge and information efficiently as well as effectively.

Exercising *ba* is defined by interactions between explicit knowledge and actions. It offers mainly a context for internalization. By acting on explicit knowledge, which is communicated through such media as text and/or video manuals, simulation programs, or any combination of them, individuals can embody it into tacit operational knowledge. In other words, individuals learn explicit knowledge by actually or virtually doing it. In exercising *ba*, action initiates individual reflection and then enables individual transcendence, while in dialoguing *ba* thought starts collective reflection and then enables collective transcendence (for more discussion, see Nonaka and Konno 1998, Nonaka, Toyama, and Konno 2000).

Forming *Ba* at NTT East

The Business Communications Headquarters (BCH) of NTT East,[7] a local telecommunications services provider in the eastern part of Japan, is notable for its innovative KM program that combines a real *ba* (i.e., an original office layout) and a virtual *ba* (i.e., numerous intranet-based homepages built by every individual, section, department, and the BCH itself) to create new knowledge solutions for its business clients. The innovative KM program is the brainchild of Kunio Ushioda, executive deputy-director of the BCH. He devised a concept called "Kaichi" or his own Japanese translation of the English term "education," which originally means extraction of human capabilities. His idea is to extract human capabilities with the new office environment and the intranet.

Ushioda has also devised another concept, "creation by cross culture," which means that new knowledge is created through unexpected encounters and dialogues among people with dif-

Figure 25.3 Base zone. Copyright Suguru Kanazawa.

ferent knowledge and information. The new of-fice layout is designed to form a number of real *ba*, thereby promoting dialogues and interactions among 1,600 BCH members with different backgrounds. Each floor has four zones as follows:

- "Base Zone" is used mainly for project planning and characterized by "free address" (i.e., nobody has a designated desk, instead every member has a portable phone, a notebook computer, and a castered sidebox), which facilitates the quick organizing of project teams, the sharing of skills among project members (i.e., socialization), and unusual encounters with members of other project teams by taking next seats by chance. Thus, this zone is supposed to be an originating *ba* and a systemizing *ba* (see figure 25.3).
- "Creative Zone" is used for a project team to create new ideas through dialogues, assisted by personal computers and a 42-inch plasma display, which are connected to the intranet that provides almost all necessary information and knowledge. This space is located by the window and partitioned by green plants that are movable to make space necessary for each meeting. This zone is supposed to be a dialoguing *ba* (see figure 25.4).
- "Concentration Zone" is used for individuals to develop further ideas conceived in the "Creative Zone," and mainly by system engineers for programming, system design, or proposal writing. This space is partitioned for individuals who want to concentrate on their work in a quiet environment. This zone is supposed to be a systemizing *ba* and an exercising *ba* (see figure 25.5).
- "Refresh Zone" includes a smoking room, a vending-machine corner, and a magazine browsing corner, and is used either for relaxation or for informal interactions and conversations among employees with different backgrounds. This zone is supposed to be an originating *ba* (see figure 25.6).

Another system designed to utilize existing knowledge and thereby to create new knowledge is numerous intranet-based homepages as virtual *ba*. Every member of the BCH has his or her own homepage that consists of four parts referred to by such metaphors as "My Home,"

Figure 25.4 Creative zone. Copyright Suguru Kanazawa.

Figure 25.5 Concentration zone. Copyright Suguru Kanazawa.

Figure 25.6 Refresh zone. Copyright Suguru Kanazawa.

"My Study," "Second House," and "Resort House."

- "My Home" introduces the builder of the homepage with an individual profile and a photograph (or a moving picture) plus an extension phone number, an e-mail address, etc.
- "My Study" includes day-to-day work records about projects of the homepage builder, for example, proposals to business clients, all of which are accessible to every member of the BCH and can be copied for the business use with permission.
- "Second House" contains the work experience of the homepage builder, histories of past projects he or she has participated in, and his or her expertise or qualifications.
- "Resort House" provides information about such personal matters as hobbies and family members of the homepage builder, which is expected to facilitate communication among others.

The original intention of building the personal homepages has been to help each member master basic Internet skills and know each other.

Now, those personal homepages of colleagues belonging to the same project team (or others if necessary) are mutually linked for the quick access to each other's business files, thereby sharing a virtual systemizing *ba* as well as information and knowledge. Thanks to a text-mining technology,[8] moreover, members of the BCH can access any business files that contain information they want to know.

Also, each section or department has its own homepage that holds various knowledge bases. For example, the Third Sales Department has a knowledge base called the "Forest of Knowledge," which contains proposals and materials for presentations to business clients. The knowledge base, intended to promote the sharing of best sales know-how, works as follows:

1. a sales manager reads daily negotiation reports and proposals his team members submit electronically;
2. the manager selects proposals good enough to be registered with his comments on the "Forest of Knowledge" by clicking a registration button;
3. the number of access clicks to each registered proposal is counted, ranked, and

shown on the first page of the knowledge base;

4. salespeople who used the registered proposals click a "thank you" button, and the number of "thank you" clicks is counted and shown along with the ranking; and

5. the top two in the ranking, that is, two of the most popular proposals are conferred the semiannual "Best Knowledge Award."

Four Types of Knowledge Assets

Although knowledge is viewed as one of the most important assets for a firm to create a sustainable competitive advantage today, we do not have yet an effective method to measure, evaluate, or manage knowledge assets. Existing accounting systems are inadequate to capture the value of knowledge assets due to the tacit and dynamic nature of some knowledge assets, though several new measures to evaluate knowledge assets or intellectual capital have been proposed (Stewart 1997, Edvinsson and Malone 1997).

Yet, to create a knowledge strategy, we need some understanding of how knowledge assets are created, accumulated, and utilized. Nonaka and associates (Nonaka and Konno 1999, Nonaka, Toyama, and Konno 2000) have proposed a taxonomy to categorize knowledge assets into four types: (1) "experiential" knowledge assets, (2) "conceptual" knowledge assets, (3) "systemic" knowledge assets, and (4) "routine" knowledge assets.

Experiential knowledge assets are tacit knowledge that is built through shared hands-on experience among a firm's members and between them and its customers or suppliers. Skills and know-how, acquired and accumulated through work experiences, are examples of experiential knowledge assets. Other examples include affective knowledge (e.g., care, love, and trust), motor knowledge (e.g., facial expressions and gestures), energic knowledge (e.g., enthusiasm and tension), and rhythmic knowledge (e.g., improvisation and entrainment). Because experiential knowledge assets are tacit, they are difficult to capture, evaluate, or exchange for money. Only through their own experiences can firms accumulate their own experiential knowledge assets. Their tacitness makes experiential knowledge assets firm-specific and difficult-to-imitate resources that provide a sustainable competitive advantage to a firm.

Conceptual knowledge assets are explicit knowledge articulated into words, numbers, and diagrams. They are concepts that are held by members of a company and its customers. Examples include corporate strategies, product concepts, and designs, which are possessed by members of the company, and brand equity, which is perceived by customers. Since they have tangible forms, conceptual knowledge assets are easier to see than experiential knowledge assets. Still it is difficult to measure customers' and organizational members' perception.

Systemic knowledge assets consist of systemized and packaged explicit knowledge. Examples are manifestly stated technologies, product specifications, manuals, and documented and packaged information about customers or suppliers. Legally protected intellectual properties such as licenses and patents also fall into this category. Since they are most "visible" and easily digitized into IT, current KM practices focus primarily on them. Also, they can be traded and transferred with relative ease.

Routine knowledge assets are tacit knowledge that is embedded in organizational daily practices and actions. Examples include know-how (e.g., those in various corporate functions), organizational routines and cultures, as certain patterns of thinking and action that are shared among organizational members and reinforced by daily activities. Sharing narratives and stories about their own company also helps form routine knowledge assets. Note that the routine nature may become inertia and hinder the knowledge-creating process (cf. core rigidities in Leonard-Barton 1992).

Knowledge Assets Programs at Fuji Xerox, Hitachi, and Sony

Because the above taxonomy is new, no Japanese company has adopted it in practice yet. Increasingly, however, more and more Japanese companies have come to understand the importance of knowledge assets. Among them, probably Fuji Xerox understands best what KM is, since the company is very close to Professor Nonaka.[9] The leading copier-maker has instituted several programs regarding knowledge assets. Most interesting is the program called "C-class Marketing." C stands for CEO, COO, CKO, CIO, or top managers who have decision-making power. This unique program helps Fuji Xerox salespeople get access to their potential corporate clients' decision-makers by providing them with Fuji Xerox's knowledge assets, even hard-earned wisdom from its failures, that have been accumulated over a period about such issues as total quality management, sales force automation, risk management, outsourcing, human resource management, and so on. Most of the knowledge assets are explicit systemic knowledge assets, which were externalized from tacit experiential knowledge assets, and are currently in use at Fuji Xerox.

The program works as follows. A salesperson hands a sheet of paper titled "Collaboration Program" to a possible corporate customer's purchasing department. It lists the above issues that Fuji Xerox has accumulated and externalized as knowledge. He invites the possible customer's top manager to a "presentation room" (there are now five in Tokyo, one in Osaka, and one in Nagoya), where these top managers listen to presentations by experts on issues they are interested in. The presenters are specialists on those issues, and the presentations include Fuji Xerox's knowledge assets as well as general knowledge about the selected issues. According to an in-house survey of Fuji Xerox's salespeople, 95% of them either strongly agreed or agreed to the statement: "the program has helped strengthen the trust between you and your customers," and 88% of them either strongly agreed or agreed to the statement: "the program has helped your business negotiations."[10]

Rather than giving away its knowledge assets for free, Hitachi sells its systemic knowledge assets. When Etsuhiko Syoyama rose to president of Hitachi in 1998, he declared his vision that "we aim for the "Knowledge Enterprise" and demonstrate its ability to synthesize its technology and intelligence." The electronics giant has since started two knowledge assets programs. One is to sell its "systemic knowledge" that was only internally utilized until then, for example, packaged software of computer-assisted engineering (CAE), through a portal site named "i-engineering" on the Internet.

The other is a brand new management program that was instituted directly under the president in April 2000. The company has decided on a "brand platform" that shows the direction Hitachi brand aims at and a corporate statement, "Inspires the Next," that symbolizes the platform. This statement means that "the company will inspire the next generation, society, product, system, or solution, thereby realizing a rich life and a good society." Under the new brand management program, Hitachi brand is strictly managed and now 600 group companies should pay for its use. The goal of this program is to raise the image and value of Hitachi brand up to par with that of Sony.[11]

Sony's CEO and chairman Nobuyuki Idei stated in a recent newspaper interview that the company aims for the "Knowledge-Based Manufacturer" that capitalizes on its manufacturing capability, brand power, and knowledge about consumers.[12] The original Japanese term *"chishiki seizogyo"* for "knowledge-based enterprise" was coined by Nonaka and Konno (1999). Sony has its own knowledge assets programs. Known as a "maverick" for a Japanese company, Sony has a unique organizational culture. It instituted an education program called "Sony Juku" for young promising employees in their thirties. Every year, top management instill "Sony spirit" as "experiential knowledge" into 16 future leaders, who in turn are required to propose strategic plans as "conceptual knowledge" to top management. This year, four strategic plans for "Sony of the Internet Age" were proposed to then president Idei, who accepted them all and ordered their immediate implementation. Sony has a tradition that respects ideas from younger employees and nurtures mavericks. Ken Kutaragi, president of Sony Computer Entertainment that now dominates the video game industry with "PlayStation," is such a maverick.[13]

Knowledge Leadership

The knowledge-creating process cannot be managed in the traditional sense of management that centers on controlling the flow of information. By providing several "enablers," however, top and middle managers as "knowledge leaders" enable the organization to actively and dynamically create knowledge (Nonaka and Takeuchi 1995, von Krogh et al. 1997, von Krogh et al. 2000). Top managers as knowledge leaders should (1) provide the knowledge vision, (2) define and redefine knowledge assets, thereby keeping them relevant to the knowledge vision, (3) form, energize, and connect *ba*, and (4) direct, promote, and justify the SECI process.

Though middle managers also usually do the above tasks, creating the knowledge vision is a responsibility of top managers. Therefore, we label middle managers as "knowledge producers."

Being strategically situated at the intersection of the vertical and horizontal flows of information in an organization, they form, nurture, and lead multiple *ba* to create new knowledge. The "middle-up-down management" (Nonaka 1988; Nonaka and Takeuchi 1995) model is an example of such a "distributed leadership" that promotes the knowledge-creating process.

Providing the Knowledge Vision

To create knowledge continuously, a company needs a vision that orients, drives, and synchronizes its entire organization. Therefore, its top managers should create and disseminate a knowledge vision throughout and outside the company that (1) defines what kind of knowledge the company should create in what domain; (2) provides the company with a value system that evaluates, justifies, and determines the types and quality of knowledge it creates; (3) gives a sense of direction to the knowledge-creating process; (4) fosters spontaneous commitments of participants in the process; and (5) determines how the company and its knowledge base evolve over the long term.

Because knowledge itself has no boundaries, any kind of new knowledge can be created regardless of the existing business structure of the company. Therefore, it is important for top managers to provide such a knowledge vision that transcends the boundaries of existing products, divisions, organizations, or markets. Since visions are vague by their very nature, they have to be articulated by someone. It is fine for top managers to articulate their visions by themselves if they can, but usually the responsibility of articulating the vague visions fall on middle managers, who serve as a bridge between visionary ideals at the top and chaotic realities of front-line workers at the bottom. Middle managers have to break down the knowledge vision (usually expressed in an abstract grand concept) into more concrete and practical midrange concepts that guide the day-to-day knowledge-creating activities. They also serve as knowledge producers and supervise the knowledge-creating operations according to the company's vision (Nonaka, Toyama, and Konno 2000).

Defining and Redefining Knowledge Assets

More and more companies have created the position of chief knowledge officer (CKO) to supervise KM at the corporate level. So far, however, these CKOs' role has been limited mainly to managing the exploitation of *existing* knowledge assets. They have to also play a leading role in making a knowledge strategy by defining and redefining what kinds of *new* knowledge assets are needed to realize the knowledge vision. Because knowledge has no limit and can quickly become obsolete, top managers can and should redefine what kinds of knowledge assets are now relevant for the company. For such a creative strategy, they have to (1) take an inventory of knowledge assets the company owns, and (2) on that basis, make a strategy to create, accumulate, and utilize knowledge assets effectively and efficiently. For example, to develop an environmentally friendly car for the twenty-first century, Toyota studied a hybrid power system of a gasoline engine and an electric motor. The company found that it had not yet developed such major component technologies as the next-generation battery, motor, converter, and inverter to build such a hybrid power system. Shocked by the lack of such important knowledge that could determine its future, the top management of Toyota decided to invest heavily in research and development of the hybrid power system that is now used in the world's first hybrid car, the Prius.

Forming, Energizing, and Connecting Ba

Ba can be built intentionally or can emerge spontaneously. Top managers and knowledge producers can form *ba* by providing such physical space as meeting rooms, such cyber space as a computer network, or such mental space as common goals. Forming a task force is a typical example of intentional building of *ba*. Knowledge leaders have to choose the right mix of team members and promote interaction among them.

It is also important for knowledge leaders to find and utilize spontaneously emerging *ba*, which is often ephemeral and disappears very quickly. They have to read the situation in terms of how organization members are interacting with each other and with outside environments in order to secure a naturally emerging *ba*, as well as to form a *ba* effectively. To support such a fragile *ba* and drive the SECI process, *ba* should be energized by providing such enabling conditions as autonomy, creative chaos, information redundancy, requisite variety, love, care, trust, and commitment (Nonaka and Takeuchi 1995, von Krogh et al. 2000).

To realize the company's knowledge vision, moreover, various *ba* should be connected with each other to form a greater *ba*. To that purpose, knowledge leaders have to facilitate interactions among various *ba* and among participants therein. More often than not, relationships among *ba* are not predetermined. To connect various *ba*, therefore, knowledge leaders have to evaluate the situation as the relationships among them unfold.

Directing, Promoting, and Justifying the SECI Process

The most important task for top managers as knowledge leaders is to supervise (i.e., direct, promote, and justify, *not* control) the SECI process by checking always whether the knowledge-creating process at the corporate level is heading toward the knowledge vision, and whether knowledge created in the process is justifiable according to the knowledge vision. Without controlling the process and suppressing creativity, they should occasionally provide appropriate advice to participants in the process. And when the process is in serious trouble, they should view the whole situation and create their own concepts to solve the fundamental problem.

Middle managers as knowledge producers capture tacit knowledge from top managers and front-line workers or from such outside constituents as customers and suppliers and externalize it into new concepts. Directly involved in the knowledge-creating process, knowledge producers must have the ability to create new concepts and express them in their own language. Language proficiency here means communication capability to convey their mental models with a rich vocabulary, metaphorical expression, analogical reasoning, drawings as visual language, and nonverbal body language.

Knowledge Leadership at Eizai

Eizai, Japan's fifth largest pharmaceutical company, has practiced KM faithfully according to Nonaka's theory.[14] When Haruo Naito assumed the position of president in 1988, the domestic pharmaceutical industry faced such challenges as lower prices of medical drugs regulated by the government, new competitors from overseas and other industries, increases in R&D costs, and more knowledgeable users. In 1989, he posed to his employees a challenging question: "Society is changing, can you change yourself?" and started a corporate reform movement called "Eizai Innovation." Under the banner of "human health care or *hhc*," he also declared a new corporate vision: "Empathize with patients' emotions, put the highest priority on the increase in their benefits, and meet their various needs worldwide."

The *hhc* movement is divided so far into three stages. In the first stage in 1990–91, Naito himself selected 103 young employees from R&D, production, marketing, and administrative departments, who were then trained into "core managers" to lead the *hhc* movement and realize the Eizai Innovation. The second stage was from 1992 to 1996. In 1992, the core managers started 74 *hhc* projects throughout the company toward the goal of "every employee practicing *hhc* everyday." Those projects aimed to increase customers' benefits by creating knowledge or improvements of their products and customer relationships (though the company then was not aware that they were creating new knowledge).

In 1997, the *hhc* movement entered the third stage as president Naito set up a new office called "*Chisobu*" (which literally means the knowledge creation department). Now under the strong influence of Nonaka's theory, the KM office (1) disseminates Nonaka's theory of organizational knowledge creation throughout the company via lectures and the intranet-based homepage called "*Chi-no-Hiroba*" (or the Knowledge Forum); (2) conducts a questionnaire survey[15] to assess knowledge conversion capabilities (i.e., the four modes: socialization, externalization, combination, and internalization) of the company as a whole, all departments and sections, thereby suggesting remedies for their weaknesses in knowledge creation; (3) promotes the *hhc* movement, supports the *hhc* projects, and disseminates their achievements; and (4) plans and implements human resource development programs to educate "knowledge workers."

Among many *hhc* programs, the "*Chiso* Conference" (or knowledge creation conference) is notable since its mission is to educate knowledge producers. Participants in the education program are capable middle management employees selected by president Naito himself. It consists of five parts: (1) a course designed to develop knowledge creation capabilities, especially concept-making skills; (2) another course to teach management innovation and strategic thinking; (3) practice training at a hospital for the elderly to capture their tacit knowledge; (4) a session to present participants' proposals for management innovations; and (5) a correspondence course aimed at internalization of explicit knowledge that cannot be taught through the above courses due to time limitation.

Some Implications

Hansen et al. (1999) argued that there are two types of KM strategy, that is, "codification strategy," in which "knowledge is carefully codified and stored in databases, where it can be accessed and used easily by anyone in the company," and "personalization strategy," in which "knowledge is closely tied to the person who developed it and is shared mainly through direct person-to-person contacts" (p.107). They also argued that (1) the choice between the two is a central issue for KM; (2) trying to pursue both at the same time may harm corporate performance; and (3) one should be adopted as a main strategy and the other as a complementary strategy.

Having observed KM practices at Japanese companies, however, we take issue with their argument, which shows a dichotomous "either-or" type of thinking typical of Americans. The typology may be a false dichotomy. We argue that KM should pursue both strategies at the same time, because the two strategies, and explicit and tacit knowledge each focuses on, are complementary and equally important. Although they selected McKinsey and Boston Consulting Group as examples that emphasized the personalization strategy, a recent *Business Week* article says that both firms "deployed some of the world's most sophisticated—and expensive—internal databases."[16] They also selected Andersen Consulting as an example that emphasized the codification strategy, but the firm has been "most aggressive in community-building" or the personalization strategy, according to Davenport and Prusak's preface to their paperback edition.[17] The pursuit of both strategies is not only apparent in the Japanese companies we observed but also in some European companies such as Gemini Consulting and Nokia.[18] It seems that the IT-based or explicit knowledge-oriented KM popular in the United States and the human-based or tacit knowledge-oriented KM used in Japan are now converging.

With regard to this trend, Davenport and Prusak's preface argued that KM must be linked to business strategy, work processes, culture, behavior, and the physical business environment, some of which we have addressed in this chapter. Among them, linking KM to work processes has become increasingly easier thanks to advances in IT. As shown in the NTT East case, the cost of building knowledge bases has significantly decreased because day-to-day work records enter almost automatically into databases. All employees have to do is just write the usual daily reports or documents and then click a button to send them to their managers. This increase in efficiency provides more and more time for face-to-face interactions. Thus, IT helps us a lot to share and utilize existing knowledge. Yet, the goal of KM is, as we have stated at the beginning, to create *new* knowledge *continuously*, that is (*chishiki keiei*). We now have to wait for more advanced IT to assist us in our knowledge creation.

Notes

1. *Business Week*, August 28, 2000, p.71.
2. This article originated from Nonaka (1990), an award-winning book in Japanese.
3. This section draws on Nomura and Kametsu (1999).
4. http://www.fujixerox.co.jp/eng/mission/index.html.
5. The concept was originated by a Japanese philosopher Kitaro Nishida ([1921], 1990).
6. For a discussion about the importance of care, see chapter 3 of von Krogh et al. (2000).
7. This section draws on Kanazawa (2000) and CRM&CTI Promotion Office, NTT East (2000).
8. This technology extracts useful information and knowledge from a large quantity of unformalized text documents which do not need to be organized into databases.
9. Fuji Xerox and Xerox jointly endowed a chair of Distinguished Professor in Knowledge (the world's first) to the Haas School of Business, University of California at Berkeley, and Professor Nonaka is the first appointee to it.
10. *The Nikkei Sangyo Shimbun*, March 7, 2000.
11. *The Nikkei Ryutsu Shimbun*, April 25, 2000; http://www.hitachi.co.jp/inspire/.
12. *The Yomiuri Shimbun*, August 11, 2000.
13. *The Yomiuri Shimbun*, August 10, 2000. Also, for an interesting story about the "Making of PlayStation and visionaries who conquered the world of video games," see Asakura (2000).
14. This section draws on a case study manuscript which was prepared by an Eizai manager,

who was also a graduate student of Professor Nonaka's.

15. This questionnaire was first answered by 5,400 Eizai employees in Japan; 600 business units were analyzed and fedback with results and remedies for their weaknesses; later it was conducted in offices and R&D institutes overseas.

16. *Business Week,* August 28, 2000, p.71.

17. The paperback edition (2000) of Davenport and Prusak (1998), p.viii.

18. For Gemini Consulting, see chap. 10 of von Krogh, Ichijo, and Nonaka (2000). Nokia, which is also under the influence of Professor Nonaka, has a unique office structure (including a huge cafeteria and even sauna baths) that promotes interactions and dialogues among its employees and a state-of-the-art IT infrastructure that enables its global operations. The world's largest portable phone manufacturer's vision is "Connecting People," which applies to customers worldwide as well as to its employees (*Nikkei Information Strategy,* September 1999, pp. 38–41).

References

Asakura, R. (2000) *Revolutionaries at Sony.* New York: McGraw-Hill.

CRM&CTI Promotion Office, NTT East (2000) *Building Practical CRM.* Tokyo: NTT Publishing (in Japanese).

Davenport, T.H. and Prusak, L. (1998) *Working Knowledge: How Organizations Manage What They Know.* Boston: Harvard Business School Press.

Drucker, P. (1993) *Post-Capitalist Society.* London: Butterworth Heinemann.

Edvinsson, L., and Malone, M.S. (1997) *Intellectual Capital.* New York: Harper Business.

Gross, N. (2000) "Mining a Company's Mother Lode of Talent." *Business Week,* August 28, pp. 70–71.

Hansen, M.T., Nohria, N., and Tierney, T. (1999) "What's Your Strategy for Managing Knowledge?" *Harvard Business Review* (March–April): 106–117.

Kanazawa, S. (2000) "An Empirical Study of *Ba* for Knowledge Creation: A Case Study of NTT East's Business Communications Headquarters." Master's thesis, Graduate School of Knowledge Science, Japan Advanced Institute of Science and Technology.

Leonard-Barton, D. (1992) "Core Capabilities and Core Rigidities: A Paradox in Managing New Product Development," *Strategic Management Journal* 13(5):363–380.

Mita, M. (1999) "Learning from knowledge management of Scandinavian companies," *Nikkei Information Strategy,* pp.39–49 (in Japanese).

Nishida, K. (1990) *An Inquiry into the Good.* Translated by M. Abe and C. Ives. New Haven: Yale University Press. Originally published in 1921.

Nomura, T. and Kametsu, A. (1999) "A Framework for Designing Total Knowledge Management Systems." *The Annual Bulletin of Knowledge Management Society of Japan.* No.1:55–72 (in Japanese).

Nonaka, I. (1988) "Toward Middle-Up-Down Management: Accelerating Information Creation." *Sloan Management Review* 29(3):9–18.

Nonaka, I. (1990) *Chishiki-Sozo no Keiei (Management by Creating Knowledge).* Tokyo: Nihon Keizai Shimbun-sha (in Japanese).

Nonaka, I. (1991) "The Knowledge-Creating Company." *Harvard Business Review* (November–December):96–104.

Nonaka, I. (1994) "A Dynamic Theory of Organizational Knowledge Creation." *Organization Science* 5(1):14–37, also in this volume.

Nonaka, I. and Konno, N. (1998) "The Concept of 'ba': Building a Foundation for Knowledge Creation." *California Management Review* 40(3): 40–54.

Nonaka, I. and Konno, N. (1999) *Chishiki Keiei no Susume (An Introduction to Knowledge Management).* Tokyo: Chikuma Shoten (in Japanese).

Nonaka, I. and Takeuchi, H. (1995) *The Knowledge-Creating Company.* New York: Oxford University Press.

Nonaka, I., Umemoto, K., and Senoo, D. (1996) "From Information Processing to Knowledge Creation." *Technology in Society* 18(2):203–218.

Nonaka, I., Reinmoeller, P., and Senoo, D. (2000) "Integrated IT Systems to Capitalize on Market Knowledge," in G. von Krogh, I. Nonaka, and T. Nishiguchi (eds.), *Knowledge Creation: A Source of Value,* pp.89–109. London: Macmillan.

Nonaka, I., and Reinmoeller, P., and Toyama, R. (forthcoming). "Integrated Information Technology for Knowledge Creation," in M. Dierkes, et al. (eds.), *Handbook of Organizational Learning and Knowledge.* Oxford: Oxford University Press.

Nonaka, I., Toyama, R., and Konno, N. (2000) "SECI, Ba and Leadership: A Unified Model of Dynamic Knowledge Creation." *Long Range Planning* 33:5–34.

Nonaka, I., Toyama, R., and Nagata, A. (2000) "A Firm as a Knowledge-Creating Entity: A New Perspective on the Theory of the Firm." *Industrial and Corporate Change* 9(1):1–20.

Stewart, T. (1997) *Intellectual Capital: The New Wealth of Organizations.* New York: Doubleday.

Toffler, A. (1990) *Powershift: Knowledge, Wealth and Violence at the Edge of the 21st Century.* New York: Bantam Books.

von Krogh, G., Nonaka, I., and Ichijo, K. (1997) "Develop Knowledge Activists!" *European Management Journal* 15(5):475–483.

von Krogh, G., Nonaka, I., and Nishiguchi, T. (eds.) (2000) *Knowledge Creation: A Source of Value.* London: Macmillan.

von Krogh, G., Ichijo, K., and Nonaka, I. (2000) *Enabling Knowledge Creation: How to Unlock the Mystery of Tacit Knowledge and Release the Power of Innovation.* New York: Oxford University Press.

26

Knowledge Exploitation and Knowledge Exploration

Two Strategies for Knowledge Creating Companies

Kazuo Ichijo

From an Information Processing Paradigm to a Knowledge Creation Paradigm

Innovation and Knowledge

Briefly, a venture is like an expedition in the forest. They inevitably get motivated because they go there without a map and rack their brains to arrive at their destination. They have to create new wisdom and knowledge by themselves. However, large companies already have this kind of map, and the line to their goals is laid before them. If they say "we can join together at this place by going down this road at a speed of 5 km.p.h. So, let's meet there," they need not to have wisdom nor knowledge. All they have to do is just to walk as they are ordered to.

—Muneaki Masuda, CEO of
Culture Convenience Club[1]

To gain competitive advantage in a market, a company should innovate. Innovation could be achieved with a new concept of products and service by itself or with a way to bring about the concept, as well as a way to offer both. Likewise, corporate transformation is a result of innovation. This could be accomplished when a company innovates its organizational structure, business processes, management, and business models and could be achieved at various phases of the company's activities. In other words, newly created knowledge is utilized for the concept of a new product, a new manufacturing system, a new distribution system, a new sales system, and a new marketing system, to name a few.

The opportunity to create knowledge for gaining competitive advantage is spontaneous as well as deliberate. However, a company cannot innovate without knowledge, and consequently, it cannot gain competitive advantage in the market either. This means that a source of competitive advantage for a company should be knowledge. It is impossible to provide customers with new products and service with highly added value or to generate corporate innovation without knowledge. Therefore, it is reasonable to regard competition in the market as being between organizational knowledge, which is the source of the new products and service, rather than the competition which is generated by companies.

Only the company that has high knowledge and the ability to transfer it skillfully to its business activities can win in the market. Thus, as a corporate asset, knowledge or intellectual capital, which indicates how much knowledge exists in a company, what and how many resources and capabilities to create knowledge exist in a company, as well as how many knowledge workers are hired, trained, and retrained, is more important than tangible assets such as money or materials.

Although it has become a business truism that knowledge yields competitive advantage, not all managers may recognize this relationship between innovation and knowledge. Knowledge is a crucial enabler for innovation, that is, corporate transformation, which requires the involvement of all organizational members. In practice, however, the "knowledge issue" tends to become the primary responsibility of human resources, information technology groups, or corporate R&D; sometimes it is only part of isolated knowledge-management initiatives located deep within various business units. Knowledge-management initiatives require strong corporate commitment led by top management. Top management especially should recognize and focus on the strategic role of knowledge or the importance of knowledge creation for generating competitive advantage, that is, achieving superior business performance compared with its competitors.

In order to increase the intellectual capital of a firm, what we should pay attention to is whether a company is designed and managed to encourage the development of intellectual creativity of individuals, and whether a company shares the knowledge that its individual members have brought or acquired. The reason for this is that individual members are the primary source for any kind of knowledge, and that the intellectual capital will not increase unless individual knowledge is well shared among all the members of a company. In the next section, the way to develop intellectual capabilities of individual members of a company will be examined by referring to two theoretical perspectives on organization.

Two Perspectives on Organization

In the field of organizational theory, *the information processing paradigm* (Simon 1997) has been mainstream for many years. This idea is also reflected strongly in the structure and management of the actual organization. According to the information processing paradigm, uncertainty reduction is inevitable because of the cognitive limitation of individuals. To recognize this view is thought as the first step to frame the theory. People with cognitive limitations, what we call *bounded rationality*, contrast with those who can make rational decisions or *economic man* modeled in economics. Therefore, they were called *administrative man*. To process overwhelming amounts of information, within human cognitive boundaries, individual organizational members should be managed well by the division of labor through *goal specification*, *role specification*, and *formalization*, so that the rationality of the whole organization will be maintained. In short, this theory contends that the limited information processing capacity is inherent in human beings and to make up for it organizations are created. It is further contended that when an organization is divided into its functions and roles, then people in the organization could make rational decisions. This view of human beings in the information processing paradigm seems, in a sense, practical and cold at the same time.

On the other hand, a newly developed theoretical perspective on organizations advocated by Ikujiro Nonaka, *the knowledge creation paradigm,*[2] defines an organization not only as a system for information processing but also as a system for knowledge creation. This theory brought new ground to organizational theory. In the knowledge creation paradigm, members of organizations are not passive people who process information just within their given roles, but active participants who are able to think and produce new things, such as creating new concepts for businesses or products on their own. In contrast to the information processing paradigm that regards uncertainty reduction as its most important claim, the knowledge creation paradigm points out that it is necessary to increase uncertainty and create chaos for innovation so that people will try to think creatively. The knowledge creation paradigm sees the significance of an organizational presence in affecting human creativity and the achievement of innovation by making the greatest use of this intellectual capability. Therefore, this paradigm seems ideal and warm and appeals to people working in an organization.

Justification for the Knowledge Creation Perspective

In a knowledge-based society, it seems appropriate to understand the organization not only as an information processing system but also as a knowledge creation system. Needless to say, the information processing paradigm ought not to be overlooked in its entirety. Organization is practically based on sharing various roles and functions. However, environmental changes are very rapid, and as a consequence, organizational members may encounter a situation they did not anticipate in advance. If they neglect to cope with it because there is no mention of it in manuals or office guidelines, the organization will not adjust to this new situation. Instead, it is important that members voluntarily judge every situation on a given occasion and deal with environmental changes improvisationally if necessary. It is essential for organizational members to develop their capability to think creatively and take action voluntarily; and management, structure, and processes should be coordinated so as to develop the knowledge creating capabilities of individual organizational members.

Viewed in this light, we can say that it is better to design organizational management, structure, and processes in accordance with the knowledge creation paradigm, which pursues the development of human intellectual capability, rather than the information processing paradigm, which is based on the limits of individual cognition. Therefore, it is necessary for more companies to learn how to operate as knowledge creating companies due to recent radical environmental changes caused by such forces as globalization and the Internet. In the next section, two strategies for knowledge creating companies, knowledge exploitation and knowledge exploration, will be described. Special attention will be paid to two different categories of knowledge—public knowledge and unique private knowledge.

Knowledge Exploitation and Knowledge Exploration

We call it time machine management.[3] *As the background of business development using the Internet, both access to the Internet and the capabilities of people using the Internet are making steady progress in America more than in Japan. As a result, new business initiatives for the Internet in the U.S. advance two or three years ahead, so do the capabilities of the Internet users. Because of this fact, with regard to business development for the Internet we can see what it will be like in Japan two or three years later by watching what is happen-*

ing in America. It is like going to the future by using a time machine. We run a present Japanese business, seeing what will come about in our future.*

Masahiro Inoue,
CEO of Yahoo Japan[4]

Two Kinds of Knowledge

In terms of the knowledge creation perspective on organization, what is essential for organizational activities is to try to improve the intellectual capital of organization consistently and systematically through knowledge exploitation and knowledge exploration.[5] These two strategies are necessary since a company has to deal with two different categories of knowledge to increase its intellectual capability.

In a business context, knowledge can be separated into two broad categories: unique knowledge held exclusively by a company and public knowledge held by several competitors.[6] Both categories of knowledge are valuable if they can be successfully applied to value-creating tasks (competence), and if they can be used to capitalize on existing business opportunities. Therefore, managers either need to ensure the creation of unique knowledge that can be unleashed in value-creating activity in their organization or establish better use of public knowledge that is generally available to their organization and its competitors. Given these two different categories of knowledge, a company should deploy two different strategies to increase its intellectual capital. Both knowledge exploitation and knowledge exploration should be executed consistently and systematically so that the intellectual capital of a company will be increased.

Knowledge Exploitation for Public Knowledge

Knowledge exploitation means enhancing the intellectual capital of a company with existing knowledge, that is, public knowledge. Public knowledge is the technical sort shared in research reports, engineering drawings, conference publications, textbooks, consulting manuals, and classrooms; often it represents general technical solutions that are freely available in the market. It is predominantly social explicit knowledge or individual tacit knowledge with the potential of becoming social in easily documented forms. Some public knowledge is of a narrative kind, in which managers tell, hear, and retell stories about the industry, their competitors, the company, and themselves. *Time machine management,* found in the statement of Inoue cited earlier, is a kind of knowledge exploitation management. With knowledge exploitation, strategic activities such as knowledge acquisition and propagation play a key role.

Incidentally, we have to pay careful attention to the interpretation of knowledge exploitation. This term does not mean that we are allowed to use existing knowledge just as it is. In this case, exploitation is based on the analysis in which we examine existing knowledge and also how to make better use of it. Knowledge exploitation differs from mimicking, that is, *imitation* without doubt, and is a strategy for organizational learning.

In addition, management capability for finding, acquiring, and sharing private knowledge is crucial for the execution of knowledge exploitation, since private knowledge is widely available in the market. Widely available private knowledge can allow a company to achieve a sustainable competitive advantage if the management capability for applying it to value-creating tasks of the company is efficient and effective. The ability to transfer generic knowledge to various areas of a business may play a key role in a company's success, and the process itself may be unique, valuable, difficult to imitate, and difficult to substitute. Shared public knowledge across business units in different products, markets, or businesses can improve innovation and ultimately secure the sources of competitive advantage. This point will be highlighted in the GE case described later. The value of management to a company, and hence justify executive compensation, should depend on the extent to which managers and executives are able to generate and exploit an "asset" like knowledge more effectively than their counterparts at competing companies.

Knowledge Exploration for Unique Knowledge

Since competitors, in developing their own survival strategies, are likely to benchmark themselves against the industry leader to level out performance, knowledge, especially unique private knowledge utilized in high performance, must also be difficult to imitate. Tacit social or individual knowledge, moreover, is typically more difficult to imitate than explicit knowledge captured in documents and manuals. Of course, unique private knowledge can be explicit. How-

ever, in this case, either the knowledge should be actually impossible to replicate, or the imitation process should be so costly that it deprives the imitator of the cost parity it set out to achieve.

Knowledge exploration is a strategy for a company to increase its intellectual capital by creating its unique private knowledge within its organizational boundary. This unique knowledge must be valuable, difficult for competitors to imitate, and difficult to substitute (Barney 1991). In other words, knowledge exploration means enrichment of the intellectual capital that a company achieves by itself. By distinguishing unique private knowledge from public knowledge, managers and executives can begin to grasp the necessity for the two different strategies. They will also recognize why tacit knowledge has so much potential for increasing the intellectual capital of a company.

Summary

Both knowledge exploitation and knowledge exploration are indispensable for a company to increase its competitive advantage. Companies should try to increase their intellectual capital by executing both strategies. Executing only one of them will not increase its intellectual capital. For example, if a company relies only on knowledge exploitation, that is, it just uses its resources to obtain available public knowledge, the company would run a risk of worsening the quality of its intellectual capital. The effort to produce knowledge in a company would enable it to acquire the ability to tell whether knowledge created by other companies is useful for increasing its competitive advantage or not. Without this capability, a company could not find useful public knowledge or use it efficiently and effectively. By the same token, a company that just focuses on acquiring knowledge from other firms but does not produce or offer knowledge voluntarily would be considered an *intellectual free rider*, which means a company that steals a ride on knowledge created by other companies. Therefore, it would become difficult for the company to access knowledge created by other firms. Sooner or later, knowledge will not be offered to those companies that do not reciprocate.

On the other hand, if a company focuses on using its resources just for knowledge exploration and neglects knowledge exploitation, the company would run a risk of suffering from NIH syndrome ("Not Invented Here"), as well as cause high expense and risk. In brief, it indicates a conservative, inward-looking corporate culture that looks down on knowledge created by other firms. If a company has an introverted demeanor and regards the products made by itself as the best and does not pay any attention to other firms, it could cause an inability to adjust to environmental changes. In general, companies that stick only to manufacturing are apt to consider knowledge exploitation negatively. This, however, is incorrect because solely developing every technology, product, service, and operational and management activity can cause high cost as well as high risk to a company. It is not easy at all to create new knowledge, but it is not necessarily correct to develop everything alone.

There has to be a good balance between knowledge exploitation and knowledge exploration. Needless to say, some companies' strategy for knowledge creation tilts in favor of the former and others to the latter. However, they should not favor one strategy too much. In the next section, I will present a case to illustrate how General Electric has been dealing with these two strategies.

Case: Knowledge Exploitation and Knowledge Exploration at GE

GE, which is evaluated as the best company in the world,[7] is often analyzed as a company using the knowledge exploitation model, since it is widely recognized that GE has improved its performance by means of benchmarking, that is, best practices initiatives, encouraging learning from others. Benchmarking is learning the best practices of high performance companies, and it is conducted according to the knowledge exploitation strategy. However, GE has actually been improving its performance not only by knowledge exploitation but also by knowledge exploration, as described below.

Knowledge Exploitation at GE

GE itself has recognized that it has been trying to demonstrate its competitive advantage by becoming a learning organization since around 1989.[8] In order to encourage its organizational members to acquire knowledge actively and share it with their colleagues, GE values were prescribed. In these values, nine behavioral principles were described for GE managers to promote sharing knowledge among them, to make every effort to create a "boundaryless" (i.e., no barrier

TABLE 26.1 GE Values (1989–1999)

- Have a passion for excellence and hate bureaucracy
- Are open to ideas from anywhere and committed to Work-Out
- Live quality and drive cost and speed for competitive advantage
- Have the self-confidence to involve everyone and behave in a boundaryless fashion
- Create a clear, simple, reality-based vision and communicate it to all constituencies
- Have enormous energy and the ability to energize others
- Stretch, set aggressive goals and reward progress, yet understand accountability and commitment
- See change as opportunity, not threat
- Have global brains and build diverse and global teams

Source: http://www.ge.com

to information and knowledge sharing) organization, to be open minded to every idea irrespective of its source ("Are open to ideas from anywhere"), to pay more attention to quality, cost, and speed ("Live quality and drive cost and speed for competitive advantage") (see table 26.1). A reference to quality in these GE values draws special attention since GE later launched its Six Sigma initiative. As discussed below, Six Sigma is a quality improvement initiative that GE learned from Motorola. Additionally, as a specialized division for knowledge exploitation, the *corporate initiatives section* was established at corporate headquarters. This section has been trying to gather "best practices" for corporate performance improvement inside and outside GE and develop corporate initiatives, that is, corporatewide transformation projects, so that these best practices will be shared in the entire GE organization.

As a result of these series of activities, GE tried to improve its competitive advantage by learning from "best practices" of other companies. Included in these "best practices" were *Six Sigma*,[9] initiated by Motorola and *quick market intelligence*,[10] initiated by Wal-mart. Above all, it is well known that Six Sigma has contributed greatly to operational effectiveness at GE. GE started its Six Sigma initiative in 1996, and as early as 1997, the cost saving effect of Six Sigma outweighed its cost. From its start, with no financial benefit to GE, Six Sigma has flourished to the point where it produced more than $2 billion in benefits in 1999.[11] As we have seen, it is one of GE's core competences that once it had decided to become a learning organization, it had actually carried it out comprehensively and achieved better business performance than any other competitor. This management capability promises long-lasting growth for GE.

New Focus on Knowledge Exploration at GE

Knowledge exploited by GE has contributed to its excellent performance, and a learning culture has been established at GE. However, at the Operating Manager Meeting[12] held by GE in January 2000, the presence and importance of GE's original technologies were emphasized by GE's chairman and CEO John F. Welch, Jr. In other words, the results of knowledge exploration by GE were demonstrated to its top managers.

As the revenues and earnings from hardware businesses has been decreasing due to severe competition with rival firms, *after market service*[13] has become an important revenue and earning source for GE. In 1980, service businesses occupied only a 15% share in GE's entire revenues, whereas in 1998, 67% of GE's entire revenue came from service businesses. As recently as 1995, when this initiative was launched, GE derived $8 billion a year in revenues from product services. In 2000, this number will double to $17 billion.[14] Therefore, in GE's *1998 Annual Report*, we can find the following remark: "GE is today a global service company, and in 1998 more than two-thirds of its revenues will come from financial, information and product services."[15] However, while service businesses have still been growing steadily,[16] it was confirmed at the Operating Manager Meeting 2000 that service businesses would not be successful without the most advanced technology in an industry developed by GE. This statement warned senior managers not to rely only on service or to neglect technological innovation as a precondition for successful service businesses.

At GE Operating Manager Meeting 2000, a strong message from the chairman and CEO was sent to GE senior managers that knowledge exploitation could not be meaningful without knowledge exploration, and that innovative service is based on innovative technology. It was strongly suggested that, even though the importance of business performance shifts from hardware to service, they should not forget to seek knowledge exploration. Incidentally, in 2000 GE has renewed its nine values (table 26.2). While

TABLE 26.2 GE Values (2000)

- Are passionately focused on driving customer success
- Live Six Sigma Quality . . . ensure that the customer is always its first beneficiary . . . and use it to accelerate growth
- Insist on excellence and are intolerant of bureaucracy
- Act in a boundaryless fashion . . . always search for and apply the best ideas regardless of their source
- Prize global intellectual capital and the people that provide it . . . build diverse teams to maximize it
- See change for the growth opportunities it brings . . . i.e., "e-Business"
- Create a clear, simple, customer-centered vision . . . and continually renew and refresh its execution
- Create an environment of "stretch," excitement, informality and trust . . . reward improvements . . . and celebrate results
- Demonstrate . . . always with infectious enthusiasm for the customer . . . the "4-E's" of GE leadership: the personal Energy to welcome and deal with the speed of change . . . the ability to create an atmosphere that Energizes others . . . the Edge to make difficult decisions . . . and the ability to consistently Execute

Source: http://www.ge.com

the old GE values are those for transforming GE to a learning organization, the new GE values are those for transforming GE to an e-company. In order to utilize new growth opportunities generated by the Internet ("See change for the growth opportunities it brings . . . i.e., 'e-Business'"), a new e-culture is being created at GE.

Conclusion

A company must enhance its intellectual capital by executing both knowledge exploitation and knowledge exploration thoroughly. Organizational learning is very important and knowledge exploitation can be used for that purpose. Just as GE has demonstrated, creating a culture that values learning is critically important for increasing the knowledge creating capabilities of a company. However, the important fact about knowledge is that knowledge is both explicit and tacit. Some knowledge can be put on paper, formulated in sentences, or captured in drawings. Other kinds of knowledge are tied to the senses, skills in bodily movement, individual perception, physical experiences, rules of thumb, and intuition. Such tacit knowledge is often very difficult to describe to others (von Krogh et al. 2000) and therefore is not obtainable only by the exploitation strategy. By means of knowledge exploitation, it is not easy to acquire tacit knowledge because it might be either impossible or cost-inefficient and time-consuming.

While the idea of tacit knowledge makes sense intuitively to most people, managers often have a hard time coming to grips with it on a practical level. Recognizing the value of tacit knowledge and figuring out how to use it is the key challenge for a company operating in the current knowledge-based society. Executing knowledge exploration means valuing tacit knowledge and pursuing innovation by consistently and systematically executing "tacit-explicit conversion," that is, making tacit knowledge explicit and sharing explicit knowledge among organizational members.

Notes

1. Culture Convenience Club is a company which sells CDs, videos, and books. It was founded in 1983 by a young entrepreneur, Muneaki Masuda.

2. Nonaka and Takeuchi (1995). As the sequel to *The Knowledge Creating Company*, see von Krogh et al. (2000). In this book, the operationalization of the generic model of knowledge creation developed by Nonaka and Takeuchi is intensively discussed.

3. *Time machine management* is one of the management strategies to introduce a network business successful in America immediately to Japan.

4. Yahoo Japan was funded in 1996 by Yahoo Corporation and Soft Bank, Japan's leading Internet investment company.

5. Seminal work about exploitation and exploration is in March (1991).

6. More detailed discussion about public knowledge and private knowledge can be found in chapter 4 of *Enabling Knowledge Creation* by von Krogh et al. (2000).

7. GE was selected as world's most admired company by *Fortune* and *Financial Times* in 1998 and 1999.

8. Letter to shareholders, *GE Annual Report* 1999.

9. *Six Sigma* is a set of quality improvement initiatives to maximize customer values. By means of a very sophisticated statistical management system, defect is reduced to a ratio of three and four tenths over one million. Six Sigma initiatives have been conducted in every function including design, manufacturing, sales, service, and even among corporate staff.

10. *Quick market intelligence* is an efficient system to gather information in the market swiftly.

11. Letter to shareholders, *GE Annual Report* 1999.

12. This meeting is held at the beginning of every year. Approximately five hundred senior managers of GE attend it to review business performance in the previous year and share strategic problems.

13. *After market service* refers to various service activities after selling products, e.g., trouble shooting via network access.

14. Letter to shareholders, *GE Annual Report* 1999.

15. Letter to shareholders and employees, *GE Annual Report 1998*.

16. It is estimated service revenue will be more than $16 billion in fiscal year 2000.

References

Barney, J.B. (1991) "Firm resources and sustained competitive advantage." *Journal of Management* 17(1):99–120.

March, J.G. (1991) "Exploration and exploitation in organizational learning." *Organization Science* 2(1):71–85.

Nonaka, I. and Takeuchi H. (1995) *The Knowledge Creating Company: How Japanese Companies Create the Dynamics of Innovation*. New York: Oxford University Press.

Simon, H.A. (1997) *Administrative Behavior: A Study of Decision-Making Processes in Administrative Organizations*. 4th ed. New York: Free Press.

von Krogh, G., Ichijo, K., and Nonaka, I. (2000) *Enabling Knowledge Creation: How to Unlock the Mystery of Tacit Knowledge and Release the Power of Innovation*. New York: Oxford University Press.

The Role of Tacit Knowledge in Group Innovation

Dorothy Leonard and Sylvia Sensiper

Innovation, the source of sustained advantage for most companies, depends upon the individual and collective expertise of employees. Some of this expertise is captured and codified in software, hardware, and processes. Yet tacit knowledge also underlies many competitive capabilities—a fact driven home to some companies in the wake of aggressive downsizing, when undervalued knowledge walked out the door.

The marvelous capacity of the human mind to make sense of a lifetime's collection of experience and to connect patterns from the past to the present and future is, by its very nature, hard to capture. However, it is essential to the innovation process. The management of tacit knowledge is relatively unexplored—particularly when compared to the work on explicit knowledge. Moreover, while individual creativity is important, exciting, and even crucial to business, the creativity of groups is equally important. The creation of today's complex systems of products and services requires the merging of knowledge from diverse national, disciplinary, and personal skill-based perspectives. Innovation—whether it be revealed in new products and services, new processes, or new organizational forms—is rarely an individual undertaking. Creative cooperation is critical.

What Is Tacit Knowledge?

In the business context, we define knowledge as *information that is relevant, actionable, and based at least partially on experience*. Knowledge is a subset of information; it is subjective; it is linked to meaningful behavior; and it has tacit elements born of experience. Business theorists have, for the sake of convenience, contrasted tacit knowledge with explicit knowledge as if they were distinct categories. J.C. Spender defines tacit knowledge as "not yet explicated."[1] Ikujiro Nonaka and Hirotaka Takeuchi use this distinction to explain how an interaction between the two categories forms a knowledge spiral: explicit knowledge is shared through a combination process and becomes tacit through internalization; tacit knowledge is shared through a socialization process and becomes explicit through externalization.

In this chapter, we build on Michael Polanyi's original, messier assumption: that all knowledge has tacit dimensions.[2] Knowledge exists on a spectrum. At one extreme it is almost completely tacit, that is, semiconscious and unconscious knowledge held in peoples' heads and bodies. At the other end of the spectrum, knowledge is almost completely explicit, or codified, structured, and accessible to people other than the individuals originating it. Most knowledge, of course, exists in between the extremes. Explicit elements are objective, rational, and created in the "then and there" while the tacit elements are subjective, experiential, and created in the "here and now."[3]

Although Spender notes that "tacit does not mean knowledge that *cannot* be codified,"[4] some dimensions of knowledge are unlikely *ever* to be wholly explicated, whether embedded in cognition or in physical abilities. Semiconscious or unconscious tacit knowledge produces insight, intuition, and decisions based on "gut feel." For example, the coordination and motor skills to run a large crane are largely tacit, as are the negotiation skills required in a corporate meeting or the artistic vision embodied in the design of a new computer program interface. The common element in such knowing is the *inability* of the knower to totally articulate all that he or she knows. Tacit knowing that is embodied in physical skills resides in the body's muscles, nerves, and reflexes and is learned through practice, that is, through trial and error. Tacit knowing embodied in cognitive skills is likewise learned through experience and resides in the unconscious or semiconscious. While Polanyi addressed tacit knowledge at an individual level, others have suggested it exists in group settings. In fact, Richard Nelson and Sidney Winter suggest that organizations maintain their structure and coherency through tacit knowledge embedded in "organizational routines" that no single person understands completely.[5]

Much knowledge remains tacit for various reasons. Perhaps its explication would not be beneficial. Unless an incentive is created, there is little reason for an individual or group possessing tacit knowledge that provides an important competitive advantage to explicate "away" that advantage. More commonly, however, people are unaware of the tacit dimensions of their knowledge or are unable to articulate them. Spender notes various types of "automatic knowledge," such as skilled use of tools (e.g., a computer keyboard) or instinctive reactions (e.g., catching a falling object) or "action slips," as when one starts out to drive on an errand and ends up at the office instead.[6] In all these cases, the physical and mental reflexes operate without conscious direction (or without what Polanyi termed "focal" awareness).

Moreover, as psychological research has demonstrated, the acquisition of knowledge can occur through nonconscious processes, through "implicit learning."[7] That is, we can acquire knowledge and an understanding of how to navigate our environment "independently of conscious attempts to do so."[8] One intriguing implication is that not only can we "know more than we can tell,"[9] but also we often know more than we realize. Furthermore, our efforts to rationalize and explain nonconscious behavior may be futile, if not counterproductive. "Knowledge acquired from implicit learning procedures is knowledge that, in some raw fashion, is always ahead of the capability if its possessor to explicate it."[10] Researchers stimulating implicit learning found, in fact, that forcing individuals to describe what they thought they understood about implicitly learned processes often resulted in poorer performance than if the individuals were allowed to utilize their tacit knowledge without explicit explanation.[11]

Studies on creativity, intuition, and nonanalytical behavior suggest three ways that tacit knowledge potentially is exercised in the service of innovation. We speculate that they represent a hierarchy of increasingly radical departures from the obvious and the expected and therefore are of increasing value to innovative efforts.

Problem Solving

The most common application of tacit knowledge is to problem solving. Herbert Simon has argued that the reason experts on a given subject can solve a problem more readily than novices is that the experts have in mind a pattern born of experience, which they can overlay on a particular problem and use to quickly detect a solution. "The expert recognizes not only the situation in which he finds himself, but also what action might be appropriate for dealing with it."[12] Others writing on the topic note that "intuition may be most usefully viewed as a form of unconscious pattern-matching cognition."[13] "Only those matches that meet certain criteria enter consciousness."[14,15]

Problem Finding

A second application of tacit knowledge is to the framing of problems. Some authors distinguish between problem *finding* and problem *solving;* linking the latter to "a relatively clearly formulated problem" within an accepted paradigm and the former, which "confronts the person with a general sense of intellectual or existential unease" about the way the problem is being considered,[16] to more radical innovation. Creative problem framing allows the rejection of the "obvious" or usual answer to a problem in favor of asking a wholly different question. "Intuitive discovery is often not simply an answer to the specific problem but is an insight into the real nature of the dilemma."[17] Consultants are familiar with the situation which a client identifies a problem and sets out specifications for its solution, whereas the real value for the client may lie in reformulating the problem. Of course, the more that the consultant's unease with the current formulation derives from his or her semiconscious or unconscious knowledge, the more difficult it is to express and rationalize.

Prediction and Anticipation

Finally, the deep study of phenomena seems to provide an understanding, only partially conscious, of how something *works*, allowing an individual to anticipate and predict occurrences that are then subsequently explored very consciously. Histories of important scientific discoveries suggest that this kind of anticipation and reliance on inexplicable mental processes can be very important in invention. In stories about prominent scientists, there are frequent references to the "hunches" that occur to the prepared mind, sometimes in dreams, as in the case of Watson and Crick's formulation of the double helix. Authors writing about the stages of creative thought often refer to the preparation and incubation that precede flashes of insight. "Darwin prepared himself for his insights into evolution through a childhood interest in collecting insects, the reading of geology, and the painstaking observations he made during the voyage of the *Beagle*."[18]

Similarly, literature on nursing is full of references to the importance of listening to intuition and hunches in caring for patients. For example, the medical team at Methodist Hospital in Indianapolis was able to revive a three-year-old boy in respiratory distress because his nurse listened to her "insistent inner voice" and checked on the patient—despite the fact that "logically" nothing should be wrong.[19]

As these examples suggest, much of the research on tacit knowledge focuses on the individual—perhaps because most investigators are psychologists, for whom the single mind is of primary interest, or perhaps because writers can always probe their own experience for data. For

similar reasons, the literature on creativity likewise highlights individual expressions of innovativeness. However, as previously noted, innovation in business is usually a group process. Therefore, we need to examine more closely both tacit knowing and creativity as they are expressed by members of groups—singly and collectively.

Creativity and Social Interaction

Creative ideas do not arise spontaneously from the air but are born out of conscious, semiconscious, and unconscious mental sorting, grouping, matching, and melding. Moreover, interpersonal interactions at the conscious level stimulate and enhance these activities; interplay among individuals appears essential to the innovation process. In some businesses—notably advertising, games, and entertainment—"the creatives" or "the talent" are separated from the rest of the corporation because it is assumed that creativity and innovation bloom in isolation. However, even in businesses where "creatives" have held elite positions for years, some managers are beginning to question why *all* employees cannot contribute to innovation. One manager in a toy manufacturing company complained that in a recent meeting with 20 people, "nineteen thought they didn't need to be creative."

Studies of people selected because of individually demonstrated creativity refer consistently to their interactions with others as an essential element in their process. One study elicited comments such as: "I develop a lot of my ideas in dialogue,"[20] or "it's only by interacting with other people in the building that you get anything interesting done; it's essentially a communal enterprise."[21] The authors of this particular study conclude that "even in the most solitary, private moment—the moment of insight itself—many creative individuals are aware of the deeply social nature of their creative process."[22]

This social interaction is especially critical for teams of individuals responsible for delivering new products, services, and organizational processes. Before turning to a discussion of how tacit knowledge is utilized by such groups, we present a brief description of the innovation process.

The Nature of Innovation

The process of innovation is a rhythm of search and selection, exploration and synthesis, cycles

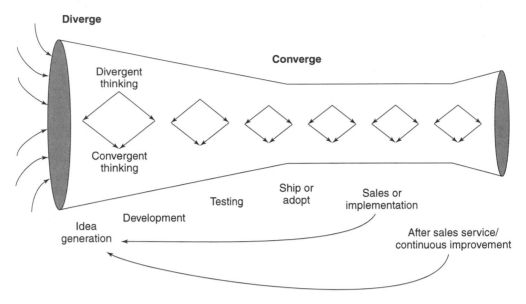

Figure 27.1 The innovation funnel: Incremental cycles. Based partially on "The Developmental Funnel," in Wheelwright and Clark, *Revolutionizing Product Development*, 1992.

of divergent thinking followed by convergence. At the highest level of abstraction, innovation is often presented as linear: idea generation is followed by development, then by adoption or testing, and finally by implementation or after-sales service. However, within this overall pattern, the stages of idea generation through implementation recur at a smaller scale at each step (see figure 27.1). The innovation pattern thus occurs as fractals, with small decision cycles embedded in larger, but very similarly structured ones, and with individual choices made within the confines of a hierarchy of prior, larger scope individual or group choices.[23]

The process by which a group or individual first creates options and then chooses one on which to focus efforts occurs during the testing and implementation stages as well as during idea generation and development. Thus, creative group activity is not confined to the initial stages of the overall innovative effort but, in fact, is essential to such downstream activities as launching a new product, implementing a new compensation system in an organization, or improving after-sales service to customers. At any point in an innovation process, then, managers need to manage both the expansion of thought that gives rise to potentially creative alternatives and the homing in on a viable option. Tacit knowledge has an important role in both stimulating the "requisite variety" of ideas and then

in the convergence that permits focus on actionable next steps.[24]

Divergence

One definition of creative synthesis (which underlies the development of many new products, services, or ways of organizing) is the "interlocking of two previously unrelated skills, or matrices of thought."[25] However, research suggests that deep skill takes at least a decade to develop.[26] Therefore, while a particularly talented or ambitious individual may develop deep skills in two or more arenas, most of us will build a single bank of expertise in our lifetimes. This expertise accrues as we experience education, work, and life in general.[27]

In working groups, individuals from different backgrounds (cultures, organizational experience, disciplinary training, preferred cognitive styles) draw upon their pools of tacit, as well as explicit knowledge, to contribute. In fact, it is the tacit dimensions of their knowledge bases that make such individuals especially valuable contributors to group projects; perspectives based on such knowledge cannot be obtained any other way, except through interaction. Inaccessible from written documents or explicit expositions, tacit knowledge is protected from competitors unless key individuals leave or are hired away. Moreover, even individuals' explicit statements or suggestions carry with them the weight of unspoken knowledge—mental models, life examples, perhaps physical skills, even unrecognized patterns of experience which people draw upon to increase the wealth of possible solutions to a problem. This experience, stored as tacit knowledge, often reaches consciousness in the form of insights, intuitions, and flashes of inspiration.

When a group of diverse individuals addresses a common challenge, each skilled person frames both the problem and its solution by applying mental schemata and patterns he or she understands best. The result is a cacophony of perspectives. In a well-managed development process, these varying perspectives foster *creative abrasion*, intellectual conflict between diverse viewpoints producing energy that is channeled into new ideas and products.[28]

The creation of such intellectual ferment is important to innovation for a number of reasons. First, the more options offered (up to a point, of course), the more likely that a frame-breaking perspective will be available for selection. A certain "requisite variety" is desirable for innovation.[29] Moreover, experimental research has demonstrated that a minority opinion offered during group decision making stimulates more innovative solutions to problems—even if the ultimate selection was not one specifically proposed from a minority viewpoint.[30] Apparently, just hearing a very different perspective challenges the mindset of those in the majority sufficiently that they will search beyond what initially appears to be an obvious solution. This may be one reason that *intellectually* heterogeneous groups are more innovative than homogeneous ones.[31] As a recent review of different types of group diversity concludes, "the diversity of information [that] functionally dissimilar individuals bring to the group improves performance in terms of creativity."[32] If all individuals in the group approach a task with highly overlapping experiential backgrounds, they may be subject to "groupthink," that is, a comfortable common viewpoint leading to closed-mindedness and pressures toward uniformity.[33] Their tacit as well as their explicit knowledge is similar enough that they neither produce a wide variety of options nor expend much effort on searching.

A popular technique for capitalizing on the respective insights and intuitions of a group of individuals is to conduct a brainstorming session.[34] At IDEO, an international product development firm, brainstorming sessions occur at crucial stages in the product development process and have been shown to lead to important consequences for the organization as a whole.

An IDEO "brainstorm" gathers together a set of staff with diverse skills—human factors, mechanical engineering, and industrial design—to generate product design ideas, often in tandem with the client. The meeting is run by a facilitator and is always held face-to-face. The "rules" are well known to IDEO designers but are posted visibly: defer judgment; build on the ideas of others; one conversation at a time; stay focused on the topic; and encourage wild ideas. All concepts and ideas elicited during a brainstorming session are recorded on a white board. The principal way that participants share their tacit knowledge is through sketching designs or through visual analogies. For example, an idea for an appliance hinge might be derived from the way in which a boat rudder is maneuvered. Because the IDEO employees share a deep understanding of process, they are generally comfortable both with the highly divergent thinking encouraged in the brainstorming itself and with the vagueness of the initial sketches and analogies as modes of communication. IDEO managers find that their clients tend to underestimate the power of brainstorming—that is, until they have experienced it. Then they are likely to walk away impressed with the profusion of ideas presented.

We may have no choice about managing divergent viewpoints in the creation of today's complex systems of products and services. In a 1992 study of three product lines (cellular phones, optical fiber systems, and refrigerators), Ove Granstrand and others found that the number of technologies and disciplinary bases required to produce these products increased between each successive product generation. For example, the first generation of cellular phones in the early 1980s, required only electrical engineering skills. By the mid-1990s, the third generation of these phones called for a knowledge of physics as well as electrical, mechanical, and computer engineering.[35]

As if the proliferation in requirements for different types of expertise were not sufficient, the design of global products today *also* demands a sensitivity to diverse norms and attitudes. Innovation knows no national bounds. When San Diego, California-based Nissan Design International designers were wrestling with the configuration of the Infiniti J-30, they discovered that their Japanese colleagues were far more sensitive to the front-end or "face" of the car than they, although translating the Japanese tacit knowledge about consumer preferences into information explicit enough for communication (mostly through sketches) took some time and a lot of effort. At last the California-based designers came to understand that the proposed design of a slightly down-turned grill and narrow headlights gave the car's persona a sour appearance to the Japanese designers, reducing its appeal. Very slight adjustments—almost indiscernible to the American designers—raised the design to "a higher level of cultural intelligence," noted NDI President Gerald Hirshberg.[36]

Perspectives at a *group* level can also be brought into juxtaposition so as to increase divergent thinking. John Seely Brown and Paul Duguid point out that when large organizations are conceived as "a collective of communities" with each community having a particular culture and viewpoint, "separate community perspectives can be amplified by interchanges. . . . Out of this friction of competing ideas can come the sort of improvisational sparks necessary for igniting organizational innovation."[37]

Whether we seek to increase the divergence of perspectives as a deliberate strategy for innovation or have the diversity thrust upon us as a necessity, we need to manage that rich profusion.[38] Much of the richness derives from the tacit dimensions of the knowledge possessed by individuals in the group. Although diverse explicit knowledge is challenging to harness and direct toward a common goal, it is easier to generate, analyze, and share than tacit knowledge.

Convergence

At every stage, innovation requires solution, convergence upon acceptable action—and again, tacit knowledge plays an important role. The *process* of innovation has a tremendous effect on the integrity and the system integration of any resultant product or service.[39] In turn, the aggregate knowledge of project members involved in the innovation process has to be coordinated and focused. The degree to which knowledge needs to be actually shared depends upon the nature of the innovation task and how much interdependency exists among subgroups or individuals. Again confining the discussion here to managing the tacit dimensions of knowledge, we suggest that three different types of tacit knowledge need to be managed: *overlapping specific*, *collective*, and *guiding*. These three form a rough hierarchy from low to high in terms of abstraction.

Overlapping Specific Knowledge

Groups or subgroups of individuals involved in an innovation project may build up shared *specific* knowledge at the interfaces between them—as, for example, of client preferences and attitudes or of particular steps in a production process. This knowledge is overlapping in that only part of each individual's tacit knowledge about the undertaking is shared—that which is essential to the completion of their interdependent tasks. The mechanisms for creating the tacit dimensions of such collective knowledge include shared experiences and apprenticeships.

Observational visits—to customers, to customers' customers, or to potential users of the general class of a given service or product produced by an organization—can stimulate innovative ideas.[40] Such "empathic design" expeditions are essentially anthropological in nature. A multifunctional team of individuals who carry with them an acute understanding of their organization's capabilities are directly exposed to the world of potential users and observe how those users interact with their environment. This observation identifies needs about which the users may be unaware and/or are unlikely to articulate. Although the empathic design team members return from the field with very different perceptions (and that, in fact, is the value of sending diverse observers), their observations overlap to create some common—to some degree tacit—understanding of the environment for which they are designing. Individuals from teams that have conducted such anthropological expeditions can explicate some of their observations about the work or home life of those observed, but clearly more knowledge is shared than can be expressed. So, for instance, members' comments about "the pace of work" or the "sporadic communication" are laden with tacit understanding. Such phrases call up specific mental images of routines around the office, household, or factory that are inaccessible to someone who has not shared visits to those same sites.

Apprenticeships are a time-honored way of building shared specific tacit knowledge. Although today most production processes are moved as rapidly as possible from art toward science, even in quite sophisticated processes, some art often remains.[41] A decade ago, a study of the transmission of hybridoma technology revealed that "the *unsaid* is indeed a part of conscious scientific practice."[42] The researchers found that the production of monoclonal antibodies was an artisanal technique. Manuals purporting to instruct in the methodology explicitly recognized the need for apprenticeship:

> The newcomer to hybridization is well advised to learn the technique in a laboratory which is already practicing fusion . . . newcomers to the technique are relatively unsuccessful initially and obtain many hybrids after some practice, although an experienced observer cannot see any difference between the technique used on the first day and in subsequent, successful experiments. The best approach is therefore to learn from an experienced laboratory and practice until hybrids are obtained.[43]

Researchers engaged in the production of the hybridomas talked about getting "a feeling for just what the cells are doing, and how healthy they are by looking at them" and reported gaining that understanding by association with experienced individuals. "The professor says: these are healthy, those are not. You learn by association, without knowing what you are looking at."[44] In such an apprenticeship, much explicit knowledge is conveyed from expert to novice, but tacit knowledge grows through shared observation and from mimicking behavior, even without knowing why.

The newer such technologies are to the world, the more important apprentices are to the innovation process. The faster the innovation cycle, the less likely that knowledge will be captured explicitly. The director of an advanced development group commented that his researchers were likely to be "stuck for life" with a technology they created because the knowledge base moves so fast it is never totally captured in any explicit form. Once responsible for a given technology, the researchers remain the key repository for not only the original concepts but also for undocumented refinements of the technology made by downstream recipients. Of course, observers may aver that all aspects of the technology *should* be captured explicitly, but as the pace of innovation accelerates, such capture is increasingly difficult. Not only has knowledge not progressed to the point of easy codification (i.e., the process is still an art), but also tacit knowledge that is a prerequisite to exploiting the technology can constitute a competitive advantage.

Collective: System Knowledge

Collective tacit knowledge is developed communally, over time, in interactions among individuals in the group. It exists more or less complete in the head of each group member who has been completely socialized into the group. One form of collective tacit knowledge encompasses the entire production system, allowing individuals to contribute to innovation without explicit communication because they understand at a systemic level how all the individual operations in an organization fit together. The more that tacit knowledge about operations is diffused and shared, the harder is imitation. This is why companies such as Chaparral Steel or Oticon invite competitors to visit and observe, convinced that no one could imitate their success from absorbing explicit knowledge.[45] Even if some individuals leave the organization, a shared "net of expectations" created through organizational routines and accepted standards remains.[46] Moreover, these expectations are conveyed through artifacts as well as through behavior. Thus, for instance, in any design shop, one sees models and prototypes embodying tacit knowledge about successful and unsuccessful attempts at innovation.

"Taken-for-granted" collective tacit knowledge often appears in the form of unconscious norms; individuals draw on it unawares. Members of a "community of practice" develop implicit ways of working and learning together.[47] Researchers at the Institute for Research on Learning noted in one study a particular norm of behavior that aided informal communication: they called it "storking," the practice of sticking one's head up over the office cubicle to query someone in a nearby cubicle.[48] Adding a few inches to the cubicles could have provided more privacy—but would have interfered with the behavioral norms of the group. While such "communities" often go unnoticed, much work depends on their informal, shared use of "noncanonical" practices,[49] that is, norms of behavior and activities that are unacknowledged by the larger organization. According to John Challenger (executive vice president of Challenger, Gray & Christmas, a Chicago-based consultancy) this kind of collective tacit knowledge is essential to how people communicate and, by extension, how they innovate. He claims that downsizing presents a particular risk for "company Alzheimer's." A firm's success depends not only on the skills and knowledge at any given point in time, but also on "memories," the intangibles of collective business experience, triumphs and failures, culture and vision.[50]

Perhaps the purest form of collective tacit knowledge is that possessed by a team or group whose process *is* the product.[51] Their individual knowledge bases are complementary but have to be shared and merged for innovation to occur. An orchestra or a sports team that plays so far beyond the ordinary that their performance constitutes an act of innovation, harnesses their individual tacit knowledge to serve a shared mental model of perfection.[52] Such groups of people (including business teams) feel bonds of shared accomplishment that are inexpressible except in exultation and excitement in the mutual achievement. Together they have created something that no one of them (or even the group of them, absent this collective tacit knowledge) could have—but that is nevertheless dependent upon their individual contributions.

Guiding Tacit Knowledge

The more innovative the new product, process, service, or organizational form, the less likely that the objectives have been spelled out in detailed specifications, simply because it is more difficult to anticipate all needs and possible interactions in a radically new product or process. Individuals creating and implementing an innovation need to exercise judgment and make dozens of decisions on their own initiative about how to reach the agreed-upon objectives. Lacking guidance, individuals may rely on their own ideas about the new product or process when making a particular decision, and their efforts may go in many disparate directions. The group must be guided by an understanding of purpose that extends beyond explicitly stated goals.[53] Such a vision or product concept keeps the school of fish swimming in the same direction, as it were.

Although such guiding visions must of course be explicit, they are often highly metaphorical or presented at a high level of abstraction, so that much of their significance is tacitly understood. Ford Motor Company used the phrase "contemporary luxury" to rally their hundreds of diversely skilled development troupes around a central concept for the 1988 design of the Lincoln Continental. The word "contemporary" helped to distinguish their design from the boxy, large images associated with past concepts of luxury cars.[54] Nonaka and Takeuchi recount how

Honda project team leader Hiroo Watanabe coined the phrase "Automobile Evolution" to inspire his designers, and the team continued the metaphorical conceptualization with the product concept "Tall Boy." The process resulted in the revolutionary Honda City, a car that was both "tall" in height and "short" in length.[55]

A guiding concept need not be expressed in words to be powerful in aligning individuals during innovation. A group symbol or logo often carries significance far beyond the visible. Moreover, creative research on "totemics" has revealed the power of aesthetics to tap into collective tacit knowledge. Angela Dumas uses "visual, object-based metaphors" to help new product developers converge on a general image for a line of products. The team members find common aesthetic and functional attributes—a similar "feel"—in an otherwise disparate group of objects, for example, paintings, furniture, wine glasses. The resulting "totem" helps coordinate design decisions.[56]

Barriers to Generating and Sharing Tacit Knowledge

Were the process of eliciting and managing the flow of the tacit dimensions of knowledge easy, innovation would still not occur effortlessly—but it would be much less of a challenge. Multiple barriers exist both to the stimulation of divergent thinking and then to the coalescence of that thinking around a common aim.

Obviously, if individuals who possess tacit knowledge important to the innovation are either actively discouraged from participating or censor themselves, none of the benefits suggested above can be realized. Individuals rewarded for hoarding their tacit knowledge will do so. In organizations where expertise is highly regarded, but mentoring and assisting others is not, rational people may be unlikely to surrender the power they gain from being an important knowledge source—especially since sharing tacit knowledge requires time devoted to personal contact.

Inequality in status among participants is also a strong inhibitor to sharing, especially when exacerbated by different frameworks for assessing information. Nurses often hesitate to suggest patient treatments to physicians, not only because the doctors have higher status, but also because the nurses base their diagnoses on different knowledge bases. Dr. Richard Bohmer has speculated that nurses' ability to assess a patient is based on observation over time, that is, longitudinal data gathered from standing by a patient's bedside. In contrast, a physician makes a judgment based on cross-sectional data, such as blood tests, ultrasound results, and x-rays.[57] Thus, the nurses' intuition about a situation draws on very different tacit knowledge, and they have neither the laboratory data to back up hunches nor the status to insist on the validity of their perspective.

Distance (both physical separation and time) renders sharing the tacit dimensions of knowledge difficult. Although technology may offer a partial solution, much knowledge is generated and transferred through body language, physical demonstrations of skill, or two- and three-dimensional prototypes that can be interactively shaped by a group of people. Howard Gardner has suggested a number of "intelligences," beyond the usual ones tested, that are more difficult to express over distances: spatial, kinesthetic, and interpersonal.[58] Furthermore, although research is scanty on the topic, a certain level of personal intimacy may be necessary to establish comfortable communication of tacit knowledge. Internet-based friendships suggest that intimacy does not depend wholly on physical co-location, but it remains to be seen whether such friendships are based enough in reality to mimic the mutual understanding born of face-to-face encounters.

All these barriers operate against the generation and sharing of the explicit as well as the tacit dimensions of knowledge. Some barriers, however, specifically inhibit the growth and transfer of tacit dimensions. First, working groups often exhibit a strong preference for a particular type of communication—most often (at least in most business situations) communication that is logical, rational, and based on "hard" data. As numerous studies of thinking styles have shown, individuals have strong thinking style preferences—for particular types of information—"hard-wired" into their brains and reinforced over years of practices and self-selection into certain careers.[59] Even if an individual could make some of the tacit dimensions of his or her knowledge explicit in the form of a physical demonstration or a drawing, such information would rarely be given a hearing because such evidence is not regarded in most business settings as relevant or useful unless backed up with analysis. Imagine how difficult it is in the ordinary product development meeting to introduce relatively

inarticulate preferences that are based on largely tacit knowledge. As Microsoft's Tom Corddry noted about the design of new multimedia products, computer programmers never offer a suggestion about a product feature without telling you the rationale. In contrast, a visibly talented artist may offer several drawn options for a screen design, "tell you which one they like— and stop!"[60] Artists find it extremely difficult to explain just why a particular pattern, rhythm, or color is preferable in a product design. In many companies, only the top managers dare express a preference without data to back it up. The point is not that such unarticulated preferences, opinions, and tastes are always correct, rather that the more diverse a collection of viewpoints shared, the more likely that the eventual solution will challenge the status quo.

Individuals possessing deep knowledge may also fear trying to express the inexpressible— and failing. "No one," they may reason, "can appreciate the experience I bring to this problem; therefore, I will appear foolish and this is too high a price to pay." Operators in factories and plants sometimes hesitate to explain their apparently uncanny ability to foretell when a piece of equipment is about to fail. A lime kiln operator once interrupted an interview to hurry off, exclaiming simply "something is wrong; she [the kiln] doesn't sound right." Later pressed to explain, he could not—or would not—explicate further what sound he heard the revolving kiln make that caused him to hasten to make adjustments. "It's nothing scientific," he said somewhat defensively. "Nothing an engineer would believe. I just know."[61]

Yet another barrier of special importance to managing tacit knowledge is the uneasiness of the group members that their colleagues will draw upon life experiences to express emotional rather than intellectual disagreement. For abrasion to be creative, it must be impersonal. After a review of relevant research, Lisa Hope Pelled suggests that group diversity based upon highly visible differences (gender, race, age) leads to more emotion-based disagreements, while more subtle forms of diversity (educational background, personality) are more likely to lead to intellectual disagreements.[62] This model suggests that the more that diversity in tacit knowledge is sought from individuals selected because of readily observable differences, the more difficult it becomes to ensure that the tacit knowledge is heard, is valued, and is targeted toward the innovation.

Managerial Implications

The value of tacit knowledge to the firm has been demonstrated.[63] Although it is much easier to stimulate, combine, and communicate the explicit dimensions of knowledge than the tacit, there are numerous situations in which tacit knowledge cannot or will not be wholly converted into explicit. Managing tacit knowledge is thus a significant challenge in the business world—and it requires more than mere awareness of the barriers.

The above descriptions of tacit knowledge in divergent and convergent processes suggest some mechanisms by which such knowledge is created and tapped. Brainstorming aids in divergent thinking if participants are encouraged to make suggestions on the basis of intuition and insight—as well as analysis—and to convey their suggestions through drawings and analogies. However, much divergent thinking occurs naturally, because individuals approach a task from such different experience bases. The more radical the desired departure from status quo, the more fruitful it is to solicit discussion by individuals from varied intellectual perspectives. Managers thus can calibrate the level of divergent thinking that they encourage by varying the number and disparity of tacit knowledge bases brought to bear on the task. However, they must manage the ensuing tendency toward chaos and keep the abrasion creative by depersonalizing conflict.[64]

Managers can also use tacit knowledge to aid convergent thinking, by creating guiding visions and concepts for groups involved in innovation. Collective tacit knowledge is created through shared experiences such as trips to customer sites and deliberate apprenticeships. Some degree of natural convergence occurs in so-called communities of practice, in which unconscious work norms guide much of the interactions among members. Managers interrupt these tacit work practices at their peril, and savvy managers may make good use of them in the service of innovation.

Many of the barriers to the sharing of tacit knowledge are the same ones that inhibit innovation in general: hierarchies that implicitly assume wisdom accrues to those with the most impressive organizational titles; such strong preferences for analysis over intuition that no one dares offer an idea without "hard facts" to back it up; and penalties for failure that discourage experimentation. Managers thus can encourage the full exploitation of tacit knowledge by paying attention to the environment they are creating, by encouraging respect for different thinking styles, by understanding the distinction between intelligent failures and stupid mistakes, and by allowing their employees to "fail forward" where appropriate.

Not all tacit knowing is valuable or even accurate. Although we may not be able to judge the knowledge itself, we can certainly see the *results* of the knowledge (just as in astronomy we deduce the presence of a black hole or even a distant planet by its effects on other bodies). The effect of tacit knowledge embodied in physical skills is especially visible. In any operation, different individuals using the exact machinery may produce very different output, just as skiers or tennis players vary in performance using the same equipment. New operators in a factory are often assigned to watch particularly skilled workers so as to absorb tacit knowledge. More cognitively based skills can also be modeled. At American Management Systems, junior consultants in the Organizational Development and Change Management practice work alongside and are coached by "shadow consultants," more experienced senior consultants with years of experience. As one junior consultant said, "the hardest thing about organizational development is that people have to have their own experiences to really understand it. They have to begin to embody the processes."[65]

Cognitive skills are also open to assessment, as individuals and teams are judged by their "track record" of performance. Organizations hire individuals and groups not for their explicitly expressed knowledge alone, but also for their anticipated overall impact on the performance of the organization. Such people often have a reputation for being "good managers" or "creative artists," much of which derives from the tacit dimensions of their knowledge.

Managers may also implicitly judge the value of tacit knowing by assessing individuals' abilities to *communicate* some of the tacit dimensions of their knowledge—through prototyping, drawing, demonstrating, expressing ideas through metaphors and analogies, or mentoring, in general. At a California company producing video games, the manager in charge of product development values individuals he calls "Gepettos" (named after Pinocchio's famous puppeteer "father") because of their ability to develop other talent and to instill some of their own tacit knowledge in new employees through informal apprenticeships. Managers who wish to encourage this kind of diffusion of tacit knowledge should set up systems that encourage, enable, and reward the disseminators.

Tacit knowledge, like all knowledge, can become outdated. By the time the obsolescence is obvious and proven, the organization will be in trouble. Therefore, one reason that managers import diverse perspectives is to serve as a check on the application of tacit knowledge to current innovation. The more rapidly moving the knowledge base involved, the more critical it is to bring people in from outside the group—either as new hires or as visitors.

Conclusion

Tacit knowledge is a tremendous resource for all activities—especially for innovation. The tacit dimensions of *individual* knowledge are not publicly available, except as embodied in people to be hired, and the tacit dimensions of *collective* knowledge are woven into the very fabric of an organization and are not easily imitated. Therefore, tacit knowledge is a source of competitive advantage. The creativity necessary for innovation derives not only from obvious and visible expertise but also from invisible reservoirs of experience.

Our understanding of tacit knowledge and its relevance to innovation is nascent. This chapter presents the barest outlines of a path toward that understanding but may serve to instigate more discussion. Clearly, many different fields of inquiry are relevant, including ones as diverse as design, cognitive psychology, group dynamics, and information technology. In order to understand the potential and complexity of collective tacit knowledge, we shall need to practice what we study—interacting through metaphor as well as analysis and through mutual apprenticeship as well as structured intellectual exchanges. We shall have to confront in the field of business the delicate, imposing task known best to poets and artists—expressing enough of the inexpressible that the communication effort becomes invaluable.

Notes

We thank Walter Swap, Barbara Feinberg, and three anonymous reviewers for their helpful comments and the Harvard Business School Division of Research for supporting this work.

1. J.C. Spender, "Competitive Advantage from Tacit Knowledge? Unpacking the Concept and its Strategic Implications," in Bertrand Mosingeon and Amy Edmondson, eds., *Organizational Learning and Competitive Advantage* (London: Sage Publications 1996), pp. 56–73, 58.

2. Michael Polanyi, *The Tacit Dimension* (New York: Doubleday, 1966), p. 4.

3. Ikujiro Nonaka and Hirotaka Takeuchi, *The Knowledge Creating Company* (New York: Oxford University Press, 1995), p. 61.

4. Spender, op. cit., p. 58.

5. Richard R. Nelson and Sidney G. Winter, *An Evolutionary Theory of Economic Change* (Cambridge: The BelKnap Press of Harvard University Press, 1982)

6. Spender, op. cit.

7. Arthur S. Reber, "Implicit Learning and Tacit Knowledge," *Journal of Experimental Psychology*, 118(1989):219–235.

8. Reber, op. cit., p. 219.

9. Polanyi, op. cit., p. 4.

10. Reber, op. cit., p. 229.

11. Much depends, apparently, upon whether the underlying structure is in fact readily accessible, as participants in the experiments deduced incorrect rules from their implicitly learned skills. "Looking for rules will not work if you cannot find them," Reber notes. Furthermore, explicit instructions apparently aid learning only insofar as they match the person's idiosyncratic implicit learning structure. Reber, op. cit., p. 223.

12. Herbert Simon, *The Sciences of the Artificial* (Cambridge, MA: MIT Press, 1981), p. 106. Interestingly, when Simon first proposed this concept of expertise, he used as an example the ability of a chess professional to determine a good move after only a few seconds of deliberation because the grandmaster's memory holds innumerable patterns of chess plays and the inherent dangers and benefits associated with the various configurations. The recent match between Gary Kasparov and an IBM computer demonstrated that when all relevant patterns can be codified, a computer can sort even more efficiently than the human brain. For certain kinds of bounded problems, with known rules, explicit knowledge may be more important than implicit.

13. Allan D. Rosenblatt and James T. Thickstun, "Intuition and Consciousness," *Psychoanalytic Quarterly* 63(1994):696–714.

14. Rosenblatt and Thickstun, op. cit., p. 705.

15. Researchers have also found that people organize information into groups of relatedness, called "chunks," in order to retain the information in short-term memory. Chunks themselves are "familiar patterns" that come to be under-

stood through experience as a unit, and as learning continues become increasingly larger and more interrelated. When new stimuli is related to this stored information and recognition of a pattern occurs, ideas and actions appropriate to the situation are elicited from memory. Simon, op. cit. A related theory suggests that cognitive elements in working memory, long-term memory, and short-term memory are represented as nodes in a network. As a person gains more knowledge in an area and begins to make connections between abstract principles and actual events, links between nodes are created and strengthened. Expert's networks may be more efficient as a result of increased speed through network links. See Debra C. Hampton, "Expertise: The True Essence of Nursing Art," *Advances in Nursing Science* 17/1(September 1994):15–24.

16. Mihaly Czikszentmihalyi and Keith Sawyer, "Creative Insight: The Social Dimension of a Solitary Moment," in Robert J. Sternberg and Janet E. Davidson, eds., *The Nature of Insight* (Cambridge, MA: The MIT Press, 1995), p. 340. They also link problem solving to short time-frames and problem-finding to long time-frames in terms of the gestation period of the thinker (p. 337). This linkage may be true for scientific discoveries, but there is no evidence that particular types of tacit knowledge utilization are always tied to particular time frames.

17. Debbie A. Shirley and Janice Langan-Fox, "Intuition: A Review of the Literature" *Psychological Reports* 79(1996):563–584, 568.

18. Csikszentmihalyi and Sawyer, op. cit., pp. 339–340.

19. Lynn Rew, "Nursing Intuition: Two Powerful and Too Valuable to Ignore," *Nursing* (July 1987), pp. 43–45.

20. Csikszentmihalyi and Sawyer, op. cit., p. 342.

21. Csikszentmihalyi and Sawyer, op. cit., p. 347.

22. Csikszentmihalyi and Sawyer, op. cit., p. 349.

23. See Kim Clark, "The Interaction of Design Hierarchies and Market Concepts in Technological Evolution," *Research Policy* 14/5(1985):235–251; Dorothy Leonard-Barton, "Implementation as Mutual Adaptation of Technology and Organization," *Research Policy* 17/5 (1988).

24. See Donald Campbell, "Blind Variation and Selective Retention in Creative Thought as in Other Knowledge Processes," *Psychological Review* 67(1960):380–400.

25. Arthur Koestler, *The Act of Creation* (New York: Dell Press, 1964), p. 121.

26. Simon, op. cit, p. 106.

27. Csikszentmihalyi and Sawyer, op. cit., p. 342.

28. The term "creative abrasion" was coined by Gerald Hirshberg, president of Nissan Design International. See Dorothy Leonard-Barton, *Wellsprings of Knowledge* (Boston, MA: Harvard Business School Press, 1995), p. 63.

29. Nonaka and Takeuchi, op. cit.

30. Charlan Jeanne Nemeth, "Managing Innovation: When Less Is More," *California Management Review* 40/1 (Fall 1997):59–74; Charlan Jeanne Nemeth and Joel Wachtler, "Creative Problem Solving as a Result of Majority vs. Minority Influence," *European Journal of Social Psychology* 13(1983):45–55; Robin Martin, "Minority Influence and Argument Generation," *British Journal of Social Psychology* 35(1996):91–103.

31. In a review of literature about diversity, Susan E. Jackson, Karen E. May, and Kristina Whitney report that "there is clear support for a relationship between diversity and creativity." See Susan E. Jackson, Karen E. May, and Kristina Whitney, "Understanding the Dynamics of Diversity in Decision-Making Teams," in Susan E. Jackson et al., eds., *Diversity in the Workplace: Human Resources Initiatives* (New York: Guilford Press, 1992), p. 230.

32. Katherine Y. Williams and Charles A. O'Reilly III, "Demography and Diversity in Organizations: A Review of 40 Years of Research," *Research in Organizational Behavior* 20 (1998): 77–140. The authors note that the same cannot necessarily be said of the implementation phase of the innovation process. This review also points out that while "functional diversity has positive effects on group performance," other forms of diversity have been found to have negative effects. Information and decision theories maintain that increased diversity more likely has a positive effect on innovations, complex problems, or product designs, (which are the domains about which we are most concerned here), but social categorization and similarity/attraction theories suggest that diversity is more problematic and can have a negative effect on group process and performance. Much depends, then, not only on the task being addressed but also on exactly what kind of diversity is being researched, and through what theoretical lens the material is viewed. Clearly, some kinds of diversity can lead to disharmony. As we suggest in this article, the conflict that arises from intellectual disagreement has to be managed carefully, lest it spill over into personal anger.

33. Irving L. Janis, *Groupthink* (Boston, MA: Houghton Mifflin, 1972, 1982). Janis suggests various ways of avoiding groupthink, including assigning someone the role of devil's advocate and inviting into policy discussions outside experts or colleagues not normally included, who

would be encouraged to challenge the views of core members.

34. This technique has been much denigrated after laboratory research revealed that "nominal groups" of individuals attacking a problem produced more, and better, ideas. However, such research relied upon highly artificial problems (e.g., what could you do with a second thumb on your hand?) and enlisted individuals who had no prior knowledge of each other. The group dynamics obviously differ in real world circumstances in which participants know each other well (and therefore do not spend time and energy on self presentation), the problem is actual and urgent, and, most important, their background expertise is relevant and probably essential. In short, in the real world, tacit knowledge is critical to brainstorming and we believe that laboratory research underestimates the power of the technique. See Robert I. Sutton and Andrew Hargadon, "Brainstorming Groups in Context: Effectiveness in a Product Design Firm," *Administrative Science Quarterly* 41/4(December 1996):685–718. Sutton and Hargadon report six important consequences for design firm IDEO as a result of this practice: supporting the organizational memory of design solution; providing skills variety for designers; supporting an attitude of wisdom; creating a status auction; impressing clients; and providing income for the firm.

35. Ove Granstrand, Erik Bohlin, Christer Oskarsson, and Niklas Sjoberg, "External Technology Acquisition in Large Multi-Technology Companies," *R&D Management* 22/2(1992):111–233.

36. Interview, December 10, 1993.

37. John Seely Brown and Paul Duguid, "Organizational Learning and Communities-of-Practice: Toward a Unified View of Working, Learning, and Innovation," *Organization Science* 2/1(1991):40–57.

38. See Dorothy Leonard and Susaan Straus, "Putting Your Company's Whole Brain to Work," *Harvard Business Review* 75/4(July/August 1997):110–121.

39. Product integrity refers to an internal dimension—namely, the product's structure and function—and an external dimension—the product's performance and the expectation of customers. The process of development affects both dimensions. For a discussion of how the innovation process affects outcome, see Kim Clark and Takahiro Fujimoto, "The Power of Product Integrity," *Harvard Business Review* 68/6(November/December 1990):107–118. See also Marco Iansiti, *Technology Integration* (Boston, MA: Harvard Business School Press, 1998).

40. See Dorothy Leonard and Jeffrey Rayport, "Sparking Innovation through Empathic Design,"

Harvard Business Review 75/6(November/December 1997):102–113. The topic is also discussed in chapter 7 of Leonard-Barton (1995), op cit.

41. Moreover, even in high-volume, highly automated processes, workers' tacit knowledge about the way that particular equipment works and their ability to problem solve is critical to continuous improvement. See Gil Preuss and Dorothy Leonard-Barton, "Chaparral Steel: Rapid Product and Process Development," Harvard Business School Case 9-692-018.

42. Alberto Cambrosio and Peter Keating, "Going Monoclonal: Art, Science and Magic in the Day-to-Day Use of Hybridoma Technology," *Social Problems* 35/3(June 1988):244–260.

43. H. Zola and D. Brocks, "Techniques for the Production and Characterization of Monoclonal Hybridoma Antibodies," in John G.R. Hurrell, ed., *Monoclonal Hybridoma Antibodies: Techniques and Applications* (Boca Raton, FL: CRC Press), quoted in Cambrosio and Keating, op. cit., p. 248.

44. Cambrosio and Keating, op. cit., p. 249.

45. See Preuss and Leonard-Barton, op. cit.; John J. Kao, "Oticon (A)," Harvard Business School Case 9-395-144.

46. See Scott D.N. Cook and Dvora Yanow's account of three flute workshops in "Culture and Organizational Learning," *Journal of Management Inquiry* 2/4(1993):373–390.

47. For an explanation of "community of practice," see Jean Lave and Etienne Wenger, *Situated Learning: Legitimate Peripheral Participation* (New York: Cambridge University Press, 1991). For an application of the idea to organizations and businesses, see John Seeley Brown, "Changing the Game of Corporate Research: Learning to Thrive in the Fog of Reality," in Raghu Garud, Praveen Rattan Nayyar, and Zur Baruch Sapira, eds., *Technological Innovations: Oversights and Foresights* (Cambridge, UK: Cambridge University Press, 1997), pp. 95–110; John S. Brown and E.S. Gray, "The People Are the Company," *Fast Company*, (premier issue), pp. 78–82; Etienne Wenger, "Communities of Practice: Where Learning Happens," *Benchmark* (Fall 1991), pp. 82–84.

48. Helga Wild, Liby Bishop, and Cheryl Lynn Sullivan, "Building Environments for Learning and Innovation," *Institute for Research on Learning Report to the Hewlett-Packard IRL Project*, Menlo Park, CA (August 1996).

49. Brown and Duguid, op. cit.

50. See "Fire and Forget?" *The Economist*, U.S. Edition, April 20, 1996, p. 51. Similarly, Freda Line, the membership manager of Britain's Employers Forum on Age (EFA), points out that many down-sizing companies have had to hire

back as consultants those employees who have taken early retirement. It is not so much the skills and experience that are needed, but many of those people "understood the crucial development history of their businesses—a vital part of corporate memory." See Tim Dawson, "Firms See Downside of Down-Sizing," *The London Times*, June 1, 1997.

51. See Mihaly Csikszentmihalyi, *Flow* (New York: Harper & Row, 1990).

52. Csikszentmihalyi, op. cit.

53. See discussion of guiding visions in H. Kent Bowen, Kim B. Clark, Charles A. Holloway, and Steven C. Wheelwright, "Development Projects: The Engine of Renewal," *Harvard Business Review* 72/5(September/October, 1994):110–120.

54. H. Kent Bowen, Kim B. Clark, Charles A. Holloway, and Steven C. Wheelwright, *The Perpetual Enterprise Machine* (New York: Oxford University Press, 1994), p. 74.

55. Nonaka and Takeuchi, op. cit., pp. 12–16.

56. Angela Dumas, "Building Totems: Metaphor-Making in Product Development," *Design Management Journal* 5/1(Winter 1994):70–82.

57. Personal communication, December 1997.

58. Howard Gardner, *Frames of Mind: The Theory of Multiple Intelligences* (New York: Harper Collins, 1993).

59. Leonard and Straus, op. cit.

60. Interview, February 28, 1994.

61. Interview, November 1984.

62. Lisa Hope Pelled, "Demographic Diversity, Conflict, and Work Group Outcomes: An Intervening Process Theory," *Organization Science* 7/6(1996):615–631. Pelled lumps creative idea generation, decision making, and problem solving together in her definitions of cognitive tasks and considers group tenure, organizational tenure, education, and functional background to be job-related diversity. "The more job-related a particular type of diversity is, the stronger its relationship with substantive conflict will be. . . . The more visible a particular type of diversity is, the stronger its relationship with affective [i.e., emotional] conflict will be" (p. 3). The literature reviewed by Williams and O'Reilly (op. cit.) seems to concur. The claim that diversity is beneficial for groups is based on variation in individual attributes such as personality, ability, and functional background.

63. Especially Nonaka and Takeuchi, op. cit.; Leonard-Barton (1995), op. cit.

64. For suggested ways of producing "light instead of heat" in very disparate groups, see Leonard and Straus (1997) op. cit.

65. Dorothy Leonard and Sylvia Sensiper, "American Management Systems: The Knowledge Centers," Harvard Business School Case N9-697-068.

EPILOGUE
Dorothy Leonard

As suggested in this chapter, the tacit dimensions of knowledge are critical throughout the innovation process—from knowledge creation to knowledge implementation and transfer or diffusion. Perhaps surprisingly, we know more about how to manage the first (see *When Sparks Fly: Igniting Creativity in Groups*) than we do the last—at least if we are focused on knowledge that is principally tacit. However, we do recognize that one prominent mechanism for transferring the tacit dimensions of knowledge (not mentioned in the chapter) is mentoring, that is, informal learning by apprentices from experts. Much of the most recent research by the senior author of this article focuses on the nature of the knowledge transferred through mentoring in the innovation process and the means by which the best mentors teach.

Excellent mentors are true experts. Cognitive psychology has shown that while *competence* may develop sooner, *expertise* may take 10 years or more of experience and practice to develop. This fact places limits on how much—and how quickly—expertise can be transferred to novices. Drawing on their experience, experts are able to recognize patterns, integrate them with information about the current context, and extrapolate from the patterns to anticipate the consequences of various alternative actions. It is not clear that the process of acquiring expertise can be significantly accelerated. Nor do all experts want to teach novices, but those experts who do mentor newcomers can help them avoid the most perilous of potential mistakes. These experts leave a residue of knowledge—quite a bit of it tacit—with their protégés.

Mentoring does not convey *exclusively* tacit knowledge, of course. Mentors may pass along explicit, structured, and codified knowledge. However, the mentoring situation affords an opportunity for informal, unstructured and sometimes even nonconscious learning—the kind of learning that enables skills, norms, values, and underlying assumptions to pass from one person to another without explicit instruction. Both within organizations (e.g., the skilled systems engineer teaching the novice how to think holistically) and across organizational boundaries (e.g., the "mentor capitalist" guiding the inexperienced entrepreneur through the shoals of building a new business from scratch), we find mentors conveying knowledge not only through explicit directives and articulated rules of thumb, but also through role modeling and directed experimentation (learning by doing). These latter mechanisms tend to transfer the more tacit dimensions of the mentors' expertise.

Mentoring takes time and energy, and today's time pressures in business lessen the likelihood that pairs of mentors and protégés will fall into a natural rhythm of action and feedback. However, those managers interested in encouraging innovation would do well to note how much effort is being expended currently by mentor and venture capitalists to feed needed expertise into start-ups (see "Gurus in the Garage," *Harvard Business Review*, November/December, 2000). If we were to invest a comparable amount of time *within* large corporations to encourage fledgling innovative activities, we might be able to emulate more of the energy and passion of entrepreneurial ventures. Innovation often occurs at the intersection of different perspectives. Encouraging long-time experts to combine their deep knowledge, including its tacit dimensions, with the enthusiasm and fresh perspectives of novices, can spark more innovation.

28

Knowledge Creation
of Global Companies

Seija Kulkki

Since the beginning of the 1990s, we have witnessed a new global phenomenon: competition through rapid successive or even parallel innovation cycles that bring about a global spread of new technologies, products, and services, even on many continents at the same time.[1] The views of sequential entering into one international market after another, based on product or technology life cycles, experience-based learning curves, or cost and quality considerations of international transactions, do not fully explain this behavior. One may argue that the competitive advantages of global companies may not be based on superior technologies, products, and services only—these may even become neutralized as a competitive advantage as soon as they enter the global marketplace—but on the organizational potential to innovate continuously (Nonaka, Toyama, and Konno 2000, p. 5). This chapter argues that global companies[2] have learned to compete with innovation efficiency, derived from a global scale of knowledge creation and experimentation, as much as they compete with exploitation and implementation efficiency, derived from a global scale of branding, marketing, leveraging, or manufacturing.

Consequently, there has been a shift in strategic management thinking toward studying how organizations not only react and adapt to but also anticipate and lead the development of markets, competition, and industries (Charkravarthy and Doz 1992, Prahalad and Hamel 1994, Brown and Eisenhardt 1998, Kulkki and Kosonen 2001). The shift in emphasis is related to fundamental structural transitions in a variety of industries brought about by major catalysts such as deregulation, global competition, technological discontinuities, and changing customer expectations (Prahalad and Hamel 1994). The issue has been especially relevant to the most dynamic, volatile, and fast-paced industries in the world, for instance, the industries related to computing (Moore, 1995, Brown and Eisenhardt 1998) or to telecommunications (Kulkki and Kosonen, 2001). However, today most of the major global players from computing to steel (Brown and Eisenhardt 1998) seem to be considering new trends of strategic thinking that are also concerned with the creation of new assets and not only with the efficient utilization of existing assets in place. These considerations elaborate on (i) how a firm can adapt to speed, changes, and discontinuities, and (ii) how a firm can create speed and changes, and even benefit from discontinuities, when its capabilities may give it an option to be one of the major players in the global marketplace.

This discussion is based on the underlying assumption that the question of where the company is going is interlinked with the question of how to get there (Hamel 1996,[3] Brown and Eisenhardt 1998). From the viewpoint of innovations, strategy seems to be intertwined with structure and actions and with an overall organizational capability for growth and renewal. Nonaka et al., in turn, view that a capability for continuous innovation is dependent on a firm's ability to create, transfer, and utilize knowledge.[4] This means that the strategy has become closely interlinked with knowledge-based organizational renewal capability. Consequently, this chapter discusses how strategies may be reflections of knowledge-based managerial and organizational mechanisms of a global firm to innovate continuously, and that the dynamism of strategy may be constituently dependent on the nature of organizational dynamism and vice versa.

This chapter relates the dynamism of strategy and organization to the nature of tacit knowledge (Nonaka, Toyama, and Nagata 2000, Nonaka, Toyama, and Konno 2000, Kulkki and Kosonen 2001) and emphasizes the role of tacit knowledge as a source for organizational "movement" in time and space. Tacit knowledge may even help in "bridging" local and global innovative actions in many economically, socially, and culturally different locations of the global marketplace.

Consequently, the chapter addresses the question of how global companies create knowledge out of richness of "localities." Global companies have a wide opportunity to create and transform local knowledge into global knowledge and vice versa. They have created new organizational and managerial ways and means of linking local creative actions and of building an overall global capacity to innovate (Hedlund 1996, Doz et al. 1996, 1997, Dunning 1997, Kulkki 1996, Kulkki and Kosonen 2001). This relates to a wider discussion about global knowledge economy and consequent new knowledge-based local and global organizational and institutional forms to operate, transact, and enact knowledge and technology on a global scale (Giddens 1990, Hedlund 1993, 1996, Hagström and Hedlund 1993, Kogut and Zander 1993, Doz et al. 1996, 1997, Kulkki

1996, Dunning 1997, Hamel 1999, Buckley and Carter 1999, Kulkki and Kosonen 2001, Burton-Jones 1999).

Creating knowledge out of the richness of localities has been discussed as a challenge of the composing and recomposing of knowledge and other assets within the worldwide network of a firm (Hedlund 1996), of conducting "metanational strategies" through the orchestration of knowledge-based capabilities within and between locations (Doz et al. 1996, 1997), and of "bringing Silicon Valley inside" (Hamel 1999), while transforming a firm in search of revolutionary innovations into one that absorbs qualities of local innovativeness and turns them into an organizational quality. Brown and Eisenhardt (1998) argue that the organizational capability of "improvising" is based on time-paced creation of strategy and on an anticipation of the future for rapid implementation (Kulkki and Kosonen 2001).

These views on global knowledge creation have emphasized mostly the internal innovation efficiency of a global firm. This chapter, however, is also concerned with external innovation efficiency; that is, how a global company creates knowledge in interaction with a variety of local environments, that is, as a "boundary or interface action." In addition, this essay is about knowledge creation[5] as a creative dialectical action. A global firm may design creative contextual and dialectical ways of existing, interacting, and transacting upon its many external and internal "boundaries as interfaces" with local and global stakeholders in time and space.

The chapter further elaborates on the nature of knowledge creation in a global firm by asking the following questions:

- What is local and global knowledge?
- How do global companies create and transform local knowledge into global knowledge and vice versa?
- What are organizational and managerial ways and means that facilitate tapping into local knowledge and bringing about a global scale of innovation over many locations in the global marketplace?
- How do global companies interact with and affect their environments in knowledge creation?

Featherstone and Lash (1995) contend that the rise of globalization has created a need to consider spatial analysis instead of traditional temporal or historical analysis of development. They refer to Vattimo's (1998) argument about "the end of history" that turns the earlier national social and cultural developments into metanarratives in crisis. Giddens (1990) argues also that globalization, and especially the pace and scope of change which accompanies it, is the main factor that "plays out" histories as an overarching national, cultural, or social ground that affects people's orientation as organizing principles of mind. However, this chapter holds that the knowledge creation of global companies may be a "meeting place" of both (i) a historical phenomenon where knowledge is created over time, and (ii) a spatial[6] phenomenon where knowledge is created "now" within a certain time-space frame.

The argument proposed is that global companies may benefit from both local and global histories and local and global space in time. Local can meet global and vice versa. Global companies conduct strategies and deploy organizational mechanisms for "movement" over time, as well as in time, locally and globally.

This chapter is organized as follows. First, the relationship of local and global knowledge and knowledge creation is discussed, including global innovation efficiency based on the future-oriented and integrative nature of tacit knowledge. Second, the chapter discusses a global firm "in time and space" from the viewpoint of (i) how local knowledge may be transformed to global knowledge, and (ii) how local knowledge and actions are interlinked. This chapter argues that strategy and structure are intertwined through knowledge that may constitute an overall innovation efficiency of a firm. Third, it elaborates on how global companies build their innovation efficiency dialectically[7] on many ontological, epistemological, and practical levels,[8] in which they are in interaction with their environments simultaneously through strategies and structures, as well as through their knowledge and individual actions (Kulkki 1999). Consequently, the renewal capability of a global firm can be "anchored" even through individual actions (Kulkki and Kosonen 2001) to rhythms and speed of change, as well as to discontinuities of markets, competition, and technology within industries subject to change.

The chapter concludes on a global scale of knowledge creation that calls, among other things, for a contextual transparency and flexibility to "move" spatially in time and space. Global companies have designed forms of or-

ganizing, where their knowledge and technology are in worldwide interplay with social and cultural development, as well as with the knowledge and technology of other organizations and institutions (Giddens 1990, Featherstone and Lash 1995, Dunning 1997, Dosi et al. 1998).

Lastly, the chapter reflects on the preliminary insights of ongoing research concerning the knowledge creation of global companies (Kulkki 1998).[9]

Local and Global Knowledge

The global economy has been transformed from one that formerly largely processed raw materials and conducted manufacturing to one that currently largely processes information and knowledge (Dunning 1997, Teece 1998). As a consequence, the logic of competition has shifted from markets with decreasing returns to markets with increasing returns driven by positive feedback loops (Arthur 1996). According to Arthur, in increasing return markets, that which is ahead tends to stay ahead: "If knowledge-based companies are competing in winner-takes-most markets, then managing becomes redefined as a series of quests for the next technological winner." The knowledge-based economy benefits from the dynamic nature of knowledge; it is an intangible asset that does not have such "resource" constraints to growth as the accessing, acquiring, and possessing of tangible assets may have, as economists and management alike are taught to think (Nonaka and Teece 2001, p. 3).

Fortunately, there seems to be a wide new option for knowledge-based competition in global markets. Hedlund (1996) argues that the global knowledge economy is characterized by two major trends: increasing global knowledge intensity and extensity.[10] He discusses global knowledge intensity as an accelerated growth of new knowledge derived from increasing education worldwide. The high global knowledge intensity also includes an increasingly demanding and sophisticated content of knowledge worldwide that incorporates insights, experiences, and learning from many locations and from social and cultural diversity. Hedlund reasons that the wide global knowledge extensity reflects the capabilities of companies and other institutions to create, transfer, and exploit knowledge globally. Giddens (1990, p. 4) also sees that local and global epistemological grounds are currently deeply changing.

Giddens (1990) also discusses the consequences of globalization and argues that local transformations caused by global knowledge are more profound than most of the change characteristics of any prior period. New social and cultural interconnections span the globe and may alter even some of the most intimate and personal features of our day-to-day life (Giddens, 1990, p. 4). He views that local and global are intertwined and that local transformations in social, cultural, institutional, or economic systems are affected by global changes in time and space. Giddens also discusses how local transformations can travel over time and space and change conditions in some other place. He uses as an example (1990, p. 65), where the prosperity and richness of some places in Singapore may be direct outcomes of poor competence and noncompetitive behavior of units in Pittsburgh. Units may belong to the same global company and he regards this as a phenomenon of how social and cultural systems "bind" and are "bound" in time and space.

According to this thinking, in a "meeting place" of local and global knowledge (figure 28.1), and consequent historical and spatial developments, global companies propel technological, social, cultural, and economic changes through the global marketplace. At their best, they may design and conduct strategies and ways of organizing that help their creative actions to bring about new innovations, over time and space. First, this requires deep local presence in places where new realities are being created; local entrepreneurs[11] are creators of new realities that are walking on the boundary between destabilizing situations and actualizing implicit possibilities, and these realities may "travel" into new contexts (Steyaert 1997, p. 22). This means living with local complexities but with global competitiveness in mind. Such local complexities as entrepreneurial and innovative processes are described as follows (Steyaert 1997, pp. 15–17): firms live in a complexity of knowledge of particulars, in a process of becoming that is written on a daily basis through transactions between many stakeholders, considering multiple scenes and multiple scenarios and searching to change existing realities into new worlds through creative actions. The entrepreneurial process is never finished; it is always ongoing, a journey more with surprises than with predictable patterns. Innovative entrepreneurs within local complexities write their own stories all the time. While doing so, they also transcend their boundaries through their local creative action. They may affect what happens globally in a wider sociocultural and economic context.

Second, global companies need ways and means of interlinking local innovative processes, as well as processes of creating out of "localities" more generic, sustainable, or abstracted knowledge that is transferable and combinable globally. The meeting place of local and global knowledge is an interface where two complexities of different origins are intertwined. The more they interact, the more they may affect each other.

Figure 28.1 suggests that a dialectic boundary as an interface between local and global knowledge is in a process of mutually interactive change, where (i) local knowledge derived from innovative, entrepreneurial processes and social,

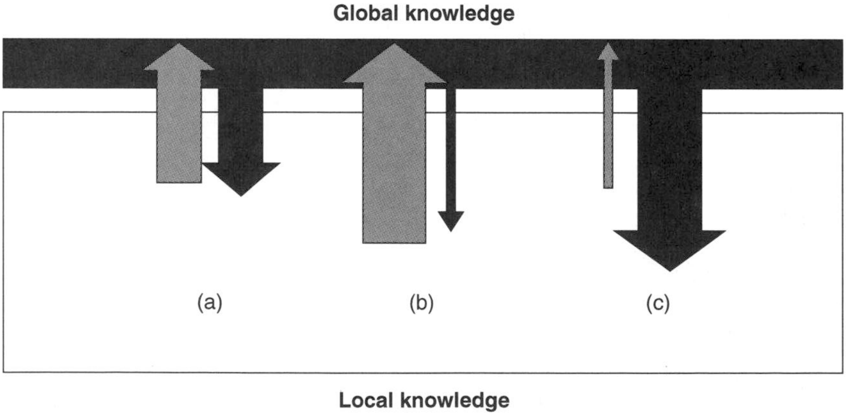

Global knowledge

Local knowledge

Figure 28.1 Intertwined local and global knowledge[16] with (a) equal impact on each other, (b) greater local impact, or (c) greater global impact.

cultural, and economic histories starts to influence global knowledge; and (ii) global knowledge based on the spatial innovation capabilities of companies over localities starts to influence local knowledge. Some localities, new "Silicon Valleys" as an innovation ecology, may have a strong impact on the worldwide knowledge base, and, in turn, some globally operating companies may affect strongly the local knowledge bases in which they are active. A tendency seems to be that both are stretching toward each other. The local innovative and entrepreneurial processes of firms are stretching over their "boundaries" in order to reach a wider applicability, generality, and mobility within the international marketplace through an understanding of global complexities. Thus, they transcend a distinction between local contexts and global context (Steyaert 1997, p. 17). The global innovative processes of companies, in turn, are stretching toward deeper understanding of local complexities.

Accordingly, local and global innovative processes are characterized by a "double-focus" competence in relation to knowledge and innovation. Companies can focus on both at the same time. This is more than Polanyi (1958, p. 56) assigns to individual performance; he argues that if a pianist shifts his attention from a piece he is playing to the observation of what he is doing with his fingers while playing it, he gets confused and may have to stop. Polanyi assigns capabilities for focal attention to particularities and global attention to the whole.[13]

Internal and External Innovation Efficiency

As global companies create knowledge out of richness of localities and, consequently, are major "change engines" of today's knowledge and technology, and even cultural and social developments, what are the sources of that change efficiency? This chapter argues for dialectic "boundary and interface efficiency" and thus follows the thinking of Bhaskar (1993), who views change and innovation as a dialectic process of content and form, where new configurations of conceptual and social interconnections may emerge. He discusses ontological, epistemological, relational, practical, and aesthetical dialectics (1993, p. 3). According to this thinking, an internal and external innovation efficiency of a global firm may be a function of (i) what a firm is, that is, in which form it "exists" in the world

(*ontological dialectic*), (ii) how it creates, transfers, and utilizes knowledge (*epistemological dialectic*), (iii) how it interacts with its internal and external "stakeholders" (*relational dialectic*), (iv) what it transacts and acts upon (*practical dialectic*), and (v) why and how it exists, interacts, and transacts (*ethical and aesthetical dialectic*). Consequently, the values, forms, and ways of existing, knowing, interacting, and transacting explain how a global company charts out possible futures and makes them happen, locally and globally. From the viewpoint of innovation efficiency, even the strategy of a firm is a reflection of its dialectic nature; that is, it is based on ontological, epistemological, and aesthetical groundings, and not only on practical and relational ones.

However, the internal and external innovation efficiency of a global firm may mostly depend on its relationship to knowledge. The knowledge-based view on innovation efficiency informs us of (i) how a firm perceives, reasons, and acts on its more or less intricate processes of conceptual and social conflict, interconnection, and change (Bhaskar 1993, p. 3) when it encounters local and global complexities, and (ii) how it transcends, through its transformative capacity of knowledge creation, beyond conflicts, polarities, and paradoxes of the local and global complexities. Bhaskar (1993, pp. 10–11) reasons for an intersubjectivity[14] of dialectics and views that it offers a "pulse of freedom" away from conflict-based reasoning and acting that is caused by subject-object perception. Accordingly, global firms may know how to overcome "conflicting" problems of local and global complexities and rather benefit from their richness through a transcending "intersubjectivity" as an attitude and approach. However, this may be dependent on whether a global firm (iii) emphasizes information and explicit knowledge or tacit knowledge as a source of its competitiveness (Teece 2001, pp. 126–127). Consequently, its (iv) dialectic relationship may be reactive and adaptive or more proactively and creatively reflexive and reflective. Global firms that base their perception, reasoning, and action solely on information or explicit knowledge may be more reactive and adaptive to changes of the global marketplace than global firms benefiting from tacit knowledge. Tacit knowledge contains qualities that give an option for sensing and anticipating future development trends (Kulkki and Kosonen 2001, Kulkki 1998). It may also leave more "space" for intersubjectivity and for transcendental creative actions.

Tacit knowledge is commonly discussed as a personal, nonarticulated, silent, hidden, experience-based, and skill-type bodily knowledge (Polanyi 1958).[15] Tacit knowledge is described as a latent, not-yet-activated reservoir of explicit knowledge, based on past experiences and practice. Consequently, tacit knowledge has been regarded as reflecting on the idiosyncratic history of a person or of an organization. This view emphasizes the experience-based stock of knowledge as derived from the past. However, Polanyi[16] also suggests that one can anticipate the future based on tacit knowledge. He discusses learning based on tacit knowledge as a heuristic act of insight, where the mind is in contact with a still-hidden reality (Polanyi and Prosch 1975, preface). In that condition, the mind may be anticipating an indeterminate range of the yet-unknown and unconceivable. Contextual learning theories discuss[17] tacit meanings[18] as providing orientation models for the future, for horizons of expectations, as well as orientation models for ambiguity, risks, and uncertainties. These may have a strong orientation toward the future,[19] dependent on the context (Kulkki 1996). Hence, tacit meanings may be prescientific and preconceptual[20] by nature (Polanyi 1958). One may argue that tacit knowledge may be a major source of innovation derived from the local creative processes of entrepreneurship which have been described as transcending current boundaries of explicit knowledge, as well as current boundaries of contexts.

Tacit knowledge also contains an ability to differentiate between space, time, direction, dimensions, sequences, entities, focus, states, moods, and feelings. With tacit knowledge individuals, and consequently organizations, can identify the beginnings and ends of the events (Kulkki 1996, Mezirow 1994). Thus, tacit knowledge integrates an experience-based, skill-type knowledge with intuitive forms to capture new ideas for future strategic lines of action. Consequently, the strategies based on tacit knowledge may not only conceive of past experiences, but they may also carry over discontinuities between the past and future. Hence, tacit knowledge may be a major source of global innovations that "travel" spatially over discontinuities in time and space.

However, global companies create rapid successive or even parallel innovation cycles with the global spread of new technologies, products, and services on many continents at the same time, a "rhythmic phenomenon" over the globe. This innovative speed to act "spatially" on many continents is dependent on a deep tacit involvement in many local complexities as histories over time in place. Paradoxically, global "spatial movements" as rapid rhythms in time and space are dependent on, and are partly outcomes of, long-term deep "existential rhythms" in many places.

Giddens (1990, pp. 16–22), in turn, challenges individuals and organizations alike and poses the question of separation of time and space. He considers that new forms of perceiving time and space also permit new time-space "zonings" of life and activities on a global scale. He tackles the issues of the disembedding social and cultural systems and the reflexive ordering and reordering of social relations; continuous new inputs of knowledge affect the actions of individuals and groups. Giddens wants to make time "empty" of space, and space "empty" of time.[21] He argues for emerging new social and technological conditions under which time and space are organized in a way that they may connect presence and absence. He sees presence and absence from the viewpoint of how to decontextualize, that is, how to "lift up" social and cultural systems and practices from the particularities of contexts of place and presence (cf. Doz et al. 1996, 1997). Giddens (1990, p. 20) discusses conditions for breaking free of local habits and practices. For him, trust may remain as a main condition of binding over time and space.[22]

Giddens (1990, pp. 14–22) also discusses even a need to distanciate or disembed or "lift out" the time and space from place. While doing so, he partly "lifts out" the social and cultural systems from their original place and lets these systems travel, interlace, and change while moving over time and space. Thus, he does not fully argue for the local social and cultural "stickiness" of knowledge (Doz et al. 1996, 1997).

Creating Knowledge Out of Localities

Nonaka (1997) discusses the knowledge creation of a firm in interaction with its local environment. Interaction may concern (i) explicit knowledge of products and services, but it may also concern (ii) tacit knowledge of hidden needs for new or revised products and services. The interaction can also be even more deeply cooperative and cocreative where (iii) new tacitly present future perspectives are sensed and anticipated. Through this interaction, the company can perceive future R&D trends, as well as trends concerning new technologies and businesses. New visions and worldviews, as well as new values, ideas, and ideals, may also be sensed, perceived, or creatively anticipated and preconceptualized. Nonaka (1997) states that this type of interorganizational and interpersonal interaction turns out to be a basis for the real-time knowledge creation of a firm. He discusses real-time knowledge creation and argues for an organic process to develop markets, not as mechanistically split segments but through an understanding of the underlying deep patterns that constitute markets. This view emphasizes the need for a tacit understanding of the constitutive powers behind the future.

Studies (Doz et al. 1996, 1997, Kulkki and Kosonen 2001) indicate that global companies have learned to organize and manage for deep involvement in many international locations in order to create and exploit new knowledge, even through deep knowledge-based interpersonal and interorganizational interaction. Companies interlink local creative actions globally through strategy, structure, and processes that are designed for the creation and exploitation of new knowledge. Doz and colleagues discuss organizational and managerial mechanisms through which companies "lift out" and de- and recontextualize local knowledge as particulars and make this knowledge travel over the global marketplace. Giddens (1990) considers that these new ways of "lifting out" and connecting local and global knowledge would have been unthinkable just a few years ago in our traditional societies.

However, Hedlund (1996) views "Silicon Valley Companies" as ones with deep involvement in only a few local environments in their development of high technology. His argument is that they are effective in creating new knowledge but not yet as effective in transferring this new knowledge over the globe. "Global Hamburgers" are effective in the transfer and exploitation of knowledge worldwide, but they are not creating new knowledge in many locations. Grant and Spender (1996, p. 8) discuss that the success of companies such as Wal-Mart and McDonald's is dependent on their ability to transfer the knowledge embodied in organizational routines from one establishment to another. "Global innovators," in turn, can conduct strategies and organize and manage deep involvement in knowledge creation in many locations, as well as transfer and exploit knowledge between many locations over many borderlines. This option is what Doz et al. (1996, 1997) present as a "metanational"

strategy, where a company acts globally as "orchestrator" of its knowledge and capabilities. Kulkki and Kosonen (2001) discuss the global innovation efficiency of the Nokia Corporation that has R&D centers in 14 countries globally with one-third of the personnel working in R&D.[23] A global firm functions as a "machinery of knowledge creation[24] in time and space."

Featherstone and Lash (1995, p. 2) think that local histories may become "replaced" by global "flows" through media-spaces, ethno-spaces, finance-spaces and techno-spaces. But they view that only in the minimalist sense can one speak yet of "global society" or "global culture," as our conceptions of society and culture are still based on traditions influenced by nation-state formation. However, Giddens has more "discontinuist" interpretations (1990, p. 3). He no longer believes in the great overarching stories that used to unite cultures, societies, and nation-states in Western thinking. Thus, he does not follow the argumentation attributed to evolutionary theories[25] that impose an orderly picture as a "story line" on the jumble of human happenings (p. 4) but instead believes that development consists of a set of discontinuities. The charting of possible, likely, and available futures becomes more important than charting the past (p. 50). Consequently, Giddens liberates people and organizations from history and holds that they should use knowledge about the past as a means of breaking with it or, at any rate, only sustaining what can be justified in the light of the future. The future is regarded as essentially open, yet counterfactually conditional upon courses of action undertaken with future possibilities in mind.

The liberation from history leads to fundamental new options of time-space stretching. This brings one to become concerned about the new formation of local and global and social and cultural life across time and space.

Local and Global Configurations

Global companies create local and global "configurations" for local involvement and global "movement" in time and space. Local processes of knowledge creation are connected to the global whole through local configurations[26] (Dunning 1997) and global linkages (Kulkki and Kosonen 2001). They are ways of acting that combine (i) deep local anchoring and (ii) wide global connectivity which provide access into otherwise

Local knowledge

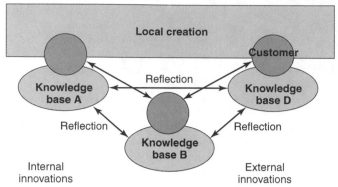

Figure 28.2 Local knowledge creation through internal and external innovative processes between units and customers and other local stakeholders of a global firm.

spatially immobile local knowledge assets that have a complementary value to the other knowledge assets of a firm (Dunning 1997). Dunning views that local anchoring may occur even through a series of on-going and "hands-on" technological and marketing relationships with new suppliers, customers, and competitors. He also holds that a firm may create a series of local configurations for various economic activities as a means of creating, exploiting, and enhancing its core competence and knowledge. Dunning further discusses the need to balance its locally anchored and globally unanchored knowledge assets.

Through such local configurations as innovative processes, a global firm anchors itself to local social, cultural, economic, and technological change and development, as well as to knowledge bases of its own firms, or of its customers, suppliers, and other stakeholders (figure 28.2). Global companies are also active in research cooperation with local universities and research institutions. Through local configurations global firms can widely and deeply create new knowledge as a "boundary or interface" action; that is, they create knowledge and innovate not only within their own local R&D and other units but also in cooperation with other organizations, institutions, and individuals. Local internal and external innovation efficiency is dependent on how reflectively and reflexively a firm acts on its internal and external boundaries.

Thus, local and global configurations reflect the dynamism of the strategy and organization of a firm: (i) how widely and deeply a firm is in-

volved in local innovation processes or local innovation ecology; (ii) how widely and deeply a firm interlinks local creative actions and brings about new generic, standardized, decontextualized, or abstracted levels of global knowledge from them; and (iii) through which means of connectivity a firm achieves speed and flexibility, as well as coherence and stability over its innovative local and global actions (figure 28.3). They also inform about the "boundary and interface efficiency" of a global firm. Csikszentmihalyi ([1988] 1995) discusses this efficiency as ways of "acting on creative fields,"[27] where promising variations are experimented with, selected, and incorporated into the domain of organization and knowledge. These configurations have a ontological dialectic and relational nature as (i) an enabling or constraining "stimulus variable" for knowledge creation, (ii) a "mediating vehicle" when interacting with the variety of its multilocational environment, (iii) a mutually constituting and creating living organism in interaction with its environment, and (iv) a resource base for knowledge creation. They may, at their best, help to transcend the "conflicts" of local and global complexities through a presensing (Scharmer 2001, pp. 72–75) and anticipating of the future.

Local and global configurations also inform us of how global firms benefit from dispersed local knowledge and transform it into global knowledge. Kulkki (1996, pp. 204–205) has found that global firms may be very efficient in solving new local and global problems and consequently in creating new knowledge and innovations. She ar-

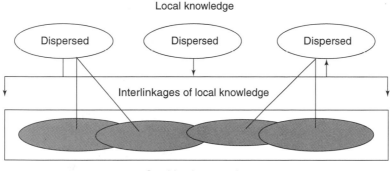

Figure 28.3 Global firms tap and interlink locally dispersed knowledge, transform it into more transferable, generic, or abstracted forms, and combine it with other local and global knowledge.

gues that some creative local processes may start with triggering problems that "push" a global firm to understand locally and globally the critical "core" of the problem. Around the critical core of the problem all necessary knowledge and competence is mobilized, including knowledge of existing worldwide experiences of analogical situations. Consequently, the complex local problems of customer and market interface may trigger within a global firm an integrated innovative process, where new businesses, technologies, products or services, or even new ways of marketing, manufacturing, supplying, and financing are developed. Buckley and Carter (2000) have found that the solving of complex local and global problems of global customers affects even the whole structure of the firm. The firm is organized around global customers and their problem solving and knowledge needs. Hamel (1996) argues that innovative companies may conduct strategies that are continually being drafted (and redrafted) according to the needs of the customer interface. Strategy is drafted within a "drafted" structure, using processes that are based on "drafting" actions.

Consequently, strategic problems and their critical "cores" may function as major organizing principles of global and local creative actions. Understanding the cores may lead to innovative processes that "naturally" combine local and global all the time. The core as a unifying aspect of the problem may even offer an option for transcendental solutions. Thus, the core, once understood, may be a "transcendental portal" to intersubjectivity between local and global in time and space. In other words, when conceptual

thinking and especially shared concepts are developed together, they may help to overcome local and global complexities and offer challenging opportunities for individual, social, and technological imagination[28] and reasoning. It is an exiting option of combining facts with visions.

Bianchi (1995) views that the conceptual capacity of a firm makes it possible to create new rules or new levels of understanding under the pressure of problem solving. Complex problems may mobilize creative processes where each step implies an innovative move in which individual minds transcend the original cognitive framework within which the problem has arisen. This may even lead to better solutions than the obvious factors of the situation might indicate and may happen if individual minds share a common interest and a strong common incentive to exploit the symbolic structure hidden in the situation. Bianchi discusses a heuristic or selective hidden rule that screens signals and reduces the ambiguity of the situation.

Global and local concept creation (figure 28.4) is based on (i) knowledge of markets and customers and (ii) knowledge of technologies. Besides local and global, individual, social, cultural, and organizational knowledge, global companies create new concepts based on their worldwide technology platforms. These technology platforms offer a wide range of opportunities for new combinations and comprise applicable and combinable technologies, and even basic technologies. Technologies are derived either from a firm's own R&D and experiences, from R&D of other organizations, or from scientific research. As "knowledge creating machineries," global

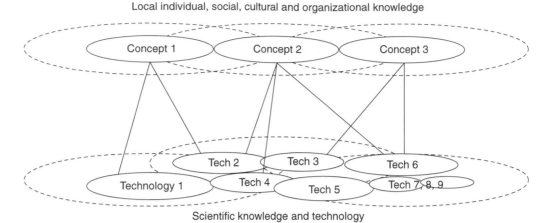

Figure 28.4 Global companies create new knowledge from (i) market and customer knowledge (individual, social, cultural and organizational knowledge) and (ii) technological knowledge (R&D and scientific research).

companies can create new concepts of businesses, products, and services that emerge out of a richness of local and global individual, social, and cultural knowledge, as well as out of a variety of new technological opportunities that make it possible to realize new ideas and make them happen. From the viewpoint of strategic management of knowledge, global companies may emphasize either market knowledge or technological knowledge or they may benefit from innovation efficiency that combines effectively both sources of knowledge. Global companies may also emphasize either local concepts or global concepts or innovations that are their combinations.

Weisberg (1995) reports that discontinuities as problems may call for thought processes that allow one to break away from the habitual, away from past experience, and thereby produce something novel, in a leap of insight. Though he argues that novel solutions to problems may also come about in an evolution, as one gradually moves away from the conception with which one began. Stacey (1994) views that complexity and creativity may call for perspectives in the organizational dynamic that focus not on equilibrium but on a far-from-equilibrium paradox, where the dynamics are both stable and unstable at the same time.

Nonaka and Takeuchi (1995, p. 56) find that when organizations innovate, they do not simply process information, from the outside in, in order to solve existing problems and adapt to a changing environment. They actually create new

knowledge and information, from the inside out, in order to redefine both problems and solutions and, in the process, to re-create their environment. Thus, Nonaka and Takeuchi view problem solving as the transcendental creation of new knowledge at the interfaces between the company and its environment. According to this thinking, local and global configurations may bring about new knowledge in a form that balances local and global aspects by being a combination of both. They carry a creative aspect of equality where the existing global solution may be at stake or become re-created at the same time with new local solutions. Through local and global innovative processes, both new local and global knowledge and new solutions may emerge.

The Global Company in Time and Space

A challenge of a global company is to create conditions where the strategy "lives" worldwide and is intertwined with the innovative processes and creative actions in time and space.

The question that remains is how a strategy is capable of giving a direction to the organizational "movement" in time and space? This section relates that question to organizational dynamism. Giddens (1984) argues that from the viewpoint of dynamic change, structures should be viewed as allowing "bindings" of time and space in social systems. He presents structures as "virtual or mental orders" of relations, which means that there is no need for structures in a traditional sense; rather, they exhibit "structural properties." The structures may only be present as "virtual entities," as memory traces, or through their time-space presence. According to this thinking, a global firm may also perceive its strategy as an organizing principle that is constitutively relying on the virtual and mental orders, shared mindsets and visions, ideas and ideals that fuel and bind the organization. This strategy is created and fueled organization-wide through "hands-on" management style and supported by global forums of dialogue and discussion, as well as by global information and communications systems in place.

Kulkki and Kosonen (2001) argue, based on the experiences of the Nokia Corporation, that innovative global companies can anticipate and create new knowledge and future markets through openness at all levels of the organization. Thus, they assign transparency as an important ontological, epistemological, relational, practical, and aesthetic quality to individual actions and the activities of teams, as well as to the action lines of the whole organization, locally and globally. They all should be open-ended and in "breathing" interaction with their environment. Kulkki and Kosonen view that transparency explains the renewal and growth capability of a firm and allows "movement" locally and globally in time and space. The multilayered openness of a firm to its environment comprises

many ways and means to sense and create future markets. Consequently, the "interface" or difference between innovative strategy and its rapid implementation may be very transparent, almost nonexistent (figure 28.5).

Figure 28.5. suggests that the speed of implementation is based on a strategy that is intertwined with local and global processes of innovation and reflective actions. They all are open to internal and external changes, locally and globally. Thus, the strategic focus and future foresights are intertwined not only with strategic innovation processes and implementation as reflective actions, but also with internal and external changes that flow widely into the organization. This leads to organization-wide, unified action, perception, and reasoning[29] in time and space and can also be translated into a capability to deploy creative and interactive strategies, processes, and ways of acting that draw their substance simultaneously from different markets and environments as well as from many technologies in place. This contextual quality helps to capture the essence of dispersed knowledge over the global marketplace. Ideally, the whole global company will be able to "breathe" and act according to the same rhythms in time. However, the role of modular processes and information systems may also be crucial for organizations in time and space, as they allow the rapid global implementation of agreed explicit actions: that is, automated implementation (Kulkki and Kosonen 2001).

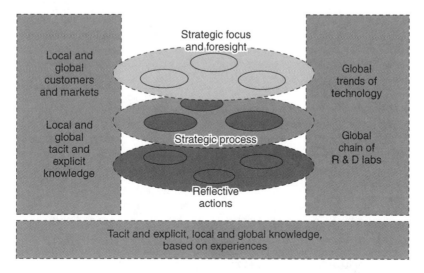

Figure 28.5 The strategic focus and foresights are intertwined with local and global innovative processes (strategic processes) and reflective actions that are based on future-oriented and experiences-based local and global knowledge.

TABLE 28.1 Strategies of Architects of Time and Followers of Time

Strategy and Knowledge	Reactive and Adaptive	Proactive and Creative
Ontology		
Of time, space, and place	Time is now with future options in mind based on historical evolutions. The firm "exists" in many local places rather than in global space.	Time is future, created from local and global histories and from being spatially "now." The firm "exists" in a global space that connects local places.
Epistemology		
Of creation and exploitation	Perceives knowledge as information or explicit knowledge. Creates new knowledge combinations of dispersed local knowledge. The emphasis is on local and global knowledge transfer and exploitation.	Benefits strongly from tacit knowledge. Creates new knowledge and innovations of local and global discontinuities. The emphasis is on market-maker behavior and the creation of new knowledge.
Interfaces		
And discontinuities	Subject-object-separation; "closed" interfaces, avoidance of discontinuities and conflicts, and an active search for balance.	Benefits from and even creates discontinuities and open interfaces, aims at mutual creation and transcendental intersubjectivity in problem solving.
Structure		
For innovative processes and actions	Emphasizes local innovative processes and actions and builds integrative global solutions out of them.	Emphasizing both local and global innovative processes and combined local and global configurations for knowledge creation. Flexibility is based on individual creative actions.
Values		
Of ethics and aesthetics	Efficiency and quality of performance and competitiveness in global marketplace	Quality and efficiency in the competitive creation of new "worlds" and markets and technologies.

The strategic focus and future foresights derive some of their content and qualities through reflective actions based on tacit knowledge. Reflective actions can have a double-focus or even multiple focuses. They may simultaneously reflect current and future tasks and local and global complexities. A global firm may create its reality through actions that are explicitly focusing on current tasks at hand, while also tacitly monitoring the flow of local and global complexities, as well as social, cultural, psychological, techno-logical, and physical aspects incorporated in them and in the contexts where a firm moves.[30] Based on this reflective and reflexive capacity, a global company has the capability to "flow" and live proactively in time all the time. This means that the future is present as an aspect, in tacit or explicit form, in every creative action of a firm, and that time is the unifying factor within the organization. Acquired insights and foresights can be sensed and shared company-wide, for instance, during the strategy process or in management development forums, R&D processes, dialogical platforms, or even in Knowledge Cafés as a dialogical place as in the case of ICL. Through dialogical processes, peoples' future foresights are converted into common visions, strategic directions, and actionable milestones and measures.[31] Global companies, being proactive and creative, can act as "architects of time," while more reactive and adaptive firms may be "followers of time" (see table 28.1).

As architects of time, global companies may enter into value-based visioning as a means of dialectic interaction with their customers, competitors, and other stakeholders. Microsoft among others has discussed its vision of a "computer that can learn, speak and even 'feel'." The Nokia Corporation has openly announced its vision of a "wireless information society" and expresses that the future has no limits. As the CEO of the Japanese Eisai Corporation states:

> human healthcare is intended to be the common mission and goal of Eisai employees worldwide, regardless of national borders, what language we speak or whether we are male or female. I do not think we can find such commonality in monetary or financial results or theories. If we, as human beings, can share thoughts that transcend borders, languages and cultures, I think those thoughts can be a kind of aesthetic, like truth, virtue or beauty. Such thoughts induce commitment. These common thoughts will be found in our mission and goals and in the knowledge creation that unfolds in our daily work towards their realization. (Naito 2001, p. 282)

Conclusions

This chapter discusses the knowledge creation of a global firm not only in the context of organization and management theories of multinational corporations but also in the context of social theories and theories of innovation, creativity, and human cognition. Kogut and Zander (1993) view that a multinational corporation is a multicultural social community, with social technology and a superior efficiency of internal knowledge management across borderlines. Dosi et al. (1998) discuss the *coevolution* of technology, business firms, and other institutions, and that development and growth is not only a matter of new technologies entering the global marketplace, but also a matter of how firms interact with other firms and institutions while they innovate. In their view (1998, p. 11), technological paradigms or regimes can be thought of as cognitive aspects of entrepreneurial processes of innovation, as entrepreneurs think about what a customer will buy. They also argue that the point of discontinuity is often the emergence of a new technological "dominant design or paradigm" (Nelson and Winter 1982). Dosi et al. also discuss (1998, p. 7) wealth creation based on technological change as being less dependent on strategizing and more on the technological, organizational, and managerial processes inside the firm. Consequently, the internal innovation efficiency of a firm is a necessary precondition for external innovation efficiency as a boundary or interface action. Internal innovation efficiency is a crucial starting point for coevolution, according to this thinking.

However, the previous discussion has had a tendency to view growth as a result of mutual adaptation to, but not as a creative interaction with, the environment. In this chapter, some global companies are architects of time; that is, firms that constitutively create their futures and their future markets with customers, partners, suppliers, etc. This cocreation is based on shared visions and foresights and on shared tacit understanding derived from experiences of creative local and global innovative actions and problem solving.

Global firms as architects of time may create their futures and future markets through accelerated growth by combining local and global innovation processes with high levels of aspiration when faced with severe competition (cf. Moore 1995, Brown and Eisenhardt 1998). The accelerated innovative processes may affect the whole company, and not only temporary teams for innovative and competitive tasks (Kulkki and Kosonen 2001). Consequently, this type of internal and external innovation efficiency may be an organization-wide quality, and as such it may strongly characterize the whole strategic behavior of a firm. Nonaka et al. (2000, p. 11) hold that the innovation efficiency of a firm is demonstrated by its capability of creating knowledge faster than the markets create.

This differs essentially from the earlier discussion on contingent, organic, evolutionary, social, or institutional views of growth (e.g., Lawrence and Lorsch 1967, Scott 1995, and Nelson and Winter 1982).[32] One may argue that, starting in the 1990s, for the first time a firm has been able to operate "as a meeting place" of local histories over time in place and global "spatialities" in time and space. In this meeting place, global companies may emphasize combined internal and external innovation efficiency and intertwined strategy with local and global innovative processes and creative and reflective actions.

Nonaka (1999)[33] considers a firm as a knowledge-creating entity with its own epistemological manner. A firm perceives and interprets reality, justifies the truth, and acts on these through a company-specific, distinctive epistemological manner. The epistemological foundations of a firm reflect its values, worldview, and visions, as well as how it perceives human beings. Nonaka and Takeuchi (1995) discuss knowledge creation and hold that organizational dynamism is based on an ongoing process of knowledge creation, where individual tacit knowledge is converted into organizational explicit knowledge by means of socialization, communication, and dialogue. They also describe knowledge creation as a process of dialogue and communication that "elevates" or "lifts" new knowledge from one ontological and epistemological level to another.

Nonaka and Takeuchi view the process of knowledge creation as a phenomenon where epistemology is intertwined with ontology; that is, the emergence of knowledge is intertwined with its social context. Nonaka, Toyama, and Konno (2000) argue that the phenomenological "place" ba[34] is a foundation of knowledge creation and has an intertwined ontological and epistemological nature; it is a shared and interactive space where knowledge is embedded. That shared space can be physical, virtual, social, or mental; the space can emerge out of shared experiences, ideas, ideals, and values, as well as out of the same office space or through the Internet and teleconferencing.

According to this thinking, ba is a foundation for knowledge creation from the individual and social viewpoints and presupposes a shared context. It is a shared phenomenological "place" that energizes individuals and groups for knowledge creation. This chapter discusses boundary efficiency and creative fields of actions from the viewpoint of a global firm and thus presupposes multiple contexts, and consequently, multiple interests, mental models, and a diversity of organizational, institutional, social, and cultural aspects. However, through local and global creative processes, a global firm may also reach transcendentally moments where multiple contexts and contents can fuse into each other and form shared contexts and contents in time and space.

In their knowledge creation, global firms are challenged by the enormous speed of change and consequent need to operate quickly in time and space. The capability to "jump over discontinuities" is needed, as well as a capability for optimal timing within the rapid pace of implementation. Thus, global firms base their speed and flexibility on strategies that rely on common values, mindsets, and ideals that bring about consistency and coherence for rapid change and renewal. One may argue that mutual trust, especially, can be the most important factor to offer stability over the discontinuities of rapid change (Kulkki and Kosonen 2001).

In the 1970s, Heidegger addressed a question about the consequences of a blind desire to develop new technologies purely instrumentally, without values and sustainable goals. He discusses the notion of humanism, individualism, and individual autonomy and how human beings relate to nature and technology. His views are that technology would promote democracy, in that it may turn what has been prerogatives of the few into necessities for the many. However, he is critical about purely "instrumental" reasoning, according to which all we are concerned with is a search for "new or improved" versions of whatever means are already available for attaining whatever goals such means make possible. What counts is doing things better than before. Whether such things are worth doing in the first place is no longer a question. He challenges the dominant Western way of thinking, where knowledge has only an instrumental value and has become identical to technology. He thinks that how we conceive of individual human beings affects our understanding of knowledge and vice versa: how we view knowledge determines where we place the individual and his or her relationship with nature and the world. There is good reason to be critical about the global knowledge creation if it ends up undermining the value of both human beings and knowledge.

However, with the help of technology, such as global information and communications technologies and technologies based on sciences of life, we have an option to experience wide social, cultural, and structural changes in organizational and institutional life, as well as in individual lives, as human beings. These may, at their best, fundamentally improve the quality of our life.

Notes

1. Kulkki and Kosonen (2001, p. 259) discuss how global companies may build time- and knowledge-based organizational and managerial capabilities for renewal and growth. The authors use the Nokia Corporation as an example of time-paced global innovation efficiency that benefits from local tacit and explicit knowledge and organizational ways and means to convert that to global knowledge for new innovations. They discuss among other things the role of company-wide shared strategic foresights, innovative ways of interacting, reflective ways of acting, and automated implementation.

2. Doz et al. (1996 and 1997), Kulkki and Kosonen (2001).

3. Hamel discusses strategies as "conducted" within a "drafted" structure and "drafting" processes. Everything is changing all the time.

4. Nonaka and Takeuchi (1995), Nonaka, Toyama, and Nagata (2000), Nonaka, Toyama, and Konno (2000).

5. Nonaka and Takeuchi (1995) and Nonaka et al. (2000) view a firm as a knowledge-creating entity and as an open system. This means a continuous flow of tacit and explicit knowledge in and out of a firm.

6. Featherstone and Lash (1995, pp. 1–2) discuss a shift from a temporal or historical analysis to spatial analysis in social sciences. They consider *global flows* of media-spaces, ethno-spaces, finance-spaces, and techno-spaces.

7. Nonaka, Toyama, and Konno (2000) discuss the dialectic nature of knowledge creation when they introduce the concept of the SECI-process (socialization, externalization, combination, and internalization of knowledge during which process tacit knowledge becomes converted to explicit and vice versa) and the concept of Ba as a founding "place" of knowledge.

8. Bhaskar (1993, p. 3) discusses the dialectical nature of development from the viewpoints of ontological, epistemological, relational, practical, and aesthetic dialectics.

9. Reference is made to an ongoing explorative, empirical study on knowledge creation of global companies conducted by interviewing Japanese, European, and U.S.-based companies.

10. Giddens (1990, p. 4) discusses increasing global knowledge and holds that it comprises intensional and extensional planes that span the globe and may alter social interconnections and even everyday lives.

11. The chapter discusses local innovators as small local firms or as units of global companies.

12. *Local knowledge* includes the historical variety of national, social, cultural, institutional, and economic development in a certain place over time, whereas *global knowledge* includes the spatial scope and pace of global social, cultural, institutional, and economic change as a consequence of the "transformative traveling" of knowledge over many locations in time and space.

13. Polanyi (1958) uses the terms focal attention and subsidiary attention. See also Dewey (1997, p. 135) regarding concrete and abstract thinking.

14. Bhaskar discusses the triunity of subjectivity, intersubjectivity, and objectivity within the language of experiences.

15. Polanyi and Prosch (1975, pp. 37–45) discuss the nature of personal knowledge from the point of view of *tacit bodily knowledge or skill*. Two kinds of skillful knowing are interwoven: a skillful handling of things must rely on our understanding them, while intellectual comprehension can be achieved only by the skillful scrutiny of a situation. The kinship between the process of tool-using and that of perceiving a whole has been so well established already by gestalt psychology that it may be taken for granted. Thus, the structure of tacit knowing includes a joint pair of constituents, i.e., a functional structure of *from-to* knowing includes jointly "from" knowing and a focal "to" or "at" knowing. Where one focuses is formed by the act of a person, who integrates one to the other.

16. Polanyi (1958, reprinted 1998, pp. 69–77) discusses among other things trick learning, sign learning, and latent learning. He discusses latent learning as an act of interpretation that may contain heuristic insights and innovations.

17. Mezirow (1994) discusses the creation of new meanings and transformative future ways of acting.

18. Contextual learning theories discuss meaning schemes and meaning perspectives. The discussion is partly based on the findings of the schema theories.

19. Polanyi (1958) discusses this in his preface based on the 1957 article, "Gestalt Psychology and the Nature of Personal Knowledge." This knowledge is derived from personal participation of the knower in all understanding. However, he argues, this does not make our understanding subjective. Comprehension is neither an arbitrary act nor a passive experience, but a responsible act claiming universal validity. Such knowing is indeed objective in the sense of establishing contact with a hidden reality, a contact that is defined as the condition for anticipating an indeterminate range of yet-unknown (and perhaps yet-unconceivable) true implications. Polanyi calls this fusion of the

personal and the objective "Personal Knowledge."
This knowledge contains intellectual commitment.
He argues that into every action of knowing there
enters a passionate contribution of the person
knowing what is being known. Thus, Polanyi describes comprehension and knowing as a passionate intellectual commitment to the yet-unknown
and unconceivable.

20. Compare Scharmer (2001) on self-
transcending knowledge and precognition.

21. Giddens gives a historical background to
time-place unification from agrarian societies that
always linked time with a certain place. "When"
was always connected to "where." Only since the
invention of the mechanical clock, from the eighteenth century onward, has the separation of time
from place been possible. The clock expressed the
uniform dimension of "empty" time (of place)
that made "time zones" possible, like a working
day. The "emptying" of time from place is in
large part the precondition for the "emptying" of
time from space. Giddens views place through the
ideal of a locale that refers to the physical settings of social activity as situated geographically.
The spatial dimensions of social life are for most
of the population dominated by presence-localized
activities. Place or localized activities are seen as
"presence," space as "absence," in term of modes
of existence and connections. Modernity increasingly tears space away from place by fostering relations between "absent" others, locationally distant from any given situation of face-to-face
interaction.

22. Giddens views (1990, p. 33) that trust is related to absence in time and space. There would
be no need to trust anyone whose activities were
continually visible and whose thought processes
were transparent, or to trust any system whose
workings were wholly known and understood.
Trust is according to him bound up, not with risk,
but with contingency. Trust carries the connotation of reliability. It is the precise link between
faith and confidence.

23. *The Nokia Annual Report 1999.*

24. *Nokia Annual Report 1999: No Limits to
the Future,* pp. 26–27.

25. Neither does he want to belong to the
school of postmodernism which views that a new
era will arrive (after modernity) that will be fragmented and disconnected from a grounding in
epistemology and faith in humanly engineered
progress (Giddens 1990, pp. 1–2). Giddens would
rather discuss postmodernity than postmodernism. He holds that postmodernity is only a
state of affairs where modernity has radicalized
itself.

26. Simonton, D.K. (1988, rev. 1995) discusses

the term *configuration* as a conformation of
structural arrangements of entities, implying that
the relative disposition of these entities is central
to the configuration's identity. For instance, a spatial placement of atoms is often called configuration. In gestalt psychology, a configuration is
taken to be a collection of sensations, emotions,
patterns, and concepts organized in such fashion
that the collection operates as a unit in thought
and behavior. The article is "Creativity, Leadership
and Change," in Robert J. Sternberg, ed., *The Nature of Creativity,* pp. 386–426 (Cambridge: Cambridge University Press).

27. Per Webster's (1996) *Encyclopedic
Unabridged Dictionary of the English Language,*
p. 528: the notion of *field* is an expanse of open
and cleared ground, devoted to sports, contests of
playing. In a field something is grown or cultivated. Field may be a sphere of activity and interest, a location remote from regular workshop facilities and offices. It may also be a sphere of
influence, the total complex of interdependent factors within which social, cognitive, and psychological events occur.

28. See, for instance, Geertz (1983) and Mills
(1959).

29. Hurley (1998) argues that the mind perceives reality while acting, and acts while perceiving. Lakoff and Johnson (1999) put forward the
view and argue that even reasoning is intertwined
with perception and action. Lakoff and Johnson
(1999, pp. 9–44) discuss cognitive consciousness
and the embodied mind. They discuss the nature
of reason as inextricably intertwined with body
and bodily experiences which both precondition
the conceptual systems of the mind, i.e., the
structures and processes of the mind to perceive
and create concepts of reality. Lakoff and Johnson
base their discussion on new discoveries of cognitive science. They discuss especially the nature of
cognitive unconsciousness and argue that cognitive unconsciousness is vast and intricately structured. Unconscious thought may be more than
95% of all thoughts. Cognitive unconsciousness
includes not only all our automatic cognitive operations but also our implicit knowledge. Lakoff
and Johnson argue that all our knowledge and beliefs are framed in terms of a conceptual system
that resides mostly in the cognitive unconsciousness and that the unconscious conceptual system
functions like a "hidden hand" that shapes how
we conceptualize all aspects of our experience.

30. Giddens (1984, pp. 2–3) views that reality,
including social structures, is neither the experience of the individual, nor the existence of any
form of societal totality. He emphasizes that the
social reality is created through mutual interplay

between individual and social, in *a series of times and spaces*, where the reflection and knowledge-ability of human beings is deeply involved in the recursive ordering of social practices and reality. Giddens discusses structuration, i.e., the chance and development of structures which has the connotation of dynamic social development based on the above mentioned interactive recursive ordering. He emphasizes the *ontology of time and space and reflection* through action and that there exists *co-presence*; individuals have the capacity *to act and tacitly reflect at the same time*; i.e., human beings can "monitor" continuously the flow of their activities, as well as the social, psychological, and physical aspects of the contexts in which they move. People routinely maintain a continuing "theoretical understanding" of the grounds of their activity.

31. Compare Nonaka and Takeuchi's (1995) discussion of how to convert tacit knowledge to explicit.

32. Brown and Eisenhardt (1998) also discuss strategy and structured chaos from the viewpoint of how global companies create strategies and new action lines while trying all the time to catch up with or even to lead rapid development. They approach the idea of renewal capability at the edge of chaos as a confluence of complexity and evolutionary theories.

33. Keynote Speech to the Knowledge Forum of the Haas School of Business at University of California at Berkeley, October 14–15, 1999.

34. Nonaka, Toyama, and Konno (2000) distinguish the concept of *ba* as a foundation of knowledge creation from the concept of communities of practice as follows. The concept of *ba* seemingly has some similarities with the concept of communities of practice (Lave and Wenger 1991, Wenger 1998). Based on the apprenticeship model, the concept of community of practice argues that a community can learn through participating in the community of practice and gradually memorizing jobs. However, there are important differences between the concepts of community of practice and *ba*. While a community of practice is a place where the members learn knowledge that is embedded in the community, *ba* is a place where new knowledge is created. While learning occurs in communities of practice, *ba* needs energy to become an active *ba* where knowledge is created. While a boundary of a community of practice is firmly set by task, culture, and history of the community, the boundary of *ba* is set by the participants and can be changed easily. Instead of being constrained by history, *ba* has a "here and now" quality. It is created, functions, and disappears according to need. While the membership of

a community of practice is fairly stable, requiring time for a new participant to learn about the community of practice and become a full participant, the membership of *ba* is not fixed; participants may come and go. While members of a community of practice belong to the community, participants of *ba* relate to the *ba*.

References

Arthur, W.B. (1996) "Increasing returns and the new world of business." *Harvard Business Review* (July–August):100–109.

Bhaskar, R. (1993) *Dialectic: The Pulse of Freedom.* London and New York: Verso.

Bianchi, M. (1995) "Markets and firms: Transaction costs versus strategic innovation." *Journal of Economic Behaviour and Organization* 28:183–202.

Brown, S.L. and Eisenhardt, K. (1998) *Competing on the Edge: Strategy as Structured Chaos.* Boston: Harvard Business School Press.

Buckley, P.J. and Carter, M.J. (1999) "International Strategies to Capture Value from Knowledge." Conference on the Global Information Revolution in International Management, October 21–23, San Francisco, GSIA, Carnegie-Mellon.

Buckley, P.J. and Carter, M.J. (2000) "Organizational Structures and Processes in Multinationals: Solving Problems of Global Integration." Proceedings of the Conference on Knowledge and Innovation, Center for Knowledge and Innovation Research/HSEBA, Helsinki, May 25–26, pp. 205–213.

Burton-Jones, A. (1999) *Knowledge Capitalism: Business, Work, and Learning in the New Economy.* Oxford University Press.

Chakravarthy, B.S. and Doz Y. (1992) "Strategy Process Research: Focusing on Corporate Self-Renewal." *Strategic Management Journal* 13: 5–14.

Csikszentmihalyi, M. ([1988] 1995) "A Systems View of Creativity," in Robert J. Sternberg, (ed.), *The Nature of Creativity*, pp. 325–339. Cambridge: Cambridge University Press.

Dewey, J. (1997) *How We Think.* Dover Publications.

Dosi, G., Teece, D., and Chytry, J. (eds.) (1998) *Technology, Organization and Competitiveness: Perspectives on Industrial and Corporate Change.* Oxford: Oxford University Press.

Doz, Y., Asakawa, K., Santos, J.F.P, and Williamsson, P. (1996, revised 1997) "The Metanational Corporation." INSEAD Working paper.

Dunning, J. (1997) "The Changing Nature of the Firm in a Knowledge-Based Globalizing Industry." Conference Paper for the Conference on

Knowledge in International Corporations, Rome, November.

Featherstone, M. and Lash, S. (1995) "Globalization, Modernity and the Spatialization of Social Theory: An Introduction," in M. Featherstone, S. Lash, and R. Robertson, (eds.), *Global Modernities*, Sage Publications.

Geertz, C. (1983) *Local Knowledge*. New York: Basic Books.

Giddens, A. (1984) *The Constitution of Society*. Oxford: Polity Press.

Giddens, A. (1990) *The Consequences of Modernity*. Oxford: Polity Press.

Hagström, P. and Hedlund, G. (1993) "The Dynamic Firm: A Three-Dimensional Model of Internal Structure," in A.D. Chandler, P. Hagström, and Ö. Söllvell (eds.), *The Dynamic Firm*. Oxford University Press (1998).

Hamel, G. (1996) "Creative Strategies Within Drafted Structures and Processes." Opening Speech for Strategic Management Society (SMS) Conference, Phoenix, October.

Hamel, G. (1999) "Bringing Silicon Valley inside." *Harvard Business Review* (September–October): 71–84.

Hedlund, G. (1993) "Assumptions on Hierarchy and Heterarchy, with Applications to the Management of the Multinational Corporation," pp. 211–236, in S. Ghoshal and D.E. Westney (eds.), *Organization Theory and Multinational Corporation*. New York: St. Martin's Press.

Hedlund, G. (1994) "A model of knowledge management and the N-form corporation." *Strategic Management Journal* 15:73–90.

Hedlund, G. (1996) "The Knowledge Intensity and Extensity and the MNCs as Nearly Recomposable Systems (NRS)." Conference Paper for the Academy of International Business Conference, Banff, Canada, Sept. 26–29.

Heidegger, M. (1976) *The Questions of Technology and Other Essays*. W. Lowitt, trans. New York: Harper and Row.

Hurley, S.L. (1998) *Consciousness in Action*. Cambridge: Harvard University Press.

Kogut, B. and Zander, U. (1993) "Knowledge of the firm and the evolutionary theory of the multinational corporation." *Journal of International Business Studies* 24(4):625–645.

Kulkki, S. (1996) "Knowledge Creation of Multinational Corporations: Knowledge Creation through Action." Doctoral diss., Helsinki School of Economics and Business Administration.

Kulkki, S. (1998) "Knowledge Creation and Dynamism of Governance Structures of Multinational Corporations: A Research Design." INSEAD Working paper, 24.2, p. 85.

Kulkki, S. (1999) "Intertwined Strategy, Actions and Structure: A Precondition for Global Knowledge Creation?" Keynote Address to the Seminar on Interactive Strategies, Sems, University of Surrey, UK, p. 26.

Kulkki, S. and Kosonen, M. (2001) "How Tacit Knowledge Explains Organizational Renewal and Growth: The Case of Nokia," in Nonaka, I. and Teece, D. (eds.), *Managing Industrial Knowledge*, pp. 244–269. London: Sage.

Lakoff, G. and Johnson, M. (1999) *Philosophy in the Flesh: The Embodied Mind and Its Challenge to Western Thought*. New York: Basic Books.

Lawrence, P.R. and Lorsch, J.W. ([1967] 1986) *Organization and Environment*. Boston: Harvard Business School Classics.

Mezirow, J. (1994) *Transformative Dimensions of Adult Learning*. San Francisco: Jossey-Bass.

Mills, C.W. (1959) *Social Imagination.*, Oxford University Press.

Moore, G.A. (1995) *Inside the Tornado. Marketing Strategies from Silicon Valley's Cutting Edge*. Capstone.

Naito, H. (2001) *Knowledge Is Commitment*. Beverly Hills: Sage Publications.

Nelson, R.A. and Winter, S. (1982) *An Evolutionary Theory of Economic Change*. Cambridge: Harvard University Press.

Nonaka, I. (1997) "Knowledge Creation and Sustainable Competitiveness of the Firm." Presentation in a seminar organized by LIFIM (the Finnish Institute of Management) on Organizational Knowledge Creation, March 23. Reported by Veijo Sahiluoma, *Kauppalehti*, April 1, 1997, no. 61, p. 32.

Nonaka, I. and Takeuchi H. (1995) *The Knowledge-Creating Company: How Japanese Companies Create the Dynamics of Innovation*. New York: Oxford University Press.

Nonaka, I. and Konno, N. (1998) "The Concept of "Ba": Building a Foundation for Knowledge Creation." *California Management Review* 40(3): 40–54.

Nonaka, I. and Teece, D. (eds.) (2001) *Managing Industrial Knowledge: Creation, Transfer, and Utilization*. Beverly Hills: Sage.

Nonaka, I., Toyama, R., and Nagata, A. (2000) "A Firm as a Knowledge-creating Entity: A New Perspective on the Theory of the Firm." *Industrial and Corporate Change* 9(1).

Nonaka, I., Toyama, R., and Konno, N. (2000) "SECI, Ba and Leadership: A Unified Model of Dynamic Knowledge Creation." *Long Range Planning* 33:5–34.

Polanyi, M. (1958) *Personal Knowledge: Towards a Post-Critical Philosophy*. London: Routledge.

Polanyi, M. and Prosch, H. (1975) *Meaning*. Chicago: University of Chicago Press.

Prahalad, C.K. and Hamel, G. (1994) "Strategy as a Field of Study: Why Search for a New Paradigm?" *Strategic Management Journal* 15:5–16.

Scott, W.R. (1995) *Institutions and Organizations.* Sage Publications.

Scharmer, C.O. (2001) "Self-transcending Knowledge: Organizing Around Emerging Realities," in I. Nonaka and D. Teece (eds.), *Managing Industrial Knowledge,* pp. 67–90. London: Sage.

Stacey, R.D. (1995) "The science of complexity: An alternative perspective for strategic change processes." *Strategic Management Journal* 16:447–495.

Steyaert, C. (1997) "A Qualitative Methodology for Process Studies of Entrepreneurship: Creating Local Knowledge Through Stories." *International Studies on Management and Organization* 27(3):13–33.

Teece, D. (1998) "Capturing Value From Knowledge Assets: The New Economy, Markets for Know-how, and Intangible Assets." *California Management Review* 40(3):55–79.

Teece, D. (2001) "Strategies for Managing Knowledge Assets: The Role of Firm Structure and Industrial Context," in I. Nonaka and D. Teece (eds.), *Managing Industrial Knowledge,* pp. 125–144.

Vattimo, G. (1988) *The End of History.* Oxford: Polity Press.

Weisberg, R.W. ([1988] rev. 1995) "Problem solving and creativity," in Robert J. Sternberg (ed.), *The Nature of Creativity,* pp. 148–176. Cambridge: Cambridge University Press.

Wenger, E. (1998) *Communities of Practice: Learning, Meaning, and Identity.* Cambridge: Cambridge University Press.

VI

Knowledge across Boundaries

29

Mobilizing Knowledge in Interorganizational Alliances

Harald M. Fischer, Joyce Brown, Joseph F. Porac,
James B. Wade, Michael DeVaughn, and Alaina Kanfer

The study of strategic alliances has blossomed over the past several years partly because the diversity of alliance forms and motivations is an interesting problem of classification and explanation. This research has revolved around definitions of alliances that concern the transfer of resources, sharing of governance structures, and the joint accomplishment of individual goals (Parkhe 1991). Inkpen (1998), for example, lists joint ventures, licensing agreements, distribution and supply agreements, research and development partnerships, and technical exchanges as among the multitude of alliance forms which can further be subclassified by governance type (e.g., equity or nonequity arrangements). Similar to alliance forms, researchers have also identified a long list of motives for alliance formation. Varadarajan and Cunningham (1995) argue, for instance, that motives underlying strategic alliance formation include market entry, changes in market structure, resource efficiency, resource acquisition, risk reduction, and skill enhancement.

While many of these known motivations for entering alliances are implicitly based on the assumption that learning and information sharing occurs among partner firms, only recently have researchers begun to focus on learning and knowledge transfer processes within strategic alliances (e.g., Inkpen and Dinur 1998, Mowery et al. 1996, Simonin 1999a). Moreover, although there has been a great deal of theorizing about features of alliances that facilitate the flow of knowledge among partner firms, relatively few empirical studies have specifically addressed and analyzed factors affecting these processes (Simonin 1999a). The purpose of this chapter is to synthesize the findings of this recent work and to establish linkages to literatures that more generally examine organizational learning and knowledge transfer.

The chapter is organized as follows: The first section will present an outline of that portion of the interorganizational alliance literature that explicitly addresses factors affecting processes of learning and knowledge transfer. The subsequent section offers what we hope might provide for an on-going discussion regarding some of the potential linkages between the research and corresponding arguments we review in the first section and those found more generally in the organizational learning and network literatures. We conclude by discussing potential areas of inquiry that might guide future empirical work in this area.

Learning and Knowledge Transfer in the Alliance Literature

The growing stream of research within the fields of strategy and organizational science exploring interorganizational alliances has been described as vast, burgeoning, and increasingly important (Grandori and Soda 1995, Gulati 1998). Stuart (2000) highlights several points on the status of this literature suggesting that we are gaining a more solid understanding of firms' motivations to enter alliances. He also observes, however, that while explanations for alliance formation are directly linked to the presumed benefits of such arrangements, surprisingly few studies have explored the conditions under which strategic alliances prove advantageous. Stuart is not alone in stating this opinion; others in the field describe the interesting questions surrounding the performance of alliances as some of the most vexing (Gulati 1998, p. 309).

As introduced, much of the large body of literature concerning strategic alliances has either explored questions surrounding a firm's motivation to enter such arrangements (e.g., Eisenhardt and Schoonhoven 1996, Grandori and Soda 1995, Pfeffer and Nowak 1976) or has presumed the positive benefits associated with alliance membership and gone on to examine performance differentials that may result for partner firms (e.g., Baum and Oliver 1991, Hamel et al. 1989). Even in the context of international cooperative ventures, the literature has been described as largely focusing on reasons behind the spread of international joint ventures and conditions under which they are likely to occur, leaving questions surrounding the search and transfer of knowledge relatively unexplored (Shenkar and Li 1999).

A strategic alliance in its general form has been aptly defined as a voluntary arrangement between two or more firms involving "exchange, sharing, or co-development of products, technologies, or services" (Gulati 1998, p. 293). Echoing Stuart, we find that relatively few studies have systematically explored these processes of "exchange" or "sharing" that so much define an alliance. Given that the opportunity to learn from partners or to transfer resources across firms has largely been cited as a primary incentive for establishing alliances in the first place (e.g., Hagedoorn 1993, Hamel 1991, Shenkar and Li 1999), it is surprising to find relatively few studies that examine the actual process of knowledge transfer within a context that is presumed to exist expressly for this purpose.

We begin by refining Stuart's question of conditions under which alliance membership proves advantageous by exploring the conditions under which learning and knowledge transfer—the presumed underlying advantage and incentive for engaging in these partnerships—is most likely to occur between and among alliance partners. In the following discussion, we will highlight some of the research that has explored questions concerning exchange or sharing (specifically) between alliance partners and the conditions under which this type of learning might be most successful. We find that the focus of this work spans the spectrum of potential levels of analysis to include features of the "knowledge" itself to the national cultures surrounding alliance partners. Following a brief summary of this literature, the subsequent portion of this chapter will be devoted to establishing explicit links between more general areas of inquiry within the strategy and organizations field, and commenting on a few of the potential directions for future research.

Knowledge Tacitness and Ambiguity

A key question that has at least been implicitly identified in the alliance literature is whether the extent to which knowledge is tacit or ambiguous affects the learning process (e.g., Inkpen 1996, Lei et al. 1997, Simonin 1999a). Varying dimensions of knowledge have been discussed based on the early work of Polanyi (1966) who classified human knowledge as either "explicit" (codified knowledge which is readily transferable via formal communications or mechanisms) or "tacit" (personal knowledge which is difficult to formalize and communicate because it is embedded in a specific context). Spender (1996) defines explicit knowledge as that which may be stored in databanks, standard operating procedures, and manuals. Tacit knowledge, however, is expressed more comprehensively (and in a more complex manner) based on individual and social levels, which may or may not be readily available or transferable to other individuals or groups.

Inkpen and Crossan (1995) build on Spender's framework by theorizing that the critical processes of transforming knowledge from an individual to a collective or shared state vary by level, from interpretation at the individual level to integration and institutionalization at the collective level. This approach is akin to the spiral of knowledge creation that moves upward in an organization, becoming more structurally embedded through the ongoing processes of sensemaking and codification (Nonaka 1994). While conceptually rich, these studies do not, however, empirically examine the effects of tacitness on outcomes reflecting knowledge transfer in broad contexts. Instead, taken together they seem to conclude that tacit knowledge, while relatively more difficult to access and communicate, is often the most desired knowledge sought via interorganizational alliance membership.

Simonin (1999a) suggests that the fundamental starting point to examining knowledge transfer in strategic alliances centers on the notion of causal ambiguity which has been a central tenet of the resource-based view and strategic management literature for some time (Barney 1991, Mozakowski 1997). Ambiguity involves barriers to imitation that make it difficult for competitors to understand which competencies are a potential source of competitive advantage. Simonin (1999a) describes tacitness, specificity, complexity, and experience as antecedents to knowledge ambiguity and tests predictions concerning the effects of ambiguity on knowledge transfer and antecedent hypotheses using complex structural equation modeling techniques. The instrument utilized in his study was a survey of primarily top executives, personally involved in the alliances under scrutiny, in approximately 150 major U.S. firms. To measure the level of knowledge ambiguity involved in a given alliance respondents were asked to assess the ease of transferability of their partners' know-how and the clarity of the association between causes and effects related to the processes held by partners. Tacitness, as a separate construct, was assessed by asking respondents how readily partners' know-how is codifiable and whether it is more explicit than tacit. Other constructs, including knowledge transfer, were measured in a similar fashion. Empirical findings include a positive and significant effect of tacitness on ambiguity and a negative and significant effect of ambiguity on knowledge transfer. Despite certain limitations addressed by the author, Simonin's work constitutes one of the first empirical attempts to highlight (and measure) the role of ambiguity in the knowledge transfer process among alliances involving large- and medium-sized firms operating in high-technology sectors. One concluding implication of this study is that the construct of ambiguity should be formally recognized and integrated into future research on knowledge transfer in the context of alliances.

A possible conclusion to be drawn from the discussion to this point is that the tacitness or ambiguity surrounding knowledge represents a potentially important contingency affecting outcomes associated with knowledge transfer. Characteristics of alliance partners such as complementarities of existing firm assets and of the governance mechanisms employed in an alliance, for example, have been assessed as having potential impacts on knowledge transfer outcomes. A more fully specified model of knowledge transfer in this context then might include the construct ambiguity as a moderator of (or, for instance, a variable moderated by) these other factors.

Firm-Level Learning Capabilities

Whereas knowledge ambiguity seems a potentially important factor in developing a model of knowledge transfer in interorganizational alliances, variance in the characteristics of alliance members themselves—most notably learning capacity—has also been explored in this literature as yielding important outcomes. The notion of absorptive capacity first suggested by Penrose (1959) and later developed by Cohen and Levinthal (1990), for example, has been shown to be both conceptually and empirically critical. Cohen and Levinthal (1990) argue that a necessary condition for a given firm's successful exploitation of new knowledge outside its own boundaries is the development within the firm of the capability to assimilate new information. This capability depends, among other things, on the firm's ability to recognize and link new knowledge to its existing in-house expertise.

In a study of biotechnology firms, Arora and Gambardella (1994) provide empirical evidence that firms differ in their ability to benefit from opportunities available through collaboration with universities and small research intensive firms. Utilizing the number of scientific papers published by the personnel of sampled firms to measure in-house scientific knowledge (representing firms' ability to evaluate external knowledge) and patent data, coupled with R&D expenditures to capture firms' ability to utilize knowledge, the authors find that both factors affect outcomes associated with alliances between large firms and smaller research intensive firms. While the ability to utilize knowledge increases the number of ventures in which a firm participates, firms with a better ability to evaluate new knowledge are more selective in that they focus on fewer alliances that generally yield more beneficial outcomes. Arora and Gambardella's findings suggest that the ability of a firm to evaluate and to utilize important sources of scientific information and capabilities depends on their in-house knowledge assets, lending general support to absorptive capacity arguments.

An extension of the absorptive capacity framework concerns the complementarity of the alliance partners in terms of the specific assets or resources possessed (or needed) by each member organization. Complementarity involves the synergy of knowledge not achievable by any single participant on its own. Shenkar and Li (1999) suggest that the desire to obtain complementary assets can be a major motivating force in the decision to pursue and forge alliances. Furthermore, Cohen and Levinthal's argument that knowledge diversity facilitates the learning process among individuals has been logically extended to encompass diversity in firms' knowledge domains, as long as the domains are complementary (Shenkar and Li 1999, p. 136). Using pre- and postalliance cross-citation rates of corresponding partners' patents and a control sample of nonallied firms, Mowery et al. (1996) empirically examine one version of this extended absorptive capacity argument. In a study of nearly 800 alliances of varying form and purpose, they find evidence suggesting that the extent of a firm's ability to absorb capabilities from its alliance partners depends on its prealliance level of technical overlap (as indicated by cross-citation measurements) with partner firms.

Related to the arguments surrounding notions of complementarity, Lane and Lubatkin (1998) further extend the absorptive capacity argument by reconceptualizing the firm-level construct as a learning dyad construct which they term "relative" absorptive capacity. This supposition is based on their dissatisfaction with prior notions of the capacity construct which seem to suggest that a given firm has an equal propensity to learn from all other organizations. Their argument is similar to Shenkar and Li's assertion that the ability of partner firms to learn from one another depends on the extent to which they share complementary assets. They extend this argument, however, by specifying that one firm's ability to learn from another depends not only on the extent to which the firms are similar regarding their respective knowledge bases, but also is impacted by similarities in other contextual features such as formalization, centralization, and compensation practices. Lane and Lubatkin find support for their arguments utilizing a sample of R&D alliances between pharmaceutical and biotechnology firms, concluding in a post hoc analysis that an absolute measure of absorptive capacity (most commonly, some form of prealliance R&D expenditures) explained little variance in interorganizational learning between partners in their sample relative to a block of similarity variables at the level of the dyad. Their overall conclusions seem to support the position that complementarity of knowledge processing systems and similarity of certain social context features, such as research decision centralization and compensation practices, strongly affect alliance partners' ability to learn from one another.

Overall, the preceding arguments may be summarized by suggesting that experience in related technical fields (in-house knowledge) and complementarity of assets positively affect a firm's capability to assimilate new information from its alliance partners, thus affecting both processes of learning and knowledge transfer. In addition, the finding that nontechnical similarities having to do with structural features and compensation practices among partner firms may positively impact knowledge transfer outcomes raises the possibility that even firms with dissimilar knowledge bases may be able to learn from each other if they have similarities in other contextual features. Understanding the conditions under which dissimilar knowledge can be assimilated may be quite important, since such knowledge is likely to be more unique and valuable to a focal firm than that which is closely related to a firm's existing knowledge base. Moreover, similarities in some of these contextual features, particularly social features such as culture, may promote trust and reduce the possibility of opportunism on the part of alliance members. Again, these arguments suggest that from a focal firm's perspective, the partner selection process is critical and that the ability to evaluate knowledge is important for identifying optimal partners.

Empirical evidence indicates that a firm's capability to learn, as described above, might moderate the dampening effects of knowledge ambiguity on transfer processes. Simonin (1999a) finds that under conditions of greater resource deployment (which he employs as one indicator of learning capacity), learning curves may be accelerated and that the effect of tacitness on ambiguity is decreased. While neither conceptually or empirically explored in great detail, the potential interactions between knowledge tacitness or ambiguity and (relative) absorptive capacity characteristics of alliance partners might serve to enhance and better specify a model of knowledge transfer in this context.

Governance and Alliance Structures

The factors affecting learning and knowledge transfer among and between alliance partners that have been discussed to this point are likely interrelated with the type of alliance structure in question. Differences among governance structures of alliances have been found in a variety of settings to affect the learning propensity of firms. Because the acquisition of new information or capabilities from partner firms is often based on tacit or ambiguous knowledge, simple contracts governing their transfer are typically inadequate and alternate forms of organization are required (Inkpen and Li 1999, Kogut 1988).

Common variants of alliance structure include licensing agreements, technology sharing or joint development agreements, and equity joint ventures, where ownership is shared by the partner firms. Together, these specific governance forms comprise about 77% of variety across all alliance forms as reported in the Cooperative Agreements and Technology Indicators Database (Mowery et al. 1996). Within the alliance literature, it is commonly asserted (and accepted) that the degree of ambiguity facing alliance partners affects the potential for learning and that opportunities for knowledge transfer afforded by different knowledge structures influences the choices made among them. It follows then that the extent of learning and knowledge transfer among partner firms is correlated with the structure of the alliance (Anand and Khanna 2000, p. 299).

Kogut (1988) is often cited as having staked the claim for the assertion that equity-based joint ventures are more effective governance structures for the transfer of tacit knowledge between alliance partners. Because of the difficulty associated with transferring organizationally embedded knowledge, other forms of transfer arrangements such as licensing are effectively ruled out (Kogut 1988, p. 323). Mowery et al. (1996) reiterate Kogut's assertions in their study of cross-citation rates for partners in varying types of bilateral alliances. They find evidence suggesting not only that equity-based joint ventures appear more effective in providing for the transfer of knowledge among alliance partners than contract-based alliances, but also that lower levels of transfer occur in unilateral contracts such as licensing agreements as compared to arrangements involving technology sharing or joint development projects. The authors describe their results as supporting elements from the "received wisdom" (Mowery et al. 1996, p. 89) on interorganizational knowledge transfers in alliances, referring to Kogut's arguments concerning equity versus nonequity based governance types.

Trust and Opportunism

Gulati (1998) proposes that the choice of governance structure is partly driven by the degree of uncertainty among potential alliance partners. In new or young alliances where partner firms have had little shared collaborative experience, a more formal governance mechanism serves to mitigate initial concerns of distrust and potential misconduct on the part of an unknown partner. Dodgson (1992) asserts that because of the length of time needed to build effective communication paths between organizations and the specific nature of what knowledge is to be shared in the context of an alliance, partner selection should be considered a strategic concern that ultimately will affect the process of mutual learning among partner firms. This point of view suggests that in the partner selection process and in subsequent collaborative activities, a great deal of emphasis should be placed on developing a high degree of trust that will, in turn, minimize opportunism.

In his study, Dodgson presents case studies of six firms experienced in R&D alliance efforts and describes strategic management problems associated with the process of collaboration. Anecdotal evidence based on these case studies suggests that firms that expend greater effort at partner selection—often spending years searching for a suitable partner or establishing a long-term negotiation period before expanding relationships—tend to enjoy relatively successful and enduring partnerships. Because prior history and duration are expected to affect the degree of trust between partners and minimize opportunistic behavior, the willingness among firms to share especially tacit knowledge also depends on these factors (Dodgson 1992, Gulati 1998).

Larsson et al. (1998) observe that in some cases one partner (a "good partner") invites exploitation by other ("bad") alliance partners who attempt to maximize their individual payoffs. In this case, opportunistic learning strategies undercut the collective knowledge development in the alliance, thereby negatively affecting the learning process and ultimately the success of the alliance. The potentially competitive nature of alliances was highlighted by Hamel et al. (1989), who argue that a firm which is able to learn the most from its partners during the alliance benefits the most in the long run. In their article, Hamel et al. suggest that many U.S. firms were left at a competitive disadvantage relative to their Japanese partners, who often learned as much as they could and then terminated alliance agreements to exploit newly learned knowledge independently. Gulati et al. (2000, p. 211) suggest that any such relationship between firms might be viewed as a learning race, in which one partner will capture the greater share of economic returns because of superior learning skills.

While the fact remains that in most strategic alliances firms intend to share information and mutually benefit from the partnership, typically they involve mixed motives with private and common interests where the access obtained to one another's knowledge may have benefits for only one partner (Gulati et al. 1994). Khanna et al. (1998) suggest specifically that a high ratio of private to common benefits leads to departures from the collaborative behaviors expected from alliance partners toward more competitive and opportunistic behavior. Dodgson (1992) concludes in his study that for firms to benefit from collaborative efforts, an understanding not only of the technological processes involved but also of the underlying motives of partners is required to affect success in garnering trust, sharing knowledge, and mutual learning.

Given that trust and opportunism (specifically, learning races) logically appear to affect learning and knowledge transfer processes, Khanna et al. (1998) suggest that the effects of these factors are also influenced by partners' activities outside the alliance. They introduce the concept of relative scope which represents each partner's portfolio of activities outside the alliance. For example, partners with fewer alliances or other activities may be more likely to perceive the benefits of continued collaboration as high relative to those firms which are able to learn quickly and exploit their newly learned knowledge across a greater number of other interests (Gulati et al. 2000). In this sense, both the external network of partner firms (representing an opportunity set for exploitation of new knowledge) and their relative levels of absorptive capacity may interact with factors associated with trust to affect learning and knowledge transfer processes among alliance partners.

Industry and Culture

Well acknowledged in the organizations and strategy literatures in general is the notion that context matters. In the case of knowledge transfer in strategic alliances, the nature of the industry is one such environmental feature that warrants consideration. Mowery et al. (1996) make the point that while strategic alliances have been important in international business for a century or more, that the environmental dynamics surrounding alliances has shifted. For example, they note that international joint ventures were originally formed as a method to exploit natural resources. More recently, however, the motivations for alliance formation have changed as the number of partnerships has increased dramatically—most notably among firms in technology-related industries.

While much of the recent research focusing on phenomena related to alliances has been conducted in technology-intensive contexts such as biotechnology (e.g., Baum et al. 2000, Lane and Lubatkin 1998, Powell et al. 1996), it is not clear that findings contained in these studies necessarily generalize to other industries. The fact that some of the research discussed to this point varies across settings or are conducted in more traditional or established industries does yield some evidence of generalizability, but relatively few studies provide such evidence. Given that degrees of knowledge tacitness, complexity, and ambiguity likely vary across different industries (Simonin, 1999a), deeper consideration of context is warranted. Appleyard (1996, chap. 30 this volume), for example, in a study comparing preferred knowledge transfer mechanisms in the steel and semiconductor industries, presents evidence that patterns of knowledge sharing across the two industries diverge significantly. Unlike the steel industry where technological change is relatively slow and knowledge transfer is predominantly facilitated by private know-how trading, Appleyard finds that public channels of communication play a central role in the transfer of knowledge among firms in the semiconductor industry.

A good deal of the alliance literature—both recent and classic—also deals with international joint ventures or other alliance agreements between firms not of the same national origin (e.g., Hamel 1991, Inkpen 1998, Mowery et al. 1996). Aside from the obvious communication issues associated with cross-national partnerships, national culture can affect preferred modes of learning, governance, and trust. In the same study comparing patterns of knowledge flows among different industries, Appleyard (1996) also asked respondents in U.S. and Japanese semiconductor firms to rate the importance of various sources of technical information. Based upon different employment systems, rules governing intellectual capital, and cultural norms, respondents diverged in the importance they placed on learning from colleagues in other firms (with U.S. employees ranking interorganizational learning higher). Levinson and Minoru (1995) further express the need to attend to how culture interacts with other factors and can either promote or hinder interorganizational learning efforts.

While the preceding discussion has focused exclusively on that portion of the alliance literature that deals with learning and knowledge transfer between and among partner firms, the following section will address some of the potential links that might be forged between the broader areas concerning organizational learning and social network theory. This discussion will highlight some areas where these broader literatures might not only inform alliance research but also where research focusing on alliances may serve to advance learning and network perspectives. Concluding comments will include discussion of some potential areas for future research.

Links to Organizational Learning and Social Network Theory

That the research and theories espoused in the strategic alliance literature regarding knowledge transfer is inextricably linked to the broader fields of organizational learning and social networks is obvious. Were it not for the fact that studies and theories devoted specifically to alliances are so vast, one might conclude that the context of alliances simply serves as an ideal setting for testing theories of learning and the dynamics of social networks. Clearly, however, this is not the case. The purpose of the following discussion then is to make explicit some of the potential links and overlaps between that work focusing narrowly on strategic alliances and a few overarching perspectives found in the strategy and organizations literatures.

Organizational Learning

The organizational learning literature, like that concerning strategic alliances, has grown rapidly during the past several years. The early work of Cyert and March (1963) views organizations as adaptive learning systems where standard operating procedures drive action and decision-making in firms. This original perspective suggests that organizational actions are adjusted through problematic search behavior where firms engage in a learning process by scanning their local environments in search of new routines. Typically, the learning processes described involve incremental adjustments made independently by the firm; that is, these processes do not necessarily involve the transfer of knowledge from one firm to another.

Following the lead of Cyert and March, however, several learning theorists (e.g., Davis 1991, Haunschild and Miner 1997, Mezias and Lant 1994) have gone on to explore how organizations learn from one another and have developed perspectives not only on vicarious learning and interorganizational imitation but also population level learning. It may be at this level that general perspectives found in the learning literature may not only inform but also be informed by concepts and research developed within the context of strategic alliances. For example, questions such as how interorganizational learning and knowledge transfer may lead to new routines altogether or how organizations actually select information to be transmitted across firms within a population might be empirically examined in the context of alliances, informing both literatures consecutively.

Recent conceptual work by Argote (1999) provides a generative framework for classifying conditions under which knowledge transfers across organizational units. While this work does not focus on formal partnerships between firms, Argote identifies four broad characteristics that condition organizational knowledge transfer, in general. These features include how knowledge transfer is affected by characteristics of the *relationship* among organizations and of the individual *organizations* concerned, features of the *knowledge* being transferred and of the *process* itself. What is notable regarding this framework is its potential usefulness for integrating the growing literature concerning learning and knowledge transfer in the context of strategic alliances. Each of the factors addressed in the preceding review of alliance-specific research arguably fits into one of the broad conditions specified by Argote. One conclusion that might be drawn from this observation, in general, is that the understanding of how knowledge is transferred across firms formally organized into an alliance may be further developed by closer examination of perspectives found within the broader organizational learning literature.

Similarly, however, the alliance literature may bring much to bear on learning perspectives. For example, in a study of franchise service organizations, Argote (1999) finds that knowledge transfer between affiliated organizations is greater than transfer between independent organizations. She concludes that future research is needed to determine why this phenomena occurs and questions whether the observed pattern of differential transfer may relate to differences in motivation or opportunities to communicate. A commonly accepted point of view within the alliance literature is that firms are compelled to enter formal alliance agreements precisely in order to learn from partner firms. While alliances and franchise-related firms are not the same, the combined views would suggest that motivation and opportunity contribute significantly to differential degrees of knowledge transfer among formally connected firms as compared to independent firms.

Argote's (1999) finding that organizations embedded in a superordinate relationship are able to increase their capacities for learning and knowledge transfer suggests that being embedded in a network improves organizational performance. These capabilities are enhanced by the respective firms' ability to draw and learn from a larger combined experience base (McEvily and Zaheer 1998). Conceptualizing the relationship between firms involved in formal arrangements as a network represents a growing trend in the broad fields of strategy and organization science, but has also recently emerged as a potential central tenet of alliance-specific studies.

Social Network Theory

Granovetter (1985) suggests that social ties or embeddedness can promote trust between actors and impact economic performance. He argues that economic activity cannot simply be understood as a competitive contest between atomistic actors, but that organizational behavior and actions are embedded in concrete, on-going systems of social interaction. This perspective stresses how the obligations inherent in personal relationships and the structure of a firm's network of social ties generate trust and discourage malfeasance. Uzzi (1996) further develops these ideas by demonstrating that a mixture of embedded and arm's length ties increased survival rates among firms in the New York apparel industry. Embedded ties promoted trust while arm's length ties proved greater access to market information. Because alliances represent a particular type of social tie, examining the overall network of ties within which a firm is embedded is likely to shed light on the effectiveness of knowledge transfer within alliances.

Gulati (1998) provides one of the first comprehensive assessments of how a social network perspective might serve to inform and extend prior research on alliances. Among his assertions is the observation that most empirical studies on the governance of alliances take a static approach and treat each alliance as independent, thereby ignoring the potential social structure resulting from prior interactions between alliance partners. In addition, Gulati highlights the important role that a social network of prior ties can play in affecting trust among partners. Not only can networks provide for strong cognitive and emotional bases for trust, but they also may serve as important mechanisms for deterrence-based trust where the anticipated utility from a tie with a given partner motivates good behavior (Powell 1990).

In exploring these concepts, Gulati (1998, p. 296) further distinguishes between two types of network embeddedness or mechanisms relevant for assessing informational advantages bestowed by networks. *Relational* embeddedness concerns the cohesion or strength of ties between actors as affecting the sharing of fine-grained information. This form of embeddedness commonly emphasizes shared understanding, the diminishment of uncertainty, and the promotion of trust among network partners in such a way that information flows are positively enhanced. *Structural* embeddedness, however, moves beyond the level of direct ties between firms to consider the position an actor occupies in the structure of its overall network. In this sense, not only are particular connections between firms important but also the pattern of strategic alliances within an industry. How firms are embedded in this overall network can affect patterns of knowledge transfer and access to information (Burt 1992, Granovetter 1985, Rowley et al. 2000).

Rowley et al. (2000) argue that the roles relational and structural embeddedness play in affecting important outcomes can only be understood by examining the interaction between these two factors. They highlight the fact that social network research has at times produced contradictory and confusing implications concerning how firms should most optimally be situated in their corresponding networks (Rowley et al. 2000, p. 369). For example, strong or cohesive ties have been shown to yield higher levels of information sharing and exchange of tacit knowledge (e.g., Uzzi 1996), as well as providing for systems of trust-based governance (e.g., Powell 1990). Weak ties, however, have been associated with gaining access to unique and novel information (e.g., Granovetter 1973), as they provide for connections to divergent regions of the overall network rather than to a densely connected set of actors.

How relational features such as the maintenance of strong or weak ties provide informational advantages to firms may be dependent on surrounding conditions, including characteristics of the relational structure and the industry (Gulati et al. 2000, Rowley et al. 2000). In a study of strategic alliance networks in the steel and semiconductor industries, Rowley et al. find that firms with strong ties to partners, who are themselves densely connected to one another, are poorly situated in the overall network. For example, strong ties between firms in the semiconductor industry negatively affected performance when the overall alliance network was comprised of otherwise tightly linked firms. In this case, strong relational ties between partner firms and dense interconnections at the network level may serve as alternate control mechanisms that when combined provide little additional benefit (Rowley et al. 2000, p. 383). In addition, the authors find that relational embeddedness effects are not only contingent on structural embeddedness but also on whether the surrounding environments demand higher degrees of exploitation of existing resources or exploration with new and uncertain routines. In relatively less-complex environments, such as the steel industry where the bulk of advantage-seeking activity is focused on exploitation of existing technologies and skills, strong ties were found to positively impact firm performance. Thus, the nature of the relationships a firm maintains among its alliance partners should be conditioned on both the structure of the overall alliance network and features affecting environmental uncertainty.

Conclusion and Future Directions

While not exhaustive, this chapter represents an attempt to integrate and synthesize research examining factors that affect learning and knowledge transfer in the context of strategic alliances and to explicitly highlight a few links to broader areas of inquiry concerning organizational learning and social networks. A deeper understanding of how important factors at varying levels of analysis affect not only the processes associated with learning outcomes but also how they interact with one another might allow future researchers in this area to more fully specify models of knowledge transfer in alliances. In addition, by explicating links to related fields of study, future work may be more grounded in and also inform broader theories and literatures. The remaining discussion in this chapter presents specific questions and topics for consideration in future empirical analyses in this area.

Future Directions

While the alliance literature in general is vast and while that portion of the literature specifically addressing learning and knowledge transfer continues to grow, several potentially interesting areas remain relatively unexplored. For example, as Zajac (1998, p. 321) points out in his commentary on the role of network analysis in studying alliances, insufficient theory and few empirical studies exist examining factors that affect the often dramatic and publicized failures of major strategic alliances. Podolny and Page (1998, p. 71) also comment that while fewer than one-third of strategic alliances might be considered successful, very few scientific studies serve to deepen our understanding of why such a large proportion of alliances do not perform the functions for which they were designed. Considering that predominant underlying motivations for alliance formation include firms' desires to develop the ability to access and utilize knowledge from alliance partners, it is reasonable to expect that the breakdown of strategic alliance agreements may be directly related to problems concerning knowledge transfer. Therefore, one perhaps obvious area for future inquiry includes detailed analyses of how the processes governing learning and knowledge transfer in alliances ultimately affects their success.

An understanding of the mechanisms of knowledge transfer among organizations in general is also not well understood. While evidence exists suggesting that firms embedded in networks often demonstrate a greater propensity to transfer information among and between its network partners (e.g., Powell et al. 1996, Uzzi 1996), the underlying mechanisms have not yet been widely explored. However, in a study of the transfer of manufacturing technology from one unit to another within the same firm, Galbraith (1990) found that productivity was positively enhanced when the engineering team from the donor unit was temporarily relocated to the recipient unit. These findings suggest that personnel movement can be a powerful mechanism for the transfer of both tacit and explicit knowledge (Argote 1999), supporting Allen's (1977) argument that individuals are the most effective carriers of information and are able to restructure knowledge in order to apply it to new contexts. Simonin (1999a) also suggests that where collaborative know-how is essential (as in alliances) but is lacking, firms may benefit by hiring personnel familiar with the partner's organization and culture.

The effects and importance of personnel transfer across firm is beginning to garner some attention across organizations and strategy research in recent years. Boeker's (1997) study of the semiconductor industry, for example, suggests that firms require new knowledge to expand operations via entrance into new product markets. The importance of interorganizational executive migration is highlighted as a primary factor affecting such an expansion. Because the transfer of personnel among and between alliance partners has not yet been explored in much detail, this specific and perhaps critical learning and knowledge transfer mechanism might be a fruitful avenue for future research.

An evolutionary approach to learning in alliances—longitudinal studies, for example, which more accurately explain partners' adaptation over the life of not only isolated alliances (Simonin 1999a) but also firms' propensity to engage in such arrangements—might suggest that firms can learn to develop specific competencies and skills associated with handling knowledge transfer in the context of alliances. Zajac (1998) observes that in some firms knowledge concerning alliances is fragmented across several business units, while in other firms this information is more centralized. He also questions whether some firms simply have developed a competency for alliances. This possibility is potentially intriguing and not inconsistent with learning and evolutionary perspectives of the firm. Nelson and Winter (1982), for example, contend that over time organizations develop not only standard operating routines but also modification routines that govern the process through which organizations search for solutions to new problems (Levitt and March 1988). Amburgey et al. (1993, p. 54), in a study of the deleterious effects of organizational change in the Finnish newspaper industry, also apply learning concepts to their argument by pointing out that to routinize the process of change (in their study) an organization must gain experience modifying their routines—in other words, learn to change by changing. This concept might be fruitfully applied in empirical analyses focusing specifically on firms' collective alliance experiences in order to assess the possibility that such a competence exists and may be learned.

A final comment relates to the difficulty of measuring underlying concepts associated with learning, knowledge, and knowledge transfer. Mowery et al. (1996, p. 90) lament the fact that despite a substantial literature on these topics, the empirical analysis of strategic alliances and interorganizational knowledge transfer relies to a great extent on case studies and poor indicators of the constructs in question. Because concepts such as absorptive capacity, knowledge ambiguity, and even whether an alliance is deemed to be "successful" are inherently difficult to measure, one potential tack would be to take a more fine-grained approach to the study of knowledge transfer by focusing on specific competencies. For example, Simonin (1999b) in a second study exploring the antecedents and effects of knowledge ambiguity focused solely on the transfer of marketing know-how within international strategic alliances. Future questions concerning access and utilization of external information and skills might benefit by first identifying specifically what competencies to examine.

Several additional areas for future consideration in this context exist. Although the study of alliances has grown substantially as a literature, the possibilities for new and insightful contributions, especially those examining learning and knowledge processes, abound. Questions regarding the development of new knowledge creation versus transfer between partners, the effects of alliance founding conditions on learning processes, and whether factors affecting these processes are applicable to other contexts (e.g., mergers and acquisitions) where knowledge transfer might play a major role are only a few additional frontiers in this area requiring additional exploration. This chapter perhaps best represents an attempt to engage discussion on the state of research on learning and knowledge transfer not only in the context of alliances but also more broadly, as well as a potential springboard for researchers interested in pursuing this promising line of inquiry.

Acknowledgment   This research was supported in part by the National Science Foundation under the Knowledge and Distributed Intelligence program (grant number 9980182), and benefited from discussions with members of the Distributed Knowledge research project <http:dkrc.org>. The chapter reflects the findings and conclusions of the authors, not the National Science Foundation.

References

Allen, T.J. (1977) *Managing the flow of technology: technology transfer and the dissemination of technological information within the R&D organization.* Cambridge, MA: MIT Press.

Amburgey, T.L., Kelly, D., and Barnett, W.P. (1993) "Resetting the clock: The dynamics of organizational change and failure." *Administrative Science Quarterly* 38:51–73.

Anand, B.N. and Khanna, T. (2000) "Do firms learn to create value? The case of the alliances." *Strategic Management Journal* 21(3):295–315.

Appleyard, M.M. (1996) "How does knowledge flow? Interfirm patterns in the semiconductor industry." *Strategic Management Journal* (Winter Special Issue) 17:137–154.

Argote, L. (1999) *Organizational Learning: Creating, Retaining, and Transferring Knowledge.* Boston: Kluwer Academic.

Arora, A. and Gambardella, A. (1994) "Evaluating technological information and utilizing it. Scientific knowledge, technological capability, and external linkages in biotechnology." *Journal of Economic Behavior and Organization* 24:91–114.

Barney, J.B. (1991) "Firm resources and sustained competitive advantage." *Journal of Management* 17:99–120.

Baum, J.A.C. and Oliver, C. (1991) "Institutional linkages and organizational mortality." *Administrative Science Quarterly* 36:187–218.

Baum, J.A.C., Calabrese, T., and Silverman, B.S. (2000) "Don't go it alone: Alliance network composition and stratup's performance in Canadian biotechnology." *Strategic Management Journal* 21(3):267–294.

Boeker, W. (1997) "Executive migration and strategic change: The effect of top manager movement on product-market entry." *Administrative Science Quarterly* 42:213–236.

Burt, R.S. (1992) *Structural Holes: The Social Structure of Competition.* Cambridge, MA: Harvard University Press.

Cohen, W.M. and Levinthal, D. (1990) "Absorptive capacity: A new perspective on learning and innovation." *Administrative Science Quarterly* 35(1):128–152.

Cyert, R.M. and March, J.G. (1963) *A Behavioral Theory of the Firm.* Englewood Cliffs, NJ: Prentice-Hall.

Davis, G.F. (1991) "Agents without principles: The spread of the poison pill through the intercorporate network." *Administrative Science Quarterly* 36:605–633.

Dodgson, M. (1992) "The strategic management of R&D collaboration." *Technology Analysis & Strategic Management* 4(3):227–244.

Eisenhardt, K.M. and Schoonhoven, C.B. (1996) "Resource-based view of strategic alliance formation: Strategic and social effects in entrepreneurial firms." *Organization Science* 7(2):136–150.

Galbraith, C.S. (1990) "Transferring core manufacturing technologies in high technology firms." *California Management Review* 32(4):56–70.

Grandori, A. and Soda, G. (1995) "Interfirm networks: antecedents, mechanisms and forms." *Organization Studies* 16(2):183–214.

Granovetter, M.S. (1973) "The strength of weak ties." *American Journal of Sociology* 78:1360–1380.

Granovetter, M.S. (1985) "Economic action and social structure: The problem of embeddedness." *American Journal of Sociology* 91:481–510.

Gulati, R. (1998) "Alliances and networks." *Strategic Management Journal* 19:293–317.

Gulati, R. (1999) "Network location and learning: The influence of network resources and the firm capabilities of alliance formation." *Strategic Management Journal* 20:397–420.

Gulati, R., Khanna, T., and Nohria, N. (1994) "Unilateral commitments and the importance of process in alliances." *Sloan Management Review* 35(3):61–70.

Gulati, R., Nohria, N., and Zaheer, A. (2000) "Strategic networks." *Strategic Management Journal* 21(3):203–215.

Hagedoorn, J. (1993) "Understanding the rationale of strategic technology partnering: Interorganizational modes of cooperation and sectoral differences." *Strategic Management Journal* 14(5): 371–385.

Hamel, G. (1991) "Competition for competence and inter-partner learning within international strategic alliances." *Strategic Management Journal* (Summer Special Issue) 12:83–103.

Hamel, G., Doz, Y.L., and Prahalad, C.K. (1989) "Collaborate with your competitors and win." *Harvard Business Review* 67(1):133–139.

Haunschild, P.R. and Miner, A.S. (1997) "Modes of imitation: The effects of outcome salience and uncertainty." *Administrative Science Quarterly* 42:472–500.

Inkpen, A.C. (1996) "Creating knowledge through collaboration." *California Management Review* 39(1):123–140.

Inkpen, A.C. (1998) "Learning knowledge acquisition and strategic alliances." *European Management Journal* 16(2):223–229.

Inkpen, A.C. and Crossan, M.M. (1995) "Believing is seeing: Joint ventures and organizational learning." *Journal of Management Studies* 32(5):595–617.

Inkpen, A.C. and Dinur, A. (1998) "Knowledge management processes and joint ventures." *Organization Science* 9(4):454–468.

Inkpen, A.C. and Li, K. (1999) "Joint venture formation: Planning and knowledge gathering for success." *Organizational Dynamics* 27(4):33–47.

Khanna, T., Gulati, R. and Nohria, N. (1998) "The dynamics of learning alliances: Competition, cooperation, and relative scope." *Strategic Management Journal* 19:193–210.

Kogut, B. (2000) "The network as knowledge: Generative rules and the emergence of structure." *Strategic Management Journal* 21(3):405–425.

Kogut, B. (1988) "Joint ventures: Theoretical and empirical perspectives." *Strategic Management Journal* 9(4):319–332.

Lane, P.J. and Lubatkin, M. (1998) "Relative absorptive capacity and interorganizational learning." *Strategic Management Journal* 21(3):405–425.

Larsson, R., Bengtsson, L., Henriksson, K., and Sparks, J. (1998) "The interorganizational learning dilemma: Collective knowledge development in strategic alliances." *Organization Science* 9(3):285–305.

Lei, D., Slocum, J.W. Jr., and Pitts, R.A. (1997) "Building cooperative advantages: Managing strategic alliances to promote organizational learning." *Journal of World Business* 33(3):203–233.

Levinson, N.S. and Minoru, A. (1995) "Cross-national alliances and interorganizational learning." *Organizational Dynamics* 24(2):50–64.

Levitt, B. and March, J.G. (1988) "Organizational learning." *Annual Review of Sociology* 14:319–340.

McEvily, B. and Zaheer, A. (1998) "Bridging Ties: A Source of Firm Heterogeneity in Competitive Capabilities." Working paper, Graduate School of Industrial Administration, Carnegie Mellon University.

Mezias, S.J. and Lant, T.K. (1994) "Mimetic learning and the evolution of organizational populations," in J. Baum and J. Singh (eds.), *Evolutionary Dynamics of Organizations*, pp. 179–198. New York: Oxford University Press.

Mowery, D.C., Oxley, J.E., and Silverman, B.S. (1996) "Strategic alliances and interfirm knowledge transfer." *Strategic Management Journal* (Winter Special Issue) 17:77–91.

Mozakowski, N. (1997) "Strategy making under causal ambiguity: Conceptual issues and empirical evidence." *Organization Science* 8(4):414–442.

Nelson, R.R. and Winter, S.G. (1982) *An Evolutionary Theory of Economic Change.* Cambridge, MA: Belknap.

Nonaka, I. (1994) "A dynamic theory of organizational knowledge creation." *Organization Science* 5(1):14–37.

Parkhe, A. (1991) "Interfirm diversity, organizational learning, and longevity in global strategic alliances." *Journal of International Business Studies* 22:579–601.

Penrose, E. (1959) *The Theory of the Growth of the Firm.* New York: Wiley.

Pfeffer, J. and Nowak, P. (1976) "Joint ventures and interorganizational dependence." *Administrative Science Quarterly* 21:398–419.

Podolny, J.M. and Page, K.L. (1998) "Network forms of organization." *Annual Review of Sociology* 24:57–76.

Polanyi, M. (1966) *The Tacit Dimension.* London: Routledge and Kegan Paul.

Powell, W. (1990) "Neither market nor hierarchy: network forms of organization," in B.M. Staw and L.L. Cummings (eds.), *Research in Organizational Behavior* 12:295–336. Greenwich, CT: JAI Press.

Powell, W., Koput, K.W., and Smith-Doerr, L. (1996) "Interorganizational collaboration and the locus of innovation: Networks of learning in biotechnology." *Administrative Science Quarterly* 41(1):116.

Rowley, T., Behrens, D., and Krackhardt, D. (2000) "Redundant governance structures: An analysis of structural and relational embeddedness in the steel and semiconductor industries." *Strategic Management Journal* 21(3):369–386.

Shenkar, O. and Li, J. (1999) "Knowledge search in international cooperative ventures." *Organization Science* 10(2):134–143.

Simonin, B.L. (1999a) "Ambiguity and the process of knowledge transfer in strategic alliances." *Strategic Management Journal* 20:595–623.

Simonin, B.L. (1999b) "Transfer of marketing know-how in international strategic alliances: An empirical investigation of the role of antecedents of knowledge ambiguity." *Journal of International Business Studies* 30(3):463–490.

Spender, J.C. (1996) "Organizational knowledge, learning, and memory: Three concepts in search of a theory." *Journal of Organizational Change* 9:63–78.

Stuart, T.E. (2000) "Interorganizational alliances and the performance of firms: A study of growth and innovation rates in a high-technology industry." *Strategic Management Journal* 21(8):791–812.

Uzzi, B. (1996) "The sources and consequences of embeddedness for the economic performance of organizations: The network effect." *American Sociological Review* 61:674–698.

Varadarajan, P.R. and Cunningham, M.H. (1995) "Strategic alliances: A synthesis of conceptual foundations." *Journal of Academy of Marketing Science* 23(4):282.

Zajac, E. (1998) "Commentary on 'Alliances and Networks' by R. Gulati." *Strategic Management Journal* 19:319–321.

30

How Does Knowledge Flow?

Interfirm Patterns in the Semiconductor Industry

Melissa M. Appleyard

This chapter examines interfirm information flows in a knowledge-intensive industry. The study looks beyond assumptions that knowledge simply "spills" across company boundaries to identify and examine the mechanisms by which technical knowledge is disseminated. Survey data on interfirm knowledge transfers in the semiconductor industry are used to explore why patterns of knowledge exchange are different both across industries and across countries. The findings offer a rare account of the primary knowledge sharing vehicles in the semiconductor industry, both in the United States and Japan, and provide a grounding for optimal strategies of knowledge management.

The chapter is organized as follows:

- The next section presents a framework for analyzing knowledge sharing decisions by firms. Distinguishing between access to knowledge and its use, the determinants of the costs and benefits from knowledge sharing are identified.
- The third section outlines the primary hypothesis regarding patterns of knowledge sharing in semiconductors compared to steel,

based upon the different characteristics of the two industries.
- The fourth section outlines the primary hypothesis concerning international differences in knowledge sharing, based upon different employment systems and intellectual property regimes found in the United States and Japan.
- The fifth section presents evidence on knowledge sharing drawn from surveys of employees in the semiconductor industry. In contrast to findings from empirical studies of the steel industry, *public* channels of communication play a *central* role in the transfer of knowledge in the semiconductor industry. The survey also finds international differences. Semiconductor employees in the United States are approached more frequently for technical information and are more likely to fulfill at least one request per year. However, Japanese workers are more likely to fulfill the majority of requests that they receive. The fieldwork provides a rare account of the primary knowledge sharing mechanisms in the semiconductor industry.
- The conclusions section draws implications

from the study for the strategic management of knowledge sharing and for public policy.

Why Would Rivals Share?

This section provides a framework for thinking about the costs and benefits derived from knowledge sharing. Knowledge sharing is defined as the transfer of useful know-how or information across company lines. Knowledge sharing decisions are made by firms which process the knowledge on the basis of anticipated costs and benefits. Figure 30.1 depicts the knowledge sharing decision faced by a firm.[1] If the firm decides to share a piece of technical knowledge, it can do so publicly or privately, and either place legal restrictions on its use or permit unrestricted use. If the firm determines that the gains to exclusive use of the technical information outweigh the gains to sharing, then the firm can resort to secrecy.[2]

The primary mechanisms of interfirm knowledge exchange are arranged in figure 30.2 in terms of *access to* and *use of* the shared knowledge. Access to knowledge can occur either through *public* channels:[3] patents, reverse engineering, newsletters, popular press, trade journals, and conference presentations; or through *private* channels: e-mail, the telephone, face-to-face meetings, visits to other companies' fabrication plants (fabs), consortia, or benchmarking studies.[4] Even if access to knowledge is public, its use may be *restricted* by legal constructs such as patents or nondisclosure agreements.

Figure 30.2 assumes that the use and dissemination of knowledge obtained by visiting other companies' fabs or participating in a consortium or benchmarking study face greater legal restrictions than do "informal" interactions via e-

Figure 30.1 Knowledge sharing decision.

	Use of the knowledge	
	Restricted	Unrestricted
Public	• Reviewing patents • Reverse engineering patented technology	• Newsletter • Popular press • Trade journals • Conferences
Private	• Visit other companies' fabs • Consortium • Benchmarking studies	• E-mail • Telephone • Face-to-face meetings

Access to the knowledge (left axis label)

Figure 30.2 Knowledge sharing mechanisms.

mail, the telephone or face-to-face conversations. Private-unrestricted knowledge sharing is similar to private-restricted knowledge sharing in that costs are incurred to search for appropriate partners and forge relationships. The two modes, though, differ in important ways. First, there is limited legal recourse if the private-unrestricted sharing relationship faces a problem such as opportunism.[5] Second, private-unrestricted transfers incur minimal transactions costs when compared to the costs of drafting a formal agreement; this transaction cost reduction may more than offset the costs of intermittent opportunism.

From the viewpoint of the firm, the decision whether or not to share knowledge with another company depends on whether the expected benefits from relinquishing the monopoly over the knowledge outweigh the expected costs.[6] Unique, useful knowledge confers monopoly rights upon the possessor allowing the firm to charge premium prices or experience lower costs than its rivals. When the firm divulges its knowledge to a competitor, it gives up the monopoly over the knowledge and must share the rents, suffering "competitive backlash" (Carter 1989, p. 156). As long as the firm expects its sharing partner to reciprocate with useful knowledge or some other form of compensation, such as a licensing fee, it can justify interfirm disclosure.

For firm i at time t, the cost and benefit comparison can be represented by the following:

$$E_{it}[B(L, R, A)] \geq E_{it}[C(D, T)]$$

The firm's expected benefit from sharing the piece of knowledge, $E_{it}B$, is an increasing function of the following: revenue from licensing, L, legal rights to use the recipient company's tech-

TABLE 30.1 Options for Knowledge Sharing

	Case	Nature of Use	Knowledge Owner's Reward
I.	Trade secret	Private	Monopoly rents
II.	Patent, no license	Private	Monopoly rents
III.	Patent and license	Private, bilateral	Duopoly rents + license fee (L)
IV.	Patent and cross-license	Private, bilateral	Duopoly rents + rights (R)
V.	Know-how trading (von Hippel 1988, Schrader 1991)	Private, bilateral	Oligopoly rents + knowledge (A)
VI.	Collective invention (Allen 1983)	Private, network	Oligopoly rents + knowledge (A)
VII.	Message-based tech transfer (Allen et al. 1983)	Private, network	Oligopoly rents + knowledge (A)
VIII.	Presenting at conferences or publishing	Public	Variable

nology, R, and/or knowledge from the recipient company, A.[7] Firm i's expected cost of knowledge sharing at time t, $E_{it}C$, increases with the decline in profitability, D, and the transaction costs, T, associated with the knowledge transfer.

Drawing on previous empirical studies, table 30.1 presents cases of knowledge sharing and associated benefits.

In addition to the benefits, firms also must consider the costs. For example, when the knowledge owner patents and licenses knowledge to a market rival, Case III, L increases while the sharer's cost advantage may fall, since the rival can legally use the knowledge.[8] Depending on pricing conditions, erosion of the sharer's cost advantage may precipitate a decline in its profitability, an increase in D, which will partially offset the benefits of L.[9] A similar outcome obtains when the knowledge owner patents and cross-licenses the knowledge, Case IV. Instead of licensing revenue the sharer receives rights of use, R, or, as many people in the semiconductor industry claim, a promise not to be sued. Finally, in the know-how trading case, Case V, the knowledge owner benefits from acquiring new knowledge, A, but must give up the monopoly rents associated with the knowledge that it shares. As for the transaction costs associated with the three cases, the cost of undertaking know-how trading is, in general, much lower than the other two, especially in the presence of legal fees charged to draft and maintain licensing agreements.

Cross-Industry Comparison of Knowledge Sharing: Semiconductors versus Steel

Previous studies of knowledge sharing behavior have focused largely on manufacturing intensive industries with a slow pace of technological change, in particular, the steel industry. However, the net benefits from knowledge sharing in an R&D intensive industry exhibit much higher variances. In the semiconductor industry, uncertainty surrounds the pay-off to a particular piece of knowledge due to difficulties in predicting: its useful life;[10] the breadth of its applicability across the industry; the ease with which it can be incorporated into another company's process flow; and whether it can be reverse engineered. Imperfect information may lead a knowledge owner to share its knowledge externally when, in fact, the *ex post* net benefit is negative. For example, if firm i licenses a processing technique to a rival, it earns L. But if the rival incorporates the technique much more quickly into its production process than firm i had anticipated, firm i may face a steeper decline in its profits, D, than initially anticipated.

The pace and nature of technological change in different industries can help explain why distinctive patterns of knowledge sharing coexist.

Hypothesis 1: If an industry experiences a rapid pace of technological change, reflected by the average time between new product or process introductions, private knowledge sharing in that industry will be less likely than in a slower paced industry.[11]

In support of the above hypothesis, von Hippel (1988) finds ample evidence that private-unrestricted know-how trading occurs in the U.S. steel minimill industry, an industry with a slow pace of technological change. He finds such activity almost nonexistent within industries that exhibit more rapid technological change such as powdered metals and biotechnology (von Hippel 1988, p. 83), although von Hippel also ob-

TABLE 30.2 Patenting Behavior in the U.S. Steel and Semiconductor Industries: Selected Companies

Company	Type	1992 Sales ($ mill)	1992 Employment (000)	Total Patents (1969–92)	Patents 1990	Patents 1991	Patents 1992	Average (1990–92)
USX	Integrated steel	5465	21.6	1367	1	3	4	3
Bethlehem Steel	Integrated steel	4899	29.6	647	13	11	13	12
Intel	Semiconductor	3921	23.9	473	45	56	73	58
Nucor	Steel minimill	1482	5.5	5	na	na	na	na
LSI Logic	Semiconductor	656	4.4	52	5	10	20	12
Chaparral	Steel minimill	404	1.0	<5	na	na	na	na
Raritan River Steel	Steel minimill	270	0.6	<5	na	na	na	na
Cirrus Logic	Semiconductor	142	0.5	8	na	na	na	na

Note: "na" represents "less than five."
Sources: Darnay (1993), U.S. Patent and Trademark Office (1993).

serves private trading in the research-intensive U.S. aerospace industry. This phenomenon may appear: (1) because much of the research is "basic," and thus falls in the bottom category of table 30.1; or (2) because of the nature of demand, which is primarily fueled by U.S. government procurement. As von Hippel observes (1988, p. 87), the aerospace companies curtail communications when government contracts come up for bid. After contracts are granted, however, informal knowledge sharing resumes. That is, when significant profits are at stake, private knowledge exchanges taper off but recommence after the spike in demand dissipates.

Inventive activity in a development-intensive industry, such as the semiconductor industry, will occur in the top range of table 30.1. New innovations often qualify for patent protection and the associated monopoly rents. In slower-paced industries, such as the steel industry, technological change is characterized by the accumulation of numerous incremental improvements over a long time horizon, thus limiting profitable patenting opportunities. Patents grant firms an enforceable claim to rents that accrue to innovations.[12] Patents also give the patent owners defined "bargaining chips"[13] for technology swapping, e.g., cross-licensing, represented by R in the expected benefits function above. Also, if an industry exhibits rapid technological change, firms in that industry may opt to share little with their competitors to maximize the size of the "technical cushion" between them. Technical cushions provide protection from a marked decline in profits, captured by a sharp rise in D in the expected costs function.

Hypothesis 1 is tested by comparing knowledge sharing in the semiconductor industry with that in steel. There is an abundance of evidence of the faster pace of technological change in semiconductors. Table 30.2 shows relative patenting activity by pairs of similarly sized steel and semiconductor companies. R&D expenditure to sales was almost 8% in semiconductors in 1994, compared with 0.5% in steel (*Business Week*, July 3, 1995). This emphasis translates into a higher incidence of patenting and a higher degree of secrecy in the semiconductor industry relative to the steel industry. A consequence of rapid product and process innovation is rapidly declining product prices, especially in memory chips (see figure 30.3). When the 16 megabit DRAM chips were introduced in late 1991, they ran nearly $300 per chip. By mid-1994, their price had plummeted to just under $50. Their current price is under $20 (*The Economist*, May 4, 1996, p. 66). Since the penalty for late entry into a product market is extremely high, semi-

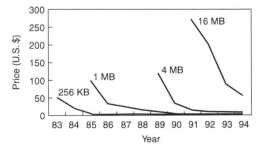

Figure 30.3 Price trends for DRAM products. *Source:* Appleyard, Hatch, and Mowery (1996)

conductor developers often are reluctant to provide specific technical information to their peers at competing firms.

Other industry characteristics, such as the nature of product markets, also distinguish the two industries. In a few major semiconductor product markets, such as microprocessors, where standards are based on firm-specific architectures, one would predict a higher level of secrecy. This is consistent with Rogers' findings in his study of microprocessor producers in Silicon Valley (Rogers 1982).

These characteristics of the semiconductor industry—active patenting, large R&D expenditures, rapid price declines—reflect the frequent introduction of new production processes and products. Given this high frequency, the hypothesis proposed above would suggest that private knowledge sharing would be *less* likely in the semiconductor industry than in the steel industry.

Knowledge-Sharing in Different Institutional Contexts: Japan versus the United States

The net expected benefits to a firm from knowledge sharing depend not only on industry characteristics but also on the institutional environment. The previous section discussed the impact of industry factors on interfirm knowledge sharing. This section extends the analysis by examining the following question: Do knowledge sharing patterns in a given industry differ across countries? Knowledge sharing among semiconductor firms in the United States and Japan is examined.

Two institutions, the intellectual property (IP) right regime and the employment system, differ markedly in the two countries, influencing the net benefit calculation. The institutional distinctions lead to the following hypothesis.

Hypothesis 2: Employees in the U.S. semiconductor industry are more likely to rely on private channels of communication than their Japanese counterparts.

Among the many differences in the IP regimes in the United States and Japan, perhaps foremost are the differences in their patenting systems. First, Japan follows a first-to-file system, whereas the United States follows a first-to-invent doctrine. Second, the patent breadth in Japan is, in general, narrower, where the "patenting of individual applications" is possible (Katz and Ordover 1990, p. 180 n.72). In contrast, the U.S. patent authorities generally require a broader range of application. Finally, in Japan, the system of *Kokai*, or "laying open," requires that all patent applications be published in the patent gazette by 18 months from the date of filing (Helfand 1991, p. 186). In the United States, only patents that are granted are made accessible to the public.[14]

When considering the variables influencing the net benefits from knowledge sharing, Japan's first-to-file patent system would likely discourage private, interfirm knowledge sharing to a greater degree than the U.S. system.[15] For example, semiconductor engineers in Japan may be reluctant to discuss ideas in early stages with competitors for fear that the competitors might try to patent the idea. If the originator of the idea is beaten to the patent office, the originator loses the patent and the expected benefits to licensing or cross-licensing, L and R, respectively. Under the first-to-invent system in the United States, however, if the originator adequately documents his or her ideas prior to sharing them, the originator can secure property rights over the ideas when they are incorporated into useful applications. Furthermore, since patent breadth in the United States is broader, it is unlikely that talking about a "small" idea related to a larger invention would disclose enough to jeopardize the originator's rights over the invention.

Both the first-to-invent provision and the broader breadth of the U.S. patent system lead to the prediction that U.S. semiconductor employees are *more* likely to share knowledge privately across company lines than their peers in Japan. The Japanese procedure of "laying open" all patent applications reinforces this conjecture, since instead of privately sharing "small" innovations, that is, ones that would not qualify for patent protection in the United States, the public has access to patent applications.

The principal difference in labor market characteristics in the two countries that may shape knowledge sharing behavior is the level of turnover. Given that turnover of personnel in the semiconductor industry is higher in the United States than in Japan, it is more likely, ceteris paribus, that U.S. workers would have relationships with people at other companies, leading to a higher incidence of cross-company communication. To some degree, attending conferences could substitute for turnover in Japan as a way of establishing cross-company relationships. However, semiconductor engineers from both countries actively engage in professional conferences.[16]

In the cost and benefit framework above, turnover would likely influence the transaction cost, T, and the estimation of the decline in profits, D. Turnover decreases transaction costs associated with knowledge sharing, since it reduces the time to develop contacts at other firms. Departed employees often feel comfortable calling on previous coworkers for technical advice. Furthermore, a departed employee often can estimate how easily his or her former company could incorporate a piece of technical knowledge, thus leading to a more accurate estimate of D. Given this ability, it seems *unlikely* that the departed employee would receive requests from former coworkers for technical knowledge that would result in "competitive backlash." Such requests would be futile under the assumptions of this chapter.[17] Therefore, the level of private knowledge exchange is predicted to be higher in the United States, since former coworkers are better able to share bits of technical knowledge without jeopardizing their employers' competitive positions.

Survey Data and Results

To determine whether knowledge sharing in the semiconductor industry differs both from patterns in the steel industry and across countries, we distributed a Learning and Communication Survey during 1994 and 1995.[18] The sample comprises questionnaire results from 134 employees of semiconductor and semiconductor equipment companies. The response rate was 40%. A total of 333 surveys were distributed to members of the following groups: engineers at participating firms in the University of California Berkeley's Sloan Competitive Semiconductor Manufacturing (CSM) Program that either recently joined the program or participated in a focus study of new process introduction; participants in the SEMICON West equipment trade show; participants in the Plasma Etch Users' Group meetings in Mountain View, California; IC and equipment vendor staff involved with the Quality and Organizational Systems group at Semiconductor Equipment and Materials International. The sample included circuit designers, development engineers, manufacturing engineers, technical sales staff, and quality control personnel.

Of the 134 respondents, 96 worked for U.S. companies, and 27 worked for Japanese companies.[19] Figure 30.4 shows that they principally worked for IC companies, and over 70% of the respondents from both countries have less than 15 years of industry experience.

The sample was not random, and there are some grounds for believing that the respondents were biased toward knowledge sharing. The majority of respondents had either previously agreed to participate in the benchmarking exercises of the CSM study or were attending an industry-related meeting when they were handed the survey. Even if the findings below overstate knowledge sharing activity in the semiconductor industry, they provide a useful reference point for both the primary mechanisms of knowledge sharing and its intensity.

Knowledge Sharing in Semiconductors versus Steel

Given the greater degree of technological change in semiconductors relative to steel, Hypothesis 1 posits that private, cross-company communication would be *less* likely in the semiconductor industry. A comparison of semiconductor survey results with results from a study of the U.S. specialty steel and minimill industry reported in Schrader (1991) supports this hypothesis, but only to a limited degree. The findings highlight that *public* sources of knowledge sharing are much more prevalent in the semiconductor industry than found by previous studies of the steel industry.

A few questions in the Learning and Communication Survey were matched to questions contained in the MIT Steel Industry Communication Survey in order to determine industry-specific communication patterns.[20] In both industries, engineers valued colleagues at other companies. The Learning and Communication Survey asked respondents to rate nine possible sources of technical information on a 7-point scale, where 1 represented "not at all important" and 7 represented "very important." For comparison with the steel study, the semiconductor sample was limited to the 53 respondents from 21 U.S. IC companies. The majority of these respondents were engineers who worked on circuit design, semiconductor process development, or equipment development and modification, although a number worked in materials procurement and manufacturing operations. The steel study drew on a much larger sample, 294 respondents, comprised of middle-level managers and engineers. In the semiconductor sample, 57% rated technologists at other companies as

	Japan	United States
Total respondents	27	96
• of which, IC:	25 (2 companies)	53 (21 companies)
• of which, vendor:	2 (1 company)	43 (26 companies)

Respondents by years in industry

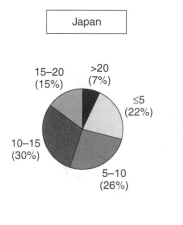

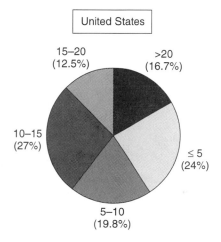

Figure 30.4 The sample.

an important source of technical information, meaning that they scored this source 5 or above on the 7-point scale. This compares with 61% of respondents from the steel study (Schrader 1991, p. 154). This finding provides only marginal evidence for the hypothesis that knowledge sharing is *less* common in semiconductors than in steel.

Although colleagues at other companies were found to be valuable in both industries, the importance of this source relative to other sources reveals a more striking difference. On average, in the semiconductor industry, technologists at other companies ranked *fourth* behind colleagues within the respondent's company, journals, books, and presentations at conferences (table 30.3). In contrast, the steel study found that technologists at other companies ranked *second*, on average, behind colleagues within the same company. This difference highlights the important role that public sources of technical information play in the semiconductor industry, a very development-intensive industry.

When comparing the frequency with which the respondents answered outside requests for specific technical information, the respondents

from the semiconductor industry were less likely to engage in knowledge sharing. A smaller percentage of the semiconductor respondents were approached by someone outside their company for technical advice or for technological infor-

TABLE 30.3 Important Sources of Technical Information for IC Respondents (1 = highest average score)

	Japan ($n = 25$)	United States ($n = 53$)
Private sources		
Colleagues in company	1	1
Technologists at other companies		4
Equipment vendors		
Materials suppliers		
Customers		
Benchmarking studies		
Public sources		
Presentations at conferences	3	3
Journals, books, etc.	2	2
Patents	4	

mation during the year prior to the survey year: 79% of the semiconductor respondents had been approached at least once versus 85% in the steel industry (Schrader 1991, p. 155). Not only were the semiconductor respondents less likely to be approached, but also a higher percentage of those approached fulfilled none of the requests for specific technical information: 10% versus only 2% in the steel study (Schrader 1991, p. 155). One interesting finding to note, however, is that 23% of the semiconductor respondents reported being approached eleven or more times, whereas 19% of the steel respondents were approached ten or more times. This may suggest that semiconductor engineers who have established their reputations through journal articles and conference presentations receive a higher number of requests per year relative to "gurus" in the steel industry who do not receive as much public exposure.

Overall, 71% of the U.S. semiconductor respondents had participated in cross-company knowledge sharing compared with 83% of the respondents from the steel study. Although this difference is not dramatic, the survey results do suggest that engineers in the U.S. semiconductor industry rely less on private contacts in other companies for technical advice than in steel.

Knowledge Sharing in Japan versus the United States

This section extends the analysis of knowledge sharing patterns by examining cross-country differences within the same industry. After limiting the sample to respondents who worked for IC companies in the United States and Japan, the findings suggest a distinctive pattern of knowledge sharing in the two countries, supporting Hypothesis 2: the Japanese respondents relied on *public* channels for external knowledge acquisition, whereas the respondents from U.S. companies gave a higher rank to *private* channels. This is supported by a similar finding reported by Almeida and Kogut (1994, p. 18): relative to semiconductor engineers in the United States, Japanese engineers possess fewer "informal contacts" at competitors. Semiconductor workers in the United States were approached more often for technical advice and were more apt to fulfill at least one request per year. According to ordered logit estimates, however, home country does not play a statistically significant role in determining participation in knowledge sharing.

TABLE 30.4 Preferred Knowledge Sharing Vehicles Linking IC Respondent with Another IC Company (1 = highest average score)

	Japan ($n = 25$)	United States ($n = 51$)
Private vehicles		
E-mail		
Telephone		4
Face-to-face meeting		3
Visit to other company's fab		
Consortium		
Benchmarking studies		
Public vehicles		
Newsletter		
Popular press	2	
Trade journals	4	1
Conferences	1	2
Reviewing patents	3	
Reverse engineering		

On average, respondents from both countries scored colleagues in company, journals, books, and presentations at conferences as the three most important sources of technical information. The U.S. respondents, though, relied on technologists at other companies and the Japanese respondents relied on patents to a greater degree (table 30.3). In terms of finding out useful technical information from "horizontal" sources, that is, from fabrication plants at other semiconductor companies, the IC respondents from Japan rated public vehicles as the most important (table 30.4). In contrast, the U.S. respondents scored personal channels of communication, namely, face-to-face meetings and telephone, in their top four.

A similar pattern was found for how IC workers find out useful technical information from equipment vendors or "vertical" sources (table 30.5). Although their most important vehicles of knowledge sharing overlapped to some degree, the Japanese respondents were more reliant on public sources than their U.S. counterparts.

Figures 30.5 and 30.6 present the opportunities for and the incidence of knowledge sharing involving the IC respondents from the United States and Japan. Consistent with the hypothesis that U.S. workers rely more heavily on private knowledge sharing, nearly 80% of the U.S. respondents versus 64% of the Japanese respondents were approached at least once in a

TABLE 30.5 Preferred Knowledge Sharing Vehicles Linking IC Respondent with Vendor (1 = highest average score)

	Japan (*n* = 20)	United States (*n* = 48)
Private vehicles		
E-mail		
Telephone		2
Face-to-face meeting		1
Use vendor's facilities		
Consortium		
Benchmarking studies		
Public vehicles		
Newsletter		
Popular press	1	
Trade journals	2	4
Conferences	4	
Reviewing patents		
Trade shows	3	3

given year by someone from another company in the industry for technical information (figure 30.5).

Approximately 90% of the respondents from both countries fulfilled at least one request (figure 30.6).

Although the Japanese respondents were less likely to be asked and slightly less likely to answer at least one request, those respondents who *did* fulfill requests were more likely to fulfill over

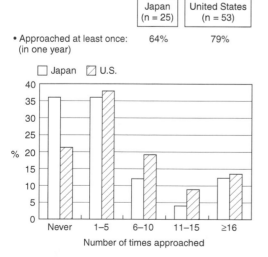

Figure 30.5 Opportunities for knowledge sharing.

	Japan (n = 25)	United States (n = 53)
• Shared at least once (in one year):	87%	90%

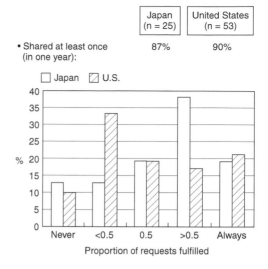

Figure 30.6 Incidence of knowledge sharing.

half the requests. This appears to counter Hypothesis 2 that workers in a labor market with higher turnover (the United States) would be more likely to fulfill requests, since they have more information with which to value the costs of knowledge sharing.[21] In the sample, the turnover rate is slightly higher in the United States: None of the Japanese respondents from IC companies had ever changed companies, whereas the U.S. respondents had worked for, on average, 1.1 other semiconductor companies and 0.3 equipment vendors.[22] In addition to turnover, conferences are another way to learn about competitors, but the attendance rate is similar across the sample: on average, the respondents from both countries attend approximately 1.5 conferences per year. Instead of refuting Hypothesis 2, the high level of request fulfillment in Japan may reflect business etiquette, whereby one would rarely request knowledge unless the knowledge owner would feel comfortable providing it (Kato and Kato 1992, p. 18).

The Profile of a Knowledge-Sharer

Using the larger sample of 123 respondents from Japanese and U.S. companies, the determinants of participating in knowledge sharing are tested using logit analysis. The characteristics of the respondents included in the ordered logit estimations are presented in table 30.6, along with their predicted signs.

In addition to testing whether the respondent's home country influenced knowledge sharing be-

TABLE 30.6 The Explanatory Variables for the Ordered Logit Analysis

Independent Variables	Values	Included in Ordered Logit with Dependent Variable "Approached"?	Included in Ordered Logit with Dependent Variable "Provided"?	Hypothesized Sign
U.S. resident	1 = United States	Yes	Yes	+
	0 = Japan			
IC Company	1 = IC	Yes	Yes	−
	0 = Eq. vendor			
Level of education	1 ≤ College			
	2 = College	Yes	Yes	+
	3 = Masters			
	4 = Ph.D			
Industry tenure	Continuous	Yes	Yes	+
Turnover	Continuous	Yes	Yes	+
Member of a professional society	1 = YES	Yes	Yes	+
	0 = NO			
Consulted outsider	1 = YES	Yes	Yes	+
	0 = NO			
Paper presentations for pay or promotion	1 = YES	Yes	Yes	+
	0 = NO			
Common technical issues	1 = YES	Yes		+
	0 = NO			
Sensitive information training	1 = YES		Yes	−
	0 = NO			

havior, the remaining independent variables fell into two general categories: the respondent's personal characteristics, and components of his or her firm's knowledge management system. First, because of institutional differences, home country is predicted to influence the likelihood of knowledge sharing, with U.S. residents exhibiting a *higher* likelihood of sharing. Second, respondents with the following characteristics were expected to engage in knowledge sharing more frequently: those who worked for equipment vendors, had a high level of education, had a long tenure in the industry, had higher levels of interfirm turnover, were members of professional societies, consulted people outside their company when solving technical problems, and worked on technical issues common to other companies or universities. These characteristics were predicted to heighten the potential for interaction with outsiders.

Finally, the components of a firm's knowledge management system can influence an employee's participation in interfirm communications. Two components considered are: training in information control, and rewards for presenting papers at professional conferences. If the respondent's company provided training on how to control sensi-

tive information, it is predicted that the respondent would be more hesitant to provide requested information. If the respondent's company included paper presentations at professional conferences in pay or promoting decisions, then the company actively encouraged external knowledge diffusion.

After eliminating respondents with missing values, 95 respondents were used in the ordered logit analyses. The categories for the first dependent variable *approached*—the number of times the respondent was approached for technical information in the year previous to the survey year—are found at the bottom of figure 30.5: *Never, 1–5, 6–10, 11–15,* or ≥ *16* times. The categories for *provided*—the number of times the respondent provided the requested information—are located at the bottom of figure 30.6: *Never, Less than Half, About Half, More than Half,* or *Always.* The estimated coefficients are reported in table 30.7.

Home country and turnover are predicted to influence the likelihood of being approached for technical information and providing such information. The results in table 30.7 show, however, that neither working in the United States nor the level of turnover confer a statistically sig-

TABLE 30.7 Ordered logit results

Independent Variable	Estimate	Standard Error
Results for "Approached for specific technical information"		
U.S. resident	0.278	0.531
IC company	−1.899***	0.432
Level of education	0.246	0.229
Industry tenure	0.045*	0.025
Turnover	0.034	0.069
Member of a professional society	0.524	0.413
Consulted outsider	−0.130	0.388
Paper presentations for pay or promotion	−0.253	0.357
Common technical issues	−0.563	0.417
Results for "Provided the requested technical information"		
U.S. resident	−0.145	0.660
IC company	−1.222***	0.460
Level of education	0.025	0.229
Industry tenure	0.056**	0.027
Turnover	−0.042	0.045
Member of a professional society	−0.060	0.477
Consulted outsider	−0.984**	0.414
Paper presentations for pay or promotion	−0.264	0.407
Sensitive information training	0.047	0.450

*Significant at the 10% level.
**Significant at the 5% level.
***Significant at the 1% level.

nificant effect. Consistent with these results, Lynn et al. (1993, p. 68) found that U.S. engineers *do* have a greater number of interfirm contacts on average, but they found "no statistically significant difference (at the 0.05 level) in the frequency with which Japanese and U.S. engineers used personal contacts at other companies for information."[23]

The only two variables that are statistically significant with the predicted sign are whether the respondent worked for an IC company and the respondent's tenure in the industry. The estimates reported in table 30.7 indicate that IC respondents are more likely to fall in the *Never* categories of both dependent variables, whereas people with long tenure in the industry are more likely to fall in the highest categories. The results are consistent with the predictions.

A surprising finding is the negative and significant coefficient on "consulted outsider" reported in the second set of results in table 30.7. The negative coefficient suggests that those who asked colleagues at other companies for assistance when problem solving were *less* likely to provide technical information when *they* were asked. This appears to counter the intuition that reciprocity drives knowledge sharing. However,

the respondents were not asked to disclose whether they had established relationships with people who approached them.[24]

To understand the rules of thumb followed by respondents when deciding whether to provide requested technical information, the questionnaire asks: "If you did not [fulfill all requests], how did you decide which requests to answer?" Grouping the answers into broad categories, the respondents replied that they share information across company lines when (1) the information is of a general sort, that is, nonconfidential or nonproprietary; (2) the information does not confer a competitive advantage; or (3) according to guidelines of the employer or a supervisor's assessment, the information may be shared. Two respondents shared information only if they anticipated reciprocation in the future, implying the existence of trading relationships and countering the negative coefficient on the "consulted outsider" variable.

Discussion and Conclusions

Knowledge creation is essential for growth in industries where the augmentation of knowledge increases at a rapid pace. The management of knowledge in an industry like semiconductors becomes a key competitive variable. Successful knowledge management hinges on optimal cross-company sharing directed by net benefit calculations. Based on survey data, this research has shown that even in a fiercely competitive industry, both public and private mechanisms are used for interfirm knowledge sharing. In Japan, semiconductor employees rely on public mechanisms. In the U.S. semiconductor industry, private channels are used to a greater extent but less so than in steel. Many of the mechanisms place limited restrictions on the use of the shared knowledge. Even when knowledge is shared through channels with limited legal recourse, for example, through face-to-face communication *not* covered by a legal contract, the benefits can have long-run pay-offs both for the firms involved and for the broader economy. As discussed below, the primary benefits accruing to firms that share include the ability to refine strategic plans, inclusion in professional networks, and coordination on industry standards. Knowledge sharing also fuels growth in regional and national economies by fostering communities of innovators and ensuring knowledge diffusion.

Implications for Firms

Input into Strategic Plan

Firms that share knowledge often receive knowledge in the process (recall A in the net benefit calculus). Knowledge gathering through public and private channels is an integral part of a firm's "competitor intelligence system" (Porter 1980, p. 71).

Through private communication channels, a development engineer often can learn about the technical problems encountered by a competitor. This information can be used by the engineer's company to alter the allocation of resources and to update expectations for future revenue streams. Depending on the progress of their competitors, technology managers may need to revise their projections for licensing revenues or cross-licensing opportunities (L and R, respectively, in the net benefit calculation). Product managers may need to release products earlier than initially planned which may compress future product planning cycles.

As companies expand their product portfolios, they benefit from learning about organizational

systems, as well as technical feats. For example, as Japanese semiconductor producers increasingly turn toward architecture-based products, such as microprocessors, and away from commodity products, such as DRAMs, they are experimenting with employment systems that increase rewards to individual creativity. They have learned about options for structuring individual rewards by talking to their U.S. counterparts.

Access to Professional Networks

Many view knowledge sharing as an "admission ticket" to the "back room" discussions of professional groups. By encouraging their engineers to gain admission to these sharing blocs, companies can access private knowledge that may not be patented or published (Hicks 1995), thus increasing the domain of their knowledge variable, A, in their net benefit calculation. For example, the results of failed experiments are rarely published in journal articles, but learning about them can prevent a firm from duplicating failures. Reflecting the importance of professional ties, over 70% of both the Japanese and American respondents to the survey discussed in this chapter noted that either they are members of professional societies or that their companies are members of an industry association.

Formation of Industry Standards

Interfirm knowledge sharing also permits the emergence of industrywide standards. Semiconductor producers have benefited from agreeing on issues such as wafer diameter and chemical purity requirements. Since these issues are precompetitive in nature, they avoid "antitrust concern" (Teece 1993, p. 15). Coordination can occur in a variety of forums—industry association meetings, industry consortia, etc.—and often requires private, informal communications to circulate technical information and build consensus.

Industrywide coordination on input standards can increase profitability. It decreases uncertainty about the quality of the knowledge variable, A, in the net benefit calculation, permitting tighter process specifications. Precise process specifications facilitate new process transfer from development to high-volume production and improve production control, thereby attracting customers with stringent reliability requirements.

Few companies adequately prepare their engineers for knowledge sharing, and even fewer internalize the technical and organizational information that their engineers gather. As discussed below, efficient knowledge sharing requires companies to train their engineers and develop information arteries through which externally gathered knowledge can circulate to strategists throughout the organization.

Preparing the Knowledge-Sharer

The important public and private knowledge sharing vehicles discussed in this chapter differ in terms of the intensity of human interaction. For example, the use of trade journals can be characterized by a low intensity of interaction relative to face-to-face meetings. Although a number of the respondents *did* receive company training in paper writing and communication skills, the training was not universally provided.

In order to protect their most strategic knowledge assets, firms must work with their employees to determine which domains of knowledge are off-limits to outsiders and which vehicles of knowledge sharing are preferred. Many semiconductor companies conduct thorough internal reviews of papers prior to submission and screen conference presentations to control knowledge diffusion. But by encouraging employees to estimate the net benefit from sharing knowledge and by hiring legal counsel to help select appropriate sharing vehicles, companies can assist their employees more explicitly. In the absence of guidance, employees will often choose knowledge sharing vehicles with very low transaction costs (T in the net benefit calculation), since they are reluctant to draw up lengthy agreements detailing permitted uses of the knowledge.

Throughout this chapter, it was assumed that agency problems do not exist. However, to ensure that the incentives of individuals align with their firms' objectives, changes to employment systems may be necessary. Rewards that emphasize certain sharing mechanisms play an important role in the knowledge management system. Based on data from the Learning and Communication Survey, Japanese engineers are more likely to rely on patents and journal articles for useful technical information than their U.S. counterparts. Their companies encourage participation in these public arenas to a greater degree: The Japanese respondents gave a higher rank to patent awards, conference presentations, and published journal articles as determinants of their pay and promotions than the U.S. respon-

dents. Because turnover is more prevalent in the United States, it is not surprising that many U.S. companies in the sample rely more heavily on individual bonuses, profit sharing, and stock options to help align their employees' incentives.

Constructing a Circulation System

Firms can bolster their knowledge stock by actively internalizing information that their employees acquire during knowledge sharing. However, engineers are notorious for their reluctance to document their work outside their personal lab books. Therefore, firms may need to dedicate people to track engineers' externally gathered knowledge. This "knowledge tracker" also can function as a resource by scanning journal articles and patents to augment the engineers' own searches. Many of the respondents noted that their companies employ people for the latter function, but the internalization of externally gathered knowledge often is neglected. Finally, after the knowledge is culled from the engineers, it must be distilled and circulated to other strategic groups within the firm in a timely fashion.

Implications for the Economy

Not only is it important for firms to understand knowledge flows, but public policy-makers should also consider the implications of knowledge sharing patterns for regional and national growth.

Regional Buoyancy

Local officials may wish to encourage active professional networks to ensure the long-term vitality of a geographic region. When comparing the success of California's Silicon Valley with the relative stagnation of Route 128 outside Boston, Saxenian (1994) finds that the tradition of interorganizational knowledge sharing in Silicon Valley has spurred the entrepreneurial activity of the region, whereas the tradition of secrecy along Route 128 has stifled such activity. Silicon Valley's regional flexibility has permitted its technical community to adapt to changing market conditions through strong professional ties. These ties link technical experts across company lines and extend across institutional boundaries to the academic communities of Stanford and the University of California at Berkeley and the investor community of local venture capitalists.

Economywide Growth

At a national level, a country's growth potential relies on idea creation and dissemination (Romer 1990, p. S72), and government policy that shapes knowledge sharing can have enduring effects. For example, the creation of a national consortium may strengthen some lines of communication but weaken others. Engineers who work for consortium members may talk face-to-face more frequently, thus strengthening their private channels of communication. However, members of the consortium may be restricted to sharing research findings only among consortium members, thus restricting knowledge diffusion.

As this research demonstrates, interfirm knowledge sharing along private and public channels is an important phenomenon in the semiconductor industry with profound implications not only for a firm's vitality but also for an economy's growth. The survey data presented show that public sources of technical information play a larger role in knowledge diffusion in Japan relative to the United States and in the semiconductor industry relative to the steel industry. Only by understanding the net benefits from knowledge sharing, which are influenced by the institutional context and the characteristics of the industry under analysis, can managers and public policy-makers pursue optimal knowledge management systems.

Notes

I am indebted to Sarah Bales, Clair Brown, Bronwyn Hall, David Mowery, Paul Romer, Stephan Schrader, the SMJ reviewers, my dissertation group, the participants in the University of California at Berkeley's Institutions and Labor seminars, the participants in the ADRES Strasbourg Conference on Innovation and many people associated with the semiconductor industry, including Tony Alvarez, Jose Arreola, Neil Berglund, Dan Flamm, Jim Nulty, John Schuler, and the late Vinay Sohoni for useful comments and insights. I gratefully acknowledge the Alfred P. Sloan Foundation for funding.

1. Throughout this chapter, it is assumed that employees' incentives are aligned with their firms', i.e., agency problems do not exist.

2. Secrecy can be achieved in a number of ways. Instead of patenting, the firm often can create a trade secret. If the knowledge is publishable, the firm can refrain from publishing details that would permit exact duplication of the research results (Hicks 1995, p. 408).

3. Particular channels of knowledge diffusion may conduct certain *types* of knowledge more efficiently. Zander (1991) analyzes the influence of knowledge type on mode of diffusion selected by multinational companies. In a study of knowledge transmission in the United States, Machlup (1962) documents the level of transmission of five types of knowledge—practical, intellectual, pastime, spiritual, unwanted—through four channels: periodicals, newspapers, radio and television.

4. Although not the focus of this study, legally enforceable, contractual agreements such as joint development and licensing agreements are common in the semiconductor industry (Kogut and Kim 1991, National Research Council 1992, Okimoto and Nishi 1994).

5. To some degree, negative reputation effects can substitute for legal actions against people who leak valuable information contrary to the wishes of their firms or knowledge sharing partners (von Hippel 1988, p. 91).

6. From the viewpoint of the policy-maker, the net benefit calculation includes the effects on the consumer surplus. See Katz and Ordover (1990) for an exposition of the influence of interfirm R&D cooperation on social surplus and the role of government-sanctioned consortia on knowledge diffusion patterns in the semiconductor industry.

7. Another potential benefit from sharing knowledge is the fostering of relationships with other companies. Hicks (1995) emphasizes the role of publication in building a firm's credibility and entry into professional networks. Furthermore, repeated knowledge sharing between two companies might serve as a testing ground for more extensive relationships like a joint venture. (See Watson [1996]) for a game theoretic treatment of this concept.) When asked about the importance of a history of knowledge sharing when selecting a partner for joint development, however, a senior U.S. semiconductor development engineer replied that technical prowess far outweighs a favorable past history.

8. The patent-license case subsumes know-how licensing. For a discussion distinguishing these two cases, see Arora (1995).

9. Schrader (1991) provides a thorough analysis of the competitive factors that knowledge traders in the specialty steel and minimill industry consider prior to sharing information. Such factors include the degree to which their companies compete and whether the knowledge falls into a highly competitive domain like product quality.

10. Although a product's lifecycle may only last two years, process technology used in its manufacture may endure decades. For example,

process chemistries used in performing anisotropic, or vertical, etches developed over a decade ago are still in use.

11. Allen *et al.* (1983, p. 203) propose a related hypothesis: "firms from industries with a more advanced degree of technological development (e.g., electrical and electronics: chemicals and pharmaceuticals) will have a higher proportion than other industries of internally generated ideas."

12. Past studies have documented, however, that patent protection is considered a weak barrier against imitation (Levin *et al.* 1987, Zander 1991).

13. Almeida and Kogut (1994, p. 23) observe that semiconductor firms often bargain with a portfolio of patents.

14. In August 1994, representatives from the United States and Japan announced a "framework" for reconciling some of the differences in their patenting systems (Riordan 1994).

15. Note that the ensuing discussion focuses on knowledge sharing within a country. Given the global nature of the semiconductor industry, U.S. and Japanese companies patent in both countries and send their engineers to many of the same conferences, but it is assumed that intranational knowledge sharing is more common than international.

16. Given the differences in the employment systems, an individual engineer's motivation to attend conferences may be very different in the two countries. U.S. engineers may be networking for a new job, whereas Japanese engineers are more likely promoting the research feats of their firms (Nishi and Kobayashi 1993). In the computer industry, Westney (1994) reports that Japanese firms encourage their employees to publish research results and participate in professional activities to a greater degree than U.S. firms.

17. Such requests would be futile unless they were accompanied by side payments to individuals, but side payments are disallowed by this chapter's assumption that agency problems do not exist.

18. Appleyard wrote the survey with Clair Brown. They received useful input from Thomas J. Allen, Adriana Kugler, and Stephan Schrader. John Schuler was very helpful in distributing the questionnaire.

19. The remaining respondents are employed by materials suppliers, national laboratories, or universities. Of the total respondents, 104 are located in the United States, 27 in Japan, 2 in Europe, and 1 in Singapore.

20. The author would like to thank Stephan Schrader for providing a copy of the MIT survey.

21. The Learning and Communication Survey, however, does not ask whether the requesters are former coworkers or not.

22. However, Almeida and Kogut (1994, p. 17) find that interfirm mobility of authors of major semiconductor patents is nearly as high in Japan as in the United States.

23. Their sample consisted of engineers who graduated from Carnegie Mellon and Tohoku University in electrical engineering and metallurgical engineering/materials science.

24. Schrader (1991) analyzes the role of previous relationships in shaping knowledge trading. He finds that ties of friendship do not play a significant role in heightening the likelihood that requested information would be provided.

References

Allen R.C. (1983) "Collective invention." *Journal of Economic Behavior and Organization* 4(1):1–24.

Allen, T.J., Hyman, D.B., and Pinckney, D.L. (1983) "Transferring technology to the small manufacturing firm: A study of technology transfer in three countries." *Research Policy* 12(4):199–211.

Almeida, P. and Kogut, B. (1994) "Technology and geography: The localization of knowledge and the mobility of patent holders." Working paper, The Wharton School, University of Pennsylvania.

Appleyard, M.M., Hatch, N.W., and Mowery, D.C. (1996) "Managing the development and transfer of new manufacturing processes in the global semiconductor industry." Working paper, University of California, Berkeley.

Arora, A. (1995) "Licensing tacit knowledge: Intellectual property rights and the market for knowhow." *Economics of Innovation and New Technology* 4:41–59.

Business Week (July 3, 1995) "R&D scoreboard," pp. 1–18.

Carter, A.P. (1989) "Knowhow trading as economic exchange." *Research Policy* 18(3):155–163.

Darnay, A.J. (ed.) (1993) *Manufacturing U.S.A.* Detroit: MI: Gale Research Inc.

The Economist (May 4, 1996) "Japanese semiconductors: Flat as a pancake." pp. 66.

Helfand, M.T. (1991) "How valid are U.S. criticisms of the Japanese patent system?" Working paper, Stanford University.

Hicks, D. (1995) "Published papers, tacit competencies and corporate management of the public/private character of knowledge." *Industrial and Corporate Change* 4(2):401–424.

Kato, H. and Kato, J. (1992) *Understanding and Working with the Japanese Business World.* Englewood Cliffs, NJ: Prentice-Hall.

Katz, M.L. and Ordover, J.A. (1990) "R&D cooperation and competition." *Brookings Papers on Economic Activity*, pp. 137–203.

Kogut, B. and Kim, D.-J. (1991) "Strategic alliances of semiconductor firms." Working paper, The Wharton School, University of Pennsylvania.

Levin, R.C., Klevorick, A.K., Nelson, R.R., and Winter, S.G. (1987) "Appropriating the returns from industrial research and development." *Brookings Papers on Economic Activity* 3:783–831.

Lynn, L.H., Piehler, H.R., and Kieler, M. (1993) "Engineering careers, job rotation, and gatekeepers in Japan and the United States." *Journal of Engineering and Technology Management* 10(1–2): 53–72.

Machlup, F. (1962) *The Production and Distribution of Knowledge in the United States*. Princeton, NJ: Princeton University Press.

National Research Council (1992) *U.S.–Japan Strategic Alliances in the Semiconductor Industry: Technology Transfer, Competition, and Public Policy*. Washington, DC: National Academy Press.

Nishi, Y. and Kobayashi, H. (1993) "A comparison between Japanese and American technology management practices," in R.S. Cutler (ed.), *Technology Management in Japan*, pp. 31–53. Boulder, CO: Westview Press.

Okimoto, D. and Nishi, Y. (1994) "R&D organization in Japanese and American semiconductor firms," in M. Aoki and R. Dore (eds.), *The Japanese Firm*, pp. 178–208. New York: Oxford University Press.

Porter, M.E. (1980) *Competitive Strategy*. New York: Free Press.

Riordan, T. (August 17, 1994) "U.S., Japan in accord on patents." *The New York Times*, pp. C1–2.

Rogers, E.M. (1982) "Information exchange and technological innovation," in D. Sahal (ed.), *The Transfer and Utilization of Technical Knowledge*, pp. 105–123. Lexington, MA: D. C. Heath.

Romer, P. (1990) "Endogenous technological change." *Journal of Political Economy* 98:S71–S102.

Saxenian, A. (1994) *Regional Advantage*. Cambridge, MA: Harvard University Press.

Schrader, S. (1991) "Informal technology transfer between firms: Cooperation through information trading." *Research Policy* 20(2):153–170.

Teece, D.J. (1993) "Information sharing, innovation, and antitrust." Working paper, University of California, Berkeley.

U.S. Patent and Trademark Office (1993) *Industrial Patent Activity in the U.S.* Washington, DC: GPO.

von Hippel, E. (1988) *The Sources of Innovation*. New York: Oxford University Press.

Watson, J. (1996) "Building a relationship." Working paper, University of California, San Diego.

Westney, D.E. (1994) "The evolution of Japan's industrial research and development," in M. Aoki and R. Dore (eds.), *The Japanese Firm*, pp. 154–177. New York: Oxford University Press.

Zander, U. (1991) *Exploiting a Technological Edge: Voluntary and Involuntary Dissemination of Technology*. Stockholm: Institute of International Business.

COMMENTARY
Melissa Appleyard

Always present but rarely spotlighted in the past, knowledge has surged on the scene as the principal competitive variable of the twenty-first century. Credited with driving the United States' "new economy" and other pockets of economic growth around the globe, knowledge is receiving its due in the academic literature, and companies are earmarking resources for managing their knowledge assets. Knowledge can be defined as the fusion of information and data with creative thinking leading to a distillate that has a useful application, for example, an innovation. In many companies, attention has shifted from the traditional supply chain to the management of the "knowledge chain"—the development, deployment, and diffusion of knowledge.

For decades, economists have sought to understand how the accumulation of knowledge contributes to economywide growth. The so-called residual, falling out of national income accounting calculations after deducting the contributions of manual labor and physical capital to growth rates, was popularized by Robert Solow (1956) but became somewhat of an enigma in the economics profession. In the economics field, recent studies have helped to make the residual much more tangible both from a theoretical and empirical perspective and have linked knowledge accumulation to firm-level payoffs (e.g., Griliches 1979, and Romer 1990). In the management field, the strategy and innovation literature has forcefully pried open the "black box" containing the residual. The contents of this book reflect some of the angles from which the residual has been poked and prodded. This chapter examines knowledge in the context of a technology-intensive industry that has grappled with resource allocation both in terms of generating new knowledge but also in terms of controlling its diffusion.

When thinking about the flow of knowledge and how companies manage the flow both within their boundaries and across boundaries, scholars often point to the special nature of knowledge—a quasi-public good—as meriting particular attention when devising a strategy for knowledge management. Knowledge exhibits the attributes of a public good in that it is "nonrival" and, to some degree, "nonexcludable" (Romer 1990). Knowledge being nonrival means that multiple users of a quantum of knowledge does not degrade its quality; and knowledge being nonexcludable means that it is difficult to perfectly cordon it off from use by others. An examination of the semiconductor industry offers ample examples of innovations that exhibit these two characteristics of knowledge.

While benchmarking best-practices in semiconductor fabrication plants, our research team came across numerous innovations on the manufacturing line. For example, at one plant a team of technicians greatly reduced the number of defects at a "bake" step through a simple modification that modulated the flow of oxygen into the furnace. This modification quickly diffused throughout the plant and then to the other plants of the two joint venture partners who owned the innovating plant, but the parties endeavored to keep the modification a secret from the equipment supplier so as to limit its diffusion to rival companies. This sort of breakthrough occurs frequently on the shop floor, and both equipment-related and process-related breakthroughs occur earlier in the knowledge chain either during process integration in the development site or scientific exploration in the research facility. The

resultant innovations vary in terms of their "excludability," largely dependent on whether they can be patented or kept secret, but they share the characteristic of being "nonrival." Their nonrival nature benefits the innovating firm in recovering its investments in R&D, as multiple pieces of equipment or plants can use the innovation simultaneously, but their nonrival nature also makes it difficult to monitor whether "nonapproved" parties have deployed the modification.

The advent of the Internet and the World Wide Web has intensified firms' awareness that scientific breakthroughs that they fund can be diffused globally nearly instantaneously. The threat of losing control of knowledge assets is greater than ever, but so are the potential gains from sharing and absorbing knowledge. As engineering-based sectors such as microelectronics encounter tremendous upfront costs in the pursuit of nanotechnologies, the sharing of knowledge across company boundaries can facilitate the pooling of complementary knowledge assets while promoting risk-sharing. As this chapter illustrates, patterns of knowledge sharing vary across industries and geographic regions. The managerial challenge is to foster knowledge sharing in light of the associated costs and benefits, while policy-makers shape institutions to encourage maximal social benefits without imposing costs that will stifle private incentives to grow the "residual."

References

Griliches, Z. (1979) "Issues in Assessing the Contribution of R&D to Productivity Growth." *Bell Journal of Economics* 10(1) (Spring):92–116.

Romer, P. (1990) "Endogenous Technological Change." *Journal of Political Economy.* 98:S71–S102.

Solow, R. (1956) "A Contribution to the Theory of Economic Growth." *Quarterly Journal of Economics* 70(February):65–94.

31

Opportunity and Constraint

Chain-to-Component Transfer Learning in Multiunit Chains of U.S. Nursing Homes, 1991–1997

Will Mitchell, Joel A.C. Baum, Jane Banaszak-Holl,
Whitney B. Berta, and Dilys Bowman

How and when do multiunit chains affect the capabilities of their component units? Chains are collections of component units that produce similar goods and services, linked together into larger "superorganizations" (Ingram and Baum 1997). This study explores how the level and similarity of capabilities of chains and their components—both existing and newly acquired—affects transfer learning across component units.[1] Transfer learning occurs when one organization causes a change in the capabilities of another, either through sharing experience or by somehow stimulating innovation. Attention to transfer learning processes is critical to understanding organizational performance because it is one of the most important routes through which organizations develop competitive advantage (Capron and Mitchell 1998). Within chains, transfer learning leads to changes in the capabilities of component units and, in turn, to changes in component performance. Past research has shown that ownership relationships, such as chain membership, influence transfer learning greatly. Changes in

capabilities are, however, typically inferred from evidence of the effects of learning on performance (e.g., Baum and Ingram 1998, Darr et al. 1995, Ingram and Baum 1997). By contrast, we focus here on changes in the underlying capabilities themselves.

Standardization of capabilities is a key motivation behind transfer learning in chains because it is critical for economies of scale and increased reliability and accountability. Chains standardize products, advertising, administration, operating procedures, equipment, and even buildings across components. Standardization raises consumers' perceptions of reliability—the ability to repeat service at a given quality level—across a chain's components (Ingram 1996). Standardization increases accountability because chains have a great incentive to monitor and pressure each component to maintain and enhance its standards. Poor quality service at any component can damage the entire chain's reputation. Reliability and accountability of chain components reduce consumer search and monitoring costs (Baum

1999). In turn, standardization enhances the performance of a chain and its components by reducing operating costs and by creating a reputation for reliability and accountability (Hannan and Freeman 1984).

Chains' strategic emphasis on standardization points to the importance of transfer learning across their components. Among a chain's existing components, transfer learning facilitates an ongoing realignment of activities. In addition, because much of chain growth occurs through acquisition, transfer learning is critically important to incorporating newly acquired components, which may be very different from the acquiring chain's existing components, into the chain's strategy.

Our empirical study examines transfer learning in almost 3,000 nursing home chains operating in the United States during the period from 1991 to 1997. Nursing homes provide an excellent context for studying transfer learning, because of the turbulent environment in which nursing homes operate and hence, the need to adjust strategies. In addition, the social implications of change in nursing home practices are substantial (Banaszak-Holl et al. 1996). The U.S. nursing home industry is known to have significant quality problems and policy-makers continue to search for ways to improve practices across facilities (Institute of Medicine 1986).

At the same time, a theory of transfer learning within chains has broader implications because the multiunit chain organizational form is coming to dominate every service industry—from retailing to healthcare—that has some direct contact between customer and organization (Ingram and Baum 1997). The results of this study thus contribute directly to our understanding of organizational change throughout the economy.

Background: Transfer Learning, Multiunit Chains, and Acquisitions

We first briefly describe the concepts of transfer learning in multiunit chains and through acquisition. We contend that chains are important organizational vehicles for learning and more specifically, that post-acquisition transfer learning within chains is particularly common. We argue that the level of chain and component capabilities and the extent of similarity between chain and component capabilities influence transfer learning.

Transfer learning requires that the "sending" organization take action to stimulate learning in the "receiving" organization. Previous studies have provided both statistical and qualitative evidence that transfer learning affects a receiver's performance (e.g., production cost) and is a function of senders' cumulative performance (e.g., total units produced in past periods), other sender characteristics (e.g., innovativeness), and recipient characteristics (e.g., size). Beyond linking sender and receiver characteristics to the receiver's subsequent performance, recent studies of transfer learning have emphasized the importance of the type of relationship between organizations that learn from each other. These studies show that ownership relationships between organizations greatly influence knowledge transfer. Darr et al. (1995), for example, present evidence that common ownership of pizza stores improved productivity, because knowledge transfer was greater between stores owned by the same franchisee. Reinforcing these findings, Baum and Ingram (1998) found evidence of transfer learning within U.S. hotel chains but not between unrelated hotels in the Manhattan hotel industry. Karim and Mitchell (2000) found that medical sector businesses undertaking change through acquiring other businesses add more new product lines than medical sector businesses that have not acquired new businesses. These results contrast with the previously dominant idea that knowledge can simply "spill over" across the boundaries of organizations into the general environment, where it is freely consumed by other firms independent of any relationship to the knowledge provider.

It is not surprising that knowledge does not transfer easily between organizations in the "open market," given the well-known difficulties and costs associated with measuring and valuing knowledge. The problems of market-type exchanges include both difficulties in coordinating the use of the knowledge and costs of protecting the value of knowledge (Capron and Mitchell 1998). Knowledge often suffers from the information paradox (Arrow 1962), such that it is difficult to protect the value of knowledge exchanged between unrelated parties.[2] Moreover, the tacit quality of knowledge may necessitate empathy and familiarity between parties to facilitate communication, so that an ongoing relationship between the parties may help preserve the nature of the knowledge, as well as its value. The need for ongoing communication to coordinate knowledge exchange leads to the need for relationship-specific investments, which are difficult and costly to sustain without some form of institutional governance (Teece 1982, 1986, Williamson 1975). Although such institutional governance sometimes requires a fully integrated hierarchy, there also exists a range of collaborative governance forms such as alliances, long-term contracts, franchises, and chains (Williamson 1991). Collaborative forms often assist transfer learning, while offering higher-powered ownership incentives and greater benefits of local focus than full integration.[3]

Darr et al. (1995) describe three mechanisms that facilitate transfer learning between their related (i.e., commonly owned) components. Regular communication increases the opportunity to share knowledge and report data to each other. Personal acquaintances create empathy, familiarity, and trust that smooth the exchange of information. And, face-to-face meetings provide opportunities to share experience and focus explicitly on common problems and their solutions. By bringing members of component organizations together for both task-oriented and social purposes, chains facilitate interorganizational transfer of experience by increasing the opportunity and motivation for transfer and the ability of organizations to successfully apply experience transferred from other organizations.

Transfer learning is particularly important following acquisition of a new component by a chain. Chain acquisitions represent a form of related diversification in which there tends to be little consolidation of operations. Transfer learning appears to be both a central motivation (Ingram and Baum 2001) and a key to success for chain acquisitions (Ingram and Baum 1997). Theoretical models of chain acquisition have emphasized the market power and social power incentives for acquiring additional units, neglecting the potential for capability development as chains transfer resources and knowledge to acquired units. Recent research in business strategy, however, has begun to emphasize the importance of acquisitions as a basic mechanism through which organizations change, reconfigure, and/or redeploy their resources and capabilities (Capron 1999, Capron et al. 1998, Capron and Mitchell 1998, Karim and Mitchell 2000). Consistent with research on transfer learning in chains, this view holds that imperfections in markets for knowledge create complications for arm's length transfer of knowledge resources. The market imperfections, which include both pricing problems and coordination difficulties,

lead to a prevalence of resource transfer through acquisitions because they provide the necessary ongoing collaborative interaction required for effective transfer learning. A key conclusion from this line of inquiry is that transfer learning is a fundamental process for chains and their acquired units.

Opportunity and Constraint in Chain-to-Component Transfer Learning

In this study, we develop and test the argument that the ability and incentives to transfer knowledge between chains and components are dependent on both the *level* and *similarity* of chains' and components' capabilities, as both direct and interactive effects. Capabilities in business organizations can be measured on multiple dimensions. After presenting our conceptual framework, we identify and measure levels of several types of capabilities for U.S. nursing home chains and their components.

Capability Level

We start by considering the level of capabilities across the chain and within focal components. This part of our argument emphasizes the importance of characteristics of both the sender and recipient. Higher levels of capabilities across a chain create greater opportunities for transfer learning to components. In contrast, a higher level of capabilities at a focal component reduces the potential of transfer learning to that particular unit. Components with lower levels of capabilities will, in contrast, have strong incentives to gain new capabilities.

Capability Similarity

We next consider how the similarity between the chain's capabilities and those of the component member influences transfer learning. We argue that capability similarity reduces transfer learning incentives, even if similarity increases learning ability. Subsequently, any benefits of similarity arise as a conditioning effect on the influence of capability level. Our arguments build on discussions that arise in the organizational learning, strategic management, and organizational ecology literatures.

These three literatures all suggest that an organization's ability to undertake transfer learning increases with similarity and decreases with dissimilarity in capabilities. An organization needs prior knowledge closely related to potential new knowledge before it can assimilate the new knowledge, and consequently, prior knowledge creates strong path-dependencies for organizations. Organizational theorists have labeled this path dependency in organizational knowledge as absorptive capacity (Cohen and Levinthal 1990). Likewise, the strategy literature, as represented in Porter's (1987) skill-transferring model, suggests that acquirers seek targets with closely related primary characteristics (e.g., logistics, operations, marketing, sales, and service) and support activities (e.g., company infrastructure, human resource management, technology development, procurement). A parallel argument also arises in the organizational ecology literature, which argues that differences in size and product mix lead organizations to compete in different ways for resources and to use different operating, management, and strategic capabilities (e.g., Aldrich 1979, Hannan and Freeman 1977, McKelvey 1982, Carroll 1985). By extension, these views suggest that chain-component differences will make transfer learning to components less likely, for two reasons. First, the chains will have less incentive to standardize currently different activities and, second, because the chains and components lack experience needed to transfer knowledge even to the extent that they wish to do so.

Despite the possibility that learning ability increases with similarity, the actual effect of similarity on knowledge transfer must be conditioned on the potential for learning benefits. The direct effect of similarity on transfer learning may well be negative, rather than positive, because similarity imposes a constraint on learning: When a component's capabilities are very similar to those of its chain, there may be little potential benefit from learning.

Consider three stylized capability levels—low, moderate, and high. Strong constraints to transfer learning incentives arise at the two extremes of chain-component similarity, low-low and high-high. When chain and component both have low capabilities, there will be little potential for transfer learning, because the chain has little to offer the component. At the other extreme, in the high-high case, a component with high levels of a capability will gain few benefits from transfer learning, even if the chain to which it belongs is also highly skilled. Although the component may gain from refinements to its ca-

pabilities, the component will be unlikely to make significant leaps to new capability levels through transfer learning.

Only in the moderate-moderate case do transfer learning ability and incentives to learn begin to converge. At moderate levels of capabilities, the component may have an experiential base on which to build, and the moderate level of capabilities at the chain may provide transfer opportunities. Even here, though, similarity may limit transfer opportunities. Moreover, some transfers may make the chain and component more dissimilar: If a moderate-capability chain attempts to create a high-capability component, it may defeat the benefits of standardization so central to the chain strategy. Thus, contrary to previous arguments, we hypothesize that similarity between the chain and component at best will only moderately increase the likelihood of transfer.

By contrast, dissimilarity can enhance transfer learning. The dissimilarity case in which chain capabilities are high and component capabilities are low is the most obvious. The main effect of the high chain capabilities will lead to substantial transfer learning. In addition, components with low initial capabilities on a particular dimension may be particularly receptive to receiving new capabilities from a chain that possesses particularly strong skills on that dimension, for two reasons. First, the component may value improving a capability area in which it is weak, while the chain may view the situation as an opportunity for improving the component in its own right and increasing standardization across components. Second, the new capabilities will tend to have less conflict with the component's existing repertoire of practices in that area than in situations in which a component is already skilled and may strongly resist disruption to what it perceives as its already successful practices. While resistance to change is common, even in situations where a firm and its staff lack skills, resistance is often less when people who must change believe that there is a problem that the change will address. Thus, the situation in which chain capabilities are high and component capabilities are low presents an opportunity for "capability infusion."

A less intuitive and somewhat more ambiguous situation is the case in which chain capabilities are low and component capabilities are high. Our earlier argument concerning capability levels suggests that transfer learning will be low when chain's capabilities are low and the component's capabilities are high. Beyond these main effects, we consider three possible outcomes given this type of dissimilarity. First, there might be no joint effect of the low chain-high component dissimilarity combination, if the main effects provide all the influences. If so, then this dissimilarity combination would inhibit transfer learning less than the similarity combination we discussed above, such that our basic prediction concerning similarity would hold. Second, the imbalance in capabilities might enhance transfer learning if the chain attempts to reinforce the component's strength with whatever parts of its own capabilities are particularly strong. Chains might be more likely to build on a component's strength if the capabilities of a newly acquired component represent an opportunity for market growth for the chain or allow the chain to move into technologically new areas of service. Again, our basic prediction concerning the main effect in which similarity reduces transfer and, conversely, dissimilarity increases transfer would hold in the reinforcement situation.

Alternatively, the combination of low chain and high component capabilities can lead to "transfer unlearning," which would weaken our prediction concerning the effect of similarity on transfer learning. By transfer unlearning, we mean that the chain might substitute some of its own strength in another capability (b) for the component's strength in the focal capability (a), pursuing the incentive of chain-wide standardization. In sum, the presence of multiple possibilities concerning similarity reinforces the ambiguity for the similarity prediction that arises at moderate levels of similarity.

Capability Similarity and Level Interactions

Unlike the main effects of similarity on transfer learning, the effect of the interaction between capability levels and similarity is more straightforward. Joint consideration of the ability and incentives for transfer learning suggests that similarity will tend to have mediating effects on the impact of capability level. In particular, two mediating effects are likely, one positive and one negative.

As a positive mediating effect, similarity may help offset the limits on transfer learning imposed by high component capabilities. Although high-capability components may have relatively little to learn, the similarity to their chain will

help create an absorptive capacity that allows the components to refine and improve shared capabilities, even if there is little potential to transfer novel capabilities from the chain.

In contrast with its positive mediating effect on component capabilities, similarity may also limit the benefits of high chain capabilities. High-capability chains will have less to offer similar components (components that already have achieved high capabilities) than dissimilar components (low capability components).

Synopsis

In summary, our arguments suggest that transfer learning outcomes and rates are a function of the opportunities and constraints resulting from the interaction of level and similarity of chain and component capabilities and from the main effects of capability levels and similarity. We expect transfer learning to increase with chain capabilities, to decrease with component capabilities, and to decrease with similarity. We also expect similarity to temper the negative effect of component capabilities and the positive effect of chain capabilities. Table 31.1 summarizes our arguments.

A Model of Chain-to-Component Transfer Learning

Our discussion of opportunity and constraint in chain-to-component transfer learning motivates the following model of transfer learning from a chain to its components:[4]

$$\Delta c = \beta_1 C - \beta_2 c - \beta_3 S_{Cc} - \beta_4 (C \times S_{Cc}) + \beta_5 (c \times S_{Cc}) \quad (1)$$

In this equation, C is the chain's capability level and c is the component's capability level, each measured at time 0. Δc is $(c_{t1} - c_{t0})$, which is the component's change in capabilities from time 0 to time 1. S_{Cc} is similarity between a chain and its component's capability levels at time 0, defined as (note that S_{Cc} takes a maximum value of 1):

$$S_{Cc} = C/c \text{ if } C < c; S_{Cc} = c/C \text{ if } c < C \quad (2)$$

The interaction terms $(C \times S_{Cc})$ and $(c \times S_{Cc})$ are multipliers of similarity with chain and component capability levels. The parameters β_1 to β_5

TABLE 31.1 Potential Influences on Transfer Learning Rate from Chains to Components, as Functions of the Level and Similarity of Chain and Component Capabilities

Component capabilities (c)	Chain capabilities (C)		
	Chain Capability High (High transfer rate, because many capabilities available)	Chain Capability Moderate (Moderate transfer rate)	Chain Capability Low (Low transfer rate, because few capabilities available)
Component Capability High (Low transfer rate, because low room for improvement)	Similar (high S_{Cc} with $C = c$): Limited transfer potential $C \times S_{Cc}$: Similarity reduces benefits of capability infusion $c \times S_{Cc}$: Absorptive capacity stemming from similarity moderates negative effect of low transfer space		Dissimilar (low S_{Cc}, with $c > C$): Transfer potential ambiguous, because neutral, reinforcement, &/or substitution by chain of component capability are possible $C \times S_{Cc}$ & $c \times S_{Cc}$: S_{Cc} is low, so interaction has little effect on transfer
Component Capability Moderate (Moderate transfer rate)		Similar (high S_{Cc} with $C = c$): Limited transfer potential, but shared experience may help take advantage	
Component Capability Low (High transfer rate, because much room for improvement)	Dissimilar (low S_{Cc}, with $C > c$): High transfer potential from infusion of chain capability $C \times S_{Cc}$ & $c \times S_{Cc}$: S_{Cc} is low, so interaction has little effect on transfer		Similar (high S_{Cc} with $C = c$): Limited transfer potential $C \times S_{Cc}$: Similarity helps find transfer opportunities, despite low chain skills $c \times S_{Cc}$: Similarity limits usage of large transfer space

are model coefficients estimating the magnitude of each effect.

The arithmetic signs in equation (1)—$\beta_1 > 0$, $\beta_2 < 0$, $\beta_3 < 0$, $\beta_4 < 0$, $\beta_5 > 0$—indicate our core predictions concerning transfer learning from chains to components. We expect that component capabilities will increase when chain capabilities (C) are high and when components with high capabilities are similar to their chains ($c \times S_{Cc}$). By contrast, component capabilities will tend to decrease when component capabilities (c) are already high, when components and chains are similar (S_{Cc}), and when chains with high capabilities are similar to the component ($C \times S_{Cc}$). In effect, the similarity interaction with high chain capability ($C \times S_{Cc}$) dampens the positive transfer learning effect of chain capabilities (C), while the similarity interaction with high component capability ($c \times S_{Cc}$) offsets the negative transfer learning effect of high component capabilities (c). We again note that the main effect of similarity (S_{Cc}) is the most ambiguous of these predictions, as similarity coupled with moderate levels of capabilities may sometimes be a fruitful occasion for transfer learning, while dissimilarity stemming from high component–low chain capabilities might inhibit transfer learning.

A notable desirable property of this model is its realistic representation of knowledge transfer as a self-damping process. If $C > c$ then c increases toward C, which also increases S_{Cc}. Increases in c and S_{Cc}, however, tend to dampen increases in c. Any further increase in c would only serve to dampen future increases in c, ultimately stabilizing c at some value that would remain unchanged so long as C did not change. This stability is the result of negative feedback, which occurs when an increase (decrease) in one variable in a model (i.e., c) sets in motion changes in other variables in the model that lead ultimately to a decrease (increase) in the initial variable. Thus, contained within the model are both conditions under which knowledge transfer is initiated and under which it ceases.

Data and Methods

We tested our model using data on nursing home chains and their components in the continental United States between January 1991 and September 1997. We draw our data from a longitudinal data set linking yearly files of the federal OSCAR (*On-line Survey Certification and Re-porting System*) data, which includes information from the state-based inspections of all Medicare and Medicaid certified nursing homes operating in the continental United States. OSCAR covers almost every nursing home in the United States. Data include facility-level information on nursing home strategy and structure (e.g., size, staffing, and services), resident case mix (e.g., % incontinent), chain membership, and any deficiencies recorded during annual inspections. In total, the data include over 105,000 records, covering nearly 20,000 unique nursing homes.

Key to our analyses is the operationalization of chain membership and the occurrence of acquisitions. The OSCAR data include the name of the multiinstitutional corporation to which a nursing home belongs. Approximately half of the nursing homes in these data report a corporate owner. We coded chain membership from names reported in the OSCAR data. We assessed inconsistencies by comparing the spelling of names, intertemporal relationships with specific homes, and geographic linkages. Finally, we checked corporate ownership for large chains using 1990–1998 volumes of the *Medical and Healthcare Marketplace Guide* (Dorland's Biomedical Publications), an annual publication providing information on commercial companies operating in the U.S. healthcare sector. We identified nearly 3,000 unique multiunit corporate owners in the data. Acquisitions—approximately 5,000 in number—were coded as a change in corporate ownership status of a nursing home. The proportion of chain nursing homes increased from 40% to 48% during the period from 1991 to 1997, although most chains tend to be quite small with less than 7% of corporate owners operating more than 10 homes.[5] Thus, extensive chaining of nursing homes exists, but it is still primarily a small-scale phenomenon.

After developing our coding scheme for corporate chains, we identified six key capabilities of nursing homes using the OSCAR data for our analyses. The capabilities variables are:

1. *Component size* (number of beds)
2. *Staff intensity* (registered nurses, practical nurses, aides, and support staff, per resident)
3. *Specialty bed intensity—Alzheimer's disease* (beds dedicated for residents with Alzheimer's disease, per total beds)
4. *Specialty bed intensity—Rehabilitation* (beds dedicated for residents requiring rehabilitation services per total beds)
5. *Specialty service intensity—Injection* (resi-

dents receiving injection services, per total residents)

6. *Specialty service intensity—Therapy* (residents receiving physical or occupational therapy, per total residents)

The size of a nursing home affects the capabilities required to operate it effectively. In this sense, home size represents an indirect measure of nursing home capabilities.

Staffing is the largest operating expense within a nursing home and any increase in the number of nurses or aides, while potentially improving resident care, also increases costs. Staffing intensity is contingent upon case mix and payment rate models, and hence represents a key part of the operating strategy for a nursing home. In this study, we include full-time equivalents (FTEs) of all employees, both nursing and ancillary, in our staffing measure. Staff intensity is a direct measure of nursing home capabilities related to operating efficiency.

The availability of beds dedicated to specialized medical services within a nursing home, such as the ability to provide care for residents with Alzheimer's disease, AIDS, Hodgkin's disease, and other special needs such as rehabilitation care, represents specialized skill sets within nursing homes. Specialty beds represent a service innovation in the health care industry in response to increasing competition driven by changing regulations, technology, and policy concerning long-term care (Banaszak-Holl et al. 1996). For instance, the period of the study was a time of great expansion and high turbulence in rehabilitation services in nursing homes, as facilities competed for the Medicare market during the 1990s.[6] Specialized units designed to treat these types of resident problems require additional skills or training among the staff, more extensive medical equipment, and even unique facility design features. Specialty bed intensity is a measure of capability differentiation because the types of equipment and staff skill requirements vary by specialty. Changes in the level of providing a particular type of specialty care bed provide a direct indicator of transfer learning from chain to component. OSCAR includes consistent information on the number of specialty-care beds for Alzheimer's and rehabilitation. These are the two most common types of specialized bed services in nursing homes, with other types of specialty care beds representing less than 1% of all nursing home beds.

In parallel with specialty beds, the availability of specialty care services such as injections,

physical- and occupational therapy, ostomy, respiratory, suction, intravenous (IV) therapy, or tracheotomy each provide direct measures of nursing home capabilities. OSCAR includes consistent information on the availability of therapy (physical and occupational) and injection services. These services require trained nursing home staff and medical technology highly specific to these services.

We computed variables for the six capability measures for each component individually (the variable c, from equation 1). As dependent variables, we calculated one-period changes for each capability for each chain component (Δc). A period is the time between state inspections, which averages about a year. We then used the individual component measures to create mean value measures for each chain as a whole (C), omitting the focal facility from these calculations. In turn, we used the component and chain measures to compute chain-component similarity (S_{Cc}) as defined in equation (2), as well as the capabilities-similarity interaction variables ($C \times S_{Cc}$ and $c \times S_{Cc}$). Table 31.2 reports summary statistics for the variables.

We estimate six specifications of our chain-to-component transfer model in equation (1), one based on each set of capability variables. Because we are interested in chain-to-component transfer learning, which, by definition, independent nursing homes cannot experience, our analyses include observations only for those nursing homes that were chain components at the start of each observation year. Moreover, new chain-component relationships formed through acquisitions are likely to be qualitatively different from established chain-component relationships, with acquisitions triggering more chain-to-component transfer. Therefore, we estimated the model separately for subsamples of components in ongoing chain relationships that started before 1991, and new chain relationships in their first two inspection periods after acquisitions.

All equations include controls (unreported) for time dependence (observation calendar year) and "cross-effects" for all five nonfocal chain and component capabilities (i.e., $C_{nonfocal}$ and $c_{nonfocal}$) to account for any complementary or substitution interactions among capabilities.[7] The "new relationship" equations also control for time since the acquisition (number of inspection periods, where each inspection period is about a year). We use conventional least-squares regression to estimate parameters for the six specifications of the model.[8]

TABLE 31.2 Summary Statistics

	Ongoing relationships ($n = 30{,}201$)				New relationships ($n = 7{,}260$)			
	mean	s.d.	min	max	mean	s.d.	min	max
1. Component size change ($c_{t1} - c_{t0}$)	0.39	8.33	−299.0	500.0	0.22	9.12	−199.0	415.0
Component size (c)	108.08	53.73	5.0	500.0	107.44	55.16	5.0	500.0
Chain mean size (C)	107.60	32.21	8.0	500.0	107.36	34.10	10.0	450.8
Component-chain similarity (S)	0.76	0.18	0.0	1.0	0.73	0.20	0.1	1.0
Component × Similarity (c × S)	83.34	40.52	0.3	500.0	79.48	40.60	0.5	321.7
Chain × Similarity (C × S)	82.52	32.40	2.1	500.0	79.06	33.59	0.9	304.0
2. Staff intensity change ($c_{t1} - c_{t0}$)	−0.07	1.27	−19.1	18.8	−0.08	1.47	−17.4	18.2
Component staff intensity (c)	1.07	1.28	0.0	20.0	1.15	1.46	0.0	19.7
Chain mean staff intensity (C)	1.21	2.04	0.0	137.9	1.48	2.52	0.2	68.2
Component-chain similarity (S)	0.78	0.22	0.0	1.0	0.73	0.24	0.0	1.0
Component × Similarity (c × S)	0.74	0.44	0.0	14.3	0.72	0.49	0.0	16.3
Chain × Similarity (C × S)	0.79	0.43	0.0	18.2	0.80	0.54	0.0	16.4
3. Alzheimer's bed intensity change ($c_{t1} - c_{t0}$)	0.00	0.06	−1.0	1.0	0.00	0.06	−1.0	1.0
Component Alzheimer's intensity (c)	0.02	0.09	0.0	1.0	0.03	0.10	0.0	1.0
Chain mean Alzheimer's intensity (C)	0.03	0.04	0.0	1.0	0.03	0.04	0.0	0.8
Component-chain similarity (S)	0.39	0.47	0.0	1.0	0.38	0.47	0.0	1.0
Component × Similarity (c × S)	0.01	0.03	0.0	1.0	0.01	0.02	0.0	0.3
Chain × Similarity (C × S)	0.00	0.02	0.0	1.0	0.00	0.01	0.0	0.3
4. Rehabilitation bed intensity change ($c_{t1} - c_{t0}$)	0.00	0.08	−1.0	1.0	0.00	0.09	−1.0	1.0
Component Rehabilitation intensity (c)	0.01	0.07	0.0	1.0	0.01	0.08	0.0	1.0
Chain mean Rehabilitation intensity (C)	0.01	0.03	0.0	1.0	0.01	0.04	0.0	1.0
Component-chain similarity (S)	0.54	0.49	0.0	1.0	0.50	0.50	0.0	1.0
Component × Similarity (c × S)	0.00	0.02	0.0	0.8	0.00	0.02	0.0	1.0
Chain × Similarity (C × S)	0.00	0.01	0.0	0.6	0.00	0.01	0.0	1.0

(continued)

TABLE 31.2 (*Continued*)

	Ongoing relationships ($n = 30{,}201$)					New relationships ($n = 7{,}260$)				
	mean	s.d.	min	max		mean	s.d.	min	max
5. Injection services intensity change ($c_{t1} - c_{t0}$)	0.00	0.09	−1.0	1.0		0.00	0.10	−0.9	0.9
Component Injection intensity (c)	0.11	0.08	0.0	1.0		0.12	0.09	0.0	1.0
Chain mean Injection intensity (C)	0.11	0.03	0.0	0.6		0.11	0.04	0.0	0.5
Component-chain similarity (S)	0.68	0.24	0.0	1.0		0.65	0.25	0.0	1.0
Component × Similarity (c × S)	0.08	0.05	0.0	0.6		0.08	0.05	0.0	0.4
Chain × Similarity (C × S)	0.07	0.03	0.0	0.5		0.07	0.04	0.0	0.4
6. Therapy services intensity change ($c_{t1} - c_{t0}$)	0.00	0.17	−1.0	1.0		0.00	0.18	−1.0	1.0
Component Therapy intensity (c)	0.17	0.21	0.0	1.0		0.20	0.23	0.0	1.0
Chain mean Therapy intensity (C)	0.16	0.11	0.0	1.0		0.18	0.13	0.0	1.0
Component-chain similarity (S)	0.54	0.29	0.0	1.0		0.51	0.29	0.0	1.0
Component × Similarity (c × S)	0.10	0.12	0.0	1.0		0.11	0.13	0.0	1.0
Chain × Similarity (C × S)	0.09	0.10	0.0	1.0		0.10	0.11	0.0	1.0

Variable definitions: 1. No. of beds, 2. Total staff per total residents, 3. Alzheimer's beds per total beds, 4. Rehabilitation beds per total beds, 5. Residents receiving injection services per total residents, 6. Residents receiving therapy services per total residents.

Results

Table 31.3 presents the model coefficients. In this table, a positive coefficient means a greater increase in component capabilities from time 0 to time 1 (i.e., between inspection periods), while a negative coefficient means a greater decrease in component capabilities. That is, positive coefficients imply greater transfer learning from chains to components.

Overall, the empirical estimates in table 31.3 provide broad support for the theoretical model, with 83% of the coefficients having the expected sign (77% significant at $p < .05$). The main effects of capability level strongly support our predictions (all 24 coefficients in the C and c columns have the expected sign and all but one is significant at $p < .05$). As expected, greater chain capabilities (C) lead to more transfer learning by components, and greater component capabilities (c) lead to less transfer learning. The interaction terms also tend to have the expected tempering effects on capability levels, although with slightly less consistency than the main effects of capability levels (20 of 24, or 83% of the interaction coefficients have the expected sign; 18 of 24, or 75% significant at $p < .05$).

The primary exceptions to the expected results are the main effects of similarity (S_{Cc}). Similarity is about as likely to be positive as it is to have the expected negative influence on transfer learning. Although similarity takes the expected negative influence in a majority of "ongoing relationships" cases (4 of 6 cases, 67%), similarity is more likely to have an unexpected positive influence on transfer learning in "new relationships" created by acquisitions (only 2 of 6, 33% similarity coefficients are negative). Therefore, the results suggest that chain-component similarity influences the rate of transfer learning most systematically as a moderator of chain and component capability level effects, rather than as a main effect.

The difference in the similarity results for ongoing relationships and newly formed relationships is instructive. The frequency of the unexpected positive influence of similarity on transfer learning following acquisition suggests that the absorptive capacity of similarity often is highly important when two organizations have recently created a relationship. In these cases, similarity may facilitate quick transfer of resources and capabilities to the target component, rather than limiting knowledge transfer opportunities. Only over time, then, as the component becomes an established part of the chain, does similarity engender the expected inhibiting effect on transfer learning. Acquisitions present important opportunities for transfer learning during which a substantial degree of buyer-target similarity may be required to achieve potential learning benefits.

Support for the model parameters other than similarity is particularly strong for newly formed relationships resulting from acquisitions. Among newly acquired firms, parameter estimates for the main and interaction effects of chain (C, $C \times S_{Cc}$) and component (c, $c \times S_{Cc}$) capabilities are significant in the predicted direction for all capabilities, except the interaction terms of rehabilitation specialty intensity (22 of 24 coefficients, 92%). By contrast, a slightly smaller number of capability coefficients are significant in the expected direction for ongoing relationships (19 of 24 coefficients, 79%). These results suggest that capabilities-driven chain-to-component transfer learning may be triggered by recent acquisitions, in contrast to more established relationships that are more likely to approach their "transfer equilibria." The lack of support for the model predictions in the equation for rehabilitation services for newly acquired components may stem from the high turbulence and relatively recent creation of the rehabilitation services market. Rather than tempering the transfer of rehabilitation knowledge, similarity may actually allow firms to expand rehabilitation capabilities more quickly in response to market demand.

Together, the comparison of the "new" and "ongoing" relationship results suggests an intriguing contrast. Capabilities matter in both types of cases but are particularly important for new relationships in which the greatest potential for capability change will tend to arise. The main effect of similarity, meanwhile, has the expected tempering of the capabilities effects in ongoing relationships but often provides a basis for rapid capability transfer in new relationships.

Although all estimated models are statistically significant ($p < .05$ or better), the models for specific capabilities provide differing levels of overall fit. The fit, as measured by the R^2 statistic, is at least moderate for all but the component size (number of beds) models. The weak fit of the component size models ($R^2 = .01$) may stem from the more limited ability to change nursing home size, which is influenced by regulatory review as well as by capital cost and chain strategy.

Beyond our simple comparison of the direction of coefficient estimates, which generally supports the theoretical model, the relative

TABLE 31.3 Empirical Estimates for Equations Predicting Change in Component Capabilities, Δc.

Capability	Chain-Component Relationship	Parameters of Equation (1) (Predicted sign)					
		$C(+)$	$c(-)$	$S_{Cc}(-)$	$C \times S_{Cc}(-)$	$c \times S_{Cc}(+)$	R^2 (D-W)
1. Component size	Ongoing	.000	−.018*	−2.191*	.011	.008	.01 (2.07)
	New	.035*	−.018*	4.603*	−.048*	.029*	.01 (2.14)
2. Staff intensity	Ongoing	.010*	−.881*	−.664*	−.163*	.553*	.52 (1.90)
	New	.018*	−.862*	−.530*	−.216*	.451*	.53 (1.95)
3. Alzheimer's bed intensity	Ongoing	.101*	−.237*	.000	−.253*	.290*	.07 (2.12)
	New	.083*	−.221*	.001	−.897*	.743*	.06 (2.09)
4. Rehabilitation bed intensity	Ongoing	.078*	−.580*	−.003*	0.336*	.154*	.23 (1.99)
	New	.129*	−.506*	.002	−.050	−.547*	.26 (1.97)
5. Injection services intensity	Ongoing	.286*	−.889*	−.008*	−.379*	.534*	.38 (2.04)
	New	.224*	−.889*	−.008	−.329*	.534*	.39 (2.09)
6. Therapy services intensity	Ongoing	.423*	−.521*	.017*	−.132*	−.007	.27 (2.19)
	New	.316*	−.485*	.001	−.141*	.106*	.25 (2.08)
% coefficients with predicted sign	Ongoing: All = 83%	100%	100%	67%	67%	83%	
	(Significant: 77%)	(83%)	(100%)	(67%)	(67%)	(67%)	
	New: All = 83%	100%	100%	33%	100%	83%	
	(Significant: 77%)	(100%)	(100%)	(17%)	(83%)	(83%)	
	Combined: All = 83%	100%	100%	50%	83%	83%	
	(Significant: 77%)	(91%)	(100%)	(42%)	(75%)	(75%)	

*$p < .05$.

D-W = Durbin–Watson statistic.

The ongoing relationship sample includes 30,201 component-year observations, the new relationship sample includes 7,260 observations.

All equations include controls for time dependence and cross-effects for the five nonfocal chain and component capabilities (i.e., C and c); new relationship equations also control for time since the acquisition.

magnitudes of the model parameters vary in several notable ways. Some parameters vary systematically in all equations. For example, the main effect coefficients for component capabilities (c) typically have larger magnitude than the main effect coefficients for chain capabilities (C), suggesting that component capability levels generally play a larger role in determining the rate of chain-to-component transfer learning in our sample. The exception to this pattern is the equation for component size, again perhaps because of the greater time and capital cost needed to change a nursing home's size.

Other parameter estimates vary in magnitude across models. For example, in the models for newly acquired components, the main versus interaction effect coefficient magnitudes for chain therapy services intensity are $C > (C \times S_{Cc})$, while for injection services equation the relative magnitudes are the opposite, $C < (C \times S_{Cc})$. And, while main versus interaction effect coefficient magnitudes for component therapy and injection services intensity are $c > (c \times S_{Cc})$, for Alzheimer's bed intensity they are $c < (c \times S_{Cc})$. When the parameter for C (or c) is smaller than the similarity interaction term parameter, the transfer "constraining" effect of similarity comes to dominate more rapidly than the "opportunity" posed by main effects of either a chain's high capability level (high C), or a component's low level (low c). Thus, when the interaction term dominates, the relationship will exhibit a greater "transfer inertia." Potentially, the differences in our findings for the specialty bed and specialty service capabilities may arise from differences in the ways in which these services are provided. State inspectors collecting data on the number of beds devoted to the care of individuals in rehabilitation or with Alzheimer's disease do not specify what treatments and staff requirements are necessary to meet the needs of these residents. Subsequently, component facilities may vary dramatically in what they actually provide for these services. On the other hand, the provision of injection and therapy services implies much more specific treatments and staff requirements within a component facility.

These variations in parameter estimates affect the shape of the relationship between chain and component capabilities and the rate of transfer learning. However, the interaction terms in our models make it difficult to intuit the impact of these variations. Therefore, to aid in interpreting our findings, we illustrate graphically the static and dynamic implications of the estimates for several representative equations. Figures 31.1 to 31.3 illustrate the relationships.

The two panels in figure 31.1 show predicted values for Δc (increase or decrease in component capability) across all possible combinations of values of C (chain capability) and c (component capability). Although not all these combinations appear in our data, we present the entire range for illustrative purposes. Figure 31.1 is based on our results for therapy (Panel A) and injection (Panel B) specialty service intensity changes for newly formed relationships. The pattern of changes in capability level (the vertical axis) across combinations of chain and component capability levels fits well with the predicted effects summarized in table 31.1. In both panels, the rate of component capability change is closest to zero (i.e., the rate of change is lowest) along the "similarity diagonal." Rates are highest where chain and component capability differences are maximal, with large increases (decreases) in component capabilities associated with conditions of high (low) chain and low (high) component capabilities. Component capability change is only slightly greater off the "similarity diagonal," however, because the main effects for similarity (S_{Cc}) are weak in the two equations represented in the figure.

The panels in figures 31.2 and 31.3 illustrate the dynamics of transfer learning over time for three initial values of C (.2, .5, and .8) across all possible starting values for c (0 to 1). Given starting values for C and c, we computed the estimated value of Δc and used this value to update c for the next period. We used parameter estimates from the model for newly formed relationships and changes in the intensity of injection services to generate this illustration. We simulated the predicted change in injection service intensity for 10 periods into the future, based on estimates for the first two periods after acquisition, to assess the implied long-term implications of the estimated initial transfer rate.

For the three panels in figure 31.2, we fixed chain capability (C) at each of the three initial values, consistent with a pure one-way, chain-to-component transfer. Each curved line within figure 31.2 represents the change in component capabilities over time, with one line for each starting point of component capabilities. As the figures show, over time (i.e., moving from left to right along each capability line within the panels), the model parameters move the transfer learning process toward equilibrium, reaching

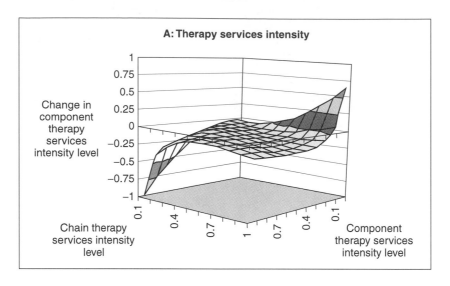

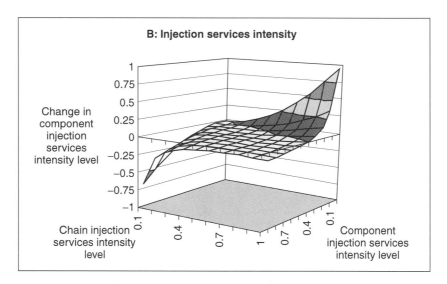

Figure 31.1 Estimated change in component level of specialty services intensity following acquisition.

higher equilibrium component values for higher chain capabilities. Note that the change in component capabilities may involve transfer learning or unlearning (the capability lines ascend or descend), depending on whether the chain or component has greater initial capability level. Moreover, regardless of the starting value for component capability level, the equilibrium component capability level is identical within each panel (i.e., in each panel, the right-hand side of the surface is flat).

For the panels in figure 31.3, we assume two-way transfer learning, such that chains can learn from components as well as components from chains. We set the rate of component-to-chain transfer equal to 10% (Panel A), 50% (Panel B), and 90% (Panel C) of the rate of estimated chain-to-component transfer. For purposes of comparison to the one-way learning patterns, we set the starting value for *C* to .5, as in figure 31.2, Panel B. Compared with Panel B of figure 31.2 (in which component-to-chain learning is 0), the component capability lines in the panels in figure 31.3 change less (ascend less via learning or descend less via unlearning), and capabilities transfer reaches equilibrium more quickly, the

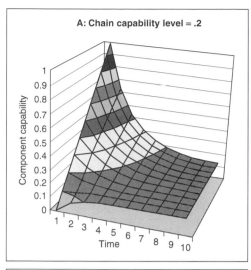

A: Chain capability level = .2

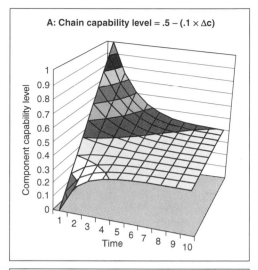

A: Chain capability level = .5 − (.1 × Δc)

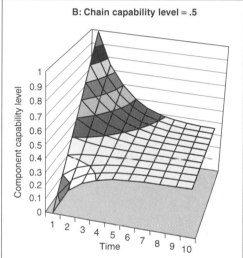

B: Chain capability level = .5

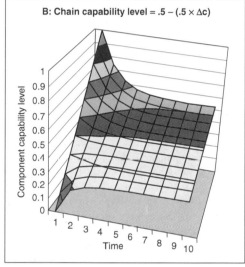

B: Chain capability level = .5 − (.5 × Δc)

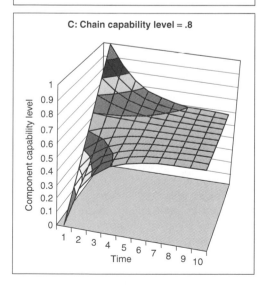

C: Chain capability level = .8

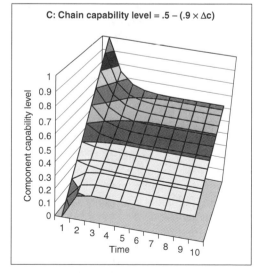

C: Chain capability level = .5 − (.9 × Δc)

Figure 31.2 Estimated change over time in component level of injection specialty services intensity following acquisition.

Figure 31.3 Estimated change over time in component injection specialty services intensity following acquisition (with two-way transfer).

faster is the rate of component-to-chain transfer. In other words, high capability components lose fewer capabilities when there is two-way transfer learning than when there is only one-way transfer learning, while low capability components gain fewer capabilities with two-way transfer learning. These differences between two-way and one-way learning occur because component-to-chain transfer leads to "mutual adjustment" of capabilities, with the speed of the adjustment increasing with the rate of component-to-chain transfer. Permitting component-to-chain transfer also causes the equilibrium component capability level to vary (the right-hand sides of the panels are sloped), such that the equilibrium now depends on both the starting value of component capability and the rate of component-to-chain transfer.

Discussion and Conclusion

We developed and estimated a model of chain-to-component transfer learning applicable to both established chain-component relationships and new relationships formed through acquisitions. We found general support for the model with intriguing variation in the main effects of similarity on post-acquisition transfer learning.

Our attention to transfer learning processes within chains is premised on the belief that how chains change and deploy their knowledge is key to their performance. A fundamental question, therefore, is what are the potential performance implications of the support for our model? Three observations are relevant here. First, the need to standardize leads chains to prefer to operate similar components, and those chains that do standardize outperform those that do not (Baum 1999, Ingram 1996, Ingram and Baum 1997). Second, capabilities may not transfer easily between chains and components that emphasize different capabilities. Forcing chain-to-component transfer of dissimilar capabilities could be worse than useless; it may be harmful if the chain's managers are unable to differentiate capabilities that apply from routines that do not (Mitchell 1992, Greve 1999, Ingram and Baum 1997). Third, chains are more knowledgeable about the nature of competition they face in their current service specialties than they are about competition in other service areas in which they would be exposed to a different and unfamiliar set of competitors. Performance often declines when chains develop new specialized services.

Taken together, these three observations suggest that the greater the variety of capabilities that chains transfer to components in chain-to-component transfer learning, the poorer the performance of the components will be. Given this conclusion, the damping effects of the similarity × capability interactions (i.e., $C \times S_{Cc}$ and $c \times S_{Cc}$) on capability transfer is consistent with the notion of absorptive capacity, the standardization benefits at the core of the chain strategy, and, in turn, with enhancing performance.

As figure 31.1 shows, however, notwithstanding the moderating effects of similarity, component capabilities changed most when chain and component were most dissimilar. High-capability chains transferred knowledge and resources to low-capability components, while low-capability chains required high-capability components to switch to capabilities with which the chain had more experience (but may not fit the component). Thus, although support for our transfer learning model is consistent with improved performance, it also points clearly to the boundary conditions within which those benefits occur, and emphasizes the greater importance of similarity for transfer learning within newly acquired components.

More broadly, our results have intriguing implications for our understanding of business dynamics, that is, how business organizations change over time in the face of constraints. Chains involve change at two levels of analysis, at the level of the component and at the level of the chain. At the component level, our model suggests that many changes occur through chain-to-component transfer learning. As an organizational form, the chain is an example of an integrated mode of organization, sharing features with fully integrated hierarchies. Like integrated hierarchies, chain ownership provides a desirable vehicle for organizational change in order to transfer capabilities that face substantial degrees of market failures.

In addition to component level change, chain-level changes can also take place, in two distinct ways. First, component-to-chain learning may occur, leading to a system-level evolution of capabilities, although we suspect that chain-to-component transfer dominates component-to-chain learning. Again, the partially integrated organizational chain form both protects and coordinates capability transfer. Second, and more common than component-to-chain transfer, chain-level change will take place as chains add and divest components. In this sense, chains are more like collaborative alliances than an integrated hierarchy. The existence of only limited points of interorganizational contact within a chain, as in most alliances, permits chains to adapt (at least partially) to changes in local markets, by adding and divesting chain components as market demand and competitive conditions change. Such corporate activity will change both the structure of the transacting chain, in terms of its size, market distribution, and pattern of capabilities, and lead to subsequent change in the individual components that the chain buys and sells. Our model shows that acquisitions and divestitures often lead to substantial component level changes that align the acquired unit with the capabilities of its new owner.

Our results, then, suggest that a chain's ability to undertake component and chain level change through capability transfer may be severely circumscribed by the performance-driven tendency toward standardization based on the chain's prior capabilities. These path-dependency constraints increase the tendency for major component-level changes to occur through acquisition and divestiture of components with heterogeneous capabilities.

By extrapolating from our model, we can thus identify how chains influence several key dimensions of business dynamics. First, chains undertake component-level changes through chain-managed capability transfer to components and the process in and of itself constrains the scope of change. Second, chains may undertake system-level changes through internal diffusion of capabilities across components, in the face of constraints on change. Third, chains facilitate both component- and system-level changes by acquiring and divesting components. Such corporate recombination helps overcome some of the system-level limits on change.

Our findings extend and reinforce two growing research streams. First, is the stream of research that characterizes multiunit chains as "interorganizational learning communities" (Darr et al. 1995, Greve 1999, Ingram and Baum 1997, 2001). In addition to supporting this characterization, our study also moves this stream forward by focusing on changes in the underlying capabilities themselves, rather than studying changes in performance and simply inferring the prior occurrence of changed capabilities. We also contribute to research that characterizes acquisitions as basic to processes of organizational change, reconfiguration, and/or capability and resource redeployment (Capron 1999, Capron et al. 1998, Capron and Mitchell 1998, Karim and Mitchell

2000). Given the prevalence of the chain organizational form across service industries, and the central roles of acquisitions and knowledge transfer in chain growth and expansion, future research combining ideas on multiunit chains, acquisitions, and transfer learning could provide new insight into the transformation of the economy.

Notes

1. Here, we focus on the tendency for components to converge toward their chains' existing capabilities, although further development of the argument could usefully consider cases in which transfer learning from components to chains causes changes in a chain's capabilities. We undertake preliminary examination of such "two-way" learning following the analysis section. We use the term "capabilities" as synonymous with the term "routines."

2. The "knowledge paradox" is that it is difficult for a potential buyer to determine the value of a piece of knowledge unless a seller discloses the knowledge to the buyer. Once the information is disclosed, however, the buyer no longer needs to purchase the knowledge. This problem creates incentives to internalize ownership, so that the creator and user of a piece of knowledge exist within the same ownership structure.

3. A discussion that discriminates the benefits of different collaborative organizational forms is beyond the scope of this study. Our summary argument is that chains will be particularly well suited as an organizational form when components tend to serve discrete local markets in which some direct contact between consumer and organization is required for service provision.

4. This model of chain-to-component transfer learning could be rewritten, symmetrically, for component-to-chain transfer as: $\Delta C = \beta_1 c - \beta_2 C - \beta_3 S_{Cc} - \beta_4 (c \times S_{Cc}) + \beta_5 (C \times S_{Cc})$. Empirically, however, it would be difficult to disentangle transfer learning from specific components within a chain when estimating this model.

5. Approximately 5% of nursing homes reported belonging to a chain and provided a corporate name, but no other facilities were found to belong to that corporation. We did not consider these nursing homes, which are sometimes part of a health provider system that includes facilities other than nursing homes (e.g., assisted living or hospital beds), as components of chains.

6. Medicare pays about four times more for nursing home care than Medicaid pays but expects rehabilitation services to be available to improve a resident's health so that the resident can

return to their previous living arrangement within 100 days. Payment for rehabilitation services was covered as an ancillary service and in this case nursing homes needed to specify within specified categories the volume of rehabilitative services residents received.

7. Empirically, effects of nonfocal capabilities measures on transfer learning of focal capabilities tended to be weak. The limited effect likely occurs because cross-effects would arise only for specialties that share related underlying operating routines. In practice, though, the capabilities we measure tend to be distinct from each other. Alzheimer's disease treatment, for instance, differs substantially from rehabilitation and therapy services, which also differ greatly from injection services. Hence, one would expect few positive or negative complementarities across those groupings other than, perhaps, from limited substitution effects.

8. Although pooling repeated observations on the same organizations can violate the assumption of independence from observation to observation and result in the model's residuals being autocorrelated, because the number of organizations is high relative to observations in our sample this should not pose too severe an estimation problem. Durbin-Watson statistics reported in table 31.3 are all close to 2.0, suggesting little autocorrelation in the data.

References

Aldrich, H.E. (1979) *Organizations and Environments*. Englewood Cliffs, NJ: Prentice-Hall.

Arrow, K.J. (1962) "Economic welfare and the allocation of resources to innovation in the rate and direction of inventive activity," in R. Nelson (ed.), *University National Bureau Conference Series* 14. New York: Arnold Press.

Banaszak-Holl, J., Zinn, J.S., and Mor, V. (1996) "The impact of market and organizational characteristics on nursing care facility service innovation: A resource dependency perspective." *Health Services Research* 31:97–109.

Baum, J.A.C. (1999) "The rise of chain nursing homes in Ontario, 1971–1996." *Social Forces* 78: 543–584.

Baum, J.A.C. and Ingram, P. (1998) "Survival-enhancing learning in the Manhattan hotel industry, 1898–1990." *Management Science* 44:996–1016.

Capron, L. (1999) "The long-term performance of horizontal acquisitions." *Strategic Management Journal* 20:987–1018.

Capron, L. and Mitchell, W. (1998) "Bilateral resource redeployment and capabilities improvement following horizontal acquisitions." *Industrial and Corporate Change* 7:453–484.

Capron, L., Dussauge, P., and Mitchell, W. (1998) "Resource redeployment following horizontal acquisitions in Europe and North America, 1988–1992." *Strategic Management Journal* 19:631–661.

Carroll, G.R. (1985) "Concentration and specialization: Dynamics of niche width in populations of organizations." *American Journal of Sociology* 90:1262–1283.

Cohen, W.M. and Levinthal, D. (1990) "Absorptive capacity: A new perspective on learning and innovation." *Administrative Science Quarterly* 35:128–152.

Darr, E., Argote, L., and Epple, D. (1995) "The acquisition, transfer and depreciation of knowledge in service organizations: Productivity in franchises." *Management Science* 41:1750–1762.

Greve, H.R. (1999) "Branch systems and nonlocal learning in organizational populations," in A.S. Miner and P.C. Anderson (eds.), *Population-Level Learning and Industry Change, Advances in Strategic Management* 16:57–80. Stamford CT: JAI Press.

Hannan, M.T., and Freeman, J. (1984) "Structural inertia and organizational change." *American Sociological Review* 49:149–164.

Hannan, M.T. and Freeman, J.H. (1977) "The population ecology of organizations." *American Journal of Sociology* 82:929–964.

Ingram, P. (1996) "Organizational form as a solution to the problem of credible commitment: The evolution of naming strategies among U.S. hotel chains, 1896–1980." *Strategic Management Journal* 17(Summer Special Issue):85–98.

Ingram, P. and Baum, J.A.C. (1997) "Chain affiliation and the failure of Manhattan hotels, 1898–1980." *Administrative Science Quarterly* 42: 68–102.

Ingram, P. and Baum, J.A.C. (2001) "Interorganizational learning and the dynamics of chain relationships," in J.A.C. Baum and H.R. Greve (eds.), *Multiunit Organization and Multimarket Strategy, Advances in Strategic Management* 18:103–139. Oxford: JAI Press.

Institute of Medicine (1986) *Improving the Quality of Care in Nursing Homes*. Washington, DC: National Academy Press.

Karim, S. and Mitchell, W. (2000) "Reconfiguring business resources following acquisitions in the U.S. medical sector, 1978–1995." *Strategic Management Journal* 21(Special Issue on the Evolution of Business Capabilities):1061–1081.

McKelvey, B. (1982) *Organizational Systematics: Taxonomy, Evolution, Classification*. Berkeley: University of California Press.

Mitchell, W. (1992) "Are more good things better, or will technical and market capabilities conflict when a firm expands?" *Industrial and Corporate Change* 1:327–346.

Porter, M.E. (1987) "From competitive advantage to corporate strategy." *Harvard Business Review* 65(3):43–59.

Teece, D.J. (1986) "Profiting from technological innovation: Implications for integration, collaboration, licensing, and public policy." *Research Policy* 15:285–305.

Teece, D.J. (1982) "Economies of scope and the scope of the enterprise." *Journal of Economic Behavior and Organization* 1:233–247.

Williamson, O.E. (1975) *Markets and Hierarchies, Analysis and Antitrust Implications: A Study in the Economics of Internal Organization.* New York: Free Press.

Williamson, O.E. (1991) "Comparative economic organization: The analysis of discrete structural alternatives." *Administrative Science Quarterly* 36:269–296.

32

Knowledge across Boundaries

Managing Knowledge in Distributed Organizations

Claudio U. Ciborra and Rafael Andreu

Organization aids knowledge.

A. Marshall

What we have to understand is the functioning of an intricate interrelated institutional structure about which we are extremely ignorant.

R. Coase

The problem of managing knowledge still needs to be set in fruitful terms before effective organizational and technical solutions are envisaged.

Not only does one have to distinguish between various forms of knowledge, like tacit or explicit, individual and collective, and how one can move from one type to another, but also what is relevant is the specific interdependence between knowledge and organizational context. Alternative ways to manage knowledge, including different systems to support knowledge management (KM) are required for different organizational contexts. For example, consider the design and implementation of a new organizational arrangement, including the tailored change of processes, the introduction of teams and other empowering mechanisms, the deployment of systems and applications to enable a richer sharing of knowledge, and so on. Suppose the new configuration of resources and policies fit perfectly the needs of the firm in question. On the other hand, if that firm, to access new knowledge or acquire new capital for growth, is forced by market or technology circumstances to enter an alliance with another firm that has its own KM systems and practices, it may well turn out that its internal KM arrangements and resources are too rigid, "closed," and incompatible. In yet another set of circumstances, the knowledge intensity of the business may oblige the firm to become a member of an open community of institutions and organizations, in which the very boundaries of the firm, its internal knowledge sources and flows and relevant property rights, are put into question and lifted up. It is obvious that KM practices and systems in these three contexts are bound to be different. Especially in the last case, multiple stakeholders, a fragmented, diversified infrastructure, and the variety of knowledge sources stay in the way of an orderly, fully controlled management policy. Not only the boundaries of the firm become more porous, but also the tracking of the knowledge property rights may be cumbersome. We will argue that the transaction costs would be too high to manage such a knowledge intensive business by adhering to models valued for the single firm.

In what follows, we spell out the differences between the three main contexts in greater detail:

- the single firm and its closed processes of KM as inspired by a resource-based view of strategy;
- an alliance between a limited number of firms and the relevant intertwining of previously separated KM processes and systems;
- a web arrangement of multiple businesses, independent research units, and institutional entities like universities, where knowledge does not belong fully to a single stakeholder, and boundaries are blurred. This is a typical context of the "new economy," where special economic principles may apply. How can a firm "manage" knowledge in this floating and rather undefined context?

We submit that the change of organizational context deeply affects the rules of KM and strategy. Specifically, an inverse relationship holds between the knowledge intensity of the business and the tightness of internal knowledge governance: what is functional and appropriate from a strategic point of view in the single-firm case becomes inadequate, if not dysfunctional, in the case of a web of organizations and institutions.

The Learning Ladder: A Model for the Single Firm

Consider first the single firm. In this context, we focus on the processes of generation and transfer of knowledge as linked to a variety of internal learning processes. In highly situated ways, people learn by doing (Williamson 1975, Nelson and Winter 1982); they learn by using systems and technologies; at times, they may engage in double-loop or radical learning (Argyris and Schön 1996); or, more in general, they are busy creating new knowledge by socializing the results of learning and converting explicit into tacit knowledge and vice versa (Nonaka and Takeuchi 1995). In a previous study, we built a "compact" representation of the main learning processes in an economic organization. Such a model has

proven to be a useful reference scheme for investigating strengths and weaknesses of organizational learning processes and, we submit, these can be of help in identifying key aspects of KM in a single firm (Andreu and Ciborra 1996).

The model, called the "learning ladder," is based on the resource-based view of strategy. According to this theory, at the heart of the firm's competitive strength is a process that develops distinctive, core capabilities (Prahalad and Hamel 1990) that is, capabilities that differentiate a company strategically and deliver competitive advantage (Leonard-Barton 1992, Barney 1991). Core capabilities develop through a series of transformations, by which standard resources available in open markets (where all firms can acquire them), are used and combined within the organizational context of a firm to produce capabilities, which in turn can become the source of competitive advantage, especially if they are rare and difficult to imitate or substitute. Such transformations are complex, situated learning processes that can play a strategic role for the firm, because (1) they imply path-dependency and specificity in the resulting core capabilities; and (2) consequently, they cause their inimitability, a crucial characteristic for obtaining competitive advantage. In order to understand the implications for a single firm organization, we analyze in more detail the major stages of the learning and transformation processes through which the firm's core capabilities are generated.

The first transformation consists of the emergence of generic capabilities from standard resources. Two different types of learning take place at this stage: one deals with mastering the use of standard resources and produces what we can call efficient work practices (Lave and Wenger 1991). Individuals and groups (or communities of practice) in the firm learn how to use resources in a given organizational situation. The quest for better work practices may even trigger a search for new resources, more appropriate to the practices under development. Or the introduction and subsequent deployment of new resources (say technological innovations) may motivate individuals and groups to "take advantage of them" through new work practices. We call such a learning loop from resources to work practices the *routinization learning loop*, since its outcome produces repertoires of constrained, routinized, and interdependent actions or moves. The environment in which learning occurs is an organizational context that influences the learning process and is in turn influenced by its result (i.e., new working practices become part of the context, thus increasing the knowledge base of the organization). Such an organizational setting has the characteristics of a formative context.[1] Work practices are "formed" within it and receive their meaning and scope from it. Work practices resulting from this learning loop are concrete, detailed, specific, and operative—in fact, they tend to lose their value when taken away from the specific situation in which they were developed and are used. From a different perspective, work practices are the first step in the firm's "internalization" of resources. Mastering the usage of a spreadsheet by an individual or a team in a specific department is an example of this type of learning.

A second transformation "abstracts" and "constructs" capabilities from existing work practices. Several characteristics connote this learning process: (1) it involves combining emerging work practices and organizational routines; (2) its outcome has a far-reaching potential impact, as capabilities convey what an organization is capable of doing if properly triggered in a variety of situations; (3) capabilities can be easily described in terms of *what* they do and *how* they do it, but *why* they do it is taken for granted, not necessarily well defined and rarely challenged; and (4) capabilities are more abstract than work practices: they are "skills without a place" that can be transferred across the organization (such as, e.g., a quality control capability). We call this the *capability learning loop*. KM at this "lower" level results in a continuously improving set of capabilities—specialized and idiosyncratic ways of using resources for given purposes. These purposes are functionally well defined and rather stable over time, although how they are attained may change, for example, with the emergence of a radically new technology (resource) or a revolutionary new use of an old resource (Penrose 1959). The driving force for continuous capability improvement is static efficiency (Ghemawat and Ricart 1993). Such learning processes tend to occur spontaneously, but the organizational climate and context, the incentive, power, and motivational systems, and, last but not least, the technology, affect deeply the learning that can be observed in different organizations. Although efficient, capabilities lack a sense of *why* they exist or at least the reasons for their existence are seldom challenged. The know-how needed to prepare "professional" sales forecasts is an example of what we mean by capabilities here. The "why" appears with

more clarity as they evolve into *core* capabilities through a third learning loop (see figure 32.1).

Thus, capabilities can evolve into core capabilities, which differentiate a company strategically (Grant 1991). There are two main factors that contribute to the selection of which capabilities have the potential to become core: the competitive environment and the business mission of the firm. When faced with its competitive environment, a firm learns whether some capabilities have strategic potential (whether they are valuable, rare, etc.). A converse influence, from core capabilities to capabilities also exists through the competitive environment, as (1) core capabilities of different firms competing in an industry define the "standards of excellence" for that industry—they can elicit which capabilities a firm should develop in order to compete effectively; (2) when confronted with a given environment, capabilities acquire a sense of *why* they are important, thus revealing more clearly their role and scope. A firm's business mission is relevant for identifying the core capabilities because it sets priorities in the alignment between them and the current mission. In turn, core capabilities can enable new business missions which, if accepted, may trigger new "capabilities—core capabilities" transformations. These interrelationships are captured by the *strategic learning loop*, which links capabilities and core capabilities (see figure 32.1). Note that also the strategic loop takes place within the firm's organizational (formative) context, and so it is "structured" by it (Giddens 1984). In turn, its outcome—core capabilities—can reshape the context itself. This subset of capabilities can be described and understood not only in terms of what they do and how they do it but also in terms of *why*: the realm of dynamic efficiency. For example, changes in the environment can make a highly efficient (in the static sense) capability worthless, because it is irrelevant for competing under new circumstances. To continue with the example above, the development of idiosyncratic ways of preparing useful sales forecasts based on the distinct strategic positioning of a firm is an illustration of a how a core capability might develop. Understanding the market and its function in "the firm's own way," resulting from its particular positioning and experience, permits it to apply forecasting capabilities (based even on standard procedures and algorithms) in a much more effective and focused way, to the point of becoming fundamental for the firm's competitive advantages. A case in point is that of Dell Com-

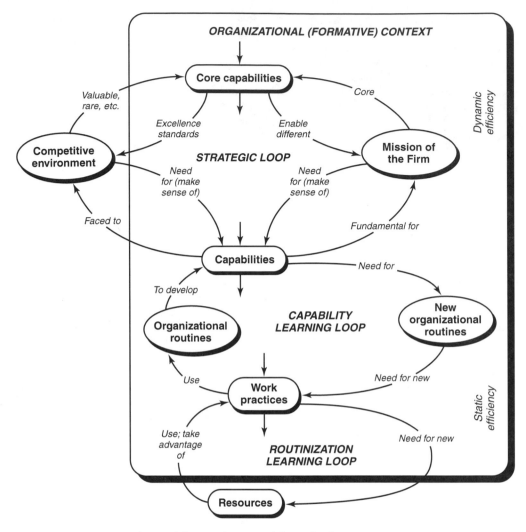

Figure 32.1 Learning in the capabilities and core capabilities development processes.

puter, which can improve significantly its relationships with suppliers because it knows its clients so well that good, detailed forecasts are the norm, while their competitors cannot do it (Dell 1998).

Finally, consider how organizational inertia can limit learning. To drastically change the context where learning takes place is a difficult endeavor, although sometimes necessary—for example, to respond to radical shifts in the environment and/or business mission. However, radical changes in the business mission are not likely to occur, as its definition and meaning correspond closely to a given organizational context. Revolutionary changes in organizational context or business mission require radical

learning, for example, becoming aware of what the extant context is and explicitly stepping out of it in order to innovate (Argyris and Schön 1996).

In sum, the ladder involves three main learning loops. One basic loop routinizes work practices and indirectly routines, while using resources; a second one combines work practices and organizational routines to form capabilities; and the third loop gives meaning to capabilities in the context of the firm's competitive environment and business mission, thus allowing the selection and elicitation of core capabilities. The knowledge of which capabilities are distinctive and fundamental to competition is strategic in nature and becomes part of the organizational (formative) context in which all the firm's activities, including learning, occur. Changing such a formative context may involve a fourth (double-loop) learning process.

The KM implications of the learning ladder for the single firm case are quite straightforward. While in the routine learning loop, the spontaneous unfolding of tacit knowledge takes place, routinization implies the systematic effort to make larger portions of this knowledge explicit for repetitive use. Thus, we find KM practices trying to strike a balance between robust, but implicit routines and routines that through formalization become standard operating procedures. Information systems can be used in various ways to enable such processes. Groupware applications can enhance the informal transfer of knowledge within specific communities of practice or teams. On the other hand, workflow applications can deal with the more formalized steps of the tasks being performed. Finally, ERP (Enterprise Resource Planning) applications take care of cross-functional and interdependent procedures. In general, we can look at KM as an activity dedicated to the transfer of useful knowledge embedded in routines throughout the organization; that is, it takes care of the cultivation and diffusion of competencies, and their selection and alignment with the prevailing business strategy. Various mechanisms can be deployed to this end.

In particular, BPR (Business Process Reengineering) and ERP can be harnessed to formalize and "freeze" capabilities into standard ways of operating. But capabilities cannot be put into software alone: organizational and educational processes may be also necessary. Knowledge management related to core capabilities focuses on creating opportunities for identifying the most competitive matches between capabilities and an adequate reading of the market and the environment in general. Knowledge management should be dedicated to create occasions for the effective mixing of inside and outside knowledge. Intelligence systems can be one important resource in this respect, together with the singling out of individuals and teams who possess "boundary spanning" roles and capabilities. Finally, KM for radical learning consists in staging activities and settings conducive to reflection in action by the key members of the organization. Education and outside consulting expertise can also play a decisive role. Attempts have been made to use simulation packages aimed at en-

hancing systems thinking and learning in action (Senge 1990).

Beyond the Borders: Interorganizational Learning Ladders

What happens to the learning ladder and to the related KM policies when two or more firms adopt a cooperative strategy and engage in some form of alliance (ranging from joint venture to merger)? In a successful alliance it is likely that the learning ladders of the partners will intertwine, almost like a DNA double helix (in the case of two firms): in this way, knowledge gets shared across separate organizations, and new knowledge is developed in the process. The learning ladder remains a useful tool to depict the ways in which such knowledge sharing and developing processes take place and to reflect on how they should be managed (see figure 32.2).

Again, the teachings and models coming from business strategy can be of help in analyzing the opportunities and outcomes of the recombination of separate knowledge processes and stocks. Specifically, the "relational" view of the strategic advantage coming from interfirm links and resources offers interesting insights (Dyer and Singh 1998). While the early resource-based view of strategy focuses on the advantage generated by key "core" assets and capabilities, the frequency of alliances, especially in very dynamic and innovative sectors, suggests that there is another source of competitive advantage. This one stems from the establishment of unique interfirm linkages, which in themselves can become a distinct source of relational quasi-rents. In other words, the firm's valuable resources do not necessarily lie only within its boundaries. They may now extend beyond them. The recombination of separate learning ladders becomes the paramount mechanism through which one can see how new knowledge, routines, and competencies are uniquely produced and exploited by the allied firms.

Under normal, arm's length market relationships, learning ladders of separate firms do not mix. Knowledge is transferred from one ladder to the other through intermediaries, who trade services and products available through the market. Standardized goods and services which embed knowledge (Demsetz 1993) are traded with minimal communication (i.e., the price) across separable technological and functional interfaces.

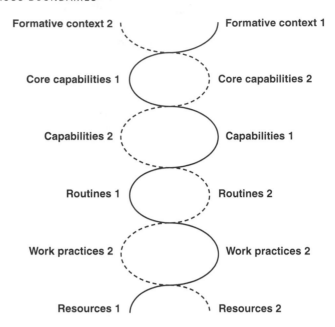

Figure 32.2 Interorganizational learning ladders.

Successful alliances, instead, transform standardized relationships into unique ones through various mechanisms, such as investments in relation-specific assets; recombination of capabilities and routines; developing distinctive know-how; establishing a common experience and joint practices; or developing a new jointly spoken language that facilitates cooperation. All these mechanisms favor the nonmarket transfer and recombination of knowledge and learning (Doz 1996). For example, close partnerships with lead users create significant opportunities for the improvement and reinvention of products and services (von Hippel 1994).

The learning ladder can become a tool to better identify such processes already pointed out by the R&D and innovation literature and highlight relevant management issues. Interlocking learning ladders can generate value in various ways by showing where the potential for knowledge sharing, recombination, and transfer is. Valuable know-how can be attained by mixing/transferring capabilities, by placing resources and routines within new contexts, or by letting existing practices being molded by different capabilities form new routines.

To be sure, governance is paramount in securing compatibility, transferability, and value generation. First, effective governance must look for a smooth interlocking process. Various aspects must be taken care of by asking questions such as: Is the core competence of one organization *compatible* with the other firm's formative context, portfolio of competencies, routines, systems, and resources? Second, can it be *transferred* to the other firm? Finally, can it lead to new mixes with existing resources and routines, leading to new combinations, to the *generation* of different practices and knowledge? One can ask these questions systematically, as shown in figure 32.3, and arrive at conclusions for every relevant cell in the table.

Once having verified this basic level of interlocking, specific aspects that may lead to relational rents should be considered. Examples are: uniqueness of the matching (due to partners scarcity or special bundling of resources); time required to achieve the fusion between the ladders; institutional factors that may favor a certain type of combination, etc. The interlocking of the ladders provides a map, like the "double helix," that points out key aspects for the governance of those knowledge transfers that can be the source of relational rents. Systems can play a crucial role, too. First, at the infrastructure or sheer resource level, issues of compatibility and data transfer emerge immediately. Many ERP or legacy systems may actually block the implementation of alliances because of incompatibility. On the other hand, IT is a resource that can be creatively reinvented by adopting another organization's competencies thanks to the alliance. Or the infrastructure might act as a carrier of a formative context, not only of procedures: this

	Formative context 2	Core capability 2	Capability 2	Routine 2	Work practice 2	Resource 2
Formative context 1						
Core capability 1						
Capability 1						
Routine 1				Compatible? Transferable? Innovation?		
Work practice 1						
Resource 1	Compatible? Transferable? Innovation?					

Figure 32.3 Governance questions for the interlocking of two learning ladders.

can have a deep and wide-ranging influence on the practices and routines of the other firm. These possibilities should be thought through as much as possible beforehand, since they may impact the level of actual collaboration between firms having different systems.

Consider as an example the evolving relationships between suppliers and customers for new product development in the car industry (Ciborra 1999). Instead of relying on huge internal design departments, most car manufacturers today subcontract partially the design of a new car to outside design firms or ateliers. Such smaller, specialized firms seem to offer to this highly qualified workforce a working environment more open to creativity and innovation. The management of the close relationship between the car manufacturer and the external design atelier consists in finding a good match between the respective CAD (computer-aided design) platforms (the level of technical resources) and between a more bureaucratic formative context (the large car manufacturer) and the team or project formative context typical of the design firm. A further challenge is combining the efficiency capability of the manufacturer with the innovation capability of the design firm. Relatedly, the creative working routines developed in the use of CAD in the design atelier need to be

made to fit with the efficiency capabilities of the manufacturer, and so on. Common computer platforms and applications can be designed only if they are compatible with the multiple balances that have to be struck between the two different learning ladders. For example, the extension of an ERP application from the manufacturer to the design firm may be difficult to execute: the idiosyncratic routines in the design firm being of a different style from the (formal) ones most frequently found in the manufacturer. On the other hand, groupware applications may be better suited for the lower level of formalization typical of the design firm routines, and they can provide useful extra channels of communication between designers and managers at the two sites.

In addition, all the activities deriving from the ladder interlocking process are bound, by their very nature, to be *collective*, in the sense of involving always more than one individual. In such a situation, collective learning and knowledge become paramount. As Andreu and Sieber (2001) point out, one important kind of collective knowledge has to do with coordination schemes, fundamental to putting collective action (routines, for example) to work. Furthermore, coordination schemes are often implicit, with the implication that their development and transfer must be based on processes that cannot be easily formalized and codified. The issue is further complicated by the fact that the routines and capabilities to be coordinated come from different contexts that puts even more pressure on the corresponding coordination schemes. Other collective bits of knowledge and capabilities have to do with how individual decisions or visions are integrated into group decisions. All these aspects point out areas where *innovation*, in the sense of generating new routines and capabilities of a collective nature, will probably have to be carefully considered. As suggested by the third type of question shown in the table of figure 32.3, it is not only a matter of compatibility or transferability, but also of how compatible and transferable practices, routines, and capabilities coming from different firms can be newly *combined* and coordinated. To be sure, systems can help to achieve this; for example, workflow-based applications and communication infrastructures can contribute to set the basis for coordination, but only to the extent that the latter can be made explicit and codified.

From the Learning Ladders to the Learning Community

A high number and density of alliances characterize knowledge intensive industries. But the emerging networks of knowledge intensive firms are much more complex and intertwined than a cluster comprising few, even if large, companies. These networks have a different shape and require distinct coordination and governance mechanisms.

Typically, firms in technology-sophisticated industries may execute every phase of their activity through some form of collaboration. This affects all the functional areas, from production to R&D, from marketing to distribution. In industries in which know-how is critical, like telecommunications, software, or pharmaceutical, companies cooperate with private research labs, universities, foundations, and other firms at the same time (Powell et al. 1996). In such an emerging pattern of relationships, it becomes more and more difficult to identify distinct clusters of recombined learning ladders. It is hard to separate the strings and their connections in this entangled, spaghetti-like configuration of resources, practices, routines, and capabilities derived from the fusion of knowledge inputs being provided by the various participants. That is, knowledge creation or recombination occur

among the members of a fluid community composed of very different organizations. The hard-to-distinguish *spillovers* or *overflows* (Callon 1998) of know-how prevail in number, volume, and importance over the *planned* or *managed transfer* of knowledge (Steinmueller 1996). Transfer is superseded by spillover through interstices. Spillovers are the knowledge by-products of activities and modes of operating of the participants. Just by being immersed in this flow and breathing its "atmosphere" (Marshall 1930) one can tap into this invisible social knowledge capital generated by the very interaction between multiple participants. Computer networks like the Internet, or the ubiquitous mobile phones, facilitate significantly such informal sharing and the rapid, uncontrollable spread of spillovers. Finally, "boundary objects" (Star and Ruhleder 1996), like standards, systems, or applications which are widely exchanged or used by members of the community, constitute an important "knowledge infrastructure" (Steinmueller 1996) that further facilitates the efficient exchange and recombination of new knowledge coming simultaneously from multiple sources and flowing to other destinations.

As for individuals, here learning takes place through the practice of membership in such an evolving community (Brown and Duguid 1991). However, it is hard to locate precisely the know-how. Knowledge is simultaneously highly sophisticated (both tacit and explicit) and widely dispersed, in the hands and minds of many, not easily produced or captured inside the boundaries of one or a few firms. Rare knowledge is neither located inside the organization nor reliably available for purchase through the market (hence, the two main mechanisms for transfer of knowledge listed by Demsetz (1993) seem to fail: only the one based on educating and learning obtains, but at a community and informal level).

As an example of this third type of KM and work organization, consider the development of the Linux operating system, and, in general, the so-called open source software. Linux is an operating system (OS), derived from a Unix kernel, that can compete on stability and reliability with current OS. Apart from the technical differences, Linux is at odds with most of the commercial OS for the way it has been developed. Huge numbers of programmers coordinating only through the Internet have been able to casually hack onto Linux. Software quality has been attained not only through hierarchical controls, as would happen in large organizations deploying structured software engineering methodologies, but also through ongoing simultaneous, multiple peer reviews over the Net. Continuous weekly releases of the software were examined and corrected by hundreds of programmers within days (Raymond 1999). This example is paradigmatic, although it involves some special features, like a final product that on the one hand, in terms of knowledge is very explicit (codified) with an internal structure (that of an OS) very well known to the participants, and on the other, being a "digital good," is very well suited not only to be transferred over the communication infrastructure but also to actually be tested and redesigned using a standard terminal device like the personal computer.

Several features of this case relate to KM and relevant organizational aspects. First, in a knowledge intensive business, one can get a quality service/product *not* through hierarchical organization but through a highly dispersed community of knowledge workers (who, however, know well the overall structure of the product). Principles like Brook's (1982) one-man month (adding another resource to a software project cuts down completion time only marginally) does not apply to a loosely connected, floating pool of numerous programmers. In this new context, instead, an added person means an extra couple of eyeballs that can scrutinize the newly released program in order to find the bugs overlooked so far. In this loosely organized community, there are no strict and explicit economic incentives at work, rather symbolic ones: for example, to be recognized as a smart person in the hacker community. Developers involved in this project have shown to be able not to be too territorial and perform "egoless programming" (Weinberg 1971). Sophisticated and innovative knowledge sharing mechanisms have been put in place, too. For example, spillovers are institutionalized through the "copyleft" practice, by which anyone is given permission to run, modify, and redistribute a program. Meeting places have been created for the explicit or informal sharing of knowledge: these are dedicated portals on the Internet (Ljunberg 2000). The formative context that molds such KM devices seems to be more inspired by the atmosphere of an academic and scientific community rather than a profit-oriented business organization.

In sum, the development of Linux challenges many of the economic assumptions that underlie the economics of strategy and organization, especially for knowledge intensive, not fully commoditized businesses, where communication, coordination, and distribution of competencies exist, and there are serious problems of robustness, reliability, and scalability. In particular, the case highlights that

- peer groups of a very large size can function without being bogged down by coordination and communication bottlenecks (thanks to the Internet and coordination tools built into the software environment);
- simultaneous or asynchronous work can take place without the need for strict sequencing or planning;
- opportunism and free riding do not seem to emerge as major issues that undermine efficient coordination. Symbolic rewards, altruism, and a gift economy seem to hold instead (Raymond 1999);
- private property of the final product is not an issue either. There are alternative business models, whereby gains can be obtained through the provision of complementary services;
- hierarchical organization does not need to come into the picture to replace a team (Alchian and Demsetz 1972) or a market arrangement (Williamson 1975). Linux has been developed by a large peer group coordinated by a "benevolent dictator," who did not appropriate the results of the cooperative effort.

The upshot is that such an Internet-based organization can defy some of the principles that keep together traditional hierarchical organizations. From a KM perspective, what emerges is an organizational form that is able to tap into the brainpower of entire communities; it is not territorial and fragmented; and it is not secretive and hostile, nor plagued by opportunism. The principles of "divide et impera" and "knowledge is power," which are pivotal in hierarchical organizations, do not seem to have a significant impact here (Fransman 1996). There are further peculiar differences. For example, from an economic perspective, the development organization of Linux is in contrast with the evolutionary theory of the firm (Nelson and Winter 1982). Such a theory takes for granted, on the basis of the feedback principle, that the firm is a repository of routines (embedding knowledge and skills) hierarchically arranged: short-run routines take care of operations; investment routines and higher-order routines modify over time the lower operating routines. Linux shows that a productive and knowledge intensive "organization" can literally consist of a knowing community, where one can identify routines and skills of the members, but these, despite their large number and the feedback processes going on all the time, are not hierarchically arranged.

To be sure, the resource-based view of strategy falters as well in this new context. According to such a view, a firm is seen as a repository of know-how and its competitive advantage is seen deriving from the possession of that know-how (the firm knows better than other firms how to organize work). Scholars point out that the distinctive competence of the firm would consist of those organizational capabilities that are able to organize, merge, and govern activities (or lower level operating routines) (Dosi et al. 1998). Instead, thanks to the new infrastructure, the knowledge intensity of the businesses and the very nature of the business itself (software production), the notion of firm as a hierarchy of routines does not hold, if not as an inefficient organization (plagued by the negative consequences of Brooks'principle).

Consequently, we are facing an altogether different business model, where the principles of doing business *à la* resource-based view of strategy seem to be turned upside down. Value in Linux (and Internet) increases with widespread use and open access. By adding (openly) new features, users increase the value of the infrastructure (a network externality typical in the "new economy" due to increasing returns to scale on the demand side), which in turn becomes the platform for new business initiatives, especially complementary services that can be sold in a market. The last characteristic is not unrelated to the fact that the primary "product" (an OS in the Linux case) is a "digital good" with high "production" costs and very low "reproduction" costs (i.e., with increasing returns to scale on the supply side; see Shapiro and Varian 1999). The latter cost structure makes the quest for complementary services a natural move to generate income.

The cases of Linux, the Internet, and the role played by the hacker community are not only confined to the software industry. One can find similar configurations and dynamics also in other research environments, like the genome project or nuclear physics. Once again, in contrast with the single firm and its closed R&D, focused on control over territoriality of results, practices, and tools, we can observe across the boundaries of the firm and its R&D activities an analogy with the industrial districts (Marshall 1930, Richardson 1972), where synergy and atmosphere caused by diffused knowledge made available to the members of the district benefits everybody. Such knowledge is the side product of a web of informal and unpredictable knowledge spillovers.

Conclusions

In this chapter we have used the learning ladder model to examine which KM and governance approaches are more appropriate in order to foster the development of key capabilities to achieve competitive advantages in different organizational settings. While in the case of a single firm the implications are straightforward and even well known, in the other two cases analyzed, namely, the interorganizational and community settings, the implications are less obvious and eye opening.

In the interorganizational setting, although consistent with ideas already set forth in the mergers and alliances literature, the learning ladder model provides a framework from which useful insights can be derived. New sources of distinctive competitive elements emerge if one assumes a relational view of strategic advantage, which conceptualizes them as rooted in unique interfirm linkages. The framework provides a basis for a detailed analysis, taking into account how the components of different learning ladders in various firms fit or don't fit. In addition, realizing that the interfirm case inevitably involves collective processes makes apparent that a new dimension has to be taken into account also at the structural level. We submit that the role that systems, applications, and technology can play in the corresponding processes may be better analyzed in the context of the proposed framework than in the common practice of today, where partnerships usually bring along surprises regarding the incompatibility of resources, skills, and systems, besides cultures. Looking at the intertwined ladders can finally help the difficult task of governance of the partnership, from a distinct KM perspective.

Finally, the knowledge community case, for which examples begin to abound in knowledge intensive industries, involves "spillover" processes rather than planned or managed transfers of know-how. This third setting suggests an interesting oxymoron: Precisely in knowledge intensive contexts, knowledge creation, deployment, and application for the purpose of attaining a sustainable competitive advantage seem to be less rooted in the basic principles that contributed to conceiving knowledge as a fundamental source of advantage in the first place. In addition, when "digital goods" are involved, some principles of the "new economy" may apply, in particular, increasing returns to scale both in the demand and the supply side. More research and better models are needed to pursue this case further, but the puzzle is served.

Notes

Many thanks to Africa Ariño, Frank Land, Sandra Sieber, Edgar Whitley and the editors of this volume for their useful comments.

1. A formative context is defined as "the set of preexisting institutional arrangements, cognitive frames and imageries that actors bring and routinely enact in a situation of action" (Ciborra and Lanzara 1994, Unger 1987). It thus comprises both the interpretive frames and the organizational routines that influence problem solving in organizations. Learning new routines is a single-loop process. Restructuring a context implies double-loop learning (Argyris and Schön 1996).

References

Alchian, A.A. and Demsetz, H. (1972) "Production, information costs and economic organization." *American Economic Review* 62:777–95.

Andreu, R. and Ciborra, C. (1996) "Core capabilities and information technology: An organizational learning approach," in B. Moingeon and A. Edmonson, (eds.), *Organizational Learning and Competitive Advantage*. London: Sage Publications.

Andreu, R. and Sieber, S. (2001) "Organizational learning and knowledge management: What is the link?" in Y. Malhotra (ed.), *Knowledge Management and Business Model Innovation*. Hershey, PA: Idea Group Publishing.

Argyris, C. and Schön, D. (1996) *Organizational Learning II: A Theory of Action Perspective*. Reading, MA: Addison-Wesley.

Barney, J. (1991) "Firm resources and sustained competitive advantage." *Journal of Management* 17(1).

Brooks, F.P. (1982) *The Mythical Man-Month*. Reading, MA: Addison-Wesley.

Brown, J.S. and Duguid, P. (1991) "Organizational learning and communities of practice: Toward a unified view of working, learning and innovation." *Organization Science* 2(1):40–57.

Callon, M. (1998) *The Laws of the Market*. Oxford: Blackwell.

Ciborra, C.U. (1999) "The transaction costs analysis of the customer-supplier relationship in product development," in A. Baskin et al. (eds.), *Cooperative Knowledge Processing*. Amsterdam: Kluwer.

Ciborra, C.U. and Lanzara, G.F. (1994) "Formative contexts and information technology." *Accounting, Management and Information Technology* 4:611–26.

Dell, M. (1998) Interview with Joan Magretta. *Harvard Business Review* (March–April).

Demsetz, H. (1993) "The theory of the firm revisited," in O.E. Williamson and S.G. Winter (eds.), *The Nature of the Firm*. Oxford: Oxford University Press.

Dosi, G., Teece, D., and Chytry, J. (eds.) (1998) *Technology, Organization and Competitiveness*. Oxford: Oxford University Press.

Doz, Y.L. (1996) "The evolution of cooperation in strategic alliances: Initial conditions or learning processes?" *Strategic Management Journal* 17: 55–83.

Dyer, J.H. and Singh, H. (1998) "The relational view: Cooperative strategy and sources of interorganizational competitive advantage." *Academy of Management Review* 23(4):660–679.

Fransman, M. (1996) "Information, knowledge, vision and the theory of the firm," in P.J. Buckley, and F.J. Michie (eds.), *Firms, Organizations and Contracts*. Oxford: Oxford University Press.

Giddens, A. (1984) *The Constitution of Society*. Berkeley: University of California Press.

Ghemawat, P. and Ricart, J.E. (1993) "The organizational tension between static and dynamic efficiency." Research paper, IESE.

Grant, R.M. (1991) "The resource-based theory of competitive advantage: Implications for strategy formulation." *California Management Review* (Spring).

Lave, J. and Wegner, E. (1991) *Situated Learning: Legitimate Peripheral Participation*. Cambridge: Cambridge University Press.

Leonard-Barton, D. (1992) "Core capabilities and core rigidities: A paradox in managing new product development." *Strategic Management Journal* 13:111–115.

Ljunberg, J. (2000) "Open source movements as a model for organizing." ECIS Proceedings, Vienna, July.

Marshall, A. (1930) *Principles of Economics*. London: Macmillan.

Nelson, R.R. and Winter, S.G. (1982) *An Evolutionary Theory of Economic Change*. Cambridge: Belknap.

Nonaka, I. and Takeuchi, K. (1995) *The Knowledge Creating Company*. New York: Oxford University Press.

Penrose, E. (1959) *The Theory of the Growth of the Firm*. London: Basil Blackwell.

Powell, W.W., Koput, K.W., and Smith-Doerr, L. (1996) "Interorganizational collaboration and the locus of innovation networks of learning in biotechnology." *Administrative Science Quarterly* 41:116–145.

Prahalad, C.K. and Hamel, G. (1990) "The core competence of the corporation." *Harvard Business Review* 68(3).

Raymond, E.S. (1999) *The Cathedral and the Bazaar*. Sebastopol, CA: O'Reilly.

Richardson, G. (1972) "The organization of industry." *Economic Journal* 82(September):883–896.

Senge, P. (1990) *The Fifth Discipline: The Art and Practice of the Learning Organization*. New York: Doubleday.

Shapiro, C.L. and Varian, H.R. (1999) *Information Rules*. Boston: Harvard Business School Press.

Star, S.L. and Ruhleder, K. (1996) "Steps towards an ecology of infrastructure: Design and access for large information spaces." *Information Systems Research* 7(1):111–34.

Steinmueller, W.E. (1996) "Technological infrastructure in information technology industries," in M. Teubal, et al. (ed.), *Technological Infrastructure Policy*. Amsterdam: Kluwer.

von Hippel, E. (1994) *Sources of Innovation*. Oxford: Oxford University Press.

Unger, R.M. (1987) *False Necessity*. Cambridge: Cambridge University Press.

Weinberg, G.M. (1971) *The Psychology of Computer Programming*. New York: Van Nostrand.

Williamson, O.E. (1975) *Markets and Hierarchies: Analysis and Antitrust Implications*. New York: Free Press.

33

Bridging Knowledge Gaps

Learning in Geographically Dispersed Cross-Functional Development Teams

Deborah Sole and Amy Edmondson

Organizational learning centrally involves an organization's ability to develop novel, innovative products and processes that respond to existing and emerging market needs. Such innovation is often accomplished through combining previously unconnected bodies of knowledge or combining existing knowledge in novel ways (Grant 1996, Schumpeter 1934). In recent years, the study and implementation of organizational forms that facilitate the exchange and combination of different kinds of knowledge has increased, and management research has paid considerable attention to different types of knowledge as a source of competitive advantage. This chapter explores geographically dispersed cross-functional teams as a way of integrating diverse knowledge in development projects.

Sources of Knowledge Diversity

In the context of product and process development, researchers have shown that the knowledge of individual contributors varies according to both what one does (occupation) and where one is (context). Individuals trained in a particular discipline, function, or occupation have substantial conceptual and practical knowledge in common with others from that discipline or occupation (e.g., Fleck 1997). They share terminology (Arrow 1974) and mental frameworks (Vicenti 1990) that act as shorthand—facilitating the efficiency of communication among them. From his in-depth study of a case of collective problem-solving—finding a cure for syphilis—Ludwig Fleck concluded that different occupations act as distinct "thought worlds" (Douglas 1986) having different *funds of knowledge* (what members know) and *systems of meaning* (how members know). Dougherty (1992) applied these concepts to organizational functions undertaking product development and noted that, even though different functional communities were exposed to the same product development circumstances, team members from different functions understood those circumstances differently, selectively perceiving certain aspects as salient and drawing different implications. Recent research (Barley and Bechky 1994, Bechky 1999) has focused on "occupational knowledge" particular to different communities such as engineers, technicians, and operators. Bechky (1999) suggested that even within the development function, occupational knowledge is sufficiently diverse as to require "translation" in order for adequate understanding to emerge.

Other organizational researchers have focused on how learning takes place in particular contexts and emphasized the unique—context specific—knowledge acquired in this way (e.g., Brown and Duguid 1991, Fleck 1997, Lave and Wenger 1990, Tyre and von Hippel 1997). The concept of situated knowledge has emerged as a way of understanding a gestalt-like awareness of a particular task situation, often involving tools and equipment, physical conditions, or even other people, within which activities are capably accomplished (e.g., Brown and Duguid 1991, Lave and Wenger 1990). In their analysis of the work of photocopier technicians, Brown and Duguid emphasized the role of *noncanonical* knowledge that emerges from the process of undertaking a task and experiencing it as "structured by the constantly changing conditions of work and the world" (1991, p. 41). Tyre and von Hippel (1997) note that organizational settings contain different kinds of clues about the underlying issues, offer different resources for generating and analyzing information, and evoke different assumptions on the part of problem solvers; thus, people learn through being physically present in a specific setting.

Contextual knowledge also pertains to the broader milieu of the working environment (Fleck 1997). Many authors have noted the existence of knowledge that resides in systemic routines or ways of interacting, describing such knowledge variously as *organizing principles* (Kogut and Zander 1992), *embedded knowledge* (Badaracco 1991, Collins 1983, Granovetter 1985), and *organizational routines* (Levitt and March 1988, Nelson and Winter 1982). Contextual knowledge is developed through repetitive collective action and is "expressed in regularities by which members cooperate in a social community (i.e., group, organization, network)" (Kogut and Zander 1992, p. 383). It comprises knowledge of appropriate methods and resources, contributing to communication and task efficiencies and task effectiveness by leveraging taken-for-granted meanings associated with particular behavior within a specific setting. These associations and behaviors are learned over time

from working in a specific setting, and so they are unlikely to be common knowledge among people who are not colocated. In addition, because contextual knowledge tends to be taken for granted by members of a community, it is not easily articulated to members of other communities.

Designing for Knowledge Diversity

Managers have employed different organizational designs to facilitate the exchange and combination of knowledge in the development process. One such design mechanism is the use of cross-functional teams—project groups with members drawn from more than one functional area such as engineering, manufacturing, and marketing (Brown and Eisenhardt 1995, p. 367). The use of cross-functional groups in product development has consistently been linked to development process performance (see review by Brown and Eisenhardt 1995, Clark and Fujimoto 1991, Dougherty 1992, Zirger and Maidique 1990). Using team members from different intellectual and occupational backgrounds increases the likelihood of combining knowledge in novel or creative ways—by bringing diverse skills, abilities, and knowledge and cognitive styles jointly to bear on an issue (Leonard 1995, Madhavan and Grover 1998). Cross-functional group composition increases the amount and variety of information available to the development project members, enabling discovery and evaluation of different design alternatives from a number of perspectives (Brown and Eisenhardt 1995). Such teams are employed to respond quickly, creatively, and flexibly to problems—capabilities considered critical in highly complex, uncertain, or nonroutine environments.

Recently, geographically dispersed cross-functional groups also have been espoused for enhancing innovation, especially in research and development activities (Boutellier et al. 1998, De Meyer 1991, 1993, Gorton and Motwani 1996, Leonard et al. 1998, Madhavan and Grover 1998, Prokesch 1997). In part, this is pragmatic. Often, assembling the ideal functionally representative group requires some degree of dispersion of its members, because commercial offices are often physically separated from production sites, and sales representatives are regularly on the road visiting clients. In addition, as industrial competence has become increasingly geographically dispersed, specialized knowledge is sought not only from different functions and occupational backgrounds but also, by design, from members in different cultural localities (Leonard et al. 1998). Input from dispersed knowledgeable resources is expected to facilitate understanding of and communication with international clients, operations, and suppliers (Boutellier et al. 1998) and to enhance learning (De Meyer 1993, Prokesch 1997). The use of *virtual teams*— geographically dispersed teams supported by communication and information technologies— is a way of responding to the dispersion of essential employees in downsized and lean organizations and of facilitating access to key expertise (Leonard et al. 1998, Townsend et al. 1998).

Effects of Knowledge Diversity

In spite of the apparent advantages of designing teams for knowledge diversity, it is by no means clear *how* team members make effective use of this knowledge. Substantial empirical evidence suggests that knowledge diversity—and member heterogeneity in general—may be both a blessing and a burden. Despite the enthusiasm for heterogeneity of team composition in the product development literature, considerable research on groups shows that heterogeneous groups face substantial hurdles to effectiveness. In particular, research in social psychology suggests that groups with member homogeneity outperform those with heterogeneous members (see Williams and O'Reilly 1998).

Difficulties in recognizing and interpreting different perspectives have been identified across functional organizational units (Dougherty 1992) and occupational workgroups (Bechky 1999). Dougherty showed that functional groups failed to effectively synthesize and leverage their expertise precisely *because* of their diversity, which acted as an "interpretive barrier." She concluded that cross-functional teams performed better when they combine their perspectives in a highly interactive, iterative fashion (Dougherty 1992). Bechky's research highlighted how technicians, juggling multiple sets of terminologies and frames of reference, fulfilled critical interpretive roles between different occupational groups. In the absence of this translating role, communications faltered between engineers and assemblers. The tactic of relying upon such translators, whose interpretive skill is drawn from working in a specific context, is unlikely to be realistic in a dispersed team setting, where members are often constrained in their opportunities to interact face to face. Similarly, research on technology transfer suggests that absorptive capacity—the ability to comprehend newly acquired information—depends heavily on the existence of prior complementary knowledge bases (Cohen and Levinthal 1990, Szulanski 1995). These findings suggest that exchange difficulties will be more prevalent across occupations than within occupations, where substantial conceptual and practical knowledge is already shared.

In addition, when knowledge is contextually embedded, it becomes increasingly difficult to share that knowledge when the type or degree of interaction cannot adequately convey the context. Knowledge that is action-oriented, such as skill in using a piece of equipment, cannot be fully codified in words, symbols, or procedural instructions. In Polanyi's words: "we can know more than we can tell" (Polanyi 1966, p. 10). Nonaka and Takeuchi (1995) emphasized the need for proximity and ongoing relationships of project participants as they share tacit knowledge through both dialogue and activity. Similarly, Tyre and von Hippel (1997) provided examples of sharing interactions that occurred only when engineers had opportunities to interact with colleagues in particular physical contexts. Therefore, although collaborators from different sites might share formal disciplinary knowledge, associated cultural meanings and ways of doing things often do not transfer intact among them. For example, in a study of collaboration between a British and a Japanese engineering firm, Lam (1997) observed that the dominant form of knowledge held, but its degree of tacitness and the way in which it was structured, utilized, and transmitted varied considerably between the two firms. The socially embedded nature of their respective engineering knowledge impeded cross-border collaborative work and knowledge transfer (Lam 1997). This study showed that regional differences in socially embedded knowledge can impede effective collaboration and suggests that intraorganizational teams also can be affected by regional or site-level differences.

The dual influences of knowledge diversity are reflected in sociological and social psychological findings on group heterogeneity as measured by demographic characteristics (Williams and O'Reilly 1998). Research in organizational demographics (e.g., O'Reilly et al. 1989, Pfeffer 1983, Tsui et al. 1992) explores how diversity in external observable traits, such as age, race, and gender, influences psychological and behavioral outcomes. Demographic diversity is not expected to be beneficial in itself, but only to the extent that it represents other diversity, such as of information, values, or perspective (Jehn et al. 1999)—although this may not always be the case (e.g., Tsui and O'Reilly 1989). Similarly, cultural diversity research studies members' social backgrounds and highlights the effects of demographic variables presupposed to relate directly to cultural attributes, values, and perceptions. Cultural diversity is often portrayed as beneficial because of the variety of perspectives, values, skills, and attributes that team members contribute as a result of their different experiences (Masnevski 1994).

Some findings do indeed suggest that demographically diverse groups outperform homogeneous groups (Hoffman 1978, Hoffman and Maier 1961), and too much similarity and group cohesion can result in groupthink with its associated performance losses (Janis 1982). Related research on minority influence also finds that, for some tasks, a "dissenting voice" leads to better group solutions (Moscovici 1976, Nemeth 1986).

In contrast, some research (Ancona and Caldwell 1992, Williams and O'Reilly 1998) concludes that increased diversity in intact working groups and project teams may have dysfunctional effects on group process and performance. In addition, member similarity in demographic characteristics has been positively associated with team effectiveness and interpersonal attraction (Hambrick and Mason 1984, Tsui et al. 1992), and homogeneous members report stronger affinity for their teams than heterogeneous team members (Ibarra 1992). In general, the relationship between group heterogeneity and performance is mixed—and most likely depends upon task and contextual factors (McGrath 1984, Williams and O'Reilly 1998).

Effects of Team Dispersion

An emerging literature on virtual teams (e.g., Alavi and Yoo 1997, Cramton 2001, Cramton and Webber 1999, Duarte and Snyder 1999, Gorton and Motwani 1996, Jarvenpaa and Leidner 1999, Leonard et al. 1998, Lewis 1998, Robey et al. 2000, Townsend et al. 1998) provides some insight into the effects of team dispersion. As much of this research stream focuses on the role of technology in supporting remote communication, team members are often selected on the basis of physical location rather than because of

specialized expertise. Even in the absence of occupational or functional diversity, however, there is evidence that geographic dispersion can aggravate the complexity of collective work. Both the frequency of distributed work and the geographic spread of members have been shown to negatively affect groups' communication and ultimately their performance (Cramton and Webber 1999). Cramton (2001) also found that dispersed student teams (connected through technology) with similar educational backgrounds lacked "mutual knowledge" of each member's local context and constraints, and this hindered their ability to work together effectively. By assuming that remote partners experienced the same circumstances they themselves experienced, team members failed to recognize the root causes of miscommunication, and so attributed their remote partners' behavior to dispositional rather than situational factors.

Virtual team research largely assumes an a priori role for technology; interaction problems thus are more readily attributed to motivational origins rather than to inherent limitations of the chosen technology to adequately represent the nature of knowledge concerned. Recommendations for effective remote interaction center around creating early opportunities to develop personal relationships and trust, which can sustain the group's interaction when members are apart (Boutellier et al. 1998, Duarte and Snyder 1999, Handy 1995, Jarvenpaa et al. 1998, Knoll and Jarvenpaa 1995, Leonard et al. 1998, Lewis 1998). The lack of research on virtual teams involving knowledge with the complexity and variety typical of development activities suggests that further research is needed to better understand how dispersed development teams access and leverage available knowledge.

In summary, research on factors that contribute to effective interaction by dispersed, heterogeneous groups is limited, and recommendations for effectively combining knowledge from diverse, dispersed sources still must be developed. Current empirical studies on dispersed or virtual groups are dominated by experimental and quasi-experimental work using student groups and thus largely exclude consideration of the effects of realistic organizational contexts, task designs, and team composition (cf. Leonard et al. 1998). Analogously, some social psychologists have advocated studying group process and performance in real-work contexts, because experimental and laboratory-based studies often exclude important sources of variance (see, e.g., Hackman 1987). This chapter thus reports on an in-depth study of two dispersed cross-functional teams, conducted to explore combined effects of occupational and contextual knowledge diversity on knowledge-sharing and learning processes in teams. The aim of this research was to understand how diverse sources of knowledge are leveraged in the development process, as well as to expand the empirical work on dispersed groups by exploring groups in a real-world organizational setting. By studying virtual teams in a real organization, we sought to gain insight about knowledge sharing practices and conditions promoting effectiveness of these teams.

Research Setting and Methodology

The present study explored the combined effects of occupational and contextual knowledge diversity on learning processes in development teams, rather than seeking to explain variance in performance. The exploratory nature of the research question reflects our observation that the literature lacks an understanding of how dispersed cross-functional teams share and combine knowledge, necessarily overcoming the barriers to doing so. Our objective of trying to understand and generate new theory about team processes in this setting required a qualitative research methodology. Thus, we sought to be guided by the data—views of knowledge and knowledge differences and instances of knowledge sharing in two teams.

Research Site

The study took place in a multinational company that relies on geographically dispersed cross-functional teams for new product and process development activities. A leading manufacturer worldwide of films used in a wide range of consumer products and industrial applications, "The Company" employed over 4,000 people worldwide, and its revenues exceeded $1 billion per year. Developing new products was an area of high priority for The Company, which set a goal of generating at least 20% of revenue from new products. All major development efforts involved representatives from research and development, sales and marketing, and manufacturing. The company had over 10 production locations in the United States, Europe, and Asia. Research and technology development activities for all products and markets were clustered at sites in all three continents. The marketing and sales organization, which included post-sale support activities, was represented throughout the Americas, Europe, and Asia.

Data Sources

Data were collected in two stages, through interviews, company documentation, and participant observation in project and team activities. In the first phase of the research, 16 semi-structured interviews were conducted with a cross-section of the development community at a single site. Interviews lasted between one and three hours and were taped and later transcribed. Interview questions were designed to elicit information about the nature of development activities and objectives; the nature and origins of knowledge drawn upon during these activities, and how, why, and with whom particular knowledge-intensive interactions and collaborations took place. The second phase of data collection involved an intensive study of two development projects identified in the first phase. Sampling of projects was theoretical, based on the opportunities they provided to observe cross-site and cross-functional interactions. We confined our sample to projects involving sites sharing a common language (English). Both projects were significant in terms of investment, risk, and complexity, and were studied during equivalent stages of the company's standard "stage-gate" development process. Both teams comprised key participants from at least three physical locations, although not all members were equally active during the period of on-site data collection. In-depth interviews and informal conversations with team members, line managers, and other project associates allowed both retrospective and prospective documentation of each project. The first author spent a month on site, during which she was able to "observe" both physical and virtual team interactions. Opportunities for collecting data about each team and project were determined by the teams' current activities, and so the sources of data for each team were quite different, although total exposure time to each was approximately equal. Finally, access to electronic repositories of project and other organization information—both during and after on-site data collection—provided the means to triangulate interview data and observed behavior.

Analytic Strategy

We reviewed tapes and notes to identify themes related to knowledge sources and patterns of knowledge sharing (team learning behaviors) over time. From each of the general interviews completed during Phase I, we isolated all quotes—expressed either positively or negatively—relating to the interviewee's or to others' knowledge. We also identified all quotes suggestive of learning or discovery, such as through a person or event influencing a development project or activity, and sought evidence of the source of insight or expertise for each learning event. Two overarching categories emerged. One category highlighted the way members of a development community characterized and labeled different bodies of knowledge, and the other encompassed observable learning behaviors.

This analysis was replicated for interviews and conversations from Phase 2. The Phase 1 categorizations facilitated identification of similar instances from other less-structured data sources—such as transcripts of team meetings, physical activities, or other recorded team interactions, as well as written documentation accessed during Phase II. These records of real-time behavior were analyzed for evidence of learning behavior—such as seeking information, experimentation, reflection, and salvaging insight from apparent failures, similar to categories identified by Edmondson (1999a).

The differences in sources and types of data for each team meant that it was not appropriate to count instances of these references to learning or drawing on identified knowledge sources; we lacked a consistent denominator that would allow meaningful comparison of tallied events across projects. Instead, we sought to carry out a detailed analysis of particular episodes of learning during the life cycle of two projects, drawing from multiple sources and perspectives. This design was appropriate for our objective of theory building rather than hypothesis testing.

Findings

Consistent with previous empirical work (Bechky 1999, Dougherty 1992), the cross-sectional interview data suggested that functional or occupational diversity was essential in development activities. At the same time, we found that locale-based or *contextual knowledge* was also a vital source of insight into development issues. Analysis of the two teams' learning episodes further revealed how different sources of knowledge can be combined and used by dispersed teams, and suggested that two kinds of knowledge sharing processes in team settings have important

implications for project performance and thus for organizational learning. In this section, we first present two case studies that portray the work of two development teams with all their attendant real-world complexity. These cases highlight the role of knowledge diversity and the way these teams used diverse knowledge to achieve project outcomes. Subsequently, we elaborate on these data to develop a framework for understanding and studying learning in dispersed cross-functional teams.

Team A

The aim of Team A's project was to develop a new product for the high-end segment of an existing, profitable market and to satisfy escalating demands for technical performance in this segment. Product performance was influenced by the chemical structure and molecular behavior of raw materials as well as by production processes, and success in the development effort required deep understanding of processing techniques, material properties, and the interactions between them. At The Company, relevant expertise and experience related to product technology and science was found in a U.S. plant facility, while process expertise was found in a UK plant, creating the opportunity to use a dispersed team to develop the product.

Team A's core members were based in four physical locations—three UK sites and one U.S. site. The project was managed by the technical lead, a chemist, based in the United Kingdom along with an experimental scientist and a processing engineer. A cotechnical lead, a senior materials specialist, was based in the United States; the production representative was based at the targeted manufacturing site, also in the United Kingdom, and the marketing lead—a manager for the market segment—worked in another UK office. Finally, several marketing liaisons on the team worked in Europe, Asia, and South America. Managerial oversight for the project came from the United States and the United Kingdom. As the project manager reported:

> It really is a global team. Myself as project manager, the commercial representative in SiteV, a production person in SiteD, a cotechnical person in SiteC, and other technical people here. Also beyond the core team there are account managers we talk to, to verify the business case, the commercial sit-

uation. We involve people from Japan, Asia-Pacific, South America, North America, and Europe. We've involved SiteH engineers for some trials.

He also explained that team members had been chosen explicitly for occupational expertise: "The way we used to work, people had special expertise. So, as Project Manager, I found that the people to pick were almost obvious—who would be the commercial person, the production person. The problem determines the expertise needed in terms of sales region, engineering, processing, etc."

Bringing in Other Contributors

Despite the diverse composition of this team, members relied regularly on additional assistance from others not formally on the team, to provide both conceptual and practical expertise. For example, the team initially missed its targeted product performance specifications and so conducted systematic experiments to eliminate possible sources of error. The project manager and a colocated team member then met with two local colleagues, who had extensive theoretical and practical experience with the problem, and then "outsourced" additional testing work to one local colleague because of her experience with particular equipment that no one on Team A possessed. The project manager explained, "If they're at the site, they tend to be flexible resources anyway. A lot of those people are available as 'resident experts'." His choice of assistance was also guided by awareness of other research activities at that site; as we observed him explaining to a particular expert, "We called you in to help, on the basis of your prior work exploring the chemistry of [particular material compositions]." Similarly, awareness of another colleague's expertise in a particular aspect of process technology led the team to involve this person in testing the team's preliminary design. In this way, the team actively drew upon the knowledge of local experts. The project manager explained his decision to involve additional local colleagues in planning subsequent experiments, " . . . he used to be the [pilot facilities] manager, he's an all-round general processing person. I asked him to join us—I said we needed an expert on [this particular stage of the process]—could he come and make sure this is okay. I also asked for an operator from the pilot facilities area. It is an example of: you see your problem and you just invite the right person—along with the usual faces."

The team's use of outside expertise thus appears casual or taken for granted. Furthermore, it was not limited to local colleagues. For instance, the team drew heavily on the expertise of one of the core members—a materials specialist with a long history in the company and a broad network of research contacts—who was not colocated with other team members. Interestingly, he, in turn, was able to access the expertise of others in his field of expertise, located in other remote sites. In this way, Team A was able to tap into sources of assistance they would have lacked awareness of and access to, without their diverse backgrounds in The Company. The project manager commented: "I [used to] struggle with their research organization. I knew there must be sources of knowledge and information but didn't know where to start. Now I have someone on the team who has good contacts into that group so I delegate him to get things done."

Similarly, the experimental scientist explained that they were intentionally "trying to use experts in their own fields." Listing names of experts from around the company, she elaborated: "We're getting down to root causes . . . acknowledging we need experts from outside [and] bringing them in from outside. . . . We're trying to get to the bottom of issues by seeking out the very best expertise."

In addition to drawing on occupational knowledge, Team A utilized site-specific production expertise of other remote colleagues. Often, this kind of contextual knowledge was critical to going beyond theoretical analysis (e.g., regarding design choices for optimal production of Team A's product) to practical expertise that determined what really worked in a given location. The team engaged the support of colleagues in operations (engineers and operators) from other business groups and sites to help them execute and analyze trials on various production options.

Integration of Different Knowledge Streams

Because Team A encompassed diverse expertise and knowledge, its members engaged in widely varying tasks and were often concerned with different priorities and issues. For example, members with commercial ties were strongly tuned to the interests of individual customers. Those from manufacturing were primarily concerned with capacity constraints in various facilities, production targets, and demands that the project might place on the chosen production facility. Thus, the team had to find a way to agree upon the implications of certain findings and conclusions, despite differing priorities and occupational knowledge bases.

Interestingly, even within occupations, we noticed that different physical locations had different, largely taken-for-granted approaches to similar work. For example, the U.S.-based materials specialist commented:

> In this site, research folk are more experimentalist; they tend to do a lot of lab work on a small scale. [In the UK] they're more involved with paper studies, concepts and ideas. They wouldn't do lab work to evaluate those. Instead, they'd design a pilot or plant line test. It had to do with the physical facilities. Here it really was a laboratory. There were lots of individual labs and lab scientists. People at my level worked in the lab everyday. There I don't think they've had the facilities nor the atmosphere. They've grown up differently.

Differences in ways of working—and the tendency to value certain methods and sources of information over others—are expected to be associated with different occupational fields (e.g., Bechky 1999). These data showed, additionally, that site-specific practices constituted another source of potential confusion, suggesting that dispersed cross-functional teams may grapple with at least two kinds of knowledge differences simultaneously—occupational and contextual.

Team A worked explicitly to integrate its differences in knowledge and perspective from different functions and locations. This appeared to pay off. We found that team members consistently recounted the same narrative of the rationale for, and the history of, the project. All team members had a clear and consistent sense of where the project was going and what were its current issues, even though all members were not directly involved in every activity. Although their different experiences affected their beliefs about how easily remaining issues might be resolved, there was little disagreement about what the issues were. One member, an experimental scientist, commented, "Collaboration to me is that, whether one's working directly on [an issue] or has a passing interest, one is kept in the communication loop—to know what's happened

and why." The project manager agreed: "In my projects, people are geographically widespread. In terms of knowledge sharing, there is a lot of knowledge created during a project, and it is vital for every team member to have access to all of that. People should know broadly what's going on in a project."

Although different members took the lead in different areas of expertise, team members explained that if anyone "needs a pair of hands or a sanity check, we're all there to help." Members also reported feeling comfortable participating, even in areas where they might not be specialists, and therefore discovered opportunities for individual learning in new domains; for instance, an experimental scientist reported: "I have learned a phenomenal amount about [the process] only through listening in on the work that [the process engineer] is doing. I watched the pilot trials, what they were measuring, what they were interested in. I found it very interesting and useful—so would hope to have a greater useful role in this area in a subsequent project."

Creating a Foundation for Integration

By focusing on the bigger picture of the project goal and establishing consistent group norms for interaction and sharing knowledge, members of Team A were able to successfully integrate their diverse streams of knowledge. This was in part driven by the explicit actions of the project manager, who expounded on the need to educate people about the business aims of the project, to try to break down site "empires" through a business focus. Thus, the project manager and other team members expended considerable effort to articulate the project's business case and frame its contribution in terms of multiple values (commercial, manufacturing, and technical).

Team A established norms of frequent communication and information sharing, both within and outside the team. The team also was systematic in documenting plans, decisions, results, and conclusions, such as through meticulous writing and distribution of minutes describing team and subteam interactions. Notes were compiled by the project manager with input from individual members. Similarly, comprehensive plans were developed, both to inform external colleagues who supported the project and also to provide a record for the team of the full history of its experimental work. Specialized team members periodically compiled focused reports summarizing the learning derived from discussions, laboratory tests, or production trials, and making conclusions drawn from these practical activities explicit. The team also "met" virtually on a regular basis through audioconferences, which enabled them to talk through issues and concerns in a more unstructured and free-flowing fashion. Thus, the team regularly engaged in a process of explicit, shared "meaning-making" that contributed to highly congruent views of the project and also to a shared sense of identity.

Team B

The aim of Team B's project was to develop a new manufacturing process in Europe for a group of products that was manufactured in the United States at the time. The team was developing a more cost-effective, environmentally friendly, single-step technique to replace an existing two-step technique. This substitution implied complex process and product changes. Analysis of The Company's products and processes had suggested the new approach might be feasible, but that significant practical knowledge had to be developed to verify the theory and implement the change.

Team B's core members were drawn from two physical locations, both UK sites, and a third manufacturing site in the United States provided substantial management influence, product knowledge, and U.S. supplier contacts. The development effort started informally at one UK site as an exploratory exercise; even at this early stage, disciplinary or occupational diversity of the team was pronounced, and a natural division of responsibility had fallen into place. The project originator and commercial lead explained, "The three of us decided to go 'offline' to try it out, with [a design engineer] providing engineering expertise, [a materials scientist] the chemistry aspect, and myself providing chemical expertise and 'air-cover'." In the initial, informal phase, the team already had an idea of where the product could be manufactured and so brought in production representatives from that plant to provide advice and insight in early trials and discussions of equipment. The advice of an experienced, remote marketing colleague also was solicited. Once the project was officially sanctioned, a production engineer and the relevant production line supervisor joined the three original members of the team, and two sales and marketing colleagues in the United Kingdom were brought in to carry out marketing aspects of the project. The production engineer assumed the role of production lead and also took on project management responsibilities. According to the materials scientist on the team, the site-based knowledge was essential for someone managing this project: "The product is going to be made there and new hardware has to be installed on a particular unit. So it was inevitable that we'd need the project manager to be at that site, because nobody here has the authority or the knowledge of their production lines to do that work."

Bringing in Other Contributors

Like Team A, Team B relied substantially on additional people, both inside and outside the company, to develop concepts and ideas and to put them to practical tests. The project's originator explained how he found it helpful to discuss his theoretical ideas with others in a similar field of expertise. The fact that they shared terminology and fundamental concepts made it possible to share unrefined thoughts and ideas, despite not being colocated; "I need kindred spirits to talk to, to discuss how and why we're doing what we're doing. I spent a lot of time talking on the phone to other scientists, mostly about the philosophy of what we're trying to do, getting moral support." He further explained that casual conversation with a local colleague, who could bring both technical knowledge and informal experience and judgment to bear on his problem, helped him develop his ideas more fully. Lacking the lead-time required to meet with remote colleagues made this an efficient avenue for focused learning, and so, "that's why I talk to [X] . . . I can go to him and say, for example, what are the technology options given this broad business scenario? Or I could say, these are the technical options—how could we move forward?"

Team members often drew on their own past contacts in the industry to gain access to equipment and materials, and this allowed them to conduct practical tests of their ideas very early in the development project. For example, three weeks after its initial meeting, the team was in contact with an equipment supplier who loaned machinery for experiments. A design engineer explained, "It moved quickly because I knew [the supplier], I had dealt with them before. We had previous trials with them six or seven years ago. They were amenable to a "look-see" trial on a small piece of equipment."

Moreover, the physical output obtained from early experiments provided a tangible manifestation of the chemical and engineering knowledge underlying the new process and was thus critical in communicating the value of the project to senior management and to other functional groups. According to the design engineer,

> we had no doubt about it—by the second trial we knew it was possible. It is important that confidence was expressed based on what we'd seen, to give other people confidence that we had a process worth supporting. . . . Experimental data makes it communicable to others. Without experimental data, people are more skeptical. The second experiment sparked the confidence that we had a method that could do the job.

The team had to move quickly in accessing new knowledge. As the materials scientist explained, "We had to be much more decisive, more sure that we'd get a good return on this risk of putting down a novel process. . . . New processes specifically to make new products are not that common (in the company)." In addition to developing the technology, the team sought to manage external perceptions, and individual members took it upon themselves to tackle key influential communities, such as the sales force and the plant management team, to build support for the project.

Team B's activities bringing diverse knowledge streams to bear on the problem-solving process exposed a serendipitous opportunity for the company as a whole. The team discovered a problem relating to the raw materials and called on a number of internal and external materials resources, including those from the current manufacturing location, to find alternative solutions. Through this exercise they realized they could manufacture suitable raw materials internally, which would eventually generate cost benefits for their own project as well as for other products.

Like Team A, Team B was composed to bring together key expertise, independent of where members were located. Again, we found that the team drew heavily on site-based knowledge, drawing from the site-based communities in which members were embedded. And like Team A, Team B also experienced challenges associated with combining diverse values and priorities. Team members' conversations suggested a persistent awareness of diverse motivations, priorities, and ways of working—both stemming from occupations and from site-based differences. For example, the design engineer highlighted occupational differences—"Perhaps that's the differ-

ence between engineering and chemistry—the discipline. . . . The chemistry folk don't see that background work that needs to be done"—while the commercial lead noted that production personnel were preoccupied with their various site-level concerns, "[New production site] folk were keen on the idea because it would be bringing new products to their site. [Current production site] folk were not happy because they would obviously lose production that stayed in this region."

Integration of Different Knowledge Streams

Again, we found that team members explicitly recognized the value of different viewpoints as well as the need to integrate them. The design engineer explained, "Overall different disciplines bring sanity into the development. This diversity is positive and essential. These different perspectives reduce the failure likelihood." We also found evidence that team members realized the often tacit or taken-for-granted nature of some kinds of knowledge; for example, a production engineer said: "We have to acknowledge the different experiences of people; we need to understand generically what matters to people. If we can't share these, can't understand these things, then we won't be able to make joint decisions on specifics."

Unlike Team A, however, Team B lacked consistency in how discoveries from different sources and locations were shared among members. Some individual members complained of not being kept informed of their colleagues' decisions and actions, and on occasion key members disputed project assumptions that other members had taken for granted. For example, in one discussion the production lead argued with the rest of the team about a critical structural requirement of the product. Later the commercial lead commented: "We were all shocked when [the production lead] said he didn't know we were using [that structure]. We've had a meeting when everyone's been there; we've all been in that room before. . . . That had been discussed—though perhaps not written down."

In this team, knowledge gaps generated by site differences appeared more significant than those generated by occupational expertise. On the one hand, the initial members of the team, though representing different functions and arguing collegially over priorities and interpretations, reported that they learned a lot from each other.

The early stages of the project had provided many opportunities for this colocated group to discuss ideas among themselves and with other colleagues. These exchanges occurred through live, face-to-face interactions (Dougherty 1992). On the other hand, psychological distance between colleagues who were not colocated remained high, not yet diminishing over time through the process of collaboration. Despite articulating confidence in the technical or task-relevant abilities of remote colleagues, team members' comments were scattered with references to "hidden agendas" and concerns about the driving motivations at other locations. In contrast to Team A, their comments suggested the absence of a coherent team identity. A materials scientist explained, "The way the team interacts is quite interesting in the respect . . . I think [the initial members] are seen sort of as a team within a team at the moment. We've been the main contingent up to a certain point and have done the majority of the footwork so far."

Lacking a Foundation for Integration

Members of Team B had not fully established themselves as a new community, with a shared sense of belonging and shared ways of working. The team's lack of shared identity and understanding appeared to be due to inadequate communication and information exchange. Team B had developed few coherent norms of communication and information sharing; it lacked the routine of "coordinate, act, then reflect" that characterized Team A. We did not find evidence that information was deliberately withheld, but that personal preferences resulted in numerous quick informational exchanges, instead of a consistent process for disseminating findings and concerns. Ad hoc one-on-one exchanges inevitably overlooked information or people who should have been informed. This occasionally frustrated expectations among colleagues from other sites or functions. For example, one Team B engineer expressed distrust of engineers at another site because he felt that he was not being kept informed of decisions made or receiving information as to how the equipment procurement was progressing. But his expectations of how to receive this information were set by norms of technology use and communication patterns established within his local engineering group. The remote engineers had different local norms and had made the information available elsewhere. Team B had not established a pattern of "meet-

ing" regularly, whether physically or virtually, at the time of data collection.

The absence of norms for consistent or extensive interaction in the team as a whole meant that shared understanding developed among colocated members, but localized subgroups (and thus pockets of knowledge) were not well integrated. On the one occasion during the period of this study that the team did get together physically—apparently for the first time since the project was formalized—it appeared that the group made significant breakthroughs in collective understanding and in developing social relationships.

Bridging Knowledge Gaps: An Organizing Framework

Figure 33.1 presents a theoretical framework abstracted from analysis of our data and reflected in the case histories. The framework suggests that, in dispersed cross-functional teams, recognizing the complexity of the development task and the value of knowledge diversity in accomplishing that task promotes collecting, exchanging, and combining knowledge. We propose that, in dispersed team settings, recognition of knowledge diversity and task complexity prompts two distinct kinds of knowledge-sharing behavior. The first is identifying and engaging knowledge from relevant diverse communities (generally carried out by individual team members reaching out to others), and the second is integrating that knowledge as a team. The framework further suggests that teams that successfully engage in both kinds of behavior will experience greater satisfaction and will more efficiently meet their development objectives than teams lacking in these behaviors. However, this proposition goes beyond the data presented here. In the following sections, we provide further evidence from Teams A and B to support this framework.

Recognizing Knowledge Needs

In both teams, both occupational and contextual knowledge sources were acknowledged and sought out. Initially, when staffing the project teams, management's focus was on occupational knowledge. Consistent with past research in product development, these teams leveraged the expertise of diverse functions and scientific fields to accomplish challenging development goals. At the same time, the tendency of both teams to ac-

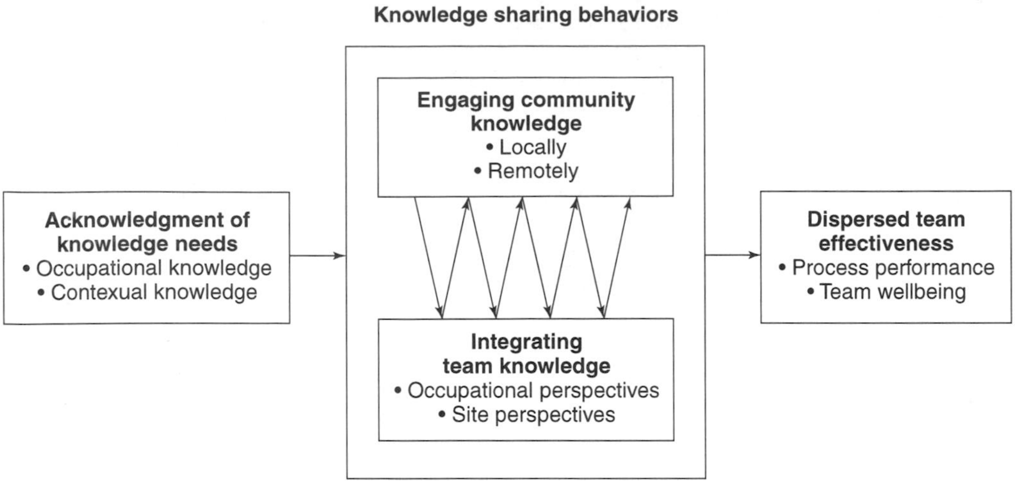

Knowledge sharing behaviors

Figure 33.1 Bridging knowledge gaps: learning in dispersed cross-functional teams.

cess help and insight particular to a specific site led us to consider locale-based or contextual knowledge as a new and distinct source of value for development teams.

Occupational Knowledge

In both teams, individuals described others or introduced themselves by their occupation, using this label as a signal of specialized knowledge. For example, "He's a processing engineer" or "I'm an experimental scientist" acted as shorthand for conveying information about distinct skills, expertise, and conceptual insights that someone might bring to bear on a problem. Thus, people in these development teams valued different occupations in developing new products and processes. A "divide and conquer" approach was used in both teams, and people tended to be comfortable with specialization of roles and responsibilities. This division happened naturally along occupational lines, with little or no discussion. As a design engineer explained, "Our roles were very clear—the engineering side definitely comes to me, the material side to [the scientist]. No overlap there. [The market manager] was definitely the commercial side. Within the small team we covered the three essential elements—looking after cash, material, and engineering."

Those recognized as knowledgeable by virtue of their occupation were sought after for formal or objective disciplinary knowledge, as well as for their informal judgment, intuition, and advice, often acquired as a result of long experience in

a domain. A process technology manager captured this distinction well, describing his group's efforts to share process expertise within the organization.

We're trying to get back to the laws of physics . . . we want to capture our knowledge in reports and math models describing relationships between equipment, process, materials. . . . We have put effort into capturing process knowledge that is primarily theoretical—but we're missing the practical knowledge. We need to gain this from operators and technicians. . . . There are great differences at the operational level and big opportunities for best practice improvement. We want to capture the truth, we want to record real experience.

Contextual Knowledge

The way in which team members in this study realized that contextual knowledge might be important and drew upon site-based differences in the team to enrich the development effort has not been anticipated in the literature. An engineer explained that deep understanding of a particular setting could prove essential in accomplishing specific activities effectively, ". . . we could learn from them—for example, the way they operate their plants is totally different to ours. They're so much more calm, more relaxed. It's good to see a unit being threaded up [there]—a totally different process. We could [also] learn lots of good things about safety—

their approach around positive personal accountability for safety, that [our product line] doesn't have."

In a similar vein, understanding the context in which the product was targeted for use was critical for making appropriate social and cultural decisions regarding its design and implementation. It was often assumed that those who were part of the relevant identity group who would use the product—whether a national, regional, cultural, or other kind of group—possessed a kind of "insider information" that permitted them to perceive design implications that might be otherwise hidden to "outsiders." Whenever possible, such people were intentionally sought to represent that unique viewpoint within a team. A marketing manager explained, "Especially important is the value of local language ability and being 'on the spot' for [a regional] project. Having a 'finger on the pulse' and 'local knowledge' is critical to the success of the development and market introduction."

Sometimes contextual knowledge simply entailed knowing who's who to contact for further advice or resources in order to accomplish certain objectives. Much of this "know-who" derived from physical proximity, because information about what other people were working on, or were capable of, diffused more easily through the physically colocated community, mostly by word of mouth (e.g., Keller and Holland 1983). However, "know-who" also extended beyond the local setting as individuals moved among organizational locations and worked closely with more and more dispersed colleagues on different projects over time. Thus, contextual knowledge can be dynamic and evolving, as an experimental scientist explained, "Production is likely to be in SiteN. So we've got [X] involved, probably because we know him; he used to be at this site. . . . He will help us identify an appropriate contact."

Electronic "who's who" directories played a part in developing this extended network, although we found in this setting that sources were rarely accessed solely on the basis of a who's who entry. Instead, personal recommendations were used as a filtering mechanism to select from the choice of potentially suitable sources. Tenure and seniority in the organization were often highly correlated with first-hand awareness of others' specialties and experience, thus senior specialist professionals were frequently sought out for their "know-who" knowledge. They were tapped both as filters to

vast bodies of codified knowledge *and* as gatekeepers into communities of expertise, in the event that they themselves could not assist a team directly.

In summary, both occupational and contextual knowledge were recognized as potentially contributing efficiencies and refinements to the development process.

Engaging Knowledge from Various Communities

Past research has highlighted the learning and innovation that can be derived from information exchanges across firm boundaries (e.g., Allen 1977, Bouty 2000, Schrader 1991, von Hippel 1987). Our data suggest that dispersed team members may also rely substantially on colleagues *within* the organizational boundary—but outside the team boundary—to help resolve immediate problems or knowledge gaps. We saw this occurring in two ways.

Engaging the Local Community

As noted above, dispersed teams are assembled primarily in response to known cross-functional or interdisciplinary needs of the development project. Because specialists in any discipline are often occupied, staffing of a project must pull from various locations to find the desired expertise. The fact of geographical dispersion is thus considered either a neutral or hindering factor. However, we found that social ties and personal relationships within a given local (physical) community were extremely effective in gaining team members "just-in-time" access to specialist knowledge and practical skills as and when the team needed it. These two teams suggested that easy access to local expertise or "an extra pair of hands" was a key determinant of team learning and project efficiency. Team members regularly pulled in their colocated colleagues for assistance with practical activities, input on decisions, as general "sounding boards," as well as for "sanity checks," all of which enabled them to proceed to the next development stage.

Furthermore, our observations and interviewees' comments hint at particular social norms for sharing expertise and time that underpin this kind of just-in-time, focused learning. We observed that subgroups were assembled to encourage skills sharing and physically arranged to encourage casual interaction. Physical proximity provided a source of common ground so that people were more willing to share their expertise and time. Quick, informal access and meaningful communication were facilitated because people knew each other personally, as well as by organizational role. "Resident experts" responded willingly to ad hoc requests for advice and their comments even suggested a sense of responsibility to facilitate access to diverse knowledge. As one materials specialist reported, "I see my own role as learning further, then sharing and disseminating. . . . Networking has become a significant component of my own activities over the last two years." Another concurred, "What I bring is a network of contacts—I have networks throughout the [company's] materials community. I'm a networker by nature, it's a skill I have. . . . I act as a conduit—I can pass information on to someone else, because of my personal contacts."

The local community thus filled knowledge gaps by contributing timely and efficient access to broad expertise and practical assistance, which were not accessible from remote team members.

Engaging the Intellectual Community

In addition to building on knowledge residing in each local community, dispersed team members also relied substantially on dispersed people throughout the organization with whom they shared an intellectual heritage. Since they were not always colocated, these colleagues were rarely called on to provide hands-on assistance; however, they played a key role in helping team members develop conceptual ideas and solutions. A materials specialist described consulting colleagues further afield, "We're always looking, for when or where our skills stop, who can we go to outside to fill the gap?" Another engineer concurred; "I have no hesitancy to contact people at [other sites]—asking them for advice or information on something."

Specific knowledge gaps were not always clearly bounded, sometimes becoming apparent only through initially loose questions and vague ideas. On these occasions, in particular, team members seemed to find it helpful to interact informally with colleagues, local or remote, with whom they already shared conceptual frameworks and terminology. A technical marketing member commented, "It's difficult to share the essential issues . . . especially in the forums that are available for sharing this kind of knowledge."

He continued, "There're a lot of "might-bes" or "possibles." And it'll be like that for a little while, because there're many, many variables in this. We've got so many outside variables to think of, at this stage we're just collating our ideas. We're trying to accommodate a commonsense view for the way forward."

His U.S. counterpart elaborated on the informal nature of their learning-oriented exchanges: "We tend to share not only what we're working on as a formal matter but we're often just constantly bouncing ideas off of each other . . . you know, have you done anything to get the material to do this or that, etc? It's not formal."

Thus, it appeared that intellectual communities filled a knowledge gap by informally contributing deeper expertise and insight into particularly problematic or fuzzy topics.

Integrating Team Knowledge

The core challenge for these dispersed teams appeared to be integrating the different insights available to them in a coherent way to meet the goals of the project. Ensuring that team members had a congruent understanding of different elements of the development effort and how these elements affect each other was an ongoing challenge. We found that dispersed teams could be successful at accessing various sources of knowledge to learn individually, without necessarily being able to integrate their knowledge into a fully shared product of the team. For example, despite progressing extremely rapidly and successfully on a number of fronts, Team B members apparently still lacked a consistent identity and shared view of its endeavor at the time of research contact. As one member commented, "On most projects, there tends to be agreement up-front on where we're going, but we haven't had that discussion earlier enough in the project—at least, not satisfactorily. I think there are people who have had very different opinions."

The data suggested that tacit values and taken-for-granted beliefs about "legitimate" ways of working, existing for both occupation and location, were at the heart of integration difficulties. These differences of perspective meant that dispersed cross-functional teams inherently lacked a common foundation from which they could engage in meaningful discussions and reach agreement on fundamental issues—appropriate problems, legitimate methods, valid sources of information, and relevant criteria—for evaluating solutions. Moreover, these differences of perspective were typically unarticulated and generally became salient only through miscommunication or misunderstanding.

The experience of these two teams suggests that integration can happen, but evidence from Team A suggests that explicitly seeking commonality in team communication and information exchange processes early can reduce such miscommunications and misunderstandings. Specifically, developing norms for how knowledge and information will be shared can simplify and streamline coordination among individual members, since the choices of communication mode, recipients, and style contain contextual information that can facilitate more meaningful communication and signal the nature of the expected response (see genre studies by Orlikowski and Yates 1994, Yates and Orlikowski 1992). Also the creation of an explicit communal memory of what work is being done and why, provides a way of keeping abreast of activities individuals have not carried out themselves. In the absence of other evidence of a collective identity, this communal memory can, in addition to promoting individual and collective effectiveness on project tasks, also help build the sense of belonging to the dispersed group.

Implications and Conclusions

One implication of this study is that dispersed cross-functional development teams provide an interesting mechanism for promoting organizational learning—not only because they are a vehicle for developing new, innovative products and processes through which the organization can better respond to emerging market trends, but also because they can give rise to residual gains in the form of knowledge dispersion in the organization. Specifically, in the process of solving problems for a specific project, team members learned "who knew what, where" and contributed to diffusion of this knowledge more broadly in the organization. Thus, following Huber's (1991) definition of organizational learning as diffusion of information within an organization, these teams were clearly agents of The Company's learning.

Individual members of these teams were simultaneously members of multiple intellectual and social communities, and working together they developed ways to integrate knowledge from these different communities. At the same time, we note that team members from different locations and functions initially lacked the shared assumptions or "background knowledge" (Nonaka 1994) that would facilitate learning from each other. Team A appears to have overcome this barrier more easily than Team B. A full explanation for this difference cannot be found in these data, but a likely factor is the well-developed and highly systematic norms for tracking and sharing information in Team A, which supported the development of a new "minicommunity," bound together by shared information and understanding. Members of a community share a sense of belonging that goes beyond task considerations.

Dispersed teams engage in two distinct kinds of knowledge-sharing or learning behavior—boundary spanning and within-team integration (Edmondson 1999b). Thus, the data in this study allow us to be more precise about the nature of team learning behaviors than earlier empirical work on team learning (e.g., Edmondson 1999a), as well as to draw inferences about how dispersed teams can vary in team learning processes. Thus, simultaneously exploring the effects of geographical dispersion and cross-functional membership introduced new insights that augment previous work in this literature.

First, we found that several team members actively drew upon membership in multiple geographical and intellectual communities and thereby brought both moral support and tangible task-related assistance from these other communities to the development project. Through such boundary-spanning (Ancona 1990), a project team gains access to broader and deeper skills and expertise that help it address specific project issues. Furthermore, these dispersed team members coopted other resources into the development effort in such a way that those additional people became an integral part of the thinking and discovery processes that led to project breakthroughs. That is, more than just seeking information or feedback across team boundaries, as discussed in earlier work (e.g., Ancona 1990, Edmondson 1999b), these dispersed teams, by virtue of being embedded in multiple and disjoint communities, had access to significant, diverse sources of support. In this way, nonteam members were brought in as temporary full participants in the project, creating a kind of virtual, just-in-time project team, expanding for a period and contracting again, as needed.

Second, it appeared that dispersed teams must actively integrate the knowledge obtained through boundary spanning, to allow shared understanding of project objectives, status, and ongoing issues. For these teams, this was easier said than done. Our analysis shows that the process of integrating different perspectives and discoveries in dispersed teams cannot be taken for granted, but instead demanded conscious ongoing attention. In particular, site-specific knowledge is easy to take for granted; "the way we do things around here" tends to seem equivalent to the way things are done (Schein 1983). Thus, dispersed team members need to learn a different way of interacting and communicating than might be adopted naturally if they were physically colocated. Discovering and developing procedural norms for interacting effectively in a dispersed team may be as important as learning related to technical aspects of a project's tasks. We speculate that teams in which members recognize these inherently tacit differences in perspective and take conscious steps to negotiate common ground will combine and use their disparate knowledge more effectively than teams lacking in such recognition.

Third, we argue that dispersed teams are more likely to benefit from these opportunities when members explicitly recognize the complexity of the organizational and interpersonal challenge in advance. In the two teams studied, discussing the role of knowledge differences appeared to prompt members to consider their own and others' skills, expertise, and experience and to seek opportunities to obtain and apply knowledge appropriate to the task at hand.

In conclusion, this study highlighted positive aspects of dispersion, beyond the convenience of utilizing resources located in multiple sites without requiring relocation. Although these teams were set up to take advantage of diverse occupational skills—in spite of facing the challenge of not being colocated—the picture that emerges in these data is not simply one of cross-functional teams struggling to overcome the inconvenience imposed by distance. Instead, it appears that dispersion is not merely a burden; it also brings unexpected benefits—if these can be utilized effectively. Dispersed teams have the advantage of incorporating multiple "local" networks of human and physical resources. That is, multiple remote resources can be local for someone on the team. On the one hand, this additional potential benefit is good news for managers who might utilize this approach for development projects. On the other hand, the data also suggested that success in this integrative process depended heavily on a dispersed team's ability to collectively diagnose both its needs and its networks, as well as to coordinate members' activities across its multiple—both obvious and subtle—boundaries.

References

Alavi, M. and Yoo, Y. (1997) *Is Learning in Virtual Teams Real?* Boston: Harvard Business School Press.

Allen, T.J. (1977) *Managing the Flow of Technology.* Cambridge, MA: MIT Press.

Ancona, D. (1990) "Outward bound: Strategies for team survival in an organization." *Academy of Management Journal* 33(2):334–365.

Ancona, D. and Caldwell, D.F. (1992) "Demography and design: Predictors of new product team performance." *Organization Science* 3:321–341.

Arrow, K. (1974) *The Limits of Organizations.* New York: Norton.

Badaracco, J.L. (1991) *The Knowledge Link: How Firms Compete through Strategic Alliances.* Boston: Harvard Business School Press.

Barley, S.R. and Bechky, B.A. (1994) "In the backrooms of science: The work of technicians in science labs." *Work and Occupations,* 21(1):85–126.

Bechky, B. (1999) "Creating Shared Meaning Across Occupational Communities: An Ethnographic Study of a Production Floor." Paper presented at the Academy of Management Conference, Chicago.

Boutellier, R., Gassmann, O., Macho, H., and Roux, M. (1998) "Management of dispersed product development teams: The role of information technologies." *R&D Management* 28(1):13–26.

Bouty, I. (2000) "Interpersonal and interaction influences of informal resource exchanges between R&D researchers across organizational boundaries." *Academy of Management Journal* 43(1): 50–65.

Brown, J.S. and Duguid, P. (1991) "Organizational learning and communities of practice: Toward a unified view of working, learning and innovation." *Organization Science* 2:40–57.

Brown, S. and Eisenhardt, K. (1995) "Product development: Past research, present findings, and future directions." *Academy of Management Review* 20(2):343–378.

Clark, K.B. and Fujimoto, T. (1991) *Product Development Performance: Strategy, Organization and Management in the World Auto Industry.* Boston: Harvard Business School Press.

Cohen, W.M. and Levinthal, D.A. (1990) "Absorptive capacity: A new perspective on learning and innovation." *Administrative Science Quarterly* 35:128–152.

Collins, H. (1983) "The structure of knowledge." *Social Research* 60:95–116.

Cramton, C.D. (2001) "The mutual knowledge problem and its consequences for dispersed collaboration." *Organization Science* 12(3):346–371.

Cramton, C.D. and Webber, S.S. (1999) "A Model of the Effects of Geographical Dispersion on Work Teams." Fairfax, VA: George Mason University.

De Meyer, A. (1991) "Tech talk: How managers are stimulating global R&D communication." *Sloan Management Review* 32(3):49–58.

De Meyer, A. (1993) "Internationalizing R&D improves a firm's technical learning." *Research Technology Management* 36(4):42–49.

Dougherty, D. (1992) "Interpretive barriers to successful product innovation in large firms. *Organization Science* 3(2):179–202.

Douglas, M. (1986) *How Institutions Think*. Syracuse, NY: Syracuse University Press.

Duarte, D.L. and Snyder, N.T. (1999) *Mastering Virtual Teams*. San Francisco: Jossey-Bass.

Edmondson, A. (1999a) "Psychological safety and learning behavior in work teams." *Administrative Science Quarterly* 44(2):350–383.

Edmondson, A. (1999b) "A safe harbor: Social psychological factors affecting boundary spanning in work teams," in B. Mannix, M. Neale, and R. Wageman (eds.), *Research on Groups and Teams*. Greenwich, CT: JAI Press.

Fleck, J. (1997) "Contingent knowledge and technology development." *Technology Analysis and Strategic Management* 9(4):383–398.

Gorton, I. and Motwani, S. (1996) "Issues in cooperative software engineering using globally distributed teams." *Information and Software Technology* 38(10):647–656.

Granovetter, M. (1985) "Economic action and social structure: The problem of embeddedness." *American Journal of Sociology* 91(3):481–510.

Grant, R. (1996) "Prospering in dynamically competitive environments: Organizational capability as knowledge integration." *Organization Science* 7(4):375–387.

Hackman, J.R. (1987) "The design of work teams," in J. Lorsch (ed.), *Handbook of Organizational Behavior*. Englewood Cliffs, NJ: Prentice-Hall.

Hambrick, D.C. and Mason, P.A. (1984) "Upper echelons: The organization as a reflection of its top managers. *Academy of Management Review* 9(2):193–206.

Handy, T. (1995) "Trust and the virtual organization." *Harvard Business Review* 73(3):40–49.

Hoffman, L.R. and Maier, N.R.F. (1961) "Quality and acceptance of problem solutions by members of homogeneous and heterogeneous groups." *Journal of Abnormal and Social Psychology* 62:401–407.

Hoffman, L.R. (1978) "The group problem-solving process," in L. Berkowitz (ed.), *Group Processes*, 101–114. New York: Academic Press.

Huber, G.P. (1991) "Organizational learning: The contributing processes and the literatures. *Organization Science* 2(1):88–115.

Ibarra, H. (1992) "Homophily and differential returns: Sex differences in network structure and access in an advertising firm." *Administrative Science Quarterly* 37(3):422–447.

Janis, I.L. (1982) *Groupthink : Psychological Studies of Policy Decisions and Fiascoes*. Boston: Houghton Mifflin.

Jarvenpaa, S., Knoll, K., and Leidner, D. (1998) "Is anybody out there? Antecedents of trust in global virtual teams." *Journal of Management Information Systems* 14(4):29–64.

Jarvenpaa, S. and Leidner, D. (1999) "Communication and trust in global virtual teams." *Organization Science* 10(6):791–815.

Jehn, K.A., Northcraft, G.B., and Neale, M.A. (1999) "Why differences make a difference: A field study of diversity, conflict, and performance in workgroups." *Administrative Science Quarterly* 44(4):741–763.

Keller and Holland (1983) "Communicators and innovators in research and development organizations." *Academy of Management Journal* 26(4): 742–749.

Knoll, K. and Jarvenpaa, S. (1995) "Learning to Work in Distributed Global Teams." Paper presented at the International Conference on Systems Science, Hawaii.

Kogut, B. and Zander, U. (1992) "Knowledge of the firm, combinative capabilities, and the replication of technology." *Organization Science* 3(3):383–397.

Lam, A. (1997) "Embedded firms, embedded knowledge: Problems of collaboration and knowledge transfer in global cooperative ventures." *Organization Studies* 18(6):973–996.

Lave, J. and Wenger, E. (1990) *Situated Learning: Legitimate Peripheral Participation*. Cambridge: Cambridge University Press.

Leonard, D. (1995) *Wellsprings of Knowledge: Building and Sustaining the Sources of Innovation*. Boston: Harvard Business School Press.

Leonard, D.A., Brands, P.A., Edmondson, A., and Fenwick, J. (1998) "Virtual teams: Using communications technology to manage geographically dispersed development groups," in S.P. Bradley and R.L. Nolan (eds.), *Sense and Respond: Capturing Value in the Network Era*, 285–298. Boston: Harvard Business School Press.

Levitt, B. and March, J.G. (1988) "Organizational learning." *Stanford University Annual Review of Sociology* 14:319–340.

Lewis, R. (1998) "Membership and management of a 'virtual' team: The perspectives of a research manager." *R&D Management* 28(1):5–12.

Madhavan, R. and Grover, R. (1998) "From embedded knowledge to embodied knowledge: New product development as knowledge management." *Journal of Marketing* 62(4):1–12.

Masnevski, M.L. (1994) "Understanding our differences: Performance in decision-making groups with diverse members." *Human Relations* 47: 531–552.

McGrath, J.E. (1984) *Groups: Interaction and Performance.* Englewood Cliffs, NJ: Prentice-Hall.

Moscovici, S. (1976) *Social Influence and Social Change.* London: Academic Press.

Nelson, R. and Winter, S. (1982) *An Evolutionary Theory of Economic Change.* Cambridge, MA: The Belknap Press of Harvard University Press.

Nemeth, C.J. (1986) "Differential contributions of majority and minority influence." *Psychological Review* 91:23–32.

Nonaka, I. (1994) "A dynamic theory of organizational knowledge creation." *Organization Science* 5(1):14–37.

Nonaka, I. and Takeuchi, H. (1995) *The Knowledge-Creating Company: How Japanese Companies Create the Dynamics of Innovation.* New York: Oxford University Press.

O'Reilly, C.A., Caldwell, D.F., and Barnett, W.P. (1989) "Workgroup demography, social integration, and turnover." *Administrative Science Quarterly* 34(1):21–37.

Orlikowski, W.J. and Yates, J. (1994) "Genre repertoire: Examining the structuring of communicative practices in organizations." *Administrative Science Quarterly* 39(4):541–574.

Pfeffer, J. (1983) "Organizational demography," in B.M. Staw and L.L. Cummings (eds.), *Research in Organizational Behavior* 44:299–357. Greenwich, CT: JAI Press.

Polanyi, M. (1966) *The Tacit Dimension.* New York: Doubleday and Company.

Prokesch, S.E. (1997) "Unleashing the power of learning: An interview with British Petroleum's John Browne." *Harvard Business Review* 75(5): 147–164.

Robey, D., Khoo, H.M., and Powers, C. (2000) "Situated learning in cross-functional virtual teams." *IEEE Transactions on Professional Communication* 43(1):51–66.

Schein, E.H. (1983) "The role of the founder in creating organizational culture." *Organizational Dynamics* 12(1):13–29.

Schrader, S. (1991) "Informal technology transfer between firms: Cooperation through information trading." *Research Policy* 20:153–170.

Szulanski, G. (1995) "Unpacking stickiness: An empirical investigation of the barriers to transfer best practice inside the firm." *Academy of Management Journal* (Best Papers Proceedings 1995): 437–441.

Townsend, A.M., DeMarie, S.M., and Hendrickson, A.R. (1998) "Virtual teams: Technology and the workplace of the future." *Academy of Management Executive* 12(3):17–29.

Tsui, A.S. and O'Reilly, C.A. (1989) "Beyond simple demographic effects: The importance of relational demography in superior-subordinate dyads." *Academy of Management Journal* 32(2): 402–423.

Tsui, A.S., Egan, T.D., and O'Reilly, C.A. (1992) "Being different: Relational demography and organizational commitment." *Administrative Science Quarterly* 37(4):549–579.

Tyre, M.J. and Hippel, E.V. (1997) "The situated nature of adaptive learning in organizations." *Organization Science* 8(1):71–83.

Vicenti, W.G. (1990) *What Engineers Know and How They Know It: Analytical Studies from Aeronautical History.* Baltimore: Johns Hopkins University Press.

von Hippel, E. (1987) "Cooperation between rivals: Informal know-how trading." *Research Policy* 16:291–302.

Williams, K.Y. and O'Reilly, C.A. (1998) "Demography and diversity in organizations," in B.M. Staw and R.M. Sutton (eds.), *Research in Organizational Behavior* 20:77–140. Stamford, CT: JAI Press.

Yates, J. and Orlikowski, W.J. (1992) "Genres of organizational communication: A structurational approach to studying communication and media." *Academy of Management Review* 17(2): 299.

Zirger, B.J. and Maidique, M. (1990) "A model of new product development: An empirical test." *Management Science* 36:867–883.

34

Managing Public and Private Firm Knowledge Within the Context of Flexible Firm Boundaries

Sharon F. Matusik

The continued growth of interfirm partnering, from strategic alliances to contingent work use in core value-creation activities to network-based competition, presents a host of complex issues surrounding how these arrangements affect firm knowledge and, ultimately, firm competitiveness. On the one hand, more porous boundaries present the firm with easier access to public knowledge resident outside of its boundaries. This may facilitate the absorption of external public knowledge and the fusion of this public knowledge with existing private firm knowledge. On the other hand, more porous boundaries may also make it easier for proprietary private firm knowledge to seep out into the external environment. This dissemination may have negative consequences particularly for firms that seek to appropriate supernormal returns from this private knowledge.

This chapter focuses on partnering for the purpose of knowledge. Although there are many other kinds of partnering arrangements—such as those dedicated only to marketing or distribution—a limited focus allows for a more detailed analysis of the partnering issues that affect core value-

creation activities of the firm. This study aims to provide a navigational chart through the large bodies of research on knowledge and on partnering to outline the issues that inform the competitive implications of knowledge-focused partnering. In so doing, this chapter draws attention to three fundamental considerations. First, it presents a framework that identifies multiple determinants of firm knowledge levels. Much of our research in this area focuses predominantly on one or a couple of determinants of firm knowledge. This chapter integrates research streams to provide a more comprehensive view of firm knowledge. This framework also draws attention to the different roles of public versus private knowledge within the firm. Second, knowledge outcomes from interfirm partnering, referred to as "flexible firm boundaries," are examined. Third, the chapter examines how the competitive context affects the relative importance of knowledge creation versus dissemination to address the question of value. As critics of the knowledge management movement have pointed out, a firm's pursuit of knowledge in and of itself may not necessarily create economic value (Herz et al. 2000). Rather, knowledge that can be put to productive use creates value. Fourth, this chapter integrates these three areas into a framework for assessing cost and implementation issues that influence the net knowledge effects of partnering. Thus, this chapter integrates research at the intersection of knowledge and strategic management around how flexible firm boundaries affect value creation.

Integrated View of Firm Knowledge

Firm knowledge levels are influenced by four processes: knowledge creation; absorption of relevant public (external) knowledge; knowledge transfers within the firm; and dissemination into the external environment of firm private proprietary knowledge. Each of these processes affects the overall level of firm knowledge. Dierickx and Cool (1989) developed the "bathtub" metaphor to distinguish between stocks and flows of resources that can be analogously applied to firm knowledge. In this metaphor, the flow of water from the faucet into the tub represents the inflow of resources and the outflow of water from the drain represents the outflow of resources. The waterline represents the stock of resources at any time. In the context of knowledge, the inflow represents the absorption of relevant external knowledge and the outflow represents dissemination of proprietary knowledge into the external environment. The water level, then, is influenced by the net inflow and outflow. In the case of knowledge, though, the intrafirm dispersion of knowledge and the process of knowledge creation also influence the knowledge level as additional spigots may increase the water level.

Figure 34.1 highlights the determinants of firm knowledge levels (knowledge creation, absorption of relevant public [external] knowledge, knowledge transfers within the firm, and dissemination into the external environment of firm private proprietary knowledge) that are discussed within this section. This section provides a brief introductory overview of the different roles public and private knowledge play in the firm. The distinction between these two kinds of knowledge forms a foundation for our understanding of how creation, absorption, and dissemination together affect overall firm knowledge. Each determinant of firm knowledge is then discussed individually.

Firms possess both private and public stocks of knowledge. Private knowledge is unique to the firm, whereas public knowledge resides in the public domain. Private—or firm-specific—knowledge can be a source of competitive advantage. It is an example of a resource that is unique, valuable, rare, and imperfectly imitable. Private knowledge includes such items as a firm's unique routines, processes, documentation, or trade secrets. Public knowledge consists of knowledge not unique to any one firm. Rather, it resides in the external environment and is, in essence, a public good.

Public knowledge includes such items as industry and occupational best practices. Total quality management (TQM), just-in-time inventory, lean manufacturing, and team-based incentives are all examples of "best practices" now in the public domain. Other examples include specific accounting practices, computer programming language skills, or the ability to use particular computer software packages. By definition, public knowledge cannot by itself be a source of competitive advantage since it is not

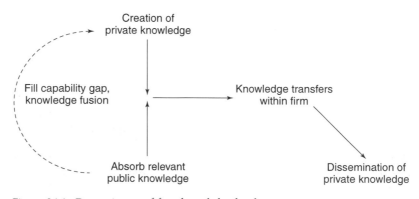

Figure 34.1. Determinants of firm knowledge levels.

unique or proprietary to any one firm. However, the failure to apply such knowledge within a given firm can be a source of competitive disadvantage. For example, computer-programming languages, such as java and html are public knowledge. For firms that write Internet-based applications, efficient use of these languages is important. A firm may have the most unique and valuable web-based application, but if the application does not use the underlying language protocols correctly, it is useless. Thus, both categories of knowledge play an important role in determining overall knowledge levels within a firm, as well as the associated value of this knowledge.

Private Knowledge Creation

Our research to date focuses primarily on private knowledge.[1] Within this research area, the process of creation and structural organizational aspects that contribute to knowledge creation have received attention. Knowledge creation results from exploration and exploitation activities within the firm's boundaries (Huber 1991, March 1991, Nonaka and Takeuchi 1995, Senge 1990), and the conversion between tacit and explicit forms of knowledge levels within the firm (Kogut and Zander 1993, Nonaka 1994, Nonaka and Takeuchi 1995, Zander and Kogut 1995). The fusion of incoming public knowledge with existing private knowledge may stimulate new knowledge creation. Public knowledge can also fuse with other existing technologies to fill capabilities gaps (Cradwell 1995, Leonard-Barton 1995, Nonaka and Takeuchi 1995). The field of innovation contains many examples of technologies that have been created by fusing together previously separate knowledge streams (Leonard-Barton 1995).

Structural aspects of private knowledge also have received attention. For example, product-development literature has long recognized the importance of within-firm formal integration mechanisms such as cross-functional teams, interdepartmental coordination, and formal rewards for sharing information in cultivating private knowledge stocks as represented by product or process innovation. Also, informal integration mechanisms such as informal advice, transmission of anecdotes, interfunctional climate, bringing together individuals with different backgrounds, intentions to acquire knowledge, attitudes toward knowledge acquisition, and cooperative behavior contribute to private knowledge (Hamel 1991,

Moenart et al. 1994, Nonaka 1994). Additionally, innovation studies examine variables such as cash flow, diversification, firm size, market concentration, stage in technological life cycle, and interdepartmental linkages to predict knowledge levels as measured by proxy variables such as patents or R&D spending and intensity (see Cohen 1995 for summary). Thus, the creation of private knowledge is influenced by elements of the formal structure, as well as the routines and processes within the firm.

Absorption of Relevant Public Knowledge

The body of research encompassing public knowledge, in comparison to that on private knowledge, is relatively small, despite observations like those of Leonard-Barton (1995) that "few, if any, companies can build core capabilities without importing knowledge from outside its boundaries" (p. 155). Benchmarking in competitor analyses, TQM implementation, and new product development practices have been discussed primarily in practitioner-oriented journals as tools to ascertain whether a firm's knowledge and practices are current. Additionally, we know that firms may imitate what they perceive as successful (DiMaggio and Powell 1983) or conduct searching and noticing activities (Huber 1991, Nonaka 1994).

Research on the effects of public knowledge within the firm comes from several different areas. The construct of absorptive capacity (Cohen and Levinthal 1989, 1990) focuses around the idea that firm expertise enables it to absorb new, related knowledge from its environment. Development of this construct has influenced many researchers to include absorptive capacity as a variable in their models (e.g., Mowery et al. 1996, Lane and Lubatkin 1998, Luo 1997, Szulanski 1996, Veugelers 1997). Also, the economic and economic geography literature on knowledge spillovers examines how firms are affected by economic activity, such as positive knowledge externalities associated with regional or technically related activity. Firms somehow benefit from the public knowledge present in their environment (Jaffe 1986, 1988, Jaffe et al. 1993). Network research makes a similar argument—that networks of relationships provide access to pools of knowledge that firms do not possess individually (Powell et al. 1996). Other studies also include the number of firm alliances or location as an indicator of the ability of the firm to assimilate surrounding public knowledge (e.g., De-Carolis and Deeds 1999). Also, Coff (1999) finds that at the industry level, there is a difference between how general knowledge gained through formal education versus hours of informal firm-specific training affects acquisition patterns. Matusik and Hill (1998) present a nested model to analyze knowledge effects associated with permeable firm boundaries. Their model takes as its first order characterization public versus private knowledge. Though there is relatively little empirical research on precisely what means firms can use to best draw in public knowledge, the absorption of this knowledge is an important consideration for firms.

Knowledge Transfers Within the Firm

The dispersion of knowledge within a firm affects who can make productive use of firm knowledge. Several detailed reviews of the research on within firm transfers exist (i.e., Argote 1999, Castaneda 2000). Broadly, within-firm transfers are affected by characteristics of the knowledge being transferred and by the transfer participants and context. Specific characteristics of the knowledge itself affect the ability to transfer knowledge within the firm. For example, Zander and Kogut (1995) find that the degree of codifiability and teachability affect the ability of the firm to transfer capabilities within the firm but across distant geographic locations. Other studies focus on specific transfer situations within a firm and examine the context and individuals involved with an intentional transfer. Lack of direct relationship or communication across subunits inhibits knowledge-sharing (Galbraith 1973, Lawrence and Lorsch 1967). Also, the stickiness of the information to be transferred and the characteristics of the individuals involved affect intentional transfers at the project level (Szulanski 1996). Hansen (1999) takes a social-networks perspective in looking at intentional knowledge transfers across subunits and finds that weak network ties are positively related to speed of transfer when the knowledge to be transferred is not complex. However, weak ties negatively affected the speed of transfer when the knowledge is complex. Thus, the complexity of the knowledge as well as the network context are important considerations. Huber (1991) also notes that the body of research on information distribution within organizations affects learning within firms (for some reviews of this area, see Huber 1991, 1982, Krone et al.

1987). Practitioner-oriented articles on knowledge management also discuss the issues involved in designing systems and processes to facilitate such transfers (e.g., Hansen et al. 1999). This well-developed and expanding research stream provides useful information about the many structural and contextual influences on effective within-firm transfers.

Preservation/Dissemination of Private Knowledge

Interestingly, few studies specifically consider dissemination of proprietary knowledge outside the firm. Classic arguments on the resource-based view of the firm articulate that a resource, such as knowledge, is a potential source of competitive advantage if it is rare, inimitable, nonsubstitutable, and valuable (Barney 1991). Certainly, the conditions of uniqueness, inimitability, and nonsubstitution suggest that dissemination of a resource such as knowledge can negatively affect competitive advantage. However, only a few studies specifically examine this process. March discusses knowledge dissemination in his simulation of the effects of turnover on knowledge and learning (March 1991). He argues that *moderate* turnover positively affects knowledge creation; there is some knowledge loss as well as gain with turnover. In March's model, those leaving take knowledge with them, while those coming in bring new ideas, so moderate turnover has a positive net knowledge effect. Also, process research on routines indicates that whenever individuals leave a routine, they take a part of that routine with them (Nelson and Winter 1982, Simon 1991). Accordingly, to the extent that individuals are embedded into the routines of an organization, their departure negatively affects the level of knowledge within the firm, regardless of whether the departing individual passes that information along to another firm. Zander and Kogut (1995) also examine imitation of innovations outside firm boundaries and find that key employee turnover is positively related to imitation. However, other characteristics of the capabilities, such as codifiability and teachability that affected within-firm transfers, did not significantly affect imitation by other firms (Zander and Kogut 1995). Though the dissemination of knowledge is recognized theoretically as important, there has been relatively little empirical examination of the mechanisms that may inhibit or accelerate it.

Synthesis

When examined together, these four processes present a comprehensive view of firm knowledge. The level of firm knowledge at any given point in time is a function of its stocks and flows of knowledge, within and across the boundaries of the firm. The following section applies these ideas to the research to date on flexible firm boundaries and the knowledge outcomes associated with such partnering.

The Case of Flexible Firm Boundaries

The model presented in the prior section has interesting implications for the research on firm partnering. Though there is a healthy body of research on antecedents to and classifications of such arrangements, there is relatively little research that examines the performance consequences of these arrangements (Gulati et al. 2000). Practitioner-focused articles also highlight the importance of structuring and managing partnering arrangements to maximize competitive gains and minimize the loss of competencies or knowledge (e.g., Bleeke and Ernst 1995, Hamel et al. 1989). However, of the relatively small group of empirical studies that examine the knowledge implications of these arrangements, there are even fewer that consider knowledge gains as well as losses. Below is an overview of research that has examined knowledge effects from partnering.

One group of studies of flexible firm boundaries examines how partnered firms intentionally transfer their proprietary knowledge to one another. Specific characteristics of alliance partners attempting to transfer knowledge affect transfer abilities at the firm level (Lane and Lubatkin 1998, Larsson et al. 1998, Lorenzoni and Lipparini 1999, Mowery et al. 1996, Simonin 1999). For example, complementarity across partners with regard to receptivity and transparency affect the ability to gain from an alliance (Larsson et al. 1998). Complementarity in compensation systems, organizational structure, and challenges faced also facilitate knowledge inflows (Lane and Lubatkin 1998). The degree of competitive collaboration, learning and bargaining power, intention to learn, organizational and skill transparency, receptivity, and firm determinants of sustainable learning are also important (Hamel 1991). Others also argue that firms seek partners with complementarities to enhance knowledge transfers and creation (Koza and Lewin 1998, Skenkar and Li 1999). Research conducted at the industry level shows that the number of alliances in an industry is positively correlated with R&D intensity (an input to the innovation process) and with technical sophistication (Freeman 1991, Hagedoorn 1995).

Knowledge effects from strategic alliances have also been investigated using patent citations. Mowery and colleagues (1996) found that arrangements with more interfirm internal overlaps (i.e., equity arrangements over contracts, and bilateral over unilateral contracts) yielded a greater post-alliance knowledge base, as measured by cross-citations. Cross-citations were also affected by complementarities between technologies in the two partnering firms. More related firms yielded greater post-alliance cross-citations. Said another way, prealliance cross-citation patterns are a predictor of post-alliance cross-citation patterns, suggesting complementary knowledge stocks are important.

Other researchers have adopted a network perspective to examine knowledge effects from interfirm partnering. Certain kinds of interorganizational linkages are positively related to the introduction of additional services in hospitals (Goes and Park 1997). This finding suggests that linkages stimulate knowledge assimilation from outside the firm. Additionally, experiences with collaborative arrangements in core functions and network centrality are positively related to future collaborations in core functions (Powell et al. 1996). In these studies, external ties enhance knowledge inflows. Network study results indicate that networks are a means of accessing knowledge that is disbursed and resides outside firm boundaries.

In sum, partnering research suggests that the more interaction and similarity there is across the partners, the greater the knowledge inflows. Knowledge dissemination from partnering has not been systematically assessed by these alliance and network research studies, despite the emphasis in areas such as transaction cost economics on potential opportunism within these arrangements. For example, perhaps in the Goes and Park study (1997), linked hospitals lost their distinctiveness and ability to exact higher rents for unique services in exchange for more external knowledge in the form of additional services. And perhaps in the Mowery et al. study (1996), increased cross-citations indicate that a firm has lost its ability to appropriate higher rents from its innovations because the innovations are no longer private knowledge.

A couple of studies have begun inquiry into potential dissemination of private knowledge. Kale et al. (2000) measure perceived learning as well as protection of proprietary assets in alliances. They find that relational capital and the ability to manage conflict are positively related to both learning and proprietary knowledge protection. Kale et al. (2000) measure relational capital as perceptions of the closeness of personal interactions, mutual respect and trust, personal friendship, and reciprocity. While the study is multiindustry and does not specify the kind of knowledge involved in partnering, the relational capital measure is positively related to perceptions of protecting core capabilities as well as learning something new from the partner. Research on alternative work arrangements presents another view of knowledge effects associated with flexible firm boundaries. Matusik (1999) examines the relationship between contract work in the core value-creation activity of software firms and the associated impact on relative levels of both public and private knowledge in the firm. Results from this study indicate that the level of contract work use does not have a direct effect on either public or private knowledge. Rather, the degree to which contract work is formally integrated into the firm (e.g., feedback sought from contractors) is positively related to both forms of knowledge. The degree to which contractors are informally integrated into the firm (e.g., high levels of social contact and access to the same resources as traditional employees) is negatively related to both kinds of knowledge. The significance of the above models that look at either knowledge outflows or relative public and private knowledge levels indicates that knowledge effects from partnering arrangements beyond inflows deserve attention.

In sum, the empirical work on knowledge effects from partnering generally focus on potential gains. These studies show that flexible boundaries have the potential to facilitate the absorption of knowledge from outside the firm. Implicit within this body of work is the idea that any firm efforts aimed at knowledge absorption or creation have positive competitive implications. Potential knowledge outflows or the relative value of knowledge gained or lost is just beginning to receive empirical attention. Furthermore, the existing research in this area does not generally measure contextual influences that may indicate whether the relative value of knowledge creation outweighs the value of protecting existing proprietary knowledge from dissemination. While the research indicates that flexible firm boundaries may facilitate the absorption of knowledge that resides outside the firm, how this is accomplished and at what competitive cost remains unanswered.

Integrating Knowledge Considerations and Flexible Boundaries Within a Context

As discussed, the existing research on flexible firm boundaries presents valuable information on how partnering arrangements may be configured to facilitate inflows of knowledge, while associated knowledge outflows have received little attention. However, the pressure on firms from the competitive landscape to either continue to develop new knowledge or products or to exploit existing proprietary information is also an important consideration (Brown and Eisenhardt 1997, Matusik and Hill 1998). Following is a review of the few studies that examine the role of the competitive environment's demands on firm knowledge. These arguments are then used as the starting point for a framework that integrates the multiple determinants of firm knowledge with what we know about partnering arrangements to address the cost and implementation considerations associated with using partnering as part of a knowledge accumulation and creation strategy.

The Role of Context

Theoretical arguments have been put forth about considering the importance of the competitive context in evaluating the potential economic benefits to knowledge creation activities. Matusik and Hill (1998) argue that the relative importance of knowledge creation activities versus the protection of proprietary knowledge from dissemination are critical in determining if, where, and how contract work should be used in firms. The relative importance of knowledge creation versus dissemination in their model is a function of the stability or dynamism in the competitive environment, as well as cost and flexibility demands. Brown and Eisenhardt (1997) use complexity theory in their inductive study of product development and continual innovation. Consistent with complexity theory, their findings suggest that firms need to keep pace with the rate of change in the competitive environment. Very high or very low levels of change relative to the rate of change in the environment have potentially negative competitive consequences. Kogut (2000) also addresses the role of the competitive context in examining the feasibility of different kinds of partnering arrangements. He argues that the strength of property rights and "bottlenecks" around the key technology (meaning one firm has a large degree of control over a key technology) affect the feasibility of certain kinds of partnering arrangements. While he does not specifically address the knowledge outcomes associated with different forms of partnering, implicit in his arguments is the notion that knowledge demands and the ability to protect knowledge is inextricably linked to partnering considerations.

Few deductive empirical studies have examined the role of the competitive context in knowledge strategies, though Rowley et al. (2000) are an exception. They look at two in-

dustries; one they classify as demanding high degrees of knowledge exploration/creation (semiconductors) and one demanding high degrees of knowledge exploitation (steel). They find that in the face of knowledge-creation demands at the industry level, weak network ties have positive performance implications. Conversely, in the face of pressures to exploit existing knowledge, strong network ties and the density of the ties has positive performance implications. Thus, industry-level factors influence the firm-level relationship between knowledge development and performance.

Decision Calculus

Integrating the above discussion of the role of context with the multiple determinants of firm knowledge and what we know about knowledge effects associated with partnering, figure 34.2

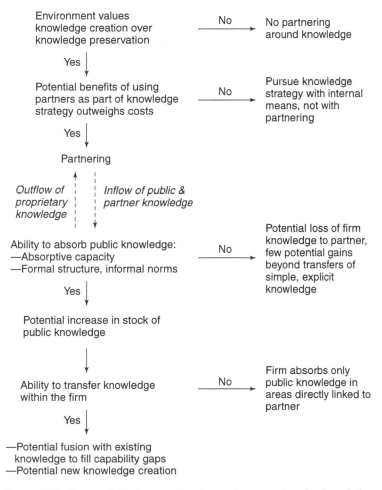

Figure 34.2. Cost and implementation issues in partnering for knowledge acquisition and creation.

presents a framework that identifies cost and implementation considerations associated with using partnering as part of a knowledge accumulation and creation strategy.

Demand for Knowledge Creation versus Knowledge Preservation Strategy

The degree to which the competitive environment values new knowledge creation over the preservation of existing knowledge that may confer a competitive advantage varies. The level of dynamism and the ability to protect and control key technologies are important considerations. The level of dynamism may reflect changes in customer preferences, the nature of necessary inputs (e.g., technology, human capital), competitor abilities, and imitation barriers. The ability to protect and control key knowledge is a function of the strength of property rights and the rare, inimitable, and nonsubstitutable nature of the knowledge. Thus, a primary consideration for firms examining knowledge-focused partnering is to what degree a knowledge creation strategy is appropriate within the competitive context. For example, in contexts where there are low levels of complexity and uncertainty, a higher focus on process-oriented research around existing technologies and skills in long-standing products and markets may have a higher value than the creation of new knowledge (Rowley et al. 2000). As Herz et al. (2000) note, the pursuit of knowledge in and of itself does not necessarily create economic value.

Costs Associated with Pursuing Knowledge Strategy Alone or Through Partnering

The literature indicates that there are many potential knowledge advantages associated with partnering. In fact, some knowledge may be obtained in no other way than through partnering with a firm that has control over an important technology. Thus, there is great potential value associated with pursuing a knowledge accumulation and creation strategy through partnering. The cost associated with pursuing a knowledge accumulation and creation strategy, either alone or through partnering, consists of building formal and informal structures that support within-firm transfers of knowledge. These costs are primarily the same, whether a firm goes it alone or partners. However, there are some additional costs associated with partnering for knowledge. There are direct costs associated with partner se-

lection, the construction of goals and intellectual property parameters, and the on-going management costs associated with partnering. There also are indirect costs associated with potential knowledge losses from being closely allied with a partner. In pursuing a partnering arrangement as part of a knowledge strategy, firms should consider the value of knowledge that may potentially be lost. In sum, the decision calculus of the firm in whether to use partnering to gain knowledge revolves around an assessment of these direct costs associated with partnering, as well as the indirect costs of the potential knowledge gains and losses.

Ability to Absorb Knowledge Through Partnering

The ability to absorb knowledge is critical in knowledge-based partnering because without it, a firm only stands to lose. Empirical results indicate that the same mechanisms that bring knowledge in also carry it out (Kale et al. 2000, Matusik 1999). Thus, the ability to absorb the knowledge brought in is essential in determining whether the net knowledge effects are positive or negative. By partnering around knowledge, the firm necessarily exposes itself to its partner. If the firm is not able to gain knowledge from its partner, then knowledge flows will be unidirectional—out of the firm. However, if the firm is able to absorb knowledge, it can increase its knowledge by bringing in some of that of its partner(s). This absorption can serve as a vehicle for bringing in best practices or partner proprietary knowledge, for example. This ability to absorb knowledge is a function of three considerations: the nature of the knowledge itself, the nature of the partnership, and firm attributes.

The first consideration is the nature of the knowledge involved in the partnering arrangement. The nature of firm knowledge has been characterized along multiple dimensions such as tacit versus explicit, component versus architectural, discrete versus systematic, and individual versus collective. The nature of knowledge affects the ease of transfer across firm boundaries. The codifiability of knowledge affects its ease of transfer because explicit knowledge is amenable to being expressed orally or in writing (Zander and Kogut 1995). Conversely, tacit knowledge, by definition, is not easily expressed. Even within a firm, the transfer of tacit knowledge is more difficult (Nonaka and Takeuchi 1995, Szulanski 1996). It follows then that explicit knowledge is easier to transfer across firm boundaries than tacit knowledge. To transfer such knowledge across firm boundaries, more intensive contact across the boundaries is necessary. Knowledge about particular parts or components of a product, project, or firm is more easily transferred than knowledge about how different parts or components are coordinated or put to product use. Component, discrete, or individually held knowledge is more limited in scope than architectural, systematic, or collectively held knowledge. Because of this more limited scope, it is easier to identify and analyze these forms of knowledge and transfer them. Knowledge about how different parts of an organization work together or systemswide knowledge requires information about a larger number of items and how these items interact. Accordingly, such knowledge is generally more complex in nature. Knowledge with greater levels of causal ambiguity (Szulanski 1996) or complexity (Galbraith 1990, Ounjian and Carne 1987) is also more difficult to transfer. Accordingly, such knowledge may be more difficult to transfer across boundaries than less complex or ambiguous knowledge. In addition, these multiple forms of knowledge intersect and further affect ease of transfer. For example, tacit architectural knowledge may be especially difficult to transmit because it is both complex and difficult to articulate, while at the other end of the spectrum, explicit component knowledge is more likely to be simple and easily expressed through formal documentation or procedures. Thus, the nature of the knowledge the firm hopes to attain affects whether those transfers will occur. If the firm hopes to obtain something like a chemical formula, such knowledge is likely to be component and explicit, so the nature of the knowledge itself should not hinder its transfer. However, if the firm hopes to attain knowledge about how its partner rapidly brings high quality new products to market, such knowledge is more likely to be architectural and at least partly tacit in nature, and so will be more difficult to transfer.

The nature of knowledge also affects what the firm may transmit to its partner, intentionally or unintentionally. The firm can most easily transfer out its own knowledge that is explicit and component in nature. If this is the intent of the firm, such transfers should be unproblematic. However, unintentional transfers may also occur. If the primary source of a firm's competitiveness is in knowledge that is explicit or component in nature, this may be more easily transmitted to a partner than knowledge that is tacit and architectural in nature which may be more impervious to dissemination outside the firm. The firm should consider the nature of the knowledge it intends to transfer as well as protect. In sum, the firm should analyze the nature of knowledge in three categories: that which it hopes to obtain through partnering; that which the firm itself is willing to transfer to its partner; and that which the firm does not intend to transfer out, but which may be exposed and vulnerable through the course of partnering.

The second consideration in the likelihood of transfer is the nature of the partnership itself. The similarities between partners are a critical part of this analysis. Studies indicate similarities across knowledge bases or skills, organizational structure, incentive systems, and dominant logics affect transfers (i.e., Hamel 1991, Lane and Lubatkin 1998, Mowery et al. 1996, Simonin 1999). Additionally, studies find that intra plant best practices transfers are more effective than inter plant transfers (Argote et al. 1990, Epple et al. 1996), and transfers within rather than between franchises are more effective (Argote 1999). In these cases, exchanges are easier within a superordinate relationship in which presumably there is constancy in much of the structure, knowledge and skill bases, incentives, and dominant logics within the plant or franchise system. These similarities, though, present a two-way street. On the one hand, selecting a similar partner means it may be easier to absorb knowledge from that partner. However, the converse is also true. A similar partner is also more likely to absorb the knowledge of the other firm. Thus, the nature of the partnership should be considered in conjunction with the nature of knowledge intended to be transferred. A symbiotic relationship is ideal when firms intend to transfer complex, tacit knowledge. However, if the intention is to transfer limited knowledge, the cost associated with exposing more firm knowledge to its partner should be weighed against the potential benefits from learning more from a partner than originally intended.

The third consideration is the within-firm capabilities: Does the firm have the ability and intent to effectively absorb knowledge? Ability is a function of related substantive knowledge (absorptive capacity) and the appropriate structures, norms, and interaction for the nature of knowledge in question. Absorptive capacity is defined as the ability to exploit external knowledge through the recognition of the value of new information, and the ability to assimilate and apply it to commercial ends. To effectively absorb knowledge from outside its boundaries, a firm must have enough related knowledge to recognize the value of new information, absorb the relevant information, and then use that information. Thus, absorptive capacity is related to partner similarity discussed above. To the extent firms have similar knowledge bases, they can more easily absorb and use new information that builds on existing knowledge.

Formal and informal structures of the firm also contribute to its ability to absorb knowledge. Incentive structures, opportunities to interact across groups, more frequent and richer communication channels, informal advice, transmission of anecdotes, personnel movement, bringing together individuals with different backgrounds, intentions to acquire knowledge, attitudes toward knowledge acquisition and cooperative behavior, and an interfunctional climate all affect absorption (Argote 1999, Hamel 1991, Moenart et al. 1994, Nonaka 1994). Other studies examines variables such as cash flow, diversification, firm size, market concentration, stage in technological life cycle, and interdepartmental linkages to predict knowledge levels as measured by proxy variables such as patents or R&D spending and intensity (see Cohen 1995 for summary). The level of commitment to learning from the partnership also influences the ability of the firm to transfer (Hamel 1991, Szulanski 1996). In addition, the type of interaction across those involved in partnering is important. Transfers of tacit or architectural knowledge require more intensive interactions than does the transfer of more simple explicit knowledge. Accordingly, the type of interaction across partners should reflect the requirements of the nature of knowledge to be transferred.

In sum, the ability to absorb knowledge from partnering is a function of the nature of knowledge, the characteristics of the partners, and the abilities within a firm to absorb external knowledge. These three considerations have implications for assessing whether a firm can benefit from its partner as well as the degree to which it is exposing its own knowledge base to intentional and unintentional transfers.

Ability to Transfer Knowledge Within the Firm

Within-firm knowledge transfers also are important indicators of the degree to which the firm can benefit from partnering. The extent to which the firm can effectively manage its within-firm knowledge flows affects its ability to fill capability gaps and create new knowledge. Capability gaps are filled when previously separate knowledge comes together. Assuming the firm effectively managed its within-firm knowledge transfers prior to partnering (see the earlier section in this study on within-firm transfers), the addition of new public knowledge from the partner can be dispersed through the firm to fill gaps that the firm was not able to bridge with its knowledge alone. Additionally, fusing previously separated knowledge stimulates new knowledge creation. Thus, the additional knowledge from partnering, if dispersed throughout the firm, can fuse with existing knowledge stocks to generate new knowledge. This fusion is especially important as it can create new knowledge at the intersection of private proprietary new knowledge and public best practices gleaned from a partner and so may be a potential source of competitive advantage. However, if a firm is unable to carry out within-firm knowledge transfers, it will then absorb knowledge from its partner only in the areas that are directly in contact with the partner. Though there are certainly gains associated with focused knowledge absorption, they are not likely to have the same magnitude as those in which knowledge is dispersed within an organization. As the innovation literature has long noted, scientific discovery and innovation are to a degree serendipitous. Nelson's seminal article (1959) on the benefits of basic research argues that the benefits from such research are most likely to accrue to firms that are active in multiple product markets because these firms can see the potential application of new ideas in a wider range of activities. Analogously, the firm that can transfer knowledge to different areas is more likely to find opportunities to apply the incoming knowledge to a wider set of challenges than the firm where the knowledge inflow is locally isolated.

Conclusion

The continued growth of knowledge-focused partnering, in its many forms, presents a host of challenges surrounding precisely how these arrangements affect knowledge outcomes and, ultimately, firm competitiveness. This chapter provides a navigational chart through the large bodies of research on knowledge and on partnering to outline the issues that inform the competitive implications of knowledge-focused partnering. The chapter makes two contributions to our understanding of the intersection of knowledge acquisition and creation with flexible firm boundaries. First, it presents a holistic picture of knowledge determinants. Though our research to date provides many useful insights into each of the determinants of knowledge levels, our understanding of how the multiple components intersect with one another to affect overall levels of knowledge is fragmented. Specifically neglected is the role of potential outflows of knowledge and the role of context in influencing the relative value of knowledge creation versus knowledge preservation strategies. Second, this chapter provides a framework to assess cost and implementation concerns that should accompany the consideration and effective use of knowledge-focused partnering.

This model also draws attention to the different roles of public versus private knowledge within the firm. While partnering can provide easier access to knowledge resident outside the boundaries of the firm, how this knowledge can help create a stronger competitive position for the firm requires close attention. After all, public knowledge cannot, by definition, be a source of competitive advantage. Rather, how this knowledge is applied within the firm to fill capability gaps and fuse with other knowledge to create new proprietary knowledge is important to consider. For example, can the firm effectively absorb this public knowledge and put it to productive use by dispersing it throughout and creating the conditions for it to fill capability gaps? And does the competitive environment reward the risk at which existing proprietary knowledge stocks are placed in attempts to let more public knowledge flow into the firm? As critics of the knowledge management movement have pointed out, a firm's pursuit of knowledge in and of itself may not necessarily create economic value. Instead, the cultivation of an agenda around either knowledge creation or preservation, coupled with an analysis of partnering that is centered on how the partnering can stimulate the creation of valuable private knowledge, can influence the effectiveness of knowledge partnering for long-run competitiveness. Thus, this chapter examines partnering considerations around the issue of how these arrangements can further knowledge-based objectives and, ultimately, firm competitiveness.

Note

1. See Floyd and Wooldridge (2000), Grant (1996), Huber (1991), Kogut and Zander (1993), and Spender (1996) for in-depth classifications and reviews of this literature.

References

Argote, L. (1999) *Organizational Learning: Creating, Retaining, and Transferring Knowledge.* Boston: Kluwer Academic Publishers.

Argote, L., Beckman, S.L., and Epple, D. (1990) "The persistence and transfer of learning in industrial settings." *Management Science* 36:140–154.

Barney, J.B. (1991) "Firm resources and sustained competitive advantage." *Journal of Management* 17:99–120.

Bleeke, J. and Ernst, D. (1995) "Is your strategic alliance really a sale?" *Harvard Business Review* 73:97–105.

Brown, S.L. and Eisenhardt, K.M. (1997) "The art of continuous change: Linking complexity theory and time-paced evolution in relentlessly shifting organization." *Administrative Science Quarterly* 42:1–34.

Castaneda, L.W. (2000) "Intrafirm knowledge transfer: A review and assessment of current research." Paper presented at the Academy of Management, Toronto, Canada.

Coff, R. (1999) "How buyers cope with uncertainty when acquiring firms in knowledge-intensive industries: Caveat emptor." *Organization Science* 10(2):144–161.

Cohen, W. (1995) "Empirical studies of innovative activity," in P. Stoneman (ed.), *Handbook of the Economics of Innovation and Technological Change*, pp. 182–264. Cambridge, MA: Blackwell.

Cohen, W. and Levinthal, D. (1989) "Innovation and learning: The two faces of R&D." *Economic Journal* 99:569–596.

Cohen, W.M. and Levinthal, D.A. (1990) "Absorptive capacity: A new perspective on learning and innovation." *Administrative Science Quarterly* 35:128–152.

Cradwell, D. (1995) *The Norton History of Technology*. London: W.W. Norton.

DeCarolis, D.M. and Deeds, D.L. (1999) "The impact of stocks and flows of organizational knowledge on firm performance: An empirical investigation of the biotechnology industry." *Strategic Management Journal* 20(10):953–968.

Dierickx, I. and Cool, K. (1989) "Asset stock accumulation and sustainability of competitive advantage." *Management Science* 35(12):1504–1511.

DiMaggio, P.J. and Powell, W.W. (1983) "The iron cage revisited: Institutional isomorphism and collective rationality in organizational fields." *American Sociological Review* 35:147–160.

Epple, D., Argote, L., and Murphy, K. (1996) "An empirical investigation of the micro structure of knowledge acquisition and transfer through learning by doing." *Organization Science* 2:58–70.

Floyd, S.W. and Wooldridge, B. (2000) *Building Strategy from the Middle: Reconceptualizing the*

Strategy Process. Thousand Oaks, CA: Sage Publications.

Freeman, C. (1991) "Networks of innovators: A synthesis." *Research Policy* 20:499–514.

Galbraith, C.S. (1990) "Transferring core manufacturing technologies in high technology firms." *California Management Review* 32(4):56–70.

Galbraith, J. (1973) *Designing Complex Organizations.* Reading, MA: Addison-Wesley.

Goes, J.B. and Park, S.H. (1997) "Interorganizational links and innovation: The case of hospital services." *Academy of Management Journal* 40: 673–697.

Grant, R.M. (1996) "Prospering in dynamically competitive environments: Organizations capability as knowledge integration." *Organization Science* 7:375–387.

Gulati, R., Nohria, N., and Zaheer, A. (2000) "Strategic networks." *Strategic Management Journal* 21:203–215.

Hagedoorn, J. (1995) "A note on international market leaders and networks of strategic technology partnering." *Strategic Management Journal* 16: 241–251.

Hamel, G. (1991) "Competition for competence and inter-partner learning within international strategic alliances." *Strategic Management Journal* 12: 83–103.

Hamel, G., Doz, Y.L., and Prahalad, C.K. (1989) "Collaborate with your competitors—and win." *Harvard Business Review*: 133–139.

Hansen, M.T. (1999) "The search-transfer problem: The role of weak ties in sharing knowledge across organizational subunits." *Administrative Science Quarterly* 44(1):82–111.

Hansen, M.T., Nohria, N., and Tierney, T. (1999) "What is your strategy for managing knowledge?" *Harvard Business Review* 77(2):106–116.

Herz, R., Amidon, D.M., Benkler, Y., Greene, D., Mayhew, J., Norton, D., O'Neill, S., Prusak, L., and Stewart, T.A. (2000) "The future course of knowledge management." Paper presented at the Knowledge: Management, measurement and organization, NYU, Stern School of Business Third Annual Intangibles Conference.

Huber, G.P. (1982) "Organizational information systems: Determinants of their performance and behavior." *Management Science* 28:135–155.

Huber, G.P. (1991) "Organizational learning: The contributing processes and the literatures." *Organization Science* 2:88–115.

Jaffe, A.B. (1986) "Technological opportunity and spillovers of R&D: Evidence from firms' patents, profits, and market value." *American Economic Review* 76:984–1001.

Jaffe, A.B. (1988) "Demand and supply influences in R&D intensity and productivity growth." *Review of Economics and Statistics* 70:431–437.

Jaffe, A.B., Trajtenberg, M., and Henderson, R. (1993) "Geographic localization of knowledge spillovers as evidenced by patent citations." *The Quarterly Journal of Economics* 108:577–598.

Kale, P., Singh, H., and Perlmutter, H. (2000) "Learning and protection of proprietary assets in strategic alliances: Building relational capital." *Strategic Management Journal* 21:217–237.

Kogut, B. (2000) "The network as knowledge: Generative rules and the emergence of structure." *Strategic Management Journal* 21:405–425.

Kogut, B., and Zander, U. (1993) "Knowledge of the firm and evolutionary theory of the multinational corporation." *Journal of International Business Studies* 24(4):625–646.

Koza, M.P. and Lewin, A.Y. (1998) "The co-evolution of strategic alliances." *Organization Science* 9(3): 255–264.

Krone, K.J., Jablin, F.M., and Putnam, L.L. (1987) "Communication theory and organizational communications: Multiple perspectives," in F.M. Jablin, L.L. Putnam, K.H. Roberts, and L.W. Porter (eds.), *Handbook of Organizational Communications.* Newbury Park, CA: Sage Publications.

Lane, P.J., and Lubatkin, M. (1998) "Relative absorptive capacity and interorganizational learning." *Strategic Management Journal* 19:461–477.

Larsson, R., Bengtsson, L., Henriksson, K., and Sparks, J. (1998) "The interorganizational learning dilemma: Collective knowledge development in strategic alliances." *Organization Science* 9(3): 285–305.

Lawrence, P.R. and Lorsch, J.W. (1967) *Organization and Environment: Managing Differentiation and Integration.* Boston: Harvard University Press.

Leonard-Barton, D. (1995) *Wellsprings of Knowledge: Building and Sustaining the Source of Innovation.* Boston: Harvard Business School Press.

Lorenzoni, G. and Lipparini, A. (1999) "The leveraging of interfirm relationships as a distinctive organizational capability: A longitudinal study." *Strategic Management Journal* 20(4):317–338.

Luo, Y. (1997) "Partner selection and venturing success: The case of joint ventures with firms in the People's Republic of China." *Organization Science* 8(6):648–662.

March, J.G. (1991) "Exploration and exploitation in organizational learning." *Organization Science* 2:71–87.

Matusik, S.F. (1999) "Ephemeral resources and firm knowledge: The case of the contingent work." Paper presented at the Academy of Management Annual Conference, BPS division, Chicago.

Matusik, S.F. and Hill, C.W.L. (1998) "The utilization of contingent work, knowledge creation, and competitive advantage." *Academy of Management Review* 23:680–697.

Moenart, R.K., Souder, W.E., Meyer, A.D., and Deschoolmeester, D. (1994) "R&D marketing integration mechanisms, communication flows, and innovation success." *Journal of Product Innovation Management* 11(1):31–46.

Mowery, D.C., Oxley, J.E., and Silverman, B.S. (1996) "Strategic alliances and interfirm knowledge transfer." *Strategic Management Journal* 17:77–92.

Nelson, R.R. (1959) "The simple economics of basic research." *Journal of Political Economy* 20: 297–306.

Nelson, R.R. and Winter, S.G. (1982) *An Evolutionary Theory of Economic Change*. Cambridge MA: The Belknap Press of Harvard University Press.

Nonaka, I. (1994) "A dynamic theory of organizational knowledge creation." *Organization Science* 5:14–37.

Nonaka, I. and Takeuchi, H. (1995) *The Knowledge-Creating Company*. New York: Oxford University Press.

Ounjian, M.L. and Carne, E.B. (1987) "A study of the factors which affect technology transfer in a multilocation multibusiness unit corporation." *IEEE Transactions on Engineering Management* EM34:194–201.

Powell, W.W., Koput, K.W., and Smith-Doerr, L. (1996) "Interorganizational collaboration and the locus of innovation: Networks of learning in biotechnology." *Administrative Science Quarterly* 41:116–145.

Rowley, T., Behrens, D., and Krackhardt, D. (2000) "Redundant governance structures: An analysis of structural and relational embeddedness in the steel and semiconductor industries." *Strategic Management Journal* 21:369–386.

Senge, P.M. (1990) *The Fifth Discipline: The Age and Practice of the Learning Organization*. London: Century Business.

Simon, H.A. (1991) "Bounded rationality and organizational learning." *Organization Science* 2(1):125–134.

Simonin, B.L. (1999) "Ambiguity and the process of knowledge transfer in strategic alliances." *Strategic Management Journal* 20(7):595–623.

Skenkar, O. and Li, J. (1999) "Knowledge search in international cooperative ventures." *Organization Science* 10(2):134–143.

Spender, J.C. (1996) "Making knowledge the basis of a dynamic theory of the firm." *Strategic Management Journal* 17(Special Issue): 45–62.

Szulanski, G. (1996) "Exploring internal stickiness: Impediments to the transfer of best practice within the firm." *Strategic Management Journal* 17(Winter):27–43.

Veugelers, R. (1997) "Internal R&D expenditures and external technology sourcing." *Research Policy* 26:303–315.

Zander, U. and Kogut, B. (1995) "Knowledge and the speed of the transfer and imitation of organizational capabilities: An empirical test." *Organization Science* 6(1):76–92.

VII

Managing Intellectual Capital

Managing Organizational Knowledge by Diagnosing Intellectual Capital

Framing and Advancing the State of the Field

Nick Bontis

He that hath knowledge spareth words; and a man of understanding is of an excellent spirit.
Proverbs 17:27

Management academics strive to conduct rigorous research from which knowledge can be transferred to future generations of managers. Thus, their role is twofold: that of theorist as well as educator. This logic has some inherent implications. First, rigorous research is required to clear the publication hurdle. This generally leads to newer academics pursuing the path of least resistance. Typically, these paths are described as having voluminous amounts of researchers and even more voluminous amounts of past research to draw on. The second implication lies in the notion that something out there exists to be to examined. The debate of whether academics lead or lag the real world has been argued for centuries. The answer, of course, rests with which group you associate with. Finally, academics must teach relevant conceptualizations in the classroom. With rising tuition costs and increas-

ing alternatives, students are in a position to carefully scrutinize where their hard-earned money will go. Within the context of the aforementioned implications, this chapter's objective is to frame and advance the field of intellectual capital. In attempting to conceptualize the phenomenon from a variety of perspectives and for different audiences, the intellectual capital field can take stock of where it has been and where it is going. This is necessary in order for it to continue its trajectory.

How has the burgeoning field of intellectual capital developed? A variety of perspectives will be used to answer this question. First, the field of intellectual capital initially started appearing in the popular press in the early 1990s (Stewart 1991, 1994). Intellectual capital was described by Stewart (1997) as a "brand new tennis ball—fuzzy, but with a lot of bounce" (p. xii). However, this statement acts as a detriment to the survival of this field in academia. Most "bouncy" topics that are researched extensively (e.g., reengineering, quality circles, management by objectives) are sometimes frowned upon in academic circles because they are considered nothing more than popular fads. Due to their temporal shortcomings, they are deemed not worthy of serious study. On the other hand, the "fuzzy" aspect of intellectual capital captures the curious interest of practitioners who are on the prowl for solutions to difficult challenges. Hence, the popularity of this topic during its genesis has been sponsored by business practitioners. It is with this audience that the conceptualization of intellectual capital resonates most.

Academics wishing to study this phenomenon face tremendous challenges. A so-called "hot topic" has no legacy, no world-renowned researchers, and no publication trajectory to follow. This becomes a very risky proposition for developing a publication portfolio. The academic state of this field is in its embryonic stage. It is being pursued by those academics who have a very strong managerial focus and a strong appetite for a field devoid of shape or direction.

The study of the field of intellectual capital is akin to the pursuit of the "elusive intangible." Academics and practitioners alike recognize and appreciate the tacit nature of organizational knowledge. Furthermore, intellectual capital is typically conceptualized as a set of subphenomena. The real problem with intellectual capital lies in its measurement. Unfortunately, an invisible conceptualization—regardless of its underlying simplicity—becomes an abyss for the academic researcher. To make matters worse, intellectual capital is conceptualized from numerous disciplines, making the field a mosaic of perspectives. Accountants are interested in how to measure it on the balance sheet, information technologists want to codify it in systems, sociologists want to balance power with it, psychologists want to develop minds because of it, human resource managers want to calculate a return on investment for it, and training and development officers want to make sure that they can build it. This field may be growing at a fantastic rate, but does anyone know where it is heading? Academics may want to ask their customers.

Students have spent decades learning how to manage scarce resources. The traditional economic model rests on the tenets of the scarcity assumption, which states that supply and demand determine market price. As all introductory economic students have learned, if supply goes down, price goes up (assuming demand is constant). However, knowledge as a resource does not comply with the scarcity assumption. The more knowledge supplied (or shared), the more highly it is valued. Furthermore, when was the last time the demand for knowledge went down? In fact, scientific folklore of the early 1900s held that all the information in the world doubled every 30 years. As the 1970s approached, that number was reduced to 7 years. Prognosticators have pushed this notion further and state that by the year 2010 all the information in the world will double every 11 hours. Do we need a better reason to appreciate the importance of educating or managing students within the intellectual capital framework?

Most if not all premier business schools around the world continue or are planning to redesign their programs. A quick scan through most course outlines yields a standard offering of functional courses with integrative modules using a variety of pedagogical techniques. One of the key issues that is being addressed is how to reflect in the classroom the onslaught of new initiatives such as intellectual capital, organizational learning, knowledge management, and other "knowledge era" initiatives. Professors continue to publish new texts to help fill the void in this new burgeoning market of course redesign. In the United States, "discussions with colleagues around the country led [professors] to conclude that [they] were not the only ones struggling to find an appropriate text for teaching the business strategy course" (Besanko et al. 1996, p. iv). Similarly, in Canada, "the primary stimulus for [revising] the book was [the program's] ongoing need for new material" (Beamish and Woodcock 1996, p. vii). Business schools that can tap into the need for managerial training that is reflective of the knowledge era will be well positioned to ride the current wave of intellectual capital interest as well.

Intellectual Capital Is an Organizational Resource

It seems that every month a new management technique emerges which CEOs, hungry for new ways to improve the performance of their business, readily devour. Companies are rightsizing, downsizing, and reengineering. They are promoting a culture of leaders and followers. They are striving to be "learning organizations" and promoting team building and self-empowerment. The options are overwhelming. But all these techniques have one thing in common: they are seeking to discover better ways to use organizational resources.

In our present economy, more and more businesses are evolving whose value is based not on their tangible resources but on their intangible resources (Itami 1987). Tangible resources are those typically found on the balance sheet of a company, such as cash, buildings, and machinery. The other category comprises intangible resources: people and their expertise, business processes, and market assets such as customer loyalty, repeat business, reputation, and so forth. The annual reports of companies such as Skandia (1994, 1995a, 1995b, 1996a, 1996b, 1997) are working toward a new balance sheet that makes more sense in today's marketplace. This new balance sheet highlights the difference between visible (explicit) accounting and invisible (implicit) accounting. Traditional annual reports have concentrated on reporting what can be explicitly calculated such as receivables, fixed assets, and so forth. Skandia has made an effort to report on their invisible assets such as intellectual capital, which provides the company with much of its market value added. Examples of other organizations that are following Skandia's lead can be found in the service sector and any enterprise where businesses rely primarily on people, such as software development start-ups, management consultants, high-technology ventures, life sciences and health care, media and entertainment and law firms (Bontis 1996a).

Although intangible assets may represent competitive advantage, organizations do not understand their nature and value (Collis 1996). Managers do not know the value of their own intellectual capital. They do not know if they have the people, resources, or business processes in place to make a success of a new strategy. They do not understand what know-how, management potential, or creativity they have access to with their employees. Because they are devoid of such information, they are rightsizing, downsizing, and reengineering in a vacuum.

That organizations are operating in a vacuum is not surprising, as they do not have any methods or tools that would enable them to analyze their intellectual capital stocks and organizational learning flows. To that end, a methodology and valuation system is required that will enable managers to identify, document, and value their knowledge management. This will enable them to make information-rich decisions

when they are planning to invest in the protection of their various intellectual properties.

In this chapter, the management of organizational knowledge encompasses two distinct but related phenomena: organizational learning flows and intellectual capital stocks. These phenomena are interrelated because organizations that have a higher capacity to absorb knowledge will also have a higher propensity to utilize and circulate it (Cohen and Levinthal 1990). The question of whether or not organizations are efficient purveyors of knowledge (Pavitt 1971) ignores the complex cognitive and behavioral changes that must occur before learning can take place. It is important to study how knowledge travels and changes in organizations (Hedlund and Nonaka 1993).

As mentioned above, intellectual capital research has primarily evolved from the desires of practitioners (Bassi and Van Buren 1998, Bontis 1996a, Darling 1996, Edvinsson and Sullivan 1996, Saint-Onge 1996). Consequently, recent developments have come largely in the form of popular press articles in business magazines and national newspapers. The challenge for academics is to frame the phenomenon using extant theories in order to develop a more rigorous conceptualization. This chapter coalesces many perspectives from numerous fields of study in an attempt to raise the understanding and importance of this phenomenon. The objective here is to conceptualize and frame the existing literature on intellectual capital as a foundation for further study.

Knowledge creation by business organizations has been virtually neglected in management studies, even though Nonaka and Takeuchi (1995) are convinced that this process has been the most important source of international competitiveness for some time. Even management guru Peter Drucker (1993) heralds the arrival of a new economy, which he refers to as the "knowledge society." He claims that in this society, knowledge is not just another resource alongside the traditional factors of production—labor, capital, and land—but the only meaningful resource today.

Until recently there has been little attempt to identify, and give structure to, the nature and role of intangible resources in the strategic management of a business. This is partly due to the fact that it is often very difficult for accountants and economists to allocate an orthodox valuation to intangibles, as they rarely have an exchange value. In consequence, intangibles usually lie outside the province of the commodity-based models of economics and accountancy (Hall 1992). As Johnson and Kaplan (1987) state:

> A company's economic value is not merely the sum of the values of its tangible assets, whether measurable at historic cost, replacement cost, or current market value prices. It also includes the value of intangible assets: the stock of innovative products, the knowledge of flexible and high-quality production processes, employee talent, and morals, customer loyalty and product awareness, reliable suppliers, efficient distribution networks and the like. Reported earnings cannot show the company's decline in value when it depletes its stock of intangible resources. Recent overemphasis on achieving superior long-term earnings performance is occurring just at the time when such performance has become a far less valid indicator of changes in the company's long-term competitive position. (p. 202)

Charles Handy (1989) suggests that the intellectual assets of a corporation are usually three to four times tangible book value. He warns that no executive would leave his cash or factory space idle, yet if CEOs are asked how much of the knowledge in their companies is used, they typically say only about 20%. The importance of this topic is also reflected in the growth of the professional services industry and the many new knowledge-based firms that have fueled our economy. Top MBA recruits no longer find as many positions in manufacturing companies as they did in the 1950s and 1960s. Nowadays, the career services offices of many business schools report that most new graduates secure positions with management consultants, accounting firms, investment banks, law firms, software developers, and information brokers. The common element found in each of these organizations is the abundance of intellectual capital.

To grasp the importance of why it is necessary to measure intellectual capital, we must understand the concept of "Tobin's q" from the accounting and finance literature. This ratio measures the relationship between a company's market value and its replacement value (i.e., the cost of replacing its assets). The ratio was developed by the Nobel Prize–winning economist James Tobin (White et al. 1994). In the long run, this

ratio will tend toward 1.00, but evidence shows that it can differ significantly from 1.00 for very long periods of time (Bodie et al. 1993). For example, companies in the software industry, where intellectual capital is abundant, tend to have a Tobin's q ratio of 7.00, whereas firms in the steel industry, noted for their large capital assets, have a q ratio of nearly 1.00.

Having discussed the importance of the intellectual capital field from multiple perspectives, we now turn to a review of the literature in order to understand the genesis of its conceptualization.

Review of the Literature

Although the importance of knowledge can be traced back to the ancient Greeks, the first evidence of codification of knowledge may have its roots in scientific management. Frederick Taylor (1911) attempted to formalize workers' experiences and tacit skills into objective rules and formulas. Barnard (1938) extended scientific management by also considering "behavioral knowledge" in management processes. As the two perspectives merged, a new synthesis of knowledge management was born that laid the foundation of organization theory. It was Herbert Simon (1945), influenced by the development of the computer and cognitive science, who recognized the nature of decision making while performing administrative functions. Simon further recognized the limitations of human cognitive capacity and coined the term "bounded rationality." Whereas traditional inputs of capital are limited by physical space or monetary constraints, intellectual capital generation may be limited by the collective "bounded rationality" of the organization.

Schumpeter (1934) was primarily concerned with the process of change in the economy as a whole. He attributed the emergence of new products and processes to new "recombinations" of knowledge. Taking this view further, Edith Penrose (1959) pointed out that the organization was considered as a "knowledge repository" and recognized the importance of experience and knowledge accumulated within the firm. Evolutionary theorists Nelson and Winter (1982) also viewed the firm as a repository of knowledge. For them, knowledge is stored as regular and predictable behavioral patterns or "routines."

Today, the nature and performance consequences of the strategies used by organizations to develop, maintain, and exploit knowledge for innovation constitute an important topic in the field of business strategy, but one that has received inadequate treatment in the extant literature (McGrath et al. 1996). Orthodox economics sidesteps the topic completely by assuming that all firms may choose from a set of universally accessible "production functions" that completely determine production cost structures and therefore do not lead to any knowledge-based performance differences (Nelson 1991, Teece 1982). The industrial organization literature on learning by doing is a partial exception (see Fudenberg and Tirole 1986).

Partly in response to this shortcoming, during the past several decades a number of theories have been developed in the field of strategy. Organizational economics and organization theory hold that firm-level differences in knowledge do exist and, moreover, that these differences play a large role in determining economic performance. These approaches include mainstream strategy (Ansoff 1965, Andrews 1971), the resource-based view of the firm (Penrose 1959, Rubin 1973, Teece 1982, Wernerfelt 1984, Barney 1986a, 1991, Dierickx and Cool 1989, Hall 1992), evolutionary theory (Nelson and Winter 1982, Winter 1987), and core competencies (Prahalad and Hamel 1990).

Economic analysis of competitive advantage focuses on how industry structure determines the profitability of firms in an industry. However, firm differences, not industry differences, are thought by many to be at the heart of strategic analysis (Nelson 1991, Rumelt 1991). Furthermore, while most formal economic tools are used to determine optimal product-market activities, the traditional concept of strategy is phrased in terms of the resource position of the firm (Learned et al. 1969, Wernerfelt 1984). Generally speaking, the indifferent treatment of knowledge in the neoclassical economics tradition endures. Firms are assumed to have the same fixed knowledge as they are jockeyed around by the invisible hand of the market. This theoretical lens is deficient in describing the phenomenon of knowledge because of two important neoclassical economics assumptions: all parties have perfect and complete information, and resources are completely mobile. These two assumptions are in conflict with the notion that individuals have limits to their cognitive abilities (Simon 1991) and that some forms of tacit knowledge are impossible to articulate (Polanyi 1967). This form of tacit knowledge that is em-

bedded in the organization can be better explained by the evolutionary theory of the firm.

Polanyi's (1967) tacit–explicit distinction was introduced into the literature by Nelson and Winter (1982) in their evolutionary theory of the firm. At the crux of their evolutionary theory are "organizational routines" that allow firms the special context in which tacit and explicit knowledge interacts:

> Organizational routines are the organization's genetic material, some explicit in bureaucratic rules, some implicit in the organization's culture. The interaction between the explicit and the tacit is evolutionary in that the choices made by individuals are selected in or out according to their utility in a specific historical and economic reality, and eventually embedded in organizational routines which then shape and constrain further individual choices. (p. 134)

Although the evolutionary theory of the firm improves on the deficiencies of the neoclassical economic tradition, it still lacks the contextual implications of a changing business environment. It may be true that organizational knowledge is embedded in routines, but evolutionary theory does not describe persistence or change of routines over time. For example, if explicit rules have been codified at one point in time, one can argue that these routines may not be appropriate at some later point in time when environmental conditions have forced an alternative strategic orientation. Pushing this notion forward, it is argued that organizational routines represent a collection of embedded rules from different times representing different environmental contexts. This internal focus on the firm's rules and resources is the basis for the resource-based view of the firm.

The resource-based view of the firm has been developed in work by Wernerfelt (1984), Barney (1986a, 1986b), Teece and colleagues (1988), Teece et al. (1994), and Prahalad and Hamel (1990), among others, largely as a reaction to the dominant competitive forces analysis of firm strategy. Other important anticipations of and contributions to this theory include Penrose (1959) and Chandler (1977, 1990). The resource-based view of the firm suggests that a business enterprise is best viewed as a collection of "sticky" and difficult-to-imitate resources and capabilities (Penrose 1959, Barney 1986a, 1986b, Wernerfelt 1984). Firm-specific resources can be physical, such as production techniques protected by patents or trade secrets, or intangible, such as brand equity or operating routines.

A confusing issue with the resource-based view begins with definitions (Nanda 1996). There is an embarrassing profusion of riches in phrases such as "distinctive competence" (Selznick 1957), "strategic firm resources" (Barney 1986b), "invisible assets" (Itami 1987), "strategic firm-specific assets" (Dierickx and Cool 1989), "core competencies" (Prahalad and Hamel 1990), "corporate capabilities" (Nohria and Eccles 1991), "dynamic capabilities" (Teece et al. 1994), "combinative capabilities" (Kogut and Zander 1992), and others just waiting to be published. Although some researchers claim differences in meanings, a few have simply found an opportunity to add their own two cents worth to a growing market of definitions. An alternate route to the nomenclature regurgitation would be to start with a general definition of resources as inputs and then to analyze the circumstances under which they are useful (Nanda 1996).

The resource-based view has other limitations. Given the emphasis on firm resources, it is argued that the only feasible unit of analysis for the resource-based view paradigm is the organization. However, past research has shown that this is somewhat limiting. Empirically, Schmalense (1985) discovered that profit differences are attributable mostly to industry effects, and firm effects are insignificant. Hansen and Wernerfelt (1989) found that both industry and firm effects were significant and independent. Kessides (1990) discovered significant firm effects, but these were dominated by industry effects. In sum, the resource-based view may have too much of an internal focus on the firm. Other researchers have taken the resource-based view further by emphasizing knowledge and learning as the critical resource. Thus, the knowledge-based view of the firm was created as an extension of the resource-based view.

Knowledge management theorists argue that knowledge is the preeminent resource of the firm (Grant 1996a, 1996b, Spender 1994, 1996, Baden-Fuller and Pitt 1996, Davenport and Prusak 1997). The knowledge-based view of the firm identifies the primary rationale for the firm as the creation and application of knowledge (Demsetz 1991, Kogut and Zander 1992, Nonaka 1994, Spender 1994, Nonaka and Takeuchi 1995, Foss 1996, Grant 1996a, 1996b, Bierly and Chakrabarti 1996, Conner and Prahalad 1996, Choi and Lee 1997). The knowledge-based view of the firm "can yield insights beyond the production-function and resource-based theories of the firm by creating a new view of the firm as a dynamic, evolving, quasi-autonomous system of knowledge production and application" (Spender 1996, p. 59). Viewing the firm as a knowledge system focuses the attention not on the allegedly given resources that the firm must use, but also, to use Penrose's (1959, p. 25) language, on the *services* rendered by a firm's resources.

Much of the literature on intellectual capital stems from an accounting and financial perspective. Many of these researchers are interested in answering two questions: (1) what causes firms to be worth so much more than their book value, and (2) what specifically is in this intangible asset. Stewart (1997) defines intellectual capital as the intellectual material that has been formalized, captured, and leveraged to create wealth by producing a higher valued asset. Following the work of Bontis (1996a, 1988), Roos et al. (1998), Stewart (1991, 1994, 1997), Sveiby (1997), Edvinsson and Malone (1997), Saint-Onge (1996), Sullivan and Edvinsson (1996), and Edvinsson and Sullivan (1996), among others, intellectual capital is defined as encompassing (a) human capital, (b) structural capital, and (c) relational capital. These subphenomena encompass the intelligence found in human beings, organizational routines, and network relationships, respectively. This field typically looks at organizational knowledge as a static asset in an organization—a so-called "stock." This concerns many theorists who are also interested in the flow of knowledge. Furthermore, intellectual capital research does not cater to changes in cognition or behavior of individuals, which is necessary for learning and improvement. The field of organizational learning has an extensive history in dealing with these limitations.

Change is the only constant variable in business today (Senge 1990). Kanter (1989) notes that organizations attempt to develop structures and systems that are more responsive to change. The field of organizational learning has thrived in this context because managers believe that the more they learn about change and learning itself, the better they will be in handling it and the better their firms will perform. However, Miller (1996) describes the organizational learning literature as maddeningly abstract and vague. Managers have little experience with organizational learning concepts (EUI and IBM 1996). Veilleux (1995) surveyed 186 human resource executives and found that although 98% of the respondents believed in the concept of organizational learning, only 52% responded that their organization had an average ability to learn. Since the seminal article by Cangelosi and Dill (1965), organizational learning has been described at three different levels: individual, group, and organization. While many organizational learning theorists have argued for the existence of learning at these levels, some researchers, especially academics in the field of international management, have extended the framework to include learning at the transorganizational level.

Individual learning is a prerequisite for organizational learning (Kim 1993). Individual level learning occurs simply by virtue of being human (McGee and Prusak 1993). As Senge (1990) puts it, "[O]rganizations learn only through individuals who learn. Individual learning does not guarantee organizational learning but without it no organizational learning occurs" (p. 139). The notion here is that organizational knowledge resides in the minds of employees. Nonaka and Takeuchi (1995) also point out that individual level learning is the foundation: "Knowledge is created only by individuals. An organization cannot create knowledge on its own without individuals. Organizational knowledge creation should be understood as a process that organizationally amplifies the knowledge created by individuals and crystallizes it at the group level through dialogue, discussion, experience sharing, or observation" (p. 239).

For the most part, researchers generally agree that individual learning is a necessary precursor to learning at a higher level (Greeno 1980). Some theorists support group-level learning as an alternative to the limitations of individual learning. Group knowledge is not a mere gathering of individual knowledge. The knowledge of individual members needs to be shared and legitimized through integrating interactions and information technology before it becomes group knowledge (Tsuchiya 1994). Learning at the organizational level starts once organizational teams integrate their own respective learning. This level of the IGO (individual–group–organizational) framework highlights the importance of the learning that resides in the organization's systems, structures, procedures, routines, and so forth (Fiol and Lyles 1985). This level of organizational learning requires the conversion of individual and group learning into a systematic base of organizational intellectual capital (Shrivastava 1986). Several other theorists concur that learning at the organizational level is an accepted component of learning in organizations

(Duncan and Weiss 1979, Hedberg 1981, Shrivastava 1983, Levitt and March 1988, Stata 1989, Huber 1991, Crossan et al. 1995, Inkpen and Crossan 1995).

Businesses are typically well versed in assessing and valuing tangible assets, such as buildings, machinery, cash, and so forth, but such measures do not include the value of the work force, their knowledge, the way they use computer systems, and so on. In an information society, such intangible assets may represent significant competitive advantage. Itami (1987) has argued that successful organizations recognize that most activities offer the potential to either enhance, or degrade, their key invisible assets, which they define as including reputation, know-how, and such. These businesses expect to accumulate invisible assets, as well as conventional assets, as they complete each turn of the business cycle.

The traditional financial performance measures worked well for the industrial era, but they are out of step with the skills and competencies companies are trying to master today (Kaplan and Norton 1992). Over the last 15 years management accounting has been redefining itself to accommodate the vast changes that have taken place in the world economy. Management accounting researchers and practitioners alike have acknowledged that many of the ways in which organizations structure and implement their management planning and control systems lack relevance for the new economy. Quinn (1992) argues that the new economy is a service-based economy where even manufacturers need to identify their core competencies as those "services" that they offer that are valued added and of a "best-in-the-world" caliber.

Many organizations are still philosophically wedded to outmoded, inward-looking management planning and control systems that use wealth measures based on physical assets and evaluation of performance linked to these. Rather than an organization's physical assets, the new economy will require the valuation of an organization's total assets, which includes its intellectual assets. Hence, to be relevant, organizations need to develop planning, control, and performance measurement systems that account for (i.e., predict, measure, and evaluate) these intellectual assets.

Kaplan and Norton (1992) proposed using what they called a "balanced scorecard" approach to performance measurement. One element of the balanced scorecard is an innovation and learning perspective that tries to assess the way in which the organization can continue to improve and create value. Vitale et al. (1994) and Vitale and Mavrinac (1995) have also developed a model and a means of evaluating a performance evaluation system on the basis of the organization's strategy, which they term "a strategic performance evaluation" system. The strategic performance evaluation system is very much an outgrowth of Kaplan and Norton's balanced scorecard concept, but it moves beyond it by providing a more direct implementation focus. Although all of these authors acknowledge the importance of learning, none of them provides specific guidance on ways in which to measure and evaluate an organization's intellectual capital stocks or organizational learning flows. Thus, while their recommendations should help organizations to bring their management planning and control systems more in line with the reality of the new economy, they still overlook the significance of knowledge management as a critical success factor of the new economic entity and its key to long-run survival.

To understand the intellectual expertise embedded in an organization requires organizational members to assess their core competencies—those areas where they can achieve or have achieved "best-in-the-world" status (Prahalad and Hamel 1990, Quinn 1992). The intellectual capital of an organization represents the wealth of ideas and ability to innovate that will determine the future of the organization. Why have management accountants and financial analysts avoided this area until recently? The most obvious answer is that intellectual capital is not only difficult to measure but also difficult to evaluate. In the past, accountants have assumed a position that either ignores the problems or writes them off as impossible to solve (Luscombe 1993). It is important to realize that intellectual capital is real and provides value. One need only look at the hackneyed example of Microsoft, whose accounting book value is significantly less than its market value based on share price, to see that there must be some explanation of this "excess" market valuation. Arguably, this "excess" is the market valuation of the intellectual capital stocks and organizational learning flows of the company.

Another measurement tool that is finding increased usage among large corporations is economic value added (EVA; Bontis 1996b). In defining and refining EVA, Stewart (1991, 1994) identified over 120 shortcomings in conventional GAAP accounting to measure real economic income. However, McConville (1994) and Ochsner

(1995) warn that although EVA makes useful adjustments for decision-making purposes, its exotic allure often leaves top executives with no clear instructions on its implementation. Accounting for such assets was also the aim in human resource accounting back in the 1960s.

As defined above, human capital represents the human factor in the organization: the combined intelligence, skills, and expertise that gives the organization its distinctive character. The human elements of the organization are those that are capable of learning, changing, innovating, and providing the creative thrust that, if properly motivated, can ensure the long-run survival of the organization. As per Lynn's (1998) overview of Human resource accounting (HRA), since Hermanson's classic study in 1964, the topic of how to and whether to value human assets has been debated by accountants and human resource theorists. Indeed, the arguments for and against HRA are especially pertinent to the valuation of intellectual assets in the new economy since they involve essentially the same issues.

According to Sackmann et al. (1989), the objective of HRA is to "quantify the economic value of people to the organization" to provide input to management and financial decisions (p. 235). Three types of HRA measurement models have been proposed by researchers:

1. Cost models: historical or acquisition cost (Brummet et al. 1968), replacement cost (Flamholtz 1973), and opportunity cost (Hekimian and Jones 1967)
2. Human resource value models: a nonmonetary behavioral emphasis model (Likert 1967) and combined nonmonetary behavioral and monetary economic value models (Likert and Bowers 1973, Gambling 1974)
3. Monetary emphasis: discounted earnings or wages approach (Morse 1973, Friedman and Lev 1974)

Sackmann et al. (1989) discuss these models extensively and also summarize the numerous attempts to apply the models in various types of organizations. While none of the experiments in HRA has been a long-run success, it is interesting to note that the majority of systems developed were in service organizations (i.e., CPA firms, banks, insurance and financial services firms) where human capital comprises a significant proportion of organizational value.

The HRA approach has always had its critics. All of the models suffer from subjectivity and uncertainty and lack reliability in that they cannot be audited with any assurance. Both of these are measurement problems. Other criticisms of HRA include whether it is morally acceptable to treat people as assets and whether such measures are too easily manipulated. Although these arguments are salient comments on HRA, they beg the question of whether human assets in organizations do have value. As said above, if intellectual capital does not exist in organizations, then why does stock price react to changes in management? Obviously, investors and financial markets attach value to the skills and expertise of CEOs and other top management. Investors value the people, their skills, and their potential in such organizations. In fact, the criticisms of HRA arise largely from the fact that such valuations of intellectual capital are "soft" measures rather than objective auditable numbers. The question thus arises: Are auditable valuations of intellectual capital necessary in the conventional sense? The answer is being debated by such bodies as the Financial Accounting Standards Board (FASB), Canadian Institute for Chartered Accountants (CICA), Securities and Exchange Commission (SEC), and International Accounting Standards Committee (IASC) right now. We

shall soon see where the accountants will lead us. In the mean time, we can continue with further development of intellectual capital's conceptualization.

Proposed Conceptualization

Adopting Kogut and Zander's (1992) perspective on higher order organizing principles, figure 35.1 proposes a conceptualization of intellectual capital. Intellectual capital is a second-order multidimensional construct. Its three subdomains include (1) human capital—the tacit knowledge embedded in the minds of the employees, (2) structural capital—the organizational routines of the business, and (3) relational capital—the knowledge embedded in the relationships established with the outside environment (Bontis 1996a, Edvinsson and Sullivan 1996).

Organizational learning, as described by Chris Argyris at Harvard (1992), among others, has been thought of as the flow of knowledge in a firm; it follows, then, that intellectual capital is the stock of knowledge in the firm. To marry the two concepts, it may be useful to consider intellectual capital as the stock unit of organizational learning. However, intellectual capital cannot necessarily be taught through education and

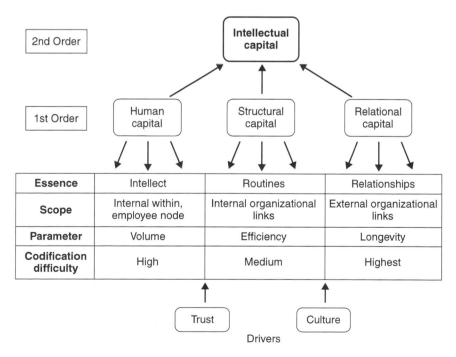

Figure 35.1 Conceptualization of intellectual capital.

training. The most precious knowledge in an organization often cannot be passed on (Levitt 1991).

Prior to continuing the conceptualization of intellectual capital stocks, it may be helpful to define *what it is not*. Intellectual capital does not include intellectual property. Intellectual property comprises assets that include copyrights, patents, semiconductor topography rights, and various design rights. It also includes trade and service marks. Undertaking an intellectual property audit is not a new idea. However, many organizations find that the results of an intellectual property audit are not particularly useful. After all, knowing that you own a patent is not a lot of use if that fact is not accompanied with information concerning its potential. Potential can be evaluated from various aspects of the patent, including return on investment, commercial potential, competitive advantage, and so on. It is important to note that intellectual property assets are usually considered from their legal perspective, which should mirror that "raison d'être." A patent for its own sake has no point or value. Therefore, intellectual property and intellectual capital are considered mutually exclusive, but the former can be considered an output of the latter.

The conceptualization of intellectual capital shall continue with an examination of the "organizational knowledge" literature. Although theories differ in their terminology and the degree to which they explicitly discuss the attributes of organizational knowledge, they all concur that superior performance, including the procurement of economic profits, results at least in part from the exploitation of distinctive process knowledge that is not articulable and that can be acquired only through experience—in short, knowledge that is "tacit" in nature (Polanyi 1967, Winter 1987). Yet, in emphasizing the positive effects of tacit knowledge on economic performance, these theories suffer from a serious shortcoming as well. While they concede that tacit knowledge limits the ability of the organization to compete in a new industrial environment in which a substantially different knowledge base is required for competitive success, they fail to recognize that tacit knowledge also limits the ability of the organization to adapt to the changing competitive requirements of the existing industry within which it already operates.

The phenomenon of intellectual capital can be dissected into three subdomains, listed above. Each is described below in the context of its essence, scope, parameter, and codification difficulty (see figure 35.1). Subsequent to that description, two drivers—"trust" and "culture"—are evaluated for their impact on intellectual capital development.

Human Capital

First, the organization's members possess individual tacit knowledge (i.e., inarticulable skills necessary to perform their functions; Nelson and Winter 1982). In order to illustrate the degree to which tacit knowledge characterizes the human capital of an organization, it is useful to conceive of the organization as a productive process that receives tangible and informational inputs from the environment, produces tangible and informational outputs that enter the environment, and is characterized internally by a series of flows among a network of nodes and ties or links (see figure 35.2).

A node represents the work performed—either pure decision making, innovative creativity, improvisation (Crossan et al. 1996), or some combination of the three—by a single member of the organization or by parallel, functionally equivalent members who do not interact with one another as part of the productive process (see figure 35.2). Thus, individual tacit knowledge, when present, exists at the nodes themselves. A tie or link is directional in nature and represents a flow of intermediate product or information from a given node. Every node has at least one tie or link originating from it, while multiple ties originating from a single node imply that the task performed at the node includes a decision about where to direct the subsequent flow. Structural tacit knowledge, when present, implies that no member of the organization has an explicit overview of these ties or, consequently, of the corresponding arrangement of nodes (see subsequent discussion on structural capital). Accordingly, a productive process characterized by a substantial degree of tacit knowledge is arranged as a hodgepodge of nodes lacking any discernible organizational logic.

Point A in figure 35.2 represents the core of human capital. Multiple nodes (human capital units) attempt to align themselves in some form of recognizable pattern so that intellectual capital becomes more readily interpretable. This point represents the lowest level of difficulty for development as well as the lowest level of externality from the core of the organization.

Human capital has also been defined on an individual level as the combination of these four

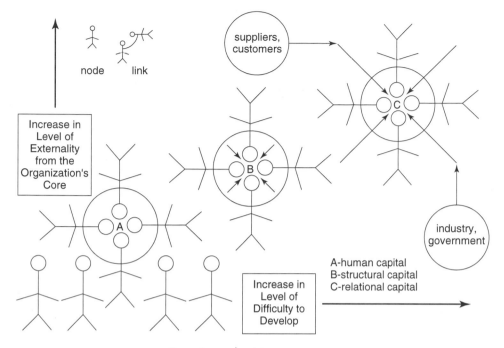

Figure 35.2 Discriminating intellectual capital subdomains.

factors: (1) your genetic inheritance, (2) your education, (3) your experience, and (4) your attitudes about life and business (Hudson 1993). Human capital is important because it is a source of innovation and strategic renewal, whether it is from brainstorming in a research lab, daydreaming at the office, throwing out old files, reengineering new processes, improving personal skills, or developing new leads in a sales representative's "little black book." The essence of human capital is the sheer intelligence of the organizational member. The scope of human capital is limited to the knowledge node (i.e., internal to the mind of the employee). It can be measured (although it is difficult) as a function of volume (i.e., a third-degree measure encompassing size, location, and time). It is also the hardest of the three subdomains of intellectual capital to codify.

Wright et al. (1994), working from a resource-based perspective, argue that in certain circumstances sustained competitive advantage can accrue from "a pool of human capital" that is larger than those groups, such as senior managers and other elites, who are traditionally identified as determining organizational success or failure. This is achieved through the human capital adding value, being unique or rare, imperfectly imitable, and not substitutable with

another resource by competing firms. Storey (1995) supports this focus: "This type of resource [human capital] can embody intangible assets such as unique configurations of complementary skills, and tacit knowledge, painstakingly accumulated, of customer wants and internal processes" (p. 4).

Structural Capital

The organization itself embodies structural tacit knowledge, which exists in "the myriad of relationships that enable the organization to function in a coordinated way [but] are reasonably understood by [at most] the participants in the relationship and a few others," which means that "the organization is . . . accomplishing its aims by following rules that are not known as such to most of the participants in the organization" (Winter 1987, p. 171).

This construct deals with the mechanisms and structures of the organization that can help support employees in their quest for optimum intellectual performance and therefore overall business performance. An individual can have a high level of intellect, but if the organization has poor systems and procedures by which to track his or her actions, the overall intellectual capital will not reach its fullest potential.

An organization with strong structural capital will have a supportive culture that allows individuals to try things, to fail, to learn, and to try again. If the culture unduly penalizes failure, its success will be minimal. Structuring intellectual assets with information systems can turn individual know-how into group property (Nicolini 1993). It is the concept of structural capital that allows intellectual capital to be measured and developed in an organization. In effect, without structural capital, intellectual capital would just be human capital. This construct therefore contains elements of efficiency, transaction times, procedural innovativeness, and access to information for codification into knowledge. It also supports elements of cost minimization and profit maximization per employee. Structural capital is the critical link that allows intellectual capital to be measured at an organizational level.

Point B in figure 35.2 illustrates the structural ties or links of human capital nodes that are required to transform human capital into structural capital. The arrows within structural capital represent the focus of intellectual capital development from the nodes into the organization's core. The essence of structural capital is the knowledge embedded within the routines of an organization. Its scope lies internal to the firm but external to the human capital nodes. It can be measured (although it is difficult) as a function of efficiency (i.e., an output function per some temporal unit). Organizational processes (such as those found in structural capital) can eventually be codified.

Infrastructure assets are those technologies, methodologies, and processes that enable the organization to function. Examples include methodologies for assessing risk, methods of managing a sales force, databases of information on the market or customers, and communication systems such as e-mail and teleconferencing systems—basically, the elements that make up the way the organization works. Such elements are peculiar to each business, and their value to the organization can be attained only by survey within the target organization. Sadly, the acquisition of infrastructure assets is frequently a result of some crisis, positioning them as a necessary evil rather than the structure that makes the organization strong. Marketing the value of infrastructure assets to the individual within the organization is also important, in order to share with them the aspects where infrastructure protects, enhances, and coordinates organizational resources.

Structural capital can be further differentiated between its technological component and architectural competencies. The technological component can be defined as the local abilities and knowledge (e.g., tacit knowledge, proprietary design rules, unique modes of working together) that are important to day-to-day technological problem solving. The architectural competencies can be defined as the ability of the firm to integrate its component competencies together in new and flexible ways and to develop new competencies as they are required (e.g., communication channels, information filters and problem-solving strategies that develop between groups, control systems, cultural values, idiosyncratic search routines). Research focusing on the architectural or integrative capabilities of firms can offer "insights into the source of enduring differences in firm performance" (Henderson and Cockburn, 1994: 64) and highlight the importance of exploring the sources of structural capital.

Relational Capital

Knowledge of market channels and of customer and supplier relationships, as well as a sound understanding of governmental or industry association impacts, is the main theme of relational capital. Frustrated managers often do not recognize that they can tap into a wealth of knowledge from their own clients and suppliers. After all, understanding what customers want in a product or a service better than anyone else is what makes someone a business leader as opposed to a follower.

Relational capital represents the potential an organization has due to ex-firm intangibles. These intangibles include the knowledge embedded in customers, suppliers, the government, or related industry associations. Point C in figure 35.2 illustrates that relational capital is the most difficult of the three subdomains to develop since it is the most external to the organization's core. The arrows represent the knowledge that must flow from sources external to the organization (i.e., its environment) into the organization's core by way of linked nodes. The essence of relational capital is knowledge embedded in relationships external to the firm. Its scope lies external to the firm and external to the human capital nodes. It can be measured (although it is difficult) as a function of longevity (i.e., relational capital becomes more valuable as time goes on). Due to its external nature, knowledge embedded in relational capital is the most difficult to codify.

One manifestation of relational capital that can be leveraged from customers is often referred to as "market orientation." There is no consensus on a definition of market orientation, but two recent definitions have become widely accepted. The first is from Kohli and Jaworski (1990), who define market orientation as the organizationwide generation of market intelligence pertaining to current and future needs of customers, dissemination of intelligence horizontally and vertically within the organization, and organizationwide action or responsiveness to market intelligence. Similar definitions are found in Deng and Dart (1994) and Lichtenthal and Wilson (1992). The second definition is from Narver and Slater (1990), who define market orientation as a one-dimension construct consisting of three behavioral components and two decision criteria—customer orientation, competitor orientation, interfunctional coordination, a long-term focus, and a profit objective. With close parallels to Kohli and Jaworski (1990), Narver and Slater (1990) include the generation and dissemination of market intelligence as well as managerial action. Hulland (1995) posits that there exist two dimensions of organizational learning in the marketing context: market orientation (as discussed above) and market learning systems (which, in the context of this particular conceptualization of intellectual capital, will be considered as a function of structural capital).

Kogut and Zander (1992) argue that what firms do better than markets is the sharing and transfer of knowledge embedded in the organizing principles of an organization. They suggest that a firm's innovative capabilities "rest in the organizing principles by which relationships among individuals, within and between groups, and among organizations are structured" (p. 384).

Teece (1988) discussed the importance of interorganizational and intraorganizational relationships and linkages to the development and profitable commercialization of new technology. He argued that as firms have moved from a serial product-delivery process (i.e., a sequential, lock-step process through the value chain) to a parallel product-delivery process (i.e., simultaneous development throughout the various functions), the need for cooperative and coordinating capabilities has increased. Pennings and Harianto (1992) also presented a theory of innovation that presumes that new technologies emerge from a firm's accumulated stock of skills (i.e., internal innovative capabilities) and its history of technological networking (i.e., external innovative capabilities). Relational capital builds on the intraorganizational relationships (Teece 1988) and technological networking (Pennings and Harianto 1992) that is available in the environment.

The organizing principles established in an innovative firm include rules by which work is coordinated and by which information is gathered and communicated. This social knowledge is not easily disseminated because it is embedded in the idiosyncratic firm-specific history and routines of the organization's entire system (Zander and Kogut 1995, Barney 1992). Companies need intelligence-gathering capabilities to keep up with technology development both inside and outside the industry. This includes not only formal processes and information systems but also informal systems based on tacit understanding by employees and senior managers that they have a responsibility to the company to gather and disseminate technological information (Hamel 1991, Kodama 1992). Effective communication among partners is essential in technology collaboration and can prove difficult to build (Dodgson 1992). However, once established, this communication channel serves as an important source of information about the other interdependent organization.

Trust and Culture as Intellectual Capital Drivers

As depicted in figure 35.1, the conceptualization of intellectual capital includes two supporting drivers for subdomain development. Trust is a very important (Barney and Hansen 1994) element of both inter- and intraorganizational cooperation. Although the importance of trust has always been evident and is widely articulated in the nonacademic literature, it has only recently become a topic of major academic concern. Organizational group members need to have mutual confidence that tasks can be delegated (i.e., that others know what to do, are motivated to do it, and are competent to do it) and that monitoring can be fairly casual. The literature on external cooperative relationships suggests that choosing an external partner with complementary technologies and strategies and building a cooperative relationship based on trust and mutual respect can be problematic (Dodgson 1992). Trust, mutual respect, and compatible modes of behavior cannot be decreed or even adequately specified as an abstract entity. That is why many firms typically begin a relationship by cooperating in less strategically central areas and build up a body of experience in working with a partner over a period of years (Gulati 1995). Generally, all participants are seen to have an affect on the trust in a relationship (Mayer et al. 1995).

As organizations become flatter, more geographically dispersed, and more prone to reorganization, traditional notions of control are being updated to reflect an increased need to trust individuals and groups to carry out critical organizational tasks without close and frequent supervision (Moingeon and Edmondson 1996). Trust is a belief (Lazaric and Lorenz 1995) related to likely outcomes, a belief that reflects an actor's cognitive representations of situational contingencies. Since researchers have tended to have difficulty separating antecedents and outcomes of trust (Mayer et al. 1995), this dual role may also be salient in the context of intellectual capital.

Organizations that have a culture that supports and encourages cooperative innovation should attempt to understand what it is about their culture that gives them a competitive advantage and develop and nurture those cultural attributes (Barney 1986a). Culture constitutes the beliefs, values, and attitudes pervasive in the organization and results in a language, symbols, and habits of behavior and thought. Increasingly it is recognized as the conscious or unconscious product of the senior management's belief (Hall 1992). Barney (1986a) discussed the potential for organizational culture to serve as a source of sustained competitive advantage. He concluded that "firms that do not have the required cultures cannot engage in activities that will modify their cultures and generate sustained superior performance because their modified cultures typically will be neither rare nor imperfectly imitable" (p. 656).

The core of culture is formed by values (Hofstede 1991). In most organizations that have pursued formalized intellectual capital management initiatives, the common component that drives the program is value alignment. Hall (1995) agrees and claims that values are the key to any successful organizational transformation because "values are basically a quality information system that when understood tell about what drives human beings and organizations and causes them to be exceptional" (p. viii). Another important element of culture within the context

of intellectual capital is the important distinction between "knowledge hoarding" versus "knowledge sharing." Unfortunately, this conflict is all too common in today's organizations, with the former outdoing the latter.

Belacso and Sayer (1994, p. 31) propose an "intellectual capitalism paradigm" that charts a changing distribution of the power of the "tools of production" from owners to managers and then to the "talents of the people." They assert that the possessors of the intellectual tools of production—organizational employees (or nodes of human capital units)—will come to exercise effective power. Hedlund (1994) proposes that a new organizational form called the "N-form corporation" builds on the interplay of tacit knowledge transfer among different levels. This is done through a variety of ways, including temporary constellations of people, lateral communication, a catalytic role for top management, and heterarchical structures.

Agency theorists (Jensen and Meckling 1976, Eisenhardt 1988) have made large inroads in the study of principal–agent relationships. For example, in the context of compensation, agency theory posits that as the proportion of outcome-based compensation (i.e., commission versus salary) increases for the agent, so does the effective management of that relationship in that their goals are now more aligned. In other words, the principle can effectively limit the divergent behavior of the agent if the latter's compensation more closely matches the former's. In the knowledge era, real power may lie in the human capital of an organization. If the nodes (employees of an organization) are the genesis of the intellectual capital in a firm, how will principles leverage off its effective utilization? This may, perhaps, become an exciting new research program for agency theorists in the future.

Recognizing that "power" is an important—some might say the most important—dynamic in organizations, it is also concerned with reviewing how knowledge management and power relate and the extent to which maximizing the potential of intellectual capital requires a radical transformation in the generation and distribution of power in organizations.

An increasingly strong case is being made that as organizations respond to environmental turbulence, particularly increased worldwide competitive pressures and swift technological and social change, they need to pay particular attention to the development and deployment of knowledge, and hence the learning needs of their employees at all levels (McGill et al. 1992, Brown et al. 1993, Parker et al. 1994, Pfeffer 1994, West 1994).

For example, Kornbluh et al. (1987) suggest that the pressure of international competition and the failure of the "technological solution" in many enterprises has focused attention on the importance of learning in order to deal with both turbulent environments and the desire of many workers for more challenging jobs. Meyer-Dohm (1992) points to the inherent errors and risks in even the most automated technology-based work systems, requiring human intervention and the design of workplaces that permit the individual a higher degree of independence.

Argyris (1994) appears to be clear on this issue that knowledgeable employees will reign supreme: "Twenty-first century corporations will find it hard to survive, let alone flourish, unless they get better work from their employees . . . employees who've learned to take active responsibility for their own behaviour, develop and share first-rate information about their jobs and make good use of genuine empowerment to shape lasting solutions to fundamental problems" (p. 77).

If these more empowering and involving managerial practices are indeed an imperative for organizational survival and growth, their implementation may lead to the employees concerned feeling more in control of their own work and lives. Being able to play a greater part in organizational decision making and development and being able to cope with increased delegation from people above them in the hierarchy may in fact be a consequence of the increased value of their intellectual capital to the organization. However, it is also possible to hypothesize the existence of counterforces, especially the response of the dominant managerial coalition, which may resist this power redistribution and, consequently, block the utilization of the full potential of the organization's intellectual capital for innovation. Before investigating these counterforces in more detail, it is important to establish the potential links between intellectual capital and innovation.

The links among learning, innovation, and organization survival have been developed by a number of writers (see, e.g., Bouwen and Fry 1991, Argyris 1992, Senge 1990). Sadler (1994) has highlighted the growth of knowledge- or talent-intensive industries and the importance of the "knowledge worker." The potential of learning and knowledge as the basis of power has been recognized by, among others, French and Raven (1959), Zimmerman (1990), Thomas and Velthouse (1990), and Townley (1993). Hence, it seems possible to posit a link among intellectual capital, innovation and power.

In his meta-analysis of the determinants of innovation at the organizational level, Damanpour (1991) reported a positive correlation between innovation and a number of variables that could be said to reflect intellectual capital and its usage, including specialization (i.e., providing a greater knowledge base), professionalization (i.e., increased boundary-spanning activity), technical knowledge resources, and external and internal communications. Centralization of decision-making authority was found to be negatively correlated as Damanpour predicted (based on the work of Thompson 1965), which suggests that a dispersion of power may be necessary for innovation. Damanpour's analysis also recognized the importance of managerial support for innovation, especially in terms of leadership and coordination. Furthermore, leadership in the form of a championing change agent has been reviewed as being an important antecedent to organizational learning (Bontis 1995).

Also of particular interest is the hypothesis by McGill et al. (1992) that in order to innovate, organizations need to employ "generative" rather than "adaptive" learning practices, which involve, among other things, a move from hierarchical position to knowledge as the dominant power base. There is an obvious need for further research to see if organizational success is related to truly empowering people and preparing and enabling them to become "highly involved" in Eccles's (1991) terms.

Research to Date

Intellectual capital research thus far has been primarily of the anecdotal variety. Most researchers have conducted case-based reviews of organizations that have established intellectual capital initiatives. Other researchers have documented the metrics that have been developed by Skandia and others. What the field needs at this point is a more concentrated focus on rigorous, metric development and quantitative evaluation.

Using survey data, Bontis (1998) has already shown a very strong and positive relationship between Likert-type measures of intellectual capital and business performance in a pilot study. The explanatory power of the final specified model was highly significant and substantive ($R^2 = 56.0\%$, p value < 0.001).

Several other researchers have also supplied evidence of a positive relationship between an organization's financial, as well as organizational performance, and its level of relational capital, one of the subdomains of intellectual capital. As discussed above, contained within the conceptualization of relational capital is market orientation. Narver and Slater (1990) find that market orientation and business performance (ROA) are strongly related. Jaworski and Kohli (1993) report on a study of 222 U.S. business units suggesting that market orientation is an important determinant of performance, regardless of market turbulence, competitive intensity, and technological turbulence. Also, Ruekert (1992) reports a positive relationship between degree of market orientation and long-run financial performance. In the United Kingdom, Greenley (1995) observed that a group of companies with higher market orientation performed better (based on return on investment) than did a group with lower market orientation. Lusch and Laczniak (1987) investigated how a company's increased emphasis on an extended marketing concept, similar to market orientation, is positively associated with financial performance. Not directly related to business performance, but yet in line with intellectual capital, Atuahene-Gima (1995) infers from an Australian sample that market orientation is an important contributor to new product success. Biemans and Harmsen (1995) have also concluded on the basis of several other studies that having a market orientation in product development has proven to be a highly critical factor for new product success.

Recent trends in organizational structure have seen a move toward "delayering," "lean production," making decisions "closer to the customer," and establishing "semi-autonomous work-groups" and an emphasis on employee involvement and empowerment (see Wellins et al. 1991, Docherty 1993, Papahristodoulou 1994, Yeatts et al. 1994). Again, it seems reasonable to hypothesize that, other things being equal, the increased intellectual capital development and thus "nodal" power generated by environmental turbulence should be more evenly distributed throughout the organization in these "leaner," "flatter" structures.

Empirical research has shown that top executives in large U.S. and Canadian businesses agree that new intellectual capital measures are required to help manage knowledge assets. Stivers et al. (1998) surveyed 253 companies among the U.S. Fortune 500 and Canadian Post 300 in their study of nonfinancial measure usage. Results showed that even though 63% of the sample felt that measuring innovation was important, only 14% were actually measuring it, and only 10% were actually using the measures for strategy development. Stivers and colleagues argue that these results show a significant measurement–use gap. This may be more significant for measures of intellectual capital. To assist managers with this gap, Bontis et al. (1999) have developed a knowledge toolbox that helps practitioners differentiate between a variety of knowledge-based tools including intellectual capital, human resource accounting, economic value added, and the balanced scorecard.

Another empirical research study conducted in this field (Bontis 1999) used a psychometrically developed survey instrument to measure knowledge stocks and flows in 32 mutual fund companies. By surveying 15 respondents across three levels of management in each organization, Bontis found that knowledge stocks and flows were closely related to business performance. He concluded that although knowledge stocks had a positive association with business performance, the misalignment of knowledge stocks with knowledge flows acted as a detriment to the overall efficiency of the organization's learning system. This research shows the importance of integrating intellectual capital with research in the knowledge management and organizational learning domains.

Conclusion

Some critics have argued that intellectual capital is just another organizational fad that will last for three to five more years, and then managers will move on to the next attempt at finding the philosophical silver bullet. In an *ASAP* feature article, Rutledge (1997) blasted the intellectual capital field and emphatically claimed that "you are a fool if you buy into this." He warned managers that if by chance they meet people with the word "knowledge" or "intellectual capital" on their business cards, they should walk quickly and quietly away. His argument centers around the fact that the driving force behind this field comes from stakeholders and not from shareholders of companies, and therefore social agendas, not performance, will drive business decisions. Although he is correct in touting the importance of the "softer stuff" related to intellectual capital, he cannot argue against its mass appeal. Dozens upon dozens of conferences, workshops, and seminars are being offered all over the world on how to measure and value intellectual capital each year. Practitioners are voting with their feet.

Although its popularity is not disputed, it is important to be skeptical when anyone claims to have found the magical formula or calculation for intellectual capital. It will never be measured in the traditional dollar terms we know. At best, we will see a slow proliferation of customized metrics that will be disclosed in traditional financial statements as addendums. Metrics such as those used by Skandia and others in the financial services industry (Bontis 1997) will continue to be developed and analyzed longitudinally. Bassi and Van Buren (1998) note that even though the stock market is already providing handsome rewards to companies that successfully leverage their intellectual capital, few firms have formalized a measurement process. The significance and lack of progress on the issue are also clear from a recent survey of 431 organizations in the United States and Europe, which ranked "measuring the value and performance of knowledge assets" highest in importance more than any other issue except "changing people's behaviour," 43% versus 54%, respectively (Skyrme and Amidon 1997).

If it is a fad, when will it end? The immense proliferation of the Internet as an information-sharing vehicle supports the argument that knowledge management and the development of intellectual capital are most sustainable as an organizational goal (Prusak 1996). As long as the economic forces embrace new knowledge-intensive industries, the field of intellectual capital will have an important place in the minds of academics and practitioners.

As with the human body's muscles, intellectual capital management may suffer from the old addage, "if you don't use it, you lose it." There is an increasing emphasis on survival of the fittest in international competitiveness. In order to stay alive, organizations must win the race (Hampden-Turner 1992). Future research in this area may want to tap into comparisons of intellectual capital characteristics by personality type with the use of the Myers-Briggs type indicator (Wiele 1993). Also, researchers could correlate intellectual capital metrics with cultural diversity and values (Hofstede 1978, 1991).

Finally, all business leaders should be appreciative of the power intellectual capital can have on business performance. The study of intellectual capital stocks and their exponential growth due to organizational learning flows produces a tremendous amount of energy, energy that can take companies far beyond their current vision (Ward 1996). It requires people to rethink their attitudes on this elusive intangible asset and to start recognizing that measuring and strategically managing intellectual capital may in fact become the most important managerial activity as we enter the third millennium.

References

Andrews, K.R. (1971) *The Concept of Corporate Strategy.* Homewood, IL: Dow Jones–Irwin.

Ansoff, H.I. (1965) *Corporate Strategy: An Analytical Approach to Business Policy for Growth and Expansion.* New York: McGraw-Hill.

Argyris, C. (1992) *On Organizational Learning.* Cambridge, MA: Blackwell.

Argyris, C. (1994) "Good communication that blocks learning." *Harvard Business Review,* July–August, pp. 77–85.

Atuahene-Gima, K. (1995) "An exploratory analysis of the impact of market orientation on new product performance. A contingency approach." *Journal of Product Innovation Management* 12: 275–293.

Baden-Fuller, C. and Pitt, M. (1996) "The nature of innovating strategic management," in C. Baden-Fuller and M. Pitt (eds.), *Strategic Innovation.* London: Routledge.

Barnard, C. (1938) *The Functions of the Executive.* Cambridge, MA: Harvard University Press.

Barney, J.B. (1986a) "Organizational culture: can it be a source of sustained competitive advantage?" *Academy of Management Review* 11(3):656–665.

Barney, J.B. (1986b) "Strategic factor markets: expectations, luck, and business strategy." *Management Science* 32(10):1231–1241.

Barney, J.B. (1991) "Firm resources and sustained competitive advantage." *Journal of Management* 17:99–120.

Barney, J.B. (1992) "Integrating organizational behavior and strategy formulation research: a resource based analysis." *Advances in Strategic Management* 8:39–62.

Barney, J.B. and Hansen, M.H. (1994) "Trustworthiness as a source of competitive advantage." *Strategic Management Journal* 15:175–190.

Bassi, L.J. and Van Buren, M.E. (1998) "Investments in Intellectual capital: creating methods for measuring impact and value." ASTD working paper, American Society of Training and Development.

Beamish, P.W. and Woodcock, C.P. (1996) *Strategic Management: Text, Readings and Cases*, 4th ed. Toronto: Irwin.

Belasco, J.A. and Sayer, R.C. (1995) "Why empowerment doesn't empower: the bankruptcy of current paradigms." *Business Horizons*, March–April, pp. 29–41.

Besanko, D., Dranove, D., and Shanley, M. (1996) *The Economics of Strategy*. New York: Wiley.

Biemans, W.G. and Harmsen, H. (1995) "Overcoming the barriers to market-oriented product development." *Journal of Marketing Practice: Applied Marketing Science* 1(2):7–25.

Bierly, P. and Chakrabarti, A. (1996) "Generic knowledge strategies in the U.S. pharmaceutical industry." *Strategic Management Journal* 17 (Winter).

Bodie Z., Kane, A., and Marcus, A.J. (1993) *Investments*. New York: Irwin.

Bontis, N. (1995) "Organizational learning and leadership: a literature review of two fields," in *Published Proceedings of ASAC '95*. Windsor, Canada.

Bontis, N. (1996a) "There's a price on your head: managing intellectual capital strategically," *Business Quarterly*, Summer.

Bontis, N. (1996b) "Economic value added," In R. Michalski and M. Sealey (eds.), *Society of Management Accountants of Canada Professional Program*, module 5, part 4.3. Toronto: Society of CMAs.

Bontis, N. (1997) "Royal bank invests in knowledge-based industries." *Knowledge Inc.* 2(8).

Bontis, N. (1998) "Intellectual capital: an exploratory study that develops measures and models." *Management Decision* 36(2).

Bontis, N. (1999) "Managing an organizational learning system by aligning stocks and flows of knowledge." *PhD diss.*, University of Western Ontario.

Bontis, N., Dragonetti, N., Jacobsen, K., and Roos, G. (1999) "The knowledge toolbox: a review of the tools available to measure and manage intangible resources." *European Management Journal* 17(4):391–402.

Bouwen, R. and Fry, R. (1991) "Organizational innovation and learning: four patterns of dialogue between the dominant logic and the new logic." *International Studies of Management and Organization* 21(4):37–51.

Brown, C., Reich, M., and Stern, D. (1993) "Becoming a high-performance work organisation: the role of security, employee involvement and training." *The International Journal of Human Resource Management* 4(2):247–275.

Brummet, R.L., Flamholtz, E.G., and Pyle, W.C. (1968) "Human resource measurement: a challenge for accountants." *The Accounting Review*, April, pp. 217–224.

Cangelosi, V. and Dill, W. (1965) "Organizational learning: observations toward a theory." *Administrative Sciences Quarterly*.

Chandler, A.D. (1977) *The Visible Hand: The Managerial Revolution in American Business*. Cambridge, MA: Belknap.

Chandler, A.D. (1990) *Scale and Scope: The Dynamics of Industrial Capitalism*. Cambridge, MA: Belknap.

Choi, C.J. and Lee, S.H. (1997) "A knowledge-based view of cooperative interorganizational relationships," in P. Beamish and J. Killing (eds.), *Cooperative Strategies: European Perspectives*. San Francisco: New Lexington Press.

Cohen, W.M. and Levinthal, D.A. (1990) "Absorptive capacity: a new perspective on learning and innovation." *Administrative Science Quarterly* 35:128–152.

Collis, D.J. (1996) "Organizational capability as a source of profit," in B. Moingeon and A. Edmondson (eds.), *Organizational Learning and Competitive Advantage*. London: Sage.

Conner, K. and Prahalad, C. (1996) "A resource-based theory of the firm: knowledge versus opportunism," *Organization Science* 7(5).

Crossan, M., Lane, H., White, R., and Djurfeldt, L. (1995) "Organizational learning: dimensions for a theory." *International Journal of Organizational Analysis* 3(4).

Crossan, M., White, R.E., Lane, H.W., and Klus, L. (1996) "The improvising organization: where planning meets opportunity." *Organization Dynamics* 24(4):20–34.

Damanpour, F. (1991) "Organizational innovation: a meta-analysis of effects of determinants and moderators." *Academy of Management Journal* 34(3):555–590.

Darling, M. (1996) "Building the knowledge organization." *Business Quarterly*, Winter.

Davenport, T. and Prusak, L. (1997) *Information Ecology: Mastering the information and Knowledge Environment*. New York: Oxford University Press.

Demsetz, H. (1991) "The theory of the firm revisited," in O. Williamson and S. Winter (eds.), *The Nature of the Firm*. New York: Oxford University Press.

Deng, S. and Dart, J. (1994) "Measuring market orientation: a multi-factor, multi-item approach." *Journal of Marketing Management* 10:725–742.

Dierickx, I. and Cool, K. (1989) "Asset stock accumulation and the sustainability of competitive advantage." *Management Science* 35:1504–1513.

Docherty, A. (1993) "Getting the best out of knowledge-workers." *Involvement and Participation* 619:6–11.

Dodgson, M. (1992) "The future for technological collaboration." *Futures*, June.

Drucker, P.F. (1993) *Post-capitalist Society*. Oxford: Butterworth Heinemann.

Duncan, R. and Weiss, A. (1979) "Organizational learning: implications for organizational design," in B. Straw (Ed.), *Research Organizational Behavior*. Greenwich: JAI Press.

Eccles, R. (1991) "The performance measurement manifesto." *Harvard Business Review*, January–February, pp. 131–137.

Economist Intelligence Unit (EIU) and IBM. (1996) "The learning organization: managing knowledge for business success." Research report, Economist Intelligence Unit and IBM Consulting Group.

Edvinsson, L. and Malone, M. (1997) *Intellectual Capital*. New York: Harper Business.

Edvinsson, L. and Sullivan, P. (1996) "Developing a model for managing intellectual capital," *European Management Journal* 14(4).

Eisenhardt, K. (1988) "Agency- and institutional-theory explanations: the case of retail sales compensation." *Academy of Management Journal* 31(3):488–511.

Fiol C. and Lyles, M. (1985) "Organizational learning." *Academy of Management Review* 10(4).

Flamholtz, E. (1973) "Human resource accounting: measuring positional replacement cost." *Human Resource Measurement*, Spring, pp. 8–16.

Foss, N. (1996) "Knowledge-based approaches to the theory of the firm: some critical comments." *Organization Science* 7(5).

French, J. and Raven, B. (1959) "The basis of social power," In D. Cartwright (ed.), *Studies in Social Power*. Ann Arbor, Michigan: Institute for Social Research.

Friedman, A. and Lev, B. (1974) "A surrogate measure for the firms investment in human resources." *Journal of Accounting Research*, Autumn, pp. 235–250.

Fudenberg, Drew and Jean Tirole. (1986). *Dynamic Models of Oligopoly*. London: Harwood.

Gambling, T.E. (1974) "A system dynamics approach to HRA." *The Accounting Review*, July, pp. 538–546.

Grant, R.M. (1996a) "Prospering in dynamically-competitive environments: organizational capability as knowledge integration." *Organization Science* 7(4).

Grant, R.M. (1996b) "Toward a knowledge-based theory of the firm." *Strategic Management Journal*, 17(Winter).

Greenly, G.E. (1995) "Forms of market orientation in UK companies." *Journal of Management Studies* 32(1):47–66.

Greeno, J. (1980) "Psychology in learning." *American Psychologist* 35(8).

Gulati, R. (1995) "Does familiarity breed trust? The implications of repeated ties for contractual choice in alliances." *Academy of Management Journal* 38(1):85–112.

Hall, Brian. (1995) *Values Shift: A Guide to Personal and Organizational Transformation*. Rockport, MA: Twin Lights.

Hall, R. (1992) "The strategic analysis of intangible resources." *Strategic Management Journal* 13:135–144.

Hamel, G. (1991) "Competition for competence and inter-partner learning within international strategic alliances." *Strategic Management Journal* 12: 83–103.

Hampden-Turner, C. (1992) *Creating Corporate Culture: From Discord to Harmony*. Reading, MA: Addison-Wesley.

Handy, C.B. (1989) *The Age of Unreason*. London: Arrow.

Hansen, G. and Wernerfelt, B. (1989) "Determinants of firm performance: the relative importance of economic and organizational factors." *Strategic Management Journal* 10.

Hedberg, B. (1981) "How organizations learn and unlearn," in P. Nystrom and W. Starbuck (eds.), *Handbook of Organizational Design*. London: Oxford University Press.

Hedlund, G. (1994) "A model of knowledge management and the N-form corporation." *Strategic Management Journal* 15.

Hedlund G. and Nonaka, I. (1993) "Models of knowledge management in the West and Japan," in P. Lorange, B. Chakravarthy, J. Roos, and A. Van de Ven (eds.), *Implementing Strategic Processes: Change, Learning, and Cooperation*. Oxford: Basil Blackwell.

Hekimian, J.S. and Jones, C. (1967) "Put people on your balance sheet." *Harvard Business Review*, January–February, pp. 105–113.

Henderson, R. and Cockburn, I. (1994) "Measuring competence? Exploring firm effects in pharmaceutical research." *Strategic Management Journal* 15:63–84.

Hermanson, R.H. (1964) "Accounting for human assets." Occasional Paper No. 14. East Lansing, MI: Bureau of Business and Economic Research, Michigan State University. Reprint Georgia State University, 1986.

Hofstede, G. (1978) "Value systems in forty countries," in *Proceedings of the 4th International Congress of the Association for Cross-Cultural Psychology*.

Hofstede, G. (1991) *Cultures and Organizations:*

Intercultural Cooperation and Its Importance to Survival. Glasgow: HarperCollins.

Huber, G. (1991) "Organizational learning: the contributing processes and the literatures." *Organization Science* 2.

Hudson, W. (1993) *Intellectual Capital: How to Build It, Enhance It, Use It.* New York: Wiley.

Hulland, J. (1995). "Market orientation and market learning systems: an environment-strategy-performance perspective." Working paper. University of Western Ontario.

Inkpen, A. and Crossan, M. (1995) "Believing is seeing: joint ventures and organizational learning." *Journal of Management Studies* 32.

Itami, H. (1987) *Mobilizing Invisible Assets.* Boston: Harvard University Press.

Jaworski, B.J. and Kohli, A.K. (1993) "Market orientation: antecedents and consequences." *Journal of Marketing* 57(July):53–70.

Jensen, M. and Meckling, W. (1976) "Theory of the firm: managerial behavior, agency costs and ownership structure." *Journal of Financial Economics* 3:305–360.

Johnson, H.T. and Kaplan, R.S. (1987) *Relevance Lost.* Boston: Harvard Business School Press.

Kanter, R. (1989) *When Giants Learn to Dance.* London: Simon and Schuster.

Kaplan, R.S. and Norton, D.P. (1992) "The balanced scorecard measures that drive performance." *Harvard Business Review*, January–February, pp. 71–79.

Kessides, I. (1990) "Internal vs. external market conditions and firm profitability: an exploratory model." *Economic Journal* 100.

Kim, D. (1993) "The link between individual and organizational learning," *Sloan Management Review*, Fall.

Kodama, F. (1992) "Technology fusion and the new R&D." *Harvard Business Review* 70(4).

Kogut, B. and Zander, U. (1992) "Knowledge of the firm, combinative capabilities, and the replication of technology." *Organization Science* 3:383–397.

Kohli, A.K. and Jaworski, B.J. (1990) "Market orientation: the construct, research propositions, and managerial implications." *Journal of Marketing* 54(April):1–18.

Kornbluh, H., Pipan, R., and Schurman, S.J. (1987) "Empowerment, learning and control in workplaces: a curricular view." *Zeitschrift für Sozialisationforschung und Etziehungssoziologie* 7(4): 253–268.

Lazaric, N. and Lorenz, E. (1995) "Trust and organizational learning during inter-firm cooperation," in *Proceedings of Seminar on Confiance, Apprentissage et Anticipation Économique.*

Learned, E., Christensen, C., Andrews, K., and Guth, W. (1969) *Business Policy: Text and Cases.* Homewood, IL: Irwin.

Levitt, B. and March, J. (1988) "Organizational learning." *Annual Review of Sociology.*

Levitt, T. (1991) *Marketing Imagination.* New York: Free Press.

Lichtenthal, J.D. and Wilson, D.T. (1992) "Becoming market oriented." *Journal of Business Research* 24:191–207.

Likert, R.M. (1967) *New Patterns of Management.* New York: McGraw-Hill.

Likert, R.M. and Bowers, D.G. (1973) "Improving the accuracy of P/L reports by estimating the changes in dollar value of the human organization." *Michigan Business Review*, March, pp. 15–24.

Lusch, R.F. and Laczniak, G.R. (1987) "The evolving marketing concept, competitive intensity and organizational performance." *Journal of the Academy of Marketing Science* 15(3).

Luscombe, N. (1993) "A learning experience." *CA Magazine*, February, p. 3.

Lynn, B. (1998) "Performance evaluation in the new economy." *International Journal of Technology Management* 16(1/2/3):162–176.

Mayer, R., Davis, J., and Schoorman, F. (1995) "An integrative model of organizational trust." *Academy of Management Review* 20(3).

McConville, D. (1994) "All about EVA." *Industry Week*, April 18.

McGee, J. and Prusak, L. (1993) *Managing Information Strategically.* New York: Wiley.

McGill, M.E., Slocum, J.W., and Lei, D. (1992) "Managerial practices in learning organizations." *Organizational Dynamics* 21(1):5–17.

McGrath, R., Tsai, M., Venkatraman, S., and MacMillan, I. (1996) "Innovation, competitive advantage and rent: a model and test." *Management Science* 42(3).

Meyer-Dohm, P. (1992) "Human resources 2020: structures of the 'learning company,' " in *Conference Proceedings of Human Resources in Europe at the Dawn of the 21st Century.* Luxembourg: Office for Official Publications of the European Communities.

Miller, D. (1996) "A preliminary typology of organizational learning: synthesizing the literature." *Journal of Management* 22(3).

Moingeon, B. and Edmondson, A. (1996) "Trust and organizational learning," in *Proceedings of Organizational Learning and Learning Organization Symposium '96.*

Morse, W.J. (1973) "A note on the relationship between human assets and human capital." *Accounting Review*, July, pp. 589–593.

Nanda, A. (1996) "Resources, capabilities and competencies," in B. Moingeon and A. Edmondson (eds.), *Organizational Learning and Competitive Advantage.* London: Sage.

Narver, J.C. and Slater, S.F. (1990) "The effect of a

market orientation on business profitability." *Journal of Marketing*, October, pp. 20–35.

Nelson, R.R. (1991) "Why do firms differ, and how does it matter?" *Strategic Management Journal* 12:61–74.

Nelson, R.R. and Winter, S.G. (1982) *An Evolutionary Theory of Economic Change*. Cambridge, MA: Belknap.

Nicolini, D. (1993) "Apprendimento organizzativo e pubblica amministrazione locale." *Autonomie Locali e Servizi Sociali* 16(2).

Nohria, N. and Eccles, R. (1991) "Corporate capability." Working paper 92-038, Harvard Business School.

Nonaka, I. (1994) "A dynamic theory of organizational knowledge." *Organization Science*, 5.

Nonaka, I. and Takeuchi, H. (1995) *The Knowledge-Creating Company*. New York: Oxford University Press.

Ochsner, R. (1995) "Welcome to the new world of economic value added." *Compensation and Benefits Review*, March–April.

Papahristodoulou, C. (1994) "Is lean production the solution?" *Economic and Industrial Democracy* 15:457–476.

Parker, S.K., Mullarkey, S., and Jackson, P.R. (1994) "Dimensions of performance effectiveness in high-involvement work organisations." *Human Resource Management Journal* 4(3):1–21.

Pavitt, K. (1971) "The multinational enterprise and the transfer of technology," in John Dunning (ed.), *The Multinational Enterprise*. London: Allen and Unwin.

Pennings, J.M. and Harianto, F. (1992) "Technological networking and innovation implementation." *Organization Science* 3(3):356–383.

Penrose, E.D. (1959) *The Theory of the Growth of the Firm*. Oxford: Basil Blackwell.

Pfeffer, J. (1994) "Competitive advantage through people." *California Management Review*. Winter, pp. 9–28.

Polanyi, M. (1967) *The Tacit Dimension*. New York: Anchor Day.

Prahalad, C.K. and Hamel, G. (1990) "The core competence of the corporation." *Harvard Business Review*, May–June, pp. 79–91.

Prusak, L. (1996) "The knowledge advantage." *Strategy and Leadership*, March/April.

Quinn, J.B. (1992). *Intelligent Enterprise*. New York: Free Press.

Roos, J., Roos, G., Dragonetti, N., and Edvinsson, L. (1998) *Intellectual Capital: Navigating in the New Business Landscape*. New York: New York University Press.

Rubin, P.H. (1973) "The expansion of firms." *Journal of Political Economy* 81:936–949.

Ruekert, R.W. (1992) "Developing a market orientation: an organizational strategy perspective." *International Journal of Research in Marketing* 9:225–245.

Rumelt, R.P. (1991) "How much does industry matter?" *Strategic Management Journal* 12:167–185.

Rutledge, J. (1997) "You're a fool if you buy into this." *ASAP*, April 7.

Sackmann, S.A., Flamholtz, E.G., and Bullen, M.L. (1989) "Human resource accounting: a state of the art review." *Journal of Accounting Literature* 8:235–264.

Sadler, P. (1994) "The management of talent." *Human Resource Management International Digest*, January–February, pp. 37–39.

Saint-Onge, H. (1996) "Tacit knowledge: the key to the strategic alignment of intellectual capital." *Strategy and Leadership*, April.

Schmalense, R. (1985) "Do markets differ much?" *American Economic Review* 75.

Schumpeter, J.A. (1934) *The Theory of Economic Development*. Cambridge, MA: Harvard University Press.

Selznick, P. (1957) *Leadership in Administration*. New York: Harper and Row.

Senge, P.M. (1990) *The Fifth Discipline: The Art and Practice of the Learning Organisation*. New York: Doubleday Currency.

Shrivastava, P. (1983) "A typology of organizational learning systems." *Journal of Management Studies* 20(1).

Shrivastava, P. (1986) "Learning structures for top management." *Human Systems Management* 6.

Simon, H.A. (1945) *Administrative Behaviour*. New York: Macmillan.

Simon, H.A. (1991) "Bounded rationality and organizational learning." *Organization Science* 2(1).

Skandia. (1994) "Visualizing intellectual capital in Skandia." A supplement to Skandia's 1994 annual report.

Skandia. (1995a). "Renewal and development: intellectual capital." A supplement to Skandia's 1995 interim annual report.

Skandia. (1995b) "Value-creating processes: intellectual capital." A supplement to Skandia's 1995 annual report.

Skandia. (1996a) "Power of innovation: intellectual capital." A supplement to Skandia's 1996 interim annual report.

Skandia. (1996b) "Customer value." A supplement to Skandia's 1996 annual report.

Skandia. (1997) "Intelligent enterprising." A supplement to Skandia's 6-month interim report.

Skyrme, D.J. and Amidon, D.M. (1997) *Creating the Knowledge-Based Business*. London: Business Intelligence.

Slater, S.F. and Narver, J.C. (1994) "Market orientation, customer value, and superior performance." *Business Horizons*, March–April, pp. 22–29.

Spender, J.-C. (1994) "Organizational knowledge, collective practice and Penrose rents." *International Business Review* 3(4).

Spender, J.-C. (1996) "Making knowledge the basis of a dynamic theory of the firm." *Strategic Management Journal*, 17(Winter).

Stata, R. (1989) "Organizational learning—the key to management innovation." *Sloan Management Review*, Spring.

Stewart, G., III. (1991) *The Quest for Value*. New York: HarperCollins.

Stewart, G., III. (1994) "EVA™: fact and fantasy." *Journal of Applied Corporate Finance*, Summer.

Stewart, T.A. (1991) "Brainpower: how intellectual capital is becoming America's most valuable asset." *Fortune*, June 3, pp. 44–60.

Stewart, T.A. (1994) "Your company's most valuable asset: intellectual capital." *Fortune*, October 3, pp. 68–74.

Stewart, T.A. (1997) *Intellectual Capital: The New Wealth of Organizations*. New York: Doubleday/Currency.

Stivers, B., Covin, J., Green Hall, N., and Smalt, S. (1998) "How nonfinancial performance measures are used," *Management Accounting*, February.

Storey, J. (1995) "HRM: still marching on, or marching out?" in Storey, J. (ed.), *Human Resource Management: A Critical Text*. London: Routledge.

Sullivan, P. and Edvinsson, L. (1996) "A model for managing intellectual capital," in R. Parr and P. Sullivan (eds.), *Technology Licensing*. New York: Wiley.

Sveiby, K.E. (1997) *The New Organizational Wealth: Managing and Measuring Knowledge-Based Assets*. New York: Berrett-Koehler.

Taylor, F. (1911) *The Principles of Scientific Management*. New York: Harper and Brothers.

Teece, D.J. (1982) "Towards an economic theory of the multiproduct firm." *Journal of Economic Behavior and Organization* 3:39–63.

Teece, D.J. (1988) "Technological change and the nature of the firm," in G. Dosi, C. Freeman, R. Nelson, G. Silverberg, and L. Soete (eds.), *Technical Change and Economic Theory*. London: Frances Pinter.

Teece, D.J., Pisano, G., and Shuen, A. (1994) "Dynamic capabilities and strategic management." Working paper, Center for Research in Management, University of California at Berkeley.

Thomas, K.W. and Velthouse, B.E. (1990) "Cognitive elements of empowerment: an interpretative model of intrinsic task motivation." *Academy of Management Review* 15(4):666–682.

Thompson, V.A. (1965) "Bureaucracy and innovation." *Administrative Science Quarterly* 10:1–20.

Townley, B. (1993) "Foucault, power/knowledge, and its relevance for human resource management." *Academy of Management Review*, 18(3): 518–545.

Tsuchiya, S. (1994) "A study of organizational knowledge," in *Proceedings of Management of Industrial and Corporate Knowledge ISMICK '94*.

Veilleux, R. (1995) "A nationwide descriptive study about the status of organizational learning in United States' businesses." Ph.D. diss., George Washington University.

Vitale, M.R. and Mavrinac, S.C. (1995) "How effective is your performance measurement system." *Management Accounting*, August, pp. 43–47.

Vitale, M.R., Mavrinac, S.C., and Hauser, M. (1994) "New process/financial scorecard: a strategic performance measurement system." *Planning Review*, July–August, pp. 12–17.

Ward, A. (1996) "Lessons learned on the knowledge highways and byways." *Strategy and Leadership*, March/April.

Wellins, R.S., Byham, W.C., and Wilson, J.M. (1991) *Empowered Teams: Creating Self-directed Groups That Improve Quality, Productivity and Participation*. San Francisco: Jossey Bass.

Wernerfelt, B. (1984) "A resource-based view of the firm." *Strategic Management Journal* 5:171–180.

West, P. (1994) "The concept of the learning organization." *Journal of European Industrial Training* 18(1).

White, G.I., Sondhi, A.C., and Fried, P. (1994) *The Analysis and Use of Financial Statements*. New York: Wiley.

Wiele, B. (1993) "Competing from the neck up." *Performance and Instruction*, March.

Winter, S.G. (1987) "Knowledge and competence as strategic assets," in D.J. Teece (ed.), *The Competitive Challenge: Strategies of Industrial Innovation and Renewal*, pp. 159–184. Cambridge, MA: Ballinger.

Wright, P.M., McMahan, G.C., and McWilliams, A. (1994) "Human resources and sustained competitive advantage: a resource-based perspective." *International Journal of Human Resource Management* 5(2):301–326.

Yeatts, D.E., Hipskind, M., and Barnes, D. (1994) "Lessons learned from self-managed work teams." *Business Horizons*, July–August, pp. 11–18.

Zander, U. and Kogut, B. (1995) "Knowledge and the speed of the transfer and imitation of organizational capabilities: an empirical test." *Organization Science* 6(1):76–92.

Zimmerman, M.A. (1990) "Towards a theory of learned hopefulness: a structural model analysis of participation and empowerment." *Journal of Research in Personality* 24.

36

Intellectual Capital

An Exploratory Study That Develops Measures and Models

Nick Bontis

All men by nature desire knowledge.
Aristotle, *Metaphysics*

*Whereas at one time the decisive factor of
production was the land, and later capital . . .
today the decisive factor is increasingly man
himself, that is, his knowledge.*
Pope John Paul II

Intellectual capital has been considered by many,
defined by some, understood by a select few, and
formally valued by practically no one (Stewart
1997, Sveiby 1997). Therein lies one of the greatest challenges facing business leaders and academic researchers today and tomorrow. Recently,
the job title of chief knowledge officer (CKO) has
been creeping up on annual reports and job ad-
vertisements with ever-increasing frequency.
These pathfinding individuals have been given
the enviable task of channeling their organizations' intellectual capital as an essential source
of competitive advantage. Knowledge officers are
responsible for justifying the value of knowledge

that is constantly being developed in their organizations (Nonaka and Takeuchi 1995). This
elusive intangible may never be evaluated in the
financial terms that we are currently accustomed
to. However, its strategic impact is never in question. From the capture, codification, and dissemination of information, through to the acquisition of new competencies via training and
development, and on to the reengineering of
business processes, present and future success in
competition will be based less on the strategic allocation of physical and financial resources and
more on the strategic management of knowledge.

Intellectual capital research has primarily
evolved from the desires of practitioners (Bontis
1996, Brooking 1996, Darling 1996, Edvinsson
and Sullivan 1996, Saint-Onge 1996). Consequently, recent developments have come largely
in the form of popular press articles in business
magazines and national newspapers. The challenge for academics is to frame the phenomenon
using extant theories in order to develop a more
rigorous conceptualization of this elusive intan-

gible. This chapter coalesces many perspectives from numerous fields of study in an attempt to raise the understanding and importance of this phenomenon. The objective here is to conceptualize and frame the existing literature on intellectual capital as a foundation for further study.

This topic is important because intellectual capital has been rarely studied or understood. In fact, managers and investors woefully neglect intellectual inputs and outputs, though these far outweigh the assets that appear on balance sheets (Stewart 1991, 1994). Handy (1989) suggests that the intellectual assets of a corporation are usually three or four times tangible book value. He warns that no executive would leave his cash or factory space idle, yet if CEOs are asked how much of the knowledge in their companies is used, they typically say only about 20%. The importance of this topic is also reflected in the increased importance of the professional services industry and the many new knowledge-based firms that have recently been launched.

This chapter is divided into five sections:

1. *Review of concepts*—a review of the recent literature, which includes definitions of terms as well as a conceptual model
2. *Research design*—the methodological approach utilized to administer the pilot study
3. *Results*—analysis of the measures and models
4. *Discussion*—highlights of the analysis, suggestions for future work, limitations of the research, and the contribution it makes to academia and managers
5. *Conclusion*—what managers can do next

Review of Concepts

Knowledge creation by business organizations has been virtually neglected in management studies even though Nonaka and Takeuchi (1995) are convinced that this process has been the most important source of international competitiveness for some time. Drucker (1993) heralds the arrival of a new economy, referred to as the knowledge society. He claims that in this society, knowledge is not just another resource alongside the traditional factors of production—labor, capital, and land—but the only meaningful resource today. Because knowledge is shared among organizational members, it is connected to the firm's history and experiences (Von Krogh et al. 1994) and soon becomes the ultimate re-

placement of other resources (Toffler 1990). This notion underpins a more general idea that economies of the future will be education led (Young 1995). What does this mean for managers? It means that the capacity to manage knowledge-based intellect is the critical skill of this era (Quinn 1992). It is up to symbolic analysts (Reich 1991) who are equipped to identify and solve intellectual capital issues that will sustain the knowledge advantage for their own organizations. If there is one distinguishing feature of the new economy that has developed as a result of powerful forces such as global competition, it is the ascendancy of intellectual capital. A shift is clearly perceptible from a manufacturing to a service-oriented economy: firms that are thriving in the new strategic environment see themselves as learning organizations pursuing the objective of continuous improvement in their knowledge assets (Senge 1990). Recently, there has been exponential growth in researching this area (Crossan and Guatto 1996). Competitive, technological, and market pressures have made continuous organizational learning a critical imperative in global strategy effectiveness (Osland and Yaprak 1995). Organizations that have been unable to enhance their knowledge assets have failed to survive (Antal et al. 1994) and are left wondering what the fuss is all about (Roos and von Krogh 1996).

The importance of this topic is also reflected in the growth of the professional services industry and the many new knowledge-based firms that have fueled our economy. Top MBA recruits no longer find as many positions in manufacturing companies as they did in the 1950s and 1960s. Nowadays, the career services offices of many business schools report that most new graduates secure positions with management consultants, accounting firms, investment banks, law firms, software developers, and information brokers. The constant requirement found in each of these positions is the importance of intellectual capital.

To grasp the importance of why it is necessary to measure this phenomenon, we must understand the concept of Tobin's q from the accounting and finance literature. This ratio measures the relationship between a company's market value and its replacement value (i.e., the cost of replacing its assets). In other words, a company with a stock market value of $100 million and a book value of $25 million will have a Tobin's q ratio of 4.00. The ratio was developed by the Nobel Prize–winning economist James

Tobin (White et al. 1994). In the long run, this ratio will tend towards 1.00, but evidence shows that it can differ significantly from 1.00 for very long periods of time (Bodie et al. 1993). For example, companies in the software industry, where intellectual capital is abundant, tend to have a Tobin's q ratio of 7.00, whereas firms in the steel industry, noted for their large capital assets, have a Tobin's q ratio of nearly 1.00. Intellectual capital valuation has become an industry on its own. For example, the Royal Bank of Canada has launched a subsidiary business that concentrates exclusively on investing in knowledge-based industries (Bontis 1997).

Sveiby (1997) highlights intellectual capital valuation by citing a familiar example of a high Tobin's q:

Shares in Microsoft, the world's largest computer software firm, changed hands at an average price of $70 during fiscal 1995 at a time when their so-called book value was just $7. In other words, for every $1 of recorded value the market saw $9 in additional value for which there was no corresponding record in Microsoft's balance sheet. (p. 3)

There are numerous other examples that make the same case. The value of intellectual capital in these firms has been cast as quasi-value by the invisible hand of the market. However, companies do not trade their intangible assets, so the value of items such as intellectual capital stocks or organizational learning flows cannot be deduced from routine market transactions like the value of traditional tangible assets. Sometimes, the value of knowledge is attributed even without the existence of any monetary transactions at all:

In August 1995 Netscape went public in one of the most oversubscribed initial public offerings in history. A company with negligible profits ended its first day of trading with a value of $2 billion—a value based entirely on intangible assets. (Sveiby 1997, p. 114)

Another popular example of a knowledge-intensive organization that is internationally known for its products is Nike. However, Nike is a shoemaker that makes no shoes—its work is research and development, design, marketing, and distribution, almost all knowledge-based activities—

but still has $334,000 in sales for each employee (Stewart 1997).

One of the purest examples of intellectual capital valuation is in the consulting industry. McKinsey, one of the industry's leaders, does not employ traditional marketing methods; it sells by having clients come knocking to purchase the best analytical knowledge available (Nicou et al. 1994). McKinsey generally sells its intellectual capital in teams of five, each led by a senior partner. Remarkably, clients are willing to pay for the transfer of this knowledge at an average annual rate of $500,000 per consultant (Sveiby 1997).

Stewart (1997) defines intellectual capital as the intellectual material—knowledge, information, intellectual property, experience—that can be put to use to create wealth." Stewart goes on to identify several organizations such as Skandia, Dow Chemical, Hughes Aircraft, and Canadian Imperial Bank of Commerce that are in the process of managing and developing this phenomenon. Stewart's major contribution was in the definition of intellectual capital and in the recognition of the difficulty to measure it. The objective of this pilot study is to explore the development of measures and models that could help both academics and practitioners more readily understand the components of intellectual capital and its impact on business performance.

Intellectual capital consists of human capital (i.e., the tacit knowledge embedded in the minds of the employees), structural capital (i.e., the organizational routines, structures and processes that contain the non-human storehouses of knowledge) and customer capital (i.e., the knowledge embedded in customer relationships which is often called relational capital). For a comprehensive review of each of these constructs, refer to chapter 35 and figures 35.1 and 35.2.

Research Design

A survey was designed that taps into the intellectual capital constructs as well as business performance within the context of the conceptual model. Many of the total design method (TDM) recommendations suggested by Dillman (1978) were adopted. A copy of the cover letter and questionnaire can be requested from the author. The questionnaire was administered to one section of MBA students as the Ivey School of Business in the University of Western Ontario. The questionnaire was designed in an easy-to-read booklet format with a total of eight pages. The cover letter was on the first page, and it introduced the concept of intellectual capital. There was no incentive to fill out the survey for the students and it was completely optional. Sixty-four students took approximately 10 minutes to complete the questionnaire.

Since this study concentrates on the firm level of analysis, each respondent was required to answer the questionnaire as a representative of the organization they worked for prior to entering the MBA program. In effect, each respondent acted as a proxy for their organization. Some students returned the questionnaires unanswered because they worked for governmental offices and felt that they could offer absolutely no feedback on the topic. Others were uncomfortable in filling out the survey because they felt that they did not know enough about the firm and were not in a position high enough to fill out the questionnaire adequately.

In designing the questionnaire, a 7-point Likert scale (strongly disagree to strongly agree) for each item with medium-length (16 to 24 words) questions was used, as suggested by Andrews (1984). A total of 63 items, designed to tap into four constructs (three constructs relating to intellectual capital plus performance), were included in the questionnaire. The items included in the survey were developed from concepts that were accentuated during the literature review phase of the study. Since this is an exploratory pilot study, no previous instruments were replicated. See appendix 36.1 for a summary of the items that were developed and used for each construct.

The results were coded in SPSS for Windows. The following items were reverse coded: human capital (H5R, H13R, H14R, H15R, H19R), customer capital (C13R, C15R), and structural capital (S13R, S16R). Of the total 4,032 data cells (63 items * 64 observations), less than 2.5% had missing values, which were assigned the means of each variable.

The following statistical tests were executed:

- Kolmogorov-Smirnov test for normality
- Cronbach's alpha test for reliability
- Principal components analysis with VARIMAX rotation, and
- Partial least squares (PLS)

Results

The 64 observations represented a variety of organizations in numerous industries. Table 36.1 highlights the profile of the data with some descriptive statistics.

Respondents were promised organizational anonymity. These industries and the number of times they were each represented show a wide cross section of businesses accounted for by the data: financial services (7), chemical (4), insurance (4), computers and software (3), and courier services (2).

Kolmogorov-Smirnov Test

The results show that most items spanned the whole range of possible responses, except for C6, C13R (customer capital), H1, H14R (human capital), S5, S6, S7, S12, S16R (structural capital), and P1, P5, P8 (performance). The Kolmogorov-Smirnov test for normality was used to see whether the responses had a normal curve about the mean. Just over half of the items (33 out of 63) were considered to have normal distributions. However, the assumption of normality is not a major issue for structural modelling. In fact, PLS is robust enough to not require normal data (Barclay et al. 1995).

Feedback from respondents highlighted certain items that were difficult to interpret and thus rejected. For example, C4 (our market share is the highest in the industry) was difficult to answer on a "strongly disagree" or "strongly agree" scale from 1 to 7. If you had the third highest market share in your industry, where would you mark your response? It would be difficult to decide in this case because respondents interpret the question differently.

TABLE 36.1 Profile of Data ($)

Item	Mean	Std. Dev.	Minimum	Maximum
Sales ($million)	588.15	931.46	1.00	4,000.00
Employees (#)	8,731	28,489	8	180,000

Cronbach's Alpha

To test the reliability of the measures, Cronbach's alpha was used as suggested by Nunnally (1978). This calculation should be the first measure one calculates to assess the quality of the instrument (Churchill 1979). A satisfactory level of reliability depends on how a measure is being used. In the early stages of research on predictor tests or hypothesized measures of a construct (as is the case with this exploratory pilot study) instruments that have reliabilities of 0.7 or greater will suffice (Nunnally 1978). The reliabilities for each of the four constructs are fine since the alpha values for each are greater than 0.85.

Principal Components Analysis

Factor analysis is a multivariate statistical method whose primary purpose is data reduction and summarization (Hair et al. 1987). By using factor analysis, a factor loading for each item and its corresponding construct was determined. In order to verify that the items tapped into their stipulated constructs, a principal components analysis with a VARIMAX rotation was executed. The items were forced into three factors, and the output was sorted and ranked based on a 0.5 loading cutoff. Typically, loadings of 0.5 or greater are considered very significant (Hair et al. 1987).

The VARIMAX rotation was used because it centers on simplifying the columns of the factor matrix. With the VARIMAX rotational approach, there tends to be some high loadings (i.e., closer to 1) and some loadings near 0 in each column of the matrix. The logic is that interpretation is easiest when the variable-factor correlations are either closer to 1, thus indicating a clear association between the variable and the factor, or 0, indicating a clear lack of association (Hair et al. 1987).

Only the items that loaded on their corresponding factors at levels of 0.5 or greater were retained for the rest of the analysis. These items are highlighted in the last column. Items were not retained because they

- did not load on any factor with a value of 0.5 or greater,
- loaded on the wrong factor, or
- had cross-loadings on two factors.

Items S12, S7, S8, and S13R were not retained because they did not load on their appropriate

factor and also cross-loaded on factor 3 at a loading of less than 0.5. The three factors had Eigenvalues and percentage of variance explained of 13.735 (25.9%), 7.634 (14.4%) and 3.289 (6.2%), respectively, with a total cumulative variance explained of 46.5%.

Partial Least Squares

Partial least squares (PLS) allows the researcher to test a model within its nomological network. Constructs derive their meaning from their underlying measures as well as their antecedent and consequent constructs giving a researcher the benefit of examining the constructs in an overall theoretical context.

The objective in PLS is to maximize the explanation variance. Thus, R^2 and the significance of relationships among constructs are measures indicative of how well a model is performing. The conceptual core of PLS is an iterative combination of principal components analysis relating measures to constructs, and path analysis permitting the construction of a system of constructs. The hypothesizing of relationships between measures and constructs, and constructs and other constructs is guided by theory. The estimation of the parameters representing the measurement and path relationships is accomplished using ordinary least squares (OLS) techniques.

The first step in PLS is for the researcher to explicitly specify both the structural model and the construct-to-measures relationships in the measurement model. The exogenous constructs are consistent with the idea of independent variables (antecedents). Similarly, the endogenous constructs are consistent with the idea of dependent variables (consequents).

The constructs can be specified as "formative" indicators or "reflective" indicators. Formative indicators imply a construct that is expressed as a function of the items (the items form or cause the construct). Reflective indicators imply a construct where the observable items are expressed as a function of the construct (the items reflect or are manifestations of the construct). One looks to theory to decide on which type of epistemic or construct-to-measure relationship to specify. In this case, all constructs were "reflective" indicators. Once specified, the measurement and structural parameters are estimated using an iterative process of OLS, simple, and multiple regressions. The process continues until the differences in the component scores converge within certain criteria.

One of the key benefits of using PLS as a structural modelling technique is that it may work with smaller samples. In general, the most complex regression will involve

1. the indicators on the most complex formative construct, or
2. the largest number of antecedent constructs leading to an endogenous construct.

Sample size requirements become at least 10 times the number of predictors from item 1 or 2, whichever is greater (Barclay et al. 1995). In this study, the sample size of 64 is high enough for PLS. There were no formative indicators, so it is the second requirement that must be met. The largest number of antecedent constructs leading to an endogenous construct is three (3 * 10 = 30 < 64).

The retained items from the previous tests were used in PLS to test their loadings within a nomological network. Nine structural combinations were examined using different relative positions for the intellectual capital constructs. The nine models represent different combinations of the intellectual capital constructs leading into performance. The R^2 figures represent the predictive power within those constructs as explained by the measures that represent the preceding constructs. The path loadings represent the causal links from one construct to the other.

The previous analysis was used to determine which of the retained items (from the original principal components analysis) were now going to be kept for further investigation. These remaining items were then placed in a structural configuration which yielded the highest original R^2 for performance at 56.0% (which is very high relatively speaking for such a construct). The selected model was then tested using PLS once more and the statistical highlights are illustrated in appendix 2.

Tests for individual item reliability, internal consistency and discriminant validity were completed for the selected model. The R^2 or predictive power in the endogenous constructs were as follows: customer capital = 24.53%, structural capital = 24.89%, and performance = 56.02%. Individual item reliability is assessed by examining the loadings, or simple correlations, of the measures with their respective construct. A rule of thumb is to accept items with loadings of 0.7 or more, which implies more shared variance between the construct and its measures than error

variance (Carmines and Zeller 1979). All lambdas (or loadings) were over the 0.7 threshold.

Internal consistency was verified since all of the items loaded at 0.7 or greater on their corresponding constructs. Internal consistency was tested using the Fornell and Larcker (1981) measure. Discriminant validity was tested using the correlation matrix of constructs. The diagonal of this matrix is the square root of the average variance extracted. For adequate discriminant validity, the diagonal elements should be significantly greater than the off-diagonal elements in the corresponding rows and columns as was the case for the selected model (see appendix 36.2).

To assess the statistical significance of the path coefficients, which are standardized betas, a jackknife analysis was performed using a program developed by Fornell and Barclay (1983). The use of jackknifing, as opposed to traditional t tests, allows the testing of the significance of parameter estimates from data which are not assumed to be multivariate normal. In this case, 32 subsamples were created by removing two cases from the total data set. The PLS analysis estimates the parameters of each subsample, and "pseudovalues" are calculated by applying the jackknife formula. Four of the five paths proved to be significant at the $p < 0.001$ level. The one path from customer capital to structural capital was not significant. Interestingly, this was also the only path to have a negative coefficient and was the least substantive of them all.

Path analysis can be used to calculate the total direct, indirect and spurious effects for each endogenous construct. Table 36.2 summarizes the results for each path highlighted in appendix 36.2:

$$1 \quad \frac{\left(\sum \lambda_{yi}\right)^2}{\left(\sum \lambda_{yi}\right)^2 + \sum \mathrm{Var}(\varepsilon_i)}$$

$$2 \quad \frac{\sum \lambda^2_{yi}}{\sum \lambda^2_{yi} + \sum \mathrm{Var}(\varepsilon_i)}$$

Discussion

The PLS procedure analyzes the measurement model and structural model concurrently. Model fit is dependent upon the integrity of the data as well as the strength of the theory. In the case of my model, the integrity of the data was fine and

TABLE 36.2 Results for Path Analysis

Path from → to	Correlation r	Direct Path (1)	Indirect Path (2)	Total Effect (1) + (2)	Spurious (3)	Total Sum (1) + (2) + (3)
Human → Customer	0.499	0.499	0	0.499	0	0.499
Human → Structural	0.492	0.524	(0.499)(−0.065)	0.492	0	0.492
Customer → Structural	0.197	−0.065	0	−0.067	(0.499)(0.524)	0.197
Customer → Performance	0.639	0.560	(−0.065)(0.398)	0.534	(0.499)(0.524)(0.398)	0.639
Structural → Performance	0.508	0.398	0	0.398	(−0.065)(0.560) + (0.524)(0.499) (0.560)	0.508

all but one of the paths proved to be significant. The strong contribution of PLS in exploratory work is that principal components analysis and path analysis are incorporated into an a priori theoretical and measurement model, and thus the parameters are estimated in this specific context.

There are numerous improvements that can be made from this pilot study for future research. First of all, the use of a convenience sample (MBAs) is a strong criticism against these data because of the appropriateness and representativeness of the respondents. Some of the MBAs mentioned that they had forgotten or were not currently close enough to the organization to respond accurately to some of the questions. Others thought that they were not in high enough positions to respond thoughtfully.

To improve on this study it would be beneficial in the future to elicit responses directly from a wide variety of organizations that include both manufacturing and service industries. By examining these two different types of organizations, one would hope to find a relatively larger concentration of intellectual capital in the professional services industry (i.e., organizations such as software developers, research laboratories, and law firms).

The objective of the study thus far has been to determine which items effectively capture the constructs of human capital, structural capital, customer capital, and performance. This was done by examining their loadings using a variety of structural model specifications. It was also noted that certain paths (i.e., the ones leading into customer capital) were neither substantive nor significant. To solve this dilemma, it may be useful in future studies to utilize model specifications that do not require paths into structural capital. Two examples of this possibility using the current pilot study data are depicted in appendix 36.3.

The Diamond specification is the optimal model encountered in the pilot study. All of the paths are substantive and significant and the R^2 of performance is high. This model also makes intuitive sense. A brilliant business school graduate that is recruited into an organization as a product manager symbolizes the human capital that starts off this model. With the advent of a supportive culture (structural capital) and market research (customer capital), the new employee can launch a very successful product (performance).

Although the Simplistic specification conjectures that the three components of intellectual capital lead into performance directly, it does not account for the interrelationships among the three. It is for this reason that it is not supported even though the R^2 value was still high for the performance construct. Given the literature review of intellectual capital, the three constructs that make up this phenomenon are known to affect each other. In other words, an intellectual employee (human capital) is practically useless without the supportive structure of an organization (structural capital) that can utilize and nurture his or her skills. This may account for the unsubstantive and insignificant path from human capital to performance.

There is an important implication for managers hidden behind appendix 36.3. What the two different model specifications are saying is that there must exist a constant interplay among human, structural and customer capital in order for an organization to leverage off its knowledge base. Isolated stocks of knowledge that reside in the employees' minds that are never codified into organizational knowledge will never positively affect business performance. In other words, it is not enough for an organization to hire and promote the brightest individuals it can find. An organization must also support and nurture bright individuals into sharing their human capital through organizational learning. Unlike normal inventory that can be found in traditional manufacturing settings, individual knowledge stocks that reside in human capital become obsolete. This obsolescence is not necessarily due to outdated knowledge. There is a behavioral explanation instead. Human beings become unmotivated when they feel they are not being utilized or challenged. That is why a stock of human capital will deteriorate if not constantly supported and nurtured.

The results of this research program should be very beneficial to both academics and practitioners. Academics in the policy and accounting areas have traditionally been very interested in how intangible assets reflect on the performance of firms. The pilot study thus far has shown that intellectual capital has a significant and substantive impact on performance. Future research may show that this causal link may be more substantive in certain specific industries. Also, future research may show that organizations with predominant home country profiles may be more in tune with intellectual capital and its effect on performance. Cross-referencing the intellectual capital data with a variety of international respondents and Hofstede's (1978) cultural dimensions may highlight some interesting relationships in this case.

For accounting researchers, intellectual capital may prove to be an important item of disclosure in the future (especially for professional services firms whose knowledge assets are not currently reflected in today's accounting procedures). Churchill's (1979) final suggestion in creating better measures is to "develop norms." Once accepted items for measuring intellectual capital are selected, organizations might be assessed by their relative positioning on each characteristic. Since respondents in this study participated anonymously, the relative positioning of actual firms was not reported.

By making periodic assessments of key intellectual capital components, their potential sale value to an outsider, and any measurable trends in these values can offer a new perspective. Another interesting calculation for accounting and finance academics is to examine what the companies actually did with their intellectual capital. For example, one might calculate a firm's "exploitation ratio" comparing the value of its intellectual capital with its actual relative performance. This would suggest how effective the organization has been in making the causal link from intellectual capital to performance.

Once managers realize the importance of measuring and developing their intellectual capital, they will invariably want to increase it since it positively affects firm performance. In recognizing the key to intellectual capital development, Professor Neil Postman (1985) of New York University believes that the most important thing one learns is always something about how one learns. This notion is similar to the idea of deutero learning as put forward by Argyris, one of the most prolific writers on organizational learning. Argyris and Schon (1978) identified three types of learning, single loop, double loop and deutero learning. Through case study analysis they examined which of the three types of learning was most prevalent in business. They concluded that most businesses follow single-loop learning, which merely detects and corrects problems as soon as possible so that the organization can continue with its regular activities. Double-loop learning, on the other hand, not only involves the detection and correction phase of problem resolution, but also attempts to modify underlying norms, policies, and objectives. Deutero learning, the most advanced of the three, involves understanding the whole process or learning how to learn. Although this concept is intuitively appealing, managers have yet to find a practical means to adopt the deutero learning process and will therefore continue to struggle to develop intellectual capital.

Conclusion

The management of intellect lies at the heart of value in the current "knowledge era" of business. Unfortunately, methods of measuring and evaluating intellectual capital have been slow to develop. There is an extremely limited literature on the study and management of intellectual capital. This is partly due to the privacy that accompanies most organizations and their discussion on intellectual capital. Continued research of this phenomenon should show that organizations with a high level of intellectual capital will be those in which the value-added service of the firm comes from deep professional knowledge, organizational learning, and protection and security of information. Managers, analysts, and researchers should also be wary of looking for a formula of intellectual capital. By definition, the tacitness of intellectual capital may not allow analysts to ever measure it using economic variables. A warning must be sent out to those accountants and financial analysts who are asking the question, How much is my intellectual capital worth? A formula may never exist. That is not to say that metric development is a waste of time. Longitudinal examination of metrics as well as benchmarking against industry norms can help managers in examining their own intellectual capital. In this case, examining the processes underlying intellectual capital development may be of more importance than ever finding out what it is all worth.

Managers who are interested in strategically managing their intellectual capital for their own organizations should follow these steps (Bontis, 1996):

1. Conduct an initial intellectual capital audit. Such an examination may consist of a survey design and administration using Likert-type scales in order to get a snapshot of the benchmark level of intellectual capital in existence. Some firms, such as Skandia (1994, 1995a, 1995b, 1996a, 1996b), use their own metrics of intellectual capital. However, each firm is different and must thrive in the context of its own industry. Each organization should design their metrics for their own strategic purposes.
2. Make knowledge management a requirement for evaluation purposes for each employee—assign personal targets to intellectual capital development. For example, companies can have each employee aim to learn something that the organization currently does not know.
3. Formally define the role of knowledge in your business and in your industry—find and secure the greatest resources of intellectual capital inside and outside your firm from places such as industry associations, academia, customers, suppliers, and the government.
4. Recruit and hire a leader responsible for the intellectual capital development of your organization. This person must have an integrated background in human resources, strategy, and information technology.
5. Classify your intellectual portfolio by producing a knowledge map of your organization—determine in which people and systems knowledge resides. For example, create a central database in which all competitive intelligence information can be accumulated and accessed.
6. Utilize information systems and sharing tools that aid in knowledge exchange and codifying, such as groupware technology, videoconferencing, intranets, corporate universities, and storytelling among employees.
7. Send employees to conferences and trade shows and have them spy. Do not pay for their travel expenses unless they share what they learned with the rest of the organization when they return.
8. Consistently conduct intellectual capital audits to reevaluate the organization's knowledge accumulation—use monetary values if at all possible, but do not be afraid to develop customized indices and metrics.
9. Identify gaps to be filled or holes to be plugged based on weaknesses relative to competitors, customers, suppliers, and best practices.
10. Assemble the organization's new knowledge portfolio in an intellectual capital addendum to the annual report.

Acknowledgment Preparation of this chapter was assisted by the financial support received from an Ontario Graduate Scholarship and an Ivey Doctoral Grant. The author gratefully acknowledges the suggestions and comments of reviewers and of Professors Mary Crossan and John Hulland. The author would also like to thank the inspirational thinking of Hubert Saint-Onge, Leif Edvinsson, and Thomas Stewart. Previous versions of certain sections of this chapter may have appeared elsewhere as a working paper, conference proceeding, or book chapter.

References

Andrews, F.M. (1984) "Construct validity and error components of survey measures: a structural modeling approach." *Public Opinion Quarterly* 48:409–442.

Antal, A.B., Dierkes, M., and Hahner, K. (1994) "Business in society: perceptions and principles in organizational learning." *Journal of General Management* 20(2):55–77.

Argyris, C. (1992) *On Organizational Learning.* Cambridge, MA: Blackwell.

Argyris, C. and Schön, D. (1978) *Organizational Learning: A Theory of Action Perspective*. Reading, MA: Addison-Wesley.

Barclay, D., Higgins, C., and Thompson, R. (1995) "The partial least squares (PLS) approach to causal modeling." *Technology Studies* 2(2).

Bodie, Z., Kane, A., and Marcus, A.J. (1993) *Investments*. New York: Irwin.

Boehnke, K., DiStefano, A., DiStefano, J., and Bontis, N. (1997) "Leadership for exceptional performance." *Business Quarterly*, Summer.

Bontis, N. (1996) "There's a price on your head: managing intellectual capital strategically." *Business Quarterly*, Summer.

Bontis, N. (1997) "Royal Bank invests in knowledge-based industries." *Knowledge Inc.* 2(8).

Brooking, A. (1996) *Intellectual Capital: Core Asset for the Third Millennium Enterprise*. London: International Thomson Business Press.

Carmines, E. and Zeller, R. (1979) "Reliability and validity assessment." Sage Paper on Quantitative Applications, No. 07-017. Beverly Hills, CA: Sage.

Churchill, G.A., Jr. (1979) "A paradigm for developing better measures of marketing constructs." *Journal of Marketing Research* 16:64–73.

Cohen, G., Kiss, G., and Le Voi, M. (1993) *Memory—Current Issues*. Buckingham. Open University.

Crossan, M. and Guatto, T. (1996) "Organizational learning research profile." *Journal of Organizational Change Management* 9(1).

Crossan, M., White, R.E., Lane, H.W., and Klus, L. (1996) "The improvising organization: where planning meets opportunity." *Organization Dynamics* 24(4):20–34.

Darling, M. (1996) "Building the knowledge organization." *Business Quarterly*, Winter.

Deng, S. and Dart, J. (1994) "Measuring market orientation: a multi-factor, multi-item approach." *Journal of Marketing Management* 10:725–742.

Dierickx, I. and Cool, K. (1989) "Asset stock accumulation and sustainability of competitive advantage." *Management Science*.

Dillman, D.A. (1978) *Mail and Telephone Surveys: The Total Design Method*. New York: Wiley.

Drucker, P.F. (1993) *Post-capitalist Society*. Oxford: Butterworth Heinemann.

Edvinsson, L. and Sullivan, P. (1996) "Developing a model for managing intellectual capital." *European Management Journal* 14(4).

Feiwal, G.R. (1975) *The Intellectual Capital of Michal Kalecki: A Study in Economic Theory and Policy*. Knoxville, TN: University of Tennessee Press.

Fornell, C. and Barclay, D. (1983) *Jackknifing: A Supplement to Lohmoller's LVPLS Program*. Ann Arbor: University of Michigan.

Fornell, C. and Larcker, D. (1981) "Evaluating structural equation models with unobservable variable and measurement error." *Journal of Marketing Research* 18:39–50.

Hair, J., Rolph, A., and Tatham, R. (1987) *Multivariate Data Analysis*, 2d ed. New York: Macmillan.

Hampden-Turner, C. (1992) *Creating Corporate Culture: From Discord to Harmony*. Reading, MA: Addison-Wesley.

Handy, C.B. (1989) *The Age of Unreason*. London: Arrow.

Hofstede, G. (1978) "Value systems in 40 countries," *Proceedings of the 4th International Congress of the Association for Cross-Cultural Psychology*.

Hudson, W. (1993) *Intellectual Capital: How to Build It, Enhance It, Use It*. New York: Wiley.

Kohli, A.K. and Jaworski, B.J. (1990) "Market orientation: the construct, research propositions, and managerial implications." *Journal of Marketing* 54:1–18.

Levitt, T. (1991) *Marketing Imagination*. New York: Free Press.

Lichtenthal, J.D. and Wilson, D.T. (1992) "Becoming market oriented." *Journal of Business Research* 24:191–207.

Narver, J.C. and Slater, S.F. (1990) "The effect of a market orientation on business profitability." *Journal of Marketing*, October, pp. 20–35.

Nelson, R.R. and Winter, S.G. (1982) *An Evolutionary Theory of Economic Change*. Cambridge, MA: Belknap Press.

Nicolini, D. (1993) "Apprendimento organizzativo e pubblica amministrazione locale." *Autonomie Locali e Servizi Sociali* 16(2).

Nicou, M., Ribbing, C., and Ading, E. (1994) *Sell Your Knowledge*. London: Kogan Page.

Nonaka, I. and Takeuchi, H. (1995) *The Knowledge-Creating Company*. New York: Oxford University Press.

Nunnally, J.C. (1978) *Psychometric Theory*, 2d ed. New York: McGraw-Hill.

Osland, G.E. and Yaprak, A. (1995) "Learning through strategic alliances: processes and factors that enhance marketing effectiveness." *European Journal of Marketing* 29:52–66.

Postman, N. (1985) *Amusing Ourselves to Death: Public Discourse in the Age of Show Business*. New York: Viking.

Prusak, L. (1996) "The knowledge advantage." *Strategy and Leadership*, March/April.

Quinn, J.B. (1992) *Intelligent Enterprise*. New York: Free Press.

Reich, R.B. (1991) *The Work of Nations*. New York: Knopf.

Roos, J. and von Krogh, G. (1996) "The epistemological challenge: managing knowledge and intellectual capital." *European Management Journal* 14(4).

Saint-Onge, H. (1996) "Tacit knowledge: the key to the strategic alignment of intellectual capital." *Strategy and Leadership*, April.

Schultz, T.W. (1981) *Investing in People: The Economics of Population Quality*. Berkeley: University of California.

Sente, P.M. (1990) *The Fifth Discipline: The Art and Practice of the Learning Organisation*. New York: Doubleday Currency.

Skandia (1994) "Visualizing intellectual capital in Skandia." A supplement to Skandia's 1994 annual report.

Skandia (1995a) "Renewal and development: intellectual capital." A supplement to Skandia's 1995 interim annual report.

Skandia (1995b) "Value-creating processes: intellectual capital." A supplement to Skandia's 1995 annual report.

Skandia (1996a) "Power of innovation: intellectual capital." A supplement to Skandia's 1996 interim annual report.

Skandia (1996b) "Customer value." A supplement to Skandia's 1996 annual report.

Stewart, T.A. (1991) "Brainpower: how intellectual capital is becoming America's most valuable asset." *Fortune*, June 3, pp. 44–60.

Stewart, T.A. (1994) "Your company's most valuable asset: intellectual capital." *Fortune*, October 3, pp. 68–74.

Stewart, T.A. (1997) *Intellectual Capital: The New Wealth of Organizations*. New York: Doubleday/Currency.

Sveiby, K.E. (1997) *The New Organizational Wealth: Managing and Measuring Knowledge Based Assets*. New York: Berrett-Koehler.

Toffler, A. (1990) *Powershift: Knowledge, Wealth and Violence at the Edge of the 21st Century*. New York: Bantam.

von Krogh, G., Roos, J., and Slocum, K. (1994) "An essay on corporate epistemology." *Strategy Management Journal*, 15.

Ward, A. (1996) "Lessons learned on the knowledge highways and byways." *Strategy and Leadership*, March/April.

White, G.I., Sondhi, A.C., and Fried, D. (1994) *The Analysis and Use of Financial Statements*. New York: Wiley.

Wiele, B. (1993) "Competing from the neck up." *Performance & Instruction*, March.

Winter, S.G. (1987) "Knowledge and competence as strategic assets," in Teece, D.J. (ed.), *The Competitive Challenge: Strategies of Industrial Innovation and Renewal*, pp. 159–184. Cambridge, MA: Ballinger.

Young, M. (1995) "Post-compulsory education and training for learning society." *Australian and New Zealand Journal of Vocational Educational Research*.

APPENDIX 36.1 SUMMARY OF SURVEY ITEMS (EXCERPTS FROM QUESTIONNAIRE)

"R" indicates reverse-coded items.

Human Capital

H1	Competence ideal level
H2	Succession training program
H3	Planners on schedule
H4	Employees cooperate in teams
H5R	No internal relationships
H6	Come up with new ideas
H7	Upgrade employees' skills
H8	Employees are bright
H9	Employees are best in industry
H10	Employees are satisfied
H11	Employees perform their best
H12	Recruitment program comprehensive
H13R	Big trouble if individuals left
H14R	Rarely think actions through
H15R	Do without thinking
H16	Individuals learn from others
H17	Employees voice opinions
H18	Get the most out of employees
H19R	Bring down to others' level
H20	Employees give it their all

Customer Capital

C1	Customers generally satisfied
C2	Reduce time to resolve problem
C3	Market share improving
C4	Market share is highest
C5	Longevity of relationships
C6	Value-added service
C7	Customers are loyal
C8	Customers increasingly select us
C9	Firm is market oriented
C10	Meet with customers
C11	Customer info disseminated
C12	Understand target markets
C13R	Do not care what customer wants
C14	Capitalize on customers' wants
C15R	Launch what customers don't want

C16	Confident of future with customer
C17	Feedback with customer

Structural Capital

S1	Lowest-cost per transaction
S2	Improving cost per revenue $
S3	Increase revenue per employee
S4	Revenue per employee is best
S5	Transaction time decreasing
S6	Transaction time is best
S7	Implement new ideas
S8	Supports development of ideas
S9	Develops most ideas in industry
S10	Firm is efficient
S11	Systems allow easy info access
S12	Procedures support innovation

S13R	Firm is bureaucratic nightmare
S14	Not too far removed from each other
S15	Atmosphere is supportive
S16R	Do not share knowledge

Performance

P1	Industry leadership
P2	Future outlook
P3	Profit
P4	Profit growth
P5	Sales growth
P6	After-tax return on assets
P7	After-tax return on sales
P8	Overall response to competition
P9	Success rate in new product launch
P10	Overall business performance

APPENDIX 36.2 STATISTICAL HIGHLIGHTS ON SELECTED MODEL SPECIFICATION

TABLE 36.A1

	Number of Items	Internal Consistency (Fornell and Larcker)	Discriminant Validity Correlation of Constructs						R Squared (%)
Human	7	0.9194	0.936						
Customer	7	0.9228	0.499	0.940					24.43
Structural	7	0.9258	0.492	0.197	0.943				24.89
Performance	9	0.9535	0.509	0.639	0.508	0.967			56.02
Human capital	H8	H15R	H9	H20	H18	H6	H11		
	0.8055	0.7855	0.8392	0.8556	0.7006	0.7059	0.8091		
Customer capital	C14	C1	C16	C9	C6	C5	C8		
	0.8189	0.7924	0.8365	0.7297	0.8205	0.7879	0.7706		
Structural capital	S10	S2	S6	S5	S1	S3	S4		
	0.8215	0.8431	0.8030	0.7368	0.7873	0.8058	0.8021		
Performance	P2	P3	P4	P5	P6	P7	P8	P9	P10
	0.7823	0.8209	0.8978	0.7977	0.8514	0.8348	0.8054	0.7406	0.9591

APPENDIX 36.3 FURTHER STATISTICAL HIGHLIGHTS ON SELECTED MODEL SPECIFICATIONS

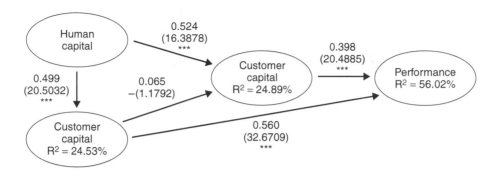

Figure 36.A2

Note: Top number is path; *t* values are in parentheses: *** = significant at $p < 0.001$.

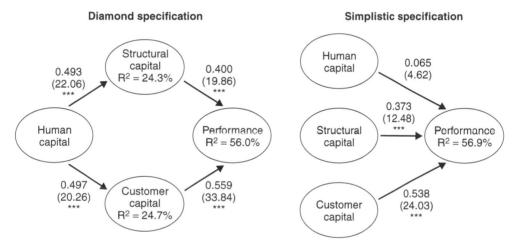

Figure 36.A1

Note: Top number is path, *t* values are in parentheses: *** = significant at $p < 0.001$.

37

Intellectual Capital Management and Disclosure

Steve Pike, Anna Rylander, and Göran Roos

Over the past decade, there has been a rapidly growing realization of the importance of intangible assets and intellectual capital as a whole in the operation of organizations. With this realization has come the need to manage companies in a new way and to measure their performance in a new way. A sharp illustration of the differences in the managerial attitudes of the industrial and postindustrial ages (Sveiby 1997) has been in the appreciation that people can no longer be considered to be costs on the profit and loss statement but are, in fact, assets to be invested in, developed, and deployed carefully. The effect of changes in business on national life has not gone unnoticed either, with governments taking a keen interest in economic development in the "new economy" (UKDTI 1998a, 1998b). In the markets, the effects of the new economy have also been startling. In early 2000 in the United States, 5% (i.e., about $1 trillion) of company capitalization is accounted for by the dotcom companies, and this valuation is not built upon profit-yielding sales or physical capital but on "stories" (Lightman 2000). In the United Kingdom the trend is similar and is expected to continue over the next decade. It is estimated that over 25% of companies that can be expected to be listed in the FTSE 100 in 2010 do not exist at present, and these will be dominated by the dotcoms and hi-techs (DTI 2000). Elsewhere it is estimated that over half of the market capitalization of all companies is due to intangible assets.

It is a well-known argument that the dominating factor in company valuation for most companies now, and especially the hi-techs and dotcoms, is intellectual capital. It is obvious that managers must be able to manage companies with these characteristics effectively. It is equally obvious that the characteristics of the underlying business and its long-term prospects have to be communicated to the investing community. Failure to do this effectively has led to the well-known problems of CEOs feeling that their market valuation is understated, that the volatility factor that applies to them is too high, and that, consequently, finance is harder to raise when needed than it should be.

Through most of the 1990s, one of the most insidious reasons why progress in describing companies' intellectual capital characteristics to others and managing them effectively internally has been slow has been the lack of a common language with which to describe and communi-

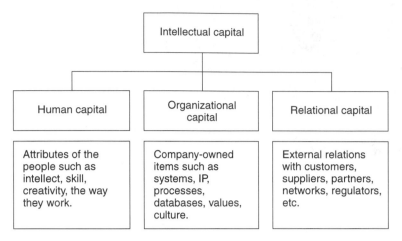

Figure 37.1 Categories of intellectual capital.

cate issues. The characteristics and potential of people, known as human capital, comprise different things to different people. Even at a detailed level where the more fundamental aspects of people and behavior emerge, there has been little evidence of the clarity that should be present when in the proximity of pure research. This is not just a problem for those concerned with intellectual capital management and disclosure; it also appears and is debated vociferously in the subsidiary area of knowledge management. For example, there are at least eight different categories for knowledge in common use. An explanation of many of them is found in Von Krogh et al. (1998). Aside from the problems of communicating meaning, management models and the results they give, and the subsequent actions managers choose to take, also lack the clarity and obvious logic that they might otherwise have if language was shared. Review documents such as those by the conferencing groups (Skyrme 1998) allow the researcher a convenient place to find, compare, and chart development from balanced scorecards and business excellence models, through the seminal works of Edvinsson and Malone (1997) and Roos et al. (1997), to Brooking (1996), Sveiby (1997), and others thereafter. Happily, in the last two years or so there has been a steady convergence in categorization and language onto a single model.

Figure 37.1 shows the emergent definitions. This diagram can be seen as indicative only of the components of intellectual capital. These elements combine and interact with each other and with traditional capital elements (physical things and monetary elements) in ways unique to in-

dividual companies to create value. Thus, the equation for intellectual capital and market value, while useful in drawing attention to intellectual capital, is incorrect from more than one point of view:

$$\text{Market value} = \text{Book value} + \text{Intellectual capital} \quad 37.1$$

Management models and new accounting schemes based upon such a model will necessarily be flawed since the variables are not separable as required by the equation. Additionally, the obvious accounting flaw is that the right-hand side of the equation does not have a single set of units: virtual and real money cannot be added to each other (Justice 1707).

The remainder of this chapter is concerned with the recent developments in intellectual capital management, measurement, and disclosure. The chapter concludes with a description of the way ahead, bearing in mind the article by Narayanan et al. (2000) demonstrating that companies able to make meaningful disclosure about their true long-term prospects achieved more satisfactory ratings and valuations than did those that could not.

Management and Measurement

Through history, man has evolved from being a hunter-gatherer, through agricultural society and industrial society, and now into a knowledge-based society. In business, some of all four sets of characteristics can be found in companies at large,

TABLE 37.1 Evolving Business Types

Business/Society	Attributes	Characteristic Statement
Hunter-gatherer	Aggressive, hand-to-mouth, meets local needs, no reserves, mobile; people are expendable.	We are a successful and profitable company. We depend on our first-rate sales force to maintain us but do not have a broad product base. We have a stable core of people to guide company development.
Agricultural	Docile, stationary, has reserves, meets local and some distant needs; people are tools.	We provide a service for customers who are always going to be there and are, in a sense, local. Our staff are broadly but not highly skilled and our procedures are well set out and adhered to. Quality is our watchword.
Industrial	Cost conscious, efficient, meets area needs; many suppliers may own distribution network; people are costs.	The company has thrived and survived recession by careful cost control, process reengineering, and careful attention to customer satisfaction. We are a volume producer with major production plants. We have a network of tied distributors. Our brands are well known.
Knowledge	Creative, agile, knows what it knows, knows customer and values, involves suppliers and distributors, electronic presence; people are assets.	We thrive through our ability to stay at the leading edge of customer needs and product design. To do this we convert our staff's talents as best we can and have an extensive network of partners. Our marketing and electronic presence give us a global position.

and this perhaps reflects the speed with which business and economics have evolved. Table 37.1 provides some examples.

It is interesting to note that as the business society has developed, the key step in value creation has ascended an intellectual staircase. This starts with selling in a hit-and-run strategic framework, to selling a defined quality product to stable customers in the agricultural society, to an efficiently produced quality product in the industrial society, and now with a customized product in the knowledge society. The key intellectual capital elements have also evolved through just being there, to physical capital dominated, to organizational capital dominated, and now to human capital dominated. It could be argued that agricultural and industrial societies required human capital, too; however, in these societies the use of humans tended to be as extensions of machines rather than as assets employing such intellectual capital attributes as intellectual agility and creativity.

The management models that have been used to guide development have also evolved, but there has been a key difference in the transition to the knowledge economy. The difference is not that yet further items have been added to the balance sheet or recorded as costs in the profit and loss statement, but that people are now also

assets with an indeterminable value as far as standard accounting is concerned. Furthermore, the knowledge they have embodied into processes has a value that may be known as far as the owning company is concerned but, when traded, has a value dependent on the context of use of the buyer, and this varies from buyer to buyer. There are now Internet-based knowledge exchanges (e.g., Knexa and IQPort), and it will be interesting indeed to watch the fate of "knowledge" traded by them.

The change in the key characteristics of companies in the knowledge era leads to one of the principal distinctions in the approaches to measurement and management. The most obvious approach is to try to retain as much of the rigor of conventional accounting by adjusting its traditional instruments. Where practitioners believe this to be impossible, they have resorted to measuring new things but retaining the forms of conventional accounting. The alternative to this is to abandon traditional accounting completely and base measurement and management on the attributes of the value generating processes of individual companies. In both methodologies, the aim is to allow managers to manage effectively internally and increase the performance and competitive position of the company, and also to communicate the performance, position, and potential of the company externally to shareholders and the investing community at large. The issue is whether either of these approaches can meet the need in an auditable, useful, and secure way. Internally, this means a measurement regime that gives managers the levers necessary to guide the business while not instilling bad behaviors through measuring the wrong things, nor imposing a heavy burden of measurement of people who have better things to do. Externally, it means providing stakeholders and potential investors with the often long-term information they need but without disclosing sensitive strategic intentions to competitors.

There are a number of intellectual capital measurement/management methodologies available now; some have been evaluated by the KnowNet group (EU/ESPRIT 2000). They could be thought of as falling roughly into the two groups described above, but precise placement is impossible. Instead, they can be thought of as being on a continuum, with finance-based models at one end and business-based models at the other. In assessing the relative effectiveness of differing approaches to measurement and management, it is necessary to have some criteria by which they may be judged. Suitable criteria to assess a model are that

1. it is auditable and reliable
2. it does not impose a large measurement overhead
3. it facilitates strategic and tactical management
4. it generates the information needed by shareholders and investors

Auditable and Reliable

The first criterion is important since if managers are to make judgments on measurements, they need confidence that the information they have can be relied upon to be a true measure of the system under consideration. Even if the interpretation of that information may differ from one manager to another, the source must be unimpeachable. Traditional accounting generally offers that quality for monetary capital and, to a considerable extent, physical capital, since quantities are simple and additive. However, valuations of physical capital are problematic since their intrinsic value is calculated through a depreciation process, which is very hard to recoup at sale, and the extrinsic value is inextricably

bound up with companies' business processes. With either physical or monetary value, the danger for managers attempting to make business decisions is that the actions they may take are based on extrapolations beyond the zone of validity for the underlying data. A common example is to equate or make some other direct link between investments costs, such as for research and development (R&D) with the value of that R&D.

Intangible assets are not additive in nature, and their measurement is open to semantic debate. It is therefore most important that a systematic approach to measurement is taken. Although serious work on measurement theory was not undertaken until as late as the nineteenth century, its completion is an even more recent event (Krantz et al. 1971). The adherence of measurement systems to the canonical requirements of measurement theory provides a means by which non-financially based measurement systems can attain the same (or better) degrees of rigor as financially based ones. There are some 13 requirements for compliance with measurement theory, but the key requirements are that the measurement system and its constituent elements are:

1. complete in coverage,
2. distinct and free from overlaps,
3. preference independent with respect to one another,
4. observable,
5. measurable, and
6. agreeable in that they are an agreed measure of the attribute.

Measurement and the consequent management of intellectual capital based on lists of attributes, which have not been thoroughly subjected to this rigor, carry with them the danger of unexpected and unwanted consequences.

Measurement Overhead

This is an entirely practical point in that measurement schemes tend to grow uncontrollably. Key attributes that have to be measured, especially the nonfinancial attributes, should be broken down only to the stage where compliance with the sixth factor listed above is satisfied. Two dangers emerge from over measurement. The first is that the cost of data collection far outweighs the benefits of having it, and that its collection also causes considerable irritation among those doing the measurement and those being measured, especially if the redundancy of the measurement is obvious. The second danger is that management based on overmeasurement leads to justified accusations of micromanagement and the tendency to instill unwanted behaviors. This latter point arises since people tend to want to improve performance and will tend to focus on many trivial elements in an overelaborate measurement system. In doing this, they loose sight of the bigger and more important picture.

Strategic Management

This category of assessment reaches to the heart of the problem. If a measurement and management scheme is to be of any real value, then it must afford management a means of translating its strategic intent into appropriate actions and feedback information showing whether these actions are working or not. A report by the Boston Consulting Group (1999) suggests that managers have only three effective levers in the creation of value: margin, asset productivity, and investment. However, Baum et al. (2000) give a more extensive list, headed by innovation, attraction of talented people, alliances, and customer satisfaction. The difference between these appraisals highlights the difference between a finance-dominated approach to management and measurement and one that includes nonfinancial measures. What appears to be clear is that managers can affect the performance of their businesses at two levels. The first of these is at the organizational level, where they affect how the processes of value creation in the company are interconnected. The second level is that they can encourage improvements in individuals or groups of processes at an operational level. Examples of the first level are strategic alliances and positioning, while examples of the second level are investments in soft assets and conditions.

It is obvious that if measurement is to support management effectively, then the measures have to be dominated by those who look forward (Van Buren 1999). This is not a new idea since a balanced approach to leading and lagging indicators was encouraged at the outset of the knowledge era by Norton and Kaplan (1996) and earlier in the Table de Bord developed in France in the 1950s. Here lies one of the principle weaknesses of accounting-based methodologies of intellectual capital management: Accounting is based on historical transactions and is thus dominated by

lagging measures. Accounting, while detailed, is also cost based rather than value based, even though some of the outcomes of past investments will have real-time and future consequences. The net present value (NPV) approach is the backbone of many financially based value assessments and can be related to the three levers in the Boston Consulting Group report. Using it to estimate company market value (MV) leads to the equation estimating market value:

$$MV = \Sigma(\text{ownership claims}) + \Sigma(\text{present operations}) + \Sigma(\text{known opportunities}) + \Sigma(\text{unknown opportunities}) + E$$
$$(47.2)$$

where E is a variable dependent on market sentiment, and other terms are expressed in terms of NPV of the free cash flow. In this equation, the cash flow from known opportunities has an element of risk, and that from unknown opportunities, which arises from current or planned R&D, has a considerable element of risk. Judging the acceptability of R&D projects using NPV as an arbiter usually results in a conservative outcome in which projects are not approved either because the NPV is too low or the projects that are approved are those that offer least risk and, consequently, usually least reward. The end result is to depress the value of the company and surrender intellectual leadership.

The flaws of NPV have been summarized by Lewis and Lippitt (1999) into problems of homogeneity, nonfinancial benefits, and problems of forecasting. The inability to address the attribution of value to elements that combine in the overall effect constitutes the homogeneity problem, while accounting for other nonfinancial spin-offs constitutes the benefits issue. Forecasting is merely a question of uncertainty in the factors needed for a calculation of value into the future. Although Lewis and Lippitt point to modifications to NPV to relieve its shortcomings, one solution might be to avoid the issue by considering alternative futures as options and hence to make this an opportunity to use real options theory. If this is done, the first two terms would remain largely the same, but the higher risk element would be calculated using the real option value of development and research (Partenen 1998). E would now include the residual value of the stock.

Real options theory is an imperfect adaptation of a financial instrument to a business application and allows the alignment of risk in projects with corporate strategy. The adaptation is explained neatly by Verity (1999) and shows that the value of an opportunity, for example, company R&D, is akin to a "call option," which gives the investor the right but not the obligation to buy something (shares) at a specified date and at a specified price. Some interpretation of the financial features is required to amass the data needed to perform the calculation in a business option context. The business parallel is that the decision to proceed with a risky R&D project is best taken later when some of the lower risk elements have been completed and a more informed view can be taken. An option is being taken on the later stages without an upfront commitment to the whole program. The most important impact is in the planning of projects to generate options and to find ways of realizing the value of the options.

In contrast, methodologies for managing intellectual capital based on a business approach should suffer from none of the intrinsic weaknesses of financially based management methods. There are, however, serious deficiencies that can considerably degrade the usefulness of the intellectual capital approach. The most common of these is the measurement of stocks of intangible assets in the belief that these constitute value. A typical example of a stock metric is the number or percentage of people with a higher degree in a company. Stocks represent the potential to create value, and unless the measurement of potential is the specific aim (Pulic 2000), management will be misguided in using such approaches to manage intellectual capital. Value is created when stocks are employed and degrades when they remain unused. If discerning the importance of the value creation pathways is the goal, the attributes that must be measured are the influences the elements of intellectual capital exert in the generation of value when they are deployed in the company. Alternatively, if some attempt is to be made at relative or even absolute value, then it will be necessary to quantify not just what is influential in the creation of value but also how large is the flow of these intellectual capital elements. The important distinction here is that what flows is not necessarily of value and what is influential in creating value might be a small flow of something very important; the estimation of value requires knowledge of the volume of flow as well as the influence that flow actually exerts. The concept of flow in intellectual capital value creation was described by Roos and Roos (1997).

Business-based models offer management many insights. Even the simpler stock models have some use in that, in the absence of other complicating factors, levels of stock and consequent performance can be benchmarked between companies. Influence models are particularly powerful since the counterpart of influence is control and control and facilitation are at the heart of management. By employing Hume's (1740) fork reasoning, what is desired in terms of a company's strategic intent ("what ought to be") can be compared with the way a company is actually operating ("what is"). The influence diagram that results from mapping the important connections between classes and subclasses of intellectual capital, usually known as a "navigator," becomes a powerful and visual tool for management to use to determine where real value is created in a company (sources) and where it is destroyed (sinks). It is not unusual to find that the value-creating pathways uncovered and prioritized by navigator analyses provide new insights for the company when seen in the context of what constitutes value in the eyes of the stakeholders (Roos and Jacobsen 1999, Roos and Lövingsson 1999). The natural counterpart of control informs management of the changes necessary and possible to improve performance. Since strategy is forward looking, then so too is the navigator approach.

There are very few influence and flow models at present. In a sense, the model of Sveiby (1997) is a step in that direction since it links subcategories of intellectual capital with a simple accounting system. However, the flows are implied, and so it could be thought of as a stock model. A reliable navigator-based approach to business management, which combines both flow and influence, remains the goal for many researchers. The holistic value added (HVA) methodology, a combination of a navigator and the axiology/measurement theory approach, is unique in the influence and flow field (see appendix 37.1).

Dotcom companies and hi-tech start-up companies require no special treatment as far as intellectual capital management methodologies are concerned. Management and measurement regimes and criteria described above remain valid. There is evidence (Bontis and Mill 2000) that Web-based measures can act as proxies for harder measures, but although the evidence appears sound, the causal links require further proofs. Dotcoms do, however, represent an extreme situation, and hence they are worthy of discussion to demonstrate that intellectual capital measurement and management models extend easily to cover them. At the same time as having few physical resources, the balance of components in relationship capital is altered, as dotcoms rely on the Internet to a far greater extent than other types of company. This means that the means they employ to develop and maintain relationship capital are different from other companies, but the need to address these issues is common to all. Real contact with customers may be rare, and so the dotcoms have to be adept at discerning the trends and signals from whatever information they glean. An example of how this is done is provided by the aftersales and analytical feedback developed and used by Amazon.com. Since the barriers to entry in dotcoms are low, the retention of key creative personnel is vital. Again, there is no fundamental difference between dotcoms and other companies; it is simply a question of balance. In launching a dotcom or adapting an existing business for operations in the electronic environment, a slightly different set of guides is required (Roos 2001), reflecting the modified management actions necessary:

1. Disaggregate and determine the existing value proposition made to customers into its key components and the transformations of intellectual capital stock, and identify the drivers of perceived value and delivered cost.
2. For each driver, identify the impact of using or incorporating e-commerce elements into the business. This will mean changing the influences in the navigator and perhaps deleting some old and creating some new transformations.
3. Create a new value proposition by reaggregating the e-business key components with the highest improvement in perceived value and delivered cost, and identify the key technology infrastructure that will yield maximum value creation and maximum differentiation in the selected market space.
4. Identify the targeted e-community and the gateway/access approach that will enable the fastest and most sustainable creation of critical mass, agility, and performance.
5. Create or modify the management model for e-business value creation, including the main classes of intellectual capital and their value exchange (cash, physical goods and services, digital goods and services, relations, brands, intellectual property, processes and systems, information, and competence embodied in the individuals).

In terms of practical management, as the intellectual capital elements are the same but with different emphasis, extra care is required in defining the measurements necessary to give managers the information needed to guide the performance and development of the company.

Shareholder Information

Leaving aside the deeper questions of disclosure for the next section, there are some comments that need to be made at this time. In order to communicate with stakeholders outside the company, the prerequisites are that you have information to communicate and that the information is in the form and language that the stakeholder understands. Any management and measurement methodology that has survived the tests so far must now be able to meet this last test.

For a long time the only information that seems to have been required by stakeholders to be reported in a standardized form in most companies has been company performance in financial terms. The exception to this has been those companies or agencies involved in delivering public services. For them, financial stability has been a key performance indicator, but along with that has been the quality, level, and extent of the service that has been provided. In the United Kingdom, however, government agencies largely started only at the end of the 1980s with the launch of the "next steps agencies." In the knowledge era, the concept of stakeholder or even shareholder value extending beyond simple financial performance measures is the crucial change. To communicate with stakeholders now requires a deeper understanding of the attributes of value from the point of view of the stakeholder groups. Internally in the company, this means that the management's strategy must be more sophisticated, and the levers that management pulls to improve its business must be that much more numerous and complex.

Understanding and being able to derive and communicate the attributes of value require that management and their models have a basing in axiology. Axiology is a branch of philosophy that developed in Germany and Austria in the nineteenth century (Rescher 1969) that, in contrast to logical positivism, states that within a well-defined context, meaningful discussion of value can take place. That is, value is not emotional but can be the subject of rational discussion. Axiology meets all four of the criteria necessary to be classified as a science:

1. It provides a standard of measure that can be used to make decisions.
2. It has universal application, regardless of time, place, or circumstance.
3. It is objective, independent of any one perspective.
4. It is quantitative and provides a mathematical means to measure objects or experiences against a standard.

The first and the last points above concern measurement, and to make practical use of axiology requires that the system of measurement meet similar criteria for rigor. Careful adherence to the canons of measurement theory provides that rigor. The fundamental idea of measurement theory, a branch of applied mathematics, is that measurements are not the same as the attribute being measured. Hence, if you want to draw conclusions about the attribute, you must take into account the nature of the correspondence between the attribute and the measurements. Measurement theory shows that strong assumptions are required for certain statistics to provide meaningful information about reality; it encourages responsible real-world data analysis (Krantz et al. 1971).

To make a practical tool requires the connection of axiology and measurement theory, and this has been achieved by M'Pherson (1996) with the Inclusive Value Methodology. This opens the way to the generation of management models that can describe and measure the attributes of value for differing stakeholder groups within an embracing context. Managers then have the potential of a methodology, measurement, and management scheme in which the impact of strategic decisions on all stakeholder groups can be assessed in advance of their implementation. This does not mean that the problems are all solved and the future is laid bare. Uncertainty in data and risk introduced by the actions of outsiders such as regulators, suppliers, partners, and governments, not to mention the actions of competitors, all conspire to make the results less than certain. The art of strategic management remains.

These, then, are the tests and requirements of a truly comprehensive intellectual capital management and measurement scheme. Although some approaches come close to providing a holistic approach by meeting most of the tests, a truly holistic model will require compliance with all tests. In practical terms this means effecting a union between navigators, which describe the practical workings of businesses, and axiology and measurement theory, which will take measures from the navigator and apply them in a rigorous model of value and financial instruments to link the nondimensional measures of value to money. Only HVA approaches this level (see appendix 37.1). However, the evolutionary process in management has a short time constant, soon models may be available that will support effectively new and modern ways of measuring all aspects of company operation. These will not only meet the tests above, but will also accommodate subsidiary aspects such as the evolving human capital practices described by Davis and Meyer (2000).

Disclosure

The preceding section deals with the provision of data and estimates of value from management systems. It is now time to consider the mechanisms of information transfer to outside stakeholders and the extent to which this can take place without compromising the security of the company. Skandia and Celemi, both Swedish companies, started independent publication of intellectual capital data in the mid 1990s, the former using Edvinsson's (1997) methodology and language, and the latter using Sveiby's (1997) methodology and language. Both have done well. Indeed, there is a growing body of evidence (Narayanan et al. 2000) that careful disclosure of information, even strategically sensitive information concerning research and development intentions, is beneficial in terms of market value. The pioneers have shown that this can be done, although the extent of disclosure has been inadequate for the purposes of the investment analyst. This is a key point. The disclosure of "intellectual capital" in the way pioneered by Skandia and Celemi may not be that helpful since they describe changes in stock or potential at a high level. The important issue is disclosure about the present and future performance of the value-creating mechanisms of the company.

The goal of disclosure is suggested by the following:

Disclosure should provide relevant, reliable, and timely information to those who need to know it so that they can make decisions concerning their relations with the company. At the same time, the information released by the company must not lead to the compromise of sensitive strategic information that would give unfair advantage to others.

Given this goal as the target, the purpose of this section is to examine current thinking on the issue of disclosure and determine the nature of the barriers to be crossed if company information disclosure on value creation is to be meaningful and commonplace.

Background

A major survey of the issues involved in the disclosure of company information on intellectual capital to the investment community was carried out by Rylander et al. (2000). The principal issues at the time were the following:

1. The information asymmetry gap is growing as the proportion of company value attributable to intangible assets increases.
2. Long-term information, particularly on strategic intent and execution, was lacking from company reporting but was considered to be of particular importance to external stakeholders, especially the investors.
3. Standards and comparability relating to the disclosure of intellectual capital would remain a major issue.
4. Value creation models could provide information to complement traditional reporting required by law.

Since the publication of that report, there have been a number of developments along the lines foreshadowed in their work. However, there have been neither solutions nor concrete proposals and hence the problem remains the same.

The U.K. government commenced a review of U.K. company law in 1998 with the aim of guiding a significant revision to the laws (Dickson 2000). The review proposes an evolutionary approach to changes in law centering on three areas: changes to the reporting calendar, the extent of information disclosure, and the role of auditors. Of them, the second is most interesting. Here, two issues where mandatory disclosure

might be considered are, first, a review of the company's last year activities focusing on market changes and positioning and, second, a statement of the company's purpose, strategy, and most interesting of all, its principle drivers of performance.

Lymer et al. (1999) have submitted a research project to the International Accounting Standards Committee suggesting the introduction of a more streamlined reporting model with minimal data interpretation between collection and the decision makers. It also points the way to a business reporting language, which has many similarities with the XML-based XFRML (extensible financial reporting markup language) introduced recently by the American Institute of Certified Public Accountants (2000).

The Financial Accounting Standards Board (FASB) has also published a report on business reporting with particular emphasis on electronic reporting (FASB 2000). This is part of a larger initiative that will be discussed further below. The key findings fall into the areas of democratization of reporting, reporting models, completeness, timeliness, content variability, and potential risk. In brief summary, the FASB found the following:

Democratization: The privileges of being "in the know" will disappear due to the ability of the Internet to disseminate information. The value is now provided by the addition of insight to this information.

Reporting models: Although companies will continue to be the prime source of information about themselves, outsiders may be able to supply supporting information, which will necessarily be of lower quality. The company will therefore have to decide whether to provide more itself.

Completeness: Old-fashioned annual reports have a specified degree of completeness and guides to interpretation. Third-party information may not have that degree of completeness and is therefore suspect.

Timeliness: If legal problems can be overcome, it is possible that information delivery can be driven from its set cycles to real time.

Content variability: There are minimum standards in reporting. While some companies provide limited information, others offer more. No opinion is offered concerning the best mix; however, Internet reporting does allow for the rapid evaluation of differences among companies.

Risks: For companies, the risks of litigation arising from Web-based disclosures are real. If disclaimers have to accompany every forward-looking statement, do the statements lose their value?

Communication Models

It is common to think that disclosure means information transmission exclusively to people or bodies external to the company. This is merely the most public mode of disclosure since many see information disclosure as a continuum problem beginning with those who collect the raw data inside the company and ending with worldwide disclosure on the Web site. In practical terms, there are a variety of discrete levels through the company and then the outside world. The outside world has two groups. The first of these is the privileged relationship that an accredited analyst has with the company, and the second and final level of disclosure is the Web site.

Such a model has two disadvantages. The first is that as the levels are ascended within the company, there is an inevitable blurring as data are interpreted and reinterpreted. The second and related disadvantage is that use of information in this way is inconsistent with the management of companies in the knowledge era (Sveiby 1997) since information is being used as a source of power in a hierarchy rather than as a company resource.

From the evidence that is amassing, it seems that the pressure on companies to report more and by electronic means is increasing. It is also clear that various levels of disclosure are possible and that companies must be clear about the distinctions if they are to proceed safely.

The Form of the Information Communicated

As stated above, the gap between what is reported and what is required is widening, although analysts constantly strive to close the gap with increasingly penetrating investigations. However, if the value creation path in a given company is invisible (and it may also be unknown in detail to the company's own management), then it is unlikely that the analysts will

get what they need. Furthermore, since no two companies are the same, even competitors with more than a superficial resemblance, intercompany comparisons by the analyst will be very difficult, and market segment-wide analysis will be impossible.

There is also concern that the information that is required is often the most difficult to provide and subject to the greatest risk. In markets dominated by institutional investors, the most valuable information concerns the long-term prospects of the market segments and the individual companies within them.

The next problem concerns the lack of time available to undertake the analysis. Anecdotal evidence suggests that the real time available to an analyst to assess the prospects and hence fair market value of a company is surprisingly short. If this evidence is true, then it means that data received by the analyst is usable only if it can be rapidly employed in some "model" preferably without any further manipulation. The satisfaction of this need is only possible if there is a common model that can be initiated quickly and that will provide guidance quickly. In the United Kingdom, the Investor Relations Society (IRS) already gives annual awards to the best annual report on the Internet (IRS 2000). BP Amoco won the December 1999 FTSE 100 award and Storehouse won the FTSE 250 award. The award panel consists of investors, academics, regulators, and Web site designers. The judging panel noted the considerable improvement in breadth and depth of disclosure over the last three years and also a considerable increase in the number of company Web sites to be evaluated. This process may lead the way to standardized elements of information delivery.

The Nature of the Information to Be Communicated

A number of concerned organizations are now seeking to determine what the nature of the information for disclosure should be. The most significant of these is the FASB. The report summarized above is one part of a larger seven-part report on disclosure commissioned in 1998 and delivered in 2001 (FASB 2001). The report on nonfinancial disclosure addresses all issues around disclosure and especially the content to be disclosed. The seven sections review operating data, performance measures, and management's analysis of changes in measures and forward-looking projections. However, they do not address projections. Various groups are also examining background information disclosure, particularly strategy statements and consequent objectives and the effect of this and industry structure on both management and the investing community.

In the United Kingdom, the Centre for Exploitation of Science and Technology (CEST) is taking a pragmatic approach to the problem of information asymmetry in their collaborative project: valuing the new intangibles (CEST 2000). Launched in the autumn of 1999 and reported in the autumn of 2000, it sets itself the goal of understanding the field of disclosure and the needs of the external and company communities. To do this it has adopted the approach of running two complementary and alternating forums, one comprising company representatives and the other the "city" investors. Through the alternating meetings, issues raised by one group can be considered by the other in a nonconfrontational and totally anonymous manner. As with the other initiatives, the key areas where more and reliable information is required are the long-term prospects and intentions of the company.

Other than a statement of the findings, the likely outcome of the CEST work will be a set of recommendations for further work based on the considerably improved understanding gained through the life of the project. This should be in line with the likely outcome of the FASB work. Although FASB recommendations will emerge on the disclosure issues highlighted above, there is unlikely to be any attempt to make them mandatory. A code of voluntary disclosure will emerge that may evolve into a set of best practices by those in the field. The hope would be that other companies would feel the need to follow the best practice.

The Canadian Institute of Chartered Accountants (CICA) published a report (Waterhouse 1999) in which they show an analysis of what was actually published at the time based on 114 responses from a field of 812. Although some of the categories of analysis may not align well with the conventional language of intellectual capital, the results are clear. The report shows that for both the CEOs and company boards, intellectual capital issues were all considered to be of above average importance in terms of reporting. Operating efficiencies head the list, but intellectual capital and corporate learning are a close second, and innovativeness and the ability

to respond to the market were third. By contrast, whereas financial reporting took place to the expected very high level, "measures of value" added were not. More usual measures of intellectual capital were not reported at all. There was no lack of data supplied to boards. Nine nonfinancial measures were surveyed, and the level of reporting from data collectors to their boards ranged from 52.7% in the case of partner and stakeholder relations to 80.4% for operating efficiencies. The intellectual capital and corporate learning metric score was 72.8%. The final report concerns the subjective level of fit between the categories chosen for analysis and the strategic needs of the respondent's companies. Here levels ranged from 55.8% for partner and stakeholder relations to 84.0% for environment, health, and safety.

There is also a major project on intangible assets measurement, monitoring, and reporting being undertaken jointly by the Brookings Institution and the Stern School of Business (Brookings 2000). The project, which will produce a report this summer, is taking a twin-track approach, with each track being addressed by a number of groups. The first track deals with trends in company investment practices in intangibles, including the effects of regulatory, tax, and reporting requirements that influence a company's investment choices. The second is a survey of the laws and regulations that impose barriers or biases.

Summary of Disclosure

The subjective impression from the evidence presented above is that, in principle, there is little to prevent real progress being made in improving the information asymmetry between companies and stakeholders. The evidence suggests that there are many benefits to be gained by a more extensive disclosure of information. There would be beneficial effects in terms of the effects on external reputation, market valuation, and the ability to raise capital, and internally in the esteem that internal stakeholders (staff) will have in the company and its management. That is not to say that there are no pitfalls; the FASB report described above highlights where some of them may lie.

Assuming that work by the FASB, CEST, and the others leads to an equitable and significant closing of the information asymmetry gap, the sticking points that remain are as follows:

1. How to provide reliable data that can be used quickly and compared across companies
2. How to address the issue of "information power" inside companies
3. How to collect and deliver the information that has been subjected to the minimum of internal interpretation but at the same time is not painfully revealing of strategic intent

None of these three issues presents an insurmountable obstacle. The challenge is therefore to find a methodology that does both of these. In addition, it must also constitute a management and measurement methodology that complies with all four criteria expressed in the section addressing management.

The Way Forward

While there is considerable work in progress concerning the separate issues of management and disclosure, there is little that brings them together. The Organisation for Economic Cooperation and Development (OECD) however, has begun investigating the area as a whole and has reinforced the expression of need to make progress in the area (OECD 1999). In Denmark, government-sponsored research determined that companies could make external statements about their intellectual capital. Unfortunately, the model that underlay their research inevitably led to the conclusion that such statements could only be general in nature, as the diversity of companies would prevent meaningful comparison (Larsen et al. 2000).

The need, therefore, remains to progress from the current position of management and measurement models to what is commonly called third-generation intellectual capital. The debate on disclosure has started to settle on the key issues and at the same time has noted the benefits of careful disclosure. The question is, Do we now have the means to bring the management, measurement, and disclosure together?

One intriguing way forward, seen in the development of the HVA (see appendix 37.1), is to generate a two-part model, with analysts using one part and company management using both.

Analysts need a model that describes the value context of the investors. This is still dominated by financial considerations, but intellectual capital, specific ethical positions, and the capabilities of management teams make significant contributions. A model that combines the attributes of value from the standpoint of the investor and analyst will have a limited range of applicability, but will allow it to be used across a market segment while not being specific to any individual company in that segment. All the analysts require, then, is input.

The company needs a measurement scheme and model that embody the management principles they wish to follow. The model must be compliant with the four criteria stated above; the most difficult to meet are the last two, which require the strategic input and the consequent generation of useful information. However, these requirements align exactly with the needs of the external community. The model and methodology must therefore expose and measure the real routes to value creation in the company and include the areas of uncertainty and risk. As there have to be strategic levers, the model must be forward looking and may include elements of real option theory in estimating values.

As the company would have both the internal model and the external model, management would have the opportunity to see in advance the possible effects of their strategic options on the stakeholder groups as well as the long-term effects on the makeup of their companies. There would inevitably be a tendency to investigate the most favorable solutions, but such is the real diversity of stakeholder groups that solutions that please everybody are usually impossible.

There are numerous additions possible to enhance capability, especially in the areas of risk and uncertainty, and also in leading-edge human capital management. But the substantial elements all now exist in the field of intellectual capital and its underlying and related sciences. It is now time to build on the work of FASB, CEST, and others and see whether the vision of people like Drucker (1994) can be made a practical reality.

APPENDIX 37.1 HOLISTIC VALUE ADDED

The main body of this chapter introduces the techniques needed to manage the modern company effectively from a measurement and modeling perspective. In most cases, old-fashioned financial modeling is found wanting, and the most promising new techniques described are described here.

Holistic value added (HVA) is a technique that combines a navigator model of the business with measurement theory and axiology to generate a nondimensional view of company value as seen from the perspective of any stakeholder. The output of this analysis is combined with a navigator-driven financial model to provide an indicative measure of dollar value for the company.

Using axiological considerations, we can postulate that a group of stakeholders can develop a comprehensive hierarchy of value that may have as its supremal an indicative relative valuation of the company in nondimensional space. The stakeholders would comprise manager, employees, shareholder, regulators, and so forth. They would also be able to agree on the nature of a small set of cardinal attributes of value even though their perceptions of their relative importance may differ. From there, the hierarchy of value can be developed until it becomes a minimum set of attributes that can be measured. This set of attributes must be compliant with the canonical requirements of measurement theory. Schematically, this takes the form shown in figure 37.A1.

The flow and influence navigator is used as a business model. Navigators showing the interconnections among intellectual capital stocks are essentially influence diagrams. The flow diagram for the company necessarily has the same structure as the influence diagram, but volume is now being measured. Conversion between one type of navigator and the other is not straightforward. In the absence of simplifying measures, tech-

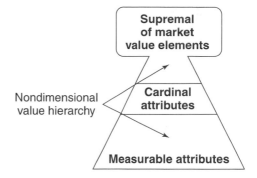

Figure 37.A1

niques such as systems dynamics have to be employed to determine flow. Both influence and flow are required outputs from the navigator, first to produce a value input to the value hierarchy and second to provide an input to financial and risk models. With a strategy input being used to modify the performance of the company, the navigator section of the HVA appears as shown in figure 37.A2.

Finally, the risk/finance model takes input from the navigator and the strategic input of management to derive a strictly financial view of company value using techniques such as NPV and real options theory. If nondimensional monetary (distinct from financial) elements appear in the value hierarchy, then since the nondimensional monetary value elements and the financial element have a common origin in the navigator, they may safely be correlated. This can then generate a dollar value for the company that will include the financial figures in the normal way but will additionally include the nonfinancial elements, weighted according to the values of the stakeholders. The complete model is as shown in figure 37.A3.

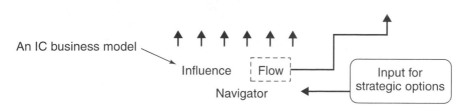

Figure 37.A2

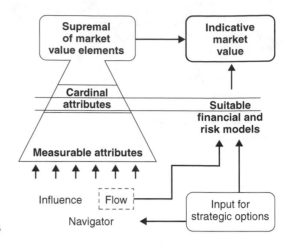

Figure 37.A3

References

American Institute of Certified Public Accountants. (2000) Web site: http://www.xfrml.org/.

Baum, G., Ittner, C., Larcker, D., Low, J., Siedfield, T., and Malone, M. (2000) "Introducing the new value creation index." *Forbes ASAP,* pp. 140–143.

Bontis, N. and Mill, J. (2000) "Web-based metrics and internet stock prices." MINT Working Paper, no. 93.

Boston Consulting Group. (1999) "The value creators: a study of the world's top performers." Available at: http://www.bcg.com/.

Brooking, A. (1996) *Intellectual Capital.* New York: International Thomson Business Press.

Brookings Institution. (2000) "Understanding intangible sources of value." Available at: http://www.brook.edu/es/intangibles/default.htm.

Centre for Exploitation of Science and Technology (CEST). (2000) Web site: http://www.cest.org.uk/.

Davis, S. and Meyer, C. (2000) *Future Wealth.* Cambridge, MA: Harvard Business School Press.

Dickson, M. (2000) "Survey—Shareholder communication: overhaul of creeky office: the Law Review." *Financial Times* June 30.

Drucker, P.F. (1994) *Post-capitalist society.* New York: HarperBusiness.

Edvinsson, L. and Malone, M.S. (1997) *Intellectual capital: The proven way to establish your company's real value by measuring its hidden brainpower.* London: Piatkus.

EU/ESPRIT 4. (2000) "KnowNet: knowledge management with intranet technologies." Project EP28928. Available at: http://www.know-net.org/.

FASB Special Report (2001) Business and Financial Reporting: Challenges from the New Economy. Available at http://accounting.rutgers.edu/raw/fasb/sr_new_economy.pdf/.

Hume, D. (1740) *Treatise on human nature,* bk. III(I)1. Reprinted in L. Selby-Bigge (ed.), *An Enquiry concerning Human Understanding.* New York: Oxford University Press, 1902.

Intellectual Capital Services Ltd. (2000) "HVA—holistic value added." Available at: http://www.intcap.com/.

Investor Relation Society. (2000) Web site: http://www.ir-soc.org.uk/.

IQPort. (2000) Web site: http://www.iqport.com/.

Justice, A. (1707) *A General Treatise on Monies and Exchanges.* London: S&J Sprint and J Nicholson.

Knexa. (2000) Web site: http://www.knexa.com/.

Krantz, D., Luce, R., Suppes, P., and Tversky, A. (1971) *Foundations of Measurement.* New York: Academic Press.

Larsen, H., Nikolaj, P., Bukh, D., and Mouritsen, J. (2000) "Intellectual capital statements—towards a guideline." Danish Agency for Trade and Industry. Available at: http://www.efs.dk/.

Lewis, E. and Lippitt, J. (1999) "Valuing intellectual assets." *Journal of Legal Economics* 9(1):31–48.

Lightman, A. (2000) "The myths that support massive Internet market caps." Available at: http://www.intellectualcapital.com/.

Lymer, A., Debreceny, R., Gray, G., and Rahman, A. (1999) "Business reporting on the Internet." Submitted to the International Accounting Standards Committee.

M'Pherson, P.K. (1996) "Business value modelling." Paper presented at 48th Conference and Congress of the International Federation for Information and Documentation, Graz, Austria.

Narayanan, V., Pinches, G., Kelm, K., and Lander, D. (2000) "The influence of voluntary disclosed qualitative information." *Strategic Management Journal* 21(7):707–722.

Norton, D. and Kaplan, R. (1996) *The Balanced Scorecard: Translating Strategy into Action*, Cambridge, MA: Harvard Business School.

(OECD). (1999) "Measuring and reporting intellectual capital: experiences. Available at: http://www.oecd.org/.

Partanen, T. (1998) "Intellectual capital accounting." Master's thesis, Helsinki School of Economics and Business Administration.

Pulic, A. (2000) "VAIC™—an accounting tool for IC management." Available at: http://www.measuring-ip.at/Papers/ham99txt.htm.

Rescher, N. (1969) *An Introduction to Value Theory*. New York: Prentice-Hall.

Roos, G. (2001) "Alliance for converging technologies." In preparation.

Roos, G. and Jacobsen, K. (1999) "Management in a complex stakeholder organisation." *Monash Mt. Eliza Business Review*, July, pp. 82–93.

Roos, G. and Lövingsson, F. (1999) "El processo CI en EL, nuevo mundo de las telecomubicaciones: experiencia de Ericsson Business Consulting Norrköping," in A.M. Güell (ed.), *Homo faber, Homo sapiens: La Gestión del Capital Intelectual*, Estade: pp. 141–169. Ediciones del Bronce.

Roos, G. and Roos, J. (1997) "Measuring your company's intellectual performance." *Journal of Long Range Planning* 30(3):413–426.

Roos, J., Roos, G., Dragonetti, N., and Edvinsson, L. (1997) *Intellectual Capital: Navigating the New Business Landscape*. New York: Macmillan.

Rylander, A., Jacobsen, K., and Roos, G. (2000) "Towards improved information disclosure on intellectual capital." *International Journal of Technology Management* 20(5–8).

Skyrme, D., Ed. (1998) "Business intelligence report: measuring the value of knowledge." Available at: http://www.business-intelligence.co.uk/.

Steering Group Report. (2000) "Business reporting research project: electronic distribution of business reporting information." Available at http://accounting.rutgers.edu/raw/fsab/brrp/brrp1.pdf/.

Sveiby, K.E. (1997) *The New Organisational Wealth: Managing and Measuring Knowledge Based Assets*. San Francisco: Berrett-Koehler.

U.K. Department of Trade and Industry (Future Unit). (1998a) "Converging technologies: consequences for the knowledge-driven economy." Available at: http://www.dti.gov.uk/future-unit/complete/index.html.

U.K. Department of Trade and Industry. (1998b) "Our competitive future: building the knowledge-driven economy." Available at: http://www.dti.gov.uk/comp/.

U.K. Department of Trade and Industry, Foresight Financial Services Panel. (2000) *Financing the Enterprise Society*. London: Her Majesty's Stationery Office.

Van Buren, M. (1999) "A yardstick for knowledge management." *American Society for Training and Development* 53(5):71–78.

Verity, D. (1999) "Real options—an analytical approach to aligning risk management and corporate strategy." *Corporate Finance Review* (Boston) 3(7). Now available at http://www.categoricalsolutions.com.av/Literature/RealOptions/RealOptions.pdf.

Von Krogh, G., Roos, J., and Kleine, D. (1998) *Knowing in Firms*. New York: Sage.

Waterhouse, J. (1999) *Measuring Up. CAMagazine*, March, pp. 41–43.

38

Social Capital, Intellectual Capital, and the Organizational Advantage

Janine Nahapiet and Sumantra Ghoshal

Kogut and Zander (1996) have proposed "that a firm be understood as a social community specializing in the speed and efficiency in the creation and transfer of knowledge" (p. 503). This is an important and relatively new perspective on the theory of the firm currently being formalized through the ongoing work of these authors (Kogut and Zander 1992, 1993, 1995, 1996, Zander and Kogut 1995) and several others (Boisot 1995, Conner and Prahalad 1996, Loasby 1991, Nonaka and Takeuchi 1995, Spender 1996). Standing in stark contrast to the more established transaction cost theory that is grounded in the assumption of human opportunism and the resulting conditions of market failure (e.g., Williamson 1975), those with this new perspective essentially argue that organizations have some particular capabilities for creating and sharing knowledge that give them their distinctive advantage over other institutional arrangements, such as markets. For strategy theory, the implications of this emerging perspective lie in a shift of focus from the historically dominant theme of value appropriation to one of value creation (Moran and Ghoshal 1996).

The particular capabilities of organizations for creating and sharing knowledge derive from a range of factors, including the special facility organizations have for the creation and transfer of tacit knowledge (Kogut and Zander 1993, 1996, Nonaka and Takeuchi 1995, Spender 1996); the organizing principles by which individual and functional expertise are structured, coordinated, and communicated, and through which individuals cooperate (Conner and Prahalad 1996, Kogut and Zander 1992, Zander and Kogut 1995); and the nature of organizations as social communities (Kogut and Zander 1992, 1996). However, notwithstanding the substantial insights we now have into the attributes of organizations as knowledge systems, we still lack a coherent theory for explaining them. In this chapter we seek to address this gap and to present a theory of how firms can enjoy what Ghoshal and Moran (1996) have called "the organizational advantage."

Our theory is rooted in the concept of social capital. Analysts of social capital are centrally concerned with the significance of relationships as a resource for social action (Baker 1990, Bourdieu 1986, Burt 1992, Coleman 1988, 1990, Jacobs 1965, Loury 1987). However, as Putnam (1995) recently has observed, social capital is not a unidimensional concept, and, while sharing a common interest in how relational resources aid the conduct of social affairs, the different authors on this topic have tended to focus on different facets of social capital. In this chapter we (1) integrate these different facets to define social capital in terms of three distinct dimensions, (2) describe how each of these dimensions facilitates the creation and exchange of knowledge, and (3) argue that organizations, as institutional settings, are able to develop high levels of social capital in terms of all three dimensions. Our primary focus, however, is on the interrelationships between social and intellectual capital since, as we have already noted, there is already a clear stream of work that identifies and elaborates the significance of knowledge processes as the foundation of such organizational advantage. Our aim here is to provide a theoretical explanation of why this is the case.

Social Capital

The term "social capital" initially appeared in community studies, highlighting the central importance—for the survival and functioning of city neighborhoods—of the networks of strong, crosscutting personal relationships developed over time that provide the basis for trust, cooperation, and collective action in such communities (Jacobs 1965). Early usage also indicated the significance of social capital for the individual: the set of resources inherent in family relations and in community social organizations useful for the development of the young child (Loury 1977). The concept has been applied since its early use to elucidate a wide range of social phenomena, although researchers increasingly have focused attention on the role of social capital as an influence not only on the development of human capital (Coleman 1988, Loury 1977, 1987) but also on the economic performance of firms (Baker 1990), geographic regions (Putnam 1993, 1995), and nations (Fukuyama 1995).

The central proposition of social capital theory is that networks of relationships constitute a valuable resource for the conduct of social affairs, providing their members with "the collectivity-owned capital, a 'credential' which entitles them to credit, in the various senses of the word" (Bourdieu 1986, p. 249). Much of this capital is embedded within networks of mutual acquaintance and recognition. Bourdieu (1986), for example, identifies the durable obligations arising from feelings of gratitude, respect, and friendship or from the institutionally guaranteed rights derived from membership in a family, a class, or a school. Other resources are available through the contacts or connections networks bring. For example, through "weak ties" (Granovetter 1973) and "friends of friends" (Boissevain 1974), network members can gain privileged access to information and to opportunities. Finally, significant social capital in the form of social status or reputation can be derived from membership in specific networks, particularly those in which such membership is relatively restricted (Bourdieu 1986, Burt 1992, D'Aveni and Kesner 1993).

Although these authors agree on the significance of relationships as a resource for social action, they lack consensus on a precise definition of social capital. Some, such as Baker (1990), limit the scope of the term to only the structure of the relationship networks, whereas others, such as Bourdieu (1986, 1993) and Putnam (1995), also include in their conceptualization of social capital the actual or potential resources that can be accessed through such networks. For our purposes here, we adopt the latter view and define social capital as the sum of the actual and potential resources embedded within, available through, and derived from the network of relationships possessed by an individual or social unit. Social capital thus comprises both the network and the assets that may be mobilized through that network (Bourdieu 1986, Burt 1992).

As a set of resources rooted in relationships, social capital has many different attributes, and Putnam (1995) has argued that a high research priority is to clarify the dimensions of social capital. In the context of our exploration of the role of social capital in the creation of intellectual capital, we suggest that it is useful to consider these facets in terms of three clusters: the structural, the relational, and the cognitive dimensions of social capital. Although we separate these three dimensions analytically, we recognize that many of the features we describe are, in fact, highly interrelated. Moreover, in our analysis we set out to indicate important facets of social capital rather than review such facets exhaustively.

In making the distinction between the structural and the relational dimensions of social capital, we draw on Granovetter's (1992) discussion of structural and relational embeddedness. Structural embeddedness concerns the properties of the social system and of the network of relations as a whole.[1] The term describes the impersonal configuration of linkages between people or units. In this chapter we use the concept of the structural dimension of social capital to refer to the overall pattern of connections among actors—that is, who you reach and how you reach them (Burt 1992). Among the most important facets of this dimension are the presence or absence of network ties among actors (Scott 1991, Wasserman and Faust 1994); network configuration (Krackhardt 1989) or morphology (Tichy et al. 1979) describing the pattern of linkages in terms of such measures as density, connectivity, and hierarchy; and appropriable organization—that is, the existence of networks created for one purpose that may be used for another (Coleman 1988).

In contrast, the term "relational embeddedness" describes the kind of personal relationships people have developed with each other through a history of interactions (Granovetter 1992). This concept focuses on the particular relations people have, such as respect and friendship, that influence their behavior. It is through these ongoing personal relationships that people fulfill such social motives as sociability, approval, and prestige. For example, two actors may occupy equivalent positions in similar network configurations, but if their personal and emotional attachments to other network members differ, their actions also are likely to differ in important respects. For instance, although one actor may choose to stay in a firm because of an attachment to fellow workers, despite economic advantages available elsewhere, another without such personal bonds may discount working relationships in making career moves. In this chapter we use the concept of the relational dimension of social capital to refer to those assets created and leveraged through relationships, and parallel to what Lindenberg (1996) describes as behavioral, as opposed to structural, embeddedness and what Hakansson and Snehota (1995) refer to as "actor bonds." Among the key facets in this cluster are trust and trustworthiness (Fukuyama 1995, Putnam 1993), norms and sanctions (Coleman 1990, Putnam 1995), obligations and expectations (Burt 1992, Coleman 1990, Granovetter 1985, Mauss 1954), and identity and identification (Hakansson and Snehota 1995, Merton 1968).

The third dimension of social capital, which we label the "cognitive dimension," refers to those resources providing shared representations, interpretations, and systems of meaning among parties (Cicourel 1973). We have identified this cluster separately because we believe it represents an important set of assets not yet discussed in the mainstream literature on social capital but the significance of which is receiving substantial attention in the strategy domain (Conner and Prahalad 1996, Grant 1996, Kogut and Zander 1992, 1996). These resources also represent facets of particular importance in the context of our consideration of intellectual capital, including shared language and codes (Arrow 1974, Cicourel 1973, Monteverde 1995) and shared narratives (Orr 1990).

Although social capital takes many forms, each of these forms has two characteristics in common: (1) they constitute some aspect of the social structure, and (2) they facilitate the actions of individuals within the structure (Coleman 1990). First, as a social-structural resource, social capital inheres in the relations between persons and among persons. Unlike other forms of capital, social capital is owned jointly by the parties in a relationship, and no one player has, or is capable of having, exclusive ownership rights (Burt 1992). Moreover, although it has value in use, social capital cannot be traded easily. Friendships and obligations do not readily pass from one person to another. Second, social capital makes possible the achievement of ends that would be impossible without it or that could be achieved only at extra cost.

In examining the consequences of social capital for action, we can identify two distinct themes. First, social capital increases the efficiency of action. For example, networks of social relations, particularly those characterized by weak ties or structural holes (i.e., disconnections or nonequivalencies among players in an arena), increase the efficiency of information diffusion through minimizing redundancy (Burt 1992). Some have also suggested that social capital in the form of high levels of trust diminishes the probability of opportunism and reduces the need for costly monitoring processes. It thus reduces the costs of transactions (Putnam 1993).

Whereas the first theme could be regarded as illustrative of what North (1990) calls "allocative efficiency," the second theme centers on the role of social capital as an aid to adaptive efficiency and to the creativity and learning it implies. In particular, researchers have found social capital to encourage cooperative behavior, thereby facilitating the development of new forms of association and innovative organization (Fukuyama 1995, Jacobs 1965, Putnam 1993). The concept, therefore, is central to the understanding of institutional dynamics, innovation, and value creation.

We should note, however, that social capital is not a universally beneficial resource. As Coleman (1990) observes, "[A] given form of social capital that is useful for facilitating certain actions may be useless or harmful for others" (p. 302). For example, the strong norms and mutual identification that may exert a powerful positive influence on group performance can, at the same time, limit its openness to information and to alternative ways of doing things, producing forms of collective blindness that sometimes have disastrous consequences (Janis 1982, Perrow 1984, Turner 1976).

The main thesis of the work we have reviewed thus far is that social capital inheres in the relations between and among persons and is a productive asset facilitating some forms of social action while inhibiting others. Social relationships within the family and wider community have been shown to be an important factor in the development of human capital (Coleman 1988). In a parallel argument we suggest that social relationships—and the social capital therein—are an important influence on the development of intellectual capital. In elaborating this argument, we focus on the firm as the primary context in which to explore the interrelationships between social and intellectual capital. Later in the chapter we consider how our analysis may be extended to a wider range of institutional settings.

Intellectual Capital

Traditionally, economists have examined physical and human capital as key resources for the firm that facilitate productive and economic activity. However, knowledge, too, has been recognized as a valuable resource by economists. Marshall (1965), for example, suggests that "capital consists in a great part of knowledge and organization.... [K]nowledge is our most powerful engine of production" (p. 115). He goes on to note that "organization aids knowledge," a perspective also central to the work of Arrow (1974). More recently, Quinn (1992) has expressed a similar view, suggesting that "with rare exceptions, the economic and producing power of the firm lies more in its intellectual and service capabilities than in its hard assets—land, plant and equipment. ... [V]irtually all public and private enterprises—including most successful corporations—are becoming dominantly repositories and coordinators of intellect" (p. 241).

In this chapter we use the term "intellectual capital" to refer to the knowledge and knowing capability of a social collectivity, such as an organization, intellectual community, or profes-

sional practice. We have elected to adopt this terminology because of its clear parallel with the concept of human capital, which embraces the acquired knowledge, skills, and capabilities that enable persons to act in new ways (Coleman 1988). Intellectual capital thus represents a valuable resource and a capability for action based on knowledge and knowing.

This orientation to intellectual capital builds on some central themes and distinctions found in the substantial and expanding literature on knowledge and knowledge processes. Many of these themes have a long history in philosophy and Western thought, dating back to Plato, Aristotle, and Descartes. Two issues are of particular relevance to our consideration of the special advantage of organizations as an institutional context for the development of intellectual capital. These are, first, debates about the different types of knowledge that may exist and, second, the issue of the level of analysis in knowledge processes, particularly the question of whether social or collective knowledge exists and in what form.

Dimensions of Intellectual Capital

Types of Knowledge

Arguably, the most persistent theme in writing about the nature of knowledge centers on the proposition that there are different types of knowledge. For example, a key distinction scholars frequently make is between practical, experience-based knowledge and the theoretical knowledge derived from reflection and abstraction from that experience—a distinction reminiscent of the debate of early philosophers between rationalism and empiricism (Giddens and Turner 1987, James 1950). Variously labeled "know-how" or "procedural knowledge," the former frequently is distinguished from know-that, know-what, or declarative knowledge (Anderson 1981, Ryle 1949). It concerns well-practiced skills and routines, whereas the latter concerns the development of facts and propositions.[2]

Perhaps the most-cited and influential distinction of this sort is Polanyi's identification of two aspects of knowledge: tacit and explicit. This is a distinction he aligns with the "knowing how" and "knowing what" of Gilbert Ryle (Polanyi 1967). Polanyi distinguishes tacit knowledge in terms of its incommunicability, and Winter (1987) has suggested that it may be useful to consider tacitness as a variable, with the degree of tacitness a function of the extent to which the knowledge is or can be codified and abstracted (see also Boisot 1995). However, close reading of Polanyi indicates that he holds the view that some knowledge will always remain tacit. In so doing, he stresses the importance of *knowing*, as well as knowledge and, in particular, the active shaping of experience performed in the pursuit of knowledge.[3] Discussing the practice of science, he observes that "science is operated by the skill of the scientist and it is through the exercise of this skill that he shapes his scientific knowledge" (Polanyi 1962, p. 49). This suggests a view both of knowledge as object and of knowing as action or enactment in which progress is made through active engagement with the world on the basis of a systematic approach to knowing.

Levels of Analysis in Knowledge and Knowing

Another equally fundamental cause for debate within philosophical and sociological circles centers on the existence, or otherwise, of particular phenomena at the collective level. That is, what is the nature of social phenomena that is different from the aggregation of individual phenomena (Durkheim 1951, Gowler and Legge 1982)? In the context of this chapter, the question concerns the degree to which it is possible to consider a concept of organizational, collective, or social knowledge that is different from that of individual organizational members.

Simon (1991a) represents one extreme of the argument, stating that "all organizational learning takes place inside human heads; an organization learns in only two ways: (a) by the learning of its members or (b) by ingesting new members who have knowledge the organization didn't previously have" (p. 176). In contrast, Nelson and Winter (1982) take a very different position, asserting that "the possession of technical 'knowledge' is an attribute of the firm as a whole, as an organized entity, and is not reducible to what any single individual knows, or even to any simple aggregation of the various competencies and capabilities of all the various individuals, equipments and installations of the firm" (p. 63).

A similar view is reflected in Brown and Duguid's (1991) analysis of communities of practice, in which shared learning is inextricably located in complex, collaborative social practices. Weick and Roberts (1993) also report research demonstrating collective knowing at the organi-

zational level.[4] Our definition of intellectual capital reflects the second of these perspectives and acknowledges the significance of socially and contextually embedded forms of knowledge and knowing as a source of value differing from the simple aggregation of the knowledge of a set of individuals.

These two dimensions of explicit/tacit and individual/social knowledge have been combined by Spender (1996), who created a matrix of four different elements of an organization's intellectual capital. Individual explicit knowledge—what Spender labels "conscious knowledge"—is typically available to the individual in the form of facts, concepts, and frameworks that can be stored and retrieved from memory or personal records. The second element, individual tacit knowledge—what Spender labels "automatic knowledge"—may take many different forms of tacit knowing, including theoretical and practical knowledge of people and the performance of different kinds of artistic, athletic, or technical skills. Availability of people with such explicit knowledge and tacit skills clearly is an important part of an organization's intellectual capital and can be a key factor in the organization's performance, particularly in contexts where the performance of individual employees is crucial, as in specialist craft work (Cooke and Yanow 1993).

The other two elements of an organization's intellectual capital are social explicit knowledge (what Spender calls "objectified knowledge") and social tacit knowledge ("collective knowledge," in Spender's terms). The former represents the shared corpus of knowledge—epitomized, for example, by scientific communities, and often regarded as the most advanced form of knowledge (Boisot 1995). Across a wide range of organizations, we are witnessing major investments in the development of such objectified knowledge as firms attempt to pool, share, and leverage their distributed knowledge and intellect (Quinn et al. 1996).

Social tacit knowledge, on the other hand, represents the knowledge that is fundamentally embedded in the forms of social and institutional practice and that resides in the tacit experiences and enactment of the collective (Brown and Duguid 1991). Such knowledge and knowing capacity may remain relatively hidden from individual actors but be accessible and sustained through their interaction (Spender 1994). It is the type of knowledge frequently distinguishing the performance of highly experienced teams. This shared knowledge has been defined as "routines" by Nelson and Winter (1982), and it appears that much important organizational knowledge may exist in this form. For example, Weick and Roberts (1993) describe the complex, tacit, but heedful interrelating they observed among members of the flight operations team on aircraft carriers, which they suggest may characterize all high-reliability organizations.

For a given firm, these four elements collectively constitute its intellectual capital. Further, the elements are not independent, as Spender (1996) notes. However, in a stylized comparison of individuals working within an organization versus the same individuals working at arm's length across a hypothetical market (in the spirit of Conner and Prahalad's [1996] analysis), we use the two categories of social knowledge to provide the crux of our distinction: as Spender (1996) argues, "[C]ollective knowledge is the most secure and strategically significant kind of organizational knowledge" (p. 52). Therefore, it is on the social explicit knowledge and the social tacit knowledge that we focus our analysis of organizational advantage. This is an important limitation of our theory because, by restricting the scope of our analysis only to social knowledge, we will be unable to capture the influences that explicit and tacit individual knowledge may have on the intellectual capital of the firm.

There is another important way in which we limit our analysis. The potential advantages of internal organization over market organization may arise from its superior abilities in both creating and exploiting intellectual capital (Kogut and Zander 1993). We focus here only on the creation of intellectual capital and ignore the exploitation aspects. We have two reasons for imposing this constraint. First, comprehensive consideration of both processes would exceed the space available. Second, and more important, the benefits of intraorganizational exploitation of knowledge stem largely from missing, incomplete, or imperfect markets for such knowledge (Arrow 1974, Teece 1988, Williamson 1975). Therefore, such advantages historically have been a part of the more traditional market-failure-based theories of the firm. Where we go beyond such theories is in our argument that internal organization may, within limits, be superior to market transactions for the creation of new knowledge.

The Creation of Intellectual Capital

How is new knowledge created? Following Schumpeter (1934), Moran and Ghoshal (1996)

have argued that all new resources, including knowledge, are created through two generic processes: combination and exchange. While this argument is yet to be widely scrutinized, and although it is possible that there may be still other processes for the creation of new knowledge (particularly at the individual level), we believe that these two, indeed, are among the key mechanisms for creating social knowledge; therefore, we adopt this framework for our purposes.

Combination and the Creation of Intellectual Capital

Combination is the process viewed by Schumpeter (1934) as the foundation for economic development—"to produce means to combine materials and forces within our reach" (p. 65)—and this perspective has become the starting point for much current work on organizations as knowledge systems (Boisot 1995, Cohen and Levinthal 1990, Kogut and Zander 1992). In this literature scholars frequently identify two types of knowledge creation. First, new knowledge can be created through incremental change and development from existing knowledge. Schumpeter (1934), for example, talks of continuous adjustment in small steps, and March and Simon (1958) identify "localized search" and "stable heuristics" as the basis for knowledge growth. Within the philosophy of science, Kuhn (1970) sees development within the paradigm as the dominant mode of progression. Second, many authors also discuss more radical change: innovation, in Schumpeter's terms; double-loop learning, according to Argyris and Schon (1978); and paradigmatic change and revolution, according to Kuhn (1970). There appears to be a consensus that both types of knowledge creation involve making new combinations—incrementally or radically—either by combining elements previously unconnected or by developing novel ways of combining elements previously associated. "Development in our sense is then defined by the carrying out of new combinations" (Schumpeter, 1934, p. 66),[5] a view endorsed by the recent research of Leonard-Barton (1995).

Exchange and the Creation of Intellectual Capital

Where resources are held by different parties, exchange is a prerequisite for resource combination. Since intellectual capital generally is created through a process of combining the knowledge and experience of different parties, it, too, is dependent upon exchange among these parties. Sometimes, this exchange involves the transfer of explicit knowledge, either individually or collectively held, as in the exchange of information within the scientific community or via the Internet. Often, new knowledge creation occurs through social interaction and coactivity. Zucker et al. (1996) recently have shown the importance of collaboration for the development and acquisition of fine-grained collective knowledge in biotechnology. Their research endorses the significance of teamwork in the creation of knowledge, as identified much earlier by Penrose (1959). In developing her theory of the growth of the firm, Penrose proposed that a firm be viewed as "a collection of individuals who have had experience in working together, for only in this way can 'teamwork' be developed" (p. 46).

There are many aspects to the learning embedded in such shared experience. They include the specific meanings and understandings subtly and extensively negotiated in the course of social interaction. Importantly, they also include an appreciation of the ways in which action may be coordinated. For, as Penrose (1959) observes, such experience "develops an increasing knowledge of the possibilities for action and the ways in which action can be taken by . . . the firm. This increase in knowledge not only causes the productive opportunity of a firm to change . . . but also contributes to the "uniqueness" of the opportunity of each individual firm" (p. 53). An interest in the ways in which such collective learning, especially concerning how to coordinate diverse production skills and to integrate several technology streams, has been at the heart of much recent discussion of core competence as the source of competence advantage (Prahalad and Hamel 1990) and is suggestive of the complex ways in which exchange contributes to the creation of intellectual capital.

The Conditions for Exchange and Combination

In their analysis of value creation, Moran and Ghoshal (1996) identify three conditions that must be satisfied for exchange and combination of resources actually to take place. We believe that these conditions apply to the creation of new intellectual capital. In addition, however, we identify a fourth factor, which we regard as a prerequisite for the creation of intellectual capital.

The first condition is that the opportunity exists to make the combination or exchange. In our context we see this condition being determined by accessibility to the objectified and collective forms of social knowledge. A fundamental requirement for the development of new intellectual capital is that it is possible to draw upon and engage in the existing and differing knowledge and knowing activities of various parties or knowing communities (Boland and Tenkasi 1995, Zucker et al. 1996). In the academic world the "invisible college" has long been recognized as an important social network giving valuable early access to distributed knowledge, facilitating its exchange and development, and thereby accelerating the advancement of science (Crane 1972). Clearly, recent developments in technology, such as Lotus Notes and the Internet, have considerably increased the opportunities for knowledge combination and exchange. In addition, however, as the history of science demonstrates, the creation of new intellectual capital also may occur through accidental rather than planned combinations and exchanges, reflecting emergent patterns of accessibility to knowledge and knowledge processes.

Second, in order for the parties involved to avail themselves of the opportunities that may exist to combine or exchange resources, value expectancy theorists suggest that those parties must expect such deployment to create value. In other words, they must anticipate that interaction, exchange, and combination will prove worthwhile, even if they remain uncertain of what will be produced or how. Writing about the anticipated outcome of a conference of business practitioners and researchers, Slocum (1994) comments, "[E]ach of us expects to learn something of value as a result of our being here. None of us knows exactly what we are going to learn or what path we will take in the pursuit of this knowledge. We are confident, however, that the process works" (p. ix). This anticipation of or receptivity to learning and new knowledge creation has been shown to be an important factor affecting the success or otherwise of strategic alliances (Hamel 1991). It exemplifies Giddens's (1984) concept of intentionality as an influence on social action and, in so doing, also acknowledges the possibility that outcomes may turn out to be different from those anticipated.

The third condition for the creation of new resources highlights the importance of motivation. Even where opportunities for exchange exist and people anticipate that value may be created through exchange or interaction, those involved must feel that their engagement in the knowledge exchange and combination will be worth their while. Moran and Ghoshal (1996) see this as the expectation that the parties engaged in exchange and combination will be able to appropriate or realize some of the new value created by their engagement, even though, as noted above, they may be uncertain about precisely what that value may be. For example, while having considerable potential, the availability of electronic knowledge exchange does not automatically induce a willingness to share information and build new intellectual capital. Quinn et al. (1996) found, in a study of Arthur Andersen Worldwide, that major changes in incentives and culture were required to stimulate use of its new electronic network, and they suggest that motivated creativity, which they describe as "care-why," is a fundamental influence in the creation of value through leveraging intellect. In his research on internal stickiness, Szulanski (1996) also found that lack of motivation may inhibit the transfer of best practice within the firm. However, Szulanski discovered that far more important as a barrier was the lack of capacity to assimilate and apply new knowledge.

Accordingly, we propose that there is a fourth precondition for the creation of new intellectual capital: combination capability. Even where the opportunities for knowledge exchange and combination exist, these opportunities are perceived as valuable, and parties are motivated to make such resource deployments or to engage in knowing activity, the capability to combine information or experience must exist. In their research on innovation, Cohen and Levinthal (1990) argue that the ability to recognize the value of new knowledge and information, and also the ability to assimilate and use it, are all vital factors in organizational learning and innovation. Their work demonstrates that all of these abilities, which they label "absorptive capacity," depend upon the existence of related prior knowledge. Moreover, they suggest that an organization's absorptive capacity does not reside in any single individual but depends, crucially, on the links across a mosaic of individual capabilities—an observation that parallels Spender's (1996) discussion of collective knowledge.

Toward a Theory of the Creation of Intellectual Capital

By way of summary, we have argued the following. First, new intellectual capital is created through combination and exchange of existing intellectual resources, which may exist in the form of explicit and tacit knowledge and knowing capability. Second, there are four conditions that affect the deployment of intellectual resources and engagement in knowing activity involving combination and exchange. Third, in reviewing the burgeoning literature on knowledge and knowing, we have encountered much evidence in support of the view that the combination and exchange of knowledge are complex social processes and that much valuable knowledge is fundamentally socially embedded—in particular situations, in coactivity, and in relationships. As yet, we have uncovered no single theoretical framework that pulls together the various strands we can identify in this literature. For example, although a growing body of work exists in which scholars adopt an evolutionary perspective and identify the special capabilities of firms in the creation and transfer of tacit knowledge, this work has not yet produced a coherent theory explaining these special capabilities. Given the social embeddedness of intellectual capital, we suggest that such a theory is likely to be one that is primarily concerned with social relationships. Accordingly, we believe that social capital theory offers a potentially valuable perspective for understanding and explaining the creation of intellectual capital. It is to this theory we now return.

Social Capital Exchange and Combination

Social capital resides in relationships, and relationships are created through exchange (Bourdieu 1986). The pattern of linkages and the relationships built through them are the foundation for social capital. What we observe is a complex and dialectical process in which social capital is created and sustained through exchange and in which, in turn, social capital facilitates exchange. For example, there is mounting evidence demonstrating that where parties trust each other, they are more willing to engage in cooperative activity through which further trust may be generated (Fukuyama 1995, Putnam 1993, Tyler and Kramer 1996). In social systems, exchange is the precursor to resource combination. Thus, social capital influences combination indirectly through exchange. However, we argue below that several facets of social capital, particularly those pertaining to the cognitive dimension, also have a direct influence on the ability of individuals to combine knowledge in the creation of intellectual capital. Although our primary objective is to explore the ways in which social capital influences the development of in-

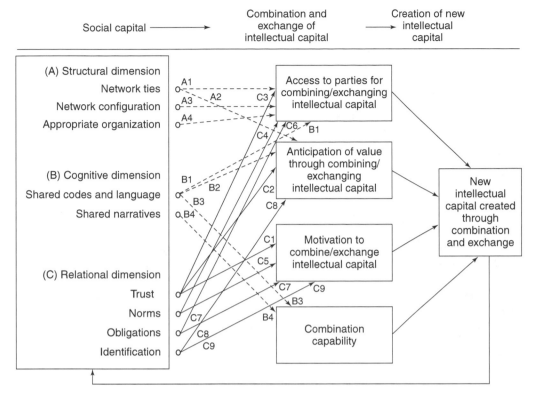

Figure 38.1 Social capital in the creation of intellectual capital.

tellectual capital, we recognize that intellectual capital may, itself, facilitate the development of social capital. Thus, later in the chapter we consider how the coevolution of these two forms of capital may underpin organizational advantage.

The main thesis we develop here is that social capital facilitates the development of intellectual capital by affecting the conditions necessary for exchange and combination to occur. To explore this proposition, we now examine some of the ways in which each of the three dimensions of social capital influence the four conditions for resource exchange and combination we presented above. The specific relationships we identify are summarized in figure 38.1.

For the sake of clarity of exposition, we consider, in the following analysis, the impact of each dimension of social capital independently of the other dimensions. We recognize, however, that both the dimensions and the several facets of social capital are likely to be interrelated in important and complex ways. For example, particular structural configurations, such as those displaying strong symmetrical ties, have consistently been shown to be associated with such relational facets as interpersonal affect and trust (Granovetter 1985, Krackhardt 1992). Similarly,

researchers have highlighted the often-complex interdependencies between social identification and shared vocabulary and language (Ashforth and Mael 1995).

Moreover, not all dimensions of social capital are mutually reinforcing. For instance, an efficient network in structural terms may not be the best way to develop the strong relational or cognitive social capital that may be necessary to ensure the effective operation of such networks. Nohria and Eccles (1992), for example, highlight important differences between face-to-face and electronic exchange and propose that using electronically mediated exchange to help create a network organization requires more, not less, face-to-face communication. Our primary focus on the independent effects of these dimensions therefore limits the richness of the present exploration and identifies an important area for future work.

Exchange, Combination, and the Structural Dimension of Social Capital

Our main argument in this section is that, within the context of the framework of combination and exchange adopted by us in this chapter, the structural dimension of social capital influences the development of intellectual capital primarily (though not exclusively) through the ways in which its various facets affect access to parties for exchanging knowledge and participating in knowing activities. While recognizing that the structural facets also may be systematically associated with other conditions for the exchange and combination of knowledge, we believe that these associations are primarily derived indirectly, through the ways in which structure influences the development of the relational and cognitive dimensions of social capital. For example, the strong, symmetrical ties frequently associated with the development of affective relationships (both positive and negative) may, in turn, influence individuals' motivation to engage in social interaction and, thereby, exchange knowledge (Krackhardt 1992, Lawler and Yoon 1996). Similarly, stable networks characterized by dense relations and high levels of interaction are conducive to the development of the different facets of the cognitive social capital we discuss in this chapter (Boisot 1995, Orr 1990).

Network Ties

The fundamental proposition of social capital theory is that network ties provide access to resources. One of the central themes in the literature is that social capital constitutes a valuable source of information benefits (i.e., "who you know" affects "what you know"). Coleman (1988) notes that information is important in providing a basis for action but is costly to gather. However, social relations, often established for other purposes, constitute information channels that reduce the amount of time and investment required to gather information.

Burt (1992) suggests that these information benefits occur in three forms: access, timing, and referrals. The term "access" refers to receiving a valuable piece of information and knowing who can use it, and it identifies the role of networks in providing an efficient information screening and distribution process for members of those networks. Thus, network ties influence both access to parties for combining and exchanging knowledge (A1 in figure 38.1) and anticipation of value through such exchange (A2 in figure 38.1). The operations of the invisible college provide an example of such networks.

"Timing" of information flows refers to the ability of personal contacts to provide information sooner than it becomes available to people without such contacts. This may well increase the anticipated value of such information (A2 in figure 38.1), as demonstrated in research on job-seeking behavior (Granovetter 1973). Such early access to information may be especially important in commercially oriented research and development, where speed to market may be a crucial factor in determining success.

"Referrals" are those processes providing information on available opportunities to people or actors in the network, hence influencing the opportunity to combine and exchange knowledge (A1 in figure 38.1). They constitute a flow of information about possibilities and also frequently include reputational endorsement for the actors involved—thereby influencing both the anticipated value of combination and exchange and the motivation for such exchange (see Granovetter 1973, Putnam 1993). However, we believe that such reputational endorsement derives more from relational than structural factors, which we explore below.

Network Configuration

Ties to provide the channels for information transmission, but the overall configuration of these ties constitutes an important facet of social capital that may impact the development of intellectual capital. For example, three properties of network structure—density, connectivity, and hierarchy—are all features associated with flexibility and ease of information exchange through their impact on the level of contact or the accessibility they provide to network members (A3 in figure 38.1; Ibarra 1992, Krackhardt 1989).

Burt (1992) notes that a player with a network rich in information benefits has contacts established in the places where useful bits of information are likely to air, who will provide a reliable flow of information to and from those places. While acknowledging the importance of trust and trustworthiness as a factor in the choice of contacts, Burt (1992) devotes much more attention to the efficiency of different relationship structures, arguing, in particular, that the sparse network, with few redundant contacts, provides more information benefits. The dense network is inefficient in the sense that it returns less diverse information for the same cost as that of the sparse network. The benefits of the latter thus derive from both the diversity of information and the lower costs of accessing it.

Jacobs (1965) and Granovetter (1973) have made similar arguments, identifying the role of "hop-and-skip" links and "loose ties" in information diffusion through communities. This aspect of diversity is very important, because it is well established that significant progress in the creation of intellectual capital often occurs by bringing together knowledge from disparate sources and disciplines. Networks and network structures thus represent facets of social capital that influence the range of information that may be accessed (A3 in figure 38.1) and that becomes available for combination. As such, these structures constitute a valuable resource as channels or conduits for knowledge diffusion and transfer.

However, there are important limitations to the conduit model, in which meaning is viewed as unproblematic and in which the primary concern is with issues of information transfer. For example, Hansen (1996) has found that weak ties facilitate search but impede transfer, especially when knowledge is not codified. Thus, whereas networks having little redundancy may be both effective and efficient for the transfer of information whose meaning is relatively unproblematic, much richer patterns of relationship and interaction are important where the meaning of information is uncertain and ambiguous or where parties to an exchange differ in their prior knowledge. For example, Cohen and Levinthal (1990) have shown that some redundancy is necessary for the development of cross-functional absorptive capacity. Nonetheless, the general point remains that the configuration of the network is an important influence on the accessibility of information resources (A3 in figure 38.1), although the appropriate level of redundancy is contingent on the degree to which the parties to knowledge exchange share a common knowledge base.

Appropriable Organization

Social capital developed in one context, such as ties, norms, and trust, can often (but not always) be transferred from one social setting to another, thus influencing patterns of social exchange. Examples include the transfer of trust from family and religious affiliations into work situations (Fukuyama 1995), the development of personal relationships into business exchanges (Coleman 1990), and the aggregation of the social capital of individuals into that of organizations (Burt 1992). This suggests that organizations created for one purpose may provide a source of valuable resources for other, different purposes (Nohria 1992, Putnam 1993, 1995). Such appropriable social organization can provide a potential network of access to people and their resources, including information and knowledge (A4 in figure 38.1), and, through its relational and cognitive dimensions, may ensure motivation and capability for exchange and combination (see below). However, such organization also may inhibit such processes; indeed, research demonstrates how organizational routines may separate rather than coordinate groups within organizations, constraining rather than enabling learning and the creation of intellectual capital (Dougherty 1996, Hedberg 1981).

Exchange, Combination, and the Cognitive Dimension of Social Capital

Earlier in this chapter, we defined intellectual capital as the knowledge and knowing capability of a social collectivity. This reflects our belief that, fundamentally, intellectual capital is a social artifact and that knowledge and meaning are always embedded in a social context—both created and sustained through ongoing relationships in such collectivities. Although scholars widely recognize that innovation generally occurs through combining different knowledge and experience and that diversity of opinion is a way of expanding knowledge, meaningful communication—an essential part of social exchange and combination processes—requires at least some sharing of context between the parties to such exchange (Boisot 1995, Boland and Tenkasi 1995, Campbell 1969). We suggest that this sharing may come about in two main ways: (1) through the existence of shared language and vocabulary and (2) through the sharing of collective narratives. Further, we suggest that these two elements constitute facets of shared cognition that facilitate the creation of intellectual capital especially through their impact on combination capability. In each case they do so by acting as both a medium and a product of social interaction.

Shared Language and Codes

There are several ways in which a shared language influences the conditions for combination and exchange. First, language has a direct and important function in social relations, for it is the means by which people discuss and exchange information, ask questions, and conduct business in society. To the extent that people share a common language, this facilitates their ability to gain access to people and their information. To the extent that their language and codes are different, this keeps people apart and restricts their access (B1 in figure 38.1).

Second, language influences our perception (Berger and Luckman 1966, Pondy and Mitroff 1979). Codes organize sensory data into perceptual categories and provide a frame of reference for observing and interpreting our environment. Thus, language filters out of awareness those events for which terms do not exist in the language and filters in those activities for which terms do exist. Shared language, therefore, may provide a common conceptual apparatus for evaluating the likely benefits of exchange and combination (B2 in figure 38.1).

Third, a shared language enhances combination capability (B3 in figure 38.1). Knowledge advances through developing new concepts and narrative forms (Nonaka and Takeuchi 1995). However, as we noted above, in order to develop such concepts and to combine the information gained through social exchange, the different parties must have some overlap in knowledge. Boland and Tenkasi (1995) identify the importance of both perspective taking and perspective making in knowledge creation, and they demonstrate how the existence of a shared vocabulary enables the combining of information. We suggest it is for all these reasons that researchers increasingly recognize group-specific communication codes as a valuable asset within firms (Arrow 1974, Kogut and Zander 1992, Monteverde 1995, Prescott and Visscher 1980).

Shared Narratives

Beyond the existence of shared language and codes, researchers have suggested that myths, stories, and metaphors also provide powerful means in communities for creating, exchanging, and preserving rich sets of meanings—a view long held by some social anthropologists (Clark 1972, Nisbet 1969). Recently, Bruner (1990) proposed that there are two different modes of cognition: (1) the information or paradigmatic mode and (2) the narrative mode. The former suggests a process of knowledge creation rooted in rational analysis and good arguments; the latter is represented in synthetic narratives, such as fairy tales, myths and legends, good stories, and metaphors. According to Bateson (1972), metaphors cut across different contexts, thus enabling the combining of both imaginative and literal observations and cognitions. Orr (1990) demonstrates how narrative in the form of stories, full

of seemingly insignificant details, facilitates the exchanging of practice and tacit experience among technicians, thereby enabling the discovery and development of improved practice. The emergence of shared narratives within a community thus enables the creation and transfer of new interpretations of events, doing so in a way that facilitates the combination of different forms of knowledge, including those largely tacit (B4 in figure 38.1).

Exchange, Combination, and the Relational Dimension of Social Capital

Much of the evidence for the relationship between social capital and intellectual capital highlights the significance of the relational dimension of social capital. Szulanski (1996) has found that one of the important barriers to the transfer of best practice within organizations is the existence of arduous relations between the source and the recipient. Whereas we have argued that the structural dimension has its primary direct impact on the condition of accessibility, and the cognitive dimension through its influence on accessibility and combination capability, research suggests that the relational dimension of social capital influences three of the conditions for exchange and combination in many ways. These are access to parties for exchange, anticipation of value through exchange and combination, and the motivation of parties to engage in knowledge creation through exchange and combination.

Trust

Misztal (1996) defines trust as the belief that the "results of somebody's intended action will be appropriate from our point of view" (pp. 9–10). A substantial body of research now exists (Fukuyama 1995, Gambetta 1988, Putnam 1993, 1995, Ring and Van de Ven 1992, 1994, Tyler and Kramer 1996) that demonstrates where relationships are high in trust, people are more willing to engage in social exchange in general, and cooperative interaction in particular (C1 in figure 38.1). Mishira (1996) argues that trust is multidimensional and indicates a willingness to be vulnerable to another party—a willingness arising from confidence in four aspects: (1) belief in the good intent and concern of exchange partners (Ouchi 1981, Pascale 1990, Ring and Van de Ven 1994), (2) belief in their competence and capability (Sako 1992, Szulanski (1996), (3) belief in their reliability (Giddens 1990, Ouchi 1981), and (4) belief in their perceived openness (Ouchi 1981).

Misztal (1996) observes that "trust, by keeping our mind open to all evidence, secures communication and dialogue" (p. 10), suggesting thereby that trust may both open up access to people for the exchange of intellectual capital (C3 in figure 38.1) and increase anticipation of value through such exchanges (C2 in figure 38.1). One can find support for this view in research demonstrating that where there are high levels of trust, people are more willing to take risks in such exchange (Nahapiet 1996, Ring and Van de Ven 1992). This may represent an increased willingness to experiment with combining different sorts of information. For example, Luhmann (1979) has shown trust to increase the potential of a system for coping with complexity and, thus, diversity—factors known to be important in the development of new intellectual capital. Trust may also indicate greater openness to the potential for value creation through exchange and combination (C2 in figure 38.1). Boisot (1995) highlights the importance of interpersonal trust for knowledge creation in contexts of high ambiguity and uncertainty: "[W]hen the message is uncodified, trust has to reside in the quality of the personal relationships that bind the parties through shared values and expectations rather than the intrinsic plausibility of the message" (p. 153).

As we noted above, there is a two-way interaction between trust and cooperation: trust lubricates cooperation, and cooperation itself breeds trust. This may lead to the development, over time, of generalized norms of cooperation, which increase yet further the willingness to engage in social exchange (Putnam 1993). In this respect, collective trust may become a potent form of "expectational asset" (Knez and Camerer 1994) that group members can rely on more generally to help solve problems of cooperation and coordination (Kramer et al. 1996).

Norms

According to Coleman (1990), a norm exists when the socially defined right to control an action is held not by the actor but by others. Thus, it represents a degree of consensus in the social system. Coleman (1988) suggests that "where a norm exists and is effective, it constitutes a powerful though sometimes fragile form of social capital" (p. S104). Norms of cooperation can es-

tablish a strong foundation for the creation of intellectual capital. Becoming in effect, "expectations that bind" (Kramer and Goldman 1995), such norms may be a significant influence on exchange processes, opening up access to parties for the exchange of knowledge (C4 in figure 38.1) and ensuring the motivation to engage in such exchange (C5 in figure 38.1; Putnam 1993).

For example, Starbuck (1992) notes the importance of social norms of openness and teamwork as key features of knowledge-intensive firms; he highlights the significance of the emphasis on cooperation rather than competition, on open disclosure of information, and on building loyalty to the firm as significant underpinnings of the success of the American law firm Wachtell, Lipton, Rosen, and Katz, which specializes in advice on nonroutine, challenging cases. Other norms of interaction that have been shown to be important in the creation of intellectual capital include a willingness to value and respond to diversity, an openness to criticism, and a tolerance of failure (Leonard-Barton 1995). Such norms may offset the tendency to "groupthink" that may emerge in strong, convergent groups and that represents the way in which high levels of social capital may be a real inhibitor for the development of intellectual capital (Janis 1982). At the same time, as Leonard-Barton (1995) has shown, norms also may have a dark side: those capabilities and values initially seen as a benefit may become, in time, a pathological rigidity.

Obligations and Expectations

Obligations represent a commitment or duty to undertake some activity in the figure. Coleman (1990) distinguishes obligations from generalized norms, viewing the former as expectations developed within particular personal relationships. He suggests that obligations operate as a "credit slip" held by A to be redeemed by some performance by B—a view reminiscent of Bourdieu's (1986) concept of credential we referred to above. In the context of the creation of intellectual capital, we suggest that such obligations and expectations are likely to influence both access to parties for exchanging and combining knowledge (C6 in figure 38.1) and the motivation to combine and exchange such knowledge (C7 in figure 38.1). The notion that "there is no such thing as a free lunch" represents a commonly held view that exchange brings with it expectations about future obligations—a view explicated in detail by Mauss (1954), Bourdieu (1977), and Cheal (1988). Fairtlough (1994) ascribes considerable importance to the formal, professional, and personal obligations that develop among those involved in cooperative research and development projects among different organizations:

> People in the two companies could rely on each other. . . . This was cooperation which certainly went beyond contractual obligations. It might also have gone beyond enlightened self interest, and beyond good professional behaviour, because the scientists liked working together, felt committed to the overall project and felt a personal obligation to help the others involved. (p. 119)

Identification

Identification is the process whereby individuals see themselves as one with another person or group of people. This may result from their membership in that group or through the group's operation as a reference group, 'in which the individual takes the values or standards of other individuals or groups as a comparative frame of reference" (Merton 1968, p. 288; see also Tajfel 1982). Kramer et al. (1996) have found that identification with a group or collective enhances concern for collective processes and outcomes, thus increasing the chances that the opportunity for exchange will be recognized. Identification, therefore, acts as a resource influencing both the anticipation of value to be achieved through combination and exchange (C8 in figure 38.1) and the motivation to combine and exchange knowledge (C9 in figure 38.1). We find support for this in the research of Lewicki and Bunker (1996), whose evidence suggests that salient group identification not only may increase the perceived opportunities for exchange but also may enhance the actual frequency of cooperation. In contrast, where groups have distinct and contradictory identities, these may constitute significant barriers to information sharing, learning, and knowledge creation (Child and Rodrigues 1996, Pettigrew 1973, Simon and Davies 1996).

Thus far, we have argued that social capital theory provides a powerful basis for understanding the creation of intellectual capital in general. The various specific links we have proposed are summarized in figure 38.1. In the next section we suggest that the theory also provides a basis for understanding the nature of organizational advantage since firms, as institutions, are likely to be relatively well endowed with social capital.

Social Capital, Intellectual Capital, and the Organizational Advantage

The last 20 years have witnessed a substantial resurgence of interest in the theory of the firm. During this period, those espousing transaction cost approaches became increasingly influential, positing, at their simplest, that the existence of firms can be explained in terms of market failure and the greater ability of firms, through hierarchy, to reduce the costs of transactions in particular (and relatively restricted) circumstances (Williamson 1975, 1981, 1985). The transaction cost theory of the firm has proved robust and has been applied across a wide range of issues, but it has also become subject to growing criticism for a range of definitional, methodological, and substantive reasons (see, e.g., Conner and Prahalad 1996, Pitelis 1993). More fundamentally, as we noted at the outset of this chapter, researchers now are seeking to develop a theory of the firm that is expressed in positive terms (Kogut and Zander 1996, Masten et al. 1991, Simon 1991b)—away from a market-failure framework to one grounded in the concept of organizational advantage (Moran and Ghoshal 1996).

Increasingly, the special capabilities of organizations for creating and transferring knowledge are being identified as a central element of organizational advantage. We suggest that social capital theory provides a sound basis for explaining why this should be the case. First, organizations as institutional settings are characterized by many of the factors known to be conducive to the development of high levels of social capital. Second, it is the coevolution of social and intellectual capital that underpins organizational advantage.

Organizations as Institutional Settings Are Conducive to the Development of Social Capital

Social capital is owned jointly by the parties to a relationship, with no exclusive ownership rights for individuals. Thus, it is fundamentally concerned with resources located within structures and processes of social exchange; as such, the development of social capital is significantly affected by those factors shaping the evolution of social relationships. We discuss four such conditions here: time, interaction, interdependence, and closure. We argue that all four are more characteristic of internal organization than of market organization as represented in neoclassical theory and that, as a result, organizations as institutional settings are conducive to the development of high levels of social capital relative to markets. However, as we subsequently note, in practice these conditions may also occur in some forms of interorganizational networks, thereby enabling such networks to become relatively well endowed with social capital.

Time and the Development of Social Capital

Like other forms of capital, social capital constitutes a form of accumulated history—here reflecting investments in social relations and social organization through time (Bourdieu 1986, Granovetter 1992). Time is important for the development of social capital, since all forms of social capital depend on stability and continuity of the social structure. The concept of embedding fundamentally means the binding of social relations in contexts of time and space (Giddens 1990). Coleman (1990) highlights the importance of continuity in social relationships: "One way in which the transactions that make up social action differ from those of the classical model of a perfect market lie in the role of time. In a model of a perfect market, transactions are both costless and instantaneous. But in the real world, transactions are consummated over a period of time" (p. 91). For example, since it takes time to build trust, relationship stability and durability are key network features associated with high levels of trust and norms of cooperation (Axelrod 1984, Granovetter 1985, Putnam 1993, Ring and Van de Ven 1992). The duration and stability of social relations also influence the clarity and visibility of mutual obligations (Misztal 1996).

Although, in the main, social capital is created as a by-product of activities engaged in for other purposes, intentional or constructed organization represents a direct, purposeful investment in social capital (Coleman 1990, 1993): "These organizations ordinarily take the form of authority structures composed of positions connected by obligations and expectations and occupied by persons" (Coleman 1990, p. 313). In contrast to the short-term transactions charac-

terizing the markets of neoclassical theory, intentional or constructed organization represents the creation and maintenance of an explicit and enduring structure of ties constituting, through organizational design, a configuration of relationships and resources usable for a variety of purposes—both formal and informal. Moreover, this commitment to continuity facilitates the other processes known to be influential in the development of social capital: interdependence, interaction, and closure.

Interdependence and the Development of Social Capital

Coleman (1990) states that social capital is eroded by factors that make people less dependent upon each other. This appears especially so for the relational dimension of social capital. For example, expectations and obligations are less significant where people have alternative sources of support. Indeed, Misztal (1996) has suggested that the recent resurgence of interest in trust can be explained by the increasingly transitional character of our present condition and the erosion of social interdependence and solidarity. Yet, most authors agree that high levels of social capital usually are developed in contexts characterized by high levels of mutual interdependence.

Whereas markets as institutional arrangements are rooted in the concept of autonomy (and institutional economists largely neglect interdependence between exchange parties; Zajac and Olsen 1993), firms fundamentally are institutions designed around the concepts and practices of specialization and interdependence and of differentiation and integration (Lawrence and Lorsch 1967, Smith 1986, Thompson 1967). Interdependence—and the coordination it implies—long has been recognized as perhaps the key attribute of business organization (Barnard 1938). Follet (1999) goes so far as to suggest that "the fair test of business administration, of industrial organization, is whether you have a business with all its parts so co-ordinated, so moving together in their closely knit and adjusting activities, so linking, interlocking and inter-relating, that they make a working unit, not a congerie of separate pieces" (p. 61). Such interdependence provides the stimulus for developing many organizationally embedded forms of social capital. For example, through providing the opportunity to create contexts characterized by the condition of interdependent viability—that is, the requirement that exchanges are positive in outcome for the system overall rather than for each individual member of the system—organizations considerably extend the circle of exchange that takes place among their members (Coleman 1993, Moran and Ghoshal 1996), thereby increasing social identification and encouraging norms of cooperation and risk taking.

Interaction and the Development of Social Capital

Social relationships generally, though not always, are strengthened through interaction but die out if not maintained. Unlike many other forms of capital, social capital increases rather than decreases with use. Interaction, thus, is a precondition for the development and maintenance of dense social capital (Bourdieu 1986). In particular, as we have noted already, scholars have shown that the cognitive and relational dimensions of social capital accumulate in network structures where linkages are strong, multidimensional, and reciprocal—features that characterize many firms but that rarely surface in pure market forms of organization. Discussing the development of language, Boland and Tenkasi (1995) note that it is "through action within communities of knowing that we make and remake both our language and our knowledge" (p. 353). According to these authors, such communities must have space for conversation, action, and interaction in order for the codes and language to develop that facilitate the creation of new intellectual capital.

In a different context, Boissevain (1974) shows how multiplex relations are more intimate than single-stranded relationships, therefore providing more accessibility and more response to pressure than single-stranded relations. Such relations typically are imbued with higher levels of obligation among network members, as well as trust-based norms (Coleman 1990). Further, Powell (1996) argues that norm-based conceptions of trust miss the extent to which cooperation is buttressed by sustained contact, regular dialogue, and constant monitoring. He adds that, without mechanisms and institutions to sustain such conversations, trust does not ensue (see also Coleman 1990). This echoes Bourdieu's (1986) earlier emphasis on the fundamental need for "an unceasing effort of sociability" (p. 250) for the reproduction of social capital in its many forms.

In neoclassical theory, markets as institutional settings are epitomized by impersonal, arm's length, spot transactions. Firms, in contrast, provide many opportunities for sustained interaction, conversations, and sociability—both by design and by accident. Formal organizations explicitly are designed to bring members together in order to undertake their primary task, to supervise activities, and to coordinate their activities, particularly in contexts requiring mutual adjustment (Mintzberg 1979, Thompson 1967), change, and innovation (Burns and Stalker 1961, Galbraith 1973). Through copresence (Giddens 1984), colocation (Fairtlough 1994), and the creation of such processes as routine choice opportunities (March and Olsen, 1976), organizations also create a myriad of contexts and occasions for the more-or-less planned coming together of people and their ideas. Finally, the literature is replete with evidence that organizational life is characterized by a substantial amount of conversation: in meetings, conferences, and social events that fill the everyday life of workers and managers (Mintzberg 1973, Prescott and Visscher 1980, Roy 1960). Together, these can be viewed as collective investment strategies for the institutional creation and maintenance of dense networks of social relationships and for the resources embedded within, available through, and derived from such networks of relationships. Alternatively, these meetings and social events provide the unplanned and unstructured opportunities for the accidental coming together of ideas that may lead to the serendipitous development of new intellectual capital.

Closure and the Development of Social Capital

Finally, there is much evidence that closure is a feature of social relationships that is conducive to the development of high levels of relational and cognitive social capital. Strong communities—the epitome of systems of dense social capital—have "identities that separate and a sense of sociological boundary that distinguishes members from nonmembers" (Etzioni 1996, p. 9; see also Bourdieu 1986). The development of norms, identity, and trust has been shown to be facilitated by network closure (Coleman 1990, Ibarra 1992), and the development of unique codes and language is assisted by the existence of community separation (Boland and Tenkasi 1995). Formal organizations, by definition, imply a measure of closure through the creation of explicit legal, financial, and social boundaries (Kogut and Zander 1996). Markets, in contrast, represent open networks that benefit from the freedom offered to individual agents but that have less access to the relational and cognitive facets of social capital.

The Coevolution of Social and Intellectual Capital Underpins Organizational Advantage

Our main argument thus far has been that social capital is influential in the development of new intellectual capital and that organizations are institutional settings conducive to the development of social capital. We have noted the significant and growing body of work that indicates organizations have some particular capabilities for creating and sharing knowledge, giving them their distinctive advantage over other institutional arrangements, such as markets. We now pull the strands of our analysis together by proposing that it is the interaction between social and intellectual capital that underpins organizational advantage.

Although our primary aim has been to suggest that social capital influences the development of intellectual capital, we recognize that the pattern of influence may be in the other direction. The view that shared knowledge forms the basis from which social order and interaction flow is a central theme in sociology, exemplified in the work of Berger and Luckman (1966) and Schultz (1970). Within organizational analysis, authors long have suggested that the firm's particular knowledge about how activities are to be coordinated underpins its capability to develop and operate as a social system (Kogut and Zander 1992, 1996, March and Simon 1958, Penrose 1959, Thompson 1967). We represent the influence of intellectual capital on social capital as a feedback relationship in figure 38.1. More important, however, we believe that it is the coevolution of social and intellectual capital that is of particular significance in explaining the source of organizational advantage.

Earlier in the chapter we noted the dialectical process by which social capital is both created and sustained through exchange and, in turn, enables such exchange to take place. As Berger and Luckman (1966) observe, "The relationship between man, the producer, and the social world, his product, is and remains a dialectical one. That is, man (not, of course, in isolation but in his collectivities) and his social world interact with each other. The product acts back upon the producer" (p. 78; see also Bourdieu, 1977). Giddens (1984), too, examines the self-reproducing quality of social practices, noting that social activities are re-

cursive—that is, "continually recreated by actors via the very means by which they express themselves as actors" (p. 2). For Giddens this implies a concept of human knowledgeability that underpins all social practice.

The discussion of knowledgeability that ensues suggests the reciprocal quality of the relationship between social and intellectual capital and is consistent with our emphasis on the social embeddedness of both forms of capital. Since both social and intellectual capital develop within and derive their significance from the social activities and social relationships within which they are located, their evolutionary paths are likely to be highly interrelated.

Consideration of the reciprocal relationship between knowledge and its social context permeates the sociology of science (Zuckerman 1988). Mullins (1973), for example, describes the joint evolution of social interaction, communication networks, and the elaboration of scientific ideas and notes that cognitive development is facilitated by the thickening of communication networks, which then leads to their further elaboration. Research within organizations offers many parallel examples (Burns and Stalker 1961, Leonard-Barton 1995, Weick 1995, Zucker et al. 1996). For instance, in a study of change in health administration, Nahapiet (1988) describes, in detail, how a new accounting calculus both shaped and was in turn shaped by the social context in which it was embedded.

Discussing Orr's (1990) influential ethnography of service technicians, Brown and Duguid (1991) provide further insight into this coevolution of knowledge and relationships. Specifically, they describe how technicians achieve two distinct forms of social construction. First, through their work, and "through cultivating connections throughout the corporation" (p. 67), technicians engage in the ongoing creation and negotiation of shared understanding—an understanding that represents their view of the world, that is their collective knowledge. The second form of social construction, which, according to Brown and Duguid (1991) is also important but less evident, is the creation of a shared identity: "In telling these stories an individual rep contributes to the construction and development of his or her own identity as a rep and reciprocally to the construction and development of the community of reps in which he or she works" (p. 68). In an analysis reminiscent of Weick and Roberts's (1993) discussion of collective mind—itself located in processes of interrelating—these authors highlight the mutually dependent and interactive ways in which social and intellectual capital coevolve.

We suggest that this emphasis on the coevolution of the two forms of capital provides a dynamic perspective on the development of organizational advantage. Spender (1996) argues that it is the collective forms of knowledge that are strategically important, and many authors claim that it is these forms of shared tacit knowledge that underpin what we have termed the "organizational advantage." It is these collective forms of knowledge, we believe, that are particularly tightly interconnected with the relational and cognitive forms of social capital with which, we have argued, organizations are relatively well endowed. Organizations thus build and retain their advantage through the dynamic and complex interrelationships between social and intellectual capital.

Discussion and Implications

The view of organizational advantage we present here is fundamentally a social one. We see the roots of intellectual capital deeply embedded in social relations and in the structure of these relations. Such a view contrasts strongly with the relatively individualistic and acontextual perspectives that characterize more transactional approaches for explaining the existence and contribution of firms. Although we have identified several ways in which facets of social capital may indeed reduce transaction costs by economizing on information and coordination costs, we believe that our theoretical propositions go much further in identifying those factors underpinning dynamic efficiency and growth.

In so doing, we note that our arguments are consistent with resource-based theory insofar as that theory highlights the competitive advantage of firms as based in their unique constellation of resources: physical, human, and organizational (Barney 1991). Those resources found to be especially valuable are those that are rare, durable, imperfectly imitable, and nontradable (Barney 1991, Dierickx and Cool 1989). Among the factors making a resource nonimitable are tacitness (Reed and DeFillippi 1990), causal ambiguity (Lippman and Rumelt 1992), time compression diseconomies, and interconnectedness (Dierickx and Cool 1989), as well as path dependence and social complexity (Barney 1991, Reed and DeFillippi 1990). All of these are features integral to the facets of social capital and to its interrela-

tionships with intellectual capital. Thus, we suggest that differences among firms, including differences in performance, may represent differences in their ability to create and exploit social capital. Moreover, at least regarding the development of intellectual capital, those firms developing particular configurations of social capital are likely to be more successful. Evidence for this suggestion is found in studies of knowledge-intensive firms that have been shown to invest heavily in resources, including physical facilities, to encourage the development of strong personal and team relationships, high levels of personal trust, norm-based control, and strong connections across porous boundaries (Alvesson 1991, 1992, Starbuck 1992, 1994, Van Maanen and Kunda 1989). The framework developed here will provide a useful basis for further testing these propositions about firm differences.

In developing our thesis, we have noted several limitations in our approach. First, regarding social capital, our analysis has concentrated primarily, although not exclusively, on how social capital assists the creation of new intellectual capital. However, we recognize that social capital also may have significant negative consequences. For example, certain norms may be antagonistic rather than supportive of cooperation, exchange, and change. Moreover, organizations high in social capital may become ossified through their relatively restricted access to diverse sources of ideas and information. But the general point underpinning our analysis is that institutions facilitate some forms of exchange and combination but limit their scope (Ghoshal and Moran 1996); thus, effective organization requires a constant balancing of potentially opposing forces (Boland and Tenkasi 1995, Etzioni 1996, Leonard-Barton 1995).

Furthermore, the creation and maintenance of some forms of social capital, particularly the relational and cognitive dimensions, are costly. The development of social capital thus represents a significant investment—conscious or unconscious—and, like all such investments, requires an understanding of the relative costs and benefits likely to be derived from such investment. These are likely to be influenced by the size and complexity of the social structure in which social capital is embedded, since the costs of maintaining linkages usually increase exponentially as a social network increases in size. Although technology may make it possible to stretch the conventional limits of networks of social capital, our arguments about the significance of interdependence, interaction, and closure suggest that there still remain important upper limits. Indeed, adding people to the network may serve to reduce certain forms of social capital, such as personal obligations or high status.

Finally, although we have responded to Putnam's challenge to progress our understanding of the various dimensions and facets of social capital, in our analysis we largely have considered these dimensions separately. Of great interest are the interrelationships among the three dimensions and, indeed, among the various facets within each dimension. We regard this as an important focus for future research.

Second, regarding intellectual capital, we have concentrated on just one aspect: its creation, rather than its diffusion and exploitation. A fuller understanding of knowledge as the source of organizational advantage will require an examination of the ways in which social capital may influence these important and complementary processes. We believe that the framework we develop here provides a sound basis for such examination. Also, we have focused very much on the types and processes of intellectual capital rather than its content—that is, the know-how rather than the know-what. Clearly, the specific knowledge content, including its quality, is an important factor to be considered when attempting to gain an understanding of the effective creation of intellectual capital.

Third, our exploration of organizational advantage began with the proposition that knowledge and knowledge processes are major foundations of such advantage. However, our discussion of the coevolution of social and intellectual capital potentially enriches this understanding of organizational advantage in important ways. For instance, our analysis elucidates resource creation within networks, concentrating particularly on the interrelated development of social and intellectual capital as key resources. As such, it is suggestive of the processes whereby organizational networks create value and that, perhaps, underpins their advantage. More generally, we believe that a detailed understanding of social capital itself may be an important element in extending our understanding of the significant, but as yet inadequately understood, concept of organizational advantage. However, we could not explore such issues in this chapter, and we recognize that much work still needs to be done to elaborate both the concept of organizational advantage and the significance of social capital therein.

Fourth and finally, we have developed our thesis about the relationships between social and intellectual capital in the context of exploring and explaining the source of organizational advantage—that is, we have made the argument regarding these interrelationships within one type of boundary: the firm. It is our view that structures of social capital fundamentally are relatively bounded, and these boundaries typically come from some external physical or social basis for grouping, such as a geographic community (Jacobs 1965, Putnam 1993), the family (Coleman 1988, Loury 1977), religion (Coleman 1990), or class (Bourdieu 1977). As we noted above, social capital is typically a by-product of other activities; thus, its development requires a "focus": an entity around which joint activities are organized (Nohria 1992) and that forms the basis for a level of network closure.

However, our analysis of the conditions conducive to the development of social capital suggests that wherever institutions operate in contexts characterized by enduring relationships—with relatively high levels of interdependence, interaction, and closure—we would expect to see these institutions emerge with relatively dense configurations of social capital. We have argued that these conditions typically occur more within organizations than in neoclassical markets, but they may also be found in particular forms of interorganizational relationship (Baker 1990, Hakansson and Snehota 1995, Larson 1992, Powell 1996, Ring and Van de Ven 1992, 1994). Therefore, we see the potential to extend our fundamental analysis to other institutional settings, including those existing among organizations.

Bourdieu (1993) argues that, by making the concept of social capital explicit, it is possible to focus rigorously on the intuitively important concept of "connections" and to establish the basis for research designed to identify the processes for social capital's creation, accumulation, dissipation, and consequence. The concept also provides a theoretical justification for the study of many social practices, such as the "social round," popularly recognized as important but frequently ignored in formal research. In particular, for Bourdieu, systematic analysis of the volume and structure of social capital enables examination of the relationships among social and other forms of capital.

In identifying the interrelationship between social and intellectual capital, we have made a similar argument. That is, by defining the concepts and developing clear propositions about their interrelationships, we have established an agenda for future research that both complements and extends existing knowledge-based theories of the firm. Moreover, we suggest that the model outlined here also provides the foundation of a viable framework to guide the investments—individual or collective—of practitioners seeking to build or extend their network of connections and, therefore, their stocks of social capital. As Bourdieu (1986) observes, "[T]he existence of connections is not a natural given, or even a social given . . . it is the product of an endless effort at institution" (p. 249).

prefer to use different terms for those forms of conversion involving tacit knowledge. However, following Polanyi (1967), we believe that all knowledge processes have a tacit dimension and that, fundamentally, the same generic processes underlie all forms of knowledge conversion. Therefore, our usage of the term "combination" in this context is more general and is rooted in our view of intellectual capital as embracing both the explicit knowledge and the tacit knowing of a collective and its members. Our view, thus, resembles more closely the concept of combinative capabilities discussed by Kogut and Zander (1992).

Notes

This research was supported in part by a grant from the Sundridge Park Research Fund. We are grateful to John Stopford, Peter Moran, Morten Hansen, Richard Pascale, Max Boisot, Wen-Pin Tsai, Nitin Nohria, Paul Willman, Anthony Hopwood, Tim Ambler, Martin Waldenstrom, and three anonymous referees for their helpful comments on earlier drafts of this article and in discussions of its subject matter.

1. We recognize that this terminology deviates from much that is customary in the field of network analysis. In particular, the focus of network analysis is relational data, but included under its heading are attributes that we label structural here. Scott (1991), for example, describes network analysis as being concerned with "the contacts, ties and connections, the group attachments and meetings which relate one agent to another. . . . These relations connect pairs of agents to larger relational systems" (p. 3). However, we justify our usage both through reference to Granovetter and because we believe this terminology captures well the personal aspect of this dimension.

2. To this recent authors have added the concept of know-why (Hamel 1991, Kogut and Zander 1992).

3. Indeed, his much-referenced chapter, in which he introduces the tacit dimension, is entitled "Tacit Knowing," not "tacit knowledge."

4. See also Walsh's (1995) comprehensive discussion of organizational cognition.

5. In their theory of the knowledge-creating company, Nonaka and Takeuchi (1995) define combination as "a process of systematizing concepts into a knowledge system. This mode of knowledge conversion involves combining different bodies of explicit knowledge" (p. 67). They

References

Alvesson, M. (1991) "Corporate culture and corporatism at the company level: a case study." *Economic and Industrial Democracy* 12:347–367.

Alvesson, M. (1992) "Leadership as a social integrative action. A study of a computer consultancy company." *Organization Studies* 13:185–209.

Andeson, J.R. (1981) *Cognitive Skills and Their Acquisition.* Hillsdale, NJ: Erlbaum.

Argyris, C. and Schon, D. (1978) *Organizational Learning: A Theory of Action Perspective.* Reading, MA: Addison-Wesley.

Arrow, K. (1974) *The Limits of Organization.* New York: Norton.

Ashforth, B.E. and Mael, F.A. (1995) "Organizational identity and strategy as a context for the individual." Paper presented at the Conference on the Embeddedness of Strategy, University of Michigan, Ann Arbor.

Axelrod, R. (1984) *The Evolution of Co-operation.* New York: Basic Books.

Baker, W. (1990) "Market networks and corporate behavior." *American Journal of Sociology* 96: 589–625.

Barnard, C.I. (1938) *The Functions of the Executive.* Cambridge, MA: Harvard University Press.

Barney, J. (1991) "Firm resources and sustained competitive advantage." *Journal of Management* 17:99–120.

Bateson, G. (1972) *Steps to an Ecology of Mind.* New York: Ballantine Books.

Berger, P.L. and Luckman, T. (1966) *The Social Construction of Reality.* London: Penguin Press.

Boisot, M. (1995) *Information Space: A Framework for Learning in Organizations, Institutions and Culture.* London: Routledge.

Boissevain, J. (1974) *Friends of Friends.* Oxford: Basil Blackwell.

Boland, R.J. and Tenkasi, R.V. (1995) "Perspective

making and perspective taking in communities of knowing." *Organization Science* 6:350–372.

Bourdieu, P. (1977) *Outline of a Theory of Practice*. Cambridge: Cambridge University Press.

Bourdieu, P. (1986) "The forms of capital," in J.G. Richardson (ed.), *Handbook of Theory and Research for the Sociology of Education*, pp. 241–258. New York: Greenwood.

Bourdieu, P. (1993) *Sociology in Question*. London: Sage.

Brown, J.S. and Duguid, P. (1991) "Organizational learning and communities-of-practice: toward a unified view of working, learning and innovation." *Organization Science* 2:40–57.

Bruner, J.S. (1990) *Acts of Meaning*. Cambridge, MA: Harvard University Press.

Burns, T. and Stalker, G. (1961) *The Management of Innovation*. London: Tavistock.

Burt, R.S. (1992) *Structural Holes: The Social Structure of Competition*. Cambridge, MA: Harvard University Press.

Campbell, D.T. (1969) "Ethnocentrism of disciplines and the fish-scale model of omniscience," in M. Sherif and C. Sherif (eds.), *Interdisciplinary Relationships in the Social Sciences*, pp. 328–348. Chicago: Aldine.

Cheal, D. (1988) *The Gift Economy*. London: Routledge.

Child, J. and Rodrigues, S. (1996) "The role of social identity in the international transfer of knowledge through joint ventures," in S.R. Clegg and G. Palmer (eds.), *The Politics of Management Knowledge*, pp. 46–68. London: Sage.

Cicourel, A.V. (1973) *Cognitive Sociology*. Harmondsworth, England: Penguin Books.

Clark, B.R. (1972) "The occupational saga in higher education." *Administrative Science Quarterly* 17:178–184.

Cohen, W.M. and Levinthal, D.A. (1990) "Absorptive capacity: a new perspective on learning and innovation." *Administrative Science Quarterly* 35:128–152.

Coleman, J.S. (1988) "Social capital in the creation of human capital." *American Journal of Sociology* 94:S95–S120.

Coleman, J.S. (1990) *Foundations of Social Theory*. Cambridge, MA: Belknap Press.

Coleman, J.S. (1993) "Properties of rational organizations," in S.M. Lindenberg and H. Schreuder (eds.), *Interdisciplinary Perspectives on Organization Studies*, pp. 79–90. Oxford: Pergamon Press.

Conner, K.R. and Prahalad, C.K. (1996) "A resource-based theory of the firm: Knowledge versus opportunism." *Organization Science* 7:477–501.

Cooke, S.D.N. and Yanow, D. (1993) "Culture and organizational learning." *Journal of Management Inquiry* 2:373–390.

Crane, D. (1972) *Invisible Colleges: Diffusion of Knowledge in Scientific Communities*. Chicago: University of Chicago Press.

D'Aveni, R.A. and Kesner, I. (1993) "Top managerial prestige, power and tender offer response: a study of elite social networks and target firm co-operation during takeovers." *Organization Science* 4:123–151.

Dierickx, I. and Cool, K. (1989) "Asset stock accumulation and sustainability of competitive advantage." *Management Science* 35:1504–1511.

Dougherty, D. (1996) "Interpretive barriers to successful product innovation in large firms," in J.R. Meindl, C. Stubbart, and J.F. Porac (eds.), *Cognition within and between Organizations*, pp. 307–340. Thousand Oaks, CA: Sage.

Durkheim, E. (1951) *Suicide: A Study in Sociology*. New York: Free Press. (First published in 1897.)

Etzioni, A. (1996) "The responsive community: a communitarian perspective." *American Sociological Review* 61:1–11.

Fairtlough, G. (1994) *Creative Compartments: A Design for Future Organization*. London: Adamantine Press.

Follet, M.P. (1949) "Coordination," In L. Urwick (ed.), *Freedom and Co-ordination: Lectures in Business Organization*, pp. 61–76. London: Management Publications Trust.

Fukuyama, F. (1995) *Trust: Social Virtues and the Creation of Prosperity*. London: Hamish Hamilton.

Galbraith, J. (1973) *Designing Complex Organizations*. Reading, MA: Addison-Wesley.

Gambetta, D., ed. (1988) *Trust: Making and Breaking Cooperative Relations*. Oxford: Basil Blackwell.

Ghoshal, S. and Moran, P. (1996) "Bad for practice: a critique of the transaction cost theory." *Academy of Management Review* 21:13–47.

Giddens, A. (1984) *The Constitution of Society: Outline of a Theory of Structuration*. Cambridge: Polity Press.

Giddens, A. (1990) *The Consequences of Modernity*. Cambridge: Polity Press.

Giddens, A. and Turner, J., eds. (1987) *Social Theory Today*. Cambridge: Polity Press.

Gowler, D. and Legge, K. (1982) "The integration of disciplinary perspectives and levels of analysis in problem-oriented research," in N. Nicholson and T. Wall (eds.), *The Theory and Practice of Organizational Psychology*, pp. 69–101. London: Academic Press.

Granovetter, M.S. (1973) "The strength of weak ties." *American Journal of Sociology* 78:1360–1380.

Granovetter, M.S. (1985) "Economic action and social structure: The problem of embeddedness." *American Journal of Sociology* 91:481–510.

Granovetter, M.S. (1992) "Problems of explanation in economic sociology," in N. Nohria and R. Eccles (eds.), *Networks and Organizations: Structure, Form and Action*, pp. 25–56. Boston: Harvard Business School Press.

Grant, R.M. (1996) "Knowledge, Strategy and the Theory of the Firm. *Strategic Management Journal* 17(S2):109–122.

Hakansson, H. and Snehota, I. (1995) *Developing Relationships in Business Networks*. London: Routledge.

Hamel, G. (1991) "Competition for competence in inter-partner learning within international strategic alliances. *Strategic Management Journal* 12: 83–103.

Hansen, M. (1996) "Using the wisdom of others: searching for and transferring knowledge." Presentation at the London Business School.

Hedberg, B. (1981) "How organizations learn and unlearn," in P.C. Nystrom and W.H. Starbuck (eds.), *Handbook of Organizational Design*, vol. 1, pp. 3–27. Oxford: Oxford University Press.

Ibarra, H. (1992) "Structural alignments, individual strategies, and managerial action: elements toward a network theory of getting things done," in N. Nohria and R.G. Eccles (eds.), *Networks and Organizations: Structure, Form and Action*, pp. 165–188. Boston: Harvard Business School Press.

Jacobs, J. (1965) *The Death and Life of Great American Cities*. London: Penguin Books.

James, W. (1950) *The Principles of Psychology*, vols. 1 and 2. New York: Dover Publications.

Janis, I.L. (1982) *Groupthink: Psychological Studies of Policy Decisions and Fiascos*. Boston: Houghton Mifflin.

Knez, M. and Camerer, C. (1994) "Creating expectational assets in the laboratory: coordination in "weakest link" games. *Strategic Management Journal* 15:101–119.

Kogut, B. and Zander, U. (1992) "Knowledge of the firm, combinative capabilities and the replication of technology." *Organization Science* 3:383–397.

Kogut, B. and Zander, U. (1993) "Knowledge of the firm and the evolutionary theory of the multinational corporation." *Journal of International Business Studies* 24:625–645.

Kogut, B. and Zander, U. (1995) "Knowledge, market failure and the multinational enterprise: a reply." *Journal of International Business Studies* 26:417–426.

Kogut, B. and Zander, U. (1996) "What do firms do? Coordination, identity and learning." *Organization Science* 7:502–518.

Krackhardt, D. (1989) "Graph theoretical dimen-sions of informal organization." Paper presented at the annual meeting of the Academy of Management, Washington, DC.

Krackhardt, D. (1992) "The strength of strong ties, in N. Nohria and R.G. Eccles (eds.), *Networks and Organizations: Structure, Form and Action*, pp. 216–239. Boston: Harvard Business School Press.

Kramer, R.M. and Goldman, L. (1995) "Helping the group or helping yourself? Social motives and group identity in resource dilemmas, in D.A. Schroeder (ed.), *Social Dilemmas*, pp. 49–68. New York: Praeger.

Kramer, R.M., Brewer, M.B., and Hanna, B.A. (1996) "Collective trust and collective action: the decision to trust as a social decision," in R.M. Kramer and T.R. Tyler (eds.), *Trust in Organizations. Frontiers of Theory and Research*, pp. 357–389. Thousand Oaks, CA: Sage.

Kuhn, T.S. (1970) *The Structure of Scientific Revolutions*, 2d ed. Chicago: University of Chicago Press.

Larson, A. (1992) "Network dyads in entrepreneurial settings: a study of the governance of exchange relations." *Administrative Science Quarterly* 37:76–104.

Lawler, E.J. and Yoon, J. (1996) "Commitment in exchange relations: Test of a theory of relational cohesion." *American Sociological Review* 61:89–108.

Lawrence, P.R. and Lorsch, J.W. (1967) *Organization and Environment: Managing Differentiation and Integration*. Boston: Division of Research, Graduate School of Business Administration, Harvard University.

Leonard-Barton, D. (1995) *Wellsprings of Knowledge: Building and Sustaining the Sources of Innovation*. Boston: Harvard Business School Press.

Lewicki, R.J. and Bunker, B.B. (1996) "Developing and maintaining trust in work relationships," in R.M. Kramer and T.M. Tyler (eds.), *Trust in Organizations: Frontiers of Theory and Research*, pp. 114–139. Thousand Oaks, CA: Sage.

Lindenberg, S. (1996) "Constitutionalism versus relationalism: two views of rational choice sociology," in J. Clark (ed.), *James S. Coleman*, pp. 229–311. London: Falmer Press.

Lippman, S.A. and Rumelt, R.P. (1982) "Uncertain imitability: an analysis of interfirm differences in efficiency under competition." *Bell Journal of Economics* 13:418–438.

Loasby, B. (1991) *Equilibrium and Evolution: An Exploration of Connecting Principles in Economics*. Manchester: Manchester University Press.

Loury, G.C. (1977) "A dynamic theory of racial income differences, in P.A. Wallace and A.M. La-

Monde (eds.), *Women, Minorities and Employment Discrimination*, pp. 153–186. Lexington, MA: Lexington Books.

Loury, G. (1987) "Why should we care about group inequality?" *Social Philosophy and Policy* 5:249–271.

Luhmann, N. (1979) *Trust and Power*. Chichester: Wiley.

March, J.G. and Olsen, J.P. (1976) *Ambiguity and Choice in Organizations*. Bergen: Universitetsforlaget.

March, J.G. and Simon, H.A. (1958) *Organizations*. New York: Wiley.

Marshall, A. (1965) *Principles of Economics*. London: Macmillan.

Masten, S.E., Meehan, J.W., and Snyder, E.A. (1991) "The costs of organization." *Journal of Law Economics and Organization* 7:1–25.

Mauss, M. (1954) *The Gift*. New York: Free Press.

Merton, R.K. (1968) *Social Theory and Social Structure*. New York: Free Press. (First published in 1948.)

Mintzberg, H. (1973) *The Nature of Managerial Work*. New York: Harper and Row.

Mintzberg, H. (1979) *The Structuring of Organizations*. Englewood Cliffs, NJ: Prentice-Hall.

Mishira, A.K. (1996) "Organizational responses to crisis. The centrality of trust," in R.M. Kramer and T.M. Tyler (eds.), *Trust in Organizations*, pp. 261–287. Thousand Oaks, CA: Sage.

Misztal, B. (1996) *Trust in Modern Societies*. Cambridge: Polity Press.

Monteverde, K. (1995) "Applying resource-based strategic analysis: Making the model more accessible to practitioners." Working paper no. 95-1, Department of Management and Information Systems, St. Joseph's University, Philadelphia.

Moran, P. and Ghoshal, S. (1996) "Value creation by firms," in J.B. Keys and L.N. Dosier (eds.), *Academy of Management Best Paper Proceedings*, pp. 41–45.

Mullins, N. (1973) *Theories and Theory Groups in Contemporary American Sociology*. New York: Harper and Row.

Nahapiet, J.E. (1988) "The rhetoric and reality of an accounting change: A study of resource allocation in the NHS." *Accounting, Organizations and Society* 13:333–358.

Nahapiet, J.E. (1996) "Managing relationships with global clients: Value creation through cross-border networks." Paper presented at the 16th annual conference of the Strategic Management Society, Phoenix, AZ.

Nelson, R.R. and Winter, S.G. (1982) *An Evolutionary Theory of Economic Change*. Boston: Belknap.

Nisbet, R.A. (1969) *Social Change and History: Aspects of the Western Theory of Development*. London: Oxford University Press.

Nohria, N. (1992) "Information and search in the creation of new business ventures," in N. Nohria and R.G. Eccles (eds.), *Networks and Organizations: Structure, Form and Action*, pp. 240–261. Boston: Harvard Business School Press.

Nohria, N. and Eccles, R.G. (1992) "Face-to-face: making network organizations work," in N. Nohria and R.G. Eccles (eds.), *Networks and Organizations: Structure, Form and Action*, pp. 288–308. Boston: Harvard Business School Press.

Nonaka, I. and Takeuchi, H. (1995) *The Knowledge Creating Company*. New York: Oxford University Press.

North, D.C. (1990) *Institutions, Institutional Change and Economic Performance*. Cambridge: Cambridge University Press.

Orr, J. (1990) "Sharing knowledge, celebrating identity: community memory in a service culture," in D. Middleton and D. Edwards (eds.), *Collective Remembering*, pp. 169–189. London: Sage.

Ouchi, W.G. (1981) *Theory Z: How American Business Can Meet the Japanese Challenge*. Reading, MA: Addison-Wesley.

Pascale, R. (1990) *Managing on the Edge: How the Smartest Companies Use Conflict to Stay Ahead*. New York: Simon and Schuster.

Penrose, E. (1959) *The Theory of the Growth of the Firm*. Oxford: Basil Blackwell.

Perrow, C. (1984) *Normal Accidents*. New York: Basic Books.

Pettigrew, A.M. (1973) *The Politics of Organizational Decision Making*. London: Tavistock.

Pitelis, C. (1993) "Transaction costs, markets and hierarchies: the issues," in C. Pitelis (ed.), *Transaction Costs, Markets and Hierarchies*, pp. 7–19. Oxford: Basil Blackwell.

Polanyi, M. (1962) *Personal Knowledge: Towards a Post-critical Philosophy*. London: Routledge and Kegan Paul. (First published in 1958.)

Polanyi, M. (1967) *The Tacit Dimension*. London: Routledge and Kegan Paul. (First published in 1966.)

Pondy, L.R. and Mitroff, I.I. (1979) "Beyond open systems models of organizations." *Research in Organization Behavior* 1:3–39.

Powell, W.W. (1996) "Trust based form of governance," in R.M. Kramer and T.R. Tyler (eds.), *Trust in Organizations: Frontiers of Theory and Research*, pp. 51–67. Thousand Oaks, CA: Sage.

Prahalad, C.K. and Hamel, G. (1990) "The core competence of the organization." *Harvard Business Review* 68:79–91.

Prescott, E.C. and Visscher, M. (1980) "Organization capital." *Journal of Political Economy* 88:446–461.

Putnam, R.D. (1993) "The prosperous community: social capital and public life." *American Prospect* 13:35–42.

Putnam, R.D. (1995) "Bowling alone: America's declining social capital." *Journal of Democracy* 6:65–78.

Quinn, J.B. (1992) *Intelligent Enterprise*. New York: Free Press.

Quinn, J.B., Anderson, P., and Finkelstein, S. (1996) Leveraging intellect. *Academy of Management Executive* 10:7–27.

Reed, R. and DeFillippi, R.J. (1990) "Causal ambiguity, barriers to imitation and sustainable competitive advantage." *Academy of Management Review* 15:88–102.

Ring, P.S. and Van de Ven, A.H. (1992) "Structuring cooperative relationships between organizations." *Strategic Management Journal* 13:483–498.

Ring, P.S. and Van de Ven, A.H. (1994) "Developmental processes of cooperative interorganizational relationships." *Academy of Management Review* 19:90–118.

Roy, D.F. (1960) "Banana time: job satisfaction and informal interaction." *Human Organization* 18:156–168.

Ryle, G. (1949) *The Concept of Mind*. London: Hutchinson.

Sako, M. (1992) *Prices, Quality and Trust: Interfirm Relations in Britain and Japan*. New York: Cambridge University Press.

Schumpeter, J.A. (1934) *The Theory of Economic Development: An Inquiry into Profits, Capital, Credit, Interest and the Business Cycle*. Cambridge, MA: Harvard University Press. (Reprinted in 1962.)

Schutz, A. (1970) *On Phenomenology and Social Relations*. Chicago: University of Chicago Press.

Scott, J. (1991) *School Network Analysis: A Handbook*. London: Sage.

Simon, H.A. (1991a) "Bounded rationality and organizational learning." *Organization Science* 2:125–134.

Simon, H.A. (1991b) "Organizations and markets." *Journal of Economic Perspectives* 5(2):25–44.

Simon, L. and Davies, G. (1996) "A contextual approach to management learning." *Organization Studies* 17:269–289.

Slocum, K.R. (1994) "Foreword," in G. von Krogh and J. Roos (eds.), *Organizational Epistemology*, p. ix. Basingstoke: Macmillan.

Smith, A. (1986) *The Wealth of Nations*, bks. 1–3. London: Penguin Books. (First published in 1776.)

Spender, J-C. (1994) "Knowing, managing and learning: a dynamic managerial epistemology." *Management Learning* 25:387–412.

Spender, J-C. (1996) "Making knowledge the basis of a dynamic theory of the firm." *Strategic Management Journal* 17(S2):45–62.

Starbuck, W.H. (1992) "Learning by knowledge intensive firms." *Journal of Management Studies* 29:713–740.

Starbuck, W.H. (1994) "Keeping a butterfly and elephant in a house of cards: the elements of exceptional success." *Journal of Management Studies* 30:885–922.

Szulanski, G. (1996) "Exploring internal stickiness: impediments to the transfer of best practice within the firm." *Strategic Management Journal* 17(S2):27–44.

Tajfel, H., ed. (1982) *Social Relations and Intergroup Relations*. Cambridge, MA: Cambridge University Press.

Teece, D.J. (1988) "Technological change and the nature of the firm," in G. Dosi, C. Freeman, R. Nelson, G. Silverberg, and L. Soete (eds.), *Technical Change and Economic Theory*, pp. 256–281. New York: Pinter.

Thompson, J.D. (1967) *Organizations in Action*. New York: McGraw-Hill.

Tichy, N.M., Tushman, M.L., and Fombrun, C. (1979) "Social network analysis for organizations." *Academy of Management Review* 4:507–519.

Turner, B.A. (1976) "The organizational and interorganizational development of disasters." *Administrative Science Quarterly* 21:378–397.

Tyler, T.R. and Kramer, R.M. (1996) "Whither trust?" in R.M. Kramer and T.R. Tyler (eds.), *Trust in Organizations: Frontiers of Theory and Research*, pp. 1–15. Thousand Oaks, CA: Sage.

Van Maanen. J. and Kunda, G. (1989) "Real feelings: emotional expression and organizational culture." *Research in Organizational Behavior* 11:43–103.

Walsh, J.P. (1995) "Managerial and organizational cognition: notes from a trip down memory lane." *Organization Science* 6:280–321.

Wasserman, S. and Faust, K. (1994) *Social Network Analysis: Methods and Applications*. Cambridge: Cambridge University Press.

Weick, K.E. (1995) *Sensemaking in Organizations*. London: Sage.

Weick, K.E. and Roberts, K.H. (1993) "Collective mind in organizations: Heedful interrelating on flight decks." *Administrative Science Quarterly* 38:357–381.

Williamson, O.E. (1975) *Markets and Hierarchies: Analysis and Antitrust Implications*. New York: Free Press.

Williamson, O.E. (1981) "The economics of organization: the transaction cost approach." *American Journal of Sociology* 87:548–577.

Williamson, O.E. (1985) *The Economic Institutions of Capitalism*. New York: Free Press.

Winter, S.G. (1987) "Knowledge and competence as strategic assets," in D.J. Teece (ed.), *The Competitive Challenge: Strategy for Industrial Innovation and Renewal*, pp. 159–184. New York: Harper and Row.

Zajac, E.J. and Olsen, C.P. (1993) "From transaction cost to transactional value analysis: implications for the study of interorganizational strategies. *Journal of Management Studies* 30: 131–146.

Zander, U. and Kogut, B. (1995) "Knowledge and the speed of transfer and imitation of organizational capabilities: an empirical test." *Organization Science* 6:76–92.

Zucker, L.G., Darby, M.R., Brewer, M.B., and Peng, Y. (1996) "Collaboration structures and information dilemmas in biotechnology: organization boundaries as trust production," in R.M. Kramer and T.R. Tyler (eds.), *Trust in Organizations: Frontiers of Theory and Research*, pp. 90–113. Thousand Oaks, CA: Sage.

Zuckerman, H. (1988) "The sociology of science," in N.J. Smelser (ed.), *Handbook of Sociology*, pp. 511–574. Beverly Hills, CA: Sage.

39

The Role of Social Capital and Organizational Knowledge in Enhancing Entrepreneurial Opportunities in High-Technology Environments

Donna Marie De Carolis

Creating, developing, and exploiting entrepreneurial opportunities in organizations comprise some of the most important and complicated managerial responsibilities. The importance lies in the fact that organizational renewal is a prerequisite for survival particularly in dynamic industry environments. The complication lies in the mystery of entrepreneurship itself, which defies traditional managerial approaches.

The challenge of managing and exploiting entrepreneurial opportunities is particularly acute in firms operating in high-technology environments. The processes and routines for generating, exchanging, and combining knowledge are in a continual state of ferment, as knowledge in the industry is changing at a fast pace. As science and technology advance, so too should the state of organizational knowledge. Consequently, while firms are struggling to establish a design or template for assimilating knowledge, the requisite knowledge itself is in a continual state of flux, leaving open the possibility that any selected design may be inappropriate. The ephemeral knowledge bases in technology-intensive environments require that firms rely in part on social capital as a capacity for action.

Social capital is being increasingly recognized as a valuable intangible asset for firms, as it provides networks of relationships that can lead to competitive advantage. Moreover, social capital is instrumental in creating organizational knowledge—the collective knowledge of the organization. Organizational knowledge contributes to the ongoing innovation processes in established capabilities and is the genesis of opportunities in new market segments and new capabilities. Unlike physical assets, organizational knowledge is intangible and fluid and resides everywhere, as it is embodied not only in the social collectivity of a firm's employees but also among its networks of suppliers, customers, and alliances.

Firms in high-technology environments must continually re-create knowledge and venture into new areas to survive, as the underlying knowledge base progresses at a rapid pace. Being "entrepreneurial" is an asset in this environment. The concept of entrepreneurship includes not only the creation of entirely new firms but also the pursuit of new opportunities by people within organizations on behalf of the organization (Shane and Venkataraman 2000). The creation, recognition, and exploitation of new ideas within organizations, particularly in dynamic environments, is a necessary ingredient for continued success.

The purpose of this chapter is to explore the relationships among social capital, organizational knowledge, and entrepreneurial opportunities in high-technology industries. In so doing, I integrate insights from the resource- and knowledge-based views of the firm, social capital and network theory literature, and a conceptual framework of entrepreneurship. A model is developed based on the premise that the strategic actions of firms are heavily influenced by the social context in which they are embedded (Baum and Dutton 1996, Dacin 1997, Oliver 1997). This social context may be conceptualized as flows of knowledge into an organization that ultimately form the substance of a firm's knowledge stocks (De Carolis and Deeds 1999, Dierickx and Cool 1989).

The chapter proceeds as follows. First, I briefly describe the concepts of social capital and organizational knowledge. Second, I review a rich framework for understanding entrepreneurship and entrepreneurial opportunities. Third, I present and describe the model based on the integration of social capital theory and the entrepreneurship conceptual framework. The chapter closes with implications for research and practice.

Social Capital

In a very general sense, the term "social capital" may be defined as the networks of strong personal relationships that are developed over time and provide the basis for trust, cooperation, and collective action in communities (Jacobs 1965). It has been applied to familial relationships, communities, and firms. Social capital is embedded in networks of acquaintances and may be conceptualized as *network resources* (Ahuja 2000). When applied to firms, network resources are the networks of ties between and among firms and individuals within firms.

Social capital theory suggests that networks of relationships are a valuable resource for the conduct of social affairs (Bourdieu 1986). Networks of relationships include feelings of gratitude, reciprocity, respect, and friendship. These networks are sources of information and opportunities and, in certain circumstances, may be used as a form of social status or reputation.

Social capital has generally been applied in two ways. First, some research views social capital only in terms of the structure of relationships in a network. The second stream of research broadens the scope of social capital to include "the sum of actual and potential resources embedded within, available through and derived from the network of relationships possessed by an individual or social unit. Social capital thus comprises both the network and the assets that may be mobilized through that network" (Nahapiet and Ghoshal 1996, p. 243). It is this second and more encompassing application of social capital that is adopted in this chapter. Social capital provides to firms the ability to *access and deploy potential capabilities*.

The importance of networks of relationships and contacts has been a persistent theme in the entrepreneurship literature. Contacts and networking are traditionally considered one of the key ingredients in the formation of new companies (Vesper 1990). Linkages with suppliers, attorneys, engineers, marketing people, inventors, associations, and the like, can be a critical asset for a new venture, whether occurring within a start-up or an established firm. As mentioned above, this form of social capital is critical to accessing and deploying potential capabilities.

Social capital may also be viewed as an intangible asset contributing to firm performance. According to the resource-based view of the firm, performance is a function of tangible and intangible assets that are rare, valuable, and inimitable (Barney 1991). Social capital manifested in network relationships is a unique resource possessed by a firm that may be difficult to imitate due to causal ambiguity (Lippman and Rumelt 1982) and social complexity (Reed and DiFillippi 1990). A firm's web of relationships accumulates and evolves over time. These relationships involve layers of connections, communication styles, and learning that are tacit in nature, making competitive duplication of these networks virtually impossible.

The importance of network resources for firms in high-technology industries cannot be understated. Network relationships provide opportunities for learning, achieving competitive parity, maintaining customer relationships, accessing complementary assets, and much more. These types of relationships may be crucial for all types of firms in these environments, both incumbents and new entrants.

Social capital is multidimensional, and various authors have chosen to focus on one facet or another (Nahapiet and Ghoshal 1996). In this chapter the focus is on the structural and cognitive aspects of social capital. The structural dimensions of social capital include the network ties and network configuration, while the cognitive dimension includes shared codes, language, and narratives. Each of these dimensions of social capital affects the development of organizational knowledge and entrepreneurial opportunities, as is elaborated upon in a subsequent section.

Organizational Knowledge

The knowledge-based view of the firm focuses on knowledge as the firm's most strategically important resource. In this sense, the knowledge-based view of the firm is an extension of the resource-based view. Organizational knowledge encompasses many types of knowledge at different levels in the firm. Moreover, organizational knowledge is certainly not limited to scientific or technological knowledge. Organizational knowledge represents all types of knowledge such as marketing, administrative, logistical, and so forth. In fact, all activities along the value chain require knowledge and expertise. Some value chain activities are more critical than others and hence form the core competencies of a firm (Prahalad and Hamel 1990).

A clear and widely cited delineation of organizational knowledge is presented by Spender (1996; see figure 39.1). Spender describes how the two most frequently discussed dimensions of knowledge intersect to create four elements of organizational knowledge. First, knowledge can be explicit or tacit. Explicit knowledge is that which is easy to transfer without loss of integrity. It is the codifiable, "blueprint" type of knowledge. Tacit knowledge (Polanyi 1967) is not easily articulated and is very difficult to communicate. Polanyi (1967) suggests that some knowledge always remains tacit, and thus, "knowing" is as important as knowledge.

The second dimension of knowledge reflects the level of analysis: individual or social. Certainly, individual members of an organization

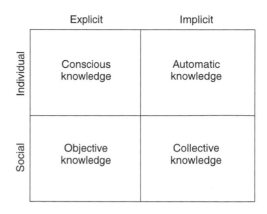

Figure 39.1 Types of organizational knowledge. Adapted from Spender (1996).

possess knowledge with different degrees of capabilities. But it is also true that knowledge resides in collectives, in groups or teams of individuals with the capacity for learning and creating knowledge. Intellectual capital comprises all four types of knowledge.

Although various definitions of "organizational knowledge" exist, I use this term in the sense of the knowledge and knowing capability of a *social collectivity*, encompassing both explicit and implicit knowledge. Organizational knowledge in this model is the collective knowledge of an organization that serves as a catalyst for action and the potential to create competitive advantage. Organizations serve as an institutional context for harnessing and developing knowledge.

A major premise of the knowledge-based view of the firm is that organizations exist to create, transfer, and transform knowledge into competitive advantage (Kogut and Zander 1992). Grant (1996) has suggested that knowledge is transferable and has the capacity to be aggregated. Knowledge resides not only within firm boundaries but also in a network of interacting firms and individual relationships (Kogut and Zander 1996). This network knowledge constitutes part of the organizational knowledge that belongs to a firm. Firms absorb both internal and external knowledge and recombine their current capabilities (Cohen and Levinthal 1990, Kogut and Zander 1992) to create new knowledge. Thus, organizational knowledge, the collective knowledge in an organization, may be viewed partly as an outcome of the knowledge generated within network relationships. This is explored in greater detail in the model that follows.

Entrepreneurship

The phenomena of entrepreneurship have been studied from various disciplines, including but not limited to economics, sociology, organizational theory, and strategic management. The field of entrepreneurship, although a distinctive domain, suffers from the lack of an agreed upon paradigm (Kuhn 1970). As a discipline, there is no generally agreed upon conceptual framework uniting and advancing research in this area.

One of the most recent and powerful conceptual frameworks for entrepreneurship has been advanced by Shane and Venkataraman (2000). They suggest that entrepreneurship may be defined as the "scholarly examination of how, by whom and with what effects opportunities to create future goods and services are discovered, evaluated and exploited. . . . [T]he field involves the study of the *sources* of opportunities; the *processes* of discovery, evaluation and exploitation of opportunities; and the set of *individuals* who discover, evaluate and exploit them" (p. 218).

In this perspective, the field of entrepreneurship encompasses situations, environment, and individuals linked together to generate future products and services. As scholars of organizations, this framework provides us with three research platforms: (1) why, when, and how opportunities for the creation of goods and services come into existence; (2) why, when, and how some people and not others discover and exploit these opportunities; and (3) why, when, and how different modes of action are used to exploit entrepreneurial opportunities. Shane and Venkataraman (2000) also emphasize that entrepreneurship includes (1) the creation of new firms, (2) the sale of opportunities to existing firms, and (3) the creation, discovery, and exploitation of opportunities by people within established firms who pursue those opportunities on behalf of the existing organization. Below I briefly describe the three dimensions of entrepreneurial opportunities.

Existence of Entrepreneurial Opportunity

Entrepreneurial opportunities are those occasions in which new goods, services, raw materials, and organizing methods may be introduced and sold at greater than their cost of production (Casson 1982). Entrepreneurial opportunities are manifested in many ways: new product markets, raw materials, new information, exploitation of market inefficiencies that result from information asymmetry, shifts in the relative costs and benefits of alternative uses for resources, as occurs with political, regulatory or demographic changes (Drucker 1985, Shane and Venkataraman 2000).

The existence of entrepreneurial opportunities depends in large part on information asymmetries. The value of particular resources or the combination of existing resources in different ways may not be apparent. Moreover, different members of society have different beliefs about the value of these resources or potential combination of resources. The entrepreneur's ideas about the existence of an opportunity should differ from others. If not, everyone would pursue the opportunity and any entrepreneurial profit would be quickly dwindled to zero.

Discovery of Entrepreneurial Opportunities

Some people will discover entrepreneurial opportunities and others will not. Two factors account for this difference. First, the discovery of entrepreneurial opportunities requires the possession of prior information necessary to identify an opportunity. To recognize an opportunity, an entrepreneur has to have prior information that is complementary with the new information, which triggers an entrepreneurial conjecture (Kaish and Gilad 1991). Second, it requires the cognitive properties necessary to value such an opportunity. These cognitive properties include the ability to combine existing concepts and information into new ideas. This proclivity varies among individuals.

Decision to Exploit Opportunities

This question addresses why, when, and how some people and not others move into the actual exploitation of the opportunities they discover. The exploitation of opportunities depends on several elements.

First is the nature of the opportunity itself. The individual has to believe that the expected value of the opportunity is greater than the opportunity cost of pursuing other alternatives. Second, individual differences both cognitive and situational are at work here. Exploitation of the opportunity will depend on the availability of financial capital. Stronger social ties to resource providers facilitate the acquisition of resources and enhance the probability of opportunity recognition (Aldrich and Zimmer 1986).

Third, if an individual is able to transfer information and capabilities from prior experience to the new opportunity, this would increase its pursuit. Finally, individuals have different risk perceptions and levels of optimism that necessarily influence their inclination to capitalize on an opportunity.

The conceptual framework of entrepreneurship as described above explains how entrepreneurial opportunities come into existence and are discovered and exploited. The model presented within enhances this framework of entrepreneurship by integrating the concepts of social capital and organizational knowledge. The phenomena of entrepreneurship are thus further elucidated by its interaction with organizational knowledge and by the social context in which it is embedded.

Entrepreneurial Opportunities: The Facilitating Role of Social Capital and Organizational Knowledge

Figure 39.2 illustrates the proposed relationships among social capital, organizational knowledge, and entrepreneurial opportunities. The model suggests that two dimensions of social capital have a direct impact on entrepreneurial opportunities and organizational knowledge (both social objective and collective knowledge). It also displays a reciprocal relationship between orga-

nizational knowledge and entrepreneurial opportunities. The following sections explain the model in detail.

The Structural Dimensions of Social Capital and Entrepreneurial Opportunities

Two structural dimensions of social capital are relevant in explaining entrepreneurial opportunities: network ties and network configuration. Network ties are the basic links from firms to both resources and information. Network configuration refers to how these ties are arranged for diffusion of information and ease of information exchange.

Network Ties and Entrepreneurial Opportunities

Entrepreneurial opportunities are partly attributable to their involvement in network ties. The exposure and interaction provided by these relationships can yield benefits in the form of access, timing, and referrals (Burt 1992). Access is being close to valuable information and know-how. Timing is getting information sooner than a firm normally would or sooner than others. Finally, being involved in a network provides referrals to people in the network who influence the opportunities to combine and exchange knowledge. The access, timing, and referrals are critical in the existence, discovery, and exploitation of opportunities.

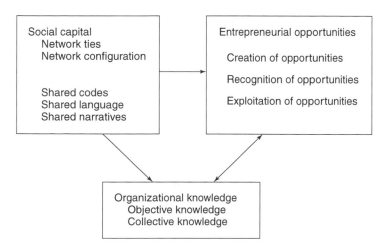

Figure 39.2 A model of the relationships among social capital, intellectual capital, and entrepreneurial opportunities.

The existence of entrepreneurial opportunities as mentioned above depends to a great extent on information asymmetry. Network ties expose firms in knowledge-intensive environments to new science and technology. Organizations exhibit absorptive capacity—the ability to assimilate and use new knowledge that is related to knowledge they already have (Cohen and Levinthal 1990). The access to new science and technology may lead to the source of an entrepreneurial opportunity, particularly if this new learning is combined with existing firm knowledge.

Social capital also exposes a firm more quickly to new knowledge. This makes it possible for firms in high-technology environments that are involved in network relationships to obtain information sooner than others. Timing is an integral part of any technology strategy, and the ability to get information before competitors is a strategic advantage.

Network ties may also directly affect the recognition of entrepreneurial opportunities. Recognition of an opportunity implies the discovery of potential profits to be made from an undervalued resource, a unique combination of resources, or an inefficiency in the industry environment. Networks facilitate information screening and information distribution for member firms. Recognition depends on existing stocks of information. When this existing stock is complementary to new information, the potential to recognize an opportunity is increased.

Referrals are the final benefit of network ties and that which relates directly to the exploitation of entrepreneurial activities. The ties to resource providers may provide avenues to financial capital, technological expertise, or "knowing who." These avenues may help firms to capitalize on an opportunity. There is also empirical evidence suggesting that social ties to resource providers enhance the exploitation of entrepreneurial opportunities (Aldrich and Zimmer 1986).

Network Configuration and Entrepreneurial Opportunities

Network configuration, as mentioned above, refers to the characteristics of the ties themselves, which enable diffusion, search, and the transfer of information among networks through the accessibility they provide to organizational members.

In dynamic industry environments where the underlying nature of science and technology is changing, the configuration of network relationships will affect the creation of new opportunities. The primary purpose of networks is to assist firms in obtaining information that they would not get in their ordinary course of affairs. How an organization's networks are configured can either broaden or limit the scope of information they receive. A network characterized by weak but diverse ties may be important in the *discovery* of entrepreneurial opportunities. Diverse or heterogeneous relationships expose a firm to different ideas, thus expanding its knowledge base (Burt 1982, Granovetter 1973, Rogers 1995). A sparse network may provide few levels of contact, but if these levels are diverse, then the firm is exposed to a diversity of information that could lead to the creation of new opportunities. This could also be the case with dense networks. However, a dense network of relationships could yield duplicative information or produce so much information that the value is diminished, thus dampening entrepreneurial opportunities (Baum et al. 2000).

As opposed to weak ties, strong ties require more attention and maintenance and so are typically fewer in number. Access to information may be constrained by strong ties. The result may, in fact, be less unique information to generate new discoveries.

On the other hand, strong ties increase the probability that tacit information may be transferred. Strong ties may facilitate more communication and intimacy, thus leading to the diffusion of more in-depth knowledge or even knowledge of a tacit nature (Uzzi 1996). Richer patterns of relationships augment the diffusion of ambiguous information (Nahapiet and Ghoshal 1998).

Recognition and exploitation of opportunities may be affected by the nature of the ties within networks. It is suggested that strong ties have a greater impact here than do weak ties. Strong ties are characterized by frequent interaction, an extended history, and mutual confiding (Granovetter 1982). Given this, strong ties promote more discussion and interaction on specific issues and facilitate exchange of detailed information. The strength of this communication then affects both recognition and exploitation of opportunities. Weak ties, although they may provide diversity of information that fosters unique discoveries, are less helpful for recognition and commercialization. The lack of interaction characteristic of weak ties does not help in interpreting the consequences of new opportunities.

The strength of network relationships also affects the exploitation of new opportunities in another way. As mentioned above, a strong network requires greater attention and maintenance, which results in more communication and relationship building. Levels of trust increase as relationships develop. Recall that exploitation of opportunities is partly a function of risk perception and optimism. People sharing similar ideas may also share similar levels of risk perception and optimism through their consistent interactions. For a particular idea or opportunity that has been discovered and recognized, its pursuit may be affected by risk perception and optimism, which may become infectious in a strong network.

To sum up, the structural aspects of social capital play an important role in the entrepreneurial process for firms in dynamic industries. They contribute substantially to the generation of new ideas or opportunities, and to the recognition and commercialization of those opportunities. Network relationships supply channels of know-how and know-who that are invaluable in high-technology environments.

The Cognitive Dimensions of Social Capital and Entrepreneurial Opportunities

Shared codes, languages, and narratives comprise the cognitive dimensions of social capital. Shared codes refer to the mental schemata that organize data into perceptual categories. People working on common projects or issues from similar or disparate backgrounds acquire a common language. Over periods of time, events occur that form the basis of common stories or narratives that serve as a bonding mechanism among people.

Entrepreneurial opportunities appear when new means–end relationships are unmasked. These revelations are a consequence of people sharing ideas and the sharing is facilitated by similar cognitive mechanisms. Common systems of meaning among individuals intensify communications and may lead to the generation of new ideas. The outcomes of interactions may be more than expected. That is, network relationships intended for one purpose may result in the creation of an unintended entrepreneurial opportunity.

The recognition of entrepreneurial opportunities depends, as described above, on information corridors and cognitive properties (Shane and Venkataraman 2000). Information corridors within individuals create stocks of information and provide a framework for recognizing new information. Cognitive properties include the ability to recognize the value of a new means–end relationship. This visualization may be difficult, as the commercial value of many inventions has gone unnoticed by their inventors.

Shared codes, languages, and narratives may have a major impact on the recognition of entrepreneurial opportunities through their interaction with individual information corridors and cognitive properties. Firms acting in isolation may develop cognitive patterns that would prohibit the recognition of opportunities. Exposure and involvement in networks may alter thinking patterns and broaden vision. Being embedded in network relationships could sharpen a firm's ability to recognize the potential of an innovation by breaking through a firm's dominant logic (Bettis and Prahalad 1995).

Finally, the cognitive facets of social capital play a pivotal role in the exploitation of entrepreneurial opportunities. Although network ties may provide the "know-who" for exploitation, it is the cognitive dimensions of social capital that facilitates communication. Risk perception and optimism about potential new opportunities may be affected by shared languages and mental schema. As people begin to think and talk about ideas in similar ways, their level of optimism is affected. So, too, will this enhanced communication influence their risk perception regarding certain opportunities. Depending on the nature of the innovation itself, the common vocabulary, ways of thinking, and history could propel or dampen the pursuit of an innovation. Being actively involved in a network of relationships facilitates risk taking and proactive behavior in high-technology environments and thus contributes to the exploitation of entrepreneurial activities (Barringer and Bluedorn 1999).

Social Capital and Organizational Knowledge

The link between social capital and organizational knowledge is direct and has been addressed by several researchers (e.g., Kogut and Zander 1992, Nahapiet and Ghoshal 1998). Being embedded in network relationships enhances a firm's knowledge by providing the mechanisms for combining and exchanging information (Nahapiet and Ghoshal 1998). The model proposed herein suggests that network relations facilitate both social objective and social collective organizational knowledge.

In high-technology environments, firms engage in environmental scanning for new ideas and trends (Barringer and Bluedorn 1999). Enhancement of social objective knowledge may depend more on the structural dimensions of social capital than on the cognitive dimensions. The impact of the cognitive properties of social capital on a firm's social objective knowledge will probably be minimal due to the nature of the knowledge itself. Objective knowledge is codifiable and easy to communicate without loss of integrity, so similar mental schemata will have minimal impact on its transfer. A firm's network relationships are tantamount to learning about technological and scientific changes in turbulent industries. Network ties will increase exposure to factual information from different sources, thus affecting a firm's objective knowledge.

The characteristics of a network also influence organizational knowledge. Density of networks may provide enormous amounts of information, but sparse networks may reduce redundancy of information (Baum et al. 2000). A loosely configured network affects information diffusion. That is, loose ties may bring together objective knowledge from different sources. Strong ties, characterized, as mentioned above, by their frequent interactions, accumulated histories, and mutual confiding, promote diffusion of ambiguous knowledge, thus directly contributing to the transfer of tacit knowledge from one party to the other.

It is the cognitive aspects of social capital that play a pivotal role in the transfer of tacit information and, consequently, the creation of "collective knowledge." Collective knowledge (Spender 1996) is organizational tacit knowledge, expertise that is d]ifficult to articulate or otherwise communicate. Shared language, codes, and narratives will influence the transfer of this type of knowledge. As members of a network share and interpret information, the flow of tacit knowledge is facilitated. Polanyi (1967) suggested that people know more than they can explain. A major premise of the knowledge-based view of the firm is that organizations are social communities that exist to transform knowledge into economically useful products (Kogut and Zander 1992). This interaction forms the basis of creating and combining knowledge.

Organizational Knowledge and Entrepreneurial Opportunities

The model depicts a reciprocal relationship between the creation of organizational knowledge and entrepreneurial opportunities. Firms have combinative capabilities (Kogut and Zander 1992) defined as the ability to combine new knowledge with existing knowledge. Through combinative capabilities, organizational knowledge is continually created and re-created. Knowledge creation is the backbone of competitive advantage and, in this model, underpins the development of entrepreneurism.

The distinction between organizational knowledge and the discovery of entrepreneurial opportunities is a fine one. In certain circumstances organizational knowledge may in fact be the same as an entrepreneurial opportunity. But, organizational knowledge also contributes to incremental innovations, organizational processes and routines, the evolution of capabilities, and surviving in existing markets. Organizational knowledge thus plays a dual role: it contributes to the evolution of existing product markets and the creation of new ones.

Recall that organizational knowledge is defined as the collective knowledge of an organization that serves as a catalyst for action and the potential to create competitive advantage. Thus, organizational knowledge may serve as a springboard for new means–ends relationships that are identified and act as major sources of new ideas. A firm's knowledge may also be the origin of information not available to other firms. The asymmetric nature of organizational knowledge is critical in the discovery of new opportunities.

Knowledge also plays a role in the recognition and exploitation of these opportunities, as it may potentially broaden cognitive perspectives of organizational actors. Organizational knowledge is manifested not only in technical or scientific knowledge but also in other areas critical to competitive advantage. As mentioned above, a firm's competencies may cover different areas of the value chain. The ability to recognize an opportunity is, in and of itself, an acquired skill that is a component of organizational knowledge, particularly in high-technology environments. Recognition of opportunities depends on an ability to visualize new means–ends relationships.

Although many new ideas or discoveries may occur, not all are recognized as having potential. The tacit dimension of organizational knowledge in particular may enhance the recognition of a discovery's potential. By communicating within specific networks, through the accumulation of learning and expression through shared languages, firms develop the expertise in recognizing opportunities that bring expected profits.

Exploitation of opportunities depends in part on the nature of the innovation itself (Shane and Venkataraman 2000). Innovations and/or new ideas will differ in their expected value. Pursuing a new idea evokes an opportunity cost. Generally, the profits expected from the commercialization of a new idea should be greater than the opportunity cost of other alternatives. Organizational knowledge provides not only the foundation for new ideas but also the wisdom and experience of judging the appropriate opportunities to pursue.

Entrepreneurial opportunities also affect a firm's organizational knowledge. New opportunities are avenues of growth. Firm capabilities evolve over time as firms engage in new activities and new product markets. This knowledge in new areas contributes to the evolution of firm capabilities. Engaging in new product development is often cited as an avenue for development of new capabilities (Leonard-Barton 1995). Even if these development projects are failures, new knowledge is gained that may be useful for future opportunities.

Also, the subsequent commercialization process is a learning experience for the firm and, as such, contributes to the creation of organizational knowledge. Learning how to strategically plan for new opportunities, to finance and market them, to scale up for production, to properly distribute—all of these may differ from project to project. Although not all pursuits will result in success, there is sufficient learning involved throughout every aspect of the commercialization process to contribute to the development of organizational knowledge.

Summary

The underlying premise of the model presented here is that entrepreneurial opportunities are in part a function of social embeddedness. The model links the concepts of social capital, organizational knowledge, and entrepreneurial opportunities in high-technology environments. It is conceptually based on the integration of social network theory and the resource-based and knowledge-based views of the firm.

Competing in high-technology industries is a continuous cycle of regeneration. Knowledge advances at a rapid pace, and product life cycles are notoriously short. Being entrepreneurial is required to survive. Entrepreneurship is defined as the process of discovering, recognizing, and exploiting new opportunities. Many of the mechanisms that advance this process may be found in network relationships and organizational knowledge.

Network ties provide exposure and interaction that yield benefits in the form of access, timing, and referrals. Contacts and relationships allow access to valuable information and know-how. They also facilitate first-mover advantages by getting information to firms more quickly. Social contacts provide referrals to people in the network who influence the opportunities to combine and exchange knowledge. The characteristics of network ties also influence new opportunities. Weak and diverse ties have benefits in terms of information variety, while strong ties create intimacies in developing relationships that can be useful in the future deployment of new capabilities.

Shared codes and languages that emerge from network relationships also affect the creation, recognition, and exploitation of entrepreneurial opportunities. As relationships develop over time, players in these networks develop common vocabularies and jargon that facilitate information sharing. These common mental schemata play critical roles in each component of the entrepreneurial process.

The influence of social capital on a firm's organizational knowledge, defined for the purposes of this chapter as social objective and collective knowledge, is also delineated. In this chapter, I have discussed the implications of the structural and cognitive dimensions of social capital on both the explicit and the implicit forms of organizational knowledge. The argument is that social capital is a strong determinant of an organization's tacit collective knowledge that includes not only scientific and technological know-how but also know-how and know-why in other areas and functions necessary to create, recognize, and pursue new opportunities.

Finally, the model depicts a reciprocal relationship between organizational knowledge and entrepreneurial opportunities. Organizational knowledge provides part of the sustenance for new ideas and aids in their recognition, and exploitation. Moreover, the discovery, recognition and pursuit of new opportunities enhance firm knowledge through the learning that takes place through this process.

There are certainly limitations to the model presented. I have focused exclusively on organizations in high-technology environments. These dynamic and turbulent industries are the perfect venue for entrepreneurial activity for both new and established firms. Clearly, other industry environments are appropriate for entrepreneurial pursuits and no doubt social capital would play a role in these environments also. Another limitation is the focus on collective intellectual capital and its relationship to social capital and entrepreneurial opportunities. There is certainly applicability of individual explicit and implicit knowledge in this model.

By focusing on the interaction of social capital, organizational knowledge, and entrepreneurial opportunities, this model lays the groundwork for further theory development and empirical research. There are numerous theoretical extensions to the model that may be pursued, most notably, as mentioned above, the role of individual knowledge in this process. Are the effects of social capital and the entrepreneurial process the same for individuals as well as the collective? Competing hypotheses could also be developed regarding the nature of the relationships between the structural and cognitive elements of social capital and the entrepreneurial process. This is an area ripe for both theoretical and empirical research.

Finally, the model has important managerial implications. In the beginning of this chapter, I noted that in high-technology industries, managing the process of "being entrepreneurial" is a challenging task. The model presented herein may assist managers in this regard. The model suggests the importance of network relationships, and it is possible for managers to manipulate, evaluate, and develop these types of relationships for key employees. It is also possible for managers to monitor the number and types of relationships and perhaps equate these relationships with the creation, recognition, and pursuit of new opportunities. The model further emphasizes the importance of all types of organizational knowledge to the enhancement of new opportunities. Likewise, the model suggests a positive impact of the pursuit of opportunities, whether a success or failure, on the development of organizational knowledge.

References

Ahuja, G. (2000) "The duality of collaboration: inducements and opportunities in the formation of interfirm linkages." *Strategic Management Journal* 21:317–343.

Aldrich, H. and Zimmer, C. (1986) "Entrepreneurship through social networks," in D. Sexton and R. Smilor (eds.), *The Art and Science of Entrepreneurship*, pp. 3–23. Cambridge, MA: Ballinger.

Barney, J. (1991) "Firm resources and sustained competitive advantage." *Journal of Management* 17:99–120.

Barringer, B.R. and Bluedorn, A.C. (1999) "The relationship between corporate entrepreneurship and strategic management." *Strategic Management Journal* 20(5):421–444.

Baum, J. and Dutton, J. (1996) "The embeddedness of strategy." *Series on Advances in Strategic Management*. Greenwich, CT: JAI Press.

Baum, J., Calabrese, T., and Silverman, B. (2000) "Don't go it alone: alliance network composition and startups' performance in Canadian biotechnology." *Strategic Management Journal* 21(3): 267–294.

Bettis, R.A. and Prahalad, C.K. (1995) The dominant logic: retrospective and extension. *Strategic Management Journal* 16:5–14.

Bourdieu, P. (1986) "The forms of capital," in J.G. Richardson (ed.), *Handbook of Theory and Research for the Sociology of Education*, pp. 241–258. New York: Greenwood.

Burt, R.S. (1982) *Toward a Structural Theory of Action*. New York: Academic Press.

Burt, R.S. (1992) *Structural Holes: The Social Structure of Competition*. Cambridge, MA: Harvard University Press.

Casson, M. (1982) *The Entrepreneur*. Totowa, NJ: Barnes and Nobles Books.

Cohen, W.M. and Levinthal, D.A. (1990) "Absorptive capacity: a new perspective on learning and innovation." *Administrative Science Quarterly* 35:1128–1152.

Dacin, M.T. (1997) "Isomorphism in context: the power and prescription of constitutional norms." *Academy of Management Journal* 40(1):46–81.

De Carolis, D.M. and Deeds, D. (1999) "The impact of stocks and flows of organizational knowledge on firm performance: an empirical investigation of the biotechnology industry." *Strategic Management Journal* 20:953–968.

Dierickx, I. and Cool, K. (1989) "Asset stock accumulation and sustainability of competitive advantage." *Management Science* 35:1504–1511.

Drucker, P. (1985) *Innovation and Entrepreneurship*. New York: Harper and Row.

Granovetter, M.S. (1973) "The strength of weak

ties." *American Journal of Sociology* 78:1360–1380.

Grant, R.M. (1996) "Toward a knowledge-based theory of the firm." *Strategic Management Journal* 17(Special Issue):109–122.

Jacobs, J. (1965) *The Death and Life of Great American Cities.* London: Penguin Books.

Kaish, S. and Gilad, B. (1991) "Characteristics of opportunities search of entrepreneurs versus executives: sources, interests and general alertness." *Journal of Business Venturing* 6:45–61.

Kogut, B. and Zander, U. (1992) "Knowledge of the firm, combinative capabilities, and the replication of technology." *Organization Science* 3:383–397.

Kuhn, T. (1970) *The Structure of Scientific Revolutions.* Chicago: University of Chicago Press.

Leonard-Barton, D. (1995) *Wellsprings of Knowledge: Building and Sustaining the Sources of Innovation.* Boston: Harvard Business School Press.

Lippman, S.A. and Rumelt, R. (1982) "Uncertainty imitability: an analysis of interfirm differences in efficiency under competition." *Bell Journal of Economics* 13:418–438.

Nahapiet, J. and Ghoshal, S. (1998) "Social capital, intellectual capital and the organizational advantage." *Academy of Management Review* 23(2): 242–266.

Oliver, C. (1997) "Sustainable competitive advantage: combining institutional and resource-based views." *Strategic Management Journal* 18(9): 697–713.

Polanyi, M. (1967) *The Tacit Dimension.* New York: Anchor Day Books.

Prahalad, C.K. and Hamel, G. (1990) "The core competence of the corporation." *Harvard Business Review,* May–June, pp. 79–91.

Reed, R. and DiFillippi, R.J. (1990) "Causal ambiguity, barriers to imitation and sustainable competitive advantage." *Academy of Management Review* 15:88–102.

Rogers, E. (1995) *Diffusion of Innovations.* New York: Free Press.

Shane, S. and Venkataraman, S. (2000) "The promise of entrepreneurship as a field of research." *Academy of Management Review* 25(1):217–226.

Spender, J.-C. (1996) "Making knowledge the basis of a dynamic theory of the firm." *Strategic Management Journal* 17(2):45–62.

Uzzi, B.D. (1996) "The sources and consequences of embeddedness for economic performance of organizations." *American Sociological Review* 61: 674–698.

Vesper, K. (1990) *New Venture Strategies.* Englewood Cliffs, NJ: Prentice Hall.

40

Leveraging Knowledge through Leadership of Organizational Learning

Mary Crossan and John Hulland

The field of strategic management has offered a variety of perspectives on the key considerations in managing the success of the enterprise. Mintzberg et al. (1998) identify organizational learning as one of the many perspectives. Within the organizational learning school, Mintzberg et al. cite the 4I organizational learning framework developed by Crossan et al. (1997) as particularly insightful. This chapter extends the 4I framework to examine how leadership affects knowledge management, organizational learning, strategy, and ultimately the performance of the enterprise. The chapter begins with a brief discussion of the critical connections between the various fields. We then use the 4I framework to anchor the discussion and demonstrate how learning, knowledge, and strategy relate. Next, the role of leadership is incorporated into the model. The methodology for testing the model is then presented and the results discussed. Finally, we address directions for future research.

Strategy, Knowledge, and Organizational Learning

It is a lofty goal to both develop and test theory linking strategy, knowledge, learning, leadership,

and performance. We see our efforts as only a preliminary thrust to connect several fields of inquiry that have much to offer one another. Our efforts are aided by the advanced state of development of the research within each field. The identified strengths and shortcomings in each field suggest the potential for cross-fertilization. This section discusses the potential that exists to link strategy, knowledge, and organizational learning. Subsequent sections extend the discussion to leadership and performance.

Mintzberg et al.'s (1998) extensive review of the strategy literature provides a comprehensive assessment of the state of the field. They identify 10 schools of strategy that fall into three groups: (1) prescriptive—design, planning, and positioning schools; (2) descriptive—entrepreneurial, cognitive, learning, power, cultural, and environmental schools; and (3) configuration—configuration school. Mintzberg et al. critique the first group of prescriptive schools for their overly analytical orientation, top management bias, lack of attention to action and learning, and neglect of the elements that lead to the creation of strategies. However, these criticisms do not negate the importance of the central message of these schools that calls for an alignment between an organization and its environment (Chandler

1962, Venkatraman 1990, Powell 1992). While we acknowledge the need for this alignment, we concur that achieving alignment is a dynamic process that both stresses (Huff et al. 1992) and stretches resources and capabilities (Hamel and Prahalad 1993).

The critique of the descriptive and configuration groups includes lack of development, conceptual vagueness, overstating the perspective, and in most instances, a disregard for the strategic elements offered up by the design, positioning, and planning schools (Mintzberg et al. 1998). The challenge remains to integrate both content and process in strategy models (Pettigrew 1992).

We believe that research on knowledge management has the potential to link strategy content and process (Spender and Grant 1996). As Tsoukas (1996) points out "in order for corporate planners to formulate a strategy they would need, among other things, to be in possession of knowledge which is, to a large extent, fundamentally dispersed" (p. 12). Grant (1996) suggests that "as the markets for resources have become subject to the same dynamically competitive conditions that have afflicted product markets, so knowledge has emerged as the most strategically significant resource of the firm" (p. 375). Although knowledge may be the most strategically significant resource, firms need to learn how to "create and transfer knowledge efficiently within an organizational context" (Kogut and Zander 1992, p. 384). The argument that knowledge management is the central competitive dimension is strikingly similar to DeGeus's (1988) observation that organizational learning may be the only sustainable competitive advantage.

While knowledge management has the potential to inform our understanding of strategy, it has two primary shortcomings. The first arises from the use of the term "knowledge," which is bound up in ontological and epistemological debates about whether anything is "knowable" (Spender 1996). Although these debates are important, they detract from the issue that whether we call something knowledge, or not, may not be the point. Individuals, groups and organizations change, or fail to change their beliefs,[1] and it is this process that we need to understand more fully. That knowledge represents "justified true belief" was first introduced by Plato and has become well accepted (Nonaka and Takeuchi 1995). Whether or not beliefs can be classified as knowl-

edge may be best assessed through the relationship with performance. Notwithstanding the inherent noise associated with performance that needs to be taken into account (time lags, intervening variables, causality), it is expected that a set of beliefs yielding strong performance is more likely to be considered "justified."

The second shortcoming, despite arguments to the contrary (e.g., Nonaka and Takeuchi 1995), is that knowledge management remains largely focused on cognition. Efforts by some theorists to stretch "knowledge" into "knowing" (Blackler 1993, 1995) have attempted to embrace behavioral components in the study of knowledge. In doing so, knowledge, knowing, and doing become more closely aligned with organizational learning. In contrast, organizational learning embraces both cognition and action (Crossan et al. 1995). Knowledge management shares common ground with organizational learning in recognizing the importance of knowledge to the success of the enterprise. Research in knowledge management informs organizational learning but does not capture the ongoing cycle of action taking and knowledge acquisition found in learning theories.

While knowledge management research has been instrumental in such areas as new product development and innovation, it has largely neglected the tension between exploration and exploitation inherent in strategic management given its predominant attention to the issues of exploration and innovation. Miller and Friesen (1982) suggest that research on innovation needs to be linked to strategy, recognizing the important role of momentum. They suggest that there can be dangerous momentum leading to too much or too little innovation. Recognizing and managing the tension between exploration and exploitation is a "primary factor in system survival and prosperity" (March 1991, p. 71). This tension has been variously described as a tension between flexibility and efficiency (Lant and Mezias 1992), variation and selection (Ashby 1960, Hannan and Freeman 1987), and innovation and cost (Tushman and O'Reilly 1996).

Organizational learning theory has also been disconnected from strategy, given its primary focus on the human elements of learning. The absence of strategy in the reviews of the organizational learning literature (Argyris and Schon 1978, 1996, Daft and Huber 1987, Fiol and Lyles 1985, Huber 1991, Levitt and March 1988) is notable. The lack of connection to strategy supports

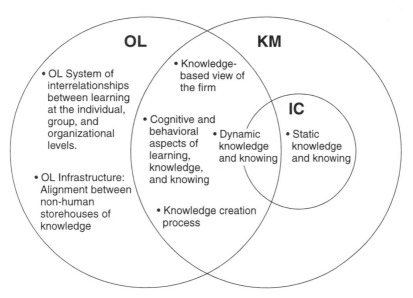

Figure 40.1 Boundaries of the organizational learning, knowledge management, and intellectual capital fields. From Vera and Crossan (2000).

Mintzberg et al.'s (1998) call for redirection of organizational learning research: "[T]he learning school should not be about learning as some kind of holy grail. Mostly it should be about learning as a discipline for elaborating a valued sense of direction—an established strategic perspective—and occasionally about changing that sense of direction, when necessary . . . and that means balancing change with continuity" (p. 226).

Vera and Crossan (2000) present the following depiction of the relationships among organizational learning (OL), knowledge management (KM), and intellectual capital (IC) (see figure 40.1). They suggest that there is significant conceptual overlap when the range of perspectives in each field of research is taken into account. However, organizational learning is less concerned about the static aspects of knowledge and knowing, yet is unique in examining the overall processes and interrelationships among the various levels of the organization.

This brief overview surfaces several key points that need to be addressed by the proposed model. There is a need to integrate content and process—the model needs to acknowledge the strengths of the design, planning, and positioning schools while also addressing their weaknesses through the descriptive theories. Although knowledge is a critical resource, a cognitive focus is insufficient. It is necessary to take into account both cognition and action inherent in learning theories. Finally, the model needs to address the fundamental tension of strategic renewal—the tension between exploration and exploitation. The following section addresses how the 4I framework of organizational learning deals with each of theses areas.

The 4I Framework of Organizational Learning

The 4I framework of organizational learning integrates content and process, addresses both cognitive and behavioral elements, and incorporates the strategic tension between exploration and exploitation. Crossan et al. (1999) describe the framework (shown in table 40.1) as follows:

Four key premises or assumptions form the underpinnings of this framework and support one central proposition.

Premise 1: Organizational learning involves a tension between assimilating new learning (exploration) and using what has been learned (exploitation).

Premise 2: Organizational learning is multi-level: individual, group, and organization.

TABLE 40.1 Learning/Renewal in Organizations: Four Processes Through Three Levels

Level	Process	Inputs/Outcomes
Individual	Intuiting	Experiences
		Images
		Metaphors
Group	Interpreting	Language
		Cognitive map
		Conversation/dialogue
Organization	Integrating	Shared understandings
		Mutual adjustment
		Interactive systems
	Institutionalizing	Routines
		Diagnostic systems
		Rules and procedures

From Crossan et al. (1999).

Premise 3: The three levels of organizational learning are linked by social and psychological processes: intuiting, interpreting, integrating, and institutionalizing (4I's).

Premise 4: Cognition affects action (and vice versa).

Proposition: The 4I's are related in feedforward and feed-back processes across the levels. (p. 523)

The learning processes are defined as follows:

Intuiting is the preconscious recognition of the pattern and/or possibilities inherent in a personal stream of experience [Weick 1995b, 25]. This process can affect the intuitive individual's actions, but it only affects others when they attempt to (inter)act with that individual. *Interpreting* is the explaining, through words and/or actions, of an insight or idea to one's self and to others. This process goes from the preverbal to the verbal resulting in the development of language. *Integrating* is the process of developing shared understanding among individuals and taking of coordinated action through mutual adjustment. Dialogue and joint action are crucial to the development of shared understanding. This process will initially be ad hoc and informal, but if the coordinated action-taking is recurring and significant, it will be

institutionalized. *Institutionalizing* is the process of ensuring that routinized actions occur. Tasks are defined, actions specified and organizational mechanisms put in place to ensure that certain actions occur. Institutionalizing is the process of embedding learning that has occurred by individuals and groups into the organization and includes systems, structures, procedures and strategy. (p. 525)

Crossan and Hulland (1998) operationalized the 4I framework in the form of the strategic learning assessment map (SLAM) shown in figure 40.2. The SLAM examines the stocks and flows of knowledge in a comprehensive organizational learning system. Consistent with the 4I framework, it suggests that knowledge resides at three levels, individual, group, and organization, with flows between the levels. Along the diagonal are the stocks of knowledge at each level: individual human capital and capability, group dynamics and shared understanding, and, at the organizational level, strategic alignment. We acknowledge that there are "flows" within a level but use the stock/flow distinction to denote the difference between flows within a level (stocks) and flows across levels (flows). Our research has suggested that it is the transference of learning across levels that is one of the greatest challenges in organizational learning, hence the importance of the stock/flow distinction.

The organization level is conceptualized as the knowledge and learning that has become embedded in the organization. It represents the repos-

LEVEL	*PROCESS*	INPUTS/OUTCOMES
INDIVIDUAL	*Intuiting*	Experiences, Images/Metaphors
GROUP	*Interpreting*	Language, Cognitive map/ Conversation, dialogue
	Integrating	Shared understandings, Mutual adjustment/ Interactive systems
ORGANIZATION	*Institutionalizing*	Routines, Diagnostic systems/ Rules & Procedures

Figure 40.2 Strategic learning assessment map. From Crossan and Hulland (1998).

itory of knowledge in such nonhuman elements as structures, systems, procedures, routines, and strategy. The organization level is consistent with the design, planning, and positioning schools of strategy noted by Mintzberg et al. (1998), since it recognizes that these nonhuman elements need to be aligned with the competitive environment.

The SLAM model recognizes that the competitive position of the firm is dynamic and therefore is modified over time by the feed-forward of knowledge from individuals and groups to the organization. The model has no top management bias on the feed-forward process. The flow across levels is not a hierarchical flow, but a flow from individuals to groups to the organization. However, as we discuss in subsequent sections, there is an important role for leadership in the feed-forward flow.

The model also recognizes the critical tension between exploration and exploitation (March 1991). While the firm innovates and renews itself through the feed-forward process, it must also exploit what it has learned through the feedback process. Organization level systems, structures, strategies, and routines can guide the learning of individuals and groups through the feedback process. For example organization level reward systems will affect individual learning by guiding and reinforcing what individuals pay attention to and how they spend their time. Organization structures will affect who talks to whom in the organization.

Crossan and Hulland (1998) have assessed the validity and reliability of SLAM and have extended the work to test several hypotheses about the relationship between the stocks and flows of organizational learning and business performance. Bontis et al. (2000) found a positive relationship between knowledge stocks at all levels and business performance, and that the misalignment of knowledge stocks and flows in an overall organizational learning system is negatively associated with business performance. This chapter extends the 4I framework and SLAM to develop conceptual links to leadership. As described in the following section, leadership is viewed as the catalyst for organizational learning.

Leadership and Organizational Learning

House and Aditya (1997) provide a comprehensive review of the leadership literature, with an overview of the prominent theories and paradigms. They discuss the leadership trait paradigm, the leader behavior paradigm, contingency theories, and several recent theoretical developments, including leader member exchange theory, implicit leadership theory, and neocharismatic theory. Yet with over 3,000 studies of leadership (Bass 1990), there still remain important questions to be addressed.

Based on their review of the literature, House and Aditya (1997) propose several questions for future research. They suggest the following as one of the more important questions: "What are the processes by which top managers have their effects on, for instance, decision choice, policy formulation and direction, development and management of infrastructures, motivation and inspiration, and representation to critical constituencies?" (p. 448). We contend that the leadership literature has not addressed this question because the lens through which leadership has been viewed does not take into account organizational learning and knowledge management.

The leadership literature has focused on leaders, followers, their interrelationship and the behaviors of leaders. For example, Yukl (1994) identifies 14 behaviors of effective leaders: supporting, consulting, delegating, recognizing, rewarding, motivating, managing conflict and team building, developing, clarifying, planning and organizing, problem solving, informing, monitoring, representing, and networking. While these behaviors may be important, the question remains, What end do they serve? At one extreme, these behaviors may be viewed as quite task or industry specific. Planning and organizing in the context of software development will be quite different than planning and organizing in oil and gas exploration, for example. Without going to the detail of industry- and task-specific behaviors, we suggest that a more general frame can be placed on these leadership behaviors by tying them to the overall management of the organizational learning infrastructure. In response to the question, What end do they serve? it can be answered that these leadership behaviors support the management of the stocks and flows of the organizational learning system. And it is this system that is the process and infrastructure for strategy formulation and implementation.

Beyond the question of the activity of leaders, there is also a question of who should be considered as a leader. In the field of organizational learning, leadership entered the discussion as a proxy for the organization. Initial concepts of leadership in organizational learning were based on the notion of the dominant coalition. Organizational learning theorists had suggested that the senior management team, or dominant coalition, was in fact the organization level of organizational learning (Duncan and Weiss 1979, Hambrick and Mason 1984). In contrast, other theorists (Hedberg 1981, Shrivastava 1983) suggested that the organization level encompassed all of the nonhuman elements of the organization, as described in SLAM.

In the initial stages of this research we wrestled with the role of leadership and its relationship to the organizational level of learning. We concurred with Duncan and Weiss (1979) that the dominant coalition has a significant impact on organizational learning, yet we also agreed with Hedberg (1981) and Shrivastava (1983) on the need to account for the embedded aspects of organizational learning. Therefore, our original conceptualization positioned leadership as a specific type of group with an impact on organizational learning. This notion was tested through case-based research and the use of survey methodology. Based on this earlier research, the theory was revised to examine leadership as it relates to the specific stocks and flows of organizational learning. The reconceptualization acknowledges that acts of leadership can occur throughout the organization, not simply at the senior management levels.

Figure 40.3 shows five leadership constructs affecting each of the five organizational learning constructs shown in SLAM. Leadership of individual and group-level learning relates to the ways in which the leader supports or undermines learning at that level. Leadership of the organization level refers to the more typical domain of strategic management. It captures whether the leader understands the competitive challenges of the industry and ensures that the systems, structure, and strategy are aligned. The leadership of the feed-forward flow represents the degree that the leader supports the flow of ideas in the organization and enables individuals to make a contribution to the organization. Leadership of the feedback flow represents the degree that the leader ensures that the nonhuman elements of the organization, such as procedures, routines, and systems, support learning at the individual and group levels.

Figure 40.3 depicts a positive relationship between each leadership construct and the corresponding organizational learning behavior construct. Strong leadership of individual learning is expected to lead to strong individual learning, for example. All of the organizational learning constructs are expected to have a positive association with performance. Performance is broken down into employee satisfaction, customer satisfaction, and financial performance. The three

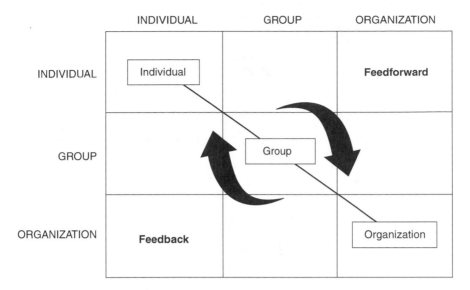

Figure 40.3 Organizational learning leadership, organizational learning behaviors, and satisfaction outcomes.

performance constructs are also expected to be interrelated. There is evidence to suggest that employee satisfaction leads to customer satisfaction, which should lead to financial performance (Rucci et al. 1998).

In summary, we suggest that the infrastructure through which knowledge flows in the organization is the mechanism for strategic renewal, enabling organizations to manage the tension between exploration (feed-forward) and exploitation (feedback). We also suggest that leadership needs to be reexamined in light of its role in managing the overall organizational learning infrastructure. In testing these relationships, we employed survey methodology to build on the previous empirical research. In the following section, we discuss the methodology.

Methodology

Survey methodology was used to test the model. Since other elements of the SLAM had undergone previous testing and analysis (Crossan and Hulland 1998), the questionnaire was expanded to include the leadership scales. Sample questionnaire items for each scale are listed in table 40.2. The questionnaire was administered to a random sample of employees (working at all levels) from one large financial institution. The survey was endorsed by the senior management team, and employees were encouraged to complete the questionnaire. Procedures were established to ensure confidentiality to all respondents. A total of 336 surveys were returned, representing a 50% response rate.

Data analysis was conducted using partial least squares (PLS), a causal modeling approach developed by Wold (1985). The main purpose of PLS is to maximize the variance explained of endogenous constructs. Like LISREL, PLS allows the researcher to analyze simultaneously all paths between constructs and the relationships between constructs and their indicators. In contrast to LISREL, PLS makes no assumptions about multivariate normality in the data, and it works with small samples. Generally speaking, PLS is ideally suited to the early stages of theory building and testing, and it has been used to explore issues of interest in many functional areas of business research (e.g., Smith and Barclay 1997, Birkinshaw et al. 1995, Staples et al. 1999). For a good introduction to PLS use, see Barclay et al. (1995).

To develop a PLS model, the structural paths, measurement model measures (indicators in PLS terminology), and construct relationships must first be specified. The constructs used in our model are shown in the figure 40.3, along with the paths between constructs to be estimated by PLS.

TABLE 40.2 Sample Items

Leadership

IIL	Management supports the learning and development of employees.
IIL	Management encourages experimentation and innovation.
GGL	Management fosters the acceptance of diversity within the group.
GGL	Management helps to create a shared mindset.
OOL	Management understands the competitive challenges of our industry.
OOL	Management ensures we have the right systems to support our strategy.
FBL	Management ensures that we have the systems, processes, and procedures we need to do our job.
FBL	Decisions made by management are well communicated to employees.
FFL	Management ensures employees can make a difference in the organization.
FFL	Employees feel they have input into the critical decisions made by management.

Behavior

IIB	Employees are current and knowledgeable about their work.
IIB	Employees have a high level of energy at work.
GGB	Different points of view are encouraged in my group.
GGB	We resolve conflict effectively in my group.
OOB	"X" has a strategy that positions us well for the future.
OOB	The organizational structure supports "X's" strategic direction.
FBB	Employees are directed by the vision and strategy of "X."
FBB	Key information is readily available through our information systems.
FFB	Ideas generated by the group are used to improve products, services, and processes.
FFB	Employees have input into strategy development.

Satisfaction

Employee	Employees are fulfilled by their work.
Employee	Employees are very satisfied working here.
Customer	"X" meets its customers' needs.
Shareholder	"X" provides a good return to its shareholders.
Shareholder	"X" meets its financial targets.

Results

Although PLS estimates parameters for both the links between measures and constructs (loadings) and between different constructs (path coefficients) simultaneously, a PLS model is usually analyzed and interpreted in two stages: (1) an assessment of the reliability and validity of the measurement model, followed by (2) an assessment of the structural model (Hulland 1999). This sequence ensures that the researcher has reliable and valid measures of constructs before attempting to draw conclusions about the nature of relationships among constructs.

The Measurement Model

Table 40.3 reports, by construct, the numbers of measurement items employed, the internal consistency (InC) of the measures, and both the average variance extracted (AVE), and root AVE values (Fornell and Larcker 1981). In general, researchers look for InC values that exceed 0.70 (Nunnally 1978). As table 40.3 shows, all of the sets of measures used in this study exceed the recommended threshold. Thus, composite reliability appears to be strong. Furthermore, the AVE values, which assess the average variance shared between a construct and its measures, appear reasonable (i.e., AVE > 0.5, and root AVE > 0.7). Taken together, these observations indicate an acceptable measurement model.

The Structural Model

The path coefficients calculated by PLS are standardized β's, like those produced by ordinary least squares regression. As already noted, the primary objective of PLS is to maximize the variance explained in the endogenous (dependent) constructs in a model. Thus, model performance is determined by examining the R^2 values on the endogenous constructs and the significance of the paths leading to these constructs.

TABLE 40.3 Composite Reliability and Average Variance
Extracted Measures, by Construct

Construct	n_{items}	IC	AVE	$\sqrt{AVE}$
Leadership				
II	4	.92	.74	.86
GG	5	.95	.80	.89
OO	3	.89	.74	.86
FB	4	.92	.73	.86
FF	3	.90	.76	.87
Behavior				
II	8	.90	.53	.73
GG	7	.88	.52	.72
OO	6	.89	.57	.76
FB	11	.92	.52	.72
FF	6	.85	.49	.70
Satisfaction				
Employee	6	.91	.63	.80
Customer	1	1.00	1.00	1.00
Shareholder	4	.86	.60	.78

The results of the structural model are summarized in tables 40.4–40.6. Tables 40.4 and 40.5 indicate the estimated direct path coefficients between constructs, whereas table 40.6 also includes indirect effects. For example, II behavior (IIB) has a direct effect on customer satisfaction (−0.06), but it also has an indirect effect via the employee satisfaction construct. This latter effect is estimated by multiplying the IIB–employee satisfaction path coefficient (0.29) by the employee satisfaction–customer satisfaction path coefficient (0.22) to determine the indirect effect (0.06). The total effect shown in table 40.6 is then simply the sum of the direct and indirect effects.

The estimated model explains a great deal of variance in all of the endogenous constructs. The five behavior constructs had R^2 (squared coefficients from table 40.4) values ranging between 31% (in the case of IIB) and 55% (FBB). Furthermore, the variances explained for the em-

ployee, customer, and shareholder satisfaction constructs were, respectively, 56%, 39%, and 55% (table 40.5). Given the fact that there are a large number of other factors that could affect these latter constructs, the variance explained by the relatively parsimonious PLS model shown in figure 40.3 is quite substantial.

Because the estimated path coefficients are standardized βs, they can be directly compared to one another. For example, the paths leading into employee satisfaction indicate that feedback behavior explains more than twice the variance in employee satisfaction than does feed-forward behavior (i.e., .34/.13 = 2.6). Thus, the results shown in table 40.6 can be used to assess the relative importance of the different drivers that can potentially affect the satisfaction constructs. Employee satisfaction is most strongly (and positively) affected by IIB, GGB, and FBB. Customer satisfaction is most heavily influenced by OOB and employee satisfaction. Finally, the key driv-

TABLE 40.4 Effects of Leadership on Organizational Learning Behaviors

Leadership Construct	OL Behavior Construct	Path Coefficient
IIL	IIB	.56
GGL	GGB	.69
OOL	OOB	.66
FBL	FBB	.74
FFL	FFB	.67

TABLE 40.5 Direct Effects of Organizational Learning Behaviors on Employee, Customer, and Shareholder Satisfaction

Organizational Learning Behavior	Employee Satisfaction	Customer Satisfaction	Shareholder Satisfaction
II	.29	−.06	.06
GG	.25	−.01	.25
OO	−.17	.40	.13
FB	.34	.10	.20
FF	.13	.05	−.19
Employee satisfaction	—	.22	—
Customer satisfaction	—	—	.43
R^2	.56	.39	.55

ers affecting shareholder satisfaction appear to be GGB, OOB, FBB, and customer satisfaction. These findings are discussed more fully in the following section.

Discussion and Conclusions

In general, our findings are consistent with the model. Leadership has a high correlation with all elements of the organizational learning system. And the organizational learning system has a high correlation with performance (employee, customer, shareholder). While each of the organizational learning constructs demonstrates high correlation with at least one of the three performance indicators, there are some notable differences. We begin by discussing the stocks and then address the flows.

Individual learning shows a high correlation of .29 with employee satisfaction, with only total effects (table 40.6) of .00 with customer satisfaction and .06 with shareholder satisfaction.

Many companies invest substantially in individual training and development, presumably based on the assumption that such investments will translate directly into superior organizational performance. Although employee satisfaction is found here to have a reasonably strong effect on customer satisfaction, it is by no means the only important driver of the latter. Thus, our results suggest that the return on investment in individual learning (IIB) may be more limited than is generally assumed.

Group learning (GGB) has a strong, positive effect on both employee and shareholder satisfaction. Given the strong effects for employee and shareholder satisfaction, it is surprising that there is only a negligible total effect (.04) for customer satisfaction. We can only speculate on why this may be the case. Strong group learning, which involves dealing with diversity, managing conflict, and developing shared understanding, may be desirable and appreciated by employees and may ultimately be good for the organization with respect to financial return to the share-

TABLE 40.6 Total Effects of Organizational Learning Behaviors on Employee, Customer, and Shareholder Satisfaction

Organizational Learning Behavior	Employee Satisfaction	Customer Satisfaction	Shareholder Satisfaction
II	.29	.00	.06
GG	.25	.04	.27
OO	−.17	.36	.28
FB	.34	.17	.28
FF	.13	.08	−.16
Employee satisfaction	—	.22	.10
Customer satisfaction	—	—	.43

holder. However, it may not appear to serve the immediate needs of customers. In fact, such learning may be disruptive to customers as they deal with the uncertainty, lack of continuity, and change associated with learning.

Organization level learning (OOB) has a very strong positive effect on both customer and shareholder satisfaction, but a *negative* effect on employee satisfaction. Thus, while it appears that an ability to learn at the organizational level is critical to a firm's financial performance, it comes at the cost of some employee dissatisfaction. Thus, investments in OOB, which relate to strategic alignment, appear to be crucial, but firms must be careful to also manage the negative consequences of such investments on employee morale (perhaps through investments in IIB, GGB, and/or FBB).

In contrast, the feedback flow (FBB) has a strong, positive effect on all three satisfaction outcomes. Indeed, it seems to be the single most important behavioral driver of satisfaction. Somewhat surprisingly (given the importance of FBB), feed-forward flow (FFB) has a moderate effect on employee satisfaction and a negative effect on shareholder satisfaction. These findings appear to support the strategic tension between exploration and exploitation. Investment in the feed-forward flow of learning (exploration) may be costly to the organization with respect to financial return. In contrast, financial performance gains are made through investment in the feedback flow (exploitation). Over time, firms need to renew themselves through the innovation generated in the feed-forward flow of learning, while also achieving financial returns through the exploitation achieved by ensuring that the institutionalized learning flows back through the organization.

In summary, organizational learning provides a process orientation to strategic management that links the knowledge and intellectual capital at the individual level with the strategic orientation of the firm at the organization level. The feed-forward and feedback flows of learning provide a dynamic infrastructure through which organizations evolve their strategies over time. Firms need to both explore (feed-forward) and exploit (feedback). Our findings suggest a strong correlation between this organizational learning infrastructure and performance. We also suggested the need to rethink the role of leadership as a means to manage the organizational learning infrastructure. The results show

a very strong correlation between this leadership task and the five elements of the organizational learning system. Leadership is a means to leverage knowledge through organizational learning.

Future Research

Although our findings are provocative, they are limited in terms of their generalizability. The approach described here clearly needs to be extended to other organizations to determine whether the pattern of results reported here is firm specific or panorganizational.

A second limitation of the present study relates to the exclusive use of perceptual measures. We believe that as this general field of inquiry grows, it will become increasingly important to use both objective and perceptual measures of organizational learning behaviors and performance/satisfaction.

The findings that suggest differential effects between the elements of the organizational learning system and the three measures of performance merit further research. In particular, it is troubling to think that investment in individual learning may have so little total effect on customer and shareholder satisfaction. As well, the tension between exploration and exploitation borne out by the results for the feed-forward and feedback flows warrants further research. This tension continues to be one of the significant challenges of strategic management and organizational learning.

Overall, the links between organizational learning and leadership appear extremely strong. Since the approach to leadership developed in this chapter departs from the more traditional view of leadership, it would be helpful to extend this research into the field. Perhaps an intervention involving training along these leadership dimensions would provide further insight into the challenges associated with this proposed approach to leadership.

In conclusion, this chapter expands on a framework of organizational learning that has been previously linked to knowledge management and strategic management, by developing critical links to leadership. Initial efforts have been made to empirically test the model. The findings support the model acknowledging critical links between leadership, organizational learning, knowledge management, strategy, and performance.

Notes

1. The use of the term "beliefs" at the organization level is meant to capture institutionalized learning such as strategy, systems, and structure.

References

Argyris, C. and D.A. Schon (1978) *Organizational Learning: A Theory of Action Perspective*. Reading, MA: Addison-Wesley.

Argyris, C. and D.A. Schon (1996) *Organizational Learning II: Theory, Method, and Practice*. Reading, MA: Addison-Wesley.

Ashby, W.R. (1960) *Design for a Brain*, 2d ed. New York: Wiley.

Barclay, D.W., Higgins, C.A., and Thompson, R.L. (1995) "The partial least squares (PLS) approach to causal modeling: personal computer adaptation and use as an illustration." *Technology Studies* 2(2):285–309.

Bass, B.M. (1990) *Bass and Stogdill's Handbook of Leadership: Theory, Research and Managerial Applications* 3d. ed. New York: Free Press.

Birkinshaw, J., Morrison, A.J., and Hulland, J. (1995) "Structural and competitive determinants of a global integration strategy." *Strategic Management Journal* 16:637–655.

Blackler, F. (1993) "Knowledge and theory of organizations: organizations as activity systems and the reframing of management." *Journal of Management Studies* 30(6):863–884.

Blackler, F. (1995) "Knowledge, knowledge work, and organizations: an overview and interpretation." *Organization Studies* 16(6):1021–1046.

Bontis, N., Crossan, M., and Hulland, J. (2000) "Managing an organizational learning system by aligning stocks and flows." *Journal of Management Studies*.

Chandler, A.D. (1962) *Strategy and Structure: Chapters in the History of the Industrial Enterprise*. Cambridge, MA: MIT Press.

Crossan, M. and Hulland, J. (1998) "Assessing the stocks and flows of organizational learning." Working paper, Richard Ivey School of Business, University of Western Ontario.

Crossan, M., Lane, H., and White, R.E. (1997) "Organizational learning: toward a theory." Working paper, Richard Ivey School of Business, University of Western Ontario.

Crossan, M., Lane, H., and White, R.E. (1999) "An organizational learning framework: from intuition to institution." *Academy of Management Review* 24(3):522–537.

Crossan, M., Lane, H., White, R.E., and Djurfeldt, L. (1995) "Organizational learning: dimensions for a theory." *The International Journal of Organizational Analysis* 3(4):337–360.

Daft, R.L. and Huber, G. (1987) "How organizations learn: a communication framework." *Research in the Sociology of Organizations* 5:1–36.

DeGeus, A.P. (1988) "Planning as learning." *Harvard Business Review*, March–April, pp. 70–74.

Duncan, R.B. and Weiss, A. (1979) "Organizational learning: implications for organizational design," in B.M. Staw (ed.), *Research in Organizational Behavior*. Greenwich, CT: JAI Press.

Fiol, C.M. and Lyles, M.A. (1985) "Organizational learning." *Academy of Management Review* 10:803–813.

Fornell, C. and Larcker, D.F. (1981) "Evaluating structural equation models with unobservable variables and measurement error." *Journal of Marketing Research* 18(February):39–50.

Grant, R.M. (1996) "Prospering in dynamically-competitive environments: organizational capability as knowledge integration." *Organization Science* 7(4):375–387.

Hambrick, D. and Mason, P.A. (1984) "Upper echelons: the organization as a reflection of its top managers." *Academy of Management Review* 9:193–206.

Hamel, G. and Prahalad, C.K. (1993) "Strategy as stretch and leverage." *Harvard Business Review* 71(2):75–83.

Hannan, M.T. and Freeman, J. (1987) "The ecology of organizational foundings: American labour unions, 1836–1985." *American Journal of Sociology* 92:910–943.

Hedberg, B. (1981) "How organizations learn and unlearn," in P.C. Nystrom and W.H. Starbuck (eds.), *Handbook of Organizational Design*, pp. 3–27. New York: Oxford University Press.

House, R.J. and Aditya, R.N. (1997) "The social scientific study of leadership: quo vadis?" *Journal of Management* 23(3):409–473.

Huber, G.P. (1991) "Organizational learning: the contributing processes and the literatures." *Organizational Science* 2(1):88–115.

Huff, J.O., Huff, A.S., and Thomas, H. (1992) "Strategic renewal and the interaction of cumulative stress and inertia." *Strategic Management Journal* 13:55–75.

Hulland, J. (1999) "Use of partial least squares (PLS) in strategic management research: a review of four recent studies." *Strategic Management Journal* 20(February):195–204.

Kogut, B. and Zander, U. (1992) "Knowledge of the firm, combinative capabilities, and the replication of technology." *Organization Science* 3:383–397.

Lant, T.K. and Mezias, S.J. (1992) "An organizational learning model of convergence and reorientation." *Organization Science* 3(1)47–71.

Levitt, B. and March, J.G. (1988) "Organizational learning." *Annual Review of Sociology* 14:319–340.

March, J.G. (1991) "Exploration and exploitation in organizational learning." *Organization Science* 12(1):71–87.

Miller, D. and Friesen, P.H. (1982) "Innovation in conservative and entrepreneurial firms: two models of strategic momentum." *Strategic Management Journal* 3:1–25.

Mintzberg, H., Ahlstrand, B., and Lampel, J. (1998) *Strategy Safari: A Guided Tour through the Wilds of Strategic Management.* New York: Free Press.

Nonaka, I. and Takeuchi, H. (1995) *The Knowledge Creating Company.* New York: Oxford University Press.

Nunnally, J.C. (1978) *Psychometric Theory*, 2d ed. New York: McGraw-Hill.

Pettigrew, A.M. (1992) "The character and significance of strategy process research." *Strategic Management Journal* 13(Winter):5–16.

Powell, T.C. (1992) "Organizational alignment as competitive advantage." *Strategic Management Journal* 13(2):119–134.

Rucci, A.J., Kirn, S.P., and Quinn, R.T. (1998) "The employee customer profit chain at Sears." *Harvard Business Review.*

Shrivastava, P. (1983) "A typology of organizational learning systems." *Journal of Management Studies* 20:7–28.

Smith, J. and Barclay, D.W. (1997) "The effects of organizational differences and trust on the effectiveness of selling partner relationships." *Journal of Marketing* 61(January):3–21.

Spender, J.-C. (1996) "Making knowledge the basis of a dynamic theory of the firm." *Strategic Management Journal* 17(Winter).

Spender, J.-C. and Grant, R.M. (1996) "Knowledge and the firm: overview." *Strategic Management Journal* 17(Winter):5–9.

Staples, S., Hulland, J., and Higgins, C.A. (1998) "A self-efficacy theory explanation for the management of remote workers in virtual organizations." *Journal of Computer Mediated Communication* 3(4).

Tsoukas, H. (1996) "The firm as a distributed knowledge system: a constructionist approach." *Strategic Management Journal* 17(Winter):11–25.

Tushman, M.L. and O'Reilly, C.A. (1996) "Ambidextrous organizations: managing evolutionary and revolutionary change." *California Management Review* 38(4):8–29.

Venkatraman, N. (1990) "Environment-strategy coalignment: an empirical test of its performance implications." *Strategic Management Journal* 11: 1–23.

Vera, D. and Crossan, M. (2000) "Organizational learning, knowledge management, and intellectual capital: an integrative conceptual model." Working Paper, Ivey Business School.

Weick, K.E. (1995) *Sensemaking in Organizations.* Thousand Oaks, CA: Sage.

Wold, H. (1985) "Systems analysis by partial least squares," in P. Nijkamp, L. Leitner, and N. Wrigley (eds.), *Measuring the Unmeasurable.* pp. 221–251. Dordrecht: Nijhoff.

Yukl, G. (1994) *Leadership in Organizations.* Englewoods Cliffs, NJ: Prentice-Hall.

41

Appendix

Beyond Knowledge Management: New Ways to Work

Brian Hackett

2000,
New York: The Conference Board

The following appendix is an excerpt from a research report published by the Conference Board and is reprinted with permission.[1] It is based on a Conference Board survey of over 150 global companies and interviews with a working group of senior executives from 12 global organizations. The survey results describe the current state of knowledge management and organizational learning from the perspective of senior line and staff executives. Two hundred senior executives at 158 global companies responded to the survey; their companies have an average of 40,000 employees, with 90% reporting revenues over $1 billion and 68% with revenues over $5 billion. The organizations that participated in the interviews are listed below:

ABN AMRO

BP Amoco

British Telecom

Clarica Life Insurance

IBM

Deere & Company

KLM Royal Dutch Airlines

PriceWaterhouseCoopers

Shell Oil

Sonera

U.S. Postal Service

Weyerhaeuser

Companies around the world are making real business contributions through practices associated with knowledge management (KM) and organizational learning (OL). A Conference Board survey of 200 senior executives shows that

- 80% of companies have some KM efforts under way,
- 6% use KM enterprisewide and 60% expect to in five years,
- 25% have a chief knowledge officer, or chief learning officer (although half are not supported with dedicated budget or staff), and
- 21% have a communicated KM strategy.

Knowledge management and OL have different distinctions and approaches at the strategic level, but they are increasingly similar in terms of tactics and tools they employ. While much of KM has been made possible by technology, many information technology–centric (IT-centric) approaches have had limited success. Rather, the most successful methods for turning knowledge into action are the result of informal employee networks and other workplace practices. For long-term success, the underlying cultural factors and support systems are key factors. And while IT-centric KM systems get media attention, changes in workplace practices and customer focus appear to be the areas where KM gets results.

While a number of firms have assigned responsibility for KM or OL to a chief knowledge officer, for example, a chief learning officer, the active participation of human resources and information technology leaders is also critical. Research and development, sales, marketing, and customer service are areas where innovative use of KM and OL has begun to deliver measurable business benefits. Implementing KM or OL on an enterprisewide basis can be expensive and politically sensitive. It should also be viewed as a long-term investment that involves all segments of the business. Leading KM and OL practitioners and observers believe that the current efforts are only a prelude to a bigger payoff—building deeper customer relationships with a fully engaged workforce.

The Conference Board and a working group of 12 global companies approached this study with the intent to define common ground for KM and OL by looking at practices that companies employed and the current barriers and future opportunities that senior executives are facing. Although each firm has evolved its own approach and methodology for managing learning and knowledge, increasingly they share comparable goals and a similar understanding of the barriers and opportunities to achieve business results.

Barriers and Opportunities

The major obstacles to successful KM are internal barriers, not issues of the market, customers, suppliers, or competitors. The main obstacle is that the need to manage knowledge is not clearly articulated. Of the 80% of companies with KM activity, only 15% had specific, stated goals for their KM objectives. Many executives have had little training or experience that prepares them for understanding how sharing knowledge relates to the bottom line. An organization must have a working definition of knowledge and

learning before it can attempt to manage it. This lack of understanding is expected to decrease over time.

A culture of hoarding knowledge is the second biggest barrier to successful KM efforts. However, overcoming that barrier is the top priority for the future, followed closely by top leadership support. Functional silos are the third most cited obstacle to sharing knowledge. A primary reason KM has grown so quickly is that it offers the means to work across functional, business unit, regional, and hierarchical boundaries. The leading practitioners of KM initiatives are working to find all the pockets of knowledge-sharing activity often hidden throughout the company. They also use KM tools and techniques to break down the walls and ceilings that often limit communication and knowledge flows. For example, GE is seeking a "boundaryless" organization with the help of a chief learning officer. Rewarding and recognizing knowledge-sharing behaviors is also a major concern. A combination of tactics, including performance management, communications, and education, are being used to combat the problems of knowledge hoarding and the "not-invented-here" syndrome.

For many cultures, motivation through pay will not work. Buckman Labs, an early leader in KM, provides an example of that kind of culture. K'Netix, the Buckman knowledge network, brings together more than 1,200 associates in over 80 countries to share knowledge in solving customer needs. It was CEO Robert Buckman's commitment to solving customers' needs that led to the creation of a broad-scale knowledge transfer capability. The ideas and solutions of one person or a group can be rapidly shared with associates wherever they are located so that customer response is fast and accurate. According to Mark Koskiniemi, vice president of human resources at Buckman:

> We do not use a lot of cash payment incentives because it is hard to track the quality of interactions. And we do not want to pay out on quantity necessarily. The rewards, recognition, and incentives are that people will be able to expand their sphere of communication, their sphere of influence in turn, and potentially their sphere of responsibility through promotion. People succeed as they use the tools to credibly advance the efforts of our company and our customers. We are moving more toward a meritocracy with this system. People who want to have a

positive global impact on the company now have another outlet for that to happen. Our knowledge-sharing systems also allow their work to be seen by management around the world.

While definitions of KM and OL are still debated, they have become common terms that span varied initiatives, new processes, and in some cases new management functions. Some organizations see KM as little more than information management, while others see it as something far more complex, involving management of knowledge in all its forms. Practitioners of KM and OL are united in their belief in the potential to increase productivity, quality, and innovation by changing the way work gets done. Regardless of their definitions KM and OL will have greater impact on organizations in the near future.

Knowledge management is an integrated, systematic approach to identifying, managing, and sharing all of an enterprise's information assets, including databases, documents, policies, and procedures, as well as previously unarticulated expertise and experience held by individual workers. Fundamentally, it is about making the collective information and experience of an enterprise available to the individual knowledge worker, who is responsible for using it wisely and for replenishing the stock. This ongoing cycle encourages a learning organization, stimulates collaboration, and empowers people to continually enhance the way they perform work.

Organizational learning is the process that enables an organization to adapt to change and move forward by acquiring new knowledge, skills, or behaviors and thereby transform itself. In successful learning organizations,

- individual learning is continuous,
- knowledge is shared,
- the company culture supports learning,
- employees are encouraged to think critically and to take risks with new ideas, and
- all individuals are valued for their contributions to the organization.

Organizations have organizational knowledge—the ability to accomplish collective tasks that individuals acting alone cannot, tasks designed to create value for the organization's stakeholders. Organizational knowledge is both explicit, such as the knowledge contained in technical drawings, manuals of procedures, and computer memories, and tacit, including judgment,

"feel," and deep understanding. Tacit knowledge is an essential part of "knowing how" and "knowing why" and is essential to making knowledge useful.

Turning tacit knowledge into explicit knowledge is part of the continuous cycle of learning, sharing, reflection, and use of that knowledge. Yet, most KM efforts focus on efficiency and sharing internal "best practices." Best practices often do not transfer. Having poor or inadequate criteria for making a best practice portable can cause such failures. Too much formalization of the "best way" could actually lead to less creativity and innovation.

Current KM efforts focused on repositories of best practice may become less and less important for four reasons:

1. Best practices are very specific to context (most learning may be learning from mistakes).
2. The repository is easier to fill than to access and reuse, for both technical and psychological reasons.
3. In a world of greater speed, firms need to look to knowledge flows more than knowledge stocks, and therefore more toward linking of people (e.g., employees, customer, and suppliers).
4. Repositories almost by definition do not link to end-to-end processes, where managers and employees can see the impact and integrate them.

The organization's strategy, culture, values, structure processes, and customer relationships are touched by KM and OL. Its practices are widespread, spanning multiple sectors, such as financial services, manufacturing, oil and chemical production, pharmaceuticals, consulting, and other service industries.

Companies report that when they better utilize knowledge they can

- make decisions faster and closer to the point of action,
- overcome internal and external barriers,
- provide more opportunities there are more opportunities to innovate,
- reduce product development time, and
- enhance customer relationships.

The most common KM goals are focused on internal practices—sharing practices and increasing efficiencies. However, innovation and cus-

TABLE 41.1 Specific Goals for KM

Share practices/increase collaboration	41%
Increase productivity/use of knowledge	18
Transfer employee knowledge	8
Increase innovation	7
Improve decision making	7
Transfer knowledge from customer	4
No specific goals	15

tomer knowledge are expected to be the areas where breakthroughs and future growth will emerge (see table 41.1).

In many ways, KM initiatives are in tune with new ways of doing business and the drivers of competition in a global economy. These drivers include the following:

- *Diffusion of technologies:* The e-mail/in-tranet/Internet infrastructure, combined with powerful database software and group-ware, has made it possible to increase the span of communication. Ideas, experiences, and problems can be shared more quickly, more often, less expensively, and more widely than ever before.
- *The marketplace:* The Internet and globaliza-tion have made discontinuous change a com-petitive fact. The rules guiding customer re-lations, competition, and the employment relationship change daily. Firms must oper-ate as adaptive systems and anticipate change under that new set of market condi-tions.
- *The customer:* Sharing knowledge with cus-tomers, potential customers, suppliers, and in some cases competitors is becoming a grow-ing business practice. For many firms shar-ing knowledge with regulators, the media and the community are equally important.
- *The workforce:* Today's workers are more technology literate, more mobile in their ca-reers, and more engaged in learning as their roles and knowledge needs change.
- *The organization:* With the spread of tech-nology infrastructures and the move to glob-alization, the roles of headquarters and com-mon workspace have been greatly reduced as the repositories of knowledge. Cross-functional teams and cross-organizational projects are an increasing part of how work gets done.

The way most people work is continuously changing. Ubiquitous and portable communica-

tions technology is a major factor in that change. People can now communicate anytime, almost anywhere, and at a relatively low cost. Work groups can capture that communication in simple-to-use but sophisticated databases. When done well, companies can mine that information so the right people can use it when they need it.

The technology that allows people to share knowledge has also put more information into the customer's head. Companies can no longer compete primarily on price. Real growth and real profit are coming from deepening the customer connection and building customer loyalty. The customer relationship can be developed most quickly and sustained most effectively if the en-tire workforce is engaged in and understands the value of building and keeping customer loyalty.

Creating a workplace where knowledge is shared and where people are encouraged to learn and to take action on those lessons learned is the surest way to compete in a market-driven econ-omy. A knowledge-sharing workplace can create more opportunities and can make retention and other workforce issues less problematic and, consequently, a relative problem for the compe-tition.

Another important factor in the adoption and effectiveness of KM is the growing experience and better understanding of the notions under-pinning the learning organization. While the practice of employee participation has been used for decades, new KM tools and techniques have given companies new ways to take further ac-tion incorporating older organizational learning principles.

Some executives feel that KM was "old wine in new bottles." The old wine that they refer to are the notions of teamwork, commitment, loy-alty, and trust. While this old wine of knowledge sharing has been around for a long time, it has not been let out of the bottle in all organizations. As Rob van der Spek, principal consultant for Kenniscentrum CIBIT, puts it, "Knowledge man-agement is common sense, but not common practice."

Implementing KM and OL

According to the survey, 21% of companies have a formally communicated knowledge sharing strategy. Among them is a diversity of strategies and approaches. Most knowledge strategies are currently based on increasing efficiencies mainly because it is easier and more immediate to ex-ploit what is known. Few firms had a strategy focused on innovation, knowledge creation, or customer loyalty.

A knowledge strategy is a function of the business strategy. Organizations with certain attributes and business challenges will opt for a certain type of knowledge strategy. For instance, in a highly decentralized organization, it would be incongruous to launch a highly centralized knowledge strategy. At IBM, the services business is rooted in competing on competence. As a result, knowledge networks, project knowledge management, and intellectual capital management are critical elements for a services knowledge strategy. Other sectors of IBM's businesses will be driven by different key processes, which can be enabled by managing transactional and operational knowledge. Basic components of any knowledge strategy, however, include the process of discovering and identifying gaps in those knowledge assets—explicit and tacit—that provide the business its competitive advantage.

The varieties of KM visible in theory and in practice may shed some light on the key findings of this study: the lack of perceived need for KM, the lack of formal planning, and the prevalence of formal KM in certain corporations but absence in others. Knowledge in an organization may be analogous to oxygen in the human body: critical to sustaining life, but not necessarily a subject for explicit management, unless the natural organic systems are failing. Very simply, KM may be implemented in two basic ways: (1) an emergent, self-organizing, "bottom-up" model or (2) a centrally designed, common shared architecture, "top-down" model.

Hard System, Bottom-Up Trial

The first KM network for British Telecom systems engineers (SEs) in the global multinational sales units was a spontaneous and organic creation of SEs who wanted to share best practices, tips, and suggestions among themselves. A surplus personal computer was liberated as a server for a simple e-mail system with a growing distribution list. Eventually this skunk works system became a victim of its own success: the time to maintain it became burdensome to the engineers, who were doing it in their spare time, and it was abandoned.

Hard System, Top-Down

Most KM literature seems devoted to IT-mediated KM systems with defined properties, planned objectives, and explicit scope and reach that require compatible technologies within that design space—centrally led and generally non-skunk works projects. Many consultants and vendors of KM "solutions" have a vested interest to focus on this end, KM, as they need a fairly centralized client concept of knowledge management before they have an "owner" to sell to.

Soft Systems—Bottom-Up and Top-Down

A high-tech firm such as Microsoft has several soft systems for knowledge management—project-release postmortems and lessons learned reports, a culture of self and mutual critique, a project team design that encourages skills overlap and competitive marketing of ideas, and concurrent engineering that serve as quick feedback loops. It also colocates its teams in one space whenever possible for intense face-to-face interaction. Despite its more than accidental access to KM tools, however, Microsoft is not known as a big advocate or user of distributed development, cross-team knowledge sharing, or sharing large databases of codified best practice.

Either the top-down or bottom-up implementation method may work and sustain positive results if it is aligned with organizational culture and local performance drivers. If there is a mismatch, however, the outcomes may be detrimental. If the culture is conditioned to have central leadership, for example, then the absence of mandate and structure typical of the emergent approach will tend to paralyze the work groups, who will be waiting for permission to act. If the various company units are historically independent silos or internally competitive (as with sales forces, e.g.), the emergent systems invented locally will not be compatible with each other.

If the emergent knowledge management is done on a skunk works basis, but the larger organizational units tighten budgets to drive out waste, then local initiatives not seen in the larger planning priorities may be closed off. The volunteer burnout syndrome is often a similar unintended result. Speed issues are multilevel and somewhat paradoxical: the highly distributed and diverse emergent approach will assist rapid evolution by "natural selection" and will speed deployment of KM initiatives in the short term but may slow their deployment of KM in the intermediate term due to lack of interoperability. Homegrown and skunk works products will probably look and feel that way. Large companies that are accustomed to more professional tools or elegant solutions may avoid their use.

If the KM arrives as a predefined package from the center, when the organization culture is more autonomous, then the positives can be supplanted with negatives:

- Psychological ownership is rejected: "This is your system, not mine." "Not invented here." "That might work for you, but it will never work here."
- The system may fall to the classic problem of "a technology in search of a problem."
- The taxonomy of best practice may not match the local needs and common language.
- The platform imposed from the top may not match local history, preference, or outside sharing potential.
- A centrally led effort often looks to financial incentives to spur use and overcome resistance, while the locally invented skunk works version was entirely voluntary and motivated by intrinsic rewards only: professionalism, the ability to contribute, peer recognition, and being part of something larger than yourself.
- Cash incentives not only cost money; they also appeal to the wrong sort of drivers for knowledge workers who should be the biggest users and beneficiaries and may ask, Why pay me to share knowledge? The intrinsic rewards are deeper, more lasting, and less open to manipulation and gaming behaviors.
- A real barrier to sustained knowledge sharing is not posting knowledge *to* a system, but rather drawing down and using the knowledge available *from* the system. In other words, it is not the *sharing* but the *receiving* of the knowledge that must also be understood.

The top-down, center-led approach may be especially prone to one-size-fits-all tunnel vision, contrary to the existing scope and priorities of the job. For example, the SEs work across several bids, while the account managers do not. By common perception, the system engineers are more collaborative and more motivated by high-quality engineering design, while the account managers are highly competitive with each other and are screened, hired, and rewarded for individual achievement, not for sharing.

Very few firms have either integrated their OL and KM initiatives. Nor have they succeeded in linking individual learning or career development to their OL or KM efforts. As Patrick Wright, chair of the department of HR studies Cornell University points out, "There is no universal consensus regarding what knowledge management is. That allows firms and local units to define it for themselves in a way that is useful to their particular context. However, there needs to be more of an understanding within firms regarding the relationship between KM and OL, both distinguishing between them and describing their interrelationships."

To adapt and anticipate the forces of discontinuous change organizations must learn. A knowledge management strategy without the link to individual and organizational learning can become a "conservative" tool if it results in standardizing and codifying current best practice. In some cases it may become an incremental change tool, such as total quality management, which can limit the chance for breakthrough thinking. Hubert Saint-Onge of Clarica states, "The connection between learning and knowledge management is generally not well understood because the two fields have been kept separate from an organization structure point of view."

Yet learning can best be served by a comprehensive knowledge strategy that includes learning modules as well as other sources of knowledge, including knowledge databases, documents, and policies. The knowledge interface we recently created allows individuals to run a search that calls upon all learning materials as well as these other sources of knowledge. Contrasting KM and OL may not be all that helpful. In fact, a knowledge-driven organization and a learning organization will ultimately end up looking very much alike.

At British Telecom and most large firms, the KM community of practitioners and the OL community of practitioners work on different problems, use different tools, rely on different authors, and base their work in different concepts. Janet McAllister, former vice president of global learning at IBM says,

Other than professional services firms, the focus on KM comes from strategy and marketing executives and the focus on learning comes from corporate training and human resources staffs. These groups do not really speak the same language, making the connection difficult. The KM movement may help overcome these old corporate politics and roadblocks that only CEOs or senior line management can break.

Approaches and Tools for KM and OL

At the strategic level, KM and OL may have different definitions and approaches at the strategic level, but they are increasingly similar in terms of tactics and tools they employ. Rapid deployment of technology (including common desktop platforms and universal access to the Internet/intranets), coupled with rapid changes in the work patterns of large companies (e.g., cross-functional teams, remote teams, interorganizational projects), has provided a fertile ground for weaving KM and OL approaches into the fabric of the enterprise. In the process, advanced KM is increasingly becoming a matter of orchestrating a package of practices that are received in their own right as having value separate from their justification as part of a learning culture or leading to best practices. Following are some of the more common tactics and IT-based tools being employed as knowledge sharing spreads in the enterprise.

Communities of Practice

The notion of a community of practice came from research at the Institute for Research on Learning and Xerox PARC in Palo Alto, California. The research discovered that learning takes place in and around communities of practice. As people find a reason to work together, they share stories and lessons learned. In short, they teach each other the practice. Communities of practice have proven to be one of the most valuable forms of knowledge sharing, yet they

- lack a formal structure, although they can fit within an existing organizational structure or may be converted to a formal structure at some point;
- are not standardized, although they can choose to set and follow standards for themselves;
- are hard to locate and define, but organizational ethnography and anthropology can help find them;
- have an exclusive membership defined by the community; and
- are early warning systems and drivers of changes in the organizational "ecosystem," if properly cultivated, not managed.

A community of practice is a group of people who share a particular practice, interest, or discipline and share information and tacit knowledge. They may be HTML programmers, service technicians, a sales team, or what have you. But not everyone agrees that a community of practice cannot be defined. IBM's Fred Schoeps says:

> We invest very systematically in communities of practice. Each has a competency leader and a core team of practitioners. We manage intellectual capital and organizational knowledge through these communities. Membership in the community includes both trained practitioners who have access to methodologies, and extended members. Decisions about training requirements, certification, methodologies, community tools, management of the communities, and intellectual capital are within the purview of the competency leader and the core team. Furthermore, communities are moving onto the intranet, using a suite of Web and Lotus applications to support the members of the community.

As part of a systematic learning effort, companies can provide resources, such as free time and meeting spaces, to support communities of practice. They can also provide opportunities for bridging across communities or even to customers or suppliers. This is done face to face and is supplemented with intranets, e-mail, or video conferencing. The value of communities of practice can go unrecognized by senior and middle management. One key role for executives is to foster such communities and explain their value but to avoid getting in their way. One example is to give the manufacturing team access to the sales forecasting information. By taking that step, the company is doing more than shortening time to market; it is creating a new bridge across communities. Other ways of aiding communities of practice include

- recognizing, acknowledging, and training the key support roles, such as facilitators, knowledge stewards, and knowledge/relationship brokers;
- helping identify communities of practice that do or could exist in the organization and supporting their attempts to cultivate an effective group with visible commitment and extra resources;
- building the cultivation and nurturing of these communities into business strategies;

- leading the cultivation and nurturing of external communities, including customers, suppliers, and the investment community;
- taping the knowledge and potential for key projects; and
- leveraging the power of communities for driving organizational change efforts.

Leadership—Relating and Sharing Values

Besides fundamentally transforming the way work is organized and carried out, knowledge management and learning help change the way organizations view leadership. As Fred Schoeps puts it, "KM is about shifting time to higher value activities, and having the right dialogue just in time with the right experts to systematically leverage expertise. Taking full advantage of collaboration, teaming, and moving away from the self-centered rugged individual."

While there will always be hierarchy and some form of command and control, shared values are becoming the anchor for generating commitment and cooperation. When values are created together and truly shared, order is achieved and decisions are made without position power and excessive rules. When the vision is articulated as a shared set of values, people have the level of trust needed to share and receive knowledge. Leadership is changing from personal and interpersonal to relational, from dominance to meaning making. And leader development is changing from preparing the leader to exercise power to increasing the capacity of the community to work smarter through collaboration.

W.L. Gore, a company known for innovation and being an employer of choice, uses four operating principles to help operationalize this type of leadership:

1. The *freedom* principle encourages associates to grow in knowledge, skill, and scope of responsibility.
2. The *waterline* principle states that mistakes made "above the waterline" are not a serious offense. However, mistakes "below the water line" can sink the ship. Therefore, before taking a serious risk or bridging an ethical standard, associates need to check with other people.
3. The *commitment* principle indicates that associates are expected to keep any commitment they make.

4. The *fairness* principle mandates that associates be fair to everyone, including suppliers and customers.

These principles lead to leadership that is not positional. Instead, leadership is expected of everyone and natural leaders are then defined by their followers. This has also helped to transfer ownership of the customer relationships to individual employees who are closest to the front lines. Relational leadership is a key issue at IBM. According to Schoeps,

> Project managers must learn to be knowledge managers and systematically leverage knowledge assets. Every manager has a role as knowledge manager responsible for the human capital entrusted to him or her as well as intellectual assets within his or her domain of responsibility. To this end we are integrating programs, skill development for KM into our leadership development.

Some of the strongest learning and KM gains have come through active championing by the CEO. There is a strong commitment at the top to change the organizational culture and begin to create values that lead to knowledge sharing across organizational boundaries. In organizations where these boundaries are very strong, CEO commitment is essential to share knowledge across the enterprise. In the absence of that commitment, even well-executed and conceived practices may remain locked within a single organizational unit for the duration of a project.

Monsanto is perhaps the best example of a company that has come closest to transforming itself to a knowledge-based company by making dramatic strategic changes and changes to the way work is organized and carried out. Monsanto looks at creating value at the individual level to improve the capability of each person. It is attempting to change the organizational culture so that the shared values of individuals lead to increased organizational capabilities. Many senior managers were skeptical about this new strategy—the most enthusiasm for the knowledge-sharing projects came from the lower levels of the company.

The organizational transformation began with Robert Shapiro's leadership in 1995. Among the changes was the establishment of a KM program and infrastructure. A director for KM helped create global learning centers and systems connecting employees to focus on innovation and growth. Shapiro's strategy called for making

Monsanto more connected and able to act like a small company. The company grew from 4 to 14 business units. To increase connections and remain decentralized, several information repositories were created on the intranet.

Monsanto's KM culture is focused on creating value by understanding how people convert information into insight. Its approach called for clearly defined roles for members of self-directed teams, particularly for the team leader who must ensure that the components of knowledge creation are occurring, champion the sharing of lessons learned, and provide the right environment.

CEOs should be role models of knowledge sharing. For example, Jacques Nasser, CEO of Ford Motor Company, personally writes a weekly e-mail to all employees with comments on his thoughts and experience for the past week. He also reads hundreds of responses each month and has a team member respond to those that need follow-up. Allan Schuman, CEO of Ecolab, does the same with a phone-mail message and in some cases audio tapes with longer messages, to all employees, generally about his lessons learned at visits with customers. This form of personal communication is usually told as a story that further ingrains the culture of the firm. These messages are timely and go beyond just making a symbolic gesture. They send practical advice, connect each employee's work to the customer, and help create the climate for others to do the same.

Chief Knowledge Officers as Leaders

Often delegated by the CEO and reporting directly or on a dotted line to the top, the role of chief knowledge officer (CKO) is commonly intended as a catalyst rather than a new organizational unit. The CKO is often an evangelist, educator, and organizer of forums, rather than a manager of KM projects per se. For the 25% of surveyed firms that have a CKO or a similar position, the power, resources, and responsibility of the job vary widely (table 41.2).

A variety of titles—chief learning officer, CKO, knowledge managers, knowledge architects, knowledge engineers—are used to describe members of this growing professional community. There are major differences in the scope of their work, why they do it, and how much influence they hold. In this chapter all will be referred to as CKOs.

Most CKOs, whether or not they have "knowledge" in their title, are working to connect their KM or OL efforts with their firm's most pressing strategic initiatives. Interviewed executives were careful not to present KM as a panacea or as a separate and new change initiative. They understand that the biggest problem for most managers and employees is the lack of time to accomplish their individual goals. These executives see KM largely as a means to alleviate those time pressures and avoid reinventing the wheel.

Individuals selected to serve as CKOs are driven by the challenge of changing how organizations think about knowledge and learning. Salary, position, or titles were not their primary motivation. The notion that their company had the latent talent, creative solutions, and capabilities to compete and change was an underlying driving philosophy.

Most CKOs focus less on technology than on the strategic aspects of knowledge that can be enabled through new ways to work in collaboration. Some CKOs have focused on the design of the workplace and social environments—more infor-

TABLE 41.2 CKOs as Members of Senior Management

	Firms with a CKO: Where are they located?	Firms without a CKO: Where would they be located?
Senior management	32%	34%
Human resources	25	21
Information technology	16	10
Management and supervision	7	5
Research and development	4	6
Information services/library	6	5
Communication	2	4
Web team	4	3
Manufacturing	3	9
Customer service	1	3

mal meeting places, retreats, learning events, and innovative development experiences—to encourage and facilitate knowledge creation, sharing and innovation.

The CKO acts as both a visionary and a bridge. There are three ways to build capability and become an integrated company: move money, move people, and move ideas throughout the firm. The CKO's job is to help break down the walls between business units, functions, and geographic locations and the ceilings between hierarchical layers. The CKOs also work at breaking down the walls to the outside—customers, suppliers, regulators, and so on. The function of the CKO team is to find and make best practices portable, but also to help motivate people to share and use knowledge.

The CKOs increasingly report to the CEO and almost always work directly with line managers. They come from various backgrounds—human resources, IT, sales, research and development, and customer service. They had experience and expertise in programming, statistics, employee involvement, organizational development, training, sales, and research. And they have a keen sense of what was happening in the marketplace in terms of e-business, the impact of rapid change, and the shifting nature of employee and customer relations.

Often overlooked as a main champion of KM is the corporate library or information services. Arian Ward points out that corporate libraries are already in the business of KM:

> Libraries have been doing KM and have been our primary repository of explicit knowledge throughout history. Doesn't it make sense to tap that existing KM expertise and team it with other disciplines within the organization to provide a comprehensive set of KM competencies? We should be transforming them into a vital component of our organizations knowledge ecosystem.

Ultimately, informal descriptions of KM professionals may be more telling than are formal job titles. These CKO roles are being filled by people who seek to bridge people's ideas across functional silos and lines of business and to make their firms adapt and react like their newer and more agile competition.

Top management increasingly cannot rely on a one-dimensional voice, whether it is from finance, human resources, IT or any other function. In conjunction with new CKO roles, the chief information officer (CIO) and senior human resources executives are providing the same strategic focus, consulting skills, and most important, the ability to work with line operations. The best results on productivity and motivation of people can come only if these executives work in close partnership as a KM team.

The CKO is the corporate knowledge strategist responsible for developing and championing a plan for transforming the company into a knowledge-creating and-sharing organization.

A standard CKO job posting may look like this:

- develops a KM strategy and architecture;
- develops KM methodologies and processes;
- builds awareness and develops training;
- collaborates with business and functional groups to implement, lead, and support KM initiatives;
- identifies opportunities for significant improvements in managing knowledge across the company, particularly in increasing profitable revenue and decreasing costs;
- coordinates KM initiatives to reduce redundancies and increase knowledge sharing;
- collaborates with HR to develop conditions that motivate knowledge contribution and sharing;
- collaborates with IT to identify and deploy the KM tools required to meet business objectives;
- assesses the effectiveness of KM strategies, practices, and initiatives;
- proposes metrics that enable the company to measure how well it leverages its intellectual capital;
- enhances sensitivity to customer needs by improving the acquisition and management of customer knowledge; and
- learns from other organizations that leverage their knowledge resources effectively.

Information Technology and Knowledge Leadership

Many of the foundation tool sets for KM come from information management. This has led many companies to try to make KM an IT-sponsored initiative. But these projects often fall short of expectations because the human component is of overriding importance. Any KM software should be designed around the way people work. Understanding how work is done requires an understanding of how knowledge flows, how ideas

TABLE 41.3 Level of IT Commitment and Degree of CIO Involvement

IT commitment to KM Has Room to Grow	
Very high	10%
High	30
Some	53
None	7
CIO Is Mostly a "Supporter" of KM	
Primary champion	15%
Supporter	54
Not involved	20
Don't know	11

are generated, how creativity is encouraged, and how customers are served. Overall, level of IT commitment and the degree of CIO involvement vary, but where it exists it is seen as a major advantage. And even though the CIO plays a greater role in KM than HR, only 40% of surveyed companies say IT has a high or very high level of commitment to KM (table 41.3).

Though KM and OL are rapidly becoming absorbed into the infrastructure and values of many organizations, the path is not yet one of spontaneous growth. Leadership and the planned dissemination of sound techniques remain the essentials for more progress. Even while the number of success stories is growing, the gap between what is happening and what remains is huge. While some companies have profited just from the basics of sharing best practices, much greater gains are coming in e-business, faster time to market, new product and service offerings, and better cross-functional coordination.

While the apparent benefits are becoming clearer, KM still needs to be justified in business terms if it is to gain widespread support. Technology costs are plummeting and most KM can be leveraged effectively on infrastructure investments that have been and are being made, but better planning and coordination are needed to get it used the right way. However, addressing the costs and benefits of KM are not the main barriers—corporate culture is.

Knowledge Culture

According to every major study on KM or OL, culture is a key barrier to success. Culture is generally defined as the beliefs, values, norms, and behaviors that are unique to an organization—in other words, "the unwritten rules" and "how work gets done around here."

The development of a knowledge-sharing culture relies on shared vision, value-based leadership at all levels, open and continuous communication, and rewards and recognition. Mark Koskiniemi of Buckman Labs says:

> Ninety percent of moving an organization to success in knowledge sharing or learning is in having the right culture. If your people are not confident that they can or should communicate freely, then all the best technology will be unable to pry knowledge out of them, or help them absorb knowledge. Buckman has been successful with our culture change efforts over the past several years. If our technology were to suddenly disappear or if we were to change systems, we would still retain the desire on the part of our associates to exchange information and share their knowledge.

A knowledge-sharing culture is based on the beliefs, attitudes, and customs that exist within an organization. Intranets can change the span of communications and provide a platform for beginning a cultural change. According to Fred Schoeps, "IBM's latest global employee survey showed that—for the first time ever—the intranet was ranked second behind coworker and just before manager as the 'best source of information.' This is a profound result." Hubert Saint-Onge of Clarica adds:

> Most practitioners in this area will agree that there is a definite requirement for a minimum threshold of trust, collaboration, and collective sense of ownership for knowledge to contribute to the creation of value. Beyond this threshold, there might very well be a mutually reinforcing relationship between the knowledge strategy and the culture of the organization. A well-conceived and effectively implemented knowledge strategy might be the most powerful transformative vehicle currently available to organizations. So, it starts to look like a two-sided Möbius strip: culture shapes knowledge strategy and knowledge strategy shapes culture.

Building a culture of trust starts with having a values-based organization. For example, at Buckman Labs a strong code of ethics is critical to proactive knowledge sharing. By having strong basic ethical guidelines, the firm needs fewer rules regarding innovation, communication, risk taking, and decision making. As Buckman's Koskiniemi points out,

> The reason why this relationship between culture and knowledge strategy is so confirming is because of its inclusive nature. Anyone in your organization can play a role in shaping and contributing to the success of the organization. Obviously, there are some initiatives a company can undertake that will alter the cultural landscape forever, and many times these are intentional undertakings. All that is done in an organization will be viewed by associates as a statement and as a shaper of the culture. Knowledge strategy is not alone in this discussion, but it has made plain the important truth—you need to have a culture that is environmentally consistent with your aims.

Individual executives can strengthen the knowledge sharing and learning culture by helping to:

- contribute to a working definition of KM and OL;
- work with human resources and IT to see that people have the tools to create and share;
- link KM and OL efforts to existing performance or change initiatives;
- gear training, performance management, and other human resources tools to KM;
- change hiring and career development to reinforce a knowledge-sharing culture;
- focus on processes that will enable cross-boundary learning and sharing;
- support, fund, and give time to learning networks;
- be a role model for good knowledge-sharing behaviors, including receiving new ideas and bad news; and
- ensure that people are held accountable and receive recognition.

Measuring the Impact on Business Results

A key question for many firms is how to measure the impact of KM on business results. Proper measurement requires that knowledge managers have the ability to communicate and demonstrate financial results, and that business managers believe in and understand the impor-

tance of what is being accomplished in KM. Customer satisfaction or customer value is the primary measure most often cited by senior executives. One milestone in integrating KM into the business is that the finance function is beginning to assume thought leadership for knowledge asset valuation and integration of these assets into financial management of the business. Another milestone is that business process managers are thinking in terms of learning loops, expert networks, and KM applications such as business intelligence, collaboration, technology-enabled learning, and process knowledge maps. In addition, many human resources personnel are changing how they think about human capital and measures of value, enabling line managers and employees to increase collaboration, and turning the human resources function itself into a knowledge-based organization (table 41.4).

Yet, despite many attempts, measuring KM return on investment is still difficult. As with training and other forms of investment in human capital, too many variables can prevent the development of a formula that leads to a proof. Most firms are relying on the evidence such as cost savings, speed to market, and customer satisfaction.

Recording the number of hits on knowledge databases or activity on a corporate intranet can be a useful proxy, but very few firms focus on that type of micromeasure. Although formal KM measurements and metrics appear relatively unimportant to most executives, they do agree on a standard measure of success for KM efforts—improved productivity at the individual and the organizational level. They consider the need for continuous on-the-job learning to be essential within a knowledge-based business environment. For example, BP's Pacesetter program links refineries across six continents to

TABLE 41.4 Survey Results: Traditional Measurements Still Determine KM Effectiveness ($n = 200$)

Customer satisfaction/value	70%
Cost reduction/savings	52
Employee attitude/morale/involvement	47
Better time to market	35
Sales effectiveness	22
New product sales	18
Number of communities of practice	12
Employee turnover	5
Number of KM initiatives	5

generate and share knowledge for performance improvement. Rick Porter, business unit leader, says, "Over the past four years, the refinery has sustained improvements of around $100 million. Over the next couple of years, we hope to generate another $70 million. Is it because of Pacesetter, per se? We don't care. We're in close enough touch with the organization that precise measurements about the Pacesetter program would be a hindrance."

The Future of Knowledge Management and Learning

Although specific approaches to KM and OL vary from firm to firm, there are many key themes and common concerns. KM and OL require a major shift in organizational culture and a commitment at all levels; build off of a series of other disciplines: organizational design and change management, process engineering, library sciences, and information management; and impacts every business discipline.

Sixty percent of surveyed companies expect to make their KM and OL initiatives enterprisewide in the next five years. Yet KM is a rapidly changing discipline in itself and even as the current initiatives are spreading, new opportunities are opening up. Two of the most important are customer knowledge and integration with e-commerce—the intercompany spread of knowledge.

Knowledge management is not the end of our learning journey, but in some sense is just the beginning. The sharing of existing best practice will raise productivity to a uniform high level, but only measured by today's standards. The real competitive threats often come from breakthrough innovation that is only dimly perceived on the radar screen of today's competitors, or indeed from new entrants who are today not classified as in your industry at all.

Viewed from this perspective, current efficiency gains are dangerous if they lock you into proven technology and traditional competitive models. Building knowledge repositories, optimizing intellectual assets, and networking human assets are not the chosen instruments to "unlearn" old knowledge, leapfrog old technology, or transform your company into a new competitive posture.

Companies are changing their focus from working *for* customers to working *with* customers. Historically, most large companies focused on what is possible—what research and development and manufacturing can come up with. Innovative companies also focus on what is needed—what it is that the customer often cannot express explicitly. Gaining that kind of customer knowledge is a growing KM discipline, but to date, very few KM efforts are being used to access and spread customer knowledge or using KM to learn from customer feedback. However, KM can play a very important role in converting customer knowledge to innovative products and services.

E-commerce, new product development, customer service, research and development, and marketing are rarely integrated with KM efforts. In certain Japanese companies and in notable examples such as Procter & Gamble, IBM, NCR, and First Union, large-scale customer knowledge efforts are just gaining ground. IBM, for instance, uses virtual teaming by client teams. The company systematically moves client teams into an electronic space to share and work in a "customer room," a virtual place, a shared electronic space for structuring relationships and working together collaboratively. Account teams manage daily customer needs working on issues, making decisions, and developing proposals and staff project plans. One of the critical success factors is not the tool, however, but the teaming service provided for 90 days to the account team to learn teaming skills and transform behavior.

Focus on E-commerce and Web-Enabled KM

Intranets and the Internet are the most important technological KM tools. It is no coincidence that the rise of KM parallels the rise of the Web—they complement each other perfectly. As Arian Ward summarizes:

> The key to the success of KM is to make both the individual and the organization win. Web technology provides the means to democratize the workplace and the marketplace. It has the potential to provide visibility for an individual and the artifacts of their work and their knowledge, as well as the accessibility to the knowledge they need to do their jobs—without having to go through traditional hierarchies.

Initiatives at leading companies focus on developing people and methods to enhance learning and improve communication, both locally and globally. The right technological infrastructure provides the tools necessary for ensuring the success of KM efforts, but it is the knowledge moving between employees and customers that counts. The tools and techniques that fall under the terms "knowledge management" or "organizational learning" are becoming key enablers of e-commerce. KM and OL as separate fields and disciplines may lose visibility and be subsumed into the e-commerce field, where the goals seem clearer and the issues less philosophical. The increase in speed will lead to enormous pressures on the remaining physical steps, especially on the linkage of work processes to technology.

This change will increasingly transcend barriers between companies and look at customers, suppliers, and other business partners as part of the shared learning and knowledge communities of the enterprise. As such, KM should become an integral part of business relationships. KM offers a set of tools and the opportunity to support the reworking of processes, yet the greatest benefits promised by KM come as innovation and creativity. Theoretically, KM is a great accelerator of innovation and creativity, but in practice, most KM projects are still conservative and focused on efficiencies. The integration of OL and KM is needed to break the old rules, unlearn outdated business models, and achieve breakthroughs.

The tools and the experience base are at hand. Perhaps what is needed now is better management of KM itself and applying the lessons learned to move to the next level, using the resources of the enterprise and KM tools and techniques to create new capabilities and deliver business value that has not yet been defined.

Note

1. Founded in 1916, The Conference Board is a not-for-profit, nonpartisan organization whose two-fold purpose is to improve the business enterprise system and to enhance the contribution of business to society. To accomplish this, The Conference Board strives to be the leading global business membership organization that enables senior executives from all industries to explore and exchange ideas of impact on business policy and practices. To support this activity, The Conference Board provides a variety of forums and a professionally managed research program that identifies and reports objectively on key areas of changing management concern, opportunity and action. The Conference Board has offices in New York and Brussels, and regional offices worldwide.

Index